Law, Business, and Society

Kiren Dosanjh Zucker
California State University, Northridge

Kristofer Neslund
Baldwin Wallace University, Retired

Nancy Neslund
St. John Fisher University, Retired

Kari Smoker
Ithaca College

Based on the work of founding author, **Tony McAdams**
University of Northern Iowa, Retired

Mc Graw Hill

LAW, BUSINESS, AND SOCIETY 2024 RELEASE

Published by McGraw Hill LLC, 1325 Avenue of the Americas, New York, NY 10019.

This book is printed on acid-free paper.

2 3 4 5 6 7 8 9 CPI 26

ISBN 978-1-266-95001-8
MHID 1-266-95001-X

Cover Image: ©*Shutterstock/Manuel Hurtado*

mheducation.com/highered

About the Authors

Kiren Dosanjh Zucker

Kiren Dosanjh Zucker is a professor in the Department of Accounting at California State University, Northridge (CSUN). She earned a BA in political science from Syracuse University and a JD from the University of Michigan. A member of the State Bar of California, she has served on its Committee of Bar Examiners and Committee on Professional Responsibility and Conduct. Her teaching and research interests focus primarily on employment law, pedagogy, and accounting ethics. Along with being named a Master Teacher by the Academy of Legal Studies in Business, she is a past recipient of the Outstanding Faculty Award from CSUN's Students with Disabilities Resources Center, the CSUN University Ambassadors' Polished Apple Award, the Harvey A. Bookstein Accounting Professor of the Year Award, and the Master of Science in Accountancy Program's Outstanding Teaching Award.

Kristofer Neslund

Kristofer Neslund retired in 2019 from Baldwin Wallace University as professor of law and accounting. He holds a BS in business administration from Bowling Green State University, a JD from Lewis and Clark College, an LLM in taxation from New York University, and a doctorate in business administration from Kent State University. He is a member of the Oregon bar and an Ohio CPA. Dr. Neslund served as associate dean of the Schools of Taxation and Accounting at Golden Gate University and was director of the graduate accounting programs at the University of San Diego and St. John Fisher University. He was president of ACBSP Region 4 (Illinois, Indiana, Minnesota, Michigan, Ohio, and Wisconsin) and president of the Great Lakes Region of the Academy of Legal Studies in Business (Indiana, Michigan, and Ohio). He was a Fulbright Scholar during 2015 at the University of Iceland where he conducted research on the collapse of the Icelandic banking system during the Great Recession and taught the capstone graduate accounting seminar. Dr. Neslund was a partner in a boutique law firm providing tax, business, and estate planning services primarily to wealthy entrepreneurs.

Nancy Ganong Neslund

Nancy Ganong Neslund retired in 2022 from St. John Fisher University in Rochester, New York. She holds a BA in economics from Willamette University, a JD from Columbia University, an LLM from New York University, and is a member of the Oregon bar. Prior to entering academia, Professor Neslund was a partner in two law firms, with a focus on administrative law and business and estate planning for entrepreneurs. She was a member of the Research Board for City Club of Portland, Oregon, and a state board member of the Women Entrepreneurs of Oregon. She was the founding academic director of the master of taxation program at Portland State University. During the academic year 2004 to 2005,

Professor Neslund was a visiting professor of law at the Europa Universität Viadrina in Germany. During her over 20 years in academia, she has been a visiting professor at the law schools of the University of Nevada-Las Vegas, the University of New Hampshire, and Lewis & Clark College in Portland, Oregon. She was an invited speaker at Singidunum University's Conference on the Impact of the Internet on Business Activities Worldwide in Belgrade, Serbia, in 2014, where she discussed the status of Bitcoin worldwide. Professor Neslund developed and for a number of years taught financial literacy for lawyers to help students become practice-ready. She is also a coauthor of the LexisNexis, *Q&A: Taxation of Business Entities.*

Kari Smoker

Kari Smoker is an associate professor of accounting and business law at Ithaca College, where she teaches legal environment of business and commercial law, as well as forensic accounting, fraud law, government and nonprofit accounting, and taxation. Previously, she was an associate professor of accounting at the State University of New York, The College at Brockport. She earned a BA in mathematics-statistics and economics from the University of Rochester, a JD from The Ohio State University, and a master of science in taxation from Golden Gate University's School of Taxation. She is also a certified fraud examiner. Prior to entering academia, she was an associate in the Tax and Business Advisory Group at Arthur Andersen and an associate attorney handling litigation and commercial and property transactions in Rochester, NY. She served as president of the Greater Rochester Association for Women Attorneys and as a member of the Rochester Business Ethics Foundation Award committee. In 2009, she received the Rochester Business Journal's *Forty under 40 Award,* and in 2014 and 2015, she received the *Faculty of the Year Award* from SUNY Brockport's School of Business and Management. She also received the *President's Award for Excellence in Teaching* at SUNY Brockport in 2017, followed by the *SUNY Chancellor's Award for Excellence in Teaching* in 2018.

Tony McAdams, Retired

Tony McAdams is professor of management emeritus at the University of Northern Iowa. He was the founding author of the first edition published in 1986 and the lead author of many subsequent editions. He earned a BA in history from the University of Northern Iowa, a JD from the University of Iowa, and an MBA from Columbia University. Professor McAdams's primary teaching interests include government regulation of business, business and society, and employment law. Professor McAdams' research interests include managerial accountability, business ethics, and employment law. His scholarly articles have appeared in such journals as *The Harvard Business Review, The Academy of Management Review, The Journal of Business Ethics,* and *The American Business Law Journal.* Professor McAdams received the Iowa Board of Regents Award for Faculty Excellence, the Distinguished Teacher of the Year Award from the student government at the University of Kentucky, and the University of Northern Iowa College of Business Administration Excellence in Teaching Award.

Preface

ACKNOWLEDGMENT AND THANK YOU

The first edition of this text was the extraordinary creation of one man. I met Tony, through his book, in my first year of full-time teaching in 1986. My associate dean, who was also a business law professor, introduced us by recommending that I consider using the first edition of *Law, Business, and Society* to teach my legal environment of business course. I think I enjoyed reading and exploring it even more than my students did and wrote to Tony to tell him so. He graciously accepted my comments and then invited me to participate with him in the second edition. I was honored to join him, along with a number of other authors over the years, in sharing his vision for orienting generations of business students to the overlapping impacts of legal directives and personal morality on their actions in the world of commerce. Although I missed participating in a number of editions along the way, this 2024 release is the eighth revision in which I have been part of the author team.

We thank you, Tony, for your unfaltering vision and long dedication to expanding the minds and elevating the discussion of four decades of students.

Nancy Ganong Neslund
Kristofer Neslund
Kari Smoker

I am honored to have been a co-author with Tony McAdams, whose vision for the text I hope we have upheld in this latest iteration.

Kiren Dosanjh Zucker

Approach

Our primary goal is to provoke student thought. To that end, we place heavy emphasis on analysis. We consider the questions we ask more important than the answers to those questions. We introduce the student to existing policy in the various substantive areas to encourage understanding and retention, as well as careful thought about the desirability of those policies.

Our book takes a strong public policy orientation. Attention in Unit I to political economy and ethics is a necessary foundation on which the student can build a logical understanding of the regulatory process. Thereafter, those business and society themes persist throughout the book. In virtually every chapter, we look beyond the law itself to other social and environmental forces. For example, in the antitrust chapters, economic philosophy is of great importance. Antitrust is explored as a matter of national social policy. We argue that antitrust has a good deal to do with the direction of American life generally. In Unit IV, law is at the heart of the fair employment practices, but we also present material from management, sociology, history, and popular culture to treat fair employment as an issue of public policy rather than as a series of narrower technical legal disputes. The law is studied in the economic, social, and political context from which it springs. These multidimensional approaches characterize most chapters as we attempt to examine the various topics as a whole and in context. At the same time, the law remains the core of the book.

Broadly, our adjustments for this 2024 release were designed to refresh the book and achieve increased reader interest by raising questions in the context of current events. This release again directs attention to the nation's ongoing debate about how much government we need in our lives, often in the context of our challenges in addressing the imperatives and impacts of climate change, the polarization of national politics, the shift in the make-up of the Supreme Court, and the growing impact of China. While this release has been in production, the Court has issued a number of decisions that have significant impact on topics covered in this text, has already accepted petitions to review many more, and has heard oral arguments in others for which decisions may be released in the near future. This illustrates the dynamic aspect of the law, even as these issues are covered in this release as of the time of its writing.

This release also notes the rise of a powerful antipathy in certain quarters of the political arena toward the consideration of ESG (environmental, social, and governmental issues) factors in investment decision making, especially by the nation's chronically underfunded public pension plans–an opposition grounded on a premise that incorporating the risks associated with such factors, such as climate change, impairs investment returns. Since the last edition, there has been a sea change with respect to the now widespread acknowledgment of imperative to address climate change, which is reflected in Chapter 17. The impact major Internet-based companies are having, not just on our individual lives, but particularly with regard to our personal privacy and possibly also on the fabric of our society, are explored in Chapter 18. In sum, although the general structure and philosophy of the book are unchanged, we have made significant revisions, including many new questions and the coverage of a number of new court cases.

WHAT'S NEW

Chapter 1 has been reorganized to streamline content and to begin by introducing the strengths, limitations, and moral implications of capitalism, as currently practiced in the United States, especially in light of the recent challenges facing American society. It asks students to consider the appropriate balance between capitalism and government regulation that best serves the needs of our nation and the world, and it examines the increasing trend of privatizing and commercializing space in the United States. It also provides an overview of the economic and political systems in China, Russia, and the EU, and the United States' relationship with each.

Chapter 2 begins with a discussion of the consulting firm McKinsey's role in promoting Purdue Pharma's opioid sales. Unethical conduct in video interviews is also explored, along with ethical questions raised by autonomous vehicles ("AVs"). Examples of whistleblowers are expanded to include a Twitter security executive. Chapter-end questions include the ethics of cryptocurrency trading, and the impersonation of a YouTube executive by an Ozy corporate officer in a fundraising call with Goldman Sachs. On the upside, it highlights Gen Z's move beyond diversity to inclusion and both Gen Z members' and Millennials' beliefs that business needs to be involved in improving society.

Chapter 3 has been reorganized and begins with a Practicing Ethics segment, setting the stage for discussing issues throughout the chapter relating to corporate social responsibility. The chapter then examines the economic, political, and social impact of corporate America and raises the question of whether big tech companies in particular–Amazon, Apple, Facebook, Google, and Microsoft–are simply too big, foreclosing the possibility of real competition and wielding too much political power. It explores the broadening appeal of corporate social responsibility, particularly among younger Americans, and compares the stakeholder versus shareholder approach as a framework for measuring corporate social performance.

Chapter 4 has been updated to include The Ending Forced Arbitration of Sexual Assault and Sexual Harassment Act signed into law in 2022, and the 2022 Gallup Poll showing trust in the U.S. Supreme Court at a record low. The class action lawsuit against the FTX founder and endorsing celebrities alleging they mislead investors is also considered. Practicing Ethics boxes consider the Jones Day defense of Abbott Laboratories in baby formula product liability cases, as well as "robot lawyers" through the ABA-award-winning DoNotPay app.

Chapter 5 discusses the Constitution's provision for the separation of powers within the federal government, highlighting issues during the Obama and Trump Administrations. The freedom of religion discussion addresses the tensions arising between the growing number of Americans in favor of LGBTQ nondiscrimination measures versus an increasingly conservative Supreme Court and the risk to LGBTQ rights in many states, and the discussion of free speech is updated to include the Supreme Court's 2021 ruling in *Mahanoy Area School District vs B.L.,* which signals an expansion of students' freedom of speech off campus, even when the speech relates to school. An update on the Redskins, officially renamed the Washington Commanders under intense public pressure in 2022, is included in the commercial speech discussion, and the section on search and seizure rules for obtaining cell phone records is updated to include the 7th Circuit's 2021 ruling in *United States v. Hammond.*

Chapter 6 begins with a description of the breach of contract dispute between a top online gamer of Fortnite and the esports organization FaZe Clan, settled in 2020, which can be used to explore various contract law principles covered in this chapter. Updates include a breach of contract claim brought against an online dating site by a male member who claimed there were not enough single ladies on the site; *force majeure* and COVID-19; University of Delaware students' breach of contract claims based on the COVID-19 campus closure; and the 2022 breach of contract claims brought against Twitter for nonpayment.

Chapter 7 has been updated in a number of ways. The discussion of defamation is illustrated by Dominion Voting Systems' suit against Fox News. Product liability concepts are raised in the context of the Supreme Court's 2021 decision upholding the jurisdiction of both Montana and Minnesota courts over product liability suits against Ford for injuries caused by its vehicles in those states, despite the fact that the vehicles were in the state as a result of resales and relocations, rather than original purchases. Product liability is also the basis for the many claims against Johnson & Johnson based on cancers attributed to asbestos in its iconic Baby Powder. After a jury case in which 22 women successfully sued Johnson & Johnson, J&J moved to contain its liability with respect to the more than 40,000 claims still pending by creating a shell company. The shell company then filed a bankruptcy petition in New Jersey, where most of the cases are pending. However, the Third Circuit held that the bankruptcy process cannot be used in that manner. It has been reported that J&J intends to seek review of the decision by the Supreme Court.

Chapter 8 covers three significant 2022 Supreme Court decisions: *West Virginia v. EPA,* in which it held that it was not within the EPA's authority under the Clean Air Act to require coal-fired plants to substitute some or all of their coal-based electricity to natural gas and/or renewables-base electricity production; *Dobbs v. Jackson Women's Health Organization,* in which it held the authority to legalize abortions is held by state governments, not the federal government; and *New York State Rifle & Pistol Association v. Bruen,* in which in announced new limits on state regulation of gun control.

Chapter 9 has been updated in several significant ways. General Partnerships incorporates the 2022 Supreme Court case, *Berfenwerfer v. Buckley,* which holds that a partner's innocence with respect to the incurrence of a partnership obligation is no defense to joint and several liability. The 2022 collapse of FTX has been added to the text box in Corporate Governance in Publicly Held Corporations. The Shareholders-Rights Movement has been updated to include the 2022 changes to the proxy rules which will allow virtually any shareholder to propose a slate of candidates for the board of directors. The powerful rising political opposition to the ESG movement, based on questionable assertions like incorporating risk factors such as climate change into investment decisions will reduce public pension plans' earnings, is discussed in Major Issues Currently Confronting Boards of Directors. New content on insider trading by Members of Congress appears in Violating Federal Securities Laws.

Chapter 10 includes coverage of a number of recent cases involving restraints of trade, including price-fixing by Visa and Mastercard, by several manufacturers in the auto parts industry, and by food industry giants like Tyson, Bumble Bee, and Sunkist. The status of the European Commission's $9 billion antitrust action against Google for illegal tying has been updated, and the discussion of Uber's "route-based pricing" (where prices vary, for example, based on pick-up and drop-off neighborhoods) and "personalized pricing" (which modifies the quoted prices based on individual data, such as type of credit card, brand of phone, and riding history) now includes empirical evidence from George Washington University that the decision-making algorithm for rideshare pricing inadvertently incorporates societal-bias, negatively impacting customers in lower-income and minority areas.

Chapter 11 refocuses the discussion of the virtues and hazards of monopoly and oligopoly on the Frightful Five high-tech colossuses: Alphabet (Google's parent), Amazon, Apple, Facebook, and Microsoft. These previously admired market disrupters are increasingly the targets of public distrust and anger. The claim that top companies have achieved abusive market power through mergers is contrasted with claims of greater efficiency and innovation. Concerns about vertical mergers are considered from the vantage of combining pay television providers and media content providers, despite the courts' dismissal of the government's anticompetition challenges in 2019 and in light of additional subsequent mergers.

Chapter 12 covers the 2023 U.S. Supreme Court decision on overtime for "highly compensated employees," the Federal Trade Commission's 2023 proposed rule to ban noncompete agreements, and the Secure Act 2.0 "Saver's Match" offering an incentive to nontraditional workers to save for retirement. The Biometric Information Privacy Acts (BINA) and Illinois Supreme Court ruling on BINA have been added, as well as an explanation of the H-2B visa.

Twitter former employees' WARN class action filed in late 2022 is also included. The confusion regarding employers' limitations on gun possession in the workplace after a 2022 U.S. Supreme Court ruling recognizing a constitutional right to carry firearms outside the home is also mentioned. "Practicing Ethics boxes on AI-powered virtual supervisors, as well as OSHA's guidelines on workplace stress and mental health, have been added. Discussions of second-chance hiring" for those with criminal backgrounds, as well as employers' COVID-19 vaccination mandates are updated. Chapter 4's discussion of the Ending Forced Arbitration of Sexual Assault and Sexual Harassment Act of 2021 is referenced.

Chapter 13 has updated its discussion of racial inequality, introducing the EEOC workshop series on Diversity, Equity, and Inclusion (DE&I), and adding recent racial harassment claims made against Tesla and other employers. The CROWN Acts addressing natural hair discrimination has been added, as well as the EEOC Guidance on Artificial Intelligence (AI) and the ADA. Updates are provided, including on the U.S. Supreme Court's 2020 rulings on ministerial exceptions for religious discrimination, and the 2022 California court decision that found California's Women on Boards law unconstitutional. The recent focus on intersectional discrimination and pay equity is also covered, along with the 2023 settlement of the EEOC's sexual harassment lawsuit against the McDonald's franchise.

Chapter 14 addresses the recent trend in union organizing across sectors, including at Amazon, Chipotle, Apple, Google, Microsoft, as well as Starbucks. A 2023 judges' order against Starbucks for labor law violations is also included. The NLRB's 2023 decision prohibiting confidentiality or disparagement clauses in severance agreements is discussed. The discussion of the U.S. Supreme Court's *Janus* ruling is updated to include note on its minimal impact on public sector unions. The Police Unions box is deleted, and the box on College Athletes is updated with NLRB 2021 General Counsel's Memo and the U.S. Supreme Court decision in *NCAA v. Alston.* The background of a pending U.S. Supreme Court decision on whether an employer can bring a state tort claim against a union for property damage suffered during a strike is explained. Chapter-end questions include a question on the Actors' Equity 2022 contract negotiations which included issues of diversity, equity, and inclusion.

Chapter 15 addresses some of the laws, both state and federal, that have been passed to protect consumers from such ills as fraud and overreaching. Part Two focuses on just four of the federal agencies–the Food and Drug Administration, Federal Trade Commission, Consumer Product Safety Commission, and Consumer Product Safety Commission, collectively charged with protecting our health, safety, and online privacy, as well as our pocketbooks from fraud. Each of these agencies has a substantial breadth of authority. Examples chosen for discussion include those that should resonate with students, such as vaping, the 2021 closure of the Abbott Laboratories' baby formula plant in Sturgis Michigan and the opening of criminal investigation of the company and the Sturgis plant. Also covered is the 2021 Supreme Court ruling in *AMG Capital Management v. FTC,* which limits the FTC's future ability to collect monetary relief from wrongdoers to compensate defrauded consumers. Part Three takes a close look at student loan debt, as well as discussing the practice of many colleges in making agreements with financial institutions for branded student credit cards that may not be in students' best interests.

Chapter 16 includes updated statistics relating to governmental requests to block content, which can raise free speech issues, directed at companies like Google and Facebook, and relating to the commercial significance of intellectual property and its theft. The chapter explores the growing challenges of effectively regulating multinational enterprises, especially those that are state-owned companies–most particularly those based in China; there are updates on actions taken by the United States as of 2022, relating to China's refusal to allow U.S. inspections of corporate financial statement audits performed by Chinese auditors and to allow the SEC to pursue fraud investigations involving Chinese actors. In addition, the antitrust section provides updates on the charges brought, and the fines assessed, against both Microsoft and Google by the EU from 2019 through 2022.

Chapter 17 has been reorganized and streamlined and begins with a discussion focused primarily on climate change, placing an appropriate emphasis on what is arguably the greatest threat facing our world today. The chapter then provides a global view of several environmentally catastrophic events. Updated statistics about the state of the environment are provided, including the percentage of the world's food irrigated with wastewater, the number of people living in water-stressed areas, and the proportion of the planet's species headed for extinction. The section on the regulation of water pollution includes an update on "covered waters" within the meaning of the Clean Water Act: the Supreme Court's 2023 ruling in *Sackett v EPA,* which severely limits the agency's ability to protect our nation's wetlands, is discussed in the afterword of the Legal Briefcase segment featuring *Solid Waste Agency of Northern Cook County.* Several updates have been provided in the discussion on regulating air pollution, including the EPA's proposal of aggressive new rules for regulating power plant emissions, the American Lung Association's 2022 "report card" on ozone and particulates, the U.S.'s significantly reduced reliance on coal-powered plants, and new U.S. Department of Transportation fuel economy standards that are being implemented for model years 2022 through 2026. Updated statistics on the Superfund program have been provided in the discussion on regulating land pollution. Finally, the discussion on international environmental treaties has been updated, reflecting the fact that the United States. rejoined the Paris Agreement on President Biden's first day in office in January 2021.

Chapter 18. Not surprisingly, there is much that has been either updated or added to this chapter. Although at the time of this writing access to generative artificial intelligence (A.I.) is only newly available to the general public, some ethical issues it may raise are presented in a new Practicing Ethics box at the outset of the chapter. Two 2022 EU laws governing the provision of Internet services, the Digital Services Act and Digital Markets Act, are discussed, both because many U.S. Internet companies are active in the EU, but also because in this area the EU laws are cutting edge and provide models that can be used in the United States, particularly at the state level. In the United States new developments in California, including amendments to the 2020 California Consumer Privacy Law, the new California Age-Appropriate Design Code (effective in 2024) providing additional protections for users under 18, as well as new rules to address child online safety are covered. Privacy concerns surrounding the Chinese company TikTok's potential misuse of users' data are discussed at several points. Two cases currently before the Supreme Court involve claims against Google, Twitter, and Facebook based on the way their algorithms magnify the messaging of terrorist organizations such as ISIS are discussed. Also before the Court are petitions for review of both an 11th Circuit decision regarding a Florida law prohibiting social media from "deplatforming" candidates for public office and 5th Circuit decision regarding a Texas statute that prohibits social media blocking any Texas Internet user from posting or receiving communications based on a viewpoint being expressed, other than those related to sexual exploitation of children, to protect survivors of sexual abuse from harassment, or those that directly incite criminal activity. A new text box discusses a federal case holding that a room scan before online exam violated the student's 4th Amendment privacy right. Data privacy is also receiving more attention as many states passed laws banning abortions following the Court's decision in *Dobbs.* The advancement in facial recognition software has also caused growing concern, caused states such as Illinois to pass biometric privacy laws, and spawned a number of lawsuits. A new section on cryptocurrencies and related intangible assets has also been added, as well as a discussion of the tax implications of creating, selling, and making purchases with cryptocurrencies.

OVERVIEW

This text is directed to courses at both the upper-division undergraduate and masters levels in the legal environment of business, government and business, and business and society. Authors of texts in these areas often rely on a single discipline (for example, law, economics, or management) as the foundation for their efforts. In this text, we take an interdisciplinary approach, using elements of law, political economy, international business, ethics, social responsibility, and management. This large task necessarily requires certain trade-offs, but we hope the product will more accurately capture the fullness of the business environment.

Our primary goal is to produce an interesting, provocative reading experience. Naturally, accuracy and reasonable comprehensiveness cannot be sacrificed. Our feeling, however, is that a law text can be both intellectually and emotionally engaging without sacrificing substantive ends. To meet our objective, we have presented the bulk of the book in the form of contemporary legal and ethical conflicts emerging from today's news. We have provided scholarly results, surveys, polls, data, anecdotes, and other specific details that lend credibility, immediacy, and interest to the reading experience.

The book is divided into five units, as follows:

Unit I–Business and Society. We do not begin with the law. Rather, in Chapter 1 (Capitalism and the Role of Government), Chapter 2 (Business Ethics), and Chapter 3 (The Corporation and Public Policy: Expanding Responsibilities), we describe some of the economic and social forces that shape our legal system.

The goals of Unit I are to (a) enhance student awareness of the many societal influences on business; (b) establish the business context from which government regulation arose; and (c) explore the roles of the free market, government intervention, and individual and corporate ethics in shaping business behavior.

The student must understand not merely the law, but the law in context. What forces have provoked government intervention in business? What alternatives to our current "mixed economy" might prove healthy? These considerations help students respond to one of the critical questions of the day: To what extent, if any, should we regulate business?

Unit II–Introduction to Law. Chapter 4 (The American Legal System) and Chapter 5 (Constitutional Law and the Bill of Rights) survey the foundations of our legal system. Here we set out the "nuts and bolts" of law, combining cases and narrative. Then with Chapter 6 (Contracts) and Chapter 7 (Business Torts and Product Liability), we examine the foundations of business law.

Unit III–Trade Regulation and Antitrust. Chapter 8 (Government Regulation of Business) raises the book's central policy inquiry: When should the government intervene in business practice? Chapter 9 (Business Organizations and Securities Regulation), Chapter 10 (Antitrust Law–Restraints of Trade), and Chapter 11 (Antitrust Law–Monopolies and Mergers) survey the core of government oversight of business.

Unit IV–Employer-Employee Relations. Chapter 12 (Employment Law I: Employee Rights), Chapter 13 (Employment Law II: Discrimination), and Chapter 14 (Employment Law III: Labor–Management Relations) are intended not only to survey the law in those areas but also to introduce some of the sensitive and provocative social issues that have led to today's extensive government intervention in the employment relationship.

Unit V–Selected Topics in Government-Business Relations. Two of the closing chapters of this book–Chapter 15 (Consumer Protection) and Chapter 17 (Environmental Protection)–emphasize the dramatic expansion of the public's demands for socially responsible conduct in business. Chapter 16 (International Ethics and Law) provides an overview of the legal and ethical issues arising out of the reality of our inextricably intertwined national economies, and Chapter 18 (Internet Law and Ethics) explores the many ethical and legal issues that arise when people can and do connect instantaneously, without the impediments or protections of location or borders.

ACCREDITATION

Our text conforms to Association to Advance Collegiate Schools of Business (AACSB) International accreditation standards.

Two chapters are devoted exclusively to ethics, and ethics themes emerge throughout the book. The chapter on employment discrimination should be quite helpful in aiding students' understanding of diversity issues. Ethics and social responsibility are at the heart of the text rather than an afterthought to meet accreditation standards.

Furthermore, as required by the rapidly changing nature of commerce and as recommended by the AACSB, the text devotes extensive attention to legal and ethical issues arising from international business. Various topics throughout the text (for example, comparative economic systems, the Foreign Corrupt Practices Act, and global pollution) afford the student a sense of the worldwide implications of American business practice, and Chapter 16 is entirely devoted to international themes.

KEY FEATURES

Approximately 180 boxed features and ethics vignettes place the law in a practical context and offer many provocative opportunities for discussion. Here are two examples:

Room for Big Ideas

The Boring Company, founded by Elon Musk (the co-creator of PayPal and the founder of Tesla, the electric car company, and SpaceX), is one of several enterprises developing Hyperloop technology that envisions passenger pods, propelled by electromagnets through a near-vacuum tube, capable of moving people from New York City to Washington, D.C.

in 30 minutes at perhaps 700 miles per hour. Boring's first project is a $48 million people mover and tunnel of less than one mile under the 200-acre Las Vegas Convention Center.

Question

Is a market-based culture of freedom and risk-taking necessary to the creation and sustenance of these very big ideas, or is a blend of the market and government more likely to succeed? Explain.

PRACTICING ETHICS Individual Social Responsibility to Humanity?

Consider the following excerpt from a speech delivered September 28, 2001, by Jose Ramos-Horta, Nobel Peace Prize Laureate (1996) and Minister for Foreign Affairs and Cooperation for the East Timor Transition Government:

> There is no dispute that abject poverty, child labor, and prostitution are a moral indictment of all humanity.
>
> However, poverty should not only touch our conscience: It is also a matter of peace and security because it destabilizes entire countries and regions. In turn it threatens the integration of the global economy that is vital if the rich are to stay rich or if the poor are to move up, if only an inch.
>
> Peace will be illusory as long as the rich ignore the clamor of the poor for a better life, as long as hundreds of millions of people live below the poverty line, cannot afford a meal a day, do not have access to clean water and a roof.

Question

Should most of us, not just active international businesses, accept a social responsibility to humanity? If we answer yes to this question, how might our actions as students, educators, employees, employers, and investors change?

Jose Ramos-Horta, "Speech to the Northern Medical Foundation Tribute to Military Medicine and Lt-Gen. P. Cosgrove," Sydney, Australia, September 28, 2001.

Approximately 200 selected websites appear throughout this release to which students can turn for more information on many of the topics discussed, including related videos.

Each chapter concludes with a Research Exercise suitable for either individual or team projects.

McGraw Hill connect®

A complete course platform

Connect enables you to build deeper connections with your students through cohesive digital content and tools, creating engaging learning experiences. We are committed to providing you with the right resources and tools to support all your students along their personal learning journeys.

65%
Less Time Grading

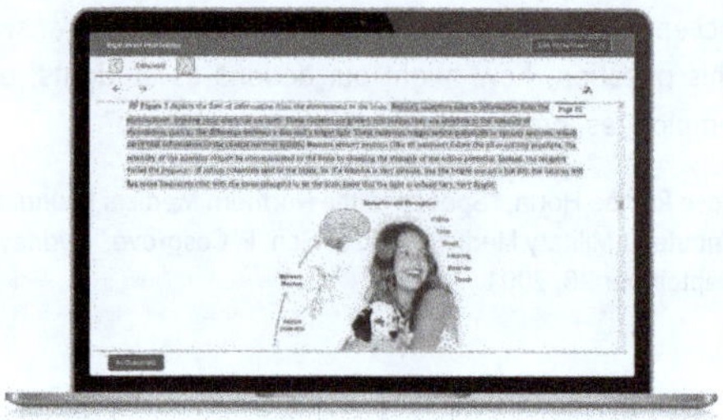
Laptop: Getty Images; Woman/dog: George Doyle/Getty Images

Every learner is unique

In Connect, instructors can assign an adaptive reading experience with SmartBook® 2.0. Rooted in advanced learning science principles, SmartBook® 2.0 delivers each student a personalized experience, focusing students on their learning gaps, ensuring that the time they spend studying is time well spent. **mheducation.com/highered/connect/smartbook**

Study anytime, anywhere

Encourage your students to download the free ReadAnywhere® app so they can access their online eBook, SmartBook® 2.0, or Adaptive Learning Assignments when it's convenient, even when they're offline. And since the app automatically syncs with their Connect account, all of their work is available every time they open it. Find out more at **mheducation.com/readanywhere**

"I really liked this app—it made it easy to study when you don't have your textbook in front of you."

Jordan Cunningham, a student at *Eastern Washington University*

Effective tools for efficient studying

Connect is designed to help students be more productive with simple, flexible, intuitive tools that maximize study time and meet students' individual learning needs. Get learning that works for everyone with Connect.

SUPPORT AT every step

Education for all

McGraw Hill works directly with Accessibility Services departments and faculty to meet the learning needs of all students. Please contact your Accessibility Services Office, and ask them to email **accessibility@mheducation.com**, or visit **mheducation.com/about/accessibility** for more information.

Affordable solutions, added value

Make technology work for you with LMS integration for single sign-on access, mobile access to the digital textbook, and reports to quickly show you how each of your students is doing. And with our Inclusive Access program, you can provide all these tools at the lowest available market price to your students. Ask your McGraw Hill representative for more information.

Solutions for your challenges

A product isn't a solution. Real solutions are affordable, reliable, and come with training and ongoing support when you need it and how you want it. Visit **supportateverystep.com** for videos and resources both you and your students can use throughout the term.

Updated and relevant content

Our new Evergreen delivery model provides the most current and relevant content for your course, hassle-free. Content, tools, and technology updates are delivered directly to your existing McGraw Hill Connect® course. Engage students and freshen up assignments with up-to-date coverage of select topics and assessments, all without having to switch editions or build a new course.

ONLINE ASSIGNMENTS AND RESOURCES

Case Analysis Exercises

Case Analysis Exercises are highly interactive, automatically graded online exercises in Connect that provide students the opportunity to dive into real-world cases. Learners are presented with the facts of a real case, asked to evaluate relevant evidence, and apply their knowledge of the law to decide on the judgement. Students are then challenged to take their knowledge of the law a step further by using their critical thinking skills to assess a similar legal scenario.

Connect's Business Law Application-Based Activities

Application-Based Activities for Business Law provide students valuable practice using problem-solving skills to apply their knowledge to realistic scenarios. Each scenario addresses key concepts and skills that students must use to work through and solve course-specific problems, resulting in improved critical thinking and relevant workplace skills. Application-Based Activities have been developed for the most often taught topics (as ranked by instructors) in the Business Law course. These unique activities are assignable and auto-gradable in Connect.

Writing Assignment

Available within McGraw Hill Connect, the Writing Assignment tool delivers a learning experience to help students improve their written communication skills and conceptual understanding. As an instructor you can assign, monitor, grade, and provide feedback on writing more efficiently and effectively.

Remote Proctoring & Browser-Locking Capabilities

Mc Graw Hill connect + proctorio

Remote proctoring and browser-locking capabilities, hosted by Proctorio within Connect, provide control of the assessment environment by enabling security options and verifying the identity of the student.

Seamlessly integrated within Connect, these services allow instructors to control students' assessment experience by restricting browser activity, recording students' activity, and verifying students are doing their own work.

Instant and detailed reporting gives instructors an at-a-glance view of potential academic integrity concerns, thereby avoiding personal bias and supporting evidence-based claims.

Test Builder in Connect

Available within Connect, Test Builder is a cloud-based tool that enables instructors to format tests that can be printed or administered within an LMS. Test Builder offers a modern, streamlined interface for easy content configuration that matches course needs, without requiring a download.

Test Builder allows you to:

- access all test bank content from a particular title.
- easily pinpoint the most relevant content through robust filtering options.

- manipulate the order of questions or scramble questions and/or answers.
- pin questions to a specific location within a test.
- determine your preferred treatment of algorithmic questions.
- choose the layout and spacing.
- add instructions and configure default settings.

Test Builder provides a secure interface for better protection of content and allows for just-in-time updates to flow directly into assessments.

Tegrity: Lectures 24/7

Tegrity in Connect is a tool that makes class time available 24/7 by automatically capturing every lecture. With a simple one-click start-and-stop process, you capture all computer screens and corresponding audio in a format that is easy to search, frame by frame. Students can replay any part of any class with easy-to-use, browser-based viewing on a PC, Mac, iPod, or other mobile device.

Educators know that the more students can see, hear, and experience class resources, the better they learn. In fact, studies prove it. Tegrity's unique search feature helps students efficiently find what they need, when they need it, across an entire semester of class recordings. Help turn your students' study time into learning moments immediately supported by your lecture. With Tegrity, you also increase intent listening and class participation by easing students' concerns about note-taking. Using Tegrity in Connect will make it more likely you will see students' faces, not the tops of their heads.

Business Law Newsletter

McGraw Hill's monthly Business Law newsletter, *Proceedings,* is designed specifically with the Business Law educator in mind. *Proceedings* incorporates "hot topics" in business law, video suggestions, an ethical dilemma, teaching tips, and a "chapter key" cross-referencing newsletter topics with the various McGraw Hill business law texts. *Proceedings* is delivered via e-mail to business law instructors each month.

Business Law Case Repository

The Case Repository is a collection of cases from the current release and previous editions.

Videos

Links to brief videos for classroom use are provided.

INSTRUCTOR RESOURCES

Instructors Manual

A package of supplementary materials is included in the instructors manual. Those materials include (1) chapter outlines, (2) general advice regarding the goals and purposes of the chapters, (3) summaries of the law cases, and (4) answers for the questions raised in the text.

PowerPoints

This release's revised PowerPoints contain an easy-to-follow lecture outline summarizing key points for every chapter.

ACKNOWLEDGMENTS

Completion of the 2024 Release of this book depended, in significant part, on the hard work of others.

The authors are pleased to acknowledge the contributions of these good people: Michele Janicek, Project Development Manager; Fran Simon and Rachael Hillebrand, Content Project Managers; Barbara Hari, Product Developer; Maragaret Haywood, Copy Editor; Kathleen Klehr, Executive Portfolio Manager; Nate Anderson, Executive Marketing Manager; and Rebecca Olson, Director, Quantitative Business.

The authors also thank the reviewers:

Steve Abraham, *State University of New York*

Wayne Anderson, *Missouri State University*

Teresa Brosnan, *Seattle University*

Nathaniel Gallegos, *Chadron State College*

Eloise Hassell, *University of North Carolina at Greensboro*

Stephanie Joseph, *Winston Salem State University*

Steven McCarty, *San Joaquin Delta College*

Susan O'Sullivan-Gavin, *Rider University*

Maria Patterson, *New York University*

Peter Shaw, *Minneapolis Community and Technical College*

Elisabeth Sperow, *California Polytechnic State University, San Luis Obispo*

Kenneth Taurman, *Indiana University Southeast*

Doula Zaharopoulos, *Phoenix College*

SUGGESTIONS

The authors welcome comments and feedback from all readers.

Nancy Ganong Neslund

Brief Contents

Contents

Chapter 2
Business Ethics 49

Chapter 3
The Corporation and Public Policy: Expanding Responsibilities 89

UNIT TWO
INTRODUCTION TO LAW 135

Chapter 4
The American Legal System 136

Chapter 17 Environmental Protection 788

Links to Brief Videos for Classroom Use

The following video links appear in the body of the text in conjunction with the subject matter of the videos.

Chapter 1

2016 Oscar-nominated movie, *The Big Short,* at **[www.youtube.com/watch?v=LWr8hbUkG9s]**

Trailer, 2011 Oscar-winning best documentary, *Inside Job,* at **[www.youtube.com/watch?v=FzrBurlJUNk]**

Steve Croft, "The Case Against Lehman Brothers," *60 Minutes,* CBS News, April 22, 2012, at **[www.cbsnews.com/news/the-case-against-lehman-brothers-23-04-2012]**.

Martin Smith, "The Untouchables," *Frontline,* PBS, January 22, 2013, at **[www.pbs.org/wgbh/pages/frontline/untouchables]**.

"Martin Shkreli on Drug Price Hikes and Playing the World's Villain" at **[www.youtube.com/watch?v=2PCb9mnrU1g]**.

Trailer, *Atlas Shrugged* documentary movie **[https://youtu.be/L-cIEcBqgaA]**.

Jane Mayer, "Ayn Rand Joins the Ticket," *The New Yorker,* August 11, 2012, at **[https://youtu.be/L-cIEcBqgaA]**.

"Is Finland Really the Happiest Country in the World?" **[www.youtube.com/watch?v=9FPU4F-Ajh8]**.

Chapter 2

2009 Harvard MBA Ethics Oath, *The Daily Show with John Stewart* **[www.cc.com/video-clips/dc3rq6/the-daily-show-with-jon-stewart-mba-ethics-oath]**.

Trailer, "The Company Men" **[youtube.com/watch?v=Pie66GR63Fc]**.

Carol Gilligan's theory, see **[www.youtube.com/watch?v=HctzZwwueL4]**.

Trailer, *Wall Street: Money Never Sleeps,* at **[www.youtube.com/watch?v=HcMFA2SHES4]**.

Chapter 3

Senator Bernie Sanders' brief 2016 speech criticizing corporate tax loopholes at **[www.youtube.com/watch?v=Sknt-UBRhxo]**.

2004 movie documentary, *The Corporation,* at **[www.youtube.com/watch?v=xHrhqtY2khc]**.

Trailer, 2018 documentary, *Dark Money,* examining how "untraceable corporate money" influences the political process, at **[www.darkmoneyfilm.com]**.

Trailer for documentary, *Starving the Beast,* at **[www.starvingthebeast.net]**.

2014 Flashmob performance of Beethoven's Ode to Joy, at **[www.youtube.com/watch?v=a23945btJYw]**.

Trailer, 2014 movie, *Bhopal: A Prayer for Rain,* at **[www.youtube.com/watch?v=rO6xCAsv4s4]**.

Trailer, *Wal-Mart: The High Cost of Low Price,* at www.bravenewfilms.org/walmartmovie].

Chapter 4

FTX crypto commercial featuring Tom Brady, see: **https://youtu.be/4p4z2wsjhmM**
"What Is Mediation?", a brief overview of mediation and arbitration, at [**https://www.youtube.com/watch?v=DWgweDmDi2Q**].

Chapter 5

Trailer: *Loving*, movie, 2016: "**http://www.youtube.com/watch?v=zRXuCY7tRgk**
Trailer, 1996 movie, *The People vs. Larry Flynt,* at [**www.youtube.com/watch?v=fR6l4D47fW8**].
Trailer, 2016 feature movie, *Loving,* at [**www.youtube.com/watch?v=zRXuCY7tRgk**].

Chapter 6

A video of the Pepsi ad that was the basis of the *Leonard v. Pepsico* lawsuit [**www.youtube.com/watch?v=ZdackF2H7Qc**].

Chapter 7

Trailer for documentary movie, "Hot Coffee," at [**http://hotcoffeethemovie.com**].

Chapter 8

Trailer, 2018 Academy Award winning movie, *The Green Book,* at [**www.youtube.com/watch?v=QkZxoko_HC0**].

Chapter 9

Ship attempting to dock in 69 mph winds, at [**https://youtu.be/gclwCFpV5IM**].

Chapter 10

Trailer, *The Informant!* movie about the ADM whistleblower, at [**www.traileraddict.com/trailer/the-informant/trailer**].

Chapter 11

"Top Ten Disastrous Mergers and Acquisitions," at [**www.youtube.com/watch?v=9dFvhq2sKfM**].

Chapter 12

Trailer, *Deepwater Horizon,* at [**www.youtube.com/watch?v=8yASbM8M2vg**].

Chapter 13

Testimony on the disproportionate impact of COVID-19 on communities of color before the House Committee of Ways and Means on May 27, 2020, at [**https://waysandmeans.house.gov/legislation/hearings/disproportionate-impact-covid-19-communities-color-0**].
"People in All 50 States Show Up for BLM Protests," see [**www.youtube.com/watch?v=SG4LiBwtWCY**].

Chapter 17

Ray Anderson, 2009 TED Talk in which he shares his story, at **[www.raycandersonfoundation.org/butterfly-effect]**.

Trailer, 2015 documentary, *The True Cost,* at **[https://truecostmovie.com]**.

Trailer, 2019 movie, *Dark Waters,* at **[www.youtube.com/watch?v=RvAOuhyunhY]**.

Trailer, 2000 movie, *Erin Brockovich,* at **[www.youtube.com/watch?v=jjqUUxIy_yk]**.

Trailer, 1998 Disney movie, *A Civil Action,* at **[www.youtube.com/watch?v=fHRXGQhpib8]**.

NASA video showing the decline in Arctic ice cover at **[www.youtube.com/watch?v=qHE0n5c6-6g]**

2012 Sundance Film Festival documentary, *Chasing Ice,* at **[www.chasingice.com]**.

UNIT ONE

Business and Society

CHAPTER ONE

Capitalism and the Role of Government

After completing this chapter, students will be able to fulfill the following learning objectives:

1-1. Describe capitalism and its relationship to individual rights.

1-2. Discuss the theory and practice of privatization.

1-3. Compare and contrast capitalism and collectivism.

1-4. Differentiate between communism and socialism as collectivist philosophies.

1-5. Discuss the current state of capitalism in China and Russia.

1-6. Evaluate arguments regarding government's proper role in the American economy.

1-7. Describe the primary characteristics of a "mixed economy."

1-8. Analyze the impact of capitalism on equality, fairness, and community in American and global society.

1-9. Describe the income and wealth gaps in America.

Part One—Introduction

Capitalism is an economic system in which business and industry are privately owned and operated for profit.

What role, if any, should the law play in your business life? How much government does America need? Is capitalism, as currently practiced, the best economic system for the challenges facing American society? What, if any, are its moral implications? These themes–examining the relationship between government and business in America–are central to this text and especially this first chapter.

Personal freedom and private property rights, combined with extraordinary human and natural resources, ignited a great American economy. The United States is among the most competitive global economies in the world (measured for business climate, innovation, strength of public institutions, and so forth).[1] Particular strengths include our labor market, financial system, and entrepreneurial culture. In advising its clients, Goldman Sachs pointed to America's attractiveness to investors: the nation's vast natural resources (especially oil, gas, and arable land), a workforce younger and more energetic than those of our chief rivals, and our continuing leadership in innovation.[2] Noted *New York Times* columnist David Brooks summarized our fundamentally commercial nature:

> Walt Whitman got America right in his essay, "Democratic Vistas." He acknowledged the vulgarity of the American success drive. He toted up its moral failings. But in the end he accepted his country's "extreme business energy," its "almost maniacal appetite for wealth." He knew that the country's dreams were all built upon that energy and drive, and eventually the spirit of commercial optimism would always prevail.[3]

Unfortunately, this appetite for wealth also meant an increase in fraud, monopolistic behaviors, and abuse of employees, and government regulations grew, in part, to curb the power of big business. The proper balance between open markets and government intervention remains, perhaps, the foremost public policy debate in American life. The disturbing example of young entrepreneur and pharmaceutical executive Martin Shkreli, an eSports and music enthusiast sometimes referred to as "Pharma Bro," illustrates both the power and the limitations of the market.

Shkreli and the 5,000 Percent Price Rise

Despite building successful drug companies in his early 30s, Shkreli's exploitation of the drug market outraged the public and some members of Congress. In 2015, his company, Turing Pharmaceuticals, bought the rights to a 50-year-old, life-saving parasitic infection medication, Daraprim. Used largely to treat HIV patients, babies, and pregnant mothers, it can be produced for pennies per pill. Patients typically need two to three pills daily for a period of weeks or months. Seemingly overnight, Shkreli raised the Daraprim price from $13.50 to $750 per pill. He then called a journalist a "moron" for asking why the price was inflated so dramatically. Rejecting charges of greed, Shkreli said he cares deeply about others, and the price increase was necessary for research.

In a civil suit alleging he engaged in anticompetitive tactics that kept other manufacturers of the drug out of the market for 18 months after the price hike, he was ordered to pay over $64 million in damages. Among the plaintiffs in that action were the Federal Trade Commission and seven states, including New York and California. In 2022, Shkreli was released from federal prison after serving five years of a seven-year sentence for securities fraud (unrelated to Daraprim). He was ordered to pay $7.36 million in penalties to the U.S. government for that offense and reportedly spent some time in solitary confinement when authorities discovered he was using a contraband cell phone in prison to continue running his drug company, Phoenixus AG (formerly Turing).

Unfortunately, the price of Daraprim, which benefits only about 2,000 Americans annually, remains in the $790 per pill range (nearly $24,000 for a supply of 30 pills), even though the U.S. Food and Drug Administration approved the first generic equivalent in early 2020.

[For a 2016 interview with Shkreli, see "Martin Shkreli on Drug Price Hikes and Playing the World's Villain" at **www.youtube.com/watch?v=2PCb9mnrU1g.**]

Critics condemn other alleged indecencies in capitalist culture. Following the 2008 financial collapse, for instance, Wall Street banks paid tens of billions of dollars in penalties for their subprime-mortgages misconduct, currency manipulations, and other wrongs. Despite evident fraud, however, the banks and bankers proved to be "too big to jail." The government criminally indicted neither major banks nor their senior executives. In his recent, colorfully titled book, *The Chickenshit Club: Why the Justice Department Fails to Prosecute Executives,*[4] author Jesse Eisinger details a general decline in white-collar prosecutions–although occasionally big banks and high-level executives have been pursued.

Capitalistic greed and inequity are also evidenced by the $18.3 million average CEO salary in 2021 for the Standard & Poor's 500. This amount–representing an increase of 18.2% from just the year before (compared to an inflation rate of about 7%)–was 324 times the median earnings paid to their companies' workers; adjusting for inflation, workers' wages fell 2.4%.[5] This CEO-worker pay gap is illustrative of broader income and wealth gaps that continue to grow, contradicting a crucial pro-capitalist claim that a healthy market generates a rising economic tide, inevitably lifting the welfare of all.

Renowned French economist Thomas Piketty has attacked this pro-capitalist claim.[6] His careful analysis of historical data, while challenged by some, finds that the rate of return on capital investments has been, in general, several times larger than the rate of wider economic growth. Hence, the gap between rich (investors) and poor (wage earners) is likely to grow, presenting greater threats to social justice and even democracy itself.

While superior performance doubtless accounts for some of the resulting inequality, less defensible forces do seem to be at work. Economist Jonathan Rothwell and other experts point, for example, to government interference in the market. Rothwell has found that much of our income inequality stems from just three economic sectors–professional services, finance and insurance, and healthcare, all of which are significantly insulated from competition by government regulation.[7] Thus, laws–the core subject of this textbook–may, in some ways, *undermine* economic fairness. Perhaps it comes as no surprise to you that our laws often benefit primarily the rich.

> Markets are vital to efficiency and freedom.

Still, Piketty has acknowledged that markets are vital to efficiency and freedom, and there are some powerful moral arguments that favor capitalism. For example, the great capitalist investor Warren Buffet recently affirmed his own view of the fundamental morality of the capitalist system, acknowledging that it produces prosperity and progress, even if it also produces inequality and is sometimes managed by unprincipled actors.[8]

What Do We Hope to Accomplish with This Text?

To this point, we have explored some of the strengths of America's capitalist system and some of its moral challenges. The balance of this chapter more carefully examines the philosophical nature of free-market capitalism, the practice of privatization, and some of the recent economic challenges. It also introduces alternatives to the free market and asks where America's political economy is headed. Chapter 1 thus serves as a foundation for the book's detailed investigation of the following questions:

1. What are the proper ethical and social roles of business in American life?
2. How much government regulation of business, if any, is necessary to fulfill those roles?

Questions—Part One

1. Journalist and lecturer Richard Doak laments what he believes to be unfair and excessive pay to executives: "Executive greed has perverted risks, rewards. . . . The American system has been rigged to over-enrich those at the top."[9] What do you think? Is greed the culprit? Has the system been "rigged," or can we continue to count on the market to distribute pay properly? Explain.
2. The John Templeton Foundation asked several prominent thinkers the following question: "Does the free market corrode moral character?" Answer that question. [See **www.templeton.org/grant/markets-and-morality-do-free-markets-corrode-moral-values**.]
3. Do you think higher taxes on the rich would be the best solution for closing the wealth gap in America? Explain.
4. Scholar Robert Skidelsky applauds capitalism for overcoming scarcity, organizing production, and lifting many out of poverty, but he thinks capitalism, at least in rich countries like the United States, has also produced a culture where our main occupation has become the production and consumption of unnecessary goods. He asks, can capitalism succeed if it continues to produce "more of the same, stimulating jaded appetites with new gadgets, thrills, and excitements?. . . Do we spend the next century wallowing in triviality?"[10] What do you think?

Part Two—The Principles of Capitalism

LO 1-1
Describe capitalism and its relationship to individual rights.

We certainly cannot understand America's system of laws without a firm appreciation for the principles of capitalism from which those laws spring. We have embraced an evolving capitalist, democratic approach to life. Other cultures have placed less faith in the market and more in government planning.

In this chapter, we explore the full economic spectrum, moving from a laissez-faire, free-market approach on the extreme right to a brief review of command economy principles on the far left. Our attention will then rest on where the world is at this moment, with most nations practicing varying combinations of markets and government regulation, or *mixed economies*. We begin, first, with an examination of the pure free-market approach.

The Pure Free-Market Approach

The pure free-market approach assumes that we can operate our business system, and our society at large, free of all but foundational legal mechanisms such as contract and criminal law. The wisdom of the market—our individual judgments, in combination with our individual consciences—should "regulate" American life. Most forms of government intervention, including regulatory agencies, consumer protection, environmental rules, occupational licensure, zoning restrictions, antitrust law, and all but the most basic government services, would be eliminated.

Free-Market Solution to the Baby Shortage?

The following ad appeared in the *Stanford Daily* (Stanford University):

> EGG DONOR WANTED $35,000 (PLUS ALL EXPENSES) Ivy League Professor and High-Tech CEO seek one truly exceptional woman who is attractive, athletic, and under the age of 29. GPA 3.5+, SAT: 1400+.

Experts estimated that about 10,000 babies annually are born in the United States from "donated" eggs and about $80 million is spent on those eggs. Fees range from a few thousand dollars to $50,000 or more. The U.S. fertility industry is lightly regulated, but most industrial nations have banned paid "donations."

Questions

1. Barnard College president Debora Spar has said, "We are selling children."
   a. Is she correct? Explain your response.
   b. Should we be doing so? Explain.
2. A *Washington Post* headline read: "How the Rise of Commercial Surrogacy Is Turning Babies into Commodities."
   a. Does capitalism encourage us to treat people as products? Explain.
   b. Are people, in fact, products? Explain.

Sources: Claire Achmad, "How the Rise of Commercial Surrogacy Is Turning Babies into Commodities," *The Washington Post,* December 31, 2014 [**www.washingtonpost.com**]; Jim Hopkins, "Egg-Donor Business Booms on Campus," *USA TODAY,* March 16, 2006 [**www.usa.com**]; and Tamar Lewin, "Egg Donors Challenge Pay Rates, Saying They Shortchange Women," *The New York Times,* October 16, 2015 [**www.nytimes.com**].

Should We Downsize Government?

Should America shrink the size of government? What combination of capitalism and government best serves the needs of America and the world? Substantially open markets have shown themselves to be the stronger vehicle for productivity, efficiency, and personal freedom. Are open markets also the stronger vehicle for improving living conditions for all citizens, for maximizing democracy, for discouraging crime and corruption, and for building strong communities? Are America and the world best served by the speed and efficiency of largely unrestrained markets, or do we still need significantly interventionist governments to correct the market's failures?

Ayn Rand and Objectivism

The controversial philosopher and novelist Ayn Rand (1905–1982) was an uncompromising advocate of capitalist, free-market principles. Rand's philosophy, labeled Objectivism, contends that only free-market principles can produce a rational, moral life. Her moral message is summarized in the challenging phrase, "The Virtue of Selfishness," the title of one of her books and an expression of her view that our own happiness is our highest moral purpose; rational selfishness–that is, maximizing one's own interests through reliance on reason and rejection of sacrifice–is the only path to a just, meaningful life. In every dimension of our lives, we should operate as traders, giving value for value. In doing so, all would be free to achieve their maximum capacity, and all would earn what they deserve–in other words, what the market rewards. We would have total responsibility for our own actions and no responsibility for others (except our children). Rand advocated complete individual freedom so long as we do not violate the rights of others.

Government and Objectivism

To Rand, the purpose of government is to protect individual rights. Therefore, the only necessary components of government are the police, the armed services, and the law courts. Governmental regulation of business would be dramatically reduced or eliminated. Agencies such as the Federal Trade Commission, the Federal Communications Commission, and the Food and Drug Administration would be eliminated. Free-market processes, along with individual and organizational morality, would guide decision making and provide the consumer protection currently afforded by those agencies. Similarly, market forces and charity would replace government in providing social security, education, welfare, and housing. Taxation would be voluntary.

Rand's Influence

Rand's views and her writing style are heavily criticized, and most philosophers are seemingly dismissive of her work, but she has been cited as a powerful influence by some of America's leading corporate and political figures, including former President Trump and many of his advisers. Her books, including *Atlas Shrugged* and *The Fountainhead,* are among the best-selling novels of all time. In fact, *Atlas Shrugged* is one of the most influential business books in history, and according to one national survey, over 8 percent of American adults had read it.[11]

[For the trailer of a 2011 documentary treatment of *Atlas Shrugged,* see **Atlas Shrugged Trailer - YouTube**.]

Big business leaders, who are often seen as villains of contemporary American life, are the great heroes in Rand's writings that champion selfishness and reject self-sacrifice. To Rand, big government suppresses individual rights and personal freedom and improperly transfers wealth from the highly productive to those who are less so. Commentator Stephen Moore explained Rand's *Atlas Shrugged* argument that big government threatens the creative and productive power of the market:

Big business leaders are the great heroes in Rand's writings.

> Politicians invariably respond to crises–that in most cases they themselves created–by spawning new government programs, laws and regulations. These, in turn, generate more havoc and poverty, which inspires the politicians to create more programs . . . and the downward spiral repeats itself until the productive sectors of the economy collapse under the collective weight of taxes and other burdens imposed in the name of fairness, equality and do-goodism.[12]

[See the Center for the Moral Defense of Capitalism at **www.moraldefense.com**. Former U.S. Speaker of the House, Paul Ryan, acknowledged an intellectual and inspirational debt to Ayn Rand. For an explanation, see Jane Mayer, "Ayn Rand Joins the Ticket," *The New Yorker,* August 11, 2012, at **www.newyorker.com**.]

Questions

1. Mark Zuckerberg and his wife Priscilla Chan announced in 2015 that they would donate 99 percent of their worth, amounting to about $45 billion, to charitable purposes. Similarly, the Bill Gates/Warren Buffett Giving Pledge asks wealthy people worldwide to give half or more of their money to philanthropy while they are alive. German billionaire Peter Kramer objected to these private gifts, which are incentivized by tax deductions, because the donors and their preferences take the place of the collective judgment of the state, which could otherwise capture at least a portion of that money in tax dollars. Thus, wealthy private Americans, rather than the government, determine what is good for the people. Should that donated money be in the hands of the government rather than the donors and their charitable foundations? Explain. See Jeff Guo, "Why a German Billionaire Says That Pledges Like Mark Zuckerberg's Are Really Bad," *The Washington Post,* December 2, 2015 [**www.washingtonpost.com**].

2. Sandy Banks, wrote in the *Los Angeles Times:*

   > The boys' faces brightened when they got to the front of the line. We're next! They'd been waiting to say it. But their smiles faded when another family was ushered in from the sidelines and slid into "their" Legoland ride. We'd been waylaid by the Premium Play Pass, Legoland's wristband version of the front-of-the-line pass.[13]

   Banks asked her readers what they thought of the fairness of paying to jump to the front of the line. Some said it was no different than flying first class or choosing to drive on a toll road. One thought the kids received a good lesson in the competitiveness of capitalism. Legoland in Carlsbad, California, said they sell only about 65 of the Premium Play wristbands daily, but those who buy them value the time saved.

   a. What do you think of the fairness of paying to jump to the head of the line at amusement parks?

   b. Do you think that drivers who pay more should be entitled to drive in a faster lane? Explain.[14]

3. Elementary schools sometimes ban tag, dodge ball, touch football, kickball, and other vigorous games from their playgrounds. One school banned touching altogether. Administrators fear physical injuries, students' reduced self-esteem, and lawsuits. As the *Los Angeles Times* editorialized, "It's hard sometimes to tell whether schools are graduating students or growing orchids."[15] Ayn Rand argued for reduced rules in life, thus relying on the market to address virtually all problems.

   a. Would you follow the rules approach or Rand's free-market approach in managing a playground? Explain.

   b. From Rand's free-market point of view, explain why we should reduce playground rules as much as possible, even at the risk of children being hurt.

Capitalism in Practice—Privatization in America and Abroad

LO 1-2
Discuss the theory and practice of privatization.

Should we sell our struggling postal system to private investors? Should we convert our interstate highway system into tollways that are leased or owned by private interests? What about "contracting out" our prison systems, schools, libraries, and parking lots? Should we turn military action over to private contractors who would replace U.S. troops? Should we replace public libraries with Amazon? In general, should we *privatize* as much as possible to increase efficiency, save money, and diminish the role of government in our lives?

Most commonly, privatization follows two patterns: (1) *contracting out,* where government, in effect, turns over a portion of its duties, such as garbage collection, to private firms and (2) the sale or lease of public assets, such as airports, to private parties. Privately operated prisons, now rather common across America, are a primary example of the privatization movement. Of course, privatization does bring worries about job losses, reduced services and responsiveness to consumers, corruption, and so on, but the underlying idea is that the market can make decisions more efficiently and effectively than government, while also maximizing personal freedom. [For a large database supportive of privatization, see **http://reason.org/areas/topic/privatization**.]

America's crumbling infrastructure is a prime area for privatization, because it requires trillions of dollars in investments for repairs, and taxpayers do not want to bear the financial burden. Several jurisdictions have turned to private companies or public–private partnerships to build toll roads or convert existing roads to toll arrangements. As would be expected, some of those projects have been highly successful, while others have led to bankruptcy.[16] Privatization critics worry about declining service, excessive tolls, too much profit for investors, pricing poorer drivers out of road access, and trading secure government jobs with benefits for low-wage private-sector jobs without benefits.[17] Nonetheless, issues with government funding are on the rise, suggesting that infrastructure privatization will continue.

A Bad Deal?

Can the government negotiate a bad deal? Consider Chicago, which leased four downtown parking garages to Morgan Stanley in 2006 for $563 million.[18] In 2008, the city entered another 75-year lease arrangement (more recently renegotiated) in which Morgan Stanley, along with other parties, paid about $1.2 billion upfront to control 36,000 parking meters, after which they raised rates.[19] An inspector general's report concluded that the parking meter lease was worth nearly one billion dollars more than Chicago received.[20] On the other hand, Morgan Stanley apparently overpaid for the garage deal and decided to turn the lease over to its lender, which subsequently sold its rights to another operator.

Challenging Moral Conventions

Privatization supporters envision major changes to daily life that challenge moral conventions. Some doctors and others, for example, argue for lifting the federal ban on organ sales as a way of addressing the current donor shortage. One recent but admittedly imprecise estimate is that some 30,000 Americans die annually from kidney failure because of the federal government ban on organ sales.[21] Critics, however, fear privatization would exploit the poor and vulnerable and discourage altruistic donors.

Firefighters Watch a House Burn

Rather than impose a fire tax, Obion County, Tennessee, contracts with local municipal governments to provide fire protection in rural areas. Those firefighters drew national attention in 2010 and 2011, when they allowed two rural family homes to burn to the ground because the families had not paid their $75 annual subscription fee to the city-operated fire department in nearby South Fulton. Apparently, no one was seriously injured in either fire. The homeowner in the 2010 blaze, Gene Cranick, said that he offered to pay the fee on the spot, but the fire department declined and engaged the fire only to the extent necessary to protect the property of a neighbor who had paid the fee.

Questions

1. Why did the fire department decline Cranick's money at the time of the fire?
2. Do you think the fire department should have extinguished the fire even though Cranick had not paid? Explain.
3. In 2012, South Fulton decided to respond to all reported fires and bill nonsubscribers $3,500 for the response. Do you think the new policy is an improvement over the original? Explain.
4. Should fire service be privatized across the nation? Explain.

Sources: Jason Hibbs, "Firefighters Watch as Home Burns to the Ground," *WPSD Local 6–News, Sports, Weather,* Paducah, KY, September 30, 2010 [**www.wpsdlocal6.com**]; Timothy W. Martin, "Putting Out Fires for a Fee," *The Wall Street Journal,* March 12, 2012 [**www.wsj.com**].

Putting aside efficiency and dollars for a moment, consider an interesting observation from writer and journalist Brian Alexander, who warns that privatization may convert us from citizens to mere customers who pay our water bill to a private company but no longer engage in thinking about, and participating in, the process of building a community, a state, or a nation. Our vital citizenship decisions would be reduced to mere consumer decisions.[22]

Abroad

Greece is pursuing the world's most aggressive privatization program. Facing a collapsing economy, Greece has been forced by its foreign lenders to sharply reduce government spending while also selling and leasing billions of euros of public property, such as land, ports, airports, roads, water and gas utilities, the national lottery, and banks. Whether the program will be economically successful and continue to serve the needs of the Greek people is unclear for years to come, but at this writing, some improvement is evidenced by a falling unemployment rate and a climbing GDP.

Questions

1. From the capitalist viewpoint, why is the private ownership of property necessary to the preservation of freedom?

2. Ayn Rand argued: "Altruism is incompatible with freedom, with capitalism, and with individual rights."
   a. Define altruism.
   b. Explain why Rand rejected altruism.
3. Responding to extreme drought conditions in 2015, California governor Jerry Brown ordered a mandatory 25 percent reduction in water use for most Californians. Commenting on the order, Steve Yuhas, a resident of the wealthy San Diego suburb Rancho Santa Fe, reportedly said: "[People] should not be forced to live on property with brown lawns, golf on brown courses or apologize for wanting their gardens to be beautiful. We pay significant property taxes based on where we live. And, no, we're not all equal when it comes to water."
   a. Should the wealthy be able to buy as much water as they wish? Explain.
   b. Explain Yuhas's argument that we're not all equal when it comes to water. See Rob Kuznia, "Rich Californians Balk at Limits: 'We're Not All Equal When It Comes to Water,'" *The Washington Post,* June 13, 2015 [**www.washingtonpost.com**].
4. *Governing Magazine* labeled golf courses "perhaps the most non-essential of the non-essential public services."[23] Studies show that payrolls for city-operated golf courses are about 13 percent higher than for privately operated courses.[24] Why do we subsidize golf, and should we continue doing so? Explain.
5. Assume the federal government removed itself from the purchase and maintenance of our national parks.
   a. Left to the private sector, what sorts of parks would develop under the profit incentive?
   b. Would Yellowstone, for example, survive in its present state? Explain.
   c. Make an argument that the federal parks are an unethical, undemocratic expropriation of private resources.
6. Assume the abolition of the federal Food and Drug Administration. How could the free market protect the citizenry from dangerous food and drug products?
7. Puritan leaders felt concern over the morality of merchants who sold goods at prices exceeding the goods' "worth." That concern was particularly grave when the goods were scarce or in great demand.
   a. Should our society develop an ethic under which goods are to be sold only "for what they are worth"? Explain.
   b. Can a seller make an accurate determination of worth? Explain.
   c. Does a product's worth differ from the price that product will bring in the marketplace? Explain.
8. Personalize the inquiry: Assume you seek to sell your Ford car for $10,000, that you know of several identical Fords in a similar state of repair that can be purchased for $9,000, and that you find a buyer willing to pay $10,000.
   a. Will you unilaterally lower your price, or direct the purchaser to the other cars? Explain.
   b. If not, have you acted justly? Explain.
9. Sports columnist Skip Bayless has argued for allowing university sports boosters to bid for the best football recruits: "Boosters should be allowed to entice recruits with whatever they want to offer–cars, signing bonuses, annual salaries, annuities." Do you agree?

Explain. See Skip Bayless, "Unleash the Boosters," ESPN.com, July 25, 2014 [**www.espn.com**]. We will examine this issue, along with historic NCAA rule changes adopted in 2021 allowing these payments, in our discussion of antitrust laws and restraints of trade in Chapter 10.

10. Gregg Williams, former defensive coordinator for the New Orleans Saints National Football League (NFL) team, was suspended by the league for one year as punishment for his alleged role in establishing a bounty system (known as "Bountygate") that paid players for injuring other players. Allegedly, many NFL teams had employed similar schemes. Williams has apologized for his "previous actions" and was subsequently hired as a defensive assistant for the Tennessee Titans for the 2013–2014 season. He was inducted into the Missouri Sports Hall of Fame in 2016. More recently, he served as interim head coach of the Cleveland Browns and as defensive coordinator for the New York Jets. In a free market, rewards for performance are helpful, both as an incentive and as a measure of contribution. Do you think bonuses for injuring opposing players should be permissible in the NFL? Explain.
11. Professor Robert E. Lane argued that the person who is motivated by the need for affiliation, rather than achievement, does less well in the market. Such a person is not rewarded as well as autonomous, achievement-oriented people.
    a. Is Lane correct? Explain.
    b. Is capitalism, in the long run, destructive of societal welfare because achievement is better rewarded than affiliation? Explain. See, Robert E. Lane, *The Loss of Happiness in Market Democracies* (New Haven: Yale University Press, 2000).
12. How would poor people be cared for in a pure free-market society?
13. Critic William Deresiewicz said, "Wall Street is capitalism in its purest form, and capitalism is predicated on bad behavior." Do you agree that capitalism is built on bad behavior? Explain. See William Deresiewicz, "Capitalists and Other Psychopaths," *The New York Times*, May 13, 2012 [**www.nytimes.com**].
14. James Shaw, Jr., disarmed a gunman at a Nashville, Tennessee, Waffle House in 2018. The gunman killed four people in the attack. Shaw dived toward the bathroom when the shooting started. With no other available exit, he took a momentary opportunity to run out of the bathroom and wrestle away the weapon. When asked about his motivation in advancing on the gunman, Shaw said: "I did that completely out of a selfish act. I was completely doing it just to save myself." Later he elaborated: "I'll say it again: I didn't really fight that man to save everybody else. . . . I took the gun so I could get myself out."
    a. Do you think acts that we label heroic are usually selfish in nature? Explain.
    b. When you help others, are your motivations primarily selfish or selfless? Explain. See Bill Chappell, "I'm Not a Hero," Says James Shaw Jr., Acclaimed as Hero of Waffle House Attack," *The Two-Way: National Public Radio*, April 23, 2018 [**www.npr.org**].

Part Three—American Capitalism Challenged

Since the fall of the Soviet Union and the general decline of communist influence, free-market reasoning has dominated worldwide economic discourse. Noted political theorist Francis Fukuyama argued in 1989 that capitalism and Western democracy had so thoroughly proven their worth that the debate about capitalism was over. Free-market liberal democracy, Fukuyama claimed, was so clearly triumphant that it would be the world's "final form of human government." Thus, he famously said, we are at the end of history. He has also acknowledged, however, the possibility of uncertainty and crisis that might lead to a "re-start" of history.[25]

Fukuyama's bold thesis continues to be widely discussed, but relatively recent events have called into question the victory of free-market liberal democracy. In particular, the COVID-19 pandemic, the subprime mortgage crisis and the Great Recession of 2008, the stunning power of the Wall Street banks and hedge funds, and globalization have shaken our faith in conventional capitalism. We will briefly touch on some of the recent economic turmoil to put doubts about the effectiveness and fairness of contemporary American capitalism in context. More details will follow in Chapter 2.

The COVID-19 Pandemic

During the COVID-19 pandemic, some big businesses and many small enterprises faced ruin. State and local governments were reeling from sharply reduced tax revenue and the heavy costs of dealing with the public health crisis. Clearly, the market alone could not adequately respond to the economic challenges, and the federal government intervened very quickly, pouring trillions of dollars in aid into America's crippled economy.

The Great Recession of 2008

In late 2008, America faced another financial crisis, one spurred not by disease but by financial markets seemingly near collapse. This situation was ignited by the subprime mortgage crisis, in which the nation's housing bubble burst and millions of Americans were no longer able to pay their home mortgages. Lending essentially froze. A powerful Wall Street investment bank, Lehman Brothers, went broke. Bear Stearns and Merrill Lynch, also Wall Street titans, faced failure and were sold. American and global financial markets panicked and appeared unable to correct themselves. Fearing another Great Depression, the George W. Bush and Barack Obama administrations flooded the market with cash, took on much of the debt held by endangered banks, and bailed out failing giants such as Goldman Sachs, General Motors, and Chrysler–companies deemed "too big to fail–through the Troubled Asset Relief Program (TARP).

Companies "too big to fail."

The ultimate cost of government expenditures to prop up the endangered economy was calculated at over $1.6 trillion. The study's authors, Alan Blinder and Mark Zandi, estimate that the government's interventions reduced the length of the recession and its job losses by about half, and its gross domestic product losses from 14 to 4 percent.[26] Critics, however, argue the bailouts were illegal extensions of federal power, dramatically increased the federal deficit, expanded the size of the federal government, set the stage for inflation, and encouraged other businesses to believe they, too, would be bailed out if necessary. Some critics also place much of the blame for the nation's housing-bubble burst on the federal government because of its policies encouraging banks to make loans to unqualified, low-income buyers.

[For a cynical look at the subprime bubble, see the trailer for the 2016 Oscar-nominated movie, *The Big Short,* at **www.youtube.com/watch?v=LWr8hbUkG9s**]. [For an overview of the Lehman Brothers banking collapse and a critique of the government's regulatory oversight, see Steve Croft, "The Case Against Lehman Brothers," *60 Minutes,* CBS News, April 22, 2012, at **www.cbsnews.com/video/the-case-against-lehman-brothers-2/**]. [For a critical examination of the broader financial meltdown, see the trailer for the 2011 Oscar-winning best documentary, *Inside Job,* at **www.youtube.com/watch?v=FzrBurlJUNk.**] [For an investigation of "why (few) Wall Street execs have been prosecuted for the financial crisis," see Martin Smith, "The Untouchables," *Frontline,* January 22, 2013, at **www.pbs.org/wgbh/pages/frontline/untouchables**.]

Banks "Too Big to Fail"?

> A bigger cushion in troubled times.

America's biggest banks were among the corporations deemed "too big to fail" during the subprime-mortgage crisis. Today, the four biggest American banks–JPMorgan Chase, Bank of America, Wells Fargo, and Citigroup–control about 42 percent of America's bank assets,[27] and their stability remains worrisome should the economy falter again. Some political leaders and economic policy experts favor breaking up the biggest banks, but reforms–including Federal Reserve rules requiring some banks to increase the amount of capital they hold (thus giving them a bigger cushion in troubled times)–have enabled the big banks to pass annual government "stress tests" indicating they may now be better situated to deal with disaster. The 2010 Dodd–Frank Wall Street Reform and Consumer Protection Act also includes provisions designed to reduce the likelihood of big bank failures.

Globalization

> "Globalization is undergoing a major crisis."

As French President Emmanuel Macron said in 2018, "Globalization is undergoing a major crisis."[28] In a "hyper-connected," "flat" world, we are all linked together in an economic and cultural intimacy scarcely imaginable a few decades back. Largely unanticipated challenges have emerged, including the rapid, global spread of COVID-19.

Donald Trump's 2016 presidential election, Brexit, and rising nationalism were, in considerable part, a backlash to globalization. The loss of American manufacturing jobs, flat or reduced wages, and the general redistribution of wealth from American and European working-class people to China and other low wage, developing nations have provoked this reaction. Critics lament the government's failure to better prepare citizens, particularly blue-collar workers, for the dislocations that have accompanied globalization, and the COVID-19 pandemic renewed arguments for rebuilding American manufacturing and reducing dependence on foreign nations, particularly China. However, some of the backlash may be misplaced. Deindustrialization, automation, and other factors have also challenged western economies.

In a positive light, globalization has significantly elevated living standards while facilitating an unprecedented sharing of cultures and lifestyles around the world. Consumers everywhere have benefited from better, cheaper products.

Is Faith in American Capitalism in Decline?

Steven Pearlstein, *Washington Post* columnist and George Mason University professor, recently raised concerns about our contemporary economy in his book: *Can American Capitalism Survive?: Why Greed Is Not Good, Opportunity Is Not Equal, and Fairness Won't Make Us Poor.*[29] Pearlstein supports capitalism, but he thinks changes are necessary. Jamie Dimon, capitalist icon and JPMorgan Chase CEO, warned in his annual letter to investors that "something

> "Is Capitalism worth saving?"

is wrong" in America, even though our nation is "exceptional."[30] *Vox Magazine* in early 2019 pointedly asked: "Is Capitalism Worth Saving?"[31] *Vox* reports that Americans' belief in the free-market economy fell from 80 percent a decade ago to about 60 percent today.[32] As we document later in this chapter, young people, in particular, seem to be losing faith in capitalism.

Some critics attribute the nation's problems to fundamental flaws in capitalism and in the American character. Michael Moore's 2009 documentary movie *Capitalism: A Love Story* assails capitalism as "evil."[33] Moore was questioned about his movie:

> *Wall Street Journal:* Why call the movie "Capitalism: A Love Story?" You don't seem to love very much about capitalism.
>
> Moore: It is a love story about the well-to-do. They happen to love their money very much. Now they love our money and they want all our money and our homes. It's about their love.[34]

Globally, the power of markets has not always produced democracy, as events in China, Russia, and the Middle East have demonstrated. Donald Trump's ascendance to power in America seemed to spring, in part, from doubts about the success and fairness of free-market liberal democracy. Those nationalist/populist sentiments favoring the "common people" and pushing back against the "elite" have also blossomed in other democratic strongholds, including the United Kingdom, France, Italy, Spain, and Austria.

Questions

1. Critics argue that the growing economic gap between the wealthy and all other Americans has resulted in a "rigged" economy that unfairly favors the wealthy and the big corporations.
   a. Do you agree? Explain.
   b. Does that economic gap threaten American democracy? Explain.
2. Quoting a fourth-century bishop, Pope Francis in 2015 referred to the unfettered pursuit of money as "the dung of the devil," but some months thereafter he referred to business as "a noble vocation, directed to producing wealth and improving the world."[35] As you study business, do you think you are primarily preparing yourself for an honorable, productive role in life or for the "evil" pursuit of money? Explain.
3. The John Templeton Foundation asked several prominent thinkers the following question: "Does the free market corrode moral character?" Answer that question. [See **www.templeton.org/grant/markets-and-morality-do-free-markets-corrode-moral-values.**]
4. Scholar Robert Skidelsky applauds capitalism for overcoming scarcity, organizing production, and lifting many out of poverty, but he thinks capitalism, at least in rich countries like the United States, has also produced a culture where our main occupation has become the production and consumption of unnecessary goods. He asks whether capitalism can succeed if it continues to produce "more of the same, stimulating jaded appetites with new gadgets, thrills, and excitements?. . . Do we spend the next century wallowing in triviality?"[36] What do you think?
5. Thomas Hoenig, a former member of the board of directors of the Federal Deposit Insurance Corporation, observed: "[Americans] realize that more must be done to address a threat that remains increasingly a part of our economy: financial institutions that are 'too big to fail.'"[37] Do you agree that our concentrated financial sector is a threat that must be addressed? Explain.

Part Four—Collectivism: Increase Government?

LO 1-3
Compare and contrast capitalism and collectivism.

The term *collectivism* embraces communism, socialism, and associated philosophies on the left side of the political/economic spectrum. Collectivist systems feature economic cooperation and varying degrees of centralized ownership and control of the means of production, as contrasted with capitalism's economic individualism and political freedom.

Communism

Although China, Cuba, North Korea, Vietnam, and Laos continue to practice communism, the balance of the world has clearly rejected Marxist–Leninist totalitarianism. Notably, China has embraced free-market practices under a communist regime.

Communist Principles

Karl Marx, despite fatal errors in his theory and his many flaws as a human being, is among history's most influential thinkers. For our purposes, his central message concerns the severe abuses that can accompany unrestrained capitalism. In fact, Marx was particularly concerned about the growing imbalance between rich and poor–an issue increasingly familiar to Americans. He also believed the pursuit of wealth and self-interest would erode society's moral core. More broadly, he espoused an economic interpretation of societal development: "the mode of production in material life determines the general character of the social, political, and spiritual processes of life."[38] Marxist principles embody a core promise of economic justice; centralized government decision-making, along with full or partial government ownership and control of the means of production, is employed to achieve economic fairness.

> Severe abuses can accompany unrestrained capitalism.

Marx's philosophy was later embraced by totalitarians, most notably Joseph Stalin in the Soviet Union and Chairman Mao in China, both of whom took millions of lives through dictatorial implementation of their versions of communism. [For an introduction to Marxist thought, see **www.cla.purdue.edu/English/theory/marxism**.]

Was Marx Correct in Some Ways?

The Economist has pointed to some of Marx's criticisms of capitalism: (1) Capitalists basically expropriate the wealth of others; (2) Capitalism is global by its nature and thus must "nestle everywhere, settle everywhere, establish connections everywhere"; (3) Capitalism has an inherent tendency toward monopoly; and (4) Capitalism produces an army of laborers basically scrambling from one job to another. *The Economist* also noted that "Marx's errors far outnumbered his insights."

Question

1. Do you agree with these assertions? Explain your answer.

Source: "Second Time, Farce; Reconsidering Marx," *The Economist,* May 5, 2018 [**www.economist.com**].

Cuba

Fidel Castro, communist leader of the 1959 Cuban Revolution and long-time Cuban president, died in 2016. Fidel's brother, Raul, assumed the presidency from 2008 until 2018, while also serving as the first secretary of the Communist Party–the most powerful figure in Cuban life–from 2011 until 2021. A new constitution was overwhelmingly approved (although critics claim the election was undemocratic) in 2019. In it, the roles of communism and socialism are affirmed, but for the first time in the communist era, the right to private property is officially recognized, and foreign investment is encouraged. Centralized economic planning and state dominance over the means of production are retained in the new constitution.[39] Planned market reforms have been slow in emerging, but Cubans are allowed to buy and sell houses and used cars freely. Cubans own cell phones and other electronic devices, Internet access is expanding, state land is being distributed for private farming, and private-sector jobs such as scooter mechanic, barber, and produce vendor are increasing. While restaurants, snack bars, and other small shops began springing up, the government placed at least a temporary halt on issuing licenses for some of those opportunities.

Most of the more than 11 million Cubans continue to lead spare, government-supported lives, much of the nation is in physical decline, and political liberty is nonexistent, although open disagreement with government policy seems to be growing. Standing in line for government rations, food, banking service, and almost everything else remains a fact of life. Nonetheless, Cubans value the security provided by communism. Gangs, guns, and drugs are uncommon in even the most impoverished neighborhoods. Cuban life expectancy and literacy are comparable to those in developed nations.

Everyone is cared for in Cuba, but maintaining satisfactory health and education services looks to be very difficult in a struggling economy. Opening trade relations with the United States during the Obama years helped Cuba considerably, especially in the tourism industry, but the Trump administration partially rescinded the Obama-era ties to Cuba. American travel to the country, in particular, is now much more restricted. As of this writing, tourism is prohibited.

Socialism

LO 1-4
Differentiate between communism and socialism as collectivist philosophies.

Communism appears to have largely run its course, both philosophically and pragmatically, but the problems that generated its appeal–poverty, oppression, the gap between rich and poor, and so on–remain. Socialism seeks to attack these problems without engaging in communist extremism. Socialism is often associated with democratic governments and peaceful change, rather than the totalitarianism and violent revolution that have characterized communism.

Historically, collective ownership of the means of production was a central socialist remedy for societal problems, but today's democratic socialists tend to accept private property and market-based economic practices, while calling for government intervention to correct the market's failures. Contemporary democratic socialist governments, therefore, are likely to be directly involved in economic planning–regulating growth, inflation, and unemployment, and using progressive taxation that results in redistribution of income.

In the contemporary Western world, Germany, Norway, Denmark, Sweden, South Africa, Finland, and France are among the nations where democratic socialist principles have maintained a significant presence.

Traditional Socialist Goals

A critical distinction between socialists and capitalists is that the former believe a society's broad directions should be carefully planned, rather than left to what some consider the whim of the market. Socialists are convinced that the free market is simply incapable of meeting the needs of all segments of society. The traditional socialist agenda, which is embraced to varying degrees by today's democratic socialists, includes these elements[40]:

1. **Liberty.** To the capitalist, individual freedom suffers under socialism. To the socialist, the freedoms of capitalism are largely an illusion, accessible only to the prosperous and powerful.
2. **Social welfare.** Socialists reserve much of their concern for the harsh conditions of the lower class–poverty, exploitation, cultural deprivation, and more. Socialists believe that the economy must be guided by the government toward the general interest, rather than left free to expand the welfare of successful capitalists. Hence, socialists tend to tolerate high taxes in order to provide income supports, free education, free health care, generous sick pay, family planning, and the like, to correct what they believe to be the failures of capitalism.
3. **Fulfilling work.** Socialists object to the harshness of working life, in which a large segment of society is chained to degrading labor.
4. **Community.** Socialists seek a communitarian approach to life, such that the excessive individualism of capitalism is muted by a concern for the welfare of all.

All humans are equally meritorious.

5. **Equality.** Class distinctions are anathema to the socialist. All humans are equally meritorious, and distinctions among them are inherently unjust.
6. **Rationality.** Socialists fear the "irrationality" of a society based on competition and unrestrained pursuit of industrial growth.

Young Socialists in America?

As we noted in the beginning of this chapter, Americans–and especially young people–seem to be losing confidence in capitalism. A 2018 poll of Americans between ages 18 and 29 found 45 percent holding a positive view of capitalism, while 51 percent felt positively about socialism. In a 2021 poll, 60 percent of Americans, overall, had positive views of capitalism, and 38 percent felt positively about socialism.

Certainly, we are not on the cusp of a socialist revolution, but many young people seem to think a form of democratic socialism that retains a less harsh free-market system and asks more of government, may be more effective than our current approach to attacking social problems, including our young people's economic prospects. What do you think?

Sources: Frank Newport, "Democrats More Positive About Socialism than Capitalism," *Gallup,* August 13, 2018 [**https://news.gallup.com**]; Jeffrey M. Jones, "Socialism, Capitalism Rating in U.S. Unchanged," *Gallup,* December 6, 2021 [**https://news.gallup.com**].

Coping with Capitalism—China and Russia

China

LO 1-5
Discuss the current state of capitalism in China and Russia.

China, firmly committed to communist principles, practices what is officially called "Socialism with Chinese Characteristics" and is sometimes labeled "state capitalism."

Economics

The Chinese government is the nation's dominant economic force, as it maintains state enterprises and intervenes in, and shapes, the market to further the state's political goals. The result has been something of an economic miracle, as China has blended its large system of state-owned enterprise with the explosive power of the free market (guided by the government) to become the globe's first- or second-ranking economy (behind the United States), depending upon the measurement employed.

State-owned firms account for about 25 percent of the Chinese economy, particularly in vital and high-profit industries.[41] China routinely affirms its commitment to private-sector growth as well as open markets for western firms, but reforms seem to have stalled.[42] The government is apparently trying to acquire a greater direct voice in the nation's biggest tech companies. Still, China's economic growth has produced notable results, as *The New York Times* summarized:

> China now leads the world in the number of homeowners, internet users, college graduates, and, by some counts, billionaires. Not so long ago, three-quarters of its population endured extreme poverty: Now it's less than 1 percent.[43]

The Fortune 500 list of global corporate giants now includes 145 Chinese companies, more than any other country, although their average profit ($4.1 billion) is less than the global average ($6.2 billion) and 2.5 times less than that of the American firms.[44] And China is aggressively expanding its worldwide commercial and political influence. China's One Belt, One Road initiative involves trillions of dollars in loans and investments to fund infrastructure projects, including roads, harbors, and railroads in some 70 mostly underdeveloped nations around the world. China hopes to knit together a global trading network, as it also builds its military and offers other countries an alternative to western-dominated capitalism.

Challenges Notwithstanding its remarkable progress, China and its 1.4 billion people face significant problems, including reduced economic growth (but still averaging three to six percent or more annually), rising labor costs, crippling pollution and corruption, a shrinking working-age labor pool, and a slower-than-hoped-for transition toward a consumer-driven growth model. Of course, COVID-19 apparently originated in China, casting a shadow over trade, travel, and other global interactions.

Politics

Law From a Western perspective, an underdeveloped ingredient in Chinese economics and governance is the stability, predictability, and fairness that comes with a comprehensive, broadly respected legal structure. China has made progress in creating a creditable legal system, but a great deal of work remains, particularly in addressing the problem of offering one set of laws for citizens and another for the Communist Party.[45]

Chinese legal protection for intellectual property is particularly vital to American business interests. China has both cybersecurity and intellectual property laws, but reluctant enforcement leaves American businesses vulnerable. Pirated movies and video games, software and trade secret theft, patent infringement, and counterfeiting fashion designs are commonplace Chinese business assaults on American interests.

Freedom Government repression remains routine in China. The government controls the media, as evidenced by censorship battles between the Chinese government and Internet news sources such as Google and *The New York Times,* as well as social media sites such as Facebook and Twitter, each of which is blocked to the Chinese public as of this writing. China uses its "Great Firewall" of Internet censors to filter search results, particularly those addressing politically sensitive themes such as official corruption, democracy, Hong Kong, Tibetan freedom, Taiwan, and the 1989 Tiananmen Square crackdown (during which troops killed many protesters engaged in pro-democracy demonstrations in Beijing).

China uses its "Great Firewall" of Internet censors to filter search results.

Religion While the Communist Party is officially atheist, the Chinese government permits religious practice, but that practice is subject to government approval and is expected to be submissive to the Communist Party. Christian religious services in unregistered "underground" or "house" churches are forbidden, and those churches are sometimes forced to close. In 2018, the government banned the online sale of the Bible. In western China, Muslim Uyghurs are reportedly subject to a government campaign of religious suppression, cultural destruction, labor camp "re-education," and even genocide.

Social Credit To further its official goals of trust and social stability, China's government is building a nationwide surveillance network to monitor the behavior of businesses and citizens, with the goal of a massive social credit (reputation) system that rewards good deeds and punishes disfavored deeds. Technology monitors individuals' conduct from the mundane (jaywalking and horn-honking) to the revolutionary (the Uyghur separatist movement).[46]

China has rejected calls to guarantee freedom of speech.

Reforms? Although China has rejected calls to guarantee freedom of speech and move toward democracy, the Communist Party leadership reportedly recognizes the need for some forms of change. Curbing corruption in a nation in which bribes are routine is a major element of President Xi's reform efforts. Drug use, gambling, and even golf (seen as a millionaires' playground and a convenient breeding ground for insider deals and official graft) are among the government's crackdown targets. At the same time, presidential term limits have been abolished. Mr. Xi is now allowed to remain president indefinitely, and recent constitutional changes have firmly entrenched Communist Party power.

Even as the government attacks corruption and misconduct, it appears to be stifling citizen dissent. For example, in 2017, President Xi called for universities to become "strongholds that adhere to party leadership."[47] Government observers are sent to universities to monitor classroom fidelity to Party ideology. [For the latest Chinese news, see **http://thebeijingnews.net.**]

Relationship with the United States

United States' dominance in global trade and economic affairs has receded in recent decades, in significant part because of China's remarkable emergence. The Trump administration responded by engaging in a trade war with China and by more directly confronting China's unfair trade practices. The consequences of those actions remain to be seen, but in recent years China's state capitalism has, in some ways, outperformed America's democratic capitalism.[48]

> Can we build a comfortable, mutually sustainable economic and political future?

Can the two countries build a comfortable, mutually sustainable economic and political future? The Chinese people mistrust American global intentions and policies and see a new day approaching. According to a 2015 survey, 67 percent of Chinese respondents said their country would replace, or already had replaced, the United States as the world's dominant power.[49] At the same time, the United States is favorably viewed, at least among the young. They admire America's free-speech tradition, and they are avid consumers of American movies, music, professional basketball, and other forms of popular culture.[50] Perhaps the current American-Chinese geopolitical rivalry is unavoidable; American fear of Chinese dominance may be inflated, as suggested by civics educator and author Eric Liu:

> America has an enduring competitive advantage over China: America makes Chinese Americans; China does not make American Chinese. China does not want to or know how to take people from around the world, welcome them, and empower them to change the very fabric of their nation's culture.[51]

But Liu, the son of Chinese immigrants, says that America can profit from a "corrective dose" of Chinese values. He argues that Americans suffer from excessive individualism, short-term thinking, and exalting rights over duties–qualities that might be improved by embracing Chinese values of shared responsibility, long-term thinking, humility, and others. Liu says that Chinese culture can bring to America "a better balance between being an individual and being in a community."[52] Do you agree with Liu?

Russia

Russia's future economic success is intimately tied to its political processes. The state needs to win over foreign investors, but those investors fear political tyranny and domestic corruption. According to *Transparency International,* Russia is the world's most corrupt major economy, ranking 136th out of 180 countries (ranking 1st meaning the least corrupt).[53]

Economics

Russia's commodity-based economy has struggled for the past decade as oil and natural gas prices have stalled worldwide and Western nations have imposed economic sanctions on Russia for its Crimean annexation and its intervention in Ukraine. Given its nuclear, military, and geopolitical might, we would expect Russia to be a dominant economic power, but in fact, the Russian economy, in nominal terms, is a bit smaller than that of Canada or Texas. The national economy was projected to contract by 6% in 2022 and is expected to remain anemic in years to come, facing what some economists have termed "economic oblivion" because of international sanctions, the exit of foreign firms, loss of long-term oil and gas markets, and diminished access to technology and other imports.[54] The average real income for Russians has been in decline for several years. Life expectancy at birth has ranked 153rd in the world.[55]

Politics

Russia exhibits democratic features, such as elections and multiple political parties, but in practice, President Vladimir Putin and his allies exert authoritarian dominance on all important matters. Freedom of speech and assembly have been curtailed, and honest treatment by the legal system often is missing. Chilling numbers of journalists and other dissenters have been imprisoned or found dead.

Former Soviet Union Notwithstanding Russia's struggles, Western visitors to modern Moscow must be hard-pressed to imagine that this energetic, consumption-happy, competitive city was once the global center of communism, the dour capital of the Union of Soviet Socialist Republics (USSR), and the home of America's primary nuclear enemy. After the fall of the USSR and the ideological defeat of communism, Russia was pushed by America and Europe toward rapid privatization. Russia developed its own form of state capitalism, featuring a new reliance on market forces blended with state intervention and direction, including extensive nationalization of industry and comprehensive economic planning. The Russian government controls about 55 percent of the nation's economy,[56] a presence that many economists believe must be reduced if Russia is to increase foreign investment and achieve a vibrant economic future.

Crony Capitalism Russia's rapid privatization program, lacking legal and regulatory institutions to guide it, opened the door for politically well-connected, super-rich oligarchs and criminal elements to capture big pieces of the economy. Thus, in some respects, Russia is still a developing nation, but it remains a superpower in terms of nuclear weaponry and rocketry and in its very formidable national natural resources.

Relationship with the United States

Russian American journalist and author Masha Gessen argues that "Russia is remaking itself as the leader of the anti-Western world."[57] Russian military intervention in Ukraine and Syria intensified concerns about Russian global intentions. A 2019 Pentagon study concluded that the United States is failing to fully counter Russia's efforts to undermine democracy in the United States and elsewhere. Russia's intervention in America's 2016 elections through cyberattacks, organizational interference, and disinformation demonstrated its determination to sow discord and achieve increased influence across the globe. The Pentagon report also noted the risk that Russia and China may become more closely aligned, which would raise grave risks for the United States.[58]

"Russia is remaking itself as the leader of the anti-Western world"

A Clash of Values Anti-Americanism is a common sentiment in Russia, a view that seems to be encouraged by the Russian government. President Putin and his government defend "traditional values," while fending off the "tolerance" and "diversity" of Western nations and the United States in particular. Gay rights are a matter of special concern in Russia. Recent legislation bans the "propaganda of nontraditional sexual relations" and imposes fines for holding gay pride rallies or providing information about the gay community to minors.[59] The Russian people express general support for President Putin, but critics question whether state capitalism as practiced in Russia can succeed in the face of political repression, routine corruption, and abuse of the rule of law.[60]

Questions

1. In assessing emerging economic trends, technology entrepreneur and academic Vivek Wadhwa asked, "Does China own the future–or does the United States?"[61] Answer Wadhwa's question.
2. Can China maintain its closed, centrally controlled political system while enjoying the benefits of its somewhat open economic markets? Explain.
3. *New York Times* columnist David Brooks wrote recently about Russia's great intellectual and spiritual traditions (think of Tolstoy, Dostoyevsky, and Chekhov):

   > The Russian ethos was not bourgeois, economically minded and pragmatic. There were radicals who believed that everything should be seen in materialistic terms. But this was a reaction to the dominant national tendency, which saw problems as primarily spiritual rather than practical, and put matters of the soul at center stage.[62]

   Today, Brooks thinks Russia's cultural impact has been diminished, as grasping for power and money have become dominant motives. In adopting elements of a more market-based economy, has Russia (as with capitalist nations) doomed its intellectual and spiritual life? Explain.

Part Five—Middle Ground? A Mixed Economy ("The Third Way")

LO 1-6 Evaluate arguments regarding government's proper role in the American economy.

LO 1-7 Describe the primary characteristics of a "mixed economy."

Pure communism has failed. Socialist principles, to the extent they require central planning, bloated bureaucracies, and restraints on personal freedom, are discredited. The state capitalism of China, Russia, and other nations has little appeal in America and Western Europe, and yet America's brand of free-market capitalism lost a great deal of luster following the Great Recession of 2008. Some left-of-center combination of free-market and welfare-state principles may be the next step. For years, the Nordic states of Sweden, Norway, Denmark, and Finland (Iceland might also be included) have practiced a form of market socialism (or social democracy) with such success that it has been labeled a "Third Way" between the harsher extremes of capitalism and communism. Their welfare states have provided generally healthy economic conditions with cradle-to-grave social care for all, in a system emphasizing the collective welfare over individual preferences. We should note, however, that the Nordic states are facing great challenges as welfare needs increase beyond the pace of economic growth.

Sweden

Life expectancy in Sweden as of 2022 was estimated at 83.33 years, as compared with 79.11 in the United States.[63] The government provides free or substantially free education, health care, childcare, parental leave, unemployment protection, and more. Incentives

Sweden provides free or substantially free education, health care, and childcare.

promote preferred behaviors. The government will pay, for example, 80 percent of a parent's salary (with a cap) for up to 480 days of paid parental leave per couple, with 90 of those days reserved for fathers. Budget concerns, however, have forced Sweden to cut back a bit in financial protections, such as public pensions and unemployment insurance.

Gender Equality

Sweden aggressively encourages gender equality.

Swedish schools strive to eradicate gender stereotypes. At Stockholm's "Egalia" (equality) preschool, for example, the staff avoids using the words "him" or "her" and addresses children as "hen" (an alternative to the male pronoun "han" and the female "hon") or as "friends." Children's books often feature gay couples, single parents, or adopted children; classics like *Cinderella* are shunned. Egalia's methods are controversial, even in Sweden.

Some Swedish theaters identify sexism in movies through the "Bechdel Test," which asks if the film in question has (A) at least two named female characters (B) who talk to each other (C) about something other than men.

Sources: Katy Scott, "These Schools Want to Wipe Away Gender Stereotypes from an Early Age," *CNN Health*, November 1, 2018 [**www.cnn.com**]; and "Putting 2017 Oscar Nominees to the 'Fun Home' Memoirist's Bechdel Test," Center Theatre Group, March 3, 2017 [**www.centertheatregroup.org**].

Taxes

To pay for its cradle-to-grave welfare benefits, high taxes are required. Sweden takes about 44 percent of its gross domestic product (GDP) in taxes. The United States, in contrast, has one of the developed world's lowest total tax burdens at about 27 percent of GDP.[64] To keep its economy healthy, Sweden has followed a policy of a comparatively low corporate tax rate of 22 percent, consistent with the U.S. rate of 21 percent at the federal level.[65]

Performance

Sweden's economy has been generally strong, although some strain has emerged in recent years. One of the results of that generally strong economy is a healthcare system that exceeds its U.S. counterpart on almost all performance measures, but costs less than half as much per person (although many Swedes are now supplementing state care with private insurance, often because of frustration over waiting times).[66]

Politics

Worries about high taxes and heavy welfare costs led the Swedes to turn, for a time, to center-right political leadership, resulting in tax cuts, reductions in welfare generosity, and expanded private enterprise. In recent years, the center-left had narrowly regained leadership until conceding defeat in the 2022 elections. Sweden's longer-term political course had been unclear as the economy slowed and welfare needs increased.

How to Explain Sweden's Success?

Active government intervention has been cleverly combined with free-market principles in Sweden. Swedish expert Nima Sanandaji argues, however, that Sweden's prosperity and social justice cannot be attributed to the nation's socialist inclinations. Rather, her research indicates that the Nordic nation's prosperity developed in periods when free-market principles were ascendant. Furthermore, centuries of commitment to healthy values including hard work, egalitarianism, and social cohesion have been crucial to Sweden's success.[67]

Could America Replicate Sweden's Policies?

We should remember that Sweden is a small, largely homogeneous nation. Replicating its policies in the United States would be difficult. And as noted, problems seem to be mounting for the Swedes. Far-right, anti-immigration political forces have gained significant strength. The country's admission of Middle East refugees, along with anger over alleged discrimination, crime, and expanding income inequality, are some of the challenges facing the nation. Some experts think Sweden will not be able to sustain its current welfare model given its aging population and increasing need for public services.[68]

Speeding Ticket

Businessman Reima Kuisla threatened to leave his homeland in Finland after he was fined about $58,000 for driving at 14 miles over the posted 50 miles per hour speed limit. Kuisla's steep fine was based on his 2013 income of more than $7 million. Finland and some other European nations impose progressive fines based upon income and/or wealth. Perhaps Kuisla felt better about Finland after an appeal, which resulted in a reduced fine of about $5,500.

Question

Would you favor penalties in America based on income and wealth? Explain.

Source: Editorial, "Can't Drive 55? Then Don't Make $$," *The Des Moines Register,* May 1, 2015, p. 14A.

American Capitalism in Europe?

LO 1-8
Analyze the impact of capitalism on equality, fairness, and community in American and global society.

Do the European Union and its 27 member nations have a better long-term vision for personal and societal welfare than the United States? Is America's more libertarian "cowboy capitalism" better adapted to meet global demands than the "coordinated, stakeholder capitalism," or "Third Way," characteristic of much of Europe? The evidence is mixed. In building entrepreneurial spirit, personal freedom, and personal wealth and income, the United States is the clear world leader, but the EU's powerful, 447-million-person bloc is an economic engine, in many ways competitive with that of the United States. For Europeans, however, quantity seems to be less important than quality. Europeans choose to work less than Americans and, as they see it, enjoy life more. Their economy is less flexible than ours and typically produces fewer jobs, but it is also less harsh. Universal healthcare, job protection, and strong unemployment benefits are part of the European identity. Of course, the EU also benefits from the security shelter provided in great part by America's military.[69]

Building a Union

From its inception, the EU successfully abolished trade barriers, energized markets, harmonized laws, and utilized a common currency (the Euro), while at the same time extending protection to farmers and other weaker economic entities. Money, in historically unprecedented quantities (nearly one trillion dollars), has been shifted from wealthy nations like Germany and France to struggling localities or nations like Poland to build infrastructure and support innovation, small businesses, transportation, training, and much more.[70] As a result, most European nations have been doing well. In recent years, however, a variety of problems have challenged the EU, including Brexit (see below), refugees from North Africa and the Middle East, nationalist and authoritarian resurgence in Hungary and other states, and economic sluggishness.

Slow Growth

Economic growth continues, but at a modest rate. Prior to COVID-19, EU unemployment had been declining and was down to about 6.3 percent (as compared with under 4 percent in the United States). Pre-COVID-19 youth unemployment (under age 25), particularly in southern Europe, was at crisis levels, with rates sometimes exceeding 30 percent in Greece, Italy, and Spain.[71] Those conditions may not improve a great deal in the near future. Certainly, the EU economy has not shown the entrepreneurial vitality that has marked the United States. Europe has many great companies, but as *The Guardian* observed in 2019, none emerged in the past 25 years; Europe does not have a Google, Facebook, or Amazon equivalent, and development initiatives in emerging technologies like artificial intelligence have been limited.[72]

France and Germany

Some nations have instituted austerity policies in the form of higher taxes and sharp cutbacks in government spending. In France, for example, significant government welfare cuts have been implemented, and privatization of state assets (such as the French National Railways) has been pursued, although resistance has slowed the process. Government spending of more than 50 percent of GDP had produced a protected population with strong family support, low poverty, and generous pensions, but for the present at least, the French government has concluded that some trimming is necessary.

Germany, on the other hand, has been able to balance a rather generous social safety net (long-term care, vacations, pensions, and more) with a very robust and highly skilled manufacturing sector. Government policies have produced job security and a comfortable life. Germany has managed its budget carefully, adopted reforms such as an increased retirement age, and maintained a strong market-based economy to support its social programs.

One measure of German excellence has been its ranking as the number one "brand" among nations. The rankings are built from interviews with over 20,000 people in 20 nations asking about their views of 50 leading nations based on governance, exports, culture, and more. The top eight nations, according to the 2022 Anholt Nation Brands Index, were (1) Germany, (2) Japan, (3) Canada, (4) Italy, (5) France, (6) United Kingdom, (7) Switzerland, and (8) the United States. The United States has often led the Index, but recent rankings in governance, in particular, have caused a decline.[73]

Brexit

Struggling to assimilate migrants, chafing under European Union regulatory oversight, and perhaps seeking a renewed sense of the United Kingdom as a proud nation-state, the British people voted by a narrow margin in 2016 to break from the EU ("Brexit"). After some 47 years of membership, the UK officially departed on January 31, 2020. Both Brexit in the UK and Donald Trump's political movement in America seem, in part, to be the result of deepening unease over globalization, which critics blame for the economic decline of blue-collar workers.[74]

Contrasting Values

Can the EU remain united? Can its system persist in a harsh, globalized world? Which vision of life–America's or Europe's–seems most promising over the long term? American commentator and social activist Jeremy Rifkin contrasted the American and European "Dreams"[75]:

American Dream	vs.	European Dream
Wealth/Individual success	vs.	Quality of life
Growth	vs.	Sustainable development
Property/Civil rights	vs.	Social/Human rights
Live to work	vs.	Work to live
Religiosity/Piety	vs.	Declining faith
Strong military	vs.	Build peace

Rifkin argues that the European "Dream" is the better one. What do you think? Which of these two lists of values is more comfortable and inspiring for you? Which is more likely to meet the demands of vigorous global competition, climate change, and race-relations evolution?

Is the Welfare State a Key to Personal Happiness?

Finland turns out to be the happiest place on Earth, according to a 2019 United Nations global study. The top five countries on the happiness list are European states with strong welfare principles: (1) Finland, (2) Denmark, (3) Norway, (4) Iceland, and (5) The Netherlands.

The United States ranks 19th on the UN list. Surveys show that only about one-third of Americans consider themselves happy. Why Americans consistently report rather low levels of happiness is unclear. Among other things, experts point to overly busy lives, decreasing trust, addictions, and financial struggles.

What qualities lead to happiness? Broadly speaking, good health, education, freedom, and wealth are associated with happiness. But wealth, at least for "average" people, seems to have a diminishing influence on happiness after incomes reach about $75,000 annually in the United States. On the other hand, a recent study suggests that the very wealthy (worth roughly $10 million or more) are modestly happier than those worth "only" one or two million dollars.

Community/Hygge

Why are the Scandinavian people particularly happy? Denmark has often been at the top of the happiness indices. Danes seek what they call "hygge," which may be thought of as coziness, intentional intimacy, trust, and the like. Simply "hanging out" with friends and family seems to be critical to happiness in Denmark. Ninety-two percent of Danes belong to some kind of social club, and the government encourages these get-togethers by helping to pay for them. Likewise, while Danes value nice things, they are said to be a "post-consumerist" society in which consumption is not a high priority. Their extraordinarily high taxes (around 50 percent of income) may also play a role in the happiness quotient, in that income is substantially leveled, allowing careers to be chosen more on the basis of interest, rather than money, and also allowing everyone to "hold his/her head high" regardless of occupational status. Finally, experts point particularly to the Danes' very high quotient of trust, which may be a product of the cradle-to-grave security provided by the government. Mothers, for example, commonly leave their babies unattended in strollers outside shops and restaurants. Of course, Denmark has the advantage of being a small, homogeneous nation largely free of America's worldwide responsibilities.

[For a skeptical view of Finnish happiness, see "Is Finland Really the Happiest Country in the World?" **[www.youtube.com/watch?v=9FPU4F-Ajh8]**.

Sources: Grant E. Donnelly and Michael Norton, "Even for the Very Rich, More Money Brings Happiness," *Wall Street Journal,* December 11, 2017 [**www.wsj.com**]; Josh Fiallo, "U.S. Falls in World Happiness Report, Finland Named Happiest Country," *Tampa Bay Times,* March 20, 2019 [**www.tampabay.com**]; Marie Helweg-Larsen, "Why Denmark Dominates the World Happiness Report Rankings Year after Year," *The Conversation,* March 20, 2018 [**https://theconversation.com**]; Christopher Ingraham, "Americans Are Becoming Less Happy, and There's Research to Prove It," *Los Angeles Times,* March 23, 2019 [**www.latimes.com**]; and Alexandra Sifferlin, "Here's How Happy Americans Are Right Now," *Time,* July 26, 2017 [**www.time.com**].

Questions

1. Billionaire investor George Soros, in his book *Open Society,* saw "market fundamentalism as a greater threat to open society today than communism." Soros feared contemporary capitalism's extreme commitment to self-interest, which results, he said, in our greatest challenge: "to establish a set of fundamental values."[76]
   a. Explain what Soros meant.
   b. Do you agree with him? Explain.
2. At a time when many Americans are questioning the free market because of societal problems like environmental damage and income inequality, Warren Buffett, Berkshire Hathaway CEO, regularly affirms his faith in capitalism, as he did at the 2019 shareholder meeting: "I believe we wouldn't be sitting here except for the market system. I don't think the country will go into socialism in 2020 or 2040 or 2060."[77] Do you agree that socialism is not in America's future? Explain.
3. Writing in *Dissent,* Joanne Barkan said, "[A]lmost all Swedes view poverty, extreme inequalities of wealth, and the degradation that comes with unemployment as unacceptable."[78]
   a. Do you agree with the Swedes? Explain.
   b. Why are Americans more tolerant of those conditions than the Swedes?

4. Scholars Daron Acemoglu, James A. Robinson, and Thierry Verdier have argued that the United States would hurt world growth if it adopted the "cuddly capitalism" of Scandinavia. For the United States to maintain its vital role as chief global innovator, Acemoglu and Verdier say that America must maintain an economic system that generously rewards successful innovators, which "implies greater inequality and greater poverty (and a weaker safety net) for a society encouraging innovation."[79] Do you agree? Explain.
5. *a.* Should an American citizen's primary duty be to themself, or to all other members of society? Explain.
   b. Should all humans be regarded as of equal value and thus equally worthy of our individual support? Explain.
   c. Can social harmony be achieved in a nation whose citizens fail to regard the state as a "super-family"? Explain.
6. According to a 2014 Pew Research survey examining opinions about the role of government, younger Americans (Millennials) favored bigger government and more services by a 53 to 38 margin, while older Americans (Gen X and Boomers) preferred smaller government and fewer services.[80] How do you account for that difference of views, by age?
7. In questioning Oakland Athletics general manager Billy Beane, the *Wall Street Journal* described professional football as "socialist" and baseball as "capitalist":

   > The NFL (National Football League) has been successful as a socialist league, equally divvying up the league's revenue among all the teams. Major league baseball, on the other hand, is a capitalist league, with a clear divide between big-market and small-market teams.[81]

   a. Do you think some of major league baseball's financial rules have to be changed to better balance the playing field? Explain.
   b. Is "socialism" or "capitalism" the better system for professional sports? Explain.
8. Swedes pay close attention to work-life balance. In 2017, Per-Erik Muskos, a politician, suggested that Overtornea, his small town in northern Sweden, with a dwindling population, should provide paid one-hour sex breaks for the town's approximately 500 employees. Muskos suggested that the one hour of the workweek already set aside for subsidized fitness activities could be devoted instead to sex. The town council rejected the proposal saying, among other things, that it was too much of an intrusion into personal lives. Do you think government policy in the United States should be more committed to encouraging and subsidizing desirable personal activities such as fitness, sex, family time, children's welfare, and so on? Explain. See Dan Bilefsky and Christina Anderson, "Swedish Town Rejects Plan to Let Workers Take a Break for Sex," *The New York Times,* May 18, 2017, p. A10 [**www.nytimes.com**].

Part Six—America's Economic Future: Where Are We Going?

How Much Government?

Should we maintain or expand our faith in free-market capitalism, or do we need to move our present mixed-economy a bit closer to the welfare state model, which itself is under great pressure? Or must a new model emerge? In sum, how much government do we need?

To help inform these questions, let's briefly examine some of the key indicators of America's economic and social health.

Good News

We are a prosperous country, although race and gender disparities are of great concern, and impacts from COVID-19 are as yet unknown. Median household income increased 21 percent between 1990 and 2018, and median household wealth rose 52 percent from 1990 to 2019.[82] The representation of women and minorities in political office, while still greatly disproportional to population, has improved meaningfully. Women now hold over 25 percent of Congressional seats, the highest percentage in U.S. history (as compared to two percent in 1965), and 29 percent of the seats in state legislatures (versus four percent in 1971). Minorities seated in Congress rose from 4 percent in 1966 to 22 percent in 2020.[83]

Much of the world strives to achieve America's blend of entrepreneurial capitalism along with intellectual and pop-culture leadership. And we should not forget that capitalist America is among the most generous of global cultures. Americans gave a record $410 billion to charity in 2017 and almost $485 billion in 2021.[84] Gallup polling data examining donations, volunteering, and aiding strangers ranked the United States first in the world in the decade from 2009 to 2018.[85]

The American Dream at Risk?

LO 1-9
Describe the income and wealth gaps in America.

America has strengths, but we are struggling in some important ways. Globalization and new technology, in the short run at least, have chipped away at our blue-collar job market. Labor unions have lost much of their power. Our multinational corporate giants often seem to be more interested in investing abroad than in America.

A 2019 Pew Research Center report found significant pessimism among Americans about what they think America will be like by the year 2050. Seventy percent are unhappy with the general direction of American life today; anxiety is increasing about retirement security, the impact of automation on jobs, and the cost of health care, among other things.[86]

American family income has stagnated for years, even though overall productivity is generally up. Wages for college graduates, averaging $51,347 for those graduating in 2019, rose only 14 percent between 1989 and 2019.[87]

The core of America–the middle class–and the very idea of the American Dream seem at risk. The portion of Americans living in middle-class circumstances declined from 61 percent in 1971 to 50 percent in 2021.[88] While the portion of upper-class Americans increased from 14 to 21 percent during that timeframe, the portion of lower-class Americans also increased from 25 to 29 percent.[89] And even though the portion of middleclass Americans remained relatively stable between 2011 and 2016 (ranging from 51 to 52 percent), the income disparity between the middle- and upper-classes increased.[90]

Overall Quality of Life

According to a U.N. 2018 report on overall quality of life (based on income, life expectancy, and education), America is doing relatively well, ranking 13th among all nations, with the Scandinavian and Western European nations generally leading the list.[91] A similar but broader study, the 2022 Social Progress Index, ranked the United States 25th in the world in general quality of life, with Norway at the top.[92] America ranked first in world-ranked universities and second in advanced access to education, but only 48th in personal safety, 33rd in inclusiveness, and 44th in nutrition and basic medical care.[93]

America ranks first in world-ranked universities.

Economics

Broadly, the United States compares well on standard economic measures, but not so well on standard social measures. Our estimated $59,800 GDP per capita in 2017 ranked 19th in the world behind smaller, more specialized economies, such as Liechtenstein (1st at $139,100) and Norway (11th at $72,100), but well ahead of our chief industrial rivals such as Germany (27th at $50,800) and Japan (42nd at $42,900).[94]

Well-Being

The United States leads the world in producing prisoners.

Among the most disappointing areas of U.S. social performance is infant mortality (the probability per 1,000 live births of dying between birth and age one). As of March 2023, infants in 54 nations have a better chance of survival than in the United States.[95] And the United States leads the world in producing prisoners, with nearly seven million incarcerated, on parole, or on probation.[96] That number has been declining in recent years, however.

A record 41 percent of households with children under 18 included a mother who is either the sole or primary source of income as of 2017.[97] Marriage itself is in decline, with 48 percent of American adults married in 2017, down from 58 percent in 1990.[98] The economically and socially productive institution of marriage with children is apparently becoming a luxury for growing numbers of Americans. In part because of fewer marriages, sexual activity is also declining. Even young people are having sex less frequently. Some experts think this suggests declining social connections, influenced perhaps by increasing time spent with video games, social media, pornography, and so on.[99]

Poverty

Prior to COVID-19, the number of Americans in poverty had been declining significantly, but 11.8 percent of the population, or about 38 million people, still fell below the official government poverty line ($25,750 annually for a family of four in 2019).[100] Economic insecurity often reaches even those who are working hard but at a low wage. About two-thirds of those living in poverty who are eligible to work are, in fact, working.[101]

A 2016 Stanford Center on Poverty and Inequality study ranked the United States 10th of 10 developed countries, on measures of poverty and inequality.[102] The result of these difficult economic conditions is that poor people, as commentator Paul Krugman explained, live in a separate America:

> Living in or near poverty has always been a form of exile, of being cut off from the larger society. . . . To be poor in America today, even more than in the past, is to be an outcast in your own country.[103]

Pets or People?

We may not take the best care of our disadvantaged fellow Americans, but we seem to be unstinting in generosity toward our pets. In 2018, Americans spent nearly $73 billion on their pets, a sum that exceeds the gross domestic products of all but about 70 nations.

Question

Would our money for pets be more wisely spent on impoverished children? Explain.

Sources: American Pet Products Association, "Americans Are Spending More on Pets than Ever Before," *PR Newswire,* March 21, 2019 [**www.prnewswire.com**] and World Bank Group, "GDP Ranking," *Development Data Hub,* 2019 [**https://datacatalog.worldbank.org**].

The Wealth and Income Gaps

Extravagant wealth, coexisting with punishing poverty, is perhaps the greatest disappointment and injustice from the critics' point of view, in the global advance of capitalist principles.

According to an Institute for Policy Studies report, America's three wealthiest people (Jeff Bezos, Bill Gates, and Warren Buffett) were worth more than the entire bottom half of the nation's population (over 160 million people), and the wealthiest 400 Americans owned more wealth than the nation's total African-American population.[104] On a global scale, the upper one percent controls about one half of the world's wealth.[105] The wealth gap is fueled by a giant divide in income earned. Fifty years ago in America, the ratio of CEO-pay to average worker pay, for example, was about 20 to 1.[106] Today, the average-CEO pay for Fortune 500 companies is 324 times the median earnings paid to their workers.[107]

Those wealth and income disparities raise concerns about a fundamental unfairness in American life that might undermine democracy and public health, reducing overall economic strength and social cohesion. These concerns might be diminished if the American Dream of upward mobility was flourishing, but the evidence suggests that such mobility has, at best, remained unchanged over the past half-century.[108] Further, a 2019 Georgetown University study indicates that Americans are better off being born rich than smart. The study found that 70 percent of kindergartners with low test scores but from wealthy families were affluent by age 25, while only 30 percent of kindergarten students with high test scores but from poor families reached affluence by their early adulthood.[109] From a free-market perspective, one would argue that the wealth and income gaps, to a significant extent, reflect productivity differences and are important spurs to excellence. [For a discussion of recent research challenging the mainstream findings on income inequality, see Thomas B. Edsall, "What If We're Looking at Inequality the Wrong Way?" *The New York Times,* June 26, 2013, at **http://opinionator.blogs.nytimes.com**.]

PRACTICING ETHICS Moral Decay in White Working-Class America?

What forces have caused the growing income and wealth gaps in America? Libertarian scholar Charles Murray, in his controversial book *Coming Apart: The State of White America, 1960–2010,* looked at the blue-collar, white working-class for some answers. He pointed to declining moral values in that group as a crucial factor in American inequality and reduced mobility. He provided evidence of an alarming fall in white working-class social capital (neighborliness and civic engagement), prompted by decreasing industry, community, religion, and marriage. Murray did not ignore similar problems in the Black working-class, but his focus was on white people.

Questions

1. Do you agree with Murray that the erosion of traditional middle-class morals and values helps explain inequality in contemporary America? Explain.
2. What other forces might have contributed to increasing inequality in American life?
3. Based on your personal sense of fairness, is a large and growing gap in income and wealth in America an ethical wrong? Explain.

Sources: Charles Murray, *Coming Apart: The State of White America, 1960–2010* (New York: Crown Forum, 2012); and Thomas B. Edsall, "What to Do about 'Coming Apart'," *The New York Times,* February 12, 2012 [**http://campaignstops.blogs.nytimes.com**].

Community

Spending money on others rather than on oneself produced greater levels of happiness.

Mounting evidence suggests that our lives are increasingly solitary, distant, and estranged. The market is driven by, and rewards, individual achievement. Could that capitalist struggle for material success be depriving us of the full satisfaction of our shared humanity? A 2013 study found that even trivial exposure to money can trigger unethical intentions and behavior,[110] while several recent studies suggest that spending money on others, rather than on oneself, produces greater levels of happiness.[111]

Whether a product of capitalist impulses or not, we do have evidence of declining social connections. Forty-six percent of Americans, according to a 2018 report, said they feel lonely sometimes or always, and younger adults were particularly lonely.[112] Only 30 percent of Americans, according to a 2008 study, reported having a close confidant at work, down from nearly 50 percent in 1985, and American workers report inviting only 32 percent of their "close" colleagues to their homes, while Polish and Indian workers report inviting more than double that percentage.[113] Similarly, Scandinavians, with their strong communitarian social welfare commitment, tend to be less troubled by social isolation than Americans.[114]

Only 30 percent of Americans reported having a close confidant at work.

Individualism Up, Morality Down?

Making use of giant, digitized databases such as Google Books, scholars can type a word in a search box and learn how frequently that word has been used in publications over the years. One study looking at 1960 to 2008 found individualistic words (such as "self," "standout," and "unique") increased in use over those 48 years, whereas communal words (such as "collective," "common," "good," and "band together") declined in use. Another study found that general moral terms (like "virtue," "decency," and "conscience") and words associated with moral excellence (like "honesty," "patience," and "compassion") receded in use over the course of the 20th century.

Questions

1. Do you see a link between increasing attention to individualism and declining attention to morality? Explain.
2. Do you think government can or should do anything about these changing social conditions? Explain.

Source: David Brooks, "What Our Words Tell Us," *The New York Times,* May 20, 2013 **[www.nytimes.com]**.

Shrinking Social Capital?

In his now-famous book, *Bowling Alone,* Robert Putnam meticulously documented the decline of what he labeled "social capital," the community and commitment bonds that seem to emerge in a culture where people regularly interact with one another.[115] Putnam's book explains that virtually every measure of social interaction, from voting to picnics to playing cards to church attendance to membership in social clubs, fell significantly from roughly 1975 to 2000. The most vivid example was a decline of 40 percent in league bowling from 1980 to 2000, although the total number of bowlers increased by about 10 percent—thus the notion of "bowling alone."

Recent evidence supports Putnam's findings. Much like bowling in previous years, today we find that movie viewing by teens is increasingly a solitary process or at least one not consumed in the shared space of a movie theater. Prior to Netflix, 70 percent of 8th and 10th graders went to the movies once a month or more, but today only about half do so.[116]

According to a 2019 poll, Americans overwhelmingly (82 percent) say that people in their neighborhoods get along well and are willing to help each other (75 percent), but only 51 percent actually talk to their neighbors weekly or more, and only 12 percent actually help their neighbors at least weekly.[117] Only one-third of Americans say most people can be trusted, down from one-half in 1972.[118] United States Senator Ben Sasse (R - Nebraska) in his 2018 book, *Them: Why We Hate Each Other–And How to Heal,*[119] points to loneliness and division in America and a resultant decline in civility. Sasse then argues that Americans should desist from demonizing their political opponents and instead join together in the common pursuit of freedom and justice. Do you think you are guilty of "demonizing" those who do not share your political views?

Questions

1. Is Putnam correct about declining social capital in America? Explain.
2. *New York Times* columnist David Brooks says that "excessive individualism" is eating away at Americans' "uniting faith," while damaging our relationships with each other. The result, he says, is that we are "distrustful and alone," opening the door to the identity politics and tribalism that divide Americans.[120]

PRACTICING ETHICS Technology and Loneliness

Since publishing *Bowling Alone,* Robert Putnam has said we need to develop new kinds of connections when old ones die. Electronic links often are considered part of the problem, but he believes they could also be part of the solution. Indeed, psychology professor Jean Twenge's analysis of survey results from one million American teens led her to conclude that the happiest teens are those who make use of digital media, but do so for only a limited amount of time.

The risks of extensive social media use are illustrated by a 2017 University of Pittsburgh national study of adults ages 19 through 32. The study found that "the more time a young adult uses social media, the more likely they are to feel socially isolated," and that "frequency of use was [also] associated with increased social isolation."[122] [Note that the study could not establish whether increased use *caused* social isolation or whether those who were already socially isolated made more extensive use of social media.]

Questions

1. On balance, do you think social media use builds social relationships or increases social isolation? Explain.
2. Facebook insiders acknowledged it was designed to be addictive. In your experience is that so? Is that strategy unethical? Explain.
3. How might our ethical standards and performances be affected by excessive reliance on social technology?

Sources: Tim Betler, "More Social Connection Online Tied to Increasing Feelings of Isolation," University of Pittsburgh Schools of the Health Sciences *Public Release,* March 6, 2017 [**www.eurekalert.org/pub_releases/2017-03/uops-msc022817.php**]; Catherine Price, "Trapped - The Secret Ways Social Media Is Built to Be Addictive (and What You Can Do to Fight Back)," *Science Focus,* October 29, 2018 [**www.sciencefocus.com**]; Jean Twenge, "What Might Explain the Unhappiness Epidemic," *The Conversation,* January 22, 2018 [**https://theconversation.com**]; and David Lee, "Facebook founding president sounds alarm," *BBC,* November 9, 2017 [**www.bbc.com**].

a. Do you practice "excessive individualism" or are you more communitarian in values and behavior?

b. Does it matter? Explain.

3. American Dan Lawton commented on his first trip to Africa:

> In Ghana, I have danced, eaten, and spoken with more strangers in six weeks than I would have in America in six years. And this paradox–that despite its material wealth and technological might America is so standoffish and lonely–has been burning a hole in my head.[121]

a. Do you agree that Americans are "standoffish and lonely"?

b. If so, do you have any explanation for that condition?

Too Much Capitalism? Or Too Little?

Has America placed too much faith in the market and too little in government? Is the alleged decline in community in some sense a product of capitalism itself? Are poverty, political corruption, and the Wall Street collapse inevitable by-products of a "selfish, greedy" market? Can we sustain an economy where a handful at the top reap enormous rewards while at least half of the population struggles for financial survival? Was a 20-year-old Cuban student and communist organizer correct when he argued: "Capitalism is more efficient. . . . But it is not more fair."[123]

Interestingly, capitalism seems to be gradually evolving in response to those criticisms. Merely maximizing short-term profits, as the best measure of business success, is increasingly

Many corporations practice ethical, socially responsible behavior.

criticized. Many corporations practice ethical, socially responsible behavior that values communities, workers, the environment, and the general welfare while maintaining the necessary commitment to profits. Perhaps the force of changing managerial ethics (see Chapter 2) and corporate social responsibility (see Chapter 3) is gradually developing a new, more just form of capitalism.

But ethical, socially responsible business practice in America cannot be achieved without a fair, effectively functioning market. Critics argue the efficiency and fairness of the market is being challenged by growing market concentration leading to monopoly and oligopoly conditions that crush the market's biggest strength: competition. What does it mean to Americans when only four airlines dominate airline traffic, where five banks hold over half of the industry's assets, or where 90 percent of the beer is controlled by two companies?[124] To the critics, it means that consumers pay more, and quality does not climb as it would in a competitive market. More alarmingly, those giant companies and industry oligopolies try to capture government, the critics say, in order to shape the law to benefit their interests.

Much of this text is devoted to questions of when we need government intervention to correct market failures (see Chapter 8) and counteract corporate power (see Chapter 3). Antitrust law (see Chapters 10 and 11) attempts to restore the market to competitive conditions when corporations have employed monopoly practices, engaged in harmful mergers and price fixing, and the like to distort the market in ways that harm consumers.

A "Remix" Needed?

America's economy is remarkable in many ways, but don't you agree that we can do better? Can we count on socially responsible business practice and current government oversight of business to strengthen productivity while enhancing justice and fairness? Or do we need more profound adjustments? As noted earlier in the chapter, socialism seems increasingly attractive to Americans, especially younger adults, but we still remain very much a free-market economy and culture. According to a 2019 Gallup Poll, 62 percent of the public wants the overall economy guided by the market rather than the government.[125]

We have many ideas, from dramatic to measured, for some kind of "remix" of the American economy. United States Senator Elizabeth Warren, for example, proposed legislation, the Accountable Capitalism Act, requiring corporations to consider the interests not only of shareholders, but of a broad range of stakeholders including customers, employees, and communities. To achieve that goal, she called for, among other things, a revolutionary change in American corporate governance wherein 40 percent of board members in large corporations would be elected by employees. Germany has successfully practiced a similar shared-governance approach for many years, but whether that system would be functional in America is entirely speculative at this moment.[126]

But perhaps wrenching change is not required? Journalist Anatole Kaletsky, author of *Capitalism 4.0: The Birth of a New Economy,*[127] reminds us that capitalism is adaptive, reinventing itself through crises.[128] Kaletsky thinks the capitalism of the future–his Capitalism 4.0–will involve closer government-business relationships with markets operating in a context prescribed to a greater extent by public officials. The business community will need to acknowledge duties beyond profit maximization. Nonetheless, Kaletsky is still a strong believer in markets.

a. List some nations that you take to be primarily useful and some that you believe to be primarily decorative. Which do you prefer?

b. Do you regard the United States as primarily useful or primarily decorative or both? Explain.

16. Which is more important to you: "freedom to pursue life's goals without state interference" or "state guarantees that nobody is in need."[146] Explain.

17. Hilda Scott wrote a book to which she affixed the provocative title, *Does Socialism Liberate Women?*[147]

    a. Answer her question. Explain.

    b. Are minority oppression and oppression of women inevitable by-products of capitalism? Explain.

18. Economist Tyler Cowen is concerned that our economy is changing in ways that encourage a reduction in personal ownership of physical objects, the "stuff" of our lives. He points particularly to the Internet and software that have allowed us to move away from ownership of reading materials. Similarly, we stream movies and TV shows rather than buying DVDs. Especially among young people, car ownership seems less important than in the past and is now replaced for many by Uber, Lyft, mass transit, and so on. As we move further toward the Internet of Things, he argues, most of the value inside our homes will reside in the companies and government that control the software that manages our homes for us.[148] Why might capitalism be threatened by Americans declining ownership of its "stuff?"

19. *a.* How do you feel about distinguished economist Gary Becker's free-market approach to America's immigration difficulties:

    > In a market economy, the way to deal with excess demand for a product or service is to raise the price. This reduces the demand and stimulates the supply. I suggest that the United States adopt a similar approach to help solve its immigration problems. Under my proposal, anyone willing to pay a specified price could enter the United States immediately.[149]

    b. What about paying students to improve standardized test score performance?

Notes

1. "Global Competitiveness Report 2019," World Economic Forum, October 9, 2019 [**www.weforum.org**]. The U.S. ranked second in 2019, ousted by Singapore from the first-place ranking it held in 2018.
2. Robert J. Samuelson, "Is America in Decline?," *The Washington Post,* January 27, 2013 [**www.washingtonpost.com**].
3. David Brooks, "The Commercial Republic," *The New York Times,* March 17, 2009 [**www.nytimes.com**].
4. Jesse Eisinger, *The Chickenshit Club: Why the Justice Department Fails to Prosecute Executives,* New York: Simon and Schuster, 2017.
5. Fred Redmond, "Runaway CEO Pay Has Created the Perfect Storm for 'Greedflation,'" July 18, 2022 [**https://aflcio.org**]. As to CEO pay, see Theo Francis and Vanessa Fuhrmans, "Big Companies Pay CEOs for Good Performance - and Bad," *The Wall Street Journal,* May 17,

2019 **[www.wsj.com]**. As to Wall Street pay, see Sarah Anderson, "Off the Deep End: The Wall Street Bonus Pool and Low-Wage Workers," Institute for Policy Studies, March 2017 **[www.ips-dc.org]**.

6. For a brief but helpful review of Thomas Piketty's book *Capital in the Twenty-First Century* (Cambridge, MA: Belknap Press, 2014), see Paul Mason, "Thomas Piketty's Capital: Everything You Need to Know about the Surprise Best Seller," *The Guardian,* April 28, 2014 **[www.theguardian.com]**.
7. Jonathan Rothwell, "Myths of the 1 Percent: What Puts People at the Top," *The New York Times,* November 17, 2017 **[www.nytimes.com]**.
8. Andrew Ross Sorkin, "Warren Buffett's Case for Capitalism," *The New York Times, May 5,* 2019 **[www.nytimes.com]**.
9. Richard Doak, "Can Capitalism Survive? Sorry, It Already Died," *The Des Moines Register,* June 21, 2009, p. 10P.
10. Robert Skidelsky, "Life After Capitalism," Project Syndicate, January 19, 2011 **[www.skidelskyr.com]**.
11. "Zogby Poll: Atlas Shrugged by Ayn Rand Read by 8.1 Percent," PRWeb, October 17, 2007 **[www.prweb.com/releases/1969/12/prweb561836.htm?tag=poll]**.
12. Stephen Moore, "Atlas Shrugged: From Fiction to Fact in 52 Years," *The Wall Street Journal,* January 9, 2009, p. W11 **[www.wsj.com]**.
13. Sandy Banks, "When Money Talks to Kids," *Los Angeles Times,* April 17, 2010 **[www.latimes.com]**.
14. See "Should Drivers Who Pay More Get a Faster Lane?" *Parade,* October 19, 2008, p. 22.
15. Editorial, "Tag–You're Illegal," *Los Angeles Times,* October 28, 2006 **[www.latimes.com]**.
16. Robert Poole, "Investor Financed Toll Roads Are Not Failures," *Reason Foundation,* September 30, 2016 **[https://reason.org]**.
17. Emily Thornton, "Roads to Riches," *BusinessWeek,* May 7, 2007, p. 50. **[www.nbc.news]**
18. Ibid.
19 Molly Ball, "The Privatization Backlash," *The Atlantic,* April 23, 2014 **[www.theatlantic.com]**.
20. Ibid.
21. Ilya Somin, "Laws Banning Organ Markets Kill Even More People than Previously Thought," *Reason,* January 3, 2019 **[https://reason.com]**.
22. Brian Alexander, "Privatization Is Changing America's Relationship with Its Physical Stuff," The Atlantic, July 12, 2017 **[www.theatlantic.com]**.
23. Charles Mahtesian, "Revenue in the Rough," *Governing,* October 1997, pp. 42–44.
24. Editorial, "City-Owned Golf Courses Cannot Be Sacred Cows," Waterloo/Cedar Falls Courier, July 13, 2003, p. C7.
25. Francis Fukuyama, "The End of History?," *The National Interest* 16, Summer 1989, pp. 3–18.
26. Alan Blinder and Mark Zandi, "The Financial Crisis: Lessons for the Next One," Center on Budget and Policy Futures, October 15, 2015, p. 5 **[www.cbpp.org]**.
27. John Maxfield, "The 4 Biggest Banks in America," *The Motley Fool,* April 23, 2016 **[www.fool.com]**.
28. Joshua Cole, "Macron Calls for a 'Global Contract' at Davos," *The Conversation,* January 26, 2018 **[https://theconversation.com]**.
29. New York: St. Martin's Press, 2018.
30. Jena McGregor, "JPMorgan's Dimon Says the US Is Exceptional, but Something Is Wrong," *The Washington Post,* April 5, 2017 **[www.washingtonpost.com]**.
31. Sean Illing, "Is Capitalism Worth Saving?" *Vox,* February 26, 2019 **[www.vox.com]**.
32. Ibid.

33. Michael Corkery, "Capitalism, Love and Mr. Moore," *The Wall Street Journal,* September 23, 2009, p. C3. [**www.wsj.com**].
34. Ibid.
35. Reuters, "Unbridled Capitalism Is the 'Dung of the Devil,' says Pope Francis," *The Guardian,* July 9, 2015 [**www.theguardian.com**] and Thomas Williams, "Pope Francis Praises Free Enterprise: A 'Noble Vocation, Directed to Producing Wealth,'" CatholicCitizens.org, February 28, 2016 [**www.catholiccitizens.org**].
36. Robert Skidelsky, "Life After Capitalism," Project Syndicate, January 19, 2011 [**www.skidelskyr.com**].
37. Thomas M. Hoenig, "Too Big to Succeed," *The New York Times,* December 1, 2010 [**www.nytimes.com**].
38. Henry Myers, "His Statues Topple, His Shadow Persists: Marx Can't Be Ignored," *The Wall Street Journal,* November 25, 1991, p. A1.
39. For a brief overview of the new Cuban constitution, see "All You Need to Know About Cuba's New Constitution," *TRT World,* March 1, 2019 [**www.trtworld.com**].
40. Elements of this list are drawn from Agnes Heller and Ferenc Feher, "Does Socialism Have a Future?" *Dissent,* Summer 1989, p. 371.
41. "State-Owned Enterprises Are a Hard Habit China Doesn't Want to Break," *Stratfor Worldview,* November 7, 2018 [**https://worldview.stratfor.com**].
42. Ibid.
43. Andrew Ross Sorkin, "Dealbook Special: China Means Business," *The New York Times,* November 25, 2018 [**www.nytimes.com**].
44. Clay Chandler, "Chinese Corporations Now Dominate the Fortune Global 500 List of Biggest Companies by Revenue–But They Are Far Less Profitable Than Their U.S. Rivals," *Fortune,* August 18, 2022 [**www.fortune.com**].
45. "Champions Chained; Chinese Law," *The Economist,* June 17, 2017, p. 16 (US).
46. John Pomfret, "China's New Surveillance State Puts Facebook's Privacy Problems in the Shade," *The Washington Post,* March 27, 2018 [**www.washingtonpost.com**] and Simon Denyer, "In China, Facial Recognition Is Sharp End of Big Data Drive for Total Surveillance," *The Washington Post,* January 7, 2018 [**www.washingtonpost.com**].
47. Te-Ping Chen, "World News: China Tests a New Kind of Class Struggle – Communist Party to Monitor Quality of Ideology Instruction at Universities as President Xi Moves to Solidify His Control," *The Wall Street Journal,* September 25, 2017, p. A13.
48. Steven Rattner, "Is China's Version of Capitalism Winning?" *The New York Times,* March 27, 2018 [**www.nytimes.com**].
49. Chris Buckley, "Chinese Embrace America's Culture but Not Its Policies," *The New York Times,* September 28, 2015 [**www.nytimes.com**].
50. Ibid.
51. Dana Milbank, "Battle Cry of the White Man," *The Washington Post,* August 5, 2014 [**www.washingtonpost.com**].
52. Ibid.
53. Transparency International, "Corruption Perceptions Index 2021" [**www.transparency.org**].
54. Elliot Smith, "Russia Faces 'Economic Oblivion' Despite Claims of Short-term Resilience, Economists Say," *CNBC,* August 2, 2022 [**https://www.cnbc.com**].
55. Joseph Stiglitz, "Stagnation in Russia," *Columbia Business School Ideas and Insights,* April 3, 2017 [**www8.gsb.columbia.edu/articles/chazen-global-insights/stagnation-russia**] and Frida Ghitis, "Is Putin Losing the Trust of Russians?" *Politico,* June 21, 2019 [**www.politico.eu**].

56. Simeon Djankov, “Russia’s Economy Under Putin: From Crony Capitalism to State Capitalism,” *Policy Brief Number 15-18* (Peterson Institute for International Economics), September 2015 [**www.piie.com**].
57. Masha Gessen, “Russia Is Remaking Itself as the Leader of the Anti-Western World,” The Washington Post, March 30, 2014 [**www.washingtonpost.com**].
58. For an overview of the Pentagon report, see Bryan Bender, “Russia Beating U.S. in Race for Global Influence, Pentagon Study Says,” *Politico,* June 30, 2019 [**www.politico.com**].
59. Associated Press, “Irked with Russia, U.S. Gays Target Vodka and Sochi,” *The Moscow Times,* July 31, 2013 [**www.themoscowtimes.com**].
60. Paul Roderick Gregory, “Leading Economist Gives Up on Putin’s Russia,” *Forbes,* May 30, 2013 [**www.forbes.com**].
61. Vivek Wadhwa, “Does China Own the Future—Or Does the U.S.?” *The Washington Post,* December 13, 2012 [**www.washingtonpost.com**].
62. David Brooks, “The Russia I Miss,” *The New York Times,* September 11, 2015 [**www.nytimes.com**].
63. “Countries Ranked by Life Expectancy,” *Worldometer* [**Life Expectancy by Country and in the World (2022) - Worldometer (worldometers.info)**].
64. Organization for Economic Co-Operation and Development, “Tax-to-GDP Ratios,” *Revenue Statistics 2018: Tax Revenue Trends in the OECD* [**www.oecd.org/tax/tax-policy/revenue-statistics-highlights-brochure.pdf**].
65. “Statutory Corporate Income Tax Rates,” *OECD.Stat,* July 15, 2019 [**https://stats.oecd.org/Index.aspx?DataSetCode=CTS_CIT**].
66. Rabah Kamal and Cynthia Cox, “How Do Healthcare Prices and Use in the U.S. Compare to Other Countries?” *Peterson-Kaiser Health System Tracker,* May 8, 2018 [**www.healthsystem-tracker.org**] and “Swedes Enjoy World-Class Healthcare–When They Get It,” *Medical Xpress,* September 3, 2018 [**https://medicalxpress.com**].
67. Jeff Jacoby, “No, Bernie Sanders, Scandinavia Is Not a Socialist Utopia,” *The Boston Globe,* October 15, 2015 [**www.bostonglobe.com**].
68. Nima Sanandaji, “So Long, Swedish Welfare State?” *Foreign Policy,* September 5, 2018 [**https://foreignpolicy.com**].
69. For an analysis of the European Union today and tomorrow, see Congressional Research Service, “The European Union: Ongoing Challenges and Future Prospects,” *CRS Report,* December 3, 2018 [**https://crsreports.congress.gov**].
70. Laurence Norman and Drew Hinshaw, “EU Finds $1 Trillion Doesn’t Buy Love–Fund for Poor Regions, Designed to Boost Unity, Instead Built Resentment,” *The Wall Street Journal,* August 9, 2018, p. A1.
71. For updated EU unemployment data, see European Commission, “Unemployment Statistics,” *Statistics Explained,* [**https://ec.europa.eu/eurostat/statistics-explained/index.php/Unemployment_statistics**].
72. Larry Elliott, “The European Union Has Bigger Problems to Deal with Than Brexit,” *The Guardian,* March 24, 2019 [**www.theguardian.com**].
73. “Nation Brand’s Index 2022: Germany Finishes First Again. . . ,” Ipsos, November 2, 2022 [**www.ipsos.com/en-us/news-polls/Germany-Retains-Top**].
74. Larry Elliott, “Brexit Is a Rejection of Globalisation,” *The Guardian,* June 26, 2016 [**www.theguardian.com**].
75. Jeremy Rifkin, “Why the European Dream Is Worth Saving,” *SpiegelOnline,* July 28, 2005 [**www.spiegel.de/international/0,1518,druck-366940,00.html**].

76. Adrian Karatnycky, quoting George Soros, in "The Merits of the Market, the Perils of 'Market Fundamentalism,'" *The Wall Street Journal,* January 9, 2001, p. A20.
77. Andrew Ross Sorkin, "Warren Buffett Still Loves Capitalism," DealBook Briefing, *The New York Time*s, May 6, 2019 [**www.nytimes.com**].
78. Joanne Barkan, "Not Yet in Paradise, But . . . ," *Dissent,* Spring 1989, pp. 147, 150.
79. Thomas B. Edsall, "Why Can't America Be Sweden?" *The New York Times,* May 29, 2013 [**http://opinionator.blogs.nytimes.com**].
80. Jonathan Chait, "No, America Is Not Turning Libertarian," *New York Magazine,* August 7, 2014 [**http://nymag.com**].
81. Jim Chairusmi, "Winning with Smaller Pockets," *The Wall Street Journal,* October 18, 2004, p. R2.
82. Juliana Menasce Horowitz, Ruth Igielnik, and Rakesh Kochhar, "Trends in income and wealth inequality," *Pew Research Center,* January 9, 2020 [**www.pewsocialtrends.org**]; and "Wealth in America: Inequality Persists in Household Wealth," *US News,* November 14, 2019 [**www.usnews.com**].
83. Anna Brown, "Despite gains, women remain underrepresented among U.S. political and business leaders," *Pew Research Center,* March 20, 2017 [**www.pewresearch.org**]; Ella Koeze, Meredith Conroy, and Amelia Thomson-DeVeaux, "More Women Are Holding Political Office--But Not Everywhere," FiveThirtyEight, January 30, 2020 [**https://fivethirtyeight.com**]; and "The 116th Congress has more women and people of color than ever–but there's still room to improve," *The Conversation,* November 8, 2018 [**https://theconversation.com**].
84. Leslie Albrecht, "The U.S. Is the No. 1 Most Generous Country in the World for the Last Decade," MarketWatch, October 26, 2019 [**www.marketwatch.com**]; National Philanthropic Trust, "Charitable Giving Statistics" [**www.nptrust.org**].
85. Jon Clifton, "The Most Generous Countries in the World," Gallup, December 12, 2018 [**https://news.gallup.com**].
86. James Hohman, "Americans Are Pessimistic About What Life Will Be Like in 2050. Here's What They Fear Most," The Daily 202, *The Washington Post,* March 22, 2019 [**www.washingtonpost.com**].
87. Sarah Min, "Sorry, Class of 2019: Paychecks for New U.S. College Grads Are Barely Rising," CBS News, May 17, 2019 [**www.cbsnews.com**].
88. Rakesh Kochhar and Stella Sechopoulos, "How the American Middle Class Has Changed in the Past Five Decades," *Pew Research Center,* April 20, 2022 [**www.pewresearch.org**].
89. Ibid.
90. Rakesh Kochhar, "The American Middle Class is Stable in Size, But Losing Ground Financially to Upper Income Families," Pew Research Center, September 6, 2018 [**www.pewresearch.org**].
91. "2018 Statistical Update," United Nations Development Programme Human Development Reports [**www.hdr.undp.org/en/2018-update**].
92. "2022 Social Progress Index - United States," Social Progress Imperative [**www.socialprogress.org**].
93. Ibid.
94. Central Intelligence Agency, "Country Comparison: GDP–Per Capita," *The World Factbook* [**www.cia.gov/library/publications/the-world-factbook/fields/211rank.html**].
95. Central Intelligence Agency, "Country Comparison-Infant Mortality Rates," *The World Factbook* [**www.cia.gov/library/publications/the-world-factbook/fields/354rank.html**]. The World Factbook updates reported statistics on a weekly basis.
96. Drew Kann, "5 Facts Behind America's High Incarceration Rate," CNN, April 21, 2019 [**www.cnn.com**] and Megan Quattlebaum and Juliene James, "As Candidates Search for Criminal

Justice Talking Points, Parole and Probation Reform Should Top List," USA Today, July 3, 2019 [**www.usatoday.com**].

97. Sarah Jane Glynn, "Breadwinning Mothers Continue to Be the U.S. Norm," Center for American Progress, May 10, 2019 [**www.americanprogress.org**].
98. Charles Fain Lehman, "Americans Are Having Less Sex," Washington Free Beacon, March 25, 2019 [**https://freebeacon.com**].
99. Ibid.
100. Jessica Semega, Melissa Kollar, John Creamer, and Abinash Mohanty, "Income and Poverty in the United States: 2018," *United States Census Bureau Library Report Number P60-266,* September 10, 2019 [**www.census.gov/library/publications/2019/demo/p60-266.html**].
101. Robert L. Fischer, "Why the War on Poverty in the US Isn't Over, in 4 Charts," *The Conversation,* July 20, 2018 [**https://theconversation.com**].
102. Stanford Center on Poverty and Inequality, "State of the Union: The Poverty and Inequality Report," *Pathways,* Special Issue 2016 [**http://inequality.stanford.edu/sites/default/files/Pathways-SOTU-2016-2.pdf**].
103. Paul Krugman, "Poverty Is Poison," *The New York Times,* February 18, 2008 [**www.nytimes.com/2008/02/18/opinion/18krugman.html?em**].
104. Noah Kirsch, "The 3 Richest Americans Hold More Wealth Than Bottom 50% of the Country, Study Finds," *Forbes,* November 9, 2017 [**www.forbes.com**] and Noah Kirsch, "Members of the Forbes 400 Hold More Wealth Than All U.S. Black Families Combined, Study Finds," *Forbes,* January 14, 2019 [**www.forbes.com**].
105. Robert Frank, "Richest 1% Now Owns Half the World's Wealth," *CNBC,* November 14, 2017 [**www.cnbc.com**].
106. Alexia Fernandez Campbell, "CEOs Made 287 Times More Money Last Year Than Their Workers Did," *Vox,* June 26, 2019 [**www.vox.com**].
107. Jim Tankersley, "Economic Mobility Hasn't Changed in a Half-Century in America, Economists Declare," The Washington Post, January 22, 2014 [**www.washingtonpost.com**].
108. Erin Richards, "7 Out of 10 Wealthy Kindergarten Students with Low Test Scores Were Affluent by Age 25, Study Finds," *USA Today,* May 15, 2019 [**www.usatoday.com**].
109. Maryam Kouchaki, Kristin Smith-Crowe, Arthur P. Brief, and Carlos Sousa, "Seeing Green: Mere Exposure to Money Triggers a Business Decision Frame and Unethical Outcomes," *Organizational Behavior and Human Decision Processes* 121, no. 1 (May 2013), p. 53.
110. Lara B. Aknin and Kate Hanniball, "Prosocial Spending and Well-Being," *Oxford Bibliographies,* June 27, 2017 [**www.oxfordbibliographies.com**].
111. Alexa Lardieri, "Study: Many Americans Report Feeling Lonely, Younger Generations More So," *U.S. News & World Report,* May 1, 2018 [**www.usnews.com**].
112. Bernie DeGroat, "Do Co-Workers Engage or Estrange after Hours," University of Michigan, *University Record,* February 11, 2008 [**www.rcgd.isr.umich.edu/news/Sanchez-Burks.univ.recrd.02.11.08.pdf**].
113. "Why Nordic countries might not be as happy as you think," BBC News, August 25, 2018 [**www.bbc.com**].
114. Robert Putnam, Bowling Alone (New York: Simon & Schuster, 2000).
115. Jean Twenge, "Why It Matters That Teens Are Reading Less," *The Conversation,* August 20, 2018 [**https://theconversation.com**].
116. Richard V. Reeves, "Feeling Good or Doing Good? Emotional Social Capital Versus Relational Social Capital," *Brookings Up Front,* April 8, 2019 [**www.brookings.edu**].

117. Connie Cass, "In God We Trust Maybe, But Not Each Other," Associated Press, November 30, 2016 [**http://ap-gfkpoll.com/featured/our-latest-poll-findings-24**].
118. New York: Macmillan Publishers, 2018.
119. David Brooks, "A Renaissance on the Right," *The New York Times,* April 13, 2018 [**www.nytimes.com**].
120. Dan Lawton, "In Ghana, No One Is a Stranger for Long," *The Christian Science Monitor,* November 9, 2009 [**www.csmonitor.com/2009/1109/p18s01-hfes.html**].
121. Tim Betler, "More Social Connection Online Tied to Increasing Feelings of Isolation," University of Pittsburgh Schools of the Health Sciences *Public Release,* March 6, 2017 [**www.eurekalert.org**].
122. David Wessel and John Harwood, "Capitalism Is Giddy with Triumph; Is It Possible to Overdo It?" *The Wall Street Journal,* May 14, 1998, p. A1.
123. See Jonathan Tepper (with Denise Hearn), *The Myth of Capitalism* (Hoboken, New Jersey: Wiley, 2018).
124. Mohamed Younis, "Four in 10 Americans Embrace Some Form of Socialism," *Gallup,* May 20, 2019 [**https://news.gallup.com**].
125. Raffaella Sadun, "Worker Representation on Boards Won't Work Without Trust," *Harvard Business Review,* August 17, 2018 [**https://hbr.org**].
126. New York: Public Affairs/Perseus, 2010.
127. Anatole Kaletsky, "Capitalism 4.0," *OECD Observer,* no. 279 (May 2010) [**www.oecdobserver.org**].
128. New York: Portfolio/Penguin, 2010.
129. Aldo Musacchio, Sergio G. Lazzarini, and Ruth V. Aguilera, "New Varieties of State Capitalism: Strategic and Governance Implications," *Academy of Management Perspectives* 29, no. 1 (2015), p. 115.
130. Mike Konczal, "Robert Reich on Why Capitalism Needs Saving," *Rolling Stone,* October 7, 2015 [**www.rollingstone.com**].
131. Roger Cohen, "Toilets and Cellphones," *The New York Times,* May 24, 2010 [**www.nytimes.com**].
132. Robert Samuelson, "Economics Made Easy," *Newsweek,* November 27, 1989, p. 64.
133. "Deliverance; The Postal Service," *The Economist,* April 21, 2018, p. 10 (US).
134. Ibid.
135. Christopher Ingraham, "Economics Professor Suggested Replacing Public Libraries with Amazon. It Didn't Go Over Well," *The Chicago Tribune,* July 24, 2018 [**www.chicagotribune.com**].
136. Carla McClain, "Dr. Spock: Restore the Family," *The Des Moines Register,* November 7, 1993, p. 3E.
137. *American Amnesia: How the War on Government Led Us to Forget What Made America Prosper* (New York: Simon & Schuster, 2016).
138. Max Ehrenfreund, "How the Scandinavians Got So Tall," *The Washington Post,* April 8, 2016 [**www.washingtonpost.com**].
139. Nolan Feeney, "Women Are Now More Likely to Have College Degree Than Men," *Time,* October 7, 2015 [**https://time.com**].
140. FIND
141. Nicholas D. Kristof, "Moonshine or the Kids?" *The New York Times,* May 22, 2010 [**http://www.nytimes.com**].
142. Ibid.
143. Thomas L. Friedman, "Foreign Affairs; Eastern Middle School," *The New York Times,* October 2, 2001 [**www.nytimes.com**].
144. Adolph Berle, *Power* (New York: Harcourt Brace Jovanovich, 1969), pp. 258–59.

145. Anne Quito, "America, the Brand, Has Fallen in World Rankings," *Quartz,* October 29, 2018 **[https://qz.com]**.

146. Roger Cohen, "Incurable American Excess," *The New York Times,* August 6, 2015 **[www.nytimes.com]**.

147. Hilda Scott, *Does Socialism Liberate Women?: Experiences from Eastern Europe* (Boston: Beacon Press, 1974).

148. Tyler Cowen, "Americans Own Less Stuff, and That's Reason to Be Nervous," *Bloomberg,* August 12, 2018 **[www.bloomberg.com]**.

149. Gary Becker, "Why Not Let Immigrants Pay for Speedy Entry?" *BusinessWeek,* March 2, 1987, p. 20.

CHAPTER TWO

Business Ethics

After completing this chapter, students will be able to fulfill the following learning objectives:

2-1. Explain the business scandals that led to legislative action in the early 21st century.

2-2. Discuss America's current moral climate.

2-3. Identify and discuss the leading ethical decision-making theories.

2-4. Compare and contrast the teleological and deontological ethical systems.

2-5. Differentiate between utilitarianism and formalism.

2-6. Explain some of the forces that encourage unethical behavior in the workplace.

2-7. Describe Kohlberg's theory of moral development.

2-8. Explain the general requirements of the Foreign Corrupt Practices Act.

2-9. Discuss some of the risks and rewards of whistleblowing.

2-10. Explain the general purpose of ethics codes in the workplace.

Part One—Introduction to Ethics

Can we count on self-regulation as a useful means of controlling behavior in the business environment? On a larger scale, can we count on the free market as discussed in Chapter 1, along with managerial and corporate ethics, to guide business conduct so that government regulation (law) can be significantly reduced?

This chapter will examine the ethical climate of business and the role of ethics in business decision making. Our goal here is not to teach morality but to sensitize the reader to the vital role integrity plays in building a sound career and a responsible life.

PRACTICING ETHICS "Turbocharging" Opioid Sales?

As opioid addiction arose into an epidemic gripping communities and claiming lives across the United States, attention turned not only to the makers of OxyContin but also to those who helped promote the drug. For example, in a 2019 lawsuit against Purdue Pharma, the Massachusetts State Attorney General disclosed communications from management consulting firm McKinsey on how to "turbocharge" sales of the opioid. McKinsey was also alleged to have been part of a team seeking to help Purdue Pharma counter the compelling statements against the drug made by grieving parents of teenagers who had died from opioid overdose.

Records uncovered in litigation revealed that McKinsey had advised Purdue Pharma to focus on selling lucrative high-dose pills, even after the drug manufacturer's 2007 guilty plea to criminally misleading physicians and government regulators about OxyContin's risks.

In a December 2020 statement on its website, McKinsey expressed regret for its efforts to boost sales of opioids: "As we look back at our client service during the opioid crisis, we recognize that we did not adequately acknowledge the epidemic unfolding in our communities or the terrible impact of opioid misuse and addiction on millions of families across the country. That is why last year we stopped doing any work on opioid-specific business, anywhere in the world."

In 2021, McKinsey entered into a multistate agreement to pay nearly $600 million to settle investigations into McKinsey's role in the opioid crisis, without admitting wrongdoing.

Questions

1. Assume that you were a McKinsey staff consultant assigned to help Purdue Pharma boost OxyContin sales (prior to the firm's 2019 decision to stop doing such work). Would you have objected to the assignment? Why or why not?
2. "Putting the client first" is said to be McKinsey's top value. Is it unethical for a management consulting firm to help a client achieve a harmful goal? Explain.
3. In their 2022 book, *When McKinsey Comes to Town: The Hidden Influence of the World's Most Powerful Consulting Firm, New York Times* reporters Walt Bogdanich and Michael Forsythe describe how McKinsey advised Juul, the e-cigarette maker, as an example of McKinsey's long history of advising companies selling addictive products. How might a management consulting firm justify advising such companies? Explain.

Sources: Michael Forsythe and Walt Bogdanich, "McKinsey Advised Purdue Pharma How to 'Turbocharge' Opioid Sales, Lawsuit Says," *The New York Times*, February 1, 2019 [**https://www.nytimes.com**]; McKinsey & Company, "Statement on Its Past Work with Purdue Pharma," December 5, 2020 [**https://www.mckinsey.com/about-us/media/mckinsey-statement-on-its-past-work-with-purdue-pharma**]; Brian Mann, "McKinsey Apologizes for Helping Purdue Pharma 'Turbocharge' Opioid Sales," *NPR*, December 9, 2020 [**https://www.npr.org**]; Michael Forsythe and Walt Bogdanich, "McKinsey Settles for Nearly $600 Million Over Role in Opioid Crisis," *The New York Times*, February 3, 2021 [**https://www.nytimes.com**]; Walt Bogdanich and Michael Forsythe, "How McKinsey Got into the Business of Addiction," *The New York Times*, September 29, 2022 [**https:www.nytimes.com**]; and Sheelah Kolhatkar, "McKinsey Is a Consulting Powerhouse. But Is It a Force for Good?" *The New York Times*, September 29, 2022 [**https:www.newyorktimes.com**].

The Moral Climate of American Business

LO 2-1
Explain the business scandals that led to legislative action in the early 21st century.

The Great Recession of 2007–2009 was triggered by the collapse of the financial services industry, which in turn was the result of decisions and actions arguably taken with short-term gain as the singular goal. Corporate greed had marked the early 2000s with business scandals. These business scandals offer sobering lessons in the importance of ethical business practices, as well as the context for the legislative responses that you will study more closely in later chapters.

Leading up to the Great Recession of 2007–2009, subprime mortgages were being aggressively issued to feed the voracious appetite of the investment banking industry, which was converting those mortgages into derivatives. These derivatives were securities comprising interests in large portfolios of mortgages. The interests (tranches) were based on the order in which investors would be paid as mortgage payments were made. For example, AAA tranche holders would be paid first. The issuers of the derivatives, the investment banks, were generating enormous fees because so many investors wanted to participate in the real estate boom by purchasing these derivatives. When the supply of high-quality mortgages ran out, the financial services industry found ways to issue mortgages to increasingly less qualified buyers (i.e., subprime mortgages), which they continued to securitize, generating additional fees. Critical to this scheme were

- Mortgage issuers willing to qualify borrowers with little capacity to make payments (receiving large fees upon the immediate sale of the mortgages to investment bankers).
- Home appraisers willing to blindly validate rapidly increasing, unrealistic market values (receiving fees while facing no realistic risk of professional disciplinary action).
- Regulators unwilling to diligently oversee the industry.
- An investment banking community that cared nothing for the consequences when, in due course, the mortgage defaults started to occur, which started happening in droves when the variable interest rates kicked in after the initial low-interest introductory rates ended.

The subprime mortgage scandal was not the first instance of morally unhinged business conduct; it is reminiscent of the savings and loan crisis of the 1980s when $150 billion evaporated, in part because of criminal behavior. The corporate greed of the Enron era (early 2000s) played out on a worldwide stage as some of the titans of American commerce were sent off to prison. Tyco International CEO Dennis Kozlowski is infamous for his wife's $2 million Sardinian birthday bash and his $6,000 shower curtain. He was released from prison in 2015 after serving less than seven years on charges of looting nearly $100 million from Tyco. Most breathtaking was Wall Street investment manager Bernard Madoff's colossal Ponzi scheme that stole as much as $65 billion from his clients before he was caught and sent to prison in 2009 to serve 150 years. (The 2016 two-part miniseries, *Madoff,* starring Richard Dreyfuss as Madoff and Blythe Danner as his wife, is available for streaming through several outlets.)

Legislative responses to these scandals, including Sarbanes-Oxley Act of 2002 and the 2010 Dodd-Frank Wall Street Reform and Consumer Protection Act discussed in later chapters, gave rise to an era of compliance **[https://www.forbes.com/sites/forbesfinancecouncil/2021/02/03/major-scandals-driving-the-rise-of-modern-compliance/?sh=1912fe24665b]**. Of course, we should not condemn the entire American business community based on the misconduct of some. **[https://www.greatworklife.com/ethical-decision-making-in-business-examples/]**.

Remote and Hybrid Workers: What's Going on Over There?

When conducting video interviews, one tech recruiter reportedly will first ask candidates to pan their cameras to prove that they are alone, since he has known job seekers who were being coached by others outside the camera's view during interviews. Some have even tried to "lip-sync" while others answer questions for them, blaming Internet connections for time lags.

Once hired, in video meetings, it's difficult for bosses to know who is paying mindful attention. Microsoft CEO Satya Nadella coined the phrase "productivity paranoia" to describe managers' concerns about remote workers' efficiency–and honesty.

1. Is it wrong to check work email while in a work video meeting? How about checking personal emails or text messages?
2. If you were being interviewed remotely for a job and were asked to scan the room with your webcam, how would you react?

Source: Callum Borchers, "Some Bosses' Trust Has Grown Remote," *The Wall Street Journal,* October 20, 2022, p. A11.

LO 2-2
Discuss America's current moral climate.

As offered in an essay published by the Center for Digital Ethics and Policy, in challenging times, "we need heroes and villains."[1] The COVID-19 pandemic created a time for heroes and villains. New York City health care workers were given a rousing salute each evening from apartment windows. Other essential workers such as grocery store clerks might have been more quietly appreciated, but they had to face those who were dubbed "covidiots" on social media, shamed for defying masks and social distancing orders, and hoarding scarce necessities like toilet paper.[2] The COVID-19 pandemic posed a "Tragedy of the Commons": when scarcity causes individuals to act in their self-interest against the common good.[3]

In recent years, the United States has been marked with deep political and social division. The common good as a moral compass might seem to be a thing of the past. The 2022 Values and Beliefs Gallup poll showed that a record-high 50 percent of Americans believe that the state of moral values in the U.S. is poor.[4] Seventy-eight percent of respondents thought U.S. moral values were getting worse; only 18 percent thought they were improving.[5] In a similar 2019 Gallup poll, political party affiliation made little difference to the beliefs held about the trajectory of our moral values.[6] However, the 2022 Gallup poll showed that Republicans are significantly more negative about the current moral state of the U.S. than Democrats, although the majorities of both parties agree that the state of moral values is getting worse.[7]

Misinformation on Social Media

In its first report posted in 2022, the Integrity Institute found that a "well-crafted lie" will attract more engagement on social media than content that tells the truth.[8]

Question

Why might misinformation garner more engagement on social media? What does the rise of misinformation reveal about America's moral climate? Explain.

Sociologist David Callahan's book, *The Cheating Culture: Why More Americans Are Doing Wrong to Get Ahead,* argues that we are a society in moral decline.[9] The result of our winner-take-all ethos, Callahan thinks, is a nation increasingly falling into two groups: a "winner class" who cheated their way to the top and an "anxious class" who fear falling behind if they too do not cheat.[10]

A third class made up of "anxious winners" seemed to appear in the 2019 college admissions scandal. Federal charges were brought against dozens in a college admissions scam driven by wealthy parents' desire to have their children gain admission to elite universities by, for example, arranging for exam proctors to correct SAT answers or submitting applications showing their children's athletic prowess in sports they had never played. Moral psychologists have offered that the wealthy and privileged may feel a sense of entitlement to their status. When that status is threatened, perhaps by the possibility that their children will not gain admission to an elite university, they are more likely to lie, steal, and cheat more to get what they want.[11]

Cheating, in one form or another, does seem to be routine in American life. But we find a glimmer of good news in scholar Dan Ariely's 2012 book, *The (Honest) Truth about Dishonesty: How We Lie to Everyone–Especially Ourselves,* which shows, through a series of experiments, that while almost all of us cheat, most of us cheat only a little.[12]

College Students

Cheating in college is commonplace.[13] In a survey of 300 students from both public and private universities, including online programs, 86 percent responded that they had cheated in school, with 54 percent indicating that cheating "was OK" and even necessary to stay competitive.[14] Mobile devices play a part, as 72 percent reported using their phone, tablet, or computer to cheat in class.[15]

PRACTICING ETHICS "Stealing the Exam" and Cheating on a Test . . . At the Office

In 2017, five accountants at KPMG, including a former managing partner for audit quality, were charged with misappropriating and using information from the Public Company Accounting Oversight Board (PCAOB) to improve the firm's performance in PCAOB inspections. Also charged was a KPMG employee who had previously been an inspections leader at the PCAOB. All six were fired. As of this writing, two have been convicted at trial, three have pleaded guilty, and one is still pending trial.

Later, in 2019, several auditors at KPMG were found to have cheated on the firm's internal tests regarding mandatory ethics, integrity, and compliance training. Senior partners shared answers with other partners and staff to help them pass the tests. In addition, one partner and other auditors at the firm manipulated the system to lower the passing score. Nearly thirty auditors engaged in this conduct on four or more occasions. In 2020, the SEC settled charges against three former KPMG audit partners who shared answers to internal training exams.

Questions

1. If you were recruiting with KPMG, how might these scandals affect your view of the firm? What questions would you have for recruiters or partners with whom you interview? Explain.
2. Which do you think is the more troubling scandal? How are these scandals similar? How are they different? Explain.
3. How different, if at all, is this behavior from cheating on college exams to raise grades and GPAs? Does successful cheating make all future representations of one's college accomplishments on resumes and job applications fraudulent? Explain.

Sources: Francine McKenna, "The KPMG Cheating Scandal Was much More Widespread than Originally Thought," *Market Watch,* June 18, 2019 [**www.marketwatch.com**]; Richard L. Cassin, "Ex-KPMG Partner Pleads Guilty in PCAOB Cheating Scandal," *FCPA Blog,* October 7, 2019 [**https://fcpablog.com**]; The New York Times Editorial Board, "Auditing the Auditors," *The New York Times,* April 14, 2017 [**www.nytimes.com**]; and Securities and Exchange Commission, "SEC Charges Three KPMG Audit Partners for Exam Sharing Misconduct," *Press Release,* May 28, 2020 [**www.sec.gov**].

Cheating in college, of course, predated mobile devices, nor are graduate business programs immune. A 2018 survey conducted by the NCAA found that more than 90 percent of U.S. college students have cheated somehow in their academic career.[16] The survey also discovered that academic cheating begins in middle school with cheating on tests and copying other students' homework answers.[17]

Questions

1. Harvard MBA students received a great deal of attention in 2009 for their voluntary campaign to sign "The MBA Oath," a pledge that they would act ethically, "serve the greater good," and avoid advancing their own "narrow ambitions" at the expense of others.[18] If you were to sign an ethics oath as a student, do you think your behavior as a student, and later as a professional, would be impacted? Explain.
2. How might the college admissions scandal described above encourage unethical conduct among college students, such as cheating? Explain.

[For a video of *The Daily Show with Jon Stewart*'s treatment of the 2009 Harvard MBA Ethics Oath, see **www.cc.com/video-clips/dc3rq6/the-daily-show-with-jon-stewart-mba-ethics-oath.** This clip contains profanity and violent rhetoric.]

Gen Z

Generation-Z, or Gen Z, roughly those born from 1996 to 2010, make up the vast majority of today's college student population. Gen Z members grew up in a digital world, with the cellphone as a fixture. Together with "the millennials" before them, Gen Z is already changing the face of the workforce.

> Inclusion is different from diversity.

> Generation Z is the most diverse generation to date. In fact, any lack of diversity in a group is what stands out to us. We are most encouraged by companies that seem interested in their employees' backgrounds, cultures and values. Inclusion is different from diversity in that a workplace might be diverse, but the office culture should also allow everyone to feel equally welcomed and valued. Inclusion is a major factor influencing how comfortable we feel in a workplace.[19]

The Deloitte Global 2022 Gen Z and Millennial Survey found that Gen Z and millennials share deep concerns about the state of the world but try to make a positive difference while managing the demands of everyday life. For example, they aim to make environmentally sustainable choices, even while facing financial anxiety.[20] Nearly 40 percent of the survey respondents said they have rejected a job or an assignment because it did not align with their values.[21] Similarly, the 2021 EY (Ernst & Young) Gen Z Segmentation Study found that working for an employer that shares their values is very or extremely important to nearly two-thirds of Gen Z.[22] A recent study by Stanford University of investors' views about companies' environmental, social, and governance initiatives found that, compared to other age groups, Gen Z and millennials are most likely to be willing to risk their savings to support companies' environmental, social, and governance initiatives.[23]

Questions

1. The Association of National Advertisers has called Gen Z "the generation of empathy" who won't purchase a product or take a job from a company with values that don't align

with their own.[24] Do you agree with this statement? Explain. Do you believe today's college students are becoming less empathetic to others? Explain.

2. How would you describe your empathy to others? [To measure your own level of empathy and to compare it with the average empathy level of college students, see **http://umichisr.qualtrics.com/SE/?SID=SV_bCvraMmZBCcov52&SVID**.]

Part Two—Analyzing Ethical Dilemmas

Ethics Theories

LO 2-3
Identify and discuss the leading ethical decision-making theories.

We have considered, in a preliminary way, some business ethics issues and America's moral climate. Now we turn to an overview of the primary philosophical theories employed in examining ethics problems. Ethics involves judgments as to good and bad, right and wrong, and what ought to be. Business ethics refers to the evaluation of business behavior based on standards of right and wrong, rather than relying entirely on principles of accounting and management. (In this discussion, the word *morals* will be used interchangeably with the word *ethics*. Distinctions between the two are not vital for our purposes.)

Finding and following the moral course is not always easy, but the difficulty may be particularly acute for the businessperson. The pressure to produce is intense, and the temptation to cheat may be great. Although the law provides useful guides and guardrails for behavior, moral answers may not be immediately revealed. The businessperson facing a difficult decision may, therefore, do what they believe to be correct at any given moment: do "what my judgment and feelings tell me is right" or "follow my gut."

Existentialism

Reliance on personal, subjective judgments to make ethical decisions, however, seems unscientific and risky. Surely well-developed standards are required? Perhaps, but before turning to those approaches, we will briefly examine *existentialism,* a highly individualized philosophy that explicitly shuns rules and, indeed, all external norms. The individual is free to find their own moral course.

Existentialists, such as Nobel Prize winner Jean-Paul Sartre, believe standards of conduct cannot be objectively discovered or rationally justified via ethical theory and reasoning. No actions are inherently right or wrong. Thus, each person may reach their own choice about ethical principles. Moral decision making–indeed, all decision making–is a solitary act. Personal freedom is the defining characteristic of every person. Each of us is, therefore, fully and exclusively responsible for our own moral decisions.[25] That view finds its roots in the notion that humans are only what we each will ourselves to be. If God does not exist, there can be no general human nature because there is no one to conceive that nature.

Existence precedes essence.

In Sartre's famous interpretation, existence precedes essence. First, humans exist; then, we individually define what we are–our essence. Therefore, each of us is free, with no rules to turn to for guidance. Just as we all choose our own natures, so must we choose our own ethical precepts. Moral responsibility belongs to each of us individually.

Responsibility

Indian spiritual, political, and civil rights leader Mahatma Gandhi viewed moral responsibility quite differently from Sartre. Gandhi's view: "All humanity is one undivided and indivisible family, and each one of us is responsible for the misdeeds of all the others."[26]

Question

Whose view makes more sense to you? Why?

Universal Truths?

Are there no rules or universal standards by which to distinguish right from wrong? Philosophers seek to provide guidance beyond the uncertainties of ethical relativism. We will survey two ethical perspectives, *teleology* and *deontology,* which form the core of the philosophical approach to ethical analysis. Before proceeding to those theories, we will note the important role of religion in ethics and take a brief look at two additional formulations—libertarianism and virtue ethics–that have been increasingly influential in contemporary moral analysis.

1. **Religion.** Judeo-Christian beliefs, Islam, Hinduism, Buddhism, Confucianism, The Baha'i Faith, and other faiths are powerful ethical voices in contemporary life. They often feature principles such as the Golden Rule to build absolute and universal standards. Scholarly studies indicate that most American managers believe in the Golden Rule and take it to be their most meaningful moral guidepost. From a religious point of view, the deity's laws are absolutes that must shape the whole of one's life, including work. Faith, rather than reason, intuition, or secular knowledge, provides the foundation for a moral life built on religion. [For worldwide coverage of ethics issues, see **www.bbc.co.uk/religion/0/**.]

2. **Libertarianism.** Contemporary philosopher Robert Nozick (1938–2002) built an ethical theory rooted in personal liberty. For him, morality coincided with the maximization of personal freedom. Justice and fairness, right and wrong are measured not by equality of results (such as wealth) for all, but from ensuring equal opportunity for all to engage in informed choices about their own welfare. Hence, Nozick took essentially a free-market stance toward ethics.

3. **Virtue ethics.** In recent years, an increasing number of philosophers have argued that the key to good ethics lies not in rules, rights, and responsibilities, but in the classic notion of character. As Plato and Aristotle argued, our attention should be given to strategies for encouraging desirable character traits such as honesty, fairness, compassion, and generosity. Aristotle believed that virtue could be taught much as any other skill. Virtue ethics applauds the person who is motivated to do the right thing and who cultivates that motivation in daily conduct. A part of the argument is that such persons are more morally reliable than those who simply follow the rules but fail to inspect, strengthen, and preserve their own personal virtues. [For an overview of virtue ethics, see **http://plato.stanford.edu/entries/ethics-virtue/**.]

Teleology and Deontology—An Overview

LO 2-4
Compare and contrast teleological and deontological ethical systems.

Religion, libertarianism, and virtue provide crucial ethical lessons. Philosophers have further clarified ethical theory by defining two broad analytical systems, *teleology* and *deontology,* that capture much of our current understanding about how to engage in careful ethical analysis.

Teleological ethical systems (often referred to as *consequentialist ethical systems*) are concerned with the consequences–the results–of an act rather than the act itself. A teleological view of life involves ends, goals, and the ultimate good. Duty and obligation are subordinated to the production of results that are good or desirable. For the teleologist/consequentialist, the end is primary, and that end or result is the measure of the ethical quality of a decision or act.

To the deontologist, on the other hand, principle is primary, and consequence is secondary or even irrelevant. Maximizing right rather than good is the deontological standard. The deontologist might well refuse to lie, as a matter of principle, even if lying would maximize good.

Deontology, derived from the Greek word meaning *duty,* is directed toward what ought to be, toward what is right. Similarly, deontology considers motives. For example, why a crime was committed may be more important than the actual consequences of the crime. Relationships among people are important from a deontological perspective primarily because they create duties. A father may be bound by duty to save his son from a burning building, rather than saving another person who could do more total good for society.

The distinction here is critical. Are we to guide our behavior by rational evaluation of the consequences of our acts, or according to duty and principle–that which ought to be? Let's take a closer look at *utilitarianism,* the principal teleological ethical theory, and *formalism,* the principal deontological ethical theory.

Teleology

Utilitarianism

LO 2-5
Differentiate utilitarianism and formalism.

In reaching an ethical decision, good is to be weighed against evil. A decision that maximizes the ratio of good over evil for all those concerned is the ethical course. Jeremy Bentham (1748–1832) and John Stuart Mill (1806–1873) were the chief intellectual forces in the development of utilitarianism. Their views and those of other utilitarian philosophers were not entirely consistent. As a result, at least two branches of utilitarianism have developed. According to *act-utilitarianism,* our moral judgment is to be guided by evaluating individual acts. The moral path is achieved by performing those *acts* that generate the greatest good; that is, the greatest overall utility in each particular situation. *Rule-utilitarianism,* on the other hand, involves following those *rules* that generate the greatest good; that is, the greatest overall utility.

Thus, the rule-utilitarian may be forced to shun a particular act that would result in greater immediate good (punishing a guilty person whose constitutional rights have been violated) in favor of upholding a broader rule that results in the greater total good over time (maintaining constitutional principles by freeing the guilty person). In sum, the principle to be followed for the utilitarian, whether examining acts or rules, is the greatest good for the greatest number. [For an extensive database exploring utilitarianism, see **www.hedweb.com/philsoph/utillink.htm**].

Deontology

Formalism

The German philosopher Immanuel Kant (1724–1804) developed perhaps the most persuasive and fully articulated vision of ethics as measured not by consequences (teleology) but by the rightness of rules. Thus, in this formalistic view of ethics, the rightness of an act depends little (or, in Kant's view, not at all) on the results of the act. Rather, Kant advocated ethical decision making based on what is right within the act itself, regardless of the consequences of the act. Moral worth springs from one's decision to discharge one's duty. Thus, the student who refuses to cheat on exams is morally worthy if their decision springs from duty or adherence to rules, but morally unworthy if the decision is merely one born of self-interest, such as fear of being caught.

How does a person of goodwill know what is right? Here Kant propounded the *categorical imperative,* the notion that every person should act on only those principles that they, as a rational person, would prescribe as universal laws to be applied to humankind. A moral rule is "categorical" rather than "hypothetical" in that its prescriptive force is independent of its consequences. The rule guides us independent of the ends we seek. Kant believed that every rational creature could act according to their categorical imperative because all such persons have "autonomous, self-legislating wills" that permit them to formulate and act on their own systems of rules. To Kant, what is right for one is right for all, and each of us can discover that "right" by exercising our rational faculties.

Questions

1. Fifty-year-old Wesley Autry, waiting with his two young daughters at a New York City subway station, saw a man collapse and fall off the passenger platform into the space between the train rails. The headlight of a train appeared. Mr. Autry immediately jumped on top of the fallen man, holding him down while the train passed over them, inches above Autry's head. Asked later why he jumped to the rescue, Autry said: "I did what I felt was right."[27] What form of ethical reasoning did Autry seem to employ in making his courageous decision?
2. British priest Tim Jones caused a big stir by telling his congregation that shoplifting is sometimes morally permissible for desperate people. In a sermon, Jones said that shoplifting can be justified when a person is in real need, is not greedy, and takes only what is necessary to get by. Later Jones said: "The point I'm making is that when we shut down every socially acceptable avenue for people in need, then the only avenue left is the socially unacceptable one."[28]

    a. Was Jones arguing from a teleological/consequentialist or a deontological/formalist point of view? Explain.

    b. Do you agree with Jones? Explain.
3. Autonomous vehicles, commonly called self-driving cars or AVs, raise ethical dilemmas. For example, suppose an AV is traveling toward a group of pedestrians on the road and must decide to either swerve off the road into a barrier, killing its passenger, or ram into the pedestrians, killing them instead. What would a utilitarian want the AV car to do? How would a deontologist choose the right option for the car? Explain.[29]

Using Ethical Reasoning: Two Cases

Obviously, ethical theories do not provide magical answers to life's most difficult questions. Those theories are useful, however, in identifying and sorting the issues that lead to better decision making. Apply those theories to the cases that follow, as you think about what kind of manager you aspire to be and how you would treat your employees.

Case One: Boss as "Jerk"

Management trainer and author Mary Donohue claims that tyrannical, authoritarian bosses are commonplace: "This is a virus that has spread far and wide." These managers, she says, rule over their employees and use fear "as their primary weapon."[30] Christine Porath, who has studied workplace civility, equates rudeness and incivility at work with secondhand smoke, permeating the workplace atmosphere and harming those other than the target.[31]

While Apple visionary Steve Jobs was celebrated for his remarkable accomplishments, he was often accused of harsh, dictatorial management practices. *Business Insider* lists 16 episodes of "Jobs Being a Huge Jerk," including allegations of lying to his partner Steve Wozniak about the money involved in a deal, firing employees without notice or severance pay, and firing a manager in front of his team.[32] Reports suggest that Jobs was often a good, charming person and leader and that he mellowed somewhat in later years.

Business journalist Jerry Useem summarized some of the scholarly evidence about tyrannical bosses in an *Atlantic Monthly* article, "Why It Pays to Be a Jerk."[33] The data are mixed, as would be expected. Stanford business professor Jeffrey Pfeffer says that "all the things we rate negatively"–like immodesty–"are the best predictors of higher salaries or getting chosen for a leadership position."[34] And research at the University of Amsterdam finds that overconfidence and some degree of obnoxiousness can make us seem more powerful and, in fact, can make us more powerful.[35] But other research by Yale professor David Rand shows that being accommodating–being nice–pays off, at least in environments where we interact with the same people on a regular basis.[36] In sum, Useem concluded that being a "jerk" is likely to fail, at least in the long run, if others do not receive spillover benefits, if the boss is dealing with the same people repeatedly, or if the boss lacks the brilliance of someone like Steve Jobs.

Wharton professor Adam Grant received a great deal of attention for his research on whether being nice pays off at work. He divides people into three categories: Takers (who look out for themselves), Givers (who are generous and expect nothing in return), and Matchers (who help others but with the expectation of reciprocal favors). In his study of engineers, salespeople, and medical school students, Grant found that Givers were overrepresented in the bottom 25 percent of their field, but also in the top 25 percent. Being too nice can hurt in the short run but pay off in the long run through engendering goodwill in others and through the learning that comes with being generous.[37] Broadly, however, Grant said: "What I've become convinced of is that nice guys and gals really do finish last."[38] Grant thinks the most effective people are those whom he labels "disagreeable givers." They are not necessarily the nicest people. They are demanding and direct, and they push others, but they do so, Grant says, with the interests of others and the organization in mind.[39]

So being an unkind, authoritarian manager might be productive, but is it the right approach? Is being a "jerk" as a manager an ethically defensible posture? Consider the following questions.

Questions

1. What ethical issues might be raised in the workplace by a leader who is a "jerk"?
2. *a.* Will your personal values require you to be a nice person at work regardless of the consequences?
   b. If so, which of the ethical theories noted above seems to be guiding your behaviors? Explain.
   c. If not, would one of the ethical theories justify your other-than-"nice" behaviors? Explain.
   d. Do you think nice people finish last? Explain.
3. Do you think the "disagreeable giver" approach to management is ethically defensible? Explain by using the ethical theories examined above.
4. The New England Patriots has a "character coach" who, among other things, checks attendance at meetings and addresses issues such as tardiness. The "character coach" has been called the Patriots' "secret weapon."[40] Do you think all organizations could use a character coach? Explain.

Sources: Olga Khazan, "It Pays to Be Nice," *The Atlantic,* June 23, 2015 [**www.theatlantic.com**]; Jerry Useem, "Why It Pays to Be a Jerk," *The Atlantic,* June 2015 [**www.theatlantic.com**]; and Lorenzo Reyes, "Is the Patriots' Secret Weapon Their Character Coach?" *USA Today,* February 2, 2018 [**www.usatoday.com**].

Case Two (Part 1): Are Layoffs Unethical? Aaron Feuerstein and Malden Mills

Fabric manufacturer Malden Mills of Lowell, Massachusetts, provided 3,100 high-paid manufacturing jobs in the Boston area when a 1995 fire destroyed most of the plant. The next morning Aaron Feuerstein, CEO of the family-controlled mill, announced that the business would be rebuilt and all employees would retain their jobs. Feuerstein said that keeping all of the workers through the rebuilding process was "the right thing to do and there's a moral imperative to do it, irrespective of the consequences."[41] Apparently, Feuerstein was significantly influenced by his Jewish heritage. In his youth, Feuerstein reportedly memorized in Hebrew the Leviticus passage: "You are not permitted to oppress the workingman because he is poor and needy."

The new plant was designed to expand production of the company's patented and very successful Polartec fabric. Following the fire, makeshift production lines were developed in warehouses, and about 85 percent of the employees returned to work, with the remaining 400 workers remaining idle but paid. The new plant, machinery, and business losses cost Feuerstein some $300 million, much of which was covered by insurance. Feuerstein was convinced that the big investment would pay in the long run and, because he had a highly successful, patent-protected product and the company was family-owned, and thus under no immediate pressure to perform, he felt he could afford to do what his long-time family investment in the community and workers seemed to require.

Questions

1. Aaron Feuerstein became something of an overnight national hero by protecting his workers. In his opinion, "It was the right thing to do and there's a moral imperative to do it, irrespective of the consequences."

   a. Was Feuerstein employing utilitarian or formalist reasoning? Explain.
   b. In your view, was he correct to say that the consequences, in this instance, did not matter? Explain.

2. Commenting on Feuerstein's approach to his employees' needs, Wharton School professor Michael Useem said, "The thinking is: employees can be seen as an ultimate competitive advantage. If you treat them well, they'll pay you back in really hard work later on."[42]
   a. Was Useem expressing formalist or utilitarian reasoning? Explain.
   b. In a pastoral letter, the U.S. Catholic bishops argued that "every economic decision and institution must be judged in light of whether it protects or undermines the dignity of the human person."[43] Does the thinking summarized by Useem undermine that dignity and, as such, require rejection under either utilitarian or formalist reasoning? Explain.
3. If you were a successful entrepreneur with the flexibility of Aaron Feuerstein, would you operate your business like an extended family? Explain.

Sources: Richard Lorant, Associated Press, "A Mill Owner's Compassion Rescues Thousands of Jobs after Devastating Fire," December 10, 1996, *Chicago Tribune*, p. 8; and Mary McGrory, "Tale of Two Bankruptcies," *Pittsburgh Post-Gazette,* December 22, 2001, p. A15.

[For a film treatment of corporate downsizing and layoffs, see *The Company Men* trailer at **www.youtube.com/watch?v=GrqP3l9iZnc**.]

Case Two (Part 2): Are Layoffs Unethical? Aaron Feuerstein, Malden Mills, and Bankruptcy

In November 2001, Malden Mills was forced to enter Chapter 11 bankruptcy proceedings (see Chapter 15) to reorganize its finances under court protection. At the time, Malden Mills was bearing a $140 million debt load. Lenders demanded the bankruptcy action as a condition for extending an additional $20 million to keep the company afloat. In late 2003, Malden Mills emerged from bankruptcy. Creditors controlled the board of directors with Aaron Feuerstein occupying the family's one seat. Malden's precarious financial position was the product of a variety of forces: Customers were lost during the rebuilding after the fire, cheaper fleece substitutes entered the market, the company took on substantial debt in rebuilding and in keeping on its employees following the fire, and the company probably overbuilt following the fire. As a result, the Malden Mills workforce shrank to 1,200 employees. Then, in 2007, Malden Mills was once again forced into bankruptcy and was purchased by Chrysalis Capital partners, a private-equity firm that renamed the company Polartec LLC. Aaron Feuerstein's association with the company ended with the sale.

Questions

1. *The Wall Street Journal* raised the question, "Are layoffs moral?"[44]
   a. Should we establish a universal, formalist rule forbidding layoffs of all hard-working, competent employees, or should we rely on utilitarian reasoning, libertarian thought, virtue theory, or religious beliefs to answer that question? Explain.
   b. Is morality irrelevant to the question of when layoffs are necessary? Explain.

2. Do you think it would be accurate and fair to say that Feuerstein's ethical choice to protect his employees led to the decline of his business? Explain.
3. Did Feuerstein make an error in judgment in relying on an absolute principle–that is, the immediate protection of his workers at all costs? Explain.
4. How might Feuerstein's workers have benefited by being laid off following the fire?
5. John MacKenzie, in a letter to *The New York Times,* said he had a duty to help Aaron Feuerstein and Malden Mills: "Of course I have an ethical obligation to buy from Malden Mills if I have a choice and if my purchase can make a difference. It would reward Mr. Feuerstein for what he has done and what he is trying to do, and the system needs more of that."[45] Do you have a duty to buy only from the most ethically responsible sellers? Explain.

Source: "Articles about Aaron M. Feuerstein," *The New York Times* [**www.topics.nytimes.com/topics/reference/timestopics/people/f/aaron_m_feuerstein/index.html**].

[For another view of the Malden Mills facts, as well as an analysis of the wisdom of Feuerstein's decision, see David W. Gill, "Was Aaron Feuerstein Wrong?" *Ethix,* June 25, 2011 **https://ethix.org/2011/06/25/was-aaron-feuerstein-wrong**.]

Part Three—Managerial Misconduct?

Can We Trust Corporate America?

Earlier in this chapter and in Chapter 1, we noted evidence of corporate misconduct. Given the subprime mortgage crisis, a strong sense of wrongdoing on Wall Street, and the ever-increasing disparity between our poorest and our richest citizens, the latter of whom often obtained their wealth through corporations they own or control, we should not be surprised that public attitudes toward big business are often not favorable. In a recent Gallup poll of confidence in major institutions, only 23 percent of Americans expressed a "great deal" or "quite a lot" of confidence in big business. For some perspective, only television news and Congress ranked lower among the 15 institutions mentioned in the Gallup survey, with only 18 and 11 percent, respectively, of Americans expressing such confidence. Interestingly, small business was second highest with a 68 percent rating. (The military was highest at 73 percent.)[46]

Another recent Gallup poll asked the American public how it rates the honesty and ethical standards of people in 22 professions. Several business categories were included, among which were bankers who were 12th on the list with 28 percent of those polled rating them "high" or "very high." Below them were labor union leaders (24 percent), business executives (20 percent), advertising practitioners (13 percent), and car salespeople (at the bottom of the list at 9 percent). (Happily, college teachers rated considerably higher, with 49 percent rating them "high" or "very high," right below police officers with 54 percent, but well below nurses, at the top of the list with 85 percent.)[47]

In a recent worldwide survey of trust in institutions,[48] the Edelman Trust Barometer shows that as trust in government has fallen, the expectation that businesses will lead on social issues has grown.[49] However, the survey also reveals that business is often seen as not doing enough on such issues as climate change.[50]

Nevertheless, as Georg Kell, founding director of the United Nations Global Compact, has observed, business has been undergoing a "silent revolution" from within to include purpose, community service, and values into their mission.[51]

In its 2019 Statement on the Purpose of a Corporation, the Business Roundtable, an association of chief executive officers of major U.S. companies, seems to have given further voice to the "silent revolution" in declaring that corporations should serve all of their stakeholders, not just of their shareholders.[52] The 181 chief executive officers who signed the statement committed to dealing fairly and ethically with suppliers, supporting communities, and investing in employees.[53] As **IBM** CEO Arvind Krishna later reflected: "Purpose and profit go together, reinforcing each other."[54]

Now we turn to an examination of what forces may encourage corporate misconduct and its accompanying trust problems.

[For "The Business Ethics Blog," see **https://businessethicsblog.com.**]

Why Do Some Managers Cheat?

Moral Development

LO 2-6
Explain some of the forces that encourage unethical behavior in the workplace.

Scholars argue that some individuals are better prepared to make ethical judgments than others. Psychologist Lawrence Kohlberg built and empirically tested a comprehensive theory of moral development in which he claimed that moral judgment, at least as applied to judgments of justice, evolves and improves primarily as a function of age and education.

Kohlberg, via interviews with children as they aged, was able to identify moral development as a movement through distinct stages, the later stages showing improvement over the earlier ones. Kohlberg identified six universal stages grouped into three levels:

LO 2-7
Describe Kohlberg's theory of moral development.

1. **Preconventional level**
   Stage 1: Obey rules to avoid punishment.
   Stage 2: Follow rules only if it is in one's own interest, but let others do the same. Conform to secure rewards.

2. **Conventional level**
   Stage 3: Conform to meet the expectations of others. Please others. Adhere to stereotypical images.
   Stage 4: Doing right is one's duty. Obey the law. Uphold the social order.

3. **Post-conventional or principled level**
   Stage 5: Current laws and values are relative. Laws and duty are obeyed based on rational calculations to serve the greatest number.

Stage 6: Follow self-chosen universal ethical principles. In the event of conflicts, principles override laws.[55]

At Level 3 the individual is able to reach independent moral judgments that may or may not conform with conventional societal wisdom. Thus, the Level 2 manager might refrain from sexual harassment because it constitutes a violation of company policy and the law. A manager at Level 3 might reach the same conclusion, but their decision would be based on independently defined universal principles of justice.

Kohlberg found that many adults never pass beyond Level 2. Consequently, if Kohlberg is correct, many managers may behave unethically simply because they have not reached the upper stages of moral maturity. Of course, some managers may achieve mature moral judgments but fail to take moral action based on those judgments.

Kohlberg's model is based on extensive longitudinal and cross-cultural studies over more than three decades. For example, one set of Chicago-area boys was interviewed at three-year intervals for 20 years. Thus, the stages of moral growth exhibit "definite empirical characteristics" such that Kohlberg was able to claim that his model had been scientifically validated.[56] Although many critics remain, the evidence, in sum, supports Kohlberg's general proposition. [For an overview on moral education, see **https://www.sciencedirect.com/topics/social-sciences/moral-education**.]

Feminine Voice

One of those lines of criticism requires a brief inspection. Kohlberg colleague Carol Gilligan contends that our conceptions of morality are, in substantial part, gender-based.[57] She claims that men typically approach morality as a function of justice, impartiality, and rights (the ethic of justice), whereas women are more likely to build a morality based on care, support, and responsiveness (the ethic of care). Men, she says, tend to take an impersonal, universal view of morality as contrasted with the feminine "voice" that rises more commonly from relationships and concern for the specific needs of others. Gilligan criticizes Kohlberg because his highest stages, 5 and 6, are structured in terms of the male approach to morality while the feminine voice falls at stage 3. Furthermore, Kohlberg's initial experimental subjects were limited to young males. The result, in Gilligan's view, is that women are underrepresented. One problem with the concept of the ethic of care is that it might be interpreted to legitimize the stereotype of women as care-giving subordinates not deserving of moral autonomy.[58] Subsequent research both challenges[59] and supports[60] Gilligan's view. [For a video outlining Gilligan's theory, see **www.youtube.com/watch?v=HctzZwwueL4**.]

Reason or Emotion?

Controlled or automatic? We have seen that Kohlberg and Gilligan (and most moral philosophers) take the position that moral decision making is the controlled product of analysis, deliberation, and experience. In recent years, however, new psychological and neuroscience evidence supports an alternative theory of morality that involves decision making by emotion or intuition. The emotion/intuition approach claims that moral decision making is an automatic, nonreflective process in which our minds, when confronted with a moral question, instantaneously generate feelings of approval or disapproval.[61] Brain-scanning experiments provide support for the automatic emotion/intuition hypothesis.[62] Some scientists speculate that controlled moral reasoning may be little more than an after-the-fact justification of conclusions already reached automatically via emotions or intuitions.

Even babies seem to make moral judgments.

Moral theorist Marc Hauser extends the emotion/intuition thesis in his book *Moral Minds.*[63] He claims that our brains are biologically endowed with a moral faculty that has evolved over eons and is designed to reach very rapid judgments about right and wrong based on unconscious processes that are involuntary and universal. Thus, when we judge an action to be morally right or wrong, Hauser says we are doing so instinctively, using our inborn moral faculty. Even babies seem to make moral judgments. Experiments show that one-year-old infants, for example, prefer taking one graham cracker from a "good" puppet rather than two from a "bad" puppet. But when the bad puppet offers eight graham crackers, infants tend to accept that offer over a single cracker from the good puppet.[64]

The emotion/intuition/biological theory provides a powerful challenge to Kohlberg and to our faith in moral reasoning generally. Psychologist Jonathan Haidt compares the intuitive, moral machinery of the brain with an elephant and conscious moral reasoning with a small rider on the elephant's back.[65] Other scholarly evidence, however, continues to support a very robust role for rational moral decision making[66]; reasoning may at times override intuitions, as Haidt himself acknowledges.[67] Overall, moral decision making may be the product of a dual-process system employing both automatic emotions (produced deep in the brain in its older structures) and controlled reasoning (produced in the newer, frontal lobes of the brain).[68] [For more, see the website **https://YourMorals.org,** where Haidt and his colleagues invite you to "learn about your own morality, ethics, and/or values, while also contributing to scientific research."]

Moral Identity?

The moral development story does not end with an understanding of moral reasoning and moral emotion/intuition. None of these forces, according to current research, adequately explains why some among us are moved, after reaching a moral judgment, to take moral action.[69] Early evidence suggests that a critical feature in total moral development, including the will to act, involves what is labeled *moral identity.* In general, moral identity involves the degree to which moral concerns are central to our sense of self. As Professor Sam Hardy explains it, a person might have a stronger sense of moral identity if that identity is centered more on moral virtue than on amoral virtues such as creativity.[70] Some studies find that those with stronger moral identities are more likely to engage in good behaviors such as volunteering or showing respect for members of "out-groups."[71] Overall, however, the evidence supporting moral identity remains quite tentative.

The White-Collar Criminal: No Regrets?

Harvard Professor Eugene Soltes, author of the book "*Why They Do It: Inside the Mind of the White-Collar Criminal,*" shared that the main challenge faced by most of the notorious white-collar criminals he interviewed, including Bernard Madoff and Dennis Kozlowski who have previously been mentioned in this text, is one we all face as humans:

> [W]e're not hardwired to detect harm that we're doing when the harm is distant. It's not enough to know the difference between right and wrong. One actually has to feel that one's actions are harmful to avoid going forward. So take something like insider trading. You don't see the victims. It's actually impossible in many instances to identify who those victims are. So it's not surprising that if you engage in insider trading, there's not going to be any internal alarm screaming out that you're engaging in some extraordinarily heinous crime.[72]

As a result, Professor Soltes remarked that he was not worried that the executives would steal five dollars from his wallet. "They're socialized. They wouldn't do that." They might, however, inflict a much greater harm taking far more from his retirement or investment accounts.

Question

Would you feel more guilty about stealing money, even a small amount, out of a classmate's backpack than you would taking far more out of the pocket of a jacket hanging in the coat room of a large conference hotel? Why or why not?

Source: Roger Parloff, "A Harvard Professor Studied Infamous White-Collar Criminals. Here's What He Learned," *Fortune.com,* October 11, 2016 [**www.fortune.com**].

Organizational Forces

Ethisphere Institute, in its recent ranking of the world's most ethical companies, identified 136 (100 of which were American) that met its standards. Ethisphere bases its rankings on what it calls an Ethics Quotient derived from nominees' codes of ethics, regulatory and legal infractions, sustainable investment policies, corporate citizenship, and more.[73] 3M, a nine-time honoree, had once described the importance of a strong ethical culture:

> It takes more than a few company policies to be held as an example of how to do business the right way. . . . What it takes is a strong ethical culture that is so fully intertwined with everyday business practices that doing the right thing is never questioned.[74]

Pressure to cheat is often cited as a measure of an organization's ethical culture, but according to the 2021 Global Business Ethics Survey, pressure on U.S. employees to compromise their standards at work had reached an all-time high in 2020.[75] Such organizational pressure can disrupt or destroy any employee's life, as illustrated by interviews several years ago with 30 young Harvard Business School graduates:

> I really feel for people who are middle management, with a wife and four kids, under financial strain. . . . You see it happen all the time, that people are indicted for fraud or larceny. You can empathize with their situation. The world is changing fast. And a lot of people have been blindsided by it–so they've done things that they don't like. I can't say that will never happen to me. It's easy for me as a single person . . . but when you're desperate, you're desperate.

"[My boss] was not willfully unethical. It was the pressure of the time."

> [My boss] was not willfully unethical. It was the pressure of the time. . . . I have no idea what pressures were on him to drive the project. It probably wasn't [his] initiative to fudge the numbers. There may have been a good intention at some point in the organization. But as it got filtered through the organization, it changed. Some executive may have said, "This is an interesting project." Unfortunately this got translated as, "The vice president really wants this project." This sort of thing can happen a lot. Things start on high. As they go down they are filtered, modified. What was a positive comment several levels above becomes "do this or die" several levels down.[76]

The Boss

Top corporate managers and executives seem to have hit a long, rough patch in American life. Many have been disgraced by scandals, and some are in prison. Wall Street executives have been accused of bringing the economy to near collapse. The vital role of senior management in setting and practicing firm ethical standards is evidenced by a recent global survey of nearly 2,000 financial professionals, over 60 percent of whom said the tone at the top of the organization is the most important determinant of behavior in the workplace.[77]

[For a film treatment of ethical issues in the business community, see the trailer *Wall Street: Money Never Sleeps,* at **www.youtube.com/watch?v=HcMFA2SHES4**.]

Wells Fargo: Rogue Employees or Systemic Fraud?

Until September 2016, Wells Fargo Bank had enjoyed a successful strategy: bank branches were a shop, and the financial products it sold were retail goods. Then Wells Fargo faced nearly $185 million in penalties for fraudulently opening depositor and credit card accounts. To meet lofty sales targets and performance expectations, Wells employees opened as many as 3.5 million accounts without customers' knowledge or authorization. In his 2016 congressional testimony, then-CEO John Stumpf blamed lower-level employees for behavior that was contrary to the bank's values and culture. Nevertheless, a 2017 internal report concluded that the leaders of Wells Fargo's community bank division took an approach to sales and performance management that "prompted low-quality sales and improper and unethical behavior." In the wake of the scandal, the bank had to pay substantial amounts in penalties and customer refunds. Stumpf was ousted as CEO, and about $75 million in executive compensation was clawed back.

Wells Fargo's woes continued. In February 2018, the central banking system of the U.S., the Federal Reserve System (the Fed), blocked Wells Fargo's ability to grow larger until it approved the bank's remediation plan. In May 2018, then-CEO Timothy Sloan asked for more time to address the Fed's feedback before submitting its plans for enhanced corporate governance, so the cap on its assets continued into 2019. Sloan stepped down as CEO in March 2019. Then, in June 2019, Wells Fargo settled class-action claims based on its auto insurance practices for approximately $390 million.

Other practices of Wells Fargo also resulted in federal action. In April 2018, the Consumer Financial Protection Bureau levied a $1 billion fine for over-charging on mortgage interest rate-lock extensions and for running a mandatory insurance program for auto loans that added costs and sometimes led to the repossession of borrowers' automobiles.

Wells Fargo's investment banking division was also subjected to scrutiny, and four bankers were fired amid both internal and regulatory investigations. An internal review revealed that Wells Fargo regularly over-charged for currency trades. Its foreign-exchange bankers relied on customers not bothering to check the charges and then blamed market fluctuation if a customer asked about the difference in trading fees.

Questions

1. Echoing then-CEO John Stumpf's congressional testimony, one observer argued that the employees, rather than the bank itself, should be held responsible for such conduct as fraudulently opening customer accounts–that regulatory fines ultimately harm the shareholders, who have already paid a price for managerial misconduct. How do you respond to this argument? Explain.
2. Another observer, who studied Wells Fargo's financial reports in the wake of these scandals, noted that Wells Fargo did not seem to be incurring costs for increased compliance and risk management and that one reason the employee incentive structure led to employees' misconduct was because the bank was not spending enough on monitoring its operations. How do you respond to this argument? Explain.
3. The Office of the Comptroller of the Currency (OCC), which in 2018 collected a $500 million penalty from Wells Fargo over its risk management practices, announced in 2018 that a review of about 40 banks showed that, over a three-year period, approximately 10,000 accounts had been opened without customer authorization. These banks were required to reimburse customers whose accounts were opened improperly. However, the OCC did not name the banks publicly. Does this change your view of Wells Fargo? What questions would you have for the OCC? Explain.

Sources: "Stick in the Mud: Wells Fargo," *The Economist,* September 9, 2017 **[www.economist.com]**; Emily Glazer, "Banking & Finance: Wells Fargo Earns New Ire from Bank's Overseers," *The Wall Street Journal,* January 6, 2018 **[www.wsj.com]**; Peter J. Hennings, "When Money Gets in the Way of Corporate Ethics," April 17, 2017, *The New York Times* **[www.nytimes.com]**; Kevin McCoy, "Fed Limits Wells Fargo's Growth, Citing 'Consumer Abuses'," *USA Today,* February 2, 2018 **[www.usatoday.com]**; Emily Glazer, "Wells Refunds Millions to Clients," *The Wall Street Journal,* July 20, 2018 **[www.wsj.com]**; Jonathan Stempel, "Wells Fargo Will Pay Customers $386 Million over Unwanted Auto Insurance," *Reuters,* June 7, 2019 **[www.reuters.com]**; Hannah Levitt; "Wells Fargo CEO Abruptly Steps Down, Succumbing to Scandals," **Bloomberg.com,** March 28, 2019 **[www.bloomberg.com]**; Renae Merle and Heather Long, "Federal Reserve Cracks Down on Wells Fargo over Scandal Involving Sham Accounts," *The Washington Post,* February 2, 2018 **[www.washingtonppost.com]**; Bill Chappell, "Wells Fargo Hit with $1 Billion in Fines Over Home and Auto Loan Abuses," *NPR,* April 20, 2018 **[www.npr.org]**; Emily Glazer, "Wells Fargo Bankers, Chasing Bonuses, Overcharged Clients – Employees Say Foreign-Currency Staff Ignored Agreed-upon Client Fees," *The Wall Street Journal,* November 28, 2017 **[www.wsj.com]**; Stephen Gandel, "Wells Fargo Earnings: Bank Still Hasn't Dealt with Its Scandal," *Bloomberg,* April 13, 2018 **[www.bloomberg.com]**; James B. Stewart, "Just Desserts, or Just Cruel?," *The New York Times,* April 20, 2018 **[www.nytimes.com]**; and Kevin McCoy, "Wells Fargo Wasn't Alone – Other US Banks also Opened Unauthorized Accounts," *USA Today,* June 14, 2018 **[wwww.usatoday.com]**.

Questions—Part Three

1. *a.* Do you think heroes are important to our character development? Explain.
   b. Do you think we have fewer heroes today than in the past? Explain.
   c. Do you have a hero? Explain.
2. Ethics expert Kirk O. Hanson has identified "six ethical dilemmas every professional faces," including "What Is Worthwhile Work?"[78] In thinking about that question,

Hanson mentions a number of considerations, including whether the work contributes to human welfare.

Will you pursue only those forms of work that contribute to human welfare? If you fail to do so, will you be committing an ethical wrong? Does all work contribute to human welfare? Explain.

3. In a 2017 *The New York Times* opinion editorial, Nicholas Kristof asserted that the opioid crisis resulted from greed, not just of drug lords, but of pharmaceutical executives who "lost their humanity" at the sight of the large profit to be gained from opioid addiction. See Nicholas Kristof, "Drug Dealers in Lab Coats," *The New York Times,* October 18, 2017 [**www.nytimes.com**].
   a. Evaluate Kristof's argument using the 2019 Business Roundtable's Statement on the Purpose of a Corporation discussed earlier.
   b. Does a corporation have a conscience? Explain. See Kenneth Goodpaster and John B. Matthews Jr., "Can a Corporation Have a Conscience?," *Harvard Business Review,* January–February 1982, p. 136.
4. Kansas City Royals pitcher Gil Meche, 32 years old and troubled by a shoulder injury, decided to retire from baseball. The decision would not have been considered particularly newsworthy beyond the sports pages except that Meche passed up the $12 million final year of his contract by doing so. Others in similar situations have reported to spring training, gone through the motions, and collected their big paychecks. Meche said, "When I signed my contract, my main goal was to earn it. Once I started to realize I wasn't earning my money, I felt bad." Meche thought he had already earned enough from the Royals: "Making that amount of money from a team that's already given me over $40 million for my life and for my kids, it just wasn't the right thing to do."[79]
   a. Would you do the same as Meche if you were similarly situated? Explain.
   b. Have you ever spurned money for reasons of principle? If so, why did you do so?
   c. Was Meche employing utilitarian or formalist reasoning? Explain. See Tyler Kepner, "Pitcher Spurns $12 Million, to Keep Self-Respect," *The New York Times,* January 26, 2011 [**www.nytimes.com**].
5. Boris Siperstein, then 38, of Austin, Texas, reported biking to meetings for his private-equity firm and estimated that he saved the firm several thousand dollars because he took his folding bike on business trips and used it in place of cabs. Siperstein also slept on the floor of the company's former Manhattan headquarters rather than exceed his personal limit of $200 for a hotel room. David Payne, then 41 and a trainer for a Brooklyn, New York, software firm, often washed his clothing in the bathtub while on the road. He traveled with detergent and used local laundromats, thus saving, he estimated, $30 to $40 in hotel service fees.[80]
   a. Will you impose frugal spending limits on yourself when you are on a company expense account? Explain.
   b. Is frugality morally required? Explain.
   c. Do employers value frugal employees? Explain.

Part Four—Business Ethics in Practice

Introduction: Corporate/White-Collar Crime

General Motors

Ignition Switch

The deaths of at least 124 people have been linked to a faulty ignition switch in some General Motors small cars. The switch, if jarred in particular ways, could shut off the engine with the vehicle in motion, resulting in a loss of power steering, airbags, and other systems. GM acknowledged it was aware of the problem by at least 2005, although some reports had emerged as early as 2001. Various adjustments were made over the years, but the problem persisted and some potential solutions reportedly were rejected on cost grounds. In 2009 GM, struggling with the Great Recession, filed for Chapter 11 bankruptcy and was "bailed out" with a $49.5 billion federal investment that made the government GM's primary owner. In 2014 GM, much improved financially and having paid back the bailout, officially notified the National Highway Traffic Safety Administration of the switch defect and ultimately recalled millions of cars. GM apologized for mishandling the problem; a number of employees, including several executives, were fired or disciplined. A $35 million civil penalty was imposed; a victim compensation fund was established; and civil lawsuits for damages followed, resulting in a $120 million settlement in 2017.[81]

Corporate Crime?

Was General Motors guilty of criminal behavior? What about its managers and officers? When does wrongful, unethical behavior become criminal? GM agreed to pay $900 million to settle a U.S. Justice Department criminal probe involving fraud and concealing a deadly safety defect. The federal government and General Motors also entered a deferred prosecution agreement under which the Justice Department, after three years, would dismiss its criminal charges without additional penalties if GM continued to satisfactorily cooperate with the government. In explaining the deal, prosecutors pointed to GM's "fairly extraordinary" cooperation in the investigation, but victims and critics were outraged. Margie Beskau, whose daughter Amy Rademaker was killed in a GM car crash, said, "I don't understand how they can basically buy their way out of it. They knew what they were doing, and they kept doing it."[82]

What about the Bosses?

To date, General Motors officers and managers have escaped prosecution by the federal government. Preet Bharara, former U.S. attorney for the Southern District of New York, explained: "There are gaps in the law. It's not a criminal violation to put into the stream of commerce an auto that might harm people."[83]

Question

Assuming they could be identified, should any of the officers, executives, and managers who knew the faulty ignition switches were causing deaths be held criminally liable, in your opinion? Explain.

Opioid Crisis: Who Is a Criminal?

As described earlier in this chapter, the epidemic of opioid addiction and its tragic consequences has drawn attention to the manufacturers of opioids. In Department of Justice filings against Purdue Pharma, members of the Sackler family, owners of Purdue Pharma whose wealth grew from the sales of OxyContin, were alleged to have helped fuel opioid addiction by approving Purdue's criminal schemes to boost opioid prescriptions, as they pressured Purdue staff to increase sales. In 2020, the company, Purdue Pharma, pleaded guilty to three federal felonies regarding the marketing and sale of OxyContin. Under a 2022 settlement agreement, the Sackler family agreed to contribute up to $6 billion to settle lawsuits brought by states and other governmental entities, creating a fund for victims and their survivors and providing resources to communities affected by the opioid crisis, and to give up control of Purdue Pharma, with profits of the new entity going to fight the opioid crisis. In a 2022 letter, a group of U.S. Senators urged the U.S. Department of Justice to open a criminal investigation of the Sackler family on its conduct relating to Purdue Pharma's admitted crimes. "Real justice in this case means holding individual lawbreakers criminally accountable," the U.S. Senators wrote. However, to date, no criminal charges have been brought against Sackler family members.

Interestingly, in September 2022, the U.S. Department of Justice announced new guidelines in corporate criminal enforcement, with "individual accountability" as a top priority.

Questions to Consider

1. In your opinion, should the Sackler family be criminally investigated for their role in the opioid crisis? Explain.
2. From an ethical perspective, compare and contrast the Sackler family's alleged role in the opioid crisis with GM officers and managers who were allegedly aware of the faulty ignition switch. How are they similar? How are they different?
3. At this writing, Walgreens and CVS pharmacies have agreed to pay more than $10 billion to settle government lawsuits regarding their role in the opioid crisis. What questions might you have for the individual executives of these corporations regarding the opioid crisis? Explain.

Sources: Sharon Terlep, "Walgreens, CVS Reach $10 Billion Deal Over Opioids," *The Wall Street Journal,* November 3, 2022 [**https://www.wsj.com**]; Geroge Frey, "Sackler Family Agrees to Pay $6 Billion in New Opioid Settlement between Purdue Pharma and States," *CNBC,* March 3, 2022 [**https://www.cnbc.com/**]; The U.S. Department of Justice, Office of Public Affairs, "Deputy Attorney General Lisa O. Monaco Delivers Remarks on Corporate Criminal Enforcement," *Justice News*, September 15, 2022 [**https://www.justice.gov/**]; Brian Mann, "Critics Want Sacklers to Face Criminal Charges for Role in Opioid Crisis," *NPR,* November 25, 2020 [**https://www.npr.org**]; and Nathaniel Weixel, "Senate Democrats Urge DOJ to Open Criminal Investigation into Sackler Family Members," *The Hill,* February 16, 2022 [**https://thehill.com/**].

Prison for Some Bosses

Nine people died and over 700 were reported as ill from salmonella poisoning linked to a Peanut Corporation of America processing plant in Georgia. Prosecutors showed that the plant did not meet federal health standards and that plant managers knowingly shipped contaminated peanut butter. The plant was shut down, the company was liquidated, and three individuals received prison terms. The CEO, Stewart Parnell, was sentenced to 28 years in prison for his crimes, including conspiracy, obstruction of justice, and introduction of adulterated food.[84]

Corporations as Crime Victims

While the headlines in recent years have often featured allegations of criminal conduct by corporations, corporate America itself can be the victim of criminals, both employees and outsiders. Cybercrime, bribery, money laundering, fraud, and outright theft harm the bottom line.

Nearly half of the organizations surveyed in a recent PricewaterhouseCoopers' (PwC) Global Economic Crime and Fraud survey reported that their organizations had suffered economic crime in the previous 24 months.[85]

Is Theft Sometimes OK?

A shopper wrote a letter to the editor explaining how he felt after observing what appeared to be a theft:

> [A]t Wal-Mart I saw a person try to put an item in their jacket. At first I thought this person was a jerk. . . . But after I returned home, I became convinced that it was OK to steal. . . . When I compare the theft of a $15 item to the grand larceny by corporate America, which ran Enron into the ground, which reaps record oil profits, . . . which occupies the seats of government and takes bribes, I now see the act of stealing a small gift . . . as heroic.[86]

Questions

1. What do you think the letter writer meant when they applied the label "heroic" to the apparent theft?
2. Should we be more aggressive in pursuing corporate fraud? Explain.

Source: Greg Wilcox, "It's All Relative," *The Des Moines Register,* December 12, 2005, p. 6A.

Prevention or Enhanced Punishment

Responding to public outrage over Enron, WorldCom, and other stunning and destructive corporate scandals, Congress and the president enacted the 2002 Sarbanes–Oxley Act (SOX) to attack crime by publicly traded companies. Among its provisions, the bill

- Established an independent board to oversee the accounting profession.
- Required senior executives to personally certify the accuracy of their financial reports.
- Created new crimes and raised penalties.
- Required auditors to attest to the efficacy of the internal control systems designed to assure the accuracy of corporate financial information.
- Required companies to disclose whether they have adopted an ethics code for senior financial management; and if not, why not.

SOX has often been criticized as a drain on company resources and an impediment to economic growth. A recent Protiviti survey said the hours that companies devoted to compliance have continued to increase.[87] Nevertheless, in an earlier survey, three out of four large company respondents said that SOX requirements had resulted in improved financial reporting processes in their organizations. Another study found that over one-third of chief financial officers believed internal control audits had greatly helped their company; just over half of chief financial officers said it had helped somewhat.[88]

Sentencing

Federal sentencing guidelines provide ranges (for example, 10–12 months' imprisonment) within which judges are advised or required to impose sentences. The guidelines are designed to provide greater predictability and consistency in punishment. Relying on the crime's "offense level" and the defendant's criminal history, a punishment range is established for each category of white-collar and street crime.

Organizational sentencing guidelines are applied to corporate crime. Companies involved in crimes may receive reduced penalties if they have effective compliance programs in place to prevent and detect crime. The programs must include ethics training and monitoring the success of compliance efforts. Responsibility for compliance rests explicitly with the board of directors and top-level executives. Directors and officers complying with the guidelines may receive leniency. Those engaging in aggravating behaviors like lending leadership support to the commission of a crime may face increased punishment. The challenges of maintaining close, effective compliance in extended, complex giants such as Walmart are formidable.

Recent Supreme Court decisions have diminished the power of the guidelines by significantly restoring federal judges' authority to deviate from them on a case-by-case basis.

Too Lenient?

Federal judge Sandra Beckwith in Ohio stretched judicial latitude to the maximum in her sentencing of Michael E. Peppel, former board chair and CEO of technology firm MCSi. Peppel pleaded guilty to fraud, which resulted in estimated damages of $18 million. The federal sentencing guidelines called for eight to ten years of incarceration, but the judge handed down a sentence of seven days in jail and three years of supervised release. The judge had responded to Peppel's 100 letters of support, strong role in the community, business expertise, five children, and other family needs. On appeal, however, the federal Sixth Circuit Court of Appeals ruled that Judge Beckwith had abused her discretion. The appeals court rejected the reasoning that Peppel's professional skills and capacity to contribute to society justified a lighter sentence and remanded the case. Judge Beckwith then sentenced Peppel to two years in prison, three years of court supervision, and a $5 million fine.

Question

Critics of increased government activism regard the free market as the best protection against corporate misconduct. They see SOX, the sentencing guidelines, and aggressive prosecution as government-inflicted drags on the economy. Do you agree? Explain. [For more on white-collar crime, see **www.fbi.gov/investigate/white-collar-crime**.]

Sources: *United States v. Peppel,* 707 F.3d 627 (6th Cir. 2013); and Walter Pavlo, "6th Circuit to Michael Peppel 'You Need More Prison Time,'" *Forbes,* February 18, 2013 [**www.forbes.com**].

Global Bribery

Door-to-door cosmetics giant Avon agreed in 2014 to pay $135 million to settle charges that its China subsidiary had paid about $8 million in bribes to various Chinese officials and that Avon's books failed to properly record those payments.[89] Former U.S. Attorney Preet Bharara said

> Avon China was in the door-to-door influence-peddling business, and for years its corporate parent, rather than putting an end to the practice, conspired to cover it up.[90]

LO 2-8 Explain the general requirements of the Foreign Corrupt Practices Act.

Polo-brand clothier Ralph Lauren paid $1.6 million in fines in 2013 to resolve federal bribery charges.[91] Ralph Lauren Corp. reportedly bribed Argentine customs officials with about $600,000 worth of perfume, dresses, and cash from 2004 to 2009 to facilitate passage of company products into the country. Lauren officials say they reported the misconduct as soon as they learned of it.

In many cultures, the payment of bribes–*baksheesh* (Middle East), *huilu* (China), *vzyatku* (Russia), *mordida* (Latin America), or *dash* (Africa)–is accepted as a necessary and, in some cases, lawful way of doing business. American firms and officers, sometimes willingly and sometimes only under great pressure, have engaged in practices that are illegal and unethical in American culture.

The Foreign Corrupt Practices Act (FCPA), the chief federal weapon against bribery abroad, was enacted in 1977 in response to disclosure of widespread bribery by American firms. In brief, the FCPA provides that U.S. nationals and businesses acting anywhere in the world, foreign nationals and companies acting in U.S. territory, and foreign companies listed on a U.S. stock exchange are engaging in criminal conduct if they offer or provide money or anything of value to foreign government officials to obtain or retain business or otherwise secure "any improper advantage." In addition, the FCPA requires rigorous internal accounting controls and careful record-keeping to ensure that bribes cannot be concealed via "slush funds" and other devices. Civil and criminal fines can be imposed on both individuals and companies, and individuals can be imprisoned. [For a "series of measures to help organizations prevent, detect and address bribery," see the International Organization for Standardization (ISO) antibribery global standard at **www.iso.org/iso/home/standards/management-standards/iso37001.htm.**]

Grease

The act does not forbid "grease" payments to foreign officials where the purpose of the payments is "to expedite or to secure the performance of a routine governmental action," such as processing papers (like visas), providing police protection, or securing phone service. Likewise a "small gift or token of esteem or gratitude" ordinarily is permissible. Those accused may offer the affirmative defense that the alleged payoff was lawful in the host country or was a normal, reasonable business expenditure directed to specific marketing and contract-performance activities. [For the FCPA Blog, see **www.fcpablog.com.**]

FCPA Controversy

The FCPA has been controversial from the outset. Some businesspeople see it as a blessing both because it is an honorable attempt at a firm moral stance and because it is often useful for an American businessperson abroad to say, "No, our laws forbid me from doing that." On the other hand, some consider the act damaging to American competitiveness. Indeed, U.S. Assistant Attorney General Leslie Caldwell recently said: "In more than half of all countries it's very difficult to do business without being faced with the potential of a FCPA violation."[92]

Recognizing that corruption is a great risk to the global economy, most industrial countries are now moving toward the zero-tolerance view held by the United States. In 2015, China, Mexico, and South Korea adopted new anticorruption reforms. In addition to the FCPA, the United States participates in several other global anticorruption initiatives. [For example, see the OECD Anti-Bribery Convention at **https://www.oecd.org/daf/anti-bribery/2021-oecd-anti-bribery-recommendation.htm**.]

U.S. Corruption

FCPA enforcement actions by the Department of Justice (DOJ) and the Securities and Exchange Commission (SEC) vary tremendously from year to year. Measured by the year an action is initiated, prior to 2007, the largest number commenced in any year totaled 14, 8 brought by the SEC and 6 by the DOJ in 2006. Since then, the lowest number has been 23 in 2014 (8 SEC and 15 DOJ) and the peak of 58 was in 2016 (29 each for the SEC and DOJ).[93]

By far the most publicized FCPA news in recent years has involved Walmart's alleged bribes in Mexico that were designed to outflank competitors by winning approval for new store construction, including one near ancient pyramids. The inquiry was broadened to include China, Brazil, and India. *The New York Times* reported that Walmart was often the aggressor in these alleged deals:

> The *Times*'s examination reveals that Wal-Mart de Mexico was not the reluctant victim of a corrupt culture that insisted on bribes as the cost of doing business. Nor did it pay bribes merely to speed up routine approvals. Rather, Wal-Mart de Mexico was an aggressive and creative corrupter, offering large payoffs to get what the law otherwise prohibited. It used bribes to subvert democratic governance—public votes, open debates, transparent procedures. It used bribes to circumvent regulatory safeguards that protect Mexican citizens from unsafe construction.[94]

The SEC charged Walmart with violations of the FCPA for "failing to operate a sufficient anti-corruption compliance program for more than a decade as the retailer experienced rapid international growth."[95] Walmart agreed to pay $114 million to settle the SEC's charges and another $138 million with regard to the criminal charges brought by the DOJ. Those payments were dwarfed by Walmart's costs for internal investigations, estimated at one to two billion dollars.[96]

> The United States ranked 23rd in Transparency International's 2019 Corruption Perceptions Index.

The United States ranked 23rd in Transparency International's 2019 Corruption Perceptions Index, which aggregates data provided by experts and business leaders to assess the perceived level of *public sector* corruption around the globe. The countries perceived to be least corrupt were Denmark, New Zealand, and Finland. Most of northern and western Europe, as well as Canada, the United Kingdom, and Australia, were perceived to be less corrupt than the United States. China (80), India (80), Brazil (106), and Russia (137) were among the nations ranking lower than the United States.[97]

Bribery's Reach

Professional soccer, the "Beautiful Game," is a great passion for hundreds of millions around the globe. The U.S. Justice Department initiated a criminal action against a number of officials in FIFA, soccer's governing body, and several corporate executives. The charges included racketeering, fraud, and money laundering involving $150 million. The wrongdoing involved kickbacks to FIFA officials from soccer marketing companies and bribes and kickbacks associated with the site selection for the World Cup and the FIFA presidential election.[98]

Beyond the FIFA scandal, bribery in many countries touches daily life in much more direct and frustrating ways:

> Nikolai can't even count the number of bribes he has paid in his life.

> Like many Russians, Nikolai can't even count the number of bribes he has paid in his life. He remembers the big ones, like the $1,000 he paid to avoid mandatory military service or the $1,200 he gave his wife's obstetrician to ensure her a place at one of Moscow's state-run maternity hospitals. But the small ones, like the dozens of $10 to $20 bribes he's handed to traffic police over the years, are instantly forgotten.[99]

PRACTICING ETHICS Bribe the Terrorists?

Banadex, a subsidiary of Cincinnati-based Chiquita Brands International, paid bribes to Colombian rebels over a period of years, including $1.7 million from 1997 to 2004 to the AUC (Autodefensas Unidas de Colombia—now disbanded), a right-wing Colombian terrorist group. Chiquita, one of the world's leading banana producers with operations in 70 nations, learned of the payments in 2000 but allowed them to continue. At the time, terrorists in Colombia were holding Americans for ransom or killing some of them, and years earlier four Chiquita employees had been killed by left-wing guerrillas. The bribes, then lawful under American and Colombian law, were thought necessary to protect employees and company property at Chiquita's Colombian operations.

In 2003, Chiquita allegedly "stumbled across" news that in 2001 the AUC had been designated a "foreign terrorist organization" by the U.S. government, which meant payments thereafter were unlawful, but the payments continued. Chiquita said it was a victim of extortion and that stopping the payments would have endangered its employees. The bribe payments were stopped in 2004, and Chiquita sold its Colombian interests. Chiquita had earned about $50 million in profits from the time AUC was designated a terrorist organization until the period when the payments ceased.

During the period of Chiquita payments to AUC, some 4,000 Colombians were killed in the banana-growing region of Colombia. An Organization of American States investigation concluded that 3,000 Central American rifles and millions of rounds of ammunition reached the terrorists after allegedly being unloaded at a Colombian port by Banadex.

In 2007, Chiquita pleaded guilty to U.S. charges of engaging in transactions with terrorists and paid a $25 million fine. U.S. Justice Department officials concluded their investigation in 2007 by deciding not to bring criminal charges against former Chiquita officials.

Families of Colombians killed or tortured by the terrorists, along with human rights groups, have filed several civil lawsuits against Chiquita. In 2014, the U.S. 11th Circuit Court of Appeals ruled that those claims could not be litigated in the United States and the U.S. Supreme Court declined to review that decision. In 2016 a federal district court in Florida ruled that the Colombian victims' lawsuits against specific Chiquita executives could go forward. However, in 2019 those lawsuits were dismissed.

Questions

1. Chiquita argued that the safety of its employees required payment of the bribes, even after learning of their illegality. What would you have done, had you been in charge? Explain.
2. Should Chiquita's corporate officers have been prosecuted by the U.S. government? Explain.
3. In 2019, more than 100 Gold Star Families sued several large U.S. defense contractors for allegedly making illegal payments to the Taliban for "protection," which the plaintiffs argue funded the Taliban's attacks on Americans in Afghanistan. What defense might the defense contractors raise? How might the plaintiffs respond? Explain.
4. In 2021, Gold Star Families sued banks such as Deutsche Bank for providing banking services to customers that it knew were dealing with terrorists. Compare the ethical culpability of the banks to the defense contractors described in the above question.

Sources: Sibylla Brodzinsky, "Chiquita Case Puts Big Firms on Notice," *The Christian Science Monitor,* April 11, 2007 [**www.csmonitor.com**]; Business & Human Rights Resource Center, "Chiquita Lawsuits (re Colombia)," 2016 [**https://business-humanrights.org**]; David J. Lynch, "Murder and Payoffs Taint Business in Colombia," *USA TODAY,* October 30, 2007, p. 1B; *Cardona v. Chiquita Brands Int'l,* 760 F.3d 1185 (11th Cir. 2014); *In re Chiquita Brands International Inc. Alien Tort Statute and Shareholder Derivative Litigation,* 08-MD-01916-KAM, U.S. District Court, Southern District of Florida (2016); The Associated Press, "Judge Throws Out Lawsuit Alleging Chiquita Funded Massacres," *ABC News,* September 14, 2019 [**https://abcnews.go.com**]; Matthew S. Schwartz, "Gold Star Families Sue Defense Contractors, Alleging They Funded the Taliban," *National Public Radio,* December 28, 2019 [**www.npr.org**]; and Emily Flitter, "Gold Star Families Accuse Major Banks of Aiding Terrorists," *The New York Times,* August 5, 2021 [**https://www.nytimes.com/**].

Whistleblowing

LO 2-9
Discuss some of the risks and rewards of whistleblowing.

In a 2022 whistleblower complaint to U.S. regulators, Peter Zatko, a former Twitter security executive, alleged that Twitter's privacy, security, and content moderation measures were seriously deficient, and that Twitter had deceitfully misled its Board of Directors and the public on Twitter's security.[100] The disclosure also claimed that one or more Twitter employees may be working for a foreign intelligence service.[101] Zatko later testified to the U.S. Senate Judiciary Committee regarding the matters raised in his whistleblower complaint.[102] In an interview, Zatko said: whistleblowing "wasn't my first choice" but after "exhausting all internal options" he had "found that ethically. . . I was obligated to follow the law" and make the disclosures, given the importance of Twitter as a social media platform.[103]

Whistleblowing wasn't his first choice.

Many federal and state statutes include whistleblower provisions, and the federal False Claims Act rewards those who help stop fraud against the government. Federal false claims recoveries in fiscal year 2021 totaled over $5.6 billion, and whistleblowers were paid over $230 million for their assistance.[104] Whistleblowers typically are entitled to 10 to 30 percent of the recovery from the wrongdoer. [For an overview of whistleblower activity and protections, see **www.whistleblowers.org** for a law firm representing whistleblowers as well as some whistleblower stories, see **www.phillipsandcohen.com**.]

Retaliation

James Nordgaard, a hedge fund trader, said his former employer, Paradigm Capital, "embarked on a campaign of retaliation" against him after he blew the whistle on what he says were "trading violations." Nordgaard says he was removed from his trading desk, isolated in a room "with little ventilation," and subsequently demoted.[105]

> Americans have long deplored "squealing."

Federal law provides varying degrees of protection from retaliation, but whistleblowers like Nordgaard often pay a high price for exercising their consciences. Americans have long deplored "squealing," and we sometimes ignore violations, partly out of fear of retribution. Based on a national survey in 2013 of employees who observed workplace misconduct in 2012, 63 percent reported what they saw, most often to a direct supervisor, but often to more than one person inside the company. Relatively few reported violations outside the organization, and only nine percent did so to a government authority.[106]

Employers sometimes discourage whistleblowing by requiring employees to sign confidentiality (also known as nondisclosure) agreements. Employers have a right to protect confidential information such as trade secrets, but in general, they cannot legally require employees to desist from legitimate whistleblowing to the government. On the other hand, some critics believe the very high recoveries available to whistleblowers may turn employees into "entrepreneurs" searching for possible wrongdoing in their companies in order to secure a financial payoff. In *Digital Realty Trust v. Somers,* the U.S. Supreme Court held that the anti-retaliation provisions of the 2010 Dodd-Frank Act protect only those who report alleged violations to the SEC, and not those who only used a company's internal compliance system.[107]

Questions

1. What might be the impact of *Digital Realty* on whistleblowers? Why might this cause concerns for corporations with internal complaint procedures? Explain.
2. *a.* How would you feel about a classmate who blew the whistle on you for cheating on an examination?

   b. Would you report cheating by a classmate if it came to your attention? Explain.

Ethics Codes

LO 2-10
Explain the general purpose of ethics codes in the workplace.

Most big companies have voluntarily developed ethics codes. Section 406 of SOX specifically requires publicly traded companies to adopt a code of ethics for senior financial officers or explain why they have not done so. Section 406 defines a code of ethics as written standards that are reasonably designed to deter wrongdoing and to promote such behaviors as honest conduct, full disclosure in reports, compliance with all applicable laws and rules, prompt reporting of violations, and methods for conforming to the code's expectations.

Responding to SOX and other pressures, an increasing number of companies have prepared more detailed codes, displayed them more prominently, required employees to read and sign the codes, and created training methods to more firmly integrate ethical expectations into company decision making. Companies that can show well-developed ethical systems, including codes of conduct and compliance with those codes, may receive more sympathetic treatment from the justice system if criminal problems emerge. [For the Ethics & Compliance Initiative, see **www.ethics.org**.]

Are codes effective in practice? The evidence is mixed, although a study of 392 international companies found a positive relationship between the quality (topics covered, tone, commitment to corporate values, nonretaliation provisions, etc.) of codes of conduct and ethical performance. Companies that established and enforced high-quality codes of conduct were found to rank highly in corporate citizenship, sustainability, ethical behavior, and public perception of the firm.[108] Likewise, a recent study supports the effectiveness of SOX 406 in that public companies with an effective ethics code for their senior financial officers improved the integrity of their financial reporting.[109] [For information on global corporate governance and citizenship, see **www.conference-board.org**.]

Research Exercise

Can ethics be taught? Many people say no. Experts at the Markkula Center for Applied Ethics at Santa Clara University explored that question. See **www.scu.edu/ethics/practicing/decision/canethicsbetaught.html.**

a. Explain their conclusion.

b. Do you agree with their conclusion? How strongly do you hold your opinion? Explain.

Chapter Questions

1. *Business Ethics* reported the following ethical dilemma submitted by an anonymous reader:

   > Mary had only a few days to earn $1,000 in sales that would allow her to reach the $1 million sales plateau when she would receive a $10,000 bonus allowing her to finance her dream home. The sales climate was tough, but she had one remaining prospect, inner-city Lincoln School, which could make especially good use of new educational materials. Lincoln had no budget for discretionary purchases, but Mary considered "donating" $1,000 to the school. In return they would make the purchases that would put her over the top. She knew her donation would help disadvantaged students and herself, but her conscience was troubled.[110]

   What should she do? Explain.

2. We are often confronted with questions about the boundaries of our personal responsibilities. Assume you are at a professional baseball game in the city in which you live.
   a. Another fan turns to you and uses a racial slur to describe the person who just sang the national anthem. What would you do? What do you think you should do? Explain.
   b. You observe fans making racial slurs and throwing bags of peanuts at a player on the visiting team. What would you do? What do you think you should do? Explain.[111]

3. *a.* With regard to the college admissions scandal discussed earlier in the chapter, are the actions of the parents involved ethically defensible? Explain.
   b. Should the children, who were admitted to the colleges based on their parents' actions, themselves face consequences? Explain.

4. *a.* In 2020, Major League Baseball Commissioner Rob Manfred issued a report on arguably the most significant scandal since the steroid abuses of the 2000s. The Houston Astros were fined $5 million, the maximum penalty allowed, and were ordered to forfeit the next two first- and second-round draft picks for illegal sign-stealing. Electronic devices had been used to provide dugout images of the opposing team's catcher

signaling pitches. The anticipated pitches were communicated to the batters by banging on a trashcan. The Commissioner, who described the Astros' culture as "very problematic," also imposed a one-year suspension from baseball on the Astros' general manager Jeff Luhnow and manager A.J. Hinch. Shortly thereafter, they were fired by team owner Jim Crane, as was bench coach Alex Cora, who was named in the report as a "mastermind" of the operation. Carlos Beltran, considered a potential Hall of Famer and was a former Astros player involved in the misconduct, agreed to leave his new position as manager of the New York Mets. Manfred had warned the entire league about cheating in 2017 after imposing a moderate fine on the Boston Red Sox for illegal sign-stealing: "future violations . . . will be subject to more serious sanctions." The Astros' conduct, Manfred's report stated, "raise[d] questions about the integrity" of baseball.[112] Should we take seriously violations of sportsmanship or is it "only a game"? Explain.

b. Does it matter whether such conduct occurs in a professional, as opposed to an amateur, setting? Explain.

5. A group of 12 employees at a real estate office in south Florida chipped in $20 each toward the purchase of lottery tickets for a Powerball drawing. One employee, Jennifer Maldanado, an administrative assistant who had been working in the office for only two weeks and had not even received her first paycheck yet, declined to join the pool. The group of 12 won $1 million, which came to over $83,000 each. Laurie Finkelstein Reader, the team leader in the office, said that winning was not going to be as much fun for the group without Maldanado, so she texted the other winners and they all agreed to give a portion (undivulged) of their winnings to Maldanado.[113]

a. Morally speaking, is sharing winnings more commendable than keeping them all for oneself? Explain.

b. Would this real estate office operate more effectively if workers shared their earnings as well as their lottery winnings? Explain.

c. Morally speaking, would sharing earnings be the more commendable approach to the office's pay policies? Explain.

d. Most of the office workers who shared with Maldanado were women. Do you think women are more inclined to share than men? If so, are women more worthy of moral approval than men? Explain.

6. According to reporting in *The New York Times,* in a 2021 fundraising call with Goldman Sachs, Ozy Media's Chief Operating Officer Samir Rao impersonated an executive from Alphabet Inc.'s YouTube.[114] Goldman Sachs, having discovered the impersonation, did not invest in Ozy, nor did Google ever invest in Ozy.[115] In October 2021, Lifeline Holdings sued Ozy Media for fraud, claiming it had invested in Ozy after being told by Ozy executives that Goldman Sachs and Google were going to invest in Ozy.[116] In announcing that Ozy's motion to dismiss would be granted, the judge reportedly said: "Not all that's shocking is illegal."[117]

a. How is an executive pretending to be a supposed investor while on a fundraising call the same as a job candidate lip-syncing another person's answers during an interview with a prospective employer? How is it different? Explain.

b. What are the limits of the law in defining ethical conduct? Explain.

7. *The Los Angeles Times* headlined a story: "Getting Brilliant Students to Seek Jobs beyond Wall Street."[118] The article examined the movement at some of the nation's top universities to encourage the brightest graduates to broaden their job search beyond high-paying Wall Street opportunities. An online campaign labeled "Stop the Brain Drain" gathered signatures and pushed for changes in campus recruiting practices. The prestigious Massachusetts Institute of Technology has an entrepreneurship center to provide support for students seeking work with start-ups and other smaller ventures. Bill Aulet, who heads the center, explained some of his reasoning: "Once it became clear that financial instruments were a big cause of the [financial] crisis, and that's what our incredibly intelligent students were being used for, we thought, 'Boy, can't they be used to do more useful things?'"[119]
   a. Would we be better off as a nation if more of our brighter students shunned Wall Street jobs? Explain.
   b. What is your ideal job? Explain.
8. A pharmacist in Lexington, Kentucky, refused to stock over-the-counter weight reducers. His reasons were: (1) the active ingredient was the same as that in nasal decongestants; (2) he feared their side effects, such as high blood pressure; and (3) he felt weight reduction should be achieved via self-discipline.[120] Assume the pharmacist manages the store for a group of owners who have given him complete authority over the products stocked. Was his decision ethical? Explain.
9. Based on a 2022 report from blockchain analysis firm Chainanalysis, $1.9 billion worth of cryptocurrency was stolen in hacks in the first seven months of 2022 alone. Arguments for restricting or banning cryptocurrency include that it is being used for illegal purposes, and that cryptocurrency trading could destabilize financial structures. Is cryptocurrency itself ethical? Is trading in cryptocurrency ethical? Explain your response.[121]
10. Risperdal, a Johnson & Johnson antipsychotic medicine, provides significant benefits, but it also can cause strokes among the elderly and generate large breasts in boys. Johnson & Johnson reportedly knew about these issues, but it manipulated and hid data about the problems and eventually pled guilty to a crime. Johnson & Johnson was expected to pay about $6 billion in penalties for its alleged wrongdoing, but it earned an estimated $18 billion in profits on the drug. The person in charge of marketing Risperdal was subsequently named CEO, a role in which he earned about $25 million in 2014.[122]
    a. Should Johnson & Johnson have been punished in an amount equal to its profits? Explain.
    b. Does corporate crime pay? Explain.
    c. Should managers who participate in serious wrongdoing be denied subsequent promotions? Explain.
11. In general, does the American value system favor "cheaters" who win in life's various competitions over virtuous individuals who "lose" with regularity? Explain.
12. If you were an executive about to hire a new manager, which of the following qualities would you consider most and least important: verbal skills, honesty and integrity, enthusiasm, appearance, or sense of humor? Explain.

13. Several CEOs withdrew from White House business advisory councils after President Trump's response to violence at a 2017 white nationalists' rally caused controversy. Merck's CEO, Kenneth Frazier, resigned from the President's manufacturing council, saying in part: "America's leaders must honor our fundamental values." Which ethics theory or theories support Mr. Frazier's statement and decision? Explain.[123]
14. You and two college classmates, both 20 years old, go to a restaurant near campus. Before paying for dinner, they both show the waitress their "AARP cards"–American Association of Retired Persons–and receive a discount on their bill. They explain that they joined AARP to receive the discounts, having completed the application form honestly, stating their correct age, and paying for their AARP membership. You question whether it is ethical for them to use their AARP cards for discounts. How might they respond?[124] Explain.
15. Can business people successfully guide their conduct by the Golden Rule? Explain.
16. Whistleblower Bradley Birkenfeld was awarded a $104 million government payment for telling the Internal Revenue Service (IRS) how his employer, Swiss bank UBS, helped thousands of Americans evade taxes. Birkenfeld's inside information helped the U.S. government crack open Swiss banking secrecy. As a result, at least 33,000 Americans voluntarily disclosed their offshore accounts, resulting in perhaps $5 billion in revenue for the federal government. Birkenfeld had been sentenced earlier to 40 months in prison for fraud in withholding information from federal investigators, but he was released early. Birkenfeld reportedly also told a court that he had smuggled diamonds for a client in a toothpaste tube. Despite those alleged misdeeds, the government decided to make the big payment to Birkenfeld to avoid discouraging other potential whistleblowers.[125] Do you think whistleblowers who committed wrongdoing themselves should be able to receive such monetary awards? Explain.
17. Self-driving cars raise ethical issues, such as who the car saves in the event of an accident: passengers, pedestrians, or the driver. Who should make such decisions regarding the design of self-driving cars? Explain.[126]
18. Assume you are working as manager of women's clothing in a large department store. You observe the manager of equivalent rank for men's clothing performing poorly in that she arrives late for work, keeps records ineptly, and is rude to customers. Her work, however, has no direct impact on your department.
    a. Do you have any responsibility either to help her or to report her poor performance? Explain.
    b. If the store as a whole performs poorly, but you have performed well, do you bear any personal responsibility for the store's failure in that you confined your efforts exclusively to your own department even though you witnessed mismanagement in the men's clothing department? Explain.

Notes

1. Bastiaan Vanacker, "Villains and Heroes in Times of Crisis," *Center for Digital Ethics and Policy,* Loyola University Chicago, May 6, 2020 [**https://www.luc.edu/digitalethics/**].
2. Ibid.

3. Ibid citing Prof. Dylan Selterman. Also cited: Prof. Garrett Hardin, "The Tragedy of the Commons," *Science*, December 13, 1968 [**https://www.science.org/**].
4. Megan Brenan and Nicole Willcoxon, "50% of Americans Rate U.S. Moral Values as 'Poor.'" *Gallup News*, June 15, 2022 [**www.news.gallup.com**].
5. Ibid.
6. Megan Brenan, "Americans Say U.S. Morals Not Good and Getting Worse," *Gallup,* May 31, 2009 [**https://news/gallup.com**].
7. Megan Brenan and Nicole Willcoxon, "50% of Americans Rate U.S. Moral Values as 'Poor.'" *Gallup News*, June 15, 2022 [**www.news.gallup.com**].
8. Steven Lee Myers, "Twitter Leads in Escalating Misinformation," *The New York Times,* October 14, 2022 [**www.newyorktimes.com**].
9. David Callahan, *The Cheating Culture: Why More Americans Are Doing Wrong to Get Ahead,* New York: Harcourt, 2004.
10. Ibid.
11. David M. Mayer, "Why Rich Parents Are More Likely to Be Unethical," *The Conversation,* March 15, 2019 [**https://theconversation.com**].
12. For a commentary on Ariely's book, see David Brooks, "The Moral Diet," *The New York Times,* June 7, 2012 [**www.nytimes.com**].
13. Margaret Barthel, "How to Stop Cheating in College," *The Atlantic,* April 20, 2016 [**www.theatlantic.com**].
14. Karen Farkas, "86 Percent of College Students Say They've Cheated. It's Easier than Ever with Mobile Devices," *Cleveland.com*, February 2, 2017 [**www.cleveland.com**].
15. Ibid.
16. Anwar Abdi, "90 Percent of College Students Have Cheated," *University Magazine,* February 20, 2018 [**https://www.universitymagazine.ca/**].
17. Ibid.
18. Leslie Wayne, "A Promise to Be Ethical in an Era of Immorality," *The New York Times,* May 30, 2009 [**www.nytimes.com**].
19. Lisa Marinelli, "Here's What Generation Z Expects From the Workplace," Business in Greater Gainesville, January 17 [**https://businessmagazinegainesville.com/heres-what-generation-z-expects-from-the-workplace/**].
20. Deloitte Touche Tohmatsu, "The Deloitte Global 2022 Gen Z and Millennial Survey," 2022 [**https://www2.deloitte.com/**].
21. Ibid.
22. EY, "2021 Gen Z Segmentation Study," EY Press Release, November 4, 2021 [**https://www.ey.com/**].
23. Lisa Ward, "Investors' Views on ESG," *The Wall Street Journal*, November 3, 2022, pp. R1–2.
24. Chris Penny, "Engaging Gen Z with Empathy," *ANA*, April 4, 2022 [**https://www.ana.net/**].
25. For more about existentialism, see Andrew West, "Sartrean Existentialism and Ethical Decision-Making in Business," *Journal of Business Ethics* 81 (2008), p. 15.
26. Carl Hausman, "Responsibility," *Ethics Newsline,* September 28, 2009 [**www.globalethics.org**].
27. Cara Buckley, "Man Is Rescued by Stranger on Subway Tracks," *The New York Times,* January 3, 2007.
28. Associated Press, "British Priest: Shoplifting Is Sometimes OK," *The Waterloo/Cedar Falls Courier,* December 23, 2009, p. 3A.

29. Teagan Ampe, "Autonomous Accidents: The Ethics of Self-Driving Car Crashes," *Viterbi* (Fall 2020) **[https: vce.usc.edu]**.
30. Mary Donohue, "Fighting Back Against the Tyranny of the Manager," *HuffPost Business Canada,* January 23, 2014 **[www.huffingtonpost.ca]**.
31. Kathy Gurchiek, "Workplace Rudeness: Put a Cork in It!," *SHRM.org,* July 15, 2015 **[www.shrm.org]**.
32. Dylan Love, "16 Examples of Steve Jobs Being a Huge Jerk," *Business Insider,* October 25, 2011 **[www.businessinsider.com]**.
33. Jerry Useem, "Why It Pays to Be a Jerk," *The Atlantic,* June 2015 **[www.theatlantic.com]**.
34. Ibid.
35. Ibid.
36. Olga Khazan, "It Pays to Be Nice," *Atlantic,* June 23, 2015 **[https://www.atlantic.com]**.
37. Tessa Berenson, "The Science Behind Why Nice People Finish Last–And How to Fix That," *Time,* September 26, 2015 **[time.com]**.
38. Ibid.
39. Ibid.
40. Lorenzo Reyes, "Is the Patriots' Secret Weapon Their Character Coach?" *USA Today,* February 2, 2018 **[www.usatoday.com]**.
41. Richard Lorant, Associated Press, "A Mill Owner's Compassion Rescues Thousands of Jobs after Devastating Fire," *Chicago Tribune,* December 10, 1996, p. 8.
42. Richard Lorant, "Rebuilding Corporate Compassion-Oath to Millworkers May Pay Off," *Seattle Times,* December 11, 1996 **[http://community.seattletimes.nwsource.com]**.
43. Timothy Schellhardt, "Are Layoffs Moral? One Firm's Answer: You Ask, We'll Sue," *The Wall Street Journal,* August 1, 1996, p. A1.
44. Ibid.
45. John P. McKenzie, "Lending a Hand if a Company Asks," *The New York Times,* February 3, 2002, Sec. 3, p. 11.
46. Justin McCarthy, "U.S. Confidence in Organized Religion Remains Low," *Gallup News*, July 8, 2019 **[www.gallup.com]**.
47. R. J. Reinhart, "Nurses Continue to Rate Highest in Honesty, Ethics," *Gallup News*, January 6, 2020 **[https://news.gallup.com]**.
48. The firm, Edelman, specializes in helping businesses and organizations promote and protect their brands and reputations. Its annual survey is called the Edelman Trust Barometer. About Us **[www.edelman.com]**.
49. Edelman, 2022 Edelman Trust Barometer **[https://www.edelman.com/trust/2022-trust-barometer]**.
50. Ibid.
51. Maureen Kline, "Why Business Leaders Need to Earn Trust, and How to Go about Doing It," Inc.com, February 18, 2016 **[www.inc.com]**.
52. Business Roundtable, "Business Roundtable Redefines the Purpose of a Corporation to Promote an Economy That Saves All Americans," August 19, 2019 **[www.businessroundtable.org]**.
53. Ibid.
54. Alan Murray and Bruce Simpson, "Purpose of 'Purpose-Washing'?" *Fortune,* November 11, 2020 **[https://fortune.com/]**.

55. For an elaboration of Kohlberg's stages, see, for example, W. D. Boyce and L. C. Jensen, *Moral Reasoning* (Lincoln, NE: University of Nebraska Press, 1978), pp. 98–109.
56. Lawrence Kohlberg, "The Cognitive-Development Approach to Moral Education," *Phi Delta Kappan* 56 (June 1975), p. 670.
57. Carol Gilligan, "In a Different Voice: Women's Conceptions of Self and Morality," *Harvard Educational Review* 47, no. 4 (November 1977), p. 481.
58. For an overview of the justice versus care debate, see Grace Clement, *Care, Autonomy, and Justice* (Boulder, CO: Westview Press, 1996).
59. James Weber and David Wasieleski, "Investigating Influences on Managers' Moral Reasoning," *Business & Society* 40, no. 1 (March 2001), pp. 79, 83.
60. Diana Robertson et al., "The Neural Processing of Moral Sensitivity to Issues of Justice and Care," *Neuropsychologia* 45 (2007), pp. 755, 763.
61. For a description of the moral intuition argument, see Jonathan Haidt, "The Emotional Dog and Its Rational Tail: A Social Intuitionist Approach to Moral Judgment," *Psychological Review* 108, no. 4 (2001), p. 814.
62. Joshua Greene and Jonathan Haidt, "How (and Where) Does Moral Judgment Work?" *Trends in Cognitive Science* 6 (2002), p. 517.
63. Marc Hauser, *Moral Minds* (New York: HarperCollins Publishers, 2006).
64. Ana Swanson, "The Disturbing Thing Scientists Learned When They Bribed Babies with Graham Crackers," *The Washington Post,* April 25, 2016 [**www.washingtonpost.com**].
65. Nicholas Wade, "Is 'Do Unto Others' Written into Our Genes?" *The New York Times,* September 18, 2007 [**www.nytimes.com**].
66. See, e.g., David Pizarro and Paul Bloom, "The Intelligence of the Moral Intuitions Comment on Haidt," *Psychological Review* 110, no. 1 (2003), p. 193.
67. David Brooks, "The End of Philosophy," *The New York Times,* April 7, 2009 [**www.nytimes.com**].
68. Benedict Carey, "Study Finds Brain Injury Changes Moral Judgment," *The New York Times,* March 21, 2007 [**www.nytimes.com**].
69. Sam A. Hardy, "Identity, Reasoning, and Emotion: An Empirical Comparison of Three Sources of Moral Motivation," *Motivation and Emotion* 30 (2006), p. 207.
70. Ibid.
71. Ruodan Shao, Karl Aquino, and Dan Freeman, "Beyond Moral Reasoning: A Review of Moral Identity Research and Its Implications for Business Ethics," *Business Ethics Quarterly* 18, no. 4 (2008), p. 513.
72. Roger Parloff, "A Harvard Professor Studied Infamous White-Collar Criminals. Here's What he Learned," *Fortune,* October 11, 2016 [**www.fortune.com**].
73. Ethisphere Institute, "The 2022 World's Most Ethical Companies Honorees List," 2022 [**https://worldsmostethicalcompanies.com/honorees/**].
74. 3M, "3M Named as a 2016 World's Most Ethical Company," press release, March 7, 2016 [**http://nws.3m.com**].
75. Ethics and Compliance Initiative, "The State of Ethics and Compliance in the Workplace: A Look at Global Trends," 2021 [**www.ethics.org**].
76. Joseph L. Badaracco Jr. and Allen P. Webb, "Business Ethics: A View from the Trenches," *California Management Review* 37, no. 2 (Winter 1995), pp. 8, 12.
77. Jo Iwasaki, "Tone at the Top," *Ethical Boardroom,* May 26, 2016 [**http://ethicalboardroom.com**].

78. Kirk O. Hanson, "The Six Ethical Dilemmas Every Professional Faces," lecture, Bentley University Verizon Visiting Professorship in Business Ethics, February 3, 2014.
79. Tyler Kepner, "Pitcher Spurns $12 Million, to Keep Self-Respect," *The New York Times,* January 26, 2011.
80. Lauren Weber, "Expense-Account Tightwads Take the Road Less Expensive," *The Wall Street Journal,* March 30, 2012, p. A1.
81. Tanyu Basu, "Timeline: A History of GM's Ignition Switch Defect," *National Public Radio,* March 31, 2014 [**www.npr.org**]; and Eric D. Lawrence, "GM Settles Deadly Ignition Cases for $120 million," *USA Today,* October 20, 2017 [**www.usatoday.com**].
82. Danielle Ivory and Bill Vlasic, "$900 Million Penalty for G.M.'s Deadly Defect Leaves Many Cold," *The New York Times,* September 17, 2015 [**www.nytimes.com**].
83. Vikas Bajaj, "The Lesson of the General Motors Settlement," *The New York Times,* September 17, 2015 [**www.nytimes.com**].
84. Kevin McCoy, "Peanut Exec in Salmonella Case Gets 28 Years," *USA Today,* September 22, 2015 [**www.usatoday.com**].
85. PricewaterhouseCoopers, "Global Economic Crime and Fraud Survey 2022," 2022 [**www.pwc.com**].
86. Greg Wilcox, "It's All Relative," *The Des Moines Register,* December 12, 2005, p. 6A.
87. Kristen Kelly, "New Survey Finds SOX Compliance Efficiency Still Eludes Many Organizations," *Protiviti Blog,* July 8, 2021 [**https://blog.protiviti.com/**].
88. John C. Coates IV and Suraj Srinivasan, "SOX after Ten Years: A Multidisciplinary Review," *Harvard Law and Economics Discussion Paper No. 758,* January 12, 2014 [**http://ssrn.com/abstract=2343108**].
89. Richard Cassin, "Avon Pays $135 Million for China FCPA Resolution," *The FCPA Blog,* December 17, 2014 [**www.fcpablog.com**].
90. Ibid.
91. Chad Bray, "Perfume, Dresses and Cash in Ralph Lauren Bribe Scheme," *The Wall Street Journal,* April 22, 2013 [**www.wsj.com**].
92. Kara Scanell, "U.S Redoubles Efforts on Foreign Bribery Cases," *Financial Times,* February 10, 2016 [**www.ft.com**].
93. Stanford Law School, "DOJ and SEC Enforcement Actions per Year," *Foreign Corrupt Practices Act Clearinghouse,* accessed August 2020 [**http://fcpa.stanford.edu**].
94. David Barstow and Alejandra Xanic von Bertrab, "How Wal-Mart Used Payoffs to Get Its Way in Mexico," *The New York Times,* December 17, 2012 [**www.nytimes.com**].
95. U.S. Securities and Exchange Commission, "Walmart Charged with FCPA Violations," press release, June 20, 2019 [**www.sec.gov**].
96. "The Anti-Bribery Business," *The Economist,* May 9, 2015 [**www.economist.com**].
97. Transparency International, "Corruption Perceptions Index 2019" [**www.transparency.org**].
98. Michael E. Miller and Fred Barbash, "U.S. Indicts World Soccer Officials in Alleged $150 Million FIFA Bribery Scandal," *The Washington Post,* May 27, 2015 [**www.washingtonpost.com**].
99. Michael Mainville, "Bribery Thrives as Big Business in Putin's Russia," *SFGate.com,* January 2, 2007 [**www.sfgate.com**].
100. Sean Lyngaas, "Meet the Former Twitter Executive Blowing the Whistle on the Company," *CNN Business,* August 24, 2022 [**https:www.cnn.com**].

101. Ibid.

102. Clare Duffy, Brian Fung, and Aditi Sangal, "Twitter's Whistleblower Testifies Before Congress," *CNN Business,* September 13, 2022 [**https://www.cnn.com**].

103. Sean Lyngaas, "Meet the Former Twitter Executive Blowing the Whistle on the Company," *CNN Business,* August 24, 2022 [**https:www.cnn.com**].

104. Department of Justice, "Justice Department's False Claims Act Settlements and Judgments Exceed $5.6 Billion in FY 2021," *Justice News,* February 1, 2022 [**www.justice.gov**].

105. Ben Protess and Nathaniel Popper, "Hazy Future for Thriving S.E.C. Whistle Blower Effort," *The New York Time*s, April 23, 2013 [**http://dealbook.nytimes.com**].

106. Dori Meinert, "Minimizing the Risk of Whistle Blower Lawsuits," *HR Magazine,* May 21, 2014 [**www.shrm.org**].

107. Dennis J. Ventry, Jr., "Digital Realty Trust, Inc. v. Somers: Bad News for Employers, Lawyers and Internal Compliance," *Justist,* March 22, 2018 [**www.jurist.org**].

108. Patrick Erwin, "Corporate Codes of Conduct: The Effects of Code Content and Quality on Ethical Performance," *Journal of Business Ethics* 99 (2011), pp. 535–548.

109. Saurabh Ahluwalia, O.C. Ferrell, and Terri L. Rittenburg, "Sarbanes–Oxley Section 406 Code of Ethics for Senior Financial Officers and Firm Behavior," *Journal of Business Ethics,* July 2016.

110. Shel Horowitz, "Should Mary Buy Her Own Bonus?" *Business Ethics,* November 11, 2009, [**www.busniess-ethics.com**].

111. Bill Shaikin, "Would You Speak Up Against Racist Taunts at the Ballpark?" *Los Angeles Times,* May 2, 2017 [**www.latimes.com**]; and Bill Chappell, "Boston Rex Sox Fan Reports A Racial Slur, and a Lifetime Ban Results," *National Public Radio,* May 4, 2017 [**www.npr.org**].

112. Tyler Kepner, "Technology, Once the Astros' Ally, Helps Do Them In," *The New York Times,* January 13, 2020 [**www.nytimes.com**]; and David Waldstein, "Carlos Beltran Out as Mets Manager after Cheating Scandal," *The New York Times,* January 16, 2020 [**www.nytimes.com**].

113. Maria Camila Bernal, "Lucky Lady: She Opted Out of Powerball Pool, but Gets a Cut of $1 Million Anyway," *The Miami Herald,* March 26, 2013 [**www.miamiherald.com**].

114. Ben Smith and Ben Protess, "Two Agencies Investigating Ozy Media," *The New York Times,* November 11, 2021, p. B4.

115. Benjamin Mullin and Suzanne Vranica, "Ozy Media Advertisers Pause Spending," *The New York Times,* October 1, 2021, p. B3.

116. Ben Smith and Ben Protess, "Two Agencies Investigating Ozy Media," *The New York Times,* November 11, 2021, p. B4.

117. Jody Godoy, "Judge to Ozy Media Investor: Not All That's Shocking Is Illegal," *Reuters*, May 4, 2022 [**https://reuters.com**].

118. Nathaniel Popper, "Getting Brilliant Students to Seek Jobs beyond Wall Street," *latimes.com,* November 4, 2011 [**www.latimes.com**].

119. Ibid.

120. Reported on WKYT TV, Channel 27, Evening News, Lexington, Kentucky, May 12, 1980.

121. Jennifer Korn, "$1.9 Billion Stolen in Crypto Hacks So Far This Year," *CNN.com,* August 16, 2022, [**https://www.cnn.com**]; Marco Quiroz-Gutierrez, "Crypto Is Fully Banned in China and 8 Other Countries," *Fortune*, January 4, 2022 [**https://fortune.com**]; McGraw-Hill Higher Educ ation, *Proceedings* (September 2022) [mheducation.com].

122. Nicholas Kristof, "When Crime Pays: J&J's Drug Risperdal," *The New York Times,* September 17, 2015 [**www.nytimes.com**].

123. Vanessa Fuhrmans, "CEOs Rethink Ties with White House," *The Wall Street Journal,* August 16, 2017 [**www.wsj.com**]; and Jennifer Rubin, "Merck, Intel and Under Armour CEOs Are Right to Leave Trump's Advisory Council," *The Washington Post,* August 15, 2017 [**www.washingtonpost.com**].

124. Veronica Dagher, "The Newest Card-Carrying Members of AARP: Twenty-Somethings," *The Wall Street Journal,* October 26, 2022, [**https://www.wsj.com/**].

125. David Kocieniewski, "Whistle-Blower Awarded $104 Million by I.R.S.," *The New York Times,* September 11, 2012 [**www.nytimes.com**].

126. Kristen Lee, "Ford Tells Feds: Autonomous Car Ethics Are On You," *The Morning Shift*, Jalopnik, June 6, 2017 [**https://jalopnik.com**].

Video icon credit: Comstock Images/Alamy Stock Photo

The Corporation and Public Policy: Expanding Responsibilities

After completing this chapter, students will be able to fulfill the following learning objectives:

3-1. Recognize the interdependent relationship between business and society at large.

3-2. Discuss whether business should play a more, or less, active role in politics, education, and other public-sector activities.

3-3. List some of the primary concerns critics have about corporate power in contemporary America.

3-4. Discuss concerns about globalization.

3-5. Make a tentative assessment regarding the proper role of business in society.

3-6. Explain the concept of corporate social responsibility.

3-7. Explain the triple bottom line/sustainability approach to corporate citizenship.

3-8. Discuss whether socially responsible business is "good business."

3-9. Contrast the stakeholder and shareholder approaches to corporate social responsibility.

PRACTICING ETHICS Yvon Chouinard and Patagonia

Outdoor adventurer Yvon Chouinard and his wife, Ellen Pennoyer, founded Patagonia, Inc., the sports clothing and outdoor gear retailer, in 1972. Fifty years later, in 2022, the couple and their family gave the $3 billion privately owned Ventura, California-based corporation, away to a special trust and nonprofit organization, set up to ensure that its annual profits of about $100 million are used to fight climate change and protect the world's undeveloped land. From the very beginning, the company was the product of entrepreneurial drive and a corporate culture practicing "green" business, "management by absence," and "saving the planet."

SOCIAL RESPONSIBILITY

Chouinard's 2005 memoir, *Let My People Go Surfing*, explains his commitment to a workplace where capitalism, ethics, and fun can coexist. Patagonia minimizes workplace monitoring, surf breaks are encouraged, health care is 100 percent paid for, and everyone takes vacations. Two-month paid leaves are offered to both parents, and Patagonia encourages a "traveling baby program," where babies accompany parents on business trips, and the company pays for an accompanying child development teacher. Patagonia is often recognized as one of the best companies to work for in America.

SUSTAINABILITY

Chouinard was an early advocate of doing business in an environmentally friendly way, including, placing notes in Patagonia catalogs that encouraged customers to buy only what they need. Since 1985, Patagonia has donated one percent of its annual sales to environmental groups. Chouinard's 2012 book, *The Responsible Company*, details methods for making money while avoiding undue societal damage.

Patagonia clothing is made in China, Thailand, Vietnam, and a number of other countries, along with limited production in the United States. When establishing ties with a new manufacturing partner, Patagonia's Social and Environmental Responsibility team engages in constant audits, visits, and corrective measures to ensure a safe, healthy, environmentally sound operation. Patagonia refuses to contract with companies employing workers under the age of 15. All workers must be paid "a legal minimum wage," and Patagonia is working toward a "living wage" for all those who make its products.

POLITICAL ACTIVISM

Patagonia has spoken out on public affairs and political issues, a controversial strategy shunned by most corporations. Patagonia endorsed two political candidates in the 2018 midterm elections, and both won. Calling President Trump's 2017 corporate tax cuts "irresponsible," Patagonia announced that its $10 million reduction in taxes would be donated to environmental groups. Patagonia also filed suit against President Trump's 2017 decision to shrink Utah's Bears Ears and Grand Staircase–Escalante national monuments.

Patagonia says the public response to its activism has been "overwhelmingly positive," while acknowledging that its status as a privately held company allows it to act more freely than its publicly traded counterparts.

Questions

1. Is Chouinard correct that companies can treat workers well, respect the environment, and still make money? Explain.
2. If he is correct, why aren't all companies following the Patagonia model?

Sources: David Gelles, "Billionaire No More: Patagonia Founder Gives Away the Company," *The New York Times*, September 14, 2022 (updated September 21, 2022) [**www.nytimes.com**]; Lindsay Blakely, "Patagonia's Unapologetically Political Strategy and the Massive Business It Has Built," *Inc.*, November 30, 2018 [**www.inc.com**]; "Employees Who March to Their Own Music," *BusinessWeek*, December 19, 2005, p. 81; Keith Garber, "Yvon Chouinard: Patagonia Founder Fights for the Environment," *U.S. News & World Report*, October 22, 2009 [**www.usnews.com**]; Hugo Martin, "Outdoor Retailer Patagonia Puts Environment Ahead of Sales Growth," *Los Angeles Times*, May 24, 2012 [**www.latimes.com**]; Brigid Schulte, "A Company That Profits as It Pampers Workers," *Washington Post*, October 25, 2014 [**www.washingtonpost.com**]; and Brad Wieners, "The Gospel of Yvon," *Men's Journal*, July 2007, p. 51.

Introduction

The Yvon Chouinard/Patagonia story expresses the central mission of this chapter: the examination of the corporation's societal duties, if any, beyond providing the best products and services at the lowest prices. Should the corporate community emulate the Patagonia model by addressing public policy challenges such as environmental decline, employee welfare, product safety, public health, poverty, discrimination, and more? Commentator Frank Bruni has argued that corporations, often out of self-interest and a sense of duty, now play crucial leadership roles in addressing these issues:

> [T]hose efforts, coupled with whatever genuine altruism and civic obligation some corporate leaders feel, have produced compelling recent examples of companies showing greater sensitivity to diversity, social justice and the changing tides of public sentiment than lawmakers often manage to.[1]

Historically, we have counted on government to identify and resolve public policy concerns, but as Bruni explains, businesses are increasingly employing their resources to help solve those concerns. In doing so, those businesses may be setting aside short-term profit maximization goals to practice what is often labeled *corporate social responsibility*. That is, they are voluntarily contributing to the general welfare in ways not necessarily required by the market and government.

In this chapter, we explore the business and society relationship in four parts: (1) criticism of corporate America, (2) emerging expectations of corporate social responsibility, (3) management of social responsibility, and (4) examination of some specific business and society issues.

Part One—Corporate Power and Its Critics

LO 3-1 Recognize the interdependent relationship between business and society at large.

Giant businesses have been crucial to America's extraordinary prosperity and its powerful place in the world. Nonetheless, critics have long argued that America's big corporations have not served the public interest well. We recognize that colossal size and the accompanying economies of scale have been critical to American competitiveness in today's tough global market. At the same time, the critics say, that very size permits continuing abuse of the American public. Part One of this chapter examines these arguments.

Corporate Giants

Measured by sales revenue, Walmart is the largest company in America (see Table 3.1), a position it has held in all but three years since 2002. It is, by a wide margin, America's number one employer, with 1.5 million workers (and some 2.2 million workers globally).[2]

By some measures of economic might, American corporations tower over most countries of the world. If we compare corporate revenue with government revenue, Walmart was the 10th largest economic entity in the world as of 2018, and 69 of the 100 largest economic entities were corporations.[3]

Exxon Mobil, number three on the 2020 *Fortune* 500 list but dropping to number six in 2022, is often cited by critics as an example of threatening and sometimes abusive corporate power. In 2012, respected investigative journalist Steve Coll released his book, *Private*

TABLE 3.1 America's Largest Corporations

Corporation	Location	Sales Revenue (in billions)
Walmart Stores	Bentonville, AR	$572.8
Amazon	Seattle, WA	469.8
Apple	Cupertino, CA	365.8
CVS Health	Woonsocket, RI	292.1
UnitedHealth Group	Minnetonka, MN	287.6

Source: *Fortune* 500 2022 Annual Ranking of America's Largest Corporations.

Empire: Exxon Mobil and American Power, detailing a company that operated much like a nation with its own foreign policy and "armies" (security forces).[4]

Big Tech

Retail and industrial giants like Walmart and Exxon represent the longstanding power of America's traditional economy, but in recent years, experts have become increasingly alarmed about the authority and behavior of America's great tech companies–Amazon, Apple, Facebook, Google, and Microsoft. Seen not long ago as frisky startups with very clever and productive new ideas, we now wonder whether those charming and much-admired newcomers are quietly reshaping the national and world economies in ways that may dangerously tilt the balance of power in their direction.

Are the big tech companies simply too big? Are they becoming increasingly immune to competition? When a new startup emerges that might constitute a challenge, we often see them gobbled up by one of the tech giants. Amazon, Apple, Facebook, Google, and Microsoft bought more than 500 companies in the 10 years ending in 2018. The Federal Trade Commission has ordered these companies to provide data for 2010–2019 relating to these acquisitions.[5] (We will further examine anti-competitive behaviors in Chapter 11.)

As a 2017 *New York Times* headline argued, "Google, Not the Government, Is Building the Future."[6] Government commitment to groundbreaking research and dramatic new projects seems to be declining, while the big tech companies are charting new paths–particularly with artificial intelligence but also with advances in cars, rockets, voice recognition technology, and so forth–that increasingly shift the course of our daily lives. We applaud this ingenuity, of course, but experts suggest we should be concerned. They ask, for example: Would we have the open, accessible Internet of today if it had been created in the private sector, rather than through government funding?[7]

Polls Predictably, we have a conflicted view of big corporations. We are grateful for corporate jobs, products, and services, but recent polls find a strong majority of Americans say too much power is concentrated in the nation's large companies.[8] Concerning big tech in particular, a 2020 poll found that 65% of likely U.S. voters agree the economic power of these companies is a problem facing the U.S. economy, and 56% support the federal government doing more to break up big tech monopolies to promote market competition.[9] In addition, 70% agreed big tech companies have too much political power.[10]

In the following sections, we examine some of the concerns critics have about the economic and political power of U.S. corporations.

The Corporate State—Economics

LO 3-2
Discuss whether business should play a more, or less, active role in politics, education, and other public-sector activities.

Perhaps the most pressing and immediate fear about corporate power is that it threatens America's long-term economic well-being. Mounting evidence shows an ongoing shift in the distribution of national income from workers to owners, and economists are increasingly concerned that this concentrated power is reducing America's legendary and crucial power to innovate and, thereby, improve life for all.[11]

One concern about the expansion of corporate power is that working life may change for the worse. Critics worry about big-company capitalism, characterized by its extraordinary achievements in efficiency and productivity but also manifesting some disturbing tendencies, as described by *Yahoo Finance:*

> You probably won't be surprised to hear that big companies could end up so powerful and influential they morph into "mini-states" that fill the void when government is unable to provide essential services. Companies will also use sensors and other gizmos to monitor employees around the clock. And workers will mostly acquiesce to this digital leash, in exchange for job security, decent pay and important benefits.[12]

Taxes

LO 3-3
List some of the primary concerns critics have about corporate power in contemporary America.

Commentator Nicholas Kristof argues that the real welfare cheats in America are not poorer citizens, but prosperous corporations that benefit from "rigged" tax laws.[13] Kristof cites a 2016 Oxfam study finding that, for each dollar they paid in federal taxes between 2008 and 2014, America's 50 largest companies received $27 in federal loans, loan guarantees, and bailouts.[14]

Congress and the Trump Administration dramatically changed America's corporate tax profile in 2017 by enacting a $1.5 trillion tax cut. It reduced America's corporate tax rate (federal and state) from nearly 39 percent (among the highest in the world) to about 24 percent (slightly above the world average).[15] The cut was expected to make American business much more competitive in global markets, thus allowing significant wage boosts for American workers. While American competitiveness has likely improved, workers have seen little direct wage benefit, at least in the short run. Americans for Tax Fairness reported that, by 2018, companies had spent over $900 billion on stock buybacks–which benefit shareholders by pushing the value of their stocks higher, but only about $7 billion on wage increases and bonuses.[16] At the same time, CEO compensation has skyrocketed, far outpacing the increase in pay for the typical worker.[17] Nonetheless, the tax cut arguably provides resources for further investment and potential job growth. As JPMorgan Chase & Co. CEO Jamie Dimon warned prior to the 2017 tax cut, "Our corporate tax system is driving capital and brains overseas."[18]

So, the tax cut may be boosting the American economy in the long run, but the benefits seem to be much greater for shareholders than the working class. Furthermore, the tax cut has likely increased our federal debt, amounting to almost $31.5 trillion in 2022, or more than $94,000 per citizen and nearly $247,000 per taxpayer.[19] Several trillions were added to cope with the economic fallout from the COVID-19 pandemic. How might that enormous debt affect your future, even if you manage your personal finances impeccably?

One partial solution to the debt problem, and to ongoing income and wealth inequality, is to raise personal income taxes on the rich. A number of America's most wealthy corporate titans, including Warren Buffet and Bill Gates, have often publicly advocated higher taxes on people like themselves. A 2019 study found that, in 2018, America's 400 wealthiest families for the first time paid taxes (to all levels of government combined) at a lower rate–just 23 percent–than any other segment of the American population; the bottom half of American households paid just over 24 percent.[20] Significantly, this decline in tax progressivity appears to be limited to a very tiny sliver of the richest American families.[21] Nevertheless, fairness and even our national welfare may call for a change in tax policy.

[See Senator Bernie Sanders' brief 2016 speech criticizing corporate tax loopholes at **www.youtube.com/watch?v=Sknt-UBRhxo**].

Monopoly and Other Misconduct

Critics argue that, in addition to the tax laws, the American economy is also "rigged," allowing a few big companies to command most industries and thereby extinguish meaningful competition. As of 2018, for example, four airlines dominated U.S. air traffic, two companies controlled about 90 percent of the beer market, and five banks held over half of the nation's banking assets.[22] The result, critics claim, is higher prices and poorer service and products. [For more detail about monopoly problems and antitrust law generally, see Chapters 11 and 12.]

Beyond monopoly concerns, complaints about the corporate role in pollution, discrimination, white-collar crime, abuse of workers, and so on remain commonplace. Banking giant Wells Fargo, for example, disgraced itself and likely further weakened Americans' faith in the banking system by engaging in a remarkable array of misconduct in recent years, as discussed in Chapter 2. Wells Fargo has paid significant penalties and punished responsible executives, but the depth of dishonesty certainly supports the critics' view that many of America's most troublesome and persistent problems are, at least in part, products of corporate misconduct. On the other hand, in a democratic, free-market society such as America's, we all must share some of the blame for our problems. If we are not happy with Wells Fargo, we are free to bank elsewhere. [For additional information on Wells Fargo, see Chapter 15.]

Globalization

LO 3-4 Discuss concerns about globalization.

Our tightly connected, highly efficient global supply chains have brought jobs, and thus vital first steps out of abject poverty, for millions of garment workers in developing nations, including Bangladesh, Vietnam, and Sri Lanka. Giant Western retail chains, such as Target and Walmart, have been under continuing international pressure to ensure that working conditions and wages improve in those factories. Progress has been achieved, but the COVID-19 crisis disrupted clothing sales and caused some retailers to renounce their clothing deals and even refuse to pay for clothing already produced for them.

In Bangladesh alone, about $3 billion in clothing orders were either canceled or put on hold by Western retail chains responding to the pandemic in early 2020. Other orders were confirmed, and in defiance of lockdown rules, hundreds of Bangladeshi garment factories re-opened, thus increasing the risk to their workforce. Those workers felt they needed to return to work or lose their jobs.

Rana Plaza

Third-world garment factories, often unsafe and unhealthy workplaces, are caught in a *race to the bottom* to provide the globe's cheapest labor. One such factory, the eight-story Rana Plaza collapsed outside Dhaka, Bangladesh, on April 24, 2013. More than 1,100 workers were killed and thousands were injured in one of the worst industrial tragedies in history. A Bangladeshi government report concluded that the building had been constructed with substandard materials and a disregard for building codes. Upper floors were illegally added to the building, and large power generators installed on those floors shook the building when they were switched on. On the day of the collapse, factory owners apparently ordered workers to enter the building, despite cracks in the walls and other evidence of safety hazards.

A *race to the bottom* to provide the globe's cheapest labor.

Who was responsible for the Rana disaster, and what should have been done? Victims and their families received small compensation awards, and some safety improvements and increased wages in the Bangladeshi garment industry followed. Further, H&M, Adidas, Walmart, and other retailers supplied by Bangladeshi garment factories entered agreements together to strengthen workers' rights, improve safety and working conditions, and blacklist unsafe factories. The agreements, however, covered only a portion of garment factories in Bangladesh. Unfortunately, money spent on safety may result in lower wages or lost jobs in a nation where the annual per capita income has been about $2,000.

According to a 2019 *Wall Street Journal* report, Amazon, Ross, TJ Maxx, and others declined to join those safety-monitoring coalitions. Amazon is among those American retailers that allegedly continued to market products produced in unsafe Bangladeshi facilities. Some were sold by Amazon directly, but about two-thirds were marketed by third-party sellers using the Amazon platform. Amazon has indicated that it does not inspect clothing factories, but it does remove products from its store if it learns of unacceptable safety and work conditions. [For more details on the *Wall Street Journal* investigation, see Justin Scheck, Jon Emont, and Alexandra Berzon, "Amazon Sells Clothes from Factories Other Retailers Blacklist," *The Wall Street Journal,* October 23, 2019 [**www.wsj.com**]. For a defense of Amazon, see Benjamin Powell, "Those Shaming Amazon About Bangladeshi Factories Should Be Ashamed of Themselves," *Washington Examiner,* November 12, 2019 [**www.washingtonexaminer.com**].

Criminal Conduct?

Criminal charges, including murder, were brought against a few dozen individuals, including the Rana Plaza owner, but progress in those cases has been limited. Civil litigation seeking damages has failed thus far. A civil claim against J.C. Penny, The Children's Place, and Walmart was dismissed in a Delaware court in 2016. A similar claim against Canadian retailer Loblaws and its Joe Fresh-brand clothing was rejected by two lower courts and the Canadian Supreme Court. The defendant companies did not have direct contractual relationships with the sub-contractors working in Rana Plaza and therefore had no duty of care for the employees of those sub-contractors, the Canadian courts reasoned.[23]

Questions

1. Prior to the legal decisions noted above, Loblaws had announced it would voluntarily pay some compensation to the families of victims. Ethics expert Chris MacDonald

responded to the tragedy by saying, "I'm still shopping at Joe Fresh . . . and with a clear conscience."[24] Can we continue to shop for cheap clothing while maintaining a clear conscience? Explain.

2. Canadian law professor David J. Doorey objected to Loblaws' legal argument that it had no duty to protect the Rana Plaza garment workers or to check building safety or to monitor supplier factories. Doorey said: "If the moral test was whether Loblaws' execs would have taken more steps to ensure the factory was safe if their own family members were working there, then surely Loblaws failed that test."[25] Do wealthy, powerful western retailers have a moral duty to protect powerless Asian workers in their supply chains who work neither for them nor for companies with which they have direct contractual relationships? Explain.

Globalization Fears

The garment factory tragedy illustrates critics' concerns that global free trade is merely an opportunity for America's giant corporations to exploit cheap, powerless labor abroad. Further, the *outsourcing* of good, high-paid factory jobs from the United States to less-developed nations has wounded the American working class. Consumers have benefited from cheaper goods, but real wages for blue-collar workers are almost unchanged over the past 35 years, even as productivity has increased significantly.

Former President Donald Trump recognized, embraced, and amplified the complaints of working-class Americans whose high-paying manufacturing jobs were abruptly swept away to Mexico and Asia, leaving behind low-paying service jobs. The world changed, and American consumers benefited immensely from higher quality yet cheaper goods. But for millions of American workers who once enjoyed a middle-class lifestyle in return for hard work in steel mills, auto plants, and appliance factories, globalization has left them without the money to take advantage of the new global order.

In general, we can see that critics' concerns about corporate domination of American life also apply worldwide. With the spread of capitalism, the world has come to understand that free markets usually are more efficient decision makers than government rules. As a result, national boundaries are receding in importance, technology is shrinking the globe, and multinational companies are treating the world as one big marketing opportunity. The universal advance of American corporate interests has produced problems; concurrently, there have been enormous gains in global standards of living, literacy, and prosperity. Is there a causal relationship between these two observations? (In Chapter 17, we will consider the differences of coincidence, correlation, and causation.)

Corporations as Psychopaths?

The 2004 movie documentary, *The Corporation,* argues that the corporation has become the dominant institution in American life, exceeding the influence of both religion and government. One result is that corporations often demonstrate the "traits of the prototypical psychopath." The contemporary corporation is depicted as an "exploitative monster" driven not by the greater good but by its first responsibility to stockholders.

Questions

1. In your view, are corporations more powerful than government, religion, our educational system, and all other American institutions? Explain.
2. According to various polls, well over half of Americans think corporations have too much power. Do you agree? Explain.

Source: Jim Keough, "Film Sees Evil in Corporations," *Worchester Telegram & Gazette,* September 29, 2004, p. C5.

[For *The Corporation* homepage, see **www.thecorporation.com**. To view the movie, visit **www.youtube.com/watch?v=xHrhqtY2khc**.]

The Corporate State—Politics

We turn now to politics where, critics argue, big money enables the business community to disproportionately influence the electoral and law-making processes.

Corporate Contributions

Lobbying

Lobbying (efforts to influence the actions of public officials) is an essential ingredient in big business strategy. Lobbying also serves the very useful role of efficiently educating busy politicians about the vast array of issues they must address but cannot possibly master without assistance. Lobbying is not confined to the business community. Labor unions, consumer and environmental interest groups, and a myriad of others battle to have their voices heard. So, lobbying serves a valuable role. Unfortunately, it also can be thoroughly corrupt.

Lobbying by the Numbers Total spending on lobbying in Washington, D.C., for 2021 was about $3.78 billion, and almost 12,200 individuals were registered and active as lobbyists.[26] The biggest spenders continue to be business groups, with the Chamber of Commerce at the top, spending more than $66 million in 2021.[27] The Chamber of Commerce was also the biggest business spender in 2016, at nearly $104 million.[28]

While the number of active, registered lobbyists has actually declined in recent years, they remain so influential in Congress that legislation is often grounded on their views. Sometimes lobbyists actually write the laws. When the House of Representatives, in 2013, passed a measure that would have rolled back part of the financial reforms in the 2010 Dodd–Frank bill (which primarily governs large banks), National Public Radio reported that 70 of the 85 lines in the final House bill reflected Citigroup (one of the nation's largest banks) recommendations, portions of which were almost word for word.[29] Furthermore, the "revolving door" between Congress and lobbying firms remains robust. Of the 48 legislators who left office after the 2016 election, one-fourth stayed in Washington and one-sixth became lobbyists. For some years, about half of departing lawmakers have become lobbyists.[30] The "swamp" resists drainage no matter which party is in charge.

Dangerous Influence? Does corporate lobbying disproportionately influence federal policy? The evidence is mixed but worrisome. A 2019 study concludes that "companies' tax bills and the probability of being audited decrease markedly when they hire a former legislator."[31] A 2014 study concluded that lobbyists from opposing camps hold each other in check about 60 percent of the time. Thus, lobbyists were successful in influencing policy about 40 percent of the time. The study also concluded that money influenced outcomes only when heavily weighted to one side.[32] A contemporaneous statistical analysis found that when economic elites and organized groups representing business interests support a new federal government policy, it has about a 45 percent chance of being adopted. It also found that average citizens, and even mass-based interest groups, have virtually no influence over federal policy.[33] The researchers concluded that democracy is threatened by "powerful business organizations and a small number of affluent Americans."[34]

On the other hand, commentator Steven Pearlstein said in 2016 that corporate influence on government was as "low as anyone can remember."[35] Corporate lobbying on narrow issues, he acknowledged, is effective, but corporate influence over big policy issues like immigration and tax reform had declined–particularly as public respect for corporations had fallen with plant closings, layoffs, extravagant executive pay, and such widely publicized corporate scandals as those which caused Enron and WorldCom to become household names in the early 2000s. In recent years, national news organizations were regularly reporting troubles surrounding Monsanto's Roundup weedkiller, Boeing's 737 MAX jets, and Big Pharma's role in the national opioid addiction crisis. One unfortunate result of such widespread coverage, Pearlstein argued, is that big business can no longer perform its traditional stabilizing role in Washington. Political extremism and gridlock, therefore, have intensified. [For the Center for Responsive Politics and its extensive database on money in politics, see **www.opensecrets.org**.]

PACs

Legally, corporate funds cannot be given directly to candidates for federal office. Corporations (as well as entities like labor unions and special interest groups) can, however, establish legally separate political action committees (PACs) to solicit contributions from employees, shareholders, and others. That money can then be disbursed by the PAC in support of the political agenda preferred by the contributors. Although PAC contributions are voluntary, corporate employees often feel pressured to participate. Unlike the federal rules, more than half of the states allow corporations to lawfully donate corporate funds to parties and candidates for state elections.

Big Money Dominance?

Are big-money contributors able to "buy" elections? More money certainly does not guarantee success. Hillary Clinton, for example, dramatically outspent Donald Trump in the 2016 presidential election and lost. Nonetheless, those who spend more generally prevail.

Does big money buy influence? Anecdotal evidence suggests well-placed contributions can be very persuasive. Prior to his presidency, for example, Donald Trump said: "As a businessman and a very substantial donor to very important people, when you give, they do whatever the hell you want them to do. . . ."[36] In a stunning burst of candor, former congressman and Trump White House Chief of Staff Mick Mulvaney told an American Bankers Association meeting in 2018,

> We had a hierarchy in my office in Congress. . . . If you're a lobbyist who never gave us money, I didn't talk to you. If you're a lobbyist who gave us money, I might talk to you.[37]

The Citizens United Case

The role of conventional PACs in the political process has receded in importance following a momentous U.S. Supreme Court decision in the 2010 *Citizens United* case.[38] The Court's highly controversial 5-4 ruling held that federal laws limiting corporate campaign contributions violated corporate free speech rights. Essentially, the decision allows corporations, labor unions, and some other entities to spend unlimited organizational funds for candidates and causes so long as they do not coordinate that spending with parties or candidates.

The five "conservative" justices in the *Citizens United* majority, treating the spending of dollars as the equivalent of the exercise of free speech, saw political spending limits as a direct denial of liberty guaranteed by the First Amendment. Corporations and labor unions were viewed by the Court as associations of individuals that should possess the same constitutional rights as the individuals themselves. The four dissenters from the "liberal" wing of the Court argued that corporations and unions, in many other ways, are not treated as people, and doing so in the case of political contributions could allow those organizations to dominate–and further corrupt–the political process.

A highly controversial 5-4 ruling

Citizens United and other court decisions have opened the door to unlimited gushers of personal and corporate money into the political arena, funneled through Independent Expenditure PACs (usually called Super PACs) and nonprofit 501(c)(4) social welfare organizations. A large portion of those funds comes from "dark money," meaning the source was not disclosed. For the November 2022 midterm elections, Super PACs collected over $2.7 billion. Some came from corporations and labor unions, but much of it came from a relative handful of individual and family mega-donors, such as Hungarian-American businessman and philanthropist George Soros, who topped the list of individual contributors at over $176 million.[39] Critics now argue that America is more accurately labeled a corporate and family *oligarchy* rather than a democracy. Do you agree?

[For an examination of "the influence of untraceable corporate money on our elections and elected officials," see the 2018 documentary movie, *Dark Money*. The trailer is at **www.darkmoneyfilm.com**.]

Change the Law? Many Americans believe we should amend the U.S. Constitution to make it clear that money does not constitute speech and that corporations are not entitled to the inalienable rights of persons, including the right to participate in the political process. In considering concerns about corporate political spending, we need to remember that labor unions, other interest groups, and wealthy individuals and families also have a large monetary voice in the political process. Thus, as *The Wall Street Journal* argues, corporations need to be sure that their voices are heard:

> [P]oliticians have created a gargantuan state that is so intrusive that businesses have no alternative than to spend money to defend themselves and their shareholders. . . . Liberals want business to disarm unilaterally.[40]

Furthermore, a recent study found that "corporate political efforts generally have positive effects on a firm's market value and its shareholder returns."[41] Arguably, then, corporations, in looking out for shareholder welfare, need to be active in politics. At the same time, big money contributions are challenging our pristine conceptions of democracy, perhaps dwarfing the voice of ordinary Americans.

The Corporate State—Social Issues and Institutions

As we've seen, the critics believe America's corporate community harms our economic and political lives, but their concerns do not end there. The corporate message, they say, pervades and shapes all dimensions of American life, including the education you are participating in as you read these words.

Schools

Higher Education A 2016 National Public Radio story was headlined: "Resisting the Corporate University."[42] Critics decry the university's hard shift away from the Liberal Arts toward vocationalism: preparing you for a job in a vast and, as they see it, controlling corporate empire. You may applaud that vocational direction, but the concern is that you are left ill-prepared to be a good citizen able to pursue a full personal, civic, intellectual, and cultural life. They say that profit-seeking has replaced the search for truth as the central goal of university aspiration and practice. Some of those critics even argue that business schools have no legitimate place on college campuses. Have these thoughts perhaps crossed your mind? If you are a business student, have you wondered at times whether your studies have failed to examine your core being and failed to sufficiently challenge your life view?

Critics accuse big business of turning college life into a marketing opportunity. Companies are employing Facebook, Instagram, TikTok, and other social media platforms to promote their commercial messages to you and millions of your peer "customers." As many as 1,000 student "campus influencers" at Virginia Tech University, for example, are paid in cash and merchandise to post commercial messages and to hold promotional events. *The New York Times* described one such student:

> Alana Clark, a 21-year-old senior at Virginia Tech, is one of more than 200 college students across the country using their Instagram accounts to promote Victoria's Secret Pink sportswear and undergarments. She also hands out free underwear on the quad.[43]

Thus, higher education, the critics argue, is increasingly viewed as a product to be marketed and consumed on the road to prosperity in the corporate state. Hunter Rawlings, former president of Cornell University, decried that trend:

> Genuine education is not a commodity, it is the awakening of a human being.[44]

[The documentary movie *Starving the Beast* examines efforts to treat education as a consumer product and to run universities more like businesses. See the trailer and more at **www.starvingthebeast.net.**]

Questions

The Wall Street Journal talked with critics, including corporate recruiters, who are increasingly skeptical about the value of an undergraduate business degree:

> [N]ow faculty members, school administrators and corporate recruiters are questioning the value of a business degree at the undergraduate level. The biggest complaint: The undergraduate degrees focus too much on the nuts and bolts of finance and accounting and don't develop enough critical thinking and problem-solving skills through long essays, in-class debates and other hallmarks of liberal-arts courses.[45]

1. Do you think your business courses should have a stronger liberal arts flavor? Explain.
2. If you are a business major, do you think you chose the wrong field of study? Explain.

PreK-Grade 12 Concerns have also emerged about the intrusion of business values, such as the growth of privatized schools, in the earliest years of education. (See Chapter 1 for a discussion of the privatization movement.) *The New York Times* has described one seemingly healthy commercial venture as a "profound shift in American education: the Googlification of the classroom."[46] More than half of America's primary and secondary students use Google apps like Docs, and more than half of the mobile devices sold to schools are Google Chromebooks.[47] Shouldn't we enthusiastically embrace this sincere effort to prepare our children for the tech world? Perhaps, but to critics, Google's success in schools has prioritized tech-based skills over traditional academic inquiry, like mathematics formulas. It has also acquired for Google the attention of millions of future adult customers, used teachers as marketing agents, raised privacy risks for students, and exploited education for sales opportunities. Is Silicon Valley helping America's kids learn to cope with the computer age, or is it distorting their education for its profit-seeking purposes? Or both?

Religion

In her book *Brands of Faith,* Professor Mara Einstein says that religion has become a product and, in consequence, churches and pastors are changing their methods and messages to suit their "market." They are branding themselves to stand out in the spiritual community.[48] Facebook and other social media platforms are now favored advertising vehicles for faith-based groups. Advertising, promotional giveaways, and marketing campaigns have become standard in many churches.

Some pastors preach the "prosperity gospel," that material success is a mark of God's favor. Televangelist Jesse Duplantis says God even told him he needs a new Falcon 7-X jet plane (about $54 million), "in one of the greatest statements the Lord ever told me," to preach to the world.[49]

God told him he needs a new jet.

Megachurch pastor David Platt, in his book *Radical: Taking Back Your Faith from the American Dream,* argues that our pursuit of the materialist American Dream cannot be reconciled with an

Americans (and the world) have clearly voted for *Dancing with the Stars.*

authentic spiritual life.[50] He asks his followers to put a cap on their consumer lives. Do you think your pursuit of the American Dream conflicts with your spiritual life?

[For a review of *Christianity Incorporated: How Big Business Is Buying the Church,* see **https://directionjournal.org/32/1/christianity-incorporated-how-big.html**].

Questions

1. Do you see any risks to religion in treating it as a product to be marketed and sold? Explain.
2. *a.* Why has religion increasingly become a product in the commercial world?
   b. Is everything a product in some sense? Explain.

Culture

Does America possess a cultural life? For decades, the concern has been that traditional high culture–classical music, opera, ballet, and the like–would be replaced by popular culture, such as rock and roll, television, and video games. Now that battle is over: Americans (and the world) have clearly voted for *Dancing with the Stars* and *The Voice.* Thus, critics assert, Corporate America's focus on the bottom line is also degrading our popular culture. While the emergence of some worthy cable television programming is encouraging, critics argue popular culture is largely a wasteland, debased not merely by a mindless market (that's us) but also by corporate greed, indifference to quality, and relentless consolidation; only a handful of giant networks, such as Comcast, Fox, Paramount, and Disney, control much of the television market.

Even the historically untamed and uncensored music festival industry (for example, Bonnaroo, Coachella, and Lollapalooza), with over 32 million customers per year, is enormously influenced–if not dominated–by just two big companies: Live Nation (producer of 60 festivals) and AEG (producer of 11 festivals).[51] The results, critics say, include excessive commercialization, uniformity of acts, and, in some cases, significant attendance declines.[52] Should we be concerned that these festivals, historically incubators of counter-cultural trends and iconic music, seem increasingly to reflect mainstream American preferences?

Music has become more homogeneous, louder, more repetitive, and less complex.

Perhaps we should applaud corporate America for effectively providing us with precisely what we want. But do we find, in the mainstream and the familiar, the challenges and innovations that stimulate us and propel us forward? Consider, for example, studies confirming what your parents have told you: Music has, indeed, become more homogeneous, louder, more repetitive, and less complex over the decades.[53] Interestingly, one of those studies found a steady increase in the use of the word "I" and a corresponding steady decline in words that suggest community and working together.[54]

But does it matter that current popular music all sounds pretty much the same? Or that reality TV is a central feature of American daily life? Or that *Sesame Street* must move from PBS to HBO to secure the finances necessary to carry on? Does it matter that the cutting-edge South by Southwest Music Festival based in Austin, Texas, is starting "to feel corporate,"[55] or that "Capitalism's Suffocating Music,"[56] as critics have argued?

[For a refreshing counter to the view that classical music is no longer attractive to younger generations, visit **www.youtube.com/watch?v=a23945btJYw** to view both the audience and the 2014 Flashmob performance of Beethoven's Ode to Joy, which has been viewed over 40 million times at the time of this writing.]

Sports

College Athletics Former Kansas State University head football coach Bill Snyder's public candor may have surprised the sports establishment:

> It's changed. I mean college athletics, football in particular, has changed dramatically over the years. . . . I think we've sold out. We're all about dollars and cents.[57]

Snyder's point of view from 2014 seems indisputable today as, seemingly, the highest-level college sports programs are in an increasingly desperate race for money. The Pac-12 (mostly West Coast schools), suffering from relatively poor on-field performance and weak television ratings, reportedly offered to sell rights to a portion of future conference media and sponsorship revenue to private investors in 2019 for a total of $750 million.[58] The National Collegiate Athletic Association (NCAA)has, for the first time, adopted new rules that allow college athletes to profit from their names, images, and likenesses.

I think we've sold out.

The University of Maryland expresses no official misgivings about its nearly $33 million, 10-year contract with Under Armour and the company's president, Kevin Plank, a Maryland graduate.[59] The school, *The New York Times* reported, was positioning itself to be the University of Under Armour, just as the University of Oregon has described itself as "the University of Nike."[60]

Much of this money, of course, is tied to and driven by another enormous industry: television. In 2011, former Colorado State University chancellor Michael Martin wryly spoke to the power of the networks by saying, "I think we could end up with two enormous conferences, one called ESPN and one called FOX."[61]

What Have We Lost? The social significance of the amateur athletics evolution from sport to business is unclear. Profit-seeking in collegiate sports is not without its benefits. Thousands of student athletes, who might otherwise not have done so, complete college every year. Funding is provided for many unprofitable sports including tennis and golf, and sports revenues often support academic programs and amenities. In 2022, new PAC-12 Commissioner George Kliavkoff encouraged college presidents to invest in football to win–not only on the field but with its return on investment.[62]

But what have we lost when the innocence and idealism of amateur sports are forfeited in favor of professionalism and profit? Is the pursuit of profit the route to a slow but sure death of honorable, meaningful sports? Perhaps the answer is becoming more evident. In 2019, an Adidas executive and several ex-NCAA college basketball coaches were sentenced for allegedly engaging in bribery schemes to recruit highly ranked high school players.[63] But are we still better off when corporate and personal profit–the free market–drives sports? And how will sports change in the wake of the financial meltdown accompanying the COVID-19 pandemic?

Are Children Next? Business values and practices have spread from professional sports to college athletics and now are rapidly emerging in youth sports as well. Kids' sports were a

$15.3 billion per year industry as of 2017; it grew to $19.2 billion as of 2019.[64] Elite youth teams travel the country to play in special events, more and more games are televised, and $60-million-plus high school football stadiums have popped up around Dallas and Houston. The National Basketball Association (NBA) now sponsors a Jr. NBA Global Championship, in hopes of developing the kind of zeal and public attention that has been so successful for Little League baseball with its World Series television contract of about $7.5 million per year.[65]

PRACTICING ETHICS The Sports Business and Compromised Values?

BEER

In the 2018 season, more than 50 of 129 Football Bowl Subdivision teams (the "big" schools) sold beer stadium-wide, about five times the number 10 years prior. Ohio State University reportedly netted over $1 million in one season from stadium beer sales, although most schools do not achieve sales of that magnitude.[66] One reason for the beer-selling trend is that college football attendance has been falling over the past decade. University brands and logos are being used in the marketing of beer products. The University of Texas Longhorns athletics department designated Mexican beer import, Corona, as its official beer and adopted the slogan, "Horns Up, Limes In."[67]

Questions

1. Do you think universities that sell beer at football games are hypocritical, in that those same schools emphatically discourage binge drinking by students? Explain.
2. Commenting on selling beer at college football games, Emily Golembiewski, a fan experience expert at Aecom, said: "[I]t's important to keep some of what people love about college and not make it a mini-NFL."[68] Do you agree? Explain.

Sources: Danny Lawhon, "Stadium-Wide Alcohol for College Football Is Growing Fast. So, Why Are Iowa Schools Resisting?," *Des Moines Register*, April 23, 2018 [**www.desmoinesregister.com**]; "Beer Sales Rake in More than $1M at Ohio Stadium," *Associated Press News*, December 12, 2017 [**https://apnews.com**]; Michael T. Nietzel, "Sobering Thoughts about Alcohol Sales at College Stadiums," *Forbes*, December 1, 2018 [**www.forbes.com**]; and Mark Tracy, "Beer Here! Beer Here?," *The New York Times*, October 8, 2015 [**www.nytimes.com**].

America's Soul?

LO 3-5
Make a tentative assessment regarding the proper role of business in society.

Critics contend that the power of the business community has become so encompassing that virtually all dimensions of American life have absorbed elements of the business ethic. Values commonly associated with businesspeople (competition, profit-seeking, reliance on technology, faith in growth) often overwhelm traditional humanist values (cooperation, individual dignity, human rights, meaningful service to society). In the name of wealth, efficiency, and productivity, the warmth, decency, and value of life have been debased. We are addicted to social media and our phones. We engage in meaningless work. Objects dominate our existence. We operate as replaceable cogs in a vast, bureaucratic machine. Indeed, we lose ourselves, the critics argue. Charles Reich, former Yale University law professor, addressed the loss of self in his influential book of the Vietnam War era, *The Greening of America:*

> Of all of the forms of impoverishment that can be seen or felt in America, loss of self, or death in life, is surely the most devastating. . . . Beginning with school, if not before, an individual is systematically stripped of his imagination, his creativity, his heritage, his dreams, and his personal uniqueness, in order to style him into a productive unit for a mass, technological society. Instinct, feeling, and spontaneity are repressed by overwhelming forces. As the

Objects dominate our existence.

individual is drawn into the meritocracy, his working life is split from his home life, and both suffer from a lack of wholeness. Eventually, people virtually become their professions, roles, or occupations, and are henceforth strangers to themselves.[69]

Some interesting empirical evidence supports Reich's view that we feel dominated by big institutions. The Harris Alienation Index measures the degree to which people feel their interests are noticed and addressed by those with power and influence. Survey questions inquire, for example, about feelings of economic inequity (the rich get richer, and the poor get poorer) and powerlessness (being left out and not counting for much). Responses are combined into an alienation "score." That score stood at a low of 29 in its first year, 1966, and has generally been rising since, with record scores around 70, the highest ever. Other Harris data, however, show recent growth in American commitment to local relationships, including communities, faith, and families.[70]

Commentator Ben Stein lamented an increasingly divided America.

Actor and commentator Ben Stein, speaking in 2006, lamented an increasingly divided America, where the interests of corporations and the wealthy are dominant and the well-being of others is in danger of being forgotten:

> The Saturday before Memorial Day I spoke to a gathering of widows and widowers, parents and children of men and women in uniform who have lost their lives in Iraq and Afghanistan. The person who spoke before me was a beautiful woman named Joanna Wroblewski, whose husband of less than two years–after four years of dating at Rutgers–had been killed in Iraq. She cried as she spoke. . . . She spoke of her devotion to her country and her husband's pride in the flag. . . .
>
> Are we keeping the faith with Joanna Wroblewski? . . . Are we maintaining an America that is not just a financial neighborhood, but also a brotherhood and a sisterhood worth losing your husband for? Is this still a community of the heart, or a looting opportunity? Will there even be a free America for Mrs. Wroblewski's descendants, or will we be a colony of the people [foreign lenders] to whom we have sold our soul?[71]

Questions

1. A 2016 *Washington Post* headline included the question: "Yosemite, Sponsored by Starbucks?" That headline stirred loud opposition and lots of jokes, such as the suggestion that Old Faithful might be used to pitch Viagra. The National Park Service (NPS) quickly indicated that the sale of national park naming rights was not in its plans, and NPS rules and guidance clearly state that "commercialization" is prohibited by law and by NPS policy. In-park recognition of donors on temporary signage, brochures, banners, and paving stones, is permitted. In response to discussions of a wider corporate role, one unidentified Park Service superintendent said: "For me as a federal employee and a taxpayer, I think it is unethical to be advertising for a corporation."[72] The national parks are significantly underfunded and have billions of dollars of deferred maintenance.
   a. Do you see anything unethical about an increased corporate presence at our national parks? Explain.
   b. Do you think an increased corporate presence at our national parks would in any way threaten those parks? Explain.

2. According to news reports, Kay Delzer, 2019 North Dakota Teacher of the Year, remodeled her third-grade classroom to capture some of the comforts and atmosphere of Starbucks. She expects daily postings by her students on Twitter and Instagram. She has her own brand, "Top Dog Teaching." She is thought of as a "teacher influencer." She and others like her become brand ambassadors who promote products online, at conferences, and elsewhere. She receives the latest technology to try in her classroom and is given inexpensive freebies such as t-shirts for herself and for handing out to other teachers who come to her very successful workshops. Do you see anything wrong with any of these teaching practices and relationships? Explain. See Natasha Singer, "Silicon Valley Courts Brand-Name Teachers, Raising Ethics Issues," *The New York Times,* September 2, 2017 [**www.nytimes.com**].
3. Facebook founder and CEO Mark Zuckerberg, in 2016, spoke about his ambitions for reaching all of the world through the Internet. Zuckerberg criticized people and nations who oppose a connected world and a global community. He envisioned Facebook as a primary vehicle for world connectivity. Do you see any problems with Mr. Zuckerberg's vision? Explain.
4. A brief analysis of social media advertising techniques employed to promote Ford, Mello Yello, Grey Poupon, and Sephora emphasized the value and power of those ads on Facebook, Twitter, and other social media platforms. The article, entitled "4 Examples of How Corporate America Is Crushing Social Media,"[73] argued that those four products were marketed online by presenting interesting content that readers would be inclined to share with their social networks.
   a. Do those corporate advertising campaigns diminish the quality of your social media experience? Explain.
   b. Do we need a social media "zone," free of corporate advertising messages? Explain.
5. *a.* Do Americans trust the business community? Do you? Explain.
   b. Does it matter? Why?
6. In your opinion, which of the following will be the biggest threat to America in the future: big government, big labor, or big business? Explain.
7. *a.* Do you think allegiance to the company will become more important than allegiance to the state? Explain.
   b. Is that a desirable direction? Raise the pros and cons.

Part Two—Corporate Social Responsibility

Introduction

The business community enjoys enormous resources and, in many ways, highly favored treatment in contemporary life. American society is burdened with a daunting array of problems: poverty, the environment, the wealth gap, drug abuse, discrimination, and much more. In addition, as we have seen, corporate America has increasingly occupied bigger and bigger parts of our shared lives. At the same time, our federal government seems, for now at least, essentially unable to effectively address the nation's needs. For these reasons, academics and social activists have for decades called upon businesses to voluntarily do more for society than providing good products and services to maximize profits.

LO 3-6
Explain the concept of corporate social responsibility.

One result of these powerful forces has been the introduction and gradual evolution of the doctrine of *corporate social responsibility* (CSR–sometimes also referred to as *corporate citizenship*). CSR raises this crucial question: Must business decision-making include consideration not merely of the welfare of the firm and its shareholder owners but of society as a whole? For most contemporary readers, the answer is self-evident–of course business bears a social responsibility. Business has enjoyed a central and favored role in American life. As such, it must assume a portion of the burden for the welfare of society at large.

The Business Roundtable, a group of the nation's top CEOs, issued a new statement of purpose in 2019 that renounces the primacy of shareholder interests and commits its companies to serving all constituents. The Roundtable pledge places socially responsible treatment of customers, employees, suppliers, the environment, and communities at the same level of importance as long-term shareholder well-being (profit maximization). In doing so, the corporate chiefs revised their 1997 statement of purpose that placed shareholders first among corporate interests. The 2019 statement was signed by CEOs from Amazon, Apple, and Walmart, among the 181 in total.[74] Time will tell whether the new expression of purpose reflects substantive change or is merely a political and marketing strategy to soothe edgy politicians and consumers.

Young people

CSR has captured broad popular appeal, particularly among younger Americans. For example, a 2016 Deloitte survey of nearly 7,700 millennials from 29 countries found that 73 percent of them thought business has a positive impact on society, but they would like employers to focus more on people and purpose and less on profits (although they recognize the necessity for long-term financial success).[75] Fifty-eight percent of respondents said that businesses "behave in an ethical manner," and 57 percent believe "their leaders are committed to helping improve society."[76] Do you agree?

Before turning to a more detailed analysis of corporate social responsibility practice, let's think for a moment about how you could direct your forthcoming professional life toward socially responsible, ethically sustainable business practices. *Social enterprise* or *social entrepreneurship* is a movement in which people launch nonprofits and businesses or take jobs using entrepreneurial and managerial skills, partly for the purpose of addressing social problems.

[To read the Business Roundtable's 2019 Statement on the Purpose of a Corporation, with signatures, see BRT-StatementonthePurposeofaCorporationwithSignaturesOctober2022.pdf, available through **https://opportunity.businessrountable.org/ourcomittment**.]

Social Enterprise/Social Entrepreneurship

Drew Chafetz, a huge soccer fan in his mid-twenties, did not turn directly to the job market following college graduation. Rather, in 2006 he cofounded love.futbol, a global nonprofit organization to help build safe soccer fields for children in impoverished nations. At this writing, love.futbol has worked with communities in 12 countries to bring soccer to more children, while helping join neighbors together to build community and combat neglect and violence.

Some profit-seeking companies are also built on the pursuit of explicit social welfare goals. Warby Parker, a for-profit enterprise, gives a free pair of eyeglasses to someone in need for every pair it sells, while also providing funding for training local entrepreneurs to sell glasses at affordable prices. Warby Parker, like Patagonia and Ben & Jerry's, is one of over 3,000 certified B Corporations in over 70 nations. B Corps are for-profit companies, certified by the nonprofit B Lab, that "are legally required to consider the impact of their decisions on their workers, customers, suppliers, community, and the environment." [For more details, see **https://bcorporation.net**.]

Some of those committed to social welfare simply seek jobs that allow them to enhance their contribution to the general good. Project manager Gail Dougherty was retiring, but before that big change, she took a $25,000 stipend from her employer, Intel, to work part-time for about a year at the Virginia Garcia Memorial Health Center in Oregon. She crunched data toward the goal of finding better ways of helping diabetes patients, many of whom are migrant workers or do not have health insurance.[77]

[To identify B Corps in your state or locality, visit **http://bcorporation.net/directory**.]

Questions

1. *a.* Do you aspire to a social enterprise/social entrepreneurship role in your future professional life?
   b. Should you? Explain.
2. Have your business school courses given sufficient attention to social responsibility issues? Explain.
3. Do consumers care whether companies are socially responsible? Explain.

A New Expectation

The ascendance of the social responsibility doctrine represents a striking ideological shift. Historically, consumers expected business to concentrate on one goal—producing and distributing the best products and services at the lowest possible prices. Thus, business was largely exempt from any affirmative duty for the resolution of social problems. Then, at least as early as the 1950s, business scholars and critics began to encourage a broader conception of corporate duty. Now in the 21st century, expectations for business in society have been radically altered. Profit-seeking remains central and essential, but for most businesspeople, the sometimes awkward ingredient of social responsibility must be another consideration. [For the Business for Social Responsibility home page, see **www.bsr.org**.]

What Is Social Responsibility?

The very broad notion of corporate social responsibility is not readily reduced to a brief definition, but Davis and Blomstrom some years ago captured the core ingredients: "The idea of social responsibility is that decision makers are obligated to take actions which protect and improve the welfare of society as a whole along with their own interests."[78]

The social role of business can be envisioned as an ideological continuum, corresponding roughly to the familiar American political spectrum of conservative/Republican views on the right, moderates in the middle, and liberal/Democrats on the left. Figure 3.1 depicts

FIGURE 3.1
A Social Responsibility Continuum

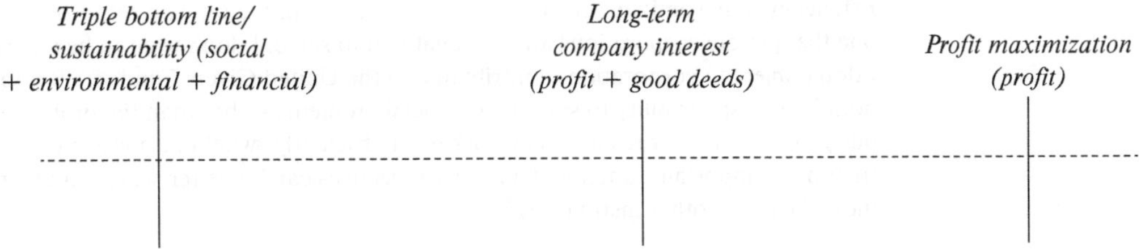

that continuum and is best understood by reading "backward" from right to left. On the right side of the spectrum lies the free-market view that *profit maximization* is the best measure of social responsibility. Across the middle (*long-term company interest*) lies a hybrid, blended perspective where profits are the first consideration, but where satisfied workers, customers, and community members are also of importance, within some reasonable limits, to secure the firm's long-term survival. On the left side of the spectrum lies the *triple bottom line/sustainability* movement that calls for a revolutionary re-visioning of corporate goals and practices, such that profit maximization is only one of three key measures of success. Triple bottom line advocates specifically call for managerial and accounting practices that respect and measure the firm's *social* and *environmental* performance, just as the firm's *financial* performance is respected and measured. The goal is to ensure the long-term viability (sustainability) of the organization and society as a whole.

[For the "Global Reporting Initiative" on sustainability practices around the world, see **www.globalreporting.org**.]

Now let's examine the continuum in a bit more detail.

Profit Maximization

On the right side of the spectrum, the dominant concern lies in maximizing shareholders' interests. Those shareholders, after all, are the owners of the firm. They are taking the financial risk. Hence, from a profit maximization point of view, the only responsible and moral course of behavior is to reap the highest return possible, within the law. Nobel prize-winning economist Milton Friedman was the most prominent advocate of the profit maximization view:

> [In a free economy] there is one and only one social responsibility of business–to use its resources and engage in activities designed to increase its profits, so long as it stays within the rules of the game, which is to say, engages in open and free competition, without deception or fraud.[79]

Friedman, employing free-market reasoning, believed the firm that maximizes its profits is necessarily maximizing its contribution to society. Furthermore, he argued that any dilution of the profit-maximizing mode–such as charitable contributions–is a misuse of the stockholders' resources. The individual stockholder, he contended, should dispose of assets according to their own wishes. Finally, he asked how managers could be expected to know what the public interest is.

Herbert Stein, former chair of the President's Council of Economic Advisers, shared Friedman's doubts about the idea of social responsibility, but Stein's concerns were of a more pragmatic nature. He argued that business is simply ill suited for solving social problems:

> Efficiency in maximizing the nation's product. . . is not the only objective of life. But it is the one that private corporations are best qualified to serve. I don't want to be a purist about this. I don't object to corporations contributing to the United Givers Fund. . . . But to rely on corporations' responsibility to solve major social problems—other than the problem of how to put our people and other resources to work most efficiently—would be a wasteful diversion from their most important function. Our other objectives can be better served in other ways, by individuals and other institutions.[80]

Long-Term Company Interest Across the middle ground of our social responsibility continuum lie those firms that believe a strong bottom line sometimes requires considerations beyond the immediate, short-run, profit-maximizing interests of the firm. In a sense, these managers are merely taking a longer-term view of profit maximization. They recognize the imperative of a strong return on the shareholder's investment, but they also believe that achieving that return may require heightened sensitivity to the welfare of employees, consumers, and the community. Furthermore, they may embrace the view that socially responsible behavior, within reasonable bounds, is simply the "right thing" to do. Karl-Johan Persson, CEO of the H&M clothing chain, explained his company's view of social responsibility: "All other things equal, profits would be higher. But we believe in the long-term business case. We sacrifice short-term gains."[81] [For the United Nations's initiative to encourage responsible corporate citizenship, see **www.unglobalcompact.org**.]

LO 3-7
Explain the triple bottom line/sustainability approach to corporate citizenship.

Triple Bottom Line/Sustainability Managers are being pushed to adopt a bigger, broader conception of social responsibility, an approach that will produce a healthy, enduring global community where our resources are not dangerously depleted or damaged. The triple bottom line calls for attention to the three Ps: people, planet, and profit. Social responsibility expert Steve Rochlin explains,

> The new corporate citizenship challenges executives to find alternatives to zero-sum solutions that often emphasize shareholder value at the cost of social and environmental welfare. Instead, the new corporate citizenship challenges companies to deliver not just financial returns but also environmental and social value—together marking the pillars of what is called a "triple bottom line." . . .[82]

The triple bottom line/sustainability approach not only employs free-market principles and recognizes the necessity for financial success but also argues that, along with profit, social and environmental responsibility are of equal importance. According to sustainability advocates, corporations giving close attention to social and economic duties, in addition to the bottom line, will enjoy a powerful competitive advantage.

Building a just, healthy, sustainable future makes a lot of sense, but reasonable people continue to differ about the most effective path to that goal. For many companies, shorter-term profit motives continue to dominate. A 2016 study of supply chain sustainability plans in 50 larger American firms concluded,

> While the survey showed many companies are thinking about and/or prioritizing supply chain optimization, few at this point seem to be embracing sustainability initiatives in a meaningful

way. Until regulations force action, many companies likely won't prioritize the resources and funding necessary to make significant change.[83]

Nonetheless, progress is evident. Some big American corporations are appointing sustainability officers and committing themselves to global sustainability projects. For example, Muhtar Kent, former CEO at Coca-Cola, spoke of his company's close attention to improved practices in water, packaging, energy conservation, and climate. He went on to specifically cite one small, but illustrative, step forward:

> Preeti Gupti, for example, is a mother of three in rural India. In the town of Agra, about 125 miles south of Delhi, she has a small store in her home which lacks reliable electrical service. With a solar-powered Coca-Cola cooler, she can now sell cold beverages, stay open later and help her children study after dark. Her income has also increased, creating still more opportunities for her children.[84]

[For a critique of triple bottom line thinking, see **www.businessethicsblog.com.**]

"Green" Jeans?

Americans' fashion-forward sensibility is sustained by globe-spanning supply chains that consume enormous amounts of water, energy, chemicals, cotton, oil, and other resources, while casting off equally enormous amounts of waste and entangling workers in often dangerous, poorly paid jobs. The Sustainable Apparel Coalition, including large, prominent brands such as Adidas, American Eagle, Kohl's, Levi, and Walmart, is working to improve sustainability throughout the global apparel industry. The Coalition developed a process to measure the apparel industry's environmental, social, and labor impact through its tool called the Higg Index. Companies can enter data about their business practices, and the Higg Index system produces a "score card" that allows those companies to compare their sustainability performance with competitors and industry standards.

Question

Think about shopping. Assume you are considering two pairs of jeans of equal style and quality, one with a favorable sustainability score, one without. Assume the jeans without the favorable score are priced at $50. How much more would you be willing to pay for the jeans with a favorable score?

a. Nothing more

b. $5

c. $10

d. $25

e. $50

Explain.

Source: The Sustainable Apparel Coalition, accessed August 2020 [**https://apparelcoalition.org**].

FIGURE 3.2
The Social Responsibility (CSR) Pyramid

Source: Archie B. Carroll, "The Pyramid of Corporate Social Responsibility: Toward the Moral Management of Organizational Stakeholders." *Business Horizons* 34, no. 4 (July–August 1991), pp. 39, 42. The Foundation for the School of Business at Indiana University.

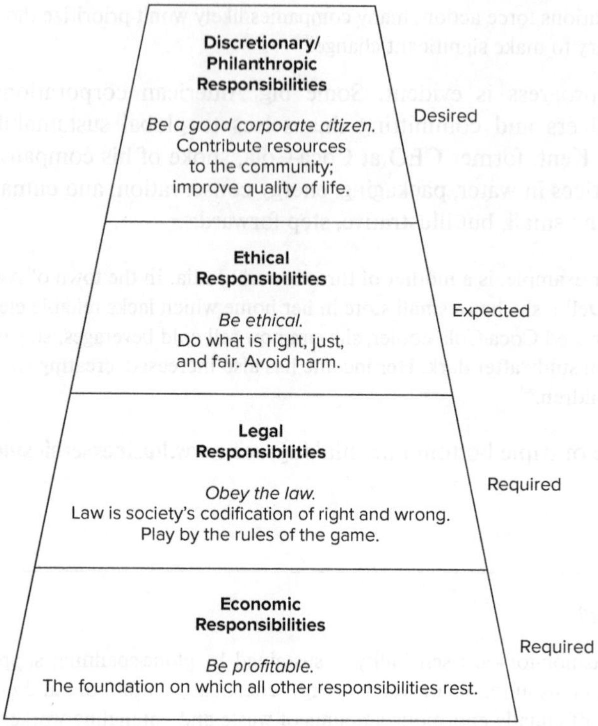

Social Responsibility Pyramid

Professor Archie Carroll's depiction of socially responsible business behavior is displayed in Figure 3.2. Successful business practice must begin with two foundational responsibilities of the pyramid: the economic responsibility of making a profit and the legal responsibility of doing so in a lawful fashion. Simultaneously, the socially responsible firm is expected to move up the pyramid beyond the fundamental demands of economics and law, to pursue the ethical course of action. In striving for profitable, lawful, ethical conduct, that company may also choose to engage in discretionary philanthropic (charitable) efforts to build a better community. While Carroll's social responsibility pyramid has been criticized and revised, it remains a useful way of thinking about corporations' expanding duties.[85] [ISO, the International Organization for Standardization, has developed a set of guidelines for socially responsible corporate behavior labeled ISO 26000. For an overview of ISO 26000, see **www.iso.org/iso/home/standards/iso26000.htm**].

Automakers and the Social Responsibility Pyramid

General Motors, Hyundai, Kia, Mitsubishi, Nissan, Suzuki, Toyota, and Volkswagen, among others, in recent years have committed moral and legal wrongs leading to deaths, environmental despoliation, and enormous economic losses.

General Motors (GM) has paid at least $2.6 billion in criminal penalties and civil claims arising from its failure to disclose an ignition defect that reportedly led to at least 124 deaths. GM employees apparently were aware of the problem for a decade or more prior to disclosure. Nissan in 2018 admitted to improperly measuring exhaust emissions and fuel economy for some of its models sold in Japan. At the same time, Nissan's ex-chairman, Carlos Ghosn, was jailed and then placed under house arrest in Japan on charges of misusing company funds, among other allegations. Prior to trial, Ghosn escaped from Japan under mysterious circumstances. Mitsubishi admitted in 2016 that its employees had intentionally inflated fuel mileage test results for some of its models. Hyundai, Kia, and Suzuki have made similar admissions. Toyota agreed to pay $1.2 billion in 2014 to settle United States criminal charges that it had failed to disclose information about a defect that caused some of its cars to accelerate suddenly, leading to at least 37 deaths. Volkswagen has paid more than $30 billion to date in various penalties and settlements to cover the costs associated with its software manipulations allegedly designed to defeat environmental emissions tests for some of its diesel vehicles.

In applying Carroll's Social Responsibility Pyramid reasoning, we see that the automakers compromised their capacity to fulfill their long-term economic responsibilities. Beyond the costs noted above, civil lawsuits, vehicle recalls, product redesigns, and other expenses will pile up for years to come. Of course, these companies also clearly failed to meet their legal and ethical responsibilities.

Some of the automakers have rather forthrightly addressed their shortcomings. Toyota president Akio Toyoda acknowledged that quality had been sacrificed for faster growth and profits. Toyoda said, "[S]ome people just got too big-headed and focused too excessively on profit."[86] [For Toyota's Corporate Social Responsibility policy, see **www.toyota-global.com/sustainability/csr/csr**].

Sources: Danielle Douglas and Michael Fletcher, "Toyota Reaches $1.2 Billion Settlement to End Probe of Accelerator Problems," *The Washington Post,* March 29, 2014 [**www.washingtonpost.com**]; "Exhausted by Scandal: 'Dieselgate' Continues to Haunt Volkswagen," *Knowledge@Wharton,* March 21, 2019 [**https://knowledge.wharton.upenn.edu**]; Eric D. Lawrence, "GM Settles Deadly Ignition Switch Cases for $120 Million," *USA TODAY,* October 20, 2017 [**www.usatoday.com**]; Norihiko Shirouzu, "Toyoda Rues Excessive Profit Focus," *The Wall Street Journal,* March 2, 2010, p. B3; and Naomi Tajitsu, "Nissan Admits to More Testing Misconduct for Cars Sold in Japan," *Reuters,* July 9, 2018 [**www.reuters.com**].

Corporate Social Responsibility in Practice

Operating in a troubled world, the corporate community is taking an increasingly active role in addressing a very wide range of social problems. Google, a zealous CSR practitioner, regularly tops the Reputation Institute's worldwide corporate responsibility rankings.[87] In 2017, for instance, Google announced its plan to award $1 billion in grants, and an additional one million volunteer hours, over a 5-year period to nonprofits that use technology and innovation to address global problems, including education, economic opportunity, and inclusion.[88]

Beyond direct giving, many social responsibility advocates believe that an entrepreneurial, profit-seeking, capitalist approach is the best route to correcting social problems. Google is one of an array of companies that have expanded their CSR efforts to include building through market mechanisms, along with giving. Many of those companies view social responsibility as workable only if it contributes to the strategic mission of the business and, ultimately, to the bottom line. Nike, for example, turned aggressively to social responsibility measures as a way of restoring its brand image after criticism for its use of global sweatshop labor.[89] Examples of corporations that practice social responsibility both as a means of "giving back" and as a strategic business practice that can contribute to the bottom line in the long term have become increasingly common:

- Several thousand Starbucks workers, many of them minorities, are receiving an online education through Arizona State University with all tuition paid by Starbucks. Thus, the company is doing good while enhancing its diversity image.[90]
- Consumer products colossus, Unilever, sells environmentally friendly detergent, installs thousands of water pumps in African villages, and removes gender stereotypes from its ads not only believing that these are the right things to do but also believing consumers will buy more from them and that brand loyalty among the global poor will increase.[91]
- Seattle's six-story Bullitt Center, the "world's greenest building," is running so efficiently after its 2013 opening that it generated 60 percent more electricity (using geothermal wells and solar panels) in 2014 than it used.[92] The $30 million building–featuring composting toilets, bike-only on-site parking, a stairway designed to allow magnificent views of Puget Sound, and no stormwater runoff–also made economic sense with a 2017 occupancy rate of 100 percent.[93]

Questions

1. In general, we understand decisions to lay off employees when companies are losing money, but how should we feel about profitable companies that lay off employees? For example, *The Washington Post* reported that 45 of the 50 biggest U.S. companies saw profits during the first six months of the COVID-19 pandemic–a time when millions of Americans were impoverished–yet 27 of those firms held layoffs and turned their profits over to their shareholders.[94] Powerful executive Barry Diller, founder of both Fox and USA broadcasting companies, has condemned "preemptive" layoffs:

   > The idea of a company that's earning money, not losing money, that's not, let's say, "industrially endangered," to have just . . . cutbacks so they can earn another $12 million or $20 million or $40 million in a year where no one's counting is really a horrible act when you think about it on every level.[95]

   a. Do you think a socially responsible company that operates at a profit would engage in layoffs? Explain.

   b. Construction, farm, and mining equipment manufacturer Vermeer Corp. suffered a 40 percent drop in revenue in 2009. To cope with the "Great Recession" of that era, Vermeer cut workers' hours, but no one lost their job. Why would Vermeer sacrifice profit to keep workers who could simply have been let go?

   c. Vermeer is privately held by the family who started the company. How might that status affect layoff decisions?

2. Was Wall Street's financial collapse in 2008–2009 due, at least in part, to a lack of diversity in the workplace? One study found that men tend to take excessive risks and women tend to be more comprehensive thinkers. Hence, some critics say, the financial community needs more women:

11. Thomas B. Edsall, "The Obama Coalition vs. Corporate America," *The New York Times,* January 9, 2013 [**http://opinionator.blogs.nytimes.com**].
12. Rich Newman, "How Your Boss Will Run Your Life in a Few Years," *Yahoo Finance,* August 19, 2014 [**http://finance.yahoo.com**].
13. Nicholas Kristof, "The Real Welfare Cheats," *The New York Times,* April 14, 2016 [**www.nytimes.com**].
14. Ibid.
15. Dan Caplinger, "How Do the New US Corporate Tax Rates Compare Globally? A Foolish Take," *USA TODAY,* July 10, 2018 [**www.usatoday.com**].
16. Kathryn Kranhold, "Big Businesses Promised Wage Hikes from Trump's Tax Cuts. What Actually Happened?," *NBC News,* February 12, 2019 [**www.nbcnews.com**].
17. Andrew Marquadt, "CEO Pay Is Skyrocketing as the Average Worker Struggles to Keep up with Inflation. Here's Who Got the Biggest Raises.," *Fortune,* April 4, 2022 (**https://www.fortune.com**).
18. Laura J. Keller, "Dimon Warns 'Something Is Wrong' with the U.S.," *Bloomberg,* April 4, 2017 [**www.bloomberg.com**].
19. Editorial, "Corporations Are Winning Big, Starving Government, with GOP Tax Break," *Des Moines Register,* April 18, 2019 [**www.desmoinesregister.com**]; and U.S. National Debt Clock: Real Time [**https://usdebtclock.org**].
20. Howard Gleckman, "Are US Billionaires Really Paying a Lower Tax Rate than Working People? Probably Not.," *Forbes,* October 11, 2019 [**www.forbes.com**].
21. Noah Smith, "The Case for Higher Taxes at the Very Top," *Bloomberg News Wire,* October 8, 2019 [**www.bnnbloomberg.ca**].
22. Jonathan Tepper (with Denise Hearn), *The Myth of Capitalism,* Hoboken, NJ: Wiley, 2018.
23. See *Abdur Rahaman v, J.C. Penney Corporation, Inc., The Children's Palace, and Wal-Mart Stores, Inc.,* C.A. No. N15C-07-174 MMJ (Del. Super. Ct., May 4, 2016); and Colin Perkel, "Loblaws Off the Hook for Rana Plaza Disaster; Bangladeshi Lawsuit Fails," *CBC News,* August 8, 2019 [**www.cbc.ca**].
24. Chris MacDonald, "Bangladesh, Joe Fresh and the Burden of Responsibility," *Canadian Business,* April 26, 2013.
25. David J. Doorey, "Vacuousness of CSR on Display in Loblaws' Victory in Rana Plaza Class Action Lawsuit," Canadian Law of Work Forum, July 12, 2017 [**http://lawofwork.ca**].
26. Center for Responsive Politics, "Lobbying Database," *OpenSecrets.org,* accessed January 2023 [**www.opensecrets.org**].
27. Center for Responsive Politics, "Top Spenders 2021," *OpenSecrets.org,* accessed January 2023 [**www.opensecrets.org**].
28. Center for Responsive Politics, "Top Spenders 2016," *OpenSecrets.org,* accessed January 2023 [**www.opensecrets.org**].
29. Ailsa Chang, "When Lobbyists Literally Write the Bill," *National Public Radio,* November 11, 2013 [**www.npr.org**].
30. Russell Berman, "An Exodus from Congress Tests the Lure of Lobbying," *The Atlantic,* May 1, 2018 [**www.theatlantic.com**].
31. Benjamin C.K. Egerod, "Study: Political Connections Lower Companies' Tax Rates and Risk of Being Audited," *ProMarket.org,* May 21, 2019 [**https://promarket.org**].
32. John Cassidy, "Is America an Oligarchy?" *The New Yorker,* April 18, 2014 [**www.newyorker.com**].

33. Ibid.
34. Ibid.
35. Steven Pearlstein, "How Big Business Lost Washington," *The Washington Post,* September 2, 2016 [**www.washingtonpost.com**].
36. James Hohmann, "The Daily 202: Mick Mulvaney's Confession Highlights the Corrosive Influence of Money in Politics," *The Washington Post,* April 25, 2018 [**www.washingtonpost.com**].
37. Ibid.
38. *Citizens United v. Federal Election Commission,* 130 S. Ct. 876 (2010).
39. Center for Responsive Politics, "Super Pacs," *OpenSecrets.org,* accessed January 2023 [**www.opensecrets.org**]; and Center for Responsive Politics, "2022 Top Donors to Outside Spending Groups," *OpenSecrets.org,* accessed January 2023 [**www.opensecrets.org**].
40. Opinion, "Political Spending Pays," *The Wall Street Journal,* June 20, 2012 [**www.wsj.com**].
41. Ibid.
42. Barbara J. King, "Resisting the Corporate University: What It Means to Be a 'Slow Professor,'" *National Public Radio,* May 12, 2016 [**www.npr.org**].
43. Claire Ballentine, "The Hot College Gig: Online Brand Promoter," *The New York Times,* August 31, 2018 [**www.nytimes.com**].
44. Hunter Rawlings, "Stop Treating College Like a Commodity," *Des Moines Register,* June 13, 2015 [**www.desmoinesregister.com**].
45. Melissa Korn, "Wealth or Waste? Rethinking the Value of a Business Major," *The Wall Street Journal,* April 5, 2012 [**www.wsj.com**].
46. Natasha Singer, "How Google Took Over the Classroom," *The New York Times,* May 13, 2017 [**www.nytimes.com**].
47. Ibid.
48. Mara Einstein, *Brands of Faith* (New York: Routledge, 2008).
49. William Cummings, "Televangelist Says God Told Him He Needs 4th Private Plane," *USA Today,* May 29, 2018 [**www.usatoday.com**].
50. David Brooks, "The Gospel of Wealth," *The New York Times,* September 6, 2010 [**www.nytimes.com**].
51. Jonathan Wynn, "Are There Too Many Music Festivals?," *The Conversation,* April 13, 2017 [**https://theconversation.com**].
52. Ibid.
53. L. R., "Same Old Song," *The Economist,* July 26, 2012 [**www.economist.com**].
54. Fraser McAlpine, "Has Pop Music Lost Its Fun?," *BBC,* January 12, 2018 [**www.bbc.co.uk**].
55. Jon Pareles, "Big Money Upends a Festival," *The New York Times,* March 16, 2014 [**www.nytimes.com**].
56. Frank Bruni, "Capitalism's Suffocating Music," *The New York Times,* October 21, 2014 [**www.nytimes.com**].
57. Associated Press, "Kansas State's Bill Snyder: College Athletics 'Sold Out,'" *USA Today,* August 6, 2014 [**www.usatoday.com**].
58. Michael Smith and John Ourand, "Pac-12 Seeking $750 M Investment for Schools, TV Networks," *Sports Business Journal,* March 21, 2019 [**www.sportsbusinessjournal.com**].
59. Mark Tracy, "Under Armor Seeks to Do for Maryland What Nike Did for Oregon," *The New York Times,* August 26, 2015 [**www.nytimes.com**].
60. Ibid.

61. Eric Crawford, "It's Time for Leagues to Pay Up," *Louisville Courier-Journal,* October 27, 2011.
62. Jon Wilner, "PAC-12 Commissioner George Kliavkoff to the University Presidents: Spend More on Football, Reap the Rewards," *The Mercury News,* January 6, 2022 [**www.mercurynews.com**].
63. Andrew Denney, "Another Ex-NCAA Coach Gets Prison Time in Bribery Scandal," *New York Post,* June 7, 2019 [**https://nypost.com**].
64. "Size of the Youth Sports Market in 2017 and 2019," *Statistica,* accessed January 2023 [**www.statistica.com**].
65. "Little League Baseball CEO Will Consider Compensating Players," *SI Wire,* August 23, 2014 [**www.si.com**].
66. Danny Lawhon, "Stadium-Wide Alcohol for College Football Is Growing Fast. So, Why Are Iowa Schools Resisting?" *Des Moines Register,* April 23, 2018 [**www.desmoinesregister.com**]; and "Beer Sales Rake in More than $1M at Ohio Stadium," *Associated Press News,* December 12, 2017 [**https://apnews.com**].
67. Michael T. Nietzel, "Sobering Thoughts about Alcohol Sales at College Stadiums," *Forbes,* December 1, 2018 [**www.forbes.com**].
68. Mark Tracy, "Beer Here! Beer Here?," *The New York Times,* October 8, 2015 [**www.nytimes.com**].
69. Charles Reich, *The Greening of America* (New York: Bantam Books, 1970), pp. 7–8.
70. "Feeling of Alienation among Americans Reaches Highest Point on Record," *The Harris Poll,* January 20, 2015 [**www.theharrispoll.com**].
71. Ben Stein, "A City on a Hill, or a Looting Opportunity," *The New York Times,* July 9, 2006 [**www.nytimes.com**].
72. Joe Davidson, "Park Service and Corporate Advertising, a Dangerous Mix." *The Washington Post,* May 9, 2016 [**www.washingtonpost.com**].
73. Joseph Pickett, "4 Examples of How Corporate America Is Crushing Social Media," *Business 2 Community,* February 8, 2013 [**www.business2community.com**].
74. Bloomberg, "Shareholder Value Isn't the Ultimate Yardstick, Top CEOs Declare," *Crain's Chicago Business,* August 19, 2019 [**www.chicagobusiness.com**].
75. "The Deloitte Millennial Survey 2016," Deloitte, accessed January 2023 [**www2.deloitte.com**].
76. Ibid.
77. Ina Jaffe, "At Intel, A Retirement Perk that Can Kick Off a New Career as a Paid Fellow," *National Public Radio,* April 17, 2017 [**www.npr.org**].
78. Keith Davis and Robert L. Blomstrom, *Business and Society: Environment and Responsibility,* 3rd ed. (New York: McGraw-Hill, 1975), p. 6.
79. Milton Friedman, *Capitalism and Freedom* (Chicago: University of Chicago Press, 1962), p. 133.
80. Herbert Stein, "Corporate America, Mind Your Own Business," *The Wall Street Journal,* July 15, 1996, p. A10.
81. Robin Givhan, "Can Cheap Clothing Generate Fair Wages? H&M Believes It Can," *The Washington Post,* November 25, 2014 [**www.washingtonpost.com**].
82. Steven A. Rochlin, "The New Corporate Citizenship," *BusinessWeek,* December 13, 2003, p. 66.
83. Yves Leclerc and David South, "Study: Prioritizing Supply Chain Sustainability, but the Real Work Remains Ahead," Stakeholder Trends and Insights, February 5, 2016 [**www.sustainablebrands.com**].
84. Muktar Kent, "Toward a Sustainable Future," Raytheon Lectureship in Business Ethics of Bentley University, April 5, 2012 [**www.bentley.edu/cbe**].

85. Archie Carroll and others have pointed to some descriptive and theoretical limitations associated with Carroll's social responsibility pyramid; and Carroll has proposed a three-domain approach of economic, legal, and ethical responsibilities arrayed in a Venn framework. The newer model appears to satisfy some of the concerns of Carroll and others about Carroll's pyramid, but for both teaching and research purposes, the pyramid remains a useful construct. For Carroll's newer construct, see Mark S. Schwartz and Archie B. Carroll, "Corporate Social Responsibility: A Three Domain Approach," *Business Ethics Quarterly* 13, no. 4 (October 2003), p. 503. For an example of research employing the Carroll pyramid and a discussion of some of the strengths and weaknesses of the pyramid, see Dane K. Peterson, "The Relationship between Perceptions of Corporate Citizenship and Organizational Commitment," *Business & Society* 43, no. 3 (September 2004), p. 296.

86. Norihiko Shirouzu, Toyoda Rues Excessive Profit Focus," *The Wall Street Journal,* March 2, 2010, p. B3.

87. Reputation Institute, "2022 Global CSR 100 RepTrak Data," [Reputation Institute | CSR Ratings (csrhub.com) and ESG Ratings & sustainability info for Google, Inc. | ESG Investing (csrhub.com)].

88. Google.org, "Our $1 Billion Commitment to Create More Opportunity for Everyone," *Press Release,* October 13, 2017 [**www.google.org**].

89. Andrea Newell, "How Nike Embraced CSR and Went from Villain to Hero," *Triple Pundit,* June 19, 2015 [**www.triplepundit.com**].

90. Jeffrey R. Young, "ASU's Starbucks Deal Was Just the Beginning," *EdSurge News,* June 21, 2017 [**www.edsurge.com**].

91. Thomas Buckley and Matthew Campbell, "If Unilever Can't Make Feel-Good Capitalism Work, Who Can?" *Bloomberg,* August 30, 2017 [**www.bloomberg.com**].

92. Sanjay Bhatt, "Bullitt Center Tops Its Green Goals, Is Making Energy to Spare," *The Seattle Times,* March 27, 2015 [**www.seattletimes.com**].

93. Washington Governor's Office, "It's Easy Being Green at the Bullitt Center in Seattle," *Press Release,* March 13, 2017 [**https://medium.com/wagovernor/its-easy-being-green-at-the-bullitt-center-in-seattle-d6f8911fd721**].

94. Douglas Macmillan, Peter Whoriskey, and Jonathan O'Connell, "America's Biggest Companies are Flourishing During the Pandemic and Putting Thousands of People Out of Work," *The Washington Post,* December 16, 2020 [**www.washingtonpost.com**].

95. Aaron Task, "Mass Layoffs by Profitable Firms a 'Horrible Act,' Diller Says," *Yahoo!* Finance, December 10, 2008.

96. Linda Basch, "More Women in Finance, a More Sustainable Economy," *The Christian Science Monitor,* June 24, 2009 [**www.csmonitor.com**].

97. For a recent, readable overview of the ESG movement, see George Kell, "The Remarkable Rise of ESG," *Forbes,* July 11, 2018 [**www.forbes.com**].

98. See Christophe Revelli and Jean-Laurent Viviani, "Financial Performance of Socially Responsible Investing: What Have We Learned? A Meta-Analysis," *Business Ethics: A European Review* 24, no. 2 (2015) p. 158; also see Joshua Margolis, Hillary Elfenbein, and James Walsh, "Does It Pay to Be Good . . . and Does It Matter? A Meta-Analysis of the Relationship between Corporate Social and Financial Performance," March 2009 [**http://ssrn.com/abstract=1866371**].

99. Timothy D. Hubbard, Dane M. Christensen, and Scott D. Graffin, "Higher Highs and Lower Lows: The Role of Corporate Social Responsibility in CEO Dismissal," *Strategic Management Journal* 38, no. 11 (November 2017), p. 2255.

100. Robert G. Eccles and Svetlana Klimenko, "The Investor Revolution," *Harvard Business Review,* May-June 2019, [**www.hbr.org**].

101. Chris MacDonald, "How Can Business 'Give Back' to Society?" *The Business Ethics Blog,* January 31, 2012 [**https://businessethicsblog.com**].
102. V. Kasturi Rangan, Lisa Chase, and Sohel Karim, "The Truth about CSR," *Harvard Business Review* 93, no. 1–2 (January–February 2015), p. 40.
103. Cedric Rose, "Q&A: A. G. Lafley," *Cincinnati Magazine,* May 1, 2013 [**www.cincinnatimagazine.com**].
104. Ibid.
105. Social Accountability International, "SA8000 Summary Statistics through 3rd Quarter 2022," accessed January 2023 [**https://si-intl.org/sa8000-search/**].
106. Mark Magnier, "Anguish Lingers in Bhopal, 25 Years after Chemical Disaster," *Los Angeles Times,* December 3, 2009 [**www.latimes.com**].
107. Susan Warren, "Chemical Companies Keep Lessons of Bhopal Spill Fresh," *The Wall Street Journal,* February 13, 2001, [**www.wsj.com**].
108. Daniel B. Kline, "Here's What Walmart Really Pays Its Workers," *Motley Fool,* May 13, 2019 [**www.fool.com**]; Melissa Repko and Lauren Thomas, "Walmart to Hike Wages for 425,000 Workers to Average Above $15 an Hour, *CNBC,* February 19, 2001 [**www.cnbc.com**]; Kelly Tyko," Costco to Increase Its Minimum Wage to $16 per Hour, But CEO Says the Average Pay for Hourly Workers is $24, *USA Today,* February 25, 2021 [**www.usatoday.com**].
109. Paul Fain, "Walmart Expands Employee Tuition Benefits," *Inside Higher Ed,* June 6, 2019 [**www.insidehighered.com**]; Lorie Konish, "Walmart Announces Plan to Pay 100% of College Tuition and Books for Its Associates," *CNBC,* July 27, 2021 [**www.cnbc.com**].
110. Walmart, "Key Takeaways from the 2022 Mid-Year Culture, Diversity, Equity, and Inclusion Report," accessed January 2023 [**https://corporate.walmart.com**].
111. Matthew Sterm, "Walmart's Customers Love Its Low Prices But Still Have Gripes," *Retail Wire,* April 29, 2022 [**https://retailwire.com**].
112. John Ballard, "Better Buy: Costco vs. Walmart," *The Motley Fool,* May 21, 2019 [**www.fool.com**]; James Brumley, "Better Buy: Costco vs. Walmart," April 11, 2021 [**www.fool.com**]; and Jennifer Saibil and Jeremy Bowman, "Better Buy: Costco vs. Walmart," *The Motley Fool,* Nov. 15, 2022 [**www.fool.com**].
113. Ibid.
114. William Beaver, "Is the Stakeholder Model Dead?" *Business Horizons* 42, no. 2 (March–April 1999), p. 8.
115. William Mellor, Lulu Yilun Chen, and Zijing Wu, "Alibaba's Jack Ma Has: $30 Billion, an Odd Relationship with Investors and No Coding Skills," *Bloomberg,* November 9, 2014 [**www.bloomberg.com**], available at [Jack Ma says Alibaba shareholders should feel love after coming third | Mint (**livemint.com**)].
116. Eliza Sydnor Romm, "Gun Makers Must Do More," *The New York Times,* April 6, 2018 [**www.nytimes.com**].
117. For a discussion of whether companies should voluntarily take gun control measures, see "Walmart and Gun Control: Should Companies Self-Regulate When the Government Doesn't Act? A New Capitalisn't Episode," *ProMarket,* September 12, 2019 [**https://promarket.org**].
118. Jacob Pramuk, "Congress Passes Most Significant Gun Reform in Decades, Sends It to Biden," *CNBC,* June 24, 2022 [**www.cnbc.com**].
119. *Donna L. Soto, et al. v. Bushmaster Firearms International,* 2019 Conn.LEXIS 66.
120. See Lois Beckett, "Families of Sandy Hook Victims Go After 'Untouchable' Gun Manufacturers," *The Guardian,* April 20, 2016 [**www.theguardian.com**]; and George Zornick, "Gunmaker in the Sandy Hook Case: Sorry, We're Immune," *The Nation,* February 23, 2016 [**www.thenation.com**].

121. Sarah Jorgensen, Jacob Hannah, and Erica Hill, "Sandy Hook Families Reach $73 Million Settlement with Gun Manufacturer Remington," *CNN,* February 16, 2022 [**www.cnn.com**].

122. Dana Radcliffe, "Gun Makers See No Problem Selling for Self-Defense and Allowing Sales to Criminals," *HuffPost,* July 9, 2013 [**www.huffpost.com**].

123. Andrew Ross Sorkin, "Guns in your 401(k)? The Push to Divest Grows," *The New York Times,* December 7, 2015 [**www.nytimes.com**].

124. Lois Beckett, "Families of Sandy Hook Victims Go After 'Untouchable' Gun Manufacturers," *The Guardian,* April 20, 2016 [**www.theguardian.com**].

125. Jim Ludema and Amber Johnson, "Gravity Payment's Dan Price on How He Measures Success After His $70K Experiment," *Forbes,* August 28, 2018 [**www.forbes.com**].

126. Ibid.

127. Dan Price, "Purpose–Not Profit–Driven Companies Will Take Over the Economy," *Huffington Post,* November 2, 2015 [**www.huffingtonpost.com**].

128. Khadeeja Safdar, "How Target Botched Its Response to the North Carolina Bathroom Law," *The Wall Street Journal,* April 5, 2017 [**www.wsj.com**].

129. Robert Kaiser, "Seminar Explores Judeo-Christian Ethics and Modern Corporations," *Toledo Blade,* April 25, 1980, p. 14.

130. Janine Puhad, "San Antonio Council Rejects Bid to Reconsider Chick-fil-A Airport Ban," *Fox News,* April 19, 2019 [**www.foxnews.com**]; and Kim Severson, "A Chicken Chain's Corporate Ethos Is Questioned by Gay Rights Advocates," *The New York Times,* January 29, 2011 [**www.nytimes.com**].

131. Iain Murray, "Businesses Already Serve a Social Purpose," *USA Today,* January 25, 2018 [**www.usatoday.com**].

132. Sam Wong, "Materialism Makes Me Feel Happy, Not Guilty," *Des Moines Register,* September 10, 2000, p. 11A.

133. Charles McCarry, *Citizen Nader* (New York: Saturday Review Press, 1972), p. 301.

134. Sarah Ullah, "How Samsung Dominates South Korea's Economy," *CNN,* February 17, 2017 [**www.cnn.com**].

135. Chico Harlan, "In S. Korea, the Republic of Samsung," *The Washington Post,* December 9, 2012 [**www.washingtonpost.com**].

136. Galaxy announced it has sold over 2 billion phones by early 2019; at the time Apple had sold somewhat less than 2 billion devises using its IOS. [**www.theverge.com**].

137. Rekha Basu, "Is It Acceptable to Do Business with Wal-Mart?" *Waterloo/Cedar Falls Courier,* June 12, 2015, p. A6.

138. Ashley Archibald, "City Council Passes Environmental Bill of Rights," *Santa Monica Daily Press,* March 14, 2013 [**http://smdp.com**].

139. David Bornstein, "Giving Capitalism a Social Conscience," *The New York Times,* October 10, 2017 [**www.nytimes.com**].

140. John Z. DeLorean with J. Patrick Wright, "Bottom-Line Fever at General Motors" (excerpted from *On a Clear Day You Can See General Motors*), The Washington Monthly, January 1980, pp. 26–27.

141. Steven N. Brenner and Earl A. Molander, "Is the Ethics of Business Changing?" *Harvard Business Review* 55, no. 1 (January–February 1977), p. 68.

Video icon credit: Comstock Images/Alamy Stock Photo

UNIT TWO

Introduction to Law

CHAPTER FOUR

The American Legal System

After completing this chapter, students will be able to fulfill the following learning objectives:

4-1. Describe the importance of law to private enterprise.

4-2. Compare and contrast the objectives of law in society.

4-3. Differentiate constitutional law, case law, and statutory law.

4-4. Differentiate the elements of a case brief.

4-5. Distinguish between substantive and procedural law.

4-6. Compare and contrast civil and criminal law.

4-7. Describe the elements of the basic court system structure.

4-8. Explain the purposes of subject matter and personal jurisdiction as requirements for a court's power to hear a dispute.

4-9. Describe the typical steps in the civil trial process.

4-10. Distinguish trials and appeals.

4-11. Identify dispute resolution alternatives to trials.

Introduction

LO 4-1
Describe the importance of law to private enterprise.

Presumably, we can agree that some business behavior is bad for society. This text examines what should be done to change that behavior. In the United States, three basic options exist: Let the market "regulate" business behavior, which means leaving choices to the ethical dictates of individual decision makers; pass a law; or rely on some combination of the market, ethics, and law. The level of market regulation in relationship to law, on a continuum from capitalism to collectivism, was discussed in Chapter 1. The degree to which self-regulation through ethics can and does impact business behavior was explored in Chapters 2 and 3. This chapter begins the discussion of the legal regulation of business with a brief outline of the American legal system. We will also look at alternative conflict resolution processes, such as negotiation, mediation, and arbitration, that do not resort to the court system. We begin by reminding ourselves of the indispensable role of law in supporting business practice.

Law and the Market

Whatever we may think about lawyers, judges, and America's dispute resolution methods, a reliable legal system in fostering and maintaining capitalism is key. Often referred to as the *rule of law,* it is the establishment of authority and influence that can constrain both individual and institutional behavior and the foundation on which vibrant societies are built and maintained.

A legal system implied by the existence of the rule of law is not just the dispute resolution infrastructure of courts and judges, but also the principles and rules of process and procedure that apply to all that come within it, as well as the fundamental principles of substantive law that are the foundation on which more complex legal rights and responsibilities are built. The concept of *due process* discussed in Chapter 5 is an example of the former, and the law governing enforceable private contracts explored in Chapter 6 is an example of the latter.

> As contemporary society becomes increasingly diverse, law grows, not diminishes, in its importance to private enterprise; and in spite of valid concerns about the impact of law on efficiency, future business managers will need to know more, not less, about how law affects business operations. No evidence suggests any other conclusion.[1]

Another layer of complexity is added when business relationships cross jurisdictional lines–between states of the United States, which converts local commerce into interstate commerce, which are addressed in Chapter 8, or across national boundaries, the complexities of which are discussed in Chapter 16, but also Chapters 17 and 18. These latter relationships can hardly exist, let alone thrive, without an effective rule of law in each jurisdiction with which a particular business transaction is associated.

Further, in democracies

> Law is important to business for another reason quite separate from its function in establishing ownership rights and facilitating promise keeping necessary to their transfer: It provides the formal expression of democratic social will. That expression implicates private enterprise in a plethora of ways, including regulation of the environment, employment laws, securities regulation, consumer protection statutes, and product liability.[2]

Question

As reported in *The New York Times,* the amount of taxes paid by corporations has been shrinking over the years, with a "revolving door" between the public and private sectors playing a role. Tax attorneys with major accounting firms are encouraged to take stints with the U.S. Department of Treasury, where they have the chance to shape tax policy in their governmental roles that could benefit their former clients. The government welcomes the expertise they offer, and the attorneys often later return to the accounting firms with greater pay and titles. What does the "revolving door" between U.S. accounting firms and the U.S. Department of Treasury, and its impact on corporate tax rates, reveal about the role of law in business and society? Should this "revolving door" be slowed down, and how? Explain.

Sources: Jesse Drucker and Danny Hakim, "How Accounting Giants Craft Favorable Tax Rules from Inside Government," *The New York Times,* September 19, 2021 [**www.meworktimes.com**]; Andrew Ross Sorkin, Jason Karaian, Sarah Kessler, Stephen Gandel, Lauren Hirsch, and Ephrat Livni, "How Tax Giants Write Their Own Rules," *The New York Times,* September 20, 2021 [nytimes.com]; and The American Legal Studies in Business Task Force Report (1998), reprinted in *American Business Law Journal* 36, no.1(Fall 1998).

Part One—Legal Foundations

Objectives of the Law

LO 4-2
Compare and contrast the objectives of law in society.

Americans differ dramatically in their views of the role the law should play in contemporary life. For some, the courts and the police primarily act as obstructions to personal freedom and to a fully efficient marketplace. Others seek much more laws to ensure that everyone in need is cared for, and everyone is sheltered from wrongdoers. Although we may argue about the law's precise import in our lives, most of us can agree on some foundational expectations for a fair, efficient legal system. Certainly, we expect the law to *maintain order* in our diverse, rapidly changing society. We also rely on the law to peacefully, fairly, and intelligently *resolve conflict.* Perhaps less obvious, but no less important, the law serves to *preserve dominant values.* Americans differ about core values, but we have reached a workable accord about our most fundamental beliefs. Some of those, such as freedom of speech, press, and religion, are guaranteed by our Bill of Rights, thus setting a steady foundation for an enduring nation. We can see that the law is a vital force in *guaranteeing freedom.* (But freedom can be confusing: Are you free to smoke wherever you wish, or do I have a right to smoke-free air?)

Justice

> We count on the law to achieve and preserve justice.

Broadly, we count on the law to *achieve and preserve justice.* The pursuit of justice often relies on honorable, efficient government. The World Justice Project's 2019 "Rule of Law Index" ranks governmental quality by such measures as criminal and civil justice, order and security, open government, and absence of corruption. Among the 126 countries studied, Denmark ranked first; the United States overall was 20.[3] Perhaps the study is correct in the sense that America still has abundant room for improvement. Nonetheless, Americans can properly be proud of a long struggle to build a more just society for all. Efforts, for example, to curb discrimination; guarantee due process; reduce violence; protect those in need; maintain order and security; build fair, efficient regulatory systems; and respect the rights of all are central practices in an extraordinarily complex and rapidly evolving American culture. It should, however, give us pause for thought that, compared to the 2018 rankings, 31 countries' rule of law performance declined by one percent or more; the decline for the United States was 2.2 percent, making it tied for the tenth largest decline with Hungary.[4] As you read this chapter, ask yourself repeatedly, "Does this rule (this procedure, this case) contribute to the search for justice?" In the end, all legal studies must involve the search for justice. (For a daily update of U.S. legal news, see **www.law.com**).

Question

When a 16-year-old girl was benched on a club volleyball team, denying her a chance to impress varsity coaches and possibly college recruiters, she and her family sued. A father in the Philadelphia suburbs sued his son's high school track coach for $40 million after his son was cut from the team, claiming that his son's chances of obtaining a college scholarship were badly hurt. Such lawsuits are increasing as families turn to the courts to resolve disputes arising from youth sports.

As a matter of justice, should club leagues, school sports programs, and coaches be subjected to such lawsuits? Explain. See Justin Jouvenal, "Teen Volleyball Player Takes Her Dispute to Another Kind of Court," *The Washington Post,* March 31, 2015 [**www.washingtonpost.com**].

Cyberbullying

Twenty-year-old Rutgers University student Dharun Ravi secretly activated the webcam in his dorm room so that he and a friend could watch his roommate, 18-year-old Tyler Clementi, engage in a romantic encounter with another male. Ravi used texts and Twitter to encourage friends to watch a second planned video that did not occur. Clementi subsequently committed suicide. Ravi was convicted of invasion of privacy and bias intimidation, among other crimes, and sentenced to 30 days in jail, 300 hours of community service, and a fine of $10,000 to be paid to hate crime victims.

The Tyler Clementi Higher Education Anti-Harassment Act, a bill that has been introduced in Congress, would require colleges and universities receiving federal student aid funding to have and distribute a policy prohibiting harassment. Prohibited harassment included cyberbullying of enrolled students by other students, faculty, and staff based on, among other things, actual or perceived sexual orientation.

Questions

1. Do you think the Tyler Clementi Higher Education Anti-Harassment Act should be enacted? Explain.
2. Although there is no federal legislation directly addressing bullying on college campuses, if the alleged conduct rises to the level of harassment under federal antidiscrimination statutes, such as the Americans with Disabilities Act, then the college or university receiving federal funding would have to take steps to resolve the harassment. Do you think further legislation is needed to address campus bullying? Explain.

Sources: Mark Trumbull, "Why Dharun Ravi Got 30 Days in Jail in Rutgers Webcam Spying Case," *The Christian Science Monitor,* May 21, 2012 [**www.christiansciencemonitor.com**]; Niels Lesniewski and Emily Bazelon, "Make the Punishment Fit the Cyber-Crime," *The New York Times,* March 19, 2012 [**www.nytimes.com**]; "Rutgers Firing Prompts New Look at Anti-Bullying Bill," *Rollcall,* April 3, 2013 [**www.rollcall.com**]; H.R.482, Tyler Clementi Higher Education Anti-Harassment Act of 2015, 114th Congress (2015–2016) [**https://www.congress.gov**]; Geoffrey Nathan, "Cyberbullying Laws, Charges, and Statues of Limitation," FederalCharges.com, 2019, [**www.federalcharges.com**]; and H.R. 5342: Tyler Clementi Higher Education Anti-Harassment Act of 2021, 117th Congress (2021-2022) [**https://www.congress.gov**].

Primary Sources of Law

U.S. law is a vast, constantly growing, and mutating body of rules and reason. That law is derived from four primary sources: constitutions, statutes, regulations, and cases (called *common law* or judge-made law).

LO 4-3 Differentiate constitutional law, case law, and statutory law.

Constitutions

These are the supreme expressions of law at both the federal and state levels of government. All other law is subordinate to federal constitutional law. Among other things, constitutions prescribe the general structure of governments and protect individual rights. Chapters 5 and 8 give extensive attention to the U.S. Constitution and the Bill of Rights.

Statutes

These are laws that are adopted by legislative bodies, particularly Congress and the state legislatures. City councils enact statutes that usually are called *ordinances*. Legislators and the statutes they enact shape the policy direction of U.S. law. Of course, legislators are not free of constraints. Federal legislation cannot conflict with the U.S. Constitution, and state legislation cannot violate either federal law or the constitutions of that state and the nation.

Regulations

Administrative agencies include such bodies as the Federal Trade Commission and the Securities and Exchange Commission at the federal level, and often a public service commission (to regulate utilities) and a human rights commission (to address discrimination problems) at the state level. Administrative agencies have the specialized expertise to carry out much of the day-to-day business of government. Among other duties, they produce and oversee regulations that add the details needed to implement the broader mandates provided by federal and state statutes. (For more detail, see Chapter 8.)

Common Law (Also Called Case Law or Judge-Made Law)

Our case law has its roots in the early English king's courts, where rules of law gradually developed out of a series of individual dispute resolutions. That body of law, the common law, was imported to America, where it has grown and evolved as our courts address the constantly changing legal requirements of our complex society.

The development of English common law and American judicial decisions into a just, ordered package is attributable in large measure to reliance on the doctrine of *stare decisis* (let the decision stand). That is, judges endeavor to follow the precedents established by previous decisions. Following precedent, however, is not mandatory. As societal beliefs and practices change, judges are called on not only to interpret precedent but also to create new law as cases reflecting these changes are brought. For example, a U.S. Supreme Court decision approving racially separate but equal education was eventually overruled by a Supreme Court decision mandating integrated schools. Nonetheless, the principle of *stare decisis* is generally adhered to because of its beneficial effect. It offers the wisdom of the past and enhances efficiency by eliminating the need for resolving every case as though it were the first of its kind. *Stare decisis* affords stability and predictability to the law.

The Case Law: Locating and Analyzing

To prepare for the *Nichols* case, which follows, a bit of practical guidance may be useful. The study of law is founded largely on the analysis of judicial opinions. Except at the federal level and in a few states, trial court decisions are filed locally for public inspection rather than being published. Appellate (appeals court) opinions, on the other hand, are generally published in volumes called *reports.* State court opinions are found in the reports of that state, as well as in a regional reporter series published by West Publishing Company that divides the United States into regions, such as South Eastern (S.E.) and Pacific (P.).

Within the appropriate reporter, the cases are cited by case name, volume, reporter name, and page number. For example, *Nichols v. Niesen,* 746 N.W.2d 220 (Wis. 2008) means that the opinion will be found in volume 746 of the *North Western Reporter,* 2nd series, on page 220, and that the decision was reached in 2008 by the Wisconsin Supreme Court. Federal court decisions are found in several reporters, including the *Federal Reporter* and the *U.S. Supreme Court Reports.* In practice, of course, those cases can most readily be found via a standard search engine or in online databases such as LexisNexis and Westlaw. (For broad databases covering many law topics, see **www.findlaw.com** and **www.justia.com.** For the National Center for State Courts, see **www.ncsconline.org**).

Briefing the Case

LO 4-4
Differentiate the elements of a case brief.

Most students find that the preparation of *case briefs* (outlines or digests) helps master the law. A brief should evolve into the form that best suits the individual student's needs. The following approach should be a useful starting point:

1. Parties — Identify the plaintiff and the defendant at the trial level. At the appeals level, identify the appellant (the party bringing the appeal; Nichols, in this instance), and the appellee (the other party on appeal; Niesen, in this instance).
2. Facts — Summarize only those facts critical to the outcome of the case.
3. Procedure — How did the case reach this court? Who won in the lower court(s)?
4. Issue — Identify the central question or questions on which the case turns.
5. Holding — How did the court resolve the issue(s)? Who won?
6. Reasoning — Explain the logic that supported the court's decision.

LEGAL BRIEFCASE

Nichols v. Niesen

746 N.W.2d 220 (Wis. 2008)

Justice N. Patrick Crooks

The court of appeals allowed the claim of Shannon, Lee, Brooke, and Brittney Nichols (the Nichols) to proceed against the Niesens for common-law negligence. The Nichols claimed that the Niesens were social hosts who did not provide any alcoholic beverages to underage guests but allegedly were aware that minors were on their property consuming alcoholic beverages. After leaving the Niesens' premises, one of these guests allegedly caused injuries while driving intoxicated. The circuit court had granted the Niesens' . . . motion to dismiss the Nichols' complaint, after concluding that the complaint failed to state a claim in common-law negligence. The primary issue upon review is whether a claim for common-law negligence should be permitted against social hosts under these circumstances.

I

On June 5, 2004, the Nichols were in a motor vehicle on County Trunk Highway J in Columbia County, Wisconsin, when that vehicle was struck by another motor vehicle, driven by Beth Carr (Carr), which had crossed the highway's center line. The Nichols alleged that the accident was caused by Carr's "failure to properly manage and control the vehicle she was operating, due in part to the voluntary ingestion by her of intoxicating beverages." As a result of the accident, Shannon Nichols "suffered very severe personal injuries," and Brittney, Brooke, and Lee Nichols "suffered injuries requiring medical care and treatment."

On the night of June 4, 2004, and into the early morning of June 5, 2004, the Nichols alleged that "a large gathering of underage high school students" congregated and consumed alcohol at the premises controlled by the Niesens. . . . (T)he Nichols alleged that "the Niesens were aware that the minors on their property were consuming alcohol." The Nichols did not allege that the Niesens knew, in advance, that the students would be consuming alcohol. The Nichols contended that the Niesens "had a duty to supervise and monitor the activities on their property" and that they were negligent because they failed to do so.

The Nichols contended that the consumption of alcohol by Carr was a substantial factor in causing the accident. Defendant Michael Shumate (Shumate), "or one or more adult residents of his household (,)" not the Niesens, was alleged to have provided the alcohol that was consumed by Carr on the Niesens' property. There was no allegation that Shumate was at the Niesens' property.

II (omitted—ed.)

III

On review, the Nichols claim that the Niesens' conduct was negligent, and that it was reasonably foreseeable that someone drinking on the Niesens' property would cause an accident. . . .

(T)he Niesens argue that knowledge of someone drinking on one's premises does not create a foreseeable risk of harm to others, and that public policy issues preclude liability in cases such as this one. The Niesens argue that the court of appeals created a new basis of liability for social hosts in Wisconsin. They argue that social hosts have never been held liable in Wisconsin solely because they were aware that an underage person had been consuming alcohol. To allow the court of appeals' decision to stand would mean that liability would apply to any social hosts who knew of underage drinking, regardless of where the alcohol was possessed or consumed, which would lead to liability with no sensible stopping point. The Niesens argue that they had limited involvement with the party outside of their alleged knowledge of underage drinking at the party, and, as a result, they should not be held liable. To hold social hosts liable in such circumstances would place an unreasonable burden on social hosts. The Niesens argue that a reasonable person would not foresee that knowledge of some unidentified underage person drinking would create an unreasonable risk to others. Rather, a reasonable person would conclude that any such risk was created by the provider of the alcohol and the underage drinker. The Niesens contend that, because they played no role in procuring or furnishing the alcohol, a negligence analysis should not be applied to their actions in this matter. Finally, the Niesens argue that the legislature, not the judiciary, is the branch of Wisconsin's government that should impose any new liability on social hosts who do not provide alcoholic beverages to underage guests.

Whether the Nichols' complaint states a claim for common-law negligence depends on whether they sufficiently pled facts, which if proven true, would establish all four required elements of an actionable negligence claim. First, the plaintiff must establish "the existence of a duty of care on the part of the defendant. . . ." Second, the plaintiff must establish that the defendant breached that duty of care. Third, the plaintiff must establish "a causal connection between the defendant's breach of the duty of care and the plaintiff's injury. . . ." Fourth, the plaintiff must establish that he or she suffered an actual loss or damage that resulted from the breach.

The court of appeals framed the issue for the first element of the test for common-law negligence as "whether the Niesens owed a duty to refrain from knowingly permitting minors to consume alcohol on their property, thus enabling them, including Carr, to drive away from their property while intoxicated." As a result, the court held that the first factor had been met because "it was reasonably foreseeable that permitting underage high school students to illegally drink alcohol on the Niesens' property would result in harm to some person or something," and because the Nichols had adequately "alleged the Niesens had a duty to refrain from knowingly permitting underage high school students from engaging in illegal alcohol consumption on their property."

(T)he court of appeals also determined that the Nichols had appropriately alleged the second factor of an actionable common-law negligence claim, which is that the Niesens had breached a duty of care that they owed to the Nichols. The court stated, "Because the Nichols' complaint alleges the Niesens knowingly permitted and failed to supervise underage alcohol consumption on their property, it alleges 'a breach of their duty to exercise ordinary care.'" . . . .

The court also held that the Nichols had established the third factor of a common-law negligence claim by showing "a causal connection between the defendant's breach of the duty of care and the plaintiff's injury. . . ." That court stated, "The Nichols have sufficiently alleged that the Niesens' permitting underage alcohol consumption on their property was a substantial factor in causing the automobile accident that resulted in their injuries."

The court of appeals further held that the Nichols had appropriately alleged the fourth factor of a common-law negligence claim, that they had suffered an actual loss or damage that resulted from the Niesens' breach. . . .

For purposes of our public policy analysis, we will assume, without deciding, that the court of appeals was correct in holding that the Nichols had stated a common-law negligence claim. (E)ven if a plaintiff adequately establishes all four elements of a common-law negligence claim, Wisconsin courts have "reserved the right to deny the existence of a negligence claim based on public policy reasons. . . ." As a result, "even if all the elements for a claim of negligence are proved, or liability for negligent conduct is assumed by the court, the court nonetheless may preclude liability based on public policy factors." This is so because "negligence and liability are distinct concepts."

In turning to our analysis of the public policy factors that bear on the Nichols' common-law negligence claim against the Niesens, it is instructive to note what is not alleged by the Nichols. The Nichols do not allege that the Niesens provided alcohol to Carr, that the Niesens were aware that Carr (specifically) was consuming alcoholic beverages, that the Niesens knew or should have known that Carr was intoxicated, or that the Niesens knew or should have known that Carr was not able to drive her motor vehicle safely at the time of the accident. We note that there also is no allegation by the Nichols that the Niesens aided, agreed to assist, or attempted to aid Carr or any other person in the procurement or consumption of alcohol on premises under their control. There also are no allegations that the Niesens knew in advance that any underage individuals would be drinking.

If one or more of the public policy "factors so dictates, the court may refuse to impose liability in a case."

The first public policy factor upon which recovery against a negligent tortfeasor may be denied is when "the injury is too remote from the negligence. . . ."

The second public policy factor upon which recovery against a negligent tortfeasor may be denied is when "the injury is too wholly out of proportion to the tortfeasor's culpability. . . ."

The third public policy factor upon which recovery against a negligent tortfeasor may be denied is when "in retrospect it appears too highly extraordinary that the negligence should have brought about the harm. . . ."

The fourth public policy factor upon which recovery against a negligent tortfeasor may be denied is when "allowing recovery would place too unreasonable a burden upon the tortfeasor. . . ."

The fifth public policy factor upon which recovery against a negligent tortfeasor may be denied is when "allowing recovery would be too likely to open the way to fraudulent claims. . . ."

The sixth, and here perhaps the most significant, public policy factor upon which recovery against a negligent tortfeasor may be denied is when "allowing recovery would have no sensible or just stopping point. . . ."

Here, the Niesens and their insurer argue that there would be no sensible or just stopping point if the court of appeals' decision stands. They claim that the decision of the court of appeals would put tort law on the path of strict liability for anyone who owns property in Wisconsin, and who knows even scant details of an underage person consuming alcohol on the property under his or her control. They argue that the next step, beyond such a proposed expansion in common-law negligence liability, may be to include in the framework of liability not just social hosts but anyone who knows that an underage person was drinking on property that is not even under their control, or to include anyone, not just property owners, who knows that any underage individual has had too much to drink.

We note that there is no allegation by the Nichols here that the Niesens knew Carr was intoxicated, impaired, or unable to safely drive a vehicle. The Niesens argue that they could not have foreseen that people coming onto their property, who already had broken the law before they arrived, would break the law again after leaving. The Niesens could not reasonably have foreseen that an underage guest who they were not specifically aware was intoxicated, and who arrived at the premises under their control with alcohol purchased elsewhere, would cause foreseeable harm to others.

We agree with the Niesens . . . that allowing recovery here would have no sensible or just stopping point.

If the Nichols' claim were allowed to proceed, the expansion of liability might also include liability for parents who allegedly should have known that drinking would occur on their property while they were absent, based on the proclivities of teenagers in a given area to consume alcohol. Imposing such liability would be only a short step away from imposing strict liability upon property owners for any underage drinking that occurs on property under their control. As Judge David G. Deininger stated in his dissent in the court of appeals, "if liability is permitted to extend to parents and property owners who fail to 'supervise and monitor the activities on their property,'" as the Nichols contend of the Niesens, "then parents or other owners of property occupied by sixteen- to twenty-year-olds" would "be well-advised to never leave home, or if they must, to ensure that all underage persons go elsewhere as well. . . ." As a result, even assuming that the Nichols had pled a viable claim for common-law negligence against the Niesens using the four-factor test, we are satisfied that the Nichols' claim should be barred on public policy considerations, since allowing recovery here would have no sensible or just stopping point.

Liability has never been applied to conduct like that of the Niesens, and liability has required active, direct and affirmative acts, such as the provision of alcohol. Neither the legislature nor this court has expanded liability to social hosts who have not provided alcohol to minors. The legislature is the appropriate governmental branch to expand liability if it desires to do so. As a result for the reasons stated herein, we reverse the court of appeals, and hold that such an expansion of liability should come from the legislature, if it is to occur at all.

Questions

1. Explain the Nichols' legal claim.
2. *a.* Who won this case and why?
   b. Do you agree with the court's decision and its reasoning? Explain.
3. LaMarre rode with his wife and their neighbors the Plummers in the Plummers' modified golf cart to have dinner at the nearby Fort Mitchell Country Club. As per Mr. Plummer's request, country club staff retrieved and chilled two bottles of champagne from Plummer's locker. During dinner, the couples consumed one of the champagne bottles, as well as a bottle of red wine that Plummer retrieved from his locker. The two couples opened the second bottle of champagne in the golf cart after dinner. After making a stop on the way home at another neighbor's house, Mr. Plummer accelerated the golf cart while Mr. LaMarre was trying to take his seat. LaMarre fell and sustained serious injuries. The LaMarres filed a lawsuit against the Plummers and the Fort Mitchell Country Club. Should the country club be liable for LaMarre's injuries? Explain. See *Fort Mitchell Country Club v. LaMarre,* 394 S.W.3d 897 (Ky. 2012).
4. Nichols, age 26, and Dobler, a minor, were guests at Maldonado's party. Dobler was served alcohol and, while intoxicated, repeatedly hit Nichols with a hammer. Nichols sued Maldanado for negligence in serving alcohol to a minor. The jury found for Nichols. Maldanado appealed. How would you rule on that appeal? Explain. See *Nichols v. Dobler,* 655 N.W.2d 787 (Mich. Ct. App. 2002).
5. Richard Paul Dube suffered serious injuries when the vehicle he was driving was struck head-on by a vehicle being driven in the wrong direction on a Massachusetts highway by Ravindra Bhoge. Bhoge had earlier in the evening consumed a number of drinks with three friends at a bar. Bhoge and his friends met regularly on Fridays after work to drink at local bars. Each person took turns paying the bill, or on some occasions, payment would be equally divided. On the night of the accident, Bhoge drank enough that the trial judge inferred that Bhoge's intoxication would have been apparent. Bhoge's three friends said they saw nothing to indicate that Bhoge was impaired, although Bhoge had left his coat behind in the bar on a particularly cold evening, and he was outside the bar for 45 minutes prior to his departure. Bhoge indicated to his friends that he was "okay" as they all prepared to leave in their vehicles. Dube sued Bhoge's three friends claiming they were social hosts and were negligent in permitting Bhoge to continue drinking. How would you rule on Dube's claim? Explain. See *Dube v. Lanphear & Others,* 868 N.E.2d 619 (2007).

Classifications of Law

We can divide the law into some categories that will help us better understand the many legal domains and processes.

LO 4-5 Distinguish between substantive and procedural law.

Substantive and Procedural Law

Substantive laws create, define, and regulate legal rights and obligations. Thus, for example, the federal Civil Rights Act of 1964 forbids discrimination in employment and other matters (see Chapter 13).

Procedural law embraces the systems and methods available to enforce the rights and obligations specified in the substantive law. So procedural law includes the judicial system and the rules by which it operates. Questions of where to hear a case, what evidence to admit, and which decisions can be appealed fall within the procedural domain. [For a "community built, freely available legal dictionary and encyclopedia," see **www.law.cornell.edu/wex**].

Law and Equity

Following the Norman conquest of England in 1066, a system of king's courts was established in which the king's representatives settled disputes. Those representatives were empowered to provide remedies of land, money, or personal property. The king's courts became known as *courts of law* and the remedies were labeled *remedies of law.* Some litigants, however, sought compensation other than the three provided. They took their pleas to the king.

Typically the chancellor, an aide to the king, would hear these petitions and, guided by the standard of fairness, could grant a remedy (such as an ***injunction*** or ***specific performance***–see the glossary of legal terms in the back of the book) specifically appropriate to the case. The chancellors' decisions accumulated over time such that a new body of remedies–and with it a new court system, known as *courts of equity*–evolved. Both court systems were adopted in the United States following the American Revolution, but today actions for law and equity are typically heard in the same court.

Public Law and Private Law

Public law deals with the relationship between a government and its citizens. Constitutional, criminal, and administrative law (such as the law relating to such government agencies as the Federal Trade Commission and the Environmental Protection Agency) fall in the public law category. ***Private law*** regulates the legal relationship among legal persons, which include individuals and entities (like corporations). Contracts, agency, and commercial paper are traditional business law topics in this category.

Civil Law and Criminal Law

LO 4-6
Compare and contrast civil and criminal law.

The legislature or other lawmaking body normally specifies whether new legislation is *civil* or *criminal* or both. Broadly, all legislation not specifically labeled criminal law falls in the civil law category. ***Civil law*** addresses the legal rights and duties arising among individuals, organizations such as corporations, and governments. Thus, for example, a person might raise a civil law claim of breach of contract or personal injury against a person or company. ***Criminal law***, on the other hand, involves wrongs against the general welfare as formulated in specific criminal statutes. Murder and theft are, of course, criminal wrongs forbidden under in specific legislation. Criminal victims may be able to bring civil law claims to compensate for their loss or injury. (For a brief discussion of business and white-collar crime and federal sentencing guidelines, see Chapter 2.)

Crimes *Crimes* are of three kinds. *Felonies* are more serious crimes, such as murder, rape, and robbery. They are typically punishable by death or by imprisonment in a federal or state penitentiary for more than one year. ***Misdemeanors*** are less serious crimes, such as petty theft, disorderly conduct, and traffic offenses. They are typically punishable by fine or by imprisonment for no more than one year. *Treason* is the special situation in which one levies war against the United States or gives aid and comfort to its enemies.

Elements of a Crime In a broad sense, crimes consist of two elements: (1) a wrongful act or omission (***actus reus***) and (2) evil intent (***mens rea***). Thus, someone who pockets a USB charger and leaves the store without paying may be charged with petty theft. The accused may defend, however, by arguing that they merely absentmindedly and unintentionally slipped it in a pocket after picking it off the shelf to read the package. Intent is a state of mind, so the jury or judge must reach a determination from the objective facts as to what the accused's state of mind must have been. Civil claims, for example, for the USB charger's return or for payment, can proceed in the absence of a criminal conviction.

Criminal Procedure In general, criminal procedure following an arrest and an initial appearance before a magistrate (and, in some cases, a preliminary hearing) is structured as follows: For misdemeanor cases, prosecutors typically file what is called an ***information***, a formal expression of the charges. The information may be reviewed by a magistrate before issuance. For felony cases, the process begins with the prosecuting officials either filing an information or seeking an ***indictment*** by bringing their charges before a grand jury of citizens to determine whether the charges have sufficient merit to justify a trial.

After an indictment or information, the individual is brought before the court for ***arraignment***, where the charges are read and a plea is entered. If the individual pleads not guilty, they will go to trial, where guilt must be established ***beyond a reasonable doubt***. In a criminal trial, the burden of proof is on the state. The defendant is, of course, presumed innocent and is entitled to a jury trial, but they may choose to have the case decided by the judge alone. If found guilty, the defendant can, among other possibilities, seek a new trial or appeal errors in the prosecution. If found innocent, the defendant may, if necessary, invoke the doctrine of ***double jeopardy***, under which a person cannot be prosecuted twice in the same tribunal for the same criminal offense. [For an extensive criminal justice database, see **www.ncjrs.gov**].

When Miranda Rights are Wronged

The 1966 *Miranda v. Arizona* U.S. Supreme Court decision provided that, under the Fifth Amendment, a suspect in police custody must be told

> You have the right to remain silent. Anything you say can and will be used against you in a court of law. You have the right to an attorney. If you cannot afford an attorney, one will be appointed for you.

If this warning is not properly provided, any statements made by the suspect and any evidence derived from those statements cannot subsequently be used in court. The *Miranda* warning has been referred to as "*Miranda* rights," but under the recent U.S. Supreme Court ruling in *Vega v. Tekoh,* being given the *Miranda* warning is not a constitutional right itself.

Vega, a Los Angeles County Sheriff, interrogated Tekoh at Tekoh's workplace about sexual assault allegations without giving Tekoh a *Miranda* warning. Vega obtained Tekoh's handwritten statement offering an apology for inappropriately touching the person who had made the complaint. At Tekoh's criminal trial for the alleged sexual assault, the prosecution introduced Tekoh's statement yielded from Vega's interrogation. The jury found Tekoh not guilty. However, Tekoh sued Vega and others for civil damages, alleging that Vega's interrogation violated his Fifth Amendment right against compelled self-incrimination. The Ninth Circuit Court of Appeals agreed, holding that the government's use of the statement given in absence of the *Miranda* warning provided a basis for Tekoh's lawsuit under a federal statute allowing government actors to be sued for violating constitutional rights.

Rejecting the Ninth Circuit's decision, the U.S. Supreme Court ruled that allowing a lawsuit for failure to give the *Miranda* warning would wrongfully extend *Miranda* from a Fifth Amendment procedural safeguard into a constitutional right. The dissenting justices reminded the majority that the iconic *Miranda* ruling had extended a right to criminal defendants to have confessions made without the *Miranda* warning excluded from criminal proceedings, which was set in "constitutional stone," and that the Court in *Miranda* had addressed violent police practices in compelling self-incrimination that existed at the time.

Questions

1. What might be the result of preventing lawsuits against police officers for failing to give the *Miranda* warning before a custodial interrogation? Do you think these lawsuits should be allowed? Explain.
2. Michigan police gave the *Miranda* warning to a murder suspect, Thompkins. After remaining silent through nearly three hours of questioning, An officer asked Thompkins: "Do you pray to God to forgive you for shooting that boy down?" Thompkins replied "yes," but said no more. Thompkins was later convicted of murder at trial where his one-word reply was admitted. Should Thompkins' reply have been admitted? Explain. See *Berghuis v. Thompkins,* 130 S. Ct. 2250 (2010).
3. In a North Carolina middle school conference room, a 13-year-old confessed to a series of home break-ins during a half hour of questioning by police officers and school administrators. The teen had not been allowed to call his grandmother, who was his guardian, and had not been given a *Miranda* warning. The state later claimed that a *Miranda* warning was not required because the teen was not in custody. Do you agree? Explain. See *J.D.B. v. North Carolina,* 564 U.S. 261 (2011).

Sources: *Vega v. Tekoh,* 142 S. Ct. 2095 (2022); *Berghuis v. Thompkins,* 130 S. Ct. 2250 (2010); *J.D.B. v. North Carolina,* 564 U.S. 261 (2011); *Miranda v. Arizona,* 86 S. Ct. 1602 (1966); Lense Herbert, "Tantamount to Nothing: *Miranda* Can(not) Be Wronged," *SCOTUSBlog,* June 27, 2022 [**https://www.scotusblog.com/**]; Jesse J. Holland, "Miranda Warning Rights Trimmed Bit by Bit by High Court," *The Christian Science Monitor,* August 2, 2010 [**www.csmonitor.com**]; and David Savage, "Supreme Court Backs Off Strict Enforcement of Miranda Rights," *Los Angeles Times,* June 2, 2010 [**https://latimes.com**].

PRACTICING ETHICS Big Law Firm vs. Sick Babies

Research studies have shown that powdered baby formula can breed a certain bacteria that causes infant meningitis, and that most infants suffering meningitis had recently consumed powdered baby formula.

New York Times investigative reporter David Enrich concluded that years before Abbott Laboratories shut down its Sturgis, Michigan, plant and voluntarily recalled its powdered baby formula in 2022, a powerful, multinational law firm's aggressive tactics had shielded Abbott from public scandal. For example, in a lawsuit brought against Abbott by Kimberly, a North Carolina house cleaner whose son, Slade, had serious brain damage after being fed allegedly tainted Abbott powdered baby formula, Jones Day got the court to remove the first two lawyers because one of them, in an unrelated matter, had been in touch with an expert witness used by Abbott in another case. Kimberly eventually was able to retain another lawyer.

Nearly ten years after Slade had fallen ill, trial was set. Abbott offered to settle confidentially for $900,000. Facing millions in ongoing medical expenses and not wanting the settlement to be kept secret, Kimberly rejected the settlement offer. Before the trial, Jones Day sought unsuccessfully to have a restraining order brought against Kimberly's family member—eight years after Slade fell ill—as evidence of why Slade may have suffered a seizure. At trial, Jones Day emphasized the unknown source of the bacteria found in Kimberly's sink. Abbott won. Upon Jones Day's request on behalf of Abbott, the court sealed trial testimony and evidence regarding Abbott's safety protocols, hiding it from public view.

Questions

1. David Enrich observed that when big law firms face each other in litigation, aggressive lawyering may be part of a "fair fight," but when the same tactics are "used against poor families and their overwhelmed lawyers, the results tend to be lopsided." What, if anything, can be done to ensure a "fair fight" between big law firms and lawyers with fewer resources? Explain.
2. What are the pros and cons of confidential settlement agreements? Explain.

Sources: David Enrich, "How Abbott Kept Sick Babies from Becoming a Scandal," *The New York Times,* September 6, 2022 [**https://www.nytimes.com**]; and Debra Cassen Weiss, "How Jones Day Protected Abbott Labs in Baby Formula Lawsuits," *ABA Journal,* September 8, 2022[**https: abajournal.com**].

Questions—Part One

1. On a February morning after receiving medical care at a Pueblo, Colorado, hospital, Mathew Jones, wearing light clothes, waited for his ride in the hospital waiting room due to cold weather. Security guards spoke with him, and then physically confronted him after he allegedly refusing to wait outside, holding him on the floor. Jones died several days later. Criminal charges against the security guards were later dropped. A lawyer for Jones' widow said: "We are going to use the civil justice system to get the justice back that Mathew's family was denied through the criminal justice system." Explain the lawyer's statement. (See Shelly Bradbury, "4 Hospital Security Guards put a Colorado man in a chokehold. He died 8 days later" *The Denver Post,* November 20, 2022 [**https://www.denverpost.com**])
2. Should we remove criminal penalties from all so-called victimless crimes, such as vagrancy and gambling? Should we regulate those behaviors in any way? Explain.
3. A 19-year-old woman who didn't pay the fare for a 30-mile cab ride was given the choice of spending 30 days in jail or taking a 30-mile walk; she chose to take the walk.[5] One Florida judge has sentenced hundreds of shoplifters to carrying a sign in public that reads: "I stole from this store." Constitutional law expert Jonathan Turley says "creative sentencing" is growing, a trend he disapproves of and regards as a strategy for entertaining the public more than deterring crime.[6]
   a. What objections would a defendant's lawyer raise to these public humiliation punishments?
   b. Would you impose a "humiliation sentence" if you were the judge? Explain.

Part Two—The Judicial Process

Most disputes are settled without resort to litigation, but when agreement cannot be reached, we can turn to the courts–a highly technical and sophisticated dispute resolution mechanism.

State Court Systems

LO 4-7
Describe the elements of the basic court system structure.

While state court systems vary substantially, a general pattern can be summarized. As shown in Figure 4.1, at the base of the court pyramid in most states is a trial court of general jurisdiction, commonly labeled a *district court* or a *superior court.* Most trials–both civil and criminal–arising out of state law are heard here, but certain classes of cases are reserved to courts of limited subject-matter jurisdiction or to various state administrative agencies (such as the state public utilities commission and the workers' compensation board). Family, small claims, juvenile, and traffic courts are examples of trial courts with limited jurisdiction. At the top of the judicial pyramid in all states is an ultimate court of appeals, ordinarily labeled the *supreme court.* A number of states also provide for an intermediate court of appeals located in the hierarchy between the trial courts and the highest appeals court.

FIGURE 4.1 **State and Federal Court Systems**

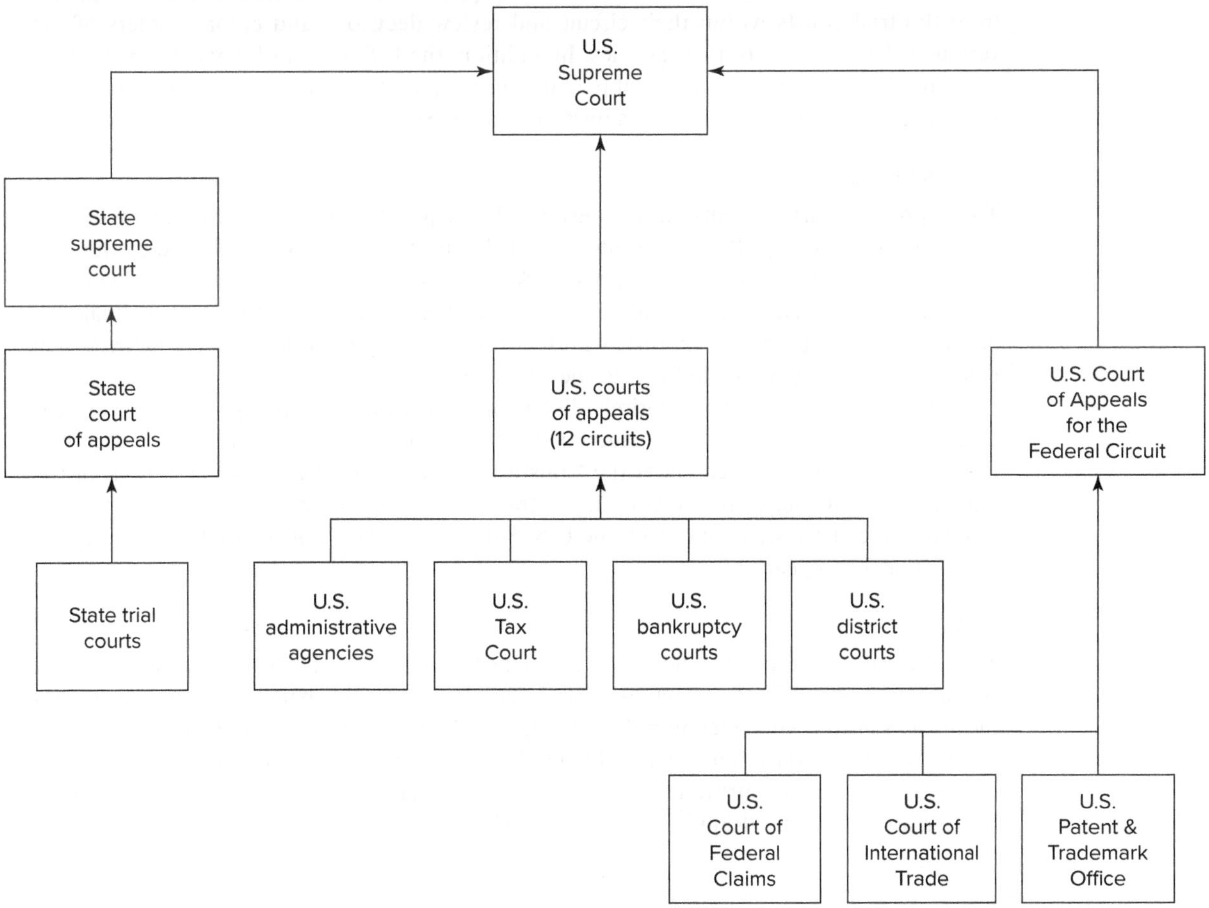

Federal Court System

District Courts

The Constitution provides for a Supreme Court and such inferior courts as Congress shall authorize. Pursuant to that authority, Congress has established at least one district court for each state and territory. The 94 district courts serve as the foundation of the federal judicial system. These are trial courts where witnesses are heard and questions of law and fact are resolved. Most federal cases begin in the district courts or in a federal administrative agency (such as the Federal Communications Commission). Congress also has provided for several trial courts of limited jurisdiction, including the U.S. Tax Court and the U.S. Court of International Trade.

[For access to all federal court websites, see the Federal Judicial Center at **www.fjc.gov**].

Courts of Appeals

Congress has divided the United States geographically into 11 judicial circuits and the District of Columbia and has established a court of appeals for each. Those courts hear appeals from the trial courts within their circuit and review decisions and enforce orders of the various federal administrative agencies. In addition, the U.S. Court of Appeals for the Federal Circuit hears, among others, all patent appeals and all appeals from the U.S. Court of Federal Claims (monetary claims against the United States).

Supreme Court

The Supreme Court has seats for nine justices. Those justices (along with the federal district and appeals court judges) are appointed for life by the president and confirmed by the Senate. Almost all of the Supreme Court's work consists of reviewing lower court decisions, primarily from the courts of appeal with a small number from state high courts. Virtually all parties seeking Supreme Court review must petition the Court for a *writ of certiorari,* which commands the lower court to forward the trial records to the Court.

Granting those petitions is entirely discretionary with the Court. Typically, it will hear cases that will resolve conflicting courts of appeal decisions, as well as those that raise questions of special significance under the Constitution or to the national welfare. Four of the nine justices must agree to the granting of the petition. The time it takes for a case to get through the court system and reach the U.S. Supreme Court is considerable; the average is approximately six years.[7]

Critics

The political nature of U.S. Supreme Court nominations has been made clear in recent years.[8] Questions of "judicial activism," the liberal/conservative balance on the Court, and the justices' own political leanings have made the Court a target for criticism.

The Supreme Court, led by Chief Justice John Roberts ("the Roberts Court"), has been criticized as being "a court of blue chambers and red chambers," referring to the color code for "Democrat" versus "Republican" or "liberal" versus "conservative."[9] Nevertheless, Chief

The new justice is not a Republican and not a Democrat [but] a member of the Supreme Court.

Justice Roberts has been seen as trying to counter the public's view of the Court as partisan. After the U.S. Senate changed its filibuster rules to confirm Justice Neil Gorsuch, Roberts said: "The new justice is not a Republican and not a Democrat" but "a member of the Supreme Court. But it's hard for people to understand"[10] when the confirmation process becomes politicized.

Ideological Rulings?

We want to believe the Supreme Court reaches its decisions in a rational, objective fashion relying on the commands of the Constitution and precedent to maintain a consistent, fair, orderly judicial system free of political influence. A study by the Brookings Institution provided "striking evidence of a relationship between the political party of the appointing president and judicial voting patterns."[11] Critics say that conservative ideological inclinations have led the Roberts Court to abandon traditional judicial restraint at times and decide issues that were broader than required by the case before it.[12]

The late Justice Scalia drew criticism for reading aloud his dissenting opinion that criticized President Obama's immigration policy; both conservative and liberal observers voiced concerns that Scalia's political pronouncements undermined the integrity of his opinion.[13]

Public trust in the Supreme Court to make decisions after dispassionate, lawyerly analysis has declined, as shown in a recent Gallup poll finding that less than half of Americans polled had some level of trust in the Supreme Court. [14] Declining respect for Supreme Court rulings could undermine the rule of law in America and perhaps threaten democracy itself.[15] [For an overview of the Supreme Court, see **www.supremecourt.gov**].

Jurisdiction

A plaintiff may not simply proceed to trial at the court of their preference. The plaintiff must go to a court with ***jurisdiction*** –that is, a court with the necessary power and authority to hear the dispute. The court must have jurisdiction over both the subject matter and the persons (or, in some instances, the property) involved in the case.

Subject-Matter Jurisdiction

LO 4-8
Explain the purposes of subject matter and personal jurisdiction as requirements for a court's power to hear a dispute.

Subject-matter jurisdiction imposes bounds on the classes of cases a court may hear. The legislation or constitution creating the court will normally specify that court's jurisdictional authority. State courts of ***general jurisdiction***, for example, may hear most types of cases, but a criminal court or probate court is limited in the subject matter it may hear.

The outer bounds of federal jurisdiction are specified in the Constitution, and Congress has further particularized those boundaries by statute. Essentially, the federal district courts may hear two types of cases: (1) those involving a federal question and (2) those involving diversity of citizenship with more than $75,000 in controversy.

Federal question jurisdiction exists in any suit where the plaintiff's claim is based on the U.S. Constitution, a U.S. treaty, or a federal statute. Thus, plaintiffs can bring cases to the federal courts involving, for example, federal antitrust statutes, federal criminal laws, Constitutional issues such as freedom of the press, and federal tax questions. Federal question jurisdiction does not require any particular amount in controversy. Furthermore, federal and state courts have *concurrent jurisdiction* over some federal questions. Thus, some federal question cases are decided in state courts applying federal law. Federal courts also can hear cases involving state laws. Congress has accorded the federal courts exclusive jurisdiction over certain subjects, including federal criminal laws, bankruptcy, and copyrights.

Under *diversity jurisdiction,* federal district courts may hear cases involving more than $75,000 where the plaintiff(s) and the defendant(s) are citizens of different states. (Corporations are treated as citizens both of their state of incorporation and the state in which their principal place of business is located.) Diversity cases also may be heard in state courts, but plaintiffs frequently prefer to bring their actions in federal courts. The quality of the federal judiciary is generally believed to be superior to that of the states, and the federal courts are considered less likely to be influenced by local bias.

Personal Jurisdiction

Judicial authority over the parties is known as *in personam jurisdiction*. In general, state court jurisdiction over a defendant can be established in three ways. First, if the defendant is a resident of the state, a summons may be served at that residence. Second, if the defendant is not a resident, a summons may be personally served on a defendant physically present in the state. Third, most states have legislated "long-arm" statutes that allow state courts to secure jurisdiction over an out-of-state defendant who has committed a tort in the state or is conducting business in the state. Hence, in an auto accident in Ohio involving both an Ohio resident and a Kentucky resident, the Ohio resident may sue in Ohio and use the long-arm statute to achieve service of process over the defendant living in Kentucky.

A state court also may acquire jurisdiction via an *in rem action.* In that instance, the defendant may be a nonresident, but the property owned by the defendant, which is the subject of the suit, is located within the state.

The following case involves a dispute about the commercial use of the name of celebrated actor and former California governor Arnold Schwarzenegger.

LEGAL BRIEFCASE

Arnold Schwarzenegger v. Fred Martin Motor Company

374 F.3d 797 (9th Cir. 2004)

Circuit Judge Fletcher

Arnold Schwarzenegger, an internationally known movie star and . . . [former] governor of California, appeals the district court's dismissal of his suit against Fred Martin Motor Company ("Fred Martin"), an Ohio car dealership, for lack of personal jurisdiction. Fred Martin had run a series of five full-page color advertisements in the *Akron Beacon Journal*, a locally circulated Ohio newspaper. Each advertisement included a small photograph of Schwarzenegger, portrayed as the "Terminator," without his permission.

Schwarzenegger brought suit in California, alleging that these unauthorized uses of his image infringed his right of publicity. We affirm the district court's dismissal for lack of personal jurisdiction.

I. BACKGROUND

Schwarzenegger is a resident of California. When Schwarzenegger brought this suit, he was a private citizen and movie star, best known for his roles as a muscle-bound hero of action films and distinctive Austrian accent. As explained in his complaint, Schwarzenegger was generally cast as the lead character in so-called star-driven films. One of Schwarzenegger's most popular and readily recognizable film roles is that of the title character in "The Terminator" (1984). . . .

Fred Martin is an automobile dealership incorporated under the laws of Ohio and located in Barberton, Ohio, a few miles southwest of Akron. There is no evidence in the record that Fred Martin has any operations or employees in California, has ever advertised in California, or has ever sold a car to anyone in California. Fred Martin maintains an Internet website that is available for viewing in California and, for that matter, from any Internet cafe in Istanbul, Bangkok, or anywhere else in the world.

In early 2002, Fred Martin engaged defendant Zimmerman & Partners Advertising, Inc. ("Zimmerman") to design and place a full-page color advertisement in the *Akron Beacon Journal,* a local Akron-based newspaper. The advertisement ran in the *Akron Beacon Journal* five times in April 2002. Most of the advertisement consists of small photographs and descriptions of various cars available for purchase or lease from Fred Martin. Just below a large-font promise that Fred Martin "WON'T BE BEAT," the advertisement includes a small, but clearly recognizable photograph of Schwarzenegger as the Terminator. A "bubble quotation," like those found in comic strips, is drawn next to Schwarzenegger's mouth, reading, "Arnold says: 'Terminate EARLY at Fred Martin!'" This part of the advertisement refers to a special offer from Fred Martin to customers, inviting them to close out their current leases before the expected termination date, and to buy or lease a new car from Fred Martin.

Neither Fred Martin nor Zimmerman ever sought or received Schwarzenegger's permission to use his photograph in the advertisement. Schwarzenegger states in his complaint that, had such a request been made, it would have been refused. The advertisement, as far as the record reveals, was never circulated outside of Ohio.

Schwarzenegger brought suit against Fred Martin and Zimmerman in Los Angeles County Superior Court alleging six state law causes of action arising out of the unauthorized use of his image in the advertisement. He claims that the defendants caused him financial harm in that the use of his photograph to endorse Fred Martin "diminishes his hard-earned reputation as a major motion picture star, and risks the potential for overexposure of his image to the public, thereby potentially diminishing the compensation he would otherwise garner from his career as a major motion picture star." According to Schwarzenegger's complaint, his compensation as the lead actor in star-driven films was based on his ability to draw crowds to the box office, and his ability to do so depended in part on the scarcity of his image. According to his complaint, if Schwarzenegger's image were to become ubiquitous—in advertisements and on television, for example—the movie-going public would be less likely to spend their money to see his films, and his compensation would diminish accordingly. Therefore, Schwarzenegger maintains, it is vital for him to avoid "oversaturation of his image." According to his complaint, he has steadfastly refused to endorse any products in the United States, despite being offered substantial sums to do so.

Defendants removed the action to federal district court in California, and Fred Martin moved to dismiss the complaint for lack of personal jurisdiction. The district court granted Fred Martin's motion, and Schwarzenegger appealed.

II. PERSONAL JURISDICTION

For a court to exercise personal jurisdiction over a nonresident defendant, that defendant must have at least "minimum contacts" with the relevant forum such that the exercise of jurisdiction "does not offend traditional notions of fair play and substantial justice." *International Shoe Co. v. Washington,* 326 U.S. 310, 316 (1945).

A. General Jurisdiction

Schwarzenegger argues, quite implausibly, that California has general personal jurisdiction over Fred Martin. For general jurisdiction to exist over a nonresident defendant such as Fred Martin, the defendant must engage in "continuous and systematic general business contacts," *Helicopteros Nacionales de Colombia, S.A. v. Hall,* 466 U.S. 408 (1984) that "approximate physical presence" in the forum state. *Bancroft & Masters,* 223 F.3d at 1086. This is an exacting standard, as it should be, because a finding of general jurisdiction permits a defendant to be haled into court in the forum state to answer for any of its activities anywhere in the world.

Schwarzenegger contends that Fred Martin's contacts with California are so extensive that it is subject to general jurisdiction. He points to the following contacts: Fred Martin regularly purchases Asian-made automobiles that are imported by California entities. However, in purchasing these automobiles, Fred Martin dealt directly with representatives in Illinois and New Jersey, but never dealt directly with the California-based importers. Some of Fred Martin's sales contracts with its automobile suppliers include a choice-of-law provision specifying California law. In addition, Fred Martin regularly retains the services of a California-based direct-mail marketing company; has hired a sales training company, incorporated in California, for consulting services; and maintains an

Internet website accessible by anyone capable of using the Internet, including people living in California.

These contacts fall well short of the "continuous and systematic" contacts that the Supreme Court and this court have held to constitute sufficient "presence" to warrant general jurisdiction. Schwarzenegger has therefore failed to establish a prima facie case of general jurisdiction.

B. Specific Jurisdiction

Alternatively, Schwarzenegger argues that Fred Martin has sufficient "minimum contacts" with California arising from, or related to, its actions in creating and distributing the advertisement such that the forum may assert specific personal jurisdiction. We have established a three-prong test for analyzing a claim of specific personal jurisdiction:

> (1) The nonresident defendant must purposefully direct his activities or consummate some transaction with the forum or resident thereof; or perform some act by which he purposefully avails himself of the privilege of conducting activities in the forum, thereby invoking the benefits and protections of its laws;
>
> (2) the claim must be one which arises out of or relates to the defendant's forum-related activities; and
>
> (3) the exercise of jurisdiction must comport with fair play and substantial justice, i.e., it must be reasonable.

The plaintiff bears the burden of satisfying the first two prongs of the test. If the plaintiff fails to satisfy either of these prongs, personal jurisdiction is not established in the forum state. If the plaintiff succeeds in satisfying both of the first two prongs, the burden then shifts to the defendant to "present a compelling case" that the exercise of jurisdiction would not be reasonable. For the reasons that follow, we hold that Schwarzenegger has failed to satisfy the first prong.

1. Purposeful Availment or Direction Generally

Under the first prong of our three-part specific jurisdiction test, Schwarzenegger must establish that Fred Martin either purposefully availed itself of the privilege of conducting activities in California, or purposefully directed its activities toward California.

A showing that a defendant purposefully availed himself of the privilege of doing business in a forum state typically consists of evidence of the defendant's actions in the forum, such as executing or performing a contract there. By taking such actions, a defendant "purposefully avails itself of the privilege of conducting activities within the forum State, thus invoking the benefits and protections of its laws." *Hanson v. Denckla,* 357 U.S. 235, 253 (1958). In return for these "benefits and protections," a defendant must—as a quid pro quo—"submit to the burdens of litigation in that forum." *Burger King,* 471 U.S. at 476.

A showing that a defendant purposefully directed his conduct toward a forum state, by contrast, usually consists of evidence of the defendant's actions outside the forum state that are directed at the forum, such as the distribution in the forum state of goods originating elsewhere.

2. Purposeful Direction

Schwarzenegger does not point to any conduct by Fred Martin in California related to the advertisement that would be readily susceptible to a purposeful availment analysis. Rather, the conduct of which Schwarzenegger complains—the unauthorized inclusion of the photograph in the advertisement and its distribution in the *Akron Beacon Journal*—took place in Ohio, not California. Fred Martin received no benefit, privilege, or protection from California in connection with the advertisement, and the traditional quid pro quo justification for finding purposeful availment thus does not apply. Therefore, to the extent that Fred Martin's conduct might justify the exercise of personal jurisdiction in California, that conduct must have been purposefully directed at California.

Here, Fred Martin's intentional act—the creation and publication of the advertisement—was expressly aimed at Ohio rather than California. The purpose of the advertisement was to entice Ohioans to buy or lease cars from Fred Martin and, in particular, to "terminate" their current car leases. The advertisement was never circulated in California, and Fred Martin had no reason to believe that any Californians would see it and pay a visit to the dealership. Fred Martin certainly had no reason to believe that a Californian had a current car lease with Fred Martin that could be "terminated" as recommended in the advertisement. It may be true that Fred Martin's intentional act eventually caused harm to Schwarzenegger in California and Fred Martin may have known that Schwarzenegger lived in California. But this does not confer jurisdiction, for Fred Martin's express aim was local. We therefore conclude that the advertisement was not expressly aimed at California.

CONCLUSION

We hold that Schwarzenegger has established neither general nor specific jurisdiction over Fred Martin in California. Schwarzenegger has not shown that Fred Martin has "continuous and systematic general business contacts," *Helicopteros,* 466 U.S. at 416, that "approximate physical presence" in California, *Bancroft & Masters,* 223 F. 3d at 1086, such that it can be sued there for any act it has committed anywhere in the world. Further, while Schwarzenegger has made out a prima facie case that Fred Martin committed intentional acts that may have caused harm to Schwarzenegger in California, he has not made out a prima facie case that Fred Martin expressly aimed its acts at California.

Affirmed.

AFTERWORD

Schwarzenegger's claim was settled out of court in 2004 when the Fred Martin Motor Company issued a written apology and agreed to pay a "substantial" sum to Arnold's All-Stars, an after-school program founded by Schwarzenegger.

Questions

1. Why was Schwarzenegger unable to sue Fred Martin in California?
2. Nicastro injured his hand while using a metal-shearing machine in New Jersey manufactured by J. McIntyre Machinery, a company incorporated and operating in England. Nicastro filed a products liability lawsuit against J. McIntyre Machinery in a New Jersey state court, basing personal jurisdiction in New Jersey on three primary facts: A U.S. distributor agreed to sell the company's machines in the United States; J. McIntyre officials attended trade shows in several other states; and four of the company's machines were located in New Jersey. J. McIntyre Machinery had not advertised in or sent goods to New Jersey.
   a. Build an argument to support the claim of jurisdiction in the New Jersey court.
   b. Decide. See *J. McIntyre Machines Ltd. v. Nicastro,* 131 S. Ct. 2780 (2011).
3. Andra, a Missouri resident, used the eBay auction site to purchase a truck from Left Gate, a company based in Texas and a vehicle dealership doing a substantial portion of its sales through eBay with no physical presence or employees in Missouri. Andra agreed to purchase the vehicle using eBay's usual process. After completing the purchase, Andra spoke several times to Left Gate representatives in Texas to discuss delivery of the vehicle. Left Gate mailed a contract and buyer's guide to him at his Missouri address. The truck was delivered to Andra in Missouri by a third-party transporter. Andra later sued Left Gate for breach of contract due to vehicle defects in a Missouri trial court. Does that court have jurisdiction over Left Gate? Explain. See *Andra v. Left Gate Property Holding, Inc.,* 453 S.W.3d 216 (Mo. 2015).
4. Burger King conducted a franchise, fast-food operation from its Miami, Florida, headquarters. John Rudzewicz and a partner, both residents of Michigan, secured a Burger King franchise in Michigan. Subsequently, the franchisees allegedly fell behind in payments and Burger King ordered the franchisees to vacate the premises. They declined to do so and continued to operate the franchise. Burger King brought suit in a federal district court in Florida. The defendant franchisees argued that the Florida court did not have personal jurisdiction over them because they were Michigan residents and the claim did not arise in Florida. The court found the defendants to be subject to Florida's "long-arm statute," which extends jurisdiction to "[a]ny person, whether or not a citizen or resident of this state," who "[b]reach[es] a contract in this state by failing to perform acts required by the contract to be performed in this state." The franchise contract provided for governance of the relationship by Florida law. Franchise policy was set in Miami, although daily supervision was managed through various district offices. The case ultimately reached the U.S. Supreme Court.
   a. What constitutional argument would you raise on behalf of the defendant franchisees?
   b. Decide. See *Burger King Corp. v. Rudzewicz,* 471 U.S. 462 (1985).

Venue

Once jurisdictional authority–that is, the power to hear the case–is established, the proper *venue* (geographic location within the court system) must be determined. Ordinarily, a case will be heard by the court geographically closest to the incident or property in question or to where the parties reside. Sometimes one of the parties may seek a *change of venue* based on considerations such as unfavorable pretrial publicity or the pursuit of a more favorable legal climate. The importance of venue is evident in a decision forcing Los Angeles–based Occidental Petroleum to defend itself in an environmental dispute in California rather than in Peru, where the conflict emerged. Members of the Achuar tribe, indigenous to the Amazon rain forest, brought a class action in Los Angeles against Occidental alleging the oil company dumped millions of gallons of wastewater into their rivers and contaminated their land with waste.[16] A California federal district court dismissed the suit, but the 9th Circuit U.S. Court of Appeals reversed. The

The Achuar tribe, indigenous to the Amazon rain forest, brought a class action in Los Angeles.

appeals court ruled, among other things, that Occidental had failed to demonstrate that Peru was the more convenient forum for the lawsuit.[17] The U.S. Supreme Court denied Occidental's petition for review.[18] The Achuar plaintiffs wanted the case tried in California, in part, because the Peruvian courts have a history of favoring corporate interests in conflicts with natives. The parties settled for an undisclosed amount to be used to fund community development projects.[19]

Standing to Sue

Not all who wish to bring a claim before a court are permitted to do so. The plaintiff must demonstrate *standing to sue.* That is, the plaintiff must show that their interest in the outcome of the controversy is sufficiently direct and substantial to justify the court's intervention. Mere interest in the issue involved is insufficient to obtain standing to sue.

The U.S. Supreme Court has underscored that standing requires a plaintiff have a "concrete and particularized" injury, although those injuries could be intangible.[20] A class action lawsuit was filed against an online "people search engine" that had provided wholly inaccurate information about the named plaintiff, including a false age and photograph, that he was a professional with a graduate degree, and was a married parent. On remand, the Ninth Circuit held Robins had standing, determining that even flattering inaccuracies could harm a job seeker, a position supported by an *amicus curiae* (often referred to as a "friend of the court") brief submitted by the Consumer Financial Protection Bureau.

We all suffer injustices. We all have complaints in life. But have we suffered an injury to a legally protected right or interest? That is the question in the *Mayer* case that arose out of "Spygate," an alleged National Football League cheating scandal.

LEGAL BRIEFCASE

Mayer v. Bill Belichick; The New England Patriots; National Football League

605 F.3d 223 (3d Cir. 2010), *cert. denied,* 562 U.S. 1271 (2011)

FACTS

In an episode popularly known as "Spygate," an employee of the New England Patriots National Football League team was caught videotaping New York Jets' sideline signals, in violation of NFL rules, during a 2007 game with the Jets. The taping was later discovered to have been part of an illicit taping program that reportedly had been ongoing since the 2000 season. The NFL penalized the Patriots and their coach, Bill Belichick. Mayer sued on behalf of himself and a class of Jets season ticketholders claiming the improper conduct violated the contractual expectations and rights of the ticketholders who had paid to observe an honest football game played in conformance with the rules. Mayer lost at trial, where the federal district court ruled that he had failed to demonstrate an actionable injury; that is, he was unable to show the court that the facts he asserted could support a right to relief under the law. Put another way, he did not have standing to sue. Mayer then appealed to the Third Circuit Federal Court of Appeals.

Circuit Judge Cowen

[I–III omitted—ed.]

IV

The District Court, while noting that Mayer alleged numerous theories of liability in this case, appropriately turned to the following dispositive question: namely, whether or not he stated an actionable injury (or, in other words, a legally protected right or interest) arising out of the alleged "dishonest" videotaping program undertaken by the Patriots and the NFL team's head coach.

Initially, we consider how tickets to sporting and other entertainment events have been treated in the past. New Jersey has generally followed a so-called "license" approach*. . . .

Although it did not use the specific term "license," the ticket stub provided by the Patriots nevertheless appears consistent with this traditional approach. For example, it unambiguously stated that "[t]his ticket only grants entry into the stadium and a spectator seat for the specified NFL game." The stub further made clear that the Jets and the owners of the stadium retain sole discretion to refuse admission or to eject a ticketholder. . . . Given that Mayer was never barred or expelled from any game at Giants Stadium, much more is needed to establish a cognizable right, interest, or injury. . . .

Mayer possessed either a license or, at best, a contractual right to enter Giants Stadium and to have a seat from which to watch a professional football game. In the clear language of the ticket stub, "[t]his ticket only grants entry into the stadium and a spectator seat for the specified NFL game." Mayer actually was allowed to enter the stadium and witnessed the "specified NFL game[s]" between the Jets and Patriots. He thereby suffered no cognizable injury to a legally protected right or interest.

Accordingly, we need not, and do not decide, whether a ticket-holder possesses nothing more than a license to enter and view whatever event, if any, happens to transpire. Here, Mayer undeniably saw *football* games played by two *NFL* teams. This therefore is not a case where, for example, the game or games were canceled, strike replacement players were used, or the professional football teams themselves did something nonsensical or absurd, such as deciding to play basketball.

Furthermore, we do recognize that Mayer alleged that he was the victim, not of mere poor performance by a team or its players, but of a team's ongoing acts of dishonesty or cheating in violation of the express rules of the game. Nevertheless, there are any number of often complicated rules and standards applicable to a variety of sports, including professional football. It appears uncontested that players often commit intentional rule infractions in order to obtain an advantage over the course of the game. . . . Mayer further does not appear to contest the fact that a team is evidently permitted by the rules to engage in a wide variety of arguably "dishonest" conduct to uncover an opponent's signals. For example, a team is apparently free to take advantage of the knowledge that a newly hired player or coach takes with him after leaving his former team, and it may even have personnel on the sidelines who try to pick up the opposing team's signals with the assistance of lip-reading, binoculars, note-taking, and other devices. In addition, even Mayer acknowledged in his amended complaint that "[t]eams are allowed to have a limited number of their own videographers on the sideline during the game."

In fact, the NFL's own commissioner did ultimately take action here. He found that the Patriots and Belichick were guilty of violating the applicable NFL rules, imposed sanctions in the form of fines and the loss of draft picks, and rather harshly characterized the whole episode as a calculated attempt to avoid well-established rules designed to encourage fair play and honest competition. At least in this specific context, it is not the role of judges and juries to be second-guessing the decision taken by a professional sports league purportedly enforcing its *own* rules. . . .

This Court refuses to countenance a course of action that would only further burden already limited judicial resources and force professional sports organizations and related individuals to expend money, time, and resources to defend against such litigation. . . .

In conclusion, this Court will affirm the dismissal of Mayer's amended complaint. Again, it bears repeating that our reasoning here is limited to the unusual and even unique circumstances presented by this appeal. We do not condone the conduct on the part of the Patriots and the team's head coach, and we likewise refrain from assessing whether the NFL's sanctions (and its alleged destruction of the videotapes themselves) were otherwise appropriate. We further recognize that professional football, like other professional sports, is a multi-billion dollar business. In turn, ticket-holders and other fans may have legitimate issues with the manner in which they are treated. . . . Significantly, our

* A license, for our purposes, is generally defined as "[a] permission . . . to commit some act that would otherwise be unlawful; esp., an agreement that it is lawful for the licensee to enter the licensor's land to do some act that would otherwise be illegal, such as hunting game." *Black's Law Dictionary* 1002 (9th ed. 2009).

ruling also does not leave Mayer and other ticketholders without any recourse. Instead, fans could speak out against the Patriots, their coach, and the NFL itself. In fact, they could even go so far as to refuse to purchase tickets or NFL-related merchandise. However, the one thing they *cannot* do is bring a legal action in a court of law.

Affirmed.

Questions

1. Why did Mayer lose this case?
2. Do you think he should have won? Why?
3. According to the court, under what circumstances might a plaintiff conceivably have an actionable claim involving a sports event gone wrong?
4. In an antitrust action brought against Apple Inc. regarding iPods, a federal judge questioned whether any of the plaintiffs had actually purchased an iPod. Why would the judge be concerned about that? How might the plaintiffs respond if they had not in fact purchased an iPod? Explain. See Jeff Elder, "Judge Questions Plaintiffs in Apple iPod Case," *The Wall Street Journal,* December 4, 2014 [**www.wsj.com**].
5. The 2019 Super Bowl win by the Los Angeles Rams was clouded by a controversial "no call" on the Rams' apparent pass interference. Two Saints fans sued on behalf of the "national fan base" to compel the NFL Commissioner to explain why he did not invoke a league rule allowing him to reverse the outcome or reschedule the game. Do the Saints fans have standing to bring this claim? Explain. (See Paul Murphy, "Can the 'no-call lawsuit' from New Orleans lawyers actually work?," 4WWL, January 23, 2019 [**www.wwltv.com**]).

Class Actions

In some instances, multiple plaintiffs may join together to represent themselves and all others who are similarly situated to file a single lawsuit alleging similar harm arising from the same, or substantially the same, wrong. The high cost of litigation, the great uncertainty of victory, and the likelihood of small individual recoveries have made the class action a very useful tool for plaintiffs. Of course, the class action also enhances judicial efficiency by bringing many claims together in one case. The Class Action Fairness Act of 2005 gave federal courts jurisdiction over class actions involving more than $5 million or where plaintiffs are from multiple states.

Several recent U.S. Supreme Court rulings have impacted the viability of the class action in business disputes. For example, a small group of Walmart employees sued the company for sex discrimination on behalf of a nationwide class of 1.5 million female employees; Walmart challenged the class action certification. The Court held that the claims against Walmart did not share enough common elements to tie together the millions of employment decisions affecting women at Walmart. As a matter of company policy, discretion over pay and promotions rested with local managers at the 4,000 or so company stores; without a specific employment practice that tied all of their claims together, the class lacked the necessary commonality.[21] The Supreme Court's decision led to regional class action suits by female Walmart workers. A federal appeals court allowed such a lawsuit to proceed, and the Supreme Court denied Walmart's petition for review.[22]

Five California women from the original suit reached a confidential settlement with Walmart and agreed to dismiss their claims. The day before they filed to dismiss, six other women filed to intervene because they could "no longer depend upon the named plaintiffs to

FIGURE 4.2 **Stages of a Lawsuit**

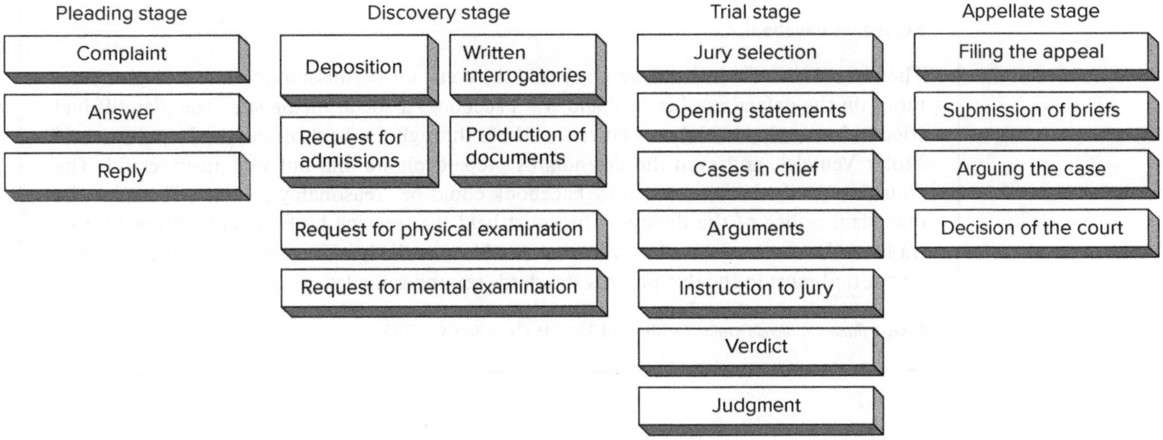

protect their interests."[23] After having received a right-to-sue letter from the Equal Employment Opportunity Commission a few months earlier, nearly 100 women in Florida filed their suit for gender discrimination against Walmart.[24]

The Civil Trial Process

Civil procedure varies by jurisdiction. The following generalizations merely typify the process (see Figure 4.2). [For a vast "catalog" of law on the Internet, see **http://catalaw.com**].

Pleadings

LO 4-9
Describe the typical steps in the civil trial process.

Pleadings are the documents by which each party sets their initial case before the court. A civil action begins when the plaintiff files their first pleading, which is labeled a ***complaint***. The complaint specifies (1) the parties to the suit, (2) evidence as to the court's jurisdiction in the case, (3) a statement of the facts, and (4) a prayer for relief (a remedy).

The complaint is filed with the clerk of the court and a summons is issued, directing the defendant to appear in court to answer the claims alleged against them. A sheriff or some other official will attempt to personally deliver the summons to the defendant. If personal delivery cannot be achieved, the summons may be left with a responsible party at the defendant's residence. Failing that, other modes of delivery are permissible, including a mailing. Publication of a notice in a newspaper will, in some instances, constitute good service of process. Ordinarily, a copy of the complaint accompanies the summons, so the defendant is apprised of the nature of the claim.

The defendant has several options. They may do nothing, but failure to respond may result in a ***default judgment*** in favor of the plaintiff. The defendant may choose to respond by filing a *demurrer* or a *motion to dismiss,* the essence of which is to argue that even if the plaintiff's recitation of the facts is accurate, a claim on which relief can be granted has not been stated.

Served on Facebook?

The plaintiff in a divorce proceeding asked the court for permission to serve a divorce summons on the defendant, her husband, via Facebook, a social media site. The plaintiff had tried to locate the defendant's current address through the post office, the Department of Motor Vehicles, and even the defendant's prepaid phone bill, but was unsuccessful. The court analyzed whether service by Facebook could be "reasonably calculated" to give the defendant notice of the divorce. The court held that service by Facebook, although non-traditional, was the form of service that would most likely offer the defendant notice and comported most to the due process standards set under the law.

Source: *Baidoo v. Blood-Dzraku,* 48 Misc. 3d 309, 311 (N.Y. Sup. Ct. 2015).

Alternatively, the defendant may file with the court an initial pleading, called an *answer*, wherein the defendant enters a denial by setting out their version of the facts and law, or in which the defendant simply concedes the validity of the plaintiff's position. The answer also may contain an *affirmative defense*, such as the statute of limitations or the statute of frauds that would bar the plaintiff's claim. The defendant's answer might include a *counterclaim* or *cross-claim.* A counterclaim is the defendant's assertion of a claim of action against the plaintiff. A cross-claim is the defendant's assertion of a claim of action against a codefendant. In some states, these would be labeled *cross-complaints.* In the event of a counterclaim or the assertion of new facts in the answer, the plaintiff will respond with a *reply.* The complaint, answer, reply, and their components are the pleadings that serve to give notice, clarify the issues, and limit the dimensions of the litigation. [For a summary of "Famous Trials" in history, see **www.famous-trials.com**].

Motions

As necessary, during and after the filing of the pleadings, either party may file motions with the court. Of special importance is a *motion for a judgment on the pleadings* or a *motion for summary judgment.* In a motion for a judgment on the pleadings, either party simply asks the judge to reach a decision based on the information in the pleadings. The judge will do so only if the defendant's answer constitutes an admission of the accuracy of the plaintiff's claim or if the plaintiff's claim clearly has no foundation in law.

In a motion for summary judgment, the party filing the motion is claiming that no facts are in dispute. Therefore, the judge may make a ruling about the law without taking the case to trial. In a summary judgment hearing, the court can look beyond the pleadings to hear evidence from affidavits, depositions, and so on. These motions avoid the time and expense of trial.

Discovery

Discovery is the primary information-gathering stage in the pretrial process. That information clarifies the trial issues, promotes pretrial settlements, and helps prevent surprises at the trial, among other things. Discovery may consist of ***depositions*** (recorded, sworn testimony), physical and mental examinations, answers to written questions (***interrogatories***), requests for access to documents and property to inspect them, and *admissions* (agreements by the parties to stipulated issues of fact or law).

Electronic communication and storage have added important new expectations and burdens to the discovery process by requiring that litigants exchange all relevant electronically stored information (ESI) during the discovery phase. Individuals and companies must be able to produce ESI from all sources, including email, files, scanned handwritten notes, stored records, voice mail, fax data, instant messages, spreadsheets, videos, PowerPoint presentations, and so on. The following case illustrates both the potential power and limitations of ESI in discovery requests.

LEGAL BRIEFCASE

Crabtree v. Angie's List 2017

U.S. Dist. LEXIS 12927 (S.D. Ind. January 31, 2017)

Magistrate Judge Mark J. Dinsmore

I. BACKGROUND

In this Fair Labor Standards Act ("FLSA") action, Plaintiffs assert they were wrongfully denied overtime compensation during a one-year period in which they worked as Senior Sales Representatives, also known as "Closers." In that position, Plaintiffs finalized sales with service providers for advertising on the Angie's List website and spent a significant portion of their workday on the telephone. Because Defendant did not provide company-issued laptops or cell phones for use outside the office, Plaintiffs often used their personal electronic devices for work purposes.

Plaintiffs believe they spent approximately 10–12 hours per day working for Defendant but were paid based upon an eight-hour day and 40-hour workweek. Defendant now seeks to obtain GPS and location services data from Plaintiffs' personal cell phones to "construct a detailed and accurate timeline of when Plaintiffs were or were not working." Plaintiffs object, arguing that the request poses significant privacy concerns and that the GPS data will not accurately portray whether Plaintiffs were working at any given time. Plaintiffs further argue that Defendant has alternative, and far less intrusive, means to identify periods of time when Plaintiffs were working.

II. LEGAL STANDARD

A party may seek an order to compel discovery when an opposing party fails to respond to discovery requests or provides evasive or incomplete responses. A party objecting to the discovery request bears the burden of showing why the request is improper.

Federal Rule of Civil Procedure 26(b)(1) defines the scope of discovery as follows:

> Parties may obtain discovery regarding any nonprivileged matter that is relevant to any party's claim or defense and proportional to the needs of the case, considering the importance of the issues at stake in the action, the amount in controversy, the parties' relative access to relevant information, the parties' resources, the importance of the discovery in resolving the issues, and whether the burden or expense of the proposed discovery outweighs its likely benefit.

Rule 26 further provides that the Court may impose additional limitations if a discovery request is cumulative, late, or out of proportion to the needs of the case:

III. DISCUSSION

A. Interrogatory No. 12 and Request for Production No. 19

Defendant initially sought the identification of all equipment used by Plaintiffs as part of their employment with Defendant and requested that Plaintiffs submit for forensic examination all such equipment. Defendant subsequently narrowed its request to the production of GPS and/or location services data between September 2014 and September 2015 from any and all computers, cellular telephones, smartphones, tablets, and other communication devices used by Plaintiffs during work time during their employment with Defendant. Defendant asserts that this data is relevant to establishing how many hours Plaintiffs worked during that yearlong period. For example, Defendant notes that Plaintiffs could remain logged in to their computers on the SalesForce software but be inactive for up to four hours. Defendant asserts the

GPS data would identify whether Plaintiffs left for the day, left for lunch or some other unpaid break during that four-hour window when they were still logged on to SalesForce. Yet if Plaintiffs were permitted, in fact expected, to work outside the office to accommodate clients in different time zones, the fact that Plaintiffs' phones had left the Angie's List building would have no meaningful impact on whether the employees were performing work at that time.

Nevertheless, Defendant cites a number of district court cases purporting to support its theory that other courts have allowed similar production requests. . . . In [citation omitted], plaintiff was permitted to obtain GPS data from trucks used in defendant's business to test the accuracy of the run data previously provided by defendant. Angie's List asserts that the GPS data in conjunction with the SalesForce data would create a more accurate picture of Plaintiffs' work hours. But Defendant is overlooking a clear distinction between its request and [the cases it cites]: Plaintiffs' privacy interests. In [citation omitted], it was plaintiff who sought the GPS data from the device in the defendant employer's truck, which presumably tracked location while the truck was being driven during the workday—a much more pointed request than seeking all GPS/location data for 24-hours a day for a one year period from a personal device that would be tracking Plaintiffs' movements well outside of their working time.

. . . In each of the other cases relied upon by Defendant, the courts compelled the production of cell phone *records*—such as the call history—not data as intrusive as GPS data that would track Plaintiffs' locations at every moment of the day for a year. Plaintiffs have already produced cell phone records that are the equivalent of those ordered to be produced in the cases cited by Defendant.

Rule 26 requires the Court to limit discovery if it can be obtained from another source that is more convenient, less burdensome, or less expensive. Additionally, the Advisory Committee Notes to the Federal Rules [of Civil Procedure] advises the courts to act with caution when evaluating requests to inspect a party's electronic devices or systems for ESI, in order to avoid unduly impinging on a party's privacy interests.

Discovery must also be "proportional to the needs of the case." In this FLSA action, the parties will need to establish when Plaintiffs were performing work for Defendant. Plaintiffs assert they have already provided Defendant with cell phone records that would allow Defendant to identify business-related calls. Defendant also has access to data from SalesForce that will show when Plaintiffs were logged into the software as well as data that will show when Plaintiffs were present at Angie's List offices such as badge swipe data and log in data from their work computers. Defendant has not demonstrated that the GPS/location services data from Plaintiffs' electronic devices will be more probative than any of the above data Defendant already has in its possession. Therefore, the Court finds that the forensic examination of Plaintiffs' electronic devices is not proportional to the needs of the case because any benefit the data might provide is outweighed by Plaintiffs' significant privacy and confidentiality interests. Defendant's Motion is DENIED as to Request for Production No. 19.

In response to Interrogatory No. 12, Plaintiffs state they have identified their cell phones by virtue of producing their cell phone records to Defendant. Plaintiffs assert that they have no other personal devices or equipment to identify that was used as part of their employment with Defendant. Consequently, Defendant's Motion is DENIED as to Interrogatory No. 12.

[B–E omitted—ed.]

F. Request for Production No. 27

This request seeks documents such as email messages, social media posts, . . . [or] text messages . . . "prepared, created, obtained, or used by" Plaintiffs from September 2014 to September 2015 that related to absences from or attendance at work. Plaintiffs respond that they did not "keep any diaries, journals, calendars, or appointment books" and have no documents responsive to the requests for those items. Plaintiffs further state that to the extent the request seeks emails, text messages, and social media posts, it is a "fishing expedition" not relevant to the claims or defenses in the case.

As Judge Posner has noted, "of course pretrial discovery is a fishing expedition and one can't know what one has caught until one fishes. But Fed. R. Civ. P. 45(c) allows the fish to object." In this instance, the Court shares Plaintiffs' concerns that Defendant casts too wide a net as it does not sufficiently justify the breadth of the request. Defendant argues that it is entitled to discovery if Plaintiffs "took 2-hour lunches, were gone running errands during the day, or remained logged in to SalesForce during periods they were not working." And on this point Defendant is correct. However, Defendant has not shown how emails, text messages or social media posts from this one year time period may be more probative as to these issues than other less intrusive data already within its control, such as the SalesForce data, computer log ins, or badge swipe data. As discussed with regard to the GPS/location services data, the Court has an obligation to guard against intrusive discovery. Defendant's broad request would encompass clearly personal communications such as an email string relating to an upcoming vacation between an employee and his or her spouse, or text messages planning a lunch date. These communications "relate to absences from work" yet have absolutely no relevance to this lawsuit. Additionally, the scope of the information sought by Defendant is plainly not proportional to the needs of this case. Therefore, Defendant's Motion is DENIED as to this request.

V. CONCLUSION

Based on the foregoing, Defendant's *Motion to Compel* is **DENIED.**

Questions

1. Why did the court distinguish between a plaintiff truck driver's request for a defendant employer's truck's GPS records and Angie's List's request for their employees' GPS data?
2. What other discovery requests might help Angie's List obtain the evidence it was seeking with the GPS data, social media posts, text messages, and so forth of the plaintiffs? Explain.
3. Should data from health monitors such as Fitbits or pedometers be discoverable in personal injury actions seeking recovery for pain and suffering? Explain. See *Bartis v. Biomet, Inc.*, Case No. 4:13-CV-00657-JAR (E.D. Mo. 2021).

Pretrial Conference

Either party may request, and many courts require, a pretrial meeting involving the attorneys, the judge, and occasionally the parties. Usually following discovery, the conference is designed to plan the course of the trial in the interests of efficiency and justice. The participants seek to define the issues and settle as much of the dispute as possible in advance of trial. If a full settlement is not reached, a trial date is set.

The Judge and Jury

The federal Constitution and most state constitutions provide for the right to a jury trial in most civil cases, unless the relief sought is only equitable (for example, an injunction). Some states place dollar minimums on that guarantee. At the federal level and in most states, unless one of the parties requests a jury, the judge alone will hear the case and decide all questions of law and fact. If the case is tried before a jury, that body will resolve questions of fact, but all questions of law will be resolved by the judge.

Jurors are selected from a jury pool composed of a cross section of the community. A panel is drawn from that pool. The individuals in that panel are questioned by the judge, by the attorneys, or by both to determine if any individual is prejudiced about the case such that they could not reach an objective decision on the merits. The questioning process is called ***voir dire***.

From an attorney's point of view, jury selection is often not so much a matter of finding jurors without bias as it is a matter of identifying those jurors who are most likely to reach a decision favorable to their client. To that end, elaborate mechanisms and strategies have been employed—particularly in criminal trials—to identify desirable jurors. For example, sophisticated, computer-assisted surveys of the trial community have been conducted to develop objective evidence by which to identify jurors who would not admit to racial prejudice but whose "profile" suggests the likelihood of such prejudice.

After questioning, the attorneys may *challenge for cause,* arguing to the judge that the individual cannot exercise the necessary objectivity of judgment. Attorneys are also afforded a limited number of ***peremptory challenges***, by which the attorney can have a potential juror dismissed without the judge's concurrence and without offering a reason. Peremptory challenges may not be used to reject jurors on the basis of race or gender.

Facebook the Jury Pool?

Social media, such as Facebook, MySpace, and Twitter, can be a valuable source of information to attorneys as they try to shape the composition of juries. Information that might not be revealed in *voir dire* sometimes comes to light online. Jury consultant Amber Yearwood in San Francisco discovered online that a member of a jury pool was highly opinionated and often dispensed medical and sex advice, a personality not well suited to the client's cause. The prospective juror was dismissed.

Source: Ana Campoy and Ashby Jones, "Searching for Details Online, Lawyers Facebook the Jury," *The New York Times,* February 22, 2011, p. A2.

The Trial

The trial begins with opening statements by the attorneys. Each is expected to outline what they intend to prove. The plaintiff, bearing the burden of proof, then presents evidence, which may include both testimony and physical evidence, such as documents and photos. Those are called *exhibits.*

The plaintiff's attorney secures testimony from their own witnesses via questioning called *direct examination.* After the plaintiff's attorney completes direct examination of a witness, the defense attorney may question that witness in a process called *cross-examination. Redirect* and *recross* may then follow. After all of the plaintiff's witnesses have been questioned, the plaintiff rests their case.

At this stage, the defense may make a motion for a ***directed verdict***, arguing, in essence, that the plaintiff has offered insufficient evidence to justify relief, so time and expense may be saved by terminating the trial. Understandably, the judge considers the motion in the light most favorable to the plaintiff. Such motions ordinarily fail and the trial goes forward with the defendant's presentation of evidence.

At the completion of the defendant's case, both parties may be permitted to offer *rebuttal* evidence, and either party may move for a directed verdict. Barring a directed verdict, the case goes forward, with each party making a closing argument. When the trial is by jury, the judge must instruct the jurors as to the law to be applied to the case. The attorneys often submit their views of the proper instructions. In most civil cases, a verdict for the plaintiff must be supported by a *preponderance of the evidence* (more likely than not). After deliberation, the verdict of the jury is rendered, and a judgment is entered by the court. [For a company providing a virtual jury in advance of trial, see **www.virtualjury.com**].

Experts

In this highly technological and scientific era, one of the biggest dilemmas facing judges and juries is the weight to give to expert testimony. Very often with cases involving medical malpractice and product liability (see Chapter 7), the testimony of experts is decisive to the outcome. But expert testimony varies wildly in its reliability and credibility. The archery case that follows investigates the theme of reliability as a basis for admission of expert testimony.

Circuit Judge E. Grady Jolly

This appeal arises from a most unfortunate, unintended, and unwitnessed death. Dr. Alan Sandifer was pierced in the head by the cable guard of his 2007 Hoyt Vulcan XT500 bow, which he was examining, and possibly modifying, while at his home. Following his death, his family members . . . ("the Sandifers") . . . filed suit against Hoyt Archery, Inc. . . . The Sandifers brought this action under the Louisiana Products Liability Act (LPLA) alleging that the compound bow was defectively designed.

The determinative issue on appeal is whether the district court erred by excluding most of the testimony of the Sandifers' primary expert, Dr. Kelkar. In disallowing Dr. Kelkar's testimony, the district court held, first, that he, as a substitute expert, exceeded the scope of the expert opinion, theory, and testimony as earlier defined by the district court when allowing him to enter the case late into the litigation. Secondly, the court excluded [Dr. Kelkar's testimony] on the grounds that Dr. Kelkar's opinion as to the causation of the accident was based on propensity evidence, relating to the character and habits of Dr. Sandifer as a hunter. Once the district court ruled on the evidentiary questions, it granted summary judgment to Hoyt . . .

Dr. Sandifer was an avid bow hunter. One evening, while at home, with his wife seated in a different room, he sat at his computer with his Hoyt compound bow. . . . [H]is wife heard a loud noise and found her husband lying unconscious on the floor with the compound bow's metal cable guard in his head through his left temple. . . . He died the next day. No one saw the accident.

How the accident occurred is confounding and is the subject of this litigation. Hoyt, the manufacturer, contends that, when modifying the bow, Dr. Sandifer voluntarily placed his head in the bow to examine it while pulling the drawstring; then, he accidentally lost control of the string, causing the cable guard to enter his head; and that such use of the bow was not a reasonably anticipated use of the instrument. The Sandifers contend that Dr. Sandifer did not voluntarily place his head into the bow but instead that the compound bow was defective, . . . [causing] the cable guard to release and enter Dr. Sandifer's brain.

. . . [T]he Sandifers asked for a continuance of the trial date that had been set. Their primary expert, Dr. Gautam Ray, a biomechanical engineer, had been diagnosed with terminal cancer and could not continue in the case. The Sandifers had employed Dr. Ray to explain how the accident occurred and to show that Dr. Sandifer's use of the compound bow was a reasonably anticipated use. . . . The district court had qualified Dr. Ray to testify at trial based upon the standards in *Daubert v. Merrell Dow Pharms. Inc.;* that is to say, his methods were reliable and his opinions helpful to the jury. Further, the court had denied Hoyt's motion for summary judgment, partially because Dr. Ray testified that Dr. Sandifer's head "most probably than not" ended up between the cable guard and the bow string involuntarily.

. . . [T]he Sandifers moved the district court to allow Dr. Ray to be replaced with another biomechanical engineer. The court granted that request. The court admonished, however, that the approval of "a substitute expert was not an opportunity for [the Sandifers] to . . . engage an expert outside the scope of expertise and methodology of Dr. Ray."

The Sandifers hired Dr. Rajeev Kelkar—an accident reconstruction expert and biomechanics consultant . . . He concluded . . . that it was most likely that Dr. Sandifer's injury resulted from a twisting of the bow string that caused Dr. Sandifer's head to involuntarily end up between the bow string and the riser due to a design defect, rather than a volitional act on his part. The basis for this opinion . . . was that Dr. Sandifer was a "meticulous" and "very safety conscious" bow hunter who would know not to flex his left elbow in a "biomechanically disadvantageous" manner and place his head in the bow.

. . . Hoyt deposed him. At that deposition, Dr. Kelkar conceded that . . . without the statements about Dr. Sandifer's careful nature as a hunter, he could not say his theory was more likely than the expert opinion offered by Hoyt.

II.

. . . Hoyt moved to exclude portions of Dr. Kelkar's report. Specifically, Hoyt argued that Dr. Kelkar's report exceeded the scope of Dr. Ray's expert report and that Dr. Kelkar's conclusions were based improperly on Dr. Sandifer's reputation for safety. Hoyt further moved for summary judgment.

The district court granted Hoyt's motions to exclude the challenged portions of Dr. Kelkar's expert report. [T]he court first observed that Dr. Kelkar's methods and conclusions were beyond the scope of Dr. Ray's report in violation of the court's instructions when allowing the substitution of experts. Second, the court . . . held that neither the Sandifers nor Dr. Kelkar demonstrated that propensity inferences were a reliable basis for an expert biomechanical opinion. . . .

After granting Hoyt's motions to exclude portions of Dr. Kelkar's report, the district court then granted Hoyt's motion for summary judgment. . . . The Sandifers timely appealed.

III.

On appeal the Sandifers make two arguments. First they argue that the district court abused its discretion by excluding the testimony of Dr. Kelkar as beyond the scope of the Sandifers' original biomechanical expert; and moreover, excluding this testimony constituted an improper discovery sanction. Secondly, the district court abused its discretion by excluding Dr. Kelkar's opinions based upon Dr. Sandifer's safe archery practices. The Sandifers argue that such evidence was not impermissible character evidence, but instead the evidence is admissible as habit evidence. Hoyt counters that the evidence was in fact character evidence and, regardless, such propensity evidence, be it character or habit, was beyond the scope of Dr. Kelkar's biomechanical expertise and formed an unreliable basis for his conclusions.

In considering the Sandifer's arguments, we need only address the district court's . . . rulings relating to propensity evidence because . . . they provide a sufficient basis for the grant of summary judgment to Hoyt.

IV.

. . . Because district courts have broad discretion in deciding the admissibility of expert testimony, "we will not find error unless the ruling is *manifestly erroneous.*" We reverse the trial court only "in 'unusual and exceptional case[s].'"

. . . [T]he district court held that Dr. Kelkar's opinion . . . did not satisfy the standards for the admissibility of expert opinion . . . because it was based upon unreliable propensity evidence. . . . [We] conclude that the district court did not abuse its discretion.

. . . The only issue we need to consider is whether the district court properly excluded Dr. Kelkar's opinion on [whether the injury arose from a] reasonably anticipated use [of the bow]. Without such testimony, the Sandifers cannot prevail.

. . . [E]xpert testimony is "admissible only if it is both relevant and reliable." . . . [The] "party seeking to have the district court admit expert testimony must demonstrate that the expert's findings and conclusions are based on the scientific method and, therefore, are reliable." The district court observed that the Sandifers "do not contend that habit or character evidence is the type of evidence reasonably relied upon in rendering a biomechanical engineering opinion." On appeal, the Sandifers have provided us with no reason to doubt this statement. Indeed, Dr. Kelkar admitted in his deposition that his statements based upon evidence of "Dr. Sandifer's habits as an individual" are not "biomechanical opinions."

With the unreliable portions excluded, Dr. Kelkar's opinion as to causation of the accident becomes ambivalent and is of no help to the jury in sorting out a reliable explanation of how the accident occurred. Without the benefit of the propensity evidence, Dr. Kelkar can only conclude that his theory is as likely as the defense theory. An expert opinion must "help the trier of fact to understand the evidence or to determine a fact in issue." . . .

. . . Dr. Kelkar's opinion, without the propensity evidence, could not help the jury decide whether Dr. Sandifer was engaged in reasonably anticipated use of the bow when the accident occurred. The district court did not abuse its discretion in excluding Dr. Kelkar's "perfectly equivocal opinion."

. . . Summary judgment was appropriate, and the judgment of the district court is

AFFIRMED.

Questions

1. Why did the court conclude that Dr. Kelkar's expert testimony was not reasonably reliable?
2. Do you agree that granting Hoyt's motion for summary judgment was necessary based on the partial exclusion of Dr. Kelkar's expert testimony? Explain.
3. Dodge slipped leaving work and claimed she suffered knee, ankle, and back injuries. Dodge sued the workplace cleaning service, but she provided no expert testimony to establish that the fall caused the injuries. Rather Dodge provided her own explanation of the fall and resulting injuries. Did the trial court err in admitting Dodge's layperson testimony? Explain. See *Dodge-Farrar v. American Cleaning Services Co.*, 54 P.3d 954 (Idaho Ct. App. 2002).

Post-trial Motions

The losing party may seek a ***judgment notwithstanding the verdict*** (judgment n.o.v) on the grounds that the jury's decision was clearly inconsistent with the law or the evidence. Such motions are rarely granted. The judge also is empowered to enter a judgment n.o.v on his or her own initiative.

Either party may move for a new trial. The winning party might do so on the grounds that the remedy provided was inferior to that warranted by the evidence. The losing party commonly claims an error of law to support a motion for a new trial. Other possible grounds for a new trial include jury misconduct or new evidence.

Appeals

LO 4-10
Distinguish trials and appeals.

After the judgment is rendered, either party may appeal the decision to a higher court. The winner may do so if the remedy is considered inadequate. Ordinarily, of course, the losing party brings the appeal. As noted, the appealing party is the ***appellant*** or *petitioner,* while the other party is the ***appellee*** or *respondent.* The appeals court does not try the case again. Its consideration is limited to mistakes of law at the trial level. The appellant will argue, for example, that a jury instruction was erroneous or that the judge erred in failing to grant a motion to strike testimony alleged to have been prejudicial. The appeals court does not hear new evidence. Its decision is based on the trial record, materials filed by the opposing attorneys, and oral arguments.

The appellate court announces its judgment and ordinarily explains that decision in an accompanying document labeled an *opinion.* (Most of the cases in this text are appellate court opinions.) If no error is found, the lower court decision is *affirmed.* If a prejudicial error is found, the appellate court may simply ***reverse*** (overrule) the lower court. Or the judgment may be to *reverse and* ***remand***, wherein the lower court decision is overruled, and the case is sent back to that court for further proceedings consistent with the appellate court's judgment. If there is no remand, a further appeal may be made by petitioning the highest court of the jurisdiction. Most such petitions are denied.

Questions—Part Two

1. What purpose is served by the concept of jurisdiction? Why do we limit the courts to which a claim can be taken?
2. Law cases often read like soap operas, even as they reveal important truths. A woman and man, each married to others, had engaged in a long-term love affair. The woman's husband died, and she pleaded with her paramour to leave his New York home to visit her in Florida. She affirmed her love for the man. They made arrangements to meet in Miami, but on his arrival at the airport, he was served a summons informing him that he was being sued. His Florida "lover" sought $500,000 for money allegedly loaned to him and for seduction inspired by a promise of marriage.
    a. Does the Florida court have jurisdiction over him? Explain.
    b. Would your answer change if he had voluntarily gone to Florida on vacation? See *Wyman v. Newhouse,* 93 F.2d 313 (2d Cir. 1937).
3. At this writing, in the wake of the FTX crypto exchange's bankruptcy filing, a lawsuit has been filed against the former FTX CEO Sam Bankman-Fried and celebrities, such as Tom Brady, Naomi Osaka, and Larry David who promoted crypto investments, for allegedly violating laws protecting investors from fraud and deception, resulting in American consumers losing more than $11 billion. The suit was filed on behalf of an individual claiming that he opened a yield-bearing account after "being exposed to some or all of the defendants' misrepresentations and omissions," and seeks class action status. Should the court certify the case as a class action, or should other investors' potential claims be brought individually? Explain. See Steven Zeitchik and Julian Mark, "FTX Investors Sue Sam Bankman-Fried and Celebrity Endorsers," *The Washington Post,* November 16, 2022 [**https://www.washingtonpost.com/**][For an FTX crypto commercial featuring Tom Brady, see: **https://youtu.be/4p4z2wsjhmM**].

Part Three—Criticism and Alternatives

Criticism

To many Americans, our system of justice is neither systematic nor just. With more than 1.33million lawyers[25] in a population of about 330[26] million people, critics argue that excessive, unproductive litigation is inevitable.

Too Many Lawyers and Lawsuits?

> "That bill shall know no limits."

Critics claim that many lawsuits are less of a search for justice and more in pursuit of big dollars for attorneys. A large law firm sued an energy industry executive for unpaid legal bills, resulting in a counterclaim asserting that the firm overbilled as a matter of practice. During discovery, emails between three attorneys at the firm surfaced that included such statements as "That bill shall know no limits." Even though the firm described the email exchange as "unfortunate banter" between colleagues, the messages may reflect a larger problem with the approaches law firms have to billing.[27] A confidential settlement ended the litigation.[28]

Legal critic Philip K. Howard argues that we need fewer lawsuits, fewer rules, and greater personal responsibility. He thinks we feel powerless in the face of rules:

> Ordinary choices–by teachers, doctors, officials, managers, even volunteers–are paralyzed by legal self-consciousness. Did you check the rules? Who will be responsible if there is an accident? . . . We have become a culture of rule followers, trained to frame every solution in terms of existing law or possible legal risk.[29]

Even the late Supreme Court Justice Antonin Scalia argued that we have too many lawyers:

> Lawyers don't dig ditches or build buildings. When a society requires such a large number of its best minds to conduct the unproductive enterprise of the law, something is wrong with the legal system.[30]

In terms of the public's view of lawyers, it may be shaped more by access than numbers. A recent study by the National Opinion Research Center at the University of Chicago found that, in the prior year, "86% of the civil legal problems reported by low-income Americans received inadequate or no legal help," even though 71 percent of such households experienced at least one civil legal problem that year. The needed services were in such areas as health care, housing, disability access, veterans' benefits, and domestic violence.[31]

The Corporate Perspective

The legal system plays an invaluable role in facilitating and stabilizing commercial practice, but for corporate America, the law is also a source of significant expense and abundant frustration. As one expert explained, dealing with legal responsibilities and problems has become a central element of management practice:

> Only a few decades ago, the law was peripheral to the core activities of doing business. When I became a business lawyer in the late 1950s, for example, our involvement was generally limited to forming a corporation or partnership for a client, providing for the investment capital, doing a lease for an office or factory, and maybe handling a key contract with a CEO or a major supplier. . . . Today the law can affect almost every action a manager takes. It has moved closer to the core activities of conducting business and succeeding in a red-hot, competitive environment. More people now have "rights" they can assert against your company, so you face claims from employees, consumers, competitors, and the government. Consequently, today's manager needs to know something about employment law, discrimination claims, sexual harassment rules, product safety issues, the rules of advertising and competition, antitrust rules, environmental law, the value of intellectual property, and more.[32]

[For critiques of the American legal system, see the U.S. Chamber Institute for Legal Reform (an affiliate of the U.S. Chamber of Commerce), **www.instituteforlegalreform.com;** and Faces of Lawsuit Abuse **www.facesoflawsuitabuse.org**]. For a critique of tort reform efforts, see Anthony Tarricone, "Do as I Say, Not as I Sue, *HuffPost,* May 25, 2011 [**https://www.huffpost.com**].

Pants: Abusing the Legal System?

Washington, D.C., administrative law judge Roy Pearson attracted the attention of journalists from around the world by suing his neighborhood laundry for $54 million, down from an earlier claim of $67 million, over the alleged loss of the pants belonging to his $1,000 suit. Pearson thought he was entitled to $18,000 per day for each day the pants were missing over a period of nearly four years. Owners Soo and Jin Chung of Custom Cleaners attempted to give Pearson a pair of pants they said were the missing item, but he said the ones offered were not his. Pearson brought claims of mental suffering, inconvenience, discomfort, and fraud (based on the "Satisfaction Guaranteed" sign at Custom Cleaners). Along the way, Pearson had rejected settlement offers that reached $12,000. The Chungs won an easy trial victory with the court, concluding that Pearson was unable to prove the pants offered to him were not his and that the "Satisfaction Guaranteed" sign did not require the Chungs to satisfy a customer's unreasonable demands. Pearson was ordered to pay the Chungs' court costs, and their legal fees for their defense were covered by contributions. The Chungs' laundry went out of business. Pearson subsequently failed in his bid to be reappointed to his judge's position. He sued for wrongful discharge and lost at the federal district court. He appealed and lost again.

Source: Henri E. Cauvin, "Court Rules for Cleaners in $54 Million Pants Suit," *The Washington Post,* June 26, 2007, p. A01; and "'Pants Judge' Roy Pearson Strikes Out in Court," *The Wall Street Journal,* May 27, 2010 [**http://blogs.wsj.com/law**].

Criticized in America; Embraced Abroad

The United States is not alone in its ongoing debate about whether more or fewer lawyers and lawsuits are needed.

Japan

Historically in Japan, lawsuits have seldom been used to settle disputes, as reflected in its relatively small number of attorneys. With the rise of international mergers, bankruptcy, patents, and other business disputes, Japan became concerned with its lawyer shortage. A government council recommended U.S.-style law schools be established. Although the number of lawyers per capita is still fewer than in the United States, the number of lawyers in Japan has increased significantly in recent years.[33] However, the number of lawsuits has not increased and bankruptcy proceedings have decreased.[34]

On the Other Hand—Litigation as a Last Resort

Almost everyone seems to be unhappy about lawyers and lawsuits, but at the same time Americans expect lawyers and the courts to settle disputes; preserve freedom and justice; and correct problems not satisfactorily addressed by the market, legislatures, and regulators. Feeling threatened by abusive bosses, corporate fraud, dangerous drugs, defective products, environmental decline, and so on, Americans count on the justice system to protect our pecuniary interests, as well as the personal freedom and democracy we prize. Lawyers and the courts often are the only available weapons to right what we believe to be wrong. So the frustration many feel about exploding litigation may be attributable to us as much as to greedy lawyers. Furthermore, laws and lawyers are central to economic efficiency. Lawyers devise and enforce the rules, processes, and structures that permit capitalism to operate effectively. As previously discussed, much of the world is coming to recognize that law and lawyers provide the foundation for economic stability and progress.

PRACTICING ETHICS Robot Lawyer

The app, DoNotPay, declares that it is "the home of the first robot lawyer" that helps its subscribers to take such legal actions as appealing a parking ticket, filing a restraining order, or suing for breach of contract.[35] Users describe their legal problem to a chatbot, "and [an AI software system] matches that with a legally correct way of saying it," explained DoNotPay founder, Josh Browder.[36]

Questions

1. How might automation of legal services resolve access to justice problems for those unable to afford a lawyer? Explain.
2. What could be ethical issues created by the use of "robot lawyers?" Explain.

Sources: Website, DoNotPay App, **https://donotpay,com**; Padraig Belton, and "Would you let a robot lawyer defend you?" BBC News, August 5, 2021 [**https://www.bbc.com**].

Trials often are an inefficient way of resolving disputes.

Fewer Trials As courts were shut down during the pandemic in 2020, despite efforts such as offering remote hearings and electronic filings were made, the number of filings in every subject area dropped.[37] In prior years, a slow but steady decline in state court caseloads had been noted, with the caseload in 2017 being "roughly the same" as in 1993.[38] Trials often are an inefficient way of resolving disputes, so these numbers might be considered good news. On the other hand, trials are visible affirmations of the indispensability of justice and these numbers may alternatively indicate growing unmet needs, perhaps driven by the cost of legal services.

Reform: Judicial Efficiency

Governments, businesses, lawyers, and judges are frustrated with the expense and inefficiency of our overburdened judicial system. Some small businesses are now buying legal services insurance or prepaid legal services for a flat monthly fee.

Some cities have taken novel approaches to adjudication, such as business courts that hear only commercial claims, thus allowing jurists to become very efficient in handling contract problems, shareholder claims, and the like. Those systems are variations on the small claims courts that have long proven effective in settling minor disputes.

Small Claims Courts

Suppose you move out of your apartment and your landlord refuses to return your $500 damage deposit even though the rooms are spotless. Hiring a lawyer doesn't make

PRACTICING ETHICS — Declining Access to Lawyers?

One of the reasons for the declining number of trials, despite increasing disputes, may be difficulty in affording a lawyer in civil suits. *The New York Times* and other publications have reported an increasing number of cases going forward with one of the parties serving as a "do-it-yourself" lawyer.[39] Pursuing a claim in a federal district court costs an average of $15,000, with more complicated cases involving scientific evidence often reaching $100,000.[40] The expense of bringing lawsuits has attracted litigation funders, who invest in business disputes in exchange for a portion of the proceeds received by the party to whom they have given capital.[41] Litigation funders assert that they are helping litigants seek justice from wealthier opponents and not supporting frivolous lawsuits, which would be risky investments.[42] Note, however, that some litigants appear to be victimized by lawsuit lenders in a lightly regulated industry where interest rates "often exceed 100 percent per year."[43]

A 2012 San Francisco ordinance created a right to civil counsel, similar to what criminal defendants receive. Those living within 200 percent of the federal poverty line and who have a case regarding such key issues as housing, safety, or child custody would be eligible for free legal assistance. Although critics may view such programs as being best left to private legal aid organizations, supporters believe that by providing legal assistance to civil litigants in need, the city will avoid the long-term costs resulting from self-represented parties, such as court delays.[44]

[For a powerful description of the realities faced by both tenants living in, and landlords providing, housing for the poorest of our citizens, see Matthew Desmond's 2016 Pulitzer Prize book, *Evicted: Poverty and Profit in the American City* (New York: Penguin Random House, 2016).]

Question

While indigent criminal defendants are assured the right to counsel under American law, the same is not true for civil disputes. Do you think San Francisco's Civil Justice initiative should be followed throughout the United States? Explain.

Sources: Matthew Goldstein and Jessica Silver-Greenberg, "Hedge Funds Pour Cash into Lending for Lawsuits, *The New York Times*, June 26, 2018 [**www.nytimes.com**]; Jennifer Smith, "Lawsuit Investors Gain in U.S.," *The Wall Street Journal*, January 13, 2014, p. B7; Mike Rosen, "Testing Civil Gideon," California Lawyer, June 2012 [**www.callawyer.com**]; Binyamin Appelbaum, "Lawsuit Loans Add New Risk for the Injured," *The New York Times*, January 16, 2011 [**www.nytimes.com**]; and Binyamin Appelbaum, "Investors Put Money on Lawsuits to Get Payouts," *The New York Times*, November 14, 2010 [**www.nytimes.com**].

financial sense and is beyond your means anyway, but a ***small claims court*** may provide an effective solution.

Small claims courts, for the most part, resolve relatively minor disputes, like your landlord-tenant problem. A wide range of problems, such as divorce or bankruptcy, cannot be litigated in small claims courts. Maximum recoveries vary from place to place, but typically range from a few thousand dollars up to $7,500 or so. To prepare for a small claims case, the key is developing and presenting to the judge as much credible evidence as possible. If you can present witnesses on your behalf, do so, but if not, clearly written narratives expressing what the witnesses would have said may be acceptable to the judge. You need not hire a lawyer, but in most states you may do so if you wish. Should the small claims litigation not work out well for you, an appeal is permitted in many states.[45]

Honda in Small Claims Court

After rejecting a class action settlement that would have paid Honda Civic hybrid owners $100 to $200 each and provided some rebates on a new Honda purchase, in 2012 Heather Peters sued Honda in small claims court. She won $9,867.19 in damages after the judge ruled that Honda misled her into thinking her hybrid could get 50 miles per gallon when its fuel economy actually dropped from approximately 42 miles per gallon to 30 miles per gallon after a software update. Honda successfully appealed to the Los Angeles County Superior Court. Even though she lost on appeal, Peters prompted other customers to file lawsuits against Honda in small claims courts across the United States, including in New Bedford, Massachusetts; St. Louis, Missouri; and Arlington, Washington.

Source: Jerry Hirsch, "Honda Loses Civic Hybrid Small Claims Court Lawsuit," *Los Angeles Times,* February 1, 2012 [**www.latimes.com**]; and Jerry Hirsch, "Honda Wins Appeal in Civic Hybrid Mileage Lawsuit," *Los Angeles Times,* May 10, 2012 [**www.latimes.com**].

Alternative Dispute Resolution

LO 4-11 Identify dispute resolution alternatives to trials.

Businesses, in particular, are increasingly looking outside the judicial system for dispute resolution strategies. Dot-com entrepreneurs are developing interesting new online mechanisms for conveniently addressing Internet-based disputes. Networks of human mediators, dispute resolution software, and PayPal dispute resolution are among the online methods of settling problems outside of court.

Cybersettle is an online system for resolving insurance disputes, often of the fender-bender or slip-and-fall variety. The parties log on to Cybersettle and type in their monetary demands or offers. The system works 24 hours a day, seven days a week. The computer compares the bids, round by round. When those numbers come within a predetermined range, the two sides are notified that a settlement has been achieved. If necessary, a telephone facilitator may join the process to help determine the final sum to be paid. Cybersettle has patented its system and says it has settled more than 200,000 transactions and has facilitated over $1.9 billion in settlements.[46] The New York City Comptroller replaced the city's

Cybersettle process with an in-house staff of claims adjusters as a more cost-effective alternative for settling small personal injury and property damages claims.[47]

What Is Alternative Dispute Resolution?

Of course, any form of negotiation and settlement would constitute an alternative to litigation, but mediation and arbitration are the most prominent of the structured substitutes. Given the expense, frustration, and risk of lawsuits, we see increased innovation in building other alternative dispute resolution (ADR) options, including private trials and minitrials. [For many ADR links, see **www.hg.org/adr.html**].

Mediation ***Mediation*** introduces a neutral third party into the dispute resolution process. Ideally, the parties devise their own solution, with the mediator as a facilitator, not a decision maker. Even if the mediator proposes solutions, they will likely be in the nature of compromises, not determinations of right and wrong. The bottom line is that only the disputing parties can adopt any particular outcome. The mediator may aid the parties in a number of ways, such as keeping communication open between the parties.

[For a brief video explaining mediation: "What Is Mediation?," see at **https://www.youtube.com/watch?v= DWgweDmDi2Q**].

Arbitration In ***arbitration***, a neutral third party is given the power to determine a binding resolution of the dispute. Depending on the situation, the resolution could be either a compromise solution or a determination of the rights of the parties with a win–lose solution. Even in the latter case, however, arbitration may be quicker and less costly than a trial. The arbitrator may be an expert in the subject area of the dispute instead of a generalist, as a judge would be. Arbitration procedures are more formal than those in mediation but less formal than court proceedings.

The Federal Arbitration Act, first enacted in 1925, supports the enforcement of most private arbitration agreements.[48] An arbitrator's decision ordinarily is legally binding and final, although an increasing but still small number of arbitration decisions are reaching court.[49]

"Rent-a-Judge"

Private Trials A number of states now permit mutually agreed-on private trials, sometimes called "rent-a-judge." Normally, a third party, such as a mediation firm makes the necessary arrangements, including hiring a retired judge and jurors. The proceedings are conducted much like a courtroom. Because the parties are paying, however, the process normally moves along more rapidly. Further, the proceeding will usually be conducted in private. Appeals to the formal judicial system are provided for in some states. Critics question the fairness of the private system and wonder if it will further erode faith in public trials, but the time and money saved can be quite substantial.

Minitrials In recent years, some corporations have agreed to settle their disputes by holding informal hearings that clarify the facts and issues that would emerge if the dispute were litigated. In a minitrial, each organization presents its version of the case to a panel of senior executives from each organization. The trial is presided over by a neutral third party, who may be expected to issue a nonbinding opinion as to the likely result were the case to be litigated. The executives then meet to attempt to negotiate a settlement. The neutral third party sometimes facilitates that discussion. Minitrials are voluntary and nonbinding, but if an agreement is reached, the parties can formalize it by entering a settlement contract.

ADR Assessed

ADR mechanisms generally have been sustained in the courts. ADR–particularly arbitration–is often the required dispute-resolution mechanism for employee complaints, such as discrimination or harassment. Mandatory arbitration clauses are often included in consumer transactions involving loans, credit cards, cable service, auto warranties, brokerage accounts, insurance, and more. Ordinarily, ADR costs less and is resolved more quickly than litigation. It is also less formal and less adversarial than the judicial process. Furthermore, the parties have more control over the proceedings in that they can choose the facilitator, when and where the dispute will be heard, and they can keep the dispute private if they wish. Despite those strengths, alternative dispute resolution has some limitations when compared with litigation.

A study of nearly 4,000 employee arbitration cases found an employee win rate of only 21.4 percent, lower than what would be expected in litigation. In cases won by employees, the median recovery was $36,500 and the mean was $109,858, both of which are substantially lower than awards reported from litigation. On the other hand, arbitration typically was both quicker and less expensive than litigation.[50]

> AT&T Mobility charged them $30.22 for a "free" phone.

Several recent U.S. Supreme Court decisions involved arbitration. One of these decisions has made arbitration less functional for consumers by allowing businesses to continue their commonplace practice of requiring arbitration of disputes, while forbidding class actions, thus compelling consumers to individually arbitrate alleged wrongdoing. Vincent and Liza Concepcion complained that AT&T Mobility charged them $30.22 in sales tax and other fees for what was advertised as a "free" phone. They sought class action status for themselves and others, but a 5–4 Supreme Court ruling denied that possibility and left the Concepcions and others similarly aggrieved to file individual claims for very small amounts of money.[51] In another 2019 case, a Lamps Plus employee who had signed an employment arbitration agreement attempted to bring a class action based on a data breach that affected approximately 1,300 employees. The U.S. Supreme Court held that individual arbitration was compelled since the employment arbitration agreement was silent on class actions.[52]

In contrast to these decisions favoring mandatory arbitration, another 2019 opinion held that a truck driver suing his truck company employer could not be forced into arbitration because the Federal Arbitration Act expressly excludes transportation workers' contracts from its coverage.[53] Similarly, in 2022, the Court held that Southwest Airlines baggage handlers could not be compelled to arbitrate their individual employment disputes.[54]

Ending Forced Arbitration of Sexual Assault and Sexual Harassment Act of 2021

Passed by Congress and signed by President Biden in March 2022, the Ending Forced Arbitration of Sexual Assault and Sexual Harassment Act of 2021 amends the Federal Arbitration Act to allow employees who otherwise would be subjected to mandatory arbitration to bring their claims of sexual assault and sexual harassment to court. Source: H.R. 4445, Ending Forced Arbitration of Sexual Assault and Sexual Harassment Act of 2021 (March 3, 2022) **[https://www.congress.gov/bill/117th-congress/house-bill/4445/text]**

The case that follows examines whether a mandatory arbitration clause in a travel agency contract to climb Mount Kilimanjaro was unconscionable under California law.

LEGAL BRIEFCASE

Lhotka v. Geographic Expeditions

181 Cal. App. 4th 816 (Cal. Ct. App. 1st Dist. 2010), *petition for review denied,* 2010 Cal. LEXIS 3320 (April 14, 2010)[55]

Judge Siggins

Geographic Expeditions, Inc. (GeoEx), appeals from an order denying its motion to compel arbitration of a wrongful death action brought by the survivors of one of its clients who died on a Mount Kilimanjaro hiking expedition. . . .

BACKGROUND

Jason Lhotka was 37 years old when he died of an altitude-related illness while on a GeoEx expedition up Mount Kilimanjaro with his mother, plaintiff Sandra Menefee. GeoEx's limitation of liability and release form, which both Lhotka and Menefee signed as a requirement of participating in the expedition, provided that each of them released GeoEx from all liability in connection with the trek and waived any claims for liability "to the maximum extent permitted by law." The release also required that the parties would submit any disputes between themselves first to mediation and then to binding arbitration. It reads: "I understand that all Trip Applications are subject to acceptance by GeoEx in San Francisco, California, USA. I agree that in the unlikely event a dispute of any kind arises between me and GeoEx, the following conditions will apply: (a) the dispute will be submitted to a neutral third-party mediator in San Francisco, California, with both parties splitting equally the cost of such mediator. If the dispute cannot be resolved through mediation, then (b) the dispute will be submitted for binding arbitration to the American Arbitration Association in San Francisco, California; (c) the dispute will be governed by California law; and (d) the maximum amount of recovery to which I will be entitled under any and all circumstances will be the sum of the land and air cost of my trip with GeoEx. I agree that this is a fair and reasonable limitation on the damages, of any sort whatsoever, that I may suffer. I agree to fully indemnify GeoEx for all of its costs (including attorneys' fees) if I commence an action or claim against GeoEx based upon claims I have previously released or waived by signing this release." Menefee paid $16,831 for herself and Lhotka to go on the trip.

A letter from GeoEx president James Sano that accompanied the limitation of liability and release explained that the form was mandatory and that, on this point, "our lawyers, insurance carriers and medical consultants give us no discretion. A signed, unmodified release form is required before any traveler may join one of our trips. Ultimately, we believe that you should choose your travel company based on its track record, not what you are asked to sign. . . . My review of other travel companies' release forms suggests that our forms are not a whole lot different from theirs."

After her son's death, Menefee sued GeoEx for wrongful death and alleged various theories of liability including fraud, gross negligence and recklessness, and intentional infliction of emotional distress. GeoEx moved to compel arbitration.

The trial court found the arbitration provision was unconscionable and on that basis denied the motion.

This appeal timely followed.

DISCUSSION

The question . . . posed here [is] whether the agreement to arbitrate is unconscionable and, therefore, unenforceable.

[I omitted—ed.]

II. *Unconscionability*

(1) We turn first to GeoEx's contention that the court erred when it found the arbitration agreement unconscionable. . . . "[U]nconscionability has generally been recognized to include an absence of meaningful choice on the part of one of the parties together with contract terms which are unreasonably favorable to the other party. Phrased another way, unconscionability has both a 'procedural' and a 'substantive' element." The

procedural element requires oppression or surprise. Oppression occurs where a contract involves lack of negotiation and meaningful choice, surprise where the allegedly unconscionable provision is hidden within a prolix printed form. The substantive element concerns whether a contractual provision reallocates risks in an objectively unreasonable or unexpected manner. Under this approach, both the procedural and substantive elements must be met before a contract or term will be deemed unconscionable. Both, however, need not be present to the same degree. A sliding scale is applied so that 'the more substantively oppressive the contract term, the less evidence of procedural unconscionability is required to come to the conclusion that the term is unenforceable, and vice versa.'" . . .

A. Procedural Unconscionability

. . . GeoEx led plaintiffs to understand not only that its terms and conditions were nonnegotiable, but that plaintiffs would encounter the same requirements with any other travel company. This is a sufficient basis for us to conclude plaintiffs lacked bargaining power.

GeoEx also contends its terms were not oppressive . . . because Menefee and Lhotka could have simply decided not to trek up Mount Kilimanjaro. It argues that contracts for recreational activities can *never* be unconscionably oppressive because, unlike agreements for necessities such as medical care or employment, a consumer of recreational activities *always* has the option of forego-ing [sic] the activity. . . .

(2) While the nonessential nature of recreational activities is a factor to be taken into account in assessing whether a contract is oppressive, it is not necessarily the dispositive factor. . . .

(3) Here, certainly, plaintiffs could have chosen not to sign on with the expedition. That option, like any availability of market alternatives, is relevant to the existence, and degree, of oppression. . . . But we must also consider the other circumstances surrounding the execution of the agreement. . . . GeoEx presented its terms as both nonnegotiable and *no different than what plaintiffs would find with any other provider.* Under these circumstances, plaintiffs made a sufficient showing to establish at least a minimal level of oppression to justify a finding of procedural unconscionability.

B. Substantive Unconscionability

With the "sliding scale" rule firmly in mind, we address whether the substantive unconscionability of the GeoEx contract warrants the trial court's ruling. . . .

The arbitration provision in GeoEx's release is . . . one-sided. . . . It guaranteed that plaintiffs could not possibly obtain anything approaching full recompense for their harm by limiting any recovery they could obtain to the amount they paid GeoEx for their trip. In addition to a limit on their recovery, plaintiffs, residents of Colorado, were required to mediate and arbitrate in San Francisco—all but guaranteeing both that GeoEx would never be out more than the amount plaintiffs had paid for their trip, and that any recovery plaintiffs might obtain would be devoured by the expense they incur in pursing their remedy. The release also required plaintiffs to indemnify GeoEx for its costs and attorney fees for defending any claims covered by the release of liability form. Notably, there is no reciprocal limitation on damages or indemnification obligations imposed on GeoEx. Rather than providing a neutral forum for dispute resolution, GeoEx's arbitration scheme provides a potent disincentive for an aggrieved client to pursue any claim, in any forum—and may well guarantee that GeoEx wins even if it loses. Absent reasonable justification for this arrangement—and none is apparent—we agree with the trial court that the arbitration clause is so one-sided as to be substantively unconscionable.

Affirmed.

Questions

1. Why was the Lhotka/Geographic Expeditions agreement to arbitrate ruled unconscionable?
2. Differentiate procedural and substantive unconscionability.
3. Kalliope and David Valchine entered court-ordered mediation to try to resolve the problems that had led them to seek a divorce. Lawyers represented both Kalliope and David at mediation. The mediation led to a marital settlement agreement between them. One month later, Kalliope sought to set aside the agreement, arguing she had been coerced by her husband, her husband's attorney, and the mediator. Kalliope testified the mediator threatened to report her to the judge for being uncooperative in refusing to sign a reasonable settlement offer. She claimed the mediator also told her she could sign the agreement and then object to its provisions at the final hearing. Should the settlement be set aside? Explain. See *Kalliope Vitakis-Valchine v. David L. Valchine,* 793 So. 2d 1094 (Fla. App. 4th Dist. 2001); and *Vitakis v. Valchine,* 34 So. 3d 17 (Fla. App. 4th Dist. 2010).
4. Is an arbitration clause as a condition of employment a fair method of alternate dispute resolution, if entered knowingly and voluntarily? Explain.
5. In an effort to reduce legal expenses, some major banks and other businesses follow policies providing that all customer complaints will be subject to arbitration. Is mandatory arbitration fair to consumers? Explain.

Research Exercise

Go to "Legal Climate: Overall Rankings by State" from the U.S. Chamber of Commerce Institute for Legal Reform (ILR) at **www.instituteforlegalreform.com/states.** Click on your state and scroll down to "All Results." Scan some of the articles discussing legal issues facing your state. Choose one and research the issue discussed. Look for counterarguments to the opinions appearing in your article. If the article discusses a lawsuit or legislation, be sure to determine what its current status is.

Chapter Questions

1. In their 2017 book *Rebooting Justice: More Technology, Fewer Lawyers, and the Future of the Law,* Benjamin H. Barton and Stephanios Bibas suggest that more technology, including online dispute resolution (ODR) and in-court help kiosks, will effectively provide access to justice. Comment. See Andie Linker, "Rebooting Justice: Another Take," *Relativity* September 18, 2019 [**www.relativity.com**].
2. The National Registry of Exonerations, a joint project of the University of California Irvine Center for Science and Society, University of Michigan Law School, and Michigan State University College of Law, shows that from January 1989 through February 2, 2020, 2,549 convicted individuals have been exonerated. In a February 2019 study, out of 2400 exonerations, 291, or 12 percent, had falsely confessed. Of those, 76 were under 18 years old at the time of the crime, and 102 were reported as having either a mental illness or intellectual disability.[56]
   a. The U.S. prison population has been estimated at somewhat above 2 million, generally viewed as the highest number of incarcerations in the world. In your opinion, what may the number of exonerations recorded in the National Registry of Exonerations compared to the U.S. prison population show about the U.S. criminal justice system? Explain.
   b. Data from the National Registry of Exonerations show that 59 percent of exonerations involved perjury or false accusations and 54 percent involved official misconduct. What conclusions might be drawn from this data? Explain.
3. The 17-year-old employee of an auto repair shop in Iowa was severely injured when a tire he was inflating on a customer's trailer exploded. The tire manufacturer is located in China but sold thousands of tires in Iowa through an American distributor. The injured employee's mother brought a product-liability claim on behalf of her son against the Chinese tire manufacturer in an Iowa state court. Can the court exercise jurisdiction over the Chinese tire manufacturer? Explain. See *Book v. Doublestar Dongfeng Tyre Co.,* 860 N.W.2d 576 (Iowa 2015).
4. Instead of sentencing five teenagers who defaced a historic Black schoolhouse with swastikas and the words "white power" and "Black power" to community service, a Virginia judge ordered that they each read from a list of books that included "Night" by Elie Wiesel, "I Know Why the Caged Bird Sings" by Maya Angelous, or "The Crucible" by Arthur Miller, and write essays.[57] What do you think about this sentence? Explain.
5. In 2013, Megan Thode, a former graduate student, sought $1.3 million in damages from Lehigh University for receiving a C+ in a class in which a B or above was needed to enroll in the next required course toward her goal of becoming a licensed professional

counselor. Thode's complaint was based on claims of breach of contract and sexual discrimination. The trial judge ruled for the defendant, Lehigh University.[58]

a. If you were the trial judge, what information would you expect to be presented at trial? Explain.

b. What could be the impact of Thode's lawsuit on student-professor relations and grading in college? Explain.

6. The California Medical Injury Compensation Reform Act (MICRA) of 1975 capped noneconomic damages such as pain and suffering at $250,000; as of this writing, the cap has never been adjusted for inflation, with a 2015 California appellate court concluding that raising the MICRA cap was a legislative matter. Such award caps have been criticized as limiting those injured from seeking legal redress, as most attorneys representing plaintiffs in medical malpractice actions work on a contingency basis. Further, plaintiffs with permanent injuries will be able to collect no more for their pain and suffering than those who will recover fully.[59]

   A 2014 California ballot measure that would have raised the MICRA cap to $1.1 million was defeated. However, at this writing, another California ballot measure has been filed for the November 2020 elections.[60]

   What are the advantages and disadvantages of limiting damages in medical malpractice suits? Explain.

7. Consider the issue of access to justice discussed in this chapter.

   a. Should the rich be entitled to better legal representation, just as they have access to better food, better medical care, better education, and so on? Explain.

   b. Should we employ a nationwide legal services program sufficient to guarantee competent legal aid to all? Explain.

8. When a Santa Clara County judge sentenced Brock Turner, a Stanford swimmer, to six months in jail for three felony counts of sexual assault, public outrage led to a successful "grass-roots" movement to remove the judge for sentencing Turner too leniently. The Santa Clara County District Attorney voiced concern that the problem was "not the judge but the law." One observer commented that the judge's recall will make the "politics of punishment" worse.[61]

   a. Do you understand these concerns? Explain.

   b. When should a judge be recalled? Explain.

9. Former workers and families of former workers of Mercedes-Benz Argentina (MBA), a subsidiary of the German corporation Daimler AG, brought a claim under the Alien Tort Claims Act and the Torture Victims Protection Act alleging that MBA had assisted the Argentine government in violating human rights in Argentina. The lawsuit against Daimler AG was brought in California. The plaintiffs argued that Daimler AG could be sued in California for the acts of its MBA subsidiary because another of its subsidiaries, Mercedes-Benz USA, operated in California. Does the California court have jurisdiction over Daimler AG in this case? Explain. See *Daimler AG v. Bauman,* 134 S. Ct. 746 (2014).

10. In 1982, a security guard was murdered during a robbery of a south Chicago McDonald's. Alton Logan was sentenced to life in prison for that murder. At the same

time, two Chicago public defenders, Dale Coventry and Jamie Kunz, were representing Andrew Wilson, who was accused of murdering two police officers. Based on a tip, Coventry and Kunz suspected that Wilson was the actual murderer in the McDonald's case. They questioned Wilson, who admitted that he, not Logan, was the murderer. Because of their duties under the attorney–client privilege, Coventry and Kunz felt they could not reveal what they knew. Logan, therefore, went to prison an innocent man, they believed. The public defenders decided to write the story in a notarized affidavit and lock it in a box in case something should happen that would allow them to reveal what they knew. When Wilson died of natural causes in 2008 in prison, Coventry and Kunz revealed their client's confession. After 26 years, Logan was released from prison. He was granted a certificate of innocence; in 2013, the city of Chicago agreed to pay Logan $10.25 million.[62]

a. Why does the legal profession expect lawyers to keep secret their clients' confidential communications?

b. Had you been Coventry and Kunz, would you have revealed what you knew in order to immediately secure justice for Logan? Explain.

11. On July 5, 1884, four sailors were cast away from their ship in a storm 1,600 miles from the Cape of Good Hope. Their lifeboat contained neither water nor much food. On the 20th day of their ordeal, Dudley and Stevens, without the assistance or agreement of Brooks, cut the throat of the fourth sailor, a 17- or 18-year-old boy. They had not eaten since day 12. Water had been available only occasionally. At the time of the death, the men were probably about 1,000 miles from land. Prior to his death, the boy was lying helplessly in the bottom of the boat. The three surviving sailors ate the boy's remains for four days, at which point they were rescued by a passing boat. They were in a seriously weakened condition.

    a. Were Dudley and Stevens guilty of murder? Explain.

    b. Should Brooks have been charged with a crime for eating the boy's flesh? Explain. See *The Queen v. Dudley and Stephens,* 14 Queen's Bench Division 273 (1884).

12. Tompkins was a citizen of Pennsylvania. While walking on a railroad footpath in that state, he was struck by an object protruding from a passing freight train owned by the Erie Railroad Company, a New York corporation. Tompkins, by virtue of diversity of citizenship, filed a negligence suit against Erie in a New York federal court. Erie argued for the application of Pennsylvania common law, in which case Tompkins would have been treated as a trespasser. Tompkins argued that the absence of a Pennsylvania statute addressing the topic meant that federal common law had to be applied to the case. Should the federal court apply the relevant Pennsylvania state law, or should the court be free to exercise its independent judgment about what the common law of the state is or should be? See *Erie Railroad v. Tompkins,* 304 U.S. 64 (1938).

13. When their 30-year-old son refused to move out of their house, a couple went to court for an eviction order. The son fought the order, arguing that as a family member he was entitled to six months' notice before being evicted. The judge asked the parents' lawyer to write an eviction order for his signature that would include a reasonable time for the son to leave the house.[63] Should courts get involved in such disputes? Explain.

14. Boschetto, a California resident, bought a 1964 Ford Galaxie 500XL advertised on eBay from Hansing, a Wisconsin resident. Hansing said the car was in excellent condition, including an "R code" classification. After delivery to California, Boschetto discovered many problems, including the fact that the car was not an "R code." The parties could not reach an out-of-court settlement, so Boschetto sued Hansing in California. Hansing moved for dismissal of the claim on the grounds of lack of personal jurisdiction. Does the fact that the transaction was conducted via eBay satisfy the jurisdictional requirement? Explain. See *Boschetto v. Hansing,* 539 F.3d 1011 (9th Cir. 2008), *cert. denied,* 129 S. Ct. 1318 (2009).
15. A boy was seriously injured when his friend with whom he was playing golf struck him with a golf club as the friend made practice swings. In the resulting personal injury lawsuit based on negligence, the defendant called Robert Boldus, a golf professional at another local golf course, as an expert witness, asking him whether "as a golf professional," he had "formed any opinions as to what had happened in this case?" Boldus testified that he believed it was an accident, and that the defendant had not violated standards of care. Questioned by the plaintiff, Boldus also testified that he did not have any training in evaluating liability or standards of care required in golf liability cases. Should Boldus have been allowed to testify as an expert witness? Explain. See *Nickles v. Schild,* 617 N.W.2d 659 (S.D. 2000).
16. Judicial reform advocates often argue that the United States should adopt the English rule providing that the losing party in a lawsuit must pay the reasonable litigation expenses of the winner.[64]

    a. In brief, what are the strengths and weaknesses of the English rule?

    b. Would you favor it? Explain.
17. Plaintiff Jonathan Gold was hired to work at defendant Deutsche Bank after completing his MBA degree at New York University. Before beginning employment, Gold signed various documents, including Form U-4, that the National Association of Securities Dealers (NASD) required all registered representatives to sign. Form U-4 provided for arbitration for all employment disputes. Gold was fired after working about one year. He then filed suit claiming sexual harassment based on his sexual orientation. Deutsche Bank moved to compel arbitration. Gold resisted arbitration, arguing, among other things, that Form U-4 was too difficult to understand and that it raised questions in his mind. Gold also showed that Deutsche Bank certified that it provided Gold with the relevant NASD rules when it had not. Was Gold required to submit his claim to arbitration? Explain. See *Gold v. Deutsche Aktiengesellschaft,* 365 F.3d 144 (2d Cir. 2004), *cert. denied,* 543 U.S. 874 (2004).

Notes

1. "The Importance of Law to the Private Enterprise System," *The Legal Studies in Business Task Force Report* (1998), reprinted in *American Business Law Journal* 36, no. 1 (Fall 1998), p. xv.
2. Ibid.
3. *The World Justice Project: Rule of Law Index 2019 Insights* [**https://worldjusticeproject.org**].
4. Ibid.

5. Avianne Tan, "Walk 30 Miles or Do Jail Time, Judge Tells Ohio Teen Who Didn't Pay Cab Fare," *ABC News,* June 2, 2015 [**http://abcnews.go.com**].
6. *Orlando Sentinel,* "More U.S. Judges Impose Creative Punishments," *Des Moines Register,* October 29, 2010, p. 10A.
7. Brent Kendall, "Why Supreme Court Cases Are Marathons," *The Wall Street Journal,* December 1, 2014 [**www.wsj.com**].
8. See, for example, Jeffrey Toobin, "Merrick Garland and the Politics of the Supreme Court," *The New Yorker,* March 28, 2016 [**www.newyorker.com/magazine**]; and Leigh Ann Caldwell, "Democrats Make their Stand at the Kavanaugh Confirmation Hearing," *nbcnews.com,* September 4, 2018 [**https://techcrunch.com**].
9. David A. Kaplan, "What's the Point of the Supreme Court?," *The New York Times,* September 5, 2018 [**www.nytimes.com**].
10. "Man in the Middle: The Supreme Court," *The Economist,* May 6, 2017 [**www.economist.com**].
11. John C. Henry, "Do You Know Who Works Here? They Can Change Your Life," *AARP. Bulletin,* November 2010, p. 26.
12. Editorial, "Our Constitutional Court," *The New York Times,* November 22, 2010 [**www.nytimes.com**].
13. Ethan Bronner, "A Dissent by Scalia Is Criticized as Political," *The New York Times,* June 27, 2012 [**www.nytimes.com**].
14. Adam Litpak and Allison Kopicki, "Approval Rating for Justices Hits Just 44% in New Poll," *The New York Times,* June 7, 2012 [**www.nytimes.com**].
15. Lincoln Caplan, "A Judge's Warning about the Legitimacy of the Supreme Court," *The New York Times,* September 26, 2010 [**www.nytimes.com**].
16. Editorial, "Case Against Oxy Hits Home," *Los Angeles Times* December 10, 2010 [**www.latimes.com**].
17. *Carijano v. Occidental Petroleum,* 626 F.3d 1137 (9th Cir. 2010).
18. *Occidental Petroleum v. Carijano,* 133 S. Ct. 1996 (2013).
19. Associated Press, "Occidental Petroleum Settles Peru Pollution Case," *Los Angeles Times,* March 5, 2015 [**www.latimes.com**].
20. Robins v. Spokeo, 136 S. Ct. 1540 (2016).
21. *Wal-Mart Stores v. Dukes,* 564 U.S. 338 (2011).
22. *Phipps v. Wal-Mart,* 792 F.3d 637 (6th Cir. 2015), *cert. denied,* 136 S. Ct. 1163 (2016).
23. Al Norman, "Sex Discrimination Wal-Mart: The 'Bitches' Story That Won't Go Away," *HuffPost,* July 20, 2016 [**www.huffpost.com**].
24. Jerry Iannelli, "Nearly 100 Women Sue Walmart for Gender-Pay Discrimination in Miami Court, *Miami New Times,* February 7, 2019 [**www.maiminewtimes.com**]; and Chavie Lieber, "Walmart just got hit with a major gender discrimination lawsuit," *Vox,* February 15, 2019 [**www.vox.com**].
25. 2022 figures were taken from "Number of lawyers in the United *States,*" *Statista,* August 16, 2022 [**www.statista.com**].
26. Neil Vigdor, "U.S. Population Makes Fewest Gains in Decades, Census Bureau Says," *The New York Times,* December 30, 2019 [**www.nytimes.com**]; United States Census Bureau, *U.S. and World Population Clock,* checked December 5, 2022 [**https://www.census.gov/popclock/**]
27. Steven J. Harper, "The Tyranny of the Billable Hour," *The New York Times,* March 28, 2013 [**www.nytimes.com**].

28. Peter Latiman, "Settling Fee Dispute, Law Firm Denounces 'Email Humor,'" *DealBook,* April 17, 2013 [**http://dealbook.nytimes.com**].
29. Philip K. Howard, "How Modern Law Makes Us Powerless," *The Wall Street Journal,* January 26, 2009 [**www.wsj.com**].
30. Lyric Wallwork Winik, "Are There Too Many Lawyers?" *Parade,* September 14, 2008, p. 9.
31. The study was commissioned by the Legal Services Corporation, the largest funder of low-income civil legal aid in the U.S. "The Justice Gap: Measuring the Unmet Civil Legal Needs of Low-income Americans," *Legal Services Corporation,* June 2017 [**www.lsc.gov**].
32. Milton Bordwin, "Your Company and the Law," *Management Review,* January 2000, p. 58.
33. People's Life, "Changes in the Number of Lawyers in Japan: 1950-2018," *Hatena Blog,* February 23, 2019 [**http://nbakki.hatenablog.com**].
34. Majirox News, "Too Many Lawyers in Japan, Says Ministry of Internal Affairs," April 23, 2012 [**www.majirrox.news.com**]; and Mitsuru Obe, "Japanese Lawyers' Problem: Too Few Cases," *The Wall Street Journal,* April 3, 2016 [**www.wsj.com**].
35. Website, DoNotPay App, **https://donotpay.com/**
36. Padraig Belton, "Would you let a robot lawyer Defend you?" *BBC News,* August 15, 2021 [**https://www.bbc.com**].
37. Diane Robinson and Sarah Gibson, "Pandemic Caseload Highlights; Court filings and dispositions, 2019-2020, *Court Statistics Project,* March 22, 2021, [**http://www.courtstatistics.org/**].
38. Court Statistics Project, "State Court Caseload Digest: 2017 Data, *National Center for State Courts,* accessed July 2020 [**www.courtstatistics.org**].
39. John T. Broderick Jr. and Ronald M. George, "A Nation of Do-It-Yourself Lawyers," *The New York Times,* January 2, 2010 [**www.nytimes.com**].
40. Binyamin Appelbaum, "Investors Put Money on Lawsuits to Get Payouts," *The New York Times,* November 14, 2010 [**www.nytimes.com**].
41. Jennifer Smith, "Lawsuit Investors Gain in U.S.," *The Wall Street Journal,* January 13, 2014, p. B7; and Matthew Goldstein and Jessica Silver-Greenberg, "Hedge Funds Pour Cash Into Lending for Lawsuits, *The New York Times,* June 26, 2018 [**www.nytimes.com**].
42. Jennifer Smith, "Lawsuit Investors Gain in U.S.," *The Wall Street Journal,* January 13, 2014, p. B7 [**www.wsj.com**].
43. Binyamin Appelbaum, "Lawsuit Loans Add New Risk for the Injured," *The New York Times,* January 16, 2011 [**www.nytimes.com**].
44. Mike Rosen, "Testing Civil Gideon," *California Lawyer,* June 2012 [**www.callawyer.com**].
45. See "Small Claims Court FAQ," NOLO [**www.nolo.com**].
46. See **www.cybersettle.com**.
47. Vanessa O'Connell, "At GE, Robo-Lawyers," *The Wall Street Journal*, October 10, 2011 [**www.wsj.com**].
48. 9 U.S.C. Sec. 1-16.
49. "Arbitration: Increasingly, It's Not Over Until the Vacatur Motion Fails," *The Wall Street Journal*, February 14, 2011 [**http://blogs.wsj.com**].
50. Alexander J. S. Colvin, "An Empirical Study of Employment Arbitration: Case Outcomes and Processes," *Journal of Empirical Legal Studies* 8, Issue 1 (March 2011), p. 1.
51. *AT&T Mobility v. Vincent Concepcion,* 131 S. Ct. 1740 (2011).
52. *Lamp Plus, Inc. v. Varela,* 139 S. Ct. 1407 (2019).

53. *New Prime v. Oliveira,* 139 S.Ct. 532 (2019).

54. Jan Wolfe, and Jess Bravin, "Supreme Court Rejects Forced Arbitration for Southwest Airlines Baggage Handlers," *The Wall Street Journal,* June 6, 2022 [**https://www.wsj.com/**].

55. See related proceedings: *Geographic Expeditions, Inc. v. Lhotka,* 2010 U.S. LEXIS 6305 (October 4, 2010).

56. National Registry of Exonerations, University of California Irvine Center for Science and Society, University of Michigan Law School, and Michigan State University College of Law [**www.law.umich.edu**].

57. Christine Hauser, "In Virginia, Vandals Finish Their Sentence. They Were Told to Read Books," *The New York Times,* April 6, 2018 [**www.nytimes.com**].

58. Carolyn Foster Segal, "The Curious Case of Megan Thode," *Inside Higher Ed,* February 19, 2013 [**www.insidehighered.com**].

59. Nora Freeman Engstrom and Robert L. Rabin, "Limiting Damages Limits Justice," *Los Angeles Times,* August 13, 2013, p. A11; and *Chan v. Curran,* 237 Cal. App. 4th 601 (Cal. Ct. App. 1st Dist. 2015).

60. "Families of Injured Patients File California Ballot Measure to Raise MICRA," *Insurance Journal,* September 26, 2019 [**www.insurancejournal.com**].

61. Jose A. Del Real, "Attempt to Recall Judge Has Detractors," *The New York Times,* February 3, 2018 [**www.nytimes.com**]; and John Pfaff, "California Ousts an Elected Judge. Everybody Loses," *The Washington Post,* June 13, 2018 [**www.washingtonpost.com**].

62. Associated Press, "Illinois Man Imprisoned for 26 Years Declared Innocent," *Springfield State Journal-Register,* April 17, 2009 [**www.sj-r.com**]; Fran Speilman, "Chicago to Pay $10.25 Million in Another Burge Case," *Chicago Sun-Times,* January 14, 2013 [**www.suntimes.com**]; and "26-Year Secret Kept Innocent Man in Prison," *60 Minutes,* March 8, 2008 [**http://truthinjustice.org/alton-logan.htm**].

63. Marwa Eltagouri, "A 30-year-old demanded notice for eviction from his parents' house. 'Outrageous,' a Judge Said," *The Washington Post,* May 23, 2018 [**www.washingtonpost.com**].

64. "Loser Pays, Everyone Wins," *The Wall Street Journal,* December 15, 2010 [**www.wsj.com**].

CHAPTER FIVE

Constitutional Law and the Bill of Rights

After completing this chapter, students will be able to fulfill the following learning objectives:

5-1. Recognize the purposes of the U.S. Constitution.

5-2. Describe the separation of powers under the U.S. Constitution.

5-3. Discuss the powerful role the Bill of Rights plays in protecting personal freedoms.

5-4. Identify the freedoms protected under the First Amendment.

5-5. Discuss the differences between First Amendment protections of commercial speech and political speech.

5-6. Describe some of the issues arising under the Fourth Amendment "search and seizure" rules.

5-7. Explain the "exclusionary rule."

5-8. Describe the law of the Fifth Amendment "Takings Clause" and the property rights controversy associated with it.

5-9. Compare and contrast substantive due process and procedural due process.

5-10. Identify some examples of the impact of the Equal Protection Clause on business and society.

Part One—Our Constitution

> *We the People of the United States, in Order to form a more perfect Union, establish Justice, insure domestic Tranquility, provide for the common defence, promote the general Welfare, and secure the Blessings of Liberty to ourselves and our Posterity, do ordain and establish this Constitution for the United States of America.*

The Preamble to the U.S. Constitution is inspiring in its expression of the founders' idealistic goals for America. In reading it, we should reflect on the Constitution's role in molding and protecting an entirely new image of a nation. That we continue to be guided by this remarkable document more than 235 years later is testimony not only to the brilliance and wisdom of its creators, but also to Americans' determination to build a free, democratic, and just society. Extraordinarily powerful in its ideas and images, it has helped shape the entire world. (See the Constitution in Appendix A at the back of this text.)

Creating a Constitution—The United States

You may recall that the Constitution grew out of the 1778 Articles of Confederation. The Revolutionary War had basically bankrupted the colonies. Currency was largely worthless, and the 13 new states fought over economic resources. Interstate disputes were routine, and the federal union that emerged under the Articles of Confederation had little real authority. As a result of this turmoil, and in an effort to strengthen the Articles, the Constitutional Convention convened in Philadelphia on May 25, 1787.

In the hot Philadelphia summer, with windows and curtains closed to assure secrecy and thereby encourage open debate, the often stout and usually heavily clothed delegates sweated their way toward a new government. All 55 delegates, our Founding Fathers, were white males, and most of them were wealthy landowners, but they were also immensely talented with a wide range of interests and experiences.

All 55 delegates, our Founding Fathers, were white males, and most of them were wealthy landowners.

The delegates agreed that a stronger central government was needed, but they were split on how far that notion should go. Virginia, led by the brilliant James Madison, favored a dominant central government with greatly diminished state authority. Alexander Hamilton (the subject of an acclaimed Broadway musical) wanted to go further yet. Among other things, he wanted to institute the presidency as a lifetime office. On the other hand, several states led by New Jersey wanted to retain strong states' rights. After weeks of debate, a middle ground began to emerge, one that eventually led to our current balance of power between all of the states, big and small, and between the states and the federal government. In the end, the delegates reached consensus on a constitution that guaranteed the revolutionary notion of rule by the people.

On September 17, 1787, the U.S. Constitution was formally signed. Following bitter disputes in some states, the Constitution was ratified, and the new government haltingly moved forward under the leadership of George Washington and John Adams.[1] [For links to national constitutions around the globe, see **https://constituteproject.org**.]

A Right to Bear Arms

Addressing one of the most contentious questions in American constitutional history, the U.S. Supreme Court, in its 2008 *District of Columbia v. Heller* decision, ruled 5–4 that the Second Amendment guarantees individual Americans a fundamental, but not unlimited, right to bear arms.[2] The Supreme Court's four conservative justices, joined by the more moderate Justice Kennedy, ruled that individuals have a constitutional right to keep loaded arms for self-defense, at least in the home. The majority view was based on its reading of the historical record associated with the Second Amendment, while the four dissenting liberal justices argued that the Second Amendment guaranteed only a collective right to bear arms in a militia.

The decision struck down a District of Columbia law that effectively banned handgun possession. Security guard Dick Heller applied for, and was denied, a permit for a handgun in his home located in a dangerous Washington, D.C., neighborhood. He sued the District, arguing that the gun ban violated his individual rights under the Second Amendment.

The Court's *Heller* ruling did preserve the constitutionality of "reasonable" gun regulations. Justice Scalia, writing for the majority, said that nothing in the ruling should "cast doubt on long-standing prohibitions on the possession of firearms by felons or the mentally ill, or laws forbidding the carrying of firearms in sensitive places such as schools and government buildings, or laws imposing conditions and qualifications on the commercial sale of arms." "Dangerous and unusual" weapons could also be banned.

In its 2010 *McDonald v. Chicago* decision,[3] the Supreme Court threw out a Chicago handgun restraint and thereby extended its *Heller* reasoning– which had applied only to federal jurisdictions– to state and city jurisdictions as well. According to an article by *The New York Times* in 2015, however, of the more than one thousand Second Amendment challenges to gun regulations that were subsequently raised, 93 percent of the decisions upheld the regulations.[4] Gun rights challenges failed, for example, when the Supreme Court declined in 2016 to review lower court decisions upholding New York and Connecticut state laws banning semiautomatic assault weapons and high-capacity magazines. Yet a national law that would ban assault weapons, like the one used in the Orlando, Florida, mass shooting in a nightclub in 2016, expired in 2004, and Congress has subsequently rejected federal gun restrictions. (On June 25, 2022, however, President Biden did sign into law the first major federal gun safety legislation in decades: the Bipartisan Safer Communities Act, Pub. Law 117-159).

According to a 2013 Rasmussen Poll, 74 percent of Americans supported the right to own a gun.[5] By 2016, however, nearly two-thirds of those polled said they wanted the next president to push for stricter gun laws,[6] and the Pew Research Center in 2019 found an increasing trend in the number of Americans favoring stricter gun control.[7] This correlates with the increase in mass shootings in the United States. According to the Gun Violence Archive, which has been tracking data since 2014, the most mass shootings on record in the United States. (690) took place in 2021, followed by the second-highest number (648) in 2022.[8]

Questions

1. As you interpret the Second Amendment, did the Supreme Court reach a *correct* decision in the *Heller* case? Explain.
2. The United States, which has the highest rate of private gun ownership among developed nations, likewise leads in gun deaths, with about 30 homicides per one million people in 2014. Switzerland had the next highest rate of about 7.7 homicides per one million people.[9] As a matter of public policy, did the Supreme Court reach a *wise* decision in the *Heller* case? Explain.
3. "When May I Shoot a Student?" was a Boise State University professor's satirical query of the Idaho state legislature just prior to its decision to permit guns on Idaho campuses.[10] At the time, eight states specifically permitted the concealed carrying of weapons on campus by students. What are your thoughts about students and faculty members carrying guns on your campus?

Structure and Purpose

LO 5-1
Recognize the purposes of the U.S. Constitution.

The Preamble to the U.S. Constitution identifies certain goals for our society, such as unity among the various states, justice, domestic tranquility (peace), defense from outsiders, the general welfare, and liberty. Articles I, II, and III then establish the three separate branches of government. Specifically, Article I creates Congress and enumerates its powers, while Article II sets up the executive branch, headed by the president. Article III provides for a federal court system.

Articles IV and VI, along with the 14th Amendment, address the relationship between the federal government and the states. Article VI, Clause 2 (the Supremacy Clause), for example, makes clear that federal law takes precedence over state law.

Article V comprises various amendments to the Constitution. The first ten amendments, known as the Bill of Rights, were ratified by the states and took effect in 1791. The remaining 17 amendments (11 through 27) were adopted at various times between 1798 and 1992.

From this brief overview, we see a number of the Constitution's broad purposes:

1. It establishes a national government.
2. It controls the relationship between the national and state governments.
3. Its provisions enable the federal government to carry out its functions.
4. It defines and preserves personal liberty.[11]

Government Power and Constitutional Restraints

The Constitution was designed to protect citizens from the government. Notably, it does not protect them from purely private concentrations of power, such as large corporations. In fact, corporations themselves are often entitled to the protections of the Constitution. (Remember the *Citizens United* discussion in Chapter 3.)

The Constitution divides power between the federal and state governments. This is done, in part, by formally limiting the federal government in Article I, Section 8 to certain *enumerated* (or specified) *powers.* For example, Article I, Section 8, Clause 3 grants Congress the authority to regulate commerce (the Commerce Clause). The 10th Amendment makes clear that all power not expressly granted to the federal government remains with the states or with the people. In addition, certain constitutional checks or restraints, including the Bill of Rights, limit Congress's reach even within the scope of its enumerated powers.

> "This Constitution, and the Laws of the United States . . . shall be the Supreme Law of the Land. . .."

Those enumerated powers have been expansively interpreted, however, giving Congress extensive authority over American life. Furthermore, in the landmark Supreme Court decision *McCulloch v. Maryland,*[12] the U.S. Supreme Court interpreted the Necessary and Proper Clause (Article I, Section 8, Clause 18) to afford Congress the *implied* powers necessary to execute its enumerated powers, thus permitting a workable national government. The *McCulloch* Court also ruled that the Constitution's Supremacy Clause (Article VI, Clause 2: "This Constitution, and the Laws of the United States . . . shall be the Supreme Law of the Land. . .") nullifies state action to the extent that it conflicts with federal law. Thus, in one sweeping decision, the Supreme Court dramatically expanded congressional power, making the federal government's authority superior to that of the states.

Too Much Government?

Has federal power and regulation gone too far? The Tea Party movement emerged in 2009, and a heated national debate ensued about the appropriate balance between individual rights, as expressed in the free market, and an interventionist federal government designed to correct market failures and protect those least able to care for themselves. Donald Trump's 2016 presidential victory, along with Republican Party dominance at both the federal and state level, may have signaled widespread voter frustration with the size of government or its ineffectiveness, or both. After President Trump took office, however, the core issue of the Tea Party–the size of the national debt–no longer generated the same intensity, even though Congress suspended the federal debt limit until after the 2020 elections and the national debt grew by more than $2 trillion.[13] Although the Tea Party is seemingly defunct, the size of the U.S. government and its proper role in American life are still important topics of political debate. [For more on the national debt, see Drew Desilver, "5 facts about the national debt," *Pew Research Center,* July 24, 2019 [**www.pewresearch.org**].]

The "Tea Party" movement emerged in 2009, and a heated national debate ensued.

Separation of Powers

LO 5-2 Describe the separation of powers under the U.S. Constitution.

As a further means of controlling power, the Constitution establishes three separate branches of federal government and a system of checks and balances. Specialized areas of authority are reserved to the president, Congress, and the courts. For instance, the president executes laws, negotiates treaties, and commands the armed forces. The Supreme Court and the inferior courts wield the power of judicial review, and Congress alone has the power to legislate and to declare war.

President Obama was harshly criticized for some of his executive orders, which his critics saw as an unconstitutional form of legislation issued by the executive branch. In one case, he sought to shield millions of undocumented immigrants from deportation. President Trump was likewise criticized for declaring a national emergency that allowed him to divert military funds to build a border wall between the United States and Mexico, for which Congress had denied funding. He was also criticized for launching an airstrike on Baghdad International Airport without first notifying Congress. The attack killed Qassem Soleimani, a top Iranian general and commander of Iran's elite special operations force, and it underscored the inherent tension between the president's role as Commander-in-Chief of the military and Congress's power to declare war.

The role of the judiciary has been a matter of particular controversy in recent years. The historic 1803 *Marbury v. Madison* decision[14] was the first time the Supreme Court declared an act of Congress unconstitutional. The decision also established the principle of judicial review: the power of the courts to consider and, if necessary, invalidate congressional and executive branch decisions. Although neither of those powers was expressly provided for in the Constitution, the Court considered them implicit in the legal structure it created. Critics today argue that the *Marbury* reasoning has been stretched too far and that courts, in effect, have been making law rather than merely interpreting it. Some critics say, for example, that federal and state judicial decisions that found, over the years, a "constitutional right" to abortion or same-sex marriage reduced the authority of our directly elected legislators and placed too much power in the hands of appointed jurists. Similarly, more recent critics claim that "a supermajority of six conservative judges" on the U.S. Supreme Court "have thrust themselves into American politics" and have "crammed decades of conservative social policy into the last three days of its term in June [2022]."[15] Others note, however, that an aggressive judiciary has historically played a crucial role in the advancement of justice and in the protection of personal freedom. [For the National Constitution Center, see **www.constitutioncenter.org**.]

Questions

1. As noted, the Constitution does not expressly authorize judicial review. Should we assume, therefore, that the framers of the Constitution did not intend to afford that power to the courts? Explain.
2. In your view, do the courts have too much power in our lives? Explain.

Federalism

The U.S. government is built on *federalism* principles; that is, the Constitution provides for shared power among national and state governments. A primary role of the Constitution is to create a balance between a central federal authority and dispersed state power. The American Civil War, driven as it was by slavery, was also provoked, in part, by differing conceptions of federalism. Southerners, in favor of *states' rights,* held the view that each state was entitled to make its own policy decisions about crucial matters like slavery, while Northerners favored a strong central government. That constitutional divide over federalism persists today. Many "conservative" Americans distrust big government and favor bringing power closer to the people. They think the federal government has often exercised authority beyond its express constitutional powers. "Liberals," on the other hand, tend to fear local biases and favor a more unified national approach to issues such as the regulation of business, education policy, medical care, and civil rights.

The Constitution and the New Federalism

Throughout American history, and especially during the Great Depression, federal power has grown, and state authority has receded. Republican Presidents Nixon and Reagan, however, took particular policy steps to revive state power. Similarly, after decades of interpreting the Constitution in a flexible, expansive manner that accorded great power to the federal government, the Supreme Court revisited the federal–state relationship in the mid-1990s, with some decisions curbing federal authority. No major federal initiative was struck down, but the Court signaled legislators and lower courts to look more closely at the federal–state balance of power.

> A long history of discrimination in voting practices against minorities

These new federalism views expressed themselves in the landmark 2013 U.S. Supreme Court decision, *Shelby County v. Holder,*[16] which examined the constitutionality of the federal Voting Rights Act of 1965. Among other things, the act subjected nine mostly southern states, as well as selected counties in other states, to federal supervision of their election processes because of a long history of discrimination against minorities in voting practices. Those states often gerrymandered election districts and imposed "voter integrity" rules (such as literacy tests, character standards, and onerous identification requirements) that were purportedly designed to assure honesty in elections but, in fact, sought to exclude minorities from voting.

Under the 1965 act, any change to voting rules in the covered states required "preclearance" from the federal government. Decades later, Shelby County, Alabama, challenged the Voting Rights Act, claiming that in reauthorizing the act in 2006, Congress exceeded its constitutional authority and violated state and local rights. By a 5-4 vote, divided on familiar conservative-liberal grounds, the Supreme Court ruled for Shelby County. It held that Section 4(b) of the Voting Rights Act, which determined the jurisdictions in which voting practices were tainted by discrimination and thus required preclearance, was based on 40-year-old discrimination data and did not necessarily speak to current conditions.

The Supreme Court acknowledged the effectiveness of the act in reducing voting discrimination but said that discriminatory practices, and the states that use them, have changed over time, requiring Congress to keep the law up to date. The act and its supporting data can be revisited, of course, but given Congress's current fractures, analysts do not expect quick action.

Texas and a number of other states rushed to enforce or enact new restrictions on voting following the *Shelby County* decision. The Texas law, ostensibly designed to prevent fraud, required presentation of a driver's license, a passport, or another approved form of photo identification prior to voting. The act was challenged in court on the grounds that its requirements were too burdensome and too expensive for those lacking such identification. The Fifth Circuit Court of Appeals ruled that the Texas law violated the Voting Rights Act,[17] and Texas agreed to modify its law for the November 2016 election.

As of 2016, fifteen states had enacted tighter voter fraud laws, even though in-person voter fraud is quite rare, and at least six of those state laws were either blocked or softened by court order. In the lead up to another presidential election year, there was a surge in legislation cutting back voter access. As of 2019, new voting restrictions had been enacted in 25 states (including Texas, Florida, and Tennessee), while other states (particularly New York, Nevada, and Colorado) enacted impactful, expansive voting laws. [For an archive of voting laws by year, see **www.brennancenter.org.**]

Immigration policy presents a conflict much like voting rights. Comprehensive, uniform federal immigration control is often at odds with state rules that address the specific needs and political preferences of those individual states. Do we need a consistent national immigration policy, or should we allow for more state-by-state preferences? The Constitution gives Congress the power to "establish a uniform Rule of Naturalization" in Article 1, Section 8.

What if a state's particular preference on an issue ultimately results in setting stricter compliance standards for an entire industry nationwide? When a state like California, known for its aggressive rules on workplace safety, consumer protection, and environmental quality, imposes new restrictions, the business community may fight back in Washington, D.C. Rather than working with an inefficient patchwork of rules differing from state to state or having to accommodate the strict preferences of a particular state, the business community may seek comprehensive federal laws applying to all states, thus preempting California's particular measures. For instance, in 2019, the Trump Administration took action to roll back California's aggressive automobile emissions standards. California responded by filing a lawsuit, joined by 22 other states, challenging that action. However, four major automobile manufacturers surprised many by supporting California's stance on emissions standards to combat climate change. This issue is discussed more fully in Chapter 17.

Nullification

Conservative activists, Republican lawmakers, and others in recent years have reasserted the historical constitutional law theory of *nullification* to attack what they take to be a broad pattern of unconstitutional usurpation of power by the federal government. Nullification advocates are furious over the imposition of national laws and court orders governing highly volatile issues like gun control, abortion, same-sex marriage, and the Affordable Care Act.

Each state, according to nullification theory, can use its own judgment to invalidate (nullify) federal laws it deems unconstitutional. For example, if Arizona believes federal immigration rules to be unconstitutional, it can, according to nullification proponents, declare the federal law unconstitutional and forbid its enforcement by the federal government in Arizona. Nullification theory is rooted in the 10th Amendment (powers not delegated to the federal government are reserved to the states or to the people) and in the reasoning that the states preceded and created the federal government, which exists only by the will of the states. Each state, therefore, can make its own decisions about which federal laws are constitutional in that state. (Nullification is related to, but is not to be confused with, neo-nullification, in which a state does not expressly declare a federal law unconstitutional but refuses to enforce that law within its jurisdiction. Neo-nullification best describes the movement to legalize marijuana at the state level.)

Nullification has become a powerful expression of states' rights and of resentment toward the federal government. No federal court decision, however, has ever validated nullification. The Supreme Court unanimously rejected a form of it in at least one instance, and it appears to be in direct conflict with the Supremacy Clause (which is discussed further in Chapter 8).

Questions

1. Constitutional law aside, do you think the federal government has asserted too much authority over issues such as same-sex marriage, abortion, marijuana use, and gun control? Explain.
2. Would the nation be improved if each state could more nearly make its own laws about those matters? Explain.

For a brief history of nullification, see Robert A. Levy, "The Limits of Nullification," *The New York Times,* September 3, 2013 [**www.nytimes.com**].

Sources: *Cooper v. Aaron,* 358 U.S. 1, 18–19 (1958) [**https://supreme.justia.com**]; and Ryan Card, "Can States 'Just Say No' to Federal Health Care Reform?" *Brigham Young University Law Review* 2010, no. 5 (2010), pp. 1795, 1808.

LO 5-3
Discuss the powerful role the Bill of Rights plays in protecting personal freedoms.

The Constitution, the Bill of Rights, and Business

The Constitution and, in particular, the Commerce Clause profoundly shape the practice of American business. Indeed, in some important ways, the Constitution is a commercial document reflecting the economic interests of the framers. We will defer further discussion of the Commerce Clause and the Supremacy Clause until Chapter 8. In this chapter, we will devote our attention primarily to the Bill of Rights, which limits the powers of the federal government and the states. When we think of the Bill of Rights, corporations ordinarily do not come to mind. Extensive litigation in recent years, however, serves notice that the relationship between the corporate "person" and the fundamental freedoms guaranteed by the Constitution is both important and unclear.

The Bill of Rights protects our personal freedoms (speech, religion, and more) from encroachment by the federal government. Furthermore, the Supreme Court has ruled that the Due Process Clause of the 14th Amendment, which is directed at the states, incorporates those fundamental freedoms and protects them against intrusion by state governments as well. [For the "Guide to Law Online," prepared by the U.S. Law Library of Congress, see **www.loc.gov/law/help/guide.php**.]

Part Two—The First Amendment

LO 5-4 Identify the freedoms protected under the First Amendment.

> Congress shall make no law respecting an establishment of religion, or prohibiting the free exercise thereof; or abridging the freedom of speech, or the press; or the right of the people peaceably to assemble, and to petition the Government for a redress of grievances.

These few words constitute one of the most powerful and noble utterances in history. Much of the magnificence that we often associate with America is embodied in the protections of the First Amendment. Surely, we must feel some sense of wonder that more than 333 million Americans continue to rely on that sentence as a cornerstone of American life. Notwithstanding the importance of the First Amendment, a 2015 nationwide survey found that one-third of Americans cannot name even one of its crucial protections.[18] [For First Amendment news, educational resources, and commentary, see **www.firstamendmentwatch.org**.]

Freedom of Religion

The First Amendment forbids both the establishment of an official state religion (the Establishment Clause) and undue government interference with religious practice (the Free Exercise Clause). Government may neither encourage nor discourage the practice of religion generally, nor may it give preference to one religion over another. Broadly, the idea of the First Amendment is to maintain a separation between church and state. The precise boundary of that separation, however, has become one of the more contentious social issues in contemporary life.

Religious Freedom Laws

Barronelle Stutzman, owner of Arlene's Flowers in Richland, Washington, declined to design custom floral arrangements for long-time customer and friend Robert Ingersoll, who was buying the flowers for his wedding to Curt Freed. Stutzman said that her Southern Baptist religious beliefs precluded her from involvement in the same-sex marriage:

> Rob was asking me to choose between my affection for him and my commitment to Christ . . .. As deeply fond as I am of Rob, my relationship with Jesus is everything to me.

The State of Washington sued Arlene's Flowers, and the trial court ruled that Stutzman had violated Washington's consumer protection laws, which forbid discrimination based on sexual orientation. The state's Supreme Court affirmed the trial court's judgment.

Was Ms. Stutzman practicing unlawful discrimination or lawfully following her religious conscience? Over the years, at least 21 states have passed "religious freedom" laws, often designed to prevent government from interfering with religious practices such as Muslim women wearing veils or Amish riding in buggies. Recently, however, religious freedom laws appear to be directed at the conflict between religious beliefs and laws forbidding discrimination against the LGBTQ community.

That conflict was inflamed by the U.S. Supreme Court's 2015 *Obergefell* ruling, which held that denial of marriage rights to same-sex couples is unconstitutional. In response, the state of Mississippi passed a bill in 2016 forbidding government agencies from acting against state employees, individuals, organizations, and private entities that deny services based on religious objections. Thus, state employees could lawfully refuse to issue same-sex marriage licenses, and private companies and religious groups could deny a lengthy list of services (weddings, for example) to LGBTQ people. (Unlike the Mississippi statute, most state religious freedom laws do not extend to the denial of private-sector services.)

Ultimately, a federal judge ruled that the Mississippi statute violates the constitutional protections of religious neutrality and equal protection under the law and ordered Mississippi and its agents to cease enforcing the state's restrictions on same-sex marriage. A number of lawsuits have emerged from this conflict, and religious freedom claimants lost in earlier cases. In its 2018 *Masterpiece Cakeshop, Ltd.* decision, however, the U.S. Supreme Court held, on narrow grounds, in favor of a Colorado baker who refused to serve same-sex couples in violation of state law. As of this writing, the Court has heard arguments in the case of another Colorado religious freedom claimant, web-designer Lorie Smith.

While the number of Americans favoring LGBTQ nondiscrimination measures has steadily increased since 2015, the U.S. Supreme Court also now comprises a greater number of conservative justices. Furthermore, no federal law directly forbids discrimination based on sexual orientation or gender identity, and only about half of the states have enacted such laws. Thus, LGBTQ rights are at risk in many states, while Americans of religious faith believe their constitutionally protected rights are likewise being compromised.

The Supreme Court did shed some light on this dilemma in 2014 in the *Hobby Lobby* case, where the Court, by a 5–4 vote, ruled in favor of the family-owned corporation's right, on religious grounds, to exclude certain contraceptives from its employee health plan despite federal law requiring employers to provide that coverage. The Court ruled that the 1993 federal Religious Freedom Restoration Act (RFRA) protected the company from the government mandate. RFRA provides that the government cannot "substantially burden a person's exercise of religion" unless it is furthering a "compelling government interest" and acting in the "least restrictive" way possible. This was the first time RFRA was extended to a corporation. Remember, however, that Hobby Lobby is privately owned by a family with strong, demonstrable religious convictions.

Sources: Public Religion Research Institute, "Americans' Support for Key LGBTQ Rights Continues to Tick Upward," March 17, 2022 [**www.prri.org**]; Camila Domonoske, "Here's Why Mississippi's 'Religious Freedom' Bill Is So Controversial, "National *Public Radio,* April 1, 2016 [**www.npr.org**]; Warren Richey, "A Florist Caught Between Faith and Financial Ruin," *The Christian Science Monitor,* July 12, 2016 [**www.csmonitor.com**]; *Barber v. Bryant,* 2016 U.S. Dist. LEXIS 86120 (June 30, 2016); *Burwell v. Hobby Lobby,* 573 U.S. 682 (2014) [**https://supreme.justia.com**]; *Obergefell v. Hodges,* 584 U.S. __ (2018) [**https://supreme.justia.com**]; and S*tate of Washington v. Arlene's Flowers,* 2017 Wash. LEXIS 216 (Wash. 2017).

Prayer, the Pledge, and Currency

Prayer in legislative settings has been routine and lawful for many years, but the U.S. Supreme Court clarified and expanded constitutional protection for that practice in a 2014 decision, *Town of Greece, New York v. Galloway.*[19] The Greece city council opened its meetings with prayers offered by a rotating group of clergy who were predominantly Christian and who sometimes invoked Jesus Christ in their remarks. Greece was sued on the grounds the prayers were an unconstitutional establishment of religion, amounting to government-sponsored worship. The Supreme Court, however, by a 5–4 margin, said ceremonial prayers at all levels of government are constitutional so long as they do not require participation and do not "denigrate nonbelievers or religious minorities, threaten damnation or preach conversion."[20]

The Pledge of Allegiance was amended to distinguish the United States from "Godless Communists."

Federal courts have reached similar conclusions about other official, but ceremonial, references to religion. In two Ninth Circuit cases, atheist Michael Newdow claimed that official references to God amount to an endorsement of religion, thus violating the First Amendment Establishment Clause. Newdow argued that the phrase "Under God" was placed in the Pledge of Allegiance for religious purposes. In fact, the Pledge was amended in 1954 to include the words "Under God," and some members of Congress at the time said it was needed to distinguish the United States from "Godless Communists."[21] The Ninth Circuit panel, however, saw the voluntary Pledge as an expression of American ideals rather than as a religious endorsement.[22] In a separate case, Newdow challenged the phrase "In God We Trust" on U.S. currency, but another Ninth Circuit panel ruled the phrase simply patriotic and ceremonial and having nothing to do with the establishment of religion.[23]

God and Student Organizations

The University of California Hastings College of the Law refused to recognize a student organization, the Christian Legal Society (CLS). Hastings said the group's faith-based rules discriminated against gays, lesbians, and others who do not share the group's religious beliefs. The organization's rules required members to pledge they would not engage in a "sexually immoral lifestyle," including "all acts of sexual conduct outside God's design for marriage between one man and one woman." Thus, to Hastings officials, the pledge represented discrimination based on religion and sexual orientation, whereas CLS members regarded it as an expression of faith. CLS challenged Hastings's policy as a violation of the member students' First Amendment rights to freedom of religion, speech, and association. In 2010, the U.S. Supreme Court ruled by a 5–4 margin in *Christian Legal Society v. Leo P. Martinez* that the students' constitutional rights were not violated; rather, the university policy was a reasonable, viewpoint-neutral condition on access to student recognition in a public university. The majority reasoned that Hastings was concerned about the group's exclusionary conduct rather than its religious beliefs. That is, all student groups must be open to all students. Dissenting justices said the decision supported suppression of unpopular and politically incorrect speech.[24]

Notwithstanding the CLS ruling, a growing number of states, including Arkansas, Iowa, and South Dakota have passed legislation allowing public college and university religious organizations to lawfully restrict membership to students who share the groups' religious beliefs.[25] The constitutionality of those statutes is untested as of this writing. The number of bills introduced in state legislatures allowing student religious organizations to restrict membership has skyrocketed in recent years. A total of three bills were introduced in 2016, 5 in 2017, and 10 in 2018, while 22 new bills were introduced during the first quarter of 2019 alone.

Veils and French Values

In 2011, France began enforcing its new law forbidding, with some exceptions, the wearing of a garment in public that hides the wearer's face. The law was promoted as a matter of security and of cultural assimilation, while it was assailed as an affront to the Muslim faith and a political move designed to appeal to voters worried about threats to traditional European values and culture. Only an estimated 2,000 women of the five million French Muslims are believed to wear burqas or niqabs covering the face. Some fines have been imposed, but enforcement has, in general, not been aggressive.

The law was challenged in court as a violation of religious and expressive freedom, but it was upheld in 2014 by the European Court of Human Rights. Notably, a U.N. Human Rights Committee subsequently issued a nonbinding decision in 2018, ruling that the ban was overly broad and violated women's freedom of religion. Nevertheless, France continued to ban the face coverings even as it mandated the public to wear face masks during the COVID-19 pandemic.

Sources: "European Court Upholds French Full Veil Ban," *BBC,* July 1, 2014 [**www.bbc.com**]; Steven Erlanger and Elvire Camus, "In a Ban, a Measure of European Tolerance," *The New York Times,* September 1, 2012 [**www.nytimes.com**]; Robert Marquand, "Face Veil Ban: Will France Take a Hard Line?" *The Christian Science Monitor,* April 11, 2011 [**www.csmonitor.com**]; "French Full-Body Veil Ban Violated Women's Freedom of Religion: UN Human Rights Committee," *UN News,* October 24, 2018 [**www.news.un.org**]; and Jason Silverstein, "France Will Still Ban Islamic Face Coverings Even After Making Masks Mandatory," *CBS News,* May 12, 2020 [**www.cbsnews.com**].

Freedom of Speech

Hustler Magazine publisher Larry Flynt: "If the First Amendment will protect a scumbag like me, then it will protect all of you. Because I am the worst."[26] [The 1996 movie *The People vs. Larry Flynt,* starring Woody Harrelson, Courtney Love, and Edward Norton, presents a bawdy, provocative view of freedom of speech. For the trailer, go to **https://www.youtube.com/watch?v=fR6l4D47fW8.**]

Freedom of speech is arguably the primary guarantor of the American approach to life. Not only is it indispensable to democracy and personal dignity, but Americans see free expression as a means of generating the best ideas. We believe in a marketplace of ideas just as we believe in a marketplace of goods. Freedom of speech is not absolute, however. We are not free to make slanderous statements about others, utter public obscenities at will, speak "fighting words" that are likely to produce a clear and present danger of violence, or yell "Fire" in a crowded theater.

We cannot freely yell "Fire" in a crowded theater.

Generally, the government cannot regulate the *content* of our speech, telling us what we can and cannot say. It does have greater authority, however, to regulate the *context* of that speech– the government may be able to restrict where, when, and how we say certain things if regulation is necessary to preserve a compelling state interest. We have broad free speech rights in so-called *public forums,* such as downtown business districts, parks, college campuses, and public plazas. Even in those places, however, the state may need to impose reasonable time and manner regulations. Thus, although the Ku Klux Klan can express hatred for Black people (the content of the message), the state may restrict where, when, and how those expressions are made (the context of the message), if necessary, for public safety.

What Is Expression?

Expression is not limited to oral and written utterances. Freedom of speech extends to messages not communicated with words. Dancing, flag burning, cross burning, artistic production, and disrobing, for example, may all be forms of protected expression. In *Tinker v. Des Moines School District,* one of the leading free speech cases in American history, the U.S. Supreme Court found First Amendment protection for wearing a black armband to a high school as a protest against the Vietnam War, where no evidence of disruption was presented.[27]

Political contributions, as we saw in the Chapter 3 discussion of the 2010 *Citizens United* case, are also a form of protected expression. The Supreme Court expanded that protection in the 2014 *McCutcheon* case, which struck down, as a violation of freedom of expression, a portion of a 1971 federal law limiting the aggregate amount of money a donor can give to all candidates or party committees.[28] Some contribution limits remain, but critics believe the decision further undermined democratic principles by expanding the political influence of wealthy individuals and organizations.

Congress may constitutionally regulate political contributions to curb corruption, but according to the Supreme Court in *Citizens United,* independent expenditures, even when made by corporations, do not promote corruption or the appearance of corruption. National polls, however, show that the American public perceives a great deal of corruption involving campaign contributions and supports limits on campaign donations.[29]

Free Speech Analysis

How do we decide when the government has violated rights to free speech? The courts have taken numerous approaches to that question. We will look briefly at cases involving content and context issues as well as the *balancing test,* which requires judges to weigh the interests of the state against the expressive rights of the individual.

Content: Vile Words

One of the most controversial Supreme Court cases of recent years involved the Topeka, Kansas, Westboro Baptist Church and its practice of protesting at the funerals of American soldiers killed in service. Pastor Fred W. Phelps and his small congregation, most of whom are family members, contend that battlefield deaths are God's punishment for America's sins, including homosexuality. The funeral protests include signs such as "Thank God for dead soldiers" and "God Hates Fags." Pastor Phelps and his family picketed the 2006 funeral of Matthew Snyder, a Marine who had been killed in Iraq.

> American soldiers killed on the battlefield: "God's punishment for America's sins."

Snyder's father sued Phelps and Westboro and won a $10.9 million damage award (reduced by the judge to $5 million) based on his claims of invasion of privacy and intentional infliction of emotional distress. That decision was reversed on appeal, and the case reached the U.S. Supreme Court in 2011, where the church's First Amendment freedom of expression argument prevailed by an 8-1 margin.[30] The quiet, nonviolent Westboro protests addressed matters of public importance on a public street at a distance from the funeral (approximately 1,000 feet) specified by authorities.

Thus, the Court's unpopular decision affirmed the long-standing position that the government ordinarily cannot restrict speech based on its content, however tasteless or valueless it may be. As lawyer and commentator Adam Cohen said about the Westboro expression: "We defend it not because these ideas are particularly worthy of being protected, but because all ideas, even the most loathsome, are."[31] Recent federal legislation requires demonstrators to be at least 300 feet from military funerals from two hours before until two hours after the ceremonies.

Context: Panhandling

Noting safety concerns about panhandlers in roadway median strips, the Portland, Maine, City Council passed an ordinance making it illegal to stand, sit, or stay on a median except to cross a road. When challenged, the ordinance was struck down by the U.S. First Circuit Court of Appeals in 2015 on First Amendment grounds, not because of the content of the message (begging) but because of its context (where the speech takes place).[32] The court went on to find that the means employed to protect public safety in Portland were broader than necessary and thus too intrusive on expression.

Some restraints on panhandling in the street or on aggressive panhandling might well be permissible. The content of the message (begging) may not be restricted, but for compelling reasons, authorities might lawfully shift the time, place, or manner (the context) of the expression.

Balancing Interests: Speech at (or about) School

Joseph Frederick, a Juneau, Alaska, high school senior, was across the street from his school, along with many other students, watching an Olympic torch parade with school permission when he and some friends unfurled a large banner reading "Bong Hits 4 Jesus." The banner was a prank designed to attract attention from television cameras. The school principal, Deborah Morse, told Frederick to lower the banner. He refused and was suspended from school. Frederick sued, and the case reached the U.S. Supreme Court. In balancing Frederick's free speech interests against the school's educational and safety duties, does the First Amendment protect Frederick? The Supreme Court said no.[33]

"Bong Hits 4 Jesus."

The U.S. Supreme Court issued a decision in 2021 in another case, this time involving ninth-grade cheerleader, Brandi Levy, who was suspended from school after posting, "f– school f– softball f– cheer f– everything," to Snapchat when she learned she did not make it onto the varsity cheerleading team.[34] She was at a convenience store when she posted the social media message. In this instance, the Court held that the school violated Levy's right to free speech,

She was suspended from school after posting, "f– school f– softball f– cheer f– everything," to Snapchat.

stating that schools will bear a heavy burden to justify intervention with off-campus speech occurring outside a school activity or program. However, it also indicated that there are certain circumstances—such as severe bullying or harassment, danger aimed at teachers or other students, and rule-breaking–where such intervention may be appropriate. These free-speech exceptions will undoubtedly be tested in future court cases.

Public Sector Workers Off the Job? On the Job?

Remember that the Constitution and Bill of Rights protect us from the government but not, for example, from our corporate employer. On the other hand, the First Amendment does generally shield *public-sector* workers' *off-the-job* expressions when speaking as citizens about matters of public concern.

Derogatory comments about her students: "frightfully dim," "utterly loathsome," and "insolent, unappreciative, selfish brats."

Nonetheless, employer restrictions necessary to effective operation of a government enterprise may be permissible, as illustrated by the 2012 dismissal of Natalie Munroe, a Pennsylvania high school English teacher. Munroe created a blog, intended for her friends but not password protected, to which she posted over 80 messages. Most of Munroe's blog comments addressed personal matters, but in several instances, she included derogatory comments about her students, such as "frightfully dim" and "utterly loathsome," and she said parents were "breeding a disgusting brood of insolent, unappreciative, selfish brats." Upon learning of the comments, parents and students were furious. Later, after poor performance reviews, Munroe was fired. Munroe sued the school claiming she was retaliated against for exercising her free speech rights. The Third Circuit Court of Appeals ruled in 2015 that she could not sue, finding that the school's interest in avoiding educational disruptions outweighed her expressive interests.[35]

Government employees' free speech rights are substantially limited *on the job.* Los Angeles Deputy District Attorney Richard Ceballos lost his job in a whistleblowing episode. Ceballos sued and, in 2006, the U.S. Supreme Court ruled that government employees who speak out "pursuant to their official duties" are speaking as employees, not as citizens, and therefore are not protected by the First Amendment regardless of the content of their message. The Court pointed to the government's need for efficiency and order in its workplace.[36]

Politically Correct Speech/Hate Speech

We are largely free of government restraints on what we can say, but should there be limits? Is free speech sometimes too hurtful to be tolerated? Are some remarks so inflammatory and insensitive that they actually undermine and obstruct discourse?

Donald Trump's 2016 presidential campaign capitalized on public frustration with so-called politically correct speech–avoiding language or behavior that might offend a particular group, especially with respect to race, gender, and sexual orientation. Charles Barkley, basketball commentator and former NBA star, challenged speech limits, as he often does, by remarks about overweight women in San Antonio, Texas: "That's a gold mine for Weight Watchers. . .. Victoria is definitely a secret [in San Antonio] . . . they can't wear no Victoria's Secret down there." Barkley later refused to apologize and said, ". . . [T]urn off your damn television. I am not going to change."[37]

Charles Barkley: "[T]urn off your damn television. I am not going to change."

Disputes about offensive language often arise in university life where the law requires policies to curb and punish civil rights violations, including racial and sexual harassment. Shouldn't we be troubled, for example, when a UCLA fraternity has a Kanye West–themed, "blackface" party? Or are we being too sensitive when students at Emory University feel threatened by "Trump 2016" campaign messages written in chalk across campus? Professors now issue "trigger warnings" that some class material might trouble students. Some recent editions of the Mark Twain novels *Adventures of Huckleberry Finn* and *Tom Sawyer* have been published with the "N-word" being replaced by the word "slave" in an effort to avoid disturbing readers. These practices have led to allegations of "The Coddling of the American Mind."[38]

At least in public spaces, racist, sexist, or hurtful speech that does not constitute a direct threat to an individual or that is not likely to provoke an imminent breach of the peace ordinarily is protected by the First Amendment. Balancing the value of free speech against the decency of curbing empty, hurtful, inflammatory remarks is difficult, however. Many universities have responded with campus speech codes designed to stop hate speech, harassment, bullying, and other offensive conduct. Those codes are sometimes denounced as mandating politically correct speech.

Speech codes may often suffer from a First Amendment problem of *overbreadth* (forbidding what should be protected speech, along with speech that can rightfully be prohibited) and/or Fifth Amendment due process of law problems relating to *vagueness* (a lack of clarity about precisely what kind of speech is, or is not, forbidden). A number of university speech codes have been invalidated as violations of First Amendment rights.[39]

Yale

Complaints of a hostile sexual environment and intimidation of female students caused Yale University to impose, in 2011, a five-year ban on all campus activities for a prestigious fraternity that counts both Bush presidents among its alumni. One of the complaints involved the fraternity's pledges chanting, "No means yes! Yes means anal!" outside a women's dormitory area. Other, more individualized and more threatening concerns were also raised. Following a federal investigation based on these complaints and on claims that the university underreported sexual harassment allegations, Yale agreed to change its harassment policy and reached a settlement that did not involve disciplinary action.[40]

Maricopa CCC

His right to send racially charged emails.

A Maricopa County Community College (Arizona) math instructor won a Ninth Circuit Court of Appeals case, involving his right to send racially charged emails over the college-maintained server to all employees with an email address. Professor Walter Kehowski sent three messages declaring, for example, "It's time to acknowledge and celebrate the superiority of Western Civilization." On his college-maintained website, he said, "[T]he only immigration reform imperative is preservation of White majority (*sic*)."

A group of Hispanic employees then sued the college district, claiming it had failed to properly respond to Kehowski's remarks, thus allowing the creation of a hostile work environment. The court of appeals, however, ruled that the emails addressed matters of public concern and were protected by the First Amendment, and therefore could not constitute illegal harassment. The court did note that some workplace harassment, such as racial insults or sexual advances toward particular individuals, may be prohibited because it lacks the expressive quality of speech directed toward a larger audience.[41]

"Be Happy, Not Gay"

Following a day designated to show support for gays and lesbians at her high school in Naperville, Illinois, student Heidi Zamecnik wore a T-shirt to school displaying the expression "Be Happy, Not Gay." The school's dean forbade the expression at the school. Another student, Alexander Nuxoll, unsuccessfully sought to wear a similar shirt. Both students objected to homosexuality on religious grounds. The two students subsequently sued the school for infringing their free speech rights. The Seventh Circuit Court of Appeals reasoned that the forbidden expression did not constitute "fighting words" or some other recognized First Amendment exception and ruled that the students had a right to wear the shirts and express their opinions.

Judge Richard Posner said

> [A] school that permits advocacy of the rights of homosexual students cannot be allowed to stifle criticism of homosexuality. The school argued (and still argues) that banning "Be Happy, Not Gay" was just a matter of protecting the "rights" of the students against whom derogatory comments are directed. But people in our society do not have a legal right to prevent criticism of their beliefs or even their way of life.

Source: *Zamecnik and Nuxoll v. Indian Prairie School District,* 636 F.3d 874 (7th Cir. 2011).

Ole Miss

Colleges and universities have sometimes been accorded considerable latitude in regulating campus speech. The Fifth Circuit Court of Appeals, for example, upheld the right of the University of Mississippi to ban flags, including the Confederate flag, at campus events.[42] Specifically banning only the Confederate flag presumably would not have met with the Court's approval.

George Mason

Many First Amendment scholars believe the correct antidote to hate speech is simply more speech; that is, they place their faith in the marketplace of ideas rather than in rules, however well-intended. The decision that follows demonstrates the First Amendment's role in resolving claims of racism, sexism, and general insensitivity springing from a George Mason University fraternity's "ugly woman contest." [For a vigorous critique of campus "political correctness," see the Foundation for Individual Rights in Education at **www.thefire.org**.]

IOTA XI Chapter v. George Mason University 993 F.2d 386 (4th Cir. 1993)

Senior Circuit Judge Sprouse

George Mason University appeals from a summary judgment granted by the district court to the IOTA XI Chapter of Sigma Chi Fraternity in its action for declaratory judgment and an injunction seeking to nullify sanctions imposed on it by the University because it conducted an "ugly woman contest" with racist and sexist overtones.

I

Sigma Chi has for two years held an annual "Derby Days" event, planned and conducted both as entertainment and as a source of funds for donations to charity. The "ugly woman contest," held on April 4, 1991, was one of the "Derby Days" events. The Fraternity staged the contest in the cafeteria of the student union. As part of the contest, eighteen Fraternity members were assigned to one of six sorority teams cooperating in events. The involved Fraternity members appeared in the contest dressed as caricatures of different types of women, including one member dressed as an offensive caricature of a black woman. He was painted black and wore stringy, black hair decorated with curlers, and his outfit was stuffed with pillows to exaggerate a woman's breasts and buttocks. He spoke in slang to parody African-Americans.

There is no direct evidence in the record concerning the subjective intent of the Fraternity members who conducted the contest. The Fraternity, which later apologized to the University officials for the presentation, conceded during the litigation that the contest was sophomoric and offensive.

Following the contest, a number of students protested to the University that the skit had been objectionably sexist and racist. Two hundred forty-seven students, many of them members of the foreign or minority student body, executed a petition, which stated, "[W]e are condemning the racist and sexist implications of this event in which male members dressed as women. One man in particular wore a black face, portraying a negative stereotype of black women."

Dean for Student Services Kenneth Bumgarner discussed the situation with representatives of the objecting students [and] student representatives of Sigma Chi. [The University decided to impose sanctions on Sigma Chi including] suspension from [most] activities for the rest of the 1991 spring semester and a two-year prohibition. . ..

On June 5, 1991, Sigma Chi brought this action against the University and Dean Bumgarner. It requested declaratory judgment and injunctive relief to nullify the sanctions as violative of the First and Fourteenth Amendments. Sigma Chi moved for summary judgment on its First Amendment claims on June 28, 1991.

. . . University President George W. Johnson . . . presented the "mission statement" of the University:

> (3) George Mason University is committed to promoting a culturally and racially diverse student body. . .. Education here is not limited to the classroom.
>
> (4) We are committed to teaching the values of equal opportunity and equal treatment, respect for diversity, and individual dignity.
>
> (5) Our mission also includes achieving the goals set forth in our affirmative action plan, a plan incorporating affirmative steps designed to attract and retain minorities to this campus.
>
> (7) George Mason University is a state institution of higher education and a recipient of federal funds.

The district court granted summary judgment to Sigma Chi on its First Amendment claim, 773 F. Supp. 792 (E.D. Va. 1991).

II [OMITTED—ED.]

III

We initially face the task of deciding whether Sigma Chi's "ugly woman contest" is sufficiently expressive to entitle it to First Amendment protection.

A

First Amendment principles governing live entertainment are relatively clear: Short of obscenity, it is generally protected. As the Supreme Court announced in *Schad v. Borough of Mount Ephraim,* 452 U.S. 61 (1981), "[e]ntertainment, as well as political and ideological speech, is protected; motion pictures, programs broadcast by radio and television, and live entertainment . . . fall within the First Amendment guarantee." Expression devoid of "ideas" but with entertainment value may also be protected because "[t]he line between the informing and the entertaining is too elusive." *Winters v. New York,* 333 U.S. 507, 510 (1948).

Even crude street skits come within the First Amendment's reach. In . . . *Schacht v. United States,* 398 U.S. 58, 61–62 (1970), . . . Justice Black [declared] that an actor participating in even a crude performance enjoys the constitutional right to freedom of speech.

Bearing on this dichotomy between low- and high-grade entertainment are the Supreme Court's holdings relating to nude dancing. See *Barnes v. Glen Theatre, Inc.,* 111 S. Ct. 2456, 2460 (1991).

[I]n *Barnes,* the Supreme Court conceded that nude dancing is expressive conduct entitled to First Amendment protection.

. . . [I]t appears that the low quality of entertainment does not necessarily weigh in the First Amendment inquiry. It would seem, therefore, that the Fraternity's skit, even as low-grade entertainment, was inherently expressive and thus entitled to First Amendment protection.

B

The University nevertheless contends that discovery will demonstrate that the contest does not merit characterization as a skit but only as mindless fraternity fun, devoid of any artistic expression. It argues further that entitlement to First Amendment protection exists only if the production was intended to convey a message likely to be understood by a particular audience. . ..

As indicated, we feel that the First Amendment protects the Fraternity's skit because it is inherently expressive entertainment. Even if this were not true, however, the skit, in our view, qualifies as expressive conduct under the test articulated in *Texas v. Johnson,* 491 U.S. 397 (1989). It is true that the *Johnson* test for determining the expressiveness of conduct requires "'[a]n intent to convey a particularized message'" and a great likelihood "'that the message would be understood by those who viewed it.'"

[T]he affidavits establish that the punishment was meted out to the Fraternity because its boorish message had interfered with the described University mission. It is manifest from these circumstances that the University officials thought the Fraternity intended to convey a message. The Fraternity members' apology and post-conduct contriteness suggest that they held the same view.

As to the second prong of the Johnson test, there was a great likelihood that at least some of the audience viewing the skit would understand the Fraternity's message of satire and humor. Some students paid to attend the performance and were entertained. . ..

. . . [W]e are persuaded that the Fraternity's "ugly woman contest" satisfies the Johnson test for expressive conduct.

IV

If this were not a sufficient response to the University's argument, the principles relating to content and viewpoint discrimination recently emphasized in *R.A.V. v. City of St. Paul,* 112 S. Ct. 2538 (1992), provide a definitive answer. Although the Court in St. Paul reviewed the constitutional effect of a city "hate speech" ordinance, and we review the constitutionality of sanctions imposed for violating University policy, *St. Paul's* rationale applies here with equal force. Noting that St. Paul's city ordinance prohibited displays of symbols that "arouse[d] anger, alarm, or resentment in others on the basis of race, color, creed, religion, or gender," but did not prohibit displays of symbols which would advance ideas of racial or religious equality, Justice Scalia stated, "The First Amendment does not permit St. Paul to impose special prohibitions on those speakers who express views on disfavored subjects."

As evidenced by their affidavits, University officials sanctioned Sigma Chi for the message conveyed by the "ugly woman contest" because it ran counter to the views the University sought to communicate to its students and the community. The mischief was the University's punishment of those who scoffed at its goals of racial integration and gender neutrality, while permitting, even encouraging, conduct that would further the viewpoint expressed in the University's goals and probably be embraced by a majority of society as well. "The First Amendment generally prevents government from proscribing . . . expressive conduct because of disapproval of the ideas expressed."

The University, however, urges us to weigh Sigma Chi's conduct against the substantial interests inherent in educational endeavors. We agree wholeheartedly that it is the University officials' responsibility, even their obligation, to achieve the goals they have set. On the other hand, a public university has many constitutionally permissible means to protect female and minority students. We must emphasize, as have other courts, that "the manner of [its action] cannot consist of selective limitations upon speech." The University should have accomplished its goals in some fashion other than silencing speech on the basis of its viewpoint.

Affirmed.

Questions

1. Is speech that consists merely of entertainment without the benefit of meaningful ideas protected by the First Amendment? Explain.
2. Explain the court's conclusion that the fraternity skit met the *Texas v. Johnson* test of "an intent to convey a particularized message" and a great likelihood "that the message would be understood by those who viewed it."
3. *a.* Should racist and sexist remarks be forbidden in college classrooms? Why?
   b. The Stanford University speech code was ruled unconstitutional. The judge in that case said, among other things, that the code was "overbroad."[43] What did he mean?
   c. Do we give too much attention to freedom of speech at the expense of community civility? Explain.
4. For an extra fee, Texas will issue specialty auto license plates, but state law allows rejection of the request if "the design might be offensive to any member of the public." The Sons of Confederate Veterans (TSCV) asked the Texas Department of Motor Vehicles Board to issue a specialty license plate displaying a Confederate battle flag, but the request was denied citing the "offensive to any member of the public" standard. TSCV sued and the case reached the Supreme Court. See *Walker v. Sons of Confederate Veterans,* 576 U.S. __ (2015) [**https://supreme.justia.com**].
   a. Is a specialty plate private speech or government speech? Explain.
   b. Were TSCV's First Amendment rights violated? Explain.
5. The U.S. Supreme Court and lower federal courts have repeatedly ruled that burning the American flag is speech protected by the First Amendment. Congress often considers a flag protection amendment to the Constitution to make flag burning illegal. Would you favor that amendment? Explain.

Commercial Speech

LO 5-5
Discuss the differences between First Amendment protections of commercial speech and political speech.

Governments often want to regulate commercial expressions ranging from advertisements and billboards to real estate "for sale" signs and circulars placed on car windshields. Does the First Amendment protect those messages from government intervention in the same manner that it protects political speech? In 1942, the U.S. Supreme Court ruled that *commercial speech* was not entitled to First Amendment protection.[44] Subsequently, the Court changed its stance and extended First Amendment rights to commercial speech, although those rights were still much more limited than for political speech. In more recent years, the Court has been gradually expanding protection for commercial speech.

Corporate Political Speech

Should corporations enjoy full First Amendment rights? Can we properly think of corporate political expressions as commercial speech? Or is commercial speech limited to those expressions that propose a commercial transaction? Experts differ on these questions, but the significance is evident if we think about the 2010 *Citizens United* decision allowing corporations to spend more freely on elections (discussed in Chapter 3).[45] In the late 1970s, Justices William Rehnquist and Byron White described corporations as "creatures of the law" possessed of wealth-creation powers but not entitled to the rights possessed by voters. By contrast, the *Citizens United* majority described corporations as "associations of citizens" deserving of free speech rights in the manner of individuals.[46] In his concurring opinion, Justice Scalia said: "[T]o exclude or impede corporate speech is to muzzle the principal agents of the modern economy. We should celebrate rather than condemn the addition of this speech to the public debate."[47] This shift in constitutional interpretation reflected, according to a *Los Angeles Times* analysis, President Ronald Reagan–era efforts to reduce government regulation of business; all five justices in the *Citizens United* majority were either appointed to the Court by Reagan or worked as young lawyers in the Reagan Administration.[48] Hence, shifting political views sometimes influence the course of judge-made law. Do you think a corporation should be regarded as a person for First Amendment purposes?

The Slants and the Redskins

The Slants is a dance-rock band comprising Asian American musicians in Portland, Oregon, who put up a legal fight to protect their group's name. The federal Lanham Act prohibits the registration of "disparaging" trademarks. The U.S. Patent and Trademark Office (PTO), considering the name an ethnic slur against Asians, refused to allow The Slants a trademark, which would strengthen the protection of the name's commercial, artistic, and expressive value. The band's leader, Simon Tam, sued, claiming the trademark denial was an unconstitutional restriction of free speech rights. Tam sought to "take ownership" of anti-Asian stereotypes and transform them to statements of pride. Tam's lawsuit reached the United States Supreme Court, which unanimously ruled in 2017 that the disparagement clause of the Lanham Act violates the First Amendment's free speech clause. The court reasoned that the public expression of ideas may not be prohibited merely because those ideas are offensive to some.

Meanwhile, in 2014, the PTO canceled the trademark held by the National Football League's Washington Redskins on grounds that it disparaged Native Americans. The

Redskins disputed the PTO finding in court. Days after the Slants decision was handed down, both the Justice Department and the Native American litigants dropped their challenge to the Redskins' trademark, acknowledging that The Slants decision had resolved the legal question in the Redskins' favor. Nevertheless, it was pressure from sponsors and businesses amid the Black Lives Matter movement that finally convinced the team in July 2020 to drop its name, and to adopt a new one–the Washington Commanders—in February 2022.

Historically, the PTO has canceled numerous other trademark names such as "Marriage Is for Fags," but it has approved marks such as "Asian Efficiency."

Questions

1. Why did the Supreme Court find that the provision forbidding registration of "disparaging trademarks" violated The Slants's First Amendment rights? Do you agree with the court? Explain.
2. The First Amendment protects speech even if it is offensive and unpopular. How did this idea ultimately play out for the Washington "Redskins"? What do you think about team's decision to finally change its name? Explain.

Sources: *Matal v. Tam,* 582 U.S. __ (2017) [**https://supreme.justia.com**]; Joe Coscarelli, "Why the Slants Took a Fight Over Their Band Name to the Supreme Court," *The New York Times,* June 19, 2017 [**www.nytimes.com**]; Josh Gerstein, "Feds Give Up Fight Against Redskins Trademark," *Politico,* June 28, 2017 [**www.politico.com**]; and Emma Bowman, "For Many Native Americans, the Washington Commanders' New Name Offers Some Closure," *NPR,* February 6, 2022 [**www.npr.org**].

Commercial Speech on Campus

The *Virginia Tech* decision below examines the constitutionality of government regulations that restrict beer advertising in college newspapers, as measured by the commercial free speech test articulated in the Supreme Court's important *Central Hudson* decision.[49]

LEGAL BRIEFCASE

Educational Media Company at Virginia Tech v. Insley

731 F.3d 291 (4th Cir. 2013)

Judge Thacker

The Virginia Alcoholic Beverage Control Board (the "ABC") prohibits college student newspapers from printing alcohol advertisements. Appellants Educational Media and the Cavalier Daily are nonprofit corporations that own student newspapers at Virginia Polytechnic Institute and State University and the University of Virginia, respectively. . ..

The district court granted summary judgment in favor of the ABC, concluding that the challenged regulation is a constitutionally appropriate restriction of commercial speech given Virginia's substantial interest in combating underage and abusive drinking on college campuses. . ..

I.

Virginia precludes college student newspapers from printing alcohol advertisements. The challenged regulation provides

> Advertisements of alcoholic beverages are not allowed in college student publications unless in reference to a dining establishment, except as provided below. A "college student

publication" is defined as any college or university publication that is prepared, edited or published primarily by students at such institution, is sanctioned as a curricular or extra-curricular activity by such institution and which is distributed or intended to be distributed primarily to persons under 21 years of age.

A.

The ABC asserts that the purpose of the challenged regulation is to combat underage and abusive college drinking. During discovery, each party proffered expert testimony. . .. Specifically, the ABC offered a declaration of Dr. Henry Saffer, an economics professor at Kean University in New Jersey. Dr. Saffer testified that, while the vast majority of studies found that alcohol advertising bans do not, in fact, reduce the overall market demand for alcohol, those studies are inapplicable here. Notably, Dr. Saffer contends that, while most scholars assume that a prohibition on alcohol advertising in one forum simply pushes alcohol advertising to other forums, according to him, (sic) this assumption only holds true where a reasonable substitute for the regulated forum exists. Dr. Saffer testified that this assumption does not hold true in the context of college student newspapers, because "[a] college newspaper is a very targeted, specific kind of media," and there is "nothing else that can replace that kind of targeted media that's specifically oriented towards and reaches college students." According to Dr. Saffer's reasoning, in the unique instance of college newspapers, alcohol advertising bans actually do have a significant effect on market demand despite the vast majority of studies that show otherwise outside of this particular context.

In contrast, the College Newspapers offered the testimony of Dr. Jon P. Nelson, an economics professor at Pennsylvania State University. Based on his research, Dr. Nelson testified that "[a]dvertising bans, partial or comprehensive, do not reduce the demand for alcohol." Rather, he explains, "[i]n a 'mature market,' such as alcohol beverages, the primary effect of advertising is to create and maintain brand loyalty[,]" as opposed to expanding overall market demand. He also notes that college students are continually exposed to alcohol advertisements in a variety of forums—including television, radio, and the Internet—which "will totally offset any possible temperance effect of the ABC regulation."

. . . Dr. Nelson noted that Dr. Saffer did not present any specific evidence in support of his proposition that targeted advertising bans in college student publications actually achieve the desired goal, that is, reduced drinking. Moreover, Dr. Saffer conceded that, in addition to the lack of empirical support for selective bans on alcohol advertising in college student publications, other methods of combating alcohol consumption on college campuses have been proven more effective. Specifically, as the district court noted, "Dr. Saffer also admits that increased taxation has been shown to reduce underage consumption in a more effective manner than advertising bans and that counter-advertising has effectively reduced levels of alcohol consumption."

The College Newspapers also established . . . that a majority of their readers are over the age of 21.

B.

[T]he district court granted summary judgment in favor of ABC.

II. [omitted—ed.]

III.

A.

While commercial speech is protected by the First Amendment, there is a "commonsense distinction" between commercial speech and other varieties of speech. [*Central Hudson Gas & Electric Corp. v. Public Service Commission of New York,* 447 U.S. 557, 562 (1980).] Thus, "[t]he Constitution . . . accords a lesser protection to commercial speech than to other constitutionally guaranteed expression. . .." [*Id.* at 562–63.] The parties agree that the challenged regulation impacts only commercial speech.

B.

Next, we consider whether the challenged regulation violates *Central Hudson* as applied to the College Newspapers. Under *Central Hudson,* a regulation of commercial speech will be upheld if (1) the regulated speech concerns lawful activity and is not misleading; (2) the regulation is supported by a substantial government interest; (3) the regulation directly advances that interest; and (4) the regulation is not more extensive than necessary to serve the government's interest. . .. We address each of the four *Central Hudson* prongs in turn.

1. LAWFUL ACTIVITY

All parties are in agreement that the first prong of *Central Hudson,* i.e., whether the regulated speech concerns lawful activity and is not misleading, is satisfied. Specifically, the challenged regulation regulates lawful activity, as alcohol advertisements—even those that reach a partially underage audience—concern the lawful activity of alcohol consumption. Additionally, the ABC has not presented any evidence that the advertisements implicated by this regulation are misleading. Thus, this prong is clearly satisfied.

2. SUBSTANTIAL GOVERNMENT INTEREST

"Next, we ask whether the asserted governmental interest is substantial." [*Id.* at 566.] As with the first prong, the parties are in agreement that Virginia's stated interest in combating underage and abusive drinking on college campuses represents a substantial governmental interest. Accordingly, the second *Central Hudson* prong is satisfied.

3. DIRECT AND MATERIAL ADVANCEMENT

a. Under *Central Hudson's* third prong, the ABC must prove that the challenged regulation directly advances the government's asserted interest. "This burden is not satisfied by mere speculation or conjecture; rather, a governmental body seeking to sustain a restriction on commercial speech must demonstrate that the harms it recites are real and that its restriction will in fact alleviate them to a material degree.' [*Edenfield v. Fane,* 507 U.S. 761, 770–71 (1993).]

In [*Educational Media Co. et al. v. Swecker,* 602 F.3d 583 (4th Cir. 2010)], we concluded that the challenged regulation satisfies the third prong because, given the general correlation between advertising of a product and demand for that product, it follows that a decrease in alcohol advertising on college campuses will necessarily result in a decrease in alcohol consumption by college students. Additionally, we concluded that the efficacy of the regulation was further substantiated by the fact that "alcohol advertisers *want* to advertise in college student publications. It is counterintuitive for alcohol vendors to spend their money on advertisements . . . if they believed that these ads would not increase demand by college students." [*Id.* at 590.]

b. . . . We agree [with *Swecker's* analysis].

4. REGULATION MORE EXTENSIVE THAN NECESSARY

. . . Under this prong of *Central Hudson,* the party defending the regulation "must demonstrate narrow tailoring of the challenged regulation to the asserted interest—a fit that is not necessarily perfect, but reasonable; that represents not necessarily the single best disposition but one whose scope is in proportion to the interest served." [*Greater New Orleans Broadcasting Association, Inc. v. United States,* 527 U.S. 173, 188 (1999).]

The ABC argues that the challenged regulation does not fail under this fourth prong because it is "reasonably tailored" to the stated aim of reducing underage and abusive alcohol consumption. Specifically, the ABC notes that the challenged regulation does not prohibit all alcohol advertisements and is but one facet of its multifaceted approach to combat the problem of underage drinking. Given the dual purpose of the regulation to combat both underage and abusive drinking, the district court agreed. Specifically, the district court held that, while the challenged regulation did have the effect of preventing the dissemination of truthful information to legal adults, this was not unduly out-of-proportion to the second half of the government's stated aim: reducing abusive alcohol consumption by college students who are 21 years of age or older.

We disagree. Instead, we conclude that . . . the challenged regulation fails under the fourth *Central Hudson* prong because it prohibits large numbers of adults who are 21 years of age or older from receiving truthful information about a product that they are legally allowed to consume.

[A] majority of the College Newspapers' readers are age 21 or older. Specifically, roughly 60% of [Virginia Tech's] *Collegiate Times's* readership is age 21 or older and the [University of Virginia's] *Cavalier Daily* reaches approximately 10,000 students, nearly 64% of whom are age 21 or older. Thus, the College Newspapers have a protected interest in printing non-misleading alcohol advertisements, just as a majority of the College Newspapers' readers have a protected interest in receiving that information. Accordingly, the challenged regulation is unconstitutionally overbroad.

[T]he portion of the challenged regulation seeking to prevent the dissemination of alcohol advertisements to readers age 21 or older . . . attempts to keep would-be drinkers in the dark based on what the ABC perceives to be their own good. Therefore, the district court erred in concluding that the challenged regulation is appropriately tailored to achieve its objective of reducing abusive college drinking.

IV.

Because a regulation of commercial speech must satisfy all four *Central Hudson* prongs in order to survive, . . . and the regulation in question here does not satisfy the fourth prong, the challenged regulation violates the First Amendment as applied to the College Newspapers.

Reversed.

DISSENT

Judge Shedd

This comprehensive plan adopted by Virginia only minimally impacts commercial speech by attempting to limit advertising aimed at a targeted market which includes a substantial percentage of readers for whom use of the product is illegal. Virginia's approach does not prohibit all advertising of alcohol which will reach this audience; it is a minor limitation on such advertising in college newspapers as part of a comprehensive plan to address a very serious problem.

Questions

1. *a.* Why did the court rule for the two college newspapers?
   b. What did the court mean in saying the alcohol advertising regulation is unconstitutionally overbroad?
2. *a.* Do you think the elimination of alcohol ads in college newspapers would be effective in reducing underage student alcohol consumption and alcohol abuse? Explain.
   b. Do you favor limits on alcohol ads in college newspapers? Explain.
   c. Do you favor higher alcohol taxes as a means of reducing underage alcohol consumption and alcohol abuse? Explain.
3. In online fantasy sports leagues, fans "draft" current professional players in baseball, football, and other sports to create their own teams that then compete based on the actual performance of those players. A Missouri company, C.B.C. Distribution and Marketing, Inc., operated a for-profit online league. In 2005, Major League Baseball changed its licensing policies and

declined to allow C.B.C. a license to continue using the names and statistics of major league baseball players. C.B.C. then sued, claiming it had a First Amendment right to use the information, while M.L.B. argued that the information was protected by the intellectual property and publicity rights of the players. Decide the case. Explain. See *C.B.C. Distribution and Marketing, Inc. v. Major League Baseball Advanced Media*, 505 F.3d 818 (8th Cir. 2007) [**https://law.justia.com**], *cert. denied sub nom. Major League Baseball v. C.B.C. Distribution & Marketing*, 553 U.S. 1090 (2008).

4. Two Rhode Island statutes prohibited all price-advertising on liquor in the state, except for in-store price tags and signs that were not visible on the street. The state sought to reduce alcohol consumption. Two licensed liquor dealers challenged the statutes' constitutionality.
   a. How would you rule on that challenge? Explain.
   b. Why would the elimination of price advertising arguably contribute to reduced alcohol consumption?

   See *44 Liquormart, Inc. v. Rhode Island*, 517 U.S. 484 (1996) [**https://supreme.justia.com**].

Part Three—The Fourth Amendment

LO 5-6
Describe some of the issues arising under the Fourth Amendment "search and seizure" rules.

David L. Riley was pulled over by the San Diego police because of an expired automobile registration. Guns were found in the car, Riley was arrested, and a warrantless search of his smartphone revealed information associating him with a gang shooting. Riley was later convicted of attempted murder. Riley sought to suppress all of the evidence secured through the cell phone search. That claim, along with a companion case, *United States v. Wurie,*[50] involving a flip phone search, reached the U.S. Supreme Court. The Court's 2014 unanimous rulings in *Riley v. California*[51] and in *Wurie* held that a warrant is required to search a cell phone, absent emergencies or a threat to officers.

Officer safety and the prevention of evidence destruction have historically been cited as justifications for warrantless searches incident to arrests, but the *Riley* Court said those concerns do not apply to cell phone searches. Furthermore, the routine role of cell phones in everyday life and their immense storage capacity make them a repository of many aspects of phone owners' lives. Such a search might be even more damaging than a warrantless search of an individual's home, the Court reasoned. The Court acknowledged the additional burden the decision places on law enforcement.

Search and Seizure Law

Authorities are under great pressure to cope with America's crime and terrorism problems. They must do so, however, within the confines of the Constitution, which is designed to protect us all–including criminals and terrorists–from the power of an unfair, overreaching government. The Fourth Amendment provides

> The right of the people to be secure in their persons, houses, papers, and effects, against unreasonable searches and seizures, shall not be violated, and no Warrants shall issue, but upon probable cause. . ..

Two crucial inquiries in search and seizure cases are whether a search has, in fact, occurred (as in the *Riley* case) and whether the search violated the subject's reasonable expectation of privacy (which is much more likely in one's home than on the street, for example).

In general, a *search warrant* issued by a judge is necessary to comply with the Constitution in making a search. A warrantless search is permissible, however, if reasonable. That could be the case if the search occurred during an arrest, or where probable cause exists to believe a crime has been committed but circumstances make securing a warrant in advance impracticable. Under the *plain view* doctrine, law enforcement officers can lawfully seize evidence of a crime (such as weapons or drugs) without a warrant if that evidence is in plain view during a lawful observation. An example would be during a vehicle stop arising from the violation of a traffic law, where an officer sees a weapon on a seat in the vehicle.

Did a Search Occur?

Antoine Jones, a nightclub owner, was suspected of being associated with an illegal narcotics operation. Police lacked a valid warrant but, nonetheless, put a GPS tracker on Jones's Jeep and followed his movements for four weeks. Jones was arrested in 2005. In a 2008 trial, a jury found him guilty of intent to distribute cocaine, for which he was sentenced to life in prison. On appeal, Jones argued that his conviction should be overturned because the warrantless use of the GPS tracker violated his Fourth Amendment right to be protected from unreasonable search and seizure. His case reached the U.S. Supreme Court, which unanimously ruled that installing a GPS device is, indeed, a *search* in constitutional law terms.[52] The Court did not resolve the question of whether a search warrant is required in such situations.

In 2018, the Court did issue a decision in *Carpenter v. United States* requiring authorities to seek a warrant for historical cellphone location records and, it implied, for other kinds of electronic information in which a person has a legitimate privacy interest.[53] In that case, the location records spanned 127 days. On the other hand, in 2021, the 7th Circuit ruled in *United States v. Hammond* that obtaining real-time cell service location information for the span of only a few hours while Hammond traveled on public roads (and during which a crime spree was being committed) did *not* constitute a search, because Hammond could not have had the same expectation of privacy as did Carpenter.[54] The Supreme Court denied certiorari.

How Far Can the Search Go?

For nearly 30 years, police officers had commonly understood that lawfully arresting an occupant of a vehicle confers the right to search the passenger compartment of that vehicle. In its 2009 decision, *Arizona v. Gant,*[55] the U.S. Supreme Court significantly diminished that authority by ruling that such searches are permissible in only two circumstances: when the individual being arrested is close enough to the vehicle to reach in for a weapon or for evidence, and when the officer can reasonably believe the vehicle contains evidence relevant to the crime for which the individual is being arrested. Thus, an arrest for a routine traffic stop would not ordinarily justify a vehicle search, but an arrest for a more serious crime might.[56]

Drug-Sniffing Dog

The Miami-Dade Police Department received a tip that the residence of Joelis Jardines was being used to grow marijuana. A drug-sniffing dog was taken to the door of the home. The dog signaled the presence of marijuana, a search warrant was obtained, and a search discovered marijuana growing in the house. Jardines was arrested.

Question

Did the use of the drug-sniffing dog render the search unconstitutional? Explain.

Source: *Florida v. Jardines,* 569 U.S. 1 (2013). **[https://supreme.justia.com]**

LO 5-7
Explain the "exclusionary rule."

Exclusionary Rule

Perhaps the most controversial aspect of Fourth Amendment interpretation is the *exclusionary rule:* as a matter of due (or *fair*) process, evidence secured in violation of the Fourth Amendment may not be used against a defendant at trial. Ultimately applied to all courts by the 1961 U.S. Supreme Court decision in *Mapp v. Ohio,*[57] the exclusionary rule is a very effective device for discouraging illegal searches, seizures, and arrests but also has the effect of freeing wrongdoers from time to time.

Fackrell arrested Strieff and found methamphetamine and drug paraphernalia.

The Supreme Court developed several exceptions to the exclusionary rule, the most recent of which was articulated in its 2016 ruling in *Utah v. Strieff.*[58] In that case, South Salt Lake City police officer Douglas Fackrell stopped Edward Strieff as he exited a house that was being observed for drug activity following an anonymous tip. Officer Fackrell detained Strieff, secured Strieff's identification, and called a police dispatcher who told Fackrell that Strieff had an outstanding arrest warrant for a minor traffic violation. With that information, Fackrell arrested Strieff, searched him, and found methamphetamine and drug paraphernalia. Strieff claimed that the drug evidence was inadmissible under the exclusionary rule since Fackrell's investigatory stop did not provide reasonable suspicion of criminal conduct.

The U.S. Supreme Court agreed that the initial stop was illegal, but ruled 5–3 that Strieff could lawfully be searched after Fackrell learned of the outstanding warrant. The discovery of the valid arrest warrant, the majority reasoned, broke the connection between the unconstitutional stop and the evidence seized incident to the lawful arrest. Justice Sonia Sotomayor, expressing particular concern for the treatment of minorities by the police, issued an angry dissent:

> [T]his case tells everyone, white and black, guilty and innocent, that an officer can verify your legal status at any time. It says that your body is subject to invasion while courts excuse the violation of your rights. It implies that you are not a citizen of a democracy but the subject of a carceral state, just waiting to be cataloged.[59]

Privacy

Hidden cameras, government surveillance, phone records, Internet exposure of personal matters, medical records, academic records, school lockers, bodily searches, and many more dimensions of our lives raise privacy concerns. Although the word *privacy* does not appear in the Constitution, courts have cited the Fourth Amendment and other constitutional provisions to firmly establish a right to privacy. Interpreting the bounds of that protection, however, is complex.

Drug testing and the disturbing photographic practice of "upskirting" are among the many situations where privacy concerns have been litigated. Drug testing clearly is a search for Fourth Amendment purposes, but when is it an unconstitutional intrusion on privacy?

Testing Students

In 1998, the school board in rural Tecumseh, Oklahoma, instituted a mandatory random urinalysis drug-testing program for all students participating in competitive extracurricular activities. The tests checked for illegal drugs but not for alcohol. Test results were not turned over to the police. An honor student, Lindsay Earls, challenged the program as a violation of her Fourth Amendment rights. A U.S. court of appeals agreed with her, ruling that school officials needed to provide evidence of an "identifiable drug abuse problem."[60]

The U.S. Supreme Court, however, reversed that decision and held, by a 5–4 margin, that the school's interest in addressing drug problems outweighed students' privacy rights.[61] The Court reasoned that those participating in extracurricular activities are subjected to many rules and restrictions that diminish their expectation of privacy, and that the program is a health and safety measure rather than an assault on personal privacy. Some state supreme courts, however, have ruled that school drug testing violates state constitutional law.[62] Nevertheless, a federal study published in 2019 indicated that 38% of school districts in the United States require drug-testing, a marked increase over the prior decade and in direct response to the opioid epidemic.[63]

Testing Welfare Applicants

At least fifteen states require welfare applicants seeking the federal government's Temporary Assistance for Needy Families (TANF) to be screened and perhaps tested for drug abuse. Some states apply testing requirements to all applicants, while others limit testing to individuals who are reasonably suspected of illegal drug-related activity.

Florida's warrantless, suspicionless drug-testing requirement for all welfare applicants was ruled unconstitutional in 2014.[64] A three-judge panel of the 11th Circuit Court of Appeals said Florida failed to show that TANF applicants differed from the general population in their drug behaviors such that the state had reason to subject them to testing. Florida failed, the court ruled, to show a "substantial need" (such as safety concerns) that would justify testing all welfare applicants rather than testing only in particularized situations of individualized suspicion.

Testing-proponents argue that substantial need does exist. They point to the unfairness in using tax dollars to subsidize drug use and argue the state has a duty to discourage drug use and, in particular, to protect children. Florida data, however, showed that only 2.6 percent of those tested were found to have used narcotics, so the program actually cost more to administer than it saved.[65] It also showed that there was no reason to believe welfare applicants in general are widely engaged in drug use.

Voyeurism and the Surveillance Society

Georgia, Massachusetts, Michigan, Texas, and Washington courts, among others in recent years, have overturned criminal convictions involving the practice of "upskirting" and similar photographic intrusions on privacy. In the Washington case, for example, Richard Sorrells and Sean Glas were found guilty of violating a state voyeurism statute for taking pictures up the skirts of some women who were working and shopping in a public mall. On appeal, their convictions were overturned because the voyeurism law did not apply, the Washington State Supreme Court unanimously ruled, to actions in public places.[66] The women had no "reasonable expectation of privacy" in the shopping mall, so their privacy could not have been invaded. A federal law, the Video Voyeurism Prevention Act (limited to situations where federal jurisdiction exists), and a number of state laws have expanded protection against photographic voyeurism. Those laws will, of course, be subject to constitutional scrutiny, particularly on First Amendment grounds because photographs are a form of expression. [For an overview of privacy issues, see **http://epic.org**.]

Questions

1. More than 13 million people become incarcerated in American jails each year. Albert Florence was mistakenly arrested for failing to pay a traffic fine that, in fact, he had paid. After arrest, he was subjected to a pair of strip searches involving showering with a delousing agent, officers lifting his genitals and looking in his body openings, and more. Does the Constitution allow authorities to strip search those admitted to jail for minor violations? Explain. See *Florence v. Board of Chosen Freeholders,* 566 U.S. 318 (2012) [**https://supreme.justia.com**].

2. Alonzo King was arrested in 2009 on an assault charge and, without first obtaining a search warrant, police swabbed the inside of his cheek for a DNA sample. Several months later his DNA was matched with a 2003 rape case. He was then convicted of that rape. He appealed his conviction arguing that he was a victim of an unreasonable search in violation of his Fourth Amendment rights. Maryland law allowed the sampling in cases where the suspect had been arrested but not yet convicted of serious crimes, including burglaries, rape, and murder. Is DNA collection simply a part of the normal criminal booking process, much like fingerprinting, and thus a minimal intrusion on privacy? Explain. See *Maryland v. King,* 569 U.S. 435 (2013) [**https://supreme.justia.com**].

3. A Connecticut resident, Paul DeFusco, was convicted of drug trafficking, based on evidence found in his home. The police conducted the home search with a warrant secured on the basis of information provided by an informant, as well as evidence (some short cut straws, glassine baggies, and prescription bottles) discovered in DeFusco's garbage.
   a. Can the police lawfully search an individual's garbage once it has been placed at the curb for disposal? Explain.

b. Explain the central issue in this case.

See *State of Connecticut v. Paul DeFusco,* 620 A.2d 746 (Conn. 1993).

4. Tucson police in Arizona, cruising in an area associated with the Crips street gang, stopped a car because its insurance coverage had been suspended. Johnson, a backseat passenger, was wearing the blue colors associated with the Crips, and Officer Trevizo saw that Johnson had a police scanner in his pocket. Trevizo questioned Johnson, learning that he was from a town frequented by the Crips gang, had recently been in prison, and had no identification with him. Trevizo asked Johnson to exit the car. He did so. Trevizo conducted a pat-down search and felt a gun. Johnson struggled, but he was arrested, and a further search revealed marijuana. Johnson was charged with unlawful possession of a gun, possession of marijuana, and resisting arrest. In court, Johnson challenged the legality of the search saying it had nothing to do with the traffic stop. Did the pat-down violate the Fourth Amendment's prohibition on unreasonable searches and seizures? Explain. See *Arizona v. Johnson,* 555 U.S. 323 (2009) [**https://supreme.justia.com**].

Business Searches

The government tries to protect us from business hazards, including pollution, defective products, and unsafe workplaces, as well as business crimes such as fraud and bribery. To do so, government agents often want to enter company buildings, observe working conditions, and examine company books. As discussed earlier, we know our homes are generally protected from searches in the absence of a warrant. Can the same be said for a place of business? The Supreme Court has answered that question:

> The Warrant Clause of the Fourth Amendment protects commercial buildings as well as private homes. To hold otherwise would belie the origin of that Amendment, and the American colonial experience. . .. "[T]he Fourth Amendment's commands grew in large measure out of the colonists' experience with the writs of assistance . . . [that] granted sweeping power to customs officials and other agents of the king to search at large for smuggled goods." Against this background, it is untenable that the ban on warrantless searches was not intended to shield places of business as well as of residence.[67]

Part Four—The Fifth Amendment

LO 5-8
Describe the law of the Fifth Amendment "Takings Clause" and the property rights controversy associated with it.

Takings—Eminent Domain

The Fifth Amendment prohibits the taking of private property for *public use* without *just compensation* for the owner. In cases where owners do not want to sell, governments often use the power of *eminent domain* to take private real property for public uses, such as highways, bike trails, and parks, while also providing just compensation.

Takings can also involve personal property. A 1937 federal law allows the government to require raisin growers to set aside a portion of their crops for the government. Farmers then share in the proceeds if the government later sells the reserve raisins. The purpose of the set-aside is to restrict supply to maintain stable raisin prices for farmers. Marvin Horne, a California raisin farmer, did not want to set aside any of his raisins, and he challenged the rule as an unlawful taking. The U.S. Supreme Court agreed with Horne, ruling in 2013 that the government must pay just compensation for taking personal property, just as for real property.[68]

What about the situation where the property claimed by the government is to be used for a *private* purpose? Communities across America, hungry for an improved tax base and more jobs, have made the practice routine– but are they violating the Fifth Amendment rights of the property owners? The following 5–4 Supreme Court decision involves a challenge to a New London, Connecticut, plan to clear a portion of the city to make way for a private-sector office and research park, along with a waterfront hotel, conference center, residences, a marina, and a river walk. Existing small businesses and residences were taken to make room for bigger, more successful private ventures, providing a stronger tax base for the city.

LEGAL BRIEFCASE

Kelo v. City of New London, Connecticut

545 U.S. 469 (2005)

Justice Stevens

In 2000, the city of New London approved a development plan that, in the words of the Supreme Court of Connecticut, was "projected to create in excess of 1,000 jobs, to increase tax and other revenues, and to revitalize an economically distressed city, including its downtown and waterfront areas" (843 A.2d 500, 507 [2004]). In assembling the land needed for this project, the city's development agent has purchased property from willing sellers and proposes to use the power of eminent domain to acquire the remainder of the property from unwilling owners in exchange for just compensation. The question presented is whether the city's proposed disposition of this property qualifies as a "public use" within the meaning of the Takings Clause of the Fifth Amendment to the Constitution.

I

The city of New London (hereinafter City) sits at the junction of the Thames River and the Long Island Sound in southeastern Connecticut. Decades of economic decline led a state agency in 1990 to designate the City a "distressed municipality." In 1996, the Federal Government closed the Naval Undersea Warfare Center, which had been located in the Fort Trumbull area of the City and had employed over 1,500 people. In 1998, the City's unemployment rate was nearly double that of the State, and its population of just under 24,000 residents was at its lowest since 1920.

These conditions prompted state and local officials to target New London, and particularly its Fort Trumbull area, for economic revitalization. To this end, respondent New London Development Corporation (NLDC), a private nonprofit entity established some years earlier to assist the City in planning economic development, was reactivated. In January 1998, the State authorized a $5.35 million bond issue to support the NLDC's planning activities and a $10 million bond issue toward the creation of a Fort Trumbull State Park. In February, the pharmaceutical company Pfizer Inc. announced that it would build a $300 million research facility on a site immediately adjacent to Fort Trumbull; local planners hoped that Pfizer would draw new business to the area. Upon obtaining state-level approval, the NLDC finalized an integrated development plan focused on 90 acres of the Fort Trumbull area.

The Fort Trumbull area is situated on a peninsula that juts into the Thames River. The area comprises approximately 115 privately owned properties, as well as the 32 acres of land formerly occupied by the naval facility (Trumbull State Park now occupies 18 of those 32 acres). The development plan encompasses seven parcels. Parcel 1 is designated for a waterfront conference hotel at the center of a "small urban village" that will include restaurants and shopping. . .. Parcel 2 will be the site of approximately 80 new residences organized into an urban neighborhood and linked by public walkway to the remainder of the development, including the state park. This parcel also includes space reserved for a new U.S. Coast Guard Museum. Parcel 3, which is located immediately north of the Pfizer facility, will contain at least 90,000 square feet of research and development office space. Parcel 4A is a 2.4-acre site that will be used either to support the adjacent state park, by providing parking or retail services for visitors, or to support the nearby marina. Parcel 4B will include a renovated marina, as well as the final stretch of the riverwalk. Parcels 5, 6, and 7 will provide land for office and retail space, parking, and water-dependent commercial uses.

The city council approved the plan in January 2000 and designated the NLDC as its development agent in charge of implementation. The city council also authorized the NLDC to purchase property or to acquire property by exercising eminent domain in the City's name. The NLDC successfully negotiated the purchase of most of the real estate in the 90-acre area, but its negotiations with petitioners failed. As a consequence, in November 2000, the NLDC initiated the condemnation proceedings that gave rise to this case.

II

Petitioner Susette Kelo has lived in the Fort Trumbull area since 1997. She has made extensive improvements to her house, which she prizes for its water view. Petitioner Wilhelmina Dery was born in her Fort Trumbull house in 1918 and has lived there her entire life. Her husband Charles has lived in the house since they married some 60 years ago. In all, the nine petitioners own 15 properties in Fort Trumbull. . .. There is no allegation that any of these properties is blighted or otherwise in poor condition; rather, they were condemned only because they happen to be located in the development area.

In December 2000, petitioners brought this action in the New London Superior Court. They claimed, among other things, that the taking of their properties would violate the "public use" restriction in the Fifth Amendment. After a seven-day bench trial, the Superior Court granted a permanent restraining order prohibiting the taking of the properties located in parcel 4A (park or marina support). It, however, denied petitioners relief as to the properties located in parcel 3 (office space).

After the Superior Court ruled, both sides took appeals to the Supreme Court of Connecticut. That court held that all of the City's proposed takings were valid.

III

Two polar propositions are perfectly clear. On the one hand, it has long been accepted that the sovereign may not take the property of A for the sole purpose of transferring it to another private party B, even though A is paid just compensation. On the other hand, it is equally clear that a State may transfer property from one private party to another if future "use by the public" is the purpose of the taking; the condemnation of land for a railroad is a familiar example. Neither of these propositions, however, determines the disposition of this case.

As for the first proposition, the City would no doubt be forbidden from taking petitioners' land for the purpose of conferring a private benefit on a particular party. Nor would the City be allowed to take property under the mere pretext of a public purpose, when its actual purpose was to bestow a private benefit. The takings before us, however, would be executed pursuant to a "carefully considered" development plan. The trial judge and all the members of the Supreme Court of Connecticut agreed that there was no evidence of an illegitimate purpose in this case.

On the other hand, this is not a case in which the City is planning to open the condemned land—at least not in its entirety—to use by the general public. Nor will the private lessees of the land in any sense be required to operate like common carriers, making their services available to all comers. But although such a projected use would be sufficient to satisfy the public use requirement, this "Court long ago rejected any literal requirement that condemned property be put into use for the general public." Indeed, while many state courts in the mid-19th century endorsed "use by the public" as the proper definition of public use, that narrow view steadily eroded over time. Not only was the "use by the public" test difficult to administer (e.g., what proportion of the public need have access to the property? at what price?), but it proved to be impractical given the diverse and always evolving needs of society. Accordingly, when this Court began applying the Fifth Amendment to the States at the close of the 19th century, it embraced the broader and more natural interpretation of public use as "public purpose."

The disposition of this case therefore turns on the question whether the City's development plan serves a "public purpose." Without exception, our cases have defined that concept broadly, reflecting our long-standing policy of deference to legislative judgments in this field.

In *Berman v. Parker,* this Court upheld a redevelopment plan targeting a blighted area of Washington, D.C., in which most of the housing for the area's 5,000 inhabitants was beyond repair. Under the plan, the area would be condemned and part of it utilized for the construction of streets, schools, and other public facilities. The remainder of the land would be leased or sold to private parties for the purpose of redevelopment, including the construction of low-cost housing.

IV

Those who govern the City were not confronted with the need to remove blight in the Fort Trumbull area, but their determination that the area was sufficiently distressed to justify a program of economic rejuvenation is entitled to our deference. The City has carefully formulated an economic development plan that it believes will provide appreciable benefits to the community, including—but by no means limited to—new jobs and increased tax revenue. . .. Given the comprehensive character of the plan, the thorough deliberation that preceded its adoption, and the limited scope of our review, it is appropriate for us to resolve the challenges of the individual owners, not on a piecemeal basis, but rather in light of the entire plan. Because that plan unquestionably serves a public purpose, the takings challenged here satisfy the public use requirement of the Fifth amendment.

To avoid this result, petitioners urge us to adopt a new bright-line rule that economic development does not qualify as a public use. Putting aside the unpersuasive suggestion that the City's plan will provide only purely economic benefits, neither precedent nor logic supports petitioners' proposal. Promoting economic development is a traditional and long-accepted function of government.

In affirming the City's authority to take petitioners' properties, we do not minimize the hardship that condemnations may entail, notwithstanding the payment of just compensation. We emphasize that nothing in our opinion precludes any State from placing further restrictions on its exercise of the takings power. Indeed, many States already impose "public use" requirements that are stricter than the federal baseline.

Affirmed.

AFTERWORD—PROPERTY RIGHTS REVOLUTION?

The *Kelo* decision was an angry disappointment for property rights advocates. A government taking of Americans' long-time homes, even for just compensation, is a powerful and frightening image. Susette Kelo eventually settled with New London, vacated her home, and received $442,000. Her "little pink house" was disassembled and moved to another lot, where it stands as something of a national symbol for property rights.

Clearly, however, governments need and have long exercised, substantial authority to take property for economic development. Of course, government planning sometimes does not work out as expected, and the Pfizer development appears to be one of those failures. In 2009, Pfizer announced it was abandoning the Fort Trumbull office complex as a cost-saving measure. Fourteen hundred jobs were departing. The hotels, stores, and condominiums planned for the lots taken from Kelo and her neighbors have yet to materialize.

Kelo produced one of the angriest backlashes to any Supreme Court decision in history. At least 44 states have passed legislation or amended their constitutions to limit eminent domain, but the effectiveness of those measures is unclear. Some of them still allow takings involving "blighted" property, an exception readily subject to abuse from the critics' point of view. [For property rights analysis and updates, and more on the *Kelo* story, see **www.ij.org**].

Questions

1. What reasoning was offered by Justice Stevens to support the majority view that the New London development complied with due process requirements?
2. *a.* What was the central question in this case, and how did the majority answer that question?
   b. How would you expect the dissent to answer that question?
3. From the dissenting point of view, what harm is likely to emerge from this decision?
4. Marilyn and James Nollan applied for a permit to replace their beachfront home with a larger structure. The California Coastal Commission agreed on the condition that the Nollans grant an easement on their beach that would allow the public to cross the property and thus facilitate movement between the public beaches that lay on both sides of the Nollan beach. The Nollans sued, claiming a violation of the Takings Clause. Decide. See *Nollan v. California Coastal Commission,* 483 U.S. 825 (1987) [**https://supreme.justia.com**].
5. Tina Bennis sued when Wayne County (Detroit), Michigan, authorities took the car she jointly owned with her husband, after police arrested him for receiving oral sex from a prostitute while parked in the car. A 1925 anti-nuisance law permitted the seizure, but Tina Bennis claimed it amounted to an unconstitutional taking because she was an innocent half owner of the 1977 Pontiac for which the couple had paid $600. Bennis's claim eventually reached the U.S. Supreme Court. Decide the case. See *Bennis v. Michigan,* 516 U.S. 442 (1996) [**https://supreme.justia.com**].

Takings—Regulatory

We have now seen how the law responds to situations in which the government uses its power of eminent domain to condemn property, for either public or private use, and pays just compensation. What happens when the government does not take the property but rather *regulates* it in a manner that deprives it of some, or all, of its economic usefulness?

For example, without providing just compensation, can a state lawfully limit the amount a landlord can charge for rent, in an effort to preserve low-income housing? Can the state forbid billboards to enhance roadside beauty?

These *regulatory takings,* whether temporary or permanent, normally do not require government compensation, because doing so would severely impair the state's ability to govern to promote the general welfare. Nonetheless, the courts have been more aggressive in recent years about requiring just compensation for some regulatory takings. Three broad classes of such takings have emerged through case law.

Total Takings

If a governmental body acts in a way that permanently extinguishes all of the economic value of a property, or physically and permanently invades the property, the taking requires just compensation unless: (1) the government is preventing a nuisance or (2) the regulation was permissible under property law at the time the property was purchased. When the South Carolina Coastal Commission passed erosion rules having the effect of preventing David Lucas from building any permanent structure on his $975,000 beachfront lots, Lucas sued, claiming a Fifth Amendment violation. The U.S. Supreme Court agreed with Lucas and held that a taking requiring just compensation had occurred because the state had deprived Lucas of *all* economically beneficial use of the property and the property did not fall within an exception.[69]

> Erosion rules–preventing Lucas from building any permanent structure on his $975,000 beachfront lots.

Exaction/Mitigation

A regulatory taking occurs in situations where the government allows land development only if the owner dedicates some property interest (called an *exaction*) or money (called a *mitigation* or *impact fee*) to the government. Thus, if you are developing land for housing, the city government might require you to devote a portion of that land to parks, or to pay a fee to help with community recreation needs.

The Supreme Court dealt with just such a case in *Dolan v. City of Tigard.*[70] Florence Dolan, owner of a plumbing and electrical supply store in Tigard, Oregon, applied for a city permit to nearly double the size of her store and to pave her parking lot. Concerned with increased traffic and water runoff due to the proposed expansion, the city granted the permit, subject to two conditions: (1) Dolan had to dedicate the portion of her property that lay within the 100-year floodplain to the city, to improve drainage for the creek that ran along her property, and (2) she had to dedicate an additional 15-foot strip of her land adjacent to the floodplain, for use as a bicycle path/walkway to relieve traffic congestion. Dolan sued and, eventually, the U.S. Supreme Court ruled that a government can compel a dedication of private property to public use where it can establish two factors: (1) a nexus or relationship between the government's legitimate purpose (flood and traffic control in *Dolan*) and the condition imposed (the land Dolan was to dedicate to public purposes), and (2) a "rough proportionality" between the burden imposed (the land given over to public use) and the impact of the development (increased water runoff and increased traffic).[71] The Supreme Court ruled that Tigard had failed to meet those standards and held for Dolan.

A 2013 U.S. Supreme Court decision expanded the *Dolan* reasoning and strengthened property rights. Coy Koontz, Sr. wanted to build on his wetland property, but the local water management district, consistent with Florida law, denied permission. Koontz was unwilling to either turn over part of his property for public purposes or pay for improvements on other public land as a way of "offsetting" the environmental damage that would have accompanied the development. Koontz sued. The Court, by a 5–4 vote, said the water management district's requirements constituted a taking and were subject to the criteria set forth in *Dolan.*[72]

Partial Takings

Government may, for example, take part of a piece of property to expand a road, install a bike path, or establish a buffer zone. These are neither total takings nor exactions, but rather fall into a case-by-case analysis as to whether compensation is required, considering the importance of the government's goals and the extent of the burden on the property owner.

Zoning in the Sixth Century

Government restraints on property development are not a modern imposition, as we learn from the following description of a zoning law in the Byzantine Empire:

> Next came the first zoning law for the beach. Coastal vistas were so cherished, and the competition for them so keen, that by the sixth century the Emperor Justinian the Great was compelled to pass an ordinance barring construction within 100 feet of the shore to protect sea views.

Source: Lena Lencek and Gideon Bosker, *The Beach: The History of Paradise on Earth* (New York: Penguin Group, 1998), p. 31.

Part Five—The 14th Amendment

Due Process

LO 5-9
Compare and contrast substantive due process and procedural due process.

The Due Process Clauses of both the Fifth Amendment (applicable to the federal government) and the 14th Amendment (applicable to the states) prohibit the government from depriving citizens of life, liberty, or property without due process of law. A **Research Exercise** at the end of this chapter provides an opportunity to explore this issue.

Substantive Due Process

Laws that arbitrarily and unfairly infringe on fundamental personal rights and liberties, such as privacy, voting, and the various freedoms specified in the Bill of Rights, may be challenged on due process grounds. Basically, the law will be struck down unless the related government interest is so compelling that it outweighs the intrusion on personal liberty. By judicial interpretation, the 14th Amendment's Due Process Clause "absorbs" the fundamental liberties (such as privacy) of the *federal* Constitution and prohibits *state* laws that abridge those fundamental liberties.

Procedural Due Process

In essence, procedural due process means that the government must provide a fair procedure, including *notice* and a *fair hearing,* before taking any action affecting a citizen's life, liberty, or property. A fair hearing typically requires, at a minimum, the right to present evidence, the right to a decision maker free of bias, and the right to appeal. The precise nature of procedural due process depends, however, on the situation. A murder trial requires meticulous attention to procedural fairness; an administrative hearing to appeal a public university decision to expel a student for disciplinary reasons, while required to meet minimal constitutional standards, can be more forgiving in its procedural niceties.

Due Process: Void for Vagueness

A statute may violate due process rights if it is so vaguely written that an ordinary person cannot understand it. The *Skilling* case that follows involves a *void for vagueness* claim arising from the infamous Enron fraud scandal that caused the former Houston, Texas, energy giant–then the seventh-largest company in America–to collapse into bankruptcy in 2001. Enron founder and board chair Ken Lay, chief executive officer Jeffrey Skilling, and chief accounting officer Richard Causey were among those indicted for various crimes associated with Enron's spectacular rise, from its founding in 1985, to its collapse a decade and a half later. Among other alleged wrongs, Skilling was convicted of depriving the corporation and the public of his "honest services" by deceiving the investors about Enron's finances. Skilling allegedly inflated Enron's share prices by failing to reveal the company's true financial condition. His appeal reached the Supreme Court in 2010, where he claimed that pretrial publicity and Enron's financial damage to Houston poisoned the jury pool and denied him his Sixth Amendment right to trial by an impartial jury. That claim was rejected by the Supreme Court, but Skilling also argued that the language of the "honest services" federal statute used to convict him was so vague that he was deprived of his due process rights.

Skilling argued that the "honest services" statute used to convict him for his role in the Enron scandal was so vague that he was deprived of his due process rights.

LEGAL BRIEFCASE

Skilling v. United States

130 S. Ct. 2896 (2010)

Justice Ginsburg

[I and II omitted—ed.]

III

We next consider whether Skilling's conspiracy conviction was premised on an improper theory of honest-services wire fraud. The honest-services statute, Section 1346, Skilling maintains, is unconstitutionally vague. . . .

A

To place Skilling's constitutional challenge in context, we first review the origin and subsequent application of the honest-services doctrine.

1

Enacted in 1872, the original mail-fraud provision, the predecessor of the modern-day mail- and wire-fraud laws, proscribed, without further elaboration, use of the mails to advance "any scheme or artifice to defraud." See *McNally v. United States,* 483 U.S. 350, 356, 107 S. Ct. 2875, 97 L. Ed. 2d 292 (1987). In 1909, Congress amended the statute to prohibit, as it does today, "any scheme or artifice to defraud, *or for obtaining money or property by means of false or fraudulent pretenses, representations, or promises.*" Section 1341 (emphasis added). Emphasizing Congress' disjunctive phrasing, the Courts of Appeals, one after the other, interpreted the term "scheme or artifice to defraud" to include deprivations not only of money or property, but also of intangible rights.

2

In 1987, this Court, in *McNally v. United States,* stopped the development of the intangible-rights doctrine in its tracks. *McNally* involved a state officer who, in selecting Kentucky's insurance agent, arranged to procure a share of the agent's commissions via kickbacks paid to companies the official partially controlled. The prosecutor did not charge that, "in the absence of the alleged scheme[,] the Commonwealth would have paid a lower premium or secured better insurance." Instead, the prosecutor maintained that the kickback scheme "defraud[ed] the citizens and government of Kentucky of their right to have the Commonwealth's affairs conducted honestly."

We held that the scheme did not qualify as mail fraud. "Rather than constru[ing] the statute in a manner that leaves its outer boundaries ambiguous and involves the Federal Government in setting standards of disclosure and good government for local and state officials," we read the statute "as limited in scope to the protection of property rights." "If Congress desires to go further," we stated, "it must speak more clearly."

3

Congress responded swiftly. The following year, it enacted a new statute "specifically to cover one of the 'intangible rights' that lower courts had protected . . . prior to *McNally:* 'the intangible right of honest services.'" In full, the honest-services statute stated:

> For the purposes of th[e] chapter [of the United States Code that prohibits, *inter alia,* mail fraud, Section 1341, and wire fraud, Section 1343], the term "scheme or artifice to defraud" includes a scheme or artifice to deprive another of the intangible right of honest services.

B

Congress, Skilling charges, reacted quickly but not clearly: He asserts that Section 1346 is unconstitutionally vague. To satisfy due process, "a penal statute [must] define the criminal offense [1] with sufficient definiteness that ordinary people can understand what conduct is prohibited and [2] in a manner that does not encourage arbitrary and discriminatory enforcement." *Kolender v. Lawson,* 461 U.S. 352, 357, 103 S. Ct. 1855, 75 L. Ed. 2d 903 (1983). The void-for-vagueness doctrine embraces these requirements.

According to Skilling, Section 1346 meets neither of the two due process essentials. First, the phrase "the intangible right of honest services," he contends, does not adequately define what behavior it bars. Second, he alleges, Section 1346's "standardless sweep allows policemen, prosecutors, and juries to pursue their personal predilections," thereby "facilitat[ing] opportunistic and arbitrary prosecutions."

In urging invalidation of Section 1346, Skilling swims against our case law's current, which requires us, if we can, to construe, not condemn, Congress' enactments.

There is no doubt that Congress intended Section 1346 to refer to and incorporate the honest-services doctrine recognized in Court of Appeals' decisions before *McNally* derailed the intangible-rights theory of fraud. . .. Congress enacted Section 1346 on the heels *of McNally* and drafted the statute using that decision's terminology.

Satisfied that Congress, by enacting Section 1346, "meant to reinstate the body of pre-*McNally* honest-services law," we have surveyed that case law. In parsing the Courts of Appeals decisions, we acknowledge that Skilling's vagueness challenge has force, for honest-services decisions preceding *McNally* were not models of clarity or consistency.

Although some applications of the pre-*McNally* honest-services doctrine occasioned disagreement among the Courts of Appeals, these cases do not cloud the doctrine's solid core: The "vast majority" of the honest-services cases involved offenders who, in violation of a fiduciary duty, participated in bribery or kickback schemes.

In view of this history, there is no doubt that Congress intended Section 1346 to reach *at least* bribes and kickbacks. Reading the statute to proscribe a wider range of offensive conduct, we acknowledge, would raise the due process concerns underlying the vagueness doctrine. To preserve the statute without transgressing constitutional limitations, we now hold that Section 1346 criminalizes *only* the bribe-and-kickback core of the pre-*McNally* case law.

Interpreted to encompass only bribery and kickback schemes, Section 1346 is not unconstitutionally vague. Recall that the void-for-vagueness doctrine addresses concerns about (1) fair notice and (2) arbitrary and discriminatory prosecutions. . ..

As to fair notice, "whatever the school of thought concerning the scope and meaning of" Section 1346, it has always been "as plain as a pikestaff that" bribes and kickbacks constitute honest-services fraud, *Williams v. United States,* 341 U.S. 97, 101, 71 S. Ct. 576, 95 L. Ed. 774 (1951). . ..

As to arbitrary prosecutions, we perceive no significant risk that the honest-services statute, as we interpret it today, will be stretched out of shape. Its prohibition on bribes and kickbacks draws content not only from the pre-*McNally* case law, but also from federal statutes proscribing—and defining—similar crimes.

C

It remains to determine whether Skilling's conduct violated Section 1346. Skilling's honest-services prosecution, the Government concedes, was not "prototypical." The Government charged Skilling with conspiring to defraud Enron's shareholders by misrepresenting the company's fiscal health, thereby artificially inflating its stock price. It was the Government's theory at trial that Skilling "profited from the fraudulent scheme . . . through the receipt of salary and bonuses, . . . and through the sale of approximately $200 million in Enron stock, which netted him $89 million."

The Government did not, at any time, allege that Skilling solicited or accepted side payments from a third party in exchange for making these misrepresentations. ("[T]he indictment does not allege, and the government's evidence did not show, that [Skilling] engaged in bribery.") It is therefore clear that, as we read Section 1346, Skilling did not commit honest-services fraud.

Affirmed in part. Vacated in part. Remanded.

AFTERWORD

The Supreme Court returned Skilling's case to the federal Fifth Circuit Court of Appeals where, in 2011, the Skilling saga appeared to be nearing its conclusion. The Fifth Circuit upheld Skilling's conviction, finding the honest-services error was "harmless," in that ample evidence unrelated to the honest-services charge supported Skilling's conviction on 19 counts of securities fraud, conspiracy, insider trading, and making false representations.[73] Skilling was released from federal custody in February 2019 after serving only 12 years of his 24-year prison sentence; his sentence was reduced because of a mistake that was made in interpreting the federal sentencing guidelines. Skilling also agreed to give up about $42 million, all of which was to go Enron fraud victims. In March 2019, only weeks after his release, Skilling began holding meetings with former Enron executives and others in the energy industry to gain backing for a new energy venture.

Questions

1. Why did the Court conclude that Skilling did not commit honest-services fraud?
2. Why did the Court conclude that the honest-services statute was unconstitutional?
3. How did the Court correct the unconstitutional infirmity in the honest-services statute?
4. Christopher Keating, a physics professor at the University of South Dakota, was involved in an ongoing conflict with a co-worker, and Keating sent an inflammatory e-mail to his department head. Keating's contract with the university was not renewed because the e-mail violated a university policy requiring civil behavior:

   > Faculty members are responsible for discharging their instructional, scholarly and service duties civilly, constructively and in an informed manner. They must treat their colleagues, staff, students and visitors with respect, and they must comport themselves at all times, even when expressing disagreement or when engaging in pedagogical exercises, in ways that will preserve and strengthen the willingness to cooperate and to give or to accept instruction, guidance or assistance.

   Keating sued the university and claimed, among other things, that the university's "civility policy" was impermissibly vague in violation of the Due Process Clause of the Fourteenth Amendment. How would you rule on his void-for-vagueness claim? Explain. See *Keating v. University of South Dakota*, 569 F. App'x 469 (8th Cir. 2014) [**https://law.justia.com**].

Equal Protection

LO 5-10
Identify some examples of the impact of the Equal Protection Clause on business and society.

The 14th Amendment provides that no state shall "deny to any person within its jurisdiction the equal protection of the laws." The Due Process Clause of the Fifth Amendment has been interpreted to provide that same protection against the power of the federal government. Fundamentally, these laws forbid a government from treating one person (including a corporation) differently from another without a purpose of furthering a legitimate governmental interest. As the law has developed, judicial scrutiny of the intrusion increases when the protected interest involves a "fundamental right" (such as procreation) or the object of the discrimination belongs to a "suspect class" (such as a particular racial group).

Notably, the Equal Protection and Due Process Clauses have played an enormous role in attacking discrimination (see Chapter 13), but they can also significantly influence routine business practice in many ways. For example, can we lawfully impose higher taxes on a gambling casino than we impose on a grocery store? Can we require the oil industry to follow more rigorous environmental standards than we expect of coal mines? In general, the answer to these questions is yes, but only if the legislation can pass the rational basis test. Otherwise, the law is unconstitutional and thus, unenforceable.

[The U.S. Supreme Court, in *Loving v. Virginia,*[74] employed due process and equal protection principles to declare Virginia's anti-miscegenation statute unconstitutional, thus ending race-based restrictions on marriage in the United States. For the 2016 *Loving* feature movie trailer, see **www.youtube.com/watch?v=zRXuCY7tRgk**].

How Many Renters?

Trying to reduce the flow of university students into certain portions of Ames, Iowa, home of Iowa State University, the city passed a zoning ordinance that permitted only single-family residences in specified areas. Under the ordinance, "family" was defined as any number of related persons or no more than three unrelated persons. The Ames Rental Property Association challenged the constitutionality of the ordinance.

Questions

1. What constitutional claim was raised by the plaintiffs?
2. Criticize the Ames approach for achieving its housing goals.
3. Decide the case. Explain.

Source: *Ames Rental Property Association v. City of Ames,* 736 N.W.2d 255 (Iowa 2007) [**https://law.justia.com**].

Same-Sex Marriage: Equal Rights?

In *Obergefell v. Hodges,* the U.S. Supreme Court in 2015 ruled 5–4 that the right to marry is guaranteed to same-sex couples by the Due Process and Equal Protection Clauses of the 14th Amendment.[75]

Marriage is one of our fundamental liberties.

Citing a well-established precedent, the Court affirmed that marriage is one of our fundamental liberties. Those liberties include choices central to individual dignity and autonomy and, as such, are protected by the Due Process Clause. Among those choices is the decision to marry. Marriage protects the sanctity of the two-person unions at the core of American life, it safeguards children and families, and it protects the social order. Because all of those principles apply equally to both opposite-sex and same-sex unions, the denial of marriage rights to same-sex couples abridges both due process of law and equal protection under the law.

The decision requires all states to issue marriage licenses to same-sex couples and to recognize the legitimacy of same-sex marriages validly performed in other states. By its ruling, the Court changed American life and reminded everyone of the Constitution's expectation of equality before the law.

The dissenting justices argued that the Constitution simply does not address the same-sex marriage issue and, therefore, should be left to each state legislature. The majority view, on the other hand, viewed the Constitution as a living document that should change with society.

In his dissent, Chief Justice Roberts noted that only 11 states and the District of Columbia permitted same-sex marriage democratically through voting booths and legislatures. He argued that the decision denied same-sex marriage supporters the opportunity to achieve "true acceptance" of their view by persuading others of the justice of their cause. Of course, Supreme Court rulings have served to educate the public, and in almost all instances (excepting, most notably, the 1973 *Roe v. Wade*[76] abortion decision and the 2022 *Dobbs v. Jackson Women's Health Organization*[77] decision that overturned Roe), controversial decisions such as those involving school integration and the right to contraception become broadly accepted by the public. The religious freedom laws noted earlier in this chapter reflect, however, stern initial resistance by some to the *Obergefell* decision.

PRACTICING ETHICS Same-Sex Marriage: How Should We Feel?

Nearly two dozen nations, mostly in the Americas and Europe, permit same-sex marriages. According to the Pew Research Center, Americans in 2004 opposed same-sex marriage 60 percent to 31 percent. But in a 2021 Gallup poll, 70 percent of Americans—a record high—responded in favor of legalizing same-sex unions. This represents an extraordinarily rapid change in views on gay and lesbian marriage. Yet, opinions vary largely by political party identification: 83 percent of Democrats support same-sex marriage, while only 53 percent of Republicans do. Those who remain opposed often object on moral and religious grounds. Consider some questions examining those concerns:

1. What issues should one consider in deciding whether same-sex marriages are morally defensible?
2. Because the American people, according to polling data, largely support same-sex marriage, can we then consider it a morally defensible practice? Explain.
3. If scholarly studies ultimately demonstrate that homosexuality is substantially the result of genetic characteristics, would we be morally required to accept same-sex marriage? Explain.

Source: Pew Research Center, "Attitudes on Same-Sex Marriage," May 14, 2019 [**www.pewforum.org**]; Gallup, "Record-High 70% in U.S. Support Same-Sex Marriage," June 8, 2021 [**https://news.gallup.com**].

Stop-and-Frisk

The New York City police department practices a "stop-and-frisk" policy by which a police officer can stop and question those the officer reasonably believes have committed, are committing, or are about to commit a felony or serious misdemeanor. Those stopped can be frisked for weapons if the officer reasonably believes they are in danger of physical injury.

The stop-and-frisk police practice is constitutionally permissible if conducted properly, but in a 2013 class-action lawsuit, *Floyd v. City of New York,* Federal District Court Judge Shira Scheindlin ruled that stop-and-frisk, as practiced in recent years in New York City, was an impermissible violation of citizens' Fourth Amendment (search and seizure) and 14th Amendment (equal protection) rights. The judge ruled that police had routinely stopped innocent people without reasonable suspicion of a crime and that the police had been engaging in racial profiling. About 83 percent of the 4.4 million stops between 2004 and 2012 involved Blacks and Hispanics, two demographics that make up slightly more than 50 percent of the city population. The city argued that the racial pattern of the stops reflected the disproportionate share of crimes committed by young minority men, but the judge rejected that reasoning, saying that factor would be valid only if all those stopped were criminals. Instead, 88 percent of those stopped were released with no finding of a justification for the stop.

Judge Scheindlin did not order a halt to stop-and-frisk, which is an important law enforcement tool if properly employed. She did, however, appoint a monitor to ensure police compliance with remedies, including new training practices and the use of body-worn cameras by some officers. From a peak of 685,000 stops in 2011, the total fell to about 24,000 in 2015. As stops declined, major crime rates in total continued to fall; however, homicides, rapes, and robberies increased in 2015.

Question

Judge Scheindlin said, "It is impermissible to subject all members of a racially defined group to heightened police enforcement because some members of that group are criminals." Would you agree with Judge Scheindlin if homicides, rapes, and robberies continue to climb? Explain.

Sources: Joseph Goldstein, "Judge Rejects New York's Stop-and-Frisk Policy," *The New York Times,* August 12, 2013 [**www.nytimes.com**]; *Floyd v. City of New York,* 959 F. Supp. 2d 540 (S.D.N.Y. 2013); Lia Eustachewich and Bob Fredericks, "Stop-and-Frisks Plunge, but Cops Struggle to Comply with Record-Keeping Rules: NYPD Monitor," *New York Post,* February 16, 2016 [**http://nypost.com**]; and Pervaiz Shallwani and Mark Morales, "NYC Officials Tout New Low in Crime, but Homicide, Rape, Robbery Rose," *The Wall Street Journal,* January 4, 2016 [**www.wsj.com**].

Research Exercise

Civil asset forfeiture is a particularly controversial, but generally lawful, police practice involving state and federal law enforcement authorities seizing property and cash from individuals who often are simply *suspected* of committing a crime. Research civil asset forfeiture cases and the passage of a historic law in California, banning the practice and paving the way for other states to do the same, at **www.aclunc.org/search?terms=civil%20forfeiture.** Then see Merrill Matthews, "Civil Asset Forfeiture and the Constitution," *IPI Ideas,* no. 70, February 18, 2016 [**www.ipi.org/ipi_issues/detail/civil-asset-forfeiture-and-the-constitution**]. Explain the constitutional challenges that might be raised against civil asset forfeitures.

Chapter Questions

1. Danny Birchfield drove into a ditch in North Dakota. Responding officers believed he was intoxicated. He failed field sobriety tests and was arrested. In violation of North Dakota law, he refused to take a chemical test. Birchfield challenged the state statute that criminalized his refusal to take the test. He argued that the statute violated the Fourth Amendment's search-and-seizure provision because the officers did not have probable cause that would have supported a search warrant. Are warrantless breath tests incident to arrest constitutionally permissible? What about warrantless blood tests? Explain. See *Birchfield v. North Dakota,* 579 U.S. 438 (2016) [**https://supreme.justia.com**].

2. Bradley Johnson, a high school mathematics teacher, posted on his classroom walls large banners with familiar phrases such as "In God We Trust," "One Nation Under God," and "God Shed His Grace on Thee." School officials told him he needed to put the phrases in context (for example, put the entire Declaration of Independence on the wall) or remove them. He did the latter and sued the school district for violating his First Amendment free speech and religious expression rights. In part, he defended his banners by pointing to displays in other classrooms that included Tibetan prayer flags, a Dalai Lama poster, and more. Decide. See *Johnson v. Poway Unified School District,* 658 F.3d 954 (9th Cir. 2011) [**https://law.justia.com**], *cert. denied,* 132 S. Ct. 1807 (2012).
3. Members of the Ku Klux Klan were distributing gun rights leaflets in Desloge, Missouri, when informed by a police officer that they were violating a city ordinance that prohibited "stand[ing] in or enter[ing] upon a roadway for the purpose of soliciting rides, employment, business or charitable contributions from, or distribut[ing] anything to, the occupant of any vehicle." The officer had observed Klan members stepping into the street to give leaflets to passing drivers. The Klan sued Desloge claiming the ordinance violated Klan members' First Amendment rights. How would you rule on that case? See *Traditionalist American Knights of the Ku Klux Klan v. City of Desloge, Missouri,* 775 F.3d 969 (8th Cir. 2014).
4. A Texas state law prohibits individuals from piloting drones above jails, petroleum refineries, sports arenas, and other specified facilities with the "intent to conduct surveillance on the individual or property captured in the image." The statute fails to define "surveillance." In addition, it provides 21 exemptions for specified activities, including policing efforts, academics pursuing scholarly research, and military activities, but journalism is not among them. Are any constitutional protections violated? Explain. See *National Press Photographers Association v. McGraw,* Case no. 1:19-cv-00946-RP, (Tex. W.D.) [**https://NPPA.org**].
5. Early in the morning hours, McNeely was stopped by Missouri police for speeding and erratic driving. He was required to take a blood test after he refused a breath test with a portable machine. His blood alcohol content was about twice the legal limit. He was charged with driving while intoxicated. Was the warrantless blood test an unreasonable search? Explain. See *Missouri v. McNeely,* 569 U.S. 141 (2013) [**https://supreme.justia.com**].
6. Police officer Hughes, from Council Bluffs, Iowa, saw 28-year-old Sorick riding his bicycle at 12:35 a.m. without lights in violation of a city ordinance. Hughes stopped Sorick, asked if he was carrying a weapon, and then frisked him, at which time he felt what he believed to be a baggie containing a hard substance. Hughes asked Sorick what the substance was and Sorick said it was marijuana. Hughes issued a citation for possession of marijuana. Sorick was found guilty at trial but appealed, claiming the frisk was an unreasonable search. Hughes testified that he searched Sorick because Hughes feared for his safety. The episode was late at night, the street was not lit, Sorick was in close proximity to Hughes, and people in that neighborhood were known to have weapons. Was the search lawful? Explain. See *Iowa v. Sorick,* 810 N.W.2d 896 (Iowa Ct. App. 2012) [**https://www.anylaw.com**].
7. James D. Harmon, Jr. owns an apartment building on West 76th Street near Central Park in New York City. Three of his apartments are subject to rent control, a long-time

city program designed to maintain affordable housing in the very expensive Manhattan market. The rent-stabilized tenants were paying rent that was 59 percent below market rates, according to Harmon.

a. Harmon called rent control "privatized welfare." Explain what he meant.

b. Harmon challenged the rent restriction. What constitutional law claim(s) was(were) raised by Harmon?

c. Who won the case? Why? See *Harmon v. Markus,* 412 F. App'x 420 (2011) [**https://casetext.com**], *cert. denied sub nom. Harmon v. Kimmel,* 132 S. Ct. 1991 (2012).

8. In June 2019, the Supreme Court issued a decision striking down as unconstitutional federal prohibitions against granting trademark protection for "immoral" or "scandalous" material. The case was brought by Erik Brunetti, who sought trademark protection for his streetwear clothing line, FUCT, which is available even in children's and infants' sizes, and includes a sweatshirt that reads, "We are fuct." Three of the justices dissented. See *Iancu v. Brunetti,* 139 S. Ct. 2294 (2019) [**https://casetext.com**]. What were their concerns? Do you agree that these are legitimate government interests warranting a denial of trademark protection?

9. An individual and a group applied to the Chicago Park District for permits to hold rallies advocating the legalization of marijuana. The Park District, a municipal agency, required a permit to conduct a public assembly, parade, or other event involving more than 50 individuals. Applications for permits had to be processed within 28 days, and denials had to be clearly explained. Denials could be appealed to the general superintendent and then to the courts. The Park District denied some of the permits for pro-marijuana rallies. Those denied filed suit, claiming the Park District permit rules were unconstitutional.

   a. What constitutional challenge was raised by the plaintiffs?

   b. Decide the case and explain. See *Thomas and Windy City Hemp Development Board v. Chicago Park District,* 534 U.S. 316 (2002) [**https://supreme.justia.com**].

10. Former U.S. Supreme Court Justice Antonin Scalia was asked if the judicial system had "gone off in error" by applying the equal protection requirements of the 14th Amendment to sex discrimination and sexual orientation discrimination. Scalia responded, "Yes, yes. . .. Certainly the Constitution does not require discrimination on the basis of sex. The only issue is whether it prohibits it. It doesn't. . .."[78]

    a. Explain why Scalia believed the 14th Amendment does not forbid discrimination based on sex and sexual orientation.

    b. Do you agree with Scalia? Explain.

11. Lancaster, California, located about 45 miles from Los Angeles, was trying to build its local economy but was tripped up by the U.S. Constitution. Costco, a big-box retailer, wanted to expand into next-door space leased to 99 Cents Only Stores. Costco told the city it would move to Palmdale if it could not expand. Lancaster tried to buy 99 Cents' lease, but the company refused. Lancaster then used its power of eminent domain to condemn the 99 Cents property for the purpose of making it available to Costco. The city noted that blight might follow if Costco left, and the city contrasted 99 Cents' under $40,000 per year in sales taxes generated with Costco's more than $400,000. 99 Cents then sued the city seeking an order blocking the effort to take the 99 Cents property.

a. How would you have ruled on the case when it was tried in 2001? Explain.

b. Would the result be any different today after the Supreme Court's 2005 decision in *Kelo v. City of New London, Connecticut,* 545 U.S.469? Explain. See *99 Cents Only Stores v. Lancaster Redevelopment Agency,* 237 F. Supp. 2d 1123 (C.D. Cal. 2001) [**https://law.justia.com**], *appeal dismissed,* 60 F. Appx. 123 (9th Cir. 2003).

12. Long Island, New York, resident Stephanie Fuller was secretly videotaped by her landlord, who had installed a video camera in the smoke detector above her bed. Fuller's landlord was found guilty of trespassing and was fined $1,500 and sentenced to 280 hours of community service.

    a. Why was the landlord not charged with a more serious felony offense?

    b. After Fuller's experience, New York enacted a criminal unlawful surveillance statute, which includes language forbidding secret surveillance in places where the victim has "a reasonable expectation of privacy." What legal significance attaches to that language?

13. Former North Carolina State University basketball stars Tom Gugliotta and Chris Corchiani were ejected from North Carolina State's arena during a 2012 game with Florida State University. Referee Karl Hess asked a police officer to eject the two men, who were seated immediately behind the scorer's table. Hess said he requested the ejections because excessive demonstration by the two men incited the crowd. Both men said they had not used inappropriate language. The Atlantic Coast Conference reprimanded Hess for not following conference protocol in the incident. Home game management officials, rather than a security officer, should have been involved in ejecting the fans. Does the First Amendment protect speech uttered at sporting events? Explain.

14. Milwaukee prostitutes, who had been arrested on multiple occasions, sued to block the city from enforcing a court-ordered injunction that permanently enjoined them from engaging in certain specified activities in certain specified areas of the city. They were prohibited from "engaging in beckoning to stop, or engaging male or female passersby in conversation, or stopping or attempting to stop motor vehicle operators by hailing, waving of arms or any other bodily gesture, or yelling in a loud voice" and other such activities. The women challenged the order on constitutional grounds.

    a. Explain the nature of that constitutional challenge.

    b. Decide the case. See *City of Milwaukee v. Burnette,* 637 N.W.2d 447 (Wis. Ct. App. 2001) [**https://law.justia.com**], *petition for rev. denied,* 638 N.W.2d 590 (Wis. 2001).

15. Jennifer O'Brien, a tenured teacher in the Paterson, New Jersey, schools with an unblemished performance record, was assigned to teach first grade in a school populated primarily by minority students. After a time, O'Brien concluded that several students in the class had behavioral problems disturbing the learning environment. Some students were hitting each other, one struck O'Brien, and another stole money from O'Brien and other students. O'Brien felt administrators had not responded adequately to her complaints, and she posted on her own Facebook page after school hours: "I'm not a teacher–I'm a warden for future criminals." Parents and others were outraged. Protests followed. O'Brien said her remarks were not a commentary on race or ethnicity but were legitimate concerns about the behavior of some students. O'Brien was dismissed from her teaching position. She sued claiming her actions, among other

things, were protected by the First Amendment. Decide the case and explain. See *In the Matter of the Tenure Hearing of Jennifer O'Brien, State Operated School District of the City of Paterson, Passaic County,* 2013 N.J. Super. Unpub. LEXIS 28 (N.J. Super. Ct. App. Div. January 11, 2013) [**https://law.justia.com**].

16. Paul Palmer submitted three shirts to his Waxahachie, Texas, school for approval under the school's dress code. Two of the shirts said "John Edwards for President" and one said "Freedom of Speech" on the front and had the text of the First Amendment on the back. The shirts were rejected as violations of the school's dress code, which did not allow shirts with printed messages, except for those related to the school and those smaller than two inches by two inches. Political messages were permitted on pins, buttons, bumper stickers, and the like. The dress code was designed to curb gang problems, reduce distractions, encourage professional dress, and maintain a safer, more orderly learning environment. Palmer sued the school claiming a violation of his First Amendment freedom of speech rights. Decide that case and explain. See *Palmer v. Waxahachie Independent School District,* 579 F.3d 502 (5th Cir. 2009), *cert. denied,* 130 S. Ct. 1055 (2010) [**https://law.justia.com**].
17. In 2020, the U.S. Supreme Court issued a decision in a challenge to the federal Telephone Consumer Protection Act, which seeks to protect consumer privacy by banning unwanted robocalls. One exception to the law was made for robocalls to collect debts guaranteed by the federal government. The law was challenged on grounds that it discriminates against certain speakers. What specific Constitutional protections are potentially at stake? Explain. What standard, if any, should be applied? What did the Supreme Court decide, and why? Do you agree? See Barr v. American Association of Political Consultants, 591 US __ (2020) [**https://supreme.justia.com**].

Notes

1. Portions of this history of the U.S. Constitution rely on Gordon Lloyd, "Introduction to the Constitutional Convention," [**https://teachingamericanhistory.org/resources/convention/intro**].
2. 554 U.S. 570 (2008) [**https://supreme.justia.com**].
3. 561 U.S. 742 (2010) [**https://supreme.justia.com**].
4. Editorial Board, "An Opening for States to Restrict Guns," *The New York Times,* December 9, 2015 [**www.nytimes.com**].
5. "74% Think Americans Have Constitutional Right to Own a Gun," *Rasmussen Reports,* January 9, 2013 [**www.rasmussenreports.com**].
6. Megan Cassella, "Majority of Americans Support Next President Pushing Tighter Gun Laws: Poll," *Reuters,* January 13, 2016 [**www.reuters.com**].
7. Katherine Schaeffer, "Share of Americans who favor stricter gun laws has increased since 2017," *Pew Research Center,* October 16, 2019 [**www.pewresearch.org**].
8. Gun Violence Archive [**www.gunviolencearchive.org**].
9. Pew Research Center, *Growing Public Support for Gun Rights,* December 10, 2014 [**www.pewresearch.org**].
10. Greg Hampikian, "When May I Shoot a Student?" *The New York Times,* February 27, 2014 [**www.nytimes.com**].
11. Jerre Williams, *Constitutional Analysis in a Nutshell* (St. Paul: West, 1979), p. 33.
12. 17 U.S. 316 (1819) [**https://supreme.justia.com**].

13. Chris Cillizza, "The day the tea party died," *CNN Politics,* July 23, 2019 **[www.cnn.com]**.
14. 5 U.S. 137 (1803) **[https://supreme.justia.com]**.
15. Brennan Center for Justice, "President Biden Should End State of the Union Silence on SCOTUS," Feb. 6, 2023 **[www.brennancenter.org]**.
16. 570 U.S. 529 (2013) **[https://supreme.justia.com]**.
17. *Veasey v. Abbott,* 815 F.3d 958 (5th Cir. 2016).
18. Editorial, "Importance of Rights Grows; So Does Ignorance," *Des Moines Register,* July 5, 2015, p. 1 OP.
19. 572 U.S. 565 (2014) **[https://supreme.justia.com]**.
20. Ibid.
21. Terence Chea, "'Under God' in Pledge of Allegiance Upheld by Court," *Cleveland.com,* March 11, 2010 **[www.cleveland.com]**.
22. *Newdow v. Rio Linda Union School District,* 597 F.3d 1007 (9th Cir. 2010).
23. *Newdow v. Lefevre,* 598 F.3d 638 (9th Cir. 2010), *cert. denied,* 131 S. Ct. 1612 (2011).
24. *Christian Legal Society v. Leo P. Martinez,* 561 U.S. 661 (2010) **[https://supreme.justia.com]**.
25. Associated Press, "New Kansas Law Lets Campus Religious Groups Restrict Membership," *The New York Times,* March 22, 2016 **[www.nytimes.com]**.
26. Cheryl Lavin, "The Redemption of Larry Flynt," *Chicago Tribune,* December 27, 1996 **[http://articles.chicagotribune.com]**.
27. 393 U.S. 503 (1969) **[https://supreme.justia.com]**.
28. *McCutcheon v. Federal Election Commission,* 572 S. Ct. 185 (2014) **[https://supreme.justia.com]**.
29. Megan Thee-Brenan, "Polls Show Broad Support for Campaign Spending Caps," *The New York Times,* April 2, 2014 **[www.nytimes.com]**.
30. *Snyder v. Phelps,* 562 U.S. 443 (2011) **[https://supreme.justia.com]**.
31. Adam Cohen, "Why Spewing Hate at Funerals Is Still Free Speech," *Time,* September 29, 2010 **[www.time.com]**.
32. *Cutting v. City of Portland, Maine,* 802 F.3d 79 (1st Cir. 2015).
33. *Deborah Morse v. Joseph Frederick,* 551 U.S. 393 (2007) **[https://supreme.justia.com]**.
34. *Mahanoy Area School District v. B. L.,* 594 U.S. ___ (2021) **[https://supreme.justia.com]**.
35. *Munroe v.* Central Bucks School District, 805 F.3d 454 (3rd Cir. 2015).
36. *Garcetti v. Ceballos,* 547 U.S. 410 (2006) **[https://supreme.justia.com]**.
37. Nick Sanchez, "Charles Barkley: San Antonio Women Won't Get Apology from Me," *Newsmax,* May 14, 2014 **[www.newsmax.com]**.
38. Greg Lukianoff and Jonathan Haidt, "The Coddling of the American Mind," *The Atlantic,* September 2015 **[www.theatlantic.com]**.
39. Erica Goldberg, "Universities' Compliance with Speech Code Decisions Leaves Much to Be Desired," September 24, 2009, *Foundation for Individual Rights in Education—The Torch* **[http://thefire.org]**.
40. David Ariosto and Leigh Remizowski, "Yale Settles Sexual Harassment Complaint," *CNN,* June 19, 2012 **[www.cnn.com]**.
41. *Rodriguez v. Maricopa County Community College,* 605 F.3d 703 (9th Cir. 2010).
42. *Barrett v. University of Mississippi,* 232 F.3d 208 (5th Cir. 2000), *cert. denied,* 531 U.S. 1052 (2000).
43. *Corry v. Stanford University,* Case No. 740309 (Cal. Super. Ct. February 27, 1995).
44. *Valentine v. Chrestensen,* 316 U.S. 52 (1942) **[https://supreme.justia.com]**.

45. *Citizens United v. FEC,* 558 U.S. 310 (2010) [**https://supreme.justia.com**].
46. David G. Savage, "Corporate Free-Speech Ruling Speaks of Shift in Supreme Court," *Los Angeles Times,* February 9, 2010 [**www.latimes.com**].
47. *Citizens United,* 558 U.S. at 7 Syllabus [**https://supreme.justia.com**].
48. Savage, "Corporate Free-Speech."
49. *Central Hudson Gas & Electric Corp. v. Public Service Commission,* 447 U.S. 557 (1980).
50. 573 U.S. 373 (2014) [**https://supreme.justia.com**].
51. Ibid.
52. *United States v. Jones,* 565 U.S. 400 (2012) [**https://supreme.justia.com**].
53. *Carpenter v. United States,* 585 U.S. __ (2018) [**https://supreme.justia.com**].
54. *United States v. Hammond,* No. 19-2357 (7th Cir. 2021) [**https://justia.com**].
55. 556 U.S. 332 (2009) [**https://supreme.justia.com**].
56. This paragraph is derived in part from Adam Liptak, "Supreme Court Cuts Back Officers' Searches of Vehicles," *The New York Times,* April 22, 2009 [**www.nytimes.com**].
57. 367 U.S. 643 (1961) [**https://supreme.justia.com**].
58. 579 U.S. 232 (2016) [**https://supreme.justia.com**].
59. *Id.,* at 2070–71 (Sotomayor, J., dissenting).
60. *Earls v. Board of Education,* 242 F.3d 1264 (10th Cir. 2001).
61. *Board of Education of Pottawatomie County v. Earls,* 536 U.S. 822 (2002) [**https://supreme.justia.com**].
62. Floralynn Einesman, "Drug Testing Students in California–Does It Violate the State Constitution?" *San Diego Law Review* 47 (Summer 2010), p. 681.
63. Laura Unger, "School Districts Double Down on Drug Testing, Targeting Even Middle Schoolers," *NBC News,* Sept. 4, 2019 [**www.nbcnews.com**].
64. *Lebron v. Secretary of the Florida Department of Children and Families,* 772 F.3d 1352 (11th Cir. 2014).
65. Frances Robles, "Florida Law on Drug Tests for Welfare Is Struck Down," *The New York Time*s, December 31, 2013 [**www.nytimes.com**].
66. *State of Washington v. Glas,* 54 P.3d 147 (Wash. 2002).
67. *Marshall v. Barlow's,* 436 U.S. 307 (1978) [**https://supreme.justia.com**].
68. *Horne v. Department of Agriculture,* 569 U.S. 513 (2013) [**https://supreme.justia.com**].
69. *Lucas v. South Carolina Coastal Council,* 505 U.S. 1003 (1992) [**https://supreme.justia.com**].
70. 512 U.S. 374 (1994) [**https://supreme.justia.com**].
71. Frank A. Vickory and Barry A. Diskin, "Advances in Private Property Protection Rights: The States in the Vanguard," *American Business Law Journal 34,* no. 4 (Summer 1997), p. 561.
72. *Koontz v. St. Johns River Water,* 570 U.S. 595 (2013) [**https://supreme.justia.com**].
73. *United States v. Skilling,* 638 F.3d 480 (5th Cir. 2011).
74. 388 U.S. 1 (1967) [**https://supreme.justia.com**].
75. 576 U.S. ___ (2015) [**https://supreme.justia.com**].
76. 410 U.S. 113 (1973) [**https://supreme.justia.com**].
77. 597 U.S. __ (2022) [**https://www.supremecourt.gov/opinions**].
78. "The Originalist," *California Lawyer,* January 2011 [**www.callawyer.com**].

Video icon credit: Comstock Images/Alamy Stock Photo

CHAPTER SIX

Contracts

After completing this chapter, students will be able to fulfill the following learning objectives:

6-1. Explain the importance of contracts in a capitalist, free-market system.

6-2. Determine whether the Uniform Commercial Code or common law governs a contract dispute.

6-3. Identify the elements of a legally enforceable contract.

6-4. Classify a contract as bilateral or unilateral, express or implied, executory or executed.

6-5. Distinguish between valid, unenforceable, void, and voidable contracts.

6-6. Describe the elements of a valid offer.

6-7. Describe the elements of a valid acceptance.

6-8. Explain the significance of consideration as an element of a legally enforceable contract.

6-9. Compare and contrast the rights and duties arising in contractual assignment and delegation.

6-10. Compare and contrast different types of third-party beneficiaries to a contract.

6-11. Explain how a contract may be discharged.

6-12. Describe the remedies available for breach of contract.

Preface: The Role of Contracts in a Complex Society

LO 6-1 Explain the importance of contracts in a capitalist, free-market system.

A free-market system cannot operate effectively and fairly without a reliable foundation in contract law. At the practical level, all buyers and sellers must be confident that the deal they are about to make will be completed as specified, or that they will have a remedy available if it is not completed. Otherwise, the legal risk in making deals would act as a drag on the commercial process, reducing certainty and undermining the extraordinary efficiency of the free market. At the philosophical level, the fundamental point of a contract is personal freedom. Contract law gives each of us a reliable mechanism for freely expressing our preferences in life. From buying a tube of toothpaste, a car, or a house, to paying tuition, to accepting an employment offer, to franchising a business, to borrowing millions of dollars, to adopting a child, and so on, the direction and value of our lives are shaped and protected to a significant degree by our contractual choices. To a considerable extent, we define ourselves by the contractual choices we make, and contract law protects those choices. The indispensable role of contract law is illustrated by the esports dispute described below.

Fortnite Star vs. Esports Contracts

When he was 20 years old, Turner "Tfue" Tenney, a top Fortnite player and a popular YouTube streamer, signed a three-year agreement with FaZe Clan, an esports organization with professional teams that compete in video games. Under the agreement, Tenney would play in FaZe Clan tournaments and training sessions and give three days a month to promotion and publicity, such as streaming videos. Further, Tenney was prevented from endorsing another gaming company or joining another Fortnite team. In exchange, he would be compensated with $2,000 a month. He could keep 80 percent of winnings from FaZe Clan tournaments, with the remainder going to FaZe Clan. Tenney was allowed to pursue brand deals but would have to split the money earned with FaZe Clan. If FaZe Clan found such deals for him, it would retain 80 percent as a finder's fee.

In 2019, Tenney sued FaZe Clan, claiming the contract was oppressive and that Tenney did not understand the agreement's terms. Further, the complaint alleged that FaZe Clan is acting as a talent agency without the talent agency license required under state law. The parties entered into a settlement in 2020.

As you study this chapter, think about the following questions:

1. How might such agreements impact esports, esports teams, and the players?
2. Was a binding contract formed between Tenney and FaZe Clan?
3. How might such a contract be breached, and what might the remedies be for such a breach?

Sources: Michael McCann, "Inside the Lawsuit that Could Shake Up the Entire eSports Industry," *Sports Illustrated,* May 30, 2019 [**www.si.com**]; Mike Snider, "Fortnite Pro Turner 'Tfue' Tenney Sues Esports Team FaZe Clan Over 'Oppressive' Contract," *USA Today,* May 20, 2019 [**www.usa.today.com**]; and **https://www.theverge.com/2020/8/26/21403052/tfue-faze-clan-lawsuit-settled-streaming-events-competition-esports**.

Part One—Building a Binding Contract

Introduction

We make promises routinely in our lives. Some of those create binding contracts; some do not. You promise, for example, to meet a friend after class, but you break your promise. Could your friend sue you in court for breach of contract? Doubtless your answer is "no," and, barring unusual circumstances, you would be correct. But why? This raises the central question in this chapter: Under what circumstances do promises become enforceable contracts? For the most part, the answer to that question has been provided by court decisions (the common law) accumulating over the many centuries of evolving contract law stretching from the ancient Middle East to England and across the Atlantic to America. Those centuries of decisions have provided a substantially fair, consistent, and predictable body of contract law, particularly in a time when the parties normally dealt with each other face-to-face, often as acquaintances.

Could your friend sue you for breach of contract?

As business transactions became more complicated, the parties more and more distant from each other, and the comparative power between individuals and corporations ever more unbalanced, the need for government intervention has increased. State legislatures began to impose new rules on what had been purely private transactions. Look, for example, at the state and federal regulation of employment contracts and relationships governing working conditions such as hours of work, safety on the job, break time, and more (see Chapter 12). State laws and court decisions resulted, to some extent, in a confusing, inefficient patchwork of laws that didn't conform to the reality of complex, contemporary business practice. As a result, the Uniform Commercial Code, a body of rules on commercial law across the United States, was developed and adopted by state legislatures.

The Uniform Commercial Code

LO 6-2 Determine whether the Uniform Commercial Code or common law governs a contract dispute.

The National Conference of Commissioners on Uniform State Laws (NCCUSL) and the American Law Institute (ALI) developed, for state-by-state approval, the Uniform Commercial Code (UCC), a body of rules designed to render commercial law consistent across the 50 states. The UCC has been adopted in 49 states, and Louisiana has adopted portions of it. With a set of uniform, predictable rules, business can be practiced with confidence and minimal legal confusion.

The UCC is divided into a series of articles addressing the multitude of potential issues that arise in complex commercial practice. For our purposes, the most important of those is Article 2, Sales, which governs all transactions involving the *sale of goods.* Section 2-105 of the UCC defines goods as tangible, movable things, such as cars, clothing, and appliances. Real estate, stocks, bonds, money, and so forth are not covered. Nor are contracts for services. Of course, many transactions involve both goods and services. Usually in determining whether the UCC applies, the courts have asked whether the dominant purpose of the contract is to provide a service or to sell a good. [For the complete Article 2, see **www.law.cornell.edu/ucc**].

In contract disputes, the first question is whether the UCC or the common law governs the situation. Throughout this chapter, you should remember that the UCC always controls if (1) the transaction is addressed by the UCC—that is, it involves a contract for the sale of goods—and (2) a UCC rule applies to the issue in question. On the other hand, the judge-made common law of contracts continues to govern transactions (1) not involving the sale of goods or (2) involving the sale of goods where no specific UCC provision applies. Increasingly, in non-UCC cases, courts analogize to UCC reasoning in arriving at their judgments, that is, the common law is absorbing UCC principles. This chapter, while focusing primarily on the common law of contracts, will introduce the role of the sales article in the practice of business.

Article 2A of the UCC governs ***leases*** of goods. In essence, Article 2A mimics the sales article except that it governs leases of goods rather than sales. Because of space constraints, Article 2A will not receive further attention in this text.

What Is a Contract?

When all of the following features are present, an enforceable contract is created, to be distinguished from an unenforceable promise. As well be explained later, some contracts must also be in writing to be enforceable.

LO 6-3 Identify the elements of a legally enforceable contract.

Agreement A meeting of the minds of the parties based on an offer by one and an acceptance by the other. The determination as to whether the parties have actually reached agreement is based on the *objective* evidence (the parties' acts, words, and so on) as a "reasonable person" would interpret it rather than on an effort to ascertain the subjective or personal intent of the parties.

Consideration The bargained-for legal value that one party agrees to pay or provide to secure the promise of another.

Capacity The parties must have the legal ability to enter the contract, that is, they must be sane, sober, and of legal age.

Genuineness of assent The parties must knowingly agree to the same thing. Their minds must meet as shown by the objective evidence. If that meeting does not occur because of, for example, mistake or fraud, or the like, a contract does not exist because the parties' assent was not real.

Legality of purpose The object of the contract must not violate the law or public policy.

Classification of Contracts

Contracts fall into a series of sometimes overlapping categories, which reveal the rather well-ordered logic of our contract system (see Figure 6.1).

LO 6-4 Classify a contract as bilateral or unilateral, express or implied, executory or executed.

LO 6-5 Distinguish between valid, unenforceable, void, and voidable contracts.

Contract formation

Bilateral and unilateral contracts A ***bilateral contract*** arises when *both* parties make promises. A ***unilateral contract*** ordinarily involves a situation in which one party makes a promise and the other *acts* in response to that promise. For example, as you establish your new restaurant, you promise a college friend that if he completes his degree, you will hire him. He can accept your promise–or offer–only by the act of completing college and not by a promise to complete college.

Express and implied contracts

When parties overtly and explicitly manifest their intention to enter an agreement, either in writing or orally, the result (if other requirements are fulfilled) is an express contract. For example, in managing the accounting department at an insurance firm, you sign a form contract with a local computer store ordering a new computer. The supplier's signature on the form creates an express, bilateral agreement. If, on the other hand, you ask your local computer service to repair a computer that is not working properly and one of the service technicians does so, you have probably entered an ***implied-in-fact contract***. A court would infer a promise by you to pay a reasonable price in return for the service's promise to make a commercially reasonable effort to repair the computer. The contract is inferred on the basis of the facts–that is, by the behavior of the parties.

Suppose, as a manager of the accounting department at the insurance firm, you receive a premium payment for a policy that was not issued by your company, but rather by your rival firm. In these circumstances, it would be unfair for you to keep the unearned money; therefore, the courts construct an implied-in-law or ***quasi-contract*** permitting the actual insurer to collect the money. This unusual situation in which the court infers the

FIGURE 6.1
Classification of Contracts.

Contract formation
1. Bilateral/unilateral
   a. Bilateral contract–a promise for a promise.
   b. Unilateral contract–a promise for an act.
2. Express/implied
   a. Express contract–explicitly stated in writing or orally.
   b. Implied-in-fact contract–inferred from the conduct of the parties.
   c. Quasi-contract–implied contract created by a court to prevent unjust enrichment.

Contract performance
1. Executory contract–not yet fully performed.
2. Executed contract–fully performed by all parties.

Contract enforceability
1. Valid contract–includes all of the necessary ingredients of a binding contract.
2. Unenforceable contract–contract exists, but a legal defense prevents enforcement.
3. Void contract–no enforceable contract at all.
4. Voidable contract–one party has the option of either enforcing or voiding the contract.

existence of a contract is employed only when necessary to prevent *unjust enrichment* (as would have been the case if you were to collect an insurance premium without having issued a policy).

Contract Performance

Executory contracts A contract is labeled *executory* until all parties fully perform.

Executed contracts When all parties have completed their performances, the contract is *executed.*

Contract Enforceability

Valid contracts A valid contract meets all of the established legal requirements and thus is enforceable in court.

Unenforceable contracts An unenforceable contract meets the basic contractual requirements but remains faulty because it fails to fulfill some other legal requirement. For example, an oral contract may be unenforceable if it falls in one of those categories of contracts, such as the sale of land, that must be in writing (see the *Statute of Frauds* later in this chapter).

Void contracts A void contract is, in fact, no contract at all because a critical legal requirement is missing, most commonly it is either an agreement to accomplish an illegal purpose (such as to commit a crime) or an agreement involving an incompetent party (such as an individual judged by a court to be insane). In either case, what is otherwise an enforceable contract is, in fact, void.

Voidable contracts A voidable contract is enforceable but can be canceled by one or more of the parties. The most common voidable contracts are those entered by minors who have the option, under the law, of either disaffirming or fulfilling most contracts, as will be explained later.

With this Ring . . .?

Christopher and Melissa had been living together for four years when Christopher proposed marriage to Melissa, buying her an engagement ring worth $10,000. After continuing to live together with their child and Melissa's other child, Melissa discovered that Christopher had cheated on her. Christopher then asked Melissa to move out with the children. Melissa had already quit her job to be a full-time mother, having assumed that Christopher would support the family as her husband. Melissa sued Christopher for "breach of promise to marry," among other claims. Christopher argued that his relationship with Melissa was illegal, making the promise to marry unenforceable. Further, he asserted he had only given Melissa a ring, but had never said the words "will you marry me?" to her. Who should win, and why? Consider these questions further as you learn about contracts in this chapter.

Source: Neetzan Zimmerman, "Georgia Man Ordered to Pay Ex $50K for 'Breach of Promise to Marry,'" ***Gawker,*** December 6, 2013 [**https://gawker.com**].

The Agreement: Offer

An offer usually consists of a promise to do something or to refrain from doing something in the future. A valid offer must include all of these elements:

LO 6-6
Describe the elements of a valid offer.

1. Present ***intent*** to enter a contract.
2. Reasonable *definiteness* of the terms of the offer.
3. *Communication* of the offer to the offeree.

Intent

Assume that you are the purchasing manager for a trucking firm, and you need a small used van to do some local light hauling. Because time is of the essence, you decide to bypass the normal bidding process and go directly to the local dealers to make a quick purchase. At the first lot, you find a suitable van. In discussing it, the sales manager says, "Well, we don't usually do this, but since you've been such a good customer, I'll tell you, we paid $10,000 for this one, so I guess we are gonna need about $11,000 to deal with you." You say, "Fine. That's reasonable. I'll take it." The manager then says, "Now wait a minute, I was just talking off the top of my head. I'll have to punch up the numbers to be sure."

Do you have a deal at that point? The core question is whether the sales manager made an ***offer***. Normally, language of that kind has been treated by the courts as preliminary negotiation lacking the necessary ***intent*** to constitute an offer. Of course, if no offer exists, you cannot accept, and no contract can emerge absent further negotiation.

Online Dating

Ian, a 29-year-old single man, paid over $9,400 for a Denver Dating Company membership after meeting with a representative of the online dating website. Ian allegedly relied on the representative's description of the company's database as including a "huge number of single women in the 25 to 35 age range," with a membership increase in that age range due to the "wave of breakups" during the COVID-19 pandemic. After joining, Ian discovered that there were only five women in the 18 to 35 age range who were active in the database.

Does Ian have a breach of contract claim? Explain. See Lily O'Neill, "Customer Sues Denver Dating Co. for lack of ladies in database," *The Denver Post,* October 21, 2021 **[https://www.denverpost.com/]**

Suppose you were responding to an ad that said, "2015 full-size Ford cargo van, $20,000." Is that ad language an offer?

Advertisements

The question of intent sometimes arises with advertisements. In buying the van for your business, suppose you were responding to an ad that said, "2015 full-size Ford cargo van, $20,000." Is that ad language an offer such that you can accept by promising to pay $20,000? Ordinarily, ads do not constitute offers but rather are treated by the courts as *invitations to deal.* Were an ad treated as an offer, it would put the seller in the commercially impracticable position of being required to provide the advertised product at the advertised price to everyone who sought it, regardless of available supply. Presumably, that open-ended duty was not the seller's intent when issuing the ad. It follows then that the buyer, in responding to an ad, is technically making an offer, with the seller free to accept or decline.

On the other hand, courts have held that some ads do manifest a present intent to make an offer. The key terms in those ads must be highly specific and complete, leaving nothing open for negotiation.

A Jet Fighter from Pepsi?

A 2022 Netflix documentary series, "Pepsi, Where's my Jet?" focuses on a 1995 Pepsi company promotion that offered merchandise in exchange for points earned by buying Pepsi-Cola. The television ad showed a teenager modeling some of the available merchandise. A Pepsi T-shirt was displayed for 75 points and a leather jacket for 1450 points. At the end of the ad, a U.S. Marine Corps Harrier "jump jet" landed outside a school, and from the cockpit, the boy said, "Sure beats the bus." The ad then stated that the jet was seven million points. John D. R. Leonard, at the time a 21-year-old business student in Seattle, Washington, joined five investors in writing a check to Pepsi for $700,008.50 and demanded the 7 million Pepsi points. Pepsi returned the check and said it had no intention of giving

Leonard the $24 million jet. Leonard sued. [To view the video of the ad **www.youtube.com/watch?v=ZdackF2H7Qc.**]

Question

Who wins? Explain.

Source: *Leonard v. Pepsico,* 210 F.3d 88 (2d Cir. 2000).

Definiteness

Suppose your friend Ken has completed a management training program for a "big box" retailer. In Ken's first assignment as an assistant manager, his boss Jane asks him to seek bids and make the other arrangements (subject to her approval) to resurface the store's large asphalt parking lot. Ken secures bids, and the lowest bidder offers to complete the work "later this summer" for $120,000. Ken briefly explains the offer to Jane, who tells Ken to take care of all the details. Ken is busy with other matters and puts off the parking lot project for a couple of weeks. When Ken gets back to the lowest bidder, he is told: "Sorry, man, we hadn't heard from you, and we got another deal." Can that contractor be held to his initial offer?

One of the requirements of a binding offer is that all of its critical terms must be sufficiently clear so that a court can determine both the intentions of the parties and their duties. In the asphalt case, many critical details–precisely when the work would be done, what surfacing material would be used, and how thickly it should be poured–had not been established. Consequently, no offer existed. In a contract for the sale of goods, UCC Section 2-204 relaxes the definiteness standard by allowing a contract to be recognized even with "one or more terms" missing if: (1) "the parties have intended to make a contract" and (2) "there is a reasonably certain basis for giving an appropriate remedy." Under the UCC, the courts can actually fill in missing terms in a sale of goods contract, such as by specifying a reasonable price. However, because asphalt resurfacing is a service contract, the UCC would not provide Ken any relief for failing to follow up with the lowest bidder. The following case involving Mariah Carey, the pop music star, demonstrates some of the problems that can arise when an understanding is indefinite.

LEGAL BRIEFCASE

Vian v. Carey

1993 U.S. Dist. Lexis 5460 (S.D.N.Y. April 26, 1993)

Judge Mukasey

Defendant Mariah Carey is a famous, successful, and apparently wealthy entertainer. Plaintiff Joseph Vian was her stepfather before she achieved stardom, but at the start of this litigation was in the process of becoming divorced from defendant's mother. He claims defendant agreed orally that he would have a license to market singing dolls in her likeness. Plaintiff claims that he and Carey had an oral contract for him to receive a license to market "Mariah dolls." These dolls would be statuettes of the singer and would play her most popular songs. Plaintiff claims that the contract was in consideration of his financial and emotional support of defendant, including picking her up from late-night recording sessions, providing her with the use of a car, paying for dental care, allowing her to use his boat for business meetings and rehearsals, and giving her various items, including unused wedding gifts from his marriage to her mother, to help furnish her apartment.

The alleged basis of the oral contract is that on at least three occasions, twice in the family car and once on Vian's boat, Vian told Carey, "Don't forget the Mariah dolls," and "I get the Mariah dolls." According to Vian, on one occasion Carey responded "okay" and on other occasions she merely smiled and nodded. Although Carey admits Vian mentioned the dolls two or three times, she testified that she thought it was a joke. For 30 years plaintiff has been in the business of designing, producing, and marketing gift and novelty items. Although it is not clear from the evidence the parties have submitted, it will be assumed that the alleged contract was formed after defendant turned 18. Under New York law, an oral agreement can form a binding contract. In determining whether a contract exists, what matters are the parties' expressed intentions, the words, and deeds that constitute objective signs in a given set of circumstances.

Therefore, the issue is whether the objective circumstances indicate that the parties intended to form a contract. Without such an intent, neither a contract nor a preliminary agreement to negotiate in good faith can exist. In making such a determination, a court may look at "whether the terms of the contract have been finally resolved." In addition, a court may consider "the context of the negotiations." Plaintiff has adduced no evidence that defendant ever intended by a nod of her head or the expression "okay" to enter into a complex commercial licensing agreement involving dolls in her likeness playing her copyrighted songs. The context in which this contract between an 18-year-old girl and her stepfather allegedly was made was an informal family setting, either in the car or on plaintiff's boat, while others were present. Vian's own version of events leads to the conclusion that there was no reason for Carey to think Vian was entirely serious, let alone that he intended to bind her to an agreement at that time. He admits he never told her he was serious. The objective circumstances do not indicate that Carey intended to form a contract with plaintiff. Although plaintiff's five-page memorandum of law fails to raise the possibility, plaintiff also has not shown that Carey intended to be bound to negotiate with plaintiff at some later date over the licensing of "Mariah dolls."

There can be no meeting of the minds, required for the formation of a contract, where essential material terms are missing. Thus, even if the parties both believe themselves to be bound, there is no contract when "the terms of the agreement are so vague and indefinite that there is no basis or standard for deciding whether the agreement had been kept or broken, or to fashion a remedy, and no means by which such terms may be made certain."

. . . The word "license" was not even used. As defendant points out, no price or royalty term was mentioned, nor was the duration or geographic scope of the license, nor was Carey's right to approve the dolls. Plaintiff admits he would not have gone ahead without defendant's approval, thus conceding the materiality of that term.

In sum, plaintiff has not raised a triable issue of fact as to the existence of a contract. Defendant's motion for summary judgment is granted.

Questions

1. Why did the court find for Carey?
2. As noted in the text, in UCC cases judges fill in contract terms where the parties clearly intended a deal. Should the court here fill in the missing terms to provide the necessary definiteness? Explain.
3. In 1961, Duke Ellington entered a copyright agreement with Mills Music, now EMI Music. Under this contract, the music publisher, defined to include "any other affiliate," agreed to pay Duke Ellington and named members of his family "fifty percent of the net revenue actually received" from foreign publication of the copyrighted music. In 2014, the New York Court of Appeals ruled on a breach of contract action brought by Ellington's grandson that claimed EMI had breached the contract by diluting the family's share of royalties in subcontracting foreign publication rights to others whose fees were deducted from the amount, then divided equally between EMI and Ellington family members. Had EMI breached the contract? Decide. *Ellington v. EMI Music, Inc.*, 997 N.Y.S.2d 339 (N.Y. 2014).

Communication

As explained, an effective offer must be the product of a present intent, it must be definite, and it must be communicated to the offeree. Communication of an offer expresses the offeror's intent to make that offer. Suppose a friend tells you that your neighbor has offered to sell his classic jukebox for $10,000. You call your neighbor and say, "I accept. I'll be right over with the $10,000." Do you have a deal? No. The owner did not communicate the offer to you. The fact that it was not communicated to you may suggest that your neighbor does not want to sell or does not want to sell to you.

Duration of an Offer

Communication of an offer affords the offeree the opportunity to create a contract by accepting that offer, but how long does that opportunity last? Here are some general rules:

1. The offeror may revoke the offer anytime prior to acceptance. (Some exceptions are explained later.) Normally, revocation is effective on receipt by the offeree. Under common law, the offeror has the right to revoke at any time prior to acceptance, even if he or she expressly promised to keep the offer open for a specified period.
2. The offer may specify that it is open for an express period (such as 10 days).
3. Where a time limit is not specified in the offer, it will be presumed to be open for a reasonable period.
4. An offer expires if rejected or on receipt of a counteroffer.

Irrevocable Offers

Some kinds of offers may not be revoked. We will note three of them:

Option contracts When an offeror promises to keep an offer open for a specified period and, in return, the offeree pays additional consideration (usually money) to secure that promise, the parties have created an option contract, which is a separate agreement and is enforceable by its terms. For example, a friend has offered to sell his customized car that you have long cherished, but you want to think about it for a few days. You might enter an option contract with your friend under which you pay $100 for the seller's promise to keep the offer open for seven days. You are under no obligation to buy the car, but the seller is under a binding obligation not to withdraw the offer or sell to another during the seven days.

Firm offers Under the UCC, if the owner of that customized car is a dealer (a merchant) and he made a written, signed offer to sell that car (a good) to you, indicating that his offer would remain open for seven days, he is bound to that promise whether you paid consideration for it or not. That situation is called a ***firm offer*** under UCC Section 2-205, which also provides that if such offers do not mention a time, then they will be kept open for a reasonable period, not exceeding three months.

Offers for unilateral contracts A problem sometimes arises when the offeror attempts to revoke a unilateral offer after the offeree has begun to perform. For example, your neighbor invites you to rake her leaves for $10, and then, when you are virtually done, she yells from the doorway, "Oh, sorry, I changed my mind. You go home now." Historically, the offeror (the neighbor, in this case) was free to revoke at any time, but the modern position holds that the offeror normally cannot revoke if the offeree (you) has commenced performance. If that performance is then completed (you ignore your neighbor's admonition to go home, and you finish the raking), the offeror (your neighbor) is bound to perform fully by paying the $10.

The Agreement: Acceptance

LO 6-7 Describe the elements of a valid acceptance.

Suppose you are in training with a large real estate firm, and your boss has authorized you to enter negotiations to buy a parcel of farmland that the company hopes to develop for housing. After preliminary discussions, you extend a written offer to the property owner indicating, among other terms, that the company is willing to pay $10,000 per acre for a 10-acre parcel. Assume the owner responds by writing, "I accept your offer at $10,000 per acre, but I need to keep the two-acre homesite." The offeree has used the word *accept,* but does the response constitute a legally binding ***acceptance***?

The general rule is that an effective acceptance must be a mirror image of the offer, that is, ordinarily, its terms must be the same as those in the offer. Here, by changing the offer's terms, the offeree has issued a ***counteroffer*** that extinguishes the original offer and constitutes a new offer, made this time by the original offeree.

Communication of Acceptance

An offer may be accepted only by the offeree–that is, the person to whom the offer was directed. Because unilateral offers are accepted by performance, no communication of acceptance beyond that performance ordinarily is necessary. In the case of a bilateral contract (a promise for a promise), acceptance is not effective until communicated.

Broadly, acceptance can be accomplished by a "yes" communicated face-to-face, by a nod of the head or some other appropriate signal, by phone, or by other unwritten means, unless the law of the state requires writing in that particular kind of transaction.

Mailbox Rule

Confusion sometimes arises when the parties are not dealing face-to-face. In general, acceptance is effective upon dispatch by whatever mode of communication has been explicitly or implicitly authorized by the offeror. This well-settled position is called the ***mailbox rule*** and means, among other things, that an acceptance is effective when sent even if never received. [For one professor's review of the mailbox rule and related rules, see **www.tomwbell.com/teaching/KMailbox.pdf**].

Authorization

The offeror controls the acceptance process and may specify an exclusive manner in which an acceptance must be communicated. If so, a contract is not created if the acceptance is communicated in anything other than the stipulated fashion. Traditionally, if the offeror did not give an ***express authorization*** to a means of communication, an acceptance by the same or faster means than that used by the offeror was implied. ***Implied authorization*** might also arise from such factors as prior dealings between the parties and custom in their industry.

Modern View

Under the UCC, the rules of acceptance have relaxed a bit. If no specific instructions for acceptance are included in the offer, the offeree is free to accept in any reasonable manner within a reasonable period, and acceptance is effective upon dispatch. Even when the means chosen are "unreasonable," acceptance is effective on dispatch under UCC 1-201(38) if it is actually received in a timely manner.

Consideration

LO 6-8
Explain the significance of consideration as an element of a legally enforceable contract.

Earlier we identified the five key ingredients in an enforceable contract: agreement, consideration, capacity, genuineness of assent, and legality of purpose. Having examined the agreement (offer and acceptance) process, we turn now to consideration. As noted earlier, consideration is the bargained-for legal value that one party agrees to pay or provide to secure another's promise. It is what the promisor demands and receives in exchange for their promise. Consideration distinguishes an enforceable contract from an unenforceable gratuitous promise. An enforceable contract requires that both the offeror and the offeree suffer a ***legal detriment***, that is, they each agree to do something they had no existing duty to do or agree to refrain from doing something they had an existing right to do. In other words, each party must pay a "price" for a contract to be enforceable.

The classic case that follows explores the idea of consideration and demonstrates that consideration can have legal value without involving monetary loss to the promisee.

LEGAL BRIEFCASE

Hamer v. Sidway 27 N.E. 256 (N.Y. 1891)

FACTS

In 1869, William E. Story Sr. promised his nephew W.E. Story II that he would pay the nephew $5,000 upon his 21st birthday if the nephew would refrain from drinking liquor, using tobacco, swearing, and playing cards or billiards for money until he reached that 21st birthday. The nephew agreed and performed his promise, but the uncle died in 1887 without paying the money, and the administrator of the estate, Sidway, declined to pay the $5,000 plus interest. The nephew had assigned (sold) his rights to the money to Louisa Hamer, who sued W.E. Story Sr.'s estate. Hamer, the plaintiff, won at the trial level, lost on appeal, and then appealed to the New York Court of Appeals.

Judge Parker

When the nephew arrived at the age of 21 years and on the 31st day of January 1875, he wrote to his uncle informing him that he had performed his part of the agreement and had thereby become entitled to the sum of $5,000. The uncle received the letter a few days later and on the sixth of February, he wrote and mailed to his nephew the following letter:

> Buffalo, February 6, 1875
> W.E. Story, Jr.
> Dear Nephew:
> Your letter of the 31st came to hand all right, saying that you had lived up to the promise made to me several years ago. I have no doubt but you have, for which you shall have five thousand dollars as I promised you. I had the money in the bank the day you was 21 years old that I intend for you, and you shall have the money certain. Now, Willie I do not intend to interfere with this money in any way till I think you are capable of taking care of it and the sooner that time comes the better it will please me. I would hate very much to have you start out in some adventure that you thought all right and lose this money in one year. The first five thousand dollars that I got together

> cost me a heap of hard work. You would hardly believe me when I tell you that to obtain this I shoved a jackplane many a day, butchered three or four years, then came to this city, and after three months' perseverance I obtained a situation in a grocery store. I opened this store early, closed late, slept in the fourth story of the building in a room 30 by 40 feet and not a human being in the building but myself. All this I done to live as cheap as I could to save something. I don't want you to take up with this kind of fare. I was here in the cholera season '49 and '52 and the deaths averaged 80 to 125 daily and plenty of smallpox. I wanted to go home, but Mr. Fisk, the gentleman I was working for, told me if I left then, after it got healthy he probably would not want me. I stayed. All the money I have saved I know just how I got it. It did not come to me in any mysterious way, and the reason I speak of this is that money got in this way stops longer with a fellow that gets it with hard knocks than it does when he finds it. Willie, you are 21 and you have many a thing to learn yet. This money you have earned much easier than I did besides acquiring good habits at the same time and you are quite welcome to the money; hope you will make good use of it. I was 10 long years getting this together after I was your age. Now, hoping this will be satisfactory, I stop . . .
>
> Truly Yours,
>
> W.E. STORY
>
> P.S.—You can consider this money on interest.

The nephew received the letter and thereafter consented that the money should remain with his uncle in accordance with the terms and conditions of the letter. The uncle died on the 29th day of January 1887, without having paid over to his nephew any portion of the said $5,000 and interest.

The defendant contends that the contract was without consideration to support it and, therefore, invalid. He asserts that the promisee by refraining from the use of liquor and tobacco was not harmed but benefited; that that which he did was best for him to do independently of his uncle's promise, and insists that it follows that unless the promisor was benefited, the contract was without consideration. A contention, which if well founded, would seem to leave open for controversy in many cases whether that which the promisee did or omitted to do was, in fact, of such benefit to him as to leave no consideration to support the enforcement of the promisor's agreement. Such a rule could not be tolerated and is without foundation in the law.

"In general a waiver of any legal right at the request of another party is a sufficient consideration for a promise" (Parsons on Contracts).

Pollock, in his work on contracts, says, "Consideration means not so much that one party is profiting as that the other abandons some legal right in the present or limits his legal freedom of action in the future as an inducement for the promise of the first."

Now, applying this rule to the facts before us, the promisee used tobacco, occasionally drank liquor, and had a legal right to do so. That right he abandoned for a period of years upon the strength of the promise of the testator that for such forbearance he would give him $5,000. We need not speculate on the effort which may have been required to give up the use of those stimulants. It is sufficient that he restricted his lawful freedom of action within certain prescribed limits upon the faith of his uncle's agreement, and now having fully performed the conditions imposed, it is of no moment whether such performance actually proved a benefit to the promisor, and the court will not inquire into it, but were it a proper subject of inquiry, we see nothing in this record that would permit a determination that the uncle was not benefited in a legal sense.

Reversed.

Questions

1. *a.* What detriment, if any, was suffered by the nephew?
   b. What benefit, if any, was secured by the uncle?
   c. As a matter of law, do we need to inquire into the uncle's benefit? Explain.
2. Lampley began work as an at-will (can be dismissed or can quit at any time) employee of Celebrity Homes in Denver, Colorado. Three months later, Celebrity announced a profit-sharing plan for all employees if the company reached its goals for the fiscal year that had begun a few weeks before. Later in the fiscal year, Lampley was dismissed. Celebrity distributed its profits after the end of the fiscal year. Lampley sued when she did not receive a share of the profits. Celebrity argued that its promise to share its profits was a gratuity, unsupported by consideration. Decide. See *Lampley v. Celebrity Homes,* 594 P.2d 605 (Colo. Ct. App. 1979).
3. An accident in the early 1960s rendered Hoffman paraplegic. At Hoffman's invitation, Thomas lived with and provided extensive physical care for Hoffman until Hoffman's death in 2004. Thomas did not pay rent, and Hoffman paid for Thomas's food, provided her with a car and cell phone, and made occasional cash payments to Thomas. While never married, the couple exchanged rings in 2002, and Thomas testified that she felt they "lived as man and wife." Thomas filed suit seeking $44,625 for services rendered to Hoffman. According to the trial court, her claim was based on the theories of "express or implied contract of employment" or "unjust enrichment." Thomas lost at the trial level. How would you rule on appeal? Explain. See *In re Estate of Hoffman,* 2006 Iowa App. LEXIS 473 (May 24, 2006).

Adequacy of Consideration

With certain exceptions, the courts do not, as Judge Parker indicated in the *Hamer* case, inquire into the economic value of the consideration in question. Legal sufficiency depends not on the value of the consideration but on whether the promisee suffered a detriment in some way. To hold otherwise would put the courts in the place of the market in deciding the value of transactions. We are all free to make both good and bad bargains.

On the other hand, the courts will rule that consideration is found wanting in situations of pretense or sham where the parties have clearly agreed on token or nominal consideration in an effort to present the transaction as a contract rather than a gift. Likewise, an extreme inadequacy of consideration will sometimes cause the court to question a contract on the grounds of ***fraud***, ***duress***, or ***unconscionability*** (all discussed later in this chapter). In these instances, the agreements would be unenforceable because of a failure of consideration. These cases are uncommon, however, and the courts infrequently inquire into the adequacy of consideration.

Appearance of Consideration

Some agreements appear to be accompanied by consideration, but, in fact, that appearance may turn out to be an illusion. Hence, if one agrees to perform a preexisting duty, consideration would be found wanting. For example, if you were to pay your neighbor $50 to keep their dog on a leash when outdoors, and a city ordinance already requires dogs to be on a leash when outdoors, your promise would be unenforceable because your neighbor already had a preexisting duty under the law to keep their dog on a leash. Performance of a preexisting legal duty does not constitute consideration because no legal detriment or benefit has arisen.

Similarly, preexisting duties sometimes arise from contracts. Suppose you hire a contractor to resurface the parking lot at your accounting firm's office. You agree on a price of $12,000. With a portion of the work completed, the contractor asks you to amend the agreement to add $2,000 because the project is requiring more time than anticipated. You agree. The work is completed. Could you then legally refuse to pay the additional $2,000? The answer is yes because the contractor failed to provide consideration for the modification of your service contract. He was under a preexisting duty to finish the contract; hence, he did not sustain an additional legal detriment under the modified agreement. Note, however, that under UCC section 2-209(1), which applies to sales of goods, "an agreement modifying a contract within this Article needs no consideration to be binding."

Suppose you are a realtor and learn from your neighbor that your friend Ames wants to sell his house. You find a buyer for the house and make all of the necessary arrangements for the sale out of regard for your friendship with Ames. Then when the transaction is complete, Ames says, "Well, this has been great of you, but I don't feel right about it. When I get my check for the sale, I'll pay you $2,000 for your hard work. I really appreciate it." What if Ames does not then pay the $2,000? Do you have recourse? No. This is a situation of ***past consideration,*** where the performance–arranging the sale of your friend's house–was not bargained for and was not given in exchange for the promise and thus cannot constitute consideration. In effect, the performance was a gift. Of course, past consideration is really not consideration at all. In some states, courts enforce promises to pay for benefits already received where doing so amounts to a moral obligation that must be enforced to prevent injustice.

Substitutes for Consideration

When necessary to achieve justice, the courts sometimes conclude that a contract exists even though consideration is clearly lacking. Moral obligation and ***quasi-contract*** (discussed earlier) are two such instances, but the most prominent of these substitutes for consideration is found in the doctrine of ***promissory estoppel***, in which the promisor is "stopped" from denying the existence of a contract where the promisee has detrimentally relied on that promise. Promissory estoppel requires the following:

1. A promise on which the promisor should expect the promisee to rely.
2. The promisee did justifiably rely on the promise.
3. Injustice can be avoided only by enforcing the promise.

Consider the following: You have been a part-time employee of a small fast-food chain restaurant while attending college. Upon graduation, you tell the restaurant manager that you think you could handle your own franchise. He says you need to get more experience and advises you to take a full-time position with the company. You do so. Everything goes well, and when you next approach the manager, he says, "If you can come up with the $50,000 and a good location, we will get you in a franchise right away. But you've gotta move on this. Maybe you better quit your job with us and concentrate on this thing." You take his advice and quit your job. You raise the $50,000 and find a vacant building to rent in a good location for a franchise. You show the building to the manager, and he agrees that it looks like a favorable location and one that can easily be converted to the company's needs. He says, "Looks like you have everything in place. If you can come up with $50,000 more we will make this thing happen." You refuse and decide to bring suit against the fast-food chain for breach of contract. The chain defends by saying that you did not provide consideration for its promise. No formal financing arrangement was ever agreed to, and you had not committed yourself to any franchising obligations. Under these circumstances, you may well prevail using a promissory estoppel claim. In brief, you would argue that you had changed your position in reliance on the franchisor's promises and that relief is necessary to prevent injustice.

Question

Now that you have learned about offer, acceptance, and consideration as requirements for a binding contract, consider again the dispute between Turner "Tfue" Tenney and FaZe Clan discussed in the Introduction. Had they formed a binding contract? Explain.

Capacity

Having examined two of the required ingredients in an enforceable contract, agreement and consideration, we turn now to a third: capacity to contract. To enter a binding agreement, one must have the legal ability to do so, that is, one's mental condition and maturity must be such that the agreement was entered with understanding and in recognition of one's own interests. The three primary areas of concern are intoxication, mental impairment, and minority (not having reached the majority), with minority being the most common area of dispute.

> The three primary areas of concern are intoxication, mental impairment, and minority (not reached age of majority).

Intoxication

Assume you have been drinking to celebrate your 21st birthday. You enter a contract with a friend to sell him your autographed Willie Mays baseball card for $200. You receive the money and turn over the card. Later, when sober, you regret the deal. Will a court nullify that contract on the grounds of your intoxication? That decision depends on whether you were sufficiently intoxicated that you did not understand the nature and purpose of the contract. If the objective evidence suggests that you did not understand the transaction, the contract would be considered voidable, in which case you could probably disaffirm the contract, demand the return of the card, and give back the $200. Note, however, that courts often are not sympathetic to people who attempt to escape contracts made while intoxicated. In most states, if you recovered the card, you would be required to return the $200 to your friend.

If, on recovering your sobriety, your friend argued that the contract was invalid because of your intoxication, and he demanded the return of his $200 in exchange for the card, you could then ***ratify*** (affirm) the contract and hold him to it. If the contract had been for one of life's ***necessaries*** (such as food, shelter, clothing, medical care, or tools of one's trade), you would have been liable for the reasonable value of the necessaries already received.

Mental Incompetence

In most cases, an agreement involving a mentally incompetent person is either *void* or *voidable.* The transaction would be void–that is, no contract would exist–if the impaired party already had been *adjudged* incompetent–for example, an individual suffering from Alzheimer's disease for whom a guardian has been appointed by a court to take care of their affairs. If the impaired party was unable to understand the purpose and effect of the contract but had not been legally adjudged incompetent, the contract would be voidable (void in some states) at the option of the impaired party. The competent party cannot void the contract, and the impaired party would have to pay the reasonable value of any necessaries already received under the contract.

Minors

Generally minors may complete their contracts if they wish, but they also have an absolute right to rescind most of those contracts until they reach adulthood, and for a reasonable time thereafter. However, many states have enacted statutes forbidding minors from disaffirming some classes of contracts, such as those for marriage, student loans, and life insurance. If rescinded, the minor has a right of recovery for everything given up in meeting the terms of the contract. Similarly, the minor must return everything that remains in their possession that was received from the contract. In many states, if nothing of the bargained-for consideration remains or if its value has been depreciated, the minor has no duty to replace it but can still recover whatever they put into the contract. If not disaffirmed within a reasonable time after the minor reaches the age of majority, the contract is considered to be ratified, and the minor is bound to its terms. Whether or not the contract is rescinded, the minor is liable for the reasonable value (not necessarily the contract price) of necessaries purchased from an adult.

Generally minors may complete their contracts if they wish, but they also have the right to rescind most of those contracts.

Despite the flexibility accorded to minors entering contracts, the adults who are parties to those contracts are bound to them and do not have the power to disaffirm. Hence, adults put themselves at risk when they choose to bargain with minors. As noted, in many states a minor need not make restitution if the consideration is lost, destroyed, or depreciated. On the other hand, courts may hold that minors who enter into a contract without undue influence have some monetary obligation, such as for the use or depreciation of the good purchased.

Comic Contracts

Reading a contract can be confusing, especially for those who are not fluent in the local language or those with learning disabilities. Comic contracts, created by Robert de Rooy, an attorney in South Africa, offer legally binding contracts, signed by the parties who are represented by characters in a comic which depicts the agreement in pictures. These comic contracts can promote transparency and help parties understand the contractual terms. Some examples of comic contracts that have been or are being created include: codes of conduct for Australian sports clubs, domestic worker contracts, employment contracts for kitchen staff workers of a hotel group, rental contracts, and loan agreements.[1]

[For examples of comic contracts, see Comic Book Contracts, **https://www.comicbookcontracts.com/overview-practical-examples**].

Genuineness of Assent

Sometimes parties appear to have concluded a binding contract, but the courts will allow them to escape that obligation because they had not, in fact, achieved an agreement. They had achieved the appearance of agreement but not the reality. That situation arises when the contract is the product of misrepresentation, fraud, duress, undue influence, or mistake. Ordinarily, such agreements are voidable and may be rescinded by the innocent party because of the absence of genuine assent, the fourth of five ingredients in a binding contract.

Misrepresentation and Fraud

An innocent untruth is a misrepresentation. Intentional untruths constitute fraud. In either case, a party to a contract who has been deceived may rescind the deal, and restitution may be secured if benefits were extended to the party issuing the untruth. The elements of fraud are

1. Misrepresentation of a material fact.
2. The misrepresentation was intentional.
3. The injured party justifiably relied on the misrepresentation.
4. Injury resulted.

Note that the test requires a misrepresented fact. In general, misrepresented opinions are not grounds for action, but many courts are now recognizing exceptions to that rule, especially when the innocent party has relied on opinion coming from an expert.

You are selling a house that allegedly is "haunted."

If you are selling a house that allegedly is "haunted," does your failure to reveal the ghostly presence constitute a misrepresentation? The *Stambovsky* case that follows addresses that unusual question.

LEGAL BRIEFCASE

Stambovsky v. Ackley et al.

169 A.D.2d 254 (N.Y. App. Div. 1991)

Justice Rubin

Plaintiff, to his horror, discovered that the house he had recently contracted to purchase was widely reputed to be possessed by poltergeists, reportedly seen by defendant seller and members of her family on numerous occasions over the last nine years. Plaintiff promptly commenced this action seeking rescission of the contract of sale.

The unusual facts of this case clearly warrant a grant of equitable relief to the buyer who, as a resident of New York City, cannot be expected to have any familiarity with the folklore of the Village of Nyack. Not being a "local," plaintiff could not readily learn that the home he had contracted to purchase is haunted. Whether the source of the spectral apparitions seen by defendant seller is parapsychic or psychogenic, having reported their presence in both a national publication (*Readers' Digest*) and the local press (in 1977 and 1982, respectively), defendant is estopped to deny their existence and, as a matter of law, the house is haunted. More to the point, however, no divination is required to conclude that it is defendant's promotional efforts in publicizing her close encounters with these spirits which fostered the home's reputation in the community. In 1989, the house was included in [a] five-home walking tour of Nyack and described in a November 27th newspaper article as "a riverfront Victorian (with ghost)." The impact of the reputation thus created goes to the very essence of the bargain between the parties, greatly impairing both the value of the property and its potential for resale.

While I agree that the real estate broker, as agent for the seller, is under no duty to disclose to a potential buyer the phantasmal reputation of the premises and that, in his pursuit of a legal remedy for fraudulent misrepresentation against the seller, plaintiff hasn't a ghost of a chance, I am nevertheless moved by the spirit of equity to allow the buyer to seek rescission of the contract of sale and recovery of his down payment. New York law fails to recognize any remedy for damages incurred as a result of the seller's mere silence, applying instead the strict rule of caveat emptor. Therefore, the theoretical basis for granting relief, even under the extraordinary facts of this case, is elusive if not ephemeral.

From the perspective of a person in the position of plaintiff herein, a very practical problem arises with respect to the discovery of a paranormal phenomenon: "Who you gonna' call?" as a title song to the movie "Ghostbusters" asks. Applying the strict rule of caveat emptor to a contract involving a house possessed by poltergeists conjures up visions of a psychic or medium routinely accompanying the structural engineer and Terminix man on an inspection of every home subject to a contract of sale. It portends that the prudent attorney will establish an escrow account lest the subject of the transaction come back to haunt him and his client—or pray that his malpractice insurance coverage extends to supernatural disasters. In the interest of avoiding such untenable consequences, the notion that a haunting is a condition which can and should be ascertained upon reasonable inspection of the premises is a hobgoblin which should be exorcised from the body of legal precedent and laid quietly to rest.

It has been suggested by a leading authority that the ancient rule which holds that mere nondisclosure does not constitute actionable misrepresentation "finds proper application in cases where the fact undisclosed is patent, or the plaintiff has equal opportunities for obtaining information which he may be expected to utilize, or the defendant has no reason to think that he is acting under any misapprehension" (Prosser, Torts Section 106, at 696 [4th ed 1971]). However, with respect to transactions in real estate, New York adheres to the doctrine of caveat emptor and imposes no duty upon the vendor to disclose any information concerning the premises unless there is a confidential or fiduciary relationship between the parties or some conduct on the part of the seller which constitutes "active concealment." Normally, some affirmative misrepresentation or partial disclosure is required to impose upon the seller a duty to communicate undisclosed conditions affecting the premises.

Common law is not moribund. . . . Where fairness and common sense dictate that an exception should be created, the evolution of the law should not be stifled by rigid application of a legal maxim.

The doctrine of caveat emptor requires that a buyer act prudently to assess the fitness and value of his purchase and operates to bar the purchaser who fails to exercise due care from seeking the equitable remedy of rescission. For the purposes of the instant motion to dismiss the action . . . plaintiff is entitled to every favorable inference which may reasonably be drawn from the pleadings, specifically, in this instance, that he met his obligation to conduct an inspection of the premises and a search of available public records with respect to title. It should be apparent, however, that the most meticulous inspection and the search would not reveal the presence of poltergeists at the premises or unearth the property's ghoulish reputation in the community. Therefore, there is no sound policy reason to deny plaintiff relief for failing to discover a state of affairs which the most prudent purchaser would not be expected to even contemplate.

Where a condition which has been created by the seller materially impairs the value of the contract and is peculiarly within the knowledge of the seller or unlikely to be discovered by a prudent purchaser exercising due care with respect to the subject transaction, nondisclosure constitutes a basis for rescission as a matter of equity. Any other outcome places upon the buyer not merely the obligation to exercise care in his purchase but rather to be omniscient with respect to any fact which may affect the bargain. No practical purpose is served by imposing such a burden upon a purchaser. To the contrary, it encourages predatory business practice. . . .

In the case at bar, defendant seller deliberately fostered the public belief that her home was possessed. Having undertaken to inform the public-at-large, to whom she has no legal relationship, about the supernatural occurrences on her property, she may be said to owe no less a duty to her contract vendee. . . . Where, as here, the seller not only takes unfair advantage of the buyer's ignorance but has created and perpetuated a condition about which he is unlikely to even inquire, enforcement of the contract (in whole or in part) is offensive to the court's sense of equity. Application of the remedy of rescission, within the bounds of the narrow exception to the doctrine of caveat emptor set forth herein, is entirely appropriate to relieve the unwitting purchaser from the consequences of a most unnatural bargain.

Accordingly, the judgment of the Supreme Court, New York County (Edward H. Lehner, J.), entered April 9, 1990, which dismissed the complaint should be modified and the first cause of action seeking rescission of the contract reinstated.

DISSENT

Justice Smith (dissenting).

I would affirm the dismissal of the complaint. . . .

"It is settled law in New York State that the seller of real property is under no duty to speak when the parties deal at arm's length. The mere silence of the seller, without some act or conduct which deceived the purchaser, does not amount to a concealment that is actionable as a fraud. . . ."

The parties herein were represented by counsel and dealt at arm's length. . . . There is no allegation that defendants, by some specific act, other than the failure to speak, deceived the plaintiff. . . .

Finally, if the doctrine of caveat emptor is to be discarded, it should be for a reason more substantive than a poltergeist. The existence of a poltergeist is no more binding upon the defendants than it is upon this court.

Based upon the foregoing, the [lower] court properly dismissed the complaint.

Questions

1. *a.* According to the court, did the defendant seller engage in a fraudulent misrepresentation in failing to disclose the "ghostly" condition of her house? Explain.
   b. The plaintiff won this case on equitable and fairness grounds. Explain the court's reasoning.
   c. Do you agree with the court's equity and fairness reasoning? Explain.
   d. Did the real estate agent engage in fraud for failing to disclose the house's haunted reputation? Explain.
2. *a.* What did the court mean by the phrase "caveat emptor"?
   b. Why did the court find for the plaintiff buyer, even though "caveat emptor" seemed to be the controlling law in this situation?
   c. Would the buyer have been successful in a misrepresentation claim if the seller had said: "This house is so peaceful. We never have any disturbances"? Why?
   d. The defendant seller had fostered the belief that her house was haunted. Did that promotional effort by the defendant influence the court's decision making? Explain.
3. Explain dissenting Justice Smith's objection to the majority's ruling.
4. In 2007, soon after moving from California into the home she had bought in Pennsylvania, Janet Milliken learned that previous occupants, Konstantinos Koumboulis and his wife, died in an apparent murder/suicide after Koumboulis allegedly shot his wife and himself in the house. The sellers, Kathleen and Joseph Jacono, had later bought the home in a real estate auction. Milliken filed a complaint against the Jaconos and the real estate firms involved in her purchase of the house, alleging fraud and misrepresentation for failure to disclose the murder/suicide. Milliken stated in her opening brief that after she and her family had moved into the home, various paranormal events had occurred. How should the court rule? Explain. See *Milliken v. Jacono,* 60 A.3d 133 (Pa. 2012).

Toy Yoda

Former Hooters waitress Jodee Berry sued Gulf Coast Wings, the corporate owner of the Hooters restaurant where she had worked, for not awarding a new Toyota as a prize for her victory in an April 2001 sales contest. Berry alleged that her manager told the waitresses in the Florida Hooters that the server selling the most beer would be entered in a drawing (involving other Hooters locations) to win a new Toyota. At one point during the contest, the manager allegedly said he did not know whether the winner would receive a Toyota car, truck, or van but knew that the winner would be required to pay registration fees. At the close of the contest, the manager told Berry she won. He blindfolded her and took her to the restaurant parking lot. He laughed when Berry found not the car she expected, but a doll based on the *Star Wars* movie character Yoda (a toy Yoda). Berry did not laugh but sued instead. The case was settled out of court. The terms of that settlement were not disclosed, but Berry's lawyer did say she would be able to afford whatever Toyota she wanted.

Questions

1. What contract-based causes of action did Berry bring in this case?
2. Defend the Hooters restaurant owner, Gulf Coast Wings.
3. Make the argument that the Hooters manager never actually made an offer to the waitresses.
4. If an offer was made, how did Berry accept that offer?
5. Make the argument that the offer and acceptance, if they existed, were not supported by consideration.

Sources: *Berry v. Gulf Coast Wings, Inc.,* Case No. 03-2001-2642-J (Fla. 14th Cir. Ct. July 24, 2001); and Keith A. Rowley, "You Asked for It, You Got It . . . Toy Yoda: Practical Jokes, Prizes, and Contract Law," *Nevada Law Journal* 3 (Spring 2003), pp. 526–559.

Duress

Sometimes genuine assent is not secured, and a contract may be rescinded because one of the parties is forced to agree. Fear lies at the heart of a duress claim. The party seeking to escape the contract must establish that a wrongful act was threatened or had occurred, causing the party to enter the contract out of fear of harm such that free will was precluded. Increasingly, courts are also setting aside contracts on the grounds of economic duress. For example, suppose you know that one of your regular customers depends on your timely delivery of steel to their factory and that they cannot expeditiously find an alternative supply. Therefore, you tell your customer that delivery will be delayed until they agree to pay a higher price for the steel. If they agree, the resulting contract probably could be rescinded on the grounds of economic duress.

Undue Influence

Under some circumstances, one party to an apparent contract can escape its terms by showing that they did not act independently because they were so dominated by the second party.

These claims are most common in cases involving those who are old or infirm and who lose their independence of thought and action to the undue influence of a caregiver or adviser.

Mistake

When starting a new job, most of us operate for a time in fear that we will make a mistake. Assume you are new to your job as an assistant manager at a custodial company and are preparing the company's bid for a general maintenance contract for a large office building. In preparing the bid, you inadvertently submit a final price of $50,000 rather than $500,000. What happens? Do you lose your job?

> You inadvertently submit a final price of $50,000 rather than $500,000. What happens?

In some cases, mistakes involving critical facts can be grounds for rescinding contracts. A ***mutual mistake*** is one in which both parties to the contract are in error about some critical fact. With exceptions, either party can rescind those contracts because genuine assent was not achieved. Your erroneous bid, however, is a ***unilateral mistake***, that is, only one party to the contract made an error. The general rule is that those contracts cannot be rescinded. Nevertheless, if you are able to show that the other party to the contract knew or should have known about your mistake, many courts would allow you to rescind. Certainly, you would make that argument in this instance because the $50,000 bid presumably is dramatically out of line with the other bids and at odds with reasonable business expectations about the value of the contract. In cases where an error is made in drafting a contract, and both parties are unaware of the error (a mutual mistake), the courts will reform the contract rather than void it. That is, the contract will be rewritten to reflect what both parties intended.

Flying for Free?

For about two hours in 2013, the Delta Airlines website advertised $6.90 round-trip flights to Hawaii. Some travelers wait for such mistaken fares, learning of them through airfare websites or social media, and quickly purchase their tickets before the obvious error is corrected. Delta honored the $6.90 airfare for purchased tickets. In 2015, the U.S. Department of Transportation (DOT) issued a temporary rule that, in cases of mistaken fares, it would not enforce a requirement prohibiting airlines from raising an airline ticket price after purchase. The airlines would be obligated to reimburse the out-of-pocket expenses of those who had already purchased their tickets under the mistaken fare, however.

Question

1. Is purchasing an airline ticket for an obviously incorrect, low fare unethical? Why or why not?
2. As a matter of contract law, what is an argument in support of the DOT's temporary rule?
3. Is it necessarily obvious in the era of competitive online sales that a low price is incorrect? For example, budget airlines in Europe often have exceedingly low fares for some seats. Explain.

Sources: Mary Forgione, "Airlines Don't Have to Honor 'Mistake' Fares, U.S. Agency Rules," *Los Angeles Times,* May 12, 2015 [**www.latimes.com**]; and Christopher Elliott, "Airlines May Be Off Hook for Mistake Fares," *USA Today,* May 31, 2015 [**www.usatoday.com**].

Question

Return once again to the dispute between Turner "Tfue" Tenney and FaZe Clan. If it could be proven that Tenney did not in fact understand the terms of the contract, would Tenney have a right to rescind? Explain.

Legality of Purpose

Having examined agreement, consideration, capacity, and genuineness of assent, we turn now to the final requirement for the creation of a binding contract: legality of purpose. *Illegality* refers to bargains to commit a crime or a tort (such as a deal with a coworker to embezzle funds from one's employer); more broadly, illegality involves bargains that are forbidden by statute or violate public policy. We can identify three general categories of illegal agreements: (1) contracts that violate statutes, (2) contracts that are unconscionable, and (3) contracts that violate public policy. In general, the effect of an illegal contract is that it cannot be enforced, and the courts will not provide a remedy if its terms are unfulfilled. With exceptions, the parties to illegal deals are left where the courts find them.

Contracts Violating Statutes

As noted, a contract to commit a crime or a tort is illegal and unenforceable. Some state laws have also specified certain other agreements that are illegal. They vary from state to state but commonly include antigambling laws, laws forbidding the conduct of certain kinds of business on Sundays (***blue laws***), laws forbidding ***usury***, and laws forbidding the practice of certain professions (law, real estate, hair care, etc.) without a license.

***Modern Family* Contract Feud**

Cast members of the Emmy Award–winning television comedy *Modern Family* filed a breach of contract lawsuit against producer 20th Century Fox, seeking to have their current contracts declared void under a California law prohibiting enforcement of a personal service contract after seven years. Shortly after the lawsuit was filed, Fox agreed to enter into new agreements with the cast members, who then dropped the lawsuit.

Questions

If the lawsuit had gone to trial, what issues would have to be decided? Who would have won? Explain.

Sources: California Labor Code Sec. 2855; and Joe Flint, "Cast of *Modern Family* Strikes New Deal," *Los Angeles Times,* July 27, 2012 [**www.latimes.com**].

Certain agreements are so thoroughly one-sided that fairness precludes enforcing them.

Unconscionable Contracts

Certain agreements are so thoroughly one-sided that fairness precludes enforcing them. Problems of unconscionability often arise in situations in which the bargaining power of one of the parties is much superior to that of the other—where one can, in effect, "twist the arm" or otherwise take advantage of the other. Both the common law of contracts and UCC Section 2-302 give the courts the power to modify or refuse to enforce such deals.

Question

Tenney claimed his contract with FaZe Clan was oppressive. Do the facts as described sound like he could claim the contract was unconscionable? Explain.

Public Policy

The courts may decline to enforce certain otherwise binding contracts because doing so would not be in the public's best interest. For example, an agreement between the local convenience stores to charge $5 for a gallon of gasoline would be a restraint of trade (price-fixing) and, as such, would be contrary to public policy and antitrust laws (see Chapter 10) and thus would be unenforceable. Similarly, suppose as a condition of being hired for a job, you must sign an agreement providing that you will not leave your employer to work for one of your employer's competitors. These *noncompete* clauses (see Chapter 12) are common and may be fully lawful, depending largely on whether the time and geographic restrictions imposed are reasonable. If unreasonable, the courts will either not enforce the clause or will alter it to achieve a fair result.

Another commonplace public policy concern arises from the ***exculpatory clause***, *limited liability clause*, or ***release***. If you participate in any potentially hazardous activity, such as attending a professional hockey game, whitewater rafting, joining a school field trip, or entering an amusement park, you may be required to agree to release others of any liability for harm that might befall you. If you own or manage a potentially hazardous enterprise such as a water slide, bungee tower, or even a health spa, you may try to protect yourself from litigation should a customer be hurt by including a release in the customer agreement. Often, such agreements are enforceable in the manner of any other contractual provision, but sometimes they are not. Many factors can influence that decision, including how sweeping the exculpation is, whether it was knowingly entered, and the relative bargaining power of the parties. The case that follows analyzes the enforceability of a liability release signed by a woman who did not speak or read English at the time she joined a gym.

LEGAL BRIEFCASE

Jimenez v. 24 Hour Fitness USA, Inc. 188 Cal. Rptr. 3d 228 (Cal. App. 4th Dist. 2015)

Justice Murray

Plaintiffs Etelvina and Pedro Jimenez appeal from summary judgment in favor of defendant 24 Hour Fitness USA, Inc. (24 Hour), in plaintiffs' negligence action stemming from a catastrophic injury sustained by Etelvina while using a treadmill at 24 Hour. Plaintiffs asserted that 24 Hour was grossly negligent in setting up the treadmill in a manner that violated the manufacturer's safety instructions.

24 Hour moved for summary judgment, contending that it was not liable as a matter of law because Etelvina signed a liability release when she joined the gym. The trial court agreed and granted summary judgment.

On appeal, plaintiffs contend that the trial court erred in granting summary judgment in 24 Hour's favor because (1) the liability release is not enforceable against plaintiffs' claim of gross negligence; [and] (2) the release was obtained by fraud and misrepresentation . . . we agree. . . . Accordingly, we reverse.

FACTUAL AND PROCEDURAL BACKGROUND

Undisputed Facts

Plaintiffs filed a complaint against 24 Hour stating causes of action for premises liability, general negligence, and loss of consortium. The action arose out of injuries Etelvina sustained on January 16, 2011, while exercising at a 24 Hour facility in Sacramento, California. Etelvina's expert opined that she fell backward off of a moving treadmill and sustained severe head injuries when she hit her head on the exposed steel foot of a leg exercise machine that 24 Hour placed approximately three feet 10 inches behind the treadmill.

24 Hour filed an answer to the complaint generally denying the allegations and claiming several affirmative defenses, including the defense that plaintiffs' claims were barred by a liability release.

At the time of her injuries, Etelvina was a member of 24 Hour. She joined 24 Hour approximately two years before the day she sustained her injury, and thereafter, she used the facilities regularly several times per week. On the day she joined, she was directed to the membership manager, Justin Wilbourn. She was then required to sign a membership agreement. However, Etelvina could not read or speak English, and Wilbourn did not speak Spanish. Wilbourn knew Etelvina did not read or speak English. Nevertheless, he did not call a Spanish-speaking employee to help him translate. Instead, he pointed to his computer screen to a figure, $24.99, indicating the membership fee, and made pumping motions with his arms like he was exercising. Etelvina understood the numbers, which are identical in Spanish, and she understood Wilbourn's physical gestures to mean that if she paid that amount, she could use the facility. She could not read anything else. Wilbourn then pointed to the lines in the agreement for Etelvina to sign.

The membership agreement contained a liability release provision, which provided: "Using the 24 Hour USA, Inc. (24 Hour) facilities involves the risk of injury to you or your guest, whether you or someone else causes it. Specific risks vary from one activity to another and the risks range from minor injuries to major injuries, such as catastrophic injuries including death. **In consideration of your participation in the activities offered by 24 Hour, *you understand and voluntarily accept this risk and agree that 24 Hour,* its officers, directors, employees, volunteers, agents and independent contractors *will not be liable for any injury,* including, without limitation, personal, bodily, or mental injury, economic loss or any damage to you, your spouse, guests, unborn child, or relatives resulting from the negligence of 24 Hour or anyone on 24 Hour's behalf or anyone using the facilities *whether related to exercise or not.*** . . . By signing below, you acknowledge and agree that you have read the foregoing and know of the nature of the activities at 24 Hour and you agree to all the terms on *pages 1 through 4* of this agreement and acknowledge that you have received a copy of it and the membership policies."

Wilbourn did not point out the release to Etelvina or make any other indications about the scope of the agreement aside from his gestures mimicking exercise and the fee. Etelvina believed she signed an agreement only to pay the monthly fee of $24.99.

In his deposition, Wilbourn, the membership manager for 24 Hour, said that he did not remember meeting Etelvina, although he identified himself as the employee who assisted her based on his signature on her membership agreement. Wilbourn testified that typically, when he encountered a potential customer who only spoke Spanish, his habit and custom was to have a Spanish-speaking employee handle the signup for that potential customer.

[A]NALYSIS

Generally, a person who signs an instrument may not avoid the impact of its terms on the ground that she failed to read it before signing. However, a release is invalid when it is procured by misrepresentation, overreaching, deception, or fraud. In cases providing the opportunity for overreaching, the releasee has a duty to act in good faith and the releaser must have a full understanding of his legal rights. Furthermore, it is the province of the jury to determine whether the circumstances afforded the opportunity for overreaching, whether the releasee engaged in overreaching and whether the releaser was misled. . . .

Here, if a jury were to be persuaded that Wilbourn made misrepresentations to Etelvina about the contents of the agreement by making nonverbal gestures indicating that what she was signing related *only* to being allowed to exercise if she paid the price on the computer screen, it would be entitled to find that Etelvina's signature on the release was produced by misrepresentation and that the release is not enforceable against her. . . .

A recent Ninth Circuit case applying California law, *Doe v. Gangland Productions, Inc.*, 730 F.3d 946 (9th Cir. 2013), is also instructive. There, the plaintiff sued two production companies for broadcasting a television documentary without concealing his identity. . . . [T]he defendants contended that the plaintiff's claims were barred because he signed a release consenting to disclosure of his real identity in the broadcast and waiving all claims for liability. . . . In a declaration, the plaintiff stated that he was dyslexic, illiterate, and that he informed the Gangland producer who asked him to sign the release that he had "'extreme difficulty reading.'" The plaintiff also stated that "when he was provided the alleged release, [the producer] told him it was 'just a receipt' for his $300 payment for the interview. Because of these representations, [the plaintiff] did not ask his girlfriend to read out loud the document before he signed it." The court reasoned that the plaintiff "made a sufficient showing of fraud in the execution of the release, which, if true, would render the release void."

In reaching its conclusion, the court in *Gangland* cited *Mairo v. Yellow Cab Co.* (1929) 208 Cal. 350. In *Mairo*, the California Supreme Court reviewed a directed verdict in the defendant's favor, where the trial court concluded that the plaintiff had waived his rights by executing several releases. The plaintiff was an illiterate Russian immigrant who understood little spoken English. He was injured after being hit by the defendant's taxicab and during the course of his medical treatment, the defendant had him sign several releases in exchange for the payment of his medical treatment. The plaintiff asserted that the defendant misrepresented the true contents of the releases and that he believed they were merely a permit to operate on him and receipts. The court held that if the true nature of the releases was "misrepresented to [the plaintiff] so that he did not know what he was really signing, they are, of course, void. But under the conflicting evidence here it is impossible to tell whether such was the fact. This also was an issue which should have gone to the jury and it was, therefore, erroneous for the trial court to direct said verdict for defendant."

. . . 24 Hour contends that these nonverbal communications cannot, as a matter of law, amount to *affirmative* misrepresentations because Etelvina "could not reasonably have relied upon anything Mr. Wilbourn said" since he spoke a different language. 24 Hour's argument implies that nonverbal communications cannot be misrepresentative or induce reasonable reliance. We reject this argument. While it may be less reasonable for a plaintiff to rely on nonverbal communications in a case where the parties speak the same language, in this case, gesturing was virtually the *only* form of communication between Wilbourn and Etelvina. It is undisputed that Etelvina did not speak English and Wilbourn did not speak Spanish. Further, Wilbourn knew Etelvina did not speak or read English. And he knew that Etelvina did not read the contract, including the terms setting forth the release, even though, as the membership manager, he must have known that the release says, "By signing below, you acknowledge and agree that *you have read* the foregoing . . ." provisions of the release. (Italics added.) Under these circumstances, already ripe for misrepresentation and overreaching, Wilbourn's gestures and pointing may very well have misrepresented the nature of the document Etelvina signed. This is an inherently factual question for a jury to decide.

DISPOSITION

Accordingly, we reverse the trial court's ruling . . . .

Questions

1. What are the similarities between *Jimenez* and *Gangland*? What are the differences? Explain the relevance of *Gangland* to the *Jimenez* court.
2. If you were on the jury having to decide the factual questions identified by this court, how would you decide? Explain.
3. What could 24 Hour Fitness do to ensure that its liability release is enforceable in such situations?
4. Ning Yan went to Vital Power Fitness Center to use a one-week complimentary pass. On each visit, he signed in on a sheet that contained a standard exculpatory clause including this language: "I also understand that Vital Power Fitness Center assumes no responsibility for any injuries and/or sicknesses incurred to me. . . ." On February 18, 1999, Yan fell from a treadmill and sustained a severe head injury. He later died from that injury. No one witnessed the fall. Yan's estate claimed he struck his head against a window ledge because the treadmill was placed too close to the window. If he did strike the window ledge, who would likely win this case? What questions might *Jimenez* raise about this case? Explain. See *Xu v. Gay*, 668 N.W.2d 166 (Mich. Ct. App. 2003).

PRACTICING ETHICS — 2010 Gulf Oil Disaster: BP Contracts Unfair/Unconscionable?

In May 2010, British Petroleum (BP) oil company was in the midst of frantic efforts to stop the oil flowing into the Gulf of Mexico from its doomed Macondo 252 well while also trying to clean up the immense quantity that escaped after the explosion of the Deepwater Horizon drilling vessel. "Several hundred" shrimpers, oyster harvesters, and others making their living from the Gulf signed contracts with BP to work as paid volunteers in the cleanup process. Among the provisions in those contracts were promises by the volunteers not to file legal claims against the oil company should they sustain damages of any kind in the cleanup process. The provisions, which many of those signing may not have fully understood, included promises not to sue in case of accident or injury and not to talk to anyone about the disaster or cleanup without BP approval. Those provisions also required a 30-day notice before pursuing legal claims against BP, even in the event of an emergency. Reportedly, BP also expected workers to add the oil giant to their personal insurance policies so that worker injuries or damages would fall to each worker's insurance rather than to BP. Commercial fisherman and United Commercial Fisherman's Association president George Barisich filed suit to block enforcement of the restrictive promises and U.S. District Judge Helen Berrigan ruled the offending provisions were overbroad and "unconscionable" and declared them null and void. BP and the Fisherman's Association soon reached an agreement removing the waiver language and agreeing not to enforce those provisions in contracts already signed. BP officials said the provisions were a "mistake," and they ordered the provisions removed as soon as they learned about them.

Questions

1. *a.* Were BP's protective provisions "wrong" as a matter of ethical business practice? Explain.
   b. If you were a manager or lawyer at BP, would you have included those protective provisions? Explain.
2. *a.* If you were a manager and you knew you could compel an employee to accept a pay cut in order to enhance an already healthy bottom line, would you do so? Explain.
   b. In your personal life, do you think you have made agreements with friends that were "one-sided" and "unconscionable" because of your possession of superior leverage of some kind?
   c. If so, were you "wrong" to do so. Explain.

Sources: Sabrina Canfield, "Judge Enjoins BP's Unconscionable Contract with Fishermen-Volunteers," *Courthouse News Service,* May 4, 2010 [**www.courthousenews.com**]; and Brendan Kirby, "Full Report: BP Backs Away from Controversial Oil Spill Settlement Language," AL.com, May 5, 2010 [**http://blog.al.com**].

Part Two—Interpreting and Enforcing Contracts

We have examined the five ingredients in a binding contract: agreement, consideration, capacity, genuineness of assent, and legality of purpose. Having established those conditions, a contract may have been created, but the door to contract problems has not been closed. Contracts sometimes must fulfill writing formalities to be enforceable. Third parties may have claims against some contracts. And what happens when a party to a contract does not perform as called for by the agreement?

Written Contracts: Requirements and Implications

Certainly a common belief is that agreements must be in writing to be enforceable; but in most cases, oral contracts are fully enforceable. The exceptions, however, are important. Oral contracts are subject to misunderstanding or to being forgotten, and fraudulent claims can readily arise from oral understandings.

> In most cases, oral contracts are fully enforceable.

Required Writings

Certain types of contracts, if not in writing, have long been known to create difficulties. In England, a ***Statute of Frauds*** was passed listing contracts that would be unenforceable unless they were written. Our states have drawn on the English Statute of Frauds in specifying the types of contracts that, in most cases, must be in writing to be enforceable.

Collateral contract Assume you have just graduated from college and you want to get started in a small printing business. You secure a bank loan on the condition that you find a creditworthy third party as a guarantor for the loan. Jacobs, a family friend, agrees with the bank to pay the debt if you fail to do so. Jacobs's promise to pay the debt must be in writing to be enforceable.

The sale of land Generally, the transfer of land includes the land's surface, its soil and minerals, and buildings permanently attached to it. Thus, if a building was permanently attached to a lot you seek for the aforementioned printing business, that building would need to be included in the written contract, but if you contracted to have a building constructed on your lot, you would not need (at least for the purposes of the Statute of Frauds) to execute a written agreement with the building contractor because you would not be contracting for an interest in land. A long-term lease (normally more than one year) for that land and building would, in most states, need to be in writing. All of these principles simply reflect the special role of land in our view of wealth and freedom.

Promises that cannot be performed within one year This requirement springs from a concern about faulty memories, deaths, and other impediments to the satisfactory conclusion of long-term contracts. The courts have interpreted this provision narrowly, in effect saying that such a contract need not be in writing if it is *possible,* according to its terms, to perform it within one year from the day of its creation. A contract for the construction of a dam that will take at least 13 months must be in writing; a contract for the construction of a building that will take from six to 13 months, depending on weather, does not.

Contracts for the sale of goods at a price of $500 or more With exceptions, under both the English-derived Statute of Frauds and UCC Section 2-201, contracts for the sale of goods (having a value of $500 or more under the UCC) must be in writing to be enforceable. Under the UCC, informal writing will suffice so long as it indicates that a contract was made, it contains a quantity term, and it was signed "by the party against whom enforcement is sought." Section 2-201 provides exceptions for certain transactions of $500 or more in goods in which a contract will be enforceable even though not in writing.

Contracts in consideration of marriage The mutual exchange of marriage promises need not be in writing, but any contract that uses marriage as the consideration to support the contract must be in writing to be enforceable. Such contracts would include, for example, prenuptial agreements that are entered prior to marriage and serve the purpose, among others, of specifying how the couple's property will be divided in the event of a divorce. Those contracts must be in writing to be enforceable.

Executor or administrator's promise When an individual dies, a personal representative (sometimes referred to as an executor or administrator) is appointed to oversee the estate. A promise by that representative to personally pay the estate's debts must be in writing to be enforceable. Thus, if the personal representative of an estate contracts with an auctioneer to dispose of the decedent's property, the representative's promise to pay the auctioneer must be in writing if the funds are to come from the representative's personal resources; the promise need not be in writing if the payment is to come from the estate.

Electronic Transactions and Statute of Frauds

The Uniform Electronic Transactions Act (UETA), widely adopted by state legislatures, gives electronic records and signatures the same legal power as paper documents and manually signed "wet signatures."[2]

Courts have held that email exchanges, and the typed name of the sender at the bottom of an email message, may satisfy the Statute of Frauds writing requirement.[3] However, the parties in the email exchange must have intended to enter into an agreement in this manner.[4] Text messaging has created a new issue under the UETA. A Massachusetts court recently ruled that a text message from a real estate broker accepting an offer to buy a client's commercial building was binding on the seller.[5]

Contract Emoji?

Suppose you are the president of your college's Business Students Club and are negotiating via text message with Dani, a t-shirt manufacturer, for the purchase of 75 t-shirts emblazoned with the club's logo. You had asked Dani how much the t-shirts will cost and received a reply: "$15 each." You then text back Dani: "How about $10 each for the 75 t-shirts?" and receive a text reply from Dani with an emoji of a "thumbs up," which signals approval.

Questions

1. Is there an enforceable contract for the sale of the t-shirts at $10 each? What questions would you need answered before deciding? Explain.
2. Consider which emojis might be used in negotiating a contract through text messages. What problems might arise? Discuss.

Failure to Comply with the Statute of Frauds

A fully performed oral contract, even though not in compliance with the Statute of Frauds, will not be rescinded by the courts. However, incomplete oral contracts that fail to comply with the statute are unenforceable. If a party to an unenforceable oral contract has provided partial performance in reliance on the contract, the courts will ordinarily provide compensation under quasi-contract principles for the reasonable value of that performance. [For more on the Statute of Frauds, see **www.expertlaw.com/library/business/statute_of_frauds.html**].

The Parol Evidence Rule

If a contract is written, whether or not a writing was required, enforcement may be affected by the existence of the writing. Suppose you are the purchasing manager for a large manufacturer. You entered a written contract for 50 new personal computers. During negotiations, the seller said it would "throw in" 10 new printers if it got the computer order, but you failed to include a provision for the printers in the contract. Is your boss about to have a fit? Perhaps, because you probably will not be able to introduce evidence of that oral understanding to alter the terms of the written contract.

In general, when a contract has been reduced to writing with the intent that the writing represents the complete and final expression of the parties' intentions, no party can introduce parol evidence (oral or written words outside the "four corners" of the agreement) to add to, change, or contradict the writing if that evidence existed at the time of, or prior to, the writing. The written agreement is presumed to be the best evidence of the parties' intentions when they entered the contract. (The parol evidence rule under UCC Section 2-202 is essentially the same as the common-law provisions discussed here.)

There are, however, a few exceptions where parol evidence may be admissible, such as

1. To add missing terms to an incomplete written contract.
2. To explain ambiguities in a written contract.
3. To prove circumstances that would invalidate a written contract, that is, to establish one of the grounds of mistake, fraud, illegality, and so forth explained earlier in this chapter.

LEGAL BRIEFCASE

Blanchard & Associates v. Lupin Pharmaceuticals, Inc. 900 F.3d 917 (7th Cir. 2018)

Judge Sykes

OPINION

In 2009 Blanchard & Associates, a Chicago law firm, provided legal services to an Indian pharmaceutical company, Lupin Ltd. ("Lupin India"), and its American subsidiary, Lupin Pharmaceuticals, Inc. ("Lupin USA"). The advice concerned the patentability of a generic birth-control drug that Lupin India planned to launch in the United States through Lupin USA. When the Lupin companies initially sought Blanchard's advice, the firm sent an engagement letter outlining its hourly fees and other terms. Neither Lupin India nor Lupin USA signed the letter, but Blanchard provided the requested legal services and the companies paid the firm for its work—at least at first. In October 2009 Blanchard sent its two final invoices but they went unpaid. Seven years later Blanchard sued the Lupin companies for breach of contract and unjust enrichment. A district judge dismissed both claims as untimely.

We agree that the unjust-enrichment claim is untimely. . . . But the contract claim is timely. Though the engagement letter is unsigned, it counts as a written contract under Illinois limitations law, and the claim for breach is therefore governed by a ten-year statute of limitations. Blanchard filed suit within that time, so we reverse and remand for further proceedings on the contract claim.

I. Background

We take the following account of the facts from the amended complaint. Blanchard is a law firm formerly based in Chicago, though its sole proprietor is a citizen of Tennessee. Lupin India is a pharmaceutical company incorporated under the laws of India. Its subsidiary, Lupin USA, is incorporated in Delaware with its principal place of business in Baltimore, Maryland. The two Lupin companies formed a joint venture to launch a generic birth-control drug in the United States. In March 2009 they turned to Blanchard for legal advice in connection with that venture—more specifically, patent reviews and related services.

Blanchard communicated with the companies through Sofia Mumtaz, who held herself out as an authorized agent for both Lupin India and Lupin USA. Blanchard sent Mumtaz an engagement letter explaining the hourly rates for the firm's attorneys and other terms of the representation. The letter also specified that payment was due on the firm's invoices within 30 days.

Mumtaz never signed the engagement letter. Nevertheless, Blanchard provided the requested services between April and August 2009. The Lupin companies accepted those services and paid the firm's first two invoices. At that point, payment stopped. On October 31, 2009, Blanchard submitted two final invoices totaling $120,835, but they went unpaid.

On August 4, 2016, Blanchard sued Lupin USA in Illinois state court alleging claims for breach of contract and unjust enrichment. After removing the case to federal court, Lupin USA moved to dismiss the complaint . . . arguing that (1) it failed to allege a valid and enforceable contract; (2) the claims were untimely; and (3) Blanchard sued the wrong party because Lupin India was responsible for any nonpayment.

Blanchard amended the complaint to add Lupin India as a defendant. . . .

Lupin USA again moved to dismiss, raising the same grounds. Lupin India neither answered nor joined the motion to dismiss, so Blanchard sought entry of default against it . . . .

The judge dismissed the suit against both defendants. . . . Turning to the contract claim, the judge held that the amended complaint sufficiently alleged the existence of a valid and enforceable contract. But she also ruled that the claim should be construed as one for breach of an *unwritten* contract because the engagement letter was never signed. Under Illinois law a five-year limitations period applies to unwritten contracts, so the judge dismissed that claim as untimely.

II. Discussion

Moving to the contract claim, here we cannot agree with the judge's analysis. She applied Illinois's five-year limitations period for unwritten agreements because the engagement letter was unsigned. That was a mistake. Though unsigned, the engagement letter qualifies as a written contract under Illinois's limitations law.

Illinois provides a five-year limitations period for actions based on unwritten contracts, but a ten-year limitations period applies to an action based on a written contract. A contract is deemed written for these purposes "if parties are identified and all the essential terms are in writing and ascertainable from the instrument itself." The essential terms include "the nature of the transaction, the amount in question and, at least by reasonable implication, an intention to repay the debt." If extrinsic evidence "is necessary to identify the parties or essential terms, the contract is considered an oral contract for purposes of the statute of limitations."

Lupin USA does not dispute that the engagement letter identifies the nature of the transaction. It argues instead that the letter does not qualify as a written contract for limitations purposes because it fails to identify the parties or the amount in question. And because the letter is unsigned, Lupin USA insists that it does not evince an intent to pay.

We disagree on all counts. The letter identifies both Blanchard & Associates and Lupin as parties to the contract. . . . "Lupin" as used here refers to the joint venture between Lupin India and Lupin USA. That's sufficient to identify the parties without resorting to extrinsic evidence. The letter also lists the hourly rates of the firm's attorneys, which establishes the amount in question to the degree necessary for a suit on a written contract. Finally, the Illinois Supreme Court has held that a contract counts as "written" for purposes of the statute of limitations even if the parties haven't signed it. . . . That forecloses Lupin USA's argument that the engagement letter doesn't evince an intent to pay. The ten-year limitations period applies, and the contract claim was timely filed.

Accordingly, we AFFIRM the dismissal of the unjust-enrichment claim, REVERSE the dismissal of the contract claim, and REMAND for further proceedings.

Questions

1. Why should there be a different, shorter statute of limitations (that is, a shorter limitation on the time to bring a lawsuit on a claim after it arises) for unwritten contracts as compared to written contracts?
2. Why did the lower court judge treat the contract between Blanchard & Associates and Lupin as unwritten? Why did this court disagree?
3. Why might Blanchard & Associates have waited for seven years after its contract claims against Lupin accrued to sue?
4. Fadal Machining Centers, a machine and machine parts manufacturer, sued Compumachine, one of its distributors, for breach of contract. Under the distributorship agreement, a hard copy of which was attached to Fadal's complaint, any legal action arising out of the contract would be heard in a California federal district court. The agreement also stated that Fadal could establish the terms of sale on occasion. Each of the 15 allegedly unpaid invoices referred to Fadal's website for the terms and conditions of sale. The terms found on the website, under the label "Contract" in large bold type, included an arbitration clause and a statement that they would prevail over any other agreement. Should Fadal's claim be heard in the California federal district court, or be submitted to arbitration? Decide and explain. See *Fadal v. Compumachine*, 461 F. App'x 630 (9th Cir. 2011).

Third Parties

We turn now to the rights and duties of those who are not parties to a contract but hold legally recognizable interests in that contract. Those interests arise when: (1) contract rights are assigned to others, (2) contract duties are delegated to others, or (3) contracts have third-party beneficiary provisions.

LO 6-9
Compare and contrast the rights and duties arising in contractual assignment and delegation.

Assignment of Rights

Ordinarily, a party to a contract is free to transfer their rights under the contract to a third party. Thus, if Ames owes Jones $500 for work performed, Jones can assign that right to Smith, who can now assert their right to collect against Ames. That transfer of rights is called an assignment (see Figure 6.2). Jones, the party making the transfer, is the assignor; Smith, the one receiving the right, is the assignee; and Ames, the party who must perform, is the obligor. Ames, the obligor, must now perform the contract for the benefit of the assignee, that is, Ames must pay the $500 to Smith. The completed assignment then extinguishes the assignor's rights under the contract.

Some contracts are not assignable without consent of the obligor. That would be the case where the obligor's duties are materially altered by the assignment. For example, if you have a contract to serve as a personal fitness trainer for a busy chief executive officer, your contract could not be assigned without your consent to another CEO, or movie star, or the like because the highly personal and specific obligations under the contract would necessarily be materially altered with a different client.

Delegation of Duties

The parties to a contract may also delegate their duties under the contract to one or more third parties. Assume Allen has secured a contract to install windows in Boyd's new office building (see Figure 6.3). Allen could delegate that duty to another contractor, Harms (although Allen would more commonly enter a subcontracting arrangement without actually transferring the underlying contract). A delegation of duty leaves Harms, the delegatee (the one to whom the duty is delegated), primarily responsible for performance, but Allen, the obligor–delegator (the one who made the delegation), remains secondarily liable in case Harms, the delegatee, fails to fulfill the duty to Boyd, the obligee (the one to whom the

FIGURE 6.2
Assignment of Rights.

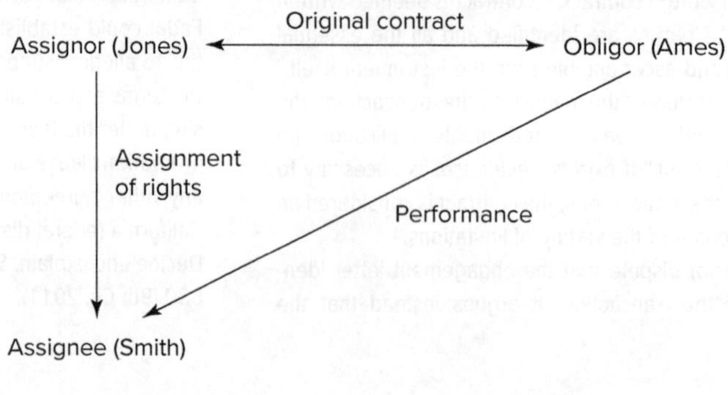

FIGURE 6.3
Delegation of Duties.

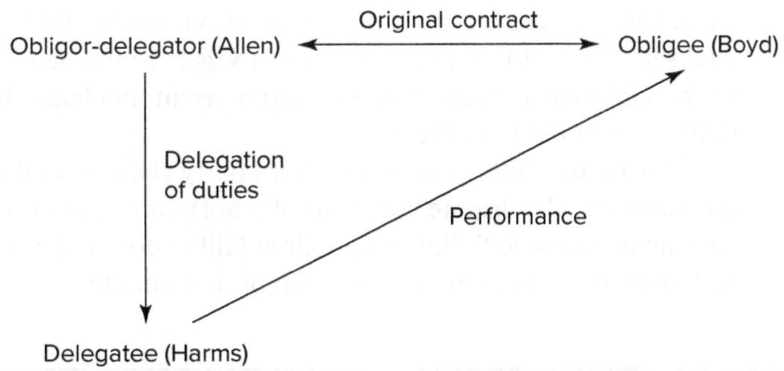

duty is owed under both the original contract and the delegation). As with the assignment of rights, some contractual duties, particularly those of a personal service nature, cannot be delegated without consent.

Third-Party Beneficiary Contracts

LO 6-10
Compare and contrast different types of third-party beneficiaries to a contract.

Normally, those not a party to a contract have no rights under that contract. As we have seen, however, third parties may be assigned rights or delegated duties under a contract. A third party may also enforce a contract where that contract was expressly intended to benefit the third party. An agreement of that nature is a third-party beneficiary contract. Third-party beneficiaries are of three kinds: creditor, donee, and incidental. In general, creditor and donee beneficiaries can enforce contracts made by others for their benefit; incidental beneficiaries cannot.

Creditor Beneficiary

Assume you decide to expand your used-car business by advertising on television. Your ads appear on TV; therefore, you owe the local television station $2,000. Rather than paying the bill directly, you transfer a used car to your friend Gleason, with the understanding that he will pay off your bill with the television station. Thus, the station becomes the creditor beneficiary of the contract between you and Gleason, and the station can sue Gleason for that money if necessary, while you remain secondarily responsible for the payment.

Donee Beneficiary

When the promisee's primary purpose in entering a contract is to make a gift to another, that third party is a donee beneficiary of the contract. The most common of these situations involves an ordinary life insurance policy for which the owner (the promisee) pays premiums to the life insurance company (the promisor), which is obliged to pay benefits to the third party upon the death of the promisee-policy owner. If necessary, the third-party beneficiary can sue the insurance company for payment.

Incidental Beneficiary

Often a third party receives benefit from a contract, although conferring that benefit was not the contracting parties' primary purpose or intent. For example, assume a General Motors car dealer enters into a contract to buy land adjacent to your used-car lot for the purpose of opening a large dealership. You would benefit immensely from the spillover effect of the large, adjacent dealership. In such a situation, you would be an incidental beneficiary of the land sale contract because that contract was not intended for your benefit. If the landowner or the GM dealer failed to perform, you, as an incidental beneficiary, would have no legal rights against either of them.

The case that follows involves a third-party claim by Gill Plumbing against its subcontractor, Jimenez. The dispute arose out of a dormitory construction contract where the general contractor, Gilbane Building, had hired Gill to do the dormitory plumbing and Gill, in turn, had hired Jimenez to install a portion of that plumbing.

LEGAL BRIEFCASE

Jimenez v. Gilbane Building Company et al. 693 S.E.2d 126 (Ga. Ct. App. 2010)

Judge Adams

. . . The background facts are that Gilbane Building Company was the general contractor for the construction of a new dormitory at Georgia Southern University. Gilbane hired Gill Plumbing as the plumbing contractor, and Gill Plumbing, in turn, hired Jose Alfredo Jimenez to perform plumbing installation work. The building was completed in July 2005, but in October, after the dormitory was occupied by students, a pipe failed causing extensive water damage to the dormitory and to some students' personal belongings. Gilbane was forced to hire Belfor USA Group, Inc., to perform remediation and repair work. Belfor's $990,060.63 bill for the services has not been paid.

Belfor filed this action against Gilbane, Gilbane filed a third-party action against Gill Plumbing, and Gill Plumbing filed a fourth-party action against Jimenez. The parties have since been realigned. Currently, both Belfor and Gilbane have claims against Gill Plumbing, and Gill Plumbing has a third-party claim against Jimenez for the costs of the remediation and repair.

In its third-party claim, Gill Plumbing asserts that it had a written agreement with Jimenez that included an indemnity agreement, and that the damages to the dormitory resulted from negligent work performed by Jimenez. Jimenez denied that he entered into a valid and enforceable contract or an indemnity agreement with Gill Plumbing and denied the negligence. The trial court granted Gill's motion for partial summary judgment against Jimenez, finding that he was liable "for indemnification to Gill Plumbing" "in the amount, if any, of damages proven to have resulted from Mr. Jimenez's defective work." Jimenez appeals this ruling and contends that "no contract existed between Mr. Jimenez and the Appellee as a matter of law" or, at least, that there are material issues of fact regarding the contract and the indemnity agreement.

Summary judgment is proper when there is no genuine issue of material fact and the movant is entitled to judgment as a matter of law. . . .

There is no question that the parties had an oral agreement. The issue before us is whether there was an enforceable written agreement and, if so, what were the terms of that agreement. The undisputed facts show that Jimenez was hired by Gill Plumbing to perform plumbing services in the "Eagle Village" construction project at Georgia Southern University, that he performed plumbing services, and that he has been paid for the work in the amount of $167,000.

Jimenez has never worked for any company other than Gill Plumbing and the two have worked together for at least 15 years. On September 15, 2004, Jimenez signed two documents, which, Gill Plumbing contends, constitute the parties' entire written agreement; Jimenez has signed other documents for Gill Plumbing in the past. The first document is contained on one page, it is dated September 15, 2004, and it has Jimenez's typewritten name and his signature. The main body of the document is as follows:

LABOR CONTRACT

Project: Eagle Village.

Item 1	Slab	50,100.00
Item 2	Rough	66,800.00
Item 3	Set Out	50,100.00

– Weekly billing to be submitted in draw format. All work must be approved by Larry Pollett.

return the parties to the positions they occupied before they entered the agreement. Generally, both parties must then make restitution to each other by returning whatever goods, property, and so forth were transferred under the contract or an equivalent amount of money.

Mitigation

Obviously the law should penalize a breaching party, as we have discussed, but you may be surprised to learn that the law also imposes expectations on the victim (the nonbreaching party). Specifically, the nonbreaching party is required to take reasonable steps toward mitigation—that is, to minimize their damages. What happens, for example, if you are wrongfully dismissed in breach of contract from your first job after college? You are expected to mitigate your damages by seeking another job. You need not take an inferior job, nor must you disturb your life by moving to another state or community, but you must take reasonable measures to minimize your claim against your former employer.

Liquidated Damages

We have reviewed both the legal penalties for breach and the duty to mitigate damages. The law also offers the opportunity to provide some control over the penalty for breach by including in the contract a liquidated damages clause. Here you and the other party to the contract agree in advance about the measure of damages should either of you default on your duties. That clause is fully enforceable so long as it is not designed to be a penalty but rather a good faith effort to assess in advance an accurate measure of damages. A valid liquidated damages clause limits the nonbreaching party to recovery of the amount provided for in that clause.

Remedies in Equity

Where justice cannot be achieved via money damages alone, the courts will sometimes impose equitable remedies. The chief forms of equitable remedy in contract cases are specific performance, injunction, reformation, and quasi-contract.

Specific Performance

In unusual circumstances, the court may order the breaching party to remedy its wrong by performing its obligations precisely as provided for in the contract. Normally that specific performance is required only where the subject matter of the contract is unique and thus cannot be adequately compensated with money. Examples of such subject matter might include a particular piece of land, artwork, or a family heirloom. By contrast, specific performance would not be available in contracts involving conventional personal property such as a television or a car unless those items were unique (for example, a one-of-a-kind Rolls Royce).

Normally the courts will not grant a specific performance remedy in personal service contracts (such as an agreement by a cosmetic surgeon to perform a face-lift). If the surgeon refused to perform, specific performance probably would not be ordered. The quality of the surgery likely would not be equal to what had been bargained for; courts do not want to be in the position of supervising the completion of contracts, and as a matter of public policy, do not want to put parties, in this case, the surgeon, in a position that amounts to involuntary servitude.

Injunction

An injunction is a court order that may either require or forbid a party to perform a specified act. Injunctions are granted only under exceptional circumstances. Perhaps the most common of those are the noncompetition agreements. For example, you take a computer programming job that will afford you access to company secrets. To protect itself, the company expects you to sign an agreement specifying that you will not take employment with a competing firm for one year after departure from your employer. If you should quit and seek to work for a competitor within one year, your former employer might be able to secure an injunction preventing you from doing so until the year has passed.

Reformation

Reformation is an equitable remedy that permits the court to rewrite the contract where it imperfectly expressed the parties' true intentions. Typically, such situations involve a mutual mistake or fraud. Thus, if the parties sign a contract to sell a lot in a housing development, but the contract is written with an incorrect street address for the lot, an equity court could simply correct the error in the contract.

Quasi-Contract

What happens if one party has conferred a benefit on another, but a contract has not been created because of a failure of consideration, the application of the Statute of Frauds, or something of the sort? As mentioned earlier, to prevent unjust enrichment, the court might then imply a contract as a matter of law. For example, assume a lawn service mistakenly trims your shrubs, and you watch them do so, knowing that they are supposed to be caring for your neighbor's lawn. You have not entered a contract with the lawn service, but a court might well require you to pay the reasonable value of trimming your shrubs. To do otherwise would unjustly enrich you.

PRACTICING ETHICS The Cost of Contracts at Twitter

At this writing, according to reporting in *The New York Times*, Elon Musk's purchase of Twitter has given rise to a number of potential contract disputes as he pursues a goal of cutting costs at the social media company.

For example, Mr. Musk's staff has refused to reimburse travel vendors for travel invoices authorized by former management, and not Mr. Musk. After Musk announced that half of the Twitter staff would be laid off, layoffs and firings continued. Mr. Musk is also reported to be hesitant to make payments on Twitter real estate leases, hoping to renegotiate or opt out of some of these agreements.

The drastic cost-cutting measures appear to be the result of Mr. Musk's concerns for Twitter's financial health as it faces competition with rivals like Facebook and concerns of advertisers over Mr. Musk's ownership of Twitter. Mr. Musk has warned that Twitter faces the possibility of bankruptcy.

Questions

1. The law of contracts aside, does Twitter have a moral duty to uphold its existing contracts, or is Twitter's reported approach to current contractual obligations an acceptable cost-cutting measure to protect the company's long-term economic security? Explain.
2. Twitter's philanthropic division, Twitter for Good, has lost many employees, and nonprofit groups have not received checks they had been promised. Should such obligations be honored before commercial vendors receive payments from Twitter? Explain.

See Mike Isaac and Ryan Mac, "As Elon Musk Cuts Costs at Twitter, Some Bills Are Going Unpaid," *The New York Times*, November 22, 2022 [**https://www.nytimes.com/**].

Research Exercise

Visit the Rocket Lawyer website's page offering sample contracts, which can be found at **www.rocketlawyer.com/legal-documents-forms.rl.** Select a type of contract–such as a lease agreement, independent contractor agreement, or business contract–and review the sample. If you were asked to enter into this agreement, what questions would you have? Be specific. Assume you have to explain to someone else, who is about to enter into the agreement as a lessee, independent contractor, buyer, etc., the importance of "reading the fine print" in a contract. Identify such a provision in the contract you selected. Use that provision to explain to the person the importance of carefully reviewing a contract's language before entering into it.

Chapter Questions

1. Wardle made a standard real estate offer to buy a house owned by Kessler. The offer contained a "time is of the essence" clause specifying that the deal had to be completed on or before 11 a.m. on September 26, 1997. Owen then submitted a backup purchase offer for the same price as offered by Wardle. Wardle's completed contract was not delivered to Kessler until approximately 11:20 a.m. on September 26, so Kessler sold to Owen. Wardle then sued Kessler. Decide. Explain. See *Owen v. Kessler,* 778 N.E.2d 953 (Mass. App. Ct. 2002).
2. In a 2013 televised interview with Oprah Winfrey, Lance Armstrong admitted to taking performance-enhancing drugs during his cycling career. Afterward, Armstrong faced several lawsuits, including one from SCA Promotions, seeking to recover approximately $12 million in bonuses it had paid Armstrong for several Tour de France victories. SCA, already suspecting Armstrong of taking performance-enhancing drugs in the 2004 Tour de France, had tried to withhold payment of his bonus for winning that race. Armstrong had sued, and the parties entered into a settlement agreement under which Armstrong received the bonus money–under the terms of that agreement, an award that "no party may challenge, appeal, or attempt to set aside." How should this case be decided? Explain.
3. Allen M. Campbell Co. sought a contract to build houses for the U.S. Navy. Approximately one-half hour before the housing bids were due, Virginia Metal Industries quoted Campbell Co. a price of $193,121 to supply the necessary doors and frames. Campbell, using the Virginia Metal quote, entered a bid and won the contract. Virginia Metal refused to supply the necessary doors, and Campbell had to secure an alternative source of supply at a price $45,562 higher than Virginia Metal's quote. Campbell sued. Explain Campbell's claim. Defend Virginia Metal. Decide. See *Allen M. Campbell Co. Inc. v. Virginia Metal Industries,* 708 F.2d 930 (4th Cir. 1983).
4. Jesse Dimmick, trying to escape police questioning in a murder investigation, burst into Jared and Lindsay Rowley's Kansas home with a knife. After gaining his trust by feeding him and watching a movie with him, the Rowleys were able to escape when Dimmick fell asleep. Police entered the house and arrested Dimmick, who was accidentally shot in the process. The Rowleys sued Dimmick for damages; Dimmick countersued for breach of contract, seeking $160,000 to cover hospital bills and $75,000 for pain and suffering. Dimmick said the Rowleys had broken their promise to keep him hidden from authorities in return for cash. What defenses could the Rowleys raise to this

claim? Explain. See "Dimmick sues couple he kidnapped," *The Topeka Capital-Journal* (November 28, 2011).

5. The motion picture *The Merry Gentleman* was considered a commercial failure despite some critical acclaim. The film's producers sued Michael Keaton, the film's lead actor and director, and Keaton's "loan-out company" that he uses for professional contracting, seeking $5.5 million in damages for breach of contract. The plaintiffs alleged that Keaton had, among other things, failed to timely prepare the first cut of the film, communicated directly with Sundance Film Festival threatening to boycott the festival if it did not accept his director's cut instead of the producers' preferred cut, failed to cooperate with the producers during the post-production process, and failed to promote the film. If you were on the jury, what questions would you want answered? Explain. *Merry Gentleman, LLC v. George & Leona Prods.*, 76 F. Supp. 3d 756 (N.D. Ill. 2014).
6. Sherwood agreed to purchase a cow, Rose 2d of Aberlone, from Walker at a price of 5.5 cents per pound (about $80). The parties believed the cow to be barren. Sherwood came to Walker's farm to collect the cow, but at that point it was obvious that Rose was pregnant. Walker refused to give over the cow, which was then worth between $750 and $1,000. Sherwood sued. Should he get the cow? Explain. See *Sherwood v. Walker,* 33 N.W. 919 (Mich. 1887).
7. Weaver leased a service station from American Oil. The lease included a clause providing that Weaver would hold American Oil harmless for any negligence by American on the premises. Weaver and an employee were burned when an American Oil employee accidentally sprayed gasoline while at Weaver's station. Weaver had one and one-half years of high school education. The trial record provides no evidence that Weaver read the lease, that American's agent asked him to read it, or that Weaver's attention was drawn to the "hold harmless" clause. The clause was in fine print and contained no title heading. Is the contract enforceable against Weaver? Explain. See *Weaver v. American Oil Co.,* 276 N.E.2d 144 (Ind. 1971).
8. Republic Bank acquired medical equipment through a lease default and contracted Tetra Financial Services to facilitate the sale of the equipment. Mark, a Tetra employee, was assigned to the task. West Penn, a large hospital system in the Pittsburgh, Pennsylvania, area, expressed an interest in purchasing the equipment and had one of its contract negotiators, Michele, handle it.

   Michele sent Mark an email on February 26, stating:

   > We are interested in the 64-slice scanner, CT workstation, ultrasound, and ultrasound table.

   Our offer is as follows:

   > Scanner: $600,000
   >
   > CT workstation: $50,000
   >
   > Ultrasound and ultrasound table: $26,500

   On March 13, Mark sent Michele an email stating:

   > Michele: I met with the bank president this morning and he gave me approval to sell West Penn the 64-slice scanner, CT workstation, and ultrasound unit with table for

> the total amount offered below [referring to Michele's February 26 email]. There is still some question regarding the cooler unit being moved to your location or left in place and a replacement provided for you. We can discuss that issue.
>
> Please let me know if you work through a purchase order system or if we need to put together a sales agreement.

Is there a contract between Republic Bank and West Penn for the purchase of the medical equipment? Decide. Explain. *See Republic Bank v. Allegheny Health,* 475 F. App'x 692 (10th Cir. 2010).

9. In 1994, California raisin grape grower Sardul Sihota allegedly promised his son Paul that, if he pursued his education, continued to work on the family's ranches, and married an Indian Sikh girl, then he and Paul's stepmother, Jitendra, would take care of him financially. Paul graduated from college in 1994. Sardul and Jitendra arranged Paul's 1996 marriage to Rajneet, an Indian Sikh girl. Paul continued to work on the family's ranches until 1999. The couple lived on the Elkhorn Ranch owned by Sardul until 2012, during which time they did not pay rent. When Sardul had to sell the Temperance Ranch in which Paul had an interest, Paul alleged that Sardul promised to put the Elkhorn Ranch in Paul's name when he was able to do so financially. Sardul denied making such a promise. Paul and Rajneet sued Sardul and Jitendra for breach of contract and fraud. Decide. Explain. See *Sihota v. Sihota,* F070363 (Cal. App. 5th Dist. 2016) (unpub'd op.).
10. The Wongs bought a hillside home in San Carlos, California, for $2.35 million from the Stolers. Several months after they moved in, the Wongs discovered they were connected to a private sewer system and not directly serviced by the city's public system. Believing they had been deceived, they sued the Stolers and the real estate agents who brokered the sale, alleging several causes of action, including rescission. After the Wongs settled their dispute with the real estate agents for $200,000, a court trial was held on the rescission claim only. Although the court found that the Stolers, with reckless disregard, made negligent misrepresentations to the Wongs, it declined to effectuate a rescission of the contract. Instead, it ordered the Stolers to be, for a limited time, indemnifiers to the Wongs for sewer maintenance and repair costs exceeding the $200,000 they obtained in their settlement with the agents. The Wongs appealed. Decide. Explain. *Wong v. Stoler,* 237 Cal. App. 4th 1375 (Cal. App. 1st Dist. 2015).
11. Preference Personnel, a North Dakota corporation, entered a contract with Peterson to help him find employment in the tax law field. The contract provided that the employer would pay the placement fee, unless Peterson voluntarily quit within 90 days, in which case he would be responsible for the fee, which was 20 percent of one year's salary. Peterson was placed in a job with an annual salary of $60,000, but he quit after one month. Peterson refused to pay the fee, and Preference sued for breach of contract. The lower court found that Peterson breached the contract, but at the time of the contract, Preference Personnel's state-required license to operate had been allowed to lapse. The court, therefore, dismissed the Preference claim, ruling that the agreement was unenforceable as a matter of public policy. Preference appealed. Rule on that appeal. Explain. See *Preference Personnel, Inc. v. Peterson,* 710 N.W.2d 383 (N.D. 2006).
12. Panera, the bakery and café chain, had a clause in its lease that prevented the White City Shopping Center in Shrewsbury, Massachusetts, from renting space to another

sandwich shop: "Landlord agrees not to enter into a lease, . . . for a bakery or restaurant reasonably expected to have annual sales of *sandwiches* (emphasis added) greater than ten percent (10%) of its total sales." Panera asked a Massachusetts Superior Court to block the shopping center from leasing space to a Qdoba Mexican Grill on the grounds that a lease with the Grill would violate the terms of the Panera lease. How should the court rule? Explain. See *White City Shopping Center, LP v. PR Restaurants, LLC,* 2006 Mass. Super. LEXIS 544 (October 31, 2006).

13. White, a 17-year-old high school sophomore, operated a trucking business, including hiring drivers, securing jobs, and so forth. He lived with his parents and received his food, clothing, and shelter from them. Valencia operated a garage and repaired White's equipment until they had a disagreement over replacement of a motor. White then disaffirmed his contract with Valencia and refused to pay what he owed. At trial, the jury found that White had caused the damage to the motor, but the court held that White could disaffirm the contract and required Valencia to refund any money paid to White under the contract. Valencia appealed.
    a. Is the fact that White was in business for himself in any way relevant to the outcome of this case? Explain.
    b. Decide the case. Explain. See *Valencia v. White,* 654 P.2d 287 (Ariz. Ct. App. 1982).

14. In 2019, movie director Woody Allen sued Amazon for wrongfully terminating their contract for the production and distribution of four films. Production on one of the films, *A Rainy Day in New York,* had finished in 2017. Allen accused Amazon of terminating the contract after the #MeToo movement, which drew attention to sexual harassment, had renewed media attention into past accusations that he molested his daughter, of which Amazon was aware before entering into the contract. Amazon responded that the termination of the contract was due to comments Allen allegedly made that were sympathetic to movie director Harvey Weinstein, as well as comments about Weinstein's accusers. Amazon asserted that the remarks undermined the value of the agreement and hurt the promotion of Allen's films. The lawsuit settled. What legal issues did this breach of contract claim against Amazon and its defense raise? How would you have decided the case? Explain. See Ilana Kaplan, "Woody Allen, Amazon Settle Wrongful Termination Lawsuit," *Rolling Stone,* November 9, 2019 [**www.rollingstone.com**]; and Joe Flint, "Woody Allen Sues Amazon Studios Claiming Breach of Contract," *The Wall Street Journal,* February 7, 2019 [**www.wsj.com**].

15. Two parties to a lawsuit exchanged e-mails for several weeks on the subject of a settlement. A lawyer for the defendant, a bank, e-mailed the plaintiff's lawyer to say that the bank had completed an internal approval process, and that the settlement would be signed shortly. However, the agreement was never signed nor was the amount agreed upon sent to the plaintiff. The defendant then claimed the settlement had never been fully executed, and was therefore invalid. Is the settlement agreement enforceable? Why or why not? See *Lehman Bros. Holdings Inc. Shinhan Bank v. Lehman Bros. Holdings, Inc.,* 739 Fed. Appx. 55 (2d Cir. 2018).

16. Stephanie Clifford, also known as Stormy Daniels, entered into a confidentiality agreement regarding her alleged sexual relationship with former President Donald Trump. That agreement was signed by Trump's lawyer, Michael Cohen, as representative of

Essential Consultants, the company he formed to transfer money under the agreement to Ms. Clifford. The contract contained a liquidated damages clause requiring her to pay $1 million for each breach. Trump has denied knowing about the agreement. See Debra Cassens Weiss, "Stormy Daniels Could Have to Pay at Least $20M in Liquidated Damages, Trump Lawyer Tells Court," *ABA Journal,* March 19, 2018 [**http://www.abajournal.com**].

a. If Donald Trump did not know about the contract, can he still be considered a beneficiary of the contract? Explain.

b. Is the liquidated damages clause valid? Explain.

17. In 2021, University of Delaware students sued the university for "breached contractual obligations" for closing the campus and moving classes online in Spring 2020.

a. Make the argument for the plaintiffs, and then offer a defense for the university.

b. What damages could the students seek? What questions would you have if you were on the jury in this case? Explain. See Randall Chase, "University of Delaware Students Can Pursue Claims over Campus Shutdown," Delaware Online, August 21, 2021[**https://www.delawareonline.com/**].

Notes

1. Kate Vitasek, "Comic Contracts: A Novel Approach to Contract Clarity and Accessibility," *Forbes,* February 14, 2017 [**www.forbes.com**].
2. Uniform Electronic Transactions Act (National Conference of Commissioners on Uniform State Laws 1999) [**www.uniformlaws.org**].
3. See *Whinfield v. Capitas Distributors,* 111 F. Supp. 3d 177 (D. Conn. 2015); and *Williamson v. Bank of N.Y. Mellon,* 947 F. Supp. 2d (N.D. Texas 2013).
4. *Waddle v. Elrod,* 367 S.W.3d 217 (Tenn. 2012).
5. *St. John's Holdings v. Two Electronics,* 2016 Mass. LCR LEXIS 166 (Mass. 2016).

Video icon credit: Comstock Images/Alamy Stock Photo

CHAPTER SEVEN

Business Torts and Product Liability

After completing this chapter, students will be able to fulfill the following learning objectives:

7-1. Compare and contrast the three fundamental kinds of torts: intentional, negligent, and strict liability.

7-2. Describe selected intentional torts against persons in business contexts, including battery, assault, false imprisonment, fraud, invasion of privacy, intentional infliction of emotional distress, and defamation.

7-3. Described selected intentional torts against property, such as trespass and nuisance, in business contexts.

7-4. Identify selected intentional tort defenses.

7-5. Discuss the impact of product liability on business practice.

7-6. Identify the requirements of a successful negligence claim.

7-7. Differentiate between the types of negligence claims emerging from defective products.

7-8. Analyze whether defenses may be successfully asserted in a negligence claim.

7-9. Compare and contrast claims based on express warranties and implied warranties.

7-10. Identify the elements of a strict liability cause of action.

7-11. Identify the defenses available in strict liability cases.

7-12. Evaluate arguments for and against tort reform.

PRACTICING ETHICS Huffing Death

Karalee Alaine Williams, an adult, entered a Baytown, Texas, Walmart on nine different occasions over a period of 27 hours in 2016 and bought, in total, at least 60 cans of aerosol dust remover. She purchased a towel and cans of dust remover during her first visit on April 10. On a second visit that day, she had soiled herself, but she bought additional cans and told the checkout employee she had suffered a seizure in the parking lot. The next morning she entered the store naked from the waist down. Several employees noticed her condition and some of them gave her a towel and a "sundress." She bought ten more cans. On subsequent visits, she bought more cans of dust remover. Early on the morning of April 12, 2016, she died in the Walmart parking lot from the effects of inhaling dust remover. Her body was discovered the next day.

Williams' mother, Deleese Allen, sued Walmart claiming, among other things, that Walmart was negligent in repeatedly selling aerosol dust remover cans to her daughter, especially after employees knew she was behaving erratically. A federal district court dismissed Allen's complaint, ruling that she had failed to state a claim upon which relief can be granted under the law, and the Fifth Circuit Court of Appeals affirmed that decision. Essentially, the courts reasoned that Walmart did not owe a duty of care to Allen to protect her daughter, and therefore, Walmart could not have any legal responsibility for her death. Furthermore, the sales were lawful since Williams was an adult. Walmart apparently did not violate either criminal or regulatory provisions of Texas law.

Questions

In responding to the following questions, consider the ethics discussions in Chapter 2, as well as public policy considerations from Chapter 3.

1. Who should be blamed for Williams's death? Explain.
2. Broadly, how do we decide where blame lies?
3. *a.* Should Walmart have refused service to Williams when she appeared in the store without clothing from the waist down? Explain.

   b. If so, how do we decide what forms of behavior, expression, and appearance would justify denial of service?
4. How do you feel about the following online comment made about the Williams case:

   > Wal-mart is a store, not a babysitter. Why should there be any liability.[sic] If someone is that deranged, or have addictive personality,[sic] let them inhale and deal with the consequences. There are warnings on the can anyways. Common sense."

Sources: *Allen v. Walmart Stores, LLC*, 907 F.3d 170 (5th Cir. 2018); and Jonathon Turley, "Fifth Circuit Rules Walmart Is not Liable for Selling 60 Cans of Fatal Dust Remover to a Clearly Deranged Addict during a 27-Hour Period," *Res Ipsa Loquitur - The Thing Itself Speaks*, October 19, 2018 [**https://jonathanturley.org**].

Part One—Torts: An Introduction

Above, the *Allen v. Walmart* case was considered as an ethics dilemma. Now we need to think about the law we employ to formally resolve personal injury claims, that is, tort claims like those raised by Allen against Walmart. ***Torts*** are civil wrongs not arising from contracts. They involve breaches of duty to particular persons causing loss or injury. ***Crimes***, by contrast, are regarded as public wrongs breaching duties to society as a whole (although the wrong is usually directed at specific persons or things). Crimes are prosecuted by the state; tort actions are initiated by individuals. Criminal law punishes wrongdoers, but the point of tort law is to make whole the injured party. Many acts can be treated as a civil wrong (a tort), a crime, or both. For example, a physical attack on another person can lead to criminal charges, but it also can support civil tort claims, most commonly ***assault*** and ***battery***.

The injured party in tort litigation can seek ***compensatory damages*** to make up for the harm suffered. Those damages may consist of medical expenses, lost income, and pain and suffering, among other possibilities. In some cases, ***punitive damages*** may be awarded to punish the wrongdoer and to discourage others from similar behavior. If the injured party dies, family members may seek damages for *wrongful death.*

Tort Categories

LO 7-1
Compare and contrast the three fundamental kinds of torts: intentional, negligent, and strict liability.

Fundamentally, torts are of three kinds: (1) intentional, (2) negligent, and (3) strict liability.

Intentional torts involve voluntary acts that harm a protected interest. Intent is established by showing the defendant meant to do the act that caused the harm. The plaintiff need not show that the harm itself was intended. The defendant is liable for all reasonably foreseeable injuries from that intentional act.

Thus, if you run an advertisement defaming a fast-food competitor by saying its food processing does not meet government standards, but you cannot prove the truth of your allegations, you may have committed the intentional tort of ***injurious falsehood*** (product disparagement).

Negligence, on the other hand, involves situations where intent is absent, but because of one party's carelessness, another has suffered injury. Suppose one of your employees, in making a delivery for the printing business you are managing, carelessly runs a red light, striking another car. The employee appears to be guilty of negligent conduct for which both they and your firm may be liable for civil damages. Furthermore, you and/or your firm might bear responsibility if, for example, you hired them knowing they had been a careless driver in the past.

A detailed discussion of negligence law follows in Part Two of this chapter, but for the moment note that negligence concerns are ubiquitous in our lives, ranging from traffic accidents to inadequate snow clearance from sidewalks, to failure to keep dangerous kitchen utensils away from children, to ill-timed golf shots, and on and on. Negligence ordinarily is the core claim for those suffering a personal injury caused by the carelessness of another. Broadly, negligence litigation involves an analysis of whether the alleged carelessness amounts to a breach of the "duty of due care." For example, can an injured party properly bring a negligence claim against homeowners when parts of their dismantled, but not yet stowed away, trampoline blow into the nearby road, causing a passing driver to crash? The Iowa Supreme Court said "yes" because the homeowners had a duty to exercise reasonable care to see that obstructions did not reach the roadway, and they breached that duty by creating a foreseeable risk in dismantling the trampoline but failing to secure the parts over the passage of several weeks' time.[1]

Did Trump Indiana, Inc., Owe a Duty to Merrill?

In 1996, Mark Merrill entered a clinic for compulsive gamblers and wrote to Trump Indiana, a casino in Gary, Indiana, asking that he be evicted if he ever entered to gamble. Merrill's name appeared on Trump Indiana's casino "eviction list." Nonetheless, Merrill later gambled at the casino, suffering substantial losses. In December 1998 and January 1999, Merrill robbed banks, apparently to cover his gambling losses. He was convicted of

The Key Highway Shipyard, formerly owned by the Bethlehem Steel Corporation, was used to repair naval ships during World War II and through the Vietnam War. A shipyard of some sort has operated at this location from the beginning of the 20th century until 1982, when Bethlehem Steel closed the facility.

The defendants demolished the original shipyard piers, which were built 40 to 50 years ago, and constructed new piers in the same location by driving piles into the Baltimore Inner Harbor. The defendants built 58 townhomes on these new piers. Pile driving was the only method of constructing the new townhomes in this particular location because the U.S. Army Corps of Engineers would not allow the Inner Harbor to be "back filled." The pile driving of which Gallagher complained occurred periodically between September 2003 and October 2004.

The plaintiff's home was constructed shortly before the War of 1812. She testified that no pile driving was conducted in the area during the years she lived in the house, beginning in 1997, until the defendants' activities commenced in September 2003. Previously, pile driving was used to build the Seagirt Marine Terminal, the Dundalk Marine Terminal, as well as the Pratt and Light Street Pavilions, which are located across from the plaintiff's residence in the Inner Harbor.

Before the defendants began their project, permits were received from the U.S. Army Corps of Engineers, the Maryland Department of the Environment, and the City of Baltimore. The permitting process took approximately two years. Pile driving on the site began only after geotechnical studies were conducted by engineering firms. During the course of actual pile driving, two permanent seismic stations and five mobile geophones were placed in the surrounding neighborhood to ensure that vibrations were monitored and did not exceed the limits established by the engineers. During the course of the defendants' activities, there was only a single recorded vibration that exceeded the limits.

The case proceeded to trial on December 15, 2006. The plaintiff testified that she heard and felt vibrations from the pile driving in her home. She further testified that cracks began to develop in her plaster walls and in other portions of her home soon after the pile driving began and that no cracks occurred once the pile driving was completed. She was not aware of any other residents in the area who made claims or filed lawsuits for damage to their homes as a result of the vibrations caused by the defendants' pile driving. No evidence of any other claims or suits on account of pile driving vibrations was presented at trial.

On December 21, 2006, the jury returned a verdict in Gallagher's favor. The jury found that: (1) pile driving caused damage to Gallagher's home, and HV Pierpont and HV Development were responsible for the pile driving; (2) the pile driving created a public nuisance; (3) the pile driving created a private nuisance; and (4) Gallagher suffered damages in the amount of $55,189.14.

After the jury's verdict was announced, the defendants renewed their motions for judgment. . . . By Order entered on August 20, 2007, the circuit court granted the defendants' motion for judgment notwithstanding the verdict [the judge overruled the jury—ed.] on all claims. Gallagher [appealed].

STRICT LIABILITY IN MARYLAND

[The Restatement of Torts,] Section 519, sets forth the general principle upon which courts have held defendants to be liable regardless of fault: "One who carries on an abnormally dangerous activity is subject to liability for harm to the person, land or chattels of another resulting from the activity, although he has exercised the utmost care to prevent the harm."

In summary, Maryland recognizes strict liability, [and] adopts the definition of abnormally dangerous activity as set forth in Section 519 of the Restatement (Second) of Torts (1977). In many, but not all cases, the "thrust of the doctrine is that the activity be abnormally dangerous in relation to the area where it occurs."

STRICT LIABILITY IN PILE DRIVING CASES

The circuit court acknowledged that "whether pile driving is an abnormally dangerous activity has yet to be determined by the Maryland Court of Appeals." The circuit court nevertheless concluded, after applying sections 519 and 520 to the facts of the case, that the Court of Appeals would hold that the pile driving activity in this case would not warrant the application of strict liability.

In the 1984 revision of Dean Prosser's landmark treatise, Professor Page Keaton observed that varying formulations of strict liability have been applied by some courts to hold that pile driving is an abnormally or unreasonably dangerous activity warranting liability without fault. The reasoning of these decisions, as well as the results, is far from uniform. Some courts consider pile driving to be no different than blasting, and therefore dangerous enough to warrant strict liability regardless of the place in which it occurs. Others have taken a more fact-based approach, considering the activity in conjunction with the locale and the type of harm that resulted.

For example, in *Caporale v. C.W. Blakeslee & Sons, Inc.,* 149 Conn. 79, 175 A.2d 561 (1961), the Supreme Court of Connecticut held that pile driving activity during the construction of the Connecticut turnpike in 1958 and 1959, in close proximity to the plaintiff's business premises, warranted the application of strict liability. The Connecticut court analogized pile driving to blasting and aligned itself with those courts that imposed strict liability not only for flying debris but also for the vibrations caused by the explosive force of the blast. The Connecticut court noted, but declined to follow, a line of New York decisions, illustrated by *Fagan v. Pathe Industries, Inc.,* 274 A.D. 703, 86 N.Y.S.2d 859, 863–64 (App. Div., 1st Dept. 1949), that rejected strict liability for pile driving where the damage was caused only by vibrations.

STRICT LIABILITY IN THIS CASE

The appellant argues that pile driving should be considered abnormally dangerous simply because it produces uncontrollable vibrations, similar to blasting. She also asserts that pile driving created an abnormal risk to persons, such as Gallagher, who have historic homes, and that damage resulting from the inevitable emission of vibration cannot be eliminated through the exercise of due care. Although some courts have adopted this view, others have declined to impose strict liability for vibrations resulting from blasting (as opposed to flying debris).

The circuit court, after reviewing the evidence presented at trial, concluded that the defendants' pile driving in the Inner Harbor did not involve a high degree of risk of harm to the person, land or chattels of another[.] We agree. Comment g to section 520 states: "The harm threatened must be major in degree, and sufficiently serious in its possible consequence to justify holding the defendant strictly liable for subjecting others to an unusual risk." The risk of harm proven in this case, relatively minor damage to a 200-year-old home from the vibrations of the pile driving, simply is not a high degree of risk which requires the application of strict liability. . . .

[A] plaintiff must show that the defendants' pile driving was likely to produce significant harm, not simply that she suffered some harm as a result of the pile driving activity.

After considering the factors of section 520 of the Restatement, we agree with the circuit court's conclusion that the pile driving in this case was not an abnormally dangerous activity.

NUISANCE

Gallagher also contends that the defendants' conduct interfered with the use and enjoyment of her land, amounting to a public and private nuisance. The circuit court disagreed, concluding that Gallagher's evidence of a private or public nuisance was insufficient as a matter of law.

Under Maryland law, to sustain a private nuisance claim "there must be a substantial interference with the plaintiff's reasonable use and enjoyment of its property." *Exxon Corp. v. Yarema*, 69 Md. App. 124, 151, 516 A.2d 990 (1986), *cert. denied*, 309 Md. 47, 522 A.2d 392 (1987). In *Yarema*, we held that the defendants' "contamination of ground water imposed crippling restrictions not only on the contaminated land but on all the property adjacent to the land." A private nuisance requires the interference to be "substantial and unreasonable and such as would be offensive or inconvenient to the normal person."

Nothing of that order occurred in this case. The defendants' activity was reasonable in time, place, manner, and duration and did not substantially interfere with Gallagher's use and enjoyment of her land. . . . Residents of Baltimore City must accept the occasional annoyance and discomforts incidental to city life.

The elements of a public nuisance were discussed by the Court of Appeals in *Tadjer v. Montgomery County*. Quoting Dean Prosser, the Court of Appeals said: "To be considered public, the nuisance must affect an interest common to the general public, rather than peculiar to one individual, or several."

The circuit court concluded that the evidence produced at trial was insufficient to prove a public nuisance under these standards. We agree.

Affirmed.

Questions

1. The plaintiff, Gallagher, brought three causes of action in her amended complaint. List them.
2. Why do you think the jury ruled in favor of Gallagher?
3. Why did Gallagher lose at the trial level even though the jury had ruled in her favor?
4. Explain why the appeals court upheld the judgment against Gallagher.
5. Who do you think should have won this case? Explain.

Selected Intentional Tort Defenses

LO 7-4 Identify selected intentional tort defenses.

The following material considers a few of the more significant defenses to the intentional torts discussed above.

Consent

Clearly, if you consent to the use of your picture in an advertising campaign and you subsequently feel that your public image has been harmed, you will have difficulty in pursuing a tort claim. However, if you gave permission under conditions of mistake, fraud, or duress, your consent was not lawfully obtained.

Mistake

As store security manager, you are radioed by a clerk to "stop the guy in the New York Yankees cap" on suspicion of shoplifting. After stopping someone fitting that description, you later discover that someone else, also wearing a Yankees cap, was the actual suspect. If the store is sued for false imprisonment, can it successfully raise a mistake defense? Unless protected under state law, probably not. Having acted intentionally, you and, by extension, your employer probably will bear responsibility. False imprisonment does not occur, however, unless the detention was unreasonable.

Mistake can be a good defense, particularly in instances in which events happen rapidly. Say, for example, a store's security personnel broke up what looked like an assault and battery in the mall parking lot, only to discover that the incident was merely horsing around by the parties. A mistake defense might be successful.

Necessity

In what we would broadly call emergency situations, one may intentionally commit a tort and yet be excused from liability. A case of necessity might occur when a person breaks into an unoccupied building late at night because they saw a fire burning inside. The same would be true if a person trespasses onto the property of another to save themself from serious physical injury.

Self-Defense

Suppose you decide to buy your own hardware store and then become frustrated by ongoing theft and vandalism. In an effort to stop the breaking, entering, and minor theft that has troubled your business, you build a trap in your store. You take up a few floorboards in a rear entryway where vandals have broken in, and you pound nails (points facing up) into those boards. Then you cover the nail points with soft felt, so they are not visible. When stepped on, the nails will pierce the felt and stab the feet of an intruder. Suppose a trespasser steps on your trap, suffers an injury, and sues you. Could you cite defense of your property as an excuse?

Perhaps it will surprise you that there is no clear answer. In general, the law allows more force used in the defense of persons than of property. Thus, the use of deadly force generally cannot be used solely for the protection of property. In the above example, you are using force to protect your property, not your person. Is it deadly force? The trespasser might be seriously injured, but death might be unlikely. Or not–what if the intruder were not found soon enough and died from loss of blood or later from blood poisoning? Alternatively, what if an innocent bystander is injured or killed, such as a police officer responding to an alarm at your business? The *Katko* case discusses the use of a spring gun to protect personal property in an unoccupied and boarded-up farmhouse.

LEGAL BRIEFCASE

Katko v. Briney

183 N.W.2d 657 (Iowa 1971)

FACTS

The Brineys, defendants/appellants in this case, owned an unoccupied farmhouse. During the period from 1957 to 1967, trespassers broke into the house, broke windows, and stole some items. The Brineys boarded windows and erected "no trespassing" signs on the land. On June 11, 1967, the Brineys attached a 20-gauge, loaded shotgun to a bed in the house, pointing the barrel toward the bedroom door. They attached a wire to the trigger and the bedroom doorknob so that the gun would fire if the door were opened. At first, Mr. Briney directed the gun so that it would hit an intruder in the stomach, but agreed with Mrs. Briney's suggestion to lower the barrel so that it would strike an intruder's legs. The gun could not be seen from the outside, and no warning about it was posted.

Katko, the plaintiff/appellee, worked in an Eddyville, Iowa, gas station. He and a friend, McDonough, had found antiques—old bottles and fruit jars—on their first trip to the Briney house, which Katko considered to be abandoned. On their second trip, they entered the house through a window. Katko opened the bedroom door and was shot in the right leg. Much of that leg, including part of the tibia, was blown away. Katko was hospitalized for 40 days. His leg was in a cast for approximately one year, and he was required to wear a brace for an additional year. His leg was permanently shortened by the trauma.

Katko sued the Brineys and secured a jury verdict of $30,000. The Brineys appealed to the Iowa Supreme Court.

CHIEF JUSTICE MOORE

The primary issue presented here is whether an owner may protect personal property in an unoccupied, boarded-up farmhouse against trespassers and thieves by a spring gun capable of inflicting death or serious injury.

We are not here concerned with a man's right to protect his home and members of his family. Defendant's home was several miles from the scene of the incident to which we refer.

Plaintiff testified he knew he had no right to break and enter the house with intent to steal bottles and fruit jars therefrom. He further testified he had entered a plea of guilty to larceny in the nighttime of property of less than $20 value [and received] a 60-day jail sentence. Other than minor traffic charges this was plaintiff's first brush with the law. . . .

The main thrust of the defendants' defense in the trial court and on this appeal is that "the law permits use of a spring gun in a dwelling or warehouse for the purpose of preventing the unlawful entry of a burglar or thief." . . . .

In the statement of issues the trial court stated plaintiff and his companion committed a felony when they broke and entered defendant's house. In instruction 2 the court referred to the early case history of the use of spring guns and stated under the law their use was prohibited except to prevent the commission of felonies of violence and where human life is in danger. The instruction included a statement that breaking and entering is not a felony of violence.

Instruction 5 stated, "You are hereby instructed that one may use reasonable force in the protection of his property, but such right is subject to the qualification that one may not use such means of force as will take human life or inflict great bodily injury. Such is the rule even though the injured party is a trespasser and is in violation of the law himself."

Instruction 6 stated, "An owner of premises is prohibited from willfully or intentionally injuring a trespasser by means of force that either takes life or inflicts great bodily injury; and therefore a person owning a premise is prohibited from setting out 'spring guns' and like dangerous devices which will likely take life or inflict great bodily injury, for the purpose of harming trespassers. The fact that the trespasser may be acting in violation of the law does not change the rule. The only time when such conduct of setting a 'spring gun' or a like dangerous device is justified would be when the trespasser was committing a felony of violence or a felony punishable by death, or where the trespasser was endangering human life by his act." . . . .

The overwhelming weight of authority, both textbook and case law, supports the trial court's statement of the applicable principles of law.

Prosser on Torts, Third Edition, pages 116–18, states,

> [T]he law has always placed a higher value upon human safety than upon mere rights in property; it is the accepted rule that there is no privilege to use any force calculated to cause death or serious bodily injury to repel the threat to land or chattels, unless there is also such a threat to the defendant's personal safety as to justify a self-defense . . . . Spring guns and other man-killing devices are not justifiable against a mere trespasser, or even a petty thief. They are privileged only against those upon whom the landowner, if he were present in person, would be free to inflict injury of the same kind.

In *Hooker v. Miller*, 37 Iowa 613, we held defendant vineyard owner liable for damages resulting from a spring gun shot although plaintiff was a trespasser and there to steal grapes. At pages 614, 615, this statement is made: "This court has held that a mere trespass against property other than a dwelling is not a sufficient justification to authorize the use of a deadly weapon by the owner in its defense; and that if death results in such a case it will be murder, though the killing be actually necessary to prevent the trespass. . . ."

Affirmed.

Questions

1. Why did the Iowa Supreme Court rule in favor of the criminal intruder, Katko?
2. What classes of people other than intruders are of concern to the courts in cases like *Katko*?
3. Did the Iowa Supreme Court reach a just verdict? Explain.

Interest in use of deadly force in the defense of property apparently increased in the summer of 2020, when many cities experienced periods of looting and rioting and, as a result, the use of such force became a topic of conversation. *The Volokh Conspiracy* is a blog on which the contributors are mostly law professors. In a series of posts, Prof. Eugene Volokh reiterated the general rules but pointed out that some states, such as Texas, may have limited exceptions to those rules. Further, according to the blog, about half the states allow the use of deadly force against robbery, defined as "theft from the person that uses modest force or a threat" without the additional requirement of "reasonable fear of death or serious bodily injury."[9]

Part Two—Product Liability

Introduction

This section addresses tort and contract claims arising from products.

How does the law handle the situation where a wheel falls off a car or a cigarette lighter explodes in a user's face? Product liability lawsuits deal with cases in which buyers, users, and in some cases bystanders are injured or killed by defective products. Those harmed may have causes of action in tort (negligence or strict liability) or contract (breach of warranty). If so, the manufacturers, distributors, and sellers of the product will have to defend themselves against often enormously large claims. [For a product liability overview, see **http://topics.law.cornell.edu/wex/Products_liability**].

Product Liability and Business Practice

LO 7-5
Discuss the impact of product liability on business practice.

Blitz USA, a manufacturer of the familiar red portable plastic gasoline cans, filed for bankruptcy in 2011 and thereafter shut its Oklahoma factory while facing dozens of product liability lawsuits. A *Wall Street Journal* commentary described Blitz and its employees as the "latest victims" of trial lawyers after Blitz spent over $30 million on the lawsuits, which, in turn, increased its product liability insurance costs.[10] Plaintiffs sought damages for serious burn injuries and deaths suffered when Blitz gas cans exploded after gasoline vapors outside the can were ignited. The claims alleged these "flashback" explosions could have been prevented had "flame arrester" shields (small mesh or plastic disks with holes) been installed in the cans.[11]

Why did Blitz decide not to add the flame arrester to its plastic gasoline cans? A lawyer representing some plaintiffs suing Blitz contended that the company dropped plans to add the arresters as a money-saving maneuver shortly before being acquired by a private equity firm.[12] Lawyers responding to the *Wall Street Journal* commentary said the shields were included in Blitz's metal gasoline cans but were omitted from their plastic containers and arguably cost less than $1 per can.[13]

Blitz asserted that adding a flame arrester would not have been effective. That defense was successful in a Texas case involving a man who died in an explosion when he poured gasoline from a Blitz can onto a fire. A federal judge subsequently ruled that internal documents later uncovered might have eliminated the ineffectiveness defense if the documents had been presented at trial.[14] For example, in 2005, Blitz CEO Rocky Flick wrote a memo entitled "My Wish List" in which he indicated his desire that Blitz cans would soon include a "device to eliminate flashback from a flame source,"[15] but Blitz was worried that the flame arresters, if installed, would cause other safety problems, such as creating a false sense of security when pouring gas on an open flame. Blitz and its chief retailer, Walmart, eventually agreed to establish a $161 million settlement fund for gas can explosion victims.[16] Then, in 2012, Scepter of Canada bought the Blitz USA site and reopened the production facilities.[17]

Whether you believe corporate greed, trial lawyers, or careless consumers were to blame, Blitz's closure demonstrates the importance of anticipating litigation expenses as part of sound business strategy. [For a general database on defective products, see **http://consumer.findlaw.com/consumer-transactions/defective-products-and-consumer-rights.html**].

Weed Killer Cancer?

A San Francisco jury in 2018 awarded a former school district groundskeeper, Dewayne Johnson, $289 million in damages ($39 million compensatory; $250 million punitive) in his lawsuit claiming that Monsanto's glyphosate weedkiller, marketed as Roundup, was a primary cause of his terminal cancer, non-Hodgkins lymphoma. In his job, Johnson had sprayed Ranger Pro, a high-concentration version of Roundup, for two or three hours, 20 or 30 times annually. The judge subsequently reduced Johnson's award to $78 million.

Johnson, age 46 in 2018, testified that he wore masks and other protective clothing, but he was exposed to windblown glyphosate nonetheless. He testified to being drenched by the liquid on two occasions when his equipment broke. After the first such episode, rashes, welts, and lesions emerged on his skin, and soon after, he was diagnosed with cancer.

The unanimous jury found that Monsanto, a subsidiary of Bayer AG, had acted with "malice" by supplying glyphosate without disclosing its allegedly life-threatening risks and by failing to return Johnson's calls after he became ill.

Many studies and decisions by government regulators, including a 2019 federal Environmental Protection Agency finding, have concluded that glyphosate is safe. One comprehensive 2017 study of 45,000 licensed pesticide applicators who had been exposed to glyphosate found no evidence of an association between the chemical and cancer. The World Health Organization, the State of California, and at least one scholarly study, on the other hand, reportedly have associated glyphosate use with cancer.

Settlement Bayer agreed in 2020 to pay up to $10.9 billion to settle an estimated 75 percent of the some 125,000 claims outstanding against Monsanto. While primarily addressing Roundup claims, the settlement also covers litigation over the Monsanto herbicide dicamba, as well as PCBs allegedly introduced into public waters by Monsanto. The settlement also provides for claims that may arise in the future. Bayer made no admission of wrongdoing. [For a detailed database on the *Johnson* case along with links to other Roundup cases and evidence, see **www.baumhedlundlaw.com/toxic-tort-law/monsanto-roundup-lawsuit/dewayne-johnson-v-monsanto-company**].

Questions

1. Can the market alone protect us satisfactorily from dangerous products? Or do you think the threat of very costly lawsuits is necessary to force American businesses

to be fully responsible in monitoring the safety of the products they produce and market? Explain.

2. Since accidents and user carelessness are inevitable and predictable with potentially hazardous products like consumer chemicals and gasoline containers, do you think manufacturers and others in the distribution chain should bear legal responsibility, regardless of fault, for injuries and deaths from those products? Explain.

Sources: *Johnson v. Monsanto,* Case No. CGC-16-550128 (Sup. Ct., Ca., San Francisco Cty, 2018); Bob Egelko and Peter Fimrite, "Judge Slashes Award by Jury in Monsanto Weed-Killer Cancer Case," *San Francisco Chronicle,* October 22, 2018 [**www.sfchronicle.com**]; and "Round Up the Usual Lawyers," *The Wall Street Journal,* August 16, 2018 [**www.wsj.com**]; and Patricia Cohen, "Roundup Maker to Pay $10 Billion to Settle Cancer Suits," The New York Times, June 24, 2020 [nytimes.com].

Negligence

The three major product liability causes of action are ***negligence***, breach of warranty, and ***strict liability***. In very simplified terms, negligence is a breach of the duty of due care. A negligent act is the failure to do (or not do) what a reasonable person would do (or not do) under a given set of circumstances. Thus, a producer or distributor has a duty to exercise reasonable care in the entire stream of events associated with the development and sale of a product. In designing, manufacturing, testing, repairing, and warning of potential dangers, those in the chain of production and distribution must meet the standard of the *reasonably prudent person.* Failure to do so constitutes negligence. Some decisions also extend potential liability to situations in which a product is being put to an unintended, but reasonably foreseeable, *misuse.*

Historically, consumers dealt face-to-face with producers and could bring breach of contract claims if injured by a defective product. However, the development in the modern era of multilayered production and distribution systems eliminated that contractual relationship between producer and consumer, making it difficult for consumers to sue producers. In a historic 1916 decision, *McPherson v. Buick Motor Co.,*[18] New York's highest court ruled that a consumer could bring a negligence claim against the manufacturer of a defective automobile even though the consumer did not purchase the car directly from the manufacturer such that there was no contractual relation. That view has since been broadly adopted, thus permitting victims of negligence to bring actions against all careless parties in the chain of production and distribution.

Such liability may continue well into a product's life cycle and cover more than the original purchaser. The rule of law at issue in the Supreme Court's 2021 decision in *Ford Motor Co. v. Montana Eighth Judicial District Court*[19] was whether product liability suits could be brought against Ford in a state in which Ford had not designed, manufactured, or sold the particular vehicles involved in the accidents. (See Chapter 4, Part Two, "Personal Jurisdiction.") The allegation in one suit was that a 1996 Ford Explorer had malfunctioned killing a woman near her home in Montana. The second suit alleged that a 1994 Crown Victoria was defective, causing an injury accident in Minnesota. As the Supreme Court stated, "Only later resales and relocations by consumers had brought the vehicles to Montana and Minnesota."[20] The Court further stated, "Ford had systematically served a market in Montana and Minnesota for the very vehicles that the plaintiffs allege malfunctioned and injured them in those States" and that "the plaintiffs are residents of the forum States, used the allegedly defective products in the forum States, and suffered injuries when those products malfunctioned there."[21]

Negligence Test

LO 7-6
Identify the requirements of a successful negligence claim.

To establish a successful negligence claim, the plaintiff must meet each of the following requirements:

- **Duty.** The plaintiff must establish that the defendant owed a duty of due care to the plaintiff. In general, the standard applied is that of the fictitious reasonable person. That a ***reasonable person*** acts prudently, sensibly, and responsibly. The standard of reasonableness depends on the circumstances of the situation. An Illinois Starbucks, for example, did not have a legal duty to protect Marcus, a three-year-old accompanied by his parents, who lost a finger when playing on heavy, cement-based stanchions and connecting ropes used to guide customers. In 2018, the federal 7th Circuit Court of Appeals reasoned that the presence of the parents lifted from Starbucks any duty that it may have had, even though the store manager had advised lower managers that the stanchions should be firmly affixed to the floor. The parents bore the duty to protect Marcus from obvious danger.[22]
- **Breach of duty.** The plaintiff must demonstrate that the defendant breached the duty of due care by engaging in conduct that did not conform to the reasonable person standard. Breach of the duty of due care may result from either the commission of a careless act or the omission of a reasonable, prudent act. Would a reasonable person discharge a firearm in a public park? Would a reasonable person foresee that failure to illuminate one's front entry steps might lead to a broken bone when a pizza is delivered? More formally, we might think of reasonable behavior as decision making that weighs the costs and benefits of acting or not acting.
- **Causation**
  a. **Actual cause.** Did the defendant's breach of the duty of due care in fact cause the harm in question? Commonly, the "but for" test is applied to determine cause-in-fact. For example, but for the defendant driver's failure to stop at the red light, the plaintiff pedestrian would not have been struck down in the crosswalk.
  b. **Proximate cause.** The plaintiff also must establish that the defendant's actions were the ***proximate cause*** of the injury. The question is whether, as a matter of policy, the defendant's conduct is sufficiently connected to the plaintiff's injury to justify imposing liability. Or is the harm so remote and so unpredictable that no one could reasonably expect the defendant to foresee it and protect against it. Many injuries arise from a series of events–some of them wildly improbable. Did the defendant's negligence lead to the plaintiff's harm, or did some intervening act break the causal link between the negligence and the harm? For example, a community's allegedly negligent maintenance resulted in a blocked road, forcing the plaintiff driver to detour. While on the detour route, the plaintiff's vehicle was struck by a plane that fell from the sky when attempting to land at a nearby airport. Was the community's negligence the proximate cause of the plaintiff's injury?[23]
- **Injury.** The plaintiff must have sustained injury, and due to problems of proof, that injury often must be physical. [For a tort law library, see **http://injury.findlaw.com/torts-and-personal-injuries.html**].

Blame Apple for Distracted Driver Accidents?

The Modisette family car was stopped on I-35 in Texas because of police activity ahead. Wilhelm crashed into the Modisettes' car, severely injuring each family member and subsequently resulting in the death of Moriah Modisette, age five. Wilhelm's iPhone 6 FaceTime application was activated at the time of the accident. Apple had previously patented lockout technology to block the use of certain iPhone functions while the user is driving. FaceTime was factory installed; it was not an optional application. The Modisettes sued Apple for its failure to design and manufacture its phones so drivers would not be able to use FaceTime when driving. The Modisettes introduced studies demonstrating the addictive and compulsive nature of mobile phone use.

Question

Based on the above requirements for a negligence claim, how would you rule in the Modisette lawsuit? Explain.

Source: *Modisette v. Apple Inc.,* 2018 Cal. App. LEXIS 1158; petition for review denied, *Modisette v. Apple Inc.,* 2019 Cal. LEXIS 1196.

Before turning specifically to negligence in a product liability context, consider the general test for negligence as applied to a bar fight.

LEGAL BRIEFCASE

Hoyt v. Gutterz Bowl & Lounge

829 N.W.2d 772 (Iowa 2013)

Justice Hecht

Defendant-appellee Gutterz Bowl & Lounge (Gutterz) is a bowling alley and tavern located in Guthrie Center, Iowa. On March 20, 2009, Curtis Hoyt and several members of his construction crew finished work and went to Gutterz for refreshments. Curtis Knapp was also a customer at Gutterz that afternoon. Hoyt soon came to believe that Knapp was scowling at him. Hoyt and Knapp had formerly been friendly, but tension had arisen between them as a result of Hoyt's alleged mistreatment of the sister of Knapp's friend.

[T]he staff of Gutterz had [no] knowledge of this history between Hoyt and Knapp.

After consuming a few beers, Hoyt and coworker Chris Brittain approached and verbally confronted Knapp. Knapp did not respond and continued to scowl at Hoyt. The waitress serving Hoyt and Brittain observed their behavior with concern and threatened to discontinue serving them unless they calmed down. Hoyt and Brittain ignored the waitress's warning, and thus she requested and secured permission from Gutterz's owner, Rodney Atkinson, to discontinue serving them. Atkinson, who had been preparing food in the kitchen, went to the bar area to assess the situation. Hoyt and Brittain complained to Atkinson that they were no longer being served and continued to taunt Knapp.

Shortly thereafter, Atkinson grew concerned that an altercation might occur. He requested that Hoyt and Brittain leave.

Hoyt finished his beer and exited the tavern. As Hoyt walked through the parking lot toward his vehicle, [Knapp] . . . . struck him in the back of the head, knocking him unconscious. Hoyt suffered several injuries including a compound fracture of his ankle. Knapp admitted to police who later arrived on the scene that he had struck Hoyt, but claimed he had done so in self-defense.

Hoyt filed this action alleging that Knapp and Gutterz were liable for the injuries he sustained when Knapp assaulted him. Gutterz moved for summary judgment, alleging Gutterz owed Hoyt no duty of reasonable care, there was no evidence of a breach of any duty, and the assault by Knapp and Hoyt's injury were not foreseeable. The district court granted Gutterz's motion for summary judgment and dismissed Gutterz from the lawsuit.

The court of appeals reversed the district court's summary judgment ruling.

III. DISCUSSION

Hoyt contends the district court erred in concluding as a matter of law that Gutterz did not breach a duty of reasonable care under these circumstances. Further, Hoyt contends, the district court erred in its consideration of foreseeability of injury to Hoyt in making its summary judgment ruling.

A. Duty

[T]he determination of whether a duty is owed under particular circumstances is a matter of law for the court's determination.

Traditionally . . . a property owner "is ordinarily under no duty to exercise any care until he knows or has reason to know that the acts of the third person are occurring, or are about to occur."

That general proposition was subject to the caveat that a duty would be imposed in scenarios where the property owner knew or had reason to know of a likelihood of third party conduct that could endanger visitors or where the place or character of the business was such that the property owner should reasonably anticipate careless or criminal conduct by third parties.

Recently . . . we examined a scenario in which the trampoline of a landowner had been blown by high winds into a nearby roadway, obstructing the travel of and causing injury to a driver. . . . We questioned and then rejected an assessment of foreseeability of risk in determining whether the landowner owed the driver a duty.

Instead . . . no-duty rulings should be limited to exceptional cases in which "an articulated countervailing principle or policy warrants denying or limiting liability in a particular class of cases."

Removing foreseeability from the duty analysis, we must consider whether some principle or strong policy consideration justifies exempting Gutterz, or the class of tavern owners in general, from the duty to exercise reasonable care. . . . [W]e cannot discern . . . any such considerations compelling exemption of tavern owners from the duty.

Accordingly, we conclude Gutterz owed Hoyt a duty of reasonable care under the circumstances presented here. We now turn to the question of whether Hoyt raised a genuine issue of material fact regarding the alleged breach of this duty.

B. Reasonable Care

While taverns are not insurers of patrons' safety against third-person criminal attacks, various jurisdictions have explained taverns must make reasonable efforts to maintain order and supervise and control patrons.

That a tavern may create a physical environment where instances of misconduct are likely to take place raises converging questions of reasonable care and the appropriate scope of liability for the defendant. . . . In a tavern, for example, the environment may foreseeably bring about the misconduct of a third party, resulting in injury to a plaintiff. While the foreseeability of misconduct raises an issue of the appropriate level of care, it also raises the issue of whether the harm suffered by the plaintiff is within the range of risks that may make the defendant's conduct negligent in failing to exercise that care.

Here, the district court found that Gutterz exercised reasonable care as a matter of law, based largely on the notion that the information available to Gutterz at the time failed to suggest any possibility of harm to Hoyt.

[W]e disagree that the record established as a matter of law that an injury to Hoyt was unforeseeable. Gutterz's duty of reasonable care applied . . . to risks arising from Hoyt's conduct, as well as those created by a third party's conduct, whether innocent, negligent, or intentional.

[B]ars are business venues in which alcohol-fueled disturbances causing injury and even death are known to occur.

Given the . . . general tenor of bar behavior, and Atkinson's own testimony regarding concern about a physical altercation, we conclude that a reasonable person might find the risk of harm to Hoyt foreseeable. Accordingly, that Hoyt may have initiated the conflict cannot serve as the basis for summary judgment that Gutterz acted reasonably under the circumstances.

Hoyt contends that Gutterz could have exercised reasonable care by any of the following: (1) calling the police when the conflict developed, (2) escorting Hoyt to his vehicle in the parking lot, or (3) verifying that Knapp was not lying in wait in the parking lot. Gutterz contends that it did escort Hoyt to his vehicle, and that its precautions here were reasonable as a matter of law. . . . [R]esolution of the factual dispute is best left to the fact finder. . . .

[Reversed]

DISSENT

WATERMAN, Justice, joined by Cady, C. J., and Mansfield, J. I respectfully dissent. . . . Uncontroverted facts establish the defendant acted reasonably as a matter of law.

There is no evidence or claim that prior fights or third-party criminal acts showed a need for a bouncer or other security at Gutterz. Bars are not insurers strictly liable for injuries on their premises inflicted by others.

Having kicked out the troublemakers–Hoyt and his companion–what else should Gutterz have done? How was the bar negligent? The majority concludes a jury could find Gutterz negligent for failing to call the police. But, no crime had (yet) been committed, and Hoyt exited the bar when told to leave. Knapp was not threatening anyone or misbehaving in any way. At that point, why call the police? From Gutterz's standpoint, the incident had been defused by Hoyt's departure. The majority also argues Atkinson should have done more to ensure Hoyt left the parking lot safely. This theory assumes Atkinson reasonably should have foreseen Knapp would attack Hoyt. Knapp had not so much as even raised his voice.

I would affirm the district court's summary judgment in favor of Gutterz.

Questions

1. Why did the Iowa Supreme Court conclude that Gutterz owed a duty of reasonable care to Hoyt?
2. According to the court, when would a property owner not owe a duty of reasonable care to a plaintiff?
3. Describe a scenario in which a property owner would not owe such a duty to an injured party.
4. Why should Hoyt, who initiated the conflict with Knapp in the Gutterz bar area, be able to recover from Gutterz for his resulting injuries? Explain.
5. Both the majority and dissenting opinions specify that taverns are not ensurers of the safety of their patrons against injury caused by third parties.
   a. On what point does the dissenting opinion disagree with the majority?
   b. Do you agree with the majority or dissenting opinion? Explain.
6. Johnny Burnett, described by his mother, Sheila Watters, as a devoted *Dungeons & Dragons* player, killed himself. (The record did not disclose his age at the time of death.) Watters blamed the death on her son's absorption in the game. She claimed that "he lost control of his own independent will and was driven to self-destruction."

   Dungeons & Dragons is an adventure game set in an imaginary ancient world; the players assume the roles of various characters as suggested by illustrated booklets. The play is orchestrated by a player labeled the "Dungeon Master." The outcome of the play is determined by using dice in conjunction with tables provided with the game. The game's materials do not mention suicide or guns. More than one million copies of the game have been sold, many to schools, where it is used as a learning tool.

   In federal district court, Watters brought a wrongful death claim against TSR, the manufacturer of *Dungeons & Dragons*. The plaintiff's complaint alleged that TSR violated its duty of care in two ways: It disseminated *Dungeons & Dragons* literature to "mentally fragile persons," and it failed to warn that the "possible consequences" of playing the game might include "loss of control of the mental processes." Decide. Explain. See *Watters v. TSR, Inc.*, 904 F.2d 378 (6th Cir. 1990).
7. Is a fireworks manufacturer liable for harm to children who ignited an explosive that had failed to detonate in the town public display the previous day? Explain.
8. An individual took his car to Quality Pontiac in Albuquerque, New Mexico, for repairs and was told to leave the car unlocked with the keys in the ignition. The lot was fenced, but the gate was unlocked. Billy Garcia entered the car lot at 9 PM, apparently looking in the cars for something to steal. Garcia stole the individual's car. The next day at approximately 11 AM, a deputy sheriff observed Garcia driving quickly through a school zone and pursued him, engaging his sirens and emergency lights. Garcia sped the car up to 90 miles an hour and collided with Herrera's car, killing one occupant and seriously injuring the other. Herrera and others sued Quality Pontiac. The complaint included an affidavit of a sociologist asserting that Albuquerque's car theft rate was the second highest in the United States and that a significant portion of cars stolen had been left unlocked with keys in the ignition. Further, stolen cars were highly likely to be involved in joy riding, and nearly 17 percent of stolen cars were involved in accidents shortly after the theft. Should Quality Pontiac be held liable? Explain. See *Herrera et al. v. Quality Pontiac*, 73 P.3d 181 (N.M. 2003).
9. Is a fireworks manufacturer liable for harm to children who ignited an explosive that had failed to detonate in the town public display the previous day? Explain.

Product Liability Negligence Claims

LO 7-7
Differentiate between the types of negligence claims emerging from defective products.

Negligence claims emerging from defective products fall into three categories of analysis: (1) manufacturing defects, (2) design defects, and (3) inadequate warnings.

Manufacturing Defects

Spilled hot coffee lawsuits are relatively common, but depending on the facts and the law of the state in question, they are difficult to win. The most famous of these cases, however, was a victory for the plaintiff, a result many applauded in sympathy for the burn victim, an elderly grandmother. But to many others worldwide, the grandmother's victory was merely further evidence of an overly litigious society.

In 1992, then-79-year-old Stella Liebeck ordered coffee at an Albuquerque, New Mexico, McDonald's drive-through. At the time, McDonald's policy reportedly was to brew its coffee at very high temperatures–often 180 to 190 degrees–to meet customer preferences. Liebeck's grandson, who was driving, pulled forward and stopped so Liebeck could add cream and sugar to her coffee. The dashboard of the car was slanted so the coffee could not be set on it. Liebeck, therefore, placed the coffee between her legs, and while trying to get the top off the container, she spilled the coffee on her lap, resulting in third-degree burns. She was hospitalized, required skin grafts, and was disabled for two years. She sought a settlement with McDonald's, but according to her family, McDonald's offered only $800.[24] Liebeck sued, accusing McDonald's of gross negligence for selling coffee that was "unreasonably dangerous" and "defectively manufactured."[25]

The number of hot coffee burns was "statistically insignificant."

Liebeck was awarded $200,000 in compensatory and $2.7 million in punitive damages. The jury found Liebeck 20 percent responsible for her own injury, thus reducing her compensatory award to $160,000. The judge subsequently reduced the punitive award to $480,000. The parties then settled out of court for an undisclosed amount. According to news reports, the jury awarded Liebeck $2.7 million in punitive damages because of what it perceived to be McDonald's callous attitude toward the accident and because of the more than 700 previous coffee-burn claims that had been filed against McDonald's. A McDonald's human-factors engineer testified that the number of hot coffee burns was "statistically insignificant" when compared with the billions of cups sold by McDonald's annually.[26]

[See the *Hot Coffee Official Trailer,* see **https://www.youtube.com/watch?v=bBKRjxeQnT4**].

A British High Court justice, however, viewed the hot coffee situation quite differently:

> Persons generally expect tea or coffee purchased to be consumed on the premises to be hot. . . . They accordingly know that care must be taken to avoid such spills.[27]

The case that follows involves another injury from hot food.

Jimenez v. Applebee's

2015 N.J. Super. Unpub. LEXIS 430 (N.J. Super. Ct. App. Div. March 4, 2015)

PER CURIAM

Plaintiff Hiram Jimenez appeals from an order entered by the Law Division on December 6, 2013, granting summary judgment in favor of defendants. We affirm.

This appeal arises from the following facts. On March 4, 2010, plaintiff met his brother Rafael at an Applebee's Neighborhood Grill ("Applebee's") in Westampton, New Jersey. After they were seated in a booth, plaintiff and his brother ordered their meals. Plaintiff ordered a steak fajita. He spoke with Rafael until a waitress brought the food to their table. According to plaintiff, his meal was served in a "sizzling skillet," which the waitress placed "right in front of [him]."

Plaintiff described the dish as "real dark," smoking, sizzling and "real hot." According to plaintiff, the waitress did not say anything when she served the food, other than to "enjoy your meal." After the waitress walked away, Rafael "reached over and said let's have prayer." Plaintiff bowed his head "[c]lose to the table." Plaintiff said he heard a loud, sizzling noise, followed by "a pop noise," and then felt a burning sensation in his left eye and on his face.

Plaintiff panicked, knocked his plate onto his lap and caused his prescription eyeglasses to fall from his face. Plaintiff said he tried to push away from the table with his right arm. He used his left arm to brush the food from his lap. He soon felt that he had "pulled" something in his right arm. He stopped applying pressure to the table, "let [his] [right] hand go because [he] felt pain," and "banged" his elbow on the table.

Rafael called for help and the restaurant's employees came to assist. A manager eventually provided Rafael with an incident report form. The description of the incident contained on the report is as follows: "[H]ot food order[ ] burned me after grease popped causing several burns to face, neck, and arms." According to plaintiff's deposition testimony, the alleged burns left no scarring.

Plaintiff thereafter filed a complaint in the trial court against defendants, alleging that defendants owned, possessed, controlled, managed, operated or supervised Applebee's. Plaintiff alleged that, on March 4, 2010, while a business invitee at Applebee's, he was injured solely as a result of defendants' negligence when he came in contact with a dangerous and hazardous condition, specifically, "a plate of hot food." Plaintiff claimed he sustained serious and permanent personal injuries for which he sought damages. Defendants filed an answer denying liability and demanding judgment dismissing the complaint.

After the completion of discovery, defendants filed a motion for summary judgment. Defendants argued that, even if plaintiff established the existence of a dangerous or hazardous condition, they were entitled to judgment as a matter of law because the condition was open, obvious and easily understood. Defendants further argued that they were entitled to summary judgment because plaintiff had not established that his damages were proximately caused by their acts or omissions. Plaintiff opposed the motion.

The motion judge . . . determined that defendants had a duty to provide their patrons with reasonably safe premises, but had no duty to warn against a danger that is open and obvious. The judge found that defendants did not breach any duty owed to plaintiff.

The judge noted that there was no dispute as to the fact that plaintiff had been served a platter of food which was sizzling, or that plaintiff opted to place his face close to the food. The judge determined that plaintiff was injured because of the actions plaintiff took with regard to a hazard that was "open and obvious." The judge concluded that defendants were entitled to summary judgment.

On appeal, plaintiff argues that: (1) the trial court erred by finding as a matter of law that defendants did not owe him a duty; (2) the trial court erroneously assumed that plaintiff placed his face within inches of the sizzling platter and issues involving the manner in which the subject incident occurred should have been reserved for the jury; and (3) the court made an erroneous finding as to the existence and extent of plaintiff's comparative negligence which was an issue for the jury.

The trial court may grant summary judgment when there are no genuine issues of material fact, and the moving party is entitled to judgment as a matter of law. . . .

Plaintiff argues that the motion judge erred by finding that defendants owed no duty to warn defendant of the danger posed by the sizzling plate of food that had been served to him.

There are three elements to a cause of action for negligence: "(1) a duty of care owed by defendant to plaintiff; (2) a breach of that duty by defendant; and (3) an injury to plaintiff proximately caused by defendant's breach." . . . .

A business owner owes its invitees "a duty of reasonable or due care to provide a safe environment for doing that which is within the scope of the invitation." "Th[is] duty of due care requires a business owner to discover and eliminate dangerous conditions, to maintain the premises in safe condition, and to avoid creating conditions that would render the premises unsafe."

Here, plaintiff does not allege that there was any dangerous condition on defendants' premises. He claims, however, that the "sizzling fajita platter" created a danger to him, and argues that the motion judge erred by finding that defendants owed him no duty to warn him of the danger.

In determining whether a person owes another a duty of reasonable care, the court considers "the foreseeability of the risk of injury." The determination of whether such a duty exists also "'involves identifying, weighing, and balancing several factors—the relationship of the parties, the nature of the attendant risk, the opportunity and ability to exercise care, and the public interest in the proposed solution.'"

Here, the risk of injury was foreseeable since the plate of food, as described by plaintiff, was sizzling, smoking and "real hot." The relationship of the parties was that of business owner and invitee. Moreover, once the platter was served, defendants had no control over it, and plaintiff had the opportunity and ability to act to protect himself from any danger that it posed, since the danger was open and obvious. We conclude that, balancing these factors, imposition of a duty upon defendants to warn plaintiff of the danger presented by the sizzling hot platter is not required as a matter of fairness and sound policy.

*****

Here, the danger posed by a plate of sizzling hot food was self-evident. Therefore, we conclude that the motion judge correctly determined that defendants had no duty to warn plaintiff that the food was sizzling hot and should be approached with due care.

*****

We conclude that the motion judge correctly determined that there was no genuine issue of material fact and defendants were entitled to judgment as a matter of law.

Affirmed.

Questions

1. Why did the appellate court affirm the trial court's decision to grant Applebee's summary judgment?
2. Sutton bought a McDonald's fried chicken sandwich at a truck stop. When he bit into the sandwich, Sutton said, "the grease from the inside of the chicken sandwich spread out all over my bottom lip, my top lip, down onto my chin." Sutton immediately dropped the sandwich. His wife dabbed his face with ice as blisters formed on his lips. Sutton reported the incident to a pair of McDonald's employees, one of whom reportedly said, "This is what happens to the sandwiches when they aren't drained completely." Sutton's lips continued to bother him. He went to a doctor who provided lip balm and told Sutton to avoid excessive exposure to sunlight. Sutton thereafter sued McDonald's and the local franchise owner for negligence, among other claims. How is this case different from *Jimenez v. Applebee's*? How is it similar? Should McDonald's and the franchise owner be held liable for Sutton's injuries? Decide. Explain. See *Sutton v. Roth*, 361 F. App'x 543 (4th Cir. 2010) (unpublished opinion).

Res Ipsa Loquitur

As we see with the McDonald's and Applebee's cases, allegedly improper manufacturing of products often generates negligence claims. However, the extremely complex process of producing, distributing, and using a product sometimes so obscures the root of the injury in question that proof of fault is nearly impossible to establish. In those circumstances, many courts have adopted the doctrine of ***res ipsa loquitur*** (the thing speaks for itself), which in some cases permits the court to infer the defendant's negligence even though that negligence cannot be proved–that is, the facts suggest that the plaintiff's injury must have resulted from the defendant's negligence, but the circumstances are such that the plaintiff is unable to prove such negligence. A showing of res ipsa loquitur requires that: (1) the injury was caused by an instrumentality under the control of the defendant, (2) the accident ordinarily would not happen absent the defendant's negligence, and (3) there is no evidence of other causes for the injury.[28]

Design Defects

From Cessna's single-engine airplanes to five-gallon buckets (which may hold liquid sufficient to drown a child) to automobile seat belts and on across the spectrum of American products, manufacturers must think about designing products to anticipate and avoid consumer injury. Two principal lines of analysis have emerged in these cases: (1) the ***risk-utility test*** holds that a product is negligently designed if the benefits of a product's design are outweighed by the risks that accompany that design and (2) the ***consumer-expectations test*** imposes on the manufacturer a duty to design its products so that they are safe not only for their intended use but also for any reasonably foreseeable use.

The *Restatement of Torts, Third,* which is published by the American Law Institute (ALI), a group of legal experts, does not constitute law but represents those experts' best judgment about what the law is and, in some cases, what the writers think it should be. The ALI has recommended to the courts a design defect standard that supports the balancing approach of the risk-utility model and gives much less attention to consumer expectations. Furthermore, a product would be considered defective in design only if its foreseeable risks could have been reduced or avoided by a reasonable alternative design and if failure to include that design makes the product not reasonably safe. That is, plaintiffs would need to show that some better design was available and was not incorporated in the product in question, While most states have adopted the risk-utility test, some have declined to do so.[29]

Warnings

Warnings seem to be everywhere. Some of them seem downright silly–so much so that for about 15 years "Wacky Warning Labels" contests were held. Leading entries one year included

> "Remove child before folding"-on a child car safety seat
> "Harmful if swallowed"-a warning on a brass fishing lure with a three-pronged hook[30]

Even though warnings can be overdone, it should be remembered that they may help protect from foreseeable dangers. For example, in 2007, the federal Consumer Product Safety Commission (CPSC) ordered warnings on all new generators and generator packaging after recording 220 deaths from generator-related carbon monoxide poisoning over three years,[31] an average of 73 per year.

A product may be considered defective because of inadequate warnings when reasonable warnings would have reduced or avoided the foreseeable risks and the failure to warn resulted in a product that was not reasonably safe. Courts also might consider the feasibility of an effective warning and the probable seriousness of the injury. The case that follows raises design-defect and failure-to-warn product liability claims.

LEGAL BRIEFCASE

Santos-Rodriguez v. Seastar Solutions

858 F.3d 695 (1st Cir. 2017)

Torruella, Circuit Judge

Plaintiff Bernardino Santos-Rodriquez ("Santos") was injured in a boating accident when a corroded rod end that was part of the boat's steering mechanism failed. Santos and several relatives sued Defendant Seastar Solutions ("Seastar"), the manufacturer of the boat's steering mechanism, alleging a design defect and a failure to warn. Santos appeals from the district court's grant of summary judgment in favor of Seastar. . . .

I. BACKGROUND

1. The Boating Accident

On June 25, 2010, Santos was riding in a twin-engine boat in a bay near Guayama, Puerto Rico. Raul Viera-Torres ("Viera") owned the boat, which was equipped with a hydraulic steering system manufactured in 2002 by Seastar. The rod connecting the steering system to the right motor had a ball-joint at the end, which broke while the boat was in motion, resulting in a loss of steering and ejecting Santos from the boat. Santos sustained extensive injuries, resulting in paraplegia. . . . Subsequent examination revealed that the rod end failed because of corrosion.

2. The Instruction Manual and the Boat's Maintenance

The Manual did not contain a specific warning about corrosion of the rod end. . . . Viera hired third-party mechanics to maintain the boat, but none of those mechanics ever brought the corroded rod end to Viera's attention.

II. ANALYSIS

A. Santos Cannot Prove That Any Failure to Warn Caused His Injuries

Here on appeal, the plaintiffs briefly summarize evidence that the Manual did not include any warnings about corrosion of the rod end and their expert's conclusion that the rod end was corroded and that this "caused loss of control of the steering of the boat," leading to the accident and Santos's injuries. They then assert, without citation, that "[u]nder Puerto Rico law, this is sufficient to raise a genuine issue of material fact." This argument does not address the district court's conclusion that "no evidence has been brought [to] the court's attention from which the trier of fact could reasonably infer that the omission of additional warnings caused Santos's injuries. Thus, even assuming that the Manual did not contain "adequate warnings or instructions," that cannot be "the proximate cause of [Santos's] injury."

B. Santos Cannot Prove That Any Design Defect in the Steering Rod Caused His Injuries

Here, the plaintiffs' expert reported that the rod end was corroded and that this corrosion "was the main cause for the failure of the subject hydraulic steering cylinder rod end." No admissible evidence shows that the corrosion was because of some defect in the product's design. In fact the plaintiff's expert report . . . does not address whether the product was properly designed.

The plaintiff's real argument is that the rod end failed, and that this is sufficient evidence of a design defect. This is precisely the type of showing rejected in *Rodriquez-Mendez,* where the plaintiffs' only evidence was that something was wrong–he had metal in his eye. Here, the plaintiffs' only showing is that something was wrong–the rod end failed. Thus, the plaintiffs did not present evidence that Seastar's design of the rod end was defective.

[Affirmed]

Questions

1. Explain why the plaintiff's failure-to-warn claim was denied.
2. Explain why the plaintiff's design-defect claim failed.
3. Based on Judge Torruella's opinion, explain why the plaintiff Santos might be disappointed in his expert witness and/or his lawyer(s).
4. Bresnahan, age 50 and 5'8" tall, was driving her Chrysler LeBaron, equipped with a driver's side air bag, at between 25 and 30 miles per hour. She was seated less than one foot from the air bag cover. Bresnahan was distracted by police lights and rear-ended a Jaguar, triggering the LeBaron air bag which broke Bresnahan's arm and caused various abrasions. The vehicle did not include a warning about the danger of sitting too close to the air bag. Was the vehicle defective because of the absence of a warning? Explain. See *Bresnahan v. Chrysler Corp.,* 65 Cal. App. 4th 1149 (1998).

As previously mentioned, the CPSC began requiring warnings on new generators and their packaging in 2007. Did those warnings make a difference? A June 2022 CPSC report covering the ten years from 2011 to 2021 found that there were at least 770 fatalities from generator-related carbon monoxide poisoning,[32] an average of 77 per year, more than the 73 average before warnings were required.

Questions

1. How often do you read the warning labels accompanying a new appliance?
2. Have you ever not purchased an appliance based on the warning labels?

Negligence Defenses: Introduction

Even if the plaintiff has established all of the necessary elements of a negligence claim, the defendant may still prevail by asserting a good defense. The two most prominent legal defenses in these cases are comparative or contributory negligence and assumption of the risk.

A trampoline at the Beta Theta Pi fraternity house at the University of Denver led to a broken neck and paralysis when a 20-year-old fraternity member, Oscar Whitlock, unsuccessfully attempted a flip at 10 PM in the dark. Whitlock had extensive experience with trampolines. On the day of the accident, he slept until 2 PM after drinking that morning until 2 AM. The trampoline was located in front of the house on university land that was leased by the fraternity. The trampoline had been used over a 10-year period by students and community members. A number of injuries had resulted. The university kept its own trampoline under lock and key because of safety concerns.

Oscar unsuccessfully attempted a trampoline flip at 10 PM in the dark.

At trial, the jury found the university 72 percent at fault, with the remainder of the blame lying with the student plaintiff. He recovered 72 percent of $7,300,000 ($5,256,000). On appeal the judgment was upheld, but the dissent argued that the university had no duty to warn against obvious risks, saying that "no reasonable person could conclude that the plaintiff was not at least as negligent as the defendant." Hence the dissent was saying, in effect, that the plaintiff had assumed the risk and, in any case, was himself arguably more negligent than the university.[33]

The Colorado State Supreme Court then reviewed the appeals court decision and reversed it on the ground that the university did not maintain a "special relationship" with the plaintiff that would have justified imposing a duty of due care on the university to ensure safe use of the trampoline.[34]

Questions

Assume you own an amusement park.

1. Would the dissent's reasoning in the *Whitlock* court of appeals decision apply to the trampoline in your amusement park business? Explain.
2. Would a warning and close supervision protect you from liability under the court of appeals decision? Explain.

Negligence Defenses: Rules

LO 7-8
Analyze whether defenses may be successfully asserted in a negligence claim.

Now the key defenses in negligence cases are considered.

Comparative Negligence

Most states have adopted *comparative negligence* as a defense, an approach that involves weighing the relative negligence of the parties. Although the formula varies from state to state, typically the plaintiff's recovery is reduced by a percentage equal to the percentage of plaintiff fault in the case. Assume a plaintiff sustained $10,000 in injuries in an accident. If the plaintiff's own negligence is found to be 20 percent responsible for the injuries, the plaintiff's recovery will be reduced to $8,000. In many states, however, when the plaintiff is more than 50 percent at fault, they will be barred from recovery.

Contributory Negligence

Rather than employing the comparative negligence doctrine, a few states continue to follow the historic rule that any contribution by the plaintiff to their own harm constitutes a complete bar to recovery. This is called ***contributory negligence***. If the plaintiff is found to have contributed in any way to their injury, even if that contribution is minuscule, they are unable to recover.

Assumption of the Risk

A plaintiff who willingly and knowingly undertakes an unreasonable risk and is injured, in many states, will be barred from recovery under the ***assumption of the risk*** defense. If a driver sees that the road ahead is flooded, he probably will not be compensated for the injuries sustained when he loses control as he attempts to drive through the water. His recovery is barred even though the road was flooded owing to operator error in opening a floodgate. The elements of the defense are: (1) knowledge of the risk and (2) the voluntary assumption of that risk. Increasingly, states that have adopted the comparative negligence doctrine do not treat assumption of the risk as a complete bar to recovery but rather as a factor in negligence balancing.

Question

In December 2022, Consumer Reports, a non-profit organization which runs independent tests on consumer products, published a report on heavy metals, specifically lead and cadmium, found in the 28 dark chocolate candy bars it tested.[35] It used California's maximum allowable dose (because no applicable federal standards exist) to determine safe levels. All of the bars tested contained both lead and cadmium; only six were below the maximum allowable dose for both metals. Frequent exposure to small amounts, such as those found in an ounce of chocolate, can lead to undesirable side effects in adults, including kidney damage, immune system suppression, and reproductive problems. But perhaps of greater concern is the impact on fetuses and young children. Heavy metals are known to cause developmental problems, affect brain development, and lead to lower IQs.

Chocolate bars currently carry no warnings about these risks.

Should chocolate companies be liable for the damage caused by their products? A **Research Exercise** at the end of this chapter provides an opportunity to investigate this issue.

Warranties

As explained previously, negligence claims are often difficult to prove. For that reason among others, a wronged consumer may wish to bring a breach-of-warranty claim in addition to, or in place of, a negligence action. A ***warranty*** is a contract-based guarantee about the character or quality of goods. If the product does not conform to the standards of the warranty, the contract is violated (breached), and the wronged party is entitled to damages.

LO 7-9
Compare and contrast claims based on express warranties and implied warranties.

Express Warranties

In the context of product liability, an express warranty exists if a seller of goods states a fact or makes a promise regarding the character or quality of the goods. Warranties are governed primarily by the Uniform Commercial Code.

UCC 2-313. Express Warranties by Affirmation, Promise, Description, Sample

1. Express warranties by the seller are created as follows:
   a. Any affirmation of fact or promise made by the seller to the buyer which relates to the goods and becomes part of the basis of the bargain creates an express warranty that the goods shall conform to the affirmation or promise.
   b. Any description of the goods which is made part of the basis of the bargain creates an express warranty that the goods shall conform to the description.
   c. Any sample or model which is made part of the basis of the bargain creates an express warranty that the whole of the goods shall conform to the sample or model.

The UCC 2-313 standard is straightforward: The seller who seeks to enhance the attractiveness of their product by offering representations as to its nature or quality must fulfill those representations or be in breach of contract and pay damages. [For the text of the Uniform Commercial Code, Article 2, Sales, see **www.law.cornell.edu/ucc**.]

Puffing

Creation of an express warranty under the UCC requires an affirmation of fact or promise. A statement of opinion is, therefore, not covered by the Code. The sales clerk who, for example, says, "Everybody agrees, this is the world's best TV," is engaging in obviously exaggerated sales talk, or *puffing,* and would not be guaranteeing that the television in question is the best available. If, on the other hand, the clerk misstates an objective fact, such as the type of display technology, a breach of warranty action might be in order. Note that an expression of opinion coming from an expert might create an express warranty because the buyer should reasonably be able to rely on the expert's affirmations.

Built Ford-Tough

In 2017, Brandon Kommer brought a class-action suit against Ford related to his purchase of a 2015 Ford F-150 XLT Super Crew truck after seeing Ford's "Built Ford-Tough" ads on television and the Internet. Soon after, while living in upstate New York, he started having problems with the doors not latching closed and the electric locks not opening in below-freezing temperatures. He alleged Ford knew of the problem but failed to disclose it, based on an April 2015 technical bulletin provided to Ford dealers titled, "Supercab/Supercrew Cab–Frozen or Inoperative Door Latch." A second bulletin was issued in November 2016, addressing the same problem, but covering even more truck models and years. The court granted Ford's motion to dismiss, based in part on the fact that the ads made no reference to the quality of the vehicles' door handles and that a Colorado court had expressly held that the "Built Ford-Tough" slogan was puffery.

When dismissing the case, however, the court gave Kommer leave to file an amended complaint if he were able to allege new facts to support the misrepresentation-by-omission claim. That, along with substantial more discovery and mediation, was apparently sufficient incentive for Ford to settle. On December 3, 2019, the parties notified the court that they had reached a preliminary agreement. Roughly a year later, Kommer filed and the court approved an unopposed motion for approval of a class-action settlement. It established a $5.3 million fund, of which $1.3 million would pay attorney's fees and expenses and a named-plaintiff service award for Kommer of $7,500. Members of the class would be notified that they could submit claims for reimbursements. When the claims process concluded, any remaining funds would be distributed to all class members.

Questions

1. Do you agree "Built Ford-Tough" is just puffery? Explain.
2. Could Ford have made a better business decision when the original technical bulletin was sent out? When the second bulletin was sent out covering even more models and years? Explain.
3. Recalling the ethics discussions in Chapter 2, do you think Ford acted ethically when the first and or second technical bulletin came out? When Kommer brought the original suit? What happened after the court's original decision and the final approval such that Ford agreed to the class action settlement?

Sources: *Kommer v. Ford Motor Company,* 1:17-CV-296 (LEK/DJS) (N.D. N.Y. Jul. 28, 2017) and *Kommer v. Ford Motor Company,* 1:17-CV-296 (LEK/DJS) (N.D. N.Y. Dec. 15, 2020).

Implied Warranties

When a seller enters a contract for the sale of goods, an implied warranty arises by operation of law. That is, an implied warranty automatically attaches to the sale of goods unless the warranty is disclaimed (disavowed) by the seller.

Important implied warranties include:

UCC 2-314. Implied Warranty: Merchantability; Usage of Trade

(1) Unless excluded or modified . . . , a warranty that the goods shall be merchantable is implied in a contract for their sale if the seller is a merchant with respect to goods of that kind. . . .

UCC 2-104. Definitions . . .

(1) "Merchant" means a person who deals in goods of the kind or otherwise by his occupation holds himself out as having knowledge or skill peculiar to the practices or goods involved in the transaction . . . .

UCC 2-315. Implied Warranty: Fitness for Particular Purpose

Where the seller at the time of contracting has reason to know any particular purpose for which the goods are required and that the buyer is relying on the seller's skill or judgment to select or furnish suitable goods, there is unless excluded or modified . . . an implied warranty that the goods shall be fit for such purpose.

The implied warranty of merchantability is a powerful tool for the wronged consumer. If the seller is a "merchant," the warranty of merchantability automatically accompanies the sale unless it is excluded via a disclaimer (explained below). The warranty arises even if the seller made no certification as to the nature or quality of the goods. UCC 2-314 enshrines the consumer's reasonable expectation that only safe goods of at least ordinary quality will appear on the market.

The implied warranty of fitness for a particular purpose likewise arises by operation of law, but only when the seller (merchant or not) knows (or has reason to know) that the goods are to be used for a specific purpose, and the seller further knows that the buyer is relying on the seller's judgment. If those conditions exist, the warranty arises automatically unless disclaimed.

Assume that a customer engages an audio products clerk in a discussion regarding the proper sound system for the customer's classic Austin Healey 3000 sports car. The customer explains the joy he expects when driving his car along the winding Kentucky roads with the convertible top down and his songs booming. Unfortunately, the audio system selected on the clerk's advice proves insufficient to be heard clearly above the rushing wind and engine noise. Should the customer be able to recover for breach of the implied warranty of fitness for a particular purpose? Of merchantability?

Disclaimers

Express warranties may be disclaimed (excluded) or modified only with great difficulty. In any contract displaying both an express warranty and language disclaiming that warranty (for example, sold "as is" or "with all faults"), the warranty will remain effective unless the warranty and the disclaimer can reasonably be read as consistent (a rare situation). It makes no sense that a seller could disclaim a promise they have just expressly made?

Implied warranties may be excluded or modified by following either of the two patterns explained in UCC Section 2-316(2) and (3)(a).

2. Subject to subsection (3), to exclude or modify the implied warranty of merchantability or any part of it the language must mention merchantability and in case of a writing must be conspicuous, and to exclude or modify any implied warranty of fitness the exclusion must be by a writing and conspicuous. . . .
3. Notwithstanding subsection (2)
   a. unless the circumstances indicate otherwise, all implied warranties are excluded by expressions like "as is", "with all faults" or other language which in common understanding calls the buyer's attention to the exclusion of warranties and makes plain that there is no implied warranty[.]

Finally, when a buyer, before entering a contract, inspects the goods (or a sample thereof) or declines to inspect, no implied warranty exists with regard to defects that should have been apparent on inspection. See UCC 2-316(3)(b).

Magnuson–Moss Warranty Act

The federal Magnuson-Moss Warranty Act extended and clarified the UCC warranty rules. Congress found that warranties were often vague, deceptive, or simply incomprehensible to the average purchaser. The act, administered by the Federal Trade Commission, applies only to consumer products and only to written warranties. It does not require offering an express written warranty, but where such a warranty is offered and the cost of the goods is more than $10, the warranty must be labeled *full* or *limited.* A full warranty requires free repair of any defect. If repair is not achieved within a reasonable time, the buyer may elect either a refund or replacement without charge. If a limited warranty is offered, the limitation must be conspicuously displayed.

If a warranty is offered on goods costing more than $15, the warrantor must "fully and conspicuously disclose in simple and readily understandable language the terms and conditions of the warranty."

The effect of the Magnuson–Moss Act has not been entirely consistent with Congress's hopes. In practice, many sellers have either offered limited warranties or eliminated them entirely.

In many states, implied warranty law has been incorporated within broader product liability actions, reflecting an emerging preference for treating personal injury and property damages as torts rather than contract-based (warranty) claims. The *Hodges* case that follows, however, finds the Kansas Supreme Court examining a breach-of-warranty claim under conventional contracts reasoning. Notice that the Kansas court struggles, as other courts have, to determine when the warranty of merchantability should apply to used goods.

LEGAL BRIEFCASE

Hodges v. Johnson

199 P.3d 1251 (Kan. 2009)

Justice Davis

FACTS

Jim Johnson owns a car dealership in Saline County that sells high-end, used vehicles. In January 2005, Johnson sold Dr. Merle Hodges and Melissa Hodges a 1995 Mercedes S320 with 135,945 miles for $17,020 (the sales price of $ 15,900 plus tax). Johnson had been driving the Mercedes as his personal vehicle for roughly 2 years before the sale. Johnson testified before the district court in this case that he told the Hodgeses when they purchased the Mercedes that it was a nice car in good condition. Dr. Hodges testified that Johnson said the car "was just pretty much a perfect car" and that Johnson "loved driving it."

At the time the Hodgeses bought the Mercedes from Johnson, there was no discussion about the operation of the air conditioning, heating, or other components of the vehicle. Both Dr. Hodges and Johnson testified that they had no reason to believe that the air conditioner did not work when the Mercedes was sold to the Hodgeses.

In February 2005, about a month after he had bought the car from Johnson, Dr. Hodges noticed that the vent in the Mercedes did not circulate cool air and that the car emitted a strange smell. In March of the same year, the Hodgeses noticed that the Mercedes' air conditioning did not work and contacted the Hodgeses' mechanic, Virgil Anderson. Anderson added Freon to the air conditioner. About a month later, the air conditioner again was not working; Anderson added more Freon. . . .

In May 2005, the air conditioner failed a third time. After checking the air conditioning system for leaks, Anderson informed the Hodgeses that the Mercedes' evaporator, condenser, and compressor needed to be replaced. Anderson explained that these repairs would cost approximately $3,000 to $ 4,000.

At some time around May 2005, a mechanic who worked for Anderson told the Hodgeses that Johnson had requested that the mechanic put a product called Super Seal into the Mercedes' air conditioner in May 2003 (when he was using the car as his personal vehicle). . . .

Johnson testified that he did not recall any problems with the Mercedes' air conditioner after the mechanics added Super Seal in May 2003, though he could not recall whether additional Freon was added during that time. Johnson further testified that the air conditioning problem in 2003 only involved the car's evaporator.

Anderson identified the condenser as the main problem with the Mercedes' air conditioner in 2005. Anderson testified during the pendency of this case that he could not determine whether the problem with the Mercedes' air conditioner existed at the time that the Hodgeses bought the car from Johnson or occurred at some time later.

The Hodgeses asked Johnson to pay to repair the air conditioning unit in the Mercedes. Johnson refused.

Shortly thereafter, the Hodgeses filed an action in small claims court against Johnson, alleging he caused them damages of $3,474–Anderson's estimate of the repair costs. The small claims court found in favor of the Hodgeses and awarded them $3,474 damages, plus $56 in costs and interest.

Johnson appealed to the district court. [T]he district court also found in favor of the Hodgeses, noting that "while [Johnson] may not have known of the failure of the air conditioning unit[,] . . . there is an implied warranty of merchantability," and Johnson "is responsible to the plaintiffs to provide a car that is merchantable." The court therefore entered a judgment in favor of the Hodgeses for $3,474, together with costs of $56 plus interest. . . .

[Both parties appealed] to the Court of Appeals. . . . The Court of Appeals reversed . . . and held as a matter of law that the implied warranty of merchantability on a used vehicle extends only to "the operation of major components that are necessary for the vehicle to operate, such as the engine and transmission." The court further held that "it is the responsibility of the buyer to ensure that the components incidental to operation are in working condition."

This court granted the Hodgeses' petition for review.

IMPLIED WARRANTY OF MERCHANTABILITY

Kansas' implied warranty of merchantability is contained in K.S.A. 84-2-314, which states that "a warranty that the goods shall be merchantable is implied in a contract for their sale if the seller is a merchant with respect to goods of that kind." K.S.A. 84-2-314(1). The statute further states that in order for goods to be "merchantable," they must be "at least such as . . . are fit for the ordinary purposes for which such goods are used." K.S.A. 84-2-314(2)(c).

ANALYSIS

The comments to K.S.A. 84-2-314 make clear that this implied warranty of merchantability applies by operation of law to "all sales by merchants" and "arises from the fact of the sale." K.S.A. 84-2-314, Kansas Comment 1. Applying this standard to the facts before us, it is clear that the transaction in this case—the sale of the Mercedes by Johnson to the Hodgeses—fits within the implied warranty. There is no dispute that Johnson is a merchant dealing in the sale of used vehicles or that the Mercedes is a "good" within the meaning of the statute. Thus, when Johnson sold the Mercedes to the Hodgeses, he implicitly warranted that the Mercedes would be "merchantable."

The Court of Appeals majority recognized that the sale of the Mercedes triggered the implied warranty but concluded as a matter of law under K.S.A. 84-2-314(2) that the vehicle's air conditioner was not covered by the warranty because the air conditioner did not affect the vehicle's merchantability. To reach this conclusion, the majority employed a three-part syllogism: First, for goods to be merchantable under the statute, they must be "fit for the ordinary purposes for which such goods are used." K.S.A. 84-2-314(2)(c). Second, the majority concluded that the primary purpose for which used vehicles are used is transportation; thus only the major components of a vehicle that bear upon its ability to effectively transport people from one location to another affect the vehicle's merchantability. Finally, the majority interpreted our past cases involving the warranty of merchantability in the sale of used vehicles to suggest that the warranty may not apply "unless a major component or several components are defective, causing the vehicle to become virtually inoperable." [*Hodges*,] 39 Kan. App. 2d at 225.

Applying this syllogism, the Court of Appeals majority determined that the air conditioner was not a major component of the Mercedes and thus did not impair the primary purpose for which used cars are employed:

"An air conditioner is not a major component of a car that is 10 years old with over 135,000 miles on it. . . . We find no implied warranty of merchantability, considering the age of the car, the high mileage, and the fact that the Hodges provided no proof that the air conditioner did not work when they purchased the vehicle." *Hodges,* 39 Kan. App. 2d at 225.

This conclusion is not supported by the case law. Although it may be that the implied warranty of merchantability does not extend to some components of a used vehicle in a particular transaction, this is a case-by-case determination in most cases—not a question of law. . . .

The Court of Appeals majority's approach is similarly unsupported by the statutes. K.S.A. 84-2-314(2)(c) defines merchantable goods as goods that are "fit for the ordinary *purposes* for which such goods are used." (Emphasis added.) The Court of Appeals interpreted this provision to mean that a used vehicle must be fit for the *primary* purpose of transportation. This interpretation is inconsistent with the plain language of K.S.A. 84-2-314(2)(c), which clearly contemplates goods that may be put to more than one use. Although there can be little doubt that the *primary* purpose of a vehicle is transportation, the Court of Appeals' opinion ignores the reality that a buyer may purchase a particular vehicle for a number of other purposes—among which may be safety, fuel economy, utility, or *comfort* in traveling to and from various destinations. . ..

The determination as to whether the implied warranty has been breached turns on a number of factors, including "[t]he buyer's knowledge that the goods are used, the extent of their prior use, and whether the goods are significantly discounted." [*International Petroleum Services*,] 230 Kan. at 457.

The broad range of used goods that may be covered by the implied warranty of merchantability underscores the wisdom of this court's previous recognition that a "late model, low mileage car, sold at a premium price, is expected to be in far better condition and to last longer than an old, high mileage, 'rough' car that is sold for little above its scrap value." *Dale,* 234 Kan. at 844. In this case, we have a 1995 Mercedes S320 with 135,945 miles selling for $17,020 in 2005. Johnson related to the buyer that it was a nice car in good condition; Dr. Hodges testified that he was told the car "was pretty much a perfect car." In short, this vehicle falls somewhere between the extremes of a "late model, low mileage car, sold at a premium price" and "an old, high mileage, 'rough' car . . . sold for little above its scrap value." 234 Kan. at 844. . . .

The question remaining to be resolved is not the existence of this warranty, but rather the *extent of the seller's obligation* under the warranty. Because this case does not involve either extreme on the spectrum of used vehicles, the resolution of this question is not a question of law, but rather a factual determination. . . .

To demonstrate a breach of the implied warranty of merchantability, a plaintiff must show that the purchased goods were defective, that the defect was present when the goods left the seller's control, and that the defect caused the injury sustained by the plaintiff. The circumstantial evidence in this case is sufficient to establish that the defect in the air conditioner existed at the time of sale. In 2003, 2 years before the Hodgeses purchased the vehicle, the Mercedes' air conditioner failed while Johnson was using it as his personal vehicle. Johnson insisted that his mechanic, against the mechanic's advice, use a product called Super Seal to fix the problem. The Hodgeses discovered that the air conditioner was again defective as soon as the weather became warm enough to require climate control. The use of the Super Seal, the strong odor emanating from the vehicle's ventilation system immediately after the sale, and the complete breakdown of the air conditioner when the buyer first attempted to use it all tend to establish that it was defective at the time of sale. While Johnson may not have known that the Mercedes' air conditioner was defective when he sold the vehicle to the Hodgeses, there is no requirement that a buyer establish that the seller knew of a defective component at the time of sale to trigger the implied warranty.

With regard to damages[:] ". . . . As concerns used or secondhand goods it is generally understood that the measure of damages is the cost of repair when repair is possible." *International Petroleum Services,* 230 Kan. at 460.

We find that there is substantial competent evidence to support the district court's conclusion that the implied warranty of merchantability in this transaction was not limited to only the Mercedes' major components affecting transportation, but rather extended at a minimum to the vehicle's air conditioning unit. We also find that there was substantial competent evidence to demonstrate that the air conditioning unit was defective at the time of sale and that the required repairs would cost $3,474. Accordingly, we reverse the Court of Appeals' reversal of the district court's judgment in favor of the Hodgeses and affirm the district court's decision.

Questions

1. Why did the court of appeals rule for Johnson?
2. Why did the Kansas Supreme Court reverse the court of appeals' judgment that the vehicle's air conditioner was not covered by a warranty?
3. What test did the Kansas Supreme Court employ to determine whether the implied warranty of merchantability had been breached?
4. How would the Kansas Supreme Court determine when a used car would be protected by the implied warranty of merchantability?
5. In buying a new motor home, Leavitt told the dealer he wanted to have plenty of power and braking capacity for driving in the mountains. He was assured by the dealer on both counts. He brought the motor home and found it unsatisfactory for mountain use. After many warranty repairs, he sued for breach of warranty.
   a. What warranty was breached, according to Leavitt?
   b. Decide the case. Explain. See *Leavitt v. Monaco Coach,* 616 N.W.2d 175 (Mich. Ct. App. 2000).
6. Douglas Kolarik alleged that he used several imported, pimento-stuffed green olives in a salad. In eating the salad, he bit down on an olive pit and fractured a tooth. The olive jar label included the words "minced pimento stuffed." The defendants were importers and wholesalers of Spanish olives that reach the defendants in barrels and are then inspected for general appearance, acid level, washed, and placed in glass jars suitable for distribution for the purpose of retail sales.
   a. What legal claim would be expected from the plaintiff based on the "minced pimento stuffed" language?
   b. Decide the case. Explain. See *Kolarik v. Cory International,* 721 N.W.2d 159 (Iowa 2006).

Skoal and Copenhagen

Bobby Hill of Canton, North Carolina, began chewing tobacco at age 13. He died of mouth cancer in 2003 at age 42. U.S. Smokeless Tobacco Co., makers of Skoal and Copenhagen, agreed in 2010 to pay Hill's family $5 million to settle the relatives' wrongful death claim. Apparently, the settlement was the first of its kind involving smokeless tobacco. Then, in 2018, the family of deceased Hall of Fame baseball player Tony Gwynn settled its wrongful death lawsuit against U.S. Smokeless Tobacco Co. for an undisclosed sum. Gwynn died at age 54 of salivary gland cancer. According to his family, Gwynn was "hopelessly addicted." He had used smokeless tobacco since 1977, about 10 years before health warnings appeared on those products.

Sources: Associated Press, "First Lawsuit Won on Chewing Tobacco," *The Des Moines Register,* December 8, 2010, p. 7A; and Brent Schrotenboer, "Tony Gwynn Family Reaches Settlement with Tobacco Company over His Death," *USA TODAY,* September 7, 2018 [**www.usatoday.com**].

Strict Liability

Sometimes things happen that businesses can neither prevent nor even explain, and yet liability may attach. Assume you operate a clothing store. A customer enters and decides to try on a pair of slacks. You show her to the dressing room. Soon after, you hear a scream from the room. Your customer has been bitten by a spider. Not surprisingly, she thinks the blame lies with your store. She sues, but her negligence and breach of warranty claims are rejected by the court. (Can you explain why those claims fail?) Finally, your customer raises a strict liability in tort argument, but the court denies that claim also. Read the overview of strict liability that follows and think about why the court denied her claim. See *Flippo v. Mode O'Day Frock Shops of Hollywood,* 449 S.W.2d 692 (Ark. 1970).

Your customer has been bitten by a spider.

Strict Liability: Overview

LO 7-10 Identify the elements of a strict liability cause of action.

Negligence and warranty claims are helpful to the harmed consumer. However, rapid changes in the nature of commercial practice, as well as an increasing societal concern for consumer protection, have led the legal community to gradually embrace yet another cause of action. Strict liability in tort offers the prospect of holding all of those in the chain of distribution liable for damages resulting from a defective product, rather than imposing the entire burden on the injured consumer. Manufacturers and sellers are best positioned to prevent the distribution of defective products, and they are best able to bear the cost of injury by spreading the loss via pricing policies and insurance coverage.

Strict liability as an independent tort emerged in 1963 in the famous California case of *Greenman v. Yuba Power Products, Inc.*[36] In the ensuing years, most states have adopted strict liability in concept. The essence of the strict liability notion is expressed in Section 402A of the *Restatement of Torts, Second.* In brief, Section 402A imposes liability where a product is sold in a defective condition and is unreasonably dangerous to the user.

Section 402A Special Liability of Seller of Product for Physical Harm to User or Consumer

1. One who sells any product in a defective condition, unreasonably dangerous to the user or consumer or to his property, is subject to liability for physical harm thereby caused to the ultimate user or consumer, or to his property, if
   a. the seller is engaged in the business of selling such a product, and,
   b. it is expected to and does reach the user or consumer without substantial change in the condition in which it is sold.
2. The rule stated in Subsection (1) applies although
   a. the seller has exercised all possible care in the preparation and sale of his product, and
   b. the user or consumer has not bought the product from or entered into any contractual relation with the seller.

Thus, strict liability does not require proof that the defendant was negligent. Strict liability law focuses on the condition of the product, rather than the conduct of the parties. Therefore, a seller who is free of actual fault may, nonetheless, be liable for injuries caused by a defective and unreasonably dangerous product. The Aim N Flame lighter case that follows considers the conditions under which a strict liability claim may be raised.

Calles v. Scripto-Tokai

864 N.E.2d 249 (Ill. 2007)

Justice Burke

On March 31, 1998, plaintiff Susan Calles resided with her four daughters, Amanda, age 11, Victoria, age 5, and twins Jenna and Jillian, age 3. At some point that night, Calles left her home with Victoria to get videos for Amanda. When she left, the twins were in bed and Amanda was watching television. Calles returned to find fire trucks and emergency vehicles around her home. It was subsequently determined by a fire investigator, Robert Finn, that Jenna had started a fire using an Aim N Flame utility lighter Calles had purchased approximately one week earlier. The Aim N Flame was ignited by pulling a trigger after an "ON/OFF" switch was slid to the "on" position. As a result of the fire, Jillian suffered smoke inhalation. She was hospitalized and died on April 21.

Calles filed suit against Tokai, designer and manufacturer of the Aim N Flame, and Scripto-Tokai, distributor (collectively Scripto), alleging that the Aim N Flame was defectively designed and unreasonably dangerous because it did not contain a child-resistant safety device. According to the complaint, a safety device was available, inexpensive, and would have reduced the risk that children could ignite the lighter. Calles's claims sounded in strict liability.

Thereafter, Scripto filed a motion for summary judgment. . . . In her deposition, Calles admitted she was aware of the risks and dangers presented by lighters in the hands of children, and for this reason, she stored the Aim N Flames on the top shelf of her kitchen cabinet. Calles further admitted that the Aim N Flame operated as intended and expected.

In opposition to Scripto's motion for summary judgment, Calles offered affidavits from several experts. . . . All of [the] experts opined that the Aim N Flame was defective and unreasonably dangerous because it lacked a child-resistant design. They also opined that a technologically and economically feasible alternative design, which included a child-resistant safety device, existed at the time the Aim N Flame was manufactured. Several of the experts averred that Scripto was aware of the desirability of a child-safety device because it knew children could operate the Aim N Flame. Further, according to these experts, Scripto owned the technology to make the Aim N Flame child resistant in 1994 and 1995.

With respect to the cost of an alternative design, . . . the Consumer Product Safety Commission, the regulatory body for lighters, estimated the increased cost of adding a safety device to the lighter would be $0.40 per unit. However [one of Calles's experts estimated], the cost would have been negligible.

Calles also offered evidence of the dangerousness of lighters in the hands of children and Scripto's awareness of such dangers. . . . Scripto admitted they had been named as defendants in 25 lawsuits filed between 1996 and 2000 for injuries that occurred between 1992 and 1999 under circumstances similar to this case.

The trial court granted summary judgment in favor of Scripto. . . .

On appeal, the appellate court . . . reversed [the trial court's summary judgment in favor of Scripto . . .].

STRICT LIABILITY

[T]his court adopted the strict liability doctrine set forth in section 402A of the Second Restatement of Torts. Under this doctrine, strict liability is imposed upon a seller of "any product in a defective condition unreasonably dangerous to the user or consumer or to his property." The test outlined in section 402A for determining whether a product is "unreasonably dangerous" is known as the consumer-expectation test. This test provides that a product is "unreasonably dangerous" when it is "dangerous to an extent beyond that which would be contemplated by the ordinary consumer who purchases it, with the ordinary knowledge common to the community as to its characteristics."

An ordinary consumer would expect that a child could obtain possession of the Aim N Flame and attempt to use it. Thus, a child is a reasonably foreseeable user. Likewise, an ordinary consumer would appreciate the consequences that would naturally flow when a child obtains possession of a lighter. . . .

Under the facts of this case, the Aim N Flame performed as an ordinary consumer would expect—it produced a flame when used in a reasonably foreseeable manner, i.e., by a child. This leads to the inescapable conclusion that the ordinary consumer's expectations were fulfilled. . . . Thus, as a matter of law, no fact finder could conclude that the Aim N Flame was unreasonably dangerous under the consumer-expectation test. Therefore, Calles cannot prevail under this theory.

This does not end our analysis, however. Though the Aim N Flame satisfies the consumer-expectation test, it may, nonetheless, be deemed unreasonably dangerous under the risk–utility test.

RISK–UTILITY TEST

Under the risk–utility test, a plaintiff may prevail in a strict liability design-defect case if he or she demonstrates that the magnitude of the danger outweighs the utility of the product, as designed. . . .

Under the risk–utility test, a court may take into consideration numerous factors. In past decisions, this court has held that a plaintiff may prove a design defect by presenting evidence of "the availability and feasibility of alternate designs at the time of its manufacture, or that the design used did not conform with the design standards of the industry. . . ."

UNIT THREE

Trade Regulation and Antitrust

CHAPTER EIGHT

Government Regulation of Business

After completing this chapter, students will be able to fulfill the following learning objectives:

8-1. Explain some of the considerations involved in deciding to impose government regulations on business practices.

8-2. Describe the concept of market failure.

8-3. Contrast the constitutional power granted to Congress under the Commerce Clause with the police powers reserved to the States.

8-4. Explain when the federal government has exceeded its authority in regulating commerce.

8-5. Explain the relationship between the Supremacy Clause and the concept of preemption.

8-6. Recognize when Congress has unconstitutionally commandeered a State's legislative function.

8-7. Identify the circumstances in which the dormant Commerce Clause principle would apply.

8-8. Describe some of the ways in which state and local regulations affect business practice.

8-9. List some of the federal agencies that regulate business practice.

8-10. Explain why administrative agencies are created.

8-11. Identify the three broad categories of federal regulatory agencies' authority.

8-12. Compare and contrast the federal agencies' executive, legislative, and judicial roles.

8-13. Describe the executive, congressional, and judicial controls placed on agency conduct to maintain appropriate "checks and balances."

Part One—An Introduction

PRACTICING ETHICS
COVID-19 and Essential Workers at America's Meat Processing Plants

By mid-April 2020, about 150 of the largest meat processing plants in the United States accounted for at least 2,200 known cases of COVID-19 and 17 deaths, becoming a national concern alongside long-term care facilities.

- Among the workers at a Wayne Farms plant in Albertville, Alabama, 75 tested positive and one death occurred.
- Smithfield's Sioux Falls, Iowa, plant had more than 200 confirmed cases before it closed. Ten days later the count was approaching 900, making it then the largest cluster of COVID-19 cases in the country.
- A JBS plant in Grand Island, Nebraska, remained open despite 237 workers having tested positive. By mid-May, one-quarter of Nebraska's confirmed COVID-19 cases were employees at meat processing plants.
- Nationally, there was a significant correlation between high countywide rates of COVID-19 infection and the presence of a meat processing plant nearby. The counties surrounding more than one third of these plants had rates of infection in the top quartile of all U.S. counties.

During this period, more than a dozen meat processing facilities were closed—not as a result of government intervention but often as attempts by companies to contain the outbreaks, and at times as a result of union pressure and worker protests. At the Tyson Foods plant in Waterloo, Iowa, closure "was forced on the company as employees refused to go to work after colleagues contacted the disease. . . . In explaining the decision [to close, the company] cited 'worker absenteeism, COVID-19 cases and community concerns.'"[1] In a statement troubling to the deeply worried workforce, Iowa's governor "warned that workers who did not return to work [when the plant reopened] would be considered a 'voluntary quit' and not be eligible for unemployment benefits."[2]

Even before the pandemic, the industry was known for its poor working conditions, with its employees having one of the highest rates of illness in the manufacturing sector at nearly 160 cases per 10,000 full-time employees, as compared to an overall sector average of 40 cases. This is grueling work accompanied by low wages—an average of $11 per hour at poultry plants. Elose Willis, the first employee to die from COVID-19 at the Tyson Foods poultry plant in Camilla, Georgia, was 56 and had spent 35 years working at the plant, five days a week, 10 hours a day, slaughtering 100,000 chickens a shift.

Federal Action?

At the federal level, the Occupational Safety and Health Administration's (OSHA) charge is "to ensure safe and healthful working conditions for working men and women by setting and enforcing standards."[3] Nonetheless, its COVID-19 standards for the meat processing industry, issued in conjunction with the Centers for Disease Control and Prevention (CDC) on May 12, 2020, were not mandatory but merely "guidance." More than a year later, OSHA still had not issued any orders with regard to, nor had it increased inspections or enforcement in light of, COVID-19's appearance in meat processing facilities [for more on OSHA, see **www.osha.gov**].

In the midst of the pandemic, while workers at poultry processing plants were struggling with the impacts of COVID-19, the U.S. Department of Agriculture (USDA) made some of their work situations even worse by granting the permission requested by 15 plants to increase their line speeds, boosting the birds per minute workers had to process above the established federal limit. Former chief of staff and senior policy advisor at OSHA Debbie Berkowitz said the USDA "did this behind closed doors with no input by the public and no consideration to the impact on food or workers' safety."[4] Increased speeds are known to increase injuries for line workers.

Just as it failed to set mandatory industry standards for the protection of workers at meat processing plants, OSHA failed to oversee even the application of its guidance by directing those plants "to work directly with appropriate state and local public health officials"[5] in developing plans for continuing operations in the wake of COVID-19 outbreaks among their workers. The results of that directive demonstrate OHSA's substantial abdication of its duty to "ensure safe and healthful working conditions."

- In Iowa, during late May 2020, a complaint was filed with the state's OSHA equivalent about a Tyson Foods plant. The regulator declined to inspect the facility, choosing instead to send an inquiry. The agency concluded, from the response it received over two weeks later, that Tyson's voluntary efforts for social distancing were satisfactory. Within a week, almost 60 percent of the Tyson workforce tested positive for the virus.

- The state of Kansas eliminated its previously required two-week quarantine for workers exposed to the virus, replacing it with OSHA's more lenient approach, which permitted companies to allow exposed workers to continue on the job as long as they have no symptoms and were using appropriate precautions.
- Internal emails from state and local government health agencies obtained in response to public records requests revealed "the deference some county officials have shown toward the giant meatpacking companies and how little power they have in pushing the companies to stem outbreaks."[6]

The CDC has an established hierarchy of controls regarding exposure to occupational hazards generally. The lowest, least effective control is the use of personal protective equipment (PPE), such as medical masks or face shields.

More effective than PPE are "administrative controls." Among those meat processing plants "should do" under the issued guidance are

- Stagger break times or provide temporary break areas and restrooms to avoid gatherings of workers during breaks;
- Stagger arrival and departure times to avoid congregations in parking areas, locker rooms, and near time clocks;
- Provide workers access to soap, clean running water, and single-use paper towels; and
- Provide hand sanitizers in multiple locations to encourage hygiene.

In addition, plants should "review" or "consider" modifying sick leave policies so ill employees do not come to work, are not penalized for taking sick leave if they have COVID-19, are permitted to draw on future sick leave, and can donate sick leave to others.

The CDC rates "engineering controls" as more effective than both administrative controls and PPE; yet in its published guidance for COVID-19, it expressed them with qualifiers, such as "if possible" and "if feasible." These controls include

- Configuring the work area so workers are spaced at least six feet apart in all directions, particularly in face-to-face settings;
- Installing impermeable dividers, such as plexiglass, between workers;
- Minimizing air flows from fans that blow from one worker directly at another; and
- Removing and rearranging chairs and tables in break rooms and adding partitions to permit proper distancing.

Listed under administrative controls in the context of performing COVID-19 risk assessments and creating control plans, "facilities should consider the appropriate role for testing and workplace contact tracing."[7]

Questions

1. If you had a family member employed at the Waterloo, Iowa, Tyson Foods plant discussed above, would you have wanted them to continue working there? How would you feel about the Governor's pronouncement that, if they didn't return to work because of health fears, they would be denied unemployment compensation?
2. Early reports of the severity of the COVID-19 outbreaks in meat processing plants implied that, as a nation, our choice was either to subject these workers (and their families and communities) to a high risk of infection, with the concomitant risk of death, or to suffer "the specter of mass meat shortages" in grocery stores.[8] For context, by the time the news media reported the gravity of the problem in meat processing plants, it had already alerted the world that the pandemic in Italy was so advanced that China had sent doctors and substantial medical supplies to help combat the outbreak.

   In your judgment, is it ethical to knowingly impose a substantially heightened risk of grave illness or death on plant workers to keep beef, pork, and chicken in supermarkets? Explain.
3. Most of the COVID-19 standards provided by federal, state, and local governments were identified as guidance only; they did not legally bind businesses to take any action. In that light, what do you think about the statement, "If these meat plants can't be held liable, there is no reason for them to take measures to ensure workers are safe. . . . If these workers are essential, protect them. They are being treated like fungible widgets instead of human beings."[9] Explain.
4. Not surprisingly, COVID-19-related issues most severely impacted our most vulnerable populations, including the working poor, who disproportionately comprise people of color and immigrants. Is it ethical for the government to

issue only nonbinding guidance, rather than enforceable standards, in circumstances in which the decision makers who will act on the guidance disproportionately come from advantaged groups? Explain.

5. As described above, OSHA's mission is "to ensure safe and healthful working conditions for working men and women by setting and enforcing standards." Yet the standards published by OSHA and the CDC during the height of the pandemic were guidelines only, without the force of law. By issuing guidance instead of enforceable standards and by leaving states or local governments to negotiate with meat processing plants, did OSHA fail in its duty to workers in those plants? Could state and local governments protect these workers as effectively as OSHA when those governments have concerns they must take into account beyond the protection of workers (such as keeping a major source of jobs and tax revenues in the community)? Explain.
6. Consider the list of "engineering controls" presented above, controls which OSHA and the CDC evaluate as "the most effective." How onerous to the meat processing companies are they? Other than the cost of workplace modifications and the revenues lost while they are put in place, what impacts might the companies experience from implementing those controls? Explain.
7. Assume that, upon reopening the economy, returning office workers across all sectors began contracting COVID-19 at rates similar to that experienced in meat processing plants at the beginning of the pandemic. Further assume that the increase is attributable, in large part, to HVAC (heating, ventilating, and air conditioning) systems and that safety could be dramatically improved by modifying or replacing those costly systems. Would you expect OSHA to issue nonbinding guidance for building owners to merely consider in responding to the outbreaks? Explain.

Sources: Kyle Bagenstose, Sky Chadde, and Matt Wynn, "Coronavirus at meatpacking plants worse than first thought," *USA Today,* April 22, 2020 [**www.usatoday.com**]; Elizabeth Merrill, "Football and the factory line: Living at risk in a heartland hot zone," *National Geographic,* May 20, 2020 [**www.nationalgeographic.com**]; Jeet Heer, "Meatpacking Plants Are a Front in the Covid-19 Class War," *The Nation,* April 29, 2020 [**www.thenation.com**]; Deena Shanker and Polly Mosendz, "America's Chicken Industry Accused of Conspiring to Keep Immigrant Wages Down," *Bloomberg,* September 3, 2019 [**www.bloomberg.com**]; "'We're modern slaves': How meat plant workers became the new frontline in Covid-19 war," *The Guardian,* May 2, 2020 [**www.theguardian.com**]; "About OSHA," Occupational Safety and Health Administration, accessed August, 2020 [**www.osha.gov**]; "Meat and Poultry Processing Workers and Employers Interim Guidance," Centers for Disease Control and Prevention, accessed July, 2020 [**www.cdc.gov**]; Amy Forliti, "Meatpacking safety recommendations are largely unenforceable," *The Spokesman-Review,* May 21, 2020 [**www.spokesman.com**]; Michael Corkery, David Yaffe-Bellany, and Derek Kravitz, "As Meatpacking Plants Reopen, Data About Worker Illness Remains Elusive," *The New York Times,* May 25, 2020 [**www.nytimes.com**]; and National Institute of Occupational Safety and Health, "Hierarchy of Controls," *Centers for Disease Control and Prevention* [**www.cdc.gov**].

Question

Workers at meat processing plants during the first year of the COVID pandemic were considered "essential" workers under the Department of Homeland Security's List of Critical Infrastructure Workers because they are "food processing workers," a subcategory of "food and agriculture workers."[10] Presumably they are essential because they perform services necessary for the well-being of the whole country. Given that, what should have been done to respond to the demands made on them to ensure their continued service on our behalf? A **Research Exercise** at the end of this chapter provides an opportunity for you to investigate this question.

How Much Government?

This chapter and all those that follow are directed to the central question of this book: How much government do we need? In the first three chapters, the roles of the free market and ethics as "regulators" of business behavior were considered. The foundations of the

American legal system were discussed in Chapters 4 through 7. Now, the role government plays in supplementing the market and business ethics is explored. The COVID-19 pandemic provides a glimpse of the complex relationships among business, government, and society. In it can be seen the juggling act involved in mitigating the impact of a microscopic viral invader on us, our families, and our communities, while balancing its effects on businesses—both those that were fully or substantially shut down and those trying to run full-out as providers of essential goods and services. All of this was made more challenging by the intertwining allocation of powers and duties among federal, state, and local governments. As discussed later, the foundation for the allocation of government power is the Constitution.

Beyond coping with pandemics, America's public policy concerns are many: economic stability; wealth, income, and opportunity inequalities; health care availability and cost; and climate change, to name a few. Do we need more, different, or fewer rules to address these problems ? Or can the invisible hand of the market, in combination with business ethics and social responsibility, provide an effective response? How do we decide when a new rule is needed? Equally important, when should an old rule be abandoned?

Why Regulation?

Market Failure

LO 8-1 Explain some of the considerations involved in deciding to impose government regulations on business practices.

In theory, government intervention in a free-enterprise economy is justified only when the market is unable to serve the public interest—that is, in instances of market failure. Market failure results from certain imperfections inherent in the market itself.

Imperfect Information

Reasoned decisions require adequate information. Because the market cannot provide perfect information and often fails to provide even adequate information, governments sometimes impose regulations to improve the available information or to diminish the unfavorable effects of inadequate information. Hence, there are, for example, mandates for labeling consumer goods, licensure requirements for many occupations, and health standards for the processing and sale of food.

LO 8-2 Describe the concept of market failure.

Are Markets Rational?

Can we make rational, efficient decisions in the absence of good information? Research demonstrates that we often face situations of *asymmetric information* where some parties to a transaction simply know more than the other parties to that transaction, with the result that optimal efficiency cannot be achieved. For example, the public has generally been unaware of the lead and cadmium found in dark chocolate, although the industry knew of the issue well before 2018. [For a court-approved settlement of a case under California's food labeling laws with regard to lead and cadmium in many widely available chocolate bars, see **www.asyousow.org/press-releases/2018/2/14/court-establishes-guidelines-for-chocolate-sold-in-california**.]

Beyond information deficiencies, the standard view of market rationality is questioned in other ways. For example, research in behavioral economics suggests that people often altruistically pursue social goals rather than simply maximizing their economic interests, as might be expected. Studies indicate that risk-taking by male financial traders increases as testosterone and cortisol levels climb, thus threatening market stability and supporting the view that financial decisions may be less rational than long believed.[11] The free market system assumes rational decision making, but people operate with *bounded rationality.* Hence, government intervention is appropriate and needed at times.

Externalities

When all the costs and/or benefits of an action or transaction are not fully internalized (absorbed) by the actor or the parties to the transaction, those costs or benefits fall elsewhere, creating what economists call *externalities, neighborhood effects,* or *spillovers.* Pollution is a classic example of a *negative externality.* The environment is often used without charge as an ingredient in the production process (commonly as a receptacle for waste). Consequently, the product is underpriced. The producer and consumer do not pay the full social cost of the product, thrusting the remaining costs on parties external to the transaction. Government regulation may step in to place the full cost on those who generated it, for example, by requiring the implementation of pollution-control practices, which should result in a decrease in pollution.

Private solutions to externalities also exist, such as through moral codes that promote a change in an actor's behavior, which reduces its impact on others. A business might, for example, voluntarily adopt sustainable business practices to reduce its environmental footprint, as have Patagonia and many other Certified B Corporations. [For more on Certified B Corporations, see **https://usca.bcorporation.net.**]

Positive externalities result when the actor or the parties to a transaction do not receive the full benefit of the action or transaction because a portion of those benefits "spills over" onto third parties who were not direct participants. For example, a positive externality results when a business decides to buy more of its inputs locally. From its point of view, production expenses are being reduced through lower transportation costs. But third parties benefit from the environmental improvement derived from reduced fossil-fuel emissions. Some positive externalities are mandated by regulation. For example, to have its development approved, a builder may be required to incorporate a bike path or significant green space into its design.

Burgers and Negative Externalities

Food journalist Mark Bittman argued that fast-food chains would have to raise prices significantly if they were forced to pay the full cost to society of their food. In 2014, he estimated that the negative externalities associated with producing one hamburger (such as carbon emissions from raising cows, obesity, and other health risks) cost between $.68 and $2.90 ($.85 and $3.62 in inflation-adjusted dollars as of this writing).

Source: *Mark Bittman,* "The True Cost of a Burger," *The New York Times,* July 15, 2014 [**www.nytimes.com**].

Public Goods

Some goods and services cannot be provided through the market's pricing system because there is no method for excluding those who choose not to pay from enjoying the benefits. These *public goods* include national defense, insect eradication, street lighting, and pollution control, as well as public schools and libraries. Presumably, most individuals would refuse to voluntarily pay for what others would receive free. Thus, in the absence of government action, public goods would not be produced in adequate quantities.

Monopoly

The government also intervenes to thwart anticompetitive behaviors (such as price-fixing and abuse of market dominance) throughout the marketplace. The concern is that the efficiency and fairness advantages of an open market will be compromised by large, powerful players and by conspiracies among competitors. The government plays the role of referee in creating and enforcing rules that curb such conduct, attempting to sustain the virtues of the free market.

Question

Which of the above market failures applied to the situation at meat packing plants at the start of the COVID pandemic?

Regulatory Life Cycle?

These market failures, and other forces explained later, sometimes lead to government intervention. Examples include the Clean Air Act and the Occupational Safety and Health Act. Dean emeritus and law school professor Joseph Tomain argued that a rather predictable pattern, or life cycle, typically emerges when the government decides to regulate an industry. Stage One is the free market itself, the period during which government regulation is absent from the industry's market. In Stage Two, a market failure is identified, suggesting the need for government intervention. In Stage Three, government regulation is imposed in the form of a rule (such as a minimum drinking age). In Stage Four, regulatory failure occurs when the benefits of the rule in question no longer exceed its costs. In Stage Five, the government may respond with regulatory reform to correct the failure, or it may move to Stage Six, simply eliminating the regulation. After Stage Six, the market has been fully deregulated, returning it to Stage One (the free market), and the regulatory life cycle is complete.[12] Note, however, that is notoriously difficult to reach Stage Six, as will be seen in Part Four of this chapter.

Tomain's regulatory cycle can be illustrated by the experience of the U.S. airline industry. Originally, the government regulated routes and fares. That regulation ended in 1978. Following deregulation, low-cost carriers entered the market. Some carriers could not compete and went out of business, but air travel became much more broadly available to the general public. In 2016, traveler advocate Charles Leocha argued that some re-regulation could benefit consumers, with which anyone caught in Southwest Airlines' debacle over the 2022 winter break might agree:[13]

> Airlines should be held to their schedules. In Europe, all are punished for delays in service and consumers are compensated. . . . Egregiously outrageous fees such as $200 to $450 for cancellation of flights should be limited to a reasonable amount. . . . The Department of Transportation should require that airlines disclose all . . . fees so consumers are able to comparison shop on more than just airfare alone.[14]

Theory and Practice

The correction of market failure is a powerful motivation for government regulation based on economic theory. But others have their own motivations for or against regulation. Many parties are involved when a regulatory regime is established or modified, whether by a legislative body, an administrative agency, or other portions of the executive branch of government. These individual motivations may be theoretical, practical, or personal. Three will be considered here: the Constitution, industry, and bureaucrats.

The Constitution The Preamble of the Constitution provides compelling motivations in the identification of its own purposes, which include the establishment of justice and promotion of the general welfare. Thus, we find the government engaging in regulatory efforts designed to achieve, for example, a more equitable distribution of income and wealth (such as Social Security and the minimum wage). Government intervention in the market has been used repeatedly to stabilize the economy, as it did during the Great Depression and the Great Recession of 2008, and as it has attempted in response to the COVID-19 pandemic; for example, in the closure of nonessential businesses. Affirmative action legislation seeks to address the historical impacts of racism and sexism. At times the government even requires people to protect themselves, both for their personal benefit and for the well-being of the larger society (consider seat belt and helmet laws, laws prohibiting the sale of tobacco and alcohol to minors, and required school attendance).

Industry Sometimes regulations are requested by an industry for its own benefit. One illustration is the licensure requirements for many professions, which not only protect the public from unqualified practitioners but also effectively reduce competition. Some public utilities, such as electric and gas companies, have even achieved the complete elimination of competitors by the creation of geographic monopolies regulated by state public utility commissions.

Bureaucrats Another motivation, which promotes regulatory expansion, is the desire of entrenched bureaucrats to secure and maintain or expand their positions of power and employment.

PRACTICING ETHICS — Revolving Doors, Regulatory Capture, and Iron Triangles?

In 2014, Rohit Bansal moved from his government job at the New York Federal Reserve Bank to Wall Street's Goldman Sachs, which is regulated by the Federal Reserve. Bansal reportedly had been coached by Goldman Sachs executive Joseph Jiampietro about how to get the new job. Then, after making the move, Bansal allegedly obtained leaked Federal Reserve documents and passed them to Jiampietro. When the leaks were discovered, Bansal was fired by Goldman Sachs. He pleaded guilty to misdemeanor criminal charges and was permanently banned from the banking industry. Goldman Sachs was fined over $86 million. Jiampietro was fired by Goldman Sachs. He denies all of the allegations against him.

Bansal's story illustrates the danger in the "revolving doors" between government and industry. Regulators, like Bansal, often leave government to work for the industry they formerly regulated, and regulators often come from the very industry they are hired to control. Troublesome as these government-industry ties may seem, close associations between government agencies and the industries being regulated are needed. Each benefits from the expertise of the other. Federal conflict-of-interest laws impose some restrictions on private-sector work following government service.

Revolving doors encourage *regulatory capture*, a form of government failure that can occur when regulators are too cozy with the industry being regulated or when industry representatives have the interest and resources to offer detailed advice on agency business while the public voice, being much less focused and less well financed, is seldom or never heard by the agency.

A recent example of regulatory capture involved a partner, Dr. Jeff Smith, at McKinsey & Company, one of the "Big Three" management consulting firms. In December 2017, Smith accepted a highly sensitive assignment for Purdue Pharma. At the time he was also working with the Food and Drug Administration (FDA) in the office that approves new drugs—the office that would rule on Purdue's new lines of drugs. Documents obtained by *The New York Times* from a group of state attorneys general as part of a 2021 settlement of an investigation into McKinsey's work with Purdue and other opioid manufacturers disclosed that:

> Dr. Smith worked on more than 40 projects for the FDA between 2007 and 2019, while also serving Purdue in at least a half-dozen initiatives–advising the drugmaker on interactions with the regulator and, in one case, helping secure approval of a new opioid product.[15]

Political scientists argue that regulatory capture of both agencies and congressional committees sometimes produces a stable, nearly impregnable *iron triangle.* Powerful interest groups (often businesses like McKinsey) occupy one corner of the triangle, congressional committees are at another corner, and agency bureaucrats (like Bansal) occupy the third. In the resulting alliance, each group cultivates its own welfare by providing political support (from interest groups to members of Congress), by writing favorable laws (from Congress to interest groups), and by agency enforcement of those laws in ways favorable to the interest groups and Congress. The likely result is diminished attention to the public welfare.

Sources: Renae Merle, "How a Goldman Sachs Executive Allegedly Stole Government Data to Woo Clients," *The Washington Post,* August 4, 2016 [**www.washingtonpost.com**]; and Chris Hamby, Walt Bogdanich, Michael Forsythe, and Jennifer Valentino-DeVries, "McKinsey Opened a Door in Its Firewall Between Pharma Clients and Regulators," *The New York Times,* April 13, 2022 [**www.nytimes.com**].

The Constitutional Foundation of Business Regulation

LO 8-3
Contrast the constitutional power granted to Congress under the Commerce Clause with the police powers reserved to the States.

The Commerce Clause, Article I, Section 8 of the U.S. Constitution broadly specifies the power accorded with the federal government to regulate business activity: "Congress shall have the Power. . . . To regulate Commerce with foreign Nations, and among the several States, and with the Indian Tribes." State authority to regulate commerce derives from the Tenth Amendment's declaration that all "powers not delegated" to the federal government are "reserved to the States." Often referred to in the aggregate as the state's *police power,* it is a reference to the right of state governments to promote the public health, safety, morals, and general welfare by regulating persons and property within their jurisdictions. The states have, in turn, delegated portions of this power to local governments.

Commerce Clause Examined

The Commerce Clause, as interpreted by the judiciary, grants Congress exclusive jurisdiction over *foreign commerce.* If a state attempts, for example, to impose a tax on foreign goods that compete with those locally grown or manufactured, that effort violates the Commerce Clause and is thus unenforceable.

Federal authority over "commerce among the several states," that is, *interstate commerce,* affords the federal government very broad power to regulate commercial activities across the United States. It was designed to create an open, effectively borderless market throughout the nation, where goods and services move freely among the states, unimpeded by state and local tariffs, duties, or other interference. The Constitution does not, however, expressly forbid state regulation of interstate commerce. States and localities have passed laws impacting interstate commerce. If passed with the intention (or impact) of favoring local economic interests, they will likely be held unconstitutional, as will be further discussed in Part Two.

Even purely *intrastate* activities can be regulated by the federal government if they have a substantial effect on interstate commerce.

The classic decision that follows illustrates the importance of Commerce Clause reasoning. In this case, Congress used its economic authority under the Clause to open public accommodations (hotels, restaurants, and the like) to all persons, thus reshaping American social and racial practices.

LEGAL BRIEFCASE

Heart of Atlanta Motel v. United States 379 U.S. 241 (1964)

Justice Clark

This is a declaratory judgment action, attacking the constitutionality of Title II of the Civil Rights Act of 1964. [The lower court found for the United States.]

1. THE FACTUAL BACKGROUND AND CONTENTIONS OF THE PARTIES

. . . Appellant owns and operates the Heart of Atlanta Motel, which has 216 rooms available to transient guests. The motel is located on Courtland Street, two blocks from downtown Peachtree Street. It is readily accessible to interstate highways 75 and 85 and state highways 23 and 41. Appellant solicits patronage from outside the State of Georgia through various national advertising media, including magazines of national circulation; it maintains over 50 billboards and highway signs within the state, soliciting patronage for the motel; it accepts convention trade from outside Georgia, and approximately 75 percent of its registered guests are from out of state. Prior to passage of the act the motel had followed a practice of refusing to rent rooms to Negroes, and it alleged that it intended to continue to do so. In an effort to perpetuate that policy this suit was filed.

The appellant contends that Congress in passing this act exceeded its power to regulate commerce under [Article I] of the Constitution of the United States. . . .

The appellees counter that the unavailability to Negroes of adequate accommodations interferes significantly with interstate travel, and that Congress, under the Commerce Clause, has power to remove such obstructions and restraints. . . .

[A]ppellees proved the refusal of the motel to accept Negro transients after the passage of the act. The district court sustained the constitutionality of the sections of the act under attack and issued a permanent injunction. . . . It restrained the appellant from "[r]efusing to accept Negroes as guests in the motel by reason of their race or color" and from "[m]aking any distinction whatever upon the basis of race or color in the availability of the goods, services, facilities, privileges, advantages, or accommodations offered or made available to the guests of the motel, or to the general public, within or upon any of the premises of the Heart of Atlanta Motel, Inc."

2. THE HISTORY OF THE ACT

. . . The act as finally adopted was most comprehensive, undertaking to prevent through peaceful and voluntary settlement discrimination in voting, as well as in places of accommodation and public facilities, federally secured programs, and in employment. Since Title II is the only portion under attack here, we confine our consideration to those public accommodation provisions.

3. TITLE II OF THE ACT

This Title is divided into seven sections beginning with Section 201(a), which provides,

> All persons shall be entitled to the full and equal enjoyment of the goods, services, facilities, privileges, advantages, and accommodations of any place of public accommodation, as defined in this section, without discrimination or segregation on the ground of race, color, religion, or national origin.

4. APPLICATION OF TITLE II TO HEART OF ATLANTA MOTEL

It is admitted that the operation of the motel brings it within the provisions of Section 201(a) of the act and that appellant refused to provide lodging for transient Negroes because of their race or color and that it intends to continue that policy unless restrained.

The sole question posed is, therefore, the constitutionality of the Civil Rights Act of 1964 as applied to these facts. . . .

5. [omitted—ed.]

6. THE BASIS OF CONGRESSIONAL ACTION

While the act as adopted carried no congressional findings, the record of its passage through each house is replete with evidence of the burdens that discrimination by race or color places upon interstate commerce. . . . This testimony included the fact that our people have become increasingly mobile with millions of people of all races traveling from state to state; that Negroes in particular have been the subject of discrimination in transient accommodations, having to travel great distances to secure the same; that often they have been unable to obtain accommodations and have had to call upon friends to put them up overnight; and that these conditions have become so acute as to require the listing of available lodging for Negroes in a special guidebook which was itself "dramatic testimony to the difficulties" Negroes encounter in travel. These exclusionary practices were found to be nationwide, the Under Secretary of Commerce testifying that there is "no question that this discrimination in the North still exists to a large degree" and in the West and Midwest as well. This testimony indicated a qualitative as well as quantitative effect on interstate travel by Negroes. The former was the obvious impairment of the Negro traveler's pleasure and convenience that resulted when he continually was uncertain of finding lodging. As for the latter, there was evidence that this uncertainty stemming from racial discrimination had the effect of discouraging travel on the part of a substantial portion of the Negro community. This was the conclusion not only of the Under Secretary of Commerce but also of the Administrator of the Federal Aviation Agency, who wrote the Chairman of the Senate Commerce Committee that it was his "belief that air commerce is adversely affected by the denial to a substantial segment of the traveling public of adequate and desegregated public accommodations." We shall not burden this opinion with further details since the voluminous testimony presents overwhelming evidence that discrimination by hotels and motels impedes interstate travel.

7. THE POWER OF CONGRESS OVER INTERSTATE TRAVEL

The power of Congress to deal with these obstructions depends on the meaning of the Commerce Clause.

In short, the determinative test of the exercise of power by the Congress under the Commerce Clause is simply whether the activity sought to be regulated is "commerce which concerns more States than one" and has a real and substantial relation to the national interest. Let us now turn to this facet of the problem.

The same interest in protecting interstate commerce which led Congress to deal with segregation in interstate carriers and the white-slave traffic has prompted it to extend the exercise of its power to gambling, to criminal enterprises, to deceptive practices in the sale of products, to fraudulent security transactions, and to racial discrimination by owners and managers of terminal restaurants. . . .

That Congress was legislating against moral wrongs in many of these areas rendered its enactments no less valid. In framing Title II of this act Congress was also dealing with what it considered a moral problem. But that fact does not detract from the overwhelming evidence of the disruptive effect the racial discrimination has had on commercial intercourse. It was this burden which empowered Congress to enact appropriate legislation, and, given this basis for the exercise of its power, Congress was not restricted by the fact that the particular obstruction to interstate commerce with which it was dealing was also deemed a moral and social wrong.

It is said that the operation of the motel here is of a purely local character. But, assuming this to be true, "[i]f it is interstate commerce that feels the pinch, it does not matter how local the operation which applies the squeeze."

Thus, the power of Congress to promote interstate commerce also includes the power to regulate the local incidents thereof, including local activities in both the states of origin and destination, which might have a substantial and harmful effect upon that commerce. One need only examine the evidence which we have discussed above to see that Congress may—as it has—prohibit racial discrimination by motels serving travelers, however "local" their operations may appear.

The only questions are (1) whether Congress had a rational basis for finding that racial discrimination by motels affected commerce, and (2) if it had such a basis, whether the means it selected to eliminate that evil are reasonable and appropriate. If they are, appellant has no "right" to select its guests as it sees fit, free from governmental regulation.

It is doubtful if in the long run appellant will suffer economic loss as a result of the act. Experience is to the contrary where discrimination is completely obliterated as to all public accommodations. But whether this be true or not is of no consequence since this Court has specifically held that the fact that a "member of the class which is regulated may suffer economic losses not shared by others . . . has never been a barrier" to such legislation. . . .

We, therefore, conclude that the action of the Congress in the adoption of the act as applied here to a motel which concededly serves interstate travelers is within the power granted it by the Commerce Clause of the Constitution, as interpreted by this Court for 140 years. . . .

Affirmed.

AFTERWORD

The "special guidebook" referred to in the sixth part of the Court's opinion provided the title for the winner of the 2018 Academy

Award for Best Picture, *The Green Book.* It was based on the concert tours through the deep south in the 1960s of Donald Shirley, a highly regarded professional classical and jazz pianist. Mahershala Ali won an Oscar for his portrayal of Shirley.

[For *The Green Book* trailer, see **www.youtube.com/watch?v=QkZxoko_HC0**.]

Questions

1. What arguments were offered by the government to establish that the Heart of Atlanta's racial policy affected interstate commerce? Are you persuaded by those arguments? Explain.
2. What test did the Court articulate to determine when Congress has the power to pass legislation based on the Commerce Clause?
3. Ollie's Barbecue, a neighborhood restaurant in Birmingham, Alabama, discriminated against Black customers. McClung brought suit to test the application of the public accommodations section of the Civil Rights Act of 1964 to his restaurant. In the suit, the government offered no evidence to show that the restaurant had ever served interstate customers or that it was likely to do so. Decide the case. See *Katzenbach v. McClung,* 379 U.S. 294 (1964).

Raich Other cases followed, including *Gonzalez v. Raich,*[16] involving the federal government's constitutional authority to regulate the use of medical marijuana. In 1996, California decriminalized the doctor-approved medical use of marijuana. The federal Controlled Substances Act (CSA), on the other hand, forbids the use, cultivation, or possession of marijuana for any purpose. A Californian, Angel Raich, whose doctor testified that "forgoing cannabis treatments would certainly cause Raich excruciating pain and could very well prove fatal," challenged the application of the CSA against California medical marijuana users. The heart of her claim was that the Commerce Clause does not give the federal government the authority to regulate the noncommercial cultivation and personal, medical use of marijuana that does not cross state lines. She won before the Ninth Circuit but lost in the U.S. Supreme Court by a 6–3 vote. Addressing the central question, the Court stated

> Angel Raich used marijuana for pain control.

> Given the enforcement difficulties that attend distinguishing between marijuana cultivated locally and marijuana grown elsewhere and concerns about diversion into illicit channels, we have no difficulty concluding that Congress had a rational basis for believing that failure to regulate the intrastate manufacture and possession of marijuana would leave a gaping hole in the CSA.[17]

In other words, once grown, even if intended for personal medicinal use, there is nothing to stop the marijuana from being sold or provided to others for nonmedicinal uses. Justice Stevens acknowledged the difficulty of Raich's situation "because, despite a congressional finding to the contrary, marijuana does have valid therapeutic purposes."[18] In closing, he referenced the possible solution of a medical necessity defense, which was raised in her complaint but was not before the Court.

Question

Gary Marbut of Missoula, Montana, hoped to manufacture .22-caliber rifles he called Montana Buckaroos. He wanted to produce and sell the guns exclusively in Montana from materials originating in Montana. He argued that Buckaroos could not be subject to federal regulation if made and sold only on an intrastate basis. Marbut (and others) brought suit seeking a court order affirming the right in Montana to manufacture and sell guns free of federal regulation. Decide. See *Montana Shooting Sports Association v. Holder,* 727 F.3d 975 (9th Cir. 2013), *cert. denied,* 134 S. Ct. 955 (2014).

Too Much Federal Power?

LO 8-4 Explain when the federal government has exceeded its authority in regulating commerce.

Dissenting in *Raich,* Supreme Court Justice Thomas warned

> If Congress can regulate this under the Commerce Clause, then it can regulate virtually anything–and the federal government is no longer one of limited and enumerated powers.[19]

Lopez Perhaps seeking to demonstrate that the Constitution does not afford unlimited power to the federal government, the Supreme Court has occasionally issued decisions expressly restraining its Commerce Clause authority. The Court clearly spoke for states' rights in the 1995 *United States v. Lopez* case.[20] In 1990, the federal government approved the Gun-Free School Zones Act, which forbade "any individual knowingly to possess a firearm at a place that [he/she] knows . . . is a school zone."[21] Congress claimed that gun possession in school zones would increase violence, delay learning, and discourage travel, thus affecting commerce. Lopez, a 12th-grade San Antonio, Texas, student, carried an unloaded, concealed gun into his high school and was charged with violating the act. His case reached the Supreme Court, where he claimed, and the Court agreed, that Congress did not have the constitutional authority to regulate the matter. By a 5–4 vote, the Court held that the possession of a gun at a school is not an economic activity that could, even if repeated elsewhere, have a substantial effect on interstate commerce.

> A 12th-grade San Antonio, Texas student carried an unloaded, concealed gun into his high school.

As an illustration of checks and balances, after *Lopez,* Congress amended the act to require that the gun in question "has moved in or otherwise affects interstate commerce." A number of post-amendment convictions have been obtained, most upheld and some overturned, but no court has found the revised act to be an unconstitutional exercise of Congress's powers under the Commerce Clause.

Brzonkala Strengthening its *Lopez* reasoning, the Supreme Court, in the 2000 *Brzonkala* case,[22] ruled by a 5–4 vote that Congress exceeded its Commerce Clause authority with regard to some provisions in the federal Violence Against Women Act (VAWA). The case involved a woman, Brzonkala, who claimed she was raped by two football players, Morrison and Crawford, when all three were students at Virginia Polytechnic Institute (VPI):

> Brzonkala alleges that soon after she met Morrison and Crawford, the two defendants pinned her down on a bed in her dormitory and forcibly raped her. Afterward, Morrison told Brzonkala, "You better not have any f***ing diseases." And, subsequently, Morrison announced publicly in the dormitory's dining hall, "I like to get girls drunk and f* * * the s* * * out of them."[23]

Congress developed a record on the aggregate economic impact of violence against women.

After Brzonkala complained to the university, Morrison was found guilty of abusive conduct by the VPI judicial committee and was suspended for one year, but that punishment was subsequently lifted. As permitted by VAWA, Brzonkala then sued for civil damages in federal court.

In debating VAWA, Congress held hearings and developed a record on the aggregate economic impact of violence against women, including driving up medical costs and discouraging women from traveling and from holding jobs, but the Supreme Court said Congress did not have the power to regulate noneconomic violent crime because it does not have a substantial effect on interstate commerce. To rule otherwise, the Court said, might "obliterate" the constitutional distinction between federal and state authority. [For the federal Office of Violence Against Women, see **www.justice.gov/ovw**.]

Supremacy Clause

LO 8-5
Explain the relationship between the Supremacy Clause and the concept of preemption.

The United States is a federalist form of government wherein authority is divided between the federal and state governments. Conflicts are inevitable, in part because the general welfare powers of state governments are broad in scope. But each level of government brings strengths to the process. State rules benefit from being enacted by bodies very close to the people themselves. On the other hand, optimal efficiency, especially for the business community, often demands one uniform federal rule rather than a patchwork of 50 state rules.[24]

Conflicts between federal law and state or local laws are most often resolved by reference to the Supremacy Clause found in the Constitution's Article VI, paragraph 2, which provides "This Constitution, and the Laws of the United States . . . shall be the Supreme Law of the Land." In the event of an irreconcilable conflict, federal law will *preempt* (supersede) state or local law, rendering the latter unconstitutional.

In general, Supreme Court decisions have affirmed the federal government's regulatory authority even when faced with conflicting state rules. Were it not so, achieving a unified national policy on any issue would be very difficult. However, recent Supreme Court preemption decisions have been split, some allowing state law to stand despite conflicts with federal law, some striking down state law.[25]

LO 8-6
Recognize when Congress has unconstitutionally commandeered a State's legislative function.

A Contrast in Cases: Betting and Marijuana

Intrastate sports betting

In 1992, Congress enacted the Professional and Amateur Sports Protection Act (PASPA), which made it unlawful for a State or any of its subdivisions "to sponsor, operate, advertise, promote, license, or authorize by law or compact . . . a lottery, sweepstakes, or other betting, gambling, or wagering scheme based . . . on competitive sporting events."[26] However, it expressly exempted the small number of states which had already legalized such activities. In 2012, after a statewide referendum to allow sports betting passed overwhelmingly, the New Jersey legislature enacted a law legalizing it. The state was sued by sports leagues and the NCAA. It lost when the Third Circuit ruled that PAPSA was a constitutional preemption of New Jersey's attempt to legalize in-state sports betting. The Supreme Court denied New Jersey's request for its review.

New Jersey tried again in 2014 to permit in-state betting on sporting events at its casinos and horse-racing tracks, this time by amending an existing state statute (rather than passing a new law). It lost again in the Third Circuit, but the Supreme Court accepted its request for review. The Court's opinion, handed down in 2018, found PAPSA to be a violation of the Tenth Amendment as an attempt by Congress to "impermissibly commandeer the regulatory power" of the state of New Jersey. In the words of the Court

> When the original States declared their independence, they claimed the powers inherent in sovereignty–in the words of the Declaration of Independence, the authority "to do all . . . Acts and Things which Independent States may of right do." The Constitution limited but did not abolish the sovereign powers of the States, which retained "a residuary and inviolable sovereignty". . . .
>
> The Constitution confers on Congress not plenary legislative power but only certain enumerated powers. Therefore, all other legislative power is reserved for the States, as the Tenth Amendment confirms. And conspicuously absent from the list of powers given to Congress is the power to issue direct orders to the governments of the States. The anticommandeering doctrine simply represents the recognition of this limit on congressional authority.[27]

The Court then explained the difference between Congress *commandeering* a state's legislative function, which is unconstitutional, and Congress *preempting* state law, which is constitutional.

> [R]egardless of the language sometimes used by Congress and this Court, every form of preemption is based on a federal law that regulates the conduct of private actors, not the States.
>
> Once this is understood, it is clear that the PASPA provision prohibiting state authorization of sports gambling is not a preemption provision because there is no way in which this provision can be understood as a regulation of private actors. It certainly does not confer any federal rights on private actors interested in conducting sports gambling operations. (It does not give them a federal right to engage in sports gambling.) Nor does it impose any federal restrictions on private actors. If a private citizen or company started a sports gambling operation, either with or without state authorization, [PASPA] would not be violated.[28]

So, at long last, New Jersey prevailed. Why was this such a hot-button issue for New Jersey? It is all about money.

> In 1897, New Jersey adopted a constitutional amendment that barred all gambling in the State. But during the Depression, the State permitted parimutuel betting on horse races as a way of increasing state revenue . . . In 1970, New Jersey became the third State to run a state lottery, and within five years, 10 other States followed suit. . . .

Thus, New Jersey once again strove to find a way to increase state revenues by creating a new stream from gambling.

Medical and recreational use of marijuana

In the 2005 *Raich* case, above, the Supreme Court held that Congress had the power to, and did, prohibit marijuana use in the Controlled Substance Act (CSA), even homegrown marijuana used exclusively for a medically prescribed use that is legal under state law. In other words, by passing the CSA, Congress *preempted* contrary state laws. By 2005, 11 states had nevertheless legalized marijuana for medical purposes. At the time of this writing, 38 states have done so.[29] Twenty-one have also legalized recreational use.[30] Nevertheless, using marijuana remains illegal under federal law.

The Obama Administration chose not to aggressively enforce federal marijuana laws, with some support from Congress in the form of a rider to an omnibus appropriations bill which Congress has reauthorized annually. As of December 2022, it was still in effect.[31] The rider, known as the Rohrabacher–Farr Amendment, provides: "None of the funds made available in this Act to the Department of Justice maybe used . . . to prevent [the] States from implementing their own State laws that authorize the use, distribution, possession, or cultivation of medical marijuana." In the 2016 case, *U.S. v. McIntosh,*[32] the Ninth Circuit held that federal criminal defendants could seek to enjoin their prosecutions by the Department of Justice based on the budget rider. In the *Sandusky v. Goetz* case, a criminal defendant raised the issue of the rider to prohibit his continued incarceration. The District Court for Colorado dismissed the case for procedural reasons, but the 10th Circuit reversed and remanded it.[33] As of this writing, there has been no final resolution of the case.

Questions

1. Review the "Law and the Market" discussion at the beginning of Chapter 4. What, if anything, do those examples indicate about the rule of law in the United States? Explain.
2. What is the difference between *preemption* and *commandeering* according to the Supreme Court?
3. As a nation, should we be concerned that Congress has passed a comprehensive law (CSA) intended to control access to, and the use of, marijuana that is not being enforced, as illustrated in the list below? Explain. In so doing, focus on the functioning of the constitutional structure, not on the substantive merits of legalizing or criminalizing marijuana use.
   - Thirty-eight states have passed laws in direct opposition to the CSA.
   - The Supreme Court has refused to hear, and redress if appropriate, claims of harm inflicted on neighboring states by the actions of states legalizing recreational use.[34]
   - Congress has undermined its own law by repeatedly reauthorizing the Rohrabacher-Farr Amendment.
4. Consider the two issues discussed above: betting on competitive sports events and legalizing recreational marijuana use. Why are they causing our legal system so many problems? Explain.

Sources: Charles P. Pierce, "Like Most Sports Controversies, the Supreme Court Gambling Case Is About Money and Control," *Sports Illustrated,* December 5, 2017 [**www.si.com**]; Jeremy Berke and Skye Gould, "States where marijuana is legal," *Business Insider,* January 1, 2020 [**www.businessinsider.com**]; "Memorandum for All United States Attorneys, Guidance Regarding Marijuana Enforcement," U.S. Department of Justice, August 29, 2013 [**www.justice.gov**]; "Tenth Circuit decision clears the way for further judicial consideration of the recently re-enacted Rohrabacher-Farr Amendment," ReedSmith, December 27, 2019 [**www.reedsmith.com**]; *U.S. v. McIntosh,* 833 F.3d 1163 (9th Cir. 2016); and *Sandusky v. Goetz,* No. 18-1483 (10th Cir. 2019).

Part Two—State Regulation of Commerce

The Tenth Amendment, as noted previously, reserves to the states any powers that are neither specifically delegated to the federal government nor prohibited to the states. Recall that this reserved power is frequently characterized by reference to the public health, safety, morals, and general welfare of the people and is often collectively referenced by the term *police power.* These powers belong to the state, which often delegates a portion of them to local governmentals. The COVID-19 pandemic has shown just how important and extensive these reserved powers are.

Stay-at-Home Orders: An Extraordinary, but Constitutional, Exercise of State Police Powers

Particularly during the first year and a half of the COVID pandemic, the vast majority of states closed their schools, many imposed face mask requirements (although varied), most had outstanding orders limiting the size of gatherings, and stay-at-home orders were in effect in some locales, at least to some extent. Essential business designations were issued in all but a few states. Eventually and gradually, all 50 states started the process of reopening. These actions were clear manifestations of the obligation and power of states to regulate for the public health, safety, and general welfare of their populations, even when such actions could have grave, if not fatal, impacts on many businesses.

In Pennsylvania, a group of business owners challenged the governor's executive order, under the state's Emergency Management Services Code, that closed the physical operations of all businesses deemed "nonlife-sustaining." The Pennsylvania Supreme Court ruled against the business owners, citing the governor's broad police powers and finding no violation of the U.S. Constitution. The business owners then petitioned the U.S. Supreme Court for an emergency stay of the state supreme court's decision. Their petition was denied.

Sources: Bernadette Meyler, "Shelter-in-Place Orders Are Perfectly Legal," *The New York Times,* April 29, 2020 [**www.nytimes.com**]; "COVID-19 State and Territory Actions Tracker," National Governors Association, accessed June 4, 2020 [**www.nga.org**]; Sarah Mervosh, Jasmine C. Lee, Lazaro Gamio, and Nadja Popovich, "See How All 50 States Are Reopening," *The New York Times,* June 4, 2020 [**www.nytimes.com**]; and Lisa Soronen, "Supreme Court Allows Pennsylvania COVID-19 Closure Executive Order to Stand," *National Conference of State Legislatures,* May 7, 2020 [**www.ncsl.org**].

The Commerce Clause grants the federal government broad authority over commerce that is interstate in nature. Purely intrastate commerce that has no significant effect on interstate commerce is within the exclusive regulatory jurisdiction of the states. However, given the inextricably interconnected national economy, purely intrastate commerce is rare.

The federal interest is in the free flow of commerce in all of its manifestations; the state's interest, broadly speaking, is in the general welfare of its citizens. Those interests often overlap, but, not infrequently, they conflict. A balancing of interests is required, although the Supremacy Clause makes it very likely that irreconcilable conflicts will be resolved in the federal government's favor.

In this section, commerce that is clearly interstate in nature but is, nonetheless, subject to concurrent state (or local) regulation is explored. The issue is whether the state regulation is unconstitutional because it either (1) *discriminates* against interstate commerce or (2) *unduly burdens* interstate commerce (that is, the burden imposed clearly exceeds the benefits derived).

Can states lawfully protect retail liquor stores from out-of-state competition?

In the case that follows, elements of the continuing conflict between federal and state control of interstate commerce, especially in health and safety matters, can be seen. At the commercial level, the case is about another classic conflict: free trade versus protectionism. Can states lawfully protect their local businesses, in this case, retail liquor stores, from out-of-state competition? The appellant is a trade association of liquor retailers, a group unusually persistent in its attempt to ward off competition from newcomers to the state. As you read *Tennessee Wine and Spirits Retailers,* pay attention to how many different government officials and institutions determined that the state regulation at issue was unconstitutional. In its 7–2 decision, the central question facing the Supreme Court was the conflict between the requirements of the Commerce Clause and the provisions of the Twenty-First Amendment to the U.S. Constitution. That amendment ended Prohibition (imposed by the Eighteenth Amendment in 1919) in 1933 and gave the states broad authority to regulate the sale of alcohol. The decision is grounded on an interpretation known as the *dormant Commerce Clause.*

LO 8-7
Identify the circumstances in which the dormant Commerce Clause principle would apply.

LEGAL BRIEFCASE

Tennessee Wine and Spirits Retailers Association v. Tennessee Alcoholic Beverage Commission 139 S. Ct. 2449 (2019)

Justice Alito

The State of Tennessee imposes demanding durational-residency requirements on all individuals and businesses seeking to obtain or renew a license to operate a liquor store. One provision precludes the renewal of a license unless the applicant has resided in the State for 10 consecutive years. Another provides that a corporation cannot obtain a license unless all of its stockholders are residents. The Court of Appeals for the Sixth Circuit struck down these provisions as blatant violations of the Commerce Clause, and neither petitioner—an association of Tennessee liquor retailers—nor the State itself defends them in this Court.

The Sixth Circuit also invalidated a provision requiring applicants for an initial license to have resided in the State for the prior two years, and petitioner does challenge that decision. But while this requirement is less extreme than the others that the Sixth Circuit found to be unconstitutional, we now hold that it also violates the Commerce Clause and is not shielded by § 2 of the Twenty-first Amendment. Section 2 was adopted as part of the scheme that ended prohibition on the national level. It gives each State leeway in choosing the alcohol-related public health and safety measures that its citizens find desirable. But § 2 is not a license to impose all manner of protectionist restrictions on commerce in alcoholic beverages. Because Tennessee's 2-year residency requirement for retail license applicants blatantly favors the State's residents and has little relationship to public health and safety, it is unconstitutional.

I. A.

Tennessee, like many other States, requires alcoholic beverages distributed in the State to pass through a specified three-tiered system. Acting through the Tennessee Alcoholic Beverage Commission (TABC), the State issues different types of licenses to producers, wholesalers, and retailers of alcoholic beverages. Producers may sell only to licensed wholesalers; wholesalers may sell only to licensed retailers or other wholesalers; and only licensed retailers may sell to consumers. No person may lawfully participate in the sale of alcohol without the appropriate license.

Included in the Tennessee scheme are onerous durational-residency requirements for all persons and companies wishing to operate "retail package stores" that sell alcoholic beverages for off-premises consumption (hereinafter liquor stores). To obtain an initial retail license, an individual must demonstrate that he or she has "been a bona fide resident" of the State for the previous two years.

In 2012, the Tennessee attorney general was asked whether the State's durational-residency requirements violate the Commerce Clause, and his answer was that the requirements constituted "trade restraints and barriers that impermissibly discriminate against interstate commerce." In light of that opinion, the TABC stopped enforcing the requirements against new applicants.

B.

In 2016, respondents Tennessee Fine Wines and Spirits, LLC dba Total Wine Spirits Beer & More (Total Wine) and Affluere Investments, Inc. . . . (Affluere) applied for licenses to own and operate liquor stores in Tennessee. At the time, neither Total Wine nor Affluere satisfied the durational-residency requirements. . . .

TABC staff recommended approval of the applications, but petitioner Tennessee Wine and Spirits Retailers Association (the Association)—a trade association of in-state liquor stores—threatened to sue the TABC if it granted them. The TABC's executive director (a respondent here) filed a declaratory judgment action in state court to settle the question of the residency requirements' constitutionality.

The case was removed to the United States District Court for the Middle District of Tennessee, and that court . . . concluded that the requirements are unconstitutional. . . .

The Association . . . took the case to the Court of Appeals for the Sixth Circuit, where a divided panel affirmed. . . .

II. A.

The Court of Appeals held that Tennessee's 2-year residency requirement violates the Commerce Clause, which provides that "[t]he Congress shall have Power . . . [t]o regulate Commerce with foreign Nations, and among the several States, and with the Indian Tribes." "Although the Clause is framed as a positive grant of power to Congress," we have long held that this Clause also prohibits state laws that unduly restrict interstate commerce. "This 'negative' aspect of the Commerce Clause" prevents the States from adopting protectionist measures and thus preserves a national market for goods and services.

This interpretation, generally known as "the dormant Commerce Clause," has a long . . . history. Its roots go back as far as *Gibbons v. Ogden* (1824), where Chief Justice Marshall found that a version of the dormant Commerce Clause argument had "great force." [B]y the latter half of the 19th century the dormant Commerce Clause was firmly established, and it played an important role in the economic history of our Nation.

[W]ithout the dormant Commerce Clause, we would be left with a constitutional scheme that those who framed and ratified the Constitution would surely find surprising.

That is so because removing state trade barriers was a principal reason for the adoption of the Constitution. Under the Articles of Confederation, States notoriously obstructed the interstate shipment of goods. "Interference with the arteries of commerce was cutting off the very life-blood of the nation." The Annapolis Convention of 1786 was convened to address this critical problem, and it culminated in a call for the Philadelphia Convention that framed the Constitution in the summer of 1787. At that Convention, discussion of the power to regulate interstate commerce was almost uniformly linked to the removal of state trade barriers, and when the Constitution was sent to the state conventions, fostering free trade among the States was prominently cited as a reason for ratification. In The Federalist No. 7, Hamilton argued that state protectionism could lead to conflict among the States, and in No. 11, he touted the benefits of a free national market. In The Federalist No. 42, Madison sounded a similar theme.

B.

Under our dormant Commerce Clause cases, if a state law discriminates against out-of-state goods or nonresident economic actors, the law can be sustained only on a showing that it is narrowly tailored to "advanc[e] a legitimate local purpose."

Tennessee's 2-year durational-residency requirement plainly favors Tennesseans over nonresidents. . . .

III. A.

Section 2 of the Twenty-first Amendment provides as follows:

> "The transportation or importation into any State, Territory, or possession of the United States for delivery or use therein of intoxicating liquors, in violation of the laws thereof, is hereby prohibited."

. . . [T]he thrust of § 2 is to "constitutionaliz[e]" the basic structure of federal-state alcohol regulatory authority that prevailed prior to the adoption of the Eighteenth Amendment [which had established prohibition]. . . .

B.

By the late 19th century, the Court was firmly of the view that the Commerce Clause by its own force restricts state regulation of interstate commerce. Dormant Commerce Clause cases from that era "advanced two distinct principles," an understanding of which is critical to gauging the States' pre-Prohibition power to regulate alcohol.

First, the Court held that the Commerce Clause prevented States from discriminating "against the citizens and products of other States" . . . .

Second, the Court "held that the Commerce Clause prevented States from passing facially neutral laws that placed an impermissible burden on interstate commerce." . . .

[IV.] C.

To summarize, the Court has acknowledged that § 2 grants States latitude with respect to the regulation of alcohol, but the Court has repeatedly declined to read § 2 as allowing the States to violate the "nondiscrimination principle" that was a central feature of the regulatory regime that the provision was meant to constitutionalize. . . .

D.

. . . [Section 2] allows each State leeway to enact the measures that its citizens believe are appropriate to address the public health and safety effects of alcohol use and to serve other legitimate interests, but it does not license the States to adopt protectionist measures with no demonstrable connection to those interests.

V.

The provision at issue here expressly discriminates against nonresidents and has at best a highly attenuated relationship to public health or safety. . . . [T]he record is devoid of any "concrete evidence" showing that the 2-year residency requirement actually promotes public health or safety; nor is there evidence that nondiscriminatory alternatives would be insufficient to further those interests. . . .

Not only is the 2-year residency requirement ill-suited to promote responsible sales and consumption practices (an interest that we recognize as legitimate . . .), but there are obvious alternatives that better serve that goal without discriminating against nonresidents. State law empowers the relevant authorities to limit both the number of retail licenses and the amount of alcohol that may be sold to an individual. The State could also mandate more extensive training for managers and employees and could even demand that they demonstrate an adequate connection with and knowledge of the local community. And the State of course remains free to monitor the practices of retailers and to take action against those who violate the law.

Given all this, the Association has fallen far short of showing that the 2-year durational-residency requirement for license applicants is valid. . . . [T]he predominant effect of the 2-year residency requirement is simply to protect the Association's members from out-of-state competition. We therefore hold that this provision violates the Commerce Clause and is not saved by the Twenty-first Amendment.

Questions

1. What was the Association's reason for challenging the TABC's recommended approval of retail liquor licenses for Total Wine and Affluere? In considering your answer, you might wish to review the section "Theory and Practice" in Part One of this chapter.
2. In general, what does the dormant Commerce Clause prohibit? Which of its two principles is relevant in this case?
3. Why did the 2-year durational-residency requirement violate the dormant Commerce Clause?
4. Both Michigan and New York permitted in-state wineries to obtain licenses that allowed them to ship directly to consumers while not permitting out-of-state wineries to do the same. At the time, 26 states allowed some form of direct shipping. Thirteen had reciprocity agreements such that shipments from out of state were allowed if the state of origin of the wine afforded similar nondiscriminatory treatment to its wineries. Two small wineries brought separate suits to challenge the direct ship rules of, in one case, Michigan and, in the other case, New York. How would you rule? Explain. See *Granholm v. Heald,* 544 U.S. 460 (2005).
5. It is not uncommon for states, seeking to entice major new business investment, to provide tax incentive packages to companies to lure them away from other states. If the deal offered by the state requires the business "to make every effort to ensure that a substantial number of employees are residents" of the state, would that provision be vulnerable to a dormant Commerce Clause challenge? Explain. See *Kopecky v. Iowa Racing and Gaming Commission,* 891 N.W.2d 439 (Iowa 2017).
   a. What if plaintiffs, residents of an adjacent state who had applied and been turned down for jobs when the facility opened, could show that the rejection rate of qualified out-of-state applicants was 90 percent, while the rejection rate of similarly qualified in-state applicants was 60 percent?
   b. What if, alternatively, the language of the deal provided that the business "will prioritize hiring of applicants who are residents" of the state? See, Julia Jacobs, "In wake of Foxconn deal, Wisconsin and Illinois vie for jobs," *Reuters,* August 24, 2017 [**www.reuters.com**].
6. Ten states require new cars be sold only through licensed franchises independent of the car manufacturers.[35] Tesla's business model is to sell direct to its customers. Does Tesla have a dormant Commerce Clause case in those states? Explain. For an example of Tesla's legal fights for the right to sell direct, see, Nick Sibilla, "Connecticut Should Be Tesla Country," *The New York Times,* July 7, 2017 [**www.nytimes.com**].

National Pork Producers Council v. Ross

California voters passed a ballot initiative in 2018 known as Proposition 12, which banned the sale in California of pork raised on farms that do not provide a minimum of 24 square feet of usable floor space per breeding pig. The National Pork Producers Council (NPPC) sued California arguing that Proposition 12 violates the dormant Commerce Clause. The federal district court dismissed the case and the Ninth Circuit affirmed that the NPPC's filing failed to state a violation of the dormant Commerce Clause. The NPPC appealed the decision to the Supreme Court and oral arguments were held on October 11, 2022. At the time of this writing, the matter is still pending.

To listen to the oral arguments before the Supreme Court, see "National Pork Producers v. Ross (212-468)," *SCOTUS-Toons,* October 11, 2022 [**www.youtube.com**].

Sources: Melia Wong, "Proposition 12: Farm Animal Confinement," *Rose Institute of State and Local Government,* accessed January 8, 2023 [**https://roseinstitute.org**]; and Yue (Wendy) Wu and Wentao Yang, "National Pork Producers Council v. Ross," *LII Supreme Court Bulletin,* accessed January 8, 2023 [**www.law.cornell.edu**].

Summary of State and Local Regulation of Business

LO 8-8
Describe some of the ways in which state and local regulations affect business practice.

The creation and modification of federal laws generally receive greater attention, but state and local laws have enormous impacts on business practice. The states are primarily responsible for regulating areas such as the insurance industry, forms of business, property use, liquor sales, and the sale and leasing of goods, to name just a few. Many businesses and professions–from engineering to funeral preparation to barbering to veterinarians to the practice of medicine, accounting, and law–require a license from the state. All states have some form of commission charged with regulating utilities in the public interest. States often seek to promote competition via antitrust legislation. Many states have passed laws forbidding usury (lending at unconscionably high interest rates), false advertising, and securities fraud. [For the Council of State Governments and updates on state law, see **www.csg.org.**]

Two 2022 decisions of the Supreme Court, one announced on June 23 and the other on June 24, have substantially altered the legal landscape of federal and state regulation in two major areas: abortions and guns.

Abortion

In *Dobbs v. Jackson Women's Health Organization,*[36] the Supreme Court held that there is no constitutional right to an abortion, overruling both its 1973 decision in *Roe v. Wade*[37] and its 1992 decision in *Planned Parenthood v. Casey.*[38] Thus, states are free to regulate access to abortions. Prior to the decision in *Dobbs,* 13 states had trigger laws ready to ban most abortions if *Roe v. Wade* were reversed, generally prohibiting most abortions, with some limited exceptions.[39] Shortly after the decision, at least 14 additional states enacted abortion laws, some expanding and some restricting access.[40] Some states have enacted protections for providers and patients that limit or prohibit interstate extraditions related to legal reproductive care services. California's law prevents state courts from enforcing judgments from other states where providing, aiding, or receiving abortion care is illegal,[41] as well as prohibiting state law enforcement from assisting abortion investigations in other states.[42] The list of state responses in the wake of the *Dobbs* case will no doubt grow longer on both sides of the issue, addressing privacy, medical services to be provided or prohibited, medical insurance coverage, and more.

Guns

States have a long history of regulating many aspects of manufacturing, selling, buying, and owning guns. In recent years, provisions in two states have come before the Supreme Court and been found unconstitutional as a violation of the Second Amendment:

> "A well regulate Militia, being necessary to the security of a free State, the right of the people to keep and bear Arms, shall not be infringed."

In 2008, in *District of Columbia v. Heller,*[43] a 5–4 Supreme Court majority held that the Second Amendment guarantees an individual right to possess firearms independent of service in a state militia and to use firearms for traditionally lawful purposes, including self-defense within the home. The District of Columbia had mostly banned the registration of handguns and made it a crime to carry unregistered firearms. However, the chief of police could issue licenses for one-year periods. The District also required that stored firearms be disassembled or locked to prevent firing. The D.C. Court of Appeals struck down the ban on registering handguns and the storage requirement. The Supreme Court affirmed, stating, among other things, that the right of self-defense is a "central component" of the Second Amendment right to bear arms and implicitly protects the right "to use arms in defense of hearth and home." This purpose would be materially impaired if the arms were inaccessible or not functional when actually needed for such a purpose.

In 2022, the issue of gun control was again before the Court. In *New York State Rifle & Pistol Association v. Bruen,*[44] a New York gun control law required those who wanted a handgun to apply for a license and enumerated the purposes which would support its approval. To carry the handgun in public, it was further necessary to show a "proper cause exists" for a permit to be issued. Without that additional showing, licensed individuals could carry a firearm only for such purposes as hunting, target shooting, or employment. Whether "proper cause" was established was left to the issuing official, although various state courts had identified "special needs" that might satisfy the rule. Decisions rejecting such requests had been reviewed under an "arbitrary and capricious" standard. The Court noted the difference between states where licenses were issued on a "may-issue" basis and those employing a "shall-issue" approach, the first being discretionary in its grant, the second being mandatory if specified requirements are met. The majority of the Court held that a government must "affirmatively prove that its firearms regulation is part of the historical tradition that delimits the outer bounds of the right to keep and bear arms." The concurring opinion by Justice Kavanaugh, joined by Justice Roberts, clarified that the ruling should not be read to prohibit objective restrictions on ownership, such as fingerprinting, background checks, mental health evaluations, and mandatory training.

Data support the proposition that gun safety laws do save lives. The Everytown for Gun Safety Support Fund is a charitable organization that states its focus as "awareness and educational work related to gun violence prevention."[45] It maintains a database that scores every state on the strength of its gun laws and its rate of gun violence. One of its key findings is the impact of a core group of laws on gun violence:

> All states should start with a core group of five foundational laws–passing background checks and/or purchase permitting, along with Extreme Risk laws and secure gun storage requirements; and rejecting Shoot First (also known as Stand Your Ground) and permitless carry laws. While each of the top 14 states in the gun law rankings has all five of these policies in place, only one of the bottom 14 states has even one of these critical protections.[46]

Extreme Risk laws, also known as Red Flag laws, generally allow loved ones or law enforcement to file a petition in court for an order to temporarily prevent someone in crisis from accessing guns.

Assault Weapons

A 10-year federal ban on assault weapons expired in 2004. Then, in 2005, the Protection of Lawful Commerce Arms Act was passed, which shielded the gun industry from civil actions "resulting from the criminal or unlawful misuse" "of a firearm or ammunition."[47] The AR-15, a popular semiautomatic rifle, was developed in the 1950s for civilian use.[48] It has been used in many mass shootings, including the shootings in Uvalde, Texas, on May 24, 2022 (just one month before the decision in *Bruen*); in Buffalo, New York, on May 14, 2022; at Marjory Stoneman Douglas High School in Parkland, Florida, in 2018; and at Sandy Hook Elementary School in Newtown, Connecticut, in 2012. "There were about 400,000 AR-15 style rifles in America before the [federal] ban went into effect in 1994. Today there are 20 million."[49]As of this writing, eight states have laws prohibiting assault weapons: California, Connecticut, Delaware, Hawaii, Maryland, Massachusetts, New Jersey, and New York.[50]

> Eight states have laws prohibiting assault weapons.

Question

What gun laws does your state have? How does your state compare on measures of rates of gun violence, such as deaths per 100,000 residents, and the strength of its gun laws with the states around yours? To find this information, you might start by accessing the current year's report, "Gun Safety Policies Save Lives," maintained by the Everytown Support Fund at **https://everytownresearch.org.** Also consider looking at what your state legislature's research department has on the subject. Other groups may maintain similar information. Are you surprised by the data you find? Do you approve of the situation in your state? Disapprove?

Sources: Sara Swann, "The history of the AR-15 and how it became a symbol of American gun culture," *Poynter,* June 29, 2022 [**https://www.poynter.org**]; Heather Cox Richardson, *Letters from an American May 26, 2022;* and "Which states prohibit assault weapons?" *Everytown Support Fund,* accessed January 9, 2023 [**https://everytownresearch.org**].

Licensure

More than 1,000 of America's occupations can be practiced, somewhere in the United States, only by those who have secured a license to do so from the appropriate federal, state, or local authorities. You would likely consider licensure an important requirement for many of them, such as medicine, law, building construction, and electrical work. You might be surprised to learn, however, that nearly one-quarter of workers in the United States now require an occupational license, as compared with five percent in 1960.[51] The list includes door repair contractors, electrical helpers, florists, funeral attendants, interior designers, makeup artists, travel guides, and upholsterers.[52]

Licensure requirements are designed to protect the public from unsafe, unhealthful, and substandard services, but they can, and often do, produce more harm than good. In the Executive Summary introducing its occupational licensing database, the National Conference of State Legislatures states: "Excessively onerous requirements . . . can create barriers to employment for individuals who may not actually pose a serious risk."[53] The following was written by former Commissioner of the Federal Trade Commission Maureen Ohlhausen:

> The burdens of excessive occupational licensing often fall disproportionately on our nation's most economically disadvantaged citizens–those working in entry-and mid-level jobs, seeking to pull themselves up the economic ladder. And even in professions where licensing makes sense, a lack of license portability across state lines poses another set of challenges, causing particular hardships for military families and others who move often.
>
> The problem of excessive occupational licensing is compounded by what I call the "Brother, May I?" situation. Too often, the members of an occupation gain effective control over the quasi-public board that regulates their profession. Once this happens, private actors wield their government-granted power to block potential competitors from entering "their" market.[54]

Do we need to license tour guides in Washington, D.C., and historic Savannah, Georgia? Should teeth-whitening services in Alabama be limited to dentists? Do Louisiana consumers need to be protected from unlicensed florists? Do women in Missouri need a licensed African-style hair braider?

[For more information on occupational licensing, see National Conference of State Legislatures, "The National Occupational Licensing Database" [**www.ncsl.org**]; and Lisa Knepper, Darwyyn Deyo, Kyle Sweetland, Jason Tiezzi, and Alec Mena, *License to Work* (3rd Edition) [**https://ij.org/report/license-to-work-3**].]

Regulation and Community Welfare

Most people would say, in the abstract, that they need less government in their lives, but when they are the victims of problems that the market is ill-suited to resolve, regulation often seems considerably more attractive. When people choose a home, the neighborhood that surrounds it often matters. Cities quite often have zoning laws, with areas authorized for commercial, residential, and mixed use. Airbnb and other short-term rental platforms have disrupted zoning restrictions. They create an opportunity for people to boost their income by engaging in the short-term rental of all or a portion of their homes to tourists and business travelers who appreciate having the comforts of home, often at less cost than a hotel or motel. It sounds like a win-win situation.

To some, however, it is a win-win-lose proposition, the losers being the members of the broader community. Zoning is a way for communities to preserve the desired characteristics (for example, aesthetics or safety) of their neighborhoods and commercial districts–the very characteristics that cause residents to love their cities and that draw tourists and business visitors. Large numbers of transitory tenants can jeopardize these values. In popular tourist destinations, like Miami Beach, Florida, residents of neighborhoods close to the beaches have found themselves living with the "endless sound of suitcases rolling down the sidewalk," noisy partying at inappropriate hours, and copious "trash left behind." In one such neighborhood, a resident remarked: "these are inns without innkeeping, and the innkeeping falls on the neighbors."[55] The mayor asserted: "We have residential areas in our community and we have zoned them so when people purchase a home they know they are in a residential community."[56]

In other cities, the issue is more immediate. Regulations intended to address escalating rents in very tight rental markets are being rendered ineffective by the reallocation of apartments to servicing tourists to the detriment of residents seeking affordable housing. Further, these rental arrangements avoid both lodging taxes and oversight. Cities have uncovered "elaborate real estate scheme[s] to make millions by circumventing state and local laws and Airbnb's own rules."[57]

In 2019, New York City uncovered just such a scheme, one that "made more than $20 million in revenue by unlawfully renting 130 Manhattan apartments to almost 76,000 guests through Airbnb."[58] Similarly impacted housing markets include San Francisco, Chicago, and New Orleans.[59]

Questions—Parts One and Two

1. Matthew Hale, a law school graduate, was denied a license to practice law in Illinois because he was an avowed racist and the leader of a white supremacist group. A state panel assessed the character and general fitness of all those who had passed the bar exam and graduated from law school and decided that Hale's active racism disqualified him. Illinois was one of 32 states with character and fitness standards. Hale appealed on First Amendment grounds, among others. Should Hale have been excluded from the practice of law, or should the market decide his fitness? Explain. See *Hale v. Committee on Character and Fitness for the State of Illinois,* 335 F.3d 678 (7th Cir. 2006).
2. The city government in Cedar Falls, Iowa, home of the University of Northern Iowa, declined to renew the liquor license of a local bar after 58 of 100 "bar checks," over nearly two years, found minors drinking illegally. One hundred seventy-four alcohol-related tickets were issued over that period.[60]
   a. Can the free market satisfactorily protect the public from the various risks associated with excessive drinking by college-age students, or are rules necessary? Explain.
   b. Would you vote to renew this bar's liquor license? Explain.
3. The National Association of Home Builders announced in 2016 that the cost of compliance with rules for home building had increased by 30 percent over the previous five years. State and local governments commonly require builders to comply with construction codes, buy storm-water discharge permits, and pay impact fees (for water, sewer, roads, parks, schools, police, fire, and sometimes open space and affordable housing). The association estimated that regulations accounted for $85,000 of the cost of the average new single-family home. One result, the association argued, was that builders were much less likely to build homes for the lower-cost, entry-level market.[61]

a. In general, do you think we should cut back on the public services paid for, in part, by impact fees in order to reduce the cost of housing? Explain.

b. Some Georgia jurisdictions impose a tree-planting requirement that reportedly raise the cost per lot by $7,500 to $15,000. How would you vote on a rule requiring tree planting on all new home lots in your local area? Why?

4. In 2012, a Connecticut woman dropped from her harness to her death while parasailing near Pompano Beach, Florida. Such deaths are unusual, apparently no more than a few dozen worldwide over the past 30 years, but Florida had seen four in recent years.

   The Florida legislature in 2014 adopted a new law governing parasailing, previously a largely unregulated commercial, recreational activity. The new rules, among other things, require insurance for operators, mandate an on-board observer, and allow operation only when winds do not exceed 20 miles per hour.

   a. Do parasailing deaths constitute a market failure? Explain.

   b. Would you vote for such a parasailing rule, or would you leave parasailing safety to the market? Explain.

Part Three—Administrative Agencies and the Regulatory Process

Assume you start a relatively simple business, perhaps a small restaurant. You will quickly come to realize that the government is going to be your partner in that business. Taxes, wages, hours, sanitation, safety, advertising, and zoning, at every turn, a government rule shapes the conduct of your business. In many cases, those rules are created and enforced by administrative agencies, a powerful subset of government little understood by the public but immensely influential in every corner of American life. So large is its impact that it is often referred to as the *fourth branch* of government.

In Part Three, the primary focus will be federal agencies, but the principles that govern, and the structure of, state agencies are essentially the same.

The Federal Agencies

LO 8-9
List some of the federal agencies that regulate business practice.

Federal law defines an *agency* as any government unit other than the legislature and the courts. Thus, the *administrative law* governing those agencies technically addresses the entire executive branch of government. Most of our attention, however, will be directed at the prominent regulatory agencies (Securities Exchange Commission Occupational Health and Safety Administration, Environmental Protection Agency, and the like) rather than at the various executive departments (Agriculture, Defense, and so on) or the nonregulatory welfare agencies (Social Security Administration and Veterans Administration). [For an online guide to federal government information and services, see **www.usa.gov**.]

Some federal agencies have a parallel at the state level. For example, a state may have a department of environmental quality. Some state agencies, however, do not have a direct federal analog, such as the state public utility commissions, as well as various state licensure boards for the professions. Planning and zoning boards can also be found at the state and local levels.

History

LO 8-10 Explain why administrative agencies are created.

In 1887, Congress established the first federal regulatory agency, the Interstate Commerce Commission (ICC), for the purpose of regulating railroad routes and rates. The Food and Drug Administration (FDA–1907) and the Federal Trade Commission (FTC–1914) followed, but federal regulation became pervasive only in response to the Great Depression of the 1930s. Congress then created the Securities and Exchange Commission (SEC–1934), the Federal Communications Commission (FCC–1934), the Civil Aeronautics Board (CAB–1940; abolished in 1985), the National Labor Relations Board (NLRB–1935), and more, as a response to the widely shared belief that the stock market crash and the Depression evidenced the failure of the free market. The government's long-standing *laissez-faire* (noninterference) policy toward business ended.

The next major burst of regulatory activity arrived in the 1960s and 1970s when Congress created such agencies as the Equal Employment Opportunity Commission (EEOC–1965), the Environmental Protection Agency (EPA–1970), the Occupational Safety and Health Administration (OSHA–1970), and the Consumer Product Safety Commission (CPSC–1972).

Most of the early agencies were designed to achieve economic goals by exerting substantial control over entire industries. With the arrival of the prosperity and social turbulence of the 1960s and 1970s, Congress established an array of new agencies directed not toward economic issues but rather toward social reform in such areas as discrimination, the environment, job safety, and product safety.

The free-market enthusiasm of the 1980s, led by President Ronald Reagan and grounded on the thinking of economics Nobel Laureate Milton Friedman, resulted in strenuous efforts to deregulate the economy and reduce the influence of federal agencies and the government generally. This carried through until the accounting and corporate governance scandals of the **dot.com** era in the early 2000s, when regulation was once again expanded to address free market failures. The near collapse in 2008 of the financial system during the Great Recession led to another regulatory burst. At this writing, the United States is once again confronting major challenges, globally as well as nationally. There seems to be little consensus on how best to go forward. It is too soon to tell what new regulatory equilibrium will be reached.

> Following the accounting and corporate governance scandals of the dot.com era in the early 2000s, we again turned to regulation to address free market failures.

Creating Agencies

Federal agencies are essentially of two kinds: executive and independent. The cabinet-level departments (Defense, Education, Energy, and so forth) are considered executive agencies, as are the subunits within them (for example, the Internal Revenue Service is an agency housed within the Treasury Department).

The primary interest here is in the independent agencies, such as the SEC, the FTC, OSHA, the EEOC, and the EPA. Congress creates an independent agency by enacting a statute called *enabling legislation,* which brings the agency into existence and grants the agency substantial authority to regulate specified segments of American life. The FTC, for example, is empowered by its enabling legislation to thwart unfair trade practices.

While the president has direct authority over executive agencies, independent agencies operate with great autonomy. For example, the president cannot remove an independent agency head at will. Nonetheless, the president and Congress have mechanisms to exert significant influence over these agencies (for example, Congress controls the agencies' budgets and the president nominates the agency head).

In creating an agency, Congress delegates a portion of its constitutionally granted legislative authority (rule-making power) to that body. Congress acknowledges the existence of a serious problem and recognizes that it has neither the resources nor the expertise needed to address it. Therefore, it creates an agency and charges it with dealing with the problem area, generally described in very broad terms. The president, with the advice and consent of the Senate, appoints the administrator or commissioners who direct each agency's affairs. Commissioners are appointed for staggered terms (typically of seven years' duration) and reflect an approximate political balance between the two major parties.

In overall effect, a fourth branch of government has been created to handle the complex issues that confront the nation, armed with the authority needed to address those issues, and staffed with the necessary expertise.

Agency Duties

LO 8-11
Identify the three broad categories of federal regulatory agencies' authority.

The authority of federal agencies falls broadly into three categories: control of supply, control of rates, and control of conduct.

Control of Supply Some agencies control entry into certain economic activities. The FCC grants radio and television licenses. The FDA decides which drugs may enter the American market, as it did in January, 2023, when it approved a second new drug for Alzheimers that may slow the cognitive decline in early stages of the disease.[62] The SEC acts as a gatekeeper, preventing the issuance of new securities for sale to the public until certain standards are met.

Control of Rates Historically, those federal agencies charged with regulating utilities and carriers (Federal Energy Regulatory Commission, the ICC, and the CAB) set the prices to be charged for the services offered within their jurisdictions, but the deregulation movement resulted in the elimination of the CAB and the ICC and a general decline in agency rate-setting. For example, the federal government decided to eliminate its authority to set the price of airline tickets and the rates charged for cable TV and long-distance telephone calls.

Control of Conduct Federal agencies may both compel and restrict business conduct.

a. Information. Agencies commonly compel companies to disclose information that would otherwise remain private. Warning labels, for example, may be mandated by the FDA about the dangers of nicotine. A lengthy list of information must be regularly provided by companies with stock traded in the public markets, such as the New York Stock Exchange.

b. Standards. Where simply requiring information is deemed inadequate for the public's needs, the government may establish minimum standards that the private sector must meet. Thus, in 2016, the FAA established rules governing the use of unmanned aircraft systems, commonly referred to as drones, and certification requirements for commercial drone operators. Hobbyists must comply with flight guidelines, but licensure is not required. Regulations became effective in 2021 which require nearly all drones to incorporate tracking technology to allow them to be monitored while flying in U.S. airspace.[63]

c. Product banishments. In rare circumstances, products can be banned from the market. In January 2020, the FDA banned the manufacture, distribution, and sale of certain flavors of cartridge-based e-cigarettes, such as fruit and mint, that appeal particularly to youth. In the press release announcing the ban, the FDA stated: "The United States has never seen an epidemic of substance use arise as quickly as our current epidemic of youth use of e-cigarettes. . . . By prioritizing enforcement against the products that are most widely used by children, our action today seeks to strike the right public health balance by maintaining e-cigarettes as a potential off-ramp for adults using combustible tobacco while ensuring these products don't provide an on-ramp to nicotine addiction for our youth."[64]

Test Your Memory!

Having come this far in the discussion of federal agencies, you might appreciate an often-used phrase describing them as "an alphabet soup of agencies." Test yourself: See how many agencies from the following list of acronyms you can accurately identify without looking back at the text!

ICC, FDA, FTC, SEC, FCC, CAB, NLRB, EEOC, EPA, OSHA, CPSC

Questions

1. The phrase *government regulation* embraces many functions. Identify them.
2. Is the federal regulatory process limited in its goals to the correction of market failures? Should it be so limited? Explain.
3. According to *The Washington Post,* self-described "drone slayer" William Merideth of Kentucky saw a drone hovering over his land, so he "grabbed his Benelli M1 Super 90 shotgun, took aim, and unleashed three rounds of birdshot." The $1,500 drone was downed and its owner, hobbyist John Boggs, who was taking pictures of the scenery, filed suit claiming Merideth had no right to shoot down the drone because the U.S. government controls all airspace. Merideth and witnesses say the drone was flying below the treeline. See Andrea Peterson and Matt McFarland, "You May Be Powerless to Stop a Drone from Hovering over Your Own Yard," *The Washington Post,* January 13, 2016. **[www.washingtonpost.com]**.

   a. Do you think Boggs was trespassing? Why?

   b. How do you feel about widespread drone use, including package delivery to housing units? By January 2022, United Parcel Service had completed 10,000 drone deliveries; Google's Wing drone delivery had completed 300,000 deliveries collectively in Virginia, Texas, Finland, Ireland, and Australia; and Walmart made 6,000 paid deliveries.[65] The Research Exercise at the end of the chapter explores possible uses of drones on your campus.

Operating the Agencies

LO 8-12
Compare and contrast the federal agencies' executive, legislative, and judicial roles.

As noted earlier, administrative agencies have broad authority involving control of supply, rates, and conduct in large segments of American life. This section will illustrate how they act as mini-governments with respect to their subject-matter charge, performing quasi-executive (enforcement), quasi-legislative (rule-making), and quasi-judicial (adjudicatory) roles. Agency action is guided generally by the Administrative Procedure Act (APA), which provides a framework for agency rule-making and details broad standards for the judicial review of agency decisions, in part to ensure that the constitutional requirements of due process are met. It is worth noting that states also have legislation similar to the APA.

Executive Functions

A major portion of the agencies' executive duties is the protection of the public by ensuring compliance with laws and regulations. Most agencies, therefore, spend a great deal of time conducting inspections and investigations and collecting information. Agencies enter into contracts, lease federal lands, register securities offerings, award grants, administer government benefits, and much more. They direct active and close attention to the industries under their supervision.

Legislative Functions

Agencies create *rules* (sometimes called *regulations*) that can be legally binding. These rules provide the details necessary to carry out the intentions of the enabling legislation. In day-to-day business practice, the rules are likely to be much more important than the original law. The Occupational Safety and Health Act, for example, calls for a safe and healthful workplace, but the rules necessary for interpreting and enforcing that general mandate come not from Congress but from the agency.

Rules Agencies enact three types of rules:

1. *Procedural rules* delineate the agency's internal operating structure and methods. For example, the Internal Revenue Service (IRS), an agency within the Treasury Department, issues Revenue Procedures providing instructions on how to seek guidance from the agency. These rules do not have force-of-law status.
2. *Interpretive rules* offer the agency's view of the law for which the agency has administrative responsibility. For example, the IRS' Revenue Ruling 87-106 describes the circumstances under which taxpayers may be able to deduct as medical expenses the costs of modifying their home to make it handicap-accessible. Courts are not bound to follow Revenue Rulings or other interpretive rules because they do not have force-of-law status.
3. *Legislative rules* are policy expressions that have force-of-law status. Those governing federal tax matters are issued not by the IRS but by the Treasury Department as Treasury Regulations. Courts are required to enforce these rules. For example, Treasury Regulation Section 1.61-14(a) makes clear that profits from illegal activities are fully taxable.

Backup Cameras

In 2007, Congress passed the Kids Transportation Act requiring the National Highway Traffic Safety Administration (NHTSA) to issue specific standards for rear-view visibility by 2011. In December 2013, after the NHTSA had delayed the deadline five times, a lawsuit was filed to force the agency to release the rule. The NHTSA did so in March 2014, one day before a hearing was scheduled to be held in the lawsuit. The rule required all new vehicles under 10,000 pounds to have rear visibility technology (typically, backup cameras) by 2018. By the time the rule was issued, nearly half of all new cars sold already had backup cameras installed.

Data supporting the new rule showed that approximately 14,000 injuries and 200 deaths occurred annually while backing up. Almost half of the victims were children under five. A government analysis indicated that back-up cameras would have reduced those numbers by half. It also determined that a back-up camera with a visual display already installed would cost between $43 and $45 per vehicle; for those without a display, the cost would be $132 to $142. Both costs are minor considering the benefits derived.

Source: Pete Bigelow, "After Years of Delays, NHTSA Issues Backup Camera Rules," *Autoblog,* March 31, 2014 [**www.autoblog.com**].

The Rule-Making Process

The APA provides for both *informal* (often called "notice-and-comment") and *formal* rule-making processes for legislative rules. Under both approaches, the process begins with the publication of a Notice of Proposed Rule Making in the *Federal Register* (a daily publication of all federal rules, regulations, and orders). Thereafter, in the case of informal rule-making, the agency must permit written comments on the proposal and hold open hearings. After receiving public comments, the agency either discontinues the process or prepares the final rule.

In the case of formal rule-making, after providing notice, the agency must hold a public hearing conducted with most of the procedural safeguards of a trial, where all interested parties may call witnesses, challenge the agency evidence, and so on.

In either process, each new rule must be subject to public comment, and agencies are required to respond to all "material" comments. In general, the standard for materiality is that the comment be unique and fact-based, and of a nature that it could "require a change" to the proposed rule. To enhance participation in the rule-making process, the federal government has provided an online portal where any member of the public can comment on any proposed rule. [To explore the data on the portal and see what rules are currently proposed, see **www.regulations.gov**.]

Final agency rules are published in the *Federal Register* and later compiled in the *Code of Federal Regulations.* [To search the *Federal Register*, see **www.federalregister.gov**. To search the current *Code of Federal Regulations*, see **https://gov.ecfr.io**. To search for past versions of the *Code of Federal Regulations*, see **https://govinfo.gov/help/cfr**.]

Challenging an Agency Rule

Even after agency rules become final, they can be challenged in court. In August 2018, the EPA published a notice of proposed rule-making that would, among other things, revoke the waiver previously granted to California to set its own vehicle emissions standards under the Clean Air Act (CAA) in light of the State's "need to address [its] extraordinary and compelling air pollution issues."[66] For 50 years, the EPA had granted more than 100 waivers for California standards, which are also used by 13 other states, which the CAA allows. California supports its power to implement higher standards not just based on the CAA but also under its state constitutional power to protect the public health, safety, and general welfare of its citizens.

> California's long-standing waiver allowing it to implement its own greenhouse gas emission standards was reinstated.

After the EPA announced its final rule to withdraw the waiver, California, joined by 22 states, the District of Columbia, and the cities of Los Angeles and New York, filed a lawsuit to contest the withdrawal. On March 9, 2022, California's long-standing waiver was finally reinstated, allowing it to implement its own greenhouse gas emission standards.[67]

Question

If the legal conflict is between California's reserved powers to protect the public health, safety, and general welfare of its population and the federal government's enumerated power to regulate interstate commerce (for example, so that car manufacturers have one uniform standard applicable across all states), which government has the more compelling argument? Explain.

Judicial Functions

Although informal procedures such as settlements are preferred, agencies commonly must turn to *quasi-judicial* proceedings to enforce agency rules. For example, the National Labor Relations Board may hold a hearing to determine if an employee was wrongfully dismissed for engaging in protected union activities. The Federal Communications Commission may decide whether to withdraw a radio license because of the holder's failure to serve the public interest. The Federal Trade Commission may judge whether a particular ad is misleading.

Rule-Making or Adjudication? Many issues facing agencies could properly be resolved either by rule-making or by adjudication. Rule-making ordinarily involves standards to be applied to the future conduct of a class of unspecified parties. An adjudication, on the other hand, characteristically addresses specific parties involved in a specific present or past dispute. The rule-making/adjudication decision is discretionary with the agency (subject to judicial review) and is based on the nature of the issue and fairness to the parties. Regardless, the agencies are, in effect, "making law" either by passing a rule that has authority much like a law enacted by Congress or by establishing a judicial-like precedent in the case of an adjudication.

Administrative Hearings After an agency investigation, a violation of a statute or regulation may be alleged. An agency, like any other government body, is bound by the Constitution. Therefore, when an agency alleges that a person has violated a statute or a regulation, the Constitution requires it to respect the procedural *due process* rights of the person charged. The APA imposes specific steps, which begin with a formal notice to the affected party. Generally, at that point, an effort is made to reach a settlement, which would likely be memorialized with a *consent order* in which the affected party agrees to actions acceptable to the agency, but makes no admission of guilt (thus, reducing the likelihood of subsequent civil liability).

Failing settlement, an administrative hearing will be held, which has much in common with a civil trial but is a *quasi-judicial* proceeding within the agency, not a *judicial* proceeding in a court. Ordinarily, the case is heard by an *administrative law judge* (ALJ). The parties have the right to present their cases, hire counsel, cross-examine, file motions, raise objections, and so on. They do not have the right to a jury trial. The ALJ decides all questions of law and fact and issues the decision, generally referred to as an *order.* That decision will be final unless appealed within the agency. After exhausting all opportunities for review within the agency, an appeal may be taken to the appropriate federal court (or state court in the case of a state agency).

Controlling the Agencies

LO 8-13 Describe the executive, congressional, and judicial controls placed on agency conduct to maintain appropriate "checks and balances."

Although agency influence in business practice and in American life is enormous, none of the agencies and their thousands of employees are directly accountable to the people. What keeps them from abusing their power or from being "captured" by special interests? Just as with our constitutional system generally, certain checks and balances constrain agency conduct while allowing the latitude necessary to achieve effectiveness.

Executive Controls

As previously noted, the president appoints the administrators (or commissioners) for both executive and independent agencies, thus significantly influencing the direction and emphasis an agency pursues. Furthermore, the president can greatly influence the agency's budget.

Recent presidents have strengthened executive oversight of agency action by requiring *cost-benefit analyses* for new rules (President Clinton) and mandating that agencies cite a specific *market failure* before issuing a new rule (President George W. Bush). President Obama maintained the cost–benefit expectation and introduced an initiative to remove what he labeled "dumb" rules. He ordered all federal agencies to eliminate outdated rules that "stifle job creation and make our economy less competitive" and asked Congress for authority to consolidate a number of federal agencies.[68] President Trump took office with a deregulatory agenda, but based on data tracked by Brookings, a nonprofit public policy organization, his "results [were] decidedly mixed."[69] President Biden asked all agencies to cut "junk fees," such as the fees and charges that appear on airline tickets and hotel bills that make it hard to compare prices or the termination fees that lock customers in and make it hard to move to a different vendor.[70] [To see reports from a nonpartisan independent "watchdog" over the federal government, explore **www.pogo.org**.]

Congressional Controls

Congress creates and it can dissolve an agency, as it did with the Interstate Commerce Commission and the Civil Aeronautics Board. It can amend the enabling legislation to alter the scope of the agency's mandate or pass laws that require agencies to take specific actions or to proceed in a specific way. Congress controls agency budgets and thus can encourage, discourage, or even prohibit particular agency actions. Recall the discussion of the conflict between many states and the federal government on the legality of marijuana in Part One of this chapter and the Rohrabacher-Farr amendment annually reauthorized by Congress, which prohibits funds provided to the Department of Justice from being used to prevent states from implementing their medical marijuana laws. Agencies often negotiate with Congress before undertaking major initiatives.

Judicial Controls

Agency rules and orders can be, and often are, challenged in court in a process known as *judicial review.* But judicial review of agency action is narrow in scope, principally confined to the two following questions:

- Did the agency have the power to take the action challenged in the lawsuit?
- Was the agency's action arbitrary, capricious, or an abuse of discretion?

Did the agency have the power to take the action challenged in the lawsuit?

One basis for asserting the lack of such power is that the delegation of rule-making authority by Congress to the agency in the enabling legislation was unconstitutional. This is well illustrated by an important 2001 Supreme Court decision involving the federal Clean Air Act (CAA). The case, *Whitman v. American Trucking Associations, Inc.,*[71] raised the question of whether Congress had improperly delegated its authority to the Environmental Protection Agency (EPA) and whether the EPA must take the cost of implementing clean air regulations into consideration when developing new rules. A unanimous Supreme Court ruled that Congress had built into the CAA constitutionally sufficient limitations on agency action. It further ruled that Congress had not required the EPA to conduct cost-benefit analyses before establishing new rules. In sum, Congress can constitutionally offer agencies broad authority to carry out Congress's general intentions.

Another ground for asserting a lack of agency power to act is that the agency exceeded the authority granted to it by the enabling legislation. The 2022 Supreme Court case, *West Virginia v. Environmental Protection Agency,* discussed below, may well make it much easier for those challenging agency action to prevail.

Can an Agency's Regulatory Power Evolve to Address Materially Changed Circumstances?

In June 2022, the Supreme Court handed down its decision (6-3) in *West Virginia v. Environmental Protection Agency,* 597 U.S. _____ (2022). The case arose when the State of West Virginia challenged the EPA's power, under its Clean Power Plan (CPP) rules, to compel coal-based electricity-generating plants to, in essence, switch some or possibly all of their electricity production to natural gas or renewable energy sources, both of which have significantly lower levels of carbon emissions. The CPP set forth three ways existing coal plants could adjust their operations to achieve the required EPA standards for CO_2 emissions:

1. Improve the technology such that more electricity is derived from the same amount of coal,
2. Substitute some or all of the coal-based electricity production with natural gas-based electricity production, and/or

3. Substitute some or all of the coal-based electricity production with renewables-based electricity production.

The EPA cited Section 111(d) of the Clean Air Act (CAA) as the source of its authority to promulgate the CPP. The Court majority described Section 111(d) as follows: "[It] operates as a gap-filler, empowering EPA to regulate harmful emissions not already controlled under the Agency's other authorities."[72]

While the Court had no problem with the first method of adjustment (improved technology), it held that the agency-mandated second and third methods were beyond the scope of the power granted under Section 111(d):

> "Capping carbon dioxide emissions at a level that will force a nationwide transition away from the use of coal to generate electricity may be a sensible 'solution to the crisis of the day.' . . . But it is not plausible that Congress gave EPA the authority to adopt on its own such a regulatory scheme in Section 111(d). A decision of such magnitude and consequence rests with Congress itself, or an agency acting pursuant to a clear delegation from that representative body."[73]

The majority based its holding unambiguously on the *major questions doctrine* (MQD), "a phrase no Supreme Court majority had previously invoked explicitly."[74] The doctrine is meant to address circumstances in which, according to the majority opinion, an "agenc[y is] asserting highly consequential power beyond what Congress could reasonably be understood to have granted."

The dissenting opinion argued that the EPA has, for decades, undertaken such sweeping actions under Section 111(d) and similar statutory grants of power without any objection from Congress that the agency was acting beyond the scope of the authority granted to it:

> The limits the majority now puts on EPA's authority fly in the face of the statute Congress wrote. The majority says it is simply "not plausible" that Congress enabled EPA to regulate power plants' emissions through generation shifting [i.e., shifting the generation of electricity from higher carbon-emission production systems to lower carbon-emission production systems]. . . . But that is just what Congress did when it broadly authorized EPA in Section 111 to select the "best system of emission reduction" for power plants. . . . The "best system" full stop–no ifs, ands, or buts of any kind relevant here. The parties do not dispute that generation shifting is indeed the "best system"–the most effective and efficient way to reduce power plants' carbon dioxide emissions. And no other provision in the Clean Air Act suggests that Congress meant to foreclose EPA from selecting that system; to the contrary, the Plan's regulatory approach fits hand-in-glove with the rest of the statute. The majority's decision rests on one claim alone: that generation shifting is just too new and too big a deal for Congress to have authorized it in Section 111's general terms. But that is wrong. A key reason Congress makes broad delegations like Section 111 is so an agency can respond, appropriately and commensurately, to new and big problems. Congress knows what it doesn't and can't know when it drafts a statute; and Congress therefore gives an expert agency the power to address issues–even significant ones–as and when they arise. That is what Congress did in enacting Section 111. The majority today overrides that legislative choice. In so doing, it deprives EPA of the power needed–and the power granted–to curb the emission of greenhouse gases.

Critics of the decision assert that the introduction of the MQD into the judicial review of whether the enabling legislation authorizes an agency to take a specific action "casts an ominous pall over the nation's regulatory future,"[75] and "turn[s] on its head the normal approach to statutory interpretation."[76] The dissent said:

> Climate change's causes and dangers are no longer subject to serious doubt. Modern science is "unequivocal that human influence"–in particular, the emission of greenhouse gases like carbon dioxide–"has warmed the atmosphere, ocean and land." . . . The rise in temperatures brings with it "increases in heat-related deaths," "coastal inundation and erosion," "more frequent and intense hurricanes, floods, and other extreme weather events," "drought," "destruction of ecosystems," and "potentially significant disruptions of food production." . . . Rising waters, scorching heat, and other severe weather conditions could force "mass migration events[,] political crises, civil unrest," and "even state failure." . . .
>
> Congress charged EPA with addressing those potentially catastrophic harms, including through regulation of fossil fuel-fired power plants. Section 111 . . . directs EPA to regulate stationary sources of any substance that "causes, or contributes significantly to, air pollution" and that "may reasonably be anticipated to endanger public health or welfare." . . . Carbon dioxide and other greenhouse gases fit that description. . . . EPA thus serves as the Nation's "primary regulator of greenhouse gas emissions." . . . And among the most significant of the entities it regulates are fossil-fuel fired (mainly coal- and natural-gas-fired) power plants. Today, those electricity-producing plants are responsible for about one quarter of the Nation's greenhouse gas emissions. . . . Curbing that output is a necessary part of any effective approach for addressing climate change. . . .
>
> Today, the Court strips the [EPA] of the power Congress gave it to respond to "the most pressing environmental challenge of our time." *Massachusetts v. EPA,* 549 U.S. 497, 505 (2007). . . .
>
> The subject matter of the regulation here makes the Court's intervention all the more troubling. Whatever else this Court may know about, it does not have a clue about how to address climate change. And let's say the obvious: The stakes here are high. Yet the Court today prevents congressionally authorized agency action to curb power plants' carbon dioxide emissions. The Court appoints itself–instead of Congress or the expert agency–the decisionmaker on climate policy. I cannot think of many things more frightening.

Supporters of the decision have asserted that "the MQD amounts to . . . an insistence that, under our overarching Constitutional system, it would be preposterous to imagine any Congress intending to create such an open-ended grant of authority, capable of justifying a significant reordering of society and later, unforeseen circumstances."[77]

The full impact of introducing the MQD into the process of judicial review of agency action will take years to determine.

Questions

1. Evaluate the prospects of Congress taking strong action to address climate change issues in the present political environment.
   a. If you believe such action is unlikely, how do you feel about the Supreme Court's curtailment of the EPA's ability to take action in this case?

2. Assume Congress is eager to take on matters related to climate change. Do you believe Congress has the expertise necessary to draft all of the precise legislation and regulations needed to achieve climate change objectives? Does Congress have the time to monitor the climate change situation and constantly adjust such legislation and regulation?

Sources: *West Virginia v. Environmental Protection Agency,* 597 U.S. ___ (2022); Philip A. Wallach, "Will West Virginia v. EPA cripple regulators? Not if Congress steps up," Brookings Institution, July 1, 2022 [**www.brookings.edu**]; and "SCOTUS Ruling in West Virginia v. EPA Threatens All Regulation," *Bloomberg Law,* July 8, 2022 [**https://news.bloomberglaw.com**].

Was the agency's action arbitrary, capricious, or an abuse of discretion?
The two primary illustrations of such actions are (1) the agency makes a decision based on factors Congress did not authorize the agency to consider and (2) the agency's action is grounded on factual determinations that are not supported by substantial evidence in the record. When none of the established grounds invalidate an agency's action, courts are directed to defer to agency expertise and not substitute their own, nonexpert, judgment. This deference is considered in the text box below:

Judicial Deference to Agency Regulations

The enabling legislation Congress enacts when creating an agency sets forth general goals to be achieved, such as protecting the environment or maintaining well-functioning securities markets. It authorizes the agency to create the regulatory structure needed to achieve these goals–a delegation of Congress's rule-making authority. The scope of that delegation is sometimes very express, but the enabling legislation will also include a general grant of power to allow the agency do the things necessary to achieve the goals expressly identified by Congress.

As discussed previously, when an agency creates regulations establishing legal rights and duties necessary or useful for the accomplishment of the goals Congress set for the agency, those regulations are legislative in nature and have force-of-law status, as long as the agency adhered to the process specified in the APA for rule promulgation.

Such regulations are often challenged by persons adversely affected. For example, in 1981 the EPA issued legislative regulations allowing factories to install equipment that increases air pollution in one part of a facility so long as emissions in other parts of the facility are collectively reduced by the same amount. An environmental advocacy group challenged those regulations, ultimately bringing the matter to the Supreme Court in the 1984 case, *Chevron v. Natural Resource Defense Council,*[78] which established the doctrine of judicial deference to legislative regulations. "*Chevron* deference" applies if (1) the statute is ambiguous on the matter in question, and (2) the regulation is grounded on a reasonable construction of the statute.

Satisfaction of the second requirement depends on whether the court concludes that the enabling legislation expressly authorized the agency to clarify the ambiguity or whether the agency's authority to do so is merely implied. In the first situation, the agency's regulation will stand unless it is arbitrary, capricious, an abuse of discretion, or is contrary to the enabling legislation. In the second situation, the regulation will stand so long as it is a reasonable interpretation of the enabling legislation, even if some other approach might be seen to be more reasonable.

Justices Gorsuch and Kavanaugh have expressed strong criticisms of *Chevron* deference. Justice Kavanaugh's appointment shifted the balance of the Court, which may eventually lead to the substantial restriction, or complete abandonment, of the doctrine. The argument is that *Chevron* deference unconstitutionally shifts power to agencies, which are part of the executive branch of government, to the detriment of the legislative and judicial branches.

Question

It is difficult to believe that the government could adequately respond to the myriad of issues confronting the United States without specialized agencies. That said, do you believe we have gone too far delegating power to the "fourth branch?" Explain.

Sources: Kimberly Strawbridge Robinson, "High Court Could Take First Step to Chevron Doctrine's Demise," *Bloomberg Law,* March 28, 2019 [**https://news.bloomberglaw.com**]; Justin Walker, "The Kavanaugh Court and the Schechter-to-Chevron Spectrum: How the New Supreme Court Will Make the Administrative State More Democratically Accountable," *University of Louisville Law Legal Studies Research Paper Series,* 2019; and Michael McConnell, "Kavanaugh and the 'Chevron Doctrine'." *Hoover Institution,* July 30, 2018 [**www.hoover.org**].

Part Four—The Federal Regulatory Process Evaluated

Agencies exist to marshal the personpower and expertise needed to deal with an advanced society's complexities, a task that is beyond the capacity of legislatures. Much of the work performed by agencies is mundane, albeit of genuine value, such as establishing building construction and water safety standards, creating the rules for securities trading and financial statement preparation, and instituting the processes for registering cars, boats, and aircraft.

Sometimes agency action is anything but mundane. For example, the Federal Reserve Board (FED) has forcefully intervened on several occasions in the last 40 years to avert national (and sometimes international) financial calamities. During the Great Recession of the late 2000s, the FED kept the financial system from imploding by, in part, injecting $2.4 trillion of liquidity.[79] It intervened again to keep the economy from collapsing during the COVID-19 pandemic.[80]

In retrospect, some interventions may have been required because of ineffective regulatory action in prior years. For example, neither the SEC nor the FED took appropriate steps in advance to rein in the financial markets in the lead-up to the Great Recession.[81] Over 8.7 million jobs were lost, 3.8 million homes were foreclosed, and 4.1 million bankruptcies were filed.[82]

> Have decades of regulatory inaction contributed to the exponentially increasing cost of addressing climate change?

In years to come, it will be revealed how much decades of regulatory inaction have contributed to the exponentially increasing cost of addressing climate change. In 2017, an article in the *Harvard Business Review* estimated the total cost between 2017 and 2025 of unmitigated climate change–including the cost of related pandemics–to be $2.2 trillion.[83]

Too Much Government?

Perhaps we should champion impact analyses of proposed and existing regulations that paint a broad picture of their environmental, social, and stakeholder impacts.

Unfortunately, at the moment, a fractured political environment and an inability to even share a common set of facts make such an approach unlikely. It seems easier to oversimplify and sustain divisiveness with politically oriented sound bytes: "Too much government!" and "Why isn't the government doing something about that?"

The question posed in this section's title has often framed the national discourse. But the context is crucial. Modern society is complex. People, businesses, and institutions cannot know the full consequences of their individual decisions, let alone the collective consequences of the actions taken by the numerous members of society. To deal with this reality, over time we have created regulatory structures, often in the form of agencies, to watch over the macro effects of our collective individual decisions.

Perhaps "Is there too much government?" is the wrong question. There will likely always be abundant examples of over-regulation, under-regulation, and ineffective regulation, some having devastating impacts on those caught up in the aftermath. Instead of focusing on whether there is too much or too little government, perhaps the approach should be championing the development of impact analyses of proposed and existing regulations which would paint a broad picture of those regulations' environmental, social, and stakeholder impacts–the tradeoffs and consequences associated with regulatory action or inaction.

The Winner: The (Carefully) Mixed Economy?

In 2008, economist and columnist Sebastian Mallaby argued that roles should be embraced for both the market and the government in the United States' mixed economy (an economic system combining private and public actors). He further called for a recognition that the American people will continue to demand more and more from their governments (protection from criminals and terrorists, clean air, safe food, good schools, retirement security, and so on).[84] Indeed, he asserted that these public goods in our prosperous society probably matter more than private pleasures such as smartphones and exotic vacations. As a result, government will likely be under great pressure to spend more, threatening the possibility of crippling fiscal deficits. Recognizing that, he believed the country must "be ruthless about making government and markets more efficient."[85]

It must also be remembered, however, that excessive regulation can kill jobs, prosperity, and ambition, so a delicate balance between market and government is necessary, as noted by *New York Times* columnist Nicholas Kristof:

> Critics are right that regulators are sometimes too zealous and bureaucratic. Sometimes regulations do curb profits and undermine jobs. But, on the whole, we need regulations to guard against human nature. The truth is that bad things usually aren't done by evil people,

> but rather by essentially decent people who go to work and get so wrapped up in the "business case" they sometimes lose their moral compass.[86]

So while freedom and prosperity require a strong free market, a healthy, just society seems to require a significant, but appropriately measured, role for government.

Research Exercise on Essential Workers

Workers at meat processing plants during the first year of the COVID pandemic were considered "essential" workers. Presumably, they are essential because they perform services necessary for the well-being of the whole country. Given that, consider what measures would have been appropriate to ensure these workers' continued service on our behalf? Be sure to identify the reasoning behind your recommendations.

Research Exercise on Campus Drones

Imagine you are interested in flying drones for fun—for example, to capture school athletic and other outdoors campus events for classmates who could not attend. To get approval from your school, you need to give a presentation to point out the benefits to the campus community and to get people excited about its possible uses. You must also brief the administration on the basic requirements that will have to be met to fly your drone. A good place to start your research on that last item will be the FAA.

Chapter Questions

1. According to a 2014 Health Policy Institute study, about 15 percent of Americans surveyed said they could not afford dental care when needed.[87] The average dentist in 2013 earned, after expenses, about $181,000, as compared with about $175,000 for family doctors. (The respective inflation-adjusted amounts are $224,000 and $217,000.) A *Washington Post* 2015 commentary argued that dentists may be overpaid, in part because they are protected from competition by law in most states. Minnesota, however, is now licensing "dental therapists," who are not dentists but are allowed to clean, fill, and pull teeth when under the "general supervision" of a dentist. One study found that dentists' income (presumably reflected in fees charged to patients) was reduced by 16 percent ($36,000, inflation-adjusted) where hygienists were allowed to offer independent care. Do you think we should allow market forces to drive down the cost of dental care by permitting less expensive dental personnel, if appropriately trained, do some of the work of dentists? Explain. See Max Ehrenfreund, "Why Dentists Are So Darn Rich," *The Washington Post,* July 29, 2015 [**www.washingtonpost.com**].
2. How would you support the argument that the "invisible hand" of the market Adam Smith envisioned is not neutral because our "hands" are not equal?
3. The Heritage Foundation's 2022 global Index of Economic Freedom generally demonstrates that the nations most successful in increasing their economic freedom (by reducing taxes and so forth) enjoy, according to the editors of the study, higher incomes and higher overall well-being.[88] When the Index was first published in 1995, the United States ranked fifth in the world but fell to eleventh in 2016, seventeenth in 2020, and twenty-fifth in 2022. Singapore ranked first in 2022. New Zealand (fourth) and Australia (twelfth) ranked above the United States, as did Iceland, Lithuania, Chile, Canada, the United Kingdom, and Estonia.

a. What do you think economic freedom is?

b. The Heritage Foundation lists 10 factors, including business freedom, in its list of inputs in measuring economic freedom. In addition to business freedom, what other factors would you include in a list designed to measure a nation's level of overall economic freedom?

c. How does economic freedom help an economy grow?

4. The expense of government regulation is not limited to the direct cost of administering the various agencies. Explain and offer examples of the other costs produced by regulation.

5. In 1995, Pulitzer Prize–winning author and presidential adviser, Arthur Schlesinger wrote

> The assault on the national government is represented as a disinterested movement to "return" power to the people. But the withdrawal of the national government does not transfer power to the people. It transfers power to the historical rival of the national government and the prime cause of its enlargement—the great corporate interests.[89]

Do you agree with Schlesinger that today we continue to need big government to counteract corporate interests and achieve fairness for all in American life? Explain.

6. Obesity contributes to the deaths of almost 500,000 Americans and costs the U.S. health care system approximately $173 million each year. It increases the risks of heart disease, Type 2 diabetes, stroke, and some cancers. According to the Centers for Disease Control and Prevention, 42 percent of adults are obese, as are 13 percent of children ages two through five and 22 percent of children 12 to 19 years old. Up to seven percent of U.S. food budgets go to sugary drinks, and as much as another 20 percent is spent on other junk food. Among adolescents, 33 to 57 percent of their calories come from junk food.[90] One strategy for reducing the health risks of obesity is to impose a tax on junk foods like soda, donuts, candy, and potato chips. At least eight cities have enacted a tax on sugary beverages. The Philadelphia tax increased prices by 34 percent and led to a 22 percent decline in purchases. Internationally, the UK's tax on such beverages increased prices by about $.25 per container. Consumption dropped 34 percent and the great majority of manufacturers lowered the sugar content of their drinks to come within the UK's dietary recommendations.[91] The World Health Organization points to Hungary's comprehensive tax on junk food as a model. Like most EU members, Hungary imposes a value-added tax on food products in general; in that country, it is 25 percent. Hungary more than doubled the tax to 52 percent for junk food. Within four years, 59 percent of its residents reduced their junk food consumption by an average of one-sixth. The reductions were much higher among the overweight and those with low incomes for whom junk food represents a much higher proportion of their diets and who are more likely to have health problems in general. Forty percent of junk food manufacturers modified their recipes to make them more healthy, and the government raised $219 million annually in taxes (about two percent of Hungary's governmental health care spending).[92]

a. Given the data presented above, would you support a significant tax, say 25 percent, on junk food? Fifty-two percent (like Hungary)? Explain.

b. As noted, lower-income people tend to be less healthy and consume more junk food as a percentage of their total diet. Any tax large enough to affect behavior will be regressive–it will represent a larger proportion of this group's disposable income. Is this fair from the low-income individual's perspective? From the country's perspective? Explain.

7. Joseph Stiglitz, the chief White House economist at the time, argued in 1996 that "a huge economic literature" supports his view that "appropriately circumscribed government programs can lead to a higher-growth economy."[93] How can government programs stimulate the economy rather than act as a drag on it? Can you think of specific examples that might have stimulated the economy?
8. *a.* In general, do you trust the federal government? Explain.

   b. More specifically, do you trust the federal agencies discussed in this chapter, including, for example, the Food and Drug Administration, the Environmental Protection Agency, and the Internal Revenue Service? Explain.
9. A bipartisan coalition called "Mayors Against Illegal Guns" released a 2010 study finding that 43,000 of the guns confiscated at crime scenes in 2009 came from out-of-state gun dealers. Georgia, Virginia, West Virginia, Alabama, Mississippi, and Alaska were among the largest gun exporters. States with strong restrictions export guns at only about one-seventh the rate of those with lax rules. In 2020, using the latest numbers available from the CDC, there were 19,384 firearm homicides out of a 24,576 total homicides.[94] Commenting on such deaths, *New York Times* columnist Nicholas Kristof said:

   > To protect the public, we regulate cars and toys, medicines and mutual funds. So, simply as a public health matter, shouldn't we take steps to reduce the toll from our domestic arms industry?[95]

   What do you think about firmer gun regulations? Explain.

Notes

1. Jeet Heer, "Meatpacking Plants Are a Front in the Covid-19 Class War," *The Nation,* April 29, 2020 [**www.thenation.com**].
2. Ibid.
3. "About OSHA," Occupational Safety and Health Administration, accessed August, 2020 [**www.osha.gov**].
4. Kyle Bagenstose, Sky Chadde, and Matt Wynn, "Coronavirus at meatpacking plants worse than first thought," *USA Today,* April 22, 2020 [**www.usatoday.com**].
5. "Meat and Poultry Processing Workers and Employers Interim Guidance," Centers for Disease Control and Prevention, accessed July, 2020 [**www.cdc.gov**].
6. Michael Corkery, David Yaffe-Bellany, and Derek Kravitz, "As Meatpacking Plants Reopen, Data About Worker Illness Remains Elusive," *The New York Times,* May 25, 2020 [**www.nytimes.com**].
7. CDC, "Meat and Poultry Processing Workers and Employers Interim Guidance."
8. Bagenstose, "Coronavirus at meatpacking plants worse than first thought."
9. Heer, "Meatpacking Plants Are a Front in the Covid-19 Class War."
10. Terry Collins, "These are the workers that the U.S. government deems 'essential' amid the coronavirus pandemic," *Fortune,* March 20, 2020 [**https://fortune.com**].

11. See, e.g., Carlos Cueva et al., "Cortisol and Testosterone Increase Financial Risk Taking and May Destablilize Markets," *Scientific Reports* 5, no. 11206 (2015), doi:10.1038/srep11206.
12. Joseph P. Tomain, "American Regulatory Policy: Have We Found the 'Third Way'?" *Kansas Law Review* 48 (May 2000), p. 829.
13. Michelle Chapman and the Associated Press, "Southwest Airlines sees quarterly loss, $825 million hit from canceled Christmas flights chaos," *Fortune,* January 6, 2023 [**www.fortune.com**].
14. Charles Leocha, "For Airlines, the Free Market Doesn't Need to Be Unfettered," *The New York Times,* May 25, 2016 [**www.nytimes.com**].
15. Chris Hamby, Walt Bogdanich, Michael Forsythe and Jennifer Valentino-DeVries, "McKinsey Opened a Door in Its Firewall Between Pharma Clients and Regulators," *The New York Times,* April 13, 2022 [**www.nytimes.com**].
16. 545 U.S. 1 (2005).
17. *Id.* at 32-33.
18. *Id.* at 8.
19. *Id.* at 57–58 (Thomas, J., dissenting).
20. 115 S. Ct. 1624 (1995).
21. 18 U.S.C. § 922(q)(1)(A).
22. *Brzonkala v. Morrison* and *United States v. Morrison,* 529 U.S. 598 (2000).
23. *Brzonkala v. Virginia Polytechnic Institute,* 169 F.3d 820, 827 (4th Cir. 1999).
24. John F. Cooney, "Federalism Spring: Evolution of the Federal-State Balance of Power," *Bloomberg Law Reports–Administrative Law,* no. 4 (2009).
25. See, e.g., *Williamson v. Mazda Motor of America, Inc.,* 131 S. Ct. 1131 (2011) [state tort suit not preempted]; *Bruesewitz v. Wyeth LLC,* 131 S. Ct. 1068 (2011) [state tort suit preempted]; and *Gobeille v. Liberty Mutual Insurance Co.,* 136 S. Ct. 936 (2016) [Employee Retirement Income Security Act (ERISA) preempts a Vermont statute requiring health insurers to report data about health care claims].
26. *Murphy v. NCAA,* 138 S. Ct. 1461, 1470 (2018).
27. *Id.* at 1475-76.
28. Ibid.
29. "State Laws," *NORML,* accessed January 7, 2023 [**https://norml.org**].
30. Ibid.
31. Rohrabacher–Farr Amendment, *Wikipedia,* accessed January 7, 2023 [**https://en.wikipedia.org**].
32. 833 F.3d 1163 (9th Cir.) 2016.
33. Matthew Clarke, "Tenth Circuit Reinstates Colorado Prisoner's Claim that Requires BOP to Release Him from Imprisonment for Marijuana Possession," *Prison Legal News,* June 1, 2020 [**www.prisonlegalnews.org**].
34. *Nebraska and Oklahoma v. Colorado,* 136 S. Ct. 1034 (2016).
35. Rob Stumpf, "Tesla's Found a Way Around Direct Sales Bans by Putting Dealerships on Tribal Lands," *The Drive,* November 8, 2022 [**www.thedrive.com**].
36. Docket no. 19-1392, 597 U.S. _____ (2022).
37. 410 U.S. 113 (1973).
38. 505 U.S. 833 (1992).

39. Nicole Dube, James Orlando, and Jessica Schaeffer-Helmecki, "State Abortion Laws Enacted Post-Dobbs Decision," *Office of Legislative Research, Connecticut General Assembly,* September 29, 2022 [**https://cga.gov**].
40. Ibid.
41. Ibid.
42. Adeel Hassan, "New Year, New (State) Rules," *The New York Times,* January 3, 2023 [**www.nytimes.com**].
43. 554 U.S. 570 (2008).
44. 42 S. Ct. 2111 (2022).
45. "Frequently Asked Questions," *Everytown Support Fund,* accessed January 9, 2023 [**https://everytownresearch.org**].
46. "Gun Safety Policies Save Lives," *Everytown Support Fund,* accessed January 9, 2023 [**https://everytownresearch.org**].
47. Sara Swann, "The history of the AR-15 and how it became a symbol of American gun culture," *Poynter,* June 29, 2022 [**https://www.poynter.org**].
48. Ibid.
49. Heather Cox Richardson, *Letters from an American,* May 26, 2022.
50. "Which states prohibit assault weapons?," *Everytown Support Fund,* accessed January 9, 2023 [**https://everytownresearch.org**].
51. Zach Herman, "The National Occupational Licensing Database Executive Summary," *National Conference of State Legislatures,* March 24, 2020 [**www.ncsl.org**].
52. Dick M. Carpenter, Lisa Knepper, Kyle Sweetland, and Jennifer McDonald, "License To Work," *Institute for Justice,* update January 1, 2020 [**https://ij.org**].
53. Herman, "The National Occupational Licensing Database."
54. Maureen K. Ohlhausen, Foreword to *License to Work, Second Edition,* Institute for Justice, accessed May 2, 2023 [**https://ij.org**].
55. Tariro Mzezewa, "Airbnb and Miami Beach Are at War. Travelers Are Caught in the Crossfire," *The New York Times,* March 9, 2019 [**www.nytimes.com**].
56. Ibid.
57. Luis Ferré-Sadurni, "Inside the Rise and Fall of a Multimillion-Dollar Airbnb Scheme," *The New York Times,* February 23, 2019 [**www.nytimes.com**].
58. Ibid.
59. Katie Benner, "Airbnb and San Francisco Settle Registration Dispute," *The New York Times,* May 2, 2017 [**www.nytimes.com**].
60. Jennifer Jacobs, "Judge Backs City's Refusal to Renew Bar's License," *The Waterloo/Cedar Falls Courier,* November 22, 1998, p. C3.
61. Chris Kirkham, "Home Builders Say They Are Squeezed by Rising Compliance Costs," *The Wall Street Journal,* May 7, 2016 [**www.wsj.com**].
62. Pam Belluck, "F.D.A. Approves New Treatment for Early Alzheimer's," *The New York Times,* January 6, 2023 [**www.nytimes.com**].
63. "UAS Remote Identification," *Federal Aviation Administration,* accessed January 9, 2023 [**www.faa.gov**].
64. PressRelease, "FDA finalizes enforcement policy on unauthorized flavored cartridge-based e-cigarettes that appeal to children, including fruit and mint," *U.S. Food & Drug Administration,* January 2, 2020 [**www.fda.gov**].

65. Jeff Link and Paresh Dave, "Amazon's Drone Delivery Dream Is Crashing," *Wired,* April 4, 2023 **[www.wired.com]**.
66. Press Release, "Attorney General Becerra Files Lawsuit Against EPA for Attacking California's Advanced Clean Car Standards," *State of California Department of Justice,* November 15, 2019 **[https://oag.ca.gov]**.
67. "EPA Restores California's Authority to Enforce Greenhouse Gas Emission Standards for Cars and Light Trucks," *Environmental Protection Agency,* March 9, 2022 **[www.epa.gov]**.
68. Lori Montgomery, "Obama Orders All Fed Agencies to Review Regulations," *The Washington Post,* January 18, 2011 **[www.washingtonpost.com]**.
69. Phillip A. Wallach and Kelly Kennedy, "Examining some of Trump's deregulation efforts: Lessons from the Brookings Regulatory Tracker," *Brookings,* March 8, 2022 **[www.brookings.edu]**.
70. Heather Cox Richardson, "October 26, 2022," *Letters from an American,* October 27, 2022.
71. 531 U.S. 457 (2001).
72. *West Virginia v. Environmental Protection Agency,* 597 U.S. _____ (2022).
73. Ibid.
74. "SCOTUS Ruling in West Virginia v. EPA Threatens All Regulation," *Bloomberg Law,* July 8, 2022 **[https:/news.bloomberglaw.com]**.
75. Ibid.
76. Ibid.
77. Philip A. Wallach, "Will West Virginia v. EPA cripple regulators? Not if Congress steps up," Brookings Institution, July 1, 2022 **[www.brookings.edu]**.
78. 467 U.S. 837 (1984).
79. "Quantitative easing," *Wikipedia,* accessed January 11, 2023 **[https://en.wikipedia.org]**.
80. Ibid.
81. Gary Gensler, "Testimony of Chairman Before the Financial Crisis Inquiry Commission," *Commodities Futures Trading Commission,* July 1, 2010 **[www.cftc.gov]**.
82. "Chart Book: The Legacy of the Great Recession," *Center on Budget and Policy Priorities,* June 6, 2019 **[www.cbpp.org]**; Sharada Dharmasankar and Bhash Mazumder, "Have Borrowers Recovered from Foreclosures during the Great Recession?," *Federal Reserve Bank of Chicago,* 2016 **[www.chicagofed.org]**; and Jay Heflin, "Pandemic likely to exceed Great Recession in number of bankruptcies," *Washington Examiner,* April 13, 2020 **[www.washingtonexaminer.com]**.
83. Dante Disparte, "If You Think Fighting Climate Change Will Be Expensive, Calculate the Cost of Letting It Happen," *Harvard Business Review,* June 12, 2017 **[https://hbr.org]**.
84. Sebastian Mallaby, "Capitalism: The Remix," **www.Washingtonpost.com,** December 4, 2008, p. A21.
85. Ibid.
86. Nicholas Kristof, "Job Crushing or Lifesaving?," *The New York Times,* April 30, 2014 **[www.nytimes.com]**.
87. Thomas Wall, Kamyar Nasseh, and Marko Vujicic, "Most Important Barriers to Dental Care Are Financial, Not Supply Related," *Health Policy Institute Research Brief,* October 2014 **[www.ada.org]**.
88. 2022 Index of Economic Freedom, "The Heritage Foundation," accessed January 2023 **[www.heritage.org]**.
89. Arthur Schlesinger Jr., "In Defense of Government," *The Wall Street Journal,* June 7, 1995, p. A14.
90. Zachary Ward et al., "Excess mortality associated with elevated body weight in the USA by state and demographic subgroup: A modelling study," *The Lancet,* Vol. 48, June 2022

[www.thelancet.com/journals/eclinm/article/PIIS2589-5370(22)00159-6/fulltext]; and "Why [Obesity] Matters, Centers for Disease Control and Prevention," accessed February 22, 2023 **[www.cdc.gov/obesity/about-obesity/why-it-matters.xhtml#:~:text=Only%202%20in%205%20young,to%20have%20obesity%20as%20adults.&text=Obesity%20costs%20the%20US%20healthcare%20system%20nearly%20%24173%20billion%20a%20year]**; Julia Belluz, "Mexico and Hungary tried junk food taxes–and they seem to be working," *Vox,* April 6, 2018 **[www.vox.com]**; Arlene Weintraub, "Should We Tax Junk Foods To Curb Obesity?," *Forbes,* January 10, 2018 **[www.forbes.com]**; and Rachel Griffith, Martin O'Connell, and Kate Smith, "Would taxes on unhealthy foods reduce obesity?" *Economics Observatory,* May 28, 2021 **[www.economicsobservatory.com/would-taxes-on-unhealthy-foods-reduce-obesity]**.

91. Julia Belluz, "Mexico and Hungary tried junk food taxes–and they seem to be working"; and Rachel Griffith et al., "Would taxes on unhealthy foods reduce obesity?"
92. Julia Belluz, "Mexico and Hungary tried junk food taxes–and they seem to be working."
93. Bob Davis, "In Presidential Race, the Key Question Is, 'What Causes Growth?'," *The Wall Street Journal,* September 27, 1996, p. A1.
94. CDC National Center for Health Statistics, "Assault or Homicide," accessed January 2022 **[www.cdc.gov/nchs/fastats/homicide.htm]**.
95. Nicholas D. Kristof, "Why Not Regulate Guns as Seriously as Toys?," *The New York Times,* January 12, 2011 **[www.nytimes.com]**.

Video icon credit: Comstock Images/Alamy Stock Photo

CHAPTER NINE

Business Organizations and Securities Regulation

After completing this chapter, students will be able to fulfill the following learning objectives:

9-1. Compare and contrast the nature, advantages, and disadvantages of corporations, general partnerships, sole proprietorships, and limited liability companies.

9-2. Explain the business judgment rule.

9-3. Explain the relationship between limited liability and the doctrine of "piercing the corporate veil."

9-4. Distinguish between equity and debt capital.

9-5. Identify the advantages and disadvantages of general partnerships.

9-6. Explain the unique features of several key hybrid forms of business.

9-7. Explain how corporations are governed.

9-8. Describe some of the challenges facing modern boards of directors, including cybersecurity, bribery, corporate political spending, international taxation, and executive compensation.

9-9. Analyze the implications of the purpose of the corporation shifting from shareholder value to stakeholder value.

9-10. Discuss board composition in light of the rapidly changing business environment in which corporations now operate.

9-11. Define the term *initial public offering* and explain the securities registration process.

9-12. Identify the purposes of the 1933 Act and the principal methods by which they are achieved.

9-13. Identify the purposes of the 1934 Act and the principal methods by which they are achieved.

9-14. Identify when a "material misrepresentation" has occurred.

9-15. Explain the due diligence defense.

9-16. Describe the fraud on the market theory of reliance and explain its importance.

9-17. Define insider trading and identify how to determine when it has occurred.

9-18. Identify the context for the passage of and the purpose of the Private Securities Litigation Reform Act.

9-19. Identify and describe the penalties the government may impose for aiding and abetting securities fraud.

9-20. Describe the tender offer process and some defenses against a hostile takeover.

9-21. Describe the impact that Brexit may have in Europe.

Introduction

This chapter provides an introduction to some of the fundamental laws governing business–including the types and characteristics of available business forms, key corporate governance issues, and business access to capital.

First, the overlap of state and federal business regulation must be addressed. State law governs most issues–such as the creation of business entities, the powers and duties of management, and capital structure. The owners of a corporation are called ***stockholders*** or ***shareholders*** because the ownership interests are called shares of ***stock***. The fundamental legal duties corporations, corporate boards, and officers owe to their shareholders are defined by the state of incorporation. Eighty percent of all publicly held companies and two-thirds of the Fortune 500 are incorporated in Delaware. Ninety-three percent of all ***initial public offerings*** (IPOs) are based in that state.[1] Thus, when state corporate law is discussed, Delaware often drives the discussion. Part One of this chapter discusses the key characteristics of the most common business forms.

Delaware: Race to the Bottom or to the Top?

Delaware generates 15 percent of its total revenue from taxes related to corporate domicile (almost 13 percent from corporate licensing fees, which is about 100 times larger than the national average of .15 percent). Delaware's success in attracting corporations is alternatively described as the fruits of a "race to the top" or as the spoils of a "race to the bottom." The most recent (2019) U.S. Chamber Institute for Legal Reform's *Lawsuit Climate Survey* ranked Delaware's legal system the best in the country for business for the 14th consecutive time. Corporate management appreciates the state's business-friendly Court of Chancery. For example, in 2013, that body upheld a bylaw restricting shareholder lawsuits to Delaware courts. Such bylaws give management the "home-field advantage" by denying jurisdiction to states that are more sympathetic to shareholders–part of the race to the bottom that favors the interests of entrenched management over those of shareholders, employees, the environment, or the community.

Historically, state corporate law was grounded in the regulation of corporate behavior in order to protect the interests of all constituencies (the shareholders, the corporation itself, the communities in which the corporation operated, and the parties with whom the corporation dealt). In 1896, New Jersey sought to undermine New York City's dominance in the incorporation market by abandoning that regulatory focus in favor of a "laissez-faire" approach that centralized power in corporate boards and management by limiting the role of shareholders. "This point of inflection [was] noticeable and dramatic[; it] 'turned corporate law inside out.'" New Jersey's incorporation revenues increased enormously, leading Delaware to join the competition in 1899. It almost immediately displaced New Jersey with its even more pro-management corporate law. Other states have unsuccessfully attempted to overtake Delaware as the jurisdiction of choice for publicly held companies. Some have taken the race to the bottom to astounding depths. For example, Nevada corporate law expressly absolves officers and directors from liability for conduct such as failing to act in good faith and receiving improper personal benefits from the corporation (for instance, charging the corporation exorbitant rent for the use of a director's property). The Nevada legislature made clear the law's objective: to reach the only incorporation market segment left open to it given Delaware's dominance among publicly held companies–persons who want to use the corporate form without being subject to the behavioral restrictions that are "axiomatic" in nearly every other state. Nevada enacted the law despite legislators' characterizations of the likely users as "scoundrels" and "sleaze balls."

For the State of Delaware's formal response to the accusations of it being the victor of the race to the bottom, see **https://corplaw.delaware.gov/facts-and-myths.**

Sources: "What Is Delaware's Franchise Tax?," *Harvard Business Services, Inc., accessed June 7, 2023* [**www.delawareinc.com**]; "Delaware Taxes: Top 5 Sources of State Revenue," *The News Journal,* May 19, 2014 [**www.delawareonline.com**]; "2019 Lawsuit Climate Survey: Ranking the States," *U.S. Chamber Institute for Legal Reform,* September 2019 [**www.instituteforlegalreform.com**]; Peg Brickley, "Allowing Firms to Restrict Suits to Delaware to Change Legal Landscape," *The Wall Street Journal,* July 7, 2013 [**www.wsj.com**]; and Michal Barzuza, "Market Segmentation: The Rise of Nevada as A Liability-Free Jurisdiction," *Virginia Law Review,* Vol. 98, No. 5 (September 2012), pp. 935-1000.

The first decade of the 21st century was scarred by two systemic failures involving corporate actors and the capital markets. The first is commonly referenced by the 2001 collapse of Enron (although it was not the largest corporate failure of that era–just the most spectacular). The second was the financial crisis that struck in the fall of 2008 (often referenced by the collapse of Lehman Brothers). Contributing to both disasters were failures of corporate governance. Congress responded each time with significant legislation imposing additional requirements on ***publicly held corporations*** (corporations with many shareholders, the shares of which are traded on the public capital markets, such as the New York Stock Exchange): the Sarbanes-Oxley Act of 2002 (SOX) and the Dodd-Frank Act of 2010. Part Two of this chapter discusses corporate governance.

Part Three will take a closer look at how businesses are financed beyond the resources of the founders. Although state law plays a role here, federal law dominates. Triggered by the 1929 stock market crash and the extended failure of the capital markets and banking system during the Great Depression, the federal government, largely under its interstate commerce powers, created the Securities and Exchange Commission (SEC) to regulate the national securities markets. Part Three will focus on this regulation.

Part One—Business Entities and Their Defining Characteristics

LO 9-1 Compare and contrast the nature, advantages, and disadvantages of corporations, general partnerships, sole proprietorships, and limited liability companies.

One of the most significant business decisions is the choice of the form in which an enterprise will be conducted. Among other things, this decision will affect the legal relationships among the owners, between them and the entity, and between various third parties and the owners and the entity. It will also affect access to outside capital and the tax treatment accorded business profits and losses. In this part of the chapter, the principal business forms are outlined, a few lesser-used forms are examined, and important new forms are discussed. The part concludes with a brief consideration of the circumstances that might favor one form over another.

The three traditional business forms are ***corporations, general partnerships,*** and ***sole proprietorships***. General partnerships and sole proprietorships are default forms. If an individual starts a business and takes no active steps to house it within a legally separate entity, the business form will, by default, be a sole proprietorship. Strictly speaking, a sole proprietorship is not a business entity–the law treats the business and the individual as the same legal person. If two or more persons join together to start a business and take no active steps to create a separate legal entity, the law will, again by default, classify the business form as a general partnership. The only way to establish a business as a corporation, or indeed as any of the other forms discussed in this part, is for its founders to take deliberate steps, specified by state law, to create the separate legal entity.

One such other entity is the ***limited liability company*** (LLC). LLCs are often referred to as a ***hybrid form*** because they are specifically designed to combine certain desired corporate characteristics with those of general partnerships. Another popular hybrid form is the ***Subchapter S corporation*** (also called an ***S corporation*** in reference to the subchapter of the Internal Revenue Code that governs the income tax treatment of such corporations and their shareholders). For state corporate law purposes, an S corporation is a corporation like any other; but for income tax purposes, the legal entity is largely ignored and virtually all of the entity's tax consequences flow through to the tax returns of its shareholders. This is similar, but not identical, to the way the tax consequences of a partnership flow through to the tax returns of the partners.

According to the latest data available (2015), and setting aside the 24 million businesses operated as sole proprietorships, more businesses are housed in these two hybrid entities, LLCs (2.3 million) and S corporations (4.3 million)–a total of 6.6 million–than in traditional corporations (1.6 million) and partnerships (1 million)–a total of 2.6 million. In terms of revenues, however, corporations ($23 trillion) and partnerships ($1.8 trillion)–a total of $24.8 trillion–overwhelm the hybrids in significance to the economy: S corporations ($6.9 trillion) and LLCs ($3.2 trillion)–$9.6 trillion combined.[2]

Each of these forms will be evaluated using the following criteria:

Formation and nontax costs: The method of, and costs related to, bringing the form into existence.

Management structure: The degree to which control of the form is exercised in a hierarchical structure.

Limited liability: The extent to which owners are personally liable for the business' obligations.

Transferability of ownership interests: Whether the law restricts owners from freely transferring their interests.

Duration of existence: The events, including those impacting the owners personally (such as death), that will end the form's existence.

Taxes: The way the choice of form affects the income tax treatment of the business and its owners.

Capital structure: The impact of form selection on the ability to access additional capital.

[For a table summarizing the key characteristics of each business form, see **www.bizfilings.com/toolkit/tools/compare-business-types**.]

Corporations

Although only 5 percent of all businesses are conducted as traditional corporations (often referred to as ***C corporations*** in reference to the subchapter of the Internal Revenue Code which governs the taxation of the corporation and its shareholders), they account for 63 percent of all business revenue. C and S corporations combined represent 18 percent of all businesses and account for 82 percent of all business revenue.[3] There are good reasons for the dominance of the corporate form, which will become evident in the discussion below.

Throughout this topic, it will be important to distinguish between the publicly held corporation and the ***closely held corporation*** (a corporation with relatively few shareholders, the stock of which has no readily available market).

Corporate constitutional rights?

Under state law, corporations are separate legal entities, sometimes referred to as *artificial persons* (as opposed to *natural persons,* which are humans). This raises the question of whether they have constitutionally protected rights. Over the years, the Supreme Court has held that sometimes they do and sometimes they do not. In 2010, the issue arose again in a profoundly significant case, *Citizens United v. Federal Election Commission,* in which the Court enunciated a wide-reaching principle that "the Government may not suppress political speech on the basis of the speaker's corporate identity." Justice Stevens, with three others, vigorously dissented:

> The real issue [is] how, not if, [Citizens United] may finance its electioneering. Citizens United is a wealthy nonprofit corporation that runs a political action committee (PAC) with millions of dollars in assets. Under [the campaign finance restriction being challenged], it could have used those assets to televise and promote *Hillary: The Movie* [a negative portrayal of the 2008 presidential candidate] wherever and whenever it wanted to . . . other than the 30 days before the last primary election. Neither Citizens United's nor any other corporation's speech has been "banned." . . . In the context of election to public office, the distinction between corporate and human speakers is significant. Although they make enormous contributions to our society, corporations are not actually members of it. They cannot vote or run for office[.] The financial resources, legal structure, and . . . orientation of corporations raise legitimate concerns about their role in the electoral process.

More recently in 2014, the Court in *Burwell v. Hobby Lobby Stores, Inc.* held in another 5–4 ruling that the portions of the Affordable Care Act of 2010 mandating the corporation's provision of certain contraception benefits "substantially burden the exercise of religion." The family that owned the company had strong religious convictions against certain approaches to contraception. The full implications of this holding are difficult to predict. For example, Justice Ginsburg asked in her dissent: "Would the exemption the Court [grants] extend to . . . religiously grounded objections to blood transfusions (Jehovah's Witnesses) . . . antidepressants (Scientologists) . . . and vaccinations (Christian Scientists . . .)?"

Sources: *Grosjean v. American Press Co.,* 297 U.S. 233 (1936); *Western & Southern Life Insurance Co. v. State Board of Equalization,* 451 U.S. 648 (1981); *Citizens United v. Federal Election Commission,* 130 S. Ct. 876 (2010); and *Burwell v. Hobby Lobby Stores, Inc.,* 134 S. Ct. 2751 (2014).

Questions

1. When a corporation funds political speech, for whom do you think it is speaking? Explain. You may wish to consider these possibilities from the *Citizens United* majority and dissenting opinions:
   a. Majority opinion: "[W]ealthy individuals and unincorporated associations can spend unlimited amounts on independent expenditures. Yet certain disfavored associations

of citizens–those that have taken on the corporate form–are penalized for engaging in the same political speech."

b. Minority opinion: "It is an interesting question 'who' is even speaking when a business corporation places an advertisement that endorses or attacks a particular candidate. Presumably it is not the customers or employees, who typically have no say in such matters. It cannot realistically be said to be the shareholders, who tend to be far removed from the day-to-day decisions of the firm and whose political preferences may be opaque to management. Perhaps the officers or directors of the corporation have the best claim to be the ones speaking, except their fiduciary duties generally prohibit them from using corporate funds for personal ends."

2. A large fast-food chain owned by evangelical Christians adopts a policy that homosexuals will not be served. Would those denied service have a cause of action based on *Hobby Lobby*? Consider the baker who was fined $135,000 for refusing to supply a wedding cake to a homosexual couple. *Klein v. Oregon Bureau of Labor and Industries,* 410 P.3d 1051 (Or. Ct. App. 2017), vacated and remanded by Supreme Court, 138 S. Ct. 1719 (2018); decision on issue of freedom of religion reaffirmed, 317 Or. Ct. App. 138 (2022). As of this writing, the Supreme Court has not ruled on the petition for certiorari submitted on September 2, 2022.

Formation and Nontax Costs

To create a corporation, an ***incorporator*** files ***articles of incorporation*** with the state. A modest fee is typically charged. The articles have mandatory elements, such as the corporation's name, the person designated to receive certain communications (for example, subpoenas), and a description of the stock to be issued. Discretionary content like voting rules may also appear.

Once the articles are filed, the corporation comes into existence. An *organizational meeting* will be held at which the initial members of the ***board of directors*** are elected. The board will then meet to undertake the corporation's initial business. Among other things, it will appoint ***officers*** and adopt ***bylaws***. Bylaws contain key policies and procedures, such as the percentage of shareholders that must approve major corporate actions like mergers. The issuance of stock will be authorized in exchange for contributions of capital, property, or services. [For a large library of business forms like bylaws, see **www.lawdepot.com**.]

At least annually, the board of directors and the shareholders must each hold meetings, and the corporation will have to make brief filings with the state to keep its records up to date, usually accompanied by a small fee. [To see how Delaware computes this fee, see **https://corp.delaware.gov/fee**.]

Corporations and general partnerships are separate accounting entities from their owners (remember: corporations are separate legal entities from their owners; partnerships are not) and, therefore, must establish their own accounting system. The cost reflects the scale of the operation. However, for reasons considered later, the accounting system of a partnership is usually much more complex and expensive to maintain than that of a corporation for any given scale of operation.

Selection and protection of corporate name, trademarks, and domains

The articles of incorporation identify the desired name for the about-to-exist corporation. States require the name to be distinguishable from those already registered. Other actions that should be considered include:

- Trademark/tradename issues—Will someone sue to stop the use of the chosen mark or name? Check with the U.S. Patent & Trademark Office (PTO) database for conflicts with existing names. If not already taken, it may be wise to protect the desired names or marks by registering them with the PTO. [For more, see **www.uspto.gov/trademarks/basics/trademark-process.**]
- Domain name—Is the desired name still available as a domain name? If yes, register it with a registrar accredited by the Internet Corporation for Assigned Names and Numbers (ICANN). If not, what name is available that will be effective for customers and others trying to find you? [For a list of registrars, see **www.icann.org/en/accredited-registrars.**]
- Doing business in other states—If business will be conducted in other states, the corporation must register as a ***foreign corporation*** in each of those states. The chosen business name must be available for use in any and all states the business expects or hopes to do business.

Management Structure

One strength of the corporate form, an attribute that has allowed it to become the Western world's most effective engine of economic growth, is its ability to separate ownership from management. Shareholders contribute the capital that allows the business to be established. In exchange, they receive stock, each share of which represents an ownership unit. Annually, the shareholders meet to elect a board of directors. All corporate powers are exercised by, or under the authority of, the board on behalf of the shareholders. Boards do not operate the business on a day-to-day basis; they are policy and oversight bodies. To actually run the company, boards appoint ***officers***, usually a CEO (chief executive officer), secretary, CFO (chief financial officer), and likely others. Officers are employees of the corporation, and they hire the other employees needed to operate the business. This hierarchy is referred to as ***centralized management***. Keep in mind that a small corporation will likely have the same formal structure, but its operational dynamics may be quite different if, as is common, a significant portion of the shareholders are also ***directors*** and/or officers—perhaps even holding multiple executive positions.

Both directors and officers have ***fiduciary duties*** to the corporation. A ***fiduciary*** is a person who acts on behalf of another (***beneficiary***) and is required to do so with great integrity. (Another fiduciary relationship is parent-to-minor child.) The ***duty of loyalty*** requires a fiduciary to act in the best interests of the beneficiary. This prohibits, for example, directors from authorizing the corporation to hire the child of the board chairman at a salary five times larger than warranted by market conditions. Directors and officers also owe the corporation a ***duty of due care***, which requires that they act toward the corporation in the manner a reasonably prudent person would employ in dealing with their own affairs under the same circumstances.

partnership law. Mrs. Bartenwerfer appealed to the Supreme Court, which affirmed the Ninth Circuit's decision. It held that the plain language and the legislative and judicial histories of the discharge exception compelled the conclusion that the "fraud of one partner . . . is the fraud of all because each partner is the agent . . . of the firm with reference to all business within the scope of the partnership." The Court stated: "Congress . . . concluded that . . . creditors' interest in recovering full payment of debts obtained by fraud outweigh[s] debtors' interest in a complete fresh start.'"

Question

In 2022, the Congressional Research Service, a highly regarded agency housed within the Library of Congress, issued a report on the U.S. Bankruptcy Code. That report's first words are:

> U.S. bankruptcy law has two central aims. First, it seeks to relieve debtors of certain financial obligations . . . by providing them with a "fresh start." Second, bankruptcy law attempts to preserve the countervailing interests of creditors . . . by maximizing total creditor return on debts in an orderly . . . fashion. Congress and the courts have established a complex system . . . intended to balance these competing interests.

Do you believe the Court's holding in *Bartenwerfer* properly balanced the two policy objectives? Explain your reasoning.

Sources: *Barfenwerfer v. Buckley,* 598 U.S. _____ (2023); Congressional Research Service, "Bankruptcy Basics: a Primer," R45137, October 2022.

Transferability of Ownership Interests

Because partnerships are mutual agencies, involve fiduciary relationships, and do not offer limited liability, without an express agreement to the contrary, the law does not allow a partner to substitute a third party for themself with the status of partner without the unanimous consent of the other partners. A partnership interest can be assigned to a third party, but the ***assignment*** entitles the ***assignee*** only to the distribution rights of the assigning partner (***assignor***). The assignee has no right to participate in control and does not have the status of partner.

Duration of Existence

Under UPA (the predecessor of RUPA; at present, UPA governs in only eight states), a partnership automatically ceases upon the death, incapacity, bankruptcy, expulsion, or withdrawal of any partner. Thus, events in the private lives of the partners can seriously impact the venture. To minimize the harm from such an automatic ***dissolution***, it is common to include a provision in the partnership agreement allowing a new, successor partnership to be formed immediately after the dissolution by the remaining partners. The ex-partner's partnership interest is valued and paid out.

Under RUPA, the only event listed above that will automatically dissolve a partnership is the withdrawal of a partner holding more than 50 percent of the partnership interests. The remaining events will result in the ***disassociation*** of the affected partner but will not dissolve the partnership nor require the formation of a new partnership by the remaining partners. The power of any partner to withdraw cannot be removed by the partnership agreement, but the right to exercise that power can be circumscribed; and a wrongfully withdrawing partner can be required to compensate the partnership for any resulting damages. The remaining partners have a statutory right to continue the business as if no dissolution had occurred.[19]

Taxes

The greatest advantage of the partnership form is the extraordinary range of economic relationships that can be crafted. Whereas a 10 percent shareholder is simply entitled to 10 percent of whatever distributions are made by the corporation, a partnership agreement can detach percentage ownership from the stream of distributions and tax consequences. To illustrate, assume L contributes land to a real estate development partnership, K contributes knowledge as the general contractor, and C contributes the cash necessary to undertake the venture. It would be acceptable to allocate the partnership cash flows as follows: C gets all of the net cash flow until C's initial cash contribution has been recouped, then L gets all of the net cash flow until the value of L's contributed land has been received, then K gets a specified amount of the net cash flow, after which all three share the remaining net cash flows equally. Note, however, that with this great flexibility comes an obligation to precisely adhere to very complex tax rules, which can materially increase the cost of operating in the partnership form.

Double taxation does not apply to partnerships because the tax law does not treat them as separate entities. The partnership's income is taxed only once–on the tax returns of the partners pursuant to the allocations specified in the partnership agreement. There is a downside risk, however; partners must pay tax annually on their share of partnership income whether or not that income has actually been distributed to them. For this reason, it is not uncommon for partnership agreements to require minimum distributions equal to the partners' expected tax liabilities. Partnership losses are generally immediately deductible on the partners' personal tax returns. However, there are a number of complex limitations that impact their deductibility.

There are two important negative tax consequences of a partnership. First, fringe benefits provided to partners are not tax-deductible. Benefits provided to employees are deductible. (Note: A partner cannot be an employee because "one cannot work for oneself," a principle that applies because a partnership is not a legal entity separate from its partners.) Second, a partner's share of the partnership's business income is generally subject to the self-employment tax. This is a two-tier system that imposes a tax at an effective rate of about 12.5 percent on the first $160,200 of earnings (as of this writing) and at an effective rate of about 2.4 percent on earnings above that level.

Capital Structure

The sole source of equity is the partners themselves, although new partners can be added to infuse additional equity capital. Debt capital can be raised based on the creditworthiness of the individual partners, as well as by offering partnership assets to lenders as collateral.

Questions

1. What characteristics of the general partnership form make it particularly desirable as a business entity?
2. What characteristics make it particularly undesirable?

LO 9-6
Explain the unique features of several key hybrid forms of business.

Limited Liability Companies—An Increasingly Popular Choice

Today, a very popular business form is the ***limited liability company*** (LLC). Beginning in 1958, the S corporation could be used to combine limited liability with the elimination of double taxation. It was not attractive to many, however, because (1) only one class of stock can be issued–no preferred stock or multiclass common stock, (2) the number of shareholders is nominally limited to 100 individuals–none of whom can be nonresident aliens, and (3) all economic and tax consequences must be shared pro rata to stock ownership. The desire for a limited-liability form with the flexibility of a partnership led to the LLC, which is now one of the most common forms of business.

Although a uniform act for LLCs was established by the NCCUSL in 1994, only three states and the Virgin Islands are governed by it. In 2006, a revised act was promulgated, which has been adopted by 21 states and the District of Columbia. At this writing, South Carolina and Missouri have introduced legislation for its adoption. In the remaining 28 states and Puerto Rico self-developed laws govern. Thus, there is still a great deal of variation in LLC law from state to state. Nonetheless, a general outline of LLC characteristics is provided below.

To create an LLC, the owners, called ***members,*** file ***articles of organization*** with the state. The ownership units are called ***members' interests***. An ***operating agreement,*** which can be oral but is most likely written, will be prepared that sets forth information similar to that found in well-drafted partnership agreements. Minor annual filings and fees are generally required, but statutes do not impose annual member meetings. The cost of setting up an accounting system will be essentially the same as for a general partnership because LLCs have the same economic and tax flexibility.

The management structure of LLCs is variable. By default, LLCs are *member-managed* (decentrally managed, similar to a general partnership). However, the operating agreement can specify that the LLC will be centrally managed like a corporation (referred to as *manager-managed*). Usually, the managers comprise a subset of the members, although nonmember managers are permitted.

LLCs are hybrids. As to limited liability and duration of existence, they closely resemble corporations. With regard to tax treatment and the opportunity for economic customization, they closely resemble general partnerships. It is still an open question whether the limited liability of LLC members can be "pierced," as is the case with corporations. But some states have spoken. Minnesota's LLC statute expressly provides for piercing the veil of LLCs.[20] The Wyoming Supreme Court has held: "We can discern no reason . . . to treat LLCs differently than we treat corporations. If the members and officers of an LLC fail to treat it as a separate entity, they should not enjoy immunity from individual liability for the LLC's acts that cause damage to third parties."[21]

Sole Proprietorships

Sole proprietorships, business ventures undertaken by a single individual, are not actually entities–they have no legal existence distinct from their owners (proprietors). It is the default form for single-owner enterprises. Seventy-two percent of all businesses are sole proprietorships, although they generate less than 4 percent of all business revenue. No legal filings or fees are required to establish a sole proprietorship; the proprietor simply starts the venture and the sole proprietorship comes into existence. Because there is only one owner, centralization of management exists automatically. Like a general partner, the proprietor is personally liable for all business obligations.

A proprietor may dispose of the proprietorship freely, but this can be accomplished only through the transfer of the individual assets that constitute the business, not by a transfer of the "business" in its own right. Further, the lack of a separate legal entity generally results in the termination of a sole proprietorship if the owner dies. In the case of the proprietor's incapacity, only the holder of a durable power of attorney, a custodian, or a guardian has the legal power to continue operations. This impractical arrangement tends to destroy the proprietorship's value in short order.

A sole proprietorship is not a taxable entity. All of its tax matters appear on the proprietor's personal tax return. Like partnerships, all business income is subject to the self-employment tax. The capital structure issues for a sole proprietorship are similar to those of a partnership–without a change in business form, new equity can only come from the proprietor. Any lending will be based on the proprietor's creditworthiness and the value of the property that can be offered as security.

Source: Internal Revenue Service, "SOI Tax Stats–Integrated Business Data" [**www.irs.gov**].

Other Hybrid Forms

Specialized Partnerships

Limited Liability Partnerships

At the same time LLCs were being conceived, the great multinational accounting firms were reeling from another episode in which the quality of their audits proved less than advertised–the savings and loan "debacle" of the 1980s. Over $1.6 billion in settlements (a staggering sum for that era) was paid out, and these firms feared extinction if professional liability damages could not be constrained. Efforts to obtain tort reform that would limit such liability failed, so a new approach was sought–the ***limited liability partnership*** (LLP). An enabling statute was first enacted in Texas in 1991 at the instigation of a number of its major law firms, which also sought relief from professional liability.[22]

All states now have some form of LLP. In spite of the similarity of the name to LLC, the LLP's closest analog is the general partnership. For example, its governing law is included as Article 10 of RUPA. To bring an LLP into existence, a document called a ***statement of qualification*** is filed with the state. Minor annual filings and fees are required. LLPs (and their partners) are taxed like a general partnership and, in all other characteristics except for limited liability, closely resemble general partnerships.

As originally conceived, an LLP partner's limited liability extended only to the negligence of the other partners. Partners retained full liability for all other partnership obligations. However, RUPA now provides full limited liability "whether arising in contract, tort, or otherwise" to all partners.[23]

Limited Partnerships

Limited partnerships have existed for a considerable time and were extremely popular until the advent of LLCs. They have two classes of owners: general partners and limited partners. ***General partners*** have the same legal benefits and burdens as the partners of a general partnership. They (often only one) are the only managers. ***Limited partners*** invest in the entity but do not participate in control (except for voting on major matters like dissolution). In exchange for having very little control, they (like shareholders) enjoy limited liability. Although unlimited liability is generally cited as the principal disadvantage of being a general partner, in practice, most general partners in limited partnerships are corporations (or LLCs) with minimal capital investments. Thus, unlimited liability is little threat unless grounds for piercing the veil exist.

Twenty-four states have adopted the initial version of the Uniform Limited Partnership Act (ULPA). The latest version (2001) has been adopted in 23 states and the District of Columbia. Three states and Puerto Rico have developed their own governing law. Limited partnerships come into existence only upon filing a ***certificate of limited partnership*** with the state. Minor annual filings and fees are required. The law of limited partnerships provides that those events involving limited partners that would terminate a general partnership under UPA have no impact on the entity's existence. Limited partnerships are generally taxed like general partnerships. Importantly, however, the income of a limited partner is not subject to self-employment tax.

Limited Liability Limited Partnerships

State legislation establishing limited liability limited partnerships (LLLPs) is generally directed at facilitating the acquisition of limited liability for the general partners of preexisting limited partnerships. In some cases, reorganizing an existing limited partnership would entail expensive or challenging hurdles. Under ULPA (2001), an LLLP is created simply by stating that the limited partnership is an LLLP in the certificate of limited partnership (an existing limited partnership would just amend its certificate).[24]

International Hybrids

Dozens of other business forms exist throughout the world. For the most part, these forms are intended to achieve various combinations of the form-of-business characteristics discussed earlier. Using these criteria, managers operating in a multinational environment should be able to evaluate form-of-business alternatives under a variety of regimes.

The closest forms of business to a U.S. publicly held corporation in other major economies are: Brazil–Sociedade por Ações Aberta (abbreviated SA),[25] Germany–Aktiengesellschaft (abbreviated AG),[26] and China–Gŭfèn yuxiàn gōngsī.[27]

Circumstances Favoring a Specific Business Form

The selection of a particular form is often driven by the founders' preferences for the characteristics previously discussed and by market realities. With the availability of LLCs, LLPs, and S corporations, under most circumstances, the disadvantages of the general partnership form are so severe that one is usually well-advised to avoid it.

Another consideration in the selection is the amount of capital needed by the enterprise. It is not rare to find someone with a great idea but with insufficient resources to take the idea to market. Some investors, such as ***venture capitalists,*** seek out such persons. They will usually insist that the venture have limited liability, as would be true with a corporation or an LLC. [For more on venture capitalists, see **www.nvca.org.**]

Similarly, ***franchisors*** normally demand that ***franchisees*** operate their franchises in a business form with limited liability. A ***franchise*** is the right to exploit the franchisor's intangible assets (such as trade names and business systems) and to partake of the franchisor's marketing, purchasing, and other services. The key advantages to the franchisee are a proven product or service, turnkey implementation, and access to support. Premium franchises can be expensive. The franchisor gains by earning fees and by achieving accelerated market penetration using the capital of others (franchisees). Unfortunately, franchisor fraud and oppression are not unusual, so careful investigation by potential franchisees is essential. [For an extensive listing of franchise opportunities and their minimum cash requirements, see **www.franchisedirect.com.**]

Large businesses need billions of dollars. Only access to global capital markets (like the New York Stock Exchange) can fulfill this need. With few exceptions, the only form that has met with success in these markets is the C corporation.

Questions-Part One

1. From initiating the process through the election of directors, describe the steps generally followed to bring a corporation into existence.
2. What are the advantages and disadvantages of dual-class common stock?
3. *a.* Why are sole proprietorships problematic if a proprietor dies or becomes disabled?
   b. Do partnerships experience similar problems?
4. *a.* What characteristics of an LLC cause it to be one of the fastest-growing business forms in the United States?
   b. What are its advantages over an S corporation? Are there any disadvantages?
5. Why are corporations the dominant form of business based on revenues in the United States?

Part Two—Corporate Governance in Publicly Held Corporations

Publicly held corporations usually have thousands of shareholders, the vast majority of whom do not plan to spend their time intimately involved with the company's business. They wish to entrust their resources to the stewardship of the corporation's management and return to their personal affairs. To ensure that the corporation is acting to further their interests, the shareholders elect a board of directors. The boards of publicly held corporations generally have both inside and outside directors. ***Inside directors*** are senior executives. ***Outside directors*** are not employed by the company. Boards govern by meeting at regular intervals to monitor the corporation's activities, establish

> Enron called the world's attention to extraordinary failings in corporate governance.

policies, hire and replace senior executives, and make major decisions such as whether to pursue a merger.

The foregoing paragraph is the textbook description of ***corporate governance***. What has become painfully evident from both the accounting scandals of the Enron era and the 2008 collapse of the financial system is that reality can be quite different. Enron called the world's attention to extraordinary failings in corporate governance, but its demise was not an isolated event. Disturbingly, the pre-Enron collapse of numerous companies failed to alert the markets and regulators, and many more implosions followed, at least two of which were actually larger (WorldCom and Parmalat). The 2008 financial crisis made clear that flaws in corporate governance persisted. The report of the Financial Crisis Inquiry Commission (the body charged by Congress to determine the causes of the so-called Great Recession) identified serious issues. The majority report stated: "We conclude dramatic failures of corporate governance and risk management at many systemically important financial institutions were a key cause of this crisis."[28] In the words of hedge fund manager and former corporate raider, Carl Icahn: "The entirely preventable financial catastrophe . . . has many culprits: reckless executives who gambled with their company's futures, feckless regulators and somnambulant boards of directors."[29]

This part of the chapter will consider corporate governance issues, including the reforms adopted in the wakes of the Enron era and the 2008 financial crisis. Several rising corporate governance issues also will be identified.

The Management Pyramid

LO 9-7
Explain how corporations are governed.

Corporations have ***centralized management***. At the apex of the pyramid is the board of directors. Immediately below is the chief executive officer (CEO). In the next echelon are the other top executives, such as the chief financial officer (CFO) and chief operating officer (COO). This classic management pyramid further expands through layers of middle management, finally coming to the base comprised of rank-and-file employees. The light shed on the boardroom by various government investigations and shareholder lawsuits during the Enron era revealed that the pyramid had become inverted at the top. Far too frequently, boards simply abdicated responsibility to their CEOs, who often held the ultimate power because of their strong influence over the board nomination process and board compensation, as well as their control over the information provided to the board. In addition, many conflicts of interest have been discovered. At Enron, for example, some directors were personal friends of senior managers, others were academics whose institutions were receiving large contributions from the company or its officers, and another was the former senior government official who was responsible for exempting Enron from the regulation of its principal line of business (dealing in energy derivatives).

Directorships can be lucrative. In 2022, the average S&P 500 outside director compensation was $316,000. In an attempt to align directors' interests with those of the investors, a substantial portion of that compensation is often in stock options or an outright grant of stock. As to the work required to earn these sums, the typical director attends only eight meetings a year.[30] Far too few directors have been willing to challenge CEO actions out of fear of forfeiting such substantial compensation.

The federal legislation passed in the aftermath of Enron, the Sarbanes–Oxley Act of 2002 (SOX), attempted to address some of these governance issues. To limit the CEO's control of audit information reaching the board, it requires a board ***audit committee*** consisting exclusively of ***independent directors***–outside directors without conflicts of interest–at least one of whom must be a financial expert. SOX gives the audit committee direct responsibility for hiring the auditing firm and setting its compensation. It further prohibits the auditor from also rendering many types of consulting services in order to promote independence. To limit the CEO's control over board membership, SOX requires a ***nominating committee*** also composed solely of independent directors.

Even after SOX, there have been serious concerns about who truly sits at the top of the pyramid. The CEO still controls much of the information that reaches the board. Shortly before the 2008 financial crisis, the Wall Street Journal published a special report headlined: "Why CEOs Need to Be Honest with Their Boards: Too Often Chief Executives Sugarcoat the Truth. That's More Dangerous Than Ever."[31] Many still wondered whether boards are active in setting policies and making major decisions or are simply following the CEO's lead. Such concerns seemed plausible. For example, immediately after Lehman Brothers' CEO announced a $3.9 billion third-quarter loss in 2008 (the prelude for the company's implosion not long thereafter), he said: "I must say the board's been wonderfully supportive."[32]

Modern corporate governance failures

WeWork (2019)

WeWork was founded in 2010, principally by CEO Adam Neumann, who was then a 30-year-old with little business experience. The company intended to disrupt the commercial office industry by acquiring real estate and converting it into "co-working" space. Large common areas with a concierge and food-infused water, lounges with music set just loud enough to allow private conversations, and individual workspaces were provided, all with Wi-Fi and printers. Sales doubled annually year after year, leading to a $47 billion valuation in January 2019–the highest of any U.S. startup. Neumann prioritized revenue growth over all things, including profit. Through the end of 2019, WeWork only had positive net income once–a meager $1.7 million in 2012.

By August 2019, the company had 527,000 tenants in 528 facilities located in 111 cities in 29 countries. It had 14,500 employees. Investment bankers, eager to win the right to participate in future stock and bond issuances that could generate hundreds of millions of dollars in fees, offered valuations of WeWork of $60 billion (JP Morgan) and $90 billion (Goldman). Revenues approached $4 billion. The balance sheet showed nearly $9 billion of assets, but it also showed a cumulative loss of over $6 billion–and the losses were growing at a remarkable rate: from $430 million in 2016 to $3 billion in 2019. Despite these losses, Neumann failed to shift attention to cost control and managing growth. Instead, he continued to rapidly add square footage.

Neumann had essentially unfettered control since his stock carried 20-to-1 voting power (dual-class stock, discussed earlier in this chapter). When he wanted a $63 million private jet, he got it. When he decided to own some of the buildings to be leased to WeWork, no one stood in the way despite the fact that such conflict-of-interest transactions are considered highly controversial.

By mid-2019, the cash hemorrhage became unsustainable. Projections showed a zero cash balance by November. It became clear that at least $10 billion of new financing was needed. The solution in August appeared to be an initial public offering. But investors turned away because of the company's large and growing losses and because of CEO Neumann's "erratic management style and behavior." By September, the company's valuation dropped to $8 billion from $47 billion in January.

The board of directors finally acted. In October, Neumann was induced to leave as CEO and board member by: (1) giving him a $185 million "consulting fee," (2) forgiving $2 million owed for personal travel on the corporate jet, (3) redeeming $1 billion of his stock, and (4) arranging for a $500 million loan to pay off borrowings he had collateralized with his stock.

The new leadership halted expansion and fired 17 percent of the workers, whose stock options had become worthless.

As to WeWork's corporate governance, *The Wall Street Journal* said scathingly:

> Little of WeWork's tragedy would have been possible were it not for the collection of veteran executives and financiers . . . who enabled Mr. Newman[.] . . . The outside board directors, all of whom had decades of experience in business and finance, voted for years to approve decisions by Mr. Newman that paved the way for WeWork's collapse. . . . [They] let Mr. Newman personally buy stakes in buildings that he would lease to WeWork. They gave him long-term voting control . . . and allowed him to sell and borrow more than $1 billion against his WeWork stock. [They failed to object when Newman] repeatedly skipped board meetings. [And some of the directors] had potential conflicts of interest themselves.

Questions

1. How did WeWork's dual-class common stock structure impair good corporate governance and significantly increase the company's financial problems at the end of Neumann's tenure as CEO and board member?
2. Consider WeWork's loss history. What would your response have been had you been a director? At what point in time would you have intervened?
3. How could a company that, essentially, never made any money be worth $47 billion? Sixty billion? Ninety billion?
4. What should the board's role be? Consider the following two opinions:
   A. "[B]oards [are] supposed to monitor risks, provide judgment and supervise managers on behalf of shareholders."[33]
   B. "Most boards meet one or two days a month and are composed of individuals who also hold demanding full-time jobs. Given those circumstances, it's absurd to believe that board members, even the most experienced and best-intentioned of them, will uncover systemic flaws or acts of malfeasance[.] That's what regulators, outside accountants, and internal controls are for—to help boards ferret out excessive risk and wrongdoing."[34]

Sources: SEC Form S-1, The We Company, August 14, 2019 [**www.sec.gov**]; Sarah E. Needleman and Eliot Brown, "WeWork to Cut Around 17% of Workforce," *The Wall Street Journal,* November 21, 2019 [**www.wsj.com**]; Eliot Brown, "WeWork's Loss Balloons to $1.25 Billion," *The Wall Street Journal,* November 13, 2019 [**www.wsj.com**]; David Benoit, Maureen Farrell, and Liz Hoffman, "As WeWork Grew, Wall Street Lent It Money and Credibility," *The Wall Street Journal,* November 8, 2019 [**www.wsj.com**]; Eliot Brown, "WeWork's CEO Makes Millions as Landlord to WeWork," *The Wall Street Journal,* January 16, 2019 [**www.wsj.com**]; Maureen Farrell and Eliot Brown, "SoftBank to Boost Stake in WeWork in Deal That Cuts Most Ties With Neumann," *The Wall Street Journal,* October 22, 2019 [**www.wsj.com**]; and Maureen Farrell and Corrie Driebusch, "WeWork to List Shares on Nasdaq, Make Governance Changes," *The Wall Street Journal,* September 13, 2019 [**www.wsj.com**].

FTX (2022)

In an event unfolding at this writing, leading cryptocurrency exchange FTX (along with some 130 related entities) has collapsed into bankruptcy owing $8 billion to over 100,000 creditors. The trigger: "How do you make a multibillion-dollar company disappear in a week? [T]he simple answer is that a leaked balance sheet leads [a major investor] to instigate a . . . 'bank run' you cannot possibly cover, exposing billions of dollars in shortfalls you apparently created by riskily investing money that wasn't yours."

The center of attention, Sam Bankman-Fried (then 25 years old with a degree in physics), established a cryptocurrency trading firm run out of his apartment in 2017. By 2019 when he founded FTX (in Hong Kong), he was handling trades of $1 billion daily. Hong Kong was selected because it allowed FTX to do things like permitting traders to engage in 100-to-1 leveraging, a level of risk-taking impossible in the U.S. FTX was moved to the Bahamas in 2021 because of its even "friendlier regulation."

There Bankman-Fried lived in a $40 million penthouse in a manner described as a "dorm situation" with several of the people who ran FTX and its related entities. The crypto industry viewed him as a "character." He wore a T-shirt and shorts, hair unkempt, while standing with former U.S. President Bill Clinton and former U.K. Prime Minister Tony Blair at a crypto conference in Nassau. He spent $130 million for the naming rights to the Miami Heat's stadium and sponsored a 2022 Super Bowl ad. He played computer games while leading video meetings with the financial community. He had a net worth of $15 billion just before the collapse ($24 billion at its peak), was the second largest contributor to a major political party in the 2022 midterm elections, and made or pledged enormous charitable contributions. (Most of the outstanding charitable pledges can no longer be honored.) In September 2022, Bankman-Fried gave an interview to Bloomberg during which "he flatly described the crypto markets as pointless speculation bordering on fraud[, with] one of the interviewers paraphrasing his summary as 'I'm in the Ponzi business.'" None of this deterred investors. Nor did Bankman-Fried's utter disregard for risk management. In an interview after the November bankruptcy filing he said: "I wasn't even . . . trying to manage risk on FTX."

He also said: "[expletive] regulators . . . they make everything worse." This typified his attitude toward regulation and corporate governance. For example, in February 2022, knowing that the Securities and Exchange Commission (SEC) was aggressively seeking to take jurisdiction over cryptocurrency trading (which the SEC chair disparagingly characterized as "the Wild West"), Bankman-Fried testified before the Senate asking Congress to grant jurisdiction to the Commodities Futures Trading Commission. He hoped to influence the enabling legislation to achieve a less stringent regulatory environment than would exist under the SEC. Additionally, when asked by investment bankers to hire more seasoned management or to add their representatives to the board of directors, Bankman-Fried threatened (sometimes in "fiery" language) to shut them out of future funding rounds, which would deprive them of the opportunity to generate potentially hundreds of millions of dollars in fees. Investors were given a choice–accept FTX's governance structure or go elsewhere.

FTX had only three board members: Bankman-Fried, an FTX employee, and an Antiguan lawyer specializing in gambling. The Bankruptcy Court fired Bankman-Fried and ousted the directors, replacing them with John J. Ray III, who led Enron and other large companies through their bankruptcy and restructuring proceedings, and who has a reputation for vigorously locating assets to settle creditors' claims. In his initial bankruptcy filing, Ray offered a "blistering" assessment of FTX's corporate governance: "Never in my career have I seen such a complete failure of corporate controls[.] From compromised systems integrity . . . to the concentration of control in the hands of a very small group of inexperienced, unsophisticated and potentially compromised individuals, this situation is unprecedented. [Among other things, this allowed FTX to] conceal the misuse of customer funds."

It will likely be years before the FTX "debacle" (Ray's word) is resolved. It will be no surprise if the FTX story ultimately bears a remarkable similarity to Enron's.

Questions

1. What similarities do you see between the WeWork and FTX collapses?
2. Why did major investors like BlackRock, Sequoia Capital, and Lightspeed Venture Partners continue to invest in FTX given Bankman-Fried's approach to management and corporate governance?
3. Assume you buy $1,000,000 of cryptocurrency using $10,000 of your savings and $990,000 of borrowed money (99-to-1 leveraging). The value rises 10% and you sell. What is your profit (for simplicity, ignore transaction fees, interest, and taxes)? Now assume that the value falls to $900,000 and you believe it will fall further and will not recover. Therefore, you sell. Describe the economic consequences to you. How do you feel about the 100-to-1 leveraging available through FTX?

Sources: Katanga Johnson and Jennifer Epstein, "Sam Bankman-Fried's Island Haven Is Drawing Scrutiny After FTX Demise," *Bloomberg,* November 18, 2022 [**www.bloomberg.com**]; David Yaffe-Bellany, "Inside a Crypto Nemesis' Campaign to Rein In the Industry,"*The New York Times,* November 21, 2022 [**www.nytimes.com**]; Olga Kharif, Yueqi Yang, and Hannah Miller, "FTX Was an Empty Black Box All Along," *Bloomberg,* November 16, 2022 [**www.bloomberg.com**]; David Yaffe-Bellany, "New Chief Calls FTX's Corporate Control a 'Complete Failure'," *The New York Times,* November 17, 2022 [**www.nytimes.com**]; David Yaffe-Bellany, "Embattled Crypto Exchange FTX Files for Bankruptcy,"*The New York Times,* November 11, 2022 [**www.nytimes.com**]; Eliot Brown, Caitlin Ostroff, and Berber Jin, "FTX's Sam Bankman-Fried Cashed Out $300 Million During Funding Spree,"*The Wall Street Journal,* November 18, 2022 [**www.wsj.com**]; David Wallace-Wells, "FTX' $32 billion valuation was a fantasy, but nobody bothered to look at it closely,"*The New York Times,* November 21, 2022 [**www.nytimes.com**]; and Richard Vanderford, "Sam Bankman-Fried 'Wasn't Even Trying' to Manage Risk at FTX, He Says," *The Wall Street Journal,* Dec. 1, 2022 [**www.wsj.com**].

Many commentators believe that corporate governance would be greatly improved, and CEO excesses curtailed, by not permitting the same person to hold the positions of board chair and CEO. "No one can reasonably expect a person to oversee himself or herself[.] . . . The CEO works for the board, not the other way around; the continuation of combined roles inhibits the board in exercising its responsibilities because it creates an insurmountable imbalance of power."[35] At the time the Great Recession unfolded in 2008, both positions were more often than not held by a single person in *Fortune* 500 companies.[36] The Dodd–Frank Act of 2010, enacted in response to the financial crisis, now requires corporations to disclose the reasons for choosing the same person for both positions, but does not prohibit the practice.

The Shareholder-Rights Movement

Although shareholders own the corporation, control rests with the board. Under the business judgment rule, discussed previously, state law significantly restricts the shareholders' ability to control management, other than indirectly through the annual election of the board.

> The notion that shareholders can actually exercise control is doubtful.

The notion that shareholders can actually exercise control through the board election process is doubtful. As stated earlier, in publicly held corporations, shareholders do not select the candidates for board positions; a committee of the existing board does. Could a dissatisfied shareholder offer a different slate of directors for the shareholders to vote on? In theory, yes; in practice, ***proxy fights*** are difficult and expensive.

Management annually solicits proxies from its shareholders. A ***proxy*** is written permission to vote a shareholder's stock on an issue, such as the election of directors. Management's solicitation is done in conjunction with its required notification to shareholders of the annual meeting. The proxy cost is thus borne by the corporation. Shareholders wanting to propose alternative candidates have to be prepared to bear the entire cost themselves. State law gives shareholders the right of access to shareholder lists maintained by the company, but a shareholder will often have to sue, at a substantial cost in time and money, to force the corporation to comply. If successful, the shareholders involved must then incur heavy costs in developing the solicitation materials for SEC review.

It is no surprise, then, that proxy fights are uncommon. Most shareholders who disagree with management's decisions simply sell their shares and invest elsewhere. From society's and the shareholders' points of view, the management of publicly held corporations proceeds largely unchecked, unless securities law violations are involved. One commentator refers to this as "the myth that boards [are] accountable to shareholders."[37]

In recent years, various proposals to give shareholders more input have gained ground, largely through the efforts of institutional investors and independent activists. Institutional investors, such as pension funds and mutual funds, have significant influence in the capital markets. When the largest public pension in the United States, the California Public Employees' Retirement System, contacts the C-suite at a company in which it holds a significant amount of stock, management is likely to listen.

Director Elections

One shareholder reform that has gained ground involves the number of votes required to elect a director. Many states, including Delaware, allow directors to be elected by just a plurality of the votes cast. If the only names before the shareholders are those on management's slate, management's nominees will generally win even if a substantial number of shareholders withhold their votes in protest. In 2006, only 16 percent of firms in the S&P 500 had any form of majority vote rule. Now, largely as a result of pressure from institutional investors, the number is 90 percent.[38]

Proxy Access

One of the most controversial issues in recent years has been ***proxy access***. As previously discussed, although it is possible for dissatisfied shareholders to wage a proxy fight, it is usually not feasible to do so. A cost-effective solution would be to require management to include shareholder nominees on the company's ballot sent to shareholders in advance of the annual meeting. In 2010, the SEC issued a new rule permitting shareholder groups (owning at least three percent of a company's stock for at least three years) to submit nominees for inclusion in the company's ballot; however, in 2011 a federal court struck down the regulation on procedural grounds. Nonetheless, pressure from a broad array of institutional investors has resulted in 71 percent of the S&P 500 voluntarily adopting the "three percent rule" as of 2018, up from one percent in 2014.

Effective September 2022, however, a new set of proxy contest rules apply. Any shareholder, regardless of how few shares held and regardless of how long those shares have been held, can offer a slate of directors which will be distributed to the shareholders along with management's slate. The new rules "constitute a seismic shift in the regulatory regime governing proxy contests at public corporations[. They] will reshape the process by which hostile bidders, activist hedge funds, social and environmental activists, and other dissident shareholders . . . utilize director elections to influence control and policy at public companies."[39]

Question

Evaluate the view that board accountability to shareholders is a myth.

Activist Investors

Shareholder activism originated in the 1980s. One form, associated with the so-called *corporate raider,* involves engaging in a ***hostile takeover*** (acquiring control of a company in the face of strong management resistance), often by encouraging other shareholders to join forces. If successful, the company is often broken up, sometimes even liquidated, because the total value of the corporation's individual components exceeds the current market value of the entity as a whole. The process was illustrated in the 1991 movie *Other Peoples' Money*. Another form is *going private,* in which the hostile takeover is accomplished by offering the current shareholders a price far above current market value (a ***tender offer***). The acquisition is often funded by *junk bonds* collateralized only with the acquired stock or with the vast majority of the target's assets (less pejoratively called a *leveraged buyout*). The bonds are characterized as "junk" because they are enormously risky, a result of the fact that the debt represents the vast majority of the corporation's value (debt-to-equity ratios of up to 80 percent have been observed).[40] In each case, the key objective is to enjoy a gain in a relatively short amount of time, either from dismantling the company or dramatically altering its operations so as to significantly increase its profitability and hence market value. The 1993 movie *Barbarians at the Gate* portrayed the leveraged buyout of RJR Nabisco. Because of their tactics and intense focus on quick profits, these activists came to be thought of as a "blight, . . . the cult of short-term shareholder value gone mad."[41]

> The cult of short-term shareholder value gone mad.

Modern shareholder activism is primarily driven by disappointment in current management's performance in developing value over a number of years. Even when the target is broken up into separate companies, the objective is to unlock intermediate- and long-term value. According to *The Economist,* "One reason [activists are a force for good] is that plenty of companies suffer from rotten management. . . . [Activists] often seek to improve [the performance of] firms' boards."[42] In sharp contrast to the SEC's views during the 1980s, in 2015 the SEC chair said that shareholder activism "can be compatible with the kind of engagement that I hope companies and shareholders can foster."[43]

> Activists can be good because plenty of companies suffer from rotten management.

Indeed, the prevailing view among observers is that activist investing is generally in the public interest. Even large shareholders cannot compel companies to respond to their concerns because boards are very difficult to displace without a proxy fight or a hostile takeover. And if a board cannot be ousted, neither can the C-suite. Activists often appear when a number of large shareholders become disgruntled because they are being ignored by the board and management. It will be the activist who launches the proxy fight or hostile takeover, the successful outcome of which will be a new board and almost certainly new senior management. A company's top management therefore has an interest in keeping large shareholders happy to avoid attracting an activist, which means that management will listen to such shareholders' concerns about poor performance and other matters directly affecting stock value. This tends to increase the value of the company's stock. Further, an activist shareholder will only profit if the company becomes more valuable. That increase in value inures to all shareholders, not just the activist.

Unsurprisingly, boards of directors and corporate management often have a different perspective. "It's a chief executive's nightmare. First an activist investor takes a stake in the company. Next they start questioning the strategy and sowing divisions between management and the board and shareholders. [CEOs] complain that activists seek short-term payouts that damage the potential for corporate growth[.]" But the investment community's response is: "Traditional activism, focused on short-term profit, stock price and total shareholder return (TSR), continues alongside a new form of activism emphasizing climate and other environmental, employee/human capital, social and governance (ESG) considerations. [D]ual purpose activists [have arisen who] combine both TSR and ESG arguments[.]"[44]

Activist "attacks" (often called "campaigns" by those sympathetic to the activist's goals) are usually dreaded by management and for good reason. Major companies have been forced to oust their CEOs (Procter & Gamble, Microsoft), break up (Motorola, eBay, Yahoo), and return enormous amounts of cash to shareholders (Apple distributed $90 billion). The CEO of a major Silicon Valley corporation said: "We think about an attack all the time."[45] As well they should: In the three years leading up to the COVID pandemic (2017–2019), there were 394 attacks on U.S. publicly traded companies with more than $500 million of market capitalization (an average of 131 per year). Attacks declined to 83 in 2020 but rose to 95 in 2021. Based on data available as of this writing, the number of attacks grew well over 30 percent in 2022. On average, 13 percent of the targeted companies' CEOs lose their position within six months of the attack; and, in 2022, activists won 44 percent of the board seats sought. "Activist funds have at least $200 billion of . . . capital [in 2022] and they have started to deploy it aggressively."[46]

LO 9-8
Describe some of the challenges facing modern boards of directors, including cybersecurity, bribery, corporate political spending, international taxation, and executive compensation.

Question

Do activist investors play a positive or negative role in the capital markets? Explain.

Major Issues Currently Confronting Boards of Directors

Cybersecurity

Corporate Board Director's 2022 "What Directors Think" survey of U.S. publicly traded corporation directors sought to determine these companies' primary crisis threat. The answer was unambiguous: cybersecurity.[47] This is no surprise given the grim statistics reported in *Forbes*:[48]

- Ninety-three percent of company networks can be penetrated by cyberattacks, usually through the poorly-protected computer systems of supply chain members. Eighty percent of businesses are attacked via such a compromised supplier account each month.

The primary reason (71 percent): simple passwords. The average time required to penetrate the target system is two days. In 2021, U.S. businesses suffered an average of 10,807 cyberattacks every week. Ten percent of those involved ransomware.

- There is a ransomware attack every 11 seconds (projected to be every 2 seconds by 2031).
- Cybercrime cost U.S. businesses $6.9 billion in 2021 and is growing rapidly (global losses increased 65 percent between 2019 and 2021). The cost worldwide could be as high as $6 *trillion* (larger than the GDP of Japan).
- In 2021, a breach at LinkedIn compromised 700 million records; another at Facebook involved 533 million records.
- Cyber defenses will have to protect 200 zettabytes ("1" followed by 21 zeros–a staggering 1,000 billion billion) of data by 2031, half of which will be in the cloud.
- Business cannot function without infrastructure. Risk to infrastructure is risk to the business. Fourteen of the U.S.'s sixteen critical infrastructure sectors were cyberattacked in 2021, including Colonial Pipeline which resulted in fuel supply disruptions across the East Coast. How was it done? A single employee's VPN password (which allowed the employee remote access to the company's systems) had been leaked on the dark web (per Wikipedia: networks that operate on the Internet that require specific software, configurations, or authorization to access) related to a company account that was no longer even in use–a failure of computer system housekeeping.[49]

Cybersecurity risks are now viewed as "an existential threat."[50] Many companies have suffered reputational and financial harm as a result of exposure to cyberattacks. The U.S., EU, China, and Australia have promulgated regulations requiring enhanced cybersecurity risk disclosures. "Corporate directors now must consider themselves on notice. . . . [Companies must disclose] how the board administers its risk oversight function. . . . Cybersecurity risk has . . . elevated itself to the top of corporate agendas and . . . boards must now engage in thoughtful and rigorous supervision[.]"[51]

Recall that, in *Marchand v. Barnhill,* senior management of Blue Bell Creameries failed to keep the board apprised of the growing risks of food safety. Boards are experiencing similar communication failures in the context of cybersecurity risk.[52] Ironically, the SEC commissioners were left in the dark for over a year about a 2017 breach of their own confidential database, EDGAR. For six months, hacker Oleksandr Ieremenko "root[ed] around the [SEC's] corporate-filing system . . . looking for information to trade on" in advance of its public disclosure. Ieremenko's stolen information from 157 companies resulted in profits of $4.1 million before he was caught. Then SEC chairman, Jay Clayton, faced embarrassing moments during testimony before Congress because the agency frequently takes companies to task for not managing and disclosing cybersecurity risks.[53] SEC guidance requires boards to "be informed immediately by the company's leadership when a cyber-incident of a serious magnitude has been identified."[54]

Bribery

Becoming the subject of a bribery investigation can lead to extraordinary reputational damage and enormous cost. Boards are, as a result, devoting great attention to detecting bribery and creating an environment in which such behavior is discouraged.

Since 1977, the Foreign Corrupt Practices Act (FCPA) has made it illegal for a U.S. company to ***bribe*** a foreign official to violate local law in order to obtain or maintain business or to secure an improper advantage. It also prohibits false accounting for payments (for example, entering a bribe on the books as a "consulting fee"). Note that it is not illegal to bribe a foreign official to do a ministerial act that is not in violation of local law (for example, bribing a corrupt foreign government clerk to actually issue the construction permits to which a company is lawfully entitled). While originally enforcing the FCPA only tepidly, Department of Justice action has been vigorous since the late 1990s.

To illustrate, for over a decade, Walmart subsidiaries in Brazil, China, India, and Mexico used intermediaries to route millions of dollars in bribes to government officials in order to further their expansion plans in those countries. Employees delivered envelopes of cash and booked other payments with misleading explanations like "professional fees." Despite concerns raised by Walmart employees and other whistleblowers, Walmart took no real action until a 2012 *New York Times* article broke a story about the company's bribery in Mexico. Propelled finally to investigate, Walmart assigned the investigation to the very attorney who was authorizing the bribery payments on behalf of the subsidiary. Unsurprisingly, the lawyer concluded that the "corruption allegations were unsubstantiated." Walmart spent at least $900 million in legal and investigatory fees trying to resolve the matter.[55]

The Organization for Economic Cooperation and Development studied 400 bribery cases.[56] Contrary to widely held views, bribes were not made primarily by rogue employees. Fifty-three percent were authorized by senior management–12 percent by the CEO. In 40 percent of the cases, the penalties exceeded the total profit generated from the transaction. Forty-seven percent of the bribes were accomplished through an intermediary (for example, a party purporting to act as a consultant, lawyer, or accountant); 35 percent were accomplished through a chain of entities housed in secrecy jurisdictions (discussed later) like the Cayman Islands.

The largest corruption fine in history was imposed on Brazil's Odebrecht in December 2016, discussed below.

Odebrecht SA–Largest corruption fine in history

On December 21, 2016, Odebrecht SA, a Brazilian company and Latin America's largest construction firm operating in 27 countries, admitted violating the FCPA and agreed to the largest anticorruption fine in history–$4.5 billion. Odebrecht built the Miami International Airport and was a major contractor for the 2014 World Cup and 2016 Rio Olympics. Over two decades, it paid $800 million in bribes to government officials in 12 countries related to more than 100 projects in order to reap $3.34 billion in illegal profits. The largest bribes occurred in Brazil ($349 million), Venezuela ($98 million), and the Dominican Republic ($92 million). The company's former CEO was sentenced to 19 years in prison and 77 other insiders have entered criminal plea bargains. Odebrecht's petrochemical subsidiary, Braskem SA, has agreed to an additional $1 billion in fines.

So rampant and extensive were its corrupt payouts that it established a department, the "Division of Structured Operations" with a separate communication system, to manage the bribery. This unit arranged for "deliveries of cash-stuffed suitcases to secret locations," in addition to wire transfers. It used banks in secrecy jurisdictions like Antigua to hide transactions. "In one case . . . Odebrecht bought the local branch of a bank, allowing other members of the conspiracy, including politicians from multiple countries, to open accounts and receive transfers without arousing attention." Upon becoming aware of the investigation, Odebrecht directed its employees to "conceal or destroy evidence" and "delete records that might reveal illegal activities."

The company issued a statement that provides insight into the environment in which such corruption flourishes: "[We apologize for our] participation in illicit actions. . . . It does not matter that we gave in to external pressure. Nor is it relevant that there are behaviors [in international dealings] that the private and public sectors must resist[.] What matters is that we acknowledge our involvement. We were complicit and did not fight these practices, as we should have."

Business plummeted in the wake of the scandal, exacerbating the financial distress of the fines and legal costs. In June 2019, Odebrecht filed for bankruptcy seeking relief from $20 billion of liabilities.

[For a complete listing of all antibribery actions, go to **https://www.sec.gov/spotlight/foreign-corrupt-practices-act#:˜:text=The%20SEC%20and%20the%20Department,its%20enforcement%20of%20the%20FCPA.**]

Questions

1. What does this incident suggest about the integrity of many international business environments?
2. Odebrecht has been described as "brazen." Does this characterization sound correct?
3. Following these events, Odebrecht's credit rating plummeted, its revenues declined precipitously, and its workforce shrank from 250,000 to 140,000. Should boards of directors be concerned about whether their executives and employees are engaged in activities that violate the Foreign Corrupt Practices Act?

Sources: "Olympus to Pay $646 Million to Settle Bribery Claims," *The New York Times,* March 1, 2016 [**www.nytimes.com**]; Ben Protess and Alexandra Stevenson, "JPMorgan Chase to Pay $264 Million to Settle Foreign Bribery Case," *The New York Times,* November 17, 2016 [**www.nytimes.com**]; Alexandra Stevenson and Matthew Goldstein, "2 Brazilian Companies Are Said to Be Settling Bribery Case," *The New York Times,* December 20, 2016 [**www.nytimes.com**]; Alexandra Stevenson and Vinod Sreeharsha, "Secret Unit Helped Brazilian Company to Bribe Government Officials," *The New York Times,* December 21, 2016 [**www.nytimes.com**]; Samuel Rubenfeld, Paul Kiernan, and Luciana Magalhaes, "Brazil's Odebrecht to Pay Up to $4.5 Billion to Settle Bribery Case," *The Wall Street Journal,* December 21, 2016 [**www.wsj.com**]; Samuel Rubenfeld and Austen Hufford, "Teva Settles Foreign Corruption Probe for $519 Million," *The Wall Street Journal,* December 22, 2016 [**www.wsj.com**]; Ryan Dube, "Odebrecht Bribery Scandal Shakes Up Latin America," *The Wall Street Journal,* December 22, 2016 [**www.wsj.com**]; and "Scandal-plagued Brazilian construction giant Odebrecht files for bankruptcy," *France24,* June 18, 2019 [**www.france24.com**].

Question

Is the Foreign Corrupt Practices Act needed? Explain.

Disclosures

Political Spending

Investors have always had some interest in the amounts corporations spend on political activities; but with the dramatic increase resulting from the 2010 Supreme Court decision in *Citizens United,*[57] many large investors are increasingly pressing for detailed disclosures. They want to be able to determine whether the spending is properly aligned with the company's stated strategy. They want to know that the spending is, in the words of the official who manages New York City's pension funds, not simply to promote "the personal political preferences of a particular executive with access to the corporate purse strings." The SEC proposed a rule in 2012 that would require clear disclosures. Despite the majority support found in the 1,200,000 comment letters, no rule followed. Under pressure from politicians, in 2013 the SEC chair assured Congress that no rule would be forthcoming; and in the federal budget enacted in December 2015, the SEC was prohibited from expending its resources on such a rule. About 75 percent of the S&P 500 companies offer voluntary disclosure, but it is limited and inconsistent.[58]

In the 2022 proxy season, 45 of the 407 shareholder proposals addressed enhanced disclosure and control of political spending. Five passed, the 45 proposals receiving an average level of support of 33 perent.[59] Many blame large institutional investors, especially the "Big 4" (BlackRock, Vanguard, State Street, and Fidelity, which collectively have $17 trillion under management), for these proposals' failure.[60] A study cited in a 2019 Harvard Law School discussion paper authored by the then Delaware Chief Justice, Leo Strine, indicated that, in the political spending disclosure proposals studied, if the largest shareholder (almost invariably an institutional investor) had voted for the proposal, 60 percent of them would have passed, rather than none. Strine said:

> Because Citizens United unleashes corporate wealth to influence who gets elected to regulate corporate conduct, . . . corporations are likely to engage in political spending solely to elect . . . candidates who favor industry-friendly regulatory policies, even though human investors have far broader concerns, including a desire to be protected from the externalities generated by corporate profit-seeking. . . . [O]ne form of nonhuman citizen that as a matter of reality controls much of the wealth of actual humans will have the ability to imbalance public policy . . . in a manner that is inconsistent with social welfare.[61]

To understand the impact of the *Citizens United* decision, consider the following statistics. In the 2008 election cycle, the last that included a presidential election before the 2010 holding in *Citizens United,* total political spending in all federal and state races was approximately $5.2 billion. In the 2016 cycle, spending reached about $6.6 billion–a new record. That record was smashed in the 2020 cycle hitting $14.4 billion. Even taking inflation into account, 2020 spending was 2.3 times the amount in 2008. In the 2020 cycle, the 100 top donors contributed $1.6 billion, political action committees (which can raise and spend unlimited sums) injected $3.3 billion, and "dark money" (political spending by anonymous donors) reached a new record of $1 billion. Both parties were beneficiaries of this unprecedented influx of money.[62] The problem is considerably worse at the state and local levels, where amounts made available by *Citizens United* that would be deemed trivial in the national context are sufficient to "totally swamp" local elections. Judges have become particularly vulnerable. U.S. Supreme Court Justice Ginsburg said: "In recent years . . . issue-oriented organizations and political action committees have spent millions of dollars opposing the reelection of judges whose decisions do not toe a party line or are alleged to be out of step with public opinion."[63] More broadly, the well-known conservative Seventh Circuit Judge Richard Posner said in a National Public Radio interview: "Our political system is pervasively corrupt due to our Supreme Court taking away campaign-contribution restrictions [in *Citizens United*] on the basis of the First Amendment." Former President Carter described the behavior permitted by *Citizens United* as "legal bribery."[64]

The public cares about this issue. A 2021 poll taken in the key political battleground states (Alaska, Arizona, Georgia, Iowa, Maine, Nevada, New Hampshire, North Carolina, Ohio, Pennsylvania, West Virginia, and Wisconsin) found that 83 percent of voters favored federal legislation to override *Citizens United.* The favorable view was consistent across gender (males 80 percent and females 86 percent), political party (Democrats 96 percent, Republicans 74 percent, and independents 73 percent), and race (white 66 percent, black 79 percent, Hispanic 71 percent, and Asian American 74 percent).[65] Previously, the Pew Research Center reported that 77 percent of the public wanted limits on political spending (71 percent of Republicans and 85 percent of Democrats).[66] The Center for Public Integrity reported 75 percent of those surveyed favored a constitutional amendment overturning *Citizens United* (85 percent of Democrats and 66 percent of Republicans).[67] Corporate boards cannot ignore the reputational risks associated with failing to be transparent about political spending.

Question

Does political spending by large corporations pose a problem for democracy? Explain.

Nontraditional Financial Metrics

Publicly held companies are required to make annual and quarterly disclosures to the public about their income, assets, liabilities and equity. When doing so, they must use a set of measurement and disclosure rules known as ***generally accepted accounting principles*** (GAAP). These rules are established by the Financial Accounting Standards Board, a private-sector organization whose promulgations have force-of-law status pursuant to authority delegated by the SEC. Disclosures that are not prepared in accordance with GAAP subjects a company to potentially draconian liability for losses sustained in the market, as well as to civil and criminal penalties. A corporation fails to adhere to GAAP at its peril.

Nonetheless, the disclosure of non-GAAP financial metrics, such as EBITDA (earnings before interest, taxes, depreciation, and amortization), is common. The closest corresponding GAAP measure is ***earnings per share*** (EPS). Ninety-seven percent of the S&P 500 made at least one such disclosure in 2018, up from 59 percent in 1996. The number of unique measures has increased threefold.[68] These disclosures do not violate the securities laws so long as: (1) the disclosures are neither misleading nor more prominent than the GAAP disclosures, and (2) every non-GAAP metric is reconciled to the closest GAAP metric. GAAP figures commonly include such things as one-time occurrences; for example, a major litigation loss in a product liability suit. Management often asserts that eliminating such items makes non-GAAP measures useful supplements to GAAP information, helping readers better perceive the company's actual operating performance and financial position, without the distortion of putatively one-off events.

In response to non-GAAP metrics that grossly distorted reality during the Enron era of the early 2000s, the SEC issued regulations in 2003 and 2010. In the years since, the SEC has grown increasingly concerned by the opportunistic manner in which non-GAAP disclosures are being prepared. For example, in April 2022 the SEC ordered Marathon Oil to revise its computation of "free cash flow" (a non-GAAP metric) because it used a formula so far afield from the way this metric is generally determined that it was deemed affirmatively misleading.[69]

The difference between GAAP and non-GAAP measures can be significant. For example, in each of the five years 2013 to 2017, Twitter suffered losses measured under GAAP cumulating to $2.3 billion. But according to its non-GAAP measure of income, it only suffered a loss in one year (2013), with an aggregate profit of $820 million—a difference of

$3.1 billion.[70] Similarly, in the second quarter of 2019, Uber reported a non-GAAP profit of $220 million despite the fact that, under GAAP, it had suffered a $5.2 billion loss.[71]

Boards of directors have been put on notice by a frustrated SEC and are increasingly under the spotlight from the financial media about the employment of metrics that exaggerate the positives and downplay the negatives. Sanctions are being imposed. For example, in December 2018, the SEC settled charges against ADT for violating the disclosure rules for non-GAAP measures. The "HIGHLIGHTS" section of its first quarter 2018 earnings disclosure indicated a 7 percent increase in non-GAAP profit. Later in the release it stated that its GAAP loss had increased 11 percent. The SEC sanctioned ADT for failing to give the comparable GAAP measure equal prominence, issuing a cease-and-desist order and levying a $100,000 penalty.[72]

Question

What are nontraditional financial metrics? In what ways are they helpful? Harmful? Explain.

Income Taxes

In its "2019 Directors' Alert," international accounting and consulting firm Deloitte said

> Once considered just another . . . cost . . . of doing business, tax has become a high-priority agenda item for both the C suite and the board. . . . Concerns now extend well beyond achieving financial targets to include managing reputational risk, weathering increased scrutiny from media and activist organizations, and addressing the impact of tax on everything[.] The pace of change in government tax policies adds complexity . . . as tax authorities grapple with the effects of digitalization, new business models[,] and globalization. [O]rganizations should be consciously shaping their tax strategies and involving senior executives [and] the board[.][73]

With respect to taxes, corporations face several risks. There is a financial risk that tax authorities will demand large cash payments after rejecting the company's determination of its tax liability. Disclosure risk can be present when the company fails to provide enough information to allow readers to evaluate the credibility of its reported ***effective tax rate*** (ETR). Companies face reputational risk when, for example, a media or government investigation reveals information creating a strong impression that the business is abusing the tax system and shifting the tax burden onto those far less able to bear it.

All of the above risks manifested for Apple when it became the poster child for using the international tax system to defeat U.S. taxation. Senator Carl Levin, chair of the Permanent Subcommittee on Investigations at the time, said: "Apple sought the Holy Grail of tax avoidance," referring to the company's claim of ***stateless income***–income that is purportedly beyond the reach of taxation by any country in the world.[74] From 2009 through 2011, Apple paid essentially no tax on $38 billion of income.[75] The result was an ETR of only 1.8 percent.[76] Apple CEO Tim Cook was summoned to appear before Congress in 2013 to defend the company's tax strategies;[77] and in April 2016, he felt it necessary to make a "personal appeal" to the European Union urging it to cease investigating Apple's tax arrangements. In due course, the EU ordered Ireland to collect about $15 billion in back taxes from the company. In mid-2020, however, Apple prevailed.[78]

> Apple sought the Holy Grail of tax avoidance–stateless income.

But this case and many others have resulted in the emergence of a new international tax regime fairly characterized as "unprecedented." Mediated through the Organization for Economic Cooperation and Development and the G20, 141 countries to date, including the U.S., the U.K.,

China, India, and virtually all of the EU, are working to implement a global minimum tax and to establish mechanisms for global information sharing and enforcement. The new system goes into effect in 2023. The Biden Administration has agreed to the plan but, as of this writing, has not secured the necessary congressional support. Nonetheless, many countries are moving forward, some vigorously, to implement the new regime. Thus, U.S. multinational corporations operating in adopting jurisdictions will be required to comply with the new laws. Governments are projected to collect an additional $240–260 billion of tax revenues annually as a result.[79]

Consider the following in terms of the reputational risk facing large corporations: A 2019 Gallup poll found that 66 percent of the American public felt that corporate taxes are too low, a figure that remained almost constant over the prior 15 years.[80] Similarly, a 2019 CBS News poll, focusing on the substantial changes made by the major tax act in 2017, found that 65 percent of Americans believe that legislation primarily benefited large corporations, with only 31 percent believing that middle-class families enjoy any tax relief from the new law. Fifty-eight percent thought the legislation would neither grow the economy nor create jobs, but rather will increase the budget deficit and imperil Medicare and Social Security.[81] Numerous media reports have appeared about the 10-year $1.35 trillion increase in the deficit attributable to the legislation's reduction in the corporate tax rate.[82]

Driving such public opinion is data like the following: in 2020, 55 of the largest U.S. corporations, despite showing high levels of profitability, collectively paid no income tax. Indeed, they received an aggregate refund of $3.5 billion. Had the 2017 tax law not included a variety of corporate tax breaks, they would have paid $8.5 billion in the aggregate—a difference of $12.5 billion for just these 55 companies. The aggregate cost of corporate tax breaks is estimated to be $180 billion annually. Without those breaks, corporate income tax revenues would have been $550 billion rather than $370 billion in 2021.[83] In 2021, 19 Fortune 100 companies paid little or no corporate income tax. A few examples make the point: Amazon reported $35.1 billion of pretax income (PTI) on its income statement, but had an effective tax rate (ETR) of only 6.1 percent. ExxonMobil had an ETR of 2.8 percent on $9.3 billion of PTI. AT&T's ETR was negative 4.1 percent despite a PTI of $29.6 billion.[84]

Public outrage over such disclosures led to the enactment of a federal corporate minimum tax in 2022 that will take effect on January 1, 2023. Any publicly held company reporting net income (before federal income tax) in their financial statements in excess of $1 billion must pay a minimum tax of 15 percent of that income. Only 80–100 companies have incomes in that range; but based on their 2022 financial statements, all three companies identified above would have been subject to the tax. They would have paid (estimates): Amazon $1.7 billion (income $11 billion), ExxonMobil $7.8 billion (income $52 billion), and AT&T $3.0 billion (income $20 billion)—a total of $12.5 billion, as opposed to an actual aggregate tax liability of about $1.2 billion (a tenfold difference). The new tax is projected to raise $22 billion annually.[85]

Stories like those above expose corporations to significant reputational risk, eliciting comments like: "The specter of big corporations avoiding all income taxes on billions in profits sends a strong and corrosive signal to Americans: that the tax system is stacked against them in favor of corporations[.]"[86]

It is no surprise, then, that 35 percent of large multinational corporations are concerned about reputational risk related to tax controversies. And as to financial and disclosure risks, the average large multinational is involved in 20 tax disputes per year, each involving an alleged tax underpayment of about $154 million. Some 30 percent of these disputes are settled rather than litigated to keep the matters out of public view, even if it costs more. Fifty-eight percent of corporate tax executives believe the volume of disputes will increase over the next several years, in significant part because of the new international tax regime. Remarkably, 24 percent say that their control systems are not adequate to manage criminal tax risks, despite 67 percent expecting more criminal investigations.[87]

Executive Compensation

Executive compensation is a lightning rod for reputational risk. Consider the following recent headlines and statements in the financial media:

- "Runaway CEO pay has Created the Perfect Storm for 'Greedflation'"[88]
- "Awaiting Layoffs, WeWork Employees Say Founder's Payout Is 'Graft'"[89]
- "CEO compensation has grown 940% since 1978–Typical worker compensation has risen only 12%"[90]
- "Abigail Disney, granddaughter of the Walt Disney Company cofounder Roy Disney, called [CEO] Bob Iger's $65 million compensation 'insane'"[91]

A *New York Times* writer said scornfully: "C.E.O.s get paid regardless of logic[,] C.E.O.s get paid extra to do the basics[,] C.E.O.s get paid regardless of scandal[, and] C.E.O.s often get paid more than companies say[.]"[92] Consider the following S&P 500 statistics from 2021:

- Median CEO compensation rose 18 percent to $18.3 million, while inflation-adjusted median worker pay declined 2.4 percent.
- The median CEO earned 364 times what the median rank-and-file employee earned, rising from 299 in 2020 and 264 in 2019.[93] Those numbers were 121 in 1995, 58 in 1989, 30 in 1978, and 20 in 1965.[94]
- Almost three dozen publicly held company CEOs had total compensation in excess of $100 million. All of the top 12 exceeded $200 million. Elon Musk's set a new record at $10.08 billion.[95]

A 2021 survey of Americans' views on business found that 87 percent think the gap between CEO and worker pay is a problem. Seventy-three percent said that CEOs are paid too much, and 72 percent felt that there should be a cap on CEO compensation regardless of performance. Eighty percent said that large corporations have undervalued workers too long.[96]

Critics point to failures on the part of the boards of directors, which are charged with overseeing executive compensation. One said

> Annual-meeting season is unfolding . . . and the script is playing out as usual–chief executive officers will get their way. They may endure the verbal lashings of a couple of shareholders, perhaps face a slightly embarrassing "say on pay" vote about their princely income[,] and then [they will] intone that after careful analysis, a compensation committee [of the board], advised by [compensation] experts, unanimously approved their ridiculous pay package.[97]

Those who see flaws in the executive compensation process identify four causal factors. First, boards may fear that the executive will depart. It is true that a successful senior executive has many opportunities, but are they always ready to move on if their pay demands are not met?[98]

Elon Musk's Unprecedented CEO Pay Package Becomes a Template

In 2018, the board of Tesla approved a compensation arrangement for CEO Elon Musk that, if fully realized, would pay out an estimated $56 billion–the largest package in history by more than order of magnitude. The board's justification: it wanted to "motivate Mr. Musk to continue to not only lead Tesla over the long-term, but particularly in light of his other business interests, to devote his time and energy in doing so." The fact that Musk's Tesla holdings (22 percent of the stock) would increase in value to $100 billion if the compensation performance targets were achieved was apparently insufficient motivation to induce his presence and attention. The package was initially reported in 2018 as $2.6 billion, still a startling amount. When the real potential payout was disclosed in 2019, a Tesla shareholder, Richard Tornetta, launched a shareholder's derivative suit against the company. The action asserts that (1) the board did not, in fact, expect Mr. Musk to depart; (2) the company already anticipated achieving several of the sales and earnings targets set for Musk when the package was offered; and (3) close relationships between Musk and members of the board's compensation committee made it unlikely that the package (which the plaintiff asserts was developed with Musk's active participation) would be seriously challenged. The lawsuit is in the testimony phase as of this writing. To date, Musk has received more than $60 billion in stock pursuant to the plan.

> *The New York Times* said: "Mr. Musk's megapackage was criticized when it was announced in 2018. . . . But pay experts say it inspired boards at other companies to concoct similar deals. . . . [T]hey see the influence of Mr. Musk's deal everywhere. . . . [M]any of last year's highest-paid executives got packages that . . . could pay out the sort of sums that would have been unthinkable a few years ago. And even as the gap between what executives and workers earn continued to widen[,] companies opened the floodgates for what they paid their leaders in 2021."

Questions:

1. If you owned stock that would increase in value to $100 billion if the performance targets you have been asked to achieve are accomplished, would you need to be offered an additional $56 billion for you to stay and actually attempt to achieve those goals?
2. How does the use of compensation consultants by boards of directors inexorably ratchet up CEO pay packages?
3. What impact do you think the spread of Musk-like pay packages will have on the ratios of CEO-to-median worker compensation?

Sources: Sissi Cao, "Elon Musk's $56 Billion Tesla Pay Package Heads to Court," *Observer,* September 23, 2019 [**https://observer.com**]; Jack Ewing, Isabella Simonetti, and Peter Eavis, "Elon Musk Tells a Court He Had Little Say in His Giant Tesla Pay," *The New York Times,* November 16, 2022 [**www.nytimes.com**]; Peter Eavis, Jack Ewing, and Isabella Simonetti, "Elon Musk Heads to Court to Defend His Billions in Tesla Pay," *The New York Times,* November 16, 2022 [**www.nytimes.com**]; Peter Eavis, "How Elon Musk Helped Lift the Ceiling on C.E.O. Pay," *The New York Times,* June 25, 2022 [**www.nytimes.com**].

The second of the four factors relates to a matter discussed earlier in this part: CEOs are more likely to control their boards than boards are to control their CEOs.[99] It is highly uncommon for directors to seriously resist the pay proposal submitted by the CEO.

Very few boards are willing to publicly suggest that their CEOs are not above average.

Third, members of the board are often CEOs of other companies (or aspirants to that position) who will not only be uncomfortable about a compensation confrontation with a fellow CEO, but who will also personally benefit from upward-moving CEO remuneration. One commentator characterizes it as "a virtueless circle in which C.E.O. pay gets ratcheted up by boards of directors stocked with other C.E.O.s who can leverage the same reasoning to justify their own ballooning salaries."[100]

Finally, there is the "Lake Wobegon effect." Garrison Keillor's closing line each week for one segment of the long-running (1974–2016) radio program, *A Prairie Home Companion,* was a description of the idyllic, fictional, small Minnesota town "where all the women are strong, all the men are good-looking, and all the children are above average." Very few boards are willing to publicly suggest that their CEOs are not above average, which inclines them to approve compensation above the median. That new data enters subsequent median computations, which fuels the relentless upward pressure on C-suite pay.[101]

The Dodd–Frank Act mandated a "say-on-pay" as of 2011—an opportunity for shareholders to vote for or against the board's proposed executive compensation arrangements. Despite the fact that, historically, the nonbinding votes have strongly been in favor of management (typically over 90 percent), executive compensation is now under intense scrutiny by important investors, with median support for pay packages being at the lowest level since voting began. For example, in 2022, shareholders refused to approve the CEO compensation proposals at Intel and Chase.[102]

In August 2022, the Securities and Exchange Commission (SEC) finalized new pay-versus-performance rules that will require certain disclosures in financial reports issued after 2022. SEC Chair Gary Gensler said: "Today's rule makes it easier for shareholders to assess a public company's decision-making with respect to its executive compensation policies." Companies will be required to provide a table which links executive compensation (especially for the CEO) to performance metrics widely used by shareholders, including total shareholder return (TSR) for the company and TSR for the company's peer group, both over the most recent five-year period. TSR is computed by summing (on a per-share basis) the total dividends paid and the increase or decrease in the stock price. The new rule is the direct result of investor discontent with "outsized CEO pay."[103]

Executive compensation arrangements should be designed to align C-suite behavior with the shareholders' interests. In the past, stock options have been the principal means by which boards have attempted to achieve this. Unfortunately, stock options are dysfunctional: if the stock price goes up, the executive wins; if the price goes down, the executive loses no investment (although there is an opportunity cost). Worse, boards repeatedly reset exercise prices downward when stock prices have declined, allowing executives to benefit even if the shareholders have suffered.[104] Since 2009, however, stock options as a percentage of total compensation at S&P 500 companies have declined by 27 percent. The emphasis has shifted to stock compensation—actual shares issued to the executive. Now executives suffer losses if the stock price declines. This form of compensation has increased 140 percent since 2009, exceeding 50 percent of total compensation for the first time in 2019.[105]

In a further effort to align C-suite conduct with the shareholders' interests, investors are pressing for "longtermism"—delaying the executive's enjoyment of performance-based compensation for a sufficient number of years to shift executives' focus away from manipulating short-term results, which is exceedingly common. One study found that the average time period for measuring most components of CEO compensation is only 1.7 years.[106] The *Harvard Business Review* reported that the best performing publicly held companies had CEOs who held their tenures for an average of 15 years. Yet the average tenure of S&P 500 CEOs is only 7 years.[107]

In October 2022, the SEC adopted new "clawback" provisions which will require executive officers to return any performance-based compensation determined by reference to quantities shown on financial statements if those statements are later required to be restated as a result of material noncompliance with the securities laws, which include the accounting rules under which financial statements are prepared (generally accepted accounting principles). If there is a restatement, all compensation paid in the prior three fiscal years is eligible for clawback. It makes no difference whether the recipient was responsible for the financial statement errors. The compensation will be redetermined using the correct numbers; and if too much was paid out, the excess must be returned. These rules are in addition to those promulgated under the Sarbanes-Oxley Act of 2002, which require the CEO and CFO to pay back any performance-based compensation received in the prior year if their own misconduct caused the financial statements to be restated. As of this writing, the final clawback rules have not been issued. Nonetheless, it is expected that they will apply to companies issuing financial statements in 2023.[108]

PRACTICING ETHICS Pacific Gas & Electric

A FUNDAMENTALLY UNETHICAL COMPANY?

Pacific Gas and Electric (PG&E) is the largest utility in the U.S., delivering electricity and natural gas to 16 million customers across 70,000 square miles of California. In 1996 and 2006, PG&E paid a total of $628 million to settle lawsuits involving its contamination of drinking water in the communities of Hinkley and Kettleman City. The 2000 movie *Erin Brockovich* was a dramatization of the Hinkley events. Despite ultimately taking responsibility, the toxic bloom is still spreading in Hinkley at a rate of 2.5 feet per day and "the entire town is threatened with extinction" because PG&E has failed to undertake the required containment.

In 1997, PG&E was convicted of 700 misdemeanors for its failure to minimize fire hazards, rerouting the money it had received for that task to other purposes.

In 2010, San Bruno was devastated when a PG&E gas line exploded with the force of a 1.1-magnitude earthquake, throwing a fireball 1,000 feet into the sky and blasting a crater 167 feet wide. Eight people were killed and dozens were injured. Thirty-eight homes were destroyed and another 66 were damaged. PG&E paid $565 million in damages. The California Public Utilities Commission (CPUC) imposed a $1.6 billion fine, and PG&E was convicted of several felonies, including obstructing the investigation. The National Transportation Safety Board concluded that the pipe was constructed in a "shoddy" fashion from "odd-shaped pieces [and] not welded properly." It also concluded that PG&E's recordkeeping system was so poor that it could not determine whether pressure levels were safe.

In 2014, mid-level managers informed supervisors that an ambitious program director was pressuring people to falsify on-time results in the marking of electricity cables and gas pipelines for pending excavation sites. PG&E transferred the managers, promoted the director, and delivered data to regulators that the company had reason not to trust. There were tens of thousands of falsifications resulting in 67 instances of excavation crews striking underground power and gas lines. In October 2019, PG&E paid a $65 million fine for this conduct.

In January 2019, PG&E filed for bankruptcy because of claims resulting from 18 wildfires in October 2017 caused by its faulty electricity transmission system. The fires burned 200,000 acres, destroyed almost 3300 structures, and killed 22 people. Then, in May 2019, regulators concluded that PG&E's electrical grid had failed again, causing the Camp Fire, which killed 85 people and destroyed the town of Paradise. Damage claims aggregating $30 billion have been filed by 80,000 parties.

The Camp Fire failure occurred on the 115,000-volt Caribou-Palermo line which stretches 56 miles across often extremely harsh terrain. Internal PG&E documents from 2010 warned that the line would soon face "thermal overload" (too much power moving through the system) because of rapid population expansion. Concerns about sagging lines and vegetation overgrowth were raised by employees. The drought-related death of millions of trees amplified the fire risk, of which PG&E was aware. The towers were, on average, 68 years old despite a life expectancy of 65 years. Some were 108 years old. In fact, portions of the line were "so old that segments were considered candidates for the National Register of Historic Places." Year after year, from 2013 through 2018, PG&E assured regulators that it would cure the problems. No material work was performed. Consultants advised physical inspections no less than every three to five years. PG&E did not implement this advice and, indeed, there was no indication that anyone had climbed the towers since at least 2001.

PG&E's recordkeeping system was so antiquated that it did not know what equipment was actually deployed, which made it impossible to assess safety risks. It had no way to prioritize projects because it lacked construction, maintenance, and inspection records. Between 2014 and 2016, $97 million was approved by regulators for updated recordkeeping systems. All but 15 percent was diverted to other uses.

PG&E's current electricity transmission system is so unsafe and unreliable that the only way PG&E can stop causing wildfires is to shut the grid down when winds reach certain levels. Since it has no capacity to turn off only small, targeted portions of the grid, PG&E must "pull the plug on a giant swath of the state's population," impacting as many as 5.4 million people for as long as five days—a scope of deliberate blackouts unprecedented in the U.S. The ill and the elderly are put at risk, many public services become unavailable, food and medical supplies requiring refrigeration perish, and businesses dependent on cooling (like hotels) lose revenues. PG&E estimates that these blackouts will be required for up to 10 years and asserts that it is under no duty to reimburse parties damaged by the power outages.

PG&E emerged from bankruptcy in July 2020. In addition to paying $11 billion to insurers, it will pay $13.5 billion to wildfire victims—half funded in cash and the rest with 22 percent of the new PG&E stock, which will be sold later to fund further payouts. The California Public Utilities Commission (CPUC) imposed a $1.6 billion fine, and the Federal Emergency Management Agency will receive $3.9 billion in reimbursements for costs incurred providing assistance. The company pleaded guilty to 84 counts of involuntary manslaughter for the Camp Fire deaths.

PG&E will be permitted to join the $20 billion wildfire fund established by the California Legislature in 2019 to provide a financial buffer for utilities operating in the state that suffer damages from future wildfires. The former CEO was forced to resign and the board was fundamentally restructured.

PG&E has been widely criticized; for example:

- Federal Judge William Alsup, supervisor of PG&E's San Bruno criminal probation, stated that the company has a "history of falsification."
- Former CPUC member Mark Ferron said PG&E played a "cat and mouse game" with regulators—doing what it wanted and waiting to see if it got caught.
- Major shareholder BlueMountain Capital Management observed that the fires were only "the latest example of how the board continues to fail the company . . . and the people of California."

The Wall Street Journal summarized:

> [We] identified repeated instances over 25 years in which PG&E misled regulatory authorities, withheld required information, didn't follow through on promised improvements, . . . or obstructed an investigation. . . . The behavior [has] persisted through multiple corrective-action plans, reorganizations and five CEOs[, which] present[s] the current problem [for decision makers]: if [PG&E] can't [be] trust[ed] to do what it says and it [isn't] chastened by penalties or public shaming, how will PG&E leadership restore both solvency and safety to this critically important institution?

Many wonder why the CPUC has allowed PG&E to get away with decades of misconduct. In January 2020, California Assemblyman Adam Gray said: "[G]overnment incompetence is part of the story. [The commission] knew about the decaying and outdated condition of PG&E's infrastructure, yet they failed to act." He asked for an extensive audit "to determine whether the regulator's lax oversight enabled neglect at [PG&E] that triggered catastrophic wildfires . . . and exasperating blackouts."

There are also suspicions that PG&E's extensive lobbying and political contributions have played a role in inattentive government oversight. A member of the San Francisco Board of Supervisors said "[PG&E's] tremendous political influence at the state and local level has led them to believe that they are above scrutiny and reproach."

Questions

1. Can PG&E be fairly characterized as a "fundamentally unethical company" or has it just acted appropriately on behalf of its shareholders? Explain.

Social Businesses Foreshadow ESG

The concept of a "social business" comes from Dr. Muhammad Yunus, an economist and winner of the 2006 Nobel Peace Prize. It occupies a unique place on the continuum running from for-profit to not-for-profit organizations. A social business is distinguished from a for-profit business in that it is formed primarily to further a specific positive social objective, rather than to seek profit-maximization. Profits are applied to the achievement of its stated social objective. Regular reporting includes both financial statements and the identification of concrete progress toward social goal attainment. A social business is distinct from a nonprofit enterprise in at least two key respects: (1) it is intended to be an economically self-sustaining enterprise (which means that it must adhere to commercially reasonable business practices) and (2) its start-up capital must be returned to its investors (although without interest).

For such ventures to become a reality, a new form of business was required. Thirty-six states, the District of Columbia, and Puerto Rico have adopted "benefit corporation" statutes and another eight are considering doing so. In such corporations, the directors' fiduciary duties require the elevation of nonfinancial interests. Well-known benefit corporations include Kickstarter, Patagonia, and KleanKanteen.

In July 2006, the nonprofit B Lab was created. "Its vision is that one day all companies compete not only to be the best in the world, but the Best for the World® and as a result society will enjoy a more shared and durable prosperity." Companies embracing this view can apply for the status "Certified B Corporation," which requires committing to a "Declaration of Interdependence." Among other things, the company must "create . . . benefit for all stakeholders, not just shareholders"; conduct its affairs "as if people and place matter"; ensure its activities "do no harm and benefit all"; and acknowledge that "we are . . . responsible for each other and future generations." As of this writing, there are over 6,000 Certified B Corporations in well over 100 countries spanning over 150 industries. Examples include Ben & Jerry's, New Seasons Market, Cascade Engineering, New Belgium Brewing, Natura & Co., Urban Green Development, and SilverChef Rentals.

[To find a benefit corporations in your state, see **https://benefitcorp.net/businesses/find-a-benefit-corp**.] [To find a Certified B Corporation in your state, see **https://bcorporation.net/directory**.]

Sources: "What is a benefit corporation?," *Benefit Corporation* [**https://benefitcorp.net**]; "Certified B Corporations: About B Corps," *Certified B Corporation* [**https://www.bcorporation.net**]; Best B Corporations, 2018, *The Green Spotlight* [**https://www.thegreenspotlight.com**]; and "B Lab announces the Best for the World 2021 B Corps," B Lab Global, July 14, 2021 [**www.bcorporation.net/en-us/news/press/b-lab-announces-2021-best-world-b-corps-performance-excellence-beyond-just-profit#:~:text=Today%20there%20are%20more%20than,%2C%20communities%2C%20and%20the%20planet**].

ESG

Definition and Measurement of ESG

One of the primary impediments to the incorporation of ESG into business and investment decision-making is the lack of solid definitions. In December 2019, SEC Commissioner Hester Peirce said: "I think the first issue is that we don't even know what ESG means."[120] One critic said: "[Metrics are] the soft underbelly of the ESG movement."[121] But a lack of precise terminology is consistent with the emergence of a new paradigm, and those attempting to incorporate ESG into their decision-making are working to formulate definitions, widely agreeing that "social" will be the most challenging.[122] S&P Global uses the following ESG factor descriptions:

- Environmental: Greenhouse gas emissions, waste and pollution, water use, land use;
- Social: Workforce and diversity, safety management, customer engagement, communities; and
- Governance: Structure and oversight, code and values, transparency and reporting, cyber risk and systems.[123]

Forbes describes ESG as "How corporations respond to climate change, treat their workers, manage their supply chains, and build trust and foster innovation."[124] KPMG enumerates key ESG factors: climate change impacts, water and waste management, natural resource scarcity, product and worker safety, supply chain management, workplace diversity and inclusion, talent management, employee relations, human rights, health, labor practices, executive compensation, political contributions, and board independence and composition.[125]

Vigorous efforts are underway to create relevant metrics for the ESG factors.

Vigorous efforts are underway to create relevant metrics for the ESG factors. They must be designed in a way that allows them to be tied to financial metrics so they can be incorporated into business and investment decision-making.[126] In 2018, the Sustainability Accounting Standards Board published 77 industry-specific standards for measuring ESG performance.[127] The Task Force on Climate-Related Financial Disclosures has produced standards specifically applicable to climate and other sustainability-related risks.[128] Fifty percent of chartered financial analysts believe that ESG metrics should be independently audited,[129] and PricewaterhouseCoopers asserts that ESG metrics will someday be as important as financial statements.[130]

At the moment, the sole guiding principle for ESG disclosures that could be construed as mandatory is the long-standing *materiality* standard enunciated in the 1976 US Supreme Court decision *TSC Industries, Inc. v. Northway, Inc.*[131] An item is material "if there is a substantial likelihood that a reasonable investor would consider it important in deciding whether to buy or sell securities or how to vote." If some ESG-related factor satisfies that standard, it must be disclosed. But the means by which that disclosure is accomplished is largely within the latitude of the company. This latitude poses a major barrier to integrating ESG factors into corporate decision-making. The SEC has said: The use of "multiple voluntary frameworks has failed to produce the consistent, comparable, and reliable information that investors need" about ESG. To redress this, at the time of this writing the SEC has circulated a proposal that would mandate a specific set of ESG disclosures in publicly traded companies' annual audited financial statements.[132] A key component is the establishment of a threshold standard: If ESG factors affect a line item on a financial statement in a magnitude of one percent or more, the company must delineate the climate-related risks.[133] The SEC had hoped the rules would become effective late in 2022, but procedural problems and the receipt of 14,000 comment letters has pushed back the timeline considerably.

Despite the lack of widely accepted ESG metrics, the increasing demand for ESG disclosures by investors in general, and institutional investors in particular (which managed

$17.1 trillion of assets at the end of 2021,[134] an amount equivalent to 18 percent of global GDP), has led to a rapid growth in voluntary disclosures over the last several years. Based on a 2022 survey of Fortune 100 companies, all of them are now making some level of ESG disclosures. Ninety-eight percent do so with respect to environmental and diversity issues (up from 88% in 2021); 94 percent make disclosures about corporate culture, especially core values (up from 88% in 2021); and 55 percent make disclosures about social impact and community relations (up from 40% in 2021).[135]

Emergence of ESG

ESG is the successor to the Socially Responsible Investment (SRI) movement, but it takes a dramatically different approach. SRI uses ethical and moral criteria to negatively screen investments; for example, not investing in firearms or tobacco. ESG is grounded on the assumption that its factors have direct impacts on financial returns. It requires companies to expressly incorporate ESG risks and opportunities into their core business strategies.

The term was coined in 2005 with the publication of a landmark study, "Who Cares Wins," by the United Nations Global Compact at the initiation of UN Secretary General Kofi Annan. The report's principal argument is that embedding ESG factors in capital markets improves financial performance and simultaneously leads to better outcomes for society.[136] Many investors agree. Forty percent of the shareholder proposals at Fortune 250 companies in the 2022 proxy season related to ESG.[137]

Millennials are twice as likely as older generations to want their pension funds invested responsibly.

Forty-three percent of financial advisors incorporate ESG factors into their investment decisions.[138] Forty-nine stock exchanges, including the London Stock Exchange, have committed to publishing ESG disclosure guidelines. None in the U.S. have yet done so, but that will change if the SEC's new ESG disclosure rules are adopted.[139]

The creation of B Lab in 2006 with its "Certified B Corporation" designation, discussed earlier, was an early attempt to promote the blending of financial and social objectives in business.

ESG Boosts Financial Performance

Corporate declarations about how seriously social and environmental issues are taken have long been viewed as disingenuous, lacking in substance, and intended merely to assuage superficial regulatory scrutiny, placate vocal critics, or function as part of a marketing campaign. Corporations strive to generate maximum returns for shareholders. They address concerns like pollution, discrimination, income inequality, and employee displacement by technology only to the extent needed to obey the law or to ameliorate the transitory rage that follows an adverse media story because doing so is viewed as a cost that negatively impacts shareholder returns. As one CEO said in an analogous context: "Almost all of our customers are interested in what we can do to clean the environment and other stuff. You can tell it's one of their core values–until you get to price."[140]

The rise in public discontent with the status quo led academics and companies to study the economic relationship between ESG and shareholder returns. The results, surprisingly to many, actually make the financial case for incorporating ESG factors into companies' core strategies. One study found that a focus on significant ESG issues increased shareholder returns in 58 percent of the companies studied. Returns declined for only 8 percent, with ESG efforts having no impact on 36 percent.[141] An examination of the stock prices of 2000 major companies over an 18-year period found that those which incorporated material ESG factors into their core strategy grew at an annual compound rate 2.3 percent higher than companies that did not.[142] Highly regarded academics determined that companies with a strategic focus on ESG enjoy annual returns 3 to 6 percent higher than companies without that focus. Downside risk is also lowered, which reduces the cost of capital and makes the company more robust in an economic downturn.[143] A study from Oxford University found that 88 percent of the companies that incorporated ESG into corporate strategy improved their profitability; 80 percent improved their stock price. Research by Dun & Bradstreet concluded "[A] business's . . . ESG . . . performance . . . increasingly affects not just its reputation, but also its operations and market position." Eighty percent of companies said that incorporating ESG into their strategies created a "significant or transformational" increase in revenue, while lowering both operational and financial risk.[144] It is now largely accepted that favorable performance on ESG factors material to the company can create a sustained competitive advantage that inures to the benefit of the owners.

Critical Link between ESG and Owner Return

An important finding in one of the previously discussed studies is that those companies which simply attempt to make ongoing incremental progress on a broad list of ESG issues realize no enhanced return for their investors. They perform no better than companies that make no claim to incorporating ESG factors into their decision-making.

Even those companies that take seriously the ESG factors material to their business, like FedEx in its attempt to reduce its carbon footprint by adopting new technologies that optimize routes and permit the use of cleaner fuels, often find little or no resulting improvement in their stock prices. The reason: when a member of an industry takes into account an ESG factor that equally impacts all other members of the industry, all that company is doing is precluding the development of a competitive disadvantage that causes it to fall behind its competitors in delivering returns to owners. Indeed, over time the approach to addressing the ESG issue simply becomes an industry-wide best practice, which conveys no competitive advantage to any individual firm. The text box that follows explains how to achieve the required linkage between ESG factors and improved financial performance.

When Does ESG Enhance Owners' Returns?

Three Harvard Business School professors, Michael Porter, George Serafeim, and Mark Kramer, make a powerful case that shared value is not created unless ESG factors are integrated into a business' core strategy. In their words

> We are entering a new stage of understanding . . . the linkage between investment performance and social impact. . . . Most corporate leaders view their sustainability efforts primarily as a way to enhance their reputations and attract socially aware consumers, employees, and investors. . . . The impact of social innovations on . . . economic-value creation [is] not fully understood or even considered. As a result, corporate executives . . . and investors alike are missing a powerful value driver. . . .

The purpose of investing is to create a virtuous cycle by allocating capital to those companies that create the greatest societal returns–both in [returns for the owners] and in improving the welfare of customers, employees, suppliers, and communities. . . .

[C]ompanies that create shared value [that is, value concurrently delivered to owners and one or more other ESG stakeholders] can outperform their peers[.] . . . [Creating shared value requires] the integration of social factors into . . . strategy[.] . . . A social purpose that is truly strategic must build on . . . the company's unique value proposition . . . that either offers better value to target customers (differentiation) or achieves structural efficiencies that support lower cost versus competitors (cost savings). . . . [Companies that do so] can outperform their peers, delivering superior returns both to society and to their shareholders. . . .

Shared value can affect strategy at three mutually reinforcing levels: (1) creating new products that address emerging social needs or open currently unserved customer segments; (2) enhancing productivity in the value chain[;] and (3) investing to improve the business environment . . . where the company operates. . . .

When shared value is integrated at all three levels, breakthrough strategies can be the result[, offering] virtually every business important new opportunities to drive growth, profitability, and competitive advantage by improving social performance.

[To read the entire article, see **www.institutionalinvestor.com/article/b1hm5ghqtxj9s7/Where-ESG-Fails**.]

Questions

1. Based on the above reading, what is shared value?
2. To achieve shared value, ESG factors must be incorporated into a business' core strategy and build on the company's value proposition. Identify the two ways this can be accomplished.
3. Give an illustration of each of the three levels at which the pursuit of shared value can affect strategy.

Source: Michael Porter, George Serafeim, and Mark Kramer, "Where ESG Fails," *Institutional Investor,* October 16, 2019 [**www.institutionalinvestor.com**].

Threats to the ESG Movement The physical realities, disenfranchisement, abuses, and other forces that have brought forth the ESG movement are not likely to abate, but threats to its success exist. Essential to the movement is trust in corporate leaders. Many commentators link the horrific corporate and financial scandals of the past 20 years to the profit-maximization mantra that took adamant hold in the 1980s. Enabled by an increasingly weak regulatory environment, bad behavior became ever-more tolerated and ineffectively punished. The moral compass of business was lost. The hope is that re-envisioning the purpose of business will steer companies in a more honorable, less damaging direction.

The forces of short-termism also pose a threat.

> Shared value, like all true competitive strategies, is a long-term proposition. Continuity in strategy enables better alignment of activities across the value chain and improvements in economic performance. The longer a company pursues shared-value creation, the more is learned

about meeting social needs in more effective and profitable ways, and the more effective it will in creating positive social impact into every aspect of its operations.[145]

Certain activists and others interested in short-term results will continue to push for outcomes achieved on the time scale of quarters, undermining the inherently long-term strategies associated with ESG. Companies striving to deliver shared value must be prepared to fend off such attacks to allow their ESG strategies to mature and yield enhanced returns for owners.

A recession in the near-term (which is widely anticipated as of this writing) would pose a risk for those companies attempting to implement ESG-based strategies. The pursuit of long-term goals is often thwarted when the focus shifts to the short-term for survival. Those companies that already have a mature ESG-based strategy should be more resilient in downturns, but this will be of no solace to companies just getting started. If the recession is severe enough, it could significantly impede the redirection of capitalism to providing profitable solutions to the world's problems. The economic battering being experienced by a number of industries during the COVID-19 pandemic is testing many companies' ESG commitments.

Another threat to the ESG movement is that only the Western world and Japan have embraced the idea that there must be a new purpose for business.[146] Asia and South America comprise a major part of the world's economy–well over 30 percent and growing.[147] If they continue with a solitary focus on profit maximization (or the achievement of a government's noneconomic objectives), those companies pursuing a loftier purpose could suffer competitive disadvantages so great that their ability to make the long-term shift to achieving more socially responsible outcomes could be jeopardized.

An increase in political instability or a further deterioration of the rule of law could introduce such chaos into the economy and government that the attempt to adopt a new purpose for business is imperiled. *Forbes* both warns and hopes: "Provided that political framework conditions based on openness and global rules do not deteriorate further, market-led changes will act as a force for good on a truly massive scale."[148]

Importantly, pushback against ESG exploded in 2022, driven by two primary factors: (1) the belief that requiring publicly held corporations to incorporate ESG factors into their decision-making results in lower returns on investment; and (2) the view held by many powerful conservative figures that ESG is "part of a broader narrative about left-wing overreach and 'wokeness' run amok[, with one state treasurer] call[ing] it 'corporate cancel culture.'" Former Vice President Pence characterized the call for enhanced ESG disclosures as a "radical ESG agenda." Elon Musk tweeted his 94 million followers that "ESG is a scam" and "the Devil incarnate." The principal economic justification underlying such assertions appears to be that "politically motivated investing strategies reduce long-term profits" (the first factor enumerated above). However, the body of research on the relationship between incorporating ESG goals into corporate strategy and financial performance, described earlier, would seem to refute that assertion. Nonetheless, many states have seriously underfunded pension plans, so a claim that ESG threatens retirement security can have a powerful impact. Florida, for example, has a public employee pension plan (2.6 million beneficiaries) that is 17 percent underfunded–its assets are $35.6 billion too little to deliver the promised retirement benefits.[149]

In retaliation against financial institutions like BlackRock (discussed earlier) that are ESG advocates, a number of states under conservative control (including as of this writing Florida, Texas, Missouri, Louisiana, South Carolina, and West Virginia) have (or are threatening to) pull their funds from those institutions' management. Florida Governor DeSantis announced in December 2022 that he has ordered the state to remove $2 billion of its assets from BlackRock. Texas passed a law forbidding municipalities to engage in business with banks that restrict funding to oil, gas, or firearm companies. As to who was harmed by Texas's action, research indicates that those municipalities will have to pay an additional $303–532 million of interest on the $32 billion of borrowing undertaken in the first eight months after the law's enactment because many municipal bond underwriters left the state.[150]

The U.S. House of Representatives, coming under Republican control in January 2023, is expected to attempt the derailment of the SEC's ESG disclosure proposal, which one Republican member of the House described as a "534-page monstrosity."[151]

Beyond these political pressures, the number of anti-ESG shareholder proposals submitted for consideration during the proxy season has increased. In 2022, the S&P 500 received a total of 642 proposals. Fifty-two (8 percent) were in opposition to current or proposed voluntary ESG disclosures. However, none received more than 3 percent support when the shares were voted.[152]

Climate Change: The Primary Driver of ESG Why has the ESG movement come to pass now? Were there fewer human rights abuses 20 or 30 years ago? Was there less gender, ethnic, or LGBT discrimination? Was corporate governance better in 2000 (as the Enron and other dot.com scandals loomed)? Was climate change not on the radar? In fact, it was, but too few took it to heart; or too many of those in control were economically adverse to considering it seriously. The Intergovernmental Panel on Climate Change (IPCC) was established in 1988 to focus the world's attention on this issue.

The World Takes Notice of Climate Change

Policy-makers concerned about climate [wanted to create] a new . . . institution. The principal impetus came from the United States[,] where the Environmental Protection Agency, the State Department and others were pushing for an international convention to restrict greenhouse gases. . . . Responding to this pressure[,] in 1988 the . . . Intergovernmental Panel on Climate Change [was created.] . . .

[C]ontrary to myths that later spread widely, the IPCC was neither an organ of the United Nations nor the creation of liberals; it was an autonomous intergovernmental body created chiefly by the conservative Reagan administration [and authorized] to issue . . . reports only with the firm agreement of essentially all the world's leading climate scientists plus the consensus of all participating governments[.]

Source: "The Discovery of Global Warming," American Institute of Physics, last accessed February 16, 2019 [**https://history.aip.org**].

The IPCC's first Assessment Report in 1990 made clear "the importance of climate change as a challenge with global consequences and requiring international cooperation."[153] Yet neither this document nor over 25 years of additional, increasingly confirmatory research brought forth an epiphany as to the purpose of business or the importance of ESG factors.

In the last several years, however, executives responsible for locating, widening, and serving markets, and for establishing and maintaining supply chains, have confronted harsh facts about climate change-driven disruptions. For example:

- The City of Coalinga, California, with its 17,000 residents, was within days of reaching Day 0 (the total absence of water) by the end of November 2022. It made an emergency water purchase sufficient to get through March 2023. The cost was $1.1 million (10 times the cost of that amount of water a year before, reflecting the fact that the entire state of California is operating under extreme water-scarcity conditions). For many local farmers, the cost of the required water exceeded the value of the crops that could be produced, leading to the abandonment of their efforts.[154]
- In 2018, commercial traffic on the Rhine, the world's busiest waterway, came to a halt for the first time when it became impassable due to a severe lack of rain for replenishment. The same happened on the Mississippi River in October 2022.[155]
- In July 2021, record temperatures were reached in Portland, Oregon, three days in a row: 108, 112, and 116 degrees. It was so hot the power cables to the street cars melted, causing transport to halt.[156]

Projections with implications for future disruption are equally stark:

- By 2030, the available fresh water supply is expected to satisfy only 60 percent of global demand.
- Forty-seven percent of the world's primary energy production facilities, which require generous access to water, are located in "highly stressed" water areas; and the available water is increasingly warm, so power generation will increasingly decline.
- $459 billion of revenues is at risk for lack of water, and another $198 billion is at risk from flooding.[157]
- Changing wave patterns and water elevations along 50 percent of the world's coastline will increase flooding and erosion.[158]
- The frequency, intensity, and impacts of extreme weather events will increase.[159]

Climate change is the ultimate long-term problem . . . a structural crisis.

Those charged with managing business risks are being forced to confront climate change head on. BlackRock CEO Lawrence Fink said in his 2020 letter to CEOs:

> We are facing the ultimate long-term problem. We don't yet know which predictions about the climate will be most accurate, nor what effects we have failed to consider. But there is no denying the direction we are heading. Every government, company, and shareholder must confront climate change. . . .
>
> Over the 40 years of my career[,] I have witnessed a number of . . . challenges[, including] the dot-com bubble . . . and the global financial crisis. Even when these episodes lasted for many

years, they were all, in the broad scheme of things, short-term in nature. Climate change is different. Even if only a fraction of the projected impacts is realized, this is a . . . structural, long-term crisis.[160]

While factors like income inequality and wage stagnation have certainly amplified public concerns about the impact corporations have had in their focused pursuit of profit, without there finally being an acknowledgment by the financial community of the inescapable, devastating impacts of climate change, there is good reason to believe that the consensus needed to break the grip of shareholder value in favor of stakeholder value would not now exist.

[To envision the potential impact of climate change on the supply chain, see **www.youtube.com/watch?v=V1kY_COMeXc** (ship attempting to dock in 69 mph winds).]

Question

Consider the industry or profession you plan to enter and the role you hope to achieve in your career. Identify two or three key ways in which these are likely to be impacted by climate change and other ESG factors. What ESG-based strategies do you think will be most important for you and that industry or profession to thrive? Explain.

Board Composition and Dynamics

LO 9-10 Discuss board composition in light of the rapidly changing business environment in which corporations now operate.

As described above, modern boards of directors are, and will continue to find themselves, confronted with a host of serious challenges. These include dealing with cybersecurity threats; precluding misconduct by employees and officers; and coping with public scrutiny of political spending, tax structures, and executive compensation. They may also need to develop contingency plans for a recession. Inflation is raging at levels not seen for 40 years. Political divisiveness permeates Western society. A war is waging in Eastern Europe. The COVID-19 pandemic is far from over. Supply chain disruptions are expected to continue for years. For example, in December 2022, Apple announced that it would be moving its iPhone production out of China because of serious supply chain concerns.[161]

Beyond all that, two fundamental and profound forces are pervasively impactful. The world is now in the midst of the Fourth Industrial Revolution, which has been described as "the marriage of the digital and the physical . . . creat[ing] exponentially greater value for far less effort[,] driven by new technologies and relentless digitalization."[162] Further, the greatest shift in core beliefs about corporate purpose in the past four decades is unfolding, driven by the recognition of critical ESG matters ranging from climate change to human rights.

Sixty-eight percent of directors believe that within five years their corporations' existing strategies will be completely irrelevant.[163] The knowledge, skills, and willingness to engage that will be needed by the board to respond will be greater than ever before. Despite the need for boardroom excellence, however, directors of public companies have reached a record level of dissatisfaction with their peers and the functionality of their boards. Forty-eight percent believe that at least one fellow director should be replaced; 19 percent think at least two should go. Among the characteristics disapproved of are a reluctance to challenge management and a lack of needed skills.[164] Director turnover is glacial–S&P 500 boards, on average, change fewer than one director per year. Boards are more likely to increase their number to bring in new views and talents than they are to take steps to remove or improve the performance of an existing director.[165]

Board independence has been a matter of serious concern since the Enron Era of the early 2000s. The New York Stock Exchange and NASDAQ now require the majority of directors to be independent. The objective is to increase the quality of corporate governance by limiting the power of the CEO.

Implications for Boards of Directors

What might be the ideal mix of individuals on a board of directors?

Diversity is increasingly deemed of great importance to ensure a full range of perspectives and capabilities. Among the types of diversity is gender. In 2019, for the first time, every S&P 500 board had at least one female director,[166] and female directors exceeded 25 percent of the board. In 2022, they held 32 percent of the seats.[167] Ethnic diversity is also deemed important. As of 2022, 22 percent of S&P 500 directors are from minority groups, up from 13 percent in 2019.[168]

Does Gender Make a Difference on Boards of Directors?

Every year, international accounting firm PricewaterhouseCoopers performs a survey of publicly held company directors. In 2022, it gave special attention to the very substantial differences in the orientation of female versus male directors. A number of those differences are summarized here.

Valuing Board Diversity	Male	Female
Gender	84%	98%
Minority	80%	92%
Age	75%	88%

Beliefs about Board Diversity	Male	Female
It's driven by political correctness	64%	29%
Shareholders are too preoccupied with it	61%	30%

ESG Issues	Male	Female
Should be incorporated into strategy	55%	65%
Reducing impact of climate change is a priority even if it impacts short-term financial performance	45%	66%

Executive Compensation Metrics Should Include	Male	Female
Diversity goals	45%	73%
Environmental goals	30%	40%

Factors that Improve Shareholder Trust	Male	Female
More disclosure	66%	81%
Board diversity	61%	74%
Commitment to environmental goals	48%	68%

Source: "Charting the course through a changing governance landscape," PricewaterhouseCoopers, 2022 [**www.pwc.com/us/en/services/governance-insights-center/assets/pwc-2022-annual-corporate-directors-survey.pdf**].

A mix of insider and independent directors will be needed. The former are intimate with the company's activities, capabilities, and weaknesses; but the latter are better able to keep the broader picture in focus.[169] Boards will need to insist that ESG is integrated into the overall enterprise risk management system[170] and that appropriate ESG metrics are developed to monitor performance improvements.[171] The achievement of ESG goals must be incorporated into executive compensation formulas to promote the effective implementation of ESG-based strategies throughout the company. This calls for ensuring that at least one member of the board is an expert in ESG matters.[172]

BlackRock and other major investors have put the boardroom on notice:

> We believe that when a company is not effectively addressing a material issue, its directors should be held accountable. . . . Where we feel companies and boards are not producing effective sustainability disclosures or implementing frameworks for managing these issues, we will hold board members accountable. [W]e will be increasingly disposed to vote against management and board directors when companies are not making sufficient progress on sustainability-related disclosures and the business practices and plans underlying them.[173]

Questions

1. Discuss the value of diversity, in its broadest sense, on boards of directors.
2. You are forming a new U.S. corporation that will be publicly held. It will operate a fleet of huge tankers that will transport crude oil from sources in 11 countries in Asia and Africa to refineries in Europe and North America. What board composition would be appropriate for this company? Explain.
3. Does minority-group representation on the board of directors make any difference in terms of corporate performance, reputation, or otherwise? The **Team Presentation Exercise** at the end of this chapter explores that question.

Questions-Part Two

1. Are activist investors good or bad for the capital markets? Explain.
2. Describe what the Foreign Corrupt Practices Act forbids.
3. Identify the arguments for and against non-traditional financial metrics.
4. What phenomenon allows some highly profitable corporations to pay essentially no income tax?
5. Identify and evaluate the arguments for and against the present level of executive compensation in publicly held corporations.
6. What are Certified B Corporations? What must a corporation do to become one?
7. Evaluate the prospects for stakeholder value displacing shareholder value. Explain why stakeholder value and a paradigm shift in the purpose of business are emerging now.

Part Three—Regulation of the Securities Markets

Part Three explores the U.S. financial markets in which businesses raise the debt and equity capital they need to come into existence, fund their operations, make acquisitions, engage in research and development, and otherwise fuel their growth and survival. These markets are impersonal–those who wish to sell their stock and bonds rarely know those interested in buying them, so personal knowledge of the parties' financial situations, character, and competency is generally absent. The capacity of an economy to grow, weather calamities, and seize opportunities is directly related to the actors' access to capital. To bring buyers and sellers confidently together, the impersonal markets require intense regulation. That regulation is the subject of this chapter.

To amass the resources needed to pursue sizable business opportunities, particularly global ventures, a large number of investors must be convinced to entrust their wealth to third-party managers. History shows that this trust has often been misplaced, vast sums having been lost in companies with incompetent or corrupt management, as can be seen in the rise and fall of WeWork and FTX discussed previously. As a result, the federal government has undertaken to promote the reliability of the U.S. securities markets through regulation. The backbone of this regulation grew out of the stock market crash of 1929 and the Great Depression that followed. Significant additional regulation followed the corporate failures of the Enron era (early 2000s) and the Great Recession of 2008. Both initial public offerings and the trading of securities already in the market are subject to substantial federal regulation. Corporations' securities may also be subject to state and international regulation.

Initial Public Offerings

LO 9-11 Define the term *initial public offering* (IPO) and explain the securities registration process.

When a corporation wants to sell a new security (whether debt or equity) through the public capital markets, if the corporation (***issuer***) and any of the persons to whom the security is offered (***offerees***) are domiciled in different states (***interstate offering***), federal law governs the sale. If the corporation and all offerees are domiciled in the same state (***intrastate offering***), state law (considered later) applies. If a company has not previously sold equity securities to the public, the issuance is referred to as an ***initial public offering*** (IPO); or, more colloquially, the corporation is said to be ***going public***. For example, DoorDash engaged in an IPO on December 9, 2020, initially placing the shares at $102. The stock began secondary trading on the New York Stock Exchange shortly thereafter, rising in two days to $190 (an 86 percent increase). Twenty days later, it was down to $143. The stock peaked at $246 on November 12, 2021 (a 141% increase over the placement price). However, as of this writing the stock is trading at $71 (30% below the placement price, and down 71% from the peak).

If a private investor, or a group of private investors, purchase all of the publicly held equity securities of a corporation that company is said to be ***going private***. Computer manufacturer Dell did an IPO in 1988, went private in 2013, and returned to the public capital markets in 2018.

Questions

1. Explain what is meant by going public. By going private.
2. Contrast intrastate and interstate offerings.

LO 9-12 Identify the purposes of the 1933 Act and the principal methods by which they are achieved.

1933 Act

The ***prospectus*** is the major component used and delivered to offerees to satisfy the requirement of pre-investment disclosure. There are three main sections in a prospectus. One contains general information about the company: the industry in which it operates, the nature of its products and services and of its management, its business plan, and so on. Another

The 1933 Act seeks to ensure full disclosure and eliminate fraud.

section contains a risk assessment of the business model, local operating conditions (such as political instability), current and potential large lawsuits, and the like. For example, when Spotify went public on April 3, 2018, its IPO registration statement disclosed the following risk: "Our corporate affairs are governed by . . . the laws of Luxembourg[.] . . . Therefore, our shareholders may have more difficulty in protecting their interests in connection with actions taken by our directors and officers . . . than they would as shareholders of a [U.S.] corporation[.]"[174]

The term ***security*** embraces not only stocks and bonds, but also the much-broader ***investment contract***. The *Howey* case that follows defines this term.

LEGAL BRIEFCASE

SEC v. W. J. Howey Co.

328 U.S. 293 (1946)

FACTS

The Howey Company owned large tracts of citrus acreage in Florida. Each prospective customer was offered both a land sales contract and a service contract by which Howey maintained the groves and marketed the produce. Purchases were usually narrow strips arranged so an acre consisted of a row of 48 trees. These tracts were not separately fenced and the purchaser had no right of entry and no right to specific fruit. All the produce was pooled. The purchasers were mostly non-residents of Florida and were predominantly professionals. They were attracted by the expectation of substantial profits.

Justice Murphy

It is admitted that the mails and instrumentalities of interstate commerce are used in the sale of the land and service contracts and that no registration statement . . . has ever been filed with the [Securities and Exchange Commission].

[The Securities Act of 1933] defines the term "security" to include the commonly known [instruments like stocks and bonds]. The definition also includes [the term] "investment contract"[.] The legal issue [is] whether the land sales contract . . . and the service contract together constitute an "investment contract" within the meaning of [the Act]. An affirmative answer brings into operation the registration requirements[.]

By including an investment contract within the scope of . . . the Securities Act, Congress was using a term the meaning of which had been crystallized by prior judicial interpretation. It is therefore reasonable to attach that meaning to the term as used by Congress, especially since such a definition is consistent with the statutory aims. In other words, an investment contract for purposes of the Securities Act means a contract, transaction or scheme whereby a person invests his money in a common enterprise and is led to expect profits solely from the efforts of the promoter or a third party[.]

The transactions in this case clearly involve investment contracts as so defined. The respondent [is] offering an opportunity to contribute money and to share in the profits of a large citrus fruit enterprise managed [by respondent, who is] offering this opportunity to persons who reside in distant localities and who lack the equipment and experience requisite to the cultivation, harvesting and marketing of the citrus products[.]

[Respondent's] failure to abide by the statutory and administrative rules in making such offerings cannot be sanctioned under the Act[.]

Questions

1. What is an investment contract?
2. Would an investment in Microsoft stock satisfy the definition of "investment contract"?
3. Why do you think Congress added the term "investment contract" to the definition of "security"?
4. Is Bitcoin a security and therefore subject to regulation by the SEC? The Team Presentation Exercise at the end of the chapter explores this issue.

AFTERWORD

Following the *Howey* case, courts have looked more closely at the final criterion, that the investor "is led to expect profits *solely* from the efforts" of others [emphasis added], and have generally taken a practical view of the requirement, essentially interpreting the term "solely" as "primarily." The goal has been to distinguish circumstances in which investors will be primarily passive from those in which there is a reasonable expectation of significant investor control and management.[175]

The third section of the prospectus is the ***audited financial statements***. An investor's goal is to make money. Investors want to know how well the corporation under consideration has accomplished this in the past so they can estimate its future economic potential. A corporation's ability to make a profit is shown on its ***income statement***, which presents the company's revenues, gains, expenses, and losses, and bottom-line net income or net loss, typically on an annual basis.

Because the income statement seeks to measure economic income, it employs accrual accounting. Revenues are recognized when earned (not when cash is received) and expenses are recognized in the period during which the related revenue is reported (regardless of when those expenses are paid). Net income is not the same as net cash inflow from carrying on business. Therefore, a ***statement of cash flows*** reconciling the beginning-of-period and end-of-period cash balances is also presented. Proper cash management is crucial to both a company's day-to-day functioning and to its ability to seize opportunities and cope with adversities.

The ***balance sheet*** presents the business's assets (economic resources), liabilities (claims against those assets held by nonowners), and equity (residual claims against the assets held by owners after all liabilities have been satisfied). Although balance sheets have numerous deficiencies (such as the use of historical cost rather than current value to measure assets), they attempt to describe the corporation's financial position as of a particular date, such as the end of the period presented in the income statement.

Technically, the financial statements are prepared by the corporation's management. To give comfort to investors that management has prepared these statements properly and honestly, independent ***certified public accountants*** (CPAs) are engaged to audit them. Audits must be performed in accordance with ***generally accepted auditing standards*** (GAAS). GAAS are intended to ensure that the procedures used to investigate the financial statements are thorough. The objective of the investigation is to determine whether the financial statements are not ***materially misleading*** in accordance with ***generally accepted accounting principles*** (GAAP). GAAP provides the rules for how revenues, gains, expenses, losses, assets, liabilities, and equity are measured and disclosed. One might paraphrase an audit: independent experts (CPAs) are supposed to "look hard" (GAAS) and decide whether the financial statements prepared by management accurately measure the income, cash flow, and financial position of the corporation (GAAP).

> The objective of the investigation is to determine whether the financial statements are n*ot materially misleading in accordance with generally accepted accounting principles.*

The ***supplemental information*** portion (the second part) of the registration statement, which is not distributed to offerees, describes such matters as how much it will cost to "float" (undertake) the offering and what major contracts exist with unions, suppliers, and customers.

The SEC vigorously enforces the 1933 Act's prescribed relationship between ***solicitation*** (offering to sell) or sales of a security and the registration process. There are three stages, referred to as "periods," briefly described here. During the ***prefiling period*** (before the registration statement has been filed with the SEC), no solicitation or sales are permitted. During the ***waiting period*** (after the registration statement has been filed, but before it has been approved by the SEC), no sales are permitted, but a limited amount of marketing is allowed. A ***tombstone ad*** (so-called because of its shape and borders) may be published in forums like *The Wall Street Journal* to make the market aware of the anticipated issuance. A ***red herring prospectus*** (name taken from the prominent red ink cautionary statement required on its first page)–the draft prospectus included with the filed registration statement–may be distributed. Once the SEC approves the registration statement, the ***post-effective period*** begins. Solicitation is permitted and sales may be consummated, but only if the offerees have first received the final prospectus.

Some companies do ***shelf registrations*** that allow them to issue securities in portions over a two-year period under a single registration statement. This allows them to float the securities when market conditions are most favorable rather than issuing them all shortly after the registration statement becomes effective.

Typically not wanting to sell the securities themselves, issuers usually employ one or more ***underwriters***. A *best-efforts underwriter* acts as the issuer's sales agent, does not take title to the securities, and earns its profit from sales commissions. A *firm-commitment underwriter* purchases the securities from the issuer at a discount, intending to profit by reselling them. Institutional investors and ***dealers*** typically purchase new offerings–the former for investment, the latter for resale to retail investors. Spotify took the highly unusual step of listing its stock without an underwriter–a *direct listing.* It issued no new stock; listing the security simply allowed existing shareholders to sell their stock to the public. The company saved $100 million in underwriting fees.[176]

Private Placement General Solicitation Ban Lifted

In July 2013, the SEC reversed a long-standing prohibition on the solicitation of unregistered securities. ***Private placements*** can now be advertised to anyone, although only accredited investors (discussed later) can make purchases. Any means of solicitation, including the Internet, is permitted. Advocates assert that the new rule promotes the ability of start-ups and small businesses to raise capital without first having to go through the onerous registration process.[177]

Questions

1. Describe the information contained in a registration statement under the 1933 Act.
2. Explain the role played by the prospectus in the registration and sale processes.
3. Describe the three primary financial statements. Explain why they are audited.

Exemptions

Neither ***exempt securities*** nor ***exempt transactions*** require full registration with the SEC. The most common exempt securities are those issued by governments, charities, and financial institutions like banks and insurance companies. Thus, they have little application to most businesses.

Depending on the exempt transaction involved, the presale disclosures and filings with the SEC range from none to something only slightly less than a full registration statement. Most exemptions prohibit general solicitation.

Some exempt transactions were created as an accommodation to small issuers to lessen the financial burden of raising capital.

Some exempt transactions were created statutorily as an accommodation to small issuers to lessen the financial burden of raising capital. For example, all intrastate offerings are exempt transactions. There is an exemption for purely private offerings, but it can sometimes be problematic determining whether a particular offering will be considered private or public. Thus, small issuers are more likely to rely on one of the regulatory exemptions created by the SEC.

Some rules, such as Rule 504 (which exempts certain transactions with an aggregate offering amount of $10 million or less) are infrequently used. The workhorse is Rule 506, for which there is no amount limitation, but which can involve only ***accredited investors*** and up to 35 ***sophisticated investors***. Accredited investors are presumed to understand, and be able to withstand the risk associated with, securities investments. They include institutional investors (like pension funds), financial institutions, directors and officers of the issuer, and individuals with annual net income of at least $200,000 and/or net worth of at least $1,000,000 (excluding the personal residence). These financial thresholds have never been adjusted for inflation since their establishment in 1982. The inflation-adjusted amounts as of this writing would be $620,000 of income or $3.1 million of net worth. The result: a nearly nine-fold increase in the individuals eligible for accredited investor status–from .56 percent of the population to 4.9 percent. Accredited investors also include individuals who fail the dollar tests but who can demonstrate a solid understanding of the financial markets, such as those holding a Series 7 (public securities broker) or Series 65 (investment advisor) license. A sophisticated investor is one who has sufficient knowledge and experience in financial matters to be able to evaluate the merits and risks of an investment (or a person advised by a party with such expertise).

Perhaps surprisingly, the total amount of capital raised privately in the U.S. is twice the amount raised on the public markets. Of the total privately raised in IPOs, 60 percent is under Rule 506.[178]

Note that even when exemptions reduce or eliminate registration under the 1933 Act, the law's sweeping antifraud provisions (discussed later) still apply.

Securities Crowdfunding Emerges

Securities crowdfunding is the use of the Internet to raise debt or equity capital, with each contributor investing a comparatively small amount. It was authorized by the 2012 JOBS Act through a new registration exemption, which became effective on May 16, 2016. Companies are allowed to raise up to $5 million annually by selling stock via the Internet using "intermediaries" (SEC-regulated third parties that manage the process). Individuals who are not accredited investors are limited in the amount they can invest each year. For example, those whose annual income and net worth (exclusive of equity in the personal residence) are both less than $124,000 are permitted to invest not more than 5 percent of the greater of those amounts (but not more than $2,500). Individuals whose income or net worth exceeds $124,000 can invest up to 10 percent of the greater of those two amounts. Companies seeking funding must disclose information about their business, their officers and directors, and how they will use the money. Audited financial statements are required if the amount to be raised exceeds $1,235,000. Nonetheless, the disclosure requirements are substantially less than those applicable to conventional IPOs.

As of 2022, about 6,200 issuances under Regulation Crowdfunding have occurred. They raised approximately $2.5 billion in capital for small ventures.

At its inception, many commentators feared that this far less-regulated sector of the U.S. capital markets would expose many financially unsophisticated individuals to fraud. These concerns now appear unfounded as only a handful of cases have been brought by regulators as of this writing.

Sources: Hannah Melotto, "How Regulation Crowdfunding Will Reach $5 Billion," *KoreConX,* January 19, 2022 [**www.koreconx.com**]; Patrick Chomczyk, "SEC Brings First Charges Involving Regulation Crowdfunding," *Inside Compliance,* Loyola University School of Law, October 19, 2021 [**http://blogs.luc.edu**]; and Ray Pellecchia, "FINRA Fines Wefunder $1.4 Million for Crowdfunding Rule Violations," Financial Industry Regulatory Authority, May 4, 2022 [**www.finra.org**].

Although the media "hype" surrounding the 2012 JOBS Act was principally directed at the above securities crowdfunding provisions, many believed it should have been focused on the act's authorization of so-called ***Regulation A+*** mini-IPOs, which went into effect on June 19, 2015.[179] Regulation A+'s predecessor, Regulation A, was limited to $5 million annually and was so inefficient a mechanism for raising capital that only about 25 companies per year used it.[180] Regulation A+ raises the annual limit to $75 million, permits individuals who are not accredited investors to participate (up to 10 percent of the greater of their income or net worth), and imposes fewer initial barriers and ongoing disclosure obligations than a traditional IPO.[181]

Question

What is the difference between an exempt security and an exempt transaction?

The Secondary Securities Markets

Once a security is issued, it can be sold repeatedly. Such sales may be accomplished on a ***physical exchange***, such as the New York Stock Exchange (NYSE), where agents of buyers and sellers deal directly with each other. Others may be made on an ***over-the-counter market***, where trades occur electronically over a computer network linking dealers across the nation. An example is NASDAQ, the National Association of Securities Dealers Automatic Quotation system. [To learn more, see **www.nyse.com** and **www.nasdaq.com**.]

The 1934 Act

LO 9-13 Identify the purposes of the 1934 Act and the principal methods by which they are achieved.

The federal law that governs post-issuance securities trades is the *Securities Exchange Act of 1934* (1934 Act), which also created the SEC. Its purposes are the same as those of its 1933 counterpart: (1) to ensure the full disclosure of all material information so investors can make sound decisions and (2) to prevent fraudulent conduct in the markets. A company is generally subject to the 1934 Act's reporting requirements if it has publicly traded securities or has both more than $10 million in assets and more than 500 nonaccredited shareholders.[182]

To promote full disclosure, the SEC requires issuers to submit a variety of reports. Annually, each must file a ***Form 10-K***, which contains information very similar to that found in a 1933 Act registration statement, including audited financial statements. To increase the timeliness of disclosures, the SEC requires additional reports, such as the quarterly ***Form 10-Q*** and ***Form 8-K***. The former is a culled-down version of Form 10-K, particularly distinguished by the fact that the included financial statements are not audited. The latter is required whenever a material event occurs, such as a change in control, a major asset acquisition or disposition, bankruptcy, a change in auditor, or the resignation of a director. [To retrieve any of these filings for specific corporations, see **www.sec.gov/edgar**.]

All corporate communications are subject to regulatory standards. Regulation Full Disclosure (usually referred to as Regulation FD) requires companies to disseminate material information in a way that rapidly reaches the general public such that no one receives a trading advantage. In April 2013, the SEC approved the use of social media such as Twitter and Facebook for such dissemination, as long as the company has previously advised the public what social media outlets it will use.[183]

Under the 1934 Act, the SEC has the power to ***suspend trading*** in any security "when it serves the public interest and will protect investors." Thus, the SEC may halt the trading of a security if it suspects price manipulation or has serious questions about a company's assets or operations.[184] The market price of a security is typically devastated by a suspension, which provides a strong incentive for corporations to avoid misconduct.

Questions

1. Explain the purposes of the 1934 Act.
2. Describe the three primary SEC filings required under the 1934 Act.

Brokers and Online Trading

When individuals want to buy or sell securities, they usually do so through an intermediary–a ***broker***. In addition to facilitating trades, brokers may provide advisory services. When they do, they must assess the suitability of investments for the particular investor. Thus, their recommendations must take into account the investor's needs, financial situation, investment objectives, and risk tolerance.

One impact of the Internet has been the shift by many investors from full-service (and full-commission) securities brokers to discount brokers who offer easy access to *online trading*. In response, most major full-service brokers have added online-trading services. Transaction costs are reduced, but investors do not receive the same level of professional guidance.[185]

One type of online trading is ***day trading***. Day traders rarely hold any security more than a few hours, earning profits by exploiting minor price volatility, not inherent value. The SEC has expressed great concern about advertising which suggests that day trading is easy and certain to be profitable. It cautions that tips and analyses are frequently false.[186] A 2019 study found that only 3 percent of those day trading 300 days or more during a year generated a profit, and only one percent of traders ended up earning more than the equivalent of minimum wage.[187]

Only 1 percent of day traders earn more than minimum wage.

Violating Federal Securities Laws

LO 9-14 Identify when a "material misrepresentation" has occurred.

LO 9-15 Explain the due diligence defense.

The consequences of noncompliance with the securities laws are potentially staggering. They include compensatory damages for losses suffered, as well as civil and criminal penalties. Some of the provisions most commonly violated by corporations and their directors and executives are discussed below.

False or Misleading Statements—1933 Act

Perhaps the greatest deterrent to misconduct in securities laws is the civil liability that can be imposed on wrongdoers by harmed investors. The 1933 Act's Section 11 establishes this liability with respect to false or misleading registration statements. The *Omnicare* case below explores whether opinions expressed by a company can rise to the status of sanctionable misrepresentations.

LEGAL BRIEFCASE

Omnicare, Inc. v. Laborers District Council Construction Industry Pension Fund

135 S. Ct. 1318 (2015)

FACTS

Omnicare, the nation's largest provider of pharmacy services to nursing homes, filed a registration statement containing several sentences of which the following is representative: "We believe our contract arrangements with . . . pharmaceutical suppliers . . . are in compliance with applicable . . . laws." Those contracts called for rebates, which were ultimately determined illegal, resulting in losses to the company. The pension fund purchased stock in the IPO and later sued, alleging that the company's opinion statement about legal compliance gave rise to liability under § 11 of the 1933 Act.

Justice Kagan

The Securities Act of 1933 protects investors by ensuring that companies . . . make a "full and fair disclosure of information" relevant to a public offering. The linchpin of the Act is its registration requirement. . . .

Section 11 . . . promotes compliance with these disclosure provisions by . . . provid[ing]:

> "[If] any part of the registration statement . . . contained an untrue statement of a material fact or omitted to state a material fact required to be stated therein or necessary to make the statements therein not misleading, any person acquiring [the] security . . . [may] sue."

[The pension fund asserts] that a statement of opinion that is ultimately found incorrect—even if believed at the time made—may count as an "untrue statement of a material fact." . . . [It claims that the] issuer's statement that "we believe we are following the law" conveys that "we in fact are following the law"—which is "materially false," no matter what the issuer thinks, if instead it is violating an anti-kickback statute.

[T]hat argument wrongly conflates facts and opinions. A fact is "a thing done or existing" or "[a]n actual happening." An opinion is "a belief[,] a view," or a "sentiment which the mind forms of persons or things." . . . [A] statement of fact expresses certainty about a thing, whereas a statement of opinion . . . does not. . . . [Congress] incorporated . . . that distinction in § 11's first part by exposing issuers to liability not for "untrue statement[s]" full stop (which would have included ones of opinion), but only for "untrue statement[s] of . . . *fact*."

[E]very [opinion] statement explicitly affirms one fact: that the speaker actually holds the stated belief. . . . "I believe our marketing practices are lawful" . . . would falsely describe [the speaker's] state of mind if she thought her company was breaking the law. In such cases, § 11's first part would subject the issuer to liability[.] . . . [T]he Funds do not contest that Omnicare's opinion was honestly held.

[T]he Funds also rely on § 11's omissions provision, alleging that Omnicare "omitted to state facts necessary" to make its opinion on legal compliance "not misleading." . . . [W]hether a statement is "misleading" depends on the perspective of a reasonable investor[.] . . .

A reasonable person understands . . . the difference . . . between a statement of fact and one of opinion. She recognizes the import of words like "I think" or "I believe," and grasps that they convey some lack of certainty as to the statement's content. . . . [T]he investor thus distinguishes between the sentences "we believe X is true" and "X is true." . . .

But . . . a reasonable investor may . . . understand an opinion statement to convey facts . . . about the speaker's basis for holding that view. . . . Consider [the] opinion . . . : "We believe our conduct is lawful." . . . In the context of the securities market, an investor, though recognizing that legal opinions can prove wrong in the end, still likely expects such an assertion to rest on some meaningful legal inquiry—rather than, say, on mere intuition[.] . . . Similarly, if the issuer made the statement in the face of its lawyers' contrary advice, or with knowledge that the Federal Government was taking the opposite view, the investor again has cause to complain: He expects not just that the issuer believes the opinion . . ., but that it fairly aligns with the information in the issuer's possession at the time. Thus, if a registration statement omits material facts about the issuer's inquiry into or knowledge concerning a statement of opinion, and if those facts conflict with what a reasonable investor would take from the statement itself, then § 11's omissions clause creates liability.

An opinion statement, however, is not necessarily misleading when an issuer knows, but fails to disclose, some fact cutting the other way. Reasonable investors understand that opinions sometimes rest on a weighing of competing facts; indeed, the presence of such facts is one reason why an issuer may frame a statement as an opinion, thus conveying uncertainty. . . .

[W]hether an omission makes an expression of opinion misleading always depends on context. Registration statements [are] filed with the SEC as a legal prerequisite for selling securities to the public. Investors do not, and are right not to, expect opinions contained in those statements to reflect baseless, off-the-cuff judgments, of the kind that an individual might communicate in daily life. At the same time, an investor reads each statement within such a document . . . in light of all its surrounding text, including hedges, disclaimers, and apparently conflicting information. . . . [Section] 11 creates liability only for the omission of material facts that cannot be squared with such a fair reading. . . .

[Remanded.]

Questions

1. Describe the pension fund's argument as to why Omnicare incurred Section 11 liability because of:
   a. What it said.
   b. What it did not say.
2. How did the Court respond to each of the pension fund's arguments?

Virtually anyone with a significant role in preparing the registration statement can be sued (the issuer, its directors, its senior officers, its underwriters, and its accountants and other experts). The liability can be vast—essentially, all damages sustained by investors while the misleading registration statements were outstanding. No proof of actual plaintiff relevance on the content of the registration statement is required—plaintiff reliance is presumed. Auditors and investment bankers, because of their "deep pockets," are often at the top of the list of defendants. Accounting firms have paid hundreds of millions of dollars to settle securities fraud suits.

The principal defense in a Section 11 action is ***due diligence***, which every defendant other than the issuer can raise. Under the general rule, the defendant must show that, based on a reasonable investigation, they reasonably believed that the registration statement was not materially misleading. What constitutes "reasonable" is determined by reference to the conduct expected of a prudent person in the management of that person's own property.

However, the due diligence standard for experts (like accountants and lawyers) is much higher. Their inquiries must rise to the standards expected of professionals, not merely of prudent persons. Thus, at an absolute minimum, the accounting firm that audits the financial statements included in the registration statement must design its audit to comport with

GAAS and must evaluate the financial statement content by reference to GAAP. Lawyers, actuaries, appraisers, and other experts whose work has a material impact on the registration statement must follow analogous rules established by their professional associations and regulators. The *BarChris* case, below, explores the due diligence defense.

LEGAL BRIEFCASE

Escott v. BarChris Construction Corporation

283 F. Supp. 643 (S.D.N.Y. 1968)

FACTS

Bowling as a leisure activity and sport grew rapidly in the 1950s. BarChris built alleys. Its revenues grew from $800,000 in 1956 to $9,165,000 in 1960 [inflation adjusted amounts: $8,120,000 and $81,940,000, respectively]. By 1962, overbuilding caused construction to halt. BarChris ran into serious financial problems. It filed a registration statement (effective May 1961) for new bonds to raise cash, and the bonds were issued. Circumstances were grave when the registration statement became effective. BarChris filed for bankruptcy in October 1962.

BarChris's financial statements dated December 31, 1960, were included in the prospectus. They were audited by Peat Marwick (a predecessor of KPMG) and contained material errors. Revenues and current assets were overstated and contingent liabilities were understated.

The prospectus overstated the demand for alley construction. It misrepresented how the proceeds would be used (a large portion would actually go to pay overdue debts and retire loans from officers). It failed to note that, because of defaults, BarChris had repossessed and was now operating several alleys. Escott and other bondholders sued under Section 11 of the 1933 Act, alleging that the prospectus was materially misleading. All defendants but BarChris raised the due diligence defense.

Judge Mclean

I turn now to the question of whether defendants have proved their due diligence defenses. The position of each defendant will be separately considered.

Russo

Russo was, to all intents and purposes, the chief executive officer of BarChris. He was a member of the executive committee. He was familiar with all aspects of the business[. He] knew all the relevant facts. He could not have believed that there were no untrue statements or material omissions in the prospectus. Russo has no due diligence defenses.

Vitolo and Pugliese

They were the founders[.] Vitolo was president and Pugliese was vice president. Despite their titles, their [control] over BarChris's affairs [was far less] than Russo's. [They are] each men of limited education. It is not hard to believe that for them the prospectus was difficult reading, if indeed they read it at all. But [the] liability of a director who signs a registration statement does not depend upon whether or not he read it or, if he did, whether or not he understood what he was reading.

And in any case, Vitolo and Pugliese were not as naive as they claim to be. They were members of BarChris's executive committee[.] They must have known what was going on. Certainly they knew of the inadequacy of cash[.] They knew of their own large advances to the company which remained unpaid. They knew that they had agreed not to deposit their checks until the financing proceeds were received. They knew and intended that part of the proceeds were to be used to pay their own loans.

All in all, [their situation] is not significantly different . . . from Russo's. They could not have believed that the registration statement was wholly true and that no material facts had been omitted[.] They have not proved their due diligence defenses.

Trilling

[Trilling was . . . a CPA and former member of Peat Marwick. He was BarChris's] controller. He signed the registration statement in that capacity, although he was not a director[.]

Trilling may well have been unaware of several of the inaccuracies in the prospectus. But he must have known of some of them[.] I cannot find that Trilling believed the entire prospectus to be true.

But even if he did, he still did not establish his due diligence defenses. He . . . failed to prove, as to the [nonaudited] parts of the prospectus . . ., that he made a reasonable investigation which afforded him a reasonable ground to believe that it was true. As far as appears, he made no investigation[.] This would have been well enough but for the fact that he signed the registration statement. As a signer, he could not avoid responsibility[. He has not proved] his due diligence defenses.

Birnbaum

Birnbaum was a young lawyer [employed as in-house counsel. He was] secretary and a director[.] He signed the later amendments [to the registration statement], thereby becoming responsible for the accuracy of the prospectus[.]

. . . He did not participate in the management of the company. As house counsel, he attended to legal matters of a routine nature[.]

One of Birnbaum's more important duties . . . was to keep the corporate minutes[.] This necessarily informed him to a considerable extent about the company's affairs[.]

It seems probable that Birnbaum did not know of many of the inaccuracies in the prospectus. He must, however, have appreciated some of them. In any case, he made no investigation[. He] was entitled to rely upon Peat Marwick for the 1960 figures[.] But he was not entitled to rely upon [anyone else] for the other portions of the prospectus. As a lawyer, he should have known his obligations[.] Having failed to make such an investigation, he did not have reasonable ground to believe that all these statements were true. Birnbaum has not established his due diligence defenses except as to the audited 1960 figures.

Auslander

Auslander was an "outside" director[.] He was chairman . . . of Valley Stream National Bank. [He became a director shortly before the sale of the bonds. He signed the registration statement.]

. . . As to the [financial statements], Auslander knew that Peat Marwick had audited [them, so he] believed them to be correct[.] He had no reasonable ground to believe otherwise.

As to the [non-audited portions of the prospectus], however, Auslander is in a different position[. He] made no investigation of the accuracy of the prospectus. He relied on the assurance of Vitolo and Russo[.]

It is true that Auslander became a director on the eve of the financing. He had little opportunity to familiarize himself with the company's affairs[.]

Section 11 imposes liability . . . upon a director, no matter how new he is. He is presumed to know his responsibility when he becomes a director. He can escape liability only by using that reasonable care to investigate the facts which a prudent man would employ in the management of his own property. In my opinion, a prudent man would not act in an important matter . . . in sole reliance upon representations of persons who are comparative strangers[.] To say that such minimal conduct measures up to the statutory standard would, to all intents and purposes, absolve new directors from responsibility merely because they are new. This is not a sensible construction of Section 11[.]

Auslander has not established his due diligence defense [except as to the financial statements].

Grant

. . . [Grant's] law firm was counsel to BarChris in matters pertaining to the registration of securities. Grant drafted the registration statement[.] As the director most directly concerned with writing [it] and assuring its accuracy, more was required of him in the way of reasonable investigation than could fairly be expected of a director who had no connection with this work[.]

. . . I find that Grant honestly believed that the registration statement was true and that no material facts had been omitted from it.

In this belief he was mistaken, and the fact is that for all his work, he never discovered any of the errors or omissions which . . . could have been detected without an audit. The question is whether, despite his failure to detect them, Grant made a reasonable effort to that end.

. . . BarChris's affairs had changed for the worse[.] Grant never discovered this. He accepted the assurances of [others] that any change which might have occurred had been for the better[.]

It is claimed that a lawyer is entitled to rely on the statements of his client[.] This is too broad a generalization. It is all a matter of degree. To require an audit would obviously be unreasonable. On the other hand, to require a check of matters easily verifiable is not unreasonable. Even honest clients can make mistakes. The statute imposes liability for untrue statements regardless of whether they are intentionally untrue[.]

. . . Grant knew that minutes of certain meetings of the BarChris executive committee held in 1961 had not been written up[.] Grant did not insist that the minutes be written up, nor did he look at Kircher's notes[.]

. . . He knew that BarChris was short of cash, but he had no idea how short. He did not know that BarChris was withholding delivery of checks already drawn and signed because there was not enough money in the bank to pay them. He did not know that the officers of the company intended to use immediately approximately one-third of the financing proceeds in a manner not disclosed in the prospectus, including approximately $1,000,000 in paying old debts[.]

Grant was entitled to rely on Peat Marwick for the 1960 figures. [But as to the rest of the prospectus, Grant] was obliged to make a reasonable investigation. I am forced to find that he did not make one[.] Grant has not established his due diligence defenses except as to the audited 1960 figures.

Peat Marwick

... The part of the registration statement ... made upon the authority of Peat Marwick as an expert was ... the 1960 [audited financial statements]. But because the statute requires the court to determine Peat Marwick's belief, and the grounds thereof, "at the time ... the registration statement became effective," ... the matter must be viewed as of May 16, 1961[.]

The 1960 Audit

[The audit] was in general charge of a member of the firm, Cummings[.] Most of the actual work was performed by a senior accountant, Berardi, [who was about thirty]. He was not yet a C.P.A. He had no previous experience with the bowling industry. This was his first job as a senior accountant[.]

The S-1 Review

The purpose of reviewing events subsequent to the date of a certified balance sheet, [an S-1 review,] is to ascertain whether any material change has occurred in the company's financial position which should be disclosed in order to prevent the ... figures from being misleading. The scope of such a review [is not] a complete audit.

Peat Marwick prepared a written program [which] conformed to generally accepted auditing standards[.]

Berardi made the S-1 review in May 1961. He devoted a little over two days to it[.] He did not discover any of the errors or omissions[.] The question is whether, despite his failure to find out anything, his investigation was reasonable within the meaning of the statute.

What Berardi did was to look at a ... trial balance as of March 31, 1961[,] compare it with the audited December 31, 1960[,] figures, discuss with Trilling certain unfavorable developments[,] and read certain minutes. He did not examine any [other] "important financial records." ...

In substance, what Berardi did is [he] asked questions, he got answers which he considered satisfactory, and he did nothing to verify them[.]

Berardi had no conception of how tight the cash position was. He did not discover that BarChris was holding up checks in substantial amounts because there was no money in the bank to cover them. He did not know of ... the officers' loans. Since he never read the prospectus, he was not even aware that there had ever been any problem about loans from officers.

There had been a material change for the worse in BarChris's financial position. That change was sufficiently serious so that the failure to disclose it made the 1960 figures misleading. Berardi did not discover it. As far as results were concerned, his S-1 review was useless.

Accountants should not be held to a standard higher than that recognized in their profession. I do not do so here. Berardi's review did not come up to that standard. He did not take some of the steps which Peat Marwick's written program prescribed. He did not spend an adequate amount of time on a task of this magnitude. Most important of all, he was too easily satisfied with glib answers to his inquiries.

... [T]here were enough danger signals in the materials which he did examine to require some further investigation on his part. Generally accepted accounting standards required such further investigation under these circumstances. It is not always sufficient merely to ask questions.

Here again, the burden of proof is on Peat Marwick. I find that that burden has not been satisfied. I conclude that Peat Marwick has not established its due diligence defense.

Questions

1. *a.* Why were so many defendants not held responsible for the misleading audited financial statements?
   b. Which defendants lost their due diligence argument with respect to these financial statements? Why?
2. Does being "new" make any difference in terms of directorial liability for a signed registration statement?
3. What would you do differently in the future if you were Peat Marwick?

Questions

1. What triggers liability under Section 11 of the 1933 Act? Can an opinion result in a violation?
2. What is the primary defense in a Section 11 action? Contrast the defense's requirements as between a director or senior officer versus an outside expert like an accountant, lawyer, or appraiser.

False or Misleading Statements Post-Issuance—1934 Act

Section 18 of the 1934 Act, relating to false or misleading statements in any filing required to maintain the registration of a security, is similar to the 1933 Act's Section 11. However, the only defense offered by Section 18 is that the defendant acted in good faith, without knowledge of the false or misleading nature of the statement. Further, unlike Section 11, where reliance by the plaintiff on the false or misleading statements is presumed, under Section 18 the plaintiff must prove they relied on the statements.

Fraud

Under the 1933 Act's Section 17(a) and the 1934 Act's Section 10(b) and its related Rule 10b-5, it is illegal, in connection with the sale or purchase of any security, to employ any scheme or to engage in any practice that defrauds another person participating in the financial markets. These provisions intentionally cast a wide net. One major example is the Ponzi scheme run by Bernard Madoff, who in 2009 was sentenced to 150 years in prison for perpetrating a $50 billion fraud. He promised very lucrative returns to investors, but those returns were in actuality payments sourced from new funds received from an ever-increasing pool of investors, not from actual earnings. When the economy weakened, the scheme collapsed. Despite the Madoff scandal's national publicity, in the decade following his conviction, SEC prosecutions for Ponzi schemes increased 50 percent. Although not matching Madoff's unprecedented theft, those schemes cost investors $31 billion–three times the amount in the pre-Madoff decade.[188]

> Prosecutions for Ponzi schemes have increased 50 percent in the decade following Madoff's conviction.

Fraudulent acts can be committed by corporate wrongdoers as well. Making misleading statements about material facts or failing to state material facts in required SEC disclosure documents or in other company communications can be fraudulent, providing powerful grounds for damage suits by harmed investors. In 2015, it was discovered that Volkswagen (VW) had knowingly deceived regulators and the public as to the level of emissions from its "clean diesel" vehicles. In March 2019, the SEC charged VW and its former CEO Martin Winterkorn with violations of Section 17(a)(2) of the 1933 Act and Section 10(b) of the 1934 Act, as well as of Rule 10b-5.[189] Winterkorn paid $14 million in civil penalties to the SEC in 2021. As of this writing, VW had paid $39 billion in penalties and damages. European regulators have charged Winterkorn with several counts of fraud in cases still in progress.[190]

> VW paid $39 billion in penalties and damages and its CEO has paid $14 million.

LO 9-16 Describe the fraud-on-the-market theory of reliance and explain its importance.

Actual reliance on the issuer's material misstatement is an element of a Section 10(b) action. Bringing forward direct evidence of reliance on fraudulent statements can be difficult, so the ***fraud-on-the-market theory*** has evolved. It is the subject of the *Basic Inc.* case below.

Basic Inc. v. Levinson et al.

485 U.S. 224 (1988)

FACTS

Prior to December 20, 1978, Basic Inc. was a publicly traded company primarily engaged in the business of manufacturing related to the steel industry. As early as 1965, Combustion Engineering, a company in the same industry, expressed some interest in acquiring Basic, but was deterred from pursuing this inclination because of antitrust concerns. Beginning in 1976, Combustion had meetings with Basic concerning the possibility of a merger. During 1977 and 1978, Basic made three public statements denying merger negotiations. On December 19, 1978, Basic's board endorsed the merger.

Respondents were former Basic shareholders who had sold their stock after Basic's first public denial in 1977 but before the December 1978 announcement. They asserted that the defendants issued three false or misleading public statements in violation of Section 10(b) and Rule 10b-5, and further that they were injured by selling Basic shares at artificially depressed prices in a market affected by petitioner's misleading statements and in reliance thereon.

Rule 10b-5 provides that it "shall be unlawful [t]o make any untrue statement of a material fact or to omit to state a material fact necessary . . . to make the statements made . . . not misleading . . . in connection with the purchase or sale of any security."

Justice Blackmun

. . . [T]o fulfill the materiality requirement "there must be a substantial likelihood that the disclosure of the omitted fact would have been viewed by the reasonable investor as having significantly altered the 'total mix' of information made available." . . .

We turn to the question of reliance and the fraud-on-the-market theory. Succinctly put:

> The fraud on the market theory is based on the hypothesis that, in an open and developed securities market, the price of a company's stock is determined by the available material information regarding the company and its business[.] Misleading statements will therefore defraud purchasers . . . even if [they] do not directly rely on the misstatements[.] The causal connection between the defendants' fraud and the plaintiffs' purchase . . . is no less significant than in a case of direct reliance on misrepresentations.

Reliance provides the requisite causal connection between a defendant's misrepresentation and a plaintiff's injury. There is, however, more than one way to demonstrate the causal connection[.]

The modern securities markets, literally involving millions of shares changing hands daily, differ from the face-to-face transactions contemplated by early fraud cases, and our understanding of Rule 10b-5's reliance requirement must encompass these differences.

With the presence of a market, the market is interposed between seller and buyer and, ideally, transmits information to the investor in the processed form of a market price. Thus, the market is performing a substantial part of the valuation process performed by the investor in a face-to-face transaction. The market is acting as the unpaid agent of the investor, informing him that given all the information available to it, the value of the stock is worth the market price.

Presumptions typically serve to assist courts in managing circumstances in which direct proof . . . is rendered difficult. The courts below accepted a presumption, created by the fraud-on-the-market theory and subject to rebuttal by petitioners, that persons who had traded Basic shares had done so in reliance on the integrity of the price set by the market, but because of petitioners' material misrepresentations that price had been fraudulently depressed. Requiring a plaintiff to show . . . how he would have acted if omitted material information had been disclosed . . . or if the misrepresentation had not been made . . . would place an unnecessarily unrealistic evidentiary burden on the Rule 10b-5 plaintiff who has traded on an impersonal market.

. . . The presumption of reliance employed in this case is consistent with [the] congressional policy embodied in the 1934 Act. In drafting that Act, Congress expressly relied on the premise that securities markets are affected by information, and enacted legislation to facilitate an investor's reliance on the integrity of those markets[.]

. . . Recent empirical studies . . . confirm Congress' premise that the market price . . . on well-developed markets reflects all publicly available information, and, hence, any material misrepresentations[.] Because most publicly available information is reflected in market price, an investor's reliance on any public material misrepresentations, therefore, may be presumed for purposes of a Rule 10b-5 action.

Any showing that severs the link between the alleged misrepresentation and [the] decision to trade will be sufficient to rebut the presumption of reliance. For example, . . . if, despite petitioners' allegedly fraudulent attempt to manipulate market price, news of the merger discussions credibly entered the market and dissipated the effects of the misstatements, those who traded Basic shares after the corrective statements would have no direct or indirect connection with the fraud[.]

. . . It is not inappropriate to apply a presumption of reliance supported by the fraud-on-the-market theory. That presumption, however, is rebuttable.

[Remanded.]

AFTERWORD

As noted by the Court in *Basic Inc.*, investors who trade with knowledge of alleged misrepresentations will not be allowed to use the fraud-on-the-market theory. Those investors have not relied on the market price as an accurate reflection of all material information.[191] In its 2014 decision in *Halliburton v. Erica P. John Fund*,[192] the Supreme Court rejected the defendant's argument that the efficient-markets hypothesis on which *Basics Inc.* is grounded had been substantially discredited by the financial crisis and various studies. The Court noted that *Basic Inc.* recognized that markets are only imperfectly efficient and "based the presumption on the fairly modest premise that 'market professionals generally consider most publicly announced material statements about companies, [which] affect[s] stock . . . prices.'"[193]

Questions

1. When is an item of undisclosed information about a company "material" for Rule 10b-5 purposes?
2. Is reliance on a misrepresentation essential in a Rule 10b-5 action?
3. *a.* Why would it be difficult for a plaintiff to demonstrate actual reliance on a material omission?
   b. What solution did the courts create to deal with this problem?
4. What is the importance of *Halliburton v. Erica P. John Fund*?

Insider Trading

LO 9-17 Define insider trading and identify the three most common contexts in which it occurs.

Classic ***insider trading*** occurs when an "insider" breaches a fiduciary duty to shareholders by buying or selling a security while in possession of material, nonpublic information. An ***insider*** is often a director, officer, or employee of an issuer but could also be someone who only temporarily has a confidential relationship with an issuer, such as an accountant or attorney. The prohibition against trading on undisclosed inside information is based on Section 10(b), which prohibits the use of any manipulative or deceptive device in connection with the purchase or sale of a security.

In recent years, prosecution of insider-trading violations has increased substantially. Publicized incidents have run from the intricate and clandestine to the inept and ridiculous:

- An executive secretary at Walt Disney and her boyfriend were charged with insider trading after sending 33 letters to investment firms offering to sell Disney's quarterly earnings reports before they were publicly released. An email stated, "I was thinking $20,000 is a fair compensation but you are free to make an offer." Multiple firms receiving the offer reported it to the SEC.[194]
- In April 2019, Tai-Cheng Yang admitted to insider trading involving Amazon's acquisition of Whole Foods. Yang's wife had a family member involved in the transaction who called her to explain why he could not be present for another family member's medical procedure–he was working on that merger. The wife told Yang, who immediately acquired call options on Whole Foods stock. When the merger was announced three days later, the Whole Foods options increased in value by 29 percent. Yang paid $57,000 in disgorgement and fines.[195]
- In January 2020, former Congressman Christopher Collins was sentenced to two years in prison for insider trading. While a congressman, he was on the board and owned 17 percent of the stock of an Australian biotech company. He received a tip from the CEO that its principal drug had just failed the clinical trial. Collins called his son, also a shareholder, and tipped him. The son then tipped his fiancée's shareholding father. The day after the son and the fiancée's father sold their shares, the news became public

and the stock fell 92 percent. Collins had been unable to sell his stock for technical reasons. The son and the fiancée's father have both pleaded guilty. Collins was sentenced to 26 months in prison and fined $200,000.[196]

- In January 2020, New York businessman Telemaque Lavidas was found guilty of insider trading in a scheme potentially involving tens of millions of dollars in illicit profits. Lavidas received substantial financial benefits for disclosing inside information about a corporation for which his father was a director. The star witness, Marc Demane, testified about a vast international conspiracy involving investment bankers, corporate executives, and traders. Demane had been extradited from Serbia in 2019 and had admitted to playing a central role in the insider-trading ring, making $70 million on illegal trades. He named specific individuals in France, London, Israel, Greece, Switzerland, Canada, and the U.S. who were all complicit. Demane said that insider trading had become a "sport" overseas, with secret information about scores of publicly traded companies being trafficked in person or by using burner cell phones. Derivatives that are illegal in the U.S. and difficult to track were used to facilitate the transactions. Lividas was sentenced to one year and a day in prison.[197]
- On July 25, 2022, former U.S. Congressman Stephen Buyer was arrested on two charges of insider trading. While in Congress, he served on the committee with oversight over the telecommunications industry. In 2018, one day after playing golf with a T-Mobile executive who told him about the then-nonpublic plan to acquire Sprint, Buyer bought $568,000 of Sprint stock. He used not only his personal account, but also joint accounts with a cousin and an acquaintance. A few weeks later, when the merger became public, he generated a profit of $107,000. After leaving Congress, Buyer established a consulting firm. Two of his clients were Navigant Consulting and Guidehouse. He became aware that the latter would acquire the former and, before the public announcement, acquired $1 million of Navigant stock. The purchases were, again, spread across multiple accounts (his own, a joint account with his wife, and the personal accounts of his wife and of the previously mentioned acquaintance). The day the acquisition was announced, Buyer sold the shares, resulting in a gain of $227,000.[198]

The SEC reports that insider-trading cases are principally related to the leak of confidential information about mergers and acquisitions (57 percent) and earnings releases (30 percent).[199]

Members of Congress Are Insider Traders?

Remarkably, federal insider-trading laws did not apply to Congress until 2012, when the STOCK Act was enacted after revelations that a number of senators and representatives had engaged in such trading during the 2008 recession and the 2010 healthcare debate.

The act has largely been a failure. In Fall 2022, a *New York Times* study found that, over the period 2019 to 2021, approximately 20 percent of Congress "trad[ed] shares of companies in industries they [were] supposed to be overseeing as part of their committee assignments . . . creating major conflicts of interest[.]" Examples include trading in Boeing and pharmaceutical giant AbbVie while those companies were under congressional investigation. Forty-four of the 50 most active congressional traders were found to have conflicts of interest. No Member of Congress has ever been prosecuted for such trading under this act.

Further, in January 2023,*Business Insider* listed 78 representatives and senators who had recently violated the STOCK Act's mandatory disclosure provisions. Such violations typically result in a meager $200 fine, which is sometimes waived by Congressional ethics officials.

Despite these recent disclosures and polls indicating that 80 percent of Americans support banning stock trading by members of Congress (views held in equal measure by Democrats, Republicans, and independents), more effective legislation has failed to result. As of this writing, the proposed bills are still languishing in committee.

Sources: Kate Kelly, Adam Playford, and Alicia Parlapiano, "Stock Trades Reported by Nearly a Fifth of Congress Show Possible Conflicts,"*The New York Times,* September 13, 2022 [**www.nytimes.com**]; James Downie, "If Dems can't even use their majority for this no-brainer, what's the point of having it?" *MSNBC,* October 3, 2022 [**www.msnbc.com**]; Lydia Moynihan, "Nearly 20% of Congress trades stocks that present conflicts of interest," *New York Post,* September 13, 2022 [**https://nypost.com**]; Mike Patton, "Congress' About-Face On Stock Trading Ban Hurts Americans' Trust In Government," *Forbes,* October 3, 2022 [**www.forbes.com**]; Dave Levinthal and Madison Hall, "78 members of Congress have violated a law designed to prevent insider trading and stop conflicts-of-interest,"*Business Insider,* January 3, 2023 [**www.businessinsider.com**]; and Dave Levinthal, "'Conflicted Congress': Key findings from Insider's five-month investigation into federal lawmakers' personal finances," *Business Insider,* December 17, 2021 [**www.businessinsider.com**].

The *Texas Gulf Sulphur* case below expresses the rule for those possessing inside information—either disclose the information or refrain from trading until the information is public.

LEGAL BRIEFCASE

SEC v. Texas Gulf Sulphur Co.

401 F.2d 833 (2d Cir. 1968)

FACTS

In November 1963, TGS [Texas Gulf Sulphur Co.] drilled a "discovery hole" in Canada that revealed possibly one of the largest ore strikes in history. Insiders began buying TGS stock at around $18. Further testing confirmed the magnitude of the strike. Rumors began to circulate. On April 12, 1964, when the stock had passed $30 and the best estimate was eight million tons, TGS issued a press release naysaying the rumors. On April 16, a Canadian mining journal story put the tonnage at 10 million. The same day a Canadian government official estimated it at 25 million and the stock passed $36. By May 15, it exceeded $58. The SEC brought an insider-trading action.

Judge Waterman

[Rule 10b-5] is based . . . on the justifiable expectation . . . that all investors trading on impersonal exchanges have relatively equal access to material information[.] The essence of the Rule is that anyone who, trading for his own account, [has access] to information intended to be available only for a corporate purpose . . . may not take "advantage of such . . . knowing it is unavailable to those with whom he is dealing," i.e., the investing public. Insiders . . . are, of course[,] precluded from so unfairly dealing, but the Rule is also applicable to one possessing the information who may not be strictly termed an "insider." . . . [A]nyone in possession of material inside information must either disclose it to the investing public [or] abstain from trading in or recommending the securities [while it] remains undisclosed[.]

An insider's duty to disclose [or] abstain . . . arises only in "those situations . . . which are reasonably certain to have a substantial effect on the market price [if] disclosed." . . . [W]hether facts are material [will depend] upon a balancing of both the indicated probability that the event will occur and the anticipated magnitude of the event[. Here,] knowledge of the possibility, which surely was more than marginal, of the existence of a mine of the vast magnitude indicated by the remarkably rich drill core . . . would certainly have been an important fact to a reasonable . . . investor in deciding whether he should buy, sell, or hold[.] . . . [A] major factor in determining whether the . . . discovery was a material fact is the importance attached to the drilling results by those who knew about it. [T]he timing . . . of their stock purchases . . . virtually compels the inference that the insiders were influenced by the drilling results[.]

We hold, therefore, that all transactions in TGS stock . . . by individuals apprised of the drilling results . . . were made in violation of Rule 10b-5[.]

Coates, who placed orders . . . immediately after the official announcement . . ., [contends that his] purchases were not proscribed purchases for the news had already been . . . disclosed. We disagree. . . . The reading of [the announcement] . . . is merely the first step in the process of dissemination required for compliance with the regulatory objective of providing all investors with an equal opportunity to make informed investment judgments[. A]t the minimum Coates should have waited until the news could reasonably have been expected to appear over the media of widest circulation, the Dow Jones broad tape, rather than hastening to insure an advantage to himself[.]

Questions

1. If you possess undisclosed inside information, what are your options for trading in the company's stock?
2. How soon after public disclosure can an insider trade in the stock?

As stated by the *Texas Gulf Sulphur* court, the rule prohibits persons who have access to information that was available to them only for a corporate purpose from trading in corporate securities with those who do not have that information. This is the *classical* theory of insider trading. Officers and employees, for example, have a fiduciary duty not to use their principal's–that is, their employer's–information for personal gain.

Tipping

The insider concept has been extended to include ***tippees***. In some cases, the ***tipper*** (the insider or an "upstream" tippee) intends to improperly convey the inside information to a third party and hopes to derive personal benefit from so doing. In such a case, both the tipper and the tippee are liable. In other cases, the tippee is deemed to "misappropriate" the inside information from the inadvertent tipper, knowing that it was confidential. This would occur, for example, if a psychiatrist learned material inside information during a session with a senior corporate executive and traded on that information. Here, the tippee, but not the tipper, would be liable. In the *O'Hagan* case, below, the Supreme Court approved the ***misappropriation theory***.

LEGAL BRIEFCASE

United States v. O'Hagan

521 U.S. 642 (1997)

FACTS

O'Hagan was a partner in a law firm. In July 1988, Grand Metropolitan retained the firm to represent it in a tender offer for Pillsbury stock. O'Hagan did no work on this matter. In August, O'Hagan began purchasing Pillsbury stock and stock options. When the tender offer was announced, O'Hagan sold his options and stock, making a profit of $4.3 million. He used the profits to conceal his previous embezzlement of unrelated client trust funds.

The SEC investigated. O'Hagan was convicted of securities fraud. The Eighth Circuit reversed, rejecting liability under the "misappropriation theory." The Supreme Court granted *certiorari*.

Section 10(b) proscribes (1) using any deceptive device (2) in connection with the purchase or sale of securities. It does not confine its coverage to deception of a purchaser or seller; rather, it reaches any deceptive device used "in connection with the purchase or sale of any security."

Justice Ginsburg

Under the . . . "classical theory" of insider trading . . ., Section 10(b) and Rule 10b-5 are violated when [an] insider trades in the securities of his corporation on the basis of material, nonpublic information. Trading on such information qualifies as a "deceptive device" . . . because "a relationship of trust [exists] between the shareholders [and the] insiders who have obtained confidential information by reason of their position with [the] corporation." That relationship . . . "gives rise to a duty to disclose [or to abstain from trading."] The classical theory applies not only to officers, directors, and other permanent insiders . . ., but also to attorneys, accountants, consultants, and others who temporarily become fiduciaries of a corporation.

The "misappropriation theory" holds that a person commits fraud "in connection with" a securities transaction . . . when he misappropriates confidential information for securities trading purposes, in breach of a duty owed to the source of the information. Under this theory, a fiduciary's undisclosed, self-serving use of a principal's information to purchase or sell securities, in breach of a duty of loyalty and confidentiality, defrauds the principal of the exclusive use of that information. In lieu of premising liability on a fiduciary relationship between company insider and purchaser or seller of the company's stock, the misappropriation theory premises liability on a fiduciary-turned-trader's deception of those who entrusted him with access to confidential information.

The two theories are complementary, each addressing efforts to capitalize on nonpublic information through the purchase or sale of securities[.]

In this case, the indictment alleged that O'Hagan, in breach of a duty of trust . . . he owed to his law firm . . . and to its client . . ., traded on the basis of nonpublic information regarding the client's tender offer[.] This conduct, the Government charged, constituted a fraudulent device in connection with the purchase and sale of securities[.]

We agree[.] We observe, first, that misappropriators . . . deal in deception. A fiduciary who "[pretends] loyalty to the principal while secretly converting the principal's information for personal gain" . . . defrauds the principal.

We turn next to the Section 10(b) requirement that the misappropriator's deceptive use of information be "in connection with the purchase or sale of [a] security." This element is satisfied because the fiduciary's fraud is consummated, not when the fiduciary gains the confidential information, but when, without disclosure to his principal, he uses the information to purchase or sell securities[.]

The misappropriation theory [is] well-tuned to an animating purpose of the [1934] Act: to insure honest securities markets and thereby promote investor confidence. Although informational disparity is inevitable in the securities markets, [an] investor's informational disadvantage vis-a-vis a misappropriator . . . stems from contrivance, not luck; it is a disadvantage that cannot be overcome with research or skill[.]

[Reversed and remanded.]

Questions

1. Are both insider-trading theories needed to fulfill the 1934 Act's desire to keep the markets "honest"?
2. Both insider-trading theories depend heavily on fiduciary relationships. Contrast the parties in the fiduciary relationships under the "classical" and "misappropriation" theories.
3. Would it have made any difference if O'Hagan had established with his broker, long before this trading, a portfolio diversification plan such that, pursuant to the plan, the identical trading would have occurred?

Does the tipper have to receive a personal benefit for liability to attach to the disclosure of confidential information? And if so, of what kind? The *Salman* case, below, considers this issue.

READING

Salman v. United States

137 S. Ct. 420 (2016)

FACTS

Maher was a Citigroup investment banker with extensive access to sensitive client information. Maher's brother, Michael, kept pestering him for information he could use to trade while the public was unaware. Maher provided such information. Unknown to him, Michael was also passing the information to Salman, Michael's friend and Maher's brother-in-law, who reaped profits of $1.5 million. Salman knew the information came from Maher. He was convicted of insider trading and sentenced to 36 months in prison and $730,000 in restitution.

On appeal to the Ninth Circuit, Salman asserted that he could not be found guilty of insider trading because Maher had received no personal benefit in the form of "a pecuniary or similarly valuable nature," as was held necessary by the Second Circuit, interpreting *Dirks v. SEC,* 463 U.S. 646 (1983), in *United States v. Newman,* 773 F.3d 438 (2014), a decision rendered while the Ninth Circuit case was pending.

Justice Alito

Section 10(b) [and] Rule 10b-5 prohibit undisclosed trading on inside corporate information by individuals who are under a duty of trust and confidence that prohibits them from secretly using such information for their personal advantage. . . . [S]ee *United States v. O'Hagan*[.] . . .

These persons also may not tip inside information to others for trading. The tippee acquires the tipper's duty to disclose or abstain from trading if the tippee knows the information was disclosed in breach of the tipper's duty[.] In *Dirks* . . . this Court explained that a tippee's liability for trading on inside information hinges on whether the tipper breached a fiduciary duty by disclosing the information. A tipper breaches such a fiduciary duty . . . when the tipper discloses the inside information for a personal benefit. [A] jury can infer a personal benefit . . . where the tipper receives something of value in exchange for the tip or "makes a gift of confidential information to a trading relative or friend."

Pointing to *Newman,* Salman argued that his conviction should be reversed [by the Ninth Circuit because] there was no evidence that Maher received anything of "a pecuniary or similarly valuable nature" in exchange [for the information.] The Ninth Circuit disagreed[.] . . .

We granted certiorari to resolve the tension between the Second Circuit's *Newman* decision and the Ninth Circuit's decision in this case.

In *Dirks,* we explained that . . . "[t]he test . . . is whether the insider personally will benefit, directly or indirectly, from his disclosure." . . . In determining whether a tipper derived a personal benefit, we instructed courts to "focus on . . . whether the insider receives a direct or indirect personal benefit from the disclosure, such as a pecuniary gain or a reputational benefit that will translate into future earnings." This personal benefit can . . . be inferred [from facts and circumstances] such as "a relationship between the insider and the recipient that suggests a *quid pro quo* from the latter, or an intention to benefit the particular recipient." In particular, we held that [insider trading occurs] "*when an insider makes a gift of confidential information to a trading relative or friend.*" In such cases, "[t]he tip and trade resemble trading by the insider followed by a gift of the profits to the recipient." . . .

. . . Maher would have breached his duty had he personally traded on the information [and] then given the proceeds as a gift to his brother. . . . But Maher . . . achieved the same result by disclosing the information to Michael, and allowing him to trade on it. . . .

To the extent the Second Circuit held that the tipper must . . . receive something of a "pecuniary or similarly valuable nature" in exchange for [the information, that] is inconsistent with *Dirks.*

[T]he Ninth Circuit's judgment is affirmed. . . .

Questions

1. Identify a range of circumstances in which a tipper would be viewed as having received sufficient personal benefit to make the tippee liable for insider trading.
2. What insider-trading scenarios are illustrated in the 1987 movie *Wall Street*? The Research Exercise at the end of the chapter examines these scenarios.

Short-Swing Profits

Short-swing profits: Any profits made by an insider through sale of company stock within six months of acquisition. Insider trading is conclusively presumed.

Closely related to insider trading is liability for ***short-swing profits***. An insider-trading case requires proof that the insider had material inside information and traded to exploit it. A short-swing profit case conclusively presumes that the insider had such information and unlawfully traded on that information any time an insider engages in a purchase and sale, or a sale and purchase, of an equity security of the insider's corporation if both transactions occur within a six-month period. The insider's actual motive is irrelevant.

Federal Securities Law Enforcement

Most of the securities law violations just discussed can be enforced against the violators by harmed private parties seeking damages, as well as by the government seeking penalties and, possibly, prison sentences. The SEC brings civil enforcement actions; the Justice Department brings criminal enforcement actions. All three actions (private damages, civil penalties, and criminal penalties) can be brought against the same defendant for the same violation.

LO 9-18 Identify the context for the passage of and the purpose of the Private Securities Litigation Reform Act.

Private Enforcement

In civil damage cases, harmed plaintiffs typically join together in a class-action lawsuit. Since the 1990s, actions taken by Congress and, more recently, decisions of the Supreme Court, have combined to make bringing, and prevailing in, such suits much more difficult. Some history may be illuminating.

As a consequence of the savings and loan debacle of the 1980s, major accounting firms paid out over $1.6 billion in class-action damages (about $4.3 billion after adjusting for inflation). Responding to these payouts, accounting firms and others began intense lobbying to curtail such suits. Among other things, they argued that it was too easy for plaintiffs to bring securities actions based solely on a significant drop in the market price of securities.

The lobbying against so-called runaway securities class-action suits paid off. In December 1995, Congress enacted the Private Securities Litigation Reform Act which eliminated joint and several liability for accountants and underwriters and precluded a presumption of fraudulent conduct from the simple fact that a security's price dropped precipitously. Plaintiffs' complaints must state with particularity the facts that constitute the alleged violation and that evidence the defendant's intention "to deceive, manipulate, or defraud."[200]

In early 2008, the Supreme Court reduced the exposure of some noncorporate defendants to claims of *aiding and abetting* securities fraud. In instances in which plaintiffs allege damage based on fraudulent representations by the corporation, third parties who may have aided the fraudulent conduct, but whose deceptive acts were not communicated to the public, are not liable to private plaintiffs.[201] As discussed below, only the government can bring such lawsuits. [For more on securities class action lawsuits, see **http://securities.stanford.edu.**]

Government Enforcement

LO 9-19 Identify and describe the penalties the government may impose for aiding and abetting securities fraud.

The government can bring suits for aiding and abetting securities fraud against third parties. The Dodd–Frank Act expanded the government's reach in such cases to any third party who, knowingly or recklessly, substantially assists the primary wrongdoer.

The SEC enforces the law by imposing *civil* penalties up to $750,000 for individuals and $15 million for corporations, as well as by requiring defendants to give up ill-gotten gains, referred to as ***disgorgement***. The SEC may impose a penalty of up to 300 percent of the profit gained or loss avoided by insider trading. In addition to imposing monetary penalties, the SEC can obtain ***injunctions*** against persons committing securities fraud, and prohibit violators in the future from serving as officers or directors of publicly traded companies.

The SEC brings civil securities actions; the Justice Department brings criminal actions.

The Department of Justice seeks *criminal* sanctions for *willful* (knowing and deliberate) violations of the 1933 and 1934 Acts, with fines of up to $25 million and imprisonment for up to 20 years. As with criminal statutes in general, the principal problem for prosecutors is convincing a jury of the defendant's guilt beyond a reasonable doubt. As a result, civil penalties are often substituted for criminal prosecutions.

For decades, the SEC permitted parties to settle without admitting guilt. In June 2013, then-SEC Chair Mary Jo White announced that those committing serious securities law violations would now be required to admit culpability as a prerequisite to settlement. JPMorgan Chase was among the first to confront this policy when, in September 2013, it was forced to admit that it had violated the securities laws by permitting an "'egregious' breakdown" in control and governance.[202]

During 2022, the SEC launched 760 enforcement actions. It ordered the collection of \$4.2 billion in civil penalties and \$2.2 billion in disgorgement.

In 2011, the SEC instituted a whistleblower program. In 2022, the agency received 12,300 tips and made 103 awards totaling \$229 million.[203]

The SEC received 12,300 tips from whistleblowers in 2022.

Unfortunately, whistleblowers often suffer after coming forward, experiencing employer retaliation and being ostracized by their industry. An SEC rule prohibits any company from taking "any action to impede an individual from communicating directly with the Commission staff about a possible securities law violation, including . . . a confidentiality agreement[.]" Despite the SEC's claims that "whistleblower protections continue to be a high priority" and that "retaliation protection remains a key tenant of the whistleblower program," there have been only about 1.2 protection enforcement actions per year since the program's creation.[204]

[For more on the SEC's whistleblower program, see **www.sec.gov/whistleblower**. For an interesting view from the vantage of actual whistleblowers and those that have aided them, see **www.whistleblowersummit.com**.]

PRACTICING ETHICS Theranos—Securities Fraud and Public Health Endangerment

In 2001, Elizabeth Holmes entered Stanford University as a chemical engineering major, dreaming of becoming the first female high-tech start-up billionaire. In the summer after her freshman year, she attended a university program in China. There she met 37-year-old Sunny Balwani, who epitomized her aspirations, having cashed out a high-tech firm he started during the dot.com bubble for \$40 million. They began a lengthy romantic relationship.

Holmes had a life-long phobia of needles and imagined revolutionizing the blood-testing industry. Instead of using a syringe to draw blood from veins sufficient to fill several three-inch vials, she envisioned a process that involved only a few drops of blood taken from a finger prick filling one to three half-inch "nanovials." She wanted the results to be available in virtually real-time and the cost to be only a fraction of the usual charge. [For a picture of Holmes and a nanovial on the cover page of *Forbes*, see **www.buzzfeednews.com/article/stephaniemlee/theranos-elizabeth-holmes-sec-charges**.]

Her ambition surging because of her relationship with Balwani, she dropped out of Stanford and founded Theranos. She hired Dr. Ian Gibbon, a highly regarded expert on processing tiny amounts of fluid, to be the company's chief scientist.

Theranos's proprietary blood-testing device went through three iterations. The first was abandoned in 2007. The second, "Edison," was written off internally in 2010, but that was never communicated to the public. The third device, "miniLab," also never worked. None of these failures, however, stopped Holmes from representing to investors, regulators, the public, physicians, and patients that Edison could perform over 200 separate tests and deliver on all of Holmes's promises. One of her early advisors was Larry Ellison, billionaire cofounder of Oracle and, thus, held by her in high regard. He told her that early in his career many told him that the ideas he was proclaiming to the public as current possibilities were either not feasible or could not be accomplished in the timeframe being touted. He said he ignored them. Holmes took this "fake it 'til you make it" strategy to heart. The big difference, however, was that Theranos was "faking" about matters that created serious health risks.

Negotiations began with Walgreens in 2011 to deploy Edison across the drugstore's thousands of retail outlets, providing in-house, inexpensive, broad scope, highly accurate, almost real-time blood tests. Fearing that if they asked too many probing questions Theranos would seek another partner, Walgreens entered the partnership without securing any proof that Edison actually worked. Despite repeated requests, no Edison was ever delivered. Nor did Theranos provide answers to questions of importance regarding the device. Nonetheless, Walgreens decided to invest $140 million in Theranos and began offering in-house tests throughout Arizona and in some locations in California in September 2013.

Holmes's convincing manner and enthralling plans induced a host of high-profile individuals to become members of Theranos's board in 2011, including former Secretaries of State George Schultz and Henry Kissinger, former Secretary of Defense William Perry, former Senator Sam Nunn, and the CEO of Bechtel Group. This provided instant credibility among high-net-worth individuals. Incredibly, Holmes got these savvy individuals and companies to agree to waive all rights to see Theranos's clinical data and financial information. They also agreed to allow her unfettered control of the company. In the aggregate, about $725 million was raised between 2011 and 2015. By 2014, Theranos was valued at $9 billion, with Holmes's majority stake worth almost $5 billion. She had become the world's first female high-tech start-up billionaire.

As part of a fundraising round in early 2014, Balwani (now Theranos's chief operating officer) told potential investors that Edison could perform 300 unique tests, 98 percent with finger-stick samples, with as many as 70 tests from a single nanovial. He also told them that the tests were being used in the field and on medevac helicopters by the military, as well as in hospitals.

In July 2015, Holmes invited then-Vice President Joe Biden to visit the Theranos lab in California. Instead of touring the actual facility, which at this point was equipped solely with conventional blood-testing machines acquired from third parties, they built a fake lab. The walls were lined from floor-to-ceiling with metal racks populated with miniLabs retrieved from storage. Immediately after his visit, Biden told a group of healthcare industry executives, "I have seen the lab of the future."

In reality, problems were rampant and long-standing. In 2009, Theranos had burned through virtually all of its $47 million of cash and was on the verge of bankruptcy. Sunny Balwani joined the company as chief operating officer, after personally guaranteeing a $12 million credit line.

From late 2013 through mid-2014, Theranos received numerous calls and emails from physicians and patients concerned about test results, and for good reason. Edison produced results that were highly unreliable, unable to be replicated in sequential tests on the same samples. The measurements were often grossly inaccurate. For example, Theranos claimed that its test for a serious sexually transmitted infectious disease was 95 percent accurate. In fact, it was only correct 65 to 80 percent of the time; a person could easily be told that they did not have the disease when, in actuality, they did.

Tyler Schultz, the grandson of director George Schultz, enthusiastically joined Theranos in 2013 after graduating with a degree in biology. He initially was assigned to the unit that verified test outcomes. Later he moved to the production team, where he quantified the variability of test results. He, thus, had firsthand knowledge of the problems and, after eight months, reported them to Holmes by email. She did not respond, but Balwani sent an email that disparaged Tyler's performance as an employee and concluded with: "The only reason I have taken so much time . . . to address this personally is because you are Mr. Schultz's grandson." Tyler quit that day and, thereafter, filed an anonymous whistleblower complaint with a healthcare laboratory regulator detailing the tampered data Theranos was sending to demonstrate Edison's safety.

After leaving, Tyler was harangued and threatened by Theranos lawyers and surveilled by company private investigators. His legal defense costs grew to $400,000. In 2015, he became a confidential source for a Wall Street Journal reporter who, on October 16, 2015, broke the stories that ultimately led to Theranos's demise. A partial list of key events, beginning with those stories and ending at the time of this writing, follows:

October 16, 2015	Two Wall Street Journal articles are published. One reveals the complete failure of Theranos's technology and the company's persistent misrepresentations about its capabilities to investors, regulators, partners, physicians, and patients. The other reports that regulators have ordered Theranos to cease using Edison.
April 2016	The SEC commences a fraud investigation.
Early May 2016	Balwani retires as COO, although employees say he was fired.
	The Department of Justice commences a criminal investigation.
May 18, 2016	Theranos voids all Edison test results for 2014 and 2015.
June 2016	Walgreens withdraws from its partnership with Theranos.
July 2016	Regulators revoke Theranos's license to operate laboratories. It bars Holmes from operating a blood-testing business for two years.
	At least eight consumer lawsuits have commenced seeking class action status.
	All of the big-name directors resign.
October 2016	Walgreens files a breach of contract action against Theranos alleging misrepresentations during partnership negotiations.
Early 2017	Fortress International Group lends Theranos $65 million to meet urgent liquidity needs. As security, Theranos pledges virtually all of its assets.
	The Fortress loan requires a "clean" audit report for 2017 (an assertion that the financial statements are correct). A new CFO discovers that the accounting records are in a state of chaos, lacking information on important matters like fixed assets. He realizes that Theranos is at serious risk of receiving a "going concern" warning from the auditor (a declaration that the company does not have enough cash to survive in the near term).
	Theranos settles the lawsuit with Walgreens for $30 million.
March 4, 2018	The SEC charges Theranos, Holmes, and Balwani with securities fraud. Theranos and Holmes settle. Holmes is fined $500,000 and banned from being a public company director or officer for 10 years. Balwani disputes the charges (but ultimately loses).
June 15, 2018	The Department of Justice files criminal charges against Theranos, Holmes, and Balwani, alleging a conspiracy to defraud financial investors. "More egregiously, this company misled doctors and patients about the reliability of medical tests that endangered health and lives." If convicted, Holmes and Balwani face up to 20 years in prison, a $250,000 fine, and an obligation to compensate all harmed parties.
September 2018	Theranos is in breach of two Fortress loan covenants: (1) The failure to obtain a clean audit report for 2017, and (2) cash falling below the minimum required. Fortress moves to seize the company's assets.
	Theranos announces that it will dissolve. Shareholders will get nothing, as will most creditors. Total losses will be nearly $1 billion.
January 2020	The criminal trial is scheduled for August 2020.
November 2022	Holmes is convicted and sentenced to 135 months in prison. She says she will appeal.
December 2022	Balwani is convicted and sentenced to 155 months in prison. His sentence is longer because he oversaw the labs, the fake test results which resulted in harm to a number of patients.

The Wall Street Journal investigative reporter who broke the story, John Carreyrou, wrote a book about Theranos, *Bad Blood.* In an interview in which he reflected on the saga, he said: "[Holmes] doesn't consider she did anything wrong. [She believes] she was led astray by her entourage . . . and that she's been the victim of [a] takedown[,] . . . instead of letting the magnitude of the wrongdoing and its consequences sink in and apologizing to patients or admitting she did something wrong."

Questions

1. How do you rate the governance provided by the board of directors? Explain.

2. Discuss whether the investors and Walgreens exercised good judgment in their decision-making.
3. For years Holmes and others lied about Theranos's technological capabilities. How did they get away with it?
4. Holmes's attorneys argued that the appropriate punishment would be 18 months of house arrest. Evaluate that proposed sentence.

Sources: John Carreyrou, "Hot Startup Theranos Has Struggled With Its Blood-Test Technology," *The Wall Street Journal,* October 16, 2015 [**www.wsj.com**]; John Carreyrou, "Hot Startup Theranos Dials Back Lab Tests at FDA's Behest," *The Wall Street Journal,* October 16, 2015 [**www.wsj.com**]; Christopher Weaver and John Carreyrou, "Craving Growth, Walgreens Dismissed Its Doubts About Theranos," *The Wall Street Journal,* May 25, 2016 [**www.wsj.com**]; John Carreyrou, Michael Siconolfi, and Christopher Weaver, "Theranos Dealt Sharp Blow as Elizabeth Holmes Is Banned From Operating Labs," *The Wall Street Journal,* July 8, 2016 [**www.wsj.com**]; John Carreyrou, "Under Fire, Theranos CEO Stifled Bad News," *The Wall Street Journal,* July 10, 2016 [**www.wsj.com**]; John Carreyrou, "Theranos Whistleblower Shook the Company—and His Family," *The Wall Street Journal,* November 18, 2016 [**www.wsj.com**]; Christopher Weaver, John Carreyrou, and Michael Siconolfi, "Big Names Take Hit on Theranos," *The Wall Street Journal,* November 28, 2016 [**www.wsj.com**]; John Carreyrou, "Theranos Inc.'s Partners in Blood," *The Wall Street Journal,* May 18, 2018 [**www.wsj.com**]; John Carreyrou, "U.S. Files Criminal Charges Against Theranos's Elizabeth Holmes, Ramesh Balwani," *The Wall Street Journal,* June 15, 2018 [**www.wsj.com**]; Julia Belluz, "How Silicon Valley got played by Theranos," *Vox,* June 15, 2018 [**www.vox.com**]; John Carreyrou, "Blood-Testing Firm Theranos to Dissolve," *The Wall Street Journal,* September 5, 2018 [**www.wsj.com**]; Francine McKenna, "The last days of Theranos — the financials were as overhyped as the blood tests," *MarketWatch,* October 20, 2018 [**www.marketwatch.com**]; Brittany Shammas, "More bad blood for Theranos founder Elizabeth Holmes–this time with her own attorneys," *Washington Post,* October 5, 2019 [**www.washingtonpost.com**]; Stephanie Pagones, "Ex-Theranos CEO Elizabeth Holmes providing own defense in civil suit," *Fox News,* January 25, 2020 [**www.foxbusiness.com**]; Kalley Huang, "No. 2 Theranos Executive Is Sentenced to Nearly 13 Years for Fraud," *The New York Times,* December 7, 2022 [**www.nytimes.com**]; and Erin Griffith, "Elizabeth Holmes Is Sentenced to More Than 11 Years for Fraud," *The New York Times,* November 18, 2022 [**www.nytimes.com**].

Tender Offers

LO 9-20 Describe the tender offer process and some defenses against a hostile takeover.

There are several ways to acquire control of a corporation. Where mergers or direct acquisitions fail, a ***tender offer*** (also called a *takeover*) can be attempted. Alternatively, the person seeking to acquire control can mount a ***proxy fight,*** as previously discussed in this chapter, by nominating an alternative slate of directors and then soliciting shareholders for their annual proxies in preference to giving their proxies to current management.

In a tender offer, the offeror announces to the public that it wishes to acquire a specific number of shares (typically the number needed to gain control). It identifies where stockholders who want to participate must tender (deliver) their shares. It also specifies the opening bid price. If fewer than the desired number of shares are tendered, the tender offeror can either walk away or increase the offering price. Every tendering shareholder receives the highest price if the offer is successful. The shares are returned if the offer fails.

When faced with a tender offer, the target corporation's management realizes that a successful offer will likely result in its dismissal because the offeror will want to put their own management in place. Often the target's management will not be eager to leave. It will resist, which accounts for the term ***hostile takeover***. Management has a problem, however, because it has a fiduciary duty to act exclusively in the shareholders' best interests and the tender offer may well be in their best interests. To avoid liability, management will generally try to style its resistance as "safeguarding the stockholders."

Management can resist in various ways. It could launch its own tender offer (that is, *go private*). Or it could start using corporate cash to buy back shares in the market, driving up the price to discourage the tender offeror. Here management has to worry that it could be sanctioned for violating Section 9 of the 1934 Act, which prohibits price manipulation. However, there is a safe harbor: each day management is permitted to purchase up to 25 percent of the security's average daily trading volume.

Another resistance tactic is ***greenmail***, in which the target's management uses corporate cash to buy the tender offeror's current stake at a significant premium to ensure the latter "goes away." Changes in the federal tax law have discouraged this technique.

Management sometimes puts takeover defenses in place by arranging "disasters" if a tender offer is attempted. Two notorious tactics are the crown jewel and poison pill defenses. In general, the ***crown jewel defense*** involves the target company selling its most attractive assets (its "crown jewels"). Management arranges for a friendly third party to purchase them at a reasonable price should a tender offer be launched, thus making the target less appealing to the hostile bidder. At the same time, management is protected because the third party will continue to make these assets available on "friendly" terms should the tender offer fail. The ***poison pill defense*** takes a variety of forms. One strategy gives current shareholders a tender offer-triggered right to buy additional stock at a discount, thus diluting the hostile bidder's shares. The trigger is commonly the acquisition by the bidder of 10 to 15 percent of the outstanding common stock.

If all else fails, the target's senior management may find comfort in the ***golden parachutes*** (generous severance pay packages) they may have negotiated to protect themselves in the event of a successful takeover bid. The Dodd–Frank Act now requires a shareholder vote on such arrangements.

Questions

1. Describe how a tender offer works.
2. What makes a tender offer a hostile takeover.
3. Why can a hostile takover make sense? The Research Exercise at the end of the chapter explores one scenario.

State Securities Regulation

After the enactment of the 1933 Act, the United States operated under a dual regulatory environment for securities. Both the state and federal governments were entitled to regulate the issuance of new securities and their subsequent purchases and sales. In 1996, the lack of regulatory uniformity among the states led Congress to enact the National Securities Markets Improvement Act, preempting state registration requirements for securities traded on national markets. Then, in 1998, Congress mandated that securities fraud claims related to national-market securities be litigated only in federal court applying only federal law. As a result, state securities regulations, known as ***blue sky laws***, now have only a shadow of their former significance, primarily applicable only to intrastate offerings. [For more on state securities regulation, see **www.nasaa.org/about/our-role**.]

International Securities Regulation

LO 9-21
Describe the impact that Brexit may have in Europe.

American securities regulation is widely considered the world's strongest, as are its capital markets. Europe has sought to close the gap for decades. Its first attempt, the Markets in Financial Instruments Directive (MiFID), went into effect in 2007. It was aimed primarily at equity securities traded on regulated markets. MiFID's performance as a regulatory foundation during the Great Recession of 2008 was so poor that the EU began efforts in 2011 to revise it, culminating in the adoption of MiFID II in 2014. MiFID II regulates virtually all debt and equity securities, commodities, derivatives, and currencies. It extends to almost all trading and imposes extensively expanded, closer-to-real-time reporting of trades.[205] The regulator, the European Securities Market Authority, recites as its purpose: "to ensure fairer, safer and more efficient markets and facilitate greater transparency for all participants." [For more on the European Securities Market Authority, see **www.esma.europa.eu**.]

> Because of Brexit, 44 percent of the U.K.'s financial services firms are shifting operations to the continent, taking with them £1.3 trillion of financial assets.

The United Kingdom's withdrawal from the EU in January 2020 has raised many questions about future financial services in Europe. The continent has long hoped to decrease the U.K.'s preeminence. Under the cloud of Brexit, 44 percent of the country's major financial services firms are in the process of moving some or most of their operations, including about 7,000 employees, to the EU, taking with them approximately £1.3 trillion of financial assets. The most popular destinations are (in order): Dublin (especially for asset and wealth managers), Luxembourg, Frankfurt, and Paris (the latter two particularly attracting banking firms). Amsterdam has displaced London as Europe's largest stock exchange.[206]

Although a huge proportion of Europe's financial transactions used to occur in the U.K., the vast majority of the underlying economic activity took place on the continent. It thus makes sense for the financial transactions to move to the continent after Brexit, and the result could be quite harmful to the United Kingdom. Financial services represent 8 percent of its GDP and 10 percent of its tax receipts. They comprise 9 percent of its total exports and are responsible for reducing its trade deficit from £73 billion to £28 billion. The sector employs 2.3 million people.[207] [For more on international securities regulation generally, see **www.iosco.org/about**.]

Research Exercise on Board Diversity

Does having gender and minority-group diversity on publicly traded companies' boards of directors really make any difference in financial performance or otherwise? Do some research and then state and explain your conclusion. You can start with the following, but try to find additional credible sources: *CNN* [**www.cnbc.com/2021/06/10/racial-diversity-stagnated-on-corporate-boards-study-finds.html**], Credit Suisse [**www.credit-suisse.com/about-us-news/en/articles/media-releases/42035-201207.html**], *Traders Magazine* (referenced in 2021 PwC corporate board survey) [**www.tradersmagazine.com/xtra/ethnic-diversity-on-boards-boosts-performance**], *Entrepreneur* [**www.entrepreneur.com/leadership/board-diversity-why-its-more-important-than-ever/398847**].

Research Exercise on Cryptocurrency as a Security

Is Bitcoin a "security" such that its trading comes under the jurisdiction of the SEC? Research the issue and state and explain your conclusion. Use as authority only content sourced from the SEC and major periodicals like *The Wall Street Journal, The New York Times, The Economist,* and *Forbes.* Locate at least four sources, no fewer than one of which must be the SEC. You may use as one source the following article from *Forbes:* "Crypto Regulation: Is Cryptocurrency A Security?" [**www.forbes.com/advisor/investing/sec-crypto-regulation**].

Research Exercise on Insider Trading

Watch the 1987 movie *Wall Street,* which portrays numerous criminal violations of the federal securities law.

1. Identify the incidents of insider trading. For each incident answer the following questions:
   a. What information was conveyed?
   b. Who was the "tipper?"
   c. Who was the "tippee?"
   d. Who would be harmed by the insiders' exploitation of the inside information?
2. Identify the incidents of stock-price manipulation involving Anacott Steel. How did Sir Lawrence eliminate Gekko's interference?
3. What was Gekko's true motivation for pursuing Bluestar Airlines?

Research Exercise on Hostile Takeovers

Watch the 1991 movie *Other People's Money,* which illustrates a hostile takeover.

1. What was the economic motivation for the takeover by the "corporate raider" portrayed by Danny DeVito?
2. What efforts did the company make to resist the takeover?
3. Ignore the fortuitous opportunity that might save the company which was introduced at the end of the movie. If you were a 15 percent holder of the company's stock, and based solely on the facts presented in the film, would you have supported the hostile takeover?

Chapter Questions

1. Modell owned 80 percent of the Cleveland Stadium Corporation (Stadium) and 53 percent of the Cleveland Browns Football Company (Browns). Gries owned 43 percent of the Browns. The Browns' board consisted of Modell, the outside lawyer for both corporations, three individuals employed by both corporations, and Gries. Modell proposed that the Browns buy the Stadium for $6 million. Gries objected, saying that the Stadium appraised for only $2 million. The Browns' board, nonetheless, approved the purchase. (All directors other than Gries voted in favor of the purchase.) Gries commenced a shareholders derivative suit seeking to rescind the purchase. Who should win? See *Gries Sports Enterprises v. Cleveland Browns Football Company,* 496 N.E.2d 959 (Ohio 1986).
2. The Patels owned the CC Motel. They formed a partnership with their son, Raj, to own and operate the motel. Title to the motel was not transferred to the partnership.

The partnership agreement required Raj to approve the motel's sale. The Patels sold the motel without telling Raj and without telling the buyers of Raj's right. He learned of the pending sale and refused to agree. The buyers asked the court to compel the sale. Who should win? See *Patel v. Patel,* 260 Cal. Rptr. 255 (Cal. Ct. App. 1989).

3. Each year many shareholder proposals are offered for inclusion in the annual meeting materials, so as to be submitted to a vote of the shareholders. Assume you have a significant investment in Corporation X and the following proposals are included in the proxy materials. Which would you vote for and why?
   a. A recommendation that any bonus and performance compensation awarded to executives be paid out evenly over the four years following the grant of the bonus and only if the performance goals continue to be met.
   b. A recommendation that the standards for all bonus and performance compensation be benchmarked against the performance of the company's market competitors, requiring superior performance for the award of any bonus.
   c. A recommendation that shareholders be permitted to vote on the selection of the state in which to reincorporate the company.
   d. A recommendation to the nominating committee that each year it include one "public director" selected in consultation with one or more nonprofit organizations whose missions encompass one or more significant activities of the corporation.
4. Ivan Landreth and his sons owned all of the stock in a lumber business they operated in Tonasket, Washington. The owners offered the stock for sale. During that time, a fire severely damaged the business, but the owners made assurances of rebuilding and modernization. The stock was sold to Dennis and Bolten, and a new organization, Landreth Timber Company, was formed with the senior Landreth remaining as a consultant on the side. The new firm was unsuccessful and was sold at a loss. The Landreth Timber Company then filed suit against Ivan Landreth and his sons seeking rescission of the first sale, alleging, among other things, that Landreth and his sons had widely offered and then sold their stock without registering it as required by the Securities Act of 1933. The district court acknowledged that stocks fit within the definition of a security and that the stock in question "possessed all of the characteristics of conventional stock." However, it held that the federal securities laws do not apply to the sale of 100 percent of the stock of a closely held corporation. Here the district court found that the purchasers had not entered into the sale with the expectation of earnings secured via the labor of others. Managerial control resided with the purchasers. Thus, the sale was a commercial venture rather than a typical investment. The court of appeals affirmed, and the case reached the Supreme Court. Decide. See *Landreth Timber Co. v. Landreth,* 471 U.S. 681 (1985).
5. A *Fortune* 500 CFO admits to having deliberately treated $4 billion in operating expenses as assets, thereby allowing the corporation to show profits instead of losses. The auditor never detected this. When the misrepresentation becomes public, the corporation's stock drops 95 percent and bond covenants governing financial statement accuracy related to billions in debt are breached causing the debt to become immediately due. At the peak price shortly before the public disclosure, the CFO sold stock (acquired through options) for $15 million, generating a $10 million gain.

a. Why might the corporation have to file for bankruptcy protection?
b. What provisions of the securities law could be the basis for a class action lawsuit by the stockholders?
c. Why will the 1995 Act probably not stop a class action lawsuit from proceeding to the discovery phase?
d. Why will the CFO be subject to criminal (as well as civil) securities sanctions?
e. Will the SEC likely ever allow the CFO to be an officer or director of a publicly traded corporation in the future?
f. Will the SEC allow the CFO to keep the $10 million gain on the stock?
g. What kind of civil penalties could the SEC impose on the CFO?

Notes

1. "2021 Annual Report," Delaware Division of Corporations [**https://corpfiles.delaware.gov**] and "Project Delaware," Urban Institute, September 2022 [**www.urban.org/policy-centers/cross-center-initiatives/state-and-local-finance-initiative/projects/state-fiscal-briefs/delaware**].
2. The data were taken from the 2015 (most recent version) "SOI Tax Stats–Integrated Business Data," Internal Revenue Service [**www.irs.gov**].
3. *Id.*
4. *Cede & Co. v. Technicolor, Inc.,* 634 A.2d 345 (Del. 1993).
5. 698 A.2d 959 (Del. Supr. Ct.1996).
6. The other was *In re Clovis Oncology,* C.A. No. 2017-0222-JRS (Del. Ch. Oct. 1, 2019).
7. "BP Deepwater Horizon costs balloon to $65 billion," *Reuters,* January16, 2018 [**www.reuters.com**].
8. "Double, Double, Oil and Trouble," *The Economist,* April 18, 2015 [**www.economist.com**].
9. "PG&E Hit With Shareholder Suit Right Before Bankruptcy," *Bloomberg Law,* Jan. 29, 2019 [**https://news.bloomberglaw.com**].
10. *ATP Tour, Inc. v. Deutscher Tennis Bund,* 91 A.3d 554 (Del. 2014); Gretchen Morgenstern, "Shareholders, Disarmed by a Delaware Court," *The New York Times,* October 25, 2014 [**www.nytimes.com**]; and Steven Solomon, "Why the Surge in Merger Litigation Fizzled," *The New York Times,* January 22, 2016 [**www.nytimes.com**].
11. Delaware General Corporate Law § 102(b)(7).
12. Gretchen Morgenstern, "Case on Mortgage Official Is Said to Be Dropped," *The New York Times,* February 19, 2011 [**www.nytimes.com**].
13. *Compania General de Tabacos de Filipinas v. Collector of Internal Revenue,* 275 U.S. 87, 100 (1927) (Holmes, J., dissenting).
14. *Commissioner v. Newman,* 159 F.2d 848, 850 (2d Cir. 1947).
15. Data come from Statista [**www.statista.com/statistics/216928/us-government-revenues-by-category** (federal tax collections) and **www.statista.com/statistics/248932/us-state-government-tax-revenue-by-state** (state tax collections)], as well as from the Bureau of Economic Analysis [**https://www.bea.gov/news/2022/gross-domestic-product-fourth-quarter-and-year-2021-second-estimate#:~:text=Current%2Ddollar%20GDP%20increased%2010.1,(tables%201%20and%203)(GDP)**].
16. 26 U.S.C. Section 11. Prior to the 2017 Tax Act, the rate was effectively a flat 35 percent for all publicly held corporations.

17. Revised Uniform Partnership Act (RUPA) § 306(a).
18. *Id.* § 307(d)(1).
19. *Id.* §§ 103(b)(6); 601(3), (4), (6), (7); 602(c); 801(1); 802(b).
20. Minnesota Statutes § 322B.303, subd. 2 (1996).
21. *Kaycee Land and Livestock v. Flahive,* 46 P.2d 323 (Wyo. 2002).
22. Robert W. Hamilton, "Registered Limited Liability Partnerships: Present at the Birth (Nearly)," *University of Colorado Law Review* 66 (1995), pp. 1065–1103.
23. RUPA § 306(c).
24. Uniform Limited Partnership Act (ULPA), §§ 102(9), 201(a)(4) (2001).
25. "Types of Company: About 4 million companies are registered in Brazil," Deloitte, accessed February 16, 2020 [**www2.deloitte.com**].
26. Julia Kagan, "AG (Aktiengesellschaft)," *Investopedia,* May 3, 2018 [**www.investopedia.com**].
27. "Key Terms in English and Chinese," How to Start a Business in Taiwan, November 1, 2018 [**https://startabusinessintaiwan.tw**].
28. Financial Crisis Inquiry Commission, *The Financial Crisis Inquiry Report,* January 2011 [**http://fcic.law.stanford.edu**].
29. Carl C. Icahn, "Corporate Boards That Do Their Job," *The Washington Post,* February 16, 2009 [**www.washingtonpost.com**].
30. Tim McLaughlin, "U.S. company directors compensated more than ever, but now risk backlash," *Reuters,* November 8, 2019 [**www.reuters.com**]; Spencer Stuart, "2022 S&P 500 Compensation Snapshot" [**www.spencerstuart.com**].
31. Kaja Whitehouse, "Why CEOs Need to Be Honest with Their Boards," *The Wall Street Journal,* January 14, 2008 [**www.wsj.com**].
32. Harry Hurt III, "Taking Away Directors' Rubber Stamps," *The New York Times,* January 17, 2010 [**www.nytimes.com**].
33. Hurt, "Taking Away Directors' Rubber Stamps."
34. Jack Welch and Suzy Welch, "How Much Blame Do Boards Deserve?," *Bloomberg Business Week,* January 14, 2009 [**www.bloomberg.com**].
35. Hurt, "Taking Away Directors' Rubber Stamps."
36. Icahn, "Corporate Boards That Do Their Job."
37. Tara Siegel Bernard, "Voting Your Shares May Start to Matter," *The New York Times,* March 5, 2010 [**www.nytimes.com**].
38. Matteo Tonello and Paul Hodgson, "Corporate Board Practices in the Russell 3000, S&P 500, and S&P Mid-Cap 400," Harvard Law School Forum on Corporate Governance, November 6, 2021 [**https://corpgov.law.harvard.edu**].
39. "The Latest on Proxy Access," Harvard Law School Forum on Corporate Governance, January 14, 2020 [**https://corpgov.law.harvard.edu**] and Kai Liekefett, Derek Zaba, and Beth Berg, "SEC Dramatically Changes the Rules for Proxy Contests," Harvard Law School Forum on Corporate Governance, November 19, 2021 [**https://corpgov.law.harvard.edu**].
40. Jonathan Olsen, "Note on Leveraged Buyouts," Tuck School of Business, Dartmouth University, 2002 [**http://pages.stern.nyu.edu**].
41. "Capitalism's Unlikely Heroes," *The Economist,* February 7, 2015 [**www.economist.com**].
42. *Ibid.*
43. Michael de la Merced, "SEC Chief Sees Virtue in Activist Investors," *The New York Times,* March 19, 2015 [**www.nytimes.com**].

44. Matt Levine, "The SEC Wants to Stop Activism," *Bloomberg,* March 24, 2022 [**www.bloomberg.com**]; Brooke Masters, "When an activist investor attack is no bad thing," *Financial Times,* January 6, 2022 [**www.ft.com**]; Martin Lipton, "Dealing with Activist Hedge Funds and Other Activist Investors," Harvard Law School Forum on Corporate Governance, September 2, 2022 [**https://corpgov.law.harvard.edu**].
45. "An Investor Calls," *The Economist,* February 7, 2015 [**www.economist.com**].
46. Jason Frankl and Brian Kushner, "The Activism Vulnerability Report | Q2 2022," Harvard Law School Forum on Corporate Governance, October 6, 2022 [**https://corpgov.law.harvard.edu**] and "2021 Review of Shareholder Activism," Lazard's Capital Markets Advisory Group, [**www.lazard.com**].
47. "What Directors Think," Corporate Board Member, 2022 [**https://boardmember.com**].
48. Chuck Brooks, "Alarming Cyber Statistics For Mid-Year 2022 That You Need To Know," *Forbes,* June 3, 2022 [**www.forbes.com**].
49. William Turton and Kartikay Mehrotra, "Hackers Breached Colonial Pipeline Using Compromised Password," *Bloomberg,* June 4, 2021 [**www.bloomberg.com**].
50. David Fontaine and John Reed Stark, "Cybersecurity: The SEC's Wake-up Call to Corporate Directors," Harvard Law School Forum on Corporate Governance, March 31, 2018 [**https://corpgov.law.harvard.edu**].
51. *Id.*
52. JP Donlon, "Boards Increasingly Challenged By Oversight Of Cyber Threats," *Corporate Board Member,* accessed June 5, 2023 [**https://boardmember.com**].
53. Dave Michaels and Gabriel Rubin, "How to Make Money Trading: Hack Into SEC, Peek at 157 Secret Earnings Reports," *The Wall Street Journal,* January 15, 2019 [**www.wsj.com**]; and Fontaine and Stark, "Cybersecurity: The SEC's Wake-up Call to Corporate Directors."
54. Fontaine and Stark, "Cybersecurity: The SEC's Wake-up Call to Corporate Directors."
55. Michael Corkery, "A 'Sorceress' in Brazil, a 'Wink' in India: Walmart Pleads Guilty After a Decade of Bribes," *The New York Times,* June 20, 2019 [**www.nytimes.com**]; and Nathaniel Meyersohn, "Walmart settles with US government over international bribery investigation," *CNN,* June 20, 2019 [**www.cnn.com**].
56. Organization for Economic Cooperation and Development, *OECD Foreign Bribery Report: An Analysis of the Crime of Bribery of Foreign Public Officials,* December 2, 2014 [**www.oecd.org**].
57. *Citizens United v. Federal Election Commission,* 130 S. Ct. 876 (2010).
58. Kate Belinski and Clayton Keir, "Corporate Political Disclosure Rankings Show 'Dramatic Gap' in Transparency Between Largest and Smaller Companies," Ballard Spahr, October 21, 2022 [**www.ballardspahr.com**].
59. Brigid Rosati, Kilian Moote, Rajeev Kumar, and Michael Maiolo, "A Look Back at the 2022 Proxy Season," Harvard Law School Forum on Corporate Governance, October 23, 2022 [**https://corpgov.law.harvard.edu**].
60. Benjamin Bain and Elizabeth Dexheimer, "Big Fund Managers Ripped for Opposing Political Cash Disclosures," *Bloomberg,* November 18, 2019 [**www.bloomberg.com**].
61. Cydney Posner, "Is It Time for Corporate Political Spending Disclosure?," Harvard Law School Forum on Corporate Governance, March 17, 2019 [**https://corpgov.lawharvard.edu**].
62. Karl Evers-Hillstrom, "Most expensive ever: 2020 election cost $14.4 billion," Open Secrets, February 11, 2021 [**www.opensecrets.org**]; Anna Massoglia and Karl Evers-Hillstrom, "'Dark money' topped $1 billion in 2020, largely boosting Democrats," Open Secrets, March 17, 2021 [**www.opensecrets.org**].

63. Emma Green, "The Local Consequences of *Citizens United,*" *The Atlantic,* July 2, 2015 [**www.theatlantic.com**].
64. Fred Wertheimer, "How Chief Justice Roberts and Four Supreme Court Colleagues Gave the Nation a System of Legalized Bribery," *The Huffington Post,* October 6, 2015 [**www.huffington-post.com**].
65. End Citizens United, "New Poll: Overwhelming Majority of Americans Across Party Lines Support The For the People Act," March 2, 2021 [**https://endcitizensunited.org**]. For full survey results see, [**https://ecuactionfund.org/wp-content/uploads/2021/03/ECU-LAV-AF-HR1-F02.26.pdf**].
66. Bradley Jones, "Most Americans want to limit campaign spending, say big donors have greater political influence," Pew Research Center, May 8, 2018 [**www.pewresearch.org**].
67. Ashley Balcerzak, "Most Americans Want to Kill 'Citizens United' with Constitutional Amendment," The Center for Public Integrity, May 10, 2018 [**https://publicintegrity.org**].
68. "Non-GAAP measures and the ongoing dialogue: What you should know," PricewaterhouseCoopers, October 2019 [**www.pwc.com**].
69. "An SEC Warning on Non-GAAP No-No's," Calbench, August 11, 2022 [**www.calcbench.com**].
70. Jian Zhang, "Learning from the Current Research on Non-GAAP Financial Measures," *The CPA Journal,* December 2019 [**www.cpajournal.com**].
71. Drew Bernstein, "Has Non-GAAP Reporting Become an Accounting Chasm?," *CFO Magazine,* September 23, 2019 [**www.cfo.com**].
72. "SEC Sanctions ADT over Non-GAAP Financial Measures in Earnings Releases," Cleary Gottlieb, January 9, 2019 [**www.clearygottlieb.com**].
73. "2019 Director's Alert," Deloitte, accessed February 16, 2020 [**www2.deloitte.com**].
74. Tim Dickinson, "The Biggest Tax Scam Ever," *Rolling Stone,* August 27, 2014 [**www.rollingstone.com**].
75. *Tax Reform: Tax Havens, Base Erosion and Profit-Shifting,* Hearing before U.S. House of Representatives Committee on Ways and Means, June 13, 2013 (Testimony of University of Southern California law professor Edward Kleinbard) [**http://waysandmeans.house.gov**].
76. Adam Satariano, "Apple May Be on the Hook for $8 Billion in Taxes in Europe Probe," *Bloomberg,* January 15, 2016 [**www.bloomberg.com**].
77. Janet Hook and Danny Yadron, "Apple CEO Tim Cook, Lawmakers Square Off Over Taxes," *The Wall Street Journal,* May 21, 2013 [**www.wsj.com**].
78. Christian Oliver, Tim Bradshaw, and Barney Jopson, "Apple's Tax Affairs Spark a Transatlantic Face-Off," *Financial Times,* April 4, 2016 [**www.ft.com**]; "Upsetting the Apple Cart," *The Economist,* September 10, 2016 [**www.economist.com**]; and Silvia Amnano, "Apple wins tax battle with EU as court annuls 2016 order to pay $15 billion in taxes," CNBC, July 15, 2020 [**www.cnbc.com**].
79. "International collaboration to end tax avoidance," Organization for Economic Cooperation and Development, accessed November 2, 2022 [**www.oecd.org**].
80. Christopher Ingraham, "Over 60 percent of voters–including half of Republicans–support Elizabeth Warren's wealth tax," *The Washington Post,* February 5, 2019 [**www.washingtonpost.com**].
81. Jennifer De Pinto and Fred Backus, "Most say new tax law helps corporations and the wealthy, not middle-class," *CBS News,* April 8, 2019 [**www.cbsnews.com**].
82. Kathryn Kranhold, "You Paid Taxes. These Corporations Didn't," The Center for Public Integrity, April 11, 2019 [**https://publicintegrity.org**].
83. Andrea Miller, "How companies like Amazon, Nike and FedEx avoid paying federal taxes," *CNBC,* April 14, 2022 [**www.cnbc.com**].

84. Ryan Koronowski, Jessica Vela, and Zahir Rasheed, "These 19 Fortune 100 Companies Paid Next to Nothing–or Nothing at All–in Taxes in 2021," Center for American Progress, April 26, 2022 [**www.americanprogress.org**].
85. Jennifer Williams-Alvarez, "Companies Seek Guidance on New U.S. Minimum Tax as Launch Date Nears," *The Wall Street Journal,* October 26, 2022 [**www.wsj.com**].
86. Kranhold, "You Paid Taxes. These Corporations Didn't."
87. Maria Azpeita, et al., "Risk Reshaped: Tax Disputes Outlook 2022-2025," Baker McKenzie, February 17, 2022 [**www.bakermckenzie.com**].
88. Fred Redmond, "CEO pay has Created the Perfect Storm for "Greedflation," AFL-CIO, July 18, 2022 [**https://aflcio.org**].
89. Noam Scheiber, Peter Eavis, and David Yaffe-Bellany, "Awaiting Layoffs, WeWork Employees Say Founder's Payout Is 'Graft,'" *The New York Times,* November 8, 2019 [**www.nytimes.com**].
90. Lawrence Mishel and Julia Wolfe, "CEO compensation has grown 940% since 1978," Economic Policy Institute, August 14, 2019 [**www.epi.org**].
91. Bill Saporito, "C.E.O. Pay, America's Economic 'Miracle,'" *The New York Times,* May 17, 2019 [**www.nytimes.com**].
92. Peter Eavis, "It's Never Been Easier to Be a C.E.O., and the Pay Keeps Rising, *The New York Times,* May 24, 2019 [**www.nytimes.com**].
93. Allison Morrow, "America's CEOs made 324 times more than you last year," *CNN,* July 19, 2022 [**www.cnn.com**].
94. Mishel and Wolfe, "CEO compensation has grown 940% since 1978."
95. Anders Melin, "Outrage at Hedge Fund Proves Futile as US CEOs Reap Record Pay," *Bloomberg,* August 18, 2022 [**www.bloomberg.com**].
96. Jennifer Tonti, "Americans Say CEO Pay Is Too High," Just Capital, May 9, 2022 [**https://justcapital.com**].
97. Bill Saporito, "C.E.O. Pay America's Economic 'Miracle,'" *The New York Times,* May 17, 2019 [**www.nytimes.com**].
98. Stan Choe, "CEOs get $800,000 pay raise, leaving workers further behind," *Associated Press,* May 24, 2019 [**https://apnews.com**].
99. Matt Pilon, "Pay-ratio disclosures put executive compensation, income inequality in spotlight," *Hartford Business Journal,* May 9, 2019 [**www.hartfordbusiness.com**].
100. Saporito, "C.E.O. Pay America's Economic 'Miracle.'"
101. Mishel and Wolfe, "CEO compensation has grown 940% since 1978."
102. Nick Popli, "Investors Are Finally Pushing Back on Massive CEO Pay Hikes," *Time,* June 9, 2022 [**https://time.com**].
103. "Investors Challenge High Executive Pay as SEC Requires More Data," *Bloomberg Law,* September 16, 2022 [**https://news.bloomberglaw.com**]; "SEC Adopts Pay Versus Performance Disclosure Rules," Securities and Exchange Commission, August 25, 2022 [**www.sec.gov**]; and Rita M. Patel et al., "New executive compensation disclosure requirement for the 2023 proxy season," DLA Piper, September 15, 2022 [**www.dlapiper.com**].
104. Mishel and Wolfe, "CEO compensation has grown 940% since 1978."
105. Roe and Papadopoulos, "2019 U.S. Executive Compensation Trends."
106. "The Risk of Rewards: Tailoring Executive Pay for Long-term Success," FCLT Global, March 8, 2021 [**www.fcltglobal.org**].
107. Adi Ignatius, "The Truth About CEO Tenure," *Harvard Business Review,* November-December 2019 [**https://hbr.org**].

108. “Statement on Final Rules Regarding Clawbacks of Erroneously Awarded Compensation,” Securities and Exchange Commission, October 26, 2022 [**www.sec.gov**]; John McCrank, “U.S. SEC adopts executive compensation clawback rules,” *Reuters,* October 26, 2022 [**www.reuters.com**]; and Brian V. Breheny et al., “SEC Adopts Final Clawback Rules and Disclosure Requirements,” Skadden, Arps, Slate, Meagher & Flom, November 2, 2022 [**www.skadden.com**].
109. Justin Fox, “The Social Responsibility of Business Is to Increase . . . What Exactly?” *Harvard Business Review,* April 18, 2012 [**https://hbr.org**].
110. Steve Denning, “The Origin of ‘The World’s Dumbest Idea’: Milton Friedman,” *Forbes,* June 26, 2013 [**www.forbes.com**].
111. Andrew Edgecliffe-Johnson, “Beyond the bottom line: should business put purpose before profit?” *Financial Times,* January 4, 2019 [**www.ft.com**].
112. *Id.*
113. “Total assets under management (AUM) of BlackRock from 2008 to 2nd quarter 2022,” Statista, accessed December 4, 2021 [**www.statista.com**].
114. “Business Roundtable Redefines the Purpose of a Corporation to Promote ‘An Economy That Serves All American,’” Business Roundtable, August 19, 2019 [**www.businessroundtable.org**].
115. Claudine Gartenberg and George Serafeim, “181 Top CEOs Have Realized Companies Need a Purpose Beyond Profit,” *Harvard Business Review,* August 20, 2019 [**www.hbr.org**].
116. Martin Lipton, Steven Rosenblum, and Karessa Cain, “Thoughts for Boards of Directors in 2020,” Harvard Law School Forum on Corporate Governance, December 10, 2019 [**https://corpgov.law.harvard.edu**].
117. Larry Fink, “A Fundamental Reshaping of Finance,” BlackRock, January 15, 2020 [**www.blackrock.com**].
118. Lipton, Rosenblum, and Cain, “Thoughts for Boards of Directors in 2020.”
119. “2020 Is a ‘Tipping Point’ for ESG, Says Nasdaq CEO Adena Friedman,” NASDAQ, January 21, 2020 [**www.nasdaq.com**].
120. Sunny Oh, “Here’s what you need to know about the $12 trillion ESG investment world,” Market Watch, December 18, 2019 [**www.marketwatch.com**].
121. Edgecliffe-Johnson, “Beyond the bottom line: should business put purpose before profit?”
122. “The ESG journey: Lessons from the boardroom and C-suite,” KPMG, accessed February 16, 2020 [**https://boardleadership.kpmg.us**].
123. “ESG: Going Beyond the Balance Sheet,” S&P Global, accessed January 30, 2020 [**www.spglobal.com**].
124. Georg Kell, “The Remarkable Rise of ESG,” *Forbes,* July 11, 2018 [**www.forbes.com**].
125. KPMG, “The ESG journey: Lessons from the boardroom and C-suite.”
126. “ESG, strategy, and the Longview: A framework for board oversight,” KPMG, accessed February 16, 2020 [**https://assets.kpmg**].
127. Oh, “Here’s what you need to know about the $12 trillion ESG investment world.”
128. Jon Hale, “Black Rock Joins Sustainable Investing Movement,” MorningStar, January 15, 2020 [**www.morningstar.co.uk**].
129. KPMG, “The ESG journey: Lessons from the boardroom and C-suite.”
130. Edgecliffe-Johnson, “Beyond the bottom line: should business put purpose before profit?”
131. *TSC Industries, Inc. v. Northway, Inc.,* 426 U.S. 438 (1976); reaffirmed in *Basic, Inc. v. Levinson,* 485 U.S. 224 (1988).

132. "Proposed SEC climate disclosure requirements," Deloitte, accessed December 4, 2022 [**www2.deloitte.com**].
133. "Proposed SEC Climate Disclosure Rule," *Bloomberg Law,* August 12, 2022 [**https://pro.bloomberglaw.com**].
134. Gary Gensler, "Statement on ESG Disclosures Proposal," Securities and Exchange Commission, May 25, 2022 [**www.sec.gov**].
135. Maia Gez, Era Anagnosti, and Taylor Pullins, "ESG Disclosure Trends in SEC Filings," Harvard Law School Forum on Corporate Governance, July 16, 2022 [**https://corpgov.law.harvard.edu**].
136. Kell, "The Remarkable Rise of ESG."
137. "ESG-Related Shareholder Proposals - Takeaways from the First Half of 2022," Orrick Herrington & Sutcliffe, July 25, 2022 [**www.orrick.com**].
138. KPMG, "The ESG journey: Lessons from the boardroom and C-suite."
139. S&P Global, "ESG: Going Beyond the Balance Sheet."
140. Edgecliffe-Johnson, "Beyond the bottom line: should business put purpose before profit?"
141. Ingo Steinhaeuser, "Financial materiality: Understanding the financial performance of ESG strategies," *Thomson Reuters,* September 7, 2022 [**www.thomsonreuters.com**].
142. Kell, "The Remarkable Rise Of ESG."
143. Michael Porter, George Serafeim, and Mark Kramer, "Where ESG Fails," *Institutional Investor,* October 16, 2019 [**www.institutionalinvestor.com**].
144. Vikram Chakravarty, et al., "Determining which factors to prioritize and the level of commitment required need not be a challenge for corporate strategists," Ernst & Young, July 30, 2022 [**www.ey.com**]; and "Failing to Meet ESG Goals Exposes Companies to Increased Operational and Financial Risks, Study Finds," *BusinessWire,* June 06, 2022 [**www.businesswire.com**].
145. Kell, "The Remarkable Rise Of ESG"; and Porter, Serafeim, and Kramer, "Where ESG Fails."
146. Edgecliffe-Johnson, "Beyond the bottom line: should business put purpose before profit?"
147. "Listof countries by GDP (nominal)," *Wikipedia,* accessed February 15, 2020 [**https://en.wikipedia.org**].
148. Kell, "The Remarkable Rise Of ESG."
149. Jeff Green and Saijel Kishan, "America's Political Right Has a New Enemy No. 1: ESG Investors," *Bloomberg,* May 20, 2022 [**www.bloomberg.com**].
150. Danielle Moran and Saijel Kishan, "Florida Will Pull $2 Billion of Assets From BlackRock Over ESG," *Bloomberg,* December 1, 2022 [**www.bloomberg.com**]; Sabrina Kharrazi, "ESG Fight Injects Fresh Risks Into Public Pension Portfolios," *Bloomberg,* November 23, 2022 [**www.bloomberg.com**]; and Jordan Wolman, "Republicans plan surge of attacks on 'woke' investing after the midterms," *Politico,* November 1, 2022 [**www.politico.com**].
151. Maxine Joselow, "Republicans to probe 'cancer' of ESG investing after midterms," *The Washington Post,* November 2, 2022 [**www.washingtonpost.com**].
152. Daniel Litowitz and Lara Aryani, "Trends in E&S Proposals in the 2022 Proxy Season," Harvard Law School Forum on Corporate Governance, November 28, 2022 [**https://corpgov.law.harvard.edu**].
153. "History of the IPCC," Intergovernmental Panel on Climate Change, accessed February 15, 2020 [**www.ipcc.ch/about/history**].
154. René Marsh, "This city paid $1.1M to keep faucets running through March as the price of water skyrockets in California, *CNN,* November 1, 2022 [**www.cnn.com**].

155. "Hot, unbothered," *The Economist,* February 23, 2019 **[www.economist.com]**; and Amanda Watts, "Another supply chain crisis: Barge traffic halted on Mississippi River by lowest water levels in a decade," *CNN,* October 8, 2022 **[www.cnn.com]**.
156. Josie Fischels, "The Record-Breaking Heat Wave That's Scorching The Pacific Northwest," *National Public Radio,* June 29, 2021 **[www.npr.org]**.
157. Deloitte, "2020 Governance Outlook;" and "Hot, unbothered," *The Economist.*
158. "Climate change will alter waves along half the world's coast," National Oceanography Centre, August 22, 2019 **[www.sciencedaily.com]**.
159. "Extreme Weather and Climate Change," Center for Climate and Energy Solutions, accessed January 30, 2020 **[www.c2es.org]**.
160. Fink, "A Fundamental Reshaping of Finance."
161. Yang Jie and Aaron Tilley, "Apple Makes Plans to Move Production Out of China," *The Wall Street Journal,* December 3, 2022 **[www.wsj.com]**.
162. Deloitte, "2019 Directors' Alert."
163. "2020 Governance Outlook," *National Association of Corporate Directors,* accessed February 16, 2020 **[www.nacdonline.org]**.
164. "Charting the course through a changing governance landscape," PricewaterhouseCoopers, 2022 **[www.pwc.com]**.
165. Jeff Green, "S&P 500 Boards Have 100 Seats Open to Add Diverse Candidates," *Bloomberg,* June 29, 2022 **[www.bloomberg.com]**.
166. Ruth Umoh, "The Last All-Male Board On The S&P 500 Just Added A Female Member," *Forbes,* July 25, 2019 **[www.forbes.com]**.
167. "Women Exceed 25% of Board Seats for First Time," *Bloomberg,* October 23, 2019 **[www.bloomberg.com]**; and Jeff Green, "S&P 500 Boards Have 100 Seats Open to Add Diverse Candidates."
168. Subodh Mishra, "U.S. Board Diversity Trends in 2019," Harvard Law School Forum on Corporate Governance, June 18, 2019 **[https://corpgov.law.harvard.edu]**; and "2022 S&P 500 Board Diversity Snapshot," Spencer Stuart, June 2022 **[www.spencerstuart.com]**.
169. Henry Wolfe, "Focus on Competency, Not Independence, to Solve Problem with Director Selection at Public Companies," Corporate Compliance Insights, March 27, 2019 **[www.corporatecomplianceinsights.com]**.
170. PwC, "ESG in the boardroom: What directors need to know."
171. Lipton, Rosenblum, and Cain, "Thoughts for Boards of Directors in 2020."
172. Tonello, "CEO and Executive Compensation Practices."
173. Fink, "A Fundamental Reshaping of Finance."
174. Spotify Technology S.A., SEC Form F-1, p. 53, *Securities and Exchange Commission,* February 28, 2018 **[www.sec.gov]**.
175. *SEC v. Aqua-Sonic Products Corp.,* 687 F.2d 577 (2d Cir. 1982).
176. Allana Akhtar, "Doing a direct listing like Slack can be a huge boon to employees and investors, but experts say it'll stay an anomaly for 1 key reason," *Business Insider,* June 21, 2019 **[www.businessinsider.com]**.
177. Peter Lattman, "SEC Lifts Advertising Ban on Private Investments," *The New York Times,* July 11, 2013 **[www.nytimes.com]** and P. Michelle Gasaway, "Private, Pre-IPO Investments Continue To Gain Influence for Companies Looking To Go Public," *Skadden Arps, et al.,* January 21, 2020 **[www.skadden.com]**.

178. Scott Bauguess, Rachita Gullapalli, and Vladimir Ivanov, "Capital Raising in the U.S.: An Analysis of the Market for Unregistered Securities Offerings, 2009–2017," *Securities and Exchange Commission Division of Economic and Risk Analysis,* August 1, 2018 [**www.sec.gov**].

179. "Raising Capital Using a Regulation A+ Mini-IPO," *SeedInvest,* October 28, 2016 [**www.seedinvest.com**].

180. "Regulation A+: Now Everyone Can Invest in Your Startup," *Forbes,* June 19, 2015 [**www.forbes.com**].

181. Kiran Lingam, "The Reg A+ Bombshell: $50M Unaccredited Equity Crowdfunding Title IV Takes Center Stage," *Crowdfund Insider,* March 25, 2015 [**https://crowdfundingtimes.wordpress.com**].

182. "Small Business and the SEC,"*U.S. Securities and Exchange Commission,* Feb. 27, 2014 [**www.sec.gov**].

183. Jessica Holzer and Greg Bensinger, "SEC Embraces Social Media," *The Wall Street Journal,* April 2, 2013 [**www.wsj.com**].

184. "Fast Answers: Trading Suspensions," *Securities and Exchange Commission,* June 7, 2011 [**www.sec.gov**].

185. Fernando Chague, Rodrigo De-Losso, and Bruno Giovannetti, "Day trading for a living?," *SSRN,* November 21, 2019 [**https://papers.ssrn.com**].

186. "Day Trading: Your Dollars at Risk," *Securities and Exchange Commission,* April 20, 2005 [**www.sec.gov**].

187. Chague, De-Losso, and Giovannetti, "Day trading for a living?"

188. Angela Wang, "In the Decade Since Madoff, Ponzi Schemers Try New Tactics," *The New York Times,* September 22, 2019 [**www.nytimes.com**] and Associated Press, "Meltdown Left Ponzi Schemes in Ashes," *Des Moines Register,* December 29, 2009.

189. "SEC Charges Volkswagen, Former CEO with Defrauding Bond Investors During 'Clean Diesel' Emissions Fraud," *Securities and Exchange Commission,* March 15, 2019 [**www.sec.gov**].

190. "SEC sues Volkswagen, ex-CEO over alleged emissions fraud on investors," *NBC News,* March 15, 2019 [**www.nbcnews.com**]; and Charles Riley, "Volkswagen's ex-CEO pays company $14 million over his role in the diesel scandal," *CNN Business,* June 9, 2021 [**www.cnn.com**].

191. *Stark Trading v. Falconbridge Ltd.,* 552 F.3d 358 (7th Cir. 2009).

192. 134 S. Ct. 2398 (2014).

193. *Halliburton v. Erica P. John Fund, Inc.,* 134 S.Ct. 2398, 2410 (2014)

194. Ethan Smith, "Disney Drama as Stock Plot Is Foiled," *The Wall Street Journal,* May 27, 2010 [**www.wsj.com**].

195. T. Gorman, "SEC Settles Whole Foods/Amazon Insider Trading Case," *SEC Actions,* April 7, 2019 [**www.secactions.com**].

196. "Former Congressman Christopher Collins Sentenced For Insider Trading Scheme And Lying To Federal Law Enforcement Agents," *Dept. of Justice,* January 17, 2020 [**www.justice.gov**].

197. Rebecca Davis O'Brien and Corinne Ramey, "New York Businessman Convicted in Insider-Trading Trial," *The Wall Street Journal,* January 15, 2020 [**www.wsj.com**]; Rebecca Davis O'Brien, "Star Witness in Insider-Trading Case Describes Far-Reaching Scheme," *The Wall Street Journal,* January 10, 2020 [**www.wsj.com**]; and Franz Wild and Matt Robinson, "Goldman VP, Poker Player and Lovers in Insider-Trading Plot," *Bloomberg,* October 23, 2019 [**www.bloomberg.com**].

198. Larry Neumeister, "Ex-US Congressman Among 9 Charged in Insider Trading Cases,"*US News & World Report,* July 25, 2022 [**www.usnews.com**] and "SEC Charges Former Indiana Congressman with Insider Trading," *Securities and Exchange Commission,* July 25, 2022 [**www.sec.gov**].
199. Division of Enforcement, "2019 Annual Report," *Securities and Exchange Commission,* February 16, 2020 [**www.sec.gov**].
200. *Tellabs, Inc. v. Makor Issues & Rights, Ltd.,* 127 S. Ct. 2499 (2007).
201. *Stoneridge Investment Partners LLC v. Scientific-Atlanta, Inc.,* 128 S. Ct. 761 (2008).
202. Jean Eaglesham, "A Historic Admission from J. P. Morgan," *The Wall Street Journal,* September 19, 2013 [**www.wsj.com**].
203. "SEC Announces Enforcement Results for FY22," *Securities and Exchange Commission,* November 15, 2022 [**www.sec.gov**].
204. Office of the Whistleblower, "2022 Annual Whistleblower Report to Congress," *Securities and Exchange Commission,* November 15, 2022 [**www.sec.gov**].
205. "MIFIDII," European Securities and Market Authority, accessed January 13, 2023 [**www.esma.europa.eu**] and Philip Stafford, "What is Mifid II and how will it affect EU's financial industry?," *Financial Times,* September 15, 2017 [**www.ft.com**].
206. Sarah Graham, "EY Financial Services Brexit Tracker: Movement within UK financial services sector stabilises five years on from Article 50 trigger," *Ernst and Young,* March 29, 2022 [**www.ey.com**]; "Government reluctant to engage with the EU on financial services says Lords Committee," *UK Parliament European Affairs Committee,* June 23, 2022 [**https://committees.parliament.uk**]; Huw Jones, "Britain kicks off post-Brexit 'transformation' of finance," *Reuters,* July 19, 2022 [**www.reuters.com**]; "Trade: Key Economic Indicators," *UK Parliament House of Commons Library,* December 22, 2022 [**https://commonslibrary.parliament.uk**]; and "Financial services: contribution to the UK economy," *UK Parliament House of Commons Library,* September 1, 2022 [**https://commonslibrary.parliament.uk**].
207. "Trade: Key Economic Indicators," *UK Parliament House of Commons Library,* December 22, 2022 [**https://commonslibrary.parliament.uk**] and "Financial services: contribution to the UK economy," *UK Parliament House of Commons Library,* September 1, 2022 [**https://commonslibrary.parliament.uk**].

Video icon credit: Comstock Images/Alamy Stock Photo

CHAPTER TEN

Antitrust Law—Restraints of Trade

After completing this chapter, students will be able to fulfill the following learning objectives:

10-1. Recognize the primary goals of antitrust law.

10-2. Describe the key antitrust statutes.

10-3. Explain the meaning of "horizontal restraints of trade."

10-4. Analyze when an unlawful price-fixing arrangement has been created.

10-5. Describe the characteristics of a group boycott.

10-6. Define resale price maintenance.

10-7. Explain the requirements for establishing an unlawful tying arrangement.

10-8. Describe the commercial advantages and disadvantages of exclusive dealing.

10-9. Contrast price discrimination and predatory pricing.

10-10. Explain how predatory pricing may be proven.

Most of us only dimly recognize the word *antitrust,* but we depend on antitrust law to maintain an open competitive economy, free of price-fixing, monopoly power, and, generally, restraints of trade. Many scholars, commentators, and politicians are now arguing, as we discussed in Chapter 3, that our economy is increasingly dominated by big corporations, thus exacerbating problems of income inequality, low wages, biased information, big-money distortion of the electoral process, and lagging entrepreneurship, among others. As you read this chapter, think about whether you believe free-market forces can safely guide our economy, or whether additional government regulation is necessary.

PRACTICING ETHICS "Pay to Play" for Student-Athletes

More than a hundred years ago, universities paid professional athletes to play on their sports teams. Football became increasingly violent, and schools that could pay their players more had an unfair competitive advantage on the field. To promote amateurism and a pro-competitive environment, the National Collegiate Athletic Association (NCAA) adopted rules limiting the payments student-athletes could receive. In particular, financial aid awards were limited to the cost of the student's attendance at the university. A group of former collegiate athletes in football, as well as men's and women's basketball, challenged the NCAA's compensation rules, claiming they constituted an agreement among competitors in an illegal restraint of trade. The NCAA, on the other hand, argued that the rules were permissible because they furthered its mission of maintaining the time-honored tradition of amateur collegiate sports. The athlete plaintiffs won at least a partial victory at the federal district court level in 2019. The court ruled that financial aid payments could extend beyond the cost of attendance, to those expenditures necessary for educational purposes (such as graduate school scholarships and the cost of computers, science equipment, and musical instruments). The NCAA could still ban other compensation, thus denying student-athletes a wholly free market in which to compete. The NCAA appealed, and the case eventually made its way to the U.S. Supreme Court. The court's final decision against the NCAA in June 2021 was damning: "To the extent [the NCAA] means to propose a sort of judicially ordained immunity from the terms of the Sherman Act for its restraints of trade—that we should overlook its restrictions because they happen to fall at the intersection of higher education, sports, and money—we cannot agree." Although the scope of the appeal was limited to the issue of education-related benefits, Justice Kavanaugh clearly signaled in a concurring opinion "that the NCAA's remaining compensation rules also raise serious questions under the antitrust laws." Meanwhile, California passed its Fair Pay to Play Act in 2019, effective 2023, granting college athletes the legal right to be paid for the commercial use of their name, image, and likeness (NIL). New York's version of the bill—the Collegiate Athletic Participation Act—was signed by its Governor in 2021. By July 2021, 24 states had passed legislation allowing for NIL compensation.

New Rules The NCAA responded to the U.S. Supreme Court's decision and to state legislation on June 30, 2021, by temporarily redacting its rules barring NIL compensation. As of February 2023, University of Miami women's basketball players—and twins—Haley and Hannah Cavinder have since earned about seven figures in NIL payments.

The NCAA Board of Governors directed its Divisions I, II, and III (levels of collegiate athletic competition) to develop new rules permitting NIL compensation but affirming that the athletes are students, not university employees, and maintaining the distinction between professional and collegiate athletics. Notably, in March 2023, the NCAA issued its first NIL-crackdown under its new compensation rules, sanctioning the University of Miami because billionaire booster John Ruiz impermissibly contacted the Cavinder twins and provided them with a meal.

O'Bannon v. NCCA In an earlier antitrust case in 2016, former UCLA and NBA basketball star Ed O'Bannon led a group of Division I college football and men's basketball players against the NCAA, seeking compensation for television broadcasts and NIL royalties. The plaintiffs prevailed, in part, when a panel of the federal 9th Circuit Court of Appeals ruled that NCAA caps on *education-related* scholarships constituted a restraint of trade. However, the court upheld the restriction on cash sums beyond the cost of attendance. The court's decision effectively defeated a settlement offer from one of the original defendants—Electronic Arts had agreed to pay about $1,200 per plaintiff to settle claims relating to its use of the players' names, images, and likenesses in its video games. The U.S. Supreme Court had declined to review that case.

Moving Forward Where this story goes next is unclear. Will the highest levels of NCAA football and basketball morph into quasi-professional, on-campus businesses? Or will Congress allow some form of a limited antitrust exemption to help maintain collegiate amateur sports?

Questions

1. Do you think the NCAA restraints on compensation for athletes constituted an ethical wrong? Explain.
2. College sports is a multibillion-dollar industry. Have former NCAA athletes, such as Ed O'Bannon, been unfairly and wrongfully denied a bigger share of the income they help generate for the sake of preserving amateurism? Explain.
3. Should college athletes be free to "sell" their services to the highest bidder among America's colleges and universities? Explain.

4. Joseph Agnew and Patrick Courtney earned college football scholarships but were injured early in their college careers. Consistent with NCAA rules, both players had received one-year scholarships with the possibility of renewal. Neither Agnew nor Courtney received scholarship renewals following their injuries. Both players sued the NCAA claiming its rules forbidding multiyear scholarships and imposing caps on the number of scholarships given per team prevented them from securing scholarships that would have covered their full college experience.
   a. Explain why the two plaintiffs thought they had been wronged by the NCAA rules.
   b. Do you agree with the two plaintiffs? Explain. See *Agnew v. National Collegiate Athletic Association,* 683 F.3d 328 (7th Cir. 2012) [**https://law.justia.com**].

Sources: *National Collegiate Athletic Association v. Alston,* 594 U.S. __ (2021) [**www.supremecourt.gov**]; *O'Bannon v. National Collegiate Athletic Association,* 802 F.3d 1049 (9th Cir. 2015), cert. denied, 137 S. Ct. 277 (2016), and Pat Forde and Ross Dellenger, "NCAA Issues Its First NIL Ruling, With Cavinder at the Center of It," *Sports Illustrated,* February 23, 2023 [**https://www.si.com**].

Part One—The Foundations of Antitrust Law

Antitrust—Early Goals

LO 10-1
Recognize the primary goals of antitrust law.

Antitrust, perhaps more than any other branch of law, is a product of changing political and economic tides. Historically, antitrust law sought to allow every American, at least in theory, the opportunity to reach the top. More specifically, antitrust advocates were concerned about the following issues:

1. **The preservation of competition.** Antitrust law was designed to provide free open markets, resulting in enhanced efficiency and increased consumer welfare. The belief was (and generally continues to be) that competition generates the best products and services at the lowest possible prices.
2. **The preservation of democracy.** Many businesses in competition meant that none of them could corner economic, political, or social power.
3. **The preservation of small businesses and, more generally, the American Dream.** Antitrust was designed to preserve the opportunity for ordinary Americans to compete with the giants.
4. **An expression of political radicalism.** At least for a segment of society, antitrust laws were meant to be tools for reshaping America to meet the needs of all people, thus counteracting, to some degree, the power of big business. [For professors' analyses of recent antitrust developments, see **http://lawprofessors.typepad.com/antitrustprof_blog**.]

Antitrust: Increase Government Intervention?

Historically, Americans have believed in the enormous power of the market to maximize freedom and general welfare, but we have also relied on government to moderate market failures. Increasingly, we see evidence that well-entrenched wealth in corporate America threatens the legitimacy of the market. Critics are particularly concerned that healthy competition is being thwarted by increasing corporate concentration. A quick glance at high-tech, airlines, telecom, hospitals, beer, and other businesses reveals that one or just a few companies dominate many American industries. While that concentration might simply suggest a victory for the most innovative, efficient, and competitive firms, increasing evidence raises doubts.

Economists Jan DeLoecker and Jan Eeckhart, for example, have found that average mark-ups (amount above cost at which products are sold) have increased from 18 percent in 1980 to nearly 70 percent in 2014, suggesting a decline in competition and a rise in market power for one or a few firms. While these findings have been challenged, a recent International Monetary Fund study found a similar trend across the globe.[1] Another recent study found that Internet access, monthly cellphone plans, and flight tickets are cheaper in Europe than America. At least a partial explanation for that divide is that Europe has maintained more aggressive antitrust and regulatory practices than the United States.[2]

In this chapter and in Chapter 11, we will learn about antitrust law, and you should consider whether we need more activist government oversight of American industry as the Roosevelt Institute recently argued:

> A forty-year assault on antitrust and competition policy—the laws and regulations meant to guard against the concentration of power in private hands—has helped tip the economy in favor of powerful corporations under the false pretense that the unencumbered ambitions of private business will align with the public good.[3]

United States' antitrust enforcement has been generally lenient since the 1980s.[4] Democrats sometimes call for more rigorous antitrust enforcement, but Republicans generally have not embraced that goal, and the Supreme Court leans toward conservative ideologies that place considerable faith in the free market. Now, however, fears about the extraordinary present and future power of the Tech giants (especially Amazon, Apple, Facebook, and Google) have produced some common ground between Democrats and Republicans such that Congress, some regulatory agencies, and the federal Justice Department seem to be moving toward more aggressive investigation of potential Big Tech monopoly behaviors. (See Chapter 11.)

Antitrust Enforcement and Statutes

The Justice Department and the Federal Trade Commission, the federal bodies responsible for antitrust enforcement, bring relatively few antitrust actions, but a government victory sends a powerful message to the business community about the risks of anticompetitive behavior. The government prefers to avoid litigation, and most cases are settled before going to court. Furthermore, the Justice Department practices leniency, sometimes allowing cooperative defendants to avoid criminal prosecution.

> A government victory sends a powerful message to the business community.

LO 10-2 Describe the key antitrust statutes.

Private parties also may sue under the antitrust laws. However, segments of the economy that are already closely regulated by the government, such as the securities industry, sometimes successfully claim they are immune from the antitrust laws. [For more on the Justice Department Antitrust Division, see **www.usdoj.gov/atr**.]

Sherman Antitrust Act, 1890

Section 1 of the Sherman Antitrust Act (Sherman Act) forbids restraints of trade, while Section 2 forbids monopolization, attempts to monopolize, and conspiracies to monopolize. Two types of enforcement options are available to the federal government:

1. **Violation of the Sherman Act opens participants to criminal penalties.** Generally, the maximum corporate fine is $100 million per violation, while individuals may be fined as much as $1 million and/or imprisoned for up to 10 years. Under some circumstances, fines can exceed those maximums.
2. **Injunctive relief is provided under civil law.** The government or a private party may secure a court order preventing continuing violations of the act and affording appropriate relief (such as dissolution or divestiture). Those harmed by a violation of the Sherman Act also may bring a civil action seeking three times the actual damages sustained (treble damages).

Clayton Act, 1914

The Clayton Act forbids price discrimination, exclusive dealing, tying arrangements, requirements contracts, mergers restraining commerce or tending to create a monopoly, and interlocking directorates. Civil enforcement of the Clayton Act is similar to that of the Sherman Act: injured parties may sue for injunctive relief and treble damages. Criminal law remedies are not available under the Clayton Act. [For links to antitrust sites worldwide, see **www.justice.gov/atr/contact/otheratr.html**.]

Federal Trade Commission Act, 1914

The Federal Trade Commission Act created the Federal Trade Commission (FTC), a powerful, independent agency designed to eliminate anticompetitive practices in American commerce. The FTC proceeds under the Sherman Act, the Clayton Act, and Section 5 of the FTC Act itself, which declares that "unfair methods of competition" and "unfair or deceptive acts or practices in or affecting commerce" are unlawful. The FTC's primary enforcement device is the cease-and-desist order, but it also may impose fines. [For the FTC Guide to Antitrust Laws, see **www.ftc.gov/bc/antitrust/index.shtm**.]

Antitrust: Other Regulatory Systems

State Law

Most states, through legislation and judicial decisions, have developed their own antitrust laws. Some states have recently become more attentive to antitrust enforcement, as illustrated by their resistance to the U.S. Supreme Court's controversial *Leegin* decision set out later in this chapter.

Patents, Copyrights, and Trademarks

These devices offer limited, government-granted, government-shielded market strength, intended to protect and encourage commercial creativity and product development.

The patent, copyright, or trademark holder is held to the terms of its government-granted privilege, thereby keeping the privilege from growing into an unlawful monopoly.

Law of Other Nations

Chapter 11 introduces the practical and ideological significance of international antitrust issues in this era of globalization. [For an antitrust database, see **www.antitrustinstitute.org**.]

Part Two—Horizontal Restraints

LO 10-3 Explain the meaning of "horizontal restraints of trade."

When competitors collude, conspire, or agree among themselves in ways that unreasonably harm competition, they are engaging in an unlawful *horizontal restraint of trade.* Instead of competing to drive prices down and quality up, competitors may be fixing prices, restricting output, dividing territories, and the like. Horizontal restraints are governed by Section 1 of the Sherman Act, which forbids contracts, combinations, or conspiracies in *restraint of trade.*

Rule of Reason

In its 1911 *Standard Oil*[5] decision, the U.S. Supreme Court articulated the *rule of reason,* which essentially provides that the Sherman Act forbids only *unreasonable* restraints of trade. To establish an unreasonable restraint, the plaintiff must provide proof of an agreement or conspiracy that has caused anticompetitive effects (often a very difficult task). If the plaintiff is successful, the defendants are then permitted to provide evidence of pro-competitive effects. The court then balances the pro- and anticompetitive effects to determine whether the agreement or conspiracy unreasonably harms competition.

Per Se

Some antitrust violations, such as horizontal price-fixing, are so injurious to competition that their mere existence ordinarily constitutes unlawful conduct. Plaintiffs must prove that the violation in question occurred, but they need not prove that the violation caused, or is likely to cause, competitive harm. These *per se* violations are simply unlawful on their face. The courts in recent years have been increasingly reluctant to find *per se* violations.

We turn now to an examination of specific categories of horizontal restraints of trade.

Horizontal Price-Fixing

Principal Legislation: Sherman Act, Section 1

> Sherman Act, Section 1. Every contract, combination in the form of trust or otherwise, or conspiracy, in restraint of trade or commerce, among the several states, or with foreign nations, is declared to be illegal.

Assume two big companies dominate the wholesale food market in their small state. Could they lawfully agree between themselves to divide their state geographically, with one

LO 10-4
Analyze when an unlawful price-fixing arrangement has been created.

supplying only the eastern half while the other supplies only the western half? Or could they lawfully allocate their customers, for example, such that one supplies all small-town grocers while the other restricts itself to grocers in the few major cities? Such arrangements ordinarily are *per se* violations of the Sherman Act because they attempt to nullify the powerful benefits of competition. [For an antitrust overview, see **http://topics.law.cornell.edu/wex/antitrust**.]

Competitors cannot lawfully agree among themselves on prices. That principle is simple and fundamental to an efficient, fair marketplace. Establishing the presence of an unlawful price-fixing arrangement, on the other hand, is anything but simple.

Proof

Establishing price-fixing and all other Sherman Act Section 1 violations requires proof that a contract, combination, or conspiracy produced the alleged wrong. Evidence of collusion arises in a variety of ways. Optimally, but uncommonly, the plaintiff can produce explicit evidence (such as a written document) of a direct agreement among the defendant parties. Failing evidence of a direct agreement, the plaintiff must present evidence of parallel business behavior among the parties, along with one or more "plus factors" that, in the aggregate, suggest the parties must have colluded.

Plus factors may include the simultaneous adoption of substantially similar pricing policies, sharing a common motive to conspire, defendants seemingly having acted against their own self-interest, signaling of intentions, or evidence of a tacit agreement or one based on mutual observation.

La Quinta Inns, for example, arguably colluded with competitors to fix prices through its "call-around" practice. Reportedly, motel managers identified their primary local competition and called them frequently to give and receive information about occupancy rates and room charges, a practice that apparently is widespread in the motel industry. The concern is that the frequent exchange of information effectively constituted collusion to fix prices. La Quinta, when challenged by the Connecticut attorney general, agreed to desist from its call-around practices throughout the United States.[6]

Question

To replace call arounds, could La Quinta lawfully check competitors' prices on the Internet, make "blind" calls to competitors, or employ "mystery" shoppers?

Poaching Employees

"If you hire a single one of these people that means war." According to court records, that was the response of Apple founder Steve Jobs when, in 2005, Google wanted to hire some Apple engineers. In 2015, a federal court in California approved a $415 million settlement of an antitrust class action claiming several Silicon Valley tech firms, including Apple and Google, had conspired to suppress job opportunities and wages by, among other practices, agreeing not to "poach" each other's employees.

At least 15 national restaurant chains (including Applebee's, Jimmy John's, and McDonald's) have agreed to drop anti-poaching policies. Those policies, however, may be lawful where important for legitimate collaborations, protection of sensitive information, increasing quality control, and the like.

In 2018, the federal Justice Department and Federal Trade Commission announced that poaching agreements would be subject to criminal prosecution.

Questions

1. Why might high-tech companies be particularly concerned about employee poaching?
2. What antitrust claims might be raised against a high-tech company that poaches employees?
3. What damages would the plaintiffs in these claims allege?

Sources: John F. Allgood, "Federal Court Approves $415 Million Settlement of Employee Antitrust Claims Against California Technology Employers," *The Hill,* September 4, 2015 [**www.thehill.com**]; "U.S. Judge Approves DOJ Settlement with eBay over Tech Hiring," *Reuters,* September 2, 2014 [**www.reuters.com**]; and Mark C. Katz, "Competition Law Considerations for H.R. Professionals," *Kluwer Competition Law Blog,* September 21, 2015 [**https://competitionlawblog.kluwercompetitionlaw.com**].

Parallel Conduct

An unlawful conspiracy must be distinguished from independent, but parallel, business behavior by competitors. So-called *conscious parallelism* is fully lawful because the competitors have not agreed either explicitly or implicitly to follow the same course of action. Rather, their business judgment has led each to independently follow parallel paths.

Valspar, in a 2017 federal Third Circuit Court of Appeals case, accused DuPont, a supplier of titanium dioxide (pigment used in paint), of conspiring with other suppliers to increase prices.[7] Among other evidence–including meetings and data sharing–Valspar pointed to 31 parallel price increases by DuPont and other suppliers in an oligopolistic (see Chapter 11) market. The court, ruling that Valspar's claim failed to provide sufficient evidence of a conspiracy, concluded that the firms were merely engaging in lawful conscious parallelism. On the other hand, Valspar's case against the other titanium dioxide defendants was heard in a Fourth Circuit federal district court, which interpreted the same set of facts to find "ample evidence" of conspiracy.[8] That case was later settled out of court.

Are We Paying Too Much?

Both government-intervention advocates and free-market champions agree that price-fixing can cripple markets and push prices higher. Consider some prominent price-fixing allegations:

- In 2018, Visa and MasterCard established a $6.2 billion settlement fund in a 13-year court battle after they were accused of engaging in a price-fixing cartel. The two allegedly set arbitrarily high interchange or "swipe" fees for processing card transactions.[9]
- A global criminal investigation of price-fixing and bid-rigging in the auto parts industry has resulted in five separate rounds of class action settlements, totaling more than $1.2 billion. Dozens of companies, including Panasonic, Lear, and Mitsubishi, and many classes of auto parts, such as door handles, air conditioners, and radiators, are involved.

The fifth and final round of settlements was being presented in early 2023 for approval in the U.S. District Court for the Eastern District of Michigan.[10] [To learn more, see **www.autopartsclass.com.**]

- Several price-fixing allegations have been made in the food industry in recent years. For instance, in 2022, Brazilian company JBS SA paid $52.5 million to settle claims that it conspired to limit the supply of beef, and thus inflate its price, in the U.S. market. The company paid a $24.5 million settlement in 2021 for similar claims relating to the sale of pork.[11] Meanwhile, Tyson Foods also agreed in 2021 to pay a $221.5 million settlement of claims alleging that it conspired to inflate the price of chicken.[12] Just two years prior, in 2019, Sunkist and Bumble Bee both agreed to plead guilty to criminal price-fixing in the canned tuna industry and were fined $100 million and $25 million, respectively. Prosecutors alleged they likewise conspired to artificially inflate prices. Chicken of the Sea cooperated with prosecutors and was shielded from penalties. StarKist declared bankruptcy.[13]
- Ending nine years of litigation over alleged conspiracies to fix corn syrup prices, Archer Daniels Midland, A. E. Staley, and others agreed in 2004 to pay $531 million to settle a class action against them.[14] [For a movie account of former ADM executive Mark Whitacre's decision to blow the whistle on the alleged conspiracy, see *The Informant!* starring Matt Damon. The trailer is available at **www.traileraddict.com/trailer/the-informant/trailer**.]
- Price-fixing behavior can touch our lives in surprising ways. A group of women reached an agreement in 2016 with the American Society for Reproductive Medicine to settle claims that the association's published guidelines on human egg donor prices constituted price-fixing. The price guidelines were not mandates, but they were widely followed. The fertility association said the guidelines were needed to prevent coercion and exploitation, but the plaintiff women said they amounted to horizontal price-fixing. The women received financial settlements, and the pricing language was removed from the association's guidelines.[15]

Question

Remember that settlements often do not constitute admissions of wrongdoing. Do you think the guidelines published by the American Society for Reproductive Medicine on human egg donor prices should constitute a per se price-fixing violation? Why or why not?

These are only a few of the many examples of alleged price-fixing conspiracies in recent years. The likely effect of these arrangements, when unlawful, is to harm competition and raise prices. Antitrust expert John M. Connor has estimated that cartels "typically push prices up at least 20 percent and sometimes much more."[16]

PRACTICING ETHICS Antitrust Law and the Price of Beer

College students spend about $5.5 billion on alcohol annually, most of that on beer. That total exceeds what students spend on books, soda, coffee, juice, and milk combined. Could antitrust law affect the consumption, or at least the price, of beer? Perhaps. A group of consumers in Madison, Wisconsin, home of the University of Wisconsin, sued some local bars and the Madison-Dane County Tavern League, Inc., for price-fixing. The plaintiffs claimed that the defendant bars had agreed to fix prices by adopting a "voluntary ban on drink specials." The plaintiffs pointed to a 2002 press release from the "Downtown Tavern Working Group" announcing that drink specials would not be offered after 8 PM on Friday and Saturday nights for "at least a year."

The defendants said the new policy was a self-imposed effort to curb binge drinking, especially by students, and that the policy was a response to pressure from the city and the University of Wisconsin. Further, the defendants said that the press release did not reflect an agreement of any kind and thus could not violate the law because all bar owners remained free to do as they wished. Eventually, the Wisconsin Supreme Court held that the policy was immune from the antitrust laws because the city effectively compelled the arrangement. Given the state legislature's broad grant of regulatory authority over alcohol to municipalities, the court concluded that the legislature must have intended the defendant taverns' actions to be exempt from the antitrust laws.

Questions

1. Is the Madison dispute too trivial and frivolous to justify court time? Explain.
2. Will the market satisfactorily protect youthful drinkers and society? Explain.
3. *a.* How would you expect the Wisconsin Supreme Court decision to have affected the consumption of beer in Madison?
   b. Explain how a "voluntary ban on drink specials" might constitute price-fixing.

Sources: *Eichenseer v. Madison-Dane County Tavern League*, 748 N.W.2d 154 (Wis. 2008) [**www.courtlistener.com**]; and "Frequently Asked Questions about College Binge Drinking," *AlcoholPolicyMD.com*, [**www.alcoholpolicymd.com**].

Real Estate Sales Commissions

The following case examines alleged horizontal price-fixing by Kentucky realtors.

LEGAL BRIEFCASE

Hyland et al. v. Homeservices of America, et al. 771 F.3d 310 (6th Cir. 2014)

Circuit Judge Norris

Class representatives Christopher and Mystic Burnette appeal three rulings by the district court that resulted in judgment for defendant real estate firms, all of which operate in Kentucky. The fourth amended complaint alleged that defendants violated Section 1 of the Sherman Antitrust Act by participating in a horizontal conspiracy to fix the commissions charged in Kentucky real estate transactions at an anti-competitive rate. The certified class consists of people who sold residential real estate in Kentucky from October 11, 2001, to October 11, 2005, and used the services of defendants. Plaintiffs contend the district court erred by granting summary judgment to defendants.

Plaintiffs filed suit in October 2005. The crux of the allegation brought by plaintiffs is that defendants violated the Sherman Act by conspiring to charge a supra-competitive real estate broker commission of 6 percent and thereby injured sellers of residential property.

To become a real estate agent in Kentucky, an individual must be licensed by the Commonwealth's Real Estate Commission (KREC). Agents typically join local realtors' boards, such as the Greater Louisville Association of Realtors, the Lexington-Bluegrass Association of Realtors, and the Kentucky Association of Realtors (KAR).

In 1991, the KREC passed a regulation (the Rebate Ban) that prohibited licensed real estate brokers in Kentucky from offering any item or thing of value, including rebates, to induce clients to retain their services. The United States Department of Justice filed suit in 2005 against the KREC alleging that the Rebate Ban violated Section 1 of the Sherman Act. That suit was settled and the Rebate Ban was abolished.

This action was filed shortly thereafter. The complaint alleges that defendants "combined, conspired and agreed to fix, maintain and inflate real estate broker commissions and associated fees and refuse to compete on the basis of price." Specifically, defendants "have charged a real estate broker commission of 6%, have described this 6% fee as the 'standard' or 'typical' fee, and have habitually refused to negotiate a lower fee." According to the complaint, this collusion resulted in sellers being forced to pay artificially inflated commissions.

EVIDENCE OF CONSPIRACY

An antitrust conspiracy can be established by either direct or circumstantial evidence.

a. Direct Evidence

The district court turned first to the public hearing that was held before the KREC on November 28, 2000. Plaintiffs maintain that the transcript of this hearing represents direct evidence of illegal collusion. The purpose of the hearing was ostensibly to share a survey of inducement laws in other states and to invite comments on the possible repeal of the KREC Rebate Ban. At the hearing, Ray Rector of Rector-Hayden expressed the opinion that the consumer pays for inducements in the form of higher fees or a decreased level of service. Jerry McMahan spoke at greater length and supported maintaining commissions. Doug Myers of Semonin echoed these sentiments: "I'd like to see our competition based on our professional performance, not upon our brokerage fees. . . ." Broker Barbara Campbell, whose agency charged only a 4.5% commission, contended that her clients were contacted by brokers who would tell them that other realtors "would not show my clients' homes to their buyers so long as they continue to do business with Campbell Realty." Another broker, Steven Gavin, reported harassment for offering only 2% to the buyer's broker.

The district court assessed this evidence and concluded that it did not constitute "direct evidence that Defendants conspired to fix real estate commissions at a supra-competitive 6%." The court observed that it had reviewed the transcript of the KREC meeting and found that plaintiffs have taken remarks made by individual realtors "out of context and construed them in a highly-strained manner."

We agree with this assessment. Like the district court, we view Jerry McMahan's statements at the hearing as ambiguous at best and they therefore do not establish direct evidence of a conspiracy. McMahan was highlighting the fact that his "full-service" firm offered more to its clients than his Internet rivals and thereby justified its higher commission rate. Also absent in the record is any comment by McMahan suggesting that brokers negotiate among themselves their respective commission rates. With respect to those who spoke about having undergone harassment for offering lower rates, the district court observed that these speakers are not parties to this action, nor did they implicate defendants.

b. Circumstantial Evidence

Evidence of "conscious parallelism," . . . can support . . . a claim based upon circumstantial evidence. . . . This court has set out the following considerations, sometimes referred to as "plus factors," in determining when circumstantial evidence amounts to a finding of concerted action: (1) whether defendants' actions, if taken independently, would be contrary to their economic interests; (2) product uniformity; (3) whether the defendants have been uniform in their actions; (4) whether the defendants have exchanged or have had the opportunity to exchange information relative to the alleged conspiracy; and (5) whether the defendants have a common motive to conspire or have engaged in a large number of communications.

The district court then reviewed evidence of parallel pricing behavior and the plus factors. It found them to be insufficient to withstand summary judgment. In reaching this conclusion, the court relied upon these conclusions:

- "Plaintiffs' evidence of parallel pricing shows merely that each Defendant had a policy of charging a minimum commission of 6% and that each Defendant occasionally deviated from its respective policy for various reasons."
- "The prevalence of the 6% rate, then, is just as consistent with independent pricing decisions. The existence of a conspiracy cannot be inferred solely on the basis that Defendants tended to charge the same amount for their services."
- "The Sixth Circuit has unequivocally proclaimed that 'setting cooperative sales-commission rates is not price fixing: it has no relation to the amount charged to clients for an agent's service.' Thus, even if it was necessary for a listing broker to offer a 3% buyer's broker commission to the cooperating broker as an incentive, the listing broker is free to charge his client 4%, 5%, 10%, or even 3% plus a flat fee. . . ."
- ". . . [C]harging a standard commission rate across the board and retaining increasing profits from the sale of higher priced homes is consistent with rational business judgment and not probative of an illegal agreement to fix commissions."
- ". . . [M]ere awareness of competitors' commissions does not support an inference that Defendants agreed to conspire."
- With respect to Jerry McMahan's comment at the 2000 KREC meeting that "the most unprofessional thing we can do in this business is cut our commissions," the court stated: ". . . A plausible inference is that Mr. McMahan thought full service brokers should not compete with the Internet brokers by offering inducements in the form of rebates, but should compete with the Internet brokers by making their services worth what they charge—whatever that may be."
- "Plaintiffs have presented no evidence of any parallel change or impact on Defendants' pricing decisions after any alleged communication or invitation that was made at the KREC public hearing or any other meeting between Defendants."

Having reviewed this evidence, which it characterized as circumstantial, the court held that "[p]laintiffs have not presented sufficient evidence to meet the stringent summary judgment standard in antitrust cases."

. . . [W]e agree with its conclusion that the circumstantial evidence is insufficient. [T]he evidence does not, as it must, eliminate a finding that the same actions are "equally consistent with independent conduct." . . .

The judgment of the district court is affirmed.

Questions

1. *a.* Who are the alleged conspirators in this price-fixing dispute, and how did they allegedly fix prices?
   b. Who won this case at the federal district court, and why did that court rule as it did?
   c. In general, is parallel pricing a lawful behavior? Explain.
2. *a.* Why did the federal district court and the 6th Circuit Court of Appeals require a showing of "plus factors" to demonstrate that the realtors had engaged in price-fixing?
   b. Why was the KREC Rebate Ban challenged by the U.S. Justice Department?
3. Why did the defendant real estate firms win this case?
4. Until late 2016, the National Football League (NFL) had required each of its 32 member teams to set minimum prices for all tickets resold on secondary markets sanctioned by the League.
   a. Why did the NFL care about the price at which game tickets were resold?
   b. Was that requirement lawful? Explain.
   c. Could the teams individually and independently set a price floor for reselling tickets on their websites? Explain.
5. The "Three Tenors"—Luciano Pavarotti, Placido Domingo, and Jose Carreras—recorded a 1990 World Cup concert, distributed by Polygram, and a 1994 World Cup concert, distributed by Warner. Polygram and Warner subsequently agreed to jointly distribute and share profits from the 1998 World Cup Three Tenors concert. The 1998 recording apparently was less "new and exciting" than had been hoped. Concerned that sales of the earlier recordings would drain interest from the 1998 recording, Polygram and Warner agreed to cease all discounting and advertising of the two earlier recordings for several weeks surrounding the release of the 1998 album. In 2001, the Federal Trade Commission issued complaints against Polygram and Warner. Those complaints eventually reached the District of Columbia Federal Circuit Court of Appeals, where Polygram and Warner defended themselves by arguing that the agreement was good for competition in that it increased the joint venture's profitability from new recordings and it eliminated free riding by each company (for the 1990 and 1994 recordings) on the joint venture's 1998 marketing.
   a. What antitrust violation was alleged by the Federal Trade Commission?
   b. What is free riding, and why is it a problem?
   c. How would you decide the case? Explain. See *Polygram v. Federal Trade Commission,* 416 F.3d 29 (D.C. Cir. 2005) [**https://law.justia.com**].
6. Assume that 10 real estate firms operate locally in the city of Gotham. Further assume that each charges a seven percent commission on all residential sales.
   a. Does that uniformity of prices, in and of itself, constitute price-fixing? Explain.
   b. Assume we have evidence that the firms agreed to set the 7 percent level. What defense would be raised against a price-fixing charge?
   c. Would that defense succeed? Explain. See *McLain v. Real Estate Board of New Orleans, Inc.,* 444 U.S. 232 (1980) [**https://supreme.justia.com**].

Refusal to Deal and Group Boycotts

Principal Legislation: Sherman Act, Section 1

LO 10-5
Describe the characteristics of a group boycott.

In America, are we free to enter into business relationships with whomever we prefer? Generally, yes, but antitrust problems sometimes emerge. When does a *refusal to deal* with another raise antitrust issues? The clearest problem is a *horizontal group boycott,* where competitors agree not to deal with a supplier, customer, or another competitor. Presumably, Ford and GM could not jointly refuse to buy tires, for example, from Bridgestone. Such arrangements so thoroughly subvert the market that they ordinarily are *per se* violations of Section 1 of the Sherman Act; thus, they do not require a detailed evaluation of competitive harm and benefits, although a showing of market power by those in the group may be required. A buyer or seller's unilateral (individual) refusal to deal sometimes raises antitrust concerns if the refusing party is a monopolist and harm to competition can be proven.[17] However, the Supreme Court has severely restricted the use of the "unilateral refusal" doctrine.[18]

A jury found a distributor-led conspiracy.

A conflict in the steel industry illustrates "refusal to deal" reasoning. Two steel industry salespeople in 2011 founded a new steel distributor, MM Steel, after leaving their sales jobs with two other steel distributors, American Alloy (AA) and Chapel. Apparently upset that their former salespeople had established a new competitor, AA and Chapel allegedly agreed to pressure steel manufacturers JSW, Nucor, and SSAB not to sell to MM. MM then sued the distributors and manufacturers, alleging an illegal group boycott. SSAB settled before trial, but the balance of the litigation continued.[19] A jury found a distributor-led conspiracy, and that decision was affirmed on appeal in 2015.[20] [For a trade regulation blog, see **http://traderegulation.blogspot.com**.]

Clarett Boycotted by the NFL?

Antitrust shapes all dimensions of our lives, as football running back Maurice Clarett learned when he tried to enter the 2004 National Football League (NFL) draft. As a freshman, Clarett led Ohio State University to an undefeated season in 2002. However, he was ineligible for college football in his sophomore year because of allegations that he accepted improper benefits and lied about doing so. Clarett then tried to enter the NFL draft but was barred by a League rule requiring players to be out of high school for at least three seasons. Clarett sued the NFL, claiming its eligibility rules violated federal antitrust laws by effectively allowing competing teams to agree among themselves to boycott certain players (including Clarett). Clarett won at the federal district court level, but he lost on appeal when the court held that the eligibility rule is exempt from the antitrust laws. The NFL eligibility rule is the product of a collective bargaining agreement between the League and the players' union, the National Football League Players Association. Antitrust promotes competition, while unions restrict it in various ways, but in balancing those competing interests, Congress and the courts have long granted unions certain exemptions from antitrust laws. The Supreme Court subsequently declined to review Clarett's case.

In 2010, Clarett was released from prison where he had served a three-and-one-half-year sentence for aggravated robbery and carrying a concealed weapon. Following his release, Clarett played football with the Omaha Nighthawks and published a book about his life. He engages in public speaking and operates "Red Zone" to provide social, behavioral, and housing services in Youngstown and Columbus, Ohio, and was featured in an ESPN *30 for 30* episode, "The Youngstown Boys."

Questions

1. Should Clarett and future football players be free to sell their services on the open market?
2. Is the NFL correct to encourage players to stay in college and mature before entering professional football? Explain.

3. Congressman Steve Cohen, Democrat of Tennessee, wrote a letter in 2009 to the National Basketball Association (NBA) and the NBA players union asking them to repeal the rule requiring players to be 19 years old and one year removed from high school before they are eligible for the NBA. The rule is part of the collective-bargaining agreement between the league and the players. Cohen labeled the law "a vestige of slavery." Discussions have been underway between the NBA and the NBA Players' Association, concerning the potential age change.
   a. What do you think Cohen meant by his "vestige of slavery" remark?
   b. Does the rule constitute an unlawful restraint of trade? Explain.
   c. Do you agree that the rule should be repealed? Explain.

Sources: *Clarett v. National Football League,* 369 F.3d 124 (2d Cir. 2004) [**https://law.justia.com**]; Colleen Marshall, "Maurice Clarett Opens Up about How He Found His Calling After Prison," *WCMH-TV,* July 23, 2018 [**www.nbc4i.com**]; Pete Thamel, "Congressman Asks N.B.A. and Union to Rescind Age Minimum for Players," *The New York Times,* June 4, 2009 [**www.nytimes.com**]; and Adam Rittenberg, "Inside the Latest Chapter of Former Ohio State Start Maurice Clarett's Life Turnaround," *ESPN,* May 12, 2020 [**www.ESPN.com**].

Questions

1. Baptist Eye Institute (BEI), a group of nonspecialized ophthalmologists in Jacksonville, Florida, controlling approximately 15 percent of the referral market, sent nearly all of its retina cases to the Florida Retina Institute. Is BEI engaging in an unlawful group boycott against plaintiff Retina Associates, a retina care provider in competition with the Florida Retina Institute? Explain. See *Retina Associates P.A. v. Southern Baptist Hospital of Florida Inc.,* 105 F.3d 1376 (11th Cir. 1997)[**https://law.justia.com**].
2. Discon, a telephone salvage company, sold services to MECo, a subsidiary of NYNEX, a phone company for the New York/New England area. MECo switched from Discon to AT&T Technologies, a Discon competitor, and paid a higher price to AT&T than it had paid to Discon. Discon claimed that the buyer and NYNEX then received a rebate from AT&T at the end of the year. Discon argued that NYNEX was able to pass on its higher costs to its customers because NYNEX was a part of a regulated phone market. Discon claimed that NYNEX, its subsidiaries, and AT&T were engaging in a group boycott in violation of the Sherman Act in order to drive Discon out of the market. How would you decide? Explain. See *NYNEX Corp. v. Discon, Inc.,* 119 S. Ct. 493 (1998) [**https://supreme.justia.com**].

Part Three—Vertical Restraints

We have been studying unfair trade practices by competitors–that is, horizontal restraints of trade. Now we turn to antitrust violations on the vertical axis–that is, restraints involving agreements between two or more members of a supply chain (such as a manufacturer and a retailer of that manufacturer's products). *Horizontal restraints* are those arising from an agreement among the *competitors* themselves, while *vertical restraints* ordinarily are those imposed by *suppliers* on their *buyers*. Horizontal restraints are sometimes *per se* unlawful, while vertical restraints are ordinarily resolved under the rule of reason. Horizontal restraints often eliminate competition, thereby undermining the power of the market, while vertical restraints may be either harmful or beneficial to competition.

American Express Vertical arrangements are sometimes of a nonprice character, as was the case in the important 2018 Supreme Court *American Express* decision, in which the credit card company was sued by the United States and a number of individual states for restraint of trade under the Sherman Act. Amex forbade merchants who accepted its card from encouraging customers to use other cards, like Discover, that charged lower fees to merchants than Amex. Encouraging consumers to use the cheaper cards presumably would, over time, increase competition and cause Amex and others to lower their fees, thus benefiting consumers. The Court, however, ruled for Amex by a 5–4 margin saying that the plaintiffs had failed to show that credit card transaction prices were higher than would be expected in a competitive market, or that Amex stifled competition. Amex's higher merchant fees, the majority reasoned, were a result of the higher value of Amex services, along with the cost of its transactions. Card fees in the United States are somewhat higher than in other markets, although rewards soften them to some extent. Critics argue that this decision may further entrench the dominant cards issuers, raise prices, and weaken antitrust enforcement across a broad range of products and services.[21]

E-Books: Apple Fixing Prices?

The following price-fixing case involves Apple's e-book marketing practices. This case illustrates some of the principles of horizontal price-fixing, as discussed above, along with elements of vertical price-fixing (resale price maintenance), as discussed below.

The Kindle e-book reader was introduced by Amazon in 2007, followed by Barnes & Noble's Nook reader (2009) and Apple's iPad (2010). Amazon priced many of its e-book best sellers at a very attractive $9.99 (often below its cost) to increase demand for the Kindle, to solidify its market position, and to encourage broader shopping at Amazon. By some measures, Amazon's share of digital book sales peaked as high as 90 percent of the market. Apple and several book publishers, including HarperCollins and Penguin—apparently fearing Amazon's expanding power in the e-book market—allegedly agreed to change e-book pricing from Amazon's "wholesale" model, where Amazon itself set e-book retail prices, to an "agency" model where the publishers themselves set the retail price of books (for example, $14.99). Retailers, including Apple and Barnes & Noble, then kept a 30 percent share. Having achieved an agreement with Apple, the publishers were allegedly able to compel Amazon to accept the same terms. Thereafter, Amazon's e-book market share reportedly fell to about 60 percent.

In 2012, the Justice Department and about 30 states filed a civil complaint against Apple and five book publishers, claiming that the defendant publishers had conspired among themselves and with Apple to fix prices in violation of the Sherman Act. The publishers denied misconduct but reached a settlement, agreeing to pay $170 million to consumers. In their defense, the publishers and Apple claimed they acted independently in implementing agency pricing, and Apple argued that its entry in the market strengthened competition.

Relying principally on horizontal price-fixing reasoning, a federal judge in 2013 found Apple guilty of colluding with the publishers to fix prices. The judge ordered Apple to modify its contracts and submit to oversight. Apple lost on appeal, and a request for Supreme Court review was denied. Apple was ordered to pay a $450 million settlement, mostly in credits to some 23 million consumers who overpaid.

Amazon has maintained its dominant position in the e-book market, but e-book sales have slipped and physical bookstores have enjoyed a considerable resurgence. Is Amazon abusing the book market?

Sources: Alexandra Alter, "The Plot Twist: E-Book Sales Slip, and Print Is Far from Dead," *The New York Times,* September 22, 2015 **[www.nytimes.com]**; Thomas Catan, Jeffrey A. Trachtenberg, and Chad Bray, "U.S. Alleges E-Book Scheme," *The Wall Street Journal,* April 11, 2012 **[www.wsj.com]**; and *United States v. Apple,* 791 F.3d 290 (2d Cir. 2015)**[https://law.justia.com]**, *cert. denied, Apple v. United States,* 136 S. Ct. 1376 (2016).

Resale Price Maintenance

Principal Legislation: Sherman Act, Section 1; Federal Trade Commission Act, Section 5

LO 10-6 Define resale price maintenance.

Manufacturers and distributors often seek to specify the price at which their customers may resell their products, a policy we might think of as vertical price-fixing but that is formally called *resale price maintenance.* Having sold its product, why should a manufacturer or distributor seek to influence the price at which the product is resold? We note five primary reasons: (1) establishing a minimum price to enhance the product's reputation, (2) helping retailers make a profit sufficient to provide customer service, (3) preventing discount stores from pricing beneath full-price retail outlets, (4) preventing *free riding,* and (5) reducing *showrooming*–where consumers educate themselves about products in brick-and-mortar stores and then buy online after making instant price comparisons.

A *unilateral* specification of a resale price, with nothing more involved, has long been permissible. Under the Supreme Court's 1919 *Colgate*[22] decision, sellers can lawfully engage in resale price maintenance if they do nothing more than announce the prices at which their products are to be resold, and unilaterally refuse to deal with anyone who does not adhere to those prices. On the other hand, an actual agreement between a seller and a buyer dictating the price at which the buyer may resell the product was, for decades, a *per se* violation of the law. Then, in 1997, the Supreme Court ruled that agreements specifying *maximum* resale prices would no longer be considered *per se* violations and must be evaluated under the rule of reason.[23] In the 2007 *Leegin* case that follows, the Supreme Court overturned a nearly 100-year-old precedent set in the *Dr. Miles* case[24] to rule that agreements specifying *minimum* resale prices also must be analyzed under the rule of reason; that is, those agreements are no longer *per se* violations of the law. Rather, they must be considered on a case-by-case basis weighing their pro- and anticompetitive effects.

Products, Inc. v. PSKS, dba Kay's Kloset 551 U.S. 877 (2007)

Justice Kennedy

I

Petitioner, Leegin Creative Leather Products, Inc. (Leegin), designs, manufactures, and distributes leather goods and accessories. In 1991, Leegin began to sell belts under the brand name "Brighton." The Brighton brand has now expanded into a variety of women's fashion accessories. It is sold across the United States in over 5,000 retail establishments, for the most part independent, small boutiques and specialty stores. . . . Leegin asserts that, at least for its products, small retailers treat customers better, provide customers more services, and make their shopping experience more satisfactory than do larger, often impersonal retailers. [Leegin's president Jerry] Kohl explained: "[W]e want the consumers to get a different experience than they get in Sam's Club or in Wal-Mart. And you can't get that kind of experience or support or customer service from a store like Wal-Mart."

Respondent PSKS, Inc., operates Kay's Kloset, a women's apparel store in Lewisville, Texas. Kay's Kloset buys from about 75 different manufacturers and at one time sold the Brighton brand. It first started purchasing Brighton goods from Leegin in 1995. Once it began selling the brand, the store promoted Brighton. For example, it ran Brighton advertisements and had Brighton days in the store. Kay's Kloset became the destination retailer in the area to buy Brighton products. Brighton was the store's most important brand and once accounted for 40 to 50 percent of its profits.

In 1997, Leegin instituted the "Brighton retail pricing and Promotion Policy." Following the policy, Leegin refused to sell to retailers that discounted Brighton goods below suggested prices. . . . In the letter to retailers establishing the policy, Leegin stated:

> In this age of mega stores like Macy's, Bloomingdales, May Co. and others, consumers are perplexed by promises of product quality and support of product which we believe is lacking in these large stores. Consumers are further confused by the ever popular sale, sale, sale, etc.
>
> We, at Leegin, choose to break away from the pack by selling [at] specialty stores; specialty stores that can offer the customer great quality merchandise, superb service, and support the Brighton product 365 days a year on a consistent basis. . . .

Leegin adopted the policy to give its retailers sufficient margins to provide customers the service central to its distribution strategy. It also expressed concern that discounting harmed Brighton's brand image and reputation.

In December 2002, Leegin discovered Kay's Kloset had been marking down Brighton's entire line by 20 percent. Kay's Kloset contended it placed Brighton products on sale to compete with nearby retailers who also were undercutting Leegin's suggested prices. Leegin, nonetheless, requested that Kay's Kloset cease discounting. Its request refused, Leegin stopped selling to the store. The loss of the Brighton brand had a considerable negative impact on the store's revenue from sales.

PSKS sued Leegin in the United States District Court for the Eastern District of Texas. It alleged, among other claims, that Leegin had violated the antitrust laws by "enter[ing] into agreements with retailers to charge only those prices fixed by Leegin."

The jury agreed with PSKS and awarded it $1.2 million.

The Court of Appeals for the Fifth Circuit affirmed. We granted certiorari to determine whether vertical minimum resale price maintenance agreements should continue to be treated as *per se* unlawful.

II

Resort to *per se* rules is confined to restraints . . . "that would always or almost always tend to restrict competition and decrease output." *Business Electronics,* 485 U.S. at 723. . . .

As a consequence, the *per se* rule is appropriate only after courts have had considerable experience with the type of restraint at issue, and only if courts can predict with confidence that it would be invalidated in all or almost all instances under the rule of reason. . . .

III

The Court has interpreted *Dr. Miles Medical Co. v. John D. Park & Sons Co.,* 220 U.S. 373 (1911), as establishing a *per se* rule against a vertical agreement between a manufacturer and its distributor to set minimum resale prices. . . .

The reasons upon which *Dr. Miles* relied do not justify a *per se* rule. As a consequence, it is necessary to examine . . . the economic effects of vertical agreements to fix minimum resale prices, and to determine whether the *per se* rule is nonetheless appropriate.

A

Though each side of the debate can find sources to support its position, it suffices to say here that economics literature is replete with procompetitive justifications for a manufacturer's use of resale price maintenance.

The justifications for vertical price restraints are similar to those for other vertical restraints. Minimum resale price maintenance can stimulate interbrand competition—the competition among manufacturers selling different brands of the same type of product—by reducing intrabrand competition—the competition among retailers selling the same brand. The promotion of interbrand competition is important because "the primary purpose of the antitrust laws is to protect [this type of] competition." *Khan,* 522 U.S. at 15. . . .

Absent vertical price restraints, the retail services that enhance interbrand competition might be under provided. This is because discounting retailers can free ride on retailers who furnish services and then capture some of the increased demand those services generate.

Resale price maintenance, in addition, can increase interbrand competition by facilitating market entry for new firms and brands. "[N]ew manufacturers and manufacturers entering new markets can use the restrictions in order to induce competent and aggressive retailers to make the kind of investment of capital and labor that is often required in the distribution of products unknown to the consumer." *GTE Sylvania,* 433 U.S. at 55. . . .

Resale price maintenance can also increase interbrand competition by encouraging retailer services that would not be provided even absent free riding. It may be difficult and inefficient for a manufacturer to make and enforce a contract with a retailer specifying the different services the retailer must perform. Offering the retailer a guaranteed margin and threatening termination if it does not live up to expectations may be the most efficient way to expand the manufacturer's market share by inducing the retailer's performance and allowing it to use its own initiative and experience in providing valuable services.

B

While vertical agreements setting minimum resale prices can have procompetitive justifications, they may have anticompetitive effects in other cases; and unlawful price fixing, designed solely to obtain monopoly profits, is an ever-present temptation. Resale price maintenance may, for example, facilitate a manufacturer cartel. An unlawful cartel will seek to discover if some manufacturers are undercutting the cartel's fixed prices. Resale price maintenance could assist the cartel in identifying price-cutting manufacturers who benefit from the lower prices they offer. Resale price maintenance, furthermore, could discourage a manufacturer from cutting prices to retailers with the concomitant benefit of cheaper prices to consumers.

Vertical price restraints also "might be used to organize cartels at the retailer level." *Business Electronics,* at 725–726. A group of retailers might collude to fix prices to consumers and then compel a manufacturer to aid the unlawful arrangement with resale price maintenance.

A horizontal cartel among competing manufacturers or competing retailers that decreases output or reduces competition in order to increase price is, and ought to be, *per se* unlawful. To the extent a vertical agreement setting minimum resale prices is entered upon to facilitate either type of cartel, it, too, would need to be held unlawful under the rule of reason.

A manufacturer with market power . . . might use resale price maintenance to give retailers an incentive not to sell the products of smaller rivals or new entrants. As should be evident, the potential anticompetitive consequences of vertical price restraints must not be ignored or underestimated.

C

Notwithstanding the risk of unlawful conduct, it cannot be stated with any degree of confidence that resale price maintenance "always or almost always tend[s] to restrict competition and decrease output." Vertical agreements establishing minimum resale prices can have either procompetitive or anticompetitive effects, depending upon the circumstances in which they are formed.

Respondent contends, nonetheless, that . . . the *per se* rule is justified because a vertical price restraint can lead to higher prices for the manufacturer's goods. . . . Respondent is mistaken in relying on pricing effects absent a further showing of anticompetitive conduct. . . . For, as has been indicated already, the antitrust laws are designed primarily to protect interbrand competition, from which lower prices can later result. . . .

Respondent's argument, furthermore, overlooks that, in general, the interests of manufacturers and consumers are aligned with respect to retailer profit margins. . . . A manufacturer has no incentive to overcompensate retailers with unjustified margins. The retailers, not the manufacturer, gain from higher retail prices. The manufacturer often loses; interbrand competition reduces its competitiveness and market share because consumers will "substitute a different brand of the same product." See *Business Electronics,* at 725. . . .

Resale price maintenance, it is true, does have economic dangers. If the rule of reason were to apply to vertical price restraints, courts would have to be diligent in eliminating their anticompetitive uses from the market. This is a realistic objective. . . .

As a final matter, that a dominant manufacturer or retailer can abuse resale price maintenance for anticompetitive purposes may not be a serious concern unless the relevant entity has market power. If a retailer lacks market power, manufacturers likely can sell their goods through rival retailers.

For all of the foregoing reasons, we think that were the Court considering the issue as an original matter, the rule of reason, not a *per se* rule of unlawfulness, would be the appropriate standard to judge vertical price restraints.

Reversed.

Questions

1. *a.* What potential pro-competitive considerations were cited by the court in supporting a rule of reason approach to resale price maintenance?
   b. What potential anticompetitive considerations were cited by the court?
2. Could we fairly conclude from the *Leegin* decision that resale price maintenance agreements are now "*per se* legal"? Explain.
3. Explain why the Court said the seller's market power is an important consideration in assessing the legality of a resale price maintenance agreement.

Leegin in Practice (the Law)

The *Leegin* ruling seems to affirm the Supreme Court's support for free-market principles and restrained judicial intervention in business practice. Accordingly, more competition and better service should follow, but critics think the decision simply allows manufacturers to pressure and cut out discounters with the result that consumers pay higher prices. Of course, if anticompetitive behavior emerges, it still can be attacked under the rule of reason, and some states continue to treat resale price maintenance as a *per se* violation of law. Similarly, the European Union generally forbids resale price maintenance, unless clear efficiencies are identified.

Leegin in Practice (the Business Response)

Many manufacturers practice resale price maintenance. Consider contact lenses. As of 2015, 40 million Americans wore them, and they spent about $4 billion annually on those lenses.[25] Approximately 90 percent of lens manufacturing is controlled by four companies: Alcon, Bausch & Lomb, Cooper Vision, and Johnson & Johnson.[26] To protect optometrists' lens sales from being undercut by discounters like Costco and 1-800-CONTACTS, those manufacturers have allegedly worked together to impose price floors on the retail sale of lenses. In response, the state of Utah (home to 1-800-CONTACTS) passed a law in 2015 forbidding any practice that "has the effect of fixing or otherwise controlling the price that a contact lens retailer charges or advertises."[27] The Utah statute has survived court challenges. Johnson & Johnson and Alcon say they have discontinued minimum pricing policies. Nationwide, several settlements have been reached in litigation against lens manufacturers.

Questions

1. Is the *Leegin* decision good or bad for consumers? Explain.
2. Krist Oil, a family-owned gasoline company with more than 70 locations, was required by Wisconsin law to mark up its retail gasoline prices in that state by a minimum of 9.18 percent above cost. Krist wanted to lower its prices. Some 26 states reportedly have minimum markup laws of one form or another.
   a. Why would some states forbid most retail sales below cost and/or require minimum markups beyond cost?
   b. Are those laws good public policy in your view? Explain. See C.J. Szafir and Patrick Gleason, "Cross Country: These Prices Are a Steal – and in Some States, That's Illegal," *The Wall Street Journal,* January 27, 2018 [**www.wsj.com**]; and Bryan Polcyn, "'How Do You Survive?' Small Station Owners Say Costco's Gas Prices Are Too Low," *Fox6Milwaukee,* February 28, 2018 [**https://fox6now.com**].

Vertical Territorial and Customer Restraints

Principal Legislation: Sherman Act, Section 1; Federal Trade Commission Act, Section 5

Manufacturers sometimes specify where and/or to whom a product may be resold. Those restrictions typically afford an exclusive sales territory to a distributor. Similarly, manufacturers may prevent distributors from selling to some classes of customers. For example, a distributor might be forbidden to sell to an unfranchised retailer. Such arrangements necessarily retard or eliminate *intrabrand* competition. Because price and service competition among dealers in the same brand ordinarily benefits the consumer, the courts have frequently struck down such arrangements. Still, those territorial and customer allocations also have merits. The *GTE Sylvania* case[28] acknowledged those virtues and established the rule that vertical restrictions are to be judged case-by-case, balancing interbrand and intrabrand competitive effects while recognizing that interbrand competition is the primary concern of antitrust law. Thus, the rule of reason is to be applied to vertical territorial and customer restraints.

Tying Arrangements

Principal Legislation: Clayton Act, Section 3; Sherman Act, Sections 1 and 2; Federal Trade Commission Act, Section 5

LO 10-7
Explain the requirements for establishing an unlawful tying arrangement.

> Clayton Act, Section 3. That it shall be unlawful for any person engaged in commerce, in the course of such commerce, to lease or make a sale or contract for sale of goods . . . or other commodities . . . or fix a price charged therefore, or discount from or rebate upon, such price, on the condition, agreement, or understanding that the lessee or purchaser thereof shall not use or deal in the goods . . . or other commodities of a competitor or competitors of the lessor or seller, where the effect of such lease, sale, or contract for sale or such condition, agreement, or understanding may be to substantially lessen competition or tend to create a monopoly in any line of commerce.

Tying arrangements (sometimes called *bundling*) are another form of nonprice vertical restraint. Typically, tying arrangements permit a customer to buy or lease a desired product (the tying product) only if the customer also buys or leases another, less desirable product (the tied product).

McDonald's does not violate antitrust law when it bundles a hamburger, fries, and soft drink as a "meal," in part because customers are also allowed to buy the three products separately, and because consumers can buy similar products at similar prices in many other stores.

But the European Commission, Europe's antitrust authority, fined Google 4.34 billion euros in 2018 for, among other things, imposing allegedly unlawful tying arrangements on makers of devices. The Commission concluded that Google stifled innovation and harmed competition by requiring makers of Android-based smartphones and tablets to pre-install Google Search and the Google Chrome browser to gain access to the Google Play store with its games, music, movies, and much more.[29] Google appealed the decision to the European General Court but lost. In September 2022, the court upheld the European Commission's finding but reduced the fine slightly from 4.34 to 4.125 billion euros (approximately $4.13 billion).[30] The case was one of three, with total fines exceeding 8 billion euros. Earlier, in May 2021, the tech giant lost the first of the three appeals.[31] Despite challenging the

EU Commission's findings, Google did change its sales practices in Europe by, for example, offering an easily accessible choice of browser and search engines to new and existing Android users.

[See Chapter 11 for a discussion of Microsoft's historic 1998 antitrust battle over its alleged practice of tying its Internet Explorer browser (the tied product) to its dominant Windows operating system (the tying product).]

The Law

Tying arrangements raise two primary antitrust concerns: (1) A party who already enjoys market power over the tying product is able to extend that power into the tied product market, and (2) competitors in the tied product market are foreclosed from equal access to that market.

The basic tying violation test has the following elements:

1. The existence of separate products; that is, there are two products present rather than two components of one product, or two entirely separate products that just happen to be elements in a single transaction.
2. A requirement that the purchase of one of the products (the tying product) is conditioned on the purchase of the other product (the tied product). Step 2 is sometimes labelled *coercion.*
3. The seller has market power in the tying product.
4. There is substantial impact on commerce in the tied product market. (Some courts require a substantial anticompetitive effect in the tied product market.)

Proof of all four elements establishes *per se* illegality. When all four cannot be satisfied, the analysis may proceed on a rule-of-reason basis, weighing pro- and anticompetitive considerations. Critics argue that tying arrangements often enhance consumer welfare and, as such, the *per se* approach should be overturned, as in the *Leegin* case set out earlier in this chapter.

Ozzy Osbourne, Tying Arrangements, and Nice Bites

Musician Ozzy Osbourne sued Anschutz Entertainment Group (AEG) for imposing an allegedly unlawful tying arrangement–it required Osbourne to schedule his Los Angeles show in the AEG-owned Los Angeles Staples Center if he wished to perform in London's O2 Arena (also owned by AEG) during his 2018–19 concert tour. Osbourne wanted to perform in the O2 Arena. However, in Los Angeles, he preferred The Forum, controlled by AEG rival Madison Square Garden Company, over the Staples Center. Osbourne argued that AEG was using its market power in the London market to harm competition in the Los Angeles market. The lawsuit was dismissed after AEG agreed to discontinue its block-booking practice. Goodwill all around did not ensue, however. In a public statement about the case, AEG appeared to disrespectfully reference Osbourne's occasional concert practice of biting the heads off of animals, to which Osbourne's wife, Sharon, said, "If you're interested, Ozzy and I have got something nice for you [to] bite on–our [. . . holes]."

Source: Kory Grow, "Adding Anschutz to Injury: Sharon Osbourne Blasts AEG over Ozzy Lawsuit," *Rolling Stone,* September 25, 2018 **[www.rollingstone.com]**.

Franchise Tying?

The following case examines tying allegations in the context of Shell and Texaco gas station franchises. The case turns, in part, on market definition, which we address more thoroughly in Chapter 11. Briefly, to establish market power in the tying product, the market itself must be defined. In doing so, we consider the geographic market (where the product is sold in commercially significant quantities) and the product market (those products that are interchangeable and thus compete, one with the other with one another).

LEGAL BRIEFCASE

Rick-Mik Enterprises, Inc. v. Equilon Enterprises, LLC

532 F.3d 963 (9th Cir. 2008)

Judge King

Equilon Enterprises, LLC ("Equilon") does business as Shell Oil Products. Equilon's standard franchise agreement requires its franchisees, Shell and Texaco gasoline stations, to use Equilon to process credit-card transactions. In addition to payment for sales of petroleum products, Equilon allegedly gets (1) transaction fees associated with the processing, or (2) some kind of unspecified "kickback" from unidentified banks that process the transactions, or both. Rick-Mik Enterprises, Inc., Mike M. Madani, and Alfred Buczkowski (collectively "Rick-Mik") are Equilon franchisees who—on behalf of themselves and other, similarly situated Equilon franchisees—allege that Equilon violated antitrust laws by illegally tying two distinct products (the franchises and the credit-card processing services). Rick-Mik contends franchisees could pay lower transaction fees from others for credit-card processing. . . .

The district court dismissed the antitrust and related state-law counts. . . .

DISCUSSION

Tying Claim

a. The market power allegations are flawed.

The alleged tying product here is gasoline franchises. Rick-Mik has a contract for an Equilon franchise to sell Shell branded gasoline and diesel. The alleged tied-product is credit-card processing services. Rick-Mik alleges it cannot get a franchise without the "tied" credit-card processing services.

Rick-Mik's complaint does not allege that Equilon has market power in the relevant market, which is the market for the tying product—gasoline franchises. Indeed, other than stating that "[Equilon] rank[s] number one in the industry in branded gasoline stations," there are no specific allegations at all as to the franchise market. The complaint alleges nothing about, for example, what percentage of gasoline franchises are Equilon's (Shell/Texaco) as compared to other franchises like Chevron, Mobil, Marathon Oil, or Union 76. There are no factual allegations as to the percentage of gasoline retail sales that are made through *non-franchise* outlets. There are no factual allegations regarding the amount of power or control that Equilon has over prospective franchisees. There are no factual allegations regarding the relative difficulty of a franchisee to switch franchise brands.

If Equilon lacks market power in the gasoline-franchise market, there can be no cognizable tying claim. For, in that case, Equilon has no power to force, exploit, or coerce a franchisee to purchase a tied-product such as credit card processing (if the processing is a distinct product for tying purposes) or to affect competition in the tied-product market. Such an arrangement would not raise antitrust concerns.

Rick-Mik argues that it alleged sufficient facts to *infer* that Equilon has sufficient economic power in the gasoline-franchise market, which has significant barriers to entry. It points to statistics indicating Equilon is an important player in the petroleum industry. According to . . . the complaint: (1) Equilon sells petroleum products to approximately 9,000 Shell and Texaco-branded retail outlets; (2) it ranks first in the industry in branded gasoline stations; (3) at 13 percent of the market, it ranks first in total gallons of gasoline sold in the United States; (4) it has annual gross revenues of approximately $24 billion; (5) it is number one or two in gasoline market share in 17 states; (6) it has four refineries, refining approximately 753,000 barrels of petroleum products per day and owns a

50 percent interest in Motiva's three refineries, refining approximately 865,000 barrels of petroleum products per day; (7) it owns an interest in approximately 10,000 miles of pipeline used to transport its petroleum products throughout the United States; and (8) it serves, on average, more than six million customers per day and sells approximately 19 billion gallons of gasoline per year, most of which is purchased by customers' credit or debit cards issued by thousands of banks, banking associations and financial institutions throughout the United States.

All of those allegations, however, relate to the *retail* gasoline market—a market where Rick-Mik is a seller—not the relevant market for franchises where it is a buyer. Further, the statistics alleged in the complaint do not distinguish between franchise-based sales and other potential types of sales (e.g., sales by directly owned outlets or sales to other distributors). Thus, the complaint fails to allege market power in the relevant market.

Nor is Rick-Mik's complaint saved by the allegation that "Shell and Texaco-branded gasolines are protected by various trademarks, copyrights and patents providing Equilon sufficient economic power over Plaintiffs in connection with its tying products to appreciably restrain competition in the tied-product market." . . . Because intellectual property rights are no longer presumed to confer market power, *see Illinois Toolworks Inc.*, 547 U.S. at 42–43, Rick-Mik's conclusory allegation that Equilon's intellectual property rights nonetheless do confer market power, unaccompanied by supporting facts, is insufficient.

Finally, the complaint's allegation of a contractual franchise relationship also fails to plead market power. A tying claim generally requires that the defendant's economic power be derived from the market, not from a contractual relationship that the plaintiff has entered into voluntarily. *See, e.g., Queen City Pizza, Inc.*, 124 F.3d at 443 ("where the defendant's 'power' to 'force' plaintiffs to purchase the alleged tying product stems not from the market, but from plaintiffs' contractual agreement to purchase the tying product, no claim will lie.")

b. Credit-card processing is not a distinct product.

There is another fatal flaw in Rick-Mik's complaint. Equilon's franchises are not a separate and distinct product from the credit-card processing services that are part of the franchise.

Franchises, almost by definition, necessarily consist of "bundled" and related products or services—not separate products.

With franchises, "the proper inquiry is . . . whether [the allegedly tied-products] are integral components of the business method being franchised. Where the challenged aggregation is an essential ingredient of the franchised system's formula for success, there is but a single product and no tie in exists as a matter of law." *Principe v. McDonald's Corp.*, 631 F.2d 303, 309 (4th Cir. 1980).

Here, Equilon's credit card services are an essential part of its franchise. Its agreement authorizes Equilon to use credit card proceeds to pay off a franchisee's account (i.e., money the franchisee owes Equilon for the gasoline Equilon delivers to the franchisee). The agreement also authorizes Equilon to charge or refund unauthorized transactions to the franchisee, helping secure the integrity of point-of-sale transactions.

Equilon points to the many other areas which are part and parcel of a franchise: signs, advertising, marketing, appearance, as well as methods of delivery and payment. Similarly, the method of receiving and processing credit transactions is an integral part of the franchise's operation. The franchise and the method of processing credit transactions are not separate products, but part of a single product (the franchise).

With franchises, the franchisee knows the contractual limitations and duties before entering into the contract. A complaint about such contractual obligations is not an antitrust matter.

Affirmed.

Questions

1. *a.* Identify the purported tying and tied products in the *Rik-Mik* case.
   b. Explain how Rik-Mik attempted to establish that Equilon had market power in the tying product.
2. How does Rik-Mik claim to have been harmed by the alleged tying arrangement?
3. Why did the court reason that a franchising contract ordinarily cannot, by itself, be the basis for an antitrust claim?
4. Who won this case and why?
5. A group of California consumers sued several television networks and cable and satellite distributors, including NBC, Fox, and Time Warner Cable. The defendant television networks sold television programming to the defendant cable distribution companies in bundles, rather than as individual channels. The distributors, in turn, sold to consumers those prepackaged bundles or on a "tier" basis. The plaintiff consumers claimed the practice of offering subscriptions only in bundles was unlawful under the Sherman Act.
   a. Explain the nature of the alleged Sherman Act violation.
   b. Who won the case? Why? See *Brantley et al. v. NBC Universal, Inc. et al.*, 675 F.3d 1192 (9th Cir. 2012) [**https://law.justia.com**]; *cert. denied*, 133 S. Ct. 573 (2012).
6. Chrysler included the price of a sound system in the base price of its cars. Chrysler's share of the auto market at the time was 10 to 12 percent. Chrysler did not reveal the "subprice" for the sound systems. Independent audio dealers objected on antitrust grounds. Explain their claim. How would you decide? See *Town Sound and Custom Tops, Inc. v. Chrysler Motor Corp.*, 959 F.2d 468 (3d Cir. 1992) [**https://law.justia.com**], *cert. denied*, 113 S. Ct. 196 (1992).

Exclusive Dealing and Requirements Contracts

Principal Legislation: Clayton Act, Section 3; Sherman Act, Section 1

LO 10-8
Describe the commercial advantages and disadvantages of exclusive dealing.

An *exclusive dealing contract* is an agreement in which a buyer commits itself to deal only with a specific seller, thereby cutting competing sellers out of that share of the market. A *requirements contract* is one in which a seller agrees to supply all of a buyer's needs, or a buyer agrees to purchase all of a seller's output, or both. Exclusive dealing and requirements contracts are typically lawful, but antitrust problems can arise depending on harm to competition. By its nature, an exclusive deal results in *market foreclosure;* that is, competitors are denied either a supply source or a sales market. Thus, antitrust issues can emerge, depending ordinarily on the market shares controlled by the parties. In general, however, manufacturers, distributors, and retailers have broad latitude in negotiating exclusive deals. We want businesses to produce and distribute their products in the manner they consider most efficient.

Music Festivals

In 2018, Soul'd Out (a Portland, Oregon, music festival) sued Coachella (the Indio, California, music festival). It alleged, among other things, that Coachella engaged in exclusive-dealing restraint of trade. A federal district court judge dismissed the case in 2019, finding that the plaintiffs failed to establish that an antitrust injury had been sustained by the festival or its artists, but the decision was reversed on appeal in May 2020. For undisclosed reasons, the parties agreed to file for a dismissal of the case in November 2020, although some speculate that the inability to hold music festivals during the COVID-19 pandemic may have been a deciding factor.

Soul'd Out, a much smaller festival than the massive Coachella, had challenged Coachella's "Radius Clause," under which Coachella performers must agree not to perform at any "Festival or Themed Event" (with some exceptions) in several nearby states (or in some cases, all of North America) for about five months before and after the Coachella music festival. The smaller Soul'd Out festival, scheduled for mid-April 2018, had signed Tank and the Bangas, but the band was required to withdraw because it was going to be playing at the sold-out Coachella in April. Radius clauses are standard to the industry, including other big festivals such as Lollapalooza. The industry argues that the restrictions are necessary to prevent others from free-riding on the big festivals' creative decisions in signing artists. Of course, acts are free to sign up with the smaller festivals if they want to give up access to Coachella and others.[32]

American Needle

The National Football League (NFL) was accused of restraint of trade for giving Reebok, in 2000, an exclusive 10-year right to produce and market nearly all NFL-trademarked headwear. The plaintiff, American Needle, a Downers Grove, Illinois, apparel manufacturer, was cut out of the premium cap market by the NFL's decision. Lower court cases found that the NFL is a single business entity and thus could not have conspired as the Sherman Act requires. The U.S. Supreme Court, however, reversed the lower

> The National Football League was accused of restraint of trade.

courts in 2010 by a 9–0 margin, saying that each of the NFL teams is independently owned and managed, and each proceeds as a separate, competing economic enterprise.[33] The case was later settled out of court.

Condoms

Church & Dwight Co. (C & D) manufactures and distributes Trojan and other brand-name latex condoms. As of 2012, C & D controlled about 75 percent of the U.S. retail condom market. The number-two seller controlled about 14 percent, and number three sold just under 10 percent. Mayer Labs, with less than 1 percent of the market, raised antitrust claims (among other causes of action) against C & D. Mayer alleged that C & D had unlawful exclusive dealing arrangements with some retail chains, including 7-Eleven, and that a C & D program granting kickbacks/rebates to retailers, based on the amount of shelf space devoted to C & D products, constituted a form of semi-exclusive dealing, in that it put a ceiling or quota on the amount of shelf space competitors could secure.

A California U.S. District Court in 2012 ruled for C & D in the exclusive dealing action, determining broadly that Mayer failed to show C & D's marketing strategies had foreclosed competition. Despite C & D's large market share, the court reasoned that Mayer failed to show C & D had market power, because no evidence was presented of restricted output, supra-competitive prices, or barriers to entry. Further, the alleged exclusive dealing arrangements were voluntary and of short duration. Finally, other channels of distribution were available to competitors. Thus, competition was not impaired.

Source: *Church & Dwight v. Mayer Laboratories,* 868 F. Supp. 2d 876 (N.D. Cal. 2012) [**https://law.justia.com**].

Price Discrimination

Principal Legislation: Clayton Act, Section 2, as amended by the Robinson–Patman Act

[For the statutory language, see **http://assembler.law.cornell.edu/uscode/15/13.html**.]

LO 10-9
Contrast price discrimination and predatory pricing.

Price discrimination involves selling substantially identical goods (not services) at reasonably contemporaneous times to different purchasers at different prices, where the effect is to harm competition. A seller may resist a claim under the Robinson–Patman Act by establishing one of the following defenses: (1) The price differential is attributable to cost savings (although, in practice, the cost savings defense has been difficult to establish); (2) the price differential is attributable to a good faith effort to meet the equally low price of a competitor; or (3) the transaction is exempt from the act. Of special note are price changes made in response to changing markets. Thus, prices may lawfully be adjusted for seasonal goods or perishables.

Uber

Have you suspected Uber of price discrimination practices? Could Uber lawfully charge you more than your friend or spouse for taking exactly the same trip at the same time and under

Could Uber lawfully charge you more than your friend or spouse. . .?

the same conditions? Uber acknowledges using "route-based pricing," reflecting artificial intelligence-based calculations of how much groups of riders are willing to pay. That willingness is measured, at least in part, on income levels of the pickup and drop-off neighborhoods or on departures from businesses likely to provide expense accounts. Some observers believe Uber has also been experimenting with "personalized pricing" (sometimes called dynamic pricing), under which fares vary based on individual differences in ability and willingness to pay. Based on individual data points, such as the credit card and phone brand used, riding history, and more, Uber could use big data analytical tools to instantaneously assess who might be willing to pay more. Personalized pricing could theoretically enhance efficiency and result in broadened service to lower-income customers, who would be subsidized by wealthier customers who do not mind paying more.[34] In practice, however, George Washington University reported in 2020 that customers in lower-income and minority areas actually paid more rather than less–not because of any conscious bias, but because of "societal bias built into the decision-making algorithm that drives rideshare pricing."[35]

So, is Uber's personalized pricing legal? An arbitrator issued a ruling in 2019 in favor of the company, in at least one challenge brought by an Uber customer alleging price discrimination.[36] Setting legal precedent on the issue is seemingly difficult because the terms of Uber's contracts require the parties to arbitrate their claims rather than proceed to litigation in federal court.

Protect Small Businesses?

The most familiar and, perhaps, poignant price discrimination allegations are brought by independent operators (such as neighborhood bookstores and local pharmacies) against rival chains (such as Barnes & Noble and big pharmaceutical firms). The independents claim that their giant competitors pay suppliers lower prices than those charged to small stores, and their complaints reflect the philosophical battle over the role of antitrust law in a rapidly changing global market. Should we use antitrust to protect small businesses, thus supporting neighborhoods, small towns, and our historic American way of life? Or should we accept the dictates of the market, where the efficiency of giants like Walmart brings low prices and high quality to all?

In the case of books, we have some evidence that the market can adjust to big sellers like Amazon. After near destruction by Internet competition, the number of independent bookstores in the United States increased by 35 percent between 2009 and 2015, and sales of physical books have increased every year since 2014, with the exception of 2018 to 2019 (although Barnes & Noble's sales declined every year between 2014 and at least 2019).[37]

Free-market advocates condemn price discrimination law as an attack on consumer-friendly discount pricing practices. Why, the critics ask, would we assault those who engage in vigorous price competition? Court decisions seem to support that view. From 2006 through 2010, plaintiffs (often small businesses) won just four percent of the Robinson–Patman cases brought in the federal courts, down from 35 percent in the years 1982 to 1993.[38] Furthermore, the federal government seldom brings a Robinson–Patman action. The following case illustrates smaller businesses' use of the Robinson–Patman Act in their ongoing struggle against what they believe to be the unfair competition of "giants."

LEGAL BRIEFCASE

Drug Mart Pharmacy Corp. v. American Home Products

2012 U.S. Dist. LEXIS 115882 (E.D.N.Y.)

U.S. Magistrate Judge Gold

[P]laintiffs are a number of individually owned retail pharmacies. Plaintiffs allege that defendants, five manufacturers of brand name prescription drugs ("BNPDs"), offered discounts and rebates to plaintiffs' competitors but not to plaintiffs, and that this constitutes price discrimination in violation of the Robinson–Patman Act.

BACKGROUND

In 2007, Senior United States District Judge I. Leo Glasser granted defendants' motion for summary judgment ". . . on the ground that plaintiffs have failed to show they are entitled to damages."

After Judge Glasser dismissed the claims of the designated parties, approximately 3,700 individual retail pharmacy plaintiffs remained. Confronted with Judge Glasser's decision, these remaining plaintiffs devised a plan to gather evidence in discovery that might show "that specific plaintiff pharmacies lost sales of BNPDs manufactured by defendants to any specific favored purchaser." Pursuant to this plan, which came to be known as the "matching process," plaintiffs compiled lists of specific BNPD customers who no longer purchased drugs from them, and then searched the databases of non-party favored purchasers (and one favored purchaser who is a party) to see whether those same individuals were obtaining the same BNPDs from those favored purchasers.

[O]nly approximately 3% (5,147 of 164,501) of the potential lost customers plaintiffs culled from their own records could be "matched" to a customer who subsequently filled the same prescriptions with one or more favored purchasers.

The de minimis nature of these results is further illustrated when they are broken down and analyzed by defendant. According to defendants, when examined in this manner, the results are that approximately 88% of plaintiffs' claims against particular defendants are based on five or fewer lost customers per year. . . . Even Klein's Pharmacy, the plaintiff with the highest number of lost transactions identified by the matching process, lost a total of only 2,521 transactions, or approximately 252 transactions per year. This amounts to only slightly more than 1% of the total BNPD transactions conducted by an average retail pharmacy during any one year (252/22,000).

In short, no matter how analyzed, the matching process identified only a de minimis number of lost customers and transactions.

DISCUSSION

. . . I now consider whether plaintiffs' evidence, revealing as it does that plaintiffs lost only a trivial number of customers and sales to favored purchasers, is nevertheless sufficient to support a Robinson-Patman Act claim. . . .

The Robinson–Patman Act

In enacting Robinson–Patman, "Congress sought to target the perceived harm to competition occasioned by powerful buyers, rather than sellers; specifically, Congress responded to the advent of large chainstores, enterprises with the clout to obtain lower prices for goods than smaller buyers could demand." *Volvo,* 546 U.S. at 175. The purpose of the Act is to prohibit "price discrimination only to the extent that it threatens to injure competition." *Brooke Grp. Ltd. v. Brown & Williamson Tobacco Corp.,* 509 U.S. 209, 220 (1993).

1. Competitive Injury

The Robinson–Patman Act prohibits price discrimination only "where the effect of such discrimination may be substantially to lessen competition." 15 U.S.C. § 13(a).

[A]fter reviewing all of the pertinent authorities, . . . I conclude that a Robinson–Patman claim requires a showing of substantial competitive injury and that the de minimis sales identified by the matching process are insufficient to establish such an injury. . . .

2. Antitrust Injury

Price discrimination does not entitle a disfavored purchaser to "automatic damages." *J. Truett Payne Co. v. Chrysler Motors Corp.,* 451 U.S. 557, 561 (1981). . . . [P]laintiffs here . . . have been unable to "match up their losses" with gains to the favored purchasers. Plaintiffs have identified less than 3% of their total lost customers as having purchased BNPDs from favored purchasers, undermining any inference that price advantages enjoyed by favored purchaser caused plaintiffs' injury.

Because they are essentially unable to match up a significant number of the customers they lost with those the favored purchasers gained, plaintiffs have failed to demonstrate antitrust injury. . . .

CONCLUSION

For all these reasons, defendants' motion for summary judgment is granted.

AFTERWORD

This district court decision was upheld on appeal at *Cash & Henderson Drugs v. Johnson & Johnson*, 799 F.3d 202 (2d Cir. 2015).

Questions

1. Why did the retail pharmacies lose this case?
2. *a.* In your opinion, have small pharmacies and small businesses generally lost significant revenue over the years to retail giants such as Walmart and Costco? Explain.

   b. If so, does that loss constitute an antitrust wrong that should be remedied by law? Explain.
3. In what sense does the Robinson–Patman Act arguably reduce efficiency, thus harming consumer welfare?
4. Texaco sold gasoline at its retail prices to Hasbrouck, an independent Texaco retailer, but granted discounts to distributors Gull and Dompier. Gull and Dompier both delivered their gas directly to retailers and did not maintain substantial storage facilities. During the period in question, sales at the stations supplied by the two distributors grew dramatically, while Hasbrouck's sales declined. Hasbrouck filed suit against Texaco, claiming that the distributor discount constituted a Robinson–Patman violation. Texaco defended, saying the discount reflected the services the distributors performed for Texaco, and that the arrangement did not harm competition. How would you decide? Explain. See *Texaco v. Ricky Hasbrouck*, 496 U.S. 543 (1990) [**https://supreme.justia.com**].
5. Utah Pie produced frozen pies in its Salt Lake City plant. Utah's competitors, Carnation, Pet, and Continental, sometimes sold pies in Salt Lake City at prices beneath those charged in other markets. Indeed, Continental's prices in Salt Lake City were beneath its direct costs plus overhead. Pet sold to Safeway using Safeway's private label at a price lower than that at which the same pies were sold under the Pet label. Pet employed an industrial spy to infiltrate Utah Pie and gather information. Utah Pie claimed that Carnation, Pet, and Continental were in violation of Robinson–Patman. How would you decide? Explain. See *Utah Pie Co. v. Continental Baking Co.*, 386 U.S. 685 (1967). For doubts about the continuing validity of the *Utah Pie* decision, see *Coastal Fuels Inc. v. Caribbean Petroleum Corp.*, 79 F.3d 182 (1st Cir. P.R. 1996) [**https://law.justia.com**].

Predatory Pricing

Principal Legislation: Sherman Act, Section 2

LO 10-10
Explain how predatory pricing may be proven.

Our core concern in this section is that a dominant firm can reduce its prices below operating costs until a competitor drops out of the market and then raise those prices to monopoly levels. In 2009, the European Commission fined Intel $1.45 billion for *predatory pricing* and other alleged misconduct. Essentially, Intel was accused of reducing prices for its chips by unlawfully paying rebates/discounts to computer manufacturers and retailers to persuade them not to use rival chips. Intel claimed, in part, that the rebates had the desirable effect of saving money for consumers, but critics say consumer choice was reduced by discouraging deals with Intel rivals, resulting in higher prices and potentially reduced quality in the long term. Intel also agreed in 2009 to pay a smaller rival chipmaker, Advanced Micro Devices (AMD), $1.25 billion to settle, among other claims, AMD's allegations of predatory pricing.[39]

Predatory pricing litigation under European precedents has a reasonable probability of success, but in the United States they are very difficult to win.

Establishing predatory pricing requires proof of two conditions:

1. Pricing below cost.
2. A "dangerous probability" of subsequently recouping the losses suffered from the below-cost pricing.[40]

Pricing Below Cost?

Amazon has become a target of predatory pricing claims. Amazon allegedly prices below cost for periods of time; particularly as it solidifies its acquisitions in new markets. The

Antitrust Law—Monopolies and Mergers

After completing this chapter, students will be able to fulfill the following learning objectives:

11-1. Identify critics' antitrust concerns about big tech companies.

11-2. Explain how Microsoft violated U.S. antitrust laws.

11-3. Analyze when a monopoly has been created.

11-4. Identify the potential benefits and hazards of mergers.

11-5. Distinguish between horizontal and vertical mergers.

11-6. Explain premerger notification requirements.

11-7. Describe remedies for mergers determined to be anticompetitive.

11-8. Analyze when a horizontal merger is anticompetitive.

11-9. Analyze when a vertical merger creates anticompetitive "market foreclosure."

11-10. Contrast antitrust enforcement in the United States and the European Union.

Introduction—Corporate Giants and Monopoly

LO 11-1
Identify critics' antitrust concerns about big tech companies.

Amazon, Apple, Exxon, Facebook, Google, Microsoft, and Walmart, products of American ingenuity, are crucial to national prosperity. At the same time, those giants and others like them can threaten societal welfare. Monopoly law addresses those threats. Single firms sometimes dominate an industry (monopoly), and more commonly in the contemporary American economy, a few big firms share that dominance (oligopoly). As journalist David Dayen explained

> [T]hink about everything you buy and every service you pay for, and how they come from concentrated suppliers. We have four airlines serving 80 percent of all passengers. We have four cable and Internet companies providing most of the nation's cell-phone and television service. . . . and a handful of producers selling every major consumer product. Even when you

think you have a choice, like in the array of online travel-booking sites, two companies (Expedia and Priceline) own all the subsidiaries.[1]

Economic concentration can reduce costs, enhance efficiency, and strengthen international competitiveness, but it can also lead to higher prices, poorer service, reduced innovation, suppressed employee wages, economic inequality, fewer startups, abuse of political power, and other problems. In 2019, New York University economist Thomas Philippon estimated the cost of excessive industry concentration at more than $5,000 per year for the typical American household.[2]

Market Failure? Historically, we have believed that the goals of private businesses operating in a free market will ordinarily align with the general good. We have believed that bigger generally signaled better and that victors in a harsh free-market battle had earned their dominance and, in the process, benefited all of America. Now, large numbers of Americans believe the economy is "rigged" in favor of big corporations and the wealthy. We are victims, critics say, of monopoly, a market failure we discussed in Chapter 8. If the critics are correct, the resulting damage may be contributing to a decline in the quality of life for many Americans. The wage and wealth inequality that we discussed in Chapter 1, for example, may be partially attributable to market concentration, where big firms continue to get bigger, and wealth increasingly is captured by executives and shareholders. Hence, monopoly power may be contributing to declining opportunities for blue-collar Americans. Concentrated industries, the argument goes, lead to reduced employment options and thus lower wages, while allowing employers to impose antipoaching (see Chapter 10), noncompete agreements (see Chapter 12), and mandatory arbitration requirements (see Chapter 12) to further restrain employee leverage.

Wealth and wage inequality, the critics claim, in turn leads to political distortion, such that laws, regulations, and law enforcement are disproportionately advantageous to the wealthy. Donald Trump's ascendancy to the presidency appears to have been powered, in part, by blue-collar anger over reduced economic prospects.

We should remember, of course, that great size and power are often earned by superior performance. Furthermore, technological shifts, reaching a new market first, returns to scale, and other legitimate economic forces can produce monopolistic results. And we have been well served, in many cases, by giant firms. Useful tools in our lives keep improving, prices often fall, entertainment options multiply, and we enjoy the comfort of predictable, steady performance by enormous banks, airlines, tech companies, and more. Giants such as Amazon, CVS, Target, and Walmart provided crucial goods and services during the COVID-19 crisis. [For a "growing movement to protect America's economy and democracy from corporate monopolies," see Citizens Against Monopoly **https://citizensagainstmonopoly.org**].

The "Frightful Five"

Alphabet (Google's parent), Amazon, Apple, Facebook, and Microsoft are, unsurprisingly, the biggest potential targets in today's antitrust universe. The Five, measured by stock market value, are half of the world's 10 largest companies, and are now positioning themselves to enter non-tech markets such as autos, finance, and health care. Furthermore, they often snap up any competition that might emerge. Facebook, for example, acquired Instagram and

WhatsApp, while Google bought Android and YouTube. In 2021, federal regulators finally allowed Google to purchase Fitbit–with its trove of personal information from 28 million users–after scrutinizing the deal for over a year.

Do the five tech giants threaten American welfare? Jeremy Phillips, general partner at Spark Capital, argued in *The New York Times* that we should keep an eye on the Big Five, but he notes that they are increasingly each other's competitor, just what we want in a free market. He points to the example of Netflix, which effectively destroyed video rental stores (Do you even remember Blockbuster?) and is itself facing intense competition from Amazon, Apple, Hulu, HBO, and others. Phillips looks at Amazon and sees a colossus, certainly, but one that is constantly threatened by tech competitors, as well as by Walmart and other traditional retailers.

Free-market arguments notwithstanding, consumers have become increasingly nervous about the dominance of these big firms. Privacy threats have grown. Personal online abuse like bullying, along with political chicanery from Russia and elsewhere, have shaken consumer faith. And the tech giants that we admired for their power to disrupt and improve commerce have become entrenched institutions, arguably using their authority to dominate and maintain rather than disrupt.

As mentioned in Chapter 10, the European Commission fined Google for alleged market abuses, but in the United States, the Federal Trade Commission (FTC) investigated Google's search practices and in 2013 declined to pursue litigation. The FTC concluded that Google's search practices were not anticompetitive, in that they were designed primarily to improve the quality of the product delivered to consumers. Search alternatives to Google are plentiful. (Google handles about two-thirds of searches and earns up to 90 percent of search revenue in the United States Internet market.)

The federal Justice Department, along with eight state attorneys general, however, filed an antitrust suit against Google in 2023 for allegedly monopolizing key Internet advertising technology products. Several other big, online platforms are apparently also under antitrust review by various government bodies.

Questions

Critics, including Facebook cofounder Chris Hughes, have campaigned for breaking up Facebook. (Hughes is no longer associated with the company.)

1. Why are the critics concerned?
2. Should we break up Facebook? Raise all of the relevant issues.

Sources: "Google's Android Fine is Not Enough to Change Its Behavior," *The Economist,* July 21, 2018 [**www.economist.com**]; Farhad Manjoo, "Tech Giants Seem Invincible. That Worries Lawmakers," *The New York Times,* January 4, 2017 [**www.nytimes.com**]; and Jeremy G. Philips, "The 'Frightful Five' Aren't So Scary, as Long as They're Competing," *The New York Times,* May 8, 2017 [**www.nytimes.com**].

Microsoft a Monopolist?

LO 11-2 Explain how Microsoft violated U.S. antitrust laws.

We learned, about 25 years ago, that even the most powerful and aggressive tech giant can be tamed by antitrust law. The U.S. Justice Department, 20 states, and the District of Columbia went to trial against Microsoft in 1998, claiming not that the software giant was too big, but that it had violated various antitrust laws in gaining and maintaining its market

> An epic legal struggle followed, with major elements of the American justice system challenging one of the world's richest men, Bill Gates.

dominance. An epic legal struggle followed, with major elements of the American justice system challenging one of the world's richest men, Bill Gates.

A federal district court in 2000 and, later, a federal court of appeals ruled that Microsoft had violated federal antitrust laws by maintaining its 95 percent share of the Intel-compatible PC operating systems market through anticompetitive means (basically, using its Windows monopoly power to coerce customers to buy other Microsoft products, such as its browser, Internet Explorer).[3] The district court judge ordered that Microsoft split into two companies as a remedy for its antitrust wrongs, but the court of appeals vacated that order. Thereafter, the case was settled out of court with Microsoft agreeing, among other things, to share some critical programming information and to be monitored to ensure compliance. Subsequent settlements with the European Union, Novell, and others cost Microsoft billions. Then, in 2013, the EU fined Microsoft $730 million for breaking the terms of their settlement. Microsoft apologized for what it said was a temporary technical problem.

Significance

The *Microsoft* case demonstrated that the power of a tech giant can be trimmed, clearing the way for new entrants and innovation while preserving Microsoft, itself, as a great tech performer. Had Microsoft continued its dominance unimpeded, would Amazon, Facebook, Google, and Netflix have found room to emerge successfully?

> Do we need to employ antitrust law to attack great concentrations of power, or are the market and ethics sufficient?

Does the *Microsoft* case suggest that we need to employ antitrust law to attack great concentrations of power, or are the market and ethics sufficient to promote economic efficiency and preserve social, economic, and political justice? At the time of its lawsuit, Microsoft stood substantially alone as a computer superpower. Today we have multiple giants, each competing with and affecting the behavior of the others. Perhaps those market pressures and a measure of corporate citizenship will do the trick–or perhaps not. Critics such as journalist Alan Murray are rather cynical about the Microsoft lesson:

> The Microsoft saga serves as a reminder of an important truth: Capitalists, for the most part, don't care much for capitalism. Their goal is to make money. And if they can do it without messy competition, so much the better.[4]

Questions

1. *a.* Do you see increasing concentrations of corporate wealth and power as threats to America's long-term welfare? Explain.

   b. If that concentration is a concern, is antitrust law the best remedy? Explain.
2. Does the *Microsoft* case stand simply for the view that bigness is bad? Explain.
3. *Bloomberg's* editorial board has argued against breaking up Facebook, saying that the social media titan has plenty of problems, but breaking it up would not solve them. Would we be better off with several smaller versions of Facebook? Explain. See Editorial Board, "Don't Break Up Facebook," *Bloomberg*, July 16, 2018 [**www.bloomberg.com**].

Part One—Monopoly

As we saw in the *Microsoft* case, monopoly lawsuits often touch and sometimes reshape our daily lives:

Apps In 2019, a class action suit was brought against Apple for alleged monopoly practices. iPhone applications (apps) can be purchased only through Apple's App Store. App developers set the retail price for their apps, but Apple then adds a commission on each sale. Plaintiff consumers argue that Apple uses its market dominance to inflate prices for customers who are forced to buy the apps only through the Apple site. The United States Supreme Court ruled in 2019 that consumers themselves can directly sue Apple on antitrust claims, thus allowing the plaintiffs to continue their monopoly action in the lower courts.[5]

Tickets StubHub, at the time an eBay-owned ticketing service, sued Ticketmaster and the Golden State Warriors National Basketball Association team in 2015 for monopoly practices. StubHub alleged that the team had threatened to cancel season ticket holders' subscriptions if they tried to resell any of their tickets on StubHub instead of Ticketmaster, the team's exclusive ticketing agent. According to StubHub's lawsuit, Ticketmaster and the Warriors monopolized the team's ticket sales and engaged in an unlawful tying arrangement by controlling both first-time and secondary ticket sales. A federal judge dismissed the lawsuit saying, basically, that although the Warriors were exerting some control over their tickets, the team's behavior was characteristic of all companies seeking to sell what they make. In a reassuring free-market response, StubHub challenged Ticketmaster in 2016 by introducing its own combined first-time and secondary ticketing platform for its role as the official ticketing partner of the Philadelphia 76ers NBA team–allowing 76ers ticket buyers to resell their unneeded tickets on StubHub or wherever they wish.

Monopoly Legislation

How do we know when an organization is an unlawful monopolist? Federal laws define the general parameters.

Principal Monopoly Legislation: Sherman Act, Section 2

> Every person who shall monopolize, or attempt to monopolize, or combine or conspire with any other person or persons, to monopolize any part of the trade or commerce among the several States, or with foreign nations, shall be deemed guilty of a felony punishable by a fine.

Section 5 of the Federal Trade Commission Act also applies to antitrust cases.

Monopoly Defined

From an economic viewpoint, a monopoly is a situation in which one firm holds the power to control prices and/or exclude competition in a particular market. The general legal test for monopolization is

1. The possession of monopoly power in the relevant market, and
2. The willful acquisition or maintenance of that power, as distinguished from growth or development as a consequence of a superior product, business acumen, or historic accident.[6]

The critical inquiries are the percentage of the market held by the alleged monopolist and the behavior that produced, maintained, or expanded that market share.

Antitrust law does not punish efficient companies that legitimately earn and maintain large market shares. Indeed, a high market concentration often promotes competition, whereas a fragmented market of many small firms may produce higher prices. (Imagine a retail food market of many corner grocery stores and no supermarkets.) The federal government relies on market concentration data (structure) in combination with evidence of actual behavior (conduct) to identify anticompetitive situations. A big market share alone is highly unlikely to lead to antitrust action, but a big market share acquired and/or maintained via abusive conduct (as alleged in *Microsoft*) may be challenged.

Oligopoly

A few firms sharing monopoly power constitute an oligopoly. As we mentioned earlier, oligopolistic markets are common in American life, and they have emerged in some global markets as well. The 2009 *New York Times* headline, "Rising Beer Prices Hint at Oligopoly,"[7] illustrates how oligopic concentration can bleed consumer pocketbooks and undermine the quality of our lives.

PRACTICING ETHICS Use Antitrust to Attack Social Wrongs?

Consumer Welfare The Supreme Court and the lower courts tend to evaluate monopolies, in particular, and antitrust problems, generally, using free-market economic principles advanced by scholars associated with the University of Chicago (now labeled the "Chicago School" of antitrust analysis). To the Chicago School, maximum consumer welfare, measured principally by prices, is the crucial test for antitrust wrongs. Under the Chicago School's assumption that the market will, in most cases, automatically correct itself if unhealthy market concentrations arise, antitrust action would be appropriate only with clear evidence of consumer injury, including increased prices, declining quality, reduced outputs, or diminished innovation. Public interests beyond low prices, including the well being of producers or of the market as a whole, are given less attention under the consumer welfare standard.

Structural Dominance Antitrust activists are now challenging the Chicago School's dominance. The activists are energized by concerns over big tech power, wealth and income inequality, the concentration of political power in the wealthy, protection for small businesses, employee abuse, and more. They are arguing for a "structural dominance" view of antitrust analysis, in which concentrations of power through monopolies and mergers might be aggressively challenged even if prices remained low and consumer welfare was unimpaired. The structuralists would continue to employ careful economic analysis, but public interest considerations in addition to price would be employed in that analysis. Thus, antitrust activists might, for example, challenge Amazon's structural dominance in the book publishing market, arguing that it has crippled mainstream publishing houses and resulted in a less diverse, less healthy, and less interesting book market. Chicago School advocates, on the other hand, point to low consumer prices and robust book sales as convincing evidence of a generally healthy book market, even if sales are dominated by one firm.

Questions

1. Do you think political and economic power in the United States is so disproportionately concentrated among a very narrow upper class that it is (a) a violation of American principles of fairness and/or (b) a significant threat to societal welfare? Explain.
2. Is antitrust law an appropriate vehicle for correcting social wrongs like income inequality and concentrated political power? Explain.

Source: Maurice E. Stucke and Ariel Ezrachi, "The Rise, Fall, and Rebirth of the U.S. Antitrust Movement," *Harvard Business Review*, December 15, 2017 [**https://hbr.org**].

Broadly, the fear is that oligopoly conditions will lead to higher prices, reduced quality and innovation, and the various social welfare and political problems previously noted. In industries such as telecommunications, food processing, credit ratings, and book publishing, we find enormous American and international markets dominated by a handful of companies. However, oligopolies often produce significant efficiencies, and smaller competitors, including startups, can sometimes find openings in the market that can restore some measure of price and quality discipline.

Monopolization Analysis

LO 11-3
Analyze when a monopoly has been created.

Monopoly lawsuits are not commonplace, but the principle that a single firm cannot lawfully dominate a market by unfair, predatory practices remains an important constraint on abusive corporate conduct. Although the case law is not a model of clarity, a rather straightforward framework for monopoly analysis has emerged:

1. Define the relevant *product market.*
2. Define the relevant *geographic market.*
3. Determine the defendant's *market power.*
4. Assess the defendant's *intent* (predatory or coercive conduct).
5. Raise any available *defenses.*

1. Product Market

Here the court seeks, effectively, to draw a circle that

1. Encompasses general categories of goods and services in which the defendant's particular products or services compete, and
2. Excludes those not in the same competitive arena.

If the products or services are *interchangeable*–that is, they are *substitutes,* one for the other–we may surmise they are in the same market. Interchangeability is determined primarily by comparing price, use, and quality among the products or services in question.

An analysis of *cross-elasticity of demand* helps us to establish interchangeability. Assume that two products, X and Y, appear to be competitors; that is, they are substitutes one for the other. Assume that the price of X doubled, and Y's sales volume was unchanged. What does that tell us about whether X and Y are, in fact, in the same product market? More specifically, if the price of potato chips, for example, falls by 10 percent, does the sales volume of salted nuts at the existing price fall? If so, we have a preliminary indication that potato chips and salted nuts may lie in the same product market and thus may be competitors.

Defining the product market is really the process we all go through in routine purchasing decisions. Assume you feel a rather undefined hunger for salty snack food. You go to the nearby convenience store. Many options confront you, but for simplicity, let's confine them to chips, nuts, and popcorn. Each of those food types has many variations. As you sort through the choices–corn chips, cheese curls, peanuts, potato chips, and so on–you employ the criteria of price, use, and quality in focusing your decision. In so doing, you are defining the product market for "salty snack food." Products closely matched in price, use, and quality are interchangeable, and are thus competitors in the same product market. But, for example, an imported salty cheese at $12 per quarter pound presumably is not in the same product market as salted sunflower seeds.

2. Geographic Market

Once the product market has been defined, we must determine where the product can be purchased. Judicial decisions offer no definitive explanation to date of the geographic market concept. A working definition might be: "any section of the country where the product is sold in commercially significant quantities." From an economic perspective, the geographic market can be defined by elasticity. If prices rise or supplies are reduced within the geographic area in question (New England, for example), and demand remains steady, will products from other areas enter the market in a quantity sufficient to affect price and/or supply? If so, the geographic market must be broadened to embrace those new sources of supply. If not, the geographic market is not larger than the area in question (New England).

3. Market Power (Market Share)

Does the market share held by the defendant threaten competition? How large that share must be to raise monopoly concerns depends on a variety of considerations, including how fragmented or concentrated the market is. The *Harvard Law Review* provides some approximate boundaries:

> Market share above 70 percent typically suffices to support an inference of monopoly power. Conversely, courts have rarely found monopoly power when a firm's market share is below 50 percent, leaving some uncertainty as to market shares between 50 and 70 percent.[8]

Market share alone, however, does not establish monopoly power. Barriers to entry, economies of scale, the strength of the competition, trends in the market, and pricing patterns all help to determine whether the market remains competitive despite a single firm's large share.

4. Intent (Predatory or Coercive Conduct)

Assuming a threatening market share is established, the next requirement is proof of an intent to monopolize. Remember that a monopoly finding requires a showing of both market power (*structure*) and willful acquisition or maintenance of that power (*conduct*). Antitrust law is not designed to attack legitimately earned market power. Rather, the concern lies with those holding monopoly power that was acquired or maintained wrongfully. Thus, a showing of deliberate predatory, coercive, or unfair conduct (such as collusion leading to price fixing) will normally suffice to establish the requisite intent.

Wrongful Conduct: An Example

Intel, the dominant microchip maker with 80 to 90 percent of the microprocessor market, allegedly engaged in wrongful conduct in building and maintaining its market dominance. Basically, Intel was accused of providing discriminatory rebates to Dell, IBM, HP, and others in return for those purchasers' agreement not to buy central processing unit chips from

Intel's rival, Advanced Micro Devices (AMD). Intel was also accused of designing its chips so that competing processors could not run efficiently with them. A 2010 settlement with the FTC prohibited those rebate and design practices. [To read more about Intel's antitrust activities, see See Edward Wyatt and Ashlee Vance, "Intel Settles with F.T.C. on Antitrust," *The New York Times,* August 4, 2010 (**www.nytimes.com**); and Stephen Labaton, "In Turnabout, Antitrust Unit Looks at Intel," *The New York Times,* June 7, 2008 (**www.nytimes.com**)].

5. Defenses

Assuming an anticompetitive monopoly is established in steps 1–4, the defendant may yet prevail if the evidence demonstrates that the monopoly was acquired via "superior skill, foresight, or industry." That is, the monopoly was earned. Sometimes a monopoly may be "thrust upon" the monopolist because the competition failed or because of "natural monopoly" conditions, where the market will support only one firm or where large economies of scale exist, as with some electrical utilities.

Questions

1. Why are the courts interested in barriers to entry?
2. Why might discounts constitute an antitrust violation?
3. Defend Intel against those charges. What arguments are available to you?

Attempted Monopolization

The Sherman Act forbids attempts to monopolize as well as anticompetitive monopoly itself. In the 1993 *Spectrum Sports* decision,[9] the Supreme Court set out a three-part test for attempted monopolization: (1) the defendant has engaged in predatory or anticompetitive conduct with (2) a specific intent to monopolize and (3) there is a dangerous probability of achieving monopoly power (meaning a "realistic" likelihood that monopoly would actually follow).

The Philadelphia Taxi Association and 80 taxi companies sued Uber in 2016 claiming that Uber's entry into the Philadelphia ride-for-hire market was an attempted monopoly. The plaintiffs argued that Uber failed to follow city regulations, including those requiring drivers to be appropriately licensed and to be paid the minimum wage, that Uber recruited 1,200 taxi drivers to its service, and that the value of taxi medallions fell from $530,000 to $80,000. Uber prevailed at both a federal district court and on appeal. The Supreme Court declined to review the decision. Basically, the two lower courts concluded that the alleged taxi harms were the result of increased competition rather than anticompetitive behavior. Prices fell, ride availability rose, and patrons were able to use a convenient, "high tech" means of hailing and paying for rides. Notice that these courts employed established consumer welfare reasoning rather than the competing structural dominance argument.[10]

Is Bob Marley a Product Market?

Music producer Rock River released remixed Bob Marley and the Wailers recordings in 2006. Universal Music Group claimed exclusive rights to those recordings and sent "cease and desist" orders to music distributors (Amazon, iTunes, and others), who immediately discontinued the sale of the Rock River remix. Rock River then sued Universal, alleging attempted monopoly of the reggae genre of sound recordings in the United States, among other claims. Rock River alleged that Universal "accounted for 81 percent of the reggae sound recordings sold, and Bob Marley recordings accounted for 76 percent of the total reggae recordings sold."

Questions

1. Is reggae music, in your judgment, an identifiable product market? Explain.
2. Universal claimed there were no significant barriers to entry in the alleged reggae music market. Explain why the absence of barriers to entry would be a significant consideration in resolving the case.
3. Assuming Universal's share of the alleged product market was correctly calculated by Rock River, who should have won this lawsuit? Explain.

Source: *Rock River Communications v. Universal Music Group,* 807 F. Supp. 2d 917 (C.D. Cal. 2011) [**https://casetext.com**], *aff'd in part and reversed in part,* 745 F.3d 343 (9th Cir. 2014) [**https://law.justia.com**].

Monopoly Case I

The case that follows is a private antitrust action involving a claim by Christy Sports, a Utah ski rental company, that Deer Valley Resort Company (DVRC), a ski resort developer and operator, had monopoly power over Deer Valley Resort's ski rental business and that DVRC abused that power to harm Christy Sports.

LEGAL BRIEFCASE

Christy Sports v. Deer Valley Resort Company

555 F.3d 1188 (10th Cir. 2009)

Circuit Judge McConnell

When the Deer Valley Resort Company ("DVRC") was developing its world-renowned ski resort in the Wasatch Mountains, it sold parcels of land within the resort village to third parties, while reserving the right of approval over the conduct of certain ancillary businesses on the property, including ski rentals. For about fifteen years, DVRC granted permission to Cole Sports and plaintiff-appellant Christy Sports to rent skis in competition with its own ski rental outlet. More recently, however, DVRC revoked that permission, presumably in order to gain more business for its own newly opened mid-mountain ski rental store. The question is whether this revocation violated the antitrust laws.

I. BACKGROUND

Deer Valley is one of three resorts in the vicinity of Park City, Utah. Many—indeed, "the vast majority," according to the Complaint—of Deer Valley's patrons are destination skiers who fly into Salt Lake City and then take a forty-five-minute bus or shuttle ride to the resort. The resort itself is divided into two areas: the base area, located at the bottom of the mountain, and the ritzier mid-mountain village, located halfway up the slope. DVRC has always been the sole provider of ski rentals at the base area, but at the mid-mountain village, Christy and Cole Sports have operated rental facilities; DVRC itself opened a mid-mountain ski rental facility in 2005.

Originally, DVRC owned all the property at the mid-mountain village, but over the years it has sold parcels to third parties.

In 1990, DVRC sold one such parcel to S.Y. and Betty Kimball, subject to a restrictive covenant that prohibited use of the property for either ski rental or real estate sales office purposes without DVRC's express written consent. The Kimballs built a commercial building and leased space in it to Christy's corporate predecessor, Bulrich Corporation. The lease expressly prohibited both the rental of skis and the operation of a real estate office. The next year, though, DVRC gave Bulrich permission to rent skis in return for 15% of the rental revenue. When Bulrich merged with another company in 1994 and formed Christy Sports, LLC, Christy continued to operate the rental business. According to the complaint, Christy stopped paying DVRC 15% of its rental revenue in 1995, though the reason for this change is unknown. Christy rented skis at the Deer Valley mid-mountain village with no objection from DVRC until 2005. During that time, DVRC was the sole purveyor of rental skis at the base area but did not have a ski rental operation at mid-mountain.

DVRC opened a mid-mountain ski rental outlet in 2005. In August of that year, the resort notified Christy that, beginning the following year's ski season, the restrictive covenant would be enforced and Christy would no longer be allowed to rent skis. Christy believes that DVRC issued the same message to Cole's, leaving DVRC as the only rental ski provider at Deer Valley, with the exception of a small operation at the Stein Eriksen Lodge, which serves its own lodgers. This leaves that majority of skiers who fly into Salt Lake City and then shuttle to Deer Valley with few choices: they can carry unwieldy ski equipment onto the plane, take a shuttle into Park City and hunt for cheaper ski rentals in town, or rent from the more conveniently located DVRC location. Christy predicts, not improbably, that most consumers will choose the third option.

Christy argues that DVRC's decision to begin enforcing its restrictive covenant is an attempt to monopolize the market of ski rentals available to destination skiers in Deer Valley, or, alternatively, to the destination skiers in the mid-mountain village itself. It alleges that by eliminating its competitors, DVRC will be able to increase prices and reduce output, thus harming consumers. The complaint states that the number of skis available for rental mid-mountain will decline by 620 pairs, and the price will increase by at least twenty-two to thirty-two percent.

The district court dismissed Christy's antitrust complaints.

II. ANALYSIS

Christy has alleged that DVRC violated Section 2 of the Sherman Act by either actual or attempted monopolization. . . . Under both types of Section 2 claims Christy must plead both power in a relevant market and anticompetitive conduct. The relevant market, according to Christy's complaint, is the market for ski rentals to destination skiers in Deer Valley in general or, even more narrowly, the market for ski rentals in the mid-mountain village. The alleged anticompetitive conduct is the enforcement of the restrictive covenant.

A great many pages in the briefs are devoted to whether the defined market set forth in the complaint—destination skiers at Deer Valley, or alternatively at Deer Valley's mid-mountain village—is too small to constitute a market for antitrust purposes, in light of the proximity of a number of ski rental outlets in Park City, just down the road. For purposes of analyzing the complaint, however, we find it not implausible that destination skiers who arrive at the resort by bus or shuttle will find it sufficiently inconvenient to travel into town to rent skis that a successful monopolist over ski rental at Deer Valley could charge supracompetitive prices. The question, we believe, is not whether DVRC might be able to raise prices and reduce output by becoming the only purveyor of rental skis at the resort, but whether such a market is legally cognizable under the antitrust laws and whether the decision of a resort owner to reserve to itself the right to provide ancillary services counts as anticompetitive conduct.

We begin our analysis with DVRC's original decision to impose the restrictive covenant.

A. IMPOSITION OF THE RESTRICTIVE COVENANT

We agree with the defendant that the creator of a resort has no obligation under the antitrust laws to allow competitive suppliers of ancillary services on its property. A theme park, for example, does not have to permit third parties to open restaurants, hotels, gift shops, or other facilities within the park; it can reserve to itself the right to conduct such businesses and receive revenues from them. Accordingly, if it sells land within the resort to third parties, the antitrust laws do not bar the resort owner from imposing a covenant against use of the property for competitive businesses. This is so even if food, rooms, gifts, or other ancillary goods and services would be cheaper and more plentiful if the resort owner allowed competition in these businesses.

This conclusion can be reached either by reference to the proper definition of a market or by reference to the absence of anticompetitive conduct. Some courts, faced with cases of this sort, have found the market definition implausible. The Seventh Circuit took this approach in *Elliott* v. *United Center,* 126 F.3d 1003 (7th Cir. 1997), when a peanut vendor challenged a sports arena's decision to ban outside food and thereby monopolize the market for food concessions within the arena. The court rejected that market definition as implausible, saying:

> The logic of [the] argument would mean that exclusive restaurants could no longer require customers to purchase their wines only at the establishment, because the restaurant would be "monopolizing" the sale of wine within its interior. Movie theaters, which traditionally (and notoriously) earn a substantial portion of their revenue from the sale of candies, popcorn, and soda, would be required by the antitrust laws to allow patrons to bring their own food.

Although discussion of sports arenas . . . seems to suggest that Christy's shortcomings lie with its alleged geographic market, the actual problem lies with its product market. In these cases the two are difficult to disentangle because the product (rental skis . . .) is intimately related to the location. Consumers do not travel to Deer Valley for rental skis. . . . The true product in these cases is the overall experience. Deer Valley offers a cluster of products that combine to create a destination ski experience; rental skis are only one small component. . . .

The complaint alleges nothing to suggest that destination skiers are choosing their ski resort based on the price of rental skis, separate and apart from the cluster of services associated with the destination-ski experience. To define one small component of the overall product as the relevant product market is simply implausible.

Alternatively, one could say that the monopolization claim would fail because the alleged conduct is not anticompetitive. Even if a firm has monopoly power in a relevant market, a plaintiff must also show "the willful acquisition or maintenance of that power as distinguished from growth or development as a consequence of a superior product, business acumen, or historic accident." *Grinnell Corp.,* 384 U.S. at 570–71. Deer Valley is not required to invite competitors onto its property to rent skis to its patrons, even if a failure to do so would mean it is the sole supplier of rental skis at the ski area.

The Supreme Court has recognized the economic value of allowing businesses to decide with whom they will deal, as it recently re-emphasized: "[A]s a general matter, the Sherman Act 'does not restrict the long recognized right of [a] trader or manufacturer engaged in an entirely private business, freely to exercise his own independent discretion as to parties with whom he will deal.'" *Verizon Commc'ns, Inc.* v. *Law Offices of Curtis V. Trinko, LLP,* 540 U.S. 398, 408 (2004). In *Trinko,* the Court acknowledged that in rare circumstances a refusal to cooperate with competitors might constitute a Section 2 violation, but that "such exceptions, because of the uncertain virtue of forced sharing and the difficulty of identifying and remedying anticompetitive conduct by a single firm," should be few.

Having invested time and money in developing a premier ski resort that attracts skiers from across the nation, DVRC could recoup its investment in a number of ways. It could increase the price of lift tickets, raise room rates, serve only high-priced food, or, as it seems to have chosen, delve more deeply into the rental ski market. . . . This does not mean consumers have no protection. The ski resort industry is competitive (and Christy does not allege otherwise). Families contemplating ski vacations have many options, and they presumably compare quality and price. If they are rational, the price they are concerned about is the sum of all of their prospective vacation costs, including not just lift ticket prices and resort lodging, but air fare, food and drink, apres-ski entertainment, ski rentals, and the like. A resort that facilitates lower ski rental prices by allowing competition is able to price other aspects of the ski vacation experience more aggressively. The competitive discipline comes not from introducing competition with respect to each component of the experience, but from competition with other ski resorts with respect to the entire package. Christy has not alleged, and it would not likely be plausible to allege, that DVRC's decision to foreclose competition in the ski rental business at the mid-mountain village will have any effect on the market for ski resort vacations as a whole.

Indeed, allowing resorts to decide for themselves what blend of vertical integration and third-party competition will produce the highest return may well increase competition in the ski resort business as a whole, and thus benefit consumers. This flexibility about business strategies induces entrants into the ski resort business by allowing them to reserve the benefits of their investments to themselves. . . .

Either line of reasoning—whether based on market definition or lack of anticompetitive conduct—leads to the same conclusion. Indeed, they are two sides of the same coin: having created a resort destination, antitrust will not force a resort developer to share its internal profit-making opportunities with competitors. The relevant market requirement reaches this result by finding implausible a market definition that singles out a small component of the cluster of services that constitutes the actual product; the anticompetitive conduct requirement reaches it by saying that it is not anticompetitive to refuse to grant access to competitors.

Although Christy insists that it has shown anticompetitive effects by its allegations of a decline in quantity and increase in price of rental skis at the mid-mountain village, this is just a repackaging of the argument rejected above. A resort operator's ability to reserve to itself the operation of ancillary businesses within the resort is not dependent on the quantity of output being as high or the price being as low as they would be if there were competition from third parties within the resort. It depends, instead, on either the proposition that a market that involves only one component of an interrelated package of services is not a relevant market for purposes of the Sherman Act or that it is not anticompetitive conduct for a resort owner to refuse to invite competitors to supply ancillary services within its resort. The fact . . . that fewer skis will be available for rental and that prices for rental skis will be higher, does not refute either of these legal propositions.

Affirmed.

Questions

1. *a.* Explain why the court concluded that "destination skiers at Deer Valley" or at "Deer Valley's mid-mountain village" constitute a market separate from ski rental outlets in nearby Park City.
   b. How did the court define the "true product" market?

2. *a.* The plaintiff failed to establish the two core elements of its case as required by the court. Explain those elements and describe why the court ruled against the plaintiff.
   b. How will consumers be protected from monopoly behavior by the defendant Deer Valley?
3. Why should Deer Valley be allowed to restrict output and raise prices by denying the plaintiff the continuing opportunity to rent skis at Deer Valley?
4. The U.S. government sued DuPont, claiming monopolization of the cellophane market. DuPont produced almost 75 percent of the cellophane sold in the United States. Cellophane constituted less than 20 percent of the "flexible packaging materials" market. The lower court found "[g]reat sensitivity of customers in the flexible packaging markets to price or quality changes."
   a. What is the relevant product market?
   b. Who wins the case? Explain. See *United States v. E.I. DuPont de Nemours & Co.*, 351 U.S. 377 (1956) [**https://supreme.justia.com**]. But see, e.g., Ramsi Woodcock, "The Elephant in the Market Power Debate," *ProMarket*, January 16, 2019 [**https://promarket.org**].

Monopoly Case II

The *Syufy* case that follows celebrates free-market principles, and it reflects acceptance of the position that dominant market shares may be earned and maintained legitimately—particularly where competition can easily enter the market. Remember, however, the *Microsoft* lesson that a dominant share gained and/or maintained by anticompetitive practices is impermissible.

> Judge Kozinski inserted nearly 200 movie titles in his opinion.

The *Syufy* case is also notable because Judge Kozinski, now retired, inserted nearly 200 movie titles in his 25-page opinion.

LEGAL BRIEFCASE

U.S. v. Syufy Enterprises

903 F.2d 659 (9th Cir. 1990)

KOZINSKI, CIRCUIT JUDGE

Suspecting that giant film distributors like Columbia, Paramount, and Twentieth Century Fox had fallen prey to Raymond Syufy, the canny operator of a chain of Las Vegas, Nevada, movie theaters, the U.S. Department of Justice brought this civil antitrust action to force Syufy to disgorge the theaters he had purchased in 1982–84 from his former competitors. The case is unusual in a number of respects: The Department of Justice concedes that moviegoers in Las Vegas suffered no direct injury as a result of the allegedly illegal transactions; nor does the record reflect complaints from Syufy's bought-out competitors, as the sales were made at fair prices and not precipitated by any monkey business; and the supposedly oppressed movie companies have weighed in on Syufy's side. The Justice Department nevertheless remains intent on rescuing this platoon of Goliaths from a single David.

After extensive discovery and an eight-and-a-half-day trial, the learned district judge entered comprehensive findings of fact and conclusions of law, holding for Syufy. He found, inter alia, that Syufy's actions did not injure competition because there are no barriers to entry—others could and did enter the market—and that Syufy therefore did not have the power to control prices or exclude the competition. . . .

FACTS

Gone are the days when a movie ticket cost a dime, popcorn a nickel, and theaters had a single screen: This is the age of the multiplex. With more than 300 new films released every year—each potentially the next Batman or E.T.—many successful theaters today run a different film on each of their 6, 12, or 18 screens. . . .

Raymond Syufy understood the formula well. In 1981 he entered the Las Vegas market with a splash by opening a six-screen theater. Newly constructed and luxuriously furnished, it put existing facilities to shame. Syufy's entry into the Las Vegas market caused a stir, precipitating a titanic bidding war. Soon theaters in Las Vegas were paying some of the highest license fees in the nation, while distributors sat back and watched the easy money roll in.

It is the nature of free enterprise that fierce, no-holds-barred competition will drive out the least effective participants in the market, providing the most efficient allocation of productive resources. And so it was in the Las Vegas movie market in 1982. After a hard-fought battle among several contenders, Syufy gained the upper hand. Two of his rivals, Mann Theatres and Plitt Theatres, saw their future as rocky and decided to sell out to Syufy. While Mann and Plitt are major exhibitors nationwide, neither had a large presence in Las Vegas. Mann operated two indoor theaters with a total of three screens; Plitt operated a single theater with three screens. Things were relatively quiet until September 1984; in September Syufy entered into earnest negotiations with Cragin Industries, his largest remaining competitor. Cragin sold out to Syufy midway through October, leaving Roberts Company, a small exhibitor of mostly second-run films, as Syufy's only competitor for first-run films in Las Vegas.

It is these three transactions—Syufy's purchases of the Mann, Plitt, and Cragin theaters—that the Justice Department claims amount to antitrust violations. As government counsel explained at oral argument, the thrust of its case is that "you may not get monopoly power by buying out your competitors.". . .

DISCUSSION

[O]f significance is the government's concession that Syufy was only a monopsonist, not a monopolist. Thus the government argues that Syufy had market power, but that he exercised this power only against suppliers (film distributors), not against consumers (moviegoers). This is consistent with the record, which demonstrates that Syufy always treated moviegoers fairly: The movie tickets, popcorn, nuts, and the Seven-Ups cost about the same in Las Vegas as in other, comparable markets. While it is theoretically possible to have a middleman who is a monopolist upstream but not downstream, this is a somewhat counterintuitive scenario. Why, if he truly had significant market power, would Raymond Syufy have chosen to take advantage of the big movie distributors while giving a fair shake to ordinary people? And why do the distributors, the alleged victims of the monopolization scheme, think that Raymond Syufy is the best thing that ever happened to the Las Vegas movie market?

There is universal agreement that monopoly power is the power to exclude competition or control prices. . . .

1. Power to Exclude Competition

It is true, of course, that when Syufy acquired Mann's, Plitt's, and Cragin's theaters he temporarily diminished the number of competitors in the Las Vegas first-run film market. But this does not necessarily indicate foul play; many legitimate market arrangements diminish the number of competitors. . . . If there are no significant barriers to entry, however, eliminating competitors will not enable the survivors to reap a monopoly profit; any attempt to raise prices above the competitive level will lure into the market new competitors able and willing to offer their commercial goods or personal services for less. . . .

The district court . . . found that there were no barriers to entry in the Las Vegas movie market. . . . [T]he district court's finding is amply supported by the record.

Immediately after Syufy bought out the last of his three competitors in October 1984, he was riding high, having captured 100 percent of the first-run film market in Las Vegas. But this utopia proved to be only a mirage. That same month, a major movie distributor, Orion, stopped doing business with Syufy, sending all of its first-run films to Roberts Company, a dark-horse competitor previously relegated to the second-run market. Roberts Company took this as an invitation to step into the major league and, against all odds, began giving Syufy serious competition in the first-run market. Fighting fire with fire, Roberts opened three multiplexes within a 13-month period, each having six or more screens. By December 1986, Roberts was operating 28 screens, trading places with Syufy, who had only 23. At the same time, Roberts was displaying a healthy portion of all first-run films. In fact, Roberts got exclusive exhibition rights to many of its films, meaning that Syufy could not show them at all.

By the end of 1987, Roberts was showing a larger percentage of first-run films than was the Redrock multiplex at the time Syufy bought it. Roberts then sold its theaters to United Artists, the largest theater chain in the country, and Syufy continued losing ground. It all boils down to this: Syufy's acquisitions did not short-circuit the operation of the natural market forces; Las Vegas's first-run film market was more competitive when this case came to trial than before Syufy bought out Mann, Plitt, and Cragin.

The Justice Department correctly points out that Syufy still has a large market share, but attributes far too much importance to this fact. In evaluating monopoly power, it is not market share that counts, but the ability to maintain market share. . . . Syufy seems unable to do this. In 1985 Syufy managed to lock up exclusive exhibition rights to 91 percent of all the first-run films in Las Vegas. By the first quarter of 1988, that percentage had fallen to 39 percent; United Artists had exclusive rights to another 25 percent, with the remaining 36 percent being played on both Syufy and UA screens.

Syufy's share of box office receipts also dropped off, albeit less precipitously. In 1985 Syufy raked in 93 percent of the gross box office from first-run films in Las Vegas. By the first quarter of 1988, that figure had fallen to 75 percent. The government insists that 75 percent is still a large number, and we are hard-pressed to disagree, but that's not the point.

The numbers reveal that Roberts/UA has steadily been eating away at Syufy's market share: In two and a half years, Syufy's percentage of exclusive exhibition rights dropped 52 percent and its percentage of box office receipts dropped 18 percent. During the same period, Roberts/UA's newly opened theaters evolved from absolute beginners, barely staying alive, into a big business.

2. Power to Control Prices

The crux of the Justice Department's case is that Syufy, top gun in the Las Vegas movie market, had the power to push around Hollywood's biggest players, dictating to them what prices they could charge for their movies. The district court found otherwise. This finding too has substantial support in the record.

Perhaps the most telling evidence of Syufy's inability to set prices came from movie distributors, Syufy's supposed victims. At the trial, distributors uniformly proclaimed their satisfaction with the way the Las Vegas first-run film market operates; none complained about the license fees paid by Syufy. . . . Particularly damaging to the government's case was the testimony of the former head of distribution for MGM/UA that his company "never had any difficulty . . . in acquiring the terms that we thought were reasonable," . . . explaining that the license fees Syufy paid "were comparable or better than any place in the United States. And in most cases better." . . .

The documentary evidence bears out this testimony. Syufy has at all times paid license fees far in excess of the national average, even higher than those paid by exhibitors in Los Angeles, the Mecca of Moviedom. In fact, Syufy paid a higher percentage of his gross receipts to distributors in 1987 and 1988 than he did during the intensely competitive period just before he acquired Cragin's Redrock.

While successful, Syufy is in no position to put the squeeze on distributors. . . .

It is a tribute to the state of competition in America that the Antitrust Division of the Department of Justice has found no worthier target than this paper tiger on which to expend limited taxpayer resources. Yet we cannot help but wonder whether bringing a lawsuit like this, and pursuing it doggedly through 27 months of pretrial proceedings, about two weeks of trial, and now the full distance on appeal, really serves the interests of free competition.

Affirmed.

Questions

1. At one point, Syufy held 100 percent of the first-run market. Why was Syufy not a monopolist?
2. Is this decision rooted more in structural (market share) or conduct (such as predatory pricing) considerations? Explain.
3. What role did the issue of Syufy's intent to monopolize play in this case? Explain.
4. Assume we have historical data showing that when the price of rolled steel has increased, the sales volume of rolled aluminum has remained constant. What, if anything, does that fact tell us about the product market for rolled steel?
5. Define the product market for championship boxing matches. See *United States v. International Boxing Club of New York, Inc.*, 358 U.S. 242 (1959) [**https://supreme.justia.com**].
6. Adidas provided cash, sporting goods, and the like to universities in exchange for various promotional rights, including the team's or coach's agreement to wear Adidas clothing in athletic activities. National Collegiate Athletic Association (NCAA) rules limited the amount of advertising that could appear on a uniform being used in competition. Adidas sued the NCAA claiming, among other things, that the advertising restrictions constituted an attempted monopoly by the NCAA. In pursuing its monopoly claim, Adidas defined the relevant market as "the market for the sale of NCAA Promotional Rights." The NCAA responded by saying that a market consisting solely of the sale of promotional rights by NCAA member institutions (colleges and universities) on athletic apparel used in intercollegiate activity was not a plausible relevant market.
   a. Define the relevant product market from the NCAA point of view.
   b. How did the court decide where the product market actually lies? See *Adidas America, Inc. v. NCAA*, 64 F. Supp. 2d 1097 (1999) [**https://law.justia.com**].

PRACTICING ETHICS Break Up the Biggest Banks?

Introducing the 2018 "Too Big to Fail, Too Big to Exist Act" in the United States Senate, Bernie Sanders, two-time presidential candidate and Vermont Independent, noted that the six largest financial institutions in America held assets equal to 50-60 percent of the national gross domestic product. Speaking with *Rolling Stone* magazine, Sanders explained that some of the banks are much bigger than they were before the government rescued them as part of the 2008 financial crisis:

> Now it turns out that our four largest financial institutions—J.P. Morgan Chase, Bank of America, Wells Fargo, and Citigroup—are on average 80 percent bigger than they were before we bailed them out. That's not right.

Questions

1. Do you believe the Wall Street banking industry operates by different ethical rules from those practiced by your hometown bankers? Explain.
2. Does the extraordinary size of the big banks, of itself, lead to wrongful practices in those banks? Put another way, is bigness bad? Explain.
3. Senator Sanders says the biggest banks' growth following the government bailout is "not right." Do you think government bailouts followed by extraordinary profits and growth constitute an ethical wrong? Explain.

Sources: Roben Farzad, "Sandy Weill's Untimely Second Thoughts," *Bloomberg Businessweek*, July 25, 2012 [**www.businessweek.com**]; and Matt Taibbi, "Taibbi: Chatting with Bernie Sanders about a Looming Financial Crisis," *Rolling Stone*, October 3, 2018 [**www.rollingstone.com**].

Questions—Part One

1. *a.* The *Harvard Law Review* argued: "In the New Economy (information technology) . . . there will inevitably be an increasing number of markets with only a few dominant players."[11] Why would that be so?
   b. Are we mistaken in pursuing Microsoft and other "new economy" giants with "old economy" antitrust principles? Explain.
2. Worldwide Basketball Sports Tours promoted early-season, NCAA-certified basketball tournaments. The National Collegiate Athletic Association's Two in Four Rule limited college basketball teams to "not more than one certified basketball event in one academic year, and not more than two certified basketball events every four years." The promoters sued the NCAA on antitrust grounds, claiming the Two in Four rule hampered their ability to make money. The NCAA argued that the limit on games was academically motivated.
   a. Does antitrust law apply to Division I collegiate basketball? Explain.
   b. Define the product market in this case. See *Worldwide Basketball & Sports Tours, Inc. v. NCAA,* 388 F.3d 955 (6th Cir. 2004) [**https://law.justia.com**], *cert. denied,* 126 S. Ct. 334 (2005).
3. *a.* A traditional concern about monopolies is that a lack of competition discourages efficiency and innovation. Argue that monopolies may actually encourage innovation.
   b. Even if monopolies do not discourage invention, we have firm economic grounds for opposing monopolies. Explain.
4. Historically, perhaps the most important interpretation of the Sherman Act's proscription of monopolization was Judge Learned Hand's opinion in the *Alcoa* case.

After finding that Alcoa controlled 90 percent of the aluminum ingot market, Hand had to determine whether Alcoa possessed a general intent to monopolize. Hand concluded that Alcoa's market dominance could have resulted only from a "persistent determination" to maintain control:

> It was not inevitable that it should always anticipate increases in the demand for ingots and be prepared to supply them. Nothing compelled it to keep doubling and redoubling its capacity before others entered the field. It insists that it never excluded competitors; but we can think of no more effective exclusion than progressively to embrace each new opportunity as it opened, and to face every newcomer with new capacity already geared into a great organization.[12]

Comment on Judge Hand's remarks.

5. Several smaller airlines sued two giants, United and American, claiming that the two violated the Sherman Act through their computerized reservation systems (CRSs). The core of the plaintiffs' position was that United and American were monopolists who violated the law by denying other airlines reasonable access to their CRSs. American and United had the largest CRSs, but other airlines also maintained CRSs. Neither had blocked any other airline's access to its CRS, but they had charged fees (in American's case, $1.75 per booking to the airline that secured a passenger through American's CRS). United and American each controlled about 12 to 14 percent of the total air transportation market. According to the court, the plaintiffs were "unhappy" about United's and American's ability to extract booking fees from them for the use of the CRSs. The U.S. Ninth Circuit Court of Appeals ruled for the defendants, and the Supreme Court declined to review the case.
   a. Explain why the plaintiffs felt wronged by American and United.
   b. Explain the defendants' argument that they could not successfully charge "excessive" prices for the use of their CRSs. See *Alaska Airlines v. United Airlines,* 948 F.2d 536 (9th Cir. 1991) [**https://law.justia.com**], *cert. denied,* 112 S. Ct. 1603 (1992).

Part Two—Mergers

LO 11-4 Identify the potential benefits and hazards of mergers.

LO 11-5 Distinguish between horizontal and vertical mergers.

We are in an era of corporate consolidation, as noted at the beginning of this chapter.[13] When promising newcomers emerge, larger competitors often simply buy them. Giants who already dominate an industry may join together. In the global agricultural seeds and chemicals markets, for example, former competitors Monsanto and Bayer have merged, as have their major competitors: Dow with DuPont and Syngenta with ChemChina.

Should we care that those six competitors are now just three and that they control perhaps two-thirds of the agricultural seed and agricultural chemicals markets both globally and in the United States? Let's remember, these products are crucial to much of the world's food supply–your food supply. And let's also remember that food security significantly shapes the world's welfare, including whether conflict or goodwill mark our future. More narrowly, we may fear that prices will rise unfairly while product quality and innovation will not achieve optimal advances.

Experts are concerned, furthermore, that the consolidated agricultural firms will control more and more of the big data and intellectual property that increasingly defines farming, with the result that the whole world will move more toward corporate farming, and the giant agriculture companies will exert increasing economic and political leverage.

United States Senator Cory Booker, New Jersey Democrat, explained some of the broader sociological implications for America:

> Consolidation has now reached a point where the top four firms in almost every sector of the food and agriculture economy have acquired abusive levels of market power. As a result, the U.S. is losing farmers at an alarming rate, agricultural jobs and wages are drying up, and rural communities are disappearing.[14]

Enhanced Efficiency

While mergers can be threatening, they often make good sense. Bayer, DowDuPont, and ChemChina see their mergers as market-driven, strategic adjustments necessary for better products, increased innovation, and an agricultural sector capable of feeding the world's billions. We must also remember that American companies are competing in a demanding international market and that mergers often bring efficiencies, such as economies of scale, that ultimately benefit consumers. Indeed, United States and European Union regulators looked very closely at these three mergers and allowed them to go forward subject to significant divestments. In some cases, enormous size is simply necessary to achieve the innovations and efficiencies needed to drive a market forward.

New Entrants

The market itself, without government intervention, frequently provides a remedy for dangerous corporate concentration. The global beer industry, for example, was shaken in 2016 when the world's largest brewer, Anheuser-Busch InBev, itself the product of a merger, acquired merged British giant SABMiller, along with a portfolio of smaller craft brewers. AB InBev's share of the worldwide beer market following the acquisitions reached approximately 30 percent with further growth and higher profits expected.[15] Those expectations, for the moment at least, have been dashed. United States beer consumption has declined, independent craft breweries have made important inroads in the beer market, and AB InBev, while still highly profitable, cut its dividend to help pay off its debt from the SABMiller purchase. Thus, while merger critics predicted increased prices and reduced innovation from industry concentration, the market–especially in the form of small, startup craft brewers–challenged AB InBev.[16] At the same time, consumer tastes had shifted toward wine and spirits.

Failing Companies

Sometimes mergers, and with them the risk of rising consumer prices, may be necessary to save failing companies, as was claimed by supporters of the U.S. Airways and American Airlines deal. The entire industry had endured big losses, and through mergers, the number of major carriers declined from seven to four firms holding the bulk of the market. That consolidation has produced higher fares on some routes where competition has declined, but the airline industry returned to profitability, smaller airlines found new spaces in the market, and record numbers of Americans were financially able to fly. A 2014 PricewaterhouseCoopers study found that airline mergers benefited the industry and helped keep fares low.[17]

In Sum

Mergers have played an important role in building American business. The merger trend remains troubling, nonetheless. A 2016 study of recent manufacturing mergers, for example, found a general increase in market power and prices with little evidence of improved efficiency or productivity.[18] *The New York Times* in 2010 cited a study finding higher prices in oil after Pennzoil acquired Quaker State, in tampons after Procter & Gamble bought Tambrands, in cereal after General Mills acquired Chex brands, and in Scotch whisky after the merger of Guinness and Grand Metropolitan.[19]

Merger Virtues

Mergers, often driven by growth opportunities, the need to cut costs, and technological change, can have an array of beneficial effects:

1. Mergers permit the replacement of inefficient management, and the threat of replacement disciplines managers to be more productive.
2. Mergers may permit stronger competition against larger rivals.
3. Mergers may improve credit access.
4. Mergers may produce efficiencies, including economies of scale.
5. Mergers frequently increase the pool of liquid assets available for expansion and innovation.
6. Mergers often offer tax advantages.
7. Growth by merger is often less expensive than internal growth.
8. Mergers help satisfy the personal ambitions and needs of management.[20]

PRACTICING ETHICS Antitrust and Personal Happiness?

Tim Wu, Columbia University law professor, big tech/media critic, and author of *The Curse of Bigness,* has called for robust application of antitrust laws to America's corporate giants. Wu thinks that the consumer welfare argument for relaxed antitrust enforcement, so long as prices are low, ignores what should be, and once was, the central goal: thwarting the pursuit of concentrated, abusive power.

From that familiar call for breaking up big corporations, Wu's argument takes a refreshingly personal, even moral, direction as he thinks about the impact of corporate power on each individual. He points to wealth and income inequality and constrained personal freedom as outcomes of corporate concentration. Ordinary Americans, he says, are being robbed of their humanity. They are, in some sense, slaves to their employers. They cannot enjoy the security of stable jobs that afford ample time off—time to find and express their humanity. They cannot become their own best selves. Wu says

> We're very materialist about the economy. We don't think about its spiritual dimensions. We don't really think about what it would mean to structure an economy that makes people happy.[21]

Questions

1. *a.* What do you think Wu meant about the "spiritual" dimension of our economy?
   b. Do you think he is right about that? Explain.
2. *a.* Do you think bigness in contemporary American business wrongly depletes ordinary Americans' personal freedom and thus their opportunities for optimal personal development? Explain.
   b. If so, is antitrust law an appropriate vehicle for enhancing those opportunities? Explain.
3. *a.* Do America's employers have a moral duty to strive for employee happiness? Explain.
   b. If so, does concentrated corporate power interfere with that goal? Explain.

Sources: Rana Foroohar, "The Curse of Bigness," *Financial Times,* November 4, 2018 [**www.ft.com**]; Christoper Shay, "Tim Wu Goes After the Titans of the New Gilded Age," *The Nation,* November 18, 2018 [**www.thenation.com**]; and Tim Wu, *The Curse of Bigness: Antitrust in the New Gilded Age,* New York: Columbia Global Reports, 2018.

Mergers fail more often than marriages.

Merger Problems

Many studies show that mergers often fail in the sense that they do not add value to the merging companies. Experts generally estimate the merger failure rate, measured in various ways, at between 50 and 80 percent. As CNN described it: "Mergers Fail More Often Than Marriages."[22] In addition to frequent financial failures, other merger hazards should be noted:

1. Too much power is being concentrated in too few hands.
2. A particular merger, although not threatening in and of itself, may trigger a merger movement among industry competitors.
3. Higher market concentration may lead to higher prices.
4. Innovation may be harmed.
5. Some companies are so large that they can significantly shape political affairs.
6. Some companies may have become so large that we cannot allow them to fail.[23]

When Should the Government Intervene?

The federal government is sometimes rather aggressive in its merger oversight. Large deals in cable, office supply, and oil drilling have been blocked in recent years by antitrust regulators. DraftKings and FanDuel, with a combined 90 percent of the daily online fantasy sports market, called off their proposed merger in 2017 after the government announced that it would sue to block the deal.

Government opposition sometimes reaches the courts. Usually, however, the government works out settlements with the merging parties. T-Mobile and Sprint, for example, received federal government approval for their horizontal merger in 2019. The two merged in 2020, creating the third largest U.S. wireless company, with T-Mobile as the surviving brand. The merger partners said the deal would allow them to better compete with larger rivals AT&T and Verizon, while also enabling increased investment in faster (5G) Internet connectivity. Government approval required the companies to sell some assets to Dish Network and guarantee Dish access to the T-Mobile network for seven years, while Dish built its own 5G network.

Critics say the merger will reduce competition and lead to higher bills for consumers. History suggests the critics may be right. In 2006, appliance giant Whirlpool was allowed to purchase prime competitor Maytag on the theory that competition from foreign appliance makers would hold prices in check. Whirlpool, however, later successfully lobbied for higher tariffs on imported appliances and prices subsequently increased.[24]

Merger Law: Overview

Mergers are addressed by the Sherman Act, Section 1; but the Clayton Act, Section 7 better expresses the legislative intent:

> That no person engaged in commerce shall acquire the whole or any part of the stock or the assets of another person engaged also in commerce where the effect of such acquisition may be substantially to lessen competition, or to tend to create a monopoly.

Technically, a merger involves the union of two or more enterprises wherein one company, the merger survivor, absorbs all of the assets and liabilities of the disappearing companies. Antitrust law, however, reaches all situations in which previously independent business entities are united–whether by merger, acquisition of stock (creating a parent-subsidiary relationship), purchase of substantially all assets, or consolidation (forming a new company into which all existing companies merge and then disappear).

Mergers take several forms, but we will mention just three categories that have been most prominent in antitrust law:

1. A horizontal merger involves firms that are in direct competition and occupy the same product and geographic markets. A merger of two vodka producers in the same geographic market would clearly fall in the horizontal category. Would the merger of a vodka producer and a gin producer constitute a horizontal merger?
2. A vertical merger involves two or more firms at different levels of the same supply chain, such as a furniture manufacturer and a fabric supplier.
3. A conglomerate merger involves firms dealing in unrelated products. Thus, the conglomerate category embraces all mergers that are neither horizontal nor vertical. An example would be the acquisition of a pet food manufacturer by a book publisher. Conglomerate mergers are of historical significance, but they currently receive little attention from the government, and we will not examine them further.

LO 11-6
Explain premerger notification requirements.

Premerger Notification

Under the Hart-Scott-Rodino Antitrust Improvements Act (HSR), a merger must be reported to the Federal Trade Commission (FTC) and the Justice Department if it exceeds a certain dollar threshold. The parties are generally barred from closing the merger until 30 days after they have made the required HSR filing, to give the government time to gather information by which to determine whether the merger should be challenged. [For more on the HSR premerger notification program, see **www.ftc.gov/bc/hsr/index.shtm**].

LO 11-7
Describe remedies for mergers determined to be anticompetitive.

Remedies

After the HSR review, the government can decide that the merger may proceed. The government may, on the other hand, conclude that the merger is anticompetitive. If the parties persist with a disfavored merger, the government can file suit. The preferred action, however, is to work out a settlement. One of the parties might sell some of its assets, or a party might agree to forgo business in some geographic segment of the market for a time. Rental car stalwart Hertz, in 2012, secured FTC approval for its $2.3 billion acquisition of Dollar Thrifty (parent of the Dollar and Thrifty car rental brands) only after agreeing to sell both its Advantage car rental business and 29 existing Dollar Thrifty on-airport locations.

In cases where negotiation fails and the government decides to sue, it can ask the court for a remedy, such as an order stopping the merger or an order requiring divestiture of certain assets. Government litigation is relatively infrequent, but the resulting message to the business community is powerful. In addition, private parties sometimes use the antitrust laws to sue for treble damages when they believe a merger has harmed them unlawfully. Government oversight, as well as the threat of occasional private action, help maintain a marketplace where consumers enjoy the benefits of vigorous competition, including lower prices, improved quality, and innovation. [For recent developments in antitrust law, see *Antitrust Today* at **https://constantinecannon.com/practice/antitrust-litigation-counseling/antitrust-today**].

[For the "Top Ten Disastrous Mergers and Acquisitions," see **www.youtube.com/watch?v=9dFvhq2sKfM**].

Horizontal Analysis

LO 11-8
Analyze when a horizontal merger is anticompetitive.

Horizontal mergers raise anticompetitive risks because they involve direct rivals seeking to join together. The courts often (but not always) follow the FTC-Justice Department merger guidelines, which focus on a pair of anticompetitive concerns:

1. **Coordinated effects/collusion.** Will the merger facilitate cooperation so that the merging parties and their competitors might fix prices, reduce output, reduce quality, or otherwise coordinate their activities rather than compete against each other? Broadly, the government takes the position that fewer firms, and thus greater market concentration, increase the likelihood of collusion–a position the courts often, but not always, embrace.
2. **Unilateral effects.** Will the merger allow the newly merged firm to unilaterally raise prices, restrict output, or control innovation? Normally, unilateral effects arise where competitors significantly restrained each other prior to the merger. By removing a rival, a merger can allow the post-merger entity to exercise market power and thereby harm consumers.

Market Power

Guidelines have been established to identify mergers that may result in market power, defined as the ability of a seller "profitably to maintain prices above competitive levels for a significant period of time." Historically, the guidelines set out a five-step methodology for analyzing horizontal mergers:

1. Definition of market.
2. Measurement of market concentration.
3. Identification of likely anticompetitive effects.
4. Likelihood of future entrants to the market.
5. Appraisal of efficiencies and other possible defenses.

1. Market Definitions

The market is defined as the smallest product and geographic market in which a monopolist could raise prices a small but significant and nontransitory amount (usually set at five percent above current prices).

2. Market Concentration

A good deal of our attention in this chapter has been directed to concerns about increasing market concentration, but how do we decide if a horizontal merger increases concentration in a way that threatens competition? The Herfindahl-Hirschman Index (HHI) is employed to measure market concentration. The HHI is useful because it measures both concentration and dispersion of market share between big and small firms. The market share of each firm is squared and the results are summed. Thus, if five companies each have 20 percent of a market, the index for that market would be 2,000. If there are 10 firms, each with 10 percent of the market, the resulting HHI would be 1,000. The larger the HHI, the more concentrated the market. In general, a postmerger HHI below 1,500 would reflect an unconcentrated market, one between 1,500 and 2,500 would be considered mildly concentrated, and one more than 2,500 is deemed a highly concentrated market. The greater the HHI and the greater the increase in the HHI, the more likely the government will be concerned about the merger. The aforementioned American Airlines-U.S. Airways merger had an HHI of 1,269 among the top four carriers in the national market (American after the merger–20 percent, Southwest–18 percent, United Continental–17 percent, and Delta–16 percent) and would be classified as "unconcentrated."[25]

3. Anticompetitive Effects

The government's concern is that the merger may permit monopoly behavior in the merged firms' market.

4. Ease of Entry

If new competitors can readily enter the post-merger market, the existing firms will be forced to charge competitive prices and otherwise conform to the discipline of the market.

5. Defenses

An otherwise unacceptable merger may be saved by certain defenses. The *failing company doctrine* permits a merger to preserve the assets of a firm that would otherwise be lost to the market. *Efficiencies* include such desirable economic results as economies of scale or reduced transportation costs as a result of the merger.

Guideline Changes

In 2010, the Justice Department and the Federal Trade Commission announced revisions to the Horizontal Merger Guidelines. Much of the analysis continues as outlined above, but strictly following the five-step structure is not expected. Market definition and market share, while still important, will receive reduced attention with adverse competitive effects coming to the forefront. The analysis will begin, not with economic theory, but with evidence of real-world competitive harm (such as customer injury, reduced innovation, or reduced product variety), at which point market definition and the balance of the analysis outlined above could be influential. This approach may, therefore, allow the government greater flexibility in proving competition problems even if large market shares cannot be established. Ongoing antitrust decisions, including the *Staples/Office Depot* case later in this chapter, will indicate how closely the courts actually follow the government's altered guidance.

Horizontal Merger Blocked

In 2011, the Justice Department successfully challenged a proposed horizontal merger between tax preparers H&R Block and TaxACT. Judge Beryl Howell at the District Court for the District of Columbia agreed with the Justice Department that the relevant product market was digital do-it-yourself (DDIY) tax preparation products (thus excluding assisted and manual tax preparation) with the three largest firms controlling 90 percent of the market (Intuit–62.2 percent, HRB–15.6 percent, and TaxACT–12.8 percent) and the remaining 10 percent split among a number of smaller firms. The merger would have increased the HHI in the DDIY market by 400 points to 4,691. The court concluded that H&R Block had failed to show that collusion would not result in what would have become a highly concentrated post-merger market.

Judge Howell also considered various company documents; in one, H&R Block allegedly said the merger would allow it to "regain control of industry pricing and avoid further price erosion." When looking at anticompetitive effects from the proposed merger, the court reasoned that TaxACT's "impressive history of innovation and competition in the DDIY market" had been important in constraining prices, a role that would have disappeared had the merger been consummated. Given these considerations and insufficient evidence that dramatic efficiencies would accompany the merger, Judge Howell ruled for the government. H&R Block did not appeal.

Sources: King & Spaulding, "DOJ Antitrust Division Wins Major Victory in H&R Block Case," *Client Alert,* November 10, 2011 [**www.lexology.com**]; Michael H. Pryor, "What the H&R Block Merger Opinion Can Tell Us about the AT&T/T-Mobile Merger Case," *LEXOLOGY,* November 16, 2011 [**www.lexology.com**]; and *United States of America v. H&R Block, Inc.,* 833 F. Supp. 2d 36 (D.D.C. 2011) [**https://law.justia.com**].

Vertical Analysis

LO 11-9

Analyze when a vertical merger creates anticompetitive "market foreclosure."

A vertical merger typically involves an alliance between a supplier and a purchaser. The primary resulting threat to competition is labeled *market foreclosure,* as illustrated in Figure 11.1. A vertical merger may deny a source of supply to a purchaser or raise prices charged to that purchaser. A vertical merger may also deny an outlet for sale to a seller. Both conditions potentially threaten competition in violation of the Clayton Act. The government looks closely at that foreclosure to determine whether it actually has an anticompetitive effect. In addition to foreclosing sources of supply or outlets for sale, the government may be concerned about other anticompetitive effects such as raising rivals' costs, facilitating collusion, and raising barriers to entry.

Vertical Merger Challenges

Vertical mergers often do not raise competitive hazards, and they can produce important efficiencies, so government challenges have been uncommon. The federal Justice Department Antitrust Division recently did, however, file a complaint to block AT&T's proposed acquisition of media content provider, Time Warner. The government argued that the vertical merger would allow AT&T, the nation's largest pay television provider, to deny video

FIGURE 11.1
Vertical Merger

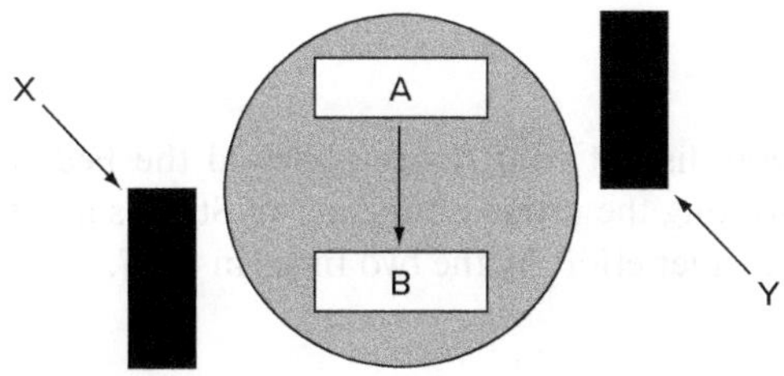

A supplies B. A and B merge. X (A's competitor) had traditionally sold to B, and Y (B's competitor) had traditionally purchased from A. Is the merger lawful? How do we decide?

content controlled by Time Warner (such as HBO, CNN, TBS, and TNT) to its competitors (for instance, Verizon and T-Mobile) or force those competitors to pay more for that content. Consumer prices would then be expected to rise. The government lost both at trial and on appeal in 2019 with the courts noting, among other things, that the pay television market has been vibrant with new competitors such as Hulu and Netflix entering and enhancing competition.[26]

Critics of the decision think it will invite more media mergers, both vertical and horizontal, as technology (streaming, in particular) forces change and companies try to get bigger to compete more effectively. Indeed, in late 2019, the merger of CBS (television network) and Viacom (which owns Paramount Pictures and MTV) was completed.

Ticketmaster

Market foreclosure concerns, as explained above, sometimes lead to government intervention. That was the case with the 2010 Ticketmaster–Live Nation merger that created a vertically integrated giant with a significant presence up and down the entertainment industry "value chain," including artist management, concert touring, concert venues, and ticketing. The merger also raised horizontal concerns in the ticketing business.

> The Ticketmaster–Live Nation merger created a vertically integrated giant.

Ticketmaster, the nation's largest ticketing company, owned a controlling share in Front Line Management, whose 200-plus clients included the Eagles and Miley Cyrus. Live Nation, the country's largest concert promoter, also owned or managed 135 major concert venues around the world, was the world's largest artist-management company, and operated related businesses, including product merchandising and online fan clubs. Live Nation was also a recent entrant to the ticketing business.

The merger partners and the Justice Department agreed to a settlement, allowing the creation of the newly merged company–to be called Live Nation Entertainment (LNE). Addressing vertical concerns, LNE agreed to Justice Department monitoring to ensure that it would not abuse its market power. The Justice Department feared that LNE might, for example, require concert venues wanting access to Ticketmaster's monopoly ticketing services to book only LNE-promoted acts, thus foreclosing other promoters from doing business with those venues. Addressing horizontal concerns, Ticketmaster agreed to divest one of its ticketing divisions while licensing its ticketing software to a competitor, thus effectively allowing the creation of two new competitors for Ticketmaster.[27]

Horizontal Merger Case

In the following case, a federal district court judge reviewed the Federal Trade Commission's request for an order blocking the proposed merger of Staples and Office Depot. The FTC had blocked a previous merger effort by the two firms in 1997.

LEGAL BRIEFCASE

Federal Trade Commission v. Staples, Inc. and Office Depot, Inc.

190 F. Supp. 3d 100 (D.D.C. 2016)

Judge Sullivan

I. INTRODUCTION

Subsequent to Defendants' announcement in February 2015 of their intent to merge, the FTC began an approximate year-long investigation into the $6.3 billion merger and its likely effects on competition. On December 7, 2015, by a unanimous vote, the FTC Commissioners found reason to believe that the proposed merger would substantially reduce competition in violation of Section 7 of the Clayton Act and Section 5 of the FTC Act. That same day, Plaintiffs commenced this action seeking a preliminary injunction to enjoin the proposed merger.

II. BACKGROUND

A. Overview

. . . To sustain employees' use of pens, Post-it notes and paperclips, large companies purchase more than two billion dollars of office supplies from Defendants annually. Companies that purchase office supplies for their own use operate in what the industry refers to as the B-to-B space. B-to-B customers prefer to work with one vendor that can meet all of the companies' office supply needs. . . .

To establish a primary vendor relationship, companies in the B-to-B space request proposals from national suppliers like Staples and Office Depot. The request for proposal (RFP) process typically results in a multi-year contract with a primary vendor that guarantees prices for specific items, includes an upfront lump-sum rebate, and a host of other services. Because the office supplies consumed by larger companies are voluminous, such companies typically pay only half the price for basic supplies as compared to the average retail consumer.

B. Defendants Staples and Office Depot

Established as big-box retail stores in the 1980s, Defendants are the primary B-to-B office supply vendors in the United States today. Plaintiffs allege that Defendants sell and distribute upwards of seventy-nine percent of office supplies in the B-to-B space. Since the 2013 merger of Office Depot and Office Max, Defendants consistently engage in head-to-head competition with each other for B-to-B contracts.

. . . Staples is the largest office supplier of consumable office supplies to large B-to-B customers in the United States. . . .

Office Depot is the second largest office supplier of consumable office supplies to large B-to-B customers in the United States. . . . [T]his case focuses on large B-to-B customers, defined by Plaintiffs as those that spend $500,000 or more per year on office supplies. Approximately 1200 corporations in the United States are included in this alleged relevant market.

C. [Omitted]

D. Regional and Local Vendors

Regional and local office supply vendors exist throughout the country. However, they typically do not bid for large B-to-B contracts.

E. Amazon Business

Amazon.com Inc.'s effort to compete in the office supply industry, including the B-to-B space, is Amazon Business. . . . Although in its infancy, Amazon's vision is for Amazon Business to be the "preferred marketplace for all professional, business and institutional customers worldwide." . . .

III. [Omitted]

IV. DISCUSSION

A. Legal Principles Considered When Defining a Relevant Market

a. Consumable office supplies as cluster market

Cluster markets allow items that are not substitutes for each other to be clustered together in one antitrust market. . . . Here plaintiffs allege that items such as pens, file folders, Post-it notes, binder clips, and paper for copiers and printers are included in this cluster market. Although a pen is not a functional substitute for a paperclip, it is possible to cluster consumable office supplies into one market for analytical convenience. Defining the market as a cluster market is justified in this case because "market shares and competitive conditions are likely to be similar for the distribution of pens to large customers and the distribution of binder clips to large customers."

B. Application of Relevant Legal Principles to Plaintiffs' Market Definition

. . . Plaintiffs argue that the relevant market is a cluster market of "consumable office supplies" which consists of "an assortment of office supplies, such as pens, paper clips, notepads and copy paper, that are used and replenished frequently." Plaintiffs' alleged relevant market is also a targeted market, limited to B-to-B customers, specifically large B-to-B customers who spend $500,000 or more on office supplies annually.

Defendants, on the other hand, argue that Plaintiffs' alleged market definition is wrong because it is a "gerrymandered and artificially narrow product market limited to *some*, but not all, consumable office supplies sold to only the most powerful companies in the world." In particular, Defendants insist that ink and toner must be included in a proper definition of the relevant product market. Defendants also argue that no evidence supports finding sales to large B-to-B customers as a distinct market.

1. *Brown Shoe* "Practical Indicia"

The *Brown Shoe* practical indicia support Plaintiffs' definition of the relevant product market . . . because there is: (a) industry or public recognition of the market as a separate economic entity; (b) B-to-B customers demand distinct prices and demonstrate a high sensitivity to price changes; and (c) B-to-B customers require specialized vendors that offer value-added services, including: (i) sophisticated information technology (IT) services; (ii) high quality customer service; and (iii) expedited delivery. . . .

2. Expert Testimony of Dr. Carl Shapiro and the Hypothetical Monopolist Test

. . . The parties agree that the main test used by economists to determine a product market is the hypothetical monopolist test (HMT). This test queries whether a hypothetical monopolist who has control over the products in an alleged market could profitably raise prices on those products. . . .

Dr. Shapiro . . . points out that Staples and Office Depot's head-to-head competition "tells us that a *monopoly* provider of consumable office supplies would charge significantly more to large customers than Staples and Office Depot today charge these same customers." Dr. Shapiro also highlights the record evidence that demonstrates Defendants compete "fiercely" for business in the large B-to-B space. Dr. Shapiro concludes that such competition implies that "the elimination of competition would lead to a significant price increase to large customers. . . ."

C. Defendants' Arguments in Opposition to Plaintiffs' Alleged Market

Defendants make two primary arguments in response to Plaintiffs' alleged market. First, Defendants . . . argue that exclusion of ink and toner, as well as "beyond office supplies" or "BOSS" products from the alleged market, is error. Second, defendants argue that no evidence supports Plaintiffs' contention that large B-to-B customers should be treated as a separate market.

1. Exclusion of ink, toner and BOSS from alleged market is proper

a. Defendants' argument for inclusion of ink and toner fails because they are not subject to the same competitive conditions as general office supplies

Competition for the sale of ink and toner has increased due to the "recent and rapid" rise of Managed Print Services (MPS). MPS vendors like Xerox, Hewlett-Packard, Lexmark, and Ricoh provide a bundle of services that includes sale of ink and toner in addition to service and maintenance of printers and copiers. There is ample record evidence to show that ink, toner, and other adjacent BOSS items are properly excluded from the relevant market because they are subject to distinct competitive conditions. For example, some large companies are shifting all of their ink and toner business to an MPS. . . . Other large companies are disaggregating ink and toner purchases between their primary vendor and an MPS. . . .

2. Antitrust laws exist to protect competition, not a particular set of consumers

Defendants' second primary argument in opposition to Plaintiffs' proposed relevant market is that "there is no evidence to support Plaintiffs' claim that large B-to-B should be treated as a separate market."

[T]he nature of how large B-to-B customers operate, including the services they demand, supports a finding that they are a targeted customer market for procurement of consumable office supplies. There is overwhelming evidence in this case that large B-to-B customers constitute a market that Defendants could target for price increases if they are allowed to merge. Significantly, Defendants themselves used the proposed merger to pressure B-to-B customers to lock in prices based on the expectation that they would lose negotiating leverage if the merger were approved. . . .

D. [Omitted]

E. Analysis of the Plaintiffs' Arguments Relating to Probable Effects on Competition Based on Market Share Calculations

Having concluded that Plaintiffs have carried their burden of establishing that the sale and distribution of consumable office supplies to large B-to-B customers in the United States is the relevant market, the Court now turns to an analysis of the likely effects of the proposed merger on competition within the relevant market. . . .

1. Concentration in the sale and distribution of consumable office supplies to large B-to-B customers

Dr. Shapiro estimated Defendants' market shares by using data collected from *Fortune* 100 companies [about their spending on consumable office supplies]. . . . Defendants' market share of the *Fortune* 100 sample as a whole is striking: Staples captures 47.3 percent and Office Depot captures 31.6 percent, for a total of 79 percent market share. The pre-merger HHI is already highly concentrated in this market, resting at 3,270. . . . If allowed to merge, the HHI would increase nearly 3,000 points, from 3,270 to 6,265. This market structure would constitute one dominant firm with a competitive fringe. Staples' proposed acquisition of Office Depot is therefore presumptively illegal because the HHI increases more than 200 points and the post-merger HHI is greater than 2,500. . . .

F. [Omitted]

G. Conclusion Regarding Plaintiffs' Market Share Analysis

Plaintiffs have met their burden of showing that the merger would result in "undue concentration" in the relevant market of the sale and distribution of consumable office supplies to large B-to-B customers in the United States. . . .

H. Plaintiffs' Evidence of Additional Harm

Sole reliance on HHI calculations cannot guarantee litigation victories. . . . The bid data . . . shows that Defendants win large B-to-B customer bids more frequently than other bidders. . . . Defendants' own documents created in the ordinary course of their business show that Defendants view themselves as the most viable office supply vendors for large businesses in the United States. . . . Large B-to-B customers view Defendants as their best option for nationwide sale and delivery of consumable office supplies. . . .

This additional evidence strengthens Plaintiffs' claim that harm will result in the form of loss of competition if Staples is permitted to acquire Office Depot.

I. Defendants' Response to Plaintiffs' *Prima Facie* Case

Defendants' sole argument in response to Plaintiffs' *prima facie* case is that the merger will not have anti-competitive effects because Amazon Business, as well as the existing patchwork of local and regional office supply companies, will expand and provide large B-to-B customers with competitive alternatives to the merged entity. . . . The relevant time frame for consideration in this forward looking exercise is two to three years.

. . . Plaintiffs point to a long list of what they view as Amazon Business' deficiencies, including, but not limited to: (1) lack of RFP experience; (2) no commitment to guaranteed pricing; (3) lack of ability to control third-party price and delivery; (4) inability to provide customer-specific pricing; (5) a lack of dedicated customer service agents dedicated to the B-to-B space; (6) no desktop delivery; (7) no proven ability to provide detailed utilization and invoice reports; and (8) lack of product variety and breadth. Although Amazon Business may successfully address some of these alleged weaknesses in the short term, the evidence . . . does not support the conclusion that Amazon Business will be in a position to restore competition lost by the proposed merger within three years.

V. CONCLUSION

As Judge Mehta observed in *Sysco,* "There can be little doubt that the acquisition of the second largest firm in the market by the largest firm in the market will tend to harm competition in that market." The Court concludes that Plaintiffs have met their burden of showing . . . that Staples' acquisition of Office Depot would lessen competition in the sale and distribution of consumable office supplies in the large B-to-B market in the United States. . . .

. . . Plaintiffs' Motion for Preliminary Injunction is GRANTED.

Questions

1. *a.* What was the court's definition of the market?
   b. How did the court arrive at that definition?
   c. Why were ink, toner, and BOSS excluded from that market?
2. *a.* What evidence supported the FTC's claim that the merger would lead to anticompetitive effects?
   b. In weighing the Federal Trade Commission's arguments and those of Staples and Office Depot, why did the court come down on the side of the government?
3. Do you think consumers will benefit from this decision? Explain.

4. Three firms controlled the $1 billion U.S. baby food market (Gerber—65 percent, Heinz—17.4 percent, and Beech-Nut—15.4 percent). Gerber was sold in over 90 percent of American supermarkets, and it had greater brand loyalty than any other product sold in the United States. Heinz was sold in 40 percent of the supermarkets and Beech-Nut in 45 percent. Heinz and Beech-Nut agreed to merge. The baby food HHI would increase from 4,755 to 5,285 if this occurred. The Federal Trade Commission opposed the merger.
   a. What other facts would you want to know to decide the legality of this proposed merger?
   b. Defend the merger.
   c. How would you decide? Explain. See *Federal Trade Commission v. H. J. Heinz Co.*, 246 F.3d 708 (D.C. Cir. 2001) [**https://law.justia.com**].
5. In 1958, Pabst Brewing Company acquired Blatz Brewing Company. Pabst was America's 10th largest brewer, while Blatz was the 18th largest. After the merger, Pabst had 4.49 percent of the nationwide beer market and was the fifth-largest brewer. In the regional market of Wisconsin, Michigan, and Illinois, the merger gave Pabst 11.32 percent of the sales. After the merger, Pabst led beer sales in Wisconsin with 23.95 percent of that statewide market. The beer market was becoming increasingly concentrated, with the total number of brewers declining from 206 to 162 during the years 1957 to 1961. In *United States v. Pabst Brewing Co.*, 384 U.S. 546 (1966) [**https://supreme.justia.com**], the Supreme Court found the merger violated the Clayton Act, Section 7. The Court did not choose among the three geographic market configurations, saying that the crucial inquiry is whether a merger may substantially lessen competition anywhere in the United States. Thus, the Court held that, under these facts, a 4.49 percent share of the market was too large. Respected scholar and jurist Richard Posner labeled the *Pabst* decision an "atrocity" and the product of a "fit of nonsense" on the part of the Supreme Court.[28] What economic arguments would support Posner's colorful complaint?

Part Three—American Antitrust Laws and the International Market

LO 11-10
Contrast antitrust enforcement in the United States and the European Union.

Antitrust questions can become extremely complex in global transactions involving multiple companies in multiple nations where those transactions are potentially governed by both U.S. and foreign antitrust laws. U.S. antitrust laws apply to foreign firms doing business in the United States, but in addition, the Sherman, Clayton, and FTC acts, among others, are all potentially applicable to business transacted abroad that directly affects America regardless of the participants' nationalities.

Extraterritoriality

The U.S. Justice Department claims authority to apply American antitrust law abroad, including the power to sue foreign firms that violate U.S. antitrust laws even when the anticompetitive actions take place overseas (extraterritorial application). America does not, however, claim unlimited antitrust authority. The 1982 Foreign Trade Antitrust Improvements Act (FTAIA) basically excludes all foreign conduct from the extraterritorial reach of the Sherman Act except conduct "involving" (1) "import commerce" and (2) nonimport commerce that has a "direct, substantial and reasonably foreseeable effect" on domestic commerce or American exporters. Claims arising from foreign commerce not falling within those two exceptions would have to be litigated in other nations.

International Antitrust Enforcement

Most antitrust enforcement occurs in the United States and the European Union, but other nations, China in particular, are taking a more aggressive stance, usually by employing laws that largely mirror those of the United States or the European Union.

European Union Antitrust Enforcement

Given the European Union's powerful global economic role, the antitrust decisions of EU regulators necessarily influence business practices worldwide and, not surprisingly, American tech firms have received particular attention.

Facebook, Google, Intel, and Qualcomm, for example, have all been fined recently for alleged anticompetitive behavior in Europe. But the fines, while relatively large, certainly are not crippling, and appeals often follow.

Similarly, European Union regulators have been willing to block mergers and force established firms to make room for startup competitors. As a result, market concentration in crucial industries is often less pronounced in Europe than in America. The four largest European airlines, for example, control about 40 percent of the market while that share is about 80 percent in the United States, and American prices reportedly are higher.[29]

Some critics believe EU antitrust policy is, in part, a commercial attack on America's high tech dominance. Nonetheless, American and European Union antitrust policies are generally compatible and are the product of constant consultation. [For EU antitrust law, see **http://ec.europa.eu/competition/index_en.html**].

Other Nations

The number of nations with competition laws totaled about 40 in 1995, but around 120 nations now have or are currently adopting competition laws, and we are seeing the beginning of a worldwide convergence of those laws led by the United States, China, and the European Union.[30]

China created its Anti-Monopoly Law in 2008. Responding to complaints about inconsistent and unpredictable antitrust enforcement, Chinese antitrust authorities, in 2014, committed to due process improvements in its antitrust practices. China agreed to treat foreign and domestic firms the same, to allow foreign companies to have legal counsel during investigative proceedings, and to publish the results of its investigations. China's official position is that aggressive antitrust enforcement is necessary to protect consumers from price gouging and other abuses, but critics suspect China uses its strengthened regulations to pursue foreign multinationals and thereby protect and promote Chinese companies.

Trade War

Antitrust laws played an important role in the Trump Administration's trade war between the United States and China. Critics believe, for example, that China has been trying to dominate the world pharmaceutical market through government-directed price fixing as well as financial subsidies to manufacturers. Some United States purchasers of Chinese-made vitamin C have been engaged for years in a lawsuit claiming that Chinese companies violate United States law by fixing the price of vitamin C for export. The Chinese Ministry of Commerce argued that Chinese law required the coordination of vitamin C prices. The defendant Chinese firms, therefore, said they were not violating United States antitrust laws because they were doing what their government required of them. In 2018, the case reached the U.S. Supreme Court, which ruled that American courts are not bound by a foreign government's interpretation of its laws, but that the interpretation must be given "respectful consideration," while other materials may also be reviewed such as "consistency with . . . past positions."[31]

Ultimately, several of the Chinese company defendants settled the case, but two defendants continued to litigate, and a judgment of approximately $150 million was entered against them. The U.S. Court of Appeals for the Second Circuit, however, ruled in favor of the Chinese defendants and reversed the judgment outright. In any event, Congress has been considering legislation designed, in part, to encourage domestic drug manufacturing and to reduce American reliance on Chinese production. For instance, the *Protecting our Pharmaceutical Supply Chain from China Act of 2022,* H.R. 7121, was introduced in the 117th Congress.

A broader discussion of the regulation of multinational corporations outside of their home countries, including anticompetitive restraints and mergers, can be found in Chapter 16.

Research Exercise

The Sherman Act was enacted in 1890, the Clayton Act and the Federal Trade Commission Act in 1914, and the Robinson-Patman Act in 1936.

a. Pick one of these acts and identify what societal conditions and events provoked its passage.

b. Are similar conditions/events occurring today? Explain.

Chapter Questions

1. The City of Chicago owned and operated the Chicago Skyway, a toll bridge connecting Chicago and Indiana. Chicago earned $52 million in tolls beyond the amount needed to meet bond payments and to maintain the Skyway. The excess was used to pay for other transportation expenses. Skyway tolls were higher than those of other area highways. Endsley, a bridge user, joined others in a class action against Chicago, claiming that the city's control of the Skyway provided monopoly power in high-speed limited access travel between Indiana and Chicago and that the city was abusing that power by collecting excessive fees. Chicago demonstrated that at least two alternative, if less desirable, routes were in competition with the Skyway. Was Chicago a monopolist? Explain. See *Endsley v. City of Chicago,* 230 F.3d 276 (7th Cir. 2000) [**https://law.justia.com**], *cert. denied,* 532 U.S. 972 (2001).

2. Major League Soccer (MLS) was the exclusive Division I professional soccer league in the United States, as recognized by the U.S. Soccer Federation (USSF), the national soccer governing body. MLS owned all of the league's 12 teams, set all schedules, negotiated all stadium leases, controlled all intellectual property rights, and controlled all player contracts. Partial control over some teams was transferred by MLS to certain investors. The investors did not hire their own players. Each employment contract was between the player and the league. MLS assigned the players in a manner designed to maintain competitive balance. MLS had been preceded in U.S. professional soccer by the North American Soccer League, which had failed financially. A group of players sued the MLS on antitrust grounds.

   a. What were the players' antitrust claims?

   b. Decide those claims. Explain. See *Fraser v. Major League Soccer,* 284 F.3d 47 (1st Cir. 2002) [**https://law.justia.com**].

3. Poplar Bluff is a city of 17,000 people in southeastern Missouri. Sikeston and Cape Girardeau, Missouri, both towns with populations of over 40,000, are 40 and 60 miles away from Poplar Bluff. Tenet Healthcare owned Lucy Lee Hospital in Poplar Bluff and proposed to buy Doctors' Regional Medical Center, also in Poplar Bluff. Both hospitals were profitable, but both were underutilized and had trouble attracting specialists. The Federal

Trade Commission filed suit to block the acquisition. The key question involved definition of the geographic market. The FTC proposed a relevant geographic market that essentially matched the service area: a 50-mile radius of downtown Poplar Bluff. Ninety percent of the two hospitals' patients came from that area. Four other hospitals were in that area. The merged hospital would have had 84 percent of the patients in that geographic market. Tenet argued that the geographic market should have encompassed a 65-mile radius from downtown Poplar Bluff. That area included 16 hospitals. Define the geographic market. See *FTC v. Tenet Health Care Corp.*, 186 F.3d 1045 (8th Cir. 1999) [**https://law.justia.com**].

4. In 2011, the U.S. Justice Department sent a letter to the National Collegiate Athletic Association raising antitrust questions about the Bowl Championship Series (BCS), which is used to determine a national college football champion. The letter asked why the BCS schools had not established a playoff system. Pressure from critics and the promise of huge payouts then pushed the BCS to establish a four-team playoff system that commenced in 2014. In your judgment, should federal antitrust law be applied to the Bowl Championship Series? Explain.
5. Lina Khan, writing in *Politico,* argued that the federal government should be concerned about threats to competition from online "platform monopolies" such as Amazon, Facebook, and Google.[32] Khan says those online giants are like the "railroads of the Internet economy" connecting buyers and sellers in an online marketplace. Khan says the online companies can use their market power, as the railroads did historically, to squeeze the suppliers and sellers that depend upon them. Explain her concern.
6. Critics worry that increasing mergers, especially those involving media firms, threaten democracy.

   a. Explain that argument.

   b. Do you agree? Explain.
7. In 1986, distinguished economist William Shepherd argued:

   > It may not be too late to turn back from this road to serfdom by reviving the case for antitrust, but the odds aren't favorable. More probably, antitrust will continue to sink.[33]

   a. What did Shepherd mean about "this road to serfdom?"

   b. In reading this chapter, do you think antitrust has been revived? Explain.

   c. Is bigness bad, or is it necessary in today's global economy? Explain.
8. Whole Foods, now a part of Amazon, in 2007 acquired its chief competitor Wild Oats Market. Whole Foods had about 12 percent of the natural foods market, and Wild Oats held about 3 percent. Whole Foods had 197 stores and added 110 by purchasing Wild Oats. About 72 percent of Wild Oats' sales were in markets where the two overlapped. Whole Foods argued that the merger was necessary to allow it to compete effectively with big chains such as Safeway and Walmart.

   Prior to the purchase, Whole Foods cofounder and CEO John Mackey allegedly said the proposed merger would end "forever or almost forever" the possibility of a big grocery chain buying an existing natural foods chain to compete with Whole Foods. Mackey also allegedly said that buying Wild Oats would prevent "nasty price wars."

   The Federal Trade Commission challenged the Whole Foods purchase of Wild Oats.

a. What was the primary issue facing the federal courts that reviewed the FTC challenge?

b. Decide the case. Explain. See *Federal Trade Commission v. Whole Foods Market,* 502 F. Supp. 2d 1 (D.D.C. 2007) [**https://law.justia.com**] and *Federal Trade Commission v. Whole Foods Market,* 533 F.3d 869 (D.C. Cir. 2008) [**https://casetext.com**]. For a brief, journalistic description of the settlement that ultimately resolved the Whole Foods–Wild Oats merger, see Diane Bartz, "Whole Foods, FTC Settle on Wild Oats Merger," *Reuters,* March 6, 2009 [**www.reuters.com**].

9. Is the influence of big business so persuasive that it nullifies the effective enforcement of the antitrust laws? Explain.

10. The central theme in this chapter is increasing corporate concentration and consolidation and the damage that arguably arises from that trend.

a. Make a list of societal harms that antitrust advocates are attributing to increasing concentration.

b. Free-market theorists are generally untroubled by concentration. Why do they hold that view?

c. What do you think about the societal risks of increasing corporate concentration and consolidation? Explain.

11. In the period 1917 to 1919, DuPont acquired 23 percent of the stock in the then-fledgling General Motors Corporation. By 1947, DuPont supplied 68 percent of GM's automotive finish needs and 38 percent of its fabric needs. In 1955, General Motors ranked first in sales and second in assets among all U.S. industrial corporations, while accounting for approximately two-fifths of the nation's annual automobile sales. In 1949, the Justice Department challenged Dupont's 1917–19 acquisitions of GM stock.

a. Why did the government challenge DuPont's acquisition?

b. May an acquisition be properly challenged 30 years after the fact as in *DuPont*? Explain.

c. Given your general understanding of finishes and fabrics, how would you defend DuPont?

d. Decide. Explain. See *United States v. E.I. DuPont de Nemours & Co.,* 353 U.S. 586 (1957) [**https://justia.com**].

12. How can a merger benefit society?

13. Which economic considerations support the view that unilateral growth is preferable to growth by merger?

14. Excel, a division of Cargill, was the second-largest firm in the beef-packing market. It sought to acquire Spencer Pack, a division of Land-O-Lakes and the third-largest beef packer. After the acquisition, Excel would have remained second-ranked in the business, but its market share would have been only slightly smaller than that of the leader, IBP. Monfort, the nation's fifth-largest beef packer, sought an injunction to block the acquisition, claiming a violation of the Clayton Act, Section 7. In effect, Monfort claimed the merger would result in a dangerous concentration of economic power in the beef-packing market, with the result that Excel would pay more for cattle and charge less for its processed beef, thus placing its competitors in a destructive and

illegal price–cost squeeze. Monfort claimed Excel's initial losses in this arrangement would be covered by its wealthy parent, Cargill. Then when the competition was driven from the market, Monfort claimed, Excel would raise its processed beef prices to supra-competitive levels. Among other defenses, Excel averred that the heavy losses Monfort claimed were merely the product of intense competition, a condition that would not constitute a violation of the antitrust laws. The district court found for Monfort, and the appeals court, considering the cost–price squeeze a form of predatory pricing, affirmed. Excel appealed to the Supreme Court. Decide. Explain. See *Cargill, Inc. v. Monfort of Colorado, Inc.*, 479 U.S. 104 (1986) [**https://justia.com**].

Notes

1. David Dayen, "The Most Important 2016 Issue You Don't Know About," *The New Republic*, March 11, 2016 [**www.newrepublic.com**].
2. David Leonhardt, "Big Business Is Overcharging You $5,000 a Year," *The New York Times*, November 10, 2019 [**www.nytimes.com**].
3. See *United States v. Microsoft Corporation*, 87 F. Supp. 2d 30 (D.D.C. 2000) [**https://law.justia.com**]; and *Microsoft v. United States*, 253 F.3d 34 (D.C. Cir. 2001) [**https://law.justia.com**], *cert. denied*, 122 S. Ct. 350 (2001).
4. Alan Murray, "Microsoft Foe Quits Antitrust Crusade–with Check in Hand," *The Wall Street Journal*, December 7, 2004 [**www.wsj.com**].
5. *Apple v. Pepper*, 587 U.S. __ (2019) [**https://supreme.justia.com**].
6. *United States v. Grinnell*, 384 U.S. 563, 570–71 (1966) [**https://supreme.justia.com**].
7. Aliza Rosenbaum, Rob Cox, and Pierre Briancon, "Rising Beer Prices Hint at Oligopoly," *The New York Times*, August 27, 2009 [**www.nytimes.com**].
8. Note, "Antitrust and the Information Age: Section 2 Monopolization Analyses in the New Economy," *Harvard Law Review* 114, no. 5 (March 2001), p. 1623 [**https://scholarlycommons.law.wlu.edu**].
9. *Spectrum Sports, Inc. v. Shirley McQuillan*, 506 U.S. 447 (1993) [**https://supreme.justia.com**].
10. *Phila. Taxi Ass'n v. Uber Techs*, 886 F.3d 332 (3d Cir. 2018) [**https://law.justia.com**], *cert. denied*, 2018 U.S. LEXIS 5311.
11. Note, "Antitrust and the Information Age," pp. 1623, 1645 [**https://scholarlycommons.law.wlu.edu**].
12. *United States v. Aluminum Co. of America*, 148 F.2d 416 (2d Cir. 1945) [**https://law.justia.com**].
13. Emmalina Glinskis, "By the Numbers: The Rise of Monopolies," *The Nation*, February 15, 2018 [**www.thenation.com**].
14. P. Scott Shearer, "Legislation Would Halt 'Large' Mergers and Acquisitions," *National Hog Farmer*, September 7, 2018 [**www.nationalhogfarmer.com**].
15. CB Information Services, "Top Brewers Place Their Bets on Craft Beer," *CB Insights*, January 2, 2018 [**www.cbinsights.com**].
16. Travis Hoium, "How the AB InBev Buyout Went Wrong," *The Motley Fool*, November 3, 2018 [**www.fool.com**].
17. Hugo Martin, "Airline Mergers Benefit Carriers and Help Keep Fares Low, Study Says," *Los Angeles Times*, January 26, 2014 [**www.latimes.com**].
18. Bruce Blonigen and Justin Pierce, "Evidence for the Effects of Mergers on Market Power and Efficiency," Finance and Economics Discussion Series 2016-082, Washington: Board of Governors of the Federal Reserve System, 2016 [**https://doi.org/10.17016/FEDS.2016.082**].
19. Editorial, "Big Food," *The New York Times*, January 25, 2010 [**www.nytimes.com**].

20. Orley Ashenfelter and Daniel Hosken, "The Effect of Mergers on Consumers Prices: Evidence from Five Selected Case Studies," *Economist's View,* April 23, 2008 **[https://economistsview.typepad.com]**.
21. Tim Wu, *The Curse of Bigness: Antitrust in the New Gilded Age,* New York: Columbia Global Reports, 2018.
22. Kevin Voigt, "Mergers Fail More Often Than Marriages," *CNN World,* May 22, 2009 **[https://edition.cnn.com]**.
23. See Michael J. Mandel, "All These Mergers Are Great, But . . .," *Bloomberg,* October 17, 1999 **[https://www.bloomberg.com]**; and Jeffrey Garten, "Megamergers Are a Clear and Present Danger," *Bloomberg,* January 25, 1999 **[https://www.bloomberg.com]**.
24. David Leonhardt, "Big Business Is Overcharging You. . .." **[www.nytimes.com]**.
25. Scott D. Thompson, "Clear Skies Seen Ahead for the American Airlines/U.S. Airways Merger," *LEXOLOGY,* February 22, 2013 **[www.lexology.com]**.
26. *United States v. AT&T, Inc.,* 916 F.3d 1029 (2019) **[https://law.justia.com]**.
27. This paragraph relies in part on Alan J. Meese and Barak D. Richman, "A Careful Examination of the Live Nation-Ticketmaster Merger," *SSRN Electronic Journal,* November 2009 **[https://ssrn.com/abstract=1542626]**.
28. Richard Posner, *Antitrust Law* (Chicago: The University of Chicago Press, 1976), p. 130.
29. David Leonhardt, "Big Business Is Overcharging You. . .." **[www.nytimes.com]**.
30. Ibid **[www.nytimes.com]**.
31. *Animal Science Products, Inc. v. Hebei Welcome Pharmaceutical Co.,* 585 U.S. __ (2018) **[https://supreme.justia.com]**.
32. Lina Kahn, "How to Reboot the FTC," *Politico,* April 13, 2016 **[www.politco.com]**.
33. William G. Shepherd, "Bust the Reagan Trustbusters," *Fortune,* August 4, 1986, pp. 225, 227.

Video icon credit: Comstock Images/Alamy Stock Photo

UNIT FOUR

Employer–Employee Relations

CHAPTER TWELVE

Employment Law I: Employee Rights

After completing this chapter, students will be able to fulfill the following learning objectives:

12-1. Distinguish between an employee and an independent contractor.

12-2. Identify potential legal challenges an employer faces in the hiring process.

12-3. Explain an employer's liability under the doctrine of *respondeat superior.*

12-4. Analyze claims of negligent hiring, supervision, and retention.

12-5. Discuss employees' rights under the Fair Labor Standards Act.

12-6. Describe the role of the Occupational Safety and Health Administration in protecting employees' health and safety at work.

12-7. Describe the benefits, coverage, and requirements for bringing a successful claim under workers' compensation laws.

12-8. Explain both employer and employee interests with regard to employee privacy rights.

12-9. Discuss workplace drug testing and the legal challenges it faces.

12-10. Describe the Family and Medical Leave Act.

12-11. Distinguish between defined benefit and defined contribution pension plans.

12-12. Analyze whether a dismissed at-will employee may bring a claim of wrongful discharge.

12-13. Recognize the purposes and requirements of the H-1B visa and the employment eligibility verification Form I-9.

Introduction

Brandon Coats is a quadriplegic who has been confined to a wheelchair since he was a teenager. Coats had been working for Dish Network (Dish) as a telephone customer service representative for approximately two years when he registered for and obtained a Colorado state-issued license to use medical marijuana to treat painful muscle spasms.

Coats consumed medical marijuana at home, after work, and in accordance with his license and Colorado state law.

The following year, Coats tested positive for tetrahydrocannabinol (THC), a component of medical marijuana, during a random workplace drug test. Coats informed Dish that he was a registered medical marijuana patient and planned to continue using medical marijuana. Dish fired Coats for violating Dish's drug policy.

Coats then filed a wrongful termination claim against Dish under a Colorado state law that generally prohibits employers from terminating employees based on their "lawful activities" conducted off the employer's premises during nonworking hours. Coats argued that his outside-of-work medical marijuana use is "lawful" under Colorado's state law allowing his medical marijuana use. Dish argued that using marijuana, even for medical purposes, was not "lawful" because it violated the federal Controlled Substances Act.

Questions

1. Should an employer be allowed to terminate an employee for using medical marijuana with a state-issued license? Explain.
2. Why would an employer prohibit employees from using marijuana at their home after work? Should employers be allowed to enforce such a policy? Explain. See *Coats v. Dish Network,* 2015 CO 44 (Colo. 2015).

Managing Lawsuits

Managers traditionally have balanced multiple responsibilities, but employment law has added complex, sometimes daunting expectations. Addressing and mitigating the risk of employment-related lawsuits has become an important consideration in management decision making. As union strength has declined (see Chapter 14), government regulations and court decisions have arguably broadened employee rights. These increased legal protections, a volatile economy, downsized workforces, weakened employer–employee loyalty, and other forces have contributed to higher levels of employee litigation.[1]

Part One—The Employment Relationship

Job Classification

Employment-related legal rights and responsibilities depend on the type of relationship the employer decides to build with the worker. The traditional, stable model of long-term direct employer–employee relationships now is often replaced with new, flexible, nontraditional staffing arrangements, including outsourcing and employee leasing, along with the use of freelancers and temporary agencies. These *contingent workers,* along with *independent contractors,* who are increasingly relied on to perform both shorter-term, nonrecurring jobs as well as those traditionally held by full- or part-time company employees, permit employers to rapidly and inexpensively expand or shrink their workforces as needed. This trend has impacted the typical relationship between a company and its workers and is reflected in the rise of the "on-demand" or "gig" economy.

Who's the Boss?

In designing a popular video game, about 70 of the 81 employees of a San Diego video game creator worked with 40 to 50 workers from its worldwide network of independent contractors. A large retailer's shipping containers are unloaded by workers provided by a trucking company, which in turn contracts with a temporary staffing agency. Companies are able to control costs and promote efficiency by outsourcing work ranging from manual labor and customer service to software testing or, in other words, "renting" high-skilled workers with needed expertise. On the other hand, the use of temporary workers has created a "parallel workforce" that is vulnerable to pay inequality as they perform the same tasks as employees for notably different compensation. Lack of traditional employment protections add to job instability. Additionally, the intangible rewards of long-term employment relationships, such as upward mobility through promotions from lower- to higher-skilled positions, may be lost as jobs that could have been "stepping stones" for outstanding employees are outsourced.

Sources: Lauren Weber, "For Videogame Makers, Hiring Is a Last Resort," *The Wall Street Journal,* April 11, 2017 [**www.wsj.com**]; and Lauren Weber, "The End of Employees," *The Wall Street Journal,* February 2, 2017 [**www.wsj.com**].

Employee or Independent Contractor?

LO 12-1 Distinguish between an employee and an independent contractor.

A key question underlying the legal issues discussed in this chapter is whether the worker in question is an employee or an independent contractor, who is generally hired to perform a specific task without an expectation of long-term continuous employment. Although there are various tests, the degree of control the employer has over the worker is a factor in the worker's classification. Where an employer can or does control how a worker performs the job, the worker is likely to be considered an employee. CBS used the distinction between "independent contractor" and "employee" to successfully appeal the Federal Communications Commission's (FCC's) fine after Justin Timberlake and Janet Jackson appeared to cooperatively expose Ms. Jackson's breast at the end of their 2004 Super Bowl halftime show performance that CBS broadcast. CBS argued that the performers were independent contractors, not employees, and therefore, CBS could not be held liable for actions taken outside their control.[2] The U.S. Supreme Court declined to review the federal appellate court's decision to reject the FCC's fine.[3]

What other advantages might a business gain from hiring an independent contractor rather than an employee? A business that hires an independent contractor generally is not required to comply with a wide range of employment and labor law standards that apply to employees. Thus, a business must provide, for example, unemployment insurance to its employees but generally does not need to do so for independent contractors. Similarly, employers are not required to pay the independent contractor overtime. Furthermore, while employers are responsible for payroll taxes, such as FICA and federal and state unemployment insurance, as well as for withholding income tax from their employees' paychecks, these tax obligations do not extend to independent contractors.

Legal Disputes Over Classification

Employers anxious to reduce financial and legal burdens sometimes improperly classify workers as independent contractors rather than employees. In 2015, Homejoy, a cleaning-service startup, went out of business after facing several lawsuits from its cleaners, who claimed they had been misclassified as independent contractors instead of employees.[4] On-demand ride services Uber and Lyft have faced similar challenges. In 2015, a California Labor Commissioner ruled that an Uber driver was an employee and entitled to reimbursement of his car expenses.[5] In 2019, however, the National Labor Relations Board (NLRB) found that Uber drivers were independent contractors and, therefore, could not form a labor union.[6] As is apparent below, job classification has not been finally settled.

Classification Standards

In 2019, California enacted a bill offering an "ABC test" for classifying workers as independent contractors. Workers could only be properly classified as an independent contractors if they were: (A) free from the control and direction of the hirer in connection with the performance of the work, both under the contract for the performance of such work and in fact; (B) performed work outside the usual course of the hiring entity's business; and (C) customarily engaged in an independently established trade, occupation, or business of the same nature as the work performed for the hiring entity. The ABC test set a higher standard for classifying workers as independent contractors, impacting several industries in the "gig economy," such as ride-hailing apps, by extending employee rights to their workers. In 2020, California voters approved Proposition 22, backed by Uber, Lyft, and DoorDash, designating drivers for app-based ride and delivery services as independent contractors, but in a 2021 California court ruling, Proposition 22 was determined to be unconstitutional.

During the Trump administration, the Department of Labor considered two factors to have the most weight in determining whether a worker is an employee or independent contractor: the degree of control the company has over the worker, and the extent to which the worker can increase their income through entrepreneurial initiative. In 2022, and as of this writing, the U.S. Department of Labor has proposed a return to the Obama Administration's multifactor approach which considers the company's control of work as well as additional factors, such as whether the work being performed is central to the company's business, and what kind of investments workers make to do their jobs, such as buying equipment, and would be applied on a case-by-case basis.

Question

Give an example of a worker who could be properly classified as an independent contractor under the ABC test. Explain how this worker meets the classification.

Sources: Larry Buhl, "New Legislation Aims to Clarify Who Is an Employee," *The American Prospect,* February 22, 2019; Margot Roosevelt and Suhauna Hussain, "Prop. 22 Ruled Unconstitutional, a Blow to California Gig Economy Law, *Los Angeles Times* (August 20, 2021) [**https://www.latimes.com/**]; and Noam Scheiber, "Proposal Would Ease Employee Status for Gig Workers," *The New York Times,* pp. B1–B4 (October 12, 2022).

Selection and Hiring

An array of potential legal problems has arisen from the increasingly complex process of choosing and employing new workers.

LO 12-2 Identify potential legal challenges an employer faces in the hiring process.

Resume Fraud

Scott Thompson, former Yahoo CEO, left the company after revelations that he falsely claimed to hold a computer science degree; he graduated with an accounting degree from a college that apparently did not have a computer science program at the time.[7] Manhattan College men's basketball coach Steve Masiello apparently lost an opportunity to coach at University of South Florida after it was discovered that his biography on Manhattan's website wrongly stated that he had graduated from the University of Kentucky; he had attended that institution but had not yet received a degree.[8] A survey of more than 2,500 hiring managers revealed that 56 percent had uncovered a lie on a resume, including exaggerations of job responsibilities and skills. About a quarter of the respondents had found applicants claiming to be currently with an employer for which they had never worked.[9]

Background Checks

Although concerns ranging from resume fraud to employee theft and workplace violence may have led to background checks becoming an expected part of the hiring process, surveys conducted by the Society for Human Resource Management have shown a decrease in the number of employers who check applicants' credit history and criminal backgrounds. One found that fewer than half of employers run credit checks on applicants for at least some positions, and another showed that only 14 percent of human resource professionals would be unwilling to hire someone with criminal record.[10]

Using credit checks in hiring arguably helps protect an employer against fraud and employee theft because applicants who have not handled their personal finances responsibly might be more likely to engage in such misconduct. However, questions about the validity and unintended impact of this practice have been raised in recent years. Not only has the connection between a bad credit report and poor job performance been disputed, but as discussed in Chapter 13, concerns have arisen that credit checks can create a discriminatory impact on certain groups' ability to gain employment.[11] Several states have passed legislation limiting the use of credit checks. The Illinois Employee Credit Privacy Act, for example, generally prohibits employers from using an employee's or applicant's credit history in making employment decisions such as hiring.[12]

The enforcement guidance of the Equal Employment Opportunity Commission (EEOC) does not ban employers from using criminal checks to screen applicants or current employees, although they should not be used to take adverse action unless the conviction is relevant to the position for which applicants are being considered. The EEOC noted that an arrest alone does not establish criminal conduct and therefore cannot be used in hiring; however, the conduct underlying the arrest could be considered by an employer in making an employment decision. [For the full text of the EEOC Enforcement Guidance on the Consideration of Arrest and Conviction Records in Employment Decisions, see **www.eeoc.gov/laws/guidance/arrest_conviction.cfm**].

A Second Chance

Unemployment rates for former inmates have traditionally been high. However, in a Society for Human Resource Management Foundation survey of human resources professionals published in 2023, 46 percent said they recruited those with criminal records more often than in the previous year. The Second Chance Business Coalition, which includes JP Morgan Chase and CVS, works to share best practices on hiring those with a criminal background. Both small businesses and big companies have said they recognize "second-chance" hiring can ease social inequities and provide more workers in a tight labor market.

Source: Allison, Prano, "More Businesses Try 'Second-Chance' Hiring," *The Wall Street Journal,* p. A3 (October 10, 2022).

Online Reputation

Employers are increasingly researching the online reputation of job applicants. One survey revealed that over 90 percent of employers browse applicants' social media profiles; nearly 80 percent have rejected an applicant because of their social media content.[13] As discussed later in this chapter, concern for privacy has led to state legislation preventing employers from requiring social media passwords as part of the application process.

Inappropriate Questions

In one survey, approximately one-third of employers did not know that they should not ask applicants about their marital status or age in an interview,[14] which expose employers to potential liability for discrimination (see Chapter 13). But what about the enormous array of awkward, intrusive, but nondiscriminatory interview questions that might leave the candidate feeling uncomfortable if not wronged? For example: "What would you do if I gave you an elephant?" has questionable relevance in a job interview.[15]

Employment Terms

Restrictive Covenants

According to one recent estimate, over 60 percent of U.S. employees are covered by a noncompete, nonsolicitation, nondisclosure agreement or a combination of these contractual obligations.[16] For example, Chris Botticella, a former executive with Bimbo Bakeries, which operates under popular brand names such as Thomas' and Entenmann's, was prohibited from taking employment at Hostess, Inc. because of the confidentiality agreement and other restrictive covenants he had signed as a condition of working for Bimbo.[17] These agreements were intended to protect Bimbo's recipes and business strategies from falling into the hands of competitors. These agreements providing that the employee will not compete with their employer, solicit its customers or employees, pass trade secrets to others, and so on, for a specified period of time after ending their current employment have been criticized as creating obstacles to professional growth as well as business development. California law prohibits such noncompete agreements, subject to certain narrow statutory exceptions.[18]

In 2023, the Federal Trade Commission (FTC) proposed a rule eliminating noncompete agreements, predicting that this would help both increase wages and opportunities for American workers; however, at this writing, the U.S. Chamber of Commerce has announced plans to challenge the FTC's proposed rule in court.[19]

Salary Transparency

Similar to several states, California requires companies with 15 or more employees to list salary ranges for all job postings, starting in 2023. New York City instituted a similar law that went into effect in 2022. These laws aim to ease pay inequities by strengthening applicants' knowledge of what others holding the job have been paid.

Question: For job applicants, what are the advantages of salary transparency in job announcements? What might be problems arising from salary transparency? Explain.

Sources: Jonah Valdez, "New California law will require job postings to include salary ranges," *Los Angeles Times,* (September 29, 2022) [**https://www.latimes.com/**]; "New York Postings to Reveal Salary Ranges, *The Wall Street Journal,* p. A1 (October 3, 2022).

Arbitration

New employees are often expected to sign agreements specifying that disputes with the employer will be settled by arbitration (see Chapter 4) rather than by litigation. A recent survey found that 56 percent of nonunion private-sector employees are subject to mandatory arbitration for employment-related disputes.[20] Employers like arbitration because it can be cheaper, faster, and less adversarial than a trial. Employees, on the other hand, argue that arbitration is stacked in favor of corporate interests and amounts to a denial of the fundamental right of access to the legal system. Employment arbitration agreements have been supported by Supreme Court decisions upholding the enforceability of legitimate, equitable employment arbitration agreements.[21] However, as noted in Chapter 4, a 2021 federal statute gives employees who are otherwise bound by mandatory arbitration agreements to bring their sexual harassment or sexual assault claims to court.[22] Further, the EEOC still retains authority to file discrimination lawsuits on behalf of employees regardless of an arbitration agreement[23] (see Chapter 13).

Firing

As a manager, you decide to fire an employee, Brown, because of what you believe to be convincing evidence that he had sexually harassed a coworker. Brown applies for a new job, and that employer seeks your evaluation of Brown's work. What should you do? If you tell what you know, you and your employer fear Brown might sue you for *defamation,* which was discussed in Chapter 7. If you fail to say what you know, you fear you might be sued for *misrepresentation* or *negligent referral* if Brown is hired and commits further

You decide to fire an employee for sexually harassing a coworker.

harassment on his new job. Because of those risks, employers often limit their references to purely factual details such as the date of hire, date of departure, and job title. Many state courts have established a qualified privilege under which legitimate business communications, with some exceptions, are shielded from liability. Similarly, a number of states have enacted legislation providing employers with immunity from liability for good faith employment references. [protection from Wrongful Discharge is discussed later in this chapter].

Questions

1. At this writing, Uber, the ride-hailing app, has agreed to pay New Jersey $100 million in back taxes after the state's labor department's audit showed that Uber had misclassified its drivers as independent contractors. How would Uber drivers be classified under U.S. Department of Labor's proposed 2022 multifactor test for job classification described in "Classification Standards"?[24]
2. As part of its selection of a Cybersecurity Technician, a software firm conducts a criminal background check of its applicants. One applicant, Tim, a former federal inmate, had been convicted of hacking into multiple corporate and governmental systems. Tim's interview went well, and the Cybersecurity Manager would like to hire Tim. If you were the software firm's Cybersecurity Director, what questions might you have about Tim's application? Explain.
3. Axe was fired from his employment at Company A after engaging in threatening behavior at work. Company B contacted Company A's human resources manager, Chris, asking if Axe is eligible for rehiring at Company A. Chris knows that Company A will not rehire Axe. How should Chris respond?[25]

Part Two—Liability

Once hired, what happens when employees make mistakes or engage in misconduct on the job that hurts others? Must the employer bear the loss in these situations? Job classification is an important first question in determining company liability for workers' job-related injuries, harm to others, and crimes. An enterprise ordinarily will not be liable for the acts of its independent contractors. Employers, on the other hand, often bear legal responsibility for employees' accidents or wrongs. That liability may spring from the doctrine of ***respondeat superior*** (let the master answer), a form of *vicarious liability* (sometimes called *imputed liability*).

Scope of Employment

LO 12-3 Explain an employer's liability under the doctrine of *respondeat superior.*

Employer liability for employee injuries, accidents, or wrongs is largely dependent on whether the employee was on the job at the time of the incident in question. Employers will be held liable under *respondeat superior* reasoning for harm to third parties caused by the intentional or negligent acts of their employees when those acts occur within the *scope of employment* (on the job). A finding of employer liability does not excuse the employee from their personal liability, but the *respondeat superior* reasoning does have the potential effect of opening the employer's deeper pockets to the plaintiff. The following questions ordinarily determine whether the harm occurred within the scope of employment:

1. Was the employee subject to the employer's supervision?
2. Was the employee motivated, at least in part, by a desire to serve the employer's business interests?
3. Did the problem arise substantially within normal working hours and in a work location?
4. Was the act in question of the general kind the employee had been hired to perform?

In *Mary M. v. City of Los Angeles,*[26] the city was held liable under the doctrine of *respondeat superior* for a sexual assault committed by a police officer. At 2:30 a.m. on October 3, 1981, Sergeant Leigh Schroyer was on duty, in uniform, carrying a gun, and patrolling in his marked police car. He stopped Mary M. for erratic driving. She pleaded not to be arrested. He ordered her to enter his patrol car and took her to her home. He entered her home and said that he expected "payment" for not arresting her. He raped her and was subsequently sentenced to a term in state prison.

> The City was held liable for a sexual assault committed by a police officer.

Mary M. sued the City of Los Angeles. The general inquiry was whether Schroyer was acting within the scope of his employment during the rape episode. The jury found for Mary M. and awarded $150,000 in damages. The court of appeals reversed, saying that Schroyer was not acting within the scope of his employment. The case went to the California Supreme Court. The city argued that Schroyer was acting on behalf of his own interests rather than those of the city, and that the city had not authorized his conduct. Therefore, Schroyer could not have been acting within the scope of employment. However, the court said that the correct question was not whether the rape was authorized but whether it happened in the course of a series of acts that were authorized. The court reversed, saying that a jury could find the city vicariously liable given the unique authority of police officers in our society.

Questions

1. Jean was carrying groceries out of the grocery store Hy-Vee when she was struck and injured by a bicycle ridden by Lewis, a 16-year-old Hy-Vee employee. Lewis was hurrying home to get a belt to complete his required Hy-Vee work uniform. He had received permission from his supervisor to return home for that purpose; Lewis had neither clocked in nor started his shift. Jean sued Hy-Vee for her resulting injuries.
   a. *What is Jean's claim?*
   b. *Decide the case. Explain. See Jean v. Hy Vee, Inc., 825 N.W.2d 327 (Iowa Ct. App. 2012).*
2. Ahern, a chef at the Heathwood Nursing and Rehabilitation Center in Chestnut Hill, Massachusetts, left work and went to the South Pacific Chinese Restaurant, where he met his supervisor, Pacitti, to socialize and discuss work-related matters. Ahern purchased two drinks and consumed at least one drink and one-half of the other before leaving to go home. On his way home, Ahern's vehicle struck Lev as he was crossing a street, causing severe and debilitating injuries. Ahern was arrested and eventually convicted of operating a motor vehicle while under the influence of intoxicating liquor. Lev sued Heathwood's owner and operator, Beverly Enterprises, alleging that Beverly was vicariously liable for Ahern's negligence based on their employment relationship.
   a. *What was the central issue in this case?*
   b. *Decide the case. Explain. See Lev v. Beverly Enterprises, 457 Mass. 234 (2010).*

3. What policy justifications support the imposition of liability on an employer for the wrongs of an employee acting within the scope of employment?

A Side Order of Pistol-Whipping?

Harris placed his order with a cashier at a Kentucky Fried Chicken (KFC) restaurant in Philadelphia, Pennsylvania, but hesitated in selecting his side orders that were part of the meal he had selected. Another KFC employee, Henry, told Harris to "hurry up." Harris replied, "I am not dealing with you." Henry then asked Harris: "Do you want the [expletive] chicken or not?" Taken aback, Harris further hesitated; Henry pulled out a gun. Harris put up his hands and asked if Henry was "going to shoot [him] over a bucket of chicken?" While another employee yelled at Henry, Harris tried to escape, but Henry followed and pistol-whipped Harris before he could leave the restaurant, causing him injuries. Harris sued KFC for negligently failing to conduct a criminal background check. In rejecting the claim, the federal district court noted that KFC was not legally required to conduct a criminal background check, and that Henry's criminal history only would have revealed two prior convictions for nonviolent crimes over five years old.

Questions

1. Do you agree with the court's ruling? Explain.
2. How else might KFC have prevented this situation? Explain.

Source: *Harris v. KFC*, 2012 U.S. Dist. LEXIS 84668 (E.D. Pa. June 18, 2012).

Hiring/Retention/Training/Supervision

PRACTICING ETHICS The "Bossy Bot"

ARTIFICIAL INTELLIGENCE (AI) AND SUPERVISION

HomeServe, a home repair service company, brought into its Tennessee call center an AI-powered virtual agent to assist its salesforce. This agent, named Charlie, answers calls, routes them to departments, and tells the human sales agents what to do. One of these sales agents is Jonathan, a top performer, who attributes his success to listening to callers and not going off a script. Although company executives find that Charlie raises efficiency to the benefit of customers, Charlie sometimes gives sales agents the wrong advice; for example, Charlie told Jonathan that a caller wanted to enroll in a repair plan, when the caller had actually been waiting for a repair. Following Charlie's suggested response led to the caller becoming irate.

HomeServe says it wants the agents to view Charlie as a "personal assistant" there to help them. To humanize Charlie, the company created an avatar of a biracial brunette woman in her 40s from Ohio who likes jazz and has two children. Reminding a *Wall Street Journal* reporter that he is a top performer, Jonathan says that "Charlie is not my supervisor."

QUESTION:

What are the ethical implications of AI-powered supervision of employees? Explain.

Source: Lisa Bannon, "AI Comes to the Office. It's Bossy, Efficient and Dehumanizing," *The Wall Street Journal* (February 18–19, 2023) (p. B1–B4).

Negligence

LO 12-4
Analyze claims of negligent hiring, supervision, and retention.

In addition to vicarious liability for employees' actions, employers may be directly liable for negligence in hiring an employee or retaining an employee who subsequently causes harm to a third party, or for careless training or supervision. Typically, the employer is liable on negligence grounds for hiring or retaining an employee whom the employer knew or should have known to be dangerous, incompetent, dishonest, or the like, where that characteristic was directly related to the injury suffered by the plaintiff. Under negligence liability, an employer may be liable for acts *outside* the scope of employment in certain circumstances. The case that follows examines the law of negligent hiring.

LEGAL BRIEFCASE

Brettman v. M&G Truck Brokerage, Inc.

127 N.E. 3d 880 (Ill. App. 2019)

Justice Jorgensen

OPINION

This matter arises out of a traffic accident between Gina Brettman and a tractor trailer driven by Isreal Vela, an employee of E.G.G. Trucking. . . . It occurred after Vela had delivered a load of cucumbers from Texana in Progresso, Texas, to a Kraft/Claussen pickling plant in Woodstock. M&G brokered the delivery of the cucumbers. Plaintiff filed a 27-count complaint against . . . various entities. . . . This appeal concerns M&G and Texana only . . .

Texana grows cucumbers in Texas and Mexico. It sells the cucumbers to processing facilities across the United States. . . . It is not a trucking company, does not own any commercial or semi-trucks, and does not have a department of transportation number or motor carrier authority. It does not contract with trucking companies. Rather, it works with shipping brokers to arrange the shipments. . . . M&G is a Texas business entity that brokers freight delivery of products. . . .

E.G.G. is a licensed motor carrier. . . . E.G.G. hired Vela, who had been working for E.G.G. for 10 years.

. . . Texana contacted M&G, asking M&G to arrange the shipment at issue. M&G, in turn, chose E.G.G. to haul the load. M&G had been working with E.G.G. since 2007. In those seven years, M&G had selected E.G.G. to haul as many as 10 loads per month without incident.

. . . The contract between M&G and E.G.G. set forth certain instructions for the trip. . . . [Vela] did not feel rushed over the course of the trip.

E.G.G. paid Vela for executing the trip. It administered Vela's drug testing and provided his safety training. E.G.G. instructed Vela to pick up the load from Texana at approximately 11 a.m. on March 9, 2014. Vela was to deliver the load to Kraft/Claussen by 5 a.m. on March 14, 2014.

After unloading the cucumbers at the Kraft/Claussen plant, Vela was no longer required to check in with M&G. E.G.G. instructed Vela to take Interstate 90 to the nearest truck stop to wait for a new load assignment, which could originate from M&G or a new broker. After delivering the load, about 25 miles from the Kraft/Claussen plant but before reaching Interstate 90, Vela collided with Brettman at an intersection. Vela was going straight, driving at the posted speed limit of 45 miles per hour, and Brettman was turning left with a green arrow. The intersection was under construction, and Vela later stated that he was confused by the traffic control signals. Vela saw that the permanent traffic signals were covered, so he assumed there were no traffic controls for drivers traveling in his direction. At the last second, he saw a temporary traffic signal hung with wire over the intersection. The temporary signal was red. He could not stop in time, and he collided with Brettman. Brettman suffered severe injuries as a result of the collision and filed the instant lawsuit.

In count II, plaintiff alleged negligent hiring against M&G. He alleged that M&G had a duty to exercise reasonable care when it selected a carrier to haul the load at issue. In his view, the exercise of reasonable care included performing an independent investigation and background check on E.G.G. and Vela. Had M&G performed an adequate investigation, it would have discovered . . . that E.G.G. was an unrated motor carrier and that Vela had a history of forging time sheets. M&G negligently hired a company it should have known to be unfit. The exercise of reasonable care in hiring also included supervising E.G.G. in the transportation and delivery of commercial product to Kraft/Claussen. M&G failed in this as well. As a result of these wrongful acts or omissions, Vela's truck collided with Brettman's automobile, causing injury.

In count IV, plaintiff alleged the same, but against Texana.

. . . [P]laintiff retained Whitney Morgan to testify to a broker's duty of care in selecting a trucking company. Morgan had worked for the United States Department of Transportation, enforcing regulations. . . . In Morgan's view, brokers should contract only with carriers that have satisfactory ratings from the Federal Motor Carrier Safety Administration (FMCSA). The FMCSA conducts compliance reviews to determine whether a carrier meets minimum safety standards. The FMCSA never conducted a compliance review on E.G.G., so E.G.G. was an "unrated" carrier. In Morgan's opinion, a broker should not contract with an unrated carrier.

Morgan posited that, if a broker were going to contract with an unrated motor carrier, it should conduct its own safety review. To do this, a broker should go to the FMCSA website to see if a given carrier has a record of accidents or safety violations. The FMCSA website showed that, while unrated overall, E.G.G. was rated at 75% on one metric measuring management controls. This was above FMCSA's "intervention threshold" of 65%. E.G.G.'s two drivers had four citations between them in the 14 months preceding the accident for falsifying time sheets and driving without enough rest. In fact, Garcia admitted in deposition that he was aware that Vela had previously falsified a time sheet. Garcia informed Vela that he would be fired if he did it again. Also, Vela previously documented average speeds of 70 miles per hour. This speed is unrealistic, given that a trip is not entirely highway driving. Either Vela was speeding, or he drove more hours than allowed by federal regulations.

According to Morgan, . . . Vela once again falsified his time sheets while performing on the contract with M&G. . . . [R]egulations require a driver to rest a minimum of 10 hours before going back on the road each day. Morgan hypothesized that, from the times and locations recorded on Vela's cell phone, it is clear he did not do this. Morgan believed that Vela drove 18 hours without proper rest before arriving at the Kraft/Claussen docking station and that he got less than 6.5 hours of sleep on the night preceding the accident. Maria Vergara, a general manager for M&G, testified in a deposition that she has used the FMCSA website to search for driver safety violations. In the past, she has disqualified certain carriers based on the FMCSA information concerning prior violations. However, she did not perform a review of E.G.G. prior to this trip. She was aware, prior to contracting with E.G.G. for this trip, that an E.G.G. driver had been in a weather-related accident within the past year. No one was hurt in that accident.

Both M&G and Texana moved for summary judgment. . . .

As to counts II and IV, negligent hiring, the court granted summary judgment to M&G and Texana, respectively. It determined that, regardless of which company had selected E.G.G., the accident occurred after the completion of the work E.G.G. was hired to perform. The court appeared to classify the issue of liability beyond the limits of the contracted-for work as determinative of the *duty* element rather than the *proximate-cause* element. . . . This appeal followed.

II. ANALYSIS

. . . The common-law tort of negligent hiring or retention finds its basis in the Restatement (Second) of Torts § 411 (1965): "One who employs an independent contractor to: (a) do work which involves risk of bodily harm unless it is skillfully and carefully done; or (b) perform a duty which the employer owes to third persons is subject to liability for physical harm to third persons caused by the failure to exercise reasonable care to employ a competent contractor. A "competent and careful contractor" is a contractor who "possesses the knowledge, skill, experience, and available equipment which a reasonable man would realize that a contractor must have in order to do the work which he is employed to do without creating unreasonable risk of injury to others, and who also possesses the personal characteristics which are equally necessary." . . . .

We begin with count II, negligent hiring against M&G. . . . [E]ven if we assume that there was sufficient evidence to raise a material factual issue as to whether M&G breached its duty of care in hiring E.G.G., plaintiff's argument ultimately fails. The remaining question is whether the failure to exercise reasonable care in hiring E.G.G. to perform the contracted-for work proximately caused the injuries. . . . This claim turns on proximate cause.

. . . Proximate cause is not a matter for the jury in this case, because the cause of action at issue sets forth a rigorous proximate-cause standard that simply cannot be met under the existing record. . . . Again, in an action for negligent hiring or retention, the injury must have occurred by virtue of the servant's employment. The employer's liability attaches "only where there was demonstrated some connection between the plaintiff's injuries and the fact of employment." . . . [A]n employer is subject to liability for harm to third persons caused by its failure to exercise reasonable care to employ a competent and careful contractor to do work that will involve a risk of harm unless *that work* is carefully done.

As a matter of public policy, the courts have set a rigorous proximate-cause standard for the cause of action. . . . [T]o support a claim for negligent hiring or retention, the injury must have occurred while the independent contractor was directly involved in the performance of the contracted-for work, as opposed to an act collateral to the work for which the contractor was engaged.

. . . And, we observed:

> [T]he purpose of the tort is to prevent injuries that occur during the term of employment and, consequently, suggests that the employer's duty of care does not extend beyond the cessation of employment.

. . . An employer *may* be liable for out-of-the-scope acts, but *only* where the employee is on the employer's premises or using the chattel of the employer and the employer has reason to know of the need and opportunity for exercising control over the employee. . . .

. . . This case is different from a scenario where a contractor's incompetent workmanship resulted in a construction failure post-job, such as a cornice falling off of a building and onto a pedestrian. . . . In that example, the work itself was not performed in a manner so as to reasonably protect third parties from harm. Here, the work itself, delivering the cucumbers, was performed without incident. Rather, it was the *worker,* not the *work,* who went on, posttermination, to injure a third party. . . .

We reject plaintiff's theory that, because E.G.G. continued to perform on its contract with M&G on the return leg of the trip, the accident did not occur posttermination. . . . [H]ere, the contract terminated upon completion of the contracted-for task, the delivery of the cucumbers. After the delivery, E.G.G. had no remaining obligations to M&G. Postdelivery meant posttermination.

We also reject plaintiff's alternate theory that, even if the accident occurred posttermination, the negligent act—driving too many hours so as to become fatigued—occurred predelivery while E.G.G. performed on its contract with M&G. . . . Here, even if we assume the independent contractor became fatigued while completing his contract for M&G, he committed the wrongful acts—failing to stop at a red light, failing to keep a reasonably careful lookout for other vehicles, failing to decrease speed, and driving too fast for conditions—posttermination.

We now turn to count IV, negligent hiring against Texana. . . . [E]ven if Texana had selected E.G.G. to haul the load, the negligence still would have occurred posttermination.

III. CONCLUSION

. . . For the reasons stated, we affirm the trial court's grant of summary judgment to M&G and Texana.

Affirmed

Questions

1. According to the court, what is the standard for proximate cause in a negligent hiring claim?
2. Why did the court affirm summary judgment for the defendants on the negligent hiring claims?
3. According to the court, how can this case be distinguished from one involving poor construction work that results in injury after the job is completed?
4. Do you agree with the court's ruling? Explain.
5. Gary Weimerskirch, assistant manager at Main Lanes Bowling Alley, walked in on David Coakley, a mechanic at the bowling alley, and Coakley's girlfriend as they were getting dressed, apparently having just engaged in sexual relations. Coakley then told Weimerskirch that he quit and he began to collect his belongings from the work area. Suddenly, Coakley grabbed a two-by-four plank, ran toward Weimerskirch, and struck him on the head with it. Coakley's criminal record included drug- and alcohol-related offenses, along with one misdemeanor assault. However, his employer did not have any knowledge of this criminal record. Furthermore, Coakley had not acted violently at work previously.
   a. What causes of action might Weimerskirch bring against the bowling alley?
   b. Decide the case. Explain. See *Weimerskirch v. Coakley et al.,* 2008 Ohio 1681 (Ohio Ct. App. 2008).

Part Three—Fair Labor Standards Act

LO 12-5 Discuss employees' rights under the Fair Labor Standards Act.

A note was passed to President Franklin D. Roosevelt in 1936 from a young girl:

> I wish you could do something to help us girls. We have been working in a sewing factory . . . getting our minimum pay of $11 a week. Today, the 200 of us girls have been cut down to $4 and $5 and $6 a week.[27]

Roosevelt reportedly remarked that something needed to be done about child labor. The depression and its tragic suffering, even of those working hard, shattered many Americans' faith in the free market and led to government intervention, including, in 1938, the Fair Labor Standards Act (FLSA), which is directed toward these major objectives:

1. The establishment of a minimum wage that provides at least the foundation for a modest standard of living for employees.
2. A flexible ceiling on hours worked weekly, the purpose of which is to increase the number of employed Americans.
3. Child labor protection.
4. Equal pay for equal work regardless of gender (see Chapter 13).

[For the U.S. Department of Labor home page, see **www.dol.gov**].

Minimum Wage

The federal minimum wage is currently $7.25 per hour, and it hasn't been increased since 2009. However, under President Biden's 2021 executive orders, federal workers and federal employees earn $15 an hour. States may set higher minimum wages. In 2023, the minimum wage in 30 states is over the federal minimum wage.[28] Critics of a federally mandated minimum wage argue that the government should not interfere in the marketplace and that increases in minimum wages threaten not only job growth but also the livelihoods of many small business owners. Supporters of minimum wage increases point to studies concluding that raising the minimum wage does not lead to the loss of low-paying jobs.[29] "Living wage" calculators have been developed that generally show current minimum wage laws do not reflect minimum living standards in light of local costs.[30] A 2020 National Low Income Housing Coalition study indicates that, on average in the United States, a full-time worker would need to earn over $23 an hour to rent a two-bedroom dwelling.[31]

Questions

1. Why might business leaders advocate for raising the federal minimum wage? The group Business for a Fair Minimum Wage, which includes business owners and executives from a range of industries, advocates for raising the federal minimum wage to at least $15. [For more on its point of view, see **www.businessforafairminimumwage.org**].
2. After the U.S. House of Representatives passed a bill in 2019 to gradually raise the federal minimum wage to $15 by 2025, the U.S. Senate Majority Leader, Sen. Mitch McConnell, said he would not take the bill to the Senate for a vote. What arguments exist against raising the minimum wage?
3. At this writing, the California FAST Recovery Act, signed into law in 2022, which would establish a state council to set the minimum wage for California fast-food workers to up to $22 an hour, has been blocked by a California court, pending a proposed referendum in opposition to the law. What are the arguments for and against the California FAST Recovery Act? Explain.

Overtime

Most workers covered under FLSA must receive overtime pay of at least 1½ times their regular pay rate for hours worked over 40 hours per week. However, FLSA also recognizes exemptions for certain occupations, such as managers, outside salespersons, administrators, and professionals with advanced degrees; these workers are referred to as "exempt" employees. *Misclassification* of "nonexempt" employees who have overtime rights under FLSA is a common basis for wage-and-hour claims against employers, which have led to high-profile settlements. For example, vision center managers and asset-protection coordinators were once considered exempt by Walmart but were then reclassified at the instigation of the Department of Labor, which ultimately ordered the company to pay $4.8 million in back wages and damages to those employees.[32] Levi-Strauss was ordered to pay over $1 million in overtime back wages to misclassified workers, including assistant store managers who were incorrectly treated as exempt, given the actual nature of their work.[33] However, a recent U.S. Supreme Court decision held that pharmaceutical sales representatives were not entitled to overtime pay.[34]

Overtime claims often involve disputes over whether the employee was actually working rather than engaging in a noncompensable activity. These *off-the-clock* claims in which employers are accused of not giving employees recorded credit for all of the time they have worked sometimes spring from advancing technology. The rise in remote and "hybrid" work arrangements, with nonexempt as well as exempt employees working from home for at least part of the workweek, has made the issue of wage and hours for nonexempt workers particularly challenging.[35]

For an employer to consider "white collar" (executive, administrative, or professional) workers exempt from overtime pay, the workers must earn at least a certain "threshold' salary. In 2016, a federal judge ordered an injunction on the enforcement of an Obama administration overtime pay rule that would have raised this salary threshold from $23,600 to $47,476 per year.[36] In 2019, the Trump administration lifted the overtime salary threshold to $35,568.[37]

Overtime and the "Highly Compensated Employee" Helix Energy Solutions Group, Inc. v. Hewitt, 598 U.S. __ (2023)

Hewitt worked for Helix Energy Solutions (Helix) on an offshore oil rig as a tool pusher and earned more than $200,000 annually. Hewitt, who often was required to work over 40 hours per week, sued Helix for overtime pay under FLSA. In defending against the claim, Helix argued that under FLSA "highly compensated employees" such as Hewitt, who the company classified as a "bona fide executive," are exempt from overtime pay. However, under FLSA, employees are exempt under the "bona fide executive" exception only if they are paid on a salary basis. Helix based Hewitt's pay on a daily rate.

The District Court agreed with Helix's view that Hewitt was compensated on a salary basis and granted Helix summary judgment. The Fifth Circuit Court of Appeals reversed, deciding that Hewitt was not paid on a salary basis and therefore could claim the FLSA's protections. On appeal, the U.S. Supreme Court considered whether Hewitt as a high-earning employee was compensated on a "salary basis" when his paycheck was based solely on a daily rate—so that he received a certain amount for each day he worked. For example, he would earn twice as much for working two days a week than working one day a week. The Court affirmed the Fifth Circuit's decision, holding that Hewitt was not an executive exempt from the FLSA's overtime pay guarantee because he was not paid on a salary basis.

Sources: Faegre Drinker, "Supreme Court Decides Helix Energy Solutions Group, Inc. v. Hewitt, *JD Supra* (February 23, 2023) [**https://www.jdsupra.com**]; and Dan Mangan, "Supreme Court rules Helix Energy Oil Rig Worker Who Makes $200,000 Is Entitled to Overtime," *CNBC.com* (February 22, 2023) [**https://www.cnbc.com/2023/**].

To address potentially abusive situations in which employers seek "free labor," the U.S. Department of Labor issued guidelines in 2010 for determining whether unpaid interns are employees with wage rights or trainees who are receiving an educational opportunity for their sole benefit and thus excluded from FLSA protection. These guidelines were updated in 2018, indicating that internships should be evaluated on case-by-case basis, and that no single factor is determinative. [For the seven factors identified by the U.S. Department of Labor regarding payment to interns, see **https://www.dol.gov/agencies/whd/fact-sheets/71-flsa-internships**].

Turning the Page on Internships: Condé Nast Paid Fellowships

Three months after being sued by former interns claiming they were unfairly compensated for their work, publishing conglomerate Condé Nast announced it was ending its internship programs. It later settled the former interns' lawsuit for $5.8 million. Two years later, Condé Nast announced it would offer six-month, full-time paid editorial fellowships.

Questions

1. What are the benefits to college students and recent graduates of the U.S. Department of Labor's student internship rules? What are the drawbacks? Explain.
2. If you were an undergraduate majoring in journalism, what obstacles would there be to participating in Condé Nast's editorial fellowship program? Would you be more likely to participate in an unpaid internship program at another publisher? Explain.

Sources: Erika Adams, "Condé Nast Replacing Internships with Paid Fellowships," *Racked,* May 19, 2015 [**www.racked.com**]; and "Condé Nast Launches Fellowship Program to Replace Internships," *News & Tech,* June 1, 2015 [**www.newsandtech.com**].

Questions

1. Answer this person's question: "I work as a pharmacist in a large discount retail store. My employer classifies me as exempt under FLSA. Like other pharmacists, I agree to work a specific number of base hours per week which determines my specific rate of pay. However, the employer has changed my base hours so frequently lately that I am effectively being treated as an hourly employee. There have been weeks I have worked more than 40 hours a week. Do I have a right to overtime?"[38]

2. Answer this person's question: "Before I resigned as a sewing manager for a small manufacturing company, where I supervised several employees and received an hourly wage, I regularly arrived at the factory 15 to 45 minutes before the start of my 5:00 am shift, spending most of that time doing such tasks as reviewing employee schedules, gathering and distributing fabric to my subordinates' workstations, cleaning work area, etc.–but without pay. Does my former employer owe me overtime pay?"[39]
3. What are the challenges posed by remote or hybrid work arrangements pose challenges to an employer's compliance with overtime regulations? How might these challenges be addressed? Explain.

Part Four—Health and Safety at Work

COVID and Vaccines

The COVID pandemic's impact on workplace health and safety entered a new phase with the availability of COVID vaccinations. In January 2022, the U.S. Supreme Court blocked the Biden Administration's COVID-19 "vaccine or testing" rules for private employers with 100 or more employees who work at central location, within days after it went into effect. These employers would have been required to have a procedure to know employees' vaccination status, track infections, and keep those who tested positive for COVID-19 away from work. While many businesses applauded the Court's ruling, some continued with their own vaccination requirements, such as Deloitte, which had already required vaccinations of its U.S. employees to access its offices. Sources: David Harrison, "Vaccine Rule Takes Effect," *The Wall Street Journal* (January 11, 2022 p. A6); Brent Kendall and Jess Bravin, "Court Blocks Biden Vaccine Rule," *The Wall Street Journal* (January 14, 2022 p. A1); and Chip Cutter, "Businesses Applaud Ruling, Even as Some Plan own Mandates," *The Wall Street Journal* (January 14, 2022, p. B5).

Deepwater Horizon

"I am here to describe the profound impact my brother's death, while working on a rig engaged in deepwater drilling, has had on our family," Chris Jones told the U.S. House Committee on Natural Resources in 2011. He was testifying as the surviving brother of Gordon Jones, one of 11 workers killed in the British Petroleum (BP) oil well explosion in the Gulf of Mexico in 2010. "[Gordon] was tragically killed aboard the Deepwater Horizon while earning his living as a mud engineer for MI SWACO, a contractor for BP. Gordon had nothing to do with this disaster. He was simply doing his job and making his way through his shift so he could get back home to his family. Instead, he never saw his family again. We can thank poor, and likely grossly negligent, decisions by many people and companies for that."[40] In 2012, BP agreed to plead guilty and pay $4.5 billion to settle criminal charges. Manslaughter charges against individual supervisors stemming from the fatal explosion were dropped in 2015.[41]

Gordon Jones was tragically killed aboard the Deepwater Horizon.

[For a trailer of the movie Deepwater Horizon, see **www.youtube.com/watch?v=8yASbM8M2vg**].

Upper Big Branch Coal Mine Disaster

Twenty-nine workers died in a 2010 mine explosion at Massey Energy's Upper Big Branch Coal Mine in West Virginia. In 2015, former CEO Don Blankenship was convicted of conspiring to violate federal mine-safety laws and sentenced to one year in prison.[42]

Deaths, Illnesses, and Injuries

A total of 4,764 workers suffered a fatal work-related injury in the United States in 2020, a slight decrease from the number reported in 2018.[43] Nonfatal workplace injuries and illnesses in the private sector also continued to decline in 2020.[44] However, in the same time period, there was a sharp rise in the number of illnesses reported, including work-related COVID-19 cases.[45]

OSHA

LO 12-6
Describe the role of the Occupational Safety and Health Administration in protecting employees' health and safety at work.

The Occupational Safety and Health Administration (OSHA) is responsible for ensuring safe workplaces. The 1970 Occupational Safety and Health Act imposes a general duty on most employers to provide a workplace free of "recognized hazards causing or likely to cause death or serious physical harm to employees." Employers have an absolute duty to remove any serious and preventable workplace hazards that are generally recognized in the industry and are known to the employer or should be known to the employer. That general duty is then supplemented with numerous specific standards. [For more on OSHA, see **www.osha.gov**].

Standards

OSHA, under the U.S. Department of Labor, promulgates and enforces health and safety standards that identify and seek to correct specific workplace hazards and problems. These can range from exposure to cancer-causing agents (such as the chemical benzene) to the surprisingly commonplace problem of one worker restarting a machine while another is servicing it. For example, a long-fought-for 2008 OSHA standard requires employers to pay for all OSHA-mandated personal protective equipment (for example, safety-specific eyewear, skin creams, and clothing).[46]

The often protracted development of OSHA regulations reflects an ongoing ideological and practical conflict over imposing additional safety rules in American workplaces. Some of the competing considerations are illustrated by disputes over ergonomics and workplace violence.

Violence

Workplace shootings have made for sadly familiar headlines, with no particular job site immune from such tragedy. In 2019, Gary Martin opened fire with a Smith & Wesson on the day he was fired from the Henry Pratt Co, in Aurora, Illinois, killing five workers, including a human resources intern, and wounding five police officers.[47] A recent study reported that workplace violence is so common in the healthcare setting that most nurses and emergency physicians believed it was part of their jobs and did not report such incidents.[48]

At this writing, OSHA is in the early stages of developing a potential standard addressing workplace violence. In developing the Prevention of Workplace Violence in Healthcare and Social Assistance (SBREFA), and is creating a small business advocacy review panel as part of this process.[49] What specific duties for employers might be developed regarding workplace violence?

The specific issue of gun possession in the workplace has been addressed at the state level. Approximately half the states prohibit employers from banning firearms in parking areas.[50] A 2022 U.S. Supreme Court decision recognizing a constitutional right to carry a firearm outside the home for self-defense did not address workplaces specifically but has caused confusion among employers with policies barring firearm possession in the workplace in states allowing such restrictions.[51]

PRACTICING ETHICS Workplace Stress

In its Safety and Health Topics Bulletin on Workplace Stress, OSHA addresses the negative impact that workplace stress and poor mental health can cause on employees' job performance and engagement, as well as daily functioning. Although OSHA does not have a standard specifically targeting workplace stress, this Topics Bulletin offers guidance and resources to employers seeking to address mental health in the workplace.

As noted by OSHA, a 2021 survey by the American Psychological Association found that more than 85% of employees reported that actions from their employer would help their mental health.

Questions to Consider

1. A supervisor notices that an employee arrived at work extremely distraught. What should the supervisor do? Why might the supervisor hesitate to act? Explain.
2. Should workplace stress be regulated through OSHA standards? Explain.

Sources: U.S. Department of Labor, "Workplace Stress," Safety and Health Topics Bulletin, **https://www.osha.gov/workplace-stress** citing American Psychological Association, "The American Workforce Faces Compounding Pressure: APA's 2021 Work and Well-being Survey [**https://www.apa.org/pubs/reports/work-well-being/compounding-pressure-2021**]; and U.S. Department of Labor, OSHA, Director of Technical Support and Emergency Management, "OSHA Injury and Illness Recordkeeping and Reporting Requirements" [**https://www.apa.org/pubs/reports/work-well-being/compounding-pressure-2021**].

Variances

Employers may seek both permanent and temporary *variances* (exceptions) from OSHA standards. A permanent variance may be granted only if the workplace will be as safe as if the standard were enforced. A temporary variance permits additional time to put in place the necessary compliance measures. Employees have a right to a hearing to contest variances.

OSHA Information Requirements

Right to Know

OSHA has adopted an employee *hazard communication standard* to protect employees from the dangers associated with chemicals and other toxins in the workplace. Chemical manufacturers and importers must develop *material safety data sheets* for all chemicals. Employers must then label all chemical containers so that employees will know about the chemical and its dangers, and employers must educate employees about chemical hazards and how to deal with them.

Records

As a general rule, businesses must maintain records listing and summarizing work-related injuries, illnesses, and deaths. A summary of those records must be posted at the job. Notice of any OSHA citations of imminent dangers on the job must also be posted at the job site. In recent years, OSHA reformed and simplified the record-keeping process, with some smaller companies, especially those engaging in nonhazardous activities, exempt from meeting the record-keeping requirements.

Go-Cart Races at Work

Does an employee's injury suffered in a go-cart race held as part of an off-site team-building event need to be reported? According to a 2009 letter from OSHA responding to this inquiry, an injury in those circumstances is work-related and, therefore, reportable even if the employee had the option to return to work or take a half-day vacation instead of participating in the go-cart race that followed a mandatory off-site meeting. A 2012 federal appellate decision suggested that requiring record keeping of all workplace injuries may be more efficient than analyzing whether such an injury is work-related.

Sources: ***OSHA*** Letter of Interpretation on Standard 1904, 1904.5(b)(1), February 24, 2009 [**www.osha.gov**]; and *Caterpillar Logistics v. Solis,* 674 F.3d 705 (7th Cir. 2012).

Enforcement

OSHA's most publicized enforcement mechanism is the unannounced on-site inspection. Inspections arise at the initiative of the agency itself or at the request of employees or their representatives. The inspections must be conducted in a reasonable manner during work hours or other reasonable times, and ordinarily, they are not required to be announced in advance. However, employers can demand a warrant prior to inspection. With proper justification, warrants can easily be secured from a federal magistrate. Employer and employee representatives may accompany the inspector.

To enhance efficiency, OSHA practices a targeted, site-specific inspection plan designed to identify and monitor the workplaces most likely to have safety and health problems. However, an employer can become exempt from such inspections under OSHA's Voluntary Protection Program (VPP), a program that drew criticism from the Office of Inspector General in 2013. An Assistant Secretary of Labor acknowledged some of the problems, but also indicated that there had been improvement in the previous four years.[52]

Citations

Citations may be issued if violations are discovered during the inspection process. Immediate, serious threats can be restrained with a court order. Following a citation, the employer may ask to meet with an area OSHA official to discuss the problem. Often a settlement emerges from these meetings. Failing a settlement, the employer can appeal to the independent OSHA Review Commission and thereafter to the federal court of appeals. Violations may lead to fines and/or imprisonment. For example, OSHA cited and fined Excel, a company packing Hershey's chocolates, $283,000 for failing to report dozens of serious injuries to its workers, after protests by hundreds of students working in the plant on an international exchange program run by the State Department.[53]

Enforcement versus Compliance?

The business community often criticizes OSHA for unfairly increasing the cost of production by imposing inflexible and overzealous expectations. Labor organizations and job safety advocates, on the other hand, have criticized OSHA as a timid, faltering safety shield. In 2023, OSHA issued new enforcement guidance designed to make its penalties more effectively deter employers from repeated, serious violations of OSHA standards. For example, regional OSHA offices now can issue "Instance-By-Instance" citations for "high-gravity" serious violations of OSHA standards specific to conditions such as falls, machine guarding, and respiratory protection.[54]

The Severe Violator Enforcement Program (SVEP) concentrates on employers who have demonstrated indifference to their safety obligations by engaging in willful, repeated, or "failure to abate" violations. SVEP uses mandatory follow-up inspections, press releases, and increased fines, among other tools, to send a clear message that such conduct will be rigorously addressed by OSHA.[55] OSHA makes public its list of severe violators. [For current SVEP logs see **www.osha.gov/enforcement**].

Workers' Compensation

LO 12-7

Describe the benefits, coverage, and requirements for bringing a successful claim under workers' compensation laws.

Korey Stringer, a 27-year-old Pro Bowl tackle, died of heatstroke complications on August 1, 2001, after going through a preseason Minnesota Vikings workout.[56] Normally, when an employee is injured or dies on the job, the employee or the estate may not sue for damages. Rather, recovery is limited to the fixed sum provided for by the workers' compensation statute, regardless of fault. Stringer's family, however, filed a wrongful death suit seeking to hold the Vikings and various individuals responsible for gross negligence and other wrongs in responding to Stringer's heatstroke. The Vikings argued that the Stringer suit was barred by the state workers' compensation law. Minnesota is one of a number of states, however, that recognize an exception to workers' compensation exclusivity provisions in cases of *gross negligence* by the defendants.[57] The Stringers' case reached the Minnesota Supreme Court, where the 4–2 majority ruled on technical grounds against the family's gross negligence claim, thus limiting their remedy to workers' compensation, a sum much lower than Stringer's projected commercial worth.[58]

Early in the 20th century, the states began enacting workers' compensation laws to provide an administrative remedy for those, like Stringer, who are injured or killed on the job.

> Korey Stringer, a 27-year-old Pro Bowl tackle, died of heatstroke complications.

Previously, employers' superior financial resources and various technical legal defenses meant that employees were often not successful suing to recover damages for their on-the-job injuries. All states now provide some form of workers' compensation that does not require a lawsuit. Instead, workers or their families apply for compensation

department-issued pager to both his then-wife and a coworker with whom he was romantically involved. Noticing a frequency in overage charges, the police department audited the content of police officers' texts to determine whether the overage charges were the result of work-related messages that might show the need to upgrade the text-messaging plan. Although a workplace policy stated that employees had no expectation of privacy in using Internet or email provided them at work, it did not address the pagers given to the police officers. As a result of the audit, Quon was disciplined for misusing the pager.

The legal question was whether the police department's review of Sargeant Quon's text messages violated his Fourth Amendment right to privacy. Acknowledging that "workplace norms" regarding technology are evolving, in 2010 the U.S. Supreme Court held in *City of Ontario v. Quon* that, even assuming Quon had a reasonable expectation of privacy in his text messages, the police department's review of the text messages did not violate Quon's Fourth Amendment rights. Ontario had a legitimate reason for the search, and the search was not excessive in scope.[69]

Employers' rights to monitor electronic messages may be defined on a case-by-case basis. A former employee had sent emails to her attorney regarding a possible workplace discrimination claim using a company laptop computer and her personal, password-protected email account rather than her business email address. After she resigned and sued, her former employer hired a computer expert who retrieved the emails between her and her attorney, which were then reviewed by the company's attorney. Holding that the employee had a reasonable expectation of privacy in those emails, the New Jersey Supreme Court also acknowledged that although employers can establish rules regarding the use of workplace computers and discipline employees; accordingly, this power did not include the right to read privileged communications between an employee and her attorney.[70]

The Law

In general, employers can lawfully monitor workers' attendance, performance, email, use of the Internet, and so on, but uncertainty remains. Having a clear, written workplace policy regarding the use and monitoring of technology is a good employment practice.

Although at this writing there is no unifying U.S. federal digital privacy law, the 1986 Electronic Communications Privacy Act prohibits private individuals and organizations from intercepting wire, oral, or electronic communications. The act provides for two exceptions, however: (1) prior consent by one of the parties to the communication and (2) employer monitoring in the "ordinary course of business" by telephone or other device furnished by a provider of wire or electronic communication service. Thus, workplace monitoring of phone calls (except for purely private conversations), workplace computers, voice mail, email, and Internet use are all likely to be considered lawful if approached in a reasonable manner.

As discussed previously in this chapter, job applicants face the possibility that their prospective employers might research their online reputations. Should the employer be allowed to require job applicants to disclose the passwords to their Facebook and other social media accounts? At this writing, 25 states have enacted legislation prohibiting an employer from requesting or requiring an employee or applicant to disclose a user name or password for a personal social media account.[71]

Requesting access to employees' social media accounts, even in the absence of legislation, still creates potential liability for the employer, as illustrated in a case involving a restaurant employee's invitation-only group on MySpace.com for coworkers to "vent" about work. Posts included sexual comments about the employer's managers and customers as well as references to illegal drug use. When one member showed the MySpace profile to a manager, she was later asked by another manager to share the password to access the profile. The employer terminated the profile's creator as well as another one of the invited coworkers, who sued for, among other claims, invasion of privacy. Given that a jury could reasonably find that the invited member of the MySpace group was coerced into providing the password, making the employer's access unauthorized, a federal district court upheld the jury's verdict against the employer.[72]

Biometrics, AI, and Employee Privacy

Prior to the emergence of Artificial Intelligence (AI)-powered bots assisting employees, discussed earlier in the chapter, AI had already been offering employers powerful tools to monitor employees. A wristband patented by Amazon tracks hand movements of warehouse workers and nudges them into efficiency through vibrations. Employers can use smart ID badges to track employees around the office and see how well they interact with their coworkers. AI can also check to make sure that workers are wearing safety gear and offer feedback on their work. Uber's algorithm monitors workers' performance, ranking them on a five-star basis. Drivers with consistently low ratings can be removed from the Uber app.

Employers can also use such technology to authenticate workers' identities through biometrics, or measurements of their unique physical characteristics, such as facial measurements. Biometrics can also include fingerprints, palmprints, voiceprints, eye measurements, and more. Several states have enacted legislation to address employees' privacy rights to their biometric data, including the Illinois Biometric Information Privacy Act (BIPA), which applies to the workplace. Typically, these laws require employers to give employees notice and obtain their consent regarding the collection, storage, and use of their biometric data. In 2022, the Illinois Supreme Court ruled that BIPA claims are not barred by the state's workers' compensation statute. In 2023, the Illinois Supreme Court ruled that BIPA claims accrue each time data are unlawfully collected and disclosed, rather than just the first time.

Questions

1. Should employers be allowed to collect, store, and use employees' biometric data? Should an employer be allowed to use biometric data to authenticate the identity of an applicant in the hiring process? Explain.
2. What are the advantages of AI-empowered surveillance? What are the disadvantages? Explain.

Sources: "Smile You're on Camera; Future Workplaces," *The Economist,* March 31, 2018 **[www.economist.com]**; "Your Boss Is Watching: How AI-Powered Surveillance Rules the Workplace," *Politico* (May 27, 2021) **[https://www.politico.eu/]**; Kohrman Jackson and Krantz, "Biometrics and AI in the Workplace: Boon or Bane?" *JDSupra* (October 12, 2022) **[https://www.jdsupra.com]**; Fox Rothschild, "Illinois Supreme Court Rules that BIPA Claims Accrue with Each Scan," *Fox Rothschild Publications* (February 17, 2023) **[https://www.foxrothschild.com/]**; and Adam S. Forman and Nathaniel M. Glasser, "Employers Take Heed: Follow Illinois Biometric Privacy Rules or Risk a Losing Battle," *Epstein Beck Green Publications* (February 16, 2022) **[https://www.ebglaw.com]**.

Koeppel v. Speirs 2010 Iowa App. LEXIS 25 (Iowa Ct. App. January 22, 2010) (unpublished op.)

EISENHAUER, P. J.

I. BACKGROUND FACTS AND PROCEEDINGS

[Sara] Koeppel and Deanna Miller were the only employees of Speirs, an insurance agent. A small (4' x 7') bathroom with a sink and toilet is located in the office. On December 27, 2005, Koeppel discovered a digital surveillance camera hidden inside the office bathroom. After contacting the Waterloo Police Department, a search warrant was obtained and officers located the camera in the bathroom. The camera was positioned to view the toilet and surrounding area. When confronted by police, Speirs produced the receiver and monitor for the camera from a locked drawer in his desk.

When questioned about the presence of the camera, Speirs admitted he had placed it in the bathroom on December 26, 2005, and stated he did so because he suspected one of his employees was abusing drugs while at work and was concerned she would embezzle money. Speirs claimed he was unable to get a signal from the camera when it was in the bathroom. At the time the officers arrived, the surveillance system was not set up to receive images from the camera. However, setup could be completed by plugging the equipment found in Speirs's desk drawer into an electrical outlet.

After connecting the equipment, the officers tested it and found it did not work. Speirs told the officers the camera battery was likely dead. After changing the battery at Speirs's suggestion, a fuzzy picture of the toilet seat and bathroom wall was visible. The image would cut in and out every few seconds. Videotapes located in Speirs's office were blank.

Speirs purchased the camera on November 26, 2005. Miller told the police, when interviewed on December 28, she saw the camera in the bathroom on November 28, 2005. Speirs, in another proceeding, testified he used the camera to monitor Miller at her desk on December 10, 2005, and in seven or ten viewings, he observed no wrongdoing.

Koeppel [sued] Speirs, alleging . . . invasion of privacy. . . .

Speirs then filed a motion for summary judgment . . . claiming there was no actual intrusion upon Koeppel's privacy because there is no evidence he viewed her in the restroom. Koeppel [argued] Speirs's act of placing the camera in the bathroom with the intent to view her was an invasion of her privacy. She also argued there was sufficient evidence for the jury to find the camera was operational. . . . [T]he district court entered its ruling, granting Speirs's motion. The court agreed Speirs intended to view Koeppel while she was in the bathroom, but concluded Koeppel could only be liable for an actual intrusion on her privacy, not an attempted intrusion. Finding no evidence Speirs viewed Koeppel in the bathroom, the court dismissed the claim.

On November 25, 2008, Koeppel appealed. . . .

III. INVASION OF PRIVACY

Koeppel first contends the court erred in granting summary judgment on her invasion of privacy claim. She contends Speirs's act of placing a camera in the bathroom with the intent to view her is sufficient to support a cause of action for invasion of privacy. In the alternative, she contends there is a question of fact as to whether there was an actual intrusion into her privacy.

Iowa has adopted the tort of invasion of privacy, as set forth in the Restatement (Second) of Torts (1977), which provides the right to privacy can be invaded by "unreasonable intrusion upon the seclusion of another." Under this theory,

> [o]ne who *intentionally intrudes*, physically or otherwise, upon the solitude or seclusion of another or his private affairs or concerns, is subject to liability to the other for invasion of privacy, if the intrusion would be *highly offensive to a reasonable person.*

To recover under this theory, Koeppel must show Speirs intentionally intruded upon her seclusion, and that a reasonable person would find the intrusion "highly offensive."

There is no question viewing or recording Koeppel while in the bathroom would be considered "highly offensive" by any reasonable person. There also can be no dispute a bathroom is a place where one enjoys seclusion. Nor is it debatable that Speirs acted intentionally in placing a recording device in the bathroom. The question presented in this case is whether there is enough evidence to create a question of fact as to whether there was an intrusion on Koeppel's privacy.

The district court concluded an actual invasion of privacy must occur for the cause of action to stand and found no facts supported an actual invasion. Koeppel argues intent to intrude on privacy is enough to maintain a cause of action. She cites *In re Marriage of Tigges* and two cases outside this jurisdiction in support of her argument.

In the case of *Tigges,* our supreme court addressed the question of unreasonable intrusion upon the seclusion of another where a husband secretly videotaped his wife in their bedroom. [*In re Marriage of*] *Tigges,* 758 N.W.2d [824,] 825 [(Iowa 2008)]. The husband argued there was no invasion of privacy because the video captured nothing "private" or "sexual" in nature. *Id.* at 829. In rejecting this claim, our supreme court stated:

> The wrongfulness of the conduct springs not from the specific nature of the recorded activities, but instead from the fact that Cathy's activities were recorded without her knowledge and consent at a time and place and under circumstances in which she had a reasonable expectation of privacy.

Id. at 830. We disagree with Koeppel's assertion that *Tigges* supports the proposition that the focus of invasion of privacy claims is on the intent of the perpetrator; as our supreme court states, it's the fact the victim was *recorded* without her knowledge and consent that results in the intrusion. *See id.*

. . . Koeppel cites *Harkey v. Abate* . . . . In that case, the plaintiffs brought an invasion of privacy suit after using a roller-skating rink restroom with see-through panels installed in the ceiling, which permitted surreptitious observation from above. The Michigan Court of Appeals stated:

> In our opinion, the installation of the hidden viewing devices alone constitutes an interference with that privacy which a reasonable person would find highly offensive. And though the absence of proof that the devices were utilized is relevant to the question of damages, it is not fatal to plaintiff's case.

Although this case does not support Koeppel's argument that mere intent to intrude on privacy is enough, it provides guidance in establishing the proof necessary to survive summary judgment on an invasion-of-privacy claim.

In its summary judgment ruling, the trial court . . . cites *Brazinski v. Amoco Petroleum Additives Co.*, where a female business invitee brought an invasion-of-privacy claim after learning the defendant had a television camera trained on the entrance of a locker room for its female employees. The court . . . concluded the plaintiff's claim could not stand because she was unable to show she had been in the locker room during the period the surveillance was being conducted. The case is distinguishable from Koeppel's case, however, because as a business invitee, the plaintiff in *Brazinski* was not presumed to have used the locker room as the defendant's female employees did. . . . Unlike *Brazinski*, there is no doubt in the present case that Koeppel used the office bathroom.

From the foregoing cases, we conclude to succeed on her claim, Koeppel must show the surveillance camera was capable of functioning while in the bathroom. Speirs claims it was not, that he was unable to receive any signal from the camera in the bathroom. Other evidence shows when a new battery was in the camera, a picture of the bathroom was visible on the monitor in Speirs's office, albeit not a clear and consistent one. The images obtained from the bathroom need not have been of high quality to establish an invasion of privacy, nor did the camera need to be pointed at the toilet—it is sufficient that the seclusion of the bathroom, a private area, was intruded upon. There is also evidence the camera was in the bathroom earlier in November.

. . . Accordingly, we reverse the district court ruling granting summary judgment in favor of Speirs on this claim.

Questions

1. At trial, how could Speirs be found liable for invasion of privacy if the bathroom camera had not been operating? Explain.
2. The court in *Koeppel* cited an additional case involving the following facts: The director of a nonprofit residential facility for neglected and abused children learned that someone was accessing pornographic websites late at night from a facility office computer located in an enclosed office. The two employees stationed in that office performed clerical work during normal business hours and were not suspected. Without telling them, the director installed a hidden camera in the office, trained on the computer in question. The camera did not operate during the day. After discovering the camera, the employees sued for invasion of privacy.
   a. How might this case support the court's decision in *Koeppel*?
   b. Decide. Explain. See *Hernandez v. Hillsides*, 47 Cal. 4th 272 (Cal. 2010).
3. Young was the pastor of Ft. Caroline United Methodist Church in Florida. Young was provided with a private office and a computer in that office. The computer was not networked to any other computers. Young and the church administrator had keys to the office. No one was permitted in the office without Young's permission, and the church administrator was not permitted to log on to the computer unless Young was present. The church administrator received notice from the church's Internet service provider that spam was linked to the church's Internet address. The administrator ran a "spybot" program on the church computers and found questionable web addresses. The church's district supervisor and bishop were contacted and permission was given to involve police officials. Officers came to the church; the administrator unlocked Young's office and signed "consent to search" forms for the office and the computer. Officers searched the office and computer and found proscribed images and websites. Young subsequently filed a trial court motion to suppress the evidence gained from the office and computer search. The trial judge granted that motion, ruling that the search violated Young's Fourth Amendment right to be free of unreasonable searches and seizures. The state appealed. Rule on that appeal. See *State v. Young*, 974 So. 2d 601 (Fla. Dist. Ct. App. 2008).

Drug Testing

Mary Wheeler decided to institute an employee drug-testing program for her Chagrin Falls, Ohio, landscaping company. One job applicant at Wheeler's company told the interviewer that he would have no problem with the drug test. Then according to Wheeler: "While filling out his paperwork, the interviewer asked the applicant for a driver's license. The applicant reached into his pocket, and by accident pulled out a small bag of cocaine."[73] That episode certainly confirmed Wheeler's judgment that workplace drug tests were necessary for her company, and the data support Wheeler's fears. According to a federal government study, nearly 1 out of 5 workers between the ages of 18 and 25 used illicit drugs in the past month, along with 1 out of 10 between the ages of 26 and 34.[74]

In an effort to address workplace drug problems, employers often provide information about drug abuse, have written policies regarding drug use at work, and offer employee assistance programs.[75] As employers faced difficulty in staffing, however, a 2021 poll found that nearly ten percent of employers were dropping drug testing as a way to attract and retain employees.[76]

Drug-Free Workplace

The Drug-Free Workplace Act of 1988 applies to employers who have contracts of $100,000 or more with the federal government or who receive aid from the government. Those employers are required to develop an anti-drug policy for employees. They must provide drug-free awareness programs for employees and must acquaint employees with available assistance for those with drug problems, while also warning them of the penalties that accompany violation of the policy. The act requires employees to adhere to the company policy and to inform their employer within five days if they are convicted of, or plead no contest to, a drug-related offense in the workplace. [For more information on the Federal Drug-Free Workplace Program, see **www.workplace.samhsa.gov**].

Drug Testing in Law and Practice

LO 12-9 Discuss workplace drug testing and the legal challenges it faces.

Drug testing is regulated primarily by state law, so generalizations are difficult. Broadly, we can say that private-sector drug testing, properly conducted, ordinarily is lawful in the following five situations:

1. *Pre-employment testing.* State and local law may impose some restrictions.
2. *In association with periodic physical examinations.* Advance notice is often required.
3. *For cause* when an employer has probable cause or reasonable suspicion.
4. *Post-accident testing* where drug use is suspected.
5. *Follow-up testing* for those returning from drug (including alcohol) rehabilitation.

Random testing, on the other hand, sometimes produces significant legal issues. A number of states forbid random drug testing or limit it to safety-sensitive situations. The U.S. Supreme Court has upheld such testing for public-sector employees where public safety is involved and for those having access to particularly sensitive information.[77] The legality of drug testing often reduces to a balancing test where the employee's right to privacy is balanced against the employer's business needs. Where safety and security are involved, and when notice is provided, the courts are more supportive of testing. Particularly intrusive or careless testing often tilts that balance toward employees. Beyond the balancing test, a number of other legal considerations influence employer drug-testing practices, particularly in public-sector jobs:

U.S. Constitution

As explained in Chapter 5, the Fourth Amendment forbids unreasonable searches and seizures. Thus, government employers ordinarily cannot conduct a search without individualized suspicion–that is, without probable cause. Certain exceptions, however, have been recognized in cases involving such issues as safety, national security, and athletic participation. Remember that the Constitution protects citizens from the government, not from private-sector employers (with limited exceptions).

State constitutions

Many state constitutions offer privacy protection, but court decisions, to date, have generally not extended those protections to private-sector employers. On the other hand, certain states, such as California and Massachusetts, explicitly offer constitutional protection to private-sector employees.

Federal statutes

Drug testing could violate Title VII of the Civil Rights Act of 1964 or the Americans with Disabilities Act (see Chapter 13) if the testing fails to treat all individuals equally. The ADA protects *recovering* drug addicts and those erroneously believed to be drug abusers, but not employees or applicants who are currently abusing drugs.

State and local statutes

Historically, most state and local drug-testing legislation placed limits on that testing, but in recent years, fears about drug use in the workplace and often intense business community lobbying have, in some cases, relaxed those testing restraints.

Common law claims

Some of the more prominent common law claims that might provide a method for challenging the use of drug testing include invasion of privacy, defamation (dissemination of erroneous information about an employee), negligence (in testing or in selecting a test provider), intentional infliction of emotional distress, and wrongful discharge (discussed later in this chapter).

Legalizing Marijuana: What's an Employer to Do?

As of February 2023, 21 states, as well as Washington, D.C., and Guam, have legalized marijuana, with several of those states prohibiting employers from refusing to hire or taking adverse action against employees based on positive marijuana test results. According to the 2022 Drugs at Work survey conducted by Current Consulting Group, most employers

(75%) said they plan to continue testing for marijuana; however, nearly 10 percent have either stopped testing for marijuana or are considering dropping it from their testing panel, and another 15 percent are unsure about testing for marijuana.

Question

What are the arguments for workplace testing for marijuana use? What are the arguments against it? Explain.

Sources: Claire Hansen, Horus Alas, and Elliott Davis, Jr., "Where is Marijuana Legal? A Guide to Marijuana Legalization," *US News & World Report* (February 16, 2023) [**https://www.usnews.com/**]; and First Advantage, "The Workplace Is a Mirror of Society, and Drug Testing Trends Reflect It," *First Advantage Blog* [**https://fadv.com/**].

Part Six—Employee Benefits and Income Maintenance

In recent years, in conjunction with the passage and implementation of the Patient Protection and Affordable Care Act (ACA or Obamacare), employee benefits have been the subject of much political debate and legislative action. The ACA survived a constitutional challenge brought by 18 Republican state attorneys general and the Trump administration when the Supreme Court ruled in 2021 that the challengers lacked standing.[78]

Under the ACA, employers with 50 or more employees that do not provide affordable health insurance coverage for their employees are subject to penalties. Those with fewer than 50 employees that do not provide health insurance will not face a penalty but are eligible for tax credits. Critics argue that this amounts to a mandate for larger employers to provide health insurance for their employees in order to avoid paying penalties, or conversely, to provide an incentive for employers for whom health care costs outweigh the penalties. [For more information on the ACA, see **www.healthcare.gov**].

The federal Consolidated Budget Reconciliation Act (COBRA) requires employers with 20 or more employees to permit departing employees to retain group health coverage at their own expense for up to 18 months as long as they are not terminated for gross misconduct. Unfortunately, the cost of COBRA policies is often too high for the former workers to keep the coverage.

Family Leave

LO 12-10
Describe the Family and Medical Leave Act.

Along with health care, another pressing social issue affecting the workplace is the care of the elderly and disabled. According to a 2021 report by the National Partnership for Women and Families, one in five working adults provided care for another person in 2020; over 60 percent of those had been employed in the prior 12 months.[79]

The Family and Medical Leave Act (FMLA) entitles eligible employees of covered employers to take job-protected, *unpaid* leave for certain family-related or medical reasons. Eligible employees are entitled to 12 weeks of FMLA leave in a 12-month period for the birth, adoption, or foster care placement of a child; to care for a child, spouse, or parent who has a serious medical condition; or for the employee's own serious medical condition.

Employees taking leave are entitled to reinstatement to the same or an equivalent job. Employers with 50 or more employees are covered by FMLA. The 2008 National Defense Authorization Act (NDAA) amended FMLA to provide military family leave to eligible employees to care for their spouse, child, or parent who is undergoing medical treatment for a serious injury or illness incurred in the line of duty or for "qualifying exigencies," including child care and counseling arising from their spouse's, child's, or parent's call to active duty status from the military reserves.[80] In its 2015 final rule defining "spouse" under the FMLA, the Department of Labor included same-sex spouses who got married in a state recognizing same-sex marriage, even if the couple does not reside in that state.[81]

Lost wages often make FMLA leave unattractive. However, approximately two-thirds of employees taking FMLA leave receive either full or partial pay, typically by using paid vacation leave, sick leave, or other forms of paid time off.[82] Employers in eleven states and the District of Columbia are required to provide paid family and medical leave.[83] In general, these programs are funded through employee-paid payroll taxes.[84] [For more on the FMLA, see **www.dol.gov/whd/fmla**].

Work Abroad?

Of the 41 countries represented in a recent study, the United States stood alone as a nation not mandating some form of paid leave for new parents. In comparison, Estonia offers 86 weeks of paid leave, and Hungary and Lithuania offer about 1 and 1/3 years. The smallest amount is about two months. In most countries providing paid leave, the government covers the cost.

In his 2021 American Families Plan, President Biden proposed "creating a national comprehensive paid family and medical leave program that will bring America in line with competitor nations that offer paid leave programs." Some of these programs were incorporated into earlier versions of the Build Back Better legislation, but not the version that eventually passed Congress as the Inflation Reduction Act of 2022.

Sources: Gretchen Livingston and Deja Thoma, "Among 41 countries, only U.S. lacks paid parental leave," *Pew Research Center,* December 16, 2019 [**www.pewresearch.org**]; and Michael Mandel, "Platform Work and the Care Economy," *Progressive Policy Institute* (November 21, 2022) [**https://www.progressivepolicy.org/publication/platform-work-and-the-care-economy/**].

Unemployment Compensation

The tragedy of the Great Depression, when up to 25 percent of the workforce was unemployed, led in 1935 to the passage of the Social Security Act, one portion of which provided for an unemployment insurance program. Today, all 50 states and the federal government are engaged in a cooperative system that helps protect the temporarily jobless. The system is mostly financed through a payroll tax paid by employers, but some states require employees to contribute as well.

The actual state tax rate for each employer varies, depending on the employer's *experience ratings*–the number of layoffs in its workforce. Thus, employers have an incentive to retain employees.

Rules vary by state, but in general, employees qualify for unemployment benefits by reaching a specified total of annual wages. Those losing their jobs must apply to a state agency for unemployment compensation, the amount of which varies by state. Benefits may be collected for a specified maximum period, usually 26 weeks. During that time, those collecting compensation must be ready to work and must make an effort to find suitable work. Workers who quit or who are fired for *misconduct* are ineligible for unemployment compensation. Examples of such misconduct are.

- A dairy worker led her coworkers in an after-hours swim in a cheese vat (filled with water at the time).[85]
- An on-patrol police officer was charged with having sex with a woman multiple times, sometimes in parking lots.[86]
- A 25-year-old hotel worker used her employer's computer to write a 300-page manuscript describing her successful efforts to avoid doing any work.[87]

As the gig economy rises, more workers are ineligible for unemployment compensation because they are classified as independent contractors rather than employees. Some states, such as Virginia, offer a way for these workers to opt into unemployment insurance programs, but most states require workers to be searching for traditional, full-time employment in order to qualify.[88]

The passage of the Coronavirus Aid, Relief, and Economic Security Act (CARES) provided additional unemployment benefits, in part by adding $600 per week to all unemployment checks and, in part, by temporarily relaxing the requirements for receiving benefits. The federal unemployment benefits programs under CARES ended on September 4, 2021.[89]

WARN

The Worker Adjustment and Retraining Notification Act (WARN) requires firms with 100 or more employees to provide 60 days' notice if they: (1) lay off one-third or more of their workers at any site employing at least 150 workers, (2) reduce the workforce at any site by 500 or more, or (3) close a site employing at least 50 workers.

Without WARNing?

Layoffs at Tech Firms

In 2022, over 1,000 tech firms laid off nearly 161,000 workers, according to the tracking site layoffs.fyi. In November 2022, five former employees of Twitter brought a class action against the company alleging that the company violated the WARN Act by laying off 3,700 workers–50% of its workforce–without providing the required 60-day warning.

Sources: Natalie Campisi, "What's the WARN Act and Why Is Twitter Being Sued for Violating It," *Forbes - Advisor* (November 23, 2022) [**https://www.nasdaq.com/**]; and layoffs.fyi [**https://layoffs.fyi/**].

Pensions

LO 12-11 Distinguish between defined benefit and defined contribution pension plans.

The Employee Benefit Research Institute's Retirement Confidence Survey is the longest-running of its kind. Its 2022 annual survey revealed that over seven in 10 workers are at least somewhat confident they will have enough money for retirement, with 8 in 10 retirees feeling confident that they will have enough money to last through their retirement. However, one-third of the workers and one-fourth of retirees surveyed felt that the COVID-19 pandemic had made them less confident in their retirement prospects. More than four out of five workers a workplace retirement savings plan are satisfied with this benefit.[90]

Pensions generally take two forms: *defined-benefit plans* and *defined-contribution plans.*

Defined-benefit plans provide specified monthly payments upon retirement. In the private sector, employers started moving away from them in the 1980s and most now offer only defined-contribution plans. The vast majority of state and local governments, however, still provide defined plans. Based on statistics provided by the Federal Reserve, in the aggregate, state pensions are underfunded by $4 trillion; they have assets sufficient to cover only 52 percent of the promised benefits.[91]

> More than four out of five workers who are offered a workplace retirement savings plan are satisfied with this benefit.

In 2006, private defined-benefit plan underfunding reached $450 billion–3.26 percent of the GDP. This led to increased funding requirements in the federal Pension Protection Act of 2006, which sought to protect retirement accounts and hold companies that underfunded existing pension accounts accountable.[92]

Defined-contribution plans, such as the popular 401(k), specify in advance the "match" the employer will provide to the employee's own contributions. The employee is offered a menu of investment options, but no promises are made about the amount that will be available upon retirement. Defined-contribution plans are attractive to employees because the money *vests*–the employer's contributions become nonforfeitable fairly quickly and can be taken by an employee who changes jobs. From an employer's point of view, defined-contribution plans are less expensive to manage, and they shift the risk of the amount available upon retirement from employer to employee.

Now millions of Americans depend on their own investment wisdom and the reliability of their 401(k) plan's third-party administration for their retirement security. The Department of Labor's disclosure guidelines are designed to assist employees in managing and investing their 401(k) plans.[93] The U.S. Supreme Court strengthened that oversight somewhat by finding that retirement account holders can sue if the administrator of their plan fails to follow their investment instructions[94] [see **www.401khelpcenter.com** and **www.ebri.org** for large databases on 401(k) and other retirement topics].

"Saver's Match" and Secure Act 2.0

Nontraditional Workers Saving for Retirement

Nontraditional workers, such as those working in the "gig economy" like ride-hailing and delivery service companies, face challenges in saving for retirement because they typically are not included in workplace retirement plans. The Secure Act 2.0, signed by President

Biden in 2022, not only focuses on enhancing workplace savings options but also offers a "saver's match" program as an incentive for these nontraditional workers to save for retirement. Effective in 2027, the federal government will deposit a 50 percent match, at a $1,000 maximum in response to up to $2,000 of an eligible worker's contribution to their workplace or individual retirement account. Eligibility is based on income, and the match is reduced over certain limits.

Source: Ann Carrns, "Freelancers Will Get Help Saving for Retirement," *The New York Times* (January 7, 2023, p. B4).

ERISA

The federal Employee Retirement Income Security Act (ERISA) regulates pension funds to help ensure their long-term financial health by reducing fraud and mismanagement. ERISA requires fund managers to keep detailed records, engage in prudent investments, and provide an annual report certified by qualified, impartial third parties. ERISA also establishes strict vesting rights to ensure that employees actually receive the pensions to which they are entitled. Employer contributions typically vest in full after three years or in a six-year, graduated system. The Pension Benefit Guaranty Corporation (PBGC), funded by employer contributions, was created under ERISA to insure defined-benefit plans so that vested persons will be paid up to a specified maximum if their plan cannot meet its obligations. Defined-contribution plans are not covered by the PBGC.

The Future?

Retirement is founded on pensions, savings, and Social Security (SS). As to the first two, it's grim. The median savings of those 55 to 64 is only $62,000, even though out-of-pocket healthcare costs alone will exceed $280,000. Twenty percent of Americans have no savings; 33 percent have less than $5,000. The reasons given: low income, large debts, housing costs, won't curtail lifestyle, too busy to plan, and cynicism about the future. For most, SS will be the primary source of retirement income. Thirty-eight percent would live in poverty without it. But median SS is only $16,308 (net of Medicare B), so 46 percent will have to work after "retiring." Social Security will be insolvent by 2035; benefits will have to be cut 25 percent. The program's economics are dubious. In 1945, 41.2 workers paid in for every retiree. The ratios have fallen: 5.1:1 (1960), 3.4:1 (1990), 2.6:1 (2020), and 1.9:1 (2035 projected). Further, the federal government has, for decades, taken Social Security's surpluses ($2.9 trillion) to reduce its reported budget deficits. The reckoning has arrived. In 1970, SS was 16 percent of the federal budget; now it's 40 percent. Paying back this $2.9 trillion (plus interest) will boost the already burgeoning national debt.[95]

The federal government owes Social Security $2.9 trillion.

Younger generations are even less prepared, despite dreams of retiring much earlier than their elders. Two-thirds have no savings; those who do have only 31 percent of the recommended amount. Forty percent will suffer a major standard of living reduction.[96]

Part Seven—Termination: Protection from Wrongful Discharge

Along with her boss and several coworkers, Catherine Wagenseller, an Arizona nurse, joined a Colorado River rafting trip where she declined to participate in a "Moon River" skit in which the group allegedly "mooned" the audience. Likewise, Wagenseller did not join her boss in the heavy drinking and similar behaviors that allegedly marked the trip. Despite favorable job evaluations preceding the trip, Wagenseller's relationship with her boss deteriorated afterward, and eventually she was terminated. Wagenseller, an at-will employee, sued, claiming she was wrongfully discharged.

> Wagenseller declined to participate in a "Moon River" skit.

An *at-will employee,* by definition, is not under contract for a definite period and as such can be fired at any time. The employee is likewise free to quit at any time. Furthermore, both the employer and the employee freely enter the bargain understanding its terms, so a court should, in general, enforce those terms. Critics, however, argue that the doctrine ignores the historic inequality of bargaining power between employers and employees. Over time, the at-will rule has been softened in most states by legislative and judicially imposed limitations. Statutory exceptions to the at-will rule include labor laws protecting union workers (see Chapter 14) and the equal employment opportunity laws that forbid the dismissal of an employee for discriminatory reasons (see Chapter 13).

Wagenseller argued that the Arizona court should adopt the *public policy exception* to the at-will doctrine. She claimed that she was fired because she refused to engage in behaviors that might have violated the Arizona indecent exposure statute. The state Supreme Court agreed with Wagenseller by finding in that statute a public policy favoring privacy and decency. It returned the case to the trial court to determine whether Wagenseller's termination violated that public policy.[97]

Judicial Limitations on At-Will Principles

LO 12-12
Analyze whether a dismissed at-will employee may bring a claim of wrongful discharge.

Court decisions have provided grounds for dismissed at-will employees to claim that they have been *wrongfully discharged.* Those judicial decisions were often provoked by transparently unjust dismissals, for example, whistleblowers who exposed their employers' misdeeds and employees who declined to commit perjury on behalf of their employers. Limitations fall into three categories: (1) express or implied contracts, (2) an implied covenant of good faith and fair dealing, and (3) the tort of violating an established public policy, as discussed above. Additional tort claims may also substitute for, or supplement, wrongful discharge claims.

Express or implied employment contracts

A number of states have adopted a contractual protection for at-will employees arising, typically, either from the employee handbook or from the employer's conduct and oral representations. For example, an employee handbook might contain a policy expecting employees to arrive on time to start their shift, and describing the progressive discipline tardy employees will face–such as an oral warning the first time they are late, a written warning for a second late arrival, and other discipline up to dismissal for continued incidents. This policy creates a contract that employees will not be terminated the first, or even the second, time they arrive late to work. Similarly, oral assurances of continued employment or an employer's practice of providing mentoring to rehabilitate employees' poor performance rather than firing them may create contracts that protect at-will employees from termination.

Implied covenant of good faith and fair dealing

A few state courts have held that neither party to a contract may act in bad faith to deprive the other of the benefits of the contract. For example, Bruce Rubenstein gave up his job with Arbor Mortgage to take an at-will position with Huntington Mortgage with the understanding that he would be the manager of a new branch office to be opened in central New Jersey. After a few weeks, however, Huntington decided on a downsizing strategy under which the new branch would not be opened. Rubenstein was offered a job as a Huntington loan originator, but he declined. He sued Huntington asserting, among other things, that Huntington had breached the covenant of good faith and fair dealing. Reubenstein believed that Huntington knew of the possibility of downsizing before hiring him. The court agreed that Rubenstein could have a viable claim for breach of the implied covenant of good faith and fair dealing if the facts, at trial, proved to be as Rubenstein alleged.[98]

Public policy

As seen in the example involving Wagenseller discussed above, most states have now adopted some form of "public policy" exception to at-will employment, under which a dismissal is wrongful if it results from employee conduct that is consistent with a public good or the public interest as expressed in legislation, constitutional protections, and the like. The exception often protects, for example, employees fired for pursuing a lawful claim against their employer (for example, workers' compensation or wage claims) or fulfilling a civic responsibility such as jury duty. These exceptions are established case by case and may differ from state to state.

The public policy exception to the at-will employment rule is not without its limitations, however. In 2017, Juli Briskman, a marketing analyst in Virginia, was photographed making an obscene gesture at President Trump's motorcade as it drove past her as she biked. The photographs were published and shared on social media. Briskman posted the photograph to her Facebook page and informed her employer, a government contractor. She was told she was being fired for fear of governmental retaliation, and for her violation of company policy banning obscene content on social media. In dismissing her subsequent wrongful termination suit, the court agreed with the employer that Virginia does not recognize a free-speech public policy exception to at-will employment.[99]

Only Funny until Someone Quits: The Firing Contest

The owner of a chain of QC Mart convenience stores in Bettendorf, Iowa, offered a $10 cash prize to workers who could predict which of them would be the next to be fired. A memo distributed to all employees asked them to write down and seal in an envelope the name of the coworker they thought would be fired next. The owner explained that secret shoppers would visit the store to see which cashiers were committing such offenses as wearing a hat, talking on a cell phone, and not wearing a QC Mart shirt. Once a firing occurred, the contest would begin again. After receiving the memo, QC Mart cashier Misty Shelsky, along with her store manager and a few other employees, quit. When Shelsky applied for unemployment benefits, the owner challenged the claim, asserting that she had left the job voluntarily. As defined by the Department of Labor, a constructive discharge (treated as a termination) occurs when a worker's resignation may be found not to be voluntary because the employer has created a hostile or intolerable work environment, or has applied other forms of pressure or coercion, that forced the employee to quit or resign.

Question

Should Shelsky be viewed as a terminated employee? Explain your decision.

Sources: Clark Kauffman, "Firing Contest by Boss Leads Employees to Quit," *Des Moines Register,* October 2, 2011, p. 1B; and U.S. Department of Labor, "WARN Advisor Glossary: Constructive Discharge," accessed September 2020 [**https://webapps.dol.gov/elaws**].

Additional Torts

Dismissed employees are increasingly turning to a variety of tort actions, often labeled "tag-along torts," seeking compensatory and punitive damages. These claims include defamation, intentional infliction of emotional distress, interference with contract, and invasion of privacy. The following case addresses whether at-will employees may bring an action for fraud based on their employer's alleged inducement to join a business unit that was being sold off.

LEGAL BRIEFCASE

Sawyer v. E. I. Du Pont de Nemours & Co. 430 S.W.3d 396 (Tex. 2014)

Justice Nathan L. Hecht

[The question] certified to us by the United States Court of Appeals for the Fifth Circuit ask[s] whether, under Texas law, at-will employees . . . can sue their corporate employer for fraudulently inducing them to move to a wholly owned subsidiary. We conclude that while an employee can sue an employer for fraud in some situations, in the context in which the certified [question] arise[s], the answer . . . is no.

I

The factual background . . . may be summarized as follows.

In February 2002, E. I. du Pont de Nemours and Company announced plans to spin off part of its operations, including its Terathane Products Unit in La Porte, into a wholly owned subsidiary, DuPont Textiles and Interiors ("DTI"). Most of the Unit employees were covered by a collective bargaining agreement ("CBA"), which gave them the right to transfer to other DuPont jobs rather than move to the new DTI subsidiary. DTI's employees were to be covered by an identical CBA and would continue to receive the same pay and benefits they had at DuPont. But the Unit employees, who had worked for DuPont many years, were afraid DuPont would sell DTI, and that such a sale would adversely affect their compensation and retirement packages. DuPont wanted the Unit employees to go to DTI to avoid significant training expenses—both for transferring employees in their new DuPont jobs and for their DTI replacements—and layoffs of people displaced by more senior transferring employees.

DuPont and the union agreed that the Unit employees would be given a deadline to decide whether to move to DTI, and the fate of those who decided to stay would be subject to further bargaining. DuPont allegedly assured the Unit employees, to persuade them to move to DTI, that DuPont would keep DTI, even though, unbeknownst to the employees, DuPont had already discussed selling DTI with a potential buyer, Koch Industries. Effective February 1, 2003, almost all of the Unit employees moved to DTI. A few weeks later, on April 14, DuPont announced it was negotiating a sale of DTI to Koch. The sale was finalized on May 1, 2004. Koch subsequently reduced the former DuPont employees' compensation and retirement benefits.

In November 2006, 63 of the former DuPont employees ("the Employees") sued DuPont for fraudulently inducing them to terminate their employment and accept employment with DTI by misrepresenting that DTI would not be sold. The Employees claim over $23 million in damages. DuPont contends that the Employees were all at will and therefore cannot sue for fraud. The 59 Employees covered by DuPont's CBA argue that they were not at will because the CBA prohibited discharge except for "just cause." DuPont responds, in part, that because the CBA could be terminated on 60 days' notice, the CBA's requirement of "just cause" for discharge did not modify the at-will status of covered employees.

The Fifth Circuit asks:

1. Under Texas law, may at-will employees bring fraud claims against their employers for loss of their employment?

II

"For well over a century, the general rule in this State, as in most American jurisdictions, has been that absent a specific agreement to the contrary, employment may be terminated by the employer or the employee at will, for good cause, bad cause, or no cause at all." The Legislature has created a few narrow exceptions, prohibiting, for example, discharge based on certain forms of discrimination or in retaliation for engaging in certain protected conduct. But Texas courts have created only one: prohibiting an employee from being discharged for refusing to perform an illegal act. Otherwise, "[t]he courts of Texas have steadfastly refused to vary from [the general rule]."

Thus, we have repeatedly refused to recognize common-law whistleblower liability. We have refused to impose on employers a duty to exercise ordinary care in investigating employee misconduct because such a duty "would significantly damage the at-will employment relationship that Texas has so carefully guarded." And we have refused to impose a duty of good faith and fair dealing on employers, noting that it would "completely alter the nature of the at-will employment relationship."

We have not determined whether an at-will employee can sue his employer for fraud, but the courts of appeals have dealt with the issue and have almost all held that a fraud claim cannot be based on illusory promises of continued at-will employment. . . .

This does not mean that at-will employees can never sue for fraud. Recovery of expenses incurred in reliance on a fraudulent promise of prospective employment has been allowed because neither the injury nor the recovery depends on continued employment. The distinction is similar to one we have drawn in determining whether an at-will employee's contract with his employer is valid. "At-will employment does not preclude employers and employees from forming subsequent contracts, 'so long as neither party relies on continued employment as consideration for the contract.'" An employer and employee may agree, for example, to arbitrate their disputes, or for reasonable restrictions on post-discharge competition, as long as other consideration is given. But if the employer or employee can avoid performance of a promise by exercising a right to terminate the at-will relationship, which each is perfectly free to do with or without reason at any time, the promise is illusory and cannot support an enforceable agreement.

Such an illusory promise can no more support an action for fraud than one for breach of contract. To recover for fraud, one must prove justifiable reliance on a material misrepresentation. A representation dependent on continued at-will employment cannot be material because employment can terminate at any time. Nor can one justifiably rely on the continuation of employment that can be terminated at will. "I will if I want to" is not fraud. And no one can claim recovery of damages for the loss of an employment relationship he had no right to continue.

To allow a promise that is contingent on continued at-will employment to be enforced in a suit for fraud would mock the refusal of enforcement in a suit for breach of contract, making the non-existence of a contract action largely irrelevant, and would significantly impair the at-will rule. An employee who could not show consideration for an enforceable contract could simply sue for fraud and recover not only the same actual damages but punitive damages as well.

. . . Although common-law fraud is certainly not new, allowing it to be asserted to alter or conflict with at-will employment would be. For all these reasons, we answer the Fifth Circuit's question: an at-will employee cannot bring an action for fraud that is dependent on continued employment.

Questions

1. Why did the plaintiffs lose their fraud claim? Explain.
2. Did the court bar all fraud claims that might be brought by at-will employees against their former employers after their employment is terminated? Explain.
3. In 2004, Touchstone Television Productions hired Nicollette Sheridan to play Edie Britt in the television series *Desperate Housewives.* Touchstone's agreement with Sheridan gave it the exclusive option to renew her services on an annual basis for up to an additional six seasons; Touchstone exercised this option for seasons 2 through 5. In February 2009, Touchstone informed the actress that it would not exercise its option for season 6 and that Edie Britt would be killed in a car accident

during season 5. Sheridan alleged that Touchstone's decision was motivated by her complaint regarding a September 2008 incident in which Marc Cherry, the show's creator, allegedly hit her, amounting to a wrongful termination in breach of public policy. Decide. Explain. *Touchstone Television Productions v. Sheridan,* 208 Cal. App. 4th 676 (2012).

4. IBP operated a large hog-processing plant in Storm Lake, Iowa. IBP prohibited possession of "look-alike drugs" on company property. An employee, Michael Huegerich, was randomly and lawfully inspected as he was entering the plant. The inspection revealed an asthma medication, Maxalert, which was identical in appearance to an illegal street drug, "speed." Maxalert contained the stimulant ephedrine. The pills actually belonged to his girlfriend and were in his possession by accident. Huegerich was terminated for possessing a look-alike drug in violation of company policy. Huegerich admitted that he was generally aware of IBP drug policies, but because he was a transfer from another IBP division, he had not gone through the company orientation program where new employees were advised of the policy against look-alike drugs. About six months after his dismissal, two IBP employees told Huegerich that they had heard he was fired for possessing speed. Huegerich then sued IBP for, among other claims, wrongful discharge and defamation. At trial, Huegerich provided no evidence as to how, when, and from whom the IBP employees had heard that he was terminated for possession of speed. The district court found for Huegerich in the amount of $24,000 on the wrongful discharge claim and $20,000 on the defamation claim. The court said that IBP was guilty of negligent discharge in failing to inform Huegerich about its drug policy. IBP appealed to the Iowa Supreme Court. Iowa law recognizes the doctrine of at-will employment with "narrow" exceptions for public policy violations and where a contract is created by an employer's handbook. Decide. Explain. See *Huegerich v. IBP,* 547 N.W.2d 216 (Iowa 1996).

5. Freeman, a television anchorperson, gave birth to her second child. On the day she returned from the hospital, she was notified that she had been dismissed. Six weeks later, she became unable to lactate. She sued the station for wrongful discharge, tortious interference with contract, and negligent infliction of emotional distress. Decide. Explain. See *Freeman v. Medevac Midamerica of Kansas, Inc.,* 719 F. Supp. 995 (D. Kan. 1989).

PRACTICING ETHICS Hearing the Whistle Blow?

Kevin Lamson was a sales manager for an Oregon car dealership, Crater Lake Motors. Crater Lake hired Real Performance Marketing Company (RPM) to conduct a five-day sales promotion at the dealership. During the first few days of the sales event, Lamson observed or was informed of a number of activities that he considered to be unethical and possibly unlawful, such as misrepresenting the event as a bank sale and including various insurance and service agreements in the sales contract without the knowledge of the customer. Lamson complained to the Crater Lake Motors General Manager, Shevlin, who told him to "just go home." The next week, Lamson again expressed his concerns at a Crater Lake Motors meeting.

About a month later, Shevlin criticized Lamson's attitude and recent performance, stating that Lamson "wasn't getting the job done." Shevlin also told Lamson of another planned RPM sales event and asked if Lamson intended to quit. Lamson replied that he did not intend to quit but that it seemed like Shevlin did not want him to work at Crater Lake Motors anymore. Shevlin replied that he did not want the Lamson he had seen recently.

Lamson later complained to the Crater Lake Motors owner, Coleman, about RPM. Coleman told Lamson that working at the second RPM event was mandatory and that failure to attend could result in dismissal. Lamson told Coleman that he could not participate because doing so would condone unethical behavior. Coleman said the agreement with RPM had been amended to explicitly forbid misrepresentations. Lamson did not attend the second RPM event and was fired. Lamson then sued Crater Lake Motors for wrongful discharge.

Questions

1. Was Crater Lake Motors wrong to hire RPM? Why?
2. Was Lamson wrong to refuse to work at the second RPM event? Why?
3. Did Lamson have a duty to complain about the conduct he had observed during the first RPM event? Explain.
4. Was Crater Lake wrong to terminate Lamson? Explain.
5. Who won the wrongful termination lawsuit?

Source: *Lamson v. Crater Lake Motors,* 346 Or. 628 (2009).

Part Eight—Immigration

Immigration is a vital fuel for America's economic and cultural growth, but immigration is also a source of deep political and public policy divisions. A 2022 Gallup Poll found that when Americans are asked whether U.S. current immigration levels should increase, stay the same, or decrease, 31 percent respond that they would like to see the immigration levels increase, 27 percent would like immigration levels to stay the same, while the largest number of respondents, 38 percent, would like the immigration levels to decrease.[100] U.S. Citizen and Immigration Services (USCIS) observed in its 2021 Annual Statistical Report that the number of applications for naturalization generally spikes in an election year and decreases the following year; for example, there was a spike in applications in 2020, but in 2021, the USCIS received the lowest number of such applications than in the preceding five years.[101]

As reported by the U.S. Citizenship and Immigration Services (USCIS): "During the last decade, [the] U.S. . . . welcomed more than 7.2 million naturalized citizens into the fabric of our nation. In fiscal year 2021, 809,000 people took the oath of allegiance for naturalization.[102] The most common countries of origin of these new citizens were China, Cuba, India, Mexico, and the Philippines.[103] Once naturalized, of course, these new American citizens enjoy all of the rights and privileges of U.S.-born citizens. [To find out how long it takes to become a naturalized citizen, see **www.fileright.com/blog/how-long-does-the-u-s-citizenship-process-take** and **www.boundless.com/immigration-resources/how-long-does-it-take-to-get-citizenship-after-applying**].

At this point, it may be useful to clarify terminology. It is probably frequently the case that, in common parlance in the United States, the word "immigrant" is used to refer to anyone not born in America and is likely intended to include children who were born in the United States, but whose parents were not. This can create misunderstandings because, as a legal matter, once one is naturalized, one is no longer an *immigrant,* but a *citizen.* Where place of origin is still relevant, the appropriate term is *naturalized citizen.* Birth in the United States also makes one a U.S. citizen. It also is worthwhile to point out that one cannot know whether a particular individual is a U.S.-born citizen, a naturalized citizen, or an immigrant other than by looking at the appropriate official document. That said, in the materials that follow, the term *immigrant* is intended to refer to a non-U.S. born individual.

According to a recent Pew Research Center report, while some jobs, such as sewing machine operators, are more likely to be filled by immigrants than U.S.-born workers, no specific industry has more immigrants than native-born U.S. employees.[104] Immigrants work in a broad range of jobs, many of which require highly skilled individuals, who often enter the country under the H-1B visa program discussed below. Nearly one-third of U.S. immigrants age 25 or older have a bachelor's degree.[105]

With the increased scrutiny on, and longer processing times for, admission under the current administration, corporate employers are concerned about losing foreign talent to other countries such as Canada that have a more welcoming immigration policy.[106] Seasonal businesses, such as hotels and landscaping, have also been negatively impacted by the reduced number of foreign workers, necessitating either restricting offered services or turning away customers.[107] Nevertheless, some raise concerns about the negative impact that large immigrant populations, entering both legally and illegally, may have on low-income native-born Americans.[108]

In 2021, immigrants totaled approximately 17 percent of the U.S. workforce, with unauthorized immigrants representing less than 5 percent of the U.S. workforce.[109] On a long-term basis, due to our aging population and low birthrate, without immigrants adding to the U.S. workforce, the working-age population could fall by almost 8 million by 2035.[110] [For more on immigration to the United States, see **www.uscis.gov**].

American Immigration Law in the Workplace

LO 12-13 Recognize the purposes and requirements of the H-1B visa and the employment eligibility verification Form I-9.

The Immigration and Nationality Act (INA), as amended by the Immigration Act of 1990 (IMMACT), created the H-1B visa program. In seeking an H-1B visa, an employer must affirm to the U.S. Department of Labor that the hiring will not harm the wages and working conditions of employees in similar jobs.[111]

The H-2B provisions of the Immigration and Nationality Act (INA) provide for the admission of nonimmigrants to the United States to perform temporary and seasonal nonagricultural labor. The employer must not offer terms, wages, and working conditions to U.S. workers that are less favorable than what the employer offers or provides to H-2B workers. Also, the employer must not impose restrictions or obligations on U.S. workers that are not imposed on H-2B workers.[112]

Federal immigration law now requires all employers to verify that every new hire is a U.S. citizen, a permanent resident, or a foreign national with permission to work in this country. A Form I-9 must be completed for each new employee. The prospective employee must present documents establishing both their identity and their eligibility to work in the United States. The employer must examine the documents and complete the I-9 if the documents appear legitimate.

Employers cannot knowingly hire illegal immigrants, but neither can they discriminate against legal immigrants because of national origin and similar factors. [For links to the I-9 form and other immigration information, see **www.uscis.gov/portal/site/uscis**].

Enforcement

Enforcement of our immigration laws focuses primarily on two issues: the hiring of illegal immigrants and illegal discrimination against applicants based on citizenship status or national origin. Critics charge that these policies create a conflict for employers: on one hand, employers must be sure to verify applicants' ability to work in the United States, but, on the other hand, they must take care not to place extra burdens on applicants because they are of a particular national origin or are U.S. legal residents with the right to work, as opposed to citizens.[113] For example, under a settlement reached with the U.S. Department of Justice, a California company, American Education and Travel Services Inc., agreed to pay $10,000 in back pay and compensatory damages to a lawful permanent resident who was denied a residential counselor position because he was not a U.S. citizen or native English speaker.[114]

E-Verify is a free online system run by the federal government that determines an employee's eligibility to work in the United States, comparing information reported on an employee's Form I-9 with federal records. Since 2009, the federal government mandates certain federal contractors to use the program. However, critics note that E-Verify does not address whether the identity provided is authentic, which could encourage identity theft to help illegal workers clear this employment hurdle.[115] [For overviews of many of the employment law topics in this chapter, see **http://topics.law.cornell.edu/wex/category/employment_law**].

Last Call at London Pubs?

Brexit, Closed Borders, and U.K.'s Labor Shortage

Along with the impact of the COVID pandemic and high energy prices, London's restaurant owners face a labor shortage resulting largely from the UK's closed borders under Brexit. Waiters, chefs, and bartenders from Italy, Greece, and Spain used to offer these businesses a talent pool moving freely to the UK. Brexit was meant to generate higher wages and more training for UK resident workers. However, restaurant owners are now struggling to find waiters and kitchen workers. According to a 2022 survey by UKHospitality and the British Beer and Pub Association, about 4 in 10 British pubs and restaurants have curtailed their hours, and about 3 in 10 restaurants, pubs, and hotels could become insolvent.

Source: Mark Landler, "U.K. Restaurants in Crunch as Post-Brexit Labor Shortage Worsens," *The New York Times* (December 22, 2022, p. A4).

Research Exercise

Visit the Privacy Rights Clearinghouse at **www.privacyrights.org/consumer-guides/workplace-privacy-and-employee-monitoring.**

Think of an employer you have worked for or an employer in the career you plan to enter. After consulting the guidelines on mobile devices, GPS tracking, and social media monitoring, create employee policies addressing each of these issues for that employer.

Chapter Questions

1. In an early December 2021 Zoom webinar call, Better.com's CEO, Mr. Vishal Garg told 900 of the company's 10,000 employees: "I come to you with not great news. . . If you're on this call you are part of the unlucky group that is being laid off. Your employment here is terminated effective immediately." There had been no prior warning of the layoffs. What are the legal and ethical issues arising from Mr. Garg's Zoom webinar call? Explain. (See Emma Goldberg, "Better. com's CEO is 'Taking Time Off' After Firing 900 Employees over Zoom," *The New York Times* (December 10, 2021) [**https://www.nytimes.com**].)
2. Abplanalp, a five-year employee of Com-Co Insurance, signed an employment agreement which included a restrictive covenant providing that, should he leave Com-Co, he would not use Com-Co customer lists or solicit business from Com-Co clients for three years. Abplanalp moved to Service Insurance, where he sold insurance to some friends and relatives. He did not sell to any other persons whom he came to know while working for Com-Co. Abplanalp was sued by Com-Co for violating the restrictive covenant. Decide. Explain. See *Com-Co Insurance Agency v. Service Insurance Agency,* 748 N.E.2d 298 (Ill. App. Ct. 2001).

3. Two female music students at Boston University (BU) individually brought concerns about their male professor, a renowned musician, to the attention of administrators in the BU College of Fine Arts. One student withdrew from BU apparently as a result of the professor's conduct, but later met with a BU College of Fine Arts administrator, with whom she shared text messages she had received from the professor while a student at BU. The administrator replied that she should have asked the professor to stop sending those messages. The second student was referred by another professor to a different college administrator, who informed the student that the professor's behavior constituted sexual harassment but blamed it on the professor's "personality" and did not remove him as her instructor. The students filed a lawsuit that included claims against BU for negligent hiring, supervision, training, and retention. What questions might you have before deciding on these claims? Explain. See *Shyr v. Boston University,* 2017 U.S. Dist. LEXIS 37161 (D. Mass. March 13, 2017).
4. A group of Fargo, North Dakota, nurses were paid a subminimum wage for their "on-call" time. When on call, the nurses were required to be able to report to their hospital within 20 minutes, they were required to provide a phone number where they could be reached, and they were not to consume alcohol or drugs. After being called, nurses returned to regular pay. In three years, 36 of the 135 nurses who sued had been called in more than once. The nurses sued the hospital for violating the Fair Labor Standards Act's minimum wage provision. Decide. Explain. See *Reimer v. Champion Healthcare Corp.,* 258 F.3d 720 (8th Cir. 2001).
5. Amid a wave of downsizing of U.S. white-collar workers in early 2023, some employers chose to manage their workforces by increasing scrutiny in performance reviews, adding new limits to remote work, or requesting workers to relocate to other states as a requirement for continued employment. What legal issues might face employers taking such actions to achieve a reduction in workforce? Explain. See Chip Cutter, "Companies Trim Workforces Without Having to Use Layoffs," *The Wall Street Journal* (February 27, 2023 p. B1–B2).
6. Guz, a longtime Bechtel employee, was dismissed during what Bechtel said was a business slump. Bechtel's personnel policy included a provision saying employees "may be terminated at the option of Bechtel." Guz sued for wrongful dismissal claiming, among other things, that Bechtel breached an implied contract to be terminated only for good cause and that Bechtel breached the implied covenant of good faith and fair dealing. A lower court concluded that Guz's promotions, raises, favorable performance reviews, together with Bechtel's progressive discipline policy and Bechtel officials' statements of company practices, supported Guz's position. Bechtel appealed. Decide. Explain. See *Guz v. Bechtel National Inc.,* 8 P.3d 1089 (Cal. 2000).
7. Hershey Company Retail Sales Representatives (RSRs) were classified as exempt under the Fair Labor Standards Act (FLSA), and Hershey never paid hourly compensation to RSRs for any overtime they worked. While the RSRs received bonuses based on performance, they were not eligible to receive sales commissions. RSRs are part of teams that help sell Hershey products to retail outlets of various sizes from Walmart to independently owned shops. In a wage and hour claim seeking overtime compensation, RSRs contended that they are primarily responsible for merchandising tasks such

as delivering and setting up product displays, tagging products, and stocking shelves. Hershey defended that RSRs' job duties include selling products directly to retailers, meeting with their key decision makers to increase sales, and only occasionally assisting with merchandising at their stores. Are the RSRs nonexempt employees with rights to overtime compensation under FLSA? Decide. Explain. See *Campanelli v. Hershey Co.,* 765 F. Supp. 2d 1185 (N.D. Cal. 2011).

8. Rodrigues was fired in 2006 by The Scotts Company, the lawn care giant, because a required drug test revealed nicotine in his urine. Company policy forbade employee smoking both on and off the job. Scotts announced in 2005 that it would no longer hire smokers, and it gave its employees one year to comply with the new policy, which was designed to improve employee wellness and reduce company health care costs. Rodrigues was a pack-a-day smoker when he was hired. He was aware of the no-smoking policy, and he had been warned to quit when a supervisor saw a pack of cigarettes on the dashboard of his car. Was Rodrigues wrongfully terminated? What questions would you have before deciding? Explain. See Sacha Pfieffer, "Off-the-Job Smoker Sues over Firing," *The Boston Globe,* November 30, 2006 [**www.bostonglobe.com**].
9. Safeway in Denver hosted a picnic for its employees. Safeway bought a 40-pound gas tank to use with a grill that was designed for a 20-pound tank. A label on the grill warned against that use. The grill failed to operate properly and a manager asked Lewis to try to fix it. When Lewis did so, a "ball of fire" erupted and Lewis was badly burned. The Occupational Safety and Health Administration then issued a citation against Safeway. Safeway appealed to the courts.

    a. Defend Safeway.

    b. Decide the case. Explain. See *Safeway, Inc. v. Occupational Safety & Health Rev. Comm.,* 382 F.3d 1189 (10th Cir. 2004).
10. Lloyd was a Drake University security guard on duty at the university's annual street-painting event. A student informed Lloyd of an apparent altercation between a football player, Joseph, and a woman, Kane, the nature of which was later disputed. Seeing Joseph holding Kane in the air with her feet kicking, Lloyd ordered Joseph to release Kane twice before Joseph put Kane down and lunged angrily toward Lloyd, who then used pepper spray on Joseph and hit him on the leg with a baton. Lloyd's actions were the subject of student complaints and local media coverage, and demands from activist groups for an investigation. During the investigation, Lloyd was given a desk job and assured that he would not lose his job. However, Drake fired Lloyd. Lloyd sued for wrongful termination. Decide. Explain. See *Lloyd v. Drake University,* 686 N.W.2d 225 (Iowa 2004).
11. In 2009, Mitchell was employed at-will as an anesthesia technician at the University of Kentucky (UK) Chandler Medical Center, while also attending the university as a graduate student. He had a valid license to carry a concealed deadly weapon under Kentucky law. On April 22, 2009, several of Mitchell's coworkers were under the impression that he had a firearm in his employee locker, and they reported this to hospital administration. Hospital administrators contacted the UK police department. When questioned, Mitchell denied having a firearm in his locker. Police and hospital administrators searched Mitchell's locker with his permission but found no weapons.

Mitchell informed the police officers that he had a concealed carry license and admitted that he kept a firearm in his vehicle, which was parked on campus. Campus police escorted Mitchell to his car, where he showed them the semiautomatic pistol he had stored in his vehicle. On April 29, 2009, the university terminated Mitchell's employment for violation of its policy prohibiting possession of a deadly weapon on university property or while conducting university business. Mitchell filed suit, alleging termination in violation of public policy. Decide. Explain. See *Mitchell v. University of Kentucky,* 366 S.W.3d 895 (Ky. 2012).

12. Honeywell employed Randy Landin from 1977 to 1979 and from 1984 to 1988. From 1979 to 1984, Landin was imprisoned for the strangulation death of Nancy Miller, his Honeywell coworker. On his release from prison, Landin reapplied at Honeywell. Honeywell rehired Landin as a custodian in 1984. Because of workplace confrontations Landin was twice transferred to different Honeywell locations. Kathleen Nesser was assigned to Landin's maintenance crew in April 1988. Landin and Nesser became friends and spent time together away from work. When Landin expressed a romantic interest, Nesser stopped spending time with Landin. Landin began to harass and threaten Nesser both at work and at home. In late June 1988, Nesser requested a transfer out of that Honeywell facility.

    On July 1, 1988, Nesser found a death threat scratched on her locker door. Landin did not come to work on or after July 1, and he resigned on July 11, 1988. On July 19, approximately six hours after her Honeywell shift ended, Landin shot and killed Nesser in her driveway. Landin was convicted of first-degree murder and sentenced to life imprisonment. What claims could Nesser's estate bring against Honeywell? Analyze these claims and explain how you would decide. See *Yunker v. Honeywell, Inc.,* 496 N.W.2d 419 (Minn.Ct.App. 1993).

13. Whigham was employed as the Director of Creative Solutions at a marketing, advertising, and public relations company that sought to cultivate an enjoyable work atmosphere. Whigham proposed the idea of a company kickball game to his superior, who instructed him to proceed. Whigham then made the arrangements for a facility rental, the T-shirts, drinks, and snacks with the company funds he was authorized to use. He promoted the event, which took place on a Friday at 3:00 pm, using the company intranet. Roughly half of the company's employees were in attendance. Whigham was seriously injured in the game, and he filed a claim for workers' compensation. The Workers' Compensation Commissioner denied the claim, and Whigham appealed. Decide. Explain. See *Whigham v. Jackson Dawson Communications,* 410 S.C. 131 (2014).

14. Dancers at Club Orleans in Topeka, Kansas, who earned only tips without a regular wage, were subject to house rules that prohibited illicit or illegal conduct and regulated interaction among the dancers and between the dancers and customers. Violations of the rules could result in the dancer being fined or terminated. The rules also set minimum tips for various types of dances, which were enforced. The dancers were allowed to schedule their own shifts. One of the dancers filed an unemployment benefits claim against Milano's, the company that owned Club Orleans. Is the dancer an employee or an independent contractor? Decide. Explain. See *Milano's v. Kansas Department of Labor,* 296 Kan. 497 (2013).

15. Diana Vail, who received medical treatment for migraine headaches, worked at Raybestos, a car parts manufacturer. Raybestos had been giving Vail intermittent leave under FMLA for her migraine headaches since April 2004. From May to September 2005, Vail's requests for FMLA leave due to migraine headaches became more frequent, often falling on weekdays when her husband's mowing company was busiest. Growing suspicious that Vail's requests were not genuine, Raybestos monitored Vail's activities by hiring an off-duty police officer to conduct video surveillance. The officer reported that Vail mowed the lawns of a cemetery, her husband's client, on a day when Vail called prior to her shift to request leave. Vail was subsequently terminated based on her performance of physical labor while on FMLA.
    a. Did Vail's termination violate FMLA? Explain.
    b. Did the employer's surveillance of Vail interfere with her rights under FMLA? Explain. See *Vail v. Raybestos,* 533 F.3d 904 (7th Cir. 2008).
    c. An employee who had been on FMLA leave for incapacitating back pain posted photos to her Facebook page (as did her friend) showing her drinking and dancing over a period of at least eight hours at a local festival. Several of the employees' coworkers who were her Facebook friends told management what they had seen on the employee's page; the employee was fired as a result. The employee sued the employer for retaliation and interference with her FMLA rights. Decide. Explain. See *Jaszczyszyn v. Advantage Health Physician Network,* 504 F. App'x 440 (6th Cir. 2012) (unpublished op.).
16. An employee of Triple B Cleaning in Texas requested personal protective equipment while performing dry cleaning duties. Triple B denied the request. The employee notified the media, and after a reporter contacted the employee's supervisor, the employee was demoted and assigned menial tasks. Following the airing of the employee's complaint by local news, the employee was terminated. After being terminated, the employee filed a whistleblower complaint alleging that Triple B acted in retaliation for contacting the media about unsafe working conditions. OSHA investigated the complaint and determined that Triple B Cleaning's decision to terminate the employee was in violation of the whistleblower provisions of the Occupational Safety and Health Act.

    The company entered into a consent judgment under which it paid the employee $30,000 for lost wages, agreed to an injunction prohibiting future discrimination, and posted a notice advising its employees of their rights under OSHA's whistleblower protection provision.
    a. What public policy–or policies–are at issue in this situation?
    b. Did Triple B act ethically? Did the employee act ethically? Explain.
    c. In OSHA's press release regarding the settlement, OSHA Regional Administrator Dean McDaniel stated: "Employees should be free to exercise their rights under the law without fear of retaliation by their employers . . ." What consequences might be expected to accompany the fear of retaliation employees often feel when exercising their rights?

    See OSHA, "U.S. Department of Labor Settles Whistleblower Case Against Commercial and Industrial Steam Cleaning Company in Houston," regional news release, April 6, 2009 [**www.osha.gov**].

17. Carr alleged that her coworker at Sanderson Farms, Webb, deliberately struck her with a pallet jack multiple times. Carr also alleged that prior to this incident, while she and Webb were away from work, Webb had threatened her with bodily harm. After Carr allegedly told Sanderson Farms about the threats, the employer responded that it would take no action since the threats were not made on its property. Carr sued Sanderson Farms for negligence. Analyze this claim and explain how you would decide. See *Carr v. Sanderson Farms Inc.,* 215 So.3d 437 (Ct. App.1st Cir. 2017).

Notes

1. Johnathan D. Glater, "Layoffs Herald a Heyday for Employee Lawsuits," *The New York Times,* January 30, 2009 [**www.nytimes.com**].
2. *CBS v. FCC,* 535 F.3d 167 (3d Cir. 2008).
3. *FCC v. CBS,* 132 S. Ct. 2677 (2012), *cert. denied.*
4. Ellen Huet, "Cleaning Startup Homejoy Shuts Down, Citing Worker Misclassification Lawsuits," *Forbes,* July 17, 2015 [**www.forbes.com**].
5. James Surowiecki, "Gigs with Benefits," *The New Yorker,* June 29, 2015 [**www.newyorker.com**].
6. Vanessa Romo, "Uber Drivers Are Not Employees, National Relations Board Rules. Drivers Saw It Coming," *National Public Radio,* May 15, 2019 [**www.npr.org**].
7. James B. Stewart, "In the Undoing of a CEO, a Puzzle," *The New York Times,* May 18, 2012 [**www.nytimes.com**].
8. Zach Schonbrun and Matt Krupnick, "Manhattan Coach Is Denied South Florida Job after Resumé Check," *The New York Times,* March 26, 2014 [**www.nytimes.com**].
9. Martha C. White, "You Won't Believe How Many People Lie on Their Resumes," *Time,* August 13, 2015 [**https://time.com**].
10. Society for Human Resource Management, "SHRM Finds Fewer Employers Using Background Checks in Hiring," press release, July 19, 2012 [**www.shrm.org**]; and Society for Human Resource Management and Charles Koch Institute, "Workers with Criminal Records: A Survey by SHRM and CKI," SHRM Issue Brief, May 17, 2018 [**www.shrm.org**].
11. Sara Murray, "Credit Checks on Job Seekers by Employers Attract Scrutiny," *The Wall Street Journal,* October 21, 2010 [**www.wsj.com**].
12. Chris Dettro, "New Law Bars Most Credit Checks in Hiring," *The State Journal-Register,* January 1, 2011 [**www.sj-r.com**].
13. Sandeep Babu, "90% of Employers Consider an Applicant's Social Media Activity During Hiring Process, *Small Business News* (May 5, 2020) [**https://smallbiztrends.com**].
14. "1 in 5 Employers Unknowingly Asked an Illegal Question in an Interview, Careerbuilder Finds," *CareerBuilder,* April 9, 2015 [**www.careerbuilder.com**].
15. Ann Howard and Johanna Johnson, White Paper: "If You Were a Tree, What Kind Would You Be?" *Catalyst*, Vol. 39 No. 2, July 2010.
16. Peter Cappelli and Liat Eldor, "Contracts Gone Wild," *The Wall Street Journal*, p. R6 (November 9, 2022).
17. *Bimbo Bakeries v. Botticella,* 613 F.3d 102 (3d Cir. 2010).
18. *Edwards v. Arthur Andersen,* 44 Cal. 4th 937 (Cal. 2008).
19. Karl Evers-Hillstrom, "US Chamber Vows Fight Against FTC Ban on Noncompete Clauses," *The Hill.com* (January 23, 2023) [**https://thehill.com/**]
20. Peter Cappelli and Liat Eldor, "Contracts Gone Wild," *The Wall Street Journal*, p. R6 (November 9, 2022).

21. *Circuit City Stores, Inc. v. Adams,* 532 U.S. 105 (2001).
22. H.R. 4445, Ending Forced Arbitration of Sexual Assault and Sexual Harassment Act of 2021 (March 3, 2022) [**https://www.congress.gov/bill/117th-congress/house-bill/4445/text**]
23. *Equal Employment Opportunity Commission v. Waffle House,* 534 U.S. 279 (2002).
24. Cade Metz, "Uber Will Pay New Jersey $100 Million in Back Taxes," *The New York Times,* p. B4 (September 13, 2022)
25. Dana Leisinger, "Employers May Be Liable for Negligent Referrals on Ex-Employees," *CalChamberAlert,* (March 20, 2015) [**https://calchamberalert.com/**].
26. 54 Cal. 3d 202, 814 P.2d 1341 (Cal. 1991).
27. Jenny B. Davis, "Still Working after All These Years," *ABA Journal,* October 2001, p. 67.
28. U.S. Department of Labor, Consolidated Minimum Wage Table [**https://www.dol.gov/agencies/whd/mw-consolidated**] (viewed January 16, 2023)
29. Holly Sklar, "Research Shows Minimum Wage Increases Do Not Cause Job Loss," Business for a Fair Minimum Wage, accessed March 2020 [**www.businessforafairminimumwage.org**]; Alexia Fernandez Campbell, "A $15 minimum wage could lift 1.3 million out of poverty-and cost 1.3 million jobs," *Vox,* July 8, 2019 [**www.vox.com**]; and Arindrajit Dube, T. William Lester, and Michael Reich, "Minimum Wage Effects across State Borders: Estimates Using Contiguous Counties," *The Review of Economics and Statistics,* September 25, 2010.
30. Amy K. Glasmeier and Massachusetts Institute of Technology, "Living Wage Calculator," Massachusetts Institute of Technology, accessed September 2020 [**https://livingwage.mit.edu**].
31. Alice Adamczyk, "Minimum Wage Workers Cannot Afford Rent in any U.S. State," C*NBC Make It,* (July 14, 2020) [**https://www.cnbc.com/**]
32. Yian Q. Mui, "Wal-Mart to Pay $4.8 Million in Back Wages," *The Washington Post,* May 1, 2012 [**www.washingtonpost.com**].
33. *Christopher v. SmithKline Beecham Corp.*, 132 S. Ct. 2156 (2012).
34. Stephen Miller, "Remote Workers Pose Wage and Hour Challenges," *SHRM* (June 21, 2022) [**https://www.shrm.org/**].
35. Ibid.
36. Jonnelle Marte, "Judge Halts Rule That Would Have Expanded Overtime Pay to Millions of Workers," *The Washington Post,* November 22, 2016 [**www.washingtonpost.com**].
37. Ben Penn and Chris Opfer, "Long-Awaited Trump Overtime Pay Requirements Unveiled," *Bloomberg News,* September 28, 2019 [**https://news.bloomberglaw.com**].
38. *Archuleta v. Wal-Mart Stores,* 543 F.3d 1226 (10th Cir. 2008).
39. *Kellar v. Summit Seating Inc.,* 664 F.3d 169 (7th Cir. 2011).
40. Christopher K. Jones, "The Effect of a Brother's Statement," Testimony before the House Committee on Natural Resources, March 16, 2011 [**http://naturalresources.house.gov**].
41. Janet McConnaughey and Michael Kunzelman, Associated Press, "Manslaughter charges dropped against 2 BP supervisors over 11 rig worker deaths," *US News & World Report,* December 2, 2015 [**www.usnews.com**].
42. Ibid.; and Doreen McCalllister, "Ex Massey Energy CEO Completes 1 Year Federal Criminal Sentence," *National Public Radio,* May 11, 2017 [**www.npr.org**].
43. U.S. Department of Labor, Bureau of Labor Statistics, TED, The Economics Daily, "A Look at Workplace Deaths, Injuries, and Illnesses on Workers' Memorial Day," April 28, 2022 [**www.bls.gov**].

44. Ibid.
45. U.S. Department of Labor, Bureau of Labor Statistics, TED, The Economics Daily, "A Look at Workplace Deaths, Injuries, and Illnesses on Workers' Memorial Day," April 28, 2022 [**www.bls.gov**].
46. Employer Payment for Personal Protective Equipment, Final Rule, 29 C.F.R. Parts 1910, 1915, 1917, et al. (2008).
47. Ray Sanchez, "Illinois Shooting Rampage Highlights Scourge of Workplace Gun Violence," *CNN.com,* February 16, 2019 [**www.cnn.com**].
48. Wallace Stephens, "Violence against Health Workers: A Rising Epidemic," *AJMC,* May 12, 2019 [**www.ajmc.com**].
49. U.S. Department of Labor, OSHA, "Workplace Violence SBREFA" [**https://www.osha.gov/workplace-violence/sbrefa**] (Last visited February 22, 2023).
50. Leah Shepard, "Changes in Gun Laws Affect the Workplace," *Society of Human Resources Management (SHRM)* (August 18, 2022) [**https://www.shrm.org/**].
51. Leah Shepard, "Changes in Gun Laws Affect the Workplace," *Society of Human Resources Management (SHRM)* (August 18, 2022) [**https://www.shrm.org/**] citing New York State Rifle and Pistol Association v. Bruen, 597 U.S. ___ (2022).
52. Roy Maurer, "OSHA's Oversight of Model-Workplace Program Criticized," *Society for Human Resource Management,* December 30, 2013 [**www.shrm.org**].
53. Julia Preston, "Hershey's Packer Is Fined over Its Safety Violations," *The New York Times,* February 21, 2012 [**www.nytimes.com**].
54. Department of Labor, OSHA National News Release, "Department of Labor announces enforcement guidance changes to save lives, target employers who put profit over safety," (January 26, 2023) [**https://www.osha.gov/news/newsreleases/national/01262023-0**].
55. U.S. Department of Labor, OSHA, Severe Violator Enforcement Program (SVEP) [**https://www.osha.gov/enforcement/svep**]/
56. Associated Press, "Stringer's Widow Settles Lawsuit with NFL," *The New York Times,* January 26, 2009 [**www.nytimes.com**]. In addition to the lawsuit against the Vikings described in the text, Kelci Stringer sued the NFL and the football equipment manufacturer, Riddell. She settled her claim against the NFL. Before her lawsuit against Riddell was settled, the federal district court ruled that Riddell had a duty to warn a football player of the risk of heat exhaustion. *Stringer v. NFL,* 749 F. Supp. 2d 680 (S.D. Ohio 2010); and Associated Press, "Lawsuit over Stringer's Death Settled," June 2, 2014 [**www.foxsports.com**].
57. *Stringer v. Minnesota Vikings,* 705 N.W. 2d 746 (Minn. S. Ct. 2005).
58. Ibid.
59. *State ex rel. Gross v. Industrial Commission of Ohio,* 115 Ohio St. 3d 249 (2007).
60. Martin Armstrong, "4 in 10 U.S. Adults Have a Tattoo," *Statista,* June 26, 2017 [**www.statista.com**].
61. HR Simple, "Dress Codes: Who, What, Wear" *HR Simple Blog* (June 12, 2018).
62. Karen Weise, "What It Looks Like Inside an Amazon Warehouse Now," *The New York Times,* June 9, 2020 [**www.nytimes.com**].
63. Marissa Plescia, "Mental Health Is a Top Priority for Employers. What Are Their Strategies?, *Medcity News* (October 26, 2022) [**https://medcitynews.com/2022/10/mental-health-is-a-top-priority-for-employers-what-are-their-strategies/**].
64. Rachel Feintzeig, "The Therapist in the Next Cubicle," *The Wall Street Journal*, pp. B1–B4, February 12, 2020.

65. Jen Wieczner, "Your Company Wants to Make You Healthy," *The Wall Street Journal,* April 8, 2013 **[ww.wsj.com]**.
66. Rachel Emma Silverman, "Suit Claims Wellness Rules Risk Privacy," *The Wall Street Journal,* October 26, 2016 **[www.wsj.com]**.
67. Dawn Lim, Steven Russolillo, and Jing Yang, "BlackRock Puts Office on Notice with Firings," *The Wall Street Journal,* February 4, 2020 **[www.wsj.com]**.
68. Sue Shellenbarger, "For Office Romance, the Secret's Out," *The Wall Street Journal,* February 10, 2010 **[www.wsj.com]**.
69. *City of Ontario v. Quon,* 130 S. Ct. 2619 (2010).
70. *Stengart v. Loving Care Agency, Inc.,* 990 A.2d 650 (2010).
71. National Conference of State Legislatures, "State Social Media Privacy Laws," January 11, 2017 **[www.ncsl.org]**.
72. *Pietrylo v. Hillstone Restaurant Group,* 2009 U.S. Dist. LEXIS 88702 (D.N.J. September 25, 2009) (unpublished op.).
73. Dalia Fahmy, "Aiming for a Drug-Free Workplace," *The New York Times,* May 10, 2007 **[www.nytimes.com]**.
74. U.S. Department of Health and Human Services, Substance Abuse and Mental Health Services Administration, "Worker Substance Abuse and Workplace Policies and Programs," 2007.
75. U.S. Department of Health and Human Services, "Worker Substance Abuse and Workplace Policies and Programs."
76. Norml, "Survey: Nearly One-in Ten Employers Dropping Drug Testing Requirements to Attract Workers," *Norml.org* (November 18, 2021) **[https://norml.org/]**.
77. *National Treasury Employees Union v. Von Raab,* 109 S. Ct 1384 (1989).
78. Center on Budget and Policy Priorities, "ACA Survives Legal Challenge, Protecting Coverage for Tens of Millions", *Center on Budget and Policy Priorities* (July 20, 2021) **[https://www.cbpp.org/]**
79. Amanda Novello, "Paid Leave Could Keep 6 Million Caregivers Connected to the Labor Force by 2030," *National Partnership for Women and Families Issue Brief* (November 2021) **[https://www.nationalpartnership.org/]**
80. U.S. Department of Labor, "FMLA: Frequently Asked Questions and Answers-Military Provisions," accessed September 2020 **[www.dol.gov]**.
81. U.S. Department of Labor, "Final Rule to Revise the Definition of 'Spouse' Under the FMLA," February 25, 2015 **[www.dol.gov]**.
82. Ibid.
83. National Conference of State Legislatures, "State Family and Medical Leave Laws," September 9, 2022 **[www.ncsl.org]**.
84. Ibid.
85. Patt Johnson, "Getting the Boot," *Des Moines Register,* May 4, 2003, p. 1D.
86. Zachary Malinowski, "Unemployment Benefits Denied for Fired Cranston Cop," *The Providence Journal,* July 26, 2010 **[http://newsblog.projo.com]**.
87. Clark Kauffman, "Diary of a Goof-Off: No Work, No Pay," *Des Moines Register,* January 19, 2007, p. 1A.
88. Annie Nova, "16 Percent of Workers Cannot Get Unemployment Insurance. How to Fix That," *CNBC,* February 22, 2018 **[www.cnbc.com]**.

89. California Employment Development Department, COVID-19: Federal Unemployment Benefits **[https://edd.ca.gov/]** (last checked February 25, 2023).
90. Employee Benefit Research Institute, "2019 Retirement Confidence Survey," **[www.ebri.org]**.
91. Board of Governors of the Federal Reserve System, "EFA: State Pensions, Funding Status," accessed June 2020 **[www.federalreserve.gov]**; and CNN Money, "Ultimate guide to retirement," accessed June 2020 **[https://money.cnn.com]**.
92. Julia Kagan, Pension Protection Act of 2006, *Investopedia* (November 27, 2020) **[https://www.investopedia.com/]**.
93. U.S. Department of Labor, "Reporting and Disclosure Guide for Employee Benefit Plans," *Department of Labor* (last checked February 25, 2023) **[www.dol.gov]**.
94. *LaRue v. DeWolff, Boberg & Associates, Inc.,* 128 S. Ct. 1020 (2008).
95. Kathleen Elkins, "The No. 1 reason millennials are struggling to save for retirement—and it's not debt," *CNBC,* September 25, 2019 **[www.cnbc.com]**; Gayle L. Reznik, Dave Shoffner, and David A. Weaver, "Coping with the Demographic Challenge: Fewer Children and Living Longer," *Social Security Bulletin,* Vol. 66, No. 4, 2005/2006 **[www.ssa.gov]**; Veronique de Rugy, "How Many Workers Support One Social Security Retiree?", Mercatus Center, George Mason University, May 22, 2012 **[www.mercatus.org]**; "Policy Basics: Top Ten Facts about Social Security," *Center on Budget and Policy Priorities*, August 13, 2020 **[www.cbpp.org]**; Emily Brandon, "How Much You Will Get From Social Security," *U.S. News & World Report,* January 21, 2020 **[https://money.usnews.com]**; Amin Dabit, "The Average 401k Balance By Age," Daily Capital, March 13, 2020 **[www.personalcapital.com]**; "Five Charts about the Future of Social Security and Medicare," Peter G. Peterson Foundation, April 23, 2019 **[www.pgpf.org]**; Matthew Cuplin, "Worried About Social Security's Future? Here's What You Should Know," *Forbes,* September 2, 2020 **[www.forbes.com]**; Peter Ferrara, "The Future of Social Security," National Affairs, Summer 2015 **[www.nationalaffairs.com]**; Press release, "80% Of Americans Nervous About Retirement Fund," insurancenewsnet.com, July 31, 2019 **[https://insurancenewsnet.com]**; Alana Semuels, "This Is What Life Without Retirement Savings Looks Like," *The Atlantic*, February 22, 2018 **[www.theatlantic.com]**; and Alessandra Malito, "Don't feel ready for retirement? You're not alone," *MarketWatch,* May 9, 2018 **[www.marketwatch.com]**.
96. Megan Leonhardt, "Here's how much millennials at every age need to have saved right now to retire at 67," *CNBC,* February 26, 2020 **[www.cnbc.com]**; Kari Paul, "Young people blame climate change for their small 401(k) balances," *MarketWatch,* August 4, 2019 **[www.marketwatch.com]**; and Mark Hulbert, "Are millennials fooling themselves with their retirement-savings strategy?" *MarketWatch,* March 12, 2020 **[www.marketwatch.com]**.
97. *Wagenseller v. Scottsdale Memorial Hospital,* 710 P.2d 1025 (Ariz. 1985).
98. *Rubenstein v. Huntington Mortgage Company,* N.J. Sup. Ct., App. Div. (1997). For a journalistic account of the case, see Pitney, Hardin, Kipp, and Szuch, "Employers Must Be Cautious about Failing to Disclose Business Plans That Will Affect the Jobs of New Hires," *New Jersey Employment Law Letter,* September 1997.
99. Debra Cassens Weiss, "Wrongful Termination Claim by Woman Forced to Resign After Flipping Off Trump Motorcade," *ABA Journal,* July 2, 2018 **[www.abajournal.com]**.
100. Lydia Saad, "U.S. Immigration Views Remain Mixed and Highly Partisan," *Gallup News* (August 8, 2022) **[https://news.gallup.com/]**.
101. United States Citizenship and Immigration Services, *FY 2021 Annual Statistics Report* (January 2022) **[https://www.uscis.gov/]**.
102. Ibid.

103. Abby Budiman, "Key Findings about U.S. Immigrants," *Pew Research Center* (August 20, 2020) [**https://www.pewresearch.org/**].
104. Drew Desilver, "Immigrants Don't Make up a Majority of Workers in Any U.S. Industry," *Pew Research Center,* March 16, 2017 [**www.pewresearch.org**].
105. Don Lee, "Trump's Immigration Plan Faces Obstacles," *Los Angeles Times,* March 20, 2017, p. A1.
106. Nelson D. Schwartz and Steve Lohr, "Companies Say Trump is Hurting Business by Limiting Legal Immigration," *The New York Times,* September 2, 2018 [**www.nytimes.com**].
107. Ibid.
108. Lawrence Harrison, "The US Should Think Long and Hard about the High Numbers of Latino Immigrants," *The Christian Science Monitor,* May 28, 2009 [**www.csmonitor.com**].
109. Abby Budiman, "Key Findings about U.S. Immigrants".
110. News Release, "Foreign-Born Workers': Labor Force Characteristics–2018," *Bureau of Labor Statistics,* May 16, 2019 [**www.bls.gov**].
111. U.S. Department of Labor, "Fact Sheet #62: What are the Requirements to Participate in the H1B Program? (last revised July 2008) [**https://www.dol.gov**].
112. U.S. Department of Labor, "Fact Sheet 78: General Information for Employers Participating in the H-2B Program" [**https://www.dol.gov**].
113. Miriam Jordan, "Policing Illegal Hires Puts Some Employers in a Bind," *The Wall Street Journal,* July 15, 2010 [**www.wsj.com**].
114. Press Release, "Justice Department Resolves Citizenship Status Discrimination Charge against California Employer," *U.S. Department of Justice,* March 8, 2011 [**www.justice.gov**].
115. Bruce A. Morrison and Paul Donnelly, "A Simple Way to Keep Illegal Immigrants from Getting Jobs," *The Washington Post,* May 1, 2010 [**www.washingtonpost.com**].

Video icon credit: Comstock Images/Alamy Stock Photo

CHAPTER THIRTEEN

Employment Law II: Discrimination

After completing this chapter, students will be able to fulfill the following learning objectives:

13-1. Discuss the purpose and history of legal protections against employment discrimination.

13-2. Compare and contrast the protections offered under the federal statutes prohibiting employment discrimination: Title VII of the Civil Rights Act of 1964, the Equal Pay Act, the Americans with Disabilities Act, and the Age Discrimination in Employment Act.

13-3. Explain the role of the Equal Employment Opportunity Commission in enforcing federal statutes prohibiting employment discrimination.

13-4. Identify the remedies available to victims of unlawful employment discrimination.

13-5. Distinguish the primary forms of employment discrimination analysis: disparate treatment and disparate impact.

13-6. List the actions of employers that violate Title VII's prohibition of workplace discrimination on the basis of sex.

13-7. Identify when unlawful sexual harassment has occurred.

13-8. Identify when employers are liable for unlawful sexual harassment.

13-9. Describe the protections against retaliation offered under the federal statutes prohibiting employment discrimination.

13-10. Discuss the purposes and development of affirmative action.

13-11. Explain the concept of reasonable accommodation as applied to religious- and disability-based discrimination claims.

Introduction

PRACTICING ETHICS ICS A Google Employee's Google Doc

Google fired a male software engineer who wrote and shared internally a lengthy memo criticizing Google's efforts to hire more women and minority engineers, and suggesting that biological differences between males and females made men better suited for tech jobs. The 28-year-old engineer shared the memo in Google Docs with a limited number of Google colleagues, but it became viral within the company, gaining criticism internally and then publicly through leaks and Google employees' social media accounts denouncing their colleague's memo. In an email to employees, Google CEO Sundar Pichai said that the memo promoted "harmful gender stereotypes in our workplace" which were "offensive and not OK." Google critics asserted that in firing the employee for violating policies against harassment and discrimination, the company had unfairly treated the male employee and shown intolerance for differing views.

Questions

1. What are the competing values at Google at work in this controversy? Explain.
2. If the memo had suggested that women are better suited for tech work than men based on biological differences, would that have violated Google's policies on harassment and discrimination? Explain.
3. Do you think the firing was fair? Why or why not?
4. Remote or hybrid work arrangements that have remained a prominent part of the employment landscape after the COVID pandemic may increase reliance on written or recorded communications to express ideas rather than informal workplace conversations. What opportunities for workplace equality does this offer? What challenges might employers face in upholding policies against harassment and discrimination as employees work remotely? Discuss.
5. In 2018, Google reported that over two-thirds of its staff are men, and that its highest attrition rates are among Black and Latinx staff members. Does this affect your view of the memo or the resulting termination of its author? Explain.

Sources: Jack Nicas and Yoree Koh, "Memo Sparks Google Firestorm," *The Wall Street Journal*, August 9, 2017 [**www.wsj.com**]; and Jamie Condliffe, "Google's Diversity Efforts, Charted," *The New York Times*, June 19, 2018 [**www.nytimes.com**].

According to a 2021 CNBC survey, almost 80 percent of workers want to work for an organization that values diversity, equity, and inclusion.[1] To encourage and support organizations' Diversity, Equity, and Inclusion (DE & I) initiatives, the Equal Employment Opportunity Commission, which is discussed later in the chapter, launched a Diversity, Equity, and Inclusion Workshop Series in 2022.[2]

Part One—Employment Discrimination: The Foundation in Law

LO 13-1 Discuss the purpose and history of legal protections against employment discrimination.

History

In the Reconstruction Era following the Civil War, Congress passed the Civil Rights Act of 1866 to provide the newly freed Black slaves the same right to make and enforce contracts as was enjoyed by white citizens. This law still exists today, with updated language emphasizing its protection against racial discrimination. The Civil Rights Act of 1866 has been interpreted to forbid discrimination on the basis of race in employment, which is essentially a contractual relationship.

LO 13-2
Compare and contrast the protections offered under the federal statutes prohibiting employment discrimination: Title VII of the Civil Rights Act of 1964, the Equal Pay Act, the Americans with Disabilities Act, and the Age Discrimination in Employment Act.

However, this legal protection did not prevent discriminatory practices in housing, education, business, or employment. In 1941, A. Philip Randolph, president of the predominantly Black Brotherhood of Sleeping Car Porters, organized Black leaders who threatened a massive march in Washington, D.C., protesting employment discrimination. In response, President Franklin Roosevelt issued Executive Order 8802, which created a Fair Employment Practice Committee. Congress limited the committee's budget, but Roosevelt's action was a striking step for the federal government in addressing racial discrimination.

The next major movement toward racial equality was the landmark *Brown v. Board of Education*[3] decision in 1954, in which the Supreme Court forbade "separate but equal" schools. Following *Brown,* citizens engaged in sit-ins, freedom rides, boycotts, and the like to press claims for racial equality. It was a turbulent, sometimes violent, era, but those activities were critical to subsequent advances for African Americans. With the passage of the 1964 Civil Rights Act, the campaign against discrimination solidified as one of the most energetic and influential social movements in American history.[4] The Civil Rights Act of 1964 changed American life by forbidding discrimination in education, housing, public accommodation, and, perhaps most importantly, employment. [For the National Civil Rights Museum, see **www.civilrightsmuseum.org**].

Civil Rights Act of 1964

Reflecting the increased diversity of the U.S. workforce, in which women had moved beyond traditional roles and immigrants from around the world could be found, Title VII of the Civil Rights Act of 1964 (Title VII) marked a new era in employment practices. Title VII forbids discrimination in employment on the basis of race, color, religion, sex, or national origin. Relying on its authority to regulate commerce, Congress applied Title VII to private-sector employers with 15 or more employees, employment agencies, labor unions with 15 or more members as well as those operating a hiring hall, state and local governments, and most of the federal government. Private clubs are exempt from Title VII, and religious organizations may discriminate in employment on the basis of religion. The U.S. Supreme Court has further recognized the "ministerial exception," discussed below. Broadly, Title VII forbids discrimination in hiring, firing, and all aspects of the employment relationship.

The Ministerial Exception

The U.S. Supreme Court has recognized a "ministerial exception" to federal employment discrimination protections in a religious institution's employment relationships. In deciding that a commissioned minister who provided religious instruction could not bring an Americans with Disabilities Act claim against a religious school, the Court held that the ministerial exception could include other employees who were not the head of a religious congregation. In a 2020 decision on a pair of cases, the U.S. Supreme Court considered whether lay teachers' may bring employment discrimination claims based on disability or age against Catholic schools, or if they are barred under the ministerial exception. In one case, a fifth-grade teacher was terminated after she informed the school she had breast cancer and would have to miss work to undergo chemotherapy. In the other case, a teacher at another Catholic school claimed that she was first demoted and then terminated after she refused to retire. The Ninth Circuit Court of Appeal had held that the teachers are not ministers within the meaning of the ministerial exception. The Supreme Court reversed, holding that the teachers' employment discrimination claims were barred under the ministerial exception.

Sources: *Hosanna-Tabor Evangelical Lutheran Church and School v. EEOC,* 565 U.S. 171 (2012); *Biel v. St. James School,* 911, F.3d 603 (9th Cir. 2018) and *Morrissey-Berru v. Our Lady of Guadalupe School,* 769 Fed. Appx. 460 (9th Cir. 2019), reversed and remanded by *Our Lady of Guadalupe Sch. v. Morrissey-Berru,* 140 S. Ct. 2049 Brent Kendall, "Discrimination Cases Test Court," *The Wall Street Journal,* May 12, 2020 [**www.wsj.com**].

Other Legislation and Orders

Title VII is the core of EEO laws in the United States. Other federal statutes, such as the Americans with Disabilities Act of 1990 (ADA) with its 2008 amendments and the Age Discrimination in Employment Act of 1967 (ADEA), have established additional protected categories. The Equal Pay Act of 1963 and the Civil Rights Act of 1991 address particular issues in employment discrimination. For example, the Civil Rights Act of 1991 provides that U.S. citizens working abroad for American-owned or American-controlled companies are protected from discrimination under Title VII and the ADA, unless such protection would require the employer to violate the laws of its host nation. Later in this chapter, these federal laws will be discussed further.

The Constitution

As explained in Chapter 5, the federal Constitution protects us from wrongful government action. The Fourteenth Amendment provides that no state shall deny any person "life, liberty, or property without due process of law" nor deny any person "the equal protection of the laws." Thus, citizens are protected from discrimination by state governments. The Supreme Court has interpreted the Due Process Clause of the Fifth Amendment ("nor shall any person . . . be deprived of life, liberty, or property, without due process of law"), which applies to the federal government, to include the requirement of equal protection of the law.

The Role of Federal and State Agencies

LO 13-3
Explain the role of the Equal Employment Opportunity Commission in enforcing federal statutes prohibiting employment discrimination.

The Equal Employment Opportunity Commission (EEOC), an independent federal agency, has the authority to issue regulations and guidelines as well as to receive, initiate, and investigate charges of discrimination against employers covered by federal antidiscrimination statutes such as Title VII. [See the Equal Employment Opportunity Commission's website at **www/eeoc.gov**].

State fair employment practices legislation often mirrors or expands the antidiscrimination protections found in federal statutes such as Title VII. State fair employment practice agencies may serve the same function as the EEOC in enforcing these laws. [For an example, see the California Department of Fair Employment and Housing's website at **www.dfeh.ca.gov**]. Municipal ordinances may also address employment discrimination, enforced by a particular branch of the city's government. [For the San Francisco Human Rights Commission, see **http://sf-hrc.org**].

Litigation

The first step in lawsuits claiming employment discrimination is not taken in a courthouse. A victim of employment discrimination, usually referred to as the "charging party," will file a complaint with either the EEOC or, where applicable, the local or state fair employment practices agency.

What if the allegedly discriminatory act is ongoing, rather than an incident occurring on a certain date? And at what moment does the clock start ticking on the victim's time to file an EEOC complaint? After 19 years as a Goodyear employee, Lily Ledbetter discovered that her wages were much lower than those of her male coworkers. She filed an EEOC complaint alleging gender discrimination and later won a jury verdict for back pay and punitive damages. In 2007, the U.S. Supreme Court held that Ledbetter's claim should have been brought within 180 days of her first paycheck.[5] Congress reacted to *Ledbetter* by passing The Lily Ledbetter Fair Pay Act of 2009, signed into law by President Obama in the first days of his administration. Under this statute, each paycheck issued by an employer engaged in pay discrimination is a discriminatory act, meaning that the clock resets on potential discrimination claim each time the affected employee is paid, with a two-year cap on back-pay damages.

Typically on receiving a complaint, the EEOC will refer the charging party and employer to its free mediation program. If mediation does not resolve the complaint, the EEOC investigates. If the investigation reveals that there is reasonable cause to believe that discrimination has occurred, the EEOC will invite the parties to engage in conciliation to resolve the matter. If conciliation fails, the EEOC will either file a civil suit on behalf of the charging party or issue a "right to sue" letter. This letter allows the party who filed the EEOC complaint to commence an action against the employer in court, but it also removes the EEOC from the matter.

Many potential employment discrimination lawsuits no longer reach the judicial system because they are resolved in arbitration. Businesses often now include binding arbitration agreements in job offers, requiring job seekers, as a condition of employment, to waive the right to trial and turn any grievance over to arbitration. A series of U.S. Supreme Court decisions has firmly established the enforceability of those agreements when the arbitration process provided for is legitimate and fair. The Court also has ruled, however, that the EEOC retains its right to sue on behalf of an employee, even if the worker has signed away their own rights.[6]

Despite headline-grabbing settlements in discrimination cases, an American Bar Foundation study found that discrimination lawsuits rarely make it to trial and usually end with a modest settlement. If cases do go to court, plaintiffs win in only one of three cases.[7] Another Bar Foundation study found that, although plaintiffs begin the process optimistically, they rarely get a final ruling based on the substantive merits of a case, causing them to view employment litigation as favoring defendant-employers. On the other hand, defendant-employers view the process as unfair because employees have the power to initiate what employers view as "meritless" suits that require the employer's response.[8]

LO 13-4
Identify remedies available to victims of unlawful employment discrimination.

Remedies

Recognizing the gravity and nature of injuries caused by intentional discrimination in the workplace, Congress expanded the available remedies in Title VII and the Americans with Disabilities Act so as to include compensatory damages, as well as punitive damages in some cases. Compensatory damages may be sought to redress, for example, emotional pain and suffering, but combined compensatory and punitive damages are capped at $50,000 to $300,000, depending on the size of the employer's workforce. Damages are not capped for front pay (awarded for future earnings) or in cases of intentional discrimination based on race. The EEOC often negotiates consent decrees that may require employers to adopt new procedures to correct wrongful practices. [For the Civil Rights Division of the U.S. Justice Department, see **www.justice.gov/crt**].

Equal Employment Opportunity and Pandemics

During the H1N1 outbreak, the EEOC created specific guidance to help employers navigate a pandemic's impact on the workplace in light of employment discrimination protections. In 2020, the EEOC updated the guidance to address COVID-19. EEOC Commissioner Janet Dhillon issued a statement addressing national origin and race discrimination against Asian Americans and people of Asian descent in the workplace during the pandemic. The EEOC guidance was updated in July 2022 to, for example, allow employers to assess whether current circumstances justified viral screening testing under the ADA's standards for medical examinations.

Source: EEOC, "What You Should Know about COVID-19 and the ADA, the Rehab Act, and Other EEO Laws," *U.S. Equal Employment Opportunity Commission,* updated July 1, 2022 [**https://www.eeoc.gov/**].

Part Two—Types of Discrimination

There are three basic types of illegal employment discrimination: disparate treatment, disparate impact, and harassment. In addition, Title VII and other anti-employment discrimination statutes also prohibit *retaliation* for opposing an employment practice reasonably believed to be discriminatory or for raising a claim of employment discrimination. Plaintiffs may raise claims of more than one type of employment discrimination in a single proceeding.

Disparate Treatment and Disparate Impact

LO 13-5 Distinguish the primary forms of employment discrimination analysis: disparate treatment and disparate impact.

Title VII of the 1964 Civil Rights Act provides two primary theories of recovery for individuals: disparate treatment and disparate impact (sometimes labeled *adverse impact*). A disparate treatment claim addresses *intentional* discrimination by an employer who has purposely treated an employee or applicant less favorably because of their race, color, religion, national origin, gender, or membership in a group under another protected category. Disparate impact claims arise in situations where an employment practice, which appears to be neutral, has the effect of adversely impacting members of a protected category more than it impacts other groups.

As we turn now to a close look at disparate treatment and disparate impact analysis, keep in mind the various constitutional, statutory, and executive order protections just outlined.

Disparate Treatment

Employees or applicants making claims of disparate treatment must prove their employers' intent to discriminate with either direct or indirect evidence. For example, a company president's remarks that "women were simply 'not tough enough' to supervise collections and that it was a 'man's job'" (even if tempered by his statement that "I felt that a woman was not competent enough to do this job, but I think maybe you're showing me that you can do it"[9]) may constitute *direct evidence* of intentional sex discrimination, as the 11th Circuit found. A warehouse company seeking truck loaders might send a letter to an employment agency stating: "Women would not be welcome as applicants for this physically taxing job." That letter could be used as direct evidence of the employer's intent to treat female applicants adversely compared with male applicants. More often, however, disparate treatment claims rely on *indirect evidence,* as illustrated below based on an applicant's rejection:

1. **Plaintiff's (employee's) prima facie case** (that is, a case sufficient to be presumed true unless proven otherwise) is established by proving each of the following elements:
   a. Plaintiff belongs to a protected class.
   b. Plaintiff applied for a job for which the defendant was seeking applicants.
   c. Plaintiff was qualified for the job.
   d. Plaintiff was denied the job.
   e. The position remained open, and the employer continued to seek applicants.
2. **Defendant's (employer's) case.** If the plaintiff establishes a prima facie case, the defendant must articulate some legitimate, nondiscriminatory reason for the employee's rejection (for example, needing greater work experience). However, the defendant need not prove that its decision not to hire the plaintiff was, in fact, based on that legitimate, nondiscriminatory reason. The defendant simply must raise a legitimate issue of fact disputing the plaintiff's discrimination claim.
3. **Plaintiff's response.** Assuming the defendant was successful in presenting a legitimate, nondiscriminatory reason for its action, the plaintiff must show that the reason offered by the defendant was false and thus was merely a pretext to hide discrimination. [For an overview of disparate treatment analysis, see **www.hr-guide.com/data/G701.htm**].

Questions

1. Younge, a Black male, was hired as a part-time technician by WPHL, a television station. He was scheduled to train with Schultz, a full-time technician who had worked for the station for over thirty years and who had been involved with two altercations at work, one that included accusations of racial bias. A heated, profanity-laced argument ensued after Schultz called Younge "Spike Lee," during which Schultz allegedly made another racially charged comment. A security guard intervened, and an investigation resulted in both Younge and Schultz being terminated for violating WPHL's conduct code and antiharassment policy. Younge claimed he was wrongfully terminated because of his race. If you had to decide the case, what questions would you have? Explain. See *Tribune Media Co. v. Younge,* 902 F.3d 384 (3rd Cir. 2018).
2. Cruz, a white male, brought a Title VII sex discrimination claim against the Department of Defense after unsuccessfully applying for two available teaching positions at an elementary school run by the Department. Cruz's only teaching experience was as a substitute teacher, which was deemed "non-creditable" experience. The women hired for the teaching vacancies had several years of non-substitute teaching positions, which were treated as "creditable" experience. In deciding the case, what questions would you have? Explain. See *Cruz v. Mattis,* 861 F.3d 22 (1st. Cir. 2017).

Spousal Discrimination?

Craig Holcomb, a white male and assistant coach for the Iona College men's basketball team, married a Black woman. While the team enjoyed a successful record for several years, its lackluster performance and player misconduct between 2001 and 2004 led to changes in the Iona basketball program, including the dismissal of Holcomb and a Black assistant coach. Another white assistant coach, who was not engaged in an interracial relationship, was not fired. Holcomb brought a Title VII claim asserting that he had been discharged because his wife is Black. Holcomb alleged that Iona College's athletic director had made several racist and derogatory remarks about Black players on the basketball team and had derided Holcomb's decision to marry his wife, whom he referred to as "Aunt Jemima." How would you rule on this case? Explain.

Source: *Holcomb v. Iona College,* 521 F.3d 130 (2d Cir. 2008).

Disparate Impact

Disparate impact analysis involves situations in which employers use legitimate employment standards that, despite their apparent neutrality, impose a heavier burden on a protected class than on other employees. For example, a preemployment test, offered with the best of intentions and constructed to be a fair measurement device, may disproportionately exclude members of a protected class and thus be unacceptable (barring an effective defense). Alternatively, an employer surreptitiously seeking to discriminate may establish an apparently neutral, superficially valid employment test that has the effect of achieving the employer's discrimination goal. For example, a tavern might require its bouncer to be at least 6 feet 2 inches tall. Generally, height is not a protected class. However, the tavern's requirement will likely disproportionately exclude women. Was this the tavern's intent? Most likely it was not, but disparate impact does not require a showing of intent to discriminate.

The Test

Disparate impact analysis requires the following:

1. The plaintiff-employee must identify the specific employment practice or policy (such as test score, skill, or height) that caused the alleged disparate impact on the protected class.
2. The plaintiff must prove (often with statistical evidence) that the protected class is suffering an adverse or disproportionate impact caused by the employment practice or policy in question. The statistical analysis to establish a disparate impact (against Black job applicants, for example) must be based on a comparison of the racial composition of the group of persons actually holding the jobs in question versus the racial composition of the job-qualified population in the relevant labor market.
3. Assuming a prima facie case is established in steps 1 and 2, the plaintiff-employee wins unless the defendant-employer demonstrates that the employment practice-policy is: (a) job related, and (b) consistent with business necessity. In the bouncer example above,

the tavern would have to demonstrate that the height and weight requirements were related to the job in accordance with the needs of taverns.

4. If the defendant-employer succeeds in demonstrating job relatedness and business necessity, the employer wins unless the plaintiff-employee demonstrates that an alternative, less discriminatory business practice is available and that the employer refuses to adopt it.

The following classic case examines disparate impact analysis.

LEGAL BRIEFCASE

Griggs v. Duke Power Co.

401 U.S. 424 (1971)

Chief Justice Burger

We granted the writ in this case to resolve the question whether an employer is prohibited by the Civil Rights Act of 1964, Title VII, from requiring a high school education or passing of a standardized general intelligence test as a condition of employment in or transfer to jobs when (a) neither standard is shown to be significantly related to successful job performance, (b) both requirements operate to disqualify Negroes at a substantially higher rate than white applicants, and (c) the jobs in question formerly had been filled only by white employees as part of a longstanding practice of giving preference to whites.

Congress provided, in Title VII of the Civil Rights Act of 1964, for class actions for enforcement of provisions of the Act and this proceeding was brought by a group of incumbent Negro employees against Duke Power Company. . . .

The district court found that prior to July 2, 1965, the effective date of the Civil Rights Act of 1964, the company openly discriminated on the basis of race in the hiring and assigning of employees at its Dan River plant. The plant was organized into five operating departments: (1) Labor, (2) Coal Handling, (3) Operations, (4) Maintenance, and (5) Laboratory and Test. Negroes were employed only in the Labor Department where the highest-paying jobs paid less than the lowest-paying jobs in the other four "operating" departments in which only whites were employed. Promotions were normally made within each department on the basis of job seniority. Transferees into a department usually began in the lowest position.

In 1955 the company instituted a policy of requiring a high school education for initial assignment to any department except Labor, and for transfer from the Coal Handling to any "inside" department (Operations, Maintenance, or Laboratory). When the company abandoned its policy of restricting Negroes to the Labor Department in 1965, completion of high school also was made a prerequisite to transfer from Labor to any other department. From the time the high school requirement was instituted to the time of trial, however, white employees hired before the time of the high school education requirement continued to perform satisfactorily and achieve promotions in the "operating" departments. Findings on this score are not challenged.

The company added a further requirement for new employees on July 2, 1965, the date on which Title VII became effective. To qualify for placement in any but the Labor Department it became necessary to register satisfactory scores on two professionally prepared aptitude tests, as well as to have a high school education. Completion of high school alone continued to render employees eligible for transfer to the four desirable departments from which Negroes had been excluded if the incumbent had been employed prior to the time of the new requirement. In September 1965 the company began to permit incumbent employees who lacked a high school education to qualify for transfer from Labor or Coal Handling to an "inside" job by passing two tests—the Wonderlic Personnel Test, which purports to measure general intelligence, and the Bennett Mechanical Comprehension Test. Neither was directed or intended to measure the ability to learn to perform a particular job or category of jobs. The requisite scores used for both initial hiring and transfer approximated the national median for high school graduates.

The District Court had found that while the company previously followed a policy of overt racial discrimination in a period prior to the Act, such conduct had ceased. The District Court also concluded that Title VII was intended to be prospective only and, consequently, the impact of prior inequities was beyond the reach of corrective action authorized by the Act.

. . . The Court of Appeals concluded there was no violation of the Act.

The objective of Congress in the enactment of Title VII is plain from the language of the statute. It was to achieve equality of employment opportunities and remove barriers that have operated in the past to favor an identifiable group of white employees over other employees. Under the Act, practices, procedures, or tests neutral on their face, and even neutral in terms of intent, cannot be maintained if they operate to "freeze" the status quo of prior discriminatory employment practices.

The Court of Appeals' opinion, and the partial dissent, agreed that, on the record in the present case, "whites register far better on the company's alternative requirements" than Negroes. This consequence would appear to be directly traceable to race. Basic intelligence must have the means of articulation to manifest itself fairly in a testing process. Because they are Negroes, petitioners have long received inferior education in segregated schools.

. . . Congress did not intend by Title VII, however, to guarantee a job to every person regardless of qualifications. In short, the Act does not command that any person be hired simply because he was formerly the subject of discrimination, or because he is a member of a minority group. Discriminatory preference for any group, minority or majority, is precisely and only what Congress has proscribed. . . .

. . . The Act proscribes not only overt discrimination but also practices that are fair in form, but discriminatory in operation. The touchstone is business necessity. If an employment practice which operates to exclude Negroes cannot be shown to be related to job performance, the practice is prohibited.

On the record before us, neither the high school completion requirement nor the general intelligence test is shown to bear a demonstrable relationship to successful performance of the jobs for which it was used. Both were adopted, as the Court of Appeals noted, without meaningful study of their relationship to job-performance ability. Rather, a vice president of the company testified, the requirements were instituted on the company's judgment that they generally would improve the overall quality of the workforce.

The evidence, however, shows that employees who have not completed high school or taken the tests have continued to perform satisfactorily and make progress in departments for which the high school and test criteria are not used. . . .

The Court of Appeals held that the company had adopted the diploma and test requirements without any "intention to discriminate against Negro employees." We do not suggest that either the District Court or the Court of Appeals erred in examining the employer's intent; but good intent or absence of discriminatory intent does not redeem employment procedures or testing mechanisms that operate as "built-in headwinds" for minority groups and are unrelated to measuring job capability.

The facts of this case demonstrate the inadequacy of broad and general testing devices as well as the infirmity of using diplomas or degrees as fixed measures of capability. . . .

The company contends that its general intelligence tests are specifically permitted by Section 703(h) of the Act. That section authorizes the use of "any professionally developed ability test" that is not "designed, intended *or used* to discriminate because of race. . . ." (Emphasis added.)

The Equal Employment Opportunity Commission, having enforcement responsibility, has issued guidelines interpreting Section 703(h) to permit only the use of job-related tests. The administrative interpretation of the Act by the enforcing agency is entitled to great deference. Since the Act and its legislative history support the commission's construction, this affords good reason to treat the guidelines as expressing the will of Congress.

. . . From the sum of the legislative history relevant in this case, the conclusion is inescapable that the EEOC's construction of Section 703(h) to require that employment tests be job related comports with congressional intent.

Nothing in the Act precludes the use of testing or measuring procedures; obviously they are useful. What Congress has forbidden is giving these devices and mechanisms controlling force unless they are demonstrably a reasonable measure of job performance. Congress has not commanded that the less qualified be preferred over the better qualified simply because of minority origins. Far from disparaging job qualifications as such, Congress has made such qualifications the controlling factor, so that race, religion, nationality, and sex become irrelevant. What Congress has commanded is that any tests used must measure the person for the job and not the person in the abstract.

The judgment of the Court of Appeals is . . . reversed.

Questions

1. According to the Supreme Court, what was Congress's objective in enacting Title VII?
2. Had Duke Power been able to establish that its reasons for adopting the diploma and test standards were entirely without discriminatory intent, would the Supreme Court have ruled differently? Explain.
3. What is the central issue in this case?
4. Why was North Carolina's social and educational history relevant to the outcome of the case?
5. Statistical evidence showed that 35 percent of new hires in grocery and produce at Lucky Stores, a retail grocery chain, were women, while 84 percent of new hires in deli, bakery, and general merchandise were women. Statistical evidence also showed that 31 percent of those promoted into apprentice jobs in grocery and produce were women, while women comprised 75 percent of those promoted into apprentice jobs in deli, bakery, and general merchandise. Grocery and produce jobs generally were higher-paying jobs than those in deli, bakery, and general merchandise. Women received significantly fewer overtime hours than men.

   Do these facts regarding Lucky Stores suggest discrimination? Explain. See *Stender v. Lucky Stores, Inc.*, 803 F. Supp. 259 (DC Cal. 1992).

6. To determine whether police officers were using illegal drugs, the Boston Police Department used hair tests. The police department took adverse employment actions against several Black police officers who had failed the test. The officers brought a Title VII action claiming the test created a disparate impact based on race; Black officers had passed the test at rates between 97 and 99 percent, while white officers' pass rate was 99 and 100 percent. However, the officers' expert offered evidence that difference between the rates of Black and white police officers were "statistically significant." The Boston Police Department asked for summary judgment. Should the disparate impact claim be allowed to proceed? Explain. *See Jones v. City of Boston,* 2012 U.S. Dist. LEXIS 141440 (D. Mass. September 28, 2012).
7. Eighty-one percent of the hires at Consolidated Service Systems, a small Chicago janitorial company, were of Korean origin. The EEOC brought a disparate treatment claim, saying the firm discriminated in favor of Koreans by relying primarily on word-of-mouth recruiting. Hwang, the owner, was Korean. Seventy-three percent of the job applicants were Korean. One percent of the Chicago-area workforce was Korean, and not more than three percent of the janitorial workforce for the area was Korean. The court found no persuasive evidence of intentional discrimination, although the government claimed that 99 applicants were denied jobs because they were not Koreans.
   a. Does restricting hiring to members of one ethnic group constitute discrimination where hiring is accomplished by word of mouth? Explain.
   b. What if a firm, using the word-of-mouth approach, hired only white applicants? Explain.
   c. In this case, the EEOC brought but dropped a disparate impact claim. Analyze the case using the disparate impact test. See *Equal Employment Opportunity Commission v. Consolidated Service Systems,* 989 F.2d 233 (7th Cir. 1993).

Statutory Defenses

In addition to the aforementioned defenses against disparate treatment and disparate impact claims, Title VII also affords specific exemptions or defenses, three of which are of particular note: (1) seniority, (2) employee testing, and (3) bona fide occupational qualification. Bona fide occupational qualifications are addressed in the next section as part of the sex discrimination discussion.

Seniority

Differences in wages and conditions of employment are permissible under the Civil Rights Act of 1964, where those differences are the result of a bona fide (good faith) seniority system, as long as the system was not intended to hide or facilitate discrimination. Seniority is important because it often determines who is laid off first and who gets promotions, vacations, and so forth. Because white employees often have greater seniority than Blacks, the result is that seniority may perpetuate the effects of historical discrimination. The Supreme Court has made it clear, however, that a bona fide seniority system that perpetuates past wrongs is illegal only if discriminatory intent is proven.[10]

Job-Related Employee Testing

Many employers use testing in making hiring and promotion decisions. The availability of online applications has contributed to an increase in this practice.[11] To avoid a disparate impact created by employee testing, an employer must be able to show that the test in question is job-related and consistent with business necessity; that is, the test must evaluate an individual's skills as they relate to the relevant employment opportunity. To prevent unlawful disparate treatment, an employer's test must be uniformly applied regardless of an applicant's or employee's race, sex, or other protected categories. For example, Title VII would prohibit an employer from testing the reading ability of Black applicants or employees while not requiring the same test of their white counterparts.[12]

The Four-Fifths Rule and Disparate Impact

The Four-Fifths Rule examines the results of an employer's selection tool, such as testing for hiring or measuring sales numbers for promotions, to determine whether the tool creates a disproportionately adverse impact on a protected class. Consider this scenario: 150 applicants apply to be gift wrappers for an online retailer. Applicants who pass a "gift wrap test" will be hired. One hundred of the applicants are female and 50 are male. Of the 100 female applicants, 75 pass the test and are hired. Of the 50 male applicants, only 10 pass the test and are hired. Instead of comparing raw numbers, or even the raw pass rate (selection rate) of male to female applicants, the "four-fifths rule" takes 80 percent–or four-fifths–of the higher selection rate and compares it to the excluded group's selection rate (see Table 13.1).

TABLE 13.1 **Four-Fifths Rule–Gift Wrapping Scenario**

Applicant	Numbers Passing Test/Hired	Selection Rate
Female	75 out of 100	75%
Male	10 out of 50	20%
75% ×.80 = 60% > 20%		

Because the selection rate of males is less than 80 percent of the higher selection rate for females, the employment practice in question will be presumed to create a disparate impact against men in violation of Title VII. The online retailer would then have to show the job-relatedness of the employment practice in question and demonstrate that a good-faith effort was made to find a selection procedure that lessened the disparate impact on the protected class.

Questions

1. While the gap between the number of Black and white inmates has decreased recently, the imprisonment rate for Black Americans is nearly six times the imprisonment rate for whites and nearly double the rate for Hispanics, according to a 2017 Pew Center study. Should employers "ban the box" on applications that ask about criminal records so that employers can first consider the applicants' qualifications before inquiring about criminal history? Discuss. See *EEOC v. Freeman,* 778 F.3d 463 (4th Cir. 2015); National Employment Law Project, "Ban the Box: U.S. Cities, Counties, and States Adopt Fair Hiring Policies," *NELP Toolkit,* February 1, 2017 [**www.nelp.org**]; John Gramlich, "Shrinking gap between number of blacks and whites in prison," *Pew Research Center,* April 30, 2019 [**www.pewresearch.org**]; and Colin Moynihan, "Target Agrees to Review its Screening of Job Applicants Amid Bias Claims," *The New York Times,* April 6, 2018 [**www.nytimes.com**].
2. Dianne Rawlinson sought employment as a prison guard in Alabama. She was a 22-year-old college graduate with a degree in correctional psychology. She was denied

employment because she failed to meet the 120-pound weight requirement for the job. The state also required such employees to be at least 5 feet 2 inches tall. Alabama operated four all-male, maximum-security prisons. The district court characterized the Alabama prison system as one of "rampant violence." Rawlinson sued, claiming employment discrimination. Decide. Explain. See *Dothard v. Rawlinson,* 97 S. Ct. 2720 (1977). See also *Ambat v. City and County of San Francisco,* 757 F.3d 1017 (9th Cir. 2014), discussed in Part Three.

National Origin

Employment discrimination often reflects larger social issues that come to influence workplace relations. As then-EEOC Chair Janet Dhillon noted, the hatred against Asian Americans during the COVID-19 pandemic made them vulnerable to unlawful employment discrimination on the basis of national origin.[13] In the aftermath of the September 11, 2001, terrorist attacks on the United States, the EEOC received a spike in national origin discrimination claims such as the one the EEOC brought on behalf of Karim El=Rahe against his former employer, Pesce, an upscale Houston-based restaurant. Before September 11, 2001, El-Raheb, then a Pesce general manager, had been told he was doing very well. After business declined following the September 11 terrorist attacks, Pesce's co-owners speculated that customers may be frightened by El-Raheb's appearance and name, suggesting that he could "pass for Hispanic" and should change his name accordingly. In November 2001, El-Raheb was fired because "things weren't working out."[14]

Under its 2017–2021 Strategic Enforcement Plan, the protection of vulnerable workers including immigrants and migrants is one of the EEOC's central enforcement priorities.[15] In 2016, the EEOC issued new guidance on national origin discrimination, along with "Questions and Answers" on workplace rights of employees who are, or are perceived to be, Muslim or Middle Eastern.[16] The EEOC cited "heightened concerns" for protecting these employees following the "attacks in Paris and San Bernardino" in late 2015. The 2016 Enforcement Guidance noted that national origin discrimination may overlap with other forms of discrimination that Title VII protects against, such as religion and race.[17] This is known as *intersectional discrimination.*

"English Only" and Other Restrictive Language Policies

Reflecting a national debate over whether English should be the official language of the United States, "Speak English Only" rules in the workplace have generated controversy as well as national origin discrimination claims, since language is closely related to "cultural or ethnic identity."[18] Similarly, other conceivable restrictive language policies, such as a "Speak Spanish Only" policy, could give rise to national origin discrimination claims.

Employers argue that the rules are necessary when needed to communicate with customers, to maintain job safety, and to encourage congenial worker relations. The EEOC guidelines prohibit a blanket ban on employees speaking their primary language in the workplace. However, an English-only rule at certain times is permissible if justified by "substantial business reasons."[19] In *Garcia v. Spun Steak Co.,* the employer, a producer of meat products, instituted an English-only rule for its bilingual employees to enhance safety and product quality and to address allegations that some employees were making rude comments in Spanish to English-speaking employees. The English-only rule applied to work, but not to lunch, breaks, or employees' own time. The employer's rule was upheld by a federal appellate court on the grounds that it was narrowly defined and did not create a discriminatory atmosphere.[20]

Question

Rodriguez, a FedEx employee of Hispanic origin, informed FedEx's regional human resources manager, Adkinson, that he wanted to obtain a promotion to a supervisory position. After applying and interviewing for an available position, Rodriguez was rejected. The manager who interviewed Rodriguez found him to be qualified but did not hire him because of Adkinson's expressed concerns that Rodriguez's "accent and speech pattern" would undermine his ability to rise through the corporate ranks. Another FedEx manager stated that when he asked Adkinson why Rodriguez had not received the promotion, Adkinson made derogatory comments about Rodriguez's "language" and "how he speaks." Is FedEx liable for national origin discrimination based on its failure to promote Rodriguez? Decide. Explain. See *Rodriguez v. FedEx Freight East, Inc.,* 487 F.3d 1001 (6th Cir. 2007).

Racial Harassment

In announcing its 2023 racial discrimination lawsuit against Exxon, alleging that five nooses had been found at the oil company's refinery in Baton Rouge, Louisiana, the EEOC quoted an EEOC senior trial attorney: the hangman's noose "is a longstanding symbol of violence associated with the lynching of African Americans. Such symbols are inherently threatening and significantly alter the workplace environment for Black Americans."[21] Additionally, a 2022 lawsuit brought by the California Department of Fair Employment and Housing against electric car manufacturer Tesla alleged that black employees at Tesla's Fremont factory faced daily racist abuse, including a noose drawn in a bathroom next to a reference to lynching and a racial slur.[22]

The hangman's noose.

In 2021, a construction company settled EEOC racial harassment charges for $420,000. According to the EEOC, a White supervisor told a Black employee that for Halloween, "You don't even have to dress up. I will dress in white and put a noose around your neck and we'll walk down the street together." Further, one white employee had bragged that his ancestors had owned slaves, and another white employee had told a Black employee he "walked funny because slaves used to walk with a bag on their shoulder picking cotton."[23]

As startling as these claims may seem, whether racially charged workplace conduct rises to the level of unlawful harassment appears to be a subject of conflict among federal courts. For example, an Arkansas federal court recently found that the use of a racial slur in the workplace was not derogatory but "at most coarse jesting."[24] However, a recent federal appellate court decision concluded that a racially hostile environment was created when a Black cocktail waitress was called "porch monkey" by a Caucasian restaurant manager twice within a 24-hour period.[25]

Natural Hair Discrimination

CROWN Acts

Recently, CROWN Acts (Creating a Respectful and Open World for Natural hair) have addressed employment discrimination based on hairstyle and hair texture. For example. workplace dress codes requiring that hair be "neat," or "professional" could be applied with an unconscious bias that deems natural Black hair, even neatly styled, to be in violation of workplace policy, leading to negative employment decisions such as declining to hire an applicant or disciplining an employee. In 2019, New York City established a policy prohibiting employers from taking adverse action against employees based on their natural hair. Later that year, California became the first state to provide workplace protection for Black employees wearing their natural hair. In February 2023, Minnesota became the 19th state to enact similar legislation, typically called CROWN Acts. (The U.S. Virgin Islands and over 40 local governments also have similar protections against hair discrimination in employment.)

Sources: Nigel Telman and Margaret Swetman, "What's Coming up in CROWN Act Legislation and How to Prepare," *Bloomberg News* (February 1, 2023) [**https://news.bloomberglaw.com/us-law-week/whats-coming-up-in-crown-act-legislation-and-how-to-prepare**"]; and Jasmine McClain, "Minnesota Will Be the 19th State to Pass the CROWN Act," *Rolling Out* (February 2, 2023) [**https://rollingout.com/2023/02/02/minnesota-will-be-the-19th-state-to-pass-the-crown-act/**].

Part Three—Sex Discrimination

Gender Equality

In 2021, the U.S. Bureau of Labor Statistics reported that the median weekly earnings of American women working full time in 2014 were about 83 percent of that earned by men.[26] While the gender gap in pay is commonly known, the #MeToo and Time's Up movements, discussed later in this chapter, have brought attention to other issues of gender inequality in the workplace.[27]

Not Just about Sex: Intersectional Pay Discrimination

As noted by President Biden in 2021, in comparing pay for full-time work, Black women earn 63 cents for each dollar earned by a white man; Native American women earn 60 cents; and Hispanic women earn 55 cents. The EEOC has acknowledged that, while some compensation disparities may be the result of legitimate factors, such as differences in occupations, skills, or experience, "persistent pay inequity is not solely an issue of sex discrimination, but an intersectional issue that cuts across race, color, national origin, and other protected classes."

The Lilly Ledbetter Fair Pay Act of 2009 amended federal employment discrimination laws to support workers' ability to bring claims of discriminatory compensation. For example, each paycheck that contains discriminatory compensation is a separate violation regardless of when the discrimination began.

Sources: Abigail Coleman, Robyn Dupont, and Nina Rivera, "In Pursuit of Pay Equity: Examining Barriers to Equal Pay, Intersectional Discrimination Theory, and Recent Pay Equity Initiatives" *EEOC Office of Federal Operations* (November 2021) [**https://www.eeoc.gov/**]; and EEOC, "Equal Pay Act of 1963 and Lilly Ledbetter Fair Pay Act of 2009" (April 29, 2014) [**https://www.eeoc.gov/**].

In a recent Women in the Workplace survey, which examined both workplace harassment and workplace inequality, LeanIn.Org and McKinsey & Co. found that women and men may enter the workforce in roughly equal numbers, but that women fall behind in promotions at early stages, with men outnumbering women two-to-one in senior management positions.[28]

The power and limits of statutory protections against sex discrimination are also evident in the Title VII class-action lawsuits that have been brought by female employees alleging disparity in pay, work assignments, and promotion, from financial services to retail. In 2011, the class-action approach to discrimination litigation suffered a setback in the Supreme Court when class certification was denied to female Walmart employees claiming sex discrimination.[29] As was discussed in more detail in Chapter Four, the Court decision did not reach the substantive merits of the discrimination complaint. Rather, it ruled that the case could not go forward as a class action because the plaintiffs did not point to specific, consistent, nationwide employment policies or practices that harmed the class members. In 2018, a federal judge denied class certification to women claiming sex discrimination in pay and promotion at KPMG, which has a national compensation strategies director, but individual pay and promotion decisions were made at the local level.[30] Nevertheless, in 2012, a class of female Costco employees alleging sex discrimination in promotions to managerial positions was certified, with a settlement later reached that included Costco's commitment to change its promotional practices.[31]

Women on Boards

California law SB 826, also known as the Women on Boards law, required every public company based in California to have a certain number of women on their Board of Directors. Companies with a five-member board were to have at least two women directors; those with boards of six or more were to have at least three women directors. In 2022, a California judge struck down the law as unconstitutional. Before California's law took effect, women held 17 percent of the seats on company boards in the state, according to the advocacy group 50/50 Women on Boards. As of September 2021, the percentage of California-based public companies' board seats held by women climbed to more than 30 percent, compared to 26 percent nationally.

Questions

1. What benefits could result from achieving gender balance on corporate boards? Explain.
2. Identify arguments both for and against requiring public companies to have a certain number of women on their boards.
3. What other strategies might be used to create gender balance on corporate boards? Explain.

Sources: Brian Melley, "California's Women on Boards Law Is Unconstitutional," *US News and World Report* (May 16, 2022) [**https://www.usnews.com/**]; Dottie Schindlinger, "Want Gender Balance in Boardrooms? Here Are Three Alternatives to Quotas," *Fortune,* April 25, 2020 [**https://fortune.com**]; and Editorial Board, "Editorial: California Law Forcing Companies to Put Women on Corporate Boards Is Coercion. But It's Working," *Los Angeles Times,* January 6, 2020 [**www.latimes.com**].

Discrimination on the Basis of Sex

The meaning of "sex"

LO 13-6
List the actions of employers that violate Title VII's prohibition of workplace discrimination on the basis of sex.

In June 2020, in a 6–3 decision on a trilogy of cases consolidated for decision under *Bostock v. Clayton County,*[32] the U.S. Supreme Court settled the question of whether Title VII prohibits employment discrimination on the basis of sexual orientation or gender identity. The Court held that Title VII's prohibition of employment discrimination on the basis of sex includes discrimination based on sexual orientation or gender identity. The Court stated:

> . . . In our time, few pieces of federal legislation rank in significance with the Civil Rights Act of 1964. There, in Title VII, Congress outlawed discrimination in the workplace on the basis of race, color, religion, sex, or national origin. Today, we must decide whether an employer can fire someone simply for being homosexual or transgender. The answer is clear. An employer who fires an individual for being homosexual or transgender fires that person for traits or actions it would not have questioned in members of a different sex. Sex plays a necessary and undisguisable role in the decision, exactly what Title VII forbids.[33]

The Bostock Trilogy

The following offers factual summaries of each of the three cases consolidated in the *Bostock v. Clayton County* decision.

Gerald Lynn Bostock v. Clayton County: Bostock had worked as a child welfare services coordinator for Clayton County in Georgia for a decade. During this time, the county won several awards for its work under his leadership. Shortly after he began participating in a gay recreational softball league, Bostock was fired for "conduct unbecoming" a county employee. He brought a Title VII action against Clayton County, arguing that Title VII's sex discrimination protections apply to sexual orientation.

Altitude Express Inc. v. Zarda: After several seasons, Zarda was terminated from his job as a skydiving instructor days after revealing his sexual orientation to a female client. Zarda's employer had allegedly displayed anti-gay animus prior to his termination.

R.G. & G.R. Harris Funeral Homes Inc. v. EEOC: Stephens, born as a male, worked for Harris Funeral Homes for nearly six years, announced in a letter that she would begin to live as a woman, wearing the appropriate attire. Two weeks later, the owner fired her. Asked in court for the "specific reason" for terminating Stephens, the owner replied: "Well, because he was no longer going to represent himself as a man. He wanted to dress as a woman."[34]

Sources: *Bostock v. Clayton County,* 590 U.S.__; 40 S. Ct. 1731 (2020); Tully Rinckey, "Supreme Court Ruling on LGBT Protections in Workplace Could Have Far-reaching Impact," *Lexology,* October 29, 2019 [**www.lexology.com**]; and Aimee Ortiz, "Aimee Stephens, Plaintiff in Transgender Case, Dies at 59," *The New York Times,* May 12, 2020 [**www.nytimes.com**].

Sex Discrimination in the United States

Each of the three cases consolidated in *Bostock* discussed above arose from disparate treatment, in which a long-term employee was fired shortly after the employee self-identified their sexual orientation or gender identity. Sex discrimination claims under Title VII may arise from either disparate treatment or disparate impact, as discussed previously, as well as from sexual harassment. Although employee training and policies targeting sex discrimination have become common in the American workplace, sex discrimination claims remained the basis for approximately 30 percent of the charges filed with the EEOC from 1997 to 2021.[35] The #MeToo and Time's Up movements have raised awareness of the obstacles women encounter in their professional lives. The #MeToo movement, which focuses on sexual violence, gained national attention after allegations of sexual assault and harassment against Hollywood producer Harvey Weinstein encouraged others in the movie industry to call for change. Time's Up aims to promote solutions for creating a safe, equitable workplace to support the right to earn a living without harassment and discrimination.[36]

High-Tech Sexism?

Silicon Valley, considered the center of the "high-tech" industry, has been the setting of recent high-profile sex discrimination claims that have brought scrutiny to the workplace culture in such companies as the ride-sharing app pioneer Uber. In a 2017 blog post, former Uber engineer Susan Fowler described Uber's systemic discrimination against women and her own experience at being sexually harassed by a supervisor. Former Uber CEO Travis Kalanick, who has been criticized for Uber's aggressive business tactics and perceived workplace culture, opened an internal investigation into Fowler's allegations and announced plans to address these concerns.

Questions

1. If you were a consultant for Uber, what steps might you suggest to mitigate the risk of discriminatory treatment of its female workers? Explain.
2. What might contribute to hostile work environments for women in the high-tech industry? Explain.
3. How might colleges and universities assist in creating more equal employment opportunities for women in Silicon Valley companies? Explain.

Sources: Mike Isaac, "Inside Uber's Aggressive, Unrestrained Workplace Culture," *The New York Times,* February 22, 2017 [**www.nytimes.com**]; Resty Woro Yuniar, "Uber Executive: Workplace Culture Needs a Lot of Work," *The Wall Street Journal,* March 2, 2017 [**www.wsj.com**]; and Jessica Guynn and Marco della Cava, "Silicon Valley's Dirty Little Secret: The Way It Treats Women," *USA TODAY,* March 3, 2017 [**www.usatoday.com**].

Bona Fide Occupational Qualification

Often in intentional sex discrimination cases, the key inquiry involves the *bona fide occupational qualification (BFOQ)* defense provided by Title VII. Discrimination is lawful where sex, religion, or national origin is a BFOQ reasonably necessary to the normal operation of that business. The exclusion of race and color from the list suggests that Congress thought those categories are always unacceptable as bona fide occupational qualifications. The BFOQ was meant to be a very limited exception applicable only in situations where specific inherent characteristics are necessary to the job (for example, wet nurse) or where authenticity (actors), privacy (nurses), or safety (guards) is required. Broadly, the BFOQ defense rests on this question: Is being a member of a particular gender necessary to perform the *essence* of the job?

Essence

An employer can lawfully insist on a woman to fill a woman's modeling role because being female goes to the essence of the job. Airlines, on the other hand, cannot hire only women as flight attendants, even if customers prefer females over males to perform the supplementary elements of the job (like charming passengers). Those duties "are tangential to the essence of the business involved."[37] The essence of a job may be maintaining safe, orderly conditions or providing a required service as needed. Presumably, for most jobs, gender has little to do with the ability to perform such essential ingredients.

Historically, many employers simply assumed that women could not perform certain tasks. For example, women were thought to be insufficiently aggressive for sales roles or were assumed to have a higher turnover rate because they would marry and have children. Those stereotypes are at the heart of sex discrimination litigation generally and do not support a BFOQ defense.

LEGAL BRIEFCASE

Ambat v. City & County of San Francisco 757 F.3d 1017 (9th Cir. 2014)

Opinion

MURGUIA, Circuit Judge:

Plaintiffs, . . . deputies of the San Francisco Sheriff's Department ("SFSD"), appeal the district court's order granting summary judgment to the City and County of San Francisco (the "County") on their challenge to SFSD's policy prohibiting male deputies from supervising female inmates in the housing units of SFSD's jails. The district court concluded that SFSD's policy did not violate Title VII's prohibition on sex discrimination because it fell within the statute's "bona fide occupational qualification" exception. We reverse the district court's grant of summary judgment to the County on the sex discrimination claims and vacate the denial of summary judgment to plaintiffs on those claims.

I. FACTS AND PROCEDURAL HISTORY

In October 2006, SFSD implemented a new policy prohibiting male deputies from supervising female inmates in the housing units of the jails operated by the County (the "Policy"). . . .

The adoption of the Policy coincided with SFSD's plan to consolidate all of its female inmates within a single facility, County Jail 8 ("CJ8"). CJ8 housing units, or "pods," are composed of cells or sleeping bays arrayed around a central congregation space. Each pod has two tiers and between 56 and 88 beds. At the center of the pod is a podium from which a deputy can see into common areas and into the cells and sleeping bays. Each pod is staffed by two deputies, one of whom remains at the podium while the other makes rounds. Female inmates fill some, but not all, of the available housing pods in CJ8. . . .

Although housing pods are single-sex, CJ8's pod for inmates receiving medical or psychiatric care is not sex-segregated. Male deputies are not permitted under the Policy to work with female inmates in the housing pods; however, male deputies may be assigned to the mixed-sex medical pod or assigned to transport female inmates between CJ8 and other locations. Male deputies may also enter female housing pods in some circumstances, such as to assist with feeding female inmates.

According to San Francisco Sheriff Michael Hennessey (the "Sheriff"), . . . he adopted the Policy for four reasons: (1) to protect the safety of female inmates from sexual misconduct perpetrated by male deputies, (2) to maintain the security of the jail in the face of female inmates' ability to manipulate male deputies and of the deputies' fear of false allegations of sexual misconduct by the inmates, (3) to protect the privacy of female inmates, and (4) to promote the successful rehabilitation of female inmates.

Of the four reasons the Sheriff claims led him to enact the Policy, he identified protecting the safety of inmates from sexual misconduct as the most important. As the County pointed out, between 2001 and 2009, SFSD investigated twelve complaints of sexual misconduct or inappropriate sexual relationships between a male deputy and a female inmate. Ten of those incidents occurred before the Policy was implemented in 2006, and two occurred after. . . .

With this concern for inmate safety in mind, the Sheriff asserts that he considered three responses, apart from enacting the Policy, to the problem of protecting female inmates from sexual misconduct: (1) implementing additional screening of male deputies to determine whether they were likely to engage in sexual misconduct with female inmates, (2) installing additional surveillance cameras to monitor activities in CJ8's housing pods, and (3) providing additional training to deputies. However, he claims to have rejected each of these alternatives as ineffective or unfeasible, so he proceeded to implement the Policy.

In July 2007, 35 deputies—a majority of whom were female—filed suit against the County, alleging that the policy constituted sex discrimination in violation of Title VII of the Civil Rights Act of 1964 ("Title VII"). . . .

. . . Although it did not dispute that the Policy discriminates against deputies on the basis of sex, the County . . . argued that the discrimination that resulted from the Policy was permissible under the "bona fide occupational qualification" ("BFOQ") exception to Title VII. . . .

[T]he district court ruled that the County was entitled to summary judgment on plaintiffs' discrimination claims because it had made out a valid BFOQ defense. . . .

II. TITLE VII CLAIM

B. Bona Fide Occupational Qualification Defense

Although Title VII prohibits employment discrimination on the basis of sex in most instances, it permits discrimination where "sex . . . is a bona fide occupational qualification reasonably necessary to the normal operation of [the defendant's] particular business or enterprise." For example, Title VII would not compel a producer to audition men for a female role in a film, because being female could be a BFOQ for playing that role.

Nevertheless, "[t]he BFOQ defense is written narrowly, and [the Supreme Court] has read it narrowly." . . .

> To justify discrimination under the BFOQ exception, an employer must "prove by a preponderance of the evidence: 1) that the job qualification justifying the discrimination is reasonably necessary to the essence of its business; and 2) that [sex] is a legitimate proxy for the qualification because (a) it has a substantial basis for believing that all or nearly all [men] lack the qualification, or . . . (b) it is impossible or highly impractical . . . to insure by individual testing that its employees will have the necessary qualifications for the job."

After "surveying . . . decisions applying the BFOQ exception in the prison context," we observed that "even in the unique context of prison employment, administrators seeking to justify a BFOQ must show 'a high correlation between sex and ability to perform job functions.'" We also recognized that it would be impossible to prove a BFOQ defense without "demonstrat[ing] that . . . alternative approaches . . . are not viable."

[W]e must first address the issue of the deference owed to the Sheriff's judgment in implementing the Policy.

1. Deference to the Sheriff's Judgment

"Judgments by prison administrators that 'are the product of a reasoned decision-making process, based on available information and experience,' are entitled to some deference."

Here, the record demonstrates that there are genuine issues of material fact as to whether or not such a process led to the Sheriff's adoption of the Policy. . . .

2. Job Qualifications Reasonably Necessary to the Essence of Operating San Francisco's Jails

Although deference to the Sheriff's judgment cannot play a role in our analysis, it is still necessary for us to consider each rationale that has been offered by the County in order to determine whether the County is able to satisfy our BFOQ inquiry based solely on the evidence in the record. We must consider each of the four rationales offered by the County in order to determine (1) whether any rationale suggests a job qualification reasonably necessary to the essence of operating SFSD's jails, and, if so, (2) whether sex is a legitimate proxy for determining whether a deputy actually has that qualification.

[T]he County easily meets its burden . . . of demonstrating that there are job qualifications derived from the four justifications that are reasonably necessary to the essence of operating SFSD's jails. Each of the four justifications that the Sheriff claims drove his decision to implement the Policy . . . is essential to the operation of a corrections facility. . . .

Based on these important rationales for the Policy, we have no difficulty in identifying four "job qualification[s] . . . reasonably necessary to the essence of" operating SFSD's jails, any of which would satisfy the first prong of our test. These qualifications corresponding to the four rationales are (1) not posing a threat to the safety of female inmates due to a likelihood of perpetrating sexual misconduct against them; (2) not posing a threat to jail security; (3) not posing a threat to female inmates' privacy; and (4) not posing a threat to female inmates' ability to rehabilitate. We now consider each of these four qualifications under the second prong of our test to determine whether there is any genuine dispute of material fact as to whether being male is a "legitimate proxy" for any of them.

3. Whether Sex Is a Legitimate Proxy for Reasonably Necessary Job Qualifications

The County may show that excluding all male deputies is a "legitimate proxy" for excluding deputies who lack one of the four qualifications if there is (a) "a substantial basis for believing that all or nearly all [men] lack the qualification" or (b) "it is impossible or highly impractical . . . to insure by individual testing" whether or not a male deputy has the qualification. . . .

The County asserts that the primary reason for the Sheriff's adoption of the Policy was to protect the safety of female inmates by reducing the possibility of sexual harassment and abuse by male deputies. While . . . this is an extremely important interest, . . . the County has not shown that the Sheriff had "a substantial basis for believing that all or nearly all" male deputies were likely to engage in sexual misconduct with female inmates, nor has it shown that "it is impossible or highly impractical . . . to insure by individual testing" that a male deputy does not pose such a threat.

The statistics on sexual misconduct perpetrated by male deputies against female inmates in SFSD's jails are deeply troubling. . . .

Nevertheless, these statistics by themselves do not prove that "all or substantially all" male deputies are likely to perpetrate sexual misconduct. . . .

[T]he County is also unable to show that . . . it is impossible or highly impractical to insure by individual testing that a male deputy does not have a propensity to perpetrate sexual misconduct. . . . As the County points out, peace officer candidates must also undergo psychological examinations.

While conceding that background checks and psychological testing are used for the purpose of screening for a propensity to perpetrate sexual misconduct, the County suggests that such screening mechanisms are inadequate because they are unable to detect *all* potential perpetrators. Removing every deputy with any potential for engaging in misconduct may be a laudable goal, but that goal is insufficient to justify a policy that discriminates in such broad strokes. Rather, . . . a BFOQ defense cannot be maintained if available testing offers "a practical reliable differentiation of the unqualified from the qualified applicant, [even if it is] not a perfect differentiation." The record before us does not resolve the genuine dispute over whether the tests that are presently used or that could be used by SFSD would permit it to make a practical reliable differentiation between those who are likely to engage in sexual misconduct and those who are not.

The County also argues that employing male deputies in the female housing pods poses a threat to jail security. In so arguing, it points to two specific assertions offered by the Sheriff. First, the Sheriff expressed concern that male deputies were particularly vulnerable to manipulation by female inmates, potentially leading them to overlook conduct in violation of jail regulations, such as smuggling contraband into the jail. Second, he claimed that the consequence of male deputies' fear of being accused of sexual misconduct could be that those deputies would be unwilling to supervise female inmates as closely as necessary, leading to an even greater risk of female inmates being able to violate jail rules.

However, the record on summary judgment is insufficient to demonstrate that there is no genuine dispute as to whether "all or substantially all" male deputies would be vulnerable to manipulation by female inmates or as to whether it would be "impossible or highly impractical" to test for whether a male deputy is manipulable. . . .

The County's third justification for the Policy is protecting the privacy interests of female inmates. However, the record does not demonstrate that there is an actual risk of female inmates' privacy being compromised by male deputies. SFSD has policies in place to prevent male deputies from taking on duties, such as strip searches, that might violate the privacy of female inmates. The inmates are required to remain clothed at all times, except when showering. When showering or using the toilet, inmates' bodies are covered by a privacy screen.

The Sheriff claims that the use of privacy screens compromises jail security, but there is a genuine dispute as to whether privacy screens actually do compromise jail security where, as here, the screens remained in use even after the Policy was adopted.

The County's final justification for the Policy is promoting the rehabilitation of female inmates. The Sheriff asserts that he was concerned that surveillance by male deputies could traumatize female inmates, particularly those who had suffered physical or sexual abuse in the past. The County introduced evidence that a disproportionately high number of female inmates had suffered such abuse. Nevertheless, there is a genuine dispute over whether excluding male deputies is a legitimate proxy for excluding deputies who would interfere with female inmates' rehabilitation.

. . . Further, there is no evidence in the record that the individuals staffing the rehabilitative programs . . . are themselves required to be female. If female inmates were supervised by men in their rehabilitative programs while the Policy was in effect, that fact alone would defeat the County's argument that excluding men from supervisory roles was necessary to promote female inmates' rehabilitation. . . .

C. Conclusion

The justifications offered by the County in support of the Policy each speak to extremely important concerns. . . . However, the fact that the Policy seeks to advance such important goals as inmate safety is not, by itself, sufficient to permit discrimination on the basis of sex. . . .

. . . The district court's grant of summary judgment as to plaintiffs' sex discrimination claims and other claims predicated thereon is REVERSED.

. . . This case is REMANDED for further proceedings on these claims.

Questions

1. What is the two-prong test to justify a BFOQ exception to Title VII's protection against sex discrimination?
   a. Which prong did the County of San Francisco satisfy? Explain.
   b. Which prong did the County of San Francisco fail to satisfy? Explain.
2. Should Women's Workout World, a health and exercise club, be able to lawfully decline to accept men as customers and/or employees? Decide the case. Explain. See *U.S. EEOC v. Sedita,* 816 F. Supp. 1291 (N.D. Ill. 1993).
3. Can the Hooters restaurant chain lawfully decline to hire men to be food servers? Scantily clad "Hooters girls" serve food and beverages to Hooters restaurant customers. Explain. See Matthew Heller, "Would-Be Hooters Guy Sues for Gender Bias," *Courthouse News Service,* January 13, 2009 [**www.courthousenews.com**].

"Looks" Discrimination

Harrah's Reno, Nevada, casino instituted a "Personal Best" appearance policy requiring its female bartenders to wear makeup while prohibiting their male counterparts from wearing any. After a successful 20-year career as a Harrah's bartender, Darlene Jespersen was fired for refusing to wear makeup under the policy.

Brenna Lewis staffed the front desks of Heartland Inn motels near Des Moines, Iowa. Her performance was excellent, earning her compliments from customers and merit raises. A new Heartland executive, Barbara Cullinan, had approved hiring Lewis for a full-time position staffing one motel's front desk during the day, but Cullinan became dissatisfied after seeing Lewis in person. Cullinan was heard saying that Heartland staff should be "pretty," especially those working at the front desk. Lewis was self-described as "slightly more masculine," avoiding makeup and wearing her hair short. The Heartland front desk job description did not mention appearance, stating only that a guest service representative must create "a warm, inviting atmosphere" and perform tasks such as relaying information and receiving reservations. Over the protests of her direct manager, Lewis was eventually fired.

Both Jespersen and Lewis brought Title VII claims against their former employers.

Questions

1. What do these cases have in common? How do they differ? Explain. Decide each case.
2. Should the law recognize a separate cause of action for "looks discrimination"? Explain.

Sources: *Jespersen v. Harrah's,* 444 F.3d 1104 (9th Cir. 2006); and *Lewis v. Heartland Inns,* 591 F.3d 1033 (8th Cir. 2010).

Work–Life Balance and Sex Discrimination

Antidiscrimination law has been critical in allowing women to pursue careers and in providing some refuge from the professional disadvantages of pregnancy experienced at some workplaces.

Pregnancy Discrimination

The Pregnancy Discrimination Act (PDA) amended Title VII of the Civil Rights Act of 1964 making discrimination with respect to pregnancy a form of sex discrimination. Broadly, the PDA requires that pregnant employees be treated the same as all other employees with temporary disabilities. In general, an employer should not ask job applicants about pregnancy, and applicants have no duty to reveal their pregnancy. A pregnant employee cannot be forced to take time off or be forced to quit due to pregnancy. An employer also may not discriminate against female applicants or employees because they might start a family. [For the 2015 EEOC enforcement guidance on pregnancy discrimination, see "EEOC Enforcement Guidance on Pregnancy Discrimination and Related Issues" at **www.eeoc.gov/laws/guidance/pregnancy_guidance.cfm**].

Family Responsibilities Discrimination

"Family Responsibilities Discrimination" (FRD) has achieved increased recognition in recent years. While no express antidiscrimination statutory protection is afforded to parents or caregivers, FRD claims may be based on existing statutes such as Title VII. For example, a federal appeals court allowed the mother of six-year-old triplets and an older child to bring a Title VII claim alleging that she was rejected for a promotion in favor of a less-qualified woman as a result of a sex-based stereotype that mothers with young children neglect their careers.[38] [For the EEOC enforcement guidance on FRD, see "EEOC Enforcement Guidance: Unlawful Disparate Treatment of Workers with Caregiving Responsibilities" at **www.eeoc.gov/policy/docs/caregiving.html**].

A sex-based stereotype that mothers with young children neglect their careers.

Questions

1. Waitresses at the Rustic Inn were prohibited under a written policy from waiting tables past their fifth month of pregnancy and were required either to suspend working or to switch to positions as cashiers or hostesses, whose pay was less because of the absence of gratuities. The EEOC filed a lawsuit against the employer on behalf of a class of three aggrieved employees, alleging that the policy violated the PDA. Decide. See *EEOC v. W&O Inc.,* 213 F.3d 600 (11th Cir. 2000).
2. According to the Bureau of Labor Statistics, nearly 75 percent of mothers and more than 90 percent of fathers work. The Coronavirus pandemic put work–life balance on full view as schools and offices closed. How might this result in family responsibilities discrimination and the recognition of FRD protections? Explain your answer. See Meghan McCarty Carino, "Struggles of working parents on full display amid pandemic," *Marketplace,* March 26, 2020 [**www.marketplace.org**].

Equal Pay

Title VII affords broad protection from discrimination in pay because of sex. The Equal Pay Act of 1963 directly forbids discrimination on the basis of sex by paying wages to employees of one sex at a rate less than the rate paid to employees of the opposite sex for equal work on jobs requiring equal skill, effort, and responsibility and performed under similar working conditions. Equal has been interpreted to mean "substantially equal." The act provides for certain exceptions. Unequal wage payments are lawful if paid pursuant to: (1) a seniority system, (2) a merit system, (3) a system that measures earnings by quantity or quality of production, or (4) a differential based on "any other factor other than sex." The employer seeking to avoid a violation of the Equal Pay Act can adjust its wage structure by raising the pay of the disfavored sex performing equal work. Lowering the pay of the favored sex violates the act.

It has been held that, if a male employee has a greater skill set–such as accounting skills–than his female coworker doing "equal work," the employer may pay the man at a higher rate, as long as the male employee's superior skills are actually considered in making the pay decision.[39]

Prior Pay and the EPA

After three years of working as a math consultant for the Fresno County Office of Education, Rizo discovered that a newly hired male math consultant was being paid a significantly higher salary than she was earning. The county used a pay schedule that was based on the employee's prior wages, which had set Rizo at a relatively low salary. Rizo filed a complaint that included an Equal Pay Act claim. A federal appellate court held that prior salary could not be used to justify this pay differential, finding that the "other factors other than sex" must be job-related.

Source: *Rizo v. Yovino,* 950 F.3d 1217 (9th Cir. 2020).

Sexual Harassment

The #MeToo movement gained attention in the wake of allegations of sexual assault and harassment against Hollywood producer Harvey Weinstein for abusing his power in the movie industry. A typical and reasonable response to a request for an example of sexual harassment might be "a male boss making unwanted sexual advances to a female employee, telling her that such conduct is a job requirement." However, this example does not provide a full picture of sexual harassment claims. As a form of sex discrimination actionable under Title VII, sexual harassment protection covers both men and women and strives to maintain equal opportunity in the workplace.

Questions

1. Women with authority seem to be particularly susceptible to sexual harassment from senior leaders, as well as from their subordinates. A 2020 study of women in Sweden, the United States, and Japan showed that women in leadership were 30 percent to 100 percent more likely to be harassed than women in subordinate positions.[40] Why might women in powerful positions be more likely to experience sexual harassment? How might an employer address this issue?

2. In 2023, the EEOC announced a McDonald's franchise would pay nearly $2 million to resolve the EEOC's sexual harassment lawsuit against it. The lawsuit alleged that the franchise had known of harassing conduct at various McDonald's restaurants, mainly directed at young, teenaged employees, that included frequent unwanted touching, offensive comments, unwelcome sexual advances, and intimidation by supervisors, managers, and coworkers and allowed it to continue, unabated. In announcing the settlement, the EEOC indicated that "employers should be mindful of the demographics of their workforce, including whether employees may be more vulnerable to being targeted [for sexual harassment] because of their age." Along with young workers, which groups may be more vulnerable to sexual harassment? What can an employer do to protect them? Explain. See: EEOC, "McDonald's Franchise to Pay Nearly $2 Million to Settle EEOC Sexual Harassment Lawsuit," (January 6, 2023) [**https://www.eeoc.gov/**].

The Customer Is Not Always Right

Two female cashiers at Love's truck stop in Buckeye, Arizona, ages 18 and 20, were allegedly subjected to unwanted sexual touching and pressing, crude and obscene remarks, sexual demands and innuendos, and demands for personal information–by customers and sometimes in front of other customers. The EEOC filed a claim asserting that Love's management knew about and tolerated this sexually hostile work environment caused by its customers. Further, at least one manager allegedly laughed about it, and another manager said the harassment was to be expected because it was a truck stop. Managers also told the two cashiers to "deal with it," especially the misconduct of one repeat customer because "he's always like that." Should the employer be held liable for workplace harassment by its customers? Explain.

Source: Press Release, "Arizona Truck Stop to Pay $70,000 to Settle EEOC Suit Charging Sex Harassment by Customers," *U.S. Equal Employment Opportunity Commission,* August 3, 2010 [**www.eeoc.gov**].

The Law of Sexual Harassment

Sexual harassment, as a form of discrimination, consists of unwelcome sexual advances, requests for sexual favors, and other verbal or physical conduct of a sexual nature that: (1) becomes a condition of employment, (2) becomes a basis for employment decisions, or (3) unreasonably interferes with work performance or creates a hostile working environment.

There are two types of sexual harassment: quid pro quo ("this for that," such as a sexual favor in exchange for keeping one's job) and hostile work environment (a workplace rendered offensive and abusive by such conduct as sexual comments, pictures, jokes, sexual aggression, and the like, where no employment benefit is gained or lost). As discussed earlier in this chapter, hostile work environments may be created by offensive or abusive conduct involving protected categories other than sex, including race, religion, national origin, and disability. The law of sexual harassment, particularly in regard to hostile work environments, may apply to these cases.

As a preliminary matter, let us consider first who the defendant is when a sexual harassment claim is made. Although the question is not settled, most federal courts have ruled that victims of sexual harassment seeking recovery under Title VII cannot sue the person who actually committed the harassment. The victim might be able to sue the wrongdoer under a state statute or by using a tort claim such as assault, but under Title VII, personal liability appears not to be available. This result, if the current judicial pattern continues, is not as unfair as it might at first appear because well-settled principles of justice hold the employer, and not the employer's agents or employees, generally responsible for workplace wrongdoing. The victim, therefore, can seek damages from the employer as the responsible party.

The Test

LO 13-7 Identify when unlawful sexual harassment has occurred.

LO 13-8 Identify when employers are liable for unlawful sexual harassment.

A pair of 1998 U.S. Supreme Court decisions, *Burlington Industries* and *Faragher,*[41] considerably clarified the circumstances under which an employer is liable for sexual harassment in the workplace. The analysis proceeds as follows:

1. **Proof of sexual harassment**–The plaintiff-employee-victim must prove the following:
   a. The harassing conduct is unwelcome.
   b. The harassing conduct is because of sex.
   c. The harassing conduct resulted in a tangible employment action, or was sufficiently severe or pervasive as to unreasonably alter the conditions of employment and create a hostile, abusive work environment.

   If a plaintiff is unable to prove all of these items, their claim fails. If a plaintiff does proves all of them, the inquiry then turns to the question of whether the employer bears responsibility for the harassment, the second step proceeds.
2. **Employer liability and the affirmative defense**
   a. If the wrongdoer is a coworker, the plaintiff-employee-victim can bring a negligence claim seeking to prove that the employer unreasonably failed to prevent or remedy the discriminatory harassment where management knew or should have known about it.
   b. If the wrongdoer is a supervisor with authority over the plaintiff, and if the plaintiff suffered a *tangible employment action* (such as job loss or demotion) as a result of the harassment, the employer is vicariously liable for the plaintiff's losses. See the discussion of indirect liability in Chapter 12. The employer will be strictly liable for the supervisor's wrongdoing and no defense is available, regardless of lack of knowledge, absence of negligence, or any other factor.
   c. If the wrongdoer is a supervisor with authority over the plaintiff, but the employee suffered no tangible employment action, the employer can avoid liability by proving both elements of the following affirmative defense: (1) the employer exercised reasonable care to prevent and correct the harassment promptly (for example, by instituting antiharassment training programs or having a policy for reporting harassment), and (2) the plaintiff unreasonably failed to take advantage of those opportunities.

In its 2013 decision on a Title VII sexual harassment claim, *Vance v. Ball State University,* the U.S. Supreme Court restricted the definition of *supervisor* to one who could take a tangible employment action against the allegedly harassed employee.[42] The impact of that decision is illustrated in the case that follows.

McCormack v. Safeway 2014 U.S. Dist. LEXIS 17805 (D. Ariz. February 12, 2014)

David G. Campbell

I. BACKGROUND

Plaintiffs are two women, Mary McCormack and Samantha Stabenchek, who worked as cashiers for a Safeway store in Scottsdale, Arizona. McCormack is the mother of Stabenchek. Stabenchek was 17 years old when she started work at Safeway and appears to have been a minor during the events at issue in this case.

On March 3, 2011, Jose Lopez, a general clerk at the store, cornered Ms. Stabenchek, grabbed her buttocks, and kissed her. Plaintiffs allege that the assault was the culmination of months of sexual harassment in which Lopez made inappropriate comments to Stabenchek in the workplace and sent her sexually explicit text messages. After the assault, McCormack reported Lopez's conduct. Stabenchek participated in Safeway's internal investigation of the assault, which led to Lopez's termination on March 26, 2011.

Less than a month after reporting the sexual assault, Plaintiffs were both interviewed about McCormack's alleged violation of Safeway's coupon policy. Safeway alleges that in late December 2010, a Safeway security analyst reported that it appeared as though McCormack was violating the company's coupon policies. The analyst allegedly discovered more evidence of coupon abuse, which she reported to a loss prevention investigator in April 2011. The investigator confronted Stabenchek and McCormack in connection with his investigation. McCormack was suspended pending further investigation. Feeling that their honesty was impugned "on the heels" of their reports about Lopez's misconduct, Plaintiffs resigned on April 13, 2011.

Stabenchek has asserted [a] sexual harassment . . . [claim] against Safeway under Title VII of the Civil Rights Act of 1964 . . . ("Title VII"). . . .

III. HARASSMENT CLAIMS

Title VII provides that an employer may not "discriminate against an individual with respect to [her] compensation, terms, conditions, or privileges of employment because of [her] . . . sex[.]" Sexual harassment constitutes unlawful discrimination under Title VII. *Meritor Sav. Bank v. Vinson*. . . . If the harassing employee is the victim's coworker, the employer may be held liable only if it was negligent in controlling working conditions. *Vance v. Ball State Univ.* . . . "In cases in which the harasser is a 'supervisor,' however, different rules apply," and the employer may be held vicariously liable."

A. Vicarious Liability

Safeway asserts that it cannot be held vicariously liable for Lopez's harassment because Lopez was not Stabenchek's supervisor. "[A]n employee is a 'supervisor' for purposes of vicarious liability under Title VII if he or she is empowered by the employer to take tangible employment actions against the victim." *Vance*. . . . "The ability to direct another employee's tasks is simply not sufficient" to give rise to "supervisor" status. Instead, supervisors are a "*distinct class* of agent [empowered] to make economic decisions affecting other employees under his or her control. . . . Tangible employment actions are the means by which the supervisor brings the official power of the enterprise to bear on subordinates.". . . [internal quotation marks and citation omitted] [emphasis in original].

Lopez was a front end manager when Stabenchek became an employee at Defendant's Scottsdale location, but he had been demoted to general clerk by the time much of the alleged harassment took place, including the sexual assault. The distinction is not important, however, because neither front end managers nor general clerks qualify as supervisors under *Vance*. Front end managers and general clerks lack authority to make economic decisions affecting other employees under their control. Front end managers and general clerks are not empowered by Safeway to hire, promote, demote, fire, increase pay, decrease pay, or impose any economic change on any employees.

Plaintiffs assert that Lopez was Stabenchek's supervisor under *Vance* because he was in charge of the store during some of Stabenchek's shifts and because he sat in on Stabenchek's initial job interview and assured her that she would get her hired. Plaintiffs have presented evidence that front end managers occasionally directed other employees to sign documents that Safeway "uses to bind their employees." In addition, Plaintiffs assert that front end managers are supervisors because they have significant decision-making power, including telling employees when to clock out and when to take breaks. But Plaintiffs have provided no evidence that Lopez had any ability to influence Stabenchek's employment beyond determining the timing of her breaks and the manner in which she performed her job, and *Vance* states that "the ability to direct employee's tasks is simply not sufficient" to justify a finding that a manager is a supervisor for purposes of Title VII vicarious liability. *Vance* requires Plaintiffs to show that Lopez had power to make economic decisions affecting Stabenchek's employment at Safeway such as the ability to fire, hire, promote, or change Stabenchek's compensation. Plaintiffs have presented no evidence that Lopez possessed such authority.

Plaintiffs' reliance on *Lindquist v. Tanner* . . . is misplaced. . . . [I]n *Tanner* . . . the harasser was able to impact the plaintiff's employment status. The harasser actively recruited the plaintiff . . . [, appeared] that he had the ability to determine whether or not plaintiff would become a full-time employee, and the harasser was the most senior employee on-site. . . . Lopez participated in

Stabenchek's hiring process. Safeway has shown, however, that while Lopez sat in on Stabenchek's initial 5-minute screening interview, . . . the hiring decision was made by a different Safeway employee after an hour-long interview. . . . In addition, the fact that Lopez was occasionally the person in charge at Safeway's Scottsdale store is a far cry from the authority required by *Vance*.

Undisputed facts show that Lopez was not Stabenchek's supervisor as a matter of law. As a result, Safeway cannot be held vicariously liable for Lopez's harassment.

B. Liability in Negligence

Where harassment by a coworker is alleged, the employer can be held liable only if "its own negligence is a cause of the harassment." . . . Thus, an employer is responsible for its own actions or omissions and not for a coworker's harassment. "If the employer fails to take corrective action after learning of an employee's sexually harassing conduct, or takes inadequate action that emboldens the harasser to continue his misconduct, the employer can be deemed to have 'adopt[ed] the offending conduct and its results, quite as if they have been authorized affirmatively as the employer's policy.'"

An employer cannot be held liable for misconduct of which it is unaware. . . .

Safeway asserts that it cannot be held liable under a negligence theory because, although Stabenchek claims that Lopez had been making hundreds of sexual comments and sending thousands of sexual messages to her for months before the March 3 incident, Stabenchek never told anyone about any alleged harassment until March 5, the day before McCormack reported it to Safeway. Plaintiffs rejoin that Safeway can be liable because one of Safeway's managers observed Lopez harassing Stabenchek and did nothing to stop it.

. . . Stabenchek testified that about one month before the sexual assault, Megan Oxford, a second assistant manager, approached Stabenchek about an incident Oxford had witnessed. Oxford told Stabenchek that she saw an exchange between Lopez and Stabenchek after which Stabenchek looked at Lopez like she was disgusted. Oxford had not heard what Lopez said, but she urged Stabenchek to share anything that Stabenchek thought Oxford needed to know. Stabenchek declined to share any specific information with Oxford because she was uncomfortable and embarrassed. Oxford again asked Stabenchek if she wanted to report anything, but Stabenchek responded that Lopez was just being a "creep" and that she did not want to report anything.

Oxford's observations, and Stabenchek's subsequent responses to Oxford's questions, did not put Safeway on notice of Lopez's sexually harassing conduct toward Stabenchek. . . . Although Stabenchek told Oxford that Lopez was being a "creep," that uninformative comment was not enough to communicate that Lopez was sexually harassing Stabenchek.

Once Safeway actually learned of Lopez's sexually harassing conduct, it took prompt corrective action. Stabenchek told her mother about the Lopez's harassment on Saturday, March 5. McCormack told second assistant manager Ryan on Sunday, March 6. By Monday, March 7, the store manager, Anthony Duran, and a human resources advisor, Joyce Cameron, initiated an investigation of the incident. Lopez was interviewed later that day and was immediately suspended pending the results of the investigation. Lopez never returned to work at Safeway and was fired. . . .

IT IS ORDERED that Defendant's motion for summary judgment is granted.

Questions

1. According to the court, under *Vance,* Lopez was not Stabenchek's supervisor for purposes of Title VII sexual harassment liability. Why?
   a. What was the basis for the plaintiffs' assertion that Lopez was Stabenchek's supervisor? Explain.
   b. Do you think Lopez and others who are, for example, placed in charge of a store during shifts should be considered a supervisor for purposes of Title VII sexual harassment liability? Explain.
2. Truck driver Lesley Parkins claimed she was a victim of hostile environment sexual harassment while employed by Civil Constructors beginning in 1994. Parkins alleged that coworkers subjected her to foul language, sexual stories, and touching. Parkins complained to her dispatcher, Tim Spellman, and to one of her purported harassers, Robert Strong. She saw the job superintendent and the company EEO officer almost daily, but she did not complain to either. In 1996 Parkins filed a grievance with her union—Teamsters Local 325. The union contacted the company EEO officer, who immediately launched an investigation that led to punishment for the employees. Parkins conceded that she was not harassed following the company punishment. Parkins filed suit charging Civil Constructors with sexual harassment. Parkins claimed that two of her harassers, Strong and Charles Boeke, were foremen who supervised her work. Assuming Parkins can prove that she was, in fact, sexually harassed, what must she prove in order to hold Civil Constructors liable? See *Parkins v. Civil Constructors of Illinois,* 163 F.3d 1027 (7th Cir. 1998).
3. Eileen Craig worked for the Mahoney Group as the branch manager in Tucson and reported to Leon Byrd, the interim president. Over the course of several months, Byrd made repeated inappropriate comments to Craig about her legs and how she should wear shorter skirts. Although Craig thought the comments were obnoxious, she was not particularly offended. At Byrd's invitation, Craig met him for drinks after work at a restaurant, as they had done previously to discuss work-related matters. After Byrd made a sexual proposition, Craig laughed and shook her head but did not leave the restaurant. Byrd later

followed Craig into the restaurant's restroom, grabbed her, and kissed her. Craig did not report this incident. Byrd made further advances to Craig that she rejected. At some point, Byrd told Craig that he didn't think he could work with her anymore. Craig finally reported Byrd's conduct under the company's sexual harassment policy. The company took immediate action: Byrd was instructed to stay away from Craig and to stop making sexual comments to her, and Craig began reporting to another company executive. The investigator retained by the employer recommended, among other things, that Byrd receive a reprimand and training. At the end of the investigation, Craig began reporting again to Byrd. Eventually, Craig resigned and filed a complaint asserting a Title VII sexual harassment claim.

a. Is Mahoney liable for quid pro quo sexual harassment? What questions would you have if you were on the jury? Explain.

b. Is Mahoney liable for hostile work environment sexual harassment? What other facts might you need to know before deciding? Explain. See *Craig v. M & O Agencies, Inc.*, 496 F.3d 1047 (9th Cir. 2007).

4. A female employed as an Installation and Repairs Technician claimed a hostile work environment was created in the garage in which she worked by the routine use of profanity, crude humor, vulgar graffiti depicting sexual acts, and especially by sexually demeaning conversations conveying a profound disrespect for women. While the comments and graffiti demeaned some male employees, the conduct was directed at all the women working in the garage. In deciding whether the conduct constituted hostile environment sexual harassment, should the court evaluate the facts from the point of view of a "reasonable person" or a "reasonable woman"? Explain. See *Petrosino v. Bell Atlantic*, 385 F.3d 210 (2d Cir. 2004).

Consider the Context: Sexual Harassment at the Casino

While she was a bartender at Gold Strike Casino Resort in Tunica County, Mississippi, Debra Brockington allegedly was subjected to sexual harassment by her female supervisor Wanda Haley as well as by her former boyfriend and coworker Ed Ogden. The alleged harassment included Haley grabbing Brockington's breasts, making sexually suggestive remarks to others about Brockington, and snapping a towel against her buttocks. Brockington admitted to engaging in off-color conversations and conduct with her female coworkers. In her subsequent Title VII claim, a federal trial court, addressing Haley's behavior, held that "within the context of the plaintiff's work environment the alleged harassment in this case was neither severe nor pervasive."

Questions

1. Do you agree with the court's reasoning about the importance of workplace context in determining whether unlawful harassment has occurred? Explain.
2. In its ruling, the court said, "[C]asino bartenders have the same right as other employees to expect that they will not be subjected to unlawful harassment. . . ." What impact might the court's ruling on workplace context have on the sexual harassment protections of casino bartenders and others working in similar environments?

Source: Brockington v. Circus Circus Mississippi, 2008 U.S. Dist. LEXIS 39482 (N.D. Miss. May 15, 2008).

Same Sex?

Joseph Oncale, a heterosexual who worked on an offshore oil rig, charged a supervisor and two male coworkers with sexually harassing him, including repeated taunts and several sexual assaults, one with a bar of soap while Oncale was showering. Oncale complained to superiors, but to no avail. He then quit his job and sued his employer for sexual harassment. The case went to the U.S. Supreme Court, which unanimously ruled that same-sex harassment is actionable under Title VII.[43] Oncale then settled out of court for an undisclosed amount of money. Justice Scalia, who wrote the Supreme Court opinion, explained that the harassment must be "because of sex" (that is, gender), and that common sense and social context count. Thus, smacking a football teammate on the rear end, horseplay, roughhousing, or occasional gender-related jokes, teasing, and abusive language normally would not constitute harassment. Ordinarily, plaintiffs in same-sex harassment cases must show that the behavior was motivated by: (a) sexual desire, (b) general hostility to one or other gender, or (c) the victim's failure to conform to sexual stereotypes (such as effeminate behavior by a male). [For an analysis of the significance of the *Oncale* case, see **http://reason.com/archives/2003/01/01/man-trouble**].

What if the harasser bothers both genders equally?

Oncale settled the issue of same-sex harassment, but it raises other puzzles. For example, what if the harasser bothers both genders equally?

After *Oncale,* a husband and wife, who were also coworkers, brought a Title VII claim against their employer alleging that their supervisor had harassed both of them by soliciting sex from each of them on separate occasions. The federal appeals court affirmed the district court's dismissal, concluding that the "equal opportunity harasser" does not give rise to a Title VII sex discrimination complaint.[44]

Sexual Harassment in Other Nations

American managers working abroad must deal with international differences in attitudes toward sexual behavior in the workplace, although a general shift in harassment law in the direction of the American model is evident. This shift is significant for the American manager working abroad for a U.S.-based company or a foreign employer controlled by an American company. The Civil Rights Act of 1991 extends Title VII's protection to American employees working abroad for such employers, but offers a "foreign law defense" under which the employer would not be required to comply with Title VII if doing so would violate the host country's law. The European Union has adopted laws requiring harassment-free workplaces.[45] In Japan, sexual harassment law resembles the U.S. model.[46] In China, a woman who is sexually harassed in her workplace may file a complaint with the police under China's Protection of Rights and Interests of Women law.[47]

LO 13-9
Describe the protections against retaliation offered under the federal statutes prohibiting employment discrimination.

Retaliation

The power in an employment relationship often is unbalanced in favor of the employer. In bringing a discrimination claim, an employee is vulnerable to the employer's retaliatory action. In order to protect against an employer's abuse of power and to encourage the exercise of employees' rights, Title VII's antiretaliation provision prohibits an employer from discriminating against an employee for engaging in a protected activity. Protected activities include opposing an employment practice that is reasonably believed to violate Title VII or making a complaint under Title VII, such as filing a charge of workplace discrimination. Other civil rights laws, including the Americans with Disabilities Act, the Age Discrimination in Employment Act, and the Civil Rights Act of 1866, offer similar protections against retaliation.

A prima facie case of retaliation requires:

1. Participation in a protected activity.
2. An employment action disadvantaging the plaintiff.
3. A causal connection between the protected activity and the adverse employment action.

In several cases, the U.S. Supreme Court has addressed Title VII's antiretaliation protection. In *Crawford v. Metropolitan Government of Nashville & Davidson County,*[48] the Court held that employees who respond to questions about workplace discrimination during the employer's informal investigation are engaged in activity protected under Title VII's antiretaliation provision, even if they did not make the complaint being investigated. In *Burlington Northern & Santa Fe Railway v. White,*[49] the Court, recognizing that a broad range of employer conduct could discourage a reasonable employee from exercising Title VII rights, held that assigning a complainant to less desirable duties is an adverse employment action on which a Title VII retaliation claim may be based. In 2011, the Court held in *Thompson v. North American Stainless*[50] that an employee was protected against retaliation resulting when his fiancée and coworker filed a Title VII claim, noting that it was "obvious" that a reasonable worker might hesitate to exercise Title VII rights if it would cause the person whom they intended to marry to be fired.

After these employee-friendly rulings, the U.S. Supreme Court's 2013 decision in *University of Texas Southwestern Medical Center v. Nassar* created a higher standard for retaliation claims other than "status discrimination" claims, such as claims based on gender or national origin.[51] Dr. Naiel Nassar, a physician of Middle Eastern descent who was both a medical school faculty member and a staff physician at the school's affiliated hospital, complained to his department chair, Dr. Fitz, that one of Dr. Nassar's other supervisors, Dr. Levine, was biased against him based on national origin and religion. Dr. Nassar arranged to continue working as a hospital staff physician without being a member of the medical school's faculty, and sent a resignation letter to Dr. Fitz and several others explaining that he was resigning because of Dr. Levine's harassment. Upset at the letter's statements regarding Dr. Levine, Dr. Fitz objected to the hospital's arrangement with Dr. Nassar. Dr. Fitz asserted that it violated the hospital's affiliation agreement with the medical school, under which its staff physicians were to be composed exclusively of the school's faculty members. The offer was withdrawn. Dr. Nassar's resulting Title VII lawsuit included a retaliation claim based on Dr. Fitz's actions to stop his hospital employment. A federal appellate court affirmed the trial court's finding of retaliation, as the evidence supported the conclusion that Dr. Fitz was, at least in part, motivated to retaliate against Dr. Nassar because of his complaints. The U.S. Supreme Court reversed, interpreting Title VII's antiretaliation provision as requiring "but for" causation. Here, Dr. Nassar's continued employment with the hospital would have violated the hospital's affiliation agreement with the medical school, which arguably would have caused the medical school's objection to, and ultimate withdrawal of, Nassar's offer.

Part Four—Affirmative Action

LO 13-10
Discuss the purposes and development of affirmative action.

Some viewed the eight-year presidency of Barack Obama, the first Black President of the United States, as evidence that the racism staining the country's history was no longer a pressing issue. Therefore, it was argued, *affirmative action* efforts on behalf of minorities and women could be reduced or eliminated. Yet, a 2019 Pew Research Center survey found that 4 in 10 Americans believed that not enough progress has been made toward race equality.[52] The survey also found that 6 in 10 Americans believed race relations in the United States are generally bad.[53]

In 2020, two events, one singular and the other all too common, forced us as a nation to confront how prevalent racism still is and what will be required to truly eliminate it. Those two events were the COVID-19 pandemic, which has had a disproportionate impact on Black Americans,[54] and the simultaneous outbreak of protests across all 50 states for weeks sparked by the police killing of yet another Black man, George Floyd.[55]

For video presentations of testimony on the disproportionate impact of COVID-19 on communities of color before the House Committee of Ways and Means on May 27, 2020, see **https://www.youtube.com/watch?v=XZnFhSUMFFY**]. [For the video, "People in All 50 States Show Up for BLM Protests," see **www.youtube.com/watch?v=SG4LiBwtWCY**].

Affirmative Action Plans

In following an affirmative action plan, employers consciously take positive steps to seek out minorities and women for hiring and promotion opportunities, and they often employ goals and timetables to measure progress toward a workforce that is representative of the qualified labor pool. Affirmative action is a means of remedying past and present discriminatory wrongs in a more expeditious and thorough manner than the market might achieve on its own.

Affirmative action efforts arise in four ways: (1) courts may order the implementation of affirmative action after a finding of wrongful discrimination, (2) employers may voluntarily adopt affirmative action plans, (3) statutes might require affirmative action steps to be taken, and (4) employers may adopt affirmative action plans in order to do business with government agencies. Federal contractors must meet the affirmative action standards of the Office of Federal Contract Compliance Programs.

Early Affirmative Action Law

For nearly 20 years, judicial decisions were firmly supportive of affirmative action. A massive system of remedies emerged at all levels of government and in the private sector. In a 1979 case, *United Steelworkers of America v. Weber,*[56] the U.S. Supreme Court set out perhaps its most detailed "recipe" for those qualities that would allow a voluntary affirmative action plan in the private sector to withstand scrutiny. Weber, a white male, challenged the legality of an affirmative action plan that set aside for Black employees 50 percent of the openings in a training program until the percentage of Black craft workers in the plant equaled the percentage of Blacks in the local labor market. The plan was the product of a collective bargaining agreement between the Steelworkers and Kaiser Aluminum and Chemical. In Kaiser's Grammercy, Louisiana, plant, only five of 273 skilled craft workers were Black, whereas the local workforce was approximately 39 percent Black. In the first year of the affirmative action plan, seven Black and six white workers were admitted to the craft training program. The most junior Black employee accepted for the program had less seniority than several white employees who were not accepted. Weber was among the white males denied entry to the training program.

Weber filed suit, claiming Title VII forbade an affirmative action plan that granted a racial preference to Blacks where whites dramatically exceeded Blacks in skilled craft positions, but where there was no proof of discrimination. The federal district court and the federal court of appeals held for Weber, but the Supreme Court reversed. Several qualities of the Steelworkers' plan were instrumental in the Court's favorable ruling, including:

1. The affirmative action was part of a plan.
2. The plan was designed to open employment opportunities for Blacks in occupations, which traditionally have been closed to them.
3. The plan was temporary.
4. The plan did not unnecessarily harm the rights of white employees. That is,
   a. The plan did not require the discharge of white employees.
   b. The plan did not create an absolute bar to the advancement of white employees.

Then, in an important 1987 public-sector decision, *Johnson v. Transportation Agency,*[57] the Supreme Court approved the extension of affirmative action to women. However, the political tides were turning. The 1980s were politically conservative years. Appointments to the Supreme Court and to the lower federal courts, by President Reagan in particular, reflected that mood. Affirmative action came under attack.

Rethinking Affirmative Action

From the late 1980s to the present, a series of judicial decisions and increasing public and political skepticism have challenged the legality and wisdom of affirmative action, at least where the government is involved. The 1989 *City of Richmond v. J. A. Croson Co.*[58] case struck down Richmond, Virginia's minority "set-aside" program that required prime contractors who were doing business with the city to subcontract at least 30 percent of the work to minority businesses. The U.S. Supreme Court held that such race-conscious remedial plans were constitutional only if (1) the city or state could provide specific evidence of discrimination against a particular protected class in the past, rather than relying on proof of general societywide discrimination; and (2) its remedy was "narrowly tailored" to the needs of the situation.

Then, in *Adarand Constructors v. Pena,* a landmark 1995 decision, the Court struck down a federal highway program that extended bidding preferences to "disadvantaged" contractors.[59] The suit was brought by Randy Pech, a white contractor whose low bid on a Colorado guardrail project was rejected in favor of the bid of a minority firm. The Court ruled that the government's preference program denied Pech his right to equal protection under the law as guaranteed by the Fifth Amendment to the federal Constitution. [For a "Timeline of Affirmative Action Milestones," see **www.infoplease.com/spot/affirmativetimeline1.html**].

Affirmative Action in Employment: Where Are We?

The Supreme Court's 2009 decision in *Ricci v. DeStefano*[60] discussed and applied both arms of Title VII, disparate treatment and disparate impact. The City of New Haven, Connecticut, went to great lengths to develop a test, which would not have a disparate impact in the city's promotion decisions for its firefighters. Nevertheless, using the test results, none of the nine Blacks who sat for the exam would have been promoted. The city decided not to certify the results of the exam and was sued for disparate treatment by the individuals who were eligible for promotion based on the exam. The Supreme Court held for the plaintiffs, in essence, holding that disparate treatment was the greater ill; employers cannot cause disparate treatment out of a fear of being accused of disparate impact.

Quotas justified only by "societal discrimination" are unconstitutional.

Confusion remains after *Ricci,* particularly surrounding the differences in analysis between cases based on the Constitution and those brought under Title VII.[61] What has been made clear, however, is that both quotas and affirmative action justified only broadly by "societal discrimination" are unconstitutional.

A lawful affirmative action plan in employment cases will apparently be evaluated, in most cases, using the following considerations:

- The plan must address a compelling interest, such as remedying past or present discrimination or correcting the underutilization of women and minorities.
- The plan must be temporary.
- The plan must be narrowly tailored to minimize layoffs and other burdens.

The Supreme Court has noted that employers may make "affirmative efforts" to encourage equal opportunity in promotions.[62] If they ensure that screening procedures are not discriminatory or irrelevant,[63] employers may undertake diversity initiatives designed to create an inclusive workplace environment that supports fairness, respect, and equal opportunity.[64] [For information on diversity programs at U.S. companies, see Diversity Inc. at **http://diversityinc.com.**] [For the CEO Action for Diversity and Inclusion, see **www.ceoaction.com** with its "Check Your Blindspots Unconcious Bias Tour" at **www.ceoaction.com/tour**]. [For criticisms of affirmative action, see the Center for Equal Opportunity at **www.ceousa.org**].

Part Five—Additional Discrimination Topics

Religious Discrimination

LO 13-11
Explain the concept of reasonable accommodation as applied to religious- and disability-based discrimination claims.

Kimberly Cloutier was employed as a cashier at Costco in West Springfield, Massachusetts. The store revised its dress code to prohibit all facial jewelry other than earrings. Cloutier, a member of the "Church of Body Modification," was advised to remove her facial piercings. She declined to do, so saying that her piercings were part of her religion. The church's approximately 1,000 members engaged in such practices as piercing, tattooing, branding, and cutting. Eventually, Cloutier was fired. She sued Costco claiming she was a victim of religious discrimination in violation of Title VII of the Civil Rights Act of 1964. Costco, however, prevailed when the federal First Circuit Court of Appeals ruled that excusing Cloutier from the dress code would be an undue hardship for Costco because the company had a legitimate interest in presenting to the public a workforce that was reasonably professional in appearance.[65]

The Law

Title VII's protections against religious discrimination and harassment in the workplace include the employer's duty to reasonably accommodate employees' religious beliefs and practices. As was evident in Cloutier's conflict with Costco, reasonably accommodating religious practices often poses challenges for employers. Consider, for example, the employer who must balance an employee's religious practice of proselytizing or discussing religion in the workplace against other employees' right to be free from religious harassment.

A member of the "Church of Body Modification."

Employers need not accommodate an employee's religious practice or belief if it creates an "undue hardship" (an unreasonable burden) on the workplace. The leading religious discrimination case is *Trans World Airlines, Inc. v. Hardison,*[66] in which the plaintiff, who celebrated his religion on Saturdays, was unable to take that day off from his work in a parts warehouse. Efforts to swap shifts or change jobs were unsuccessful. The company rejected Hardison's request for a four-day week because it would have required the use of another employee at premium pay. The Supreme Court's ruling in the case reduced the employer's duty to a very modest standard: "To require TWA to bear more than a *de minimis* cost in order to give Hardison Saturdays off is an *undue hardship.*"[67] Saturdays off for Hardison would have imposed extra costs on TWA. Lower courts have differed considerably on what constitutes a *de minimis* cost versus an undue hardship. The employer suffered neither, as an Ohio court ruled, when an employee, a Seventh Day Adventist, was fired for refusing to work from sundown Friday to sundown Saturday. The employee could have been moved to an earlier shift at no cost to the employer.[68]

An employer might be unsure whether employees who request accommodation are sincere in their religious beliefs or merely seeking an advantage, such as a longer break or trying to avoid attendance or grooming policies. The EEOC defines religion broadly as "moral and ethical beliefs of what is right and wrong which are sincerely held with the strength of religious views."[69] This broad view of religious beliefs arguably indicates that employers should err in favor of moving forward to the central issue: Is an accommodation reasonable or would it create an undue hardship?

Questions

1. What challenges would you face as a manager if one of your subordinates, as an expression of her religious beliefs, wore to work an antiabortion button displaying a picture of a fetus? How would you address these challenges? See *Wilson v. U.S. West Communications,* 58 F.3d 1337 (8th Cir. 1995).
2. Yisrael worked as a dump truck driver for a North Carolina company providing paving, grading, and utility services for transportation projects. As a member of the Hebrew Israelite faith, Yisrael observed Sabbath on Saturday. After refusing to work three different Saturdays, he was terminated. The EEOC filed a lawsuit on behalf of Yisrael. What further information would you need to decide this case? Explain. See *EEOC v. Thompson Contracting, Grading, Paving, & Utilities, Inc.,* 499 F. App'x 275 (4th Cir. 2012) (unpublished opinion).
3. An Oklahoma lighting company, Voss, advertised a vacancy for an "operations supervisor" at its Tulsa location through the website of a Tulsa-area church attended by a Voss supervisor. Wolfe, who had prior operations management experience, learned about the vacancy and applied for the position, although he did not himself attend the church. Most of the job interview concerned Wolfe's religious activities and beliefs and whether he "would have a problem" coming into work early to attend Bible study before clocking in. The branch manager seemed hesitant to accept Wolf's answers as truthful. At the time Wolfe was interviewed, Voss had no viable candidates for the position being filled. Wolfe was not offered the job, and after continuing its search, the company hired an individual whose religious ideology matched that of the company's leadership. Wolfe filed an EEOC religious discrimination complaint. Decide. Explain. See Press Release, "Voss Lighting to Pay $82,500 to Settle Religious Discrimination Lawsuit," *U.S. Equal Employment Opportunity Commission,* March 19, 2013 [**www.eeoc.gov**].

The Americans with Disabilities Act

Artificial Intelligence (AI) and the ADA

The EEOC has addressed employers' use of Artificial Intelligence (AI) in hiring workers, monitoring performance, determining pay or promotions, and establishing the terms and conditions of employment. Employers may view AI as a way to save time and effort, increase objectivity, or decrease bias. However, the use of these tools may disadvantage job applicants and employees with disabilities.

As you study this chapter, consider these ways that an employer's use of algorithmic decision-making tools could violate the ADA.

- Not providing a **"reasonable accommodation"** that is necessary for a job applicant or employee to be rated fairly and accurately.
- Relying on an algorithmic decision-making tool that intentionally or unintentionally **"screens out"** an individual with a disability, even though that individual is able to do the job with a reasonable accommodation.
- Using an algorithmic decision-making tool that poses "disability-related inquiries" or seeks information that qualifies as a "medical examination" before giving the candidate a conditional offer of employment.

Source: EEOC, "The ADA and the Use of Software, Algorithms, and Artificial Intelligence to Assess Job Applicants and Employees," *EEOC Guidance* (May 12, 2022) [**https://www.eeoc.gov/**].

As a child, Edward Carmona was diagnosed with psoriasis, a skin disease causing intermittent but treatable inflammations. As an adult working as a flight attendant for Southwest Airlines, Carmona was diagnosed with psoriatic arthritis, which causes painful joint swelling and stiffness during attacks of psoriasis. Although medication eased some of his discomfort, these attacks left Carmona unable to walk without great pain for one-half to one-third of each month. After his intermittent leave under Family and Medical Leave Act (see Chapter 12) expired, he was fired for excessive absenteeism. Carmona brought a disability discrimination claim against Southwest Airlines under the Americans with Disabilities Act (ADA), winning a jury verdict that was vacated by the trial court. The Fifth Circuit Court of Appeals overturned the decision to vacate. In light of Southwest Airlines' lenient attendance policy, the jury could have reasonably concluded that nondisabled flight attendants with similar absenteeism were not being fired, and that Carmona's supervisors were annoyed by his disability-related absences.[70]

This situation illustrates the general purpose of the ADA, which seeks to remove barriers to a full, productive life for individuals with disabilities. The ADA forbids discrimination in employment, public accommodations, public services, transportation, and telecommunications for the disabled. Businesses with fewer than 15 employees are exempt from the employment portions of the ADA. The Rehabilitation Act of 1973 protects public-sector workers with disabilities from employment discrimination.

The ADA prohibits employment discrimination against a qualified individual who: (1) has a physical or mental impairment that substantially limits one or more major life activities, (2) has a record of such an impairment, or (3) is regarded as having such an impairment.

In a series of decisions, the U.S. Supreme Court narrowed the scope of the ADA, prompting a leading disabilities rights advocate to call the ADA "the incredible shrinking law."[71] In response, the Americans with Disabilities Amendments Act (ADAAA) was passed by Congress and signed into law by President George W. Bush in 2008 to overturn those decisions and establish broader definitional guidelines under the ADA.

Defining Disabilities

As amended by the ADAAA, the ADA emphasizes that "disability" should be defined broadly in offering protection from employment discrimination. Examples of disabilities include epilepsy, hypertension, asthma, diabetes, major depressive disorder, bipolar disorder, and schizophrenia. A nonexhaustive list of major life activities specified by the ADAAA includes eating, sleeping, standing, lifting, bending, concentrating, thinking, communicating, and all major bodily functions, including reproduction.

Alcoholism, drug addiction, and AIDS are disabilities under the ADA. However, the ADA excludes from its protection job applicants and employees who currently use illegal drugs. Employees with past drug or alcohol problems are protected by the ADA, as are employees with current alcohol problems who are able to perform the essential functions of the job. An employer may lawfully take an adverse employment action on the basis of, for example, a drug test showing the use of illegal controlled substances or alcohol-induced unprofessional conduct at work. Those who are rehabilitated or are currently in rehabilitation are protected from disabilities discrimination. In sum, the ADA treats alcoholism and drug addiction as medical conditions and protects those who are overcoming these impairments.

Taking medication or using a prosthetic device to overcome an impairment does not remove an individual from the ADA's protection. Episodic conditions such as epilepsy, if it creates a "substantial limitation" on an individual's major life activities, ordinarily would be covered by the ADA. In addition, an impairment in remission, such as cancer, is covered if it would substantially limit a major life activity when active.[72]

"Regarded as Having" a Disability

An individual who does not have a disability may still be protected under the ADA. If an employer incorrectly assumes that an applicant or employee has a disability, and then takes discriminatory action on that basis, the employer has violated the ADA. For example, an employer who denies an employee a promotion to a managerial position requiring extensive client contact is likely to have violated the ADA if the promotion was denied because of the employer's mistaken belief that the employee is a recovering alcoholic who would not be able to manage client meetings where alcohol is frequently served.

Accommodating Individuals with Disabilities

An employer may not discriminate in hiring or employment against a qualified person with a disability. A qualified person is one who can perform the essential job functions with or without reasonable accommodation. The ADA requires employers to make reasonable accommodations for disabled employees and applicants. Reasonable accommodations might include structural changes in the workplace, job reassignment, job restructuring, or new equipment. Employers are not required to provide an accommodation that would create an undue hardship. For example, the employer need not create a new position to reassign an employee who can no longer perform the essential job functions, but rather should place the employee in an appropriate vacant job. The employer should engage in an interactive dialogue with the employee to explore possible reasonable accommodations. [For EEOC advice about small employers and reasonable accommodation, see **www.eeoc.gov/facts/accommodation.html**].

"Getting to Work" with Reasonable Accommodation

Jeanette Colwell was hired as a part-time retail clerk at a Rite Aid store in Old Forge, Pennsylvania. She worked various shifts, including 5 PM to 9 PM, and earned supervisors' recognition for good performance. A few months after being hired, Colwell was diagnosed with "retinal vein occlusion and glaucoma in her left eye." Eventually, she became blind in that eye. Colwell informed her supervisor, Susan Chapman, that her partial blindness made it dangerous and difficult for her to drive to work at night. Bus service stopped at 6 PM, and there were no taxis serving the area where the store was located. She asked to be assigned to day shifts so that she would be able to get to work. Chapman refused the request because it "wouldn't be fair" to other workers and continued to schedule Colwell for a mix of day and evening shifts. Colwell later sent Chapman a doctor's note recommending that Colwell not drive at night, but Chapman was still unwilling to assign Colwell only to day shifts. Colwell resigned and brought an ADA claim against Rite Aid. The trial court ruled that Rite Aid had no duty to accommodate Colwell because she was able to perform all her work duties at the store. Colwell appealed.

Questions

1. Is Colwell an "individual with a disability" under the ADA? Explain.
2. How should Chapman have responded to Colwell's request? Explain.
3. Decide Colwell's claim. Explain.

Source: *Colwell v. Rite Aid*, 602 F.3d 495 (3d Cir. 2010).

The ADA in Practice

In 2019, the unemployment rate for persons with disabilities was about twice as high as the rate for those without a disability.[73] Some employers may hesitate to hire workers with disabilities out of misconceptions and fear of added costs for accommodations.[74] However, in recent years, some organizations have made efforts to increase the presence of individuals with disabilities in the professional workforce. For example, the National Business & Disability Council runs a summer internship program, "Emerging Leaders," offering business placements for college and graduate students with disabilities.[75] [For more information on the Emerging Leaders program, see **www.emerging-leaders.com**].

Tax credits to hire and provide access to individuals with disabilities, as well as tax deductions to remove architectural barriers to make its facilities more accessible, also provide incentives and remove impediments for employers to hire and retain employees with disabilities.[76]

Rosa's Law: Changing the Words

Signed by President Obama in 2010, Rosa's Law, named after Rosa Marcellino, a nine-year-old with Down Syndrome, changed the language in all federal health, education, and labor laws to remove the phrase "mentally retarded" and replace it with "intellectual disability." President Obama quoted Rosa's brother Nick as saying: "What you call people is how you treat them. If we change the words, maybe it will be the start of a new attitude towards people with disabilities."

Sources: Rosa's Law, Pub. L. No. 111-256, 124 Stat. 2643 (2010) [**www.govtrack.us**]; and President Barack Obama, "Remarks by the President at the Signing of the 21st Century Communications and Video Accessibility Act of 2010," *White House Press Office,* October 8, 2010 [**www.whitehouse.gov**].

Questions

1. Core, a social services worker, had difficulty breathing at work when she was exposed to the perfume Japanese Cherry Blossom worn by coworkers; on one occasion, she sought emergency medical treatment. Core's coworkers allegedly mocked her condition on their Facebook pages. Her employer rejected several of her accommodation requests, including a proposed fragrance-free workplace policy. The employer sent an email message to employees asking that they not enter into Core's cubicle, but instead communicate with her by telephone and email. The employer also asked Core to hold office discussions in better-ventilated areas. After exhausting her FMLA leave entitlements (see Chapter 12), Core was placed on inactive pay status. The employer offered to permit Core to return to work and make accommodations, such as instructing staff to refrain from wearing the perfume and allowing her to take breaks to get fresh air. Core rejected these offers and was effectively terminated. Core brought an ADA claim against her former employer. Decide. Explain. *Core v. Champaign County Board of Commissioners,* 2012 U.S. Dist. LEXIS 149120 (S.D. Ohio October 17, 2012).
2. Foley was terminated from his job as a financial advisor with Morgan Stanley after he removed and took off-premises the hard drive from his office computer without authorization and was not truthful about his actions for several days. Morgan Stanley's employment policies and procedures forbid the removal of its "trade secrets," defined as including computer software or hardware used in computers or word processors. Foley admitted he was terminated because of his misconduct, but claimed his actions were caused by a manic episode of bipolar disorder. Therefore, Foley argued, his termination was "because of" his disability. Decide. Explain. See *Foley v. Morgan Stanley Smith Barney,* 2013 U.S. Dist. LEXIS 28873 (S.D. Fla. March 4, 2013).

Genetic Testing

Title I of the Genetic Information Nondiscrimination Act (GINA) prohibits employers from discriminating because of genetic information. With few exceptions, employers are not allowed to gather genetic information regarding an employee or an employee's family members.[77] In the case that follows, a federal district court determines the meaning of "genetic information" as it relates to genetic testing.

LEGAL BRIEFCASE

Lowe v. Atlas Logistics Group Retail Servs. Atlanta, LLC

102 F.Supp. 3d 1360 (N.D.Ga. 2015)

Opinion

U.S. District Judge Totenberg

Atlas Logistics Group Retail Services (Atlanta), LLC ("Atlas") operates warehouses for the storage of products sold at a variety of grocery stores. So one could imagine Atlas's frustration when a mystery employee began habitually defecating in one of its warehouses. To solve the mystery of the devious defecator, Atlas requested some of its employees, including Jack Lowe and Dennis Reynolds, to submit to a cheek swab. The cheek cell samples were then sent to a lab where a technician compared the cheek cell DNA to DNA from the offending fecal matter. Lowe and Dennis were not a match. With the culprit apparently still on the loose, Lowe and Dennis filed suit under the Genetic Information Nondiscrimination Act ("GINA"), which generally prohibits employers from requesting genetic information from its employees.

Atlas attempted to remedy the defecation issue by asking its Loss Prevention Manager, Don Hill, to conduct an investigation. Mr. Hill began his investigation by comparing employee work schedules to the timing and location of the defecation episodes in order to create a list of employees who may have been responsible. Plaintiffs Jack Lowe and Dennis Reynolds were two of the employees Mr. Hill identified.

Once Mr. Hill created the list of potential suspects, he hired Speckin Forensic Laboratories ("Speckin Labs") to assist in the investigation. Hill retained Speckin Labs to perform a comparison of buccal swab samples to the fecal matter collected in the Warehouse. Atlas requested that the results of the comparison be transmitted to Atlas.

In order to perform the comparison, Speckin Labs suggested using Short Tandem Repeat analysis ("STR analysis"). STR analysis compares samples by analyzing "genetic spacers" at various sites. "Genetic spacers" are the space between an individual's genes and vary drastically from person to person. STR analysis can be used to compare DNA from one sample to another for identification purposes. STR analysis cannot, however, determine an individual's propensity for disease or disorder.

Speckin Labs sent Dr. Julie Howestine to the Warehouse in October 2012 to collect buccal swab samples from Lowe and Reynolds. . . . Dr. Howestine requested that GenQuest use the PowerPlex 21 System ("PowerPlex 21") to perform the STR analysis of Lowe's and Reynolds's buccal swab samples. The PowerPlex 21 measures the length of spaces between two genes at twenty chromosome spaces to compare various DNA samples. The PowerPlex 21 produces an electropherogram, which graphs the PowerPlex 21's analysis of DNA samples.

After performing the PowerPlex 21 analysis on Lowe's and Reynolds's DNA samples, GenQuest sent Dr. Howenstine the electropherogram with the PowerPlex 21 analysis' findings. Using the data provided in the electropherogram, Dr. Howenstine compared the DNA samples of Lowe and Reynolds to the DNA of the fecal matter and determined that neither Lowe nor Reynolds were the culprits

. . . Lowe and Reynolds filed charges of discrimination with the Equal Employment Opportunity Commission ("EEOC"). The Plaintiffs alleged that Atlas violated the Genetic Information Nondiscrimination Act. ("GINA") because Atlas illegally requested and required them to provide their genetic information and illegally disclosed their genetic information. . . .

Analysis

According to Plaintiffs Jack Lowe and Dennis Reynolds, the undisputed facts show that Atlas requested information about Speckin Labs's comparison of Lowe's and Reynolds's DNA to the fecal sample. These facts, Plaintiffs argue, demonstrate that Atlas violated [GINA], which makes it "an unlawful employment practice for an employer to request, require, or purchase genetic information with respect to an employee." . . .

Atlas responds and argues in its Motion for Summary Judgment that the information the company requested concerning Lowe's and Reynolds's DNA analysis does not constitute "genetic information" as defined in GINA. According to Defendant's interpretation of GINA, "genetic information" refers only to information related to an individual's propensity for disease. . . . The issue before the Court, therefore, is whether the term "genetic information" as used in GINA encompasses the information Atlas requested in this case.

A. The Unambiguous Statutory Language of GINA

The Court begins its analysis with the language of GINA. GINA makes it "an unlawful employment practice for an employer to request, require, or purchase genetic information with respect to an employee. . . .

GINA defines genetic information as "with respect to any individual, information about (i) such individual's genetic tests, (ii) the genetic tests of family members of such individual, and (iii) the manifestation of a disease or disorder in family members of such individual." Parts (ii) and (iii) do not apply to Lowe and Reynolds's claims, as the PowerPlex 21 analysis was not performed on DNA of their family members. Therefore, the DNA analysis would only qualify as "genetic information" under GINA if the analysis qualifies as a "genetic test."

"Genetic test" is also defined in GINA. The statute defines "genetic test" as "an analysis of human DNA, RNA, chromosomes, proteins, or metabolites, that detects genotypes, mutations, or chromosomal changes." . . .

If all the Court considers is the language of GINA, the undisputed evidence in the record establishes that the DNA analysis at issue here clearly falls within the definition of "genetic test." The parties agree that Dr. Howenstine conducted an "analysis" of Lowe's and Reynolds's DNA. And the undisputed evidence in the record shows that this analysis at a minimum detects genotypes and mutations. Because the parties agree that Atlas requested a comparison of Lowe's and Reynolds's DNA to the fecal DNA found in the warehouse, Atlas's request and course of action appear to constitute a violation of [GINA]'s prohibition against requesting genetic information from employees.

Defendant argues that this straightforward but broad interpretation of GINA is erroneous. Defendant urges the Court to interpret the "genetic test" language of GINA to exclude analyses of DNA, RNA, chromosomes, proteins, or metabolites if such analyses do not reveal an individual's propensity for disease. This proposed definition of "genetic tests"—a definition which limits genetic tests to those related to one's propensity for disease—renders other language in GINA superfluous, and should thus be rejected.

B. Evidence of Legislative Intent

Despite the plain, unambiguous language of GINA providing a broad definition of "genetic information," which covers the information Atlas requested in this case, Atlas urges the Court to adopt its narrow definition. It is true that "in rare and exceptional circumstances [a court] may decline to follow the plain meaning of a statute because overwhelming extrinsic evidence demonstrates a legislative intent contrary to the text's plain meaning. This is not such an exceptional case.

Atlas . . . cherry-picks statements made during the legislative process to support its proposition that the term "genetic test" was meant to encompass a narrower set of tests which detect one's propensity for disease. . . .

The Congressional Findings and legislative history Atlas relies upon are not remotely sufficient to justify departing from the plain meaning of the statute's text. Accordingly, the Court applies the plain terms of the statute to find that, based on this record, Atlas violated GINA when it requested the results of the PowerPlex 21 test.

C. EEOC Regulation

As the Court concludes that the statute unambiguously covers the conduct at issue in this case, its analysis is complete. Nonetheless, because so few courts have had the occasion to address GINA, the Court briefly addresses Atlas's argument that an EEOC regulation, promulgated under GINA . . . , weighs in favor its interpretation. Atlas argues, "Assuming, *arguendo,* that GINA's definition of 'genetic information' or 'genetic tests' is ambiguous, the Court should defer to the EEOC's interpretation of GINA as set forth in its regulations, which supports an order for summary judgment in Defendant's favor."

Although the EEOC's regulations define "genetic test" with exactly the same language as the statute, the regulation provide[s] a list of examples, and Atlas attempts to capitalize on this list to support its argument.

Atlas correctly points out that tests like the PowerPlex 21 analysis are absent from the list of "genetic tests" identified by the EEOC. Thus, according to Atlas, the PowerPlex21 is not the type of test contemplated by the term "genetic test."

The Court rejects Atlas's argument for three reasons. First, as noted in the regulation, this list is not meant to be exhaustive. Thus, PowerPlex 21's absence from the list is not, in itself, instructive. Second, two of the examples in the EEOC Regulation, "DNA testing to detect genetic markers that are associated with information about ancestry" and "DNA testing that reveals family relationships, such as paternity," do not determine an individual's propensity for disease. If the Court were to apply Atlas's narrow definition of "genetic tests," these two examples would go beyond the scope of the statute. Finally, the EEOC regulations identify tests and procedures which are *not* genetic tests under GINA. None of those tests resemble the PowerPlex 21 analysis or support Defendant's argument. For these reasons, the Court is unpersuaded that the EEOC's list of examples weighs in favor of Atlas's interpretation.

The Court finds Atlas's remaining arguments unpersuasive. The plain language of the statute provides that employers may not "request . . . genetic information with respect to an employee." And as GINA broadly defines it, "genetic information" includes information about an individual's "genetic tests," such as the PowerPlex test of Lowe's and Reynolds's DNA here. Thus, Atlas's request for the PowerPlex 21 results is a violation of GINA.

Conclusion

For the reasons discussed above, the Court finds Atlas liable under [GINA] and grants Plaintiffs Jack Lowe and Dennis Reynolds Partial Motion for Summary Judgment as to liability. The Court denies Defendant Atlas Logistics Group Retail Services (Atlanta), LLC Motion for Summary Judgment as to all claims.

Questions

1. Why did the court determine that the defendant employer, Atlas, had violated GINA?
2. Why did the court disagree with the definition of "genetic information" offered by Atlas?
3. What other measures could Atlas have used in its investigation? Explain.
4. If an employer asks its employees if any of their family members have been either diagnosed with COVID-19 or have tested positive for the coronavirus, would that violate GINA? Explain.[78]

Age Discrimination

Can a clothing store featuring styles designed for the college market lawfully prefer youthful salespersons? May a marketing firm reject older applicants in an effort to bring "new blood" into its workforce? While these questions are not definitively resolved, employers taking such actions might face liability for age discrimination.

ADEA Claims

The Age Discrimination in Employment Act (ADEA) protects those 40 years and older from employment discrimination based on their age. Disparate treatment and harassment claims may be brought under the ADEA, and a 2005 U.S. Supreme Court decision extended ADEA protection to disparate impact claims as well.[79]

In *Gross v. FBL,*[80] the U.S. Supreme Court made it more difficult to win an ADEA disparate treatment claim against a private-sector employer. Jack Gross had worked for FBL for over 30 years when, at age 54, he was reassigned from claims administration director to coordinator, while his former duties were transferred to a younger worker whom he had supervised. Gross filed an ADEA claim against FBL claiming the demotion violated the ADEA, and he won a jury verdict after showing that his age played a role in FBL's decision. FBL appealed. The U.S. Supreme Court held that an ADEA disparate treatment claim requires the plaintiff to show that age was not just one factor, but the deciding or "but-for" factor in the employer's decision. The proposed Protecting Older Workers Against Discrimination Act, which would have reversed *Gross,* was passed in the House of Representatives in January 2020 and referred to a Senate committee the following day. At the time of this writing, no action has as yet been taken in the Senate.

Defenses

An employer may defend against an age discrimination claim by showing that the termination was based on a legitimate, nondiscriminatory reason (such as poor performance) or that age is a bona fide occupational qualification (BFOQ). For example, if there is no test available to predict when a commercial airline pilot over 60 years of age might experience a medical emergency that could jeopardize aviation safety, then being under 60 years of age is arguably a BFOQ for that job.[81] The ADEA also provides that an employer can defeat an age discrimination claim by demonstrating that a "reasonable factor other than age" (like poor attendance) was the actual reason for terminating or otherwise disfavoring an older worker. In **2008,** the U.S. Supreme Court held that an employer using this defense in a disparate impact case carries the burden of proving a "reasonable factor other than age."[82]

OK, Boomer

The phrase, "OK, Boomer" typically is used to note a generational difference between the attitudes or experiences of those born between 1945 to 1964, and those of a younger generation. In its 2020 opinion, *Babb v. Wilkie,* the U.S. Supreme Court held that "but for" causation was not needed to prove a federal employee's age discrimination claim under the ADEA's federal sector provision, although it can be used in determining the appropriate remedy. In oral arguments, Justice Roberts asked Babb's attorney if age discrimination is shown if a younger hiring official says, in a weeks-long hiring process, "OK, Boomer" once to an older applicant.

Question

How would you answer Justice Roberts' question? Explain.

Sources: *Babb v. Wilkie,* 140 S.Ct. 1168 (2020); Lisa Nagele-Piazza, "Beware of Workplace Age Discrimination Claims Stemming from 'OK, Boomer'," *SHRM,* November 20, 2019 **[www.shrm.org]**; and Nina Totenberg, "Chief Justice Roberts: 'Is "OK, Boomer" Evidence of Age Discrimination?'," *National Public Radio,* January 15, 2020 **[www.npr.org]**.

Questions

1. Should the ADEA protect against age discrimination, regardless of age? Explain. See Dana Mattioli, "With Jobs Scarce, Age Becomes an Issue," *The Wall Street Journal,* May 19, 2009 **[www.wsj.com]**.
2. Mary, 61 years old, worked as a leasing consultant for a realty company for over two years before she was fired. The primary duty of a leasing consultant is to rent apartments. The company used phone and video evaluations to assess employees' performance. During her employment, Mary's scores allegedly were, with one exception, consistently below expectations. Allegedly, she violated company policies by showing an apartment without getting the prospective tenant's proof of identification, holding an apartment without a deposit, and showing an apartment that was not to be shown. She also allegedly had been warned and placed on probation, Mary claimed that during the

termination meeting, her supervisor made age-related comments, as she had on several prior occasions. Mary sued her former employer for discrimination under the ADEA. Assuming all of the alleged facts are true, decide the case. Explain. See *Marsh v. Associated Estates Realty Corp.,* 521 F. App'x 460 (6th Cir. 2013) (unpublished opinion).

3. The Insurance Company of North America (ICNA) sought to hire a "loss control representative." The ad called for a B.S. degree, two years of experience, and other qualities. The plaintiff, who had 30 years of loss control experience, applied for the job but was not interviewed. ICNA hired a 28-year-old woman with no loss control experience. The plaintiff sued claiming age discrimination. ICNA said the plaintiff was overqualified.
   a. Explain both the plaintiff's and defendant's arguments.
   b. Decide the case. Explain. See *EEOC v. Insurance Co. of North America,* 49 F.3d 1418 (9th Cir. 1995).

Research Exercise

At this writing, the Healthy Workplace bill, which addresses workplace bullying, has been introduced in a number of state legislatures. Using the Healthy Workplace Campaign's web page [**https://healthyworkplacebill.org/**], answer the following questions:

1. How is workplace bullying defined?
2. What is the argument supporting legislation addressing workplace bullying?
3. How is the Healthy Workplace bill different from antidiscrimination protections?
4. What arguments might be raised against the Healthy Workplace bill?

Chapter Questions

1. In a video that went viral, a white woman in Central Park's The Ramble area was shown telling a Black man, who had asked her to put her dog on a leash as was required by law, that she was going to call the police and report that a Black man was threatening her life. The man continued to video her as she approached him, asking her to stay away. She proceeded to make that call to the police, acting hysterical. After an internal investigation, the woman's employer, Franklin Templeton, fired her from her job as a portfolio manager. The former employee filed a sex discrimination claim against her former employer, alleging that she was being held to a double standard at her job because three male staffers were not fired following allegations of sexual harassment and insider trading, as well as a domestic violence conviction. What might be the employer's defense? Explain. See: Ayana Archie, "The woman who called 911 on a Black bird watch wasn't wrongfully fired, judge rules," *NPR* (September 23, 2022). [**https://www.npr.org/**] Jenni Fink, "Amy Cooper, White Woman who Called Cops on a Black Man in Central Park, Fired from Job by Franklin Templeton," *Newsweek,* May 26, 2020 [**www.newsweek.com**]; and Ted Andersen, "Franklin Templeton fires Portfolio Manager over Fallout from Viral Video," *The Business Journals,* May 27, 2020 [**www.bizjournals.com**].
2. The EEOC filed a class action against Lawry's Restaurants, including Lawry's The Prime Rib, Five Crowns, and The Tam O'Shanter Inn, on behalf of all male applicants

for server positions who were systematically rejected because of their gender. Since 1938, Lawry's had hired only females as servers and did not update their policy after the passage of Title VII. Servers' uniforms were antiquated women's costumes. What might Lawry's defense be? Will this defense be successful? Explain. See Equal Employment Opportunity Commission, "Lawry's to Pay $1 Billion for Sex Bias Against Men in Hiring," *Press Release,* November 2, 2009 [**www.eeoc.gov**].

3. Emma, a Chinese American, applied for an available server position in a Mexican restaurant and was rejected. She suspected it was because of her national origin. What might the Mexican restaurant say in defense of a national origin discrimination complaint made by Emma? Will this defense be successful? Explain. See *EEOC Compliance Manual,* Section 13: National Origin, 2002 [**www.eeoc.gov**].
4. Reeves worked as a transportation sales representative at a shipping company. She was the only woman working on the sales floor, an open area structured into a "pod" of cubicles. Six males worked with Reeves. Reeves could often hear the language of her male coworkers as they spoke over the phone or with each other. Reeves could also hear the central office radio located in the "pod" that was used by her coworkers to listen to a crude morning show. On a daily basis at work, Reeves heard vulgar language and discussions of sexual topics, including such derogatory terms as "bitch" and "whore," which her male coworkers used to describe customers. The male branch manager once asked Reeves to speak to "that stupid bitch on line 4." Reeves brought a Title VII sexual harassment claim against her employer. Decide the case. Explain. See *Reeves v. Robinson Worldwide, Inc.,* 594 F.3d 798 (11th Cir. 2010).
5. In *McCormack v. Safeway,* included as a "Legal Briefcase" in this chapter, the plaintiffs brought a retaliation claim along with their sexual harassment claims. Less than a month after reporting the sexual assault, the plaintiffs were both interviewed about McCormack's alleged violation of Safeway's coupon policy. A Safeway loss prevention investigator confronted Stabenchek and McCormack in connection with his investigation. McCormack was suspended pending further investigation. Feeling their honesty was being questioned because of their complaint, plaintiffs resigned. Decide the retaliation claim. Explain. See *McCormack v. Safeway,* 2014 U.S. Dist. LEXIS 17805 (D. Ariz. February 12, 2014).
6. A company runs credit checks on applicants for senior executive and financial positions. Among the "red flags" are bankruptcy filings, delinquent child support payments, and wage garnishments. The EEOC brought a lawsuit alleging that a disproportionate number of African Americans were adversely impacted by this credit check. What would the EEOC need to show to prove its claim, and what evidence would be needed? Explain. See *EEOC v. Kaplan Higher Education Corp.,* 748 F.3d 749 (6th Cir. 2014).
7. Hooters, a restaurant chain with scantily clad female waitresses, maintained an "Image Policy" that required waitresses' hair to be "styled and glamorous," and not appear "bizarre, outrageous or extreme," or be colored "more than two-shades in variance" from a natural color. Farryn Johnson, an African American Hooters waitress, decided to put blond highlights in her hair during the summer. She was told by her Hooters manager to take out the highlights because they were not natural to African American women, while white waitresses were allowed to keep similar hairstyles because some

white women have that color hair naturally. Has Hooters violated Title VII? Decide. Explain. See Joel Landau, "Hooters Ordered to Pay $250,000 to Black Waitress Who Was Told She Couldn't Have Blonde Streaks in Her Hair," *New York Daily News,* April 8, 2015 [**www.nydailynews.com**].

8. Thornton worked as a manager at a Connecticut retail store. In accordance with his religious beliefs, Thornton notified his manager that he could no longer work on Sundays as required by company policy. A Connecticut statute provided that: "No person who states that a particular day of the week is observed as his Sabbath may be required by his employer to work on such day. An employee's refusal to work on his Sabbath shall not constitute grounds for his dismissal." Management offered Thornton the options of transferring to a Massachusetts store where Sunday work was not required or transferring to a lower-paying supervisory job in the Connecticut store. Thornton refused both, and he was transferred to a lower-paying clerical job in the Connecticut store. Thornton claimed a violation of the Connecticut statute. The store argued that the statute violated the Establishment Clause (see Chapter 5) of the First Amendment, which forbids establishing an official state religion and giving preference to one religion over another or over none at all. Ultimately the case reached the U.S. Supreme Court.
   a. Decide. Explain.
   b. Do the religious accommodation provisions of Title VII of the Civil Rights Act violate the Establishment Clause? See *Estate of Thornton v. Caldor, Inc.,* 472 U.S. 703 (1985).
9. Dreves was terminated from her $48,500 job as a general manager of Hudson's retail operation at Burlington International Airport and replaced by Dixon, a male, at a salary of $52,500. Dreves filed an Equal Pay Act lawsuit and moved for summary judgment. In defending against the motion for summary judgment, Hudson argued that the salary difference was based on "other factors other than sex." Specifically, Dixon had to relocate his family from another state and had strong negotiating skills. Did the employer violate the Equal Pay Act? Decide. Explain. *Dreves v. Hudson Group,* 2013 U.S. Dist. LEXIS 82636 (D. Vt. June 12, 2013).
10. Jane Doe was employed by C.A.R.S. Protection Plus for nearly a year when she learned she was pregnant. After amniocentesis revealed severe defects, Doe decided to terminate her pregnancy. Doe then took one week of vacation to recuperate from the procedure. The following week, she was fired for unexcused absences and job abandonment. Doe filed a claim under the Pregnancy Discrimination Act, alleging she was fired because of her choice to undergo a surgical abortion. Decide the case. Explain. See *Doe v. C.A.R.S. Protection Plus,* 527 F.3d 358 (3d Cir. 2008).
11. Michael Cooke, a Black male, worked at Novellus Systems in Silicon Valley where he had to listen on a regular basis to a Vietnamese American coworker playing and rapping aloud to music lyrics that included racial epithets such as the "N-word." Although Cooke complained several times to his supervisors and made it clear that the language was offensive to him, the coworker continued to sing along to offensive lyrics within Cooke's earshot and to use slang including racial epithets. The EEOC, on behalf of Cooke, brought a Title VII claim against Novellus Systems for racial harassment. Decide. See Press Release, "Silicon Valley Manufacturer Novellus . . . Racial Harassment," *U.S. Equal Employment Opportunity Commission,* June 24, 2008 [**www.eeoc.gov**].

12. Victoria Pietras, a female probationary volunteer firefighter of the Farmingville Fire District, had passed the written and medical exams to become a volunteer firefighter. However, she failed a physical agility test requiring her to perform nine tasks such as dragging a water-filled hose weighing approximately 280 pounds for 150 feet in four minutes or less. The time requirement was based on the average time of the mostly male firefighters who participated in a test run. Pietras brought a Title VII sex discrimination claim that the physical test created an unlawful disparate impact against women.
    a. If you were the EEOC investigator, what questions would you have? Explain. See *Pietras v. Farmingville Fire District,* 180 F.3d 468 (2d Cir. 1999).
    b. Should physical agility or fitness tests be gender-normed so that, for example, female FBI trainees can be required to only do a minimum of 14 pushups, while male trainees must complete at least 30 pushups? Explain. See *Bauer v. Lynch,* 561 F.3d 38 (4th Cir. 2016).
13. Matthews, a Black woman, applied for a job as Economic Support Specialist in Waukesha County, Wisconsin. She was not hired. The applicants were separated into four groups based on their prior job experience. Individuals with job experience that were the most directly related to the open position were placed in Group 1, and only individuals in Group 1 were interviewed. The person hired was from that group. Matthews had been placed in Group 4. Matthews brought a Title VII disparate treatment claim alleging she was not hired because of her race. If you were Matthews' attorney, how would you argue Matthews' case? What evidence would you want to present? Explain. See *Matthews v. Waukesha County,* 759 F.3d 821 (7th Cir. 2014).
14. Reeves, who has Down Syndrome, was employed by a supermarket as a bagger for eight years. He received vocational tutoring and individual training from Jewel and a social service agency. Jewel created supervision policies that applied only to Reeves, such as a daily feedback form sent to his parents, his legal guardians, at their request. Reeves was fired after he cursed and insulted a cashier within the earshot of a customer and other employees. Reeves' parents filed an ADA claim on his behalf, alleging that Jewel discriminated against Reeves because of his disability. Decide. Explain. See *Reeves v. Jewel Stores,* 759 F.3d 698 (7th Cir. 2014).

Notes

1. WorkHuman Blog, "The Why Behind Diversity, Equity, and Inclusion Initiatives: Examples, Benefits, Definition, and More," *WorkHuman Blog* (November 4, 2022) [**https://www.workhuman.com/**] citing Susan Caminiti, "Majority of Employees Want to Work for a Company that Values DEI, survey shows," *CNBC* (April 30, 2021) [**https://www.cnbc.com/**.
2. EEOC Press Release, "EEOC Launches Diversity, Equity, and Inclusion Workshop Series," August 4, 2021 [**https://www.eeoc.gov/newsroom/eeoc-launches-diversity-equity-inclusion-dei-workshop- series**].
3. 347 U.S. 483 (1954).
4. A portion of this paragraph is drawn from William P. Murphy, Julius G. Getman, and James E. Jones Jr., *Discrimination in Employment* 4th ed. (Washington, DC: Bureau of National Affairs, 1979), pp. 1–4.
5. *Ledbetter v. Goodyear Tire & Rubber Co.,* 127 S. Ct. 2162 (2007).
6. *EEOC v. Waffle House Inc.,* 534 U.S. 279 (2002).

7. Martha Neil, "Most Job Discrimination Suits Win, at Best, Small Settlements, Study Says," *ABA Journal,* June 9, 2010 [**www.abajournal.com**].
8. Press Release, "ABF Study of Unfairness in Employment Discrimination Lawsuits Published in *Law & Society Review,*" *American Bar Foundation,* May 8, 2012 [**www.americanbarfoundation.org**].
9. *Haynes v. W.C. Caye & Co.,* 52 F.3d 926 (11th Cir. 1995).
10. See *International Brotherhood of Teamsters v. United States,* 97 S. Ct. 1843 (1977); *American Tobacco v. Patterson,* 456 U.S. 63 (1982); and *Firefighters Local Union No. 1784 v. Stotts,* 467 U.S. 561 (1984).
11. Tresa Baldas, "Employment Tests May Fail Legal Exam," *The National Law Journal,* February 18, 2008 [**www.law.com**].
12. *U.S. Equal Employment Opportunity Commission,* Fact Sheet on Employment Tests and Selection Procedures, accessed June 2020 [**www.eeoc.gov**].
13. Janet Dhillon, National Origin and Race Discrimination During COVID-19," [**https://www.eeoc.gov**].
14. Pamela Babcock, "Sample post-Sept. 11 discrimination cases filed with EEOC," *SHRM HR News,* September 1, 2006 [**www.shrm.org**].
15. *U.S. Equal Employment Opportunity Commission,* "Strategic Enforcement Plan: Fiscal Years 2017–2021," 2017 [**www.eeoc.gov**].
16. *U.S. Equal Employment Opportunity Commission,* "Questions and Answers for Employees: Workplace Rights of Employees Who Are, or Are Perceived to Be, Muslim or Middle Eastern," November 2016 [**www.eeoc.gov**].
17. *U.S. Equal Employment Opportunity Commission,* "Enforcement Guidance on National Origin Discrimination," November 18, 2016 [**www.eeoc.gov**].
18. Ibid.
19. Ibid.
20. *Garcia v. Spun Steak Co.,* 998 F.2d 1480 (9th Cir. 1993), *cert. denied,* 114 S. Ct. 2726 (1994).
21. Equal Employment Opportunity Commission, "Exxon Mobil Corporation Sued by EEOC for Race Discrimination," *EEOC Press Release* (March 2, 2023) [**https://www.eeoc.gov/**].
22. Ethan Barron, "Noose drawing, lynching reference left up for months at Tesla's Fremont factory," *The Mercury News* (February 10, 2022) [**https://www.mercurynews.com**]
23. EEOC, "CCC Group to Pay $420,000 to Settle EEOC Racial Harassment Claims", *EEOC Press Release* (August 10, 2021) [**https://www.eeoc.gov/newsroom/ccc-group-pay-420000-settle-eeoc-racial-harassment-lawsuit**].
24. *Tyrrell v. Oaklawn Jockey Club,* 2012 U.S. Dist. LEXIS 157482 (W.D. Ark. 2012).
25. *Boyer-Liberto v. Fontainebleau Corp.,* 786 F.3d 264 (4th Cir. 2015).
26. Bureau of Labor Statistics, "Median earnings for women in 2021 were 83.1% of the median for men," *TED: The Economics Daily,* January 24, 2022 [**www.bls.gov**].
27. Vanessa Furhmans, "What #MeToo Has to Do with the Workplace Gender Gap," *The Wall Street Journal,* October 23, 2018 [**www.wsj.com**].
28. Vanessa Furhmans, "What #MeToo Has to Do with the Workplace Gender Gap," *The Wall Street Journal,* October 23, 2018 [**www.wsj.com**].
29. *Walmart v. Dukes,* 564 U.S. 338 (2011).
30. Jack Taylor, "KPMG Cannot Pursue Gender, Pay Claims as a Class," *Bloomberg Law,* December 3, 2018 [**https://news.bloomberglaw.com**].

31. Impact Fund, "Update: Settlement Approved in the Costco Gender Discrimination Class-Action," accessed June 2020 [**www.impactfund.org**].
32. 590 U.S. 140 S. Ct 1731 (2020).
33. Bostock v. Clayton County, 590 U.S. 140 S. Ct 1731 (2020).
34. Aimee Ortiz, "Aimee Stephens, Plaintiff in Transgender Case, Dies at 59," *The New York Times,* May 12, 2020 [**www.nytimes.com**].
35. "Charge Statistics (Charges Filed with the EEOC) FY 1997–2019," *U.S. Economic Opportunity Employment Commission,* accessed June 2020 [**www.eeoc.gov**].
36. Alix Langone, "#MeToo and Time'sUp Founders Explain the Difference Between the Two Movements – and How They're Alike," *Time,* March 22, 2018 [**https://time.com**].
37. See, generally, *Diaz v. Pan American World Airways Inc.,* 442 F.2d 385 (5th Cir.), *cert. denied,* 404 U.S. 950 (1971).
38. *Chadwick v. Wellpoint Inc.,* 561 F.3d 38 (1st Cir. 2009).
39. *Warren v. Solo Cup,* 516 F.3d 627 (7th Cir. 2008).
40. Rachel Ranosa, "Women in Leadership Roles More Prone to Workplace Harassment," *HRD,* January 17, 2020 [**www.hcamag.com**].
41. *Burlington Industries v. Ellerth,* 524 U.S. 742 (1998) and *Faragher v. Boca Raton,* 524 U.S. 775 (1998).
42. 133 S. Ct. 2434 (2013).
43. *Oncale v. Sundowner Offshore Services,* 523 U.S. 75 (1998).
44. *Holman v. State of Indiana,* 211 F.3d 299 (7th Cir. 2000).
45. Stephen Miller, "Sexual Jokes No Laughing Matter," *Glasgow Herald,* June 7, 2002 [**www.heraldscotland.com**].
46. Gerald L. Maatman Jr., "A Global View of Sexual Harassment," *HR Magazine,* July 2000 [**www.shrm.org**].
47. "Government Laws on Sexual Harassment in Various Countries," *The Economic Times,* August 22, 2010 [**https://economictimes.indiatimes.com**].
48. 555 U.S. 271 (2009).
49. 548 U.S. 53 (2006).
50. 131 S. Ct. 863 (2011).
51. 133 S. Ct. 2517 (2013).
52. Juliana Menasce Horowitz, Anna Brown, and Kiana Cox, "Race in America 2019," *Pew Research Center,* April 9, 2019 [**www.pewsocialtrends.org**].
53. Ibid.
54. Centers for Disease Control and Prevention, "COVID-19 in Racial and Ethnic Minority Groups," 2020 [**www.cdc.gov**]; and Maria Godoy and Daniel Wood, "What Do Coronavirus Racial Disparities Look Like State By State?" *National Public Radio,* May 30, 2020 [**www.npr.org**].
55. Audra D. S. Burch, Weiyi Cai, Gabriel Gianordoli, Morrigan McCarthy, and Jugal K. Patel, "How Black Lives Matter Reached Every Corner of America," *The New York Times,* June 13, 2020 [**www.nytimes.com**].
56. 443 U.S. 193 (1979).
57. 480 U.S. 616 (1987).
58. 488 U.S. 469 (1989).
59. 115 S. Ct. 2097 (1995).

60. 129 S. Ct. 2658 (2009).
61. Charles A. Sullivan, "Circling Back to the Obvious: The Convergence of Traditional and Reverse Discrimination in Title VII Proof," *William and Mary Law Review* 46, December 2004 [**https://scholarship.law.wm.edu**].
62. *Ricci v. DeStefano,* 129 S. Ct. 2658, 2677 (2009).
63. Steven Greenhouse, "Supreme Court Ruling Offers Little Guidance on Hiring," *The New York Times,* June 30, 2009 [**www.nytimes.com**].
64. John Simons, "Workplace Diversity Efforts Get a Reboot," *The Wall Street Journal,* February 15, 2017 [**www.wsj.com**].
65. *Cloutier v. Costco,* 390 F.3d 126 (1st Cir. 2004), *cert. denied,* 545 U.S. 1131 (2005).
66. 423 U.S. 63 (1977).
67. *Trans World Airlines, Inc. v. Hardison,* 423 U.S. 63 (1977).
68. *Franks v. National Lime & Stone Co.,* 740 N.E.2d 694 (Ohio Ct. App. 2000).
69. EEOC Compliance Manual, "Section 12: Religious Discrimination," *U.S. Equal Employment Opportunity Commission,* July 22, 2008 [**www.eeoc.gov**].
70. *Carmona v. Southwest Airlines,* 604 F.3d 848 (5th Cir. 2010).
71. Joan Biskupic, "High Court Raises Bar for ADA," *USA TODAY,* January 9, 2002, p. 3A.
72. *Hoffman v. Carefirst of Fort Wayne Inc.,* 2010 U.S. Dist. LEXIS 107493 (N.D. Ind. 2010).
73. Bureau of Labor Statistics, *Persons with Disabilities: Labor Force Statistics - 2019,* February 26, 2020 [**www.bls.gov**].
74. Sara Murray, "Disabled Face Sharply Higher Jobless Rate," *The Wall Street Journal,* August 26, 2010 [**www.wsj.com**].
75. Suzanne Robitalle, "Support Grows for Disabled Job Seekers," *The Wall Street Journal,* July 22, 2008 [**www.wsj.com**].
76. "Facts About Disability-Related Tax Provisions," *U.S. Equal Employment Opportunity Commission* [**www.eeoc.gov**].
77. Pub. L. No. 110-233, 122 Stat. 881 (2008).
78. Lindsay Colvin Stone, "EEOC Issues New COVID-19 Guidance for Employers," *Sheppard Mullin Labor & Employment Law Blog,* April 2, 2020 [**www.laboremploymentlawblog.com**].
79. *Smith v. City of Jackson,* 544 U.S. 228 (2005).
80. 129 S. Ct. 2343 (2009).
81. Protecting Older Workers Against Discrimination Act, S. 2189, 112th Cong. (2012) [**www.govtrack.us**].
82. *Meacham v. Knolls Atomic Power Laboratory,* 554 U.S. 84 (2008).

Video icon credit: Comstock Images/Alamy Stock Photo

CHAPTER FOURTEEN

Employment Law III: Labor–Management Relations

After completing this chapter, students will be able to fulfill the following learning objectives:

14-1. Discuss both the decline of labor unions and their hopes for renewal.

14-2. Describe the goals of the National Labor Relations Act.

14-3. Identify unfair labor practices by management and unions.

14-4. Explain the role of the National Labor Relations Board in enforcing the NLRA.

14-5. Describe the process of union organizing and identify the related legal issues.

14-6. Explain what constitutes "bargaining in good faith."

14-7. Distinguish between "unfair labor practice strikes" and "economic strikes."

14-8. Compare and contrast "primary picketing" and "secondary picketing/boycotts."

14-9. Discuss employees' rights within or against unions.

14-10. Explain the impact of "right-to-work" laws on union security agreements.

14-11. Identify the unique laws governing public-sector unions.

Introduction

In 2020, the COVID-19 pandemic created serious health risks for grocery store workers, which led to demands for increased protections. Trader Joe's, a grocery store chain, cut hours, closed stores, and offered bonuses for working during the crisis and one week paid sick leave. However, one employee, who made a mask to match his uniform, was told not to wear the mask in front of customers and was sent to the stockroom where he was in close proximity to his unmasked co-workers. He left his shift in fear of his safety. At another store, an employee started a Facebook group for his colleagues to discuss the store's pandemic response and was subsequently fired. Other workers started a petition for "hazard pay," and a union spoke with employees. Trader Joe's managers told employees that the union was trying to take advantage of them and compared union membership with a marriage commitment.[1]

As businesses reopened, temporarily laid-off workers at a Fort Collins, Colorado, tea shop who were called back to work asked the shop's owners to meet with them to discuss workplace safety before reopening; they were permanently let go from their jobs and faced losing their unemployment benefits.[2]

In 2023, workers at the Louisville, Kentucky, Trader Joe's voted to join Trader Joe's United, an independent union also representing Trader Joe's workers in Hadley, Massachusetts, and Minneapolis, Minnesota.[3]

As you study this chapter, consider the role of unions in labor protection, as well as the rights and responsibilities of employees, unions, and management under labor laws.

Overview

Global economic shifts split America's private-sector unions into two groups: one, the old-line manufacturing organizations represented by the United Auto Workers, for example; the other, the service sector organized most notably by the Service Employees International Union, which represents approximately two million nurses, security guards, janitors, and others. Traditional union power in manufacturing has been deeply undercut by the outsourcing of jobs abroad to take advantage of cheaper wages.

The State of the Unions

According to a recent Gallup poll, 64 percent of Americans have a favorable view of labor unions, one of the highest union approval ratings that Gallup has found in the past 50 years.[4] However, in 2022, the union membership rate among wage and salary workers was only 10.1 percent, which, according to the Bureau of Labor Statistics, is the lowest on record. Since 1983, union membership has fallen nearly 50 percent. The unionization rate among public sector workers remains more than five times that of private sector workers.[5] A shift away from traditional unionized industries and mounting global competition, along with union corruption, have played a role in weakening unions and supporters say corporate resistance has impaired unionization, but as discussed later in the chapter, recent organizing efforts among workers in a wide-ranging spectrum of industries have given energy to unionization.

College Athletes

In 2019, a Maryland state legislator proposed a bill to allow college athletes around the state to unionize and collectively bargain on issues of health and safety, as well as compensation, citing the 2018 death of a University of Maryland football player after a conditioning workout and accusations of sexual abuse against NCAA coaches in recent years.

In a 2021 memo, the NLRB's General Counsel updated guidance on the issue of college athletes. The memo concluded that certain collegiate athletes are employees of their schools under the National Labor Relations Act, affording them those statutory rights and protections. These athletes provide a service under the control of the university in return for compensation. The memo also warned that referring to such players as "student-athletes" creates a chilling effect on their NLRA rights, in violation of the NLRA. The NLRB's position was in keeping with the U.S. Supreme Court's 2021 decision in *NCAA v. Alston* which recognized that collegiate sports as a profit-making enterprise.

Questions

1. Do you support the unionization of college athletes? Explain.
2. Do you think student teaching assistants, student janitors, and other student workers should be allowed to unionize? Explain.

Sources: National Labor Relations Board Office of Public Affairs, "NLRB General Counsel Jennifer Abruzzo Issues Memo on Employee Status of Players at Academic Institutions," (September 20, 2021) citing *NCAA v. Alston* 141 S. Ct. 2141 (2021) [**https://www.nlrb.gov/**]; Rick Maese, "Proposed Legislation Would Give Maryland College Athletes the Right to Unionize," *The Washington Post,* February 8, 2019 [**www.washingtonpost.com**].

Part One—History

LO 14-1
Discuss both the decline of labor unions and their hopes for renewal.

As the United States moved from an agrarian to an industrial society in the late 1880s, business competition became fierce. Costs had to be cut. People from rural areas began moving to the city to be near jobs, leaving their safety net of gardens, chickens, and cows. Similarly, immigrants streamed into the big cities. Competition for jobs became heated. Wages fell, and deplorable working conditions were the norm.[6] Some of those immigrants brought with them ideas and experiences in labor conflict and class struggle that would soon contribute to dramatic changes in the American workplace.

A Grim Picture

To say that working conditions for many people at this time were unpleasant or even dismal would be a vast understatement. The term *desperate* better describes the problem. Children were put to work as soon as they were big enough to do a job and then made to work long hours.[7] In fact, small children were employed in coal mines for 10 to 12 hours each day, at a rate of $1 to $3 per week, because they were small enough to fit in the confined spaces.[8] Young women were gathered to work in textile mills under intolerable conditions.[9]

> Children were employed in coal mines because they were small enough to fit in the confined spaces

The following firsthand report from the early 20th century reveals the grim picture:

> When I moved from the North to the South in my search for work, I entered a mill village to work in a cotton mill as a spinner. There I worked 11 hours a day, five and a half days a week, for $7 a week. In a northern mill I had done the same kind of work for $22 a week, and less hours. I worked terribly hard. . . .
>
> The sanitary conditions were ghastly. When I desired a drink of water, I had to dip my cup into a pail of water that had been brought into the mill from a spring in the fields. It tasted horrible to me. Often I saw lint from the cotton in the room floating on top of the lukewarm water. All of the men chewed tobacco, and most of the women used snuff. Little imagination is needed to judge the condition of the water which I had to drink, for working in that close, hot spinning room made me thirsty. Toilet facilities were provided three stories

> down in the basement of the mill in a room without any ventilation. Nowhere was there any running water. . . .
>
> Everything in the village is company owned. The houses look like barns on stilts, and appear to have been thrown together. When I would go inside one of them, I could see outside through the cracks in the walls. The workers do all of their trading at the company store and bank, and use the company school and library for they have no means of leaving the village.[10]

Compare those working-class conditions with the lifestyle of John D. Rockefeller, the great tycoon of the same era. Although Rockefeller was notoriously frugal, his estate at Pocantico Hills, New York, contained

> . . . more than 75 buildings. . . . Within his estate were 75 miles of private roads on which he could take his afternoon drive; private golf links on which he could play his morning game; and anywhere from 1,000 to 1,500 employees, depending on the season.
>
> . . . Rockefeller also owned an estate at Lakewood, [New Jersey] which he occupied in the spring; an estate at Ormond Beach in Florida for his winter use; a townhouse . . . in New York; an estate at Forest Hill, Cleveland which he did not visit; and a house on Euclid Avenue in Cleveland, likewise unused by him.[11]

These circumstances enable us to better understand the sense of injustice felt by many workers. [For a timeline of the labor movement, see **http://75.afscme.org/history**].

Who's the Boss?

Should a fast-food restaurant chain be held liable if one of its franchisees fires workers for trying to unionize? The answer depends on whether the restaurant chain is a "joint employer" of the franchisee's employees. In 2020, the NLRB issued a rule on the meaning of "joint employer." Under the 2020 rule, to be a joint employer, a business such as McDonald's must exert direct control over its franchisee's employees, such as scheduling them and directly determining their pay. At the time, the NLRB stated that it was restoring the definition of "joint employer" used prior to the NLRB's 2015 *Browning-Ferris* decision. *Browning-Ferris* had concluded that a business with "indirect control" over another company's employees is a "joint employer" of that company's workers.

In late 2022, however, the NLRB proposed a rule that would hold a parent company like McDonald's liable even if it only exercised "indirect control" over the franchisee's employees such as requiring the franchisee to use certain software for scheduling.

Question

1. From an ethical perspective, should a business like McDonald's be held accountable for its franchisee's labor practices? Discuss.

Sources: Noam Scheiber, "Rule Would Hold Chains Liable for Franchise Sins," *The New York Times* (p. B4); NLRB Office of Public Affairs, "NLRB Issues Joint-Employer Final Rule," *National Labor Relations Board,* February 25, 2020 [**www.nlrb.gov**]; Morgan Tanafon, "The NLRB's Final Joint-Employer Rule Will Soon Be in Effect," *JDSupra,* April 24, 2020 [**www.jdsupra.com**]; and Opinion, "NLRB Joint Employer Attack," *The Wall Street Journal,* August 28, 2015 [**www.nlrb.gov**].

Organizing Labor

The Knights of Labor, the first major labor organization in the United States, had a large following during the 1870s and 1880s.[12] The order admitted any workers to its ranks, regardless of occupation, gender, or nationality; in fact, the only people excluded from the group were gamblers, bankers, stockbrokers, and liquor dealers.[13] The Knights of Labor dedicated itself to principles of social reform, including the protection of wage and hour laws, improved health care systems, and mandatory education.[14] However, the goals of the Knights of Labor were perhaps too broad and far-reaching to bring workers any relief from their immediate problems. Great philosophical divisions within the Knights of Labor brought about its rapid decline.[15]

Skilled Workers

Samuel Gompers, who founded the American Federation of Labor (AFL), had more practical, attainable goals in mind for his organization. Gompers, a worker in the cigar industry, saw the need to organize workers along craft lines (such as plumbers, electricians, and machinists) so that each craft group could seek higher wages and better working conditions for its own workers, all of whom had the same type of skills and, presumably, shared the same occupational goals.[16] This approach, a national association of local unions directed to workers' pragmatic needs rather than the more politically motivated activities of the Knights of Labor, proved to be a successful formula for union organization.

Laborers

The Congress of Industrial Organizations (CIO) was formed in 1935 in response to the needs of ordinary laborers not working in the skilled trades to which the AFL was devoted. The CIO served assembly line workers and others who often performed repetitive, physically demanding tasks. The AFL and CIO were fierce competitors, but after years of bitter conflict, the two groups united forces in 1955. They function together today as the AFL–CIO. [For the AFL–CIO home page, see **www.aflcio.org**].

Trending: Unionizing across Sectors

In recent years, a trend of labor organizing efforts has swept through restaurants, retailers, and tech companies. An 18-year-old community college student was about to quit her job at a Lansing, Michigan, Chipotle when she joined her coworkers in organizing. The restaurant became the first Chipotle in the United States to unionize, joining the International Brotherhood of Teamsters in 2022. That same year, employees in nearly two dozen Apple stores expressed interest in unionizing; workers at a Towson, Maryland, Apple store became the first to unionize in June 2022. In January 2023, workers in that store also became the first to start collective bargaining with Apple management. In the same month, a group of quality-assurance testers in Microsoft's ZeniMax video game unit formed the company's first U.S. union. Employees at a Google Fiber contractor in Kansas City, Missouri, voted to unionize under the Alphabet Workers Union in 2022. An April 2022 vote to unionize Amazon's Staten Island, New York, warehouse was upheld by the NLRB after Amazon contested the results; however, workers at three other facilities–two in New York state and one in Alabama—voted against unionizing later in 2022. Unionizing efforts at Starbucks are discussed later in this chapter.

Questions

1. What factors may have contributed to the wave of organizing across restaurant, retail, and tech industries in recent years? Explain.
2. Employees of a Moreno Valley, California, Amazon warehouse filed for a union election in October 2022 but found that they did not have enough proof of support for the NLRB to call an election. What factors may have caused Amazon employees' unionizing efforts to stall? Explain.

Sources: Michelle Jokish Polo, "Meet the workers who unionized the first Chipotle in the nation," *Marketplace* (November 14, 2022) [**https://www.marketplace.org/**]; Tripp Mickle and Noam Scheiber, "Apple Workers at a Maryland Store Vote to Unionize, a First in the U.S.," *The New York Times* (June 19, 2022 p. A21); Catherine Thore becke, "Apple's first U.S. labor union reaches new milestone for tech industry," *CNBC* (January 11, 2023) [**https://www.cnn.com/**]; Sarah e. Needleman, "Microsoft Staff to Form Company's First U.S. Union," *The Wall Street Journal* (January 4, 2023 p. B4); Sebastian Herrera, "Amazon New York Union Vote Upheld," *The Wall Street Journal* (September 2, 2022 p. B5); and Sebastian Herrera, "Turnover, Pay at Amazon Help Stall Union Efforts," *The Wall Street Journal* (December 29, 2022 p. B3).

Unions and the Developing Law

Labor Protection

Responding to mounting public pressure, Congress passed the Norris-LaGuardia Act in 1932, making clear that the terminology "restraint of trade," which was the heart of the 1890 Sherman Antitrust Act (see Chapter 10), was not meant to include labor organizations or activities.

From 1932 to 1935, labor tensions continued to mount. The nation was still caught in the Great Depression. Believing that one element essential to economic recovery was stability in the workforce, Congress addressed the labor question with the Wagner Act of 1935. This legislation gave workers for the first time the unequivocal right to organize and engage in concerted activities for their mutual aid and benefit. To protect this right, Congress identified and made illegal a number of unfair labor practices. Through the Wagner Act, Congress also established the National Labor Relations Board, which will be discussed in Part Two.

Management Protection

Unions grew rapidly with the passage of the Wagner Act, and by 1947 Congress decided management might need a little help in coping with ever-growing labor organizations.[17] Congress enacted the Taft-Hartley Act, identifying as unfair labor practices certain activities unions used to exercise economic leverage over employers as part of the collective bargaining process. The Taft-Hartley Act also ensured employers' right to speak out in opposition to union organizing—in effect, protecting their First Amendment right to freedom of speech. Thus, the Taft-Hartley Act signaled a move by the government away from unconditional support for labor toward a balance of rights between labor and management.[18]

Corrupt Union Leaders

In response to the growing evidence that union leaders were benefiting at the expense of the membership, Congress in 1959 enacted the Landrum–Griffin Act, requiring unions to keep records of their funds. It also prohibits unions from lending money except under specified circumstances and procedures, all of which must be reported annually to the government.

Members' Rights

The Landrum–Griffin Act also contains a set of provisions often referred to as the "Bill of Rights" for individual union members. These provisions are designed to protect union members by requiring that union meetings be held, that members be permitted to speak and vote at these meetings, that every employee covered by a collective-bargaining agreement have the right to see a copy of that agreement, and that a union member be informed of the reasons and given a chance for a hearing if the union wishes to suspend or take disciplinary action against that member, unless they are being suspended for nonpayment of dues.[19]

The law has also regulated the manner in which unions represent employees in the collective-bargaining process. Because a union serves as the employees' exclusive bargaining representative, the courts have devised a *duty of fair representation*.[20] To fulfill this duty, a union must represent employees, in both negotiating and enforcing the collective-bargaining agreement, "without hostility or discrimination [and] with complete good faith and honesty [so as to] avoid arbitrary conduct."[21]

Part Two—Labor Legislation Today

Today labor–management relations are governed by the National Labor Relations Act[22] (NLRA), as enforced by the National Labor Relations Board (NLRB). This act includes within it the Wagner Act, the Taft-Hartley Act, and portions of the Landrum-Griffin Act. The remaining provisions of the Landrum–Griffin Act make up the Labor–Management Reporting and Disclosure Act and the Bill of Rights of Members of Labor Organizations.

Right to Organize and Engage in Concerted Activities

The National Labor Relations Act gives employees the right to engage in concerted activity, including strikes and collective bargaining. Section 7 of the NLRA states

LO 14-2
Describe the goals of the National Labor Relations Act.

> Employees shall have the right to self-organization, to form, join, or assist labor organizations, to bargain collectively through representatives of their own choosing, and to engage in other concerted activities for the purpose of collective bargaining or other mutual aid or protection, and shall also have the right to refrain from any and all of such activities except to the extent that such right may be affected by an agreement requiring membership in a labor organization as a condition of employment.

When political issues such as immigration become heated, employees' political advocacy efforts may affect the workplace. Political advocacy, in some circumstances, may be considered a *concerted activity* for "mutual aid or protection" under Section 7. The first question is whether there is a direct connection between the political issue at stake and a "specifically identified employment concern of the participating employees." Even if that direct connection is found, however, the employer may discipline the employees if the political activity, like attending a protest rally, for example, violates "neutrally applied" work rules such as restrictions on leaving work without permission.[23] [For a database of federal and state labor law statutes and regulations, see **http://topics.law.cornell.edu/wex/labor**].

PRACTICING ETHICS Reading Your Rights at Work

Posters from the U.S. Department of Labor (see Chapter 12) and the Equal Employment Opportunity Commission (EEOC—see Chapter 13) informing workers of their rights are familiar sights in the workplace. In 2012, the NLRB issued a Notice Posting Rule requiring most private-sector employers—regardless of whether their workers are unionized—to post a notice advising employees of their rights under the NLRA. However, two federal appellate decisions invalidated this rule, and the NLRB did not seek review by the U.S. Supreme Court. Under a federal regulation, federal contractors and subcontractors are still required to inform employees of their NLRA rights. The workplace poster remains available on the NLRB website. In addition, the NLRB has established a free NLRB mobile app for iPhone and Android users to provide the public with information about the National Labor Relations Act. [For a look at the poster, see **www.nlrb.gov/news-publications/publications/employee-rights-poster**].

Questions

1. Legal requirements aside, are employers ethically obligated to inform their workers of NLRA rights? Explain.
2. From an ethical perspective, should NLRA posting requirements be different for a nonunionized workplace versus a unionized workplace? Explain.

Sources: NLRB Office of Public Affairs, "The NLRB's Notice Posting Rule," January 6, 2014 [**www.nlrb.gov**]; U.S. Department of Labor, Executive Order 13496, Notification of Employee Rights under Federal Labor Laws, January 29, 2015 [**www.dol.gov**]; Office of Federal Compliance Programs, "Employee Notification Requirements for Contractors and Subcontractors," *U.S. Department of Labor,* accessed October 2020 [**www.dol.gov**]; and Melanie Trottman, "NLRB Rolls Out Labor Law App," *The Wall Street Journal,* August 30, 2013 [**www.wsj.com**].

Signing in Solidarity?

A grocery store cashier wrote a note to her supervisor on the break room's "whiteboard" regarding a training program known as "TIPS." The next day, she noticed that the word "TIPS" had been changed to "TITS," and a "picture of a worm or peanut urinating" on her name had been added. She hand-copied the altered whiteboard message on a piece of paper and asked her team leader and two other employees to sign the paper to confirm the accuracy of its depiction, telling each her intent to file a complaint before they signed. While she did not intend to file a joint complaint, she believed the altered message amounted to sexual harassment of other female workers as well. During the employer's investigation, the cashier was told that while she may ask other employees to be witnesses, she was to refrain from soliciting more signatures.

Questions

In seeking her coworkers' signatures, was the cashier engaged in concerted activity for "mutual aid or protection" under Section 7 of the NLRA? If so, did the employer violate that right? Decide. Explain.

Source: *Fresh & Easy Neighborhood Market,* 361 N.L.R.B. No. 12 (2014).

Unfair Labor Practices by Management

The NLRA describes and outlaws certain activities by employers that would hamper or discourage employees from exercising the rights granted to them in Section 7. Thus, Section 8(a) of the act makes it an *unfair labor practice* for an employer to:

LO 14-3

Identify unfair labor practices by management and unions.

1. Interfere with, restrain, or coerce employees in the exercise of the rights given to them by Section 7;
2. Dominate, interfere, or assist with the formation of any labor organization, including contributing financial support to it;
3. Encourage or discourage membership in any labor organization by discrimination in regard to hiring, tenure of employment, promotion, salary, or any other term of employment;
4. Discharge or take any other action against an employee because he or she has filed charges or given testimony under the act; and
5. Refuse to bargain collectively with a duly certified representative of the employees.

These five provisions are designed to allow employees to organize in an atmosphere free from intimidation by the employer. In addition, if employees have chosen a union as their exclusive collective bargaining representative, Section 8(a) regulates the bargaining between the employer and the union. The provisions also ensure that the employer will not be able to interfere with union activities by either seizing control of the union or rendering it impotent by refusing to bargain collectively.

Starbucks Order

Judge Rebukes Starbucks' Response to Union Campaign

In March 2023, an administrative law judge ruled that Starbucks had committed dozens of labor violations regarding a union campaign at its Buffalo, New York, area stores. The judge found that Starbucks had illegally monitored, disciplined, and fired employees who were engaged in union organizing; interfered with union support by promising new benefits to workers and adding workers to stores, and had "high-ranking company officials make repeated and unprecedented visits to stores in order to. . . create the impression that employees' union activities were under surveillance." In addition to mandating the reinstatement of seven discharged workers, and back pay and damages to more than two dozen workers who were determined to have been unlawfully retaliated against, the judge ordered the Starbucks chief executive, Howard Schultz, to read or be present for the reading of a notice promising to not commit these labor law violations again, and to make and distribute a video of the reading. The judge also ordered the company to bargain with the union of a Buffalo-area location that had lost a December 2021 election, concluding that the scope of the violations had tainted that vote and made a new vote an "insufficient" remedy.

From the December 2021 vote through October 2022, the NLRB certified unions in 243 of the 9,000 Starbucks U.S. stores and marked union defeats at 50 other Starbucks locations.

Sources; Noam Scheiber, "Judge Rebukes Starbucks for Labor Law Violations," *The New York Times,* (March 2, 2023 p. B5); and Heather Haddon, "Starbucks Workers' Efforts to Unionize Lose Vigor," *The Wall Street Journal* (October 31, 2022 p. B1).

Employee Handbooks

Recently, the employee handbook has been the source of complaints that employers are violating their employees' NLRA rights. For example, the at-will provision, typically signed by new employees, may state "I agree that the at-will employment relationship cannot be amended, modified, or altered in any way." This provision may be unlawful because it waives the employee's right to act with other employees to change the nature of their employment relationship.[24] However, an at-will provision declaring that managers and supervisors have no authority to alter the employment relationship's at-will status and do not restrict the employee's ability to engage in concerted activity to do so as well has been considered valid by the NLRB.[25]

Silencing Former Employees

Confidentiality and Non-disparagement Agreements

Under a 2023 NLRB ruling, an employer cannot offer its employees severance agreements that prohibit them from making disparaging statements about their former employer or from revealing details of the severance agreement. However, legal experts have noted that the NLRB's decision is limited to the former employees' rights under the NLRA, such as the right to draw attention to work conditions.

Source: Noam Scheiber, "Labor Board Curbs Rules on Silencing Ex-Employees," *The New York Times* (February 23, 2023. p. B4).

Dress Codes

In a 2018 memorandum, the NLRB offered employers guidance on employee policies which underscored employees' right to wear clothes bearing pro-union messages and logos while allowing businesses to ban apparel "with inappropriate commercial advertising or insignia."[26] A federal appellate court enforced the NLRB's decision that a car dealer's dress code prohibiting employees who have contact with the public from wearing pins, insignias, and other message clothing was unlawful.[27] However, a federal appellate court also held that AT&T was allowed to suspend employees for wearing a shirt while visiting customer homes that said "Inmate" on the front and "Prisoner of AT&T" on the back, designed to raise awareness of problematic contract negotiations, because the employer reasonably believed the message could harm its customer relations or public image.[28]

Judge Jolly

In this appeal, the National Labor Relations Board ("NLRB" or "Board") challenges certain T-Mobile workplace rules, which it contends prohibit employees from exercising unionizing rights.

T-Mobile's employee handbook (1) encouraged employees to "maintain a positive work environment"; (2) prohibited "[a]rguing or fighting," "failing to treat others with respect," and "failing to demonstrate appropriate teamwork"; (3) prohibited all photography and audio or video recording in the workplace; and (4) prohibited access to electronic information by non-approved individuals. The Board determined that all four provisions violated the National Labor Relations Act (NLRA) because each of them discouraged unionizing or other concerted activity protected by the Act. T-Mobile . . . seeks review of the Board's order.

We hold that the Board erred in finding that a reasonable employee would construe policies (1), (2), and (4) to prohibit protected activity. However, we will not upset the Board's finding that a reasonable employee would construe policy (3) to prohibit protected activity. Accordingly, we grant in part and deny in part enforcement of the Board's order.

I.

T-Mobile and Metro PCS are telecommunications companies that market cell phones and related services, with offices and retail locations located throughout the United States. In 2014, based on charges filed by the Communication Workers of America, the NLRB brought a complaint against T-Mobile alleging that several of the provisions of T-Mobile's employee handbook violated the National Labor Relations Act ("NLRA"). This appeal concerns four provisions of the handbook that the NLRB determined were forbidden under the NLRA.

A.

The "workplace conduct" policy . . . provides:

> "[T-Mobile] expects all employees to behave in a professional manner that promotes efficiency, productivity, and cooperation. Employees are expected to maintain a positive work environment by communicating in a manner that is conducive to effective working relationships with internal and external customers, clients, co-workers, and management."

The "commitment-to-integrity" policy . . . begins with the preface:

> "At T-Mobile, we expect all employees, officers and directors to exercise integrity, common sense, good judgment, and to act in a professional manner. We do not tolerate inconsistent conduct. While we cannot anticipate every situation that might arise or list all possible violations, the acts listed below are unacceptable."

The commitment-to-integrity policy then lists seventeen non-inclusive examples of "unacceptable" acts, including, in relevant part:

> "Arguing or fighting with co-workers, subordinates or supervisors; failing to treat others with respect; or failing to demonstrate appropriate teamwork."

The "recording" policy . . . provides:

> "To prevent harassment, maintain individual privacy, encourage open communication, and protect confidential information employees are prohibited from recording people or confidential information using cameras, camera phones/devices, or recording devices (audio or video) in the workplace. Apart from customer calls that are recorded for quality purposes, employees may not tape or otherwise make sound recordings of work-related or workplace discussions. Exceptions may be granted when participating in an authorized [T-Mobile] activity or with permission from an employee's Manager, HR Business Partner, or the Legal Department. If an exception is granted, employees may not take a picture, audiotape, or videotape others in the workplace without the prior notification of all participants."

Finally, the "acceptable use" policy . . . provides:

> "Users may not permit non-approved individuals access to information or information resources, or any information transmitted by, received from, printed from, or stored in these resources, without prior written approval from an authorized T-Mobile representative."

B.

. . . The Board . . . held that all four of the challenged policies violated the NLRA and issued an order to that effect.

T-Mobile timely petitioned this Court for review of the NLRB's decision. The Board has filed a cross-application for enforcement of its order.

II.

A.

Section 7 of the NLRA provides . . . "[e]mployees shall have the right to self-organization, to form, join, or assist labor organizations, to bargain collectively through representatives of their own choosing, and to engage in other concerted activities for the purpose of collective bargaining or other mutual aid or protection." . . . Section 8(a)(1) of the Act in turn provides enforcement of that policy by stating that it shall be an "unfair labor practice" to "interfere with, restrain, or coerce employees in the exercise of the rights" protected by Section 7. Here, the "appropriate inquiry" is whether T-Mobile's rules for workplace conduct violate Section 8(a)(1) by chilling a reasonable employee in the exercise of his or her Section 7 rights. . . .

In this case, where the record does not suggest that the rules have been applied in the context of union or collective activity, the "reasonable employee" is a T-Mobile employee aware of his legal rights but who also interprets work rules as they apply to the everydayness of his job. The reasonable employee does not view every employer policy through the prism of the NLRA. Indeed, "[the Board] must not presume improper interference with employee rights. The question is whether a reasonable T-Mobile employee "would reasonably construe the language to prohibit Section 7 activity."

B.

III.

The NLRB found that each of the four policies at issue . . . violated the Act because "employees would reasonably construe the language to prohibit Section 7 activity." We address each policy in turn.

A.

We first address the workplace conduct policy. . . .

To a "reasonable employee," context matters in the interpretation of these rules. The policy is titled "Workplace Conduct." The rule refers to a positive work environment and effective working relationships and requires employees to behave in a way that "promotes efficiency, productivity, and cooperation," with the obvious implication "with respect to work." In the context of the workplace presented in the record, this rule addresses a normal workplace, on a normal workday.

A reasonable employee of T-Mobile would interpret the policy as requiring professional manners, positive work environment, effective and courteous communications, getting along with everybody, common sense, and people skills. The reasonable T-Mobile employee would understand the rule to express a universally accepted guide for conduct in a responsible workplace. . . .

This reading of these workplace rules is consistent with the only other circuit to have spoken on the matter. The DC Circuit . . . addressed a policy similar to the ones at issue. There . . . the DC Circuit [said] "it is preposterous that employees are incapable of organizing a union or exercising their other statutory rights under the NLRA without resort to abusive or threatening language."

In sum, we conclude that a reasonable employee would not construe a requirement to "maintain a positive work environment by communicating in a manner that is conducive to effective working relationships" to restrict Section 7 activity. We therefore deny enforcement of the Board's order as to the workplace conduct policy.

B.

The Board also found that the commitment-to-integrity policy violated the NLRA because the policy would inhibit robust discussion of labor issues. The rule, like the workplace conduct rule, is on its face, only a common sense civility guideline.

The policy, which prohibits "arguing or fighting," "failing to treat others with respect," and "failing to demonstrate appropriate teamwork," is prefaced by the conventional, common-sense admonition that T-Mobile expects its employees to "to exercise integrity, common sense, good judgment, and to act in a professional manner." These acts appear in a long, non-inclusive list of prohibited activity, including theft, fraud, dishonesty, and sleeping on the job. These examples that define the parameters of the rule address misconduct. . . .

Here, a reasonable employee would understand the language of the commitment-to-integrity policy to refer to similar misconduct. Furthermore, a reasonable employee would be fully capable of engaging in debate over union activity or working conditions, even vigorous or heated debate, without inappropriately "arguing or fighting," "failing to treat others with respect," or "failing to demonstrate appropriate teamwork.". . .

Accordingly, we decline to enforce the Board's order as to the commitment-to-integrity policy.

C.

The Board next found that T-Mobile's recording policy violates the NLRA because it would discourage workers from engaging in protected activity.

We are primarily concerned with the broad reach of the recording ban. The ban, by its plain language, encompasses any and all photography or recording on corporate premises at any time without permission from a supervisor. This ban is, by its own terms alone, stated so broadly that a reasonable employee, generally aware of employee rights, would interpret it to discourage protected concerted activity, such as even an off-duty employee photographing a wage schedule posted on a corporate bulletin board.

T-Mobile argues that the ban's stated purposes—"[t]o prevent harassment, maintain individual privacy, encourage open communication, and protect confidential information"—are legitimate business interests that ordinarily would justify the ban. But merely reciting such justifications does not alter the fact that the operative language of the rule on its face prohibits protected Section 7 activity, including Section 7 activity wholly unrelated to those stated interests.

Unlike the "workplace conduct" policy and the "commitment-to-integrity" policy, the recording policy forbids certain forms of clearly protected activity. . . . [A] reasonable T-Mobile employee, aware of his legal rights, would read the language of the recording policy as plainly forbidding a means of engaging in protected activity.

Because a reasonable employee would construe the recording policy to prohibit forms of protected activity, we hold that the Board's determination that the recording policy violated the NLRA is supported by a reasonable interpretation of the record. Its order will be enforced in that respect.

D.

Finally, the Board found that the acceptable use policy violated the NLRA because a reasonable employee would construe it to prohibit protected activity such as accessing and sharing wage and benefit information contained in his or her email.

The NLRB's decision, however, disregards the context in which the acceptable use policy is to be read and understood. The "Scope" section of the acceptable use policy explicitly states that the policy "applies to all non-public T-Mobile information." Thus the policy only prohibits employees from sharing non-public information.

Where a company policy prohibits the disclosure of non-public information, courts presume that a reasonable employee would not construe the policy to prohibit the disclosure of information that may be properly used in protected activity, such as wage and benefit information, so long as the policy does not explicitly state that it encompasses such information. . . .

Thus the NLRB's finding that a reasonable worker would construe the acceptable use policy to discourage protected activity is unreasonable, and we deny enforcement as to that part of its order.

IV.

To sum up: We hold that the Board's findings regarding the workplace conduct policy, the commitment-to-integrity policy, and the acceptable use policy are unreasonable. The Board's order is denied enforcement as to those policies. However, the Board's findings regarding the recording policy is reasonable, and the Board's order is enforced as to that policy. The Board's order is also summarily enforced as to the eleven policies not challenged by T-Mobile on appeal.

Accordingly, T-Mobile's petition is GRANTED IN PART and DENIED IN PART.

Questions

1. Why did the court find T-Mobile's workplace conduct policy, commitment-to-integrity policy, and acceptable use policy to be acceptable under the NLRA?
2. Why did the court find T-Mobile's recording ban was unacceptable under the NLRA?
3. How could the recording ban be revised to be acceptable under the NLRA? Discuss.
4. Embarrassed over a bad haircut, Nichole Wright-Gore, a supply clerk for White Oak Manor, started wearing a hat to work. After several days, supervisors told her to remove the hat as it violated a company dress code prohibiting hats; she refused and was disciplined. Wright-Gore subsequently began to take photos of her coworkers, some with and without consent, showing them wearing hats and violating the dress code in other ways, which she shared with coworkers while discussing with them the unequal enforcement of the dress code. After employees complained about having their photos taken and shared with others without their consent, Wright-Gore was terminated for violating White Oak's policy prohibiting photos being taken in the facility. Did Wright-Gore's termination violate the NLRA? Explain. See *NLRB v. White Oak Manor,* 452 F. App'x 374 (4th Cir. 2011) (unpublished op.).

Social Media Policies

Can a Facebook posting or comment be protected activity under the NLRA? Coworkers who are "Facebook friends" or otherwise connected on social media might want to communicate about workplace issues through these venues. Employers seeking to protect their online reputation and lessen their risk of employment-related liability for, as an example, harassment (see Chapter 13) may have a "social media policy" prohibiting certain conduct on Facebook and similar sites. The NLRB's Advice Memos on social media policies state that if employees would reasonably read an employer's social media policy to mean, for example, that they are not allowed to discuss wages or ask each other about perceptions of unfair treatment, then the policy would likely violate the NLRA.[29] The NLRB has found that Costco's social media policy violated the NLRA in prohibiting employees from electronically posting statements that would, for example, "defame the Company" or "damage any person's reputation." Employees could interpret this broad policy as preventing them from engaging in such concerted activity as discussing possible mistreatment of employees.[30] The NLRB found that a clothing store wrongfully terminated several employees for posting negative comments on Facebook relating to a dispute with the store manager about closing time, given their concerns with the store's location.[31] In the case that follows, the NLRB considers whether a Facebook "like" of a coworker's post is protected concerted activity under the NLRA.

Three D, LLC (Triple Play Sports Bar and Grille) and Jillian Sanzone and Vincent Spinella

LEGAL BRIEFCASE

361 NLRB No. 31 (2014), *aff'd,* Three D, LLC v. NLRB, 629 F. App'x 33 (2d Cir. 2015)

By Members Miscimarra, Hirozawa, and Schiffer

DECISION AND ORDER

The principal issue in this case is whether the Respondent violated Section 8(a)(1) of the [National Labor Relations] Act by discharging two employees for their participation in a Facebook discussion involving claims that employees unexpectedly owed additional State income taxes because of the Respondent's withholding mistakes. We agree with the [administrative law] judge that the discharges were unlawful. . . .

I.

Section 7 of the National Labor Relations Act provides, in pertinent part, that "[e]mployees shall have the right to self-organization, to form, join, or assist labor organizations, to bargain collectively through representatives of their own choosing, and to engage in other concerted activities for the purpose of collective bargaining or other mutual aid or protection . . . ." Under Section 7, employees have a statutory right to act together "to improve terms and conditions of employment or otherwise improve their lot as employees"—including by using social media to communicate with each other and with the public for that purpose. At the same time, online employee communications can implicate legitimate employer interests, including the "right of employers to maintain discipline in their establishments." However, neither of these rights is "unlimited in the sense that [neither] can be exercised without regard to any duty which the existence of rights in others may place upon employer or employee." In this case, there is no dispute that the Facebook communications at issue constituted "concerted activities" and that they were "for the purpose of . . . mutual aid or protection." Rather, mindful of the balance to be struck between employee rights under Section 7 and legitimate employer interests, our focus here is on whether these Facebook activities, which indisputably prompted the Respondent to discharge the two employees, lost the protection of the Act. . . . [W]e agree that they did not.

A.

The Respondent, which is owned by Ralph DelBuono and Thomas Daddona, operates a bar and restaurant; DelBuono is responsible for the Respondent's accounting. The Respondent's employees are not represented by a labor organization.

The Respondent employed Jillian Sanzone as a waitress and bartender, and Vincent Spinella as a cook. In approximately January 2011, Sanzone and at least one other employee discovered that they owed more in State income taxes than they had expected. Sanzone discussed this at work with other employees, and some employees complained to the Respondent. In response to the complaints, the Respondent planned a staff meeting for February with its payroll provider to discuss the employees' concerns.

Sanzone, Spinella, and former employee Jamie LaFrance, who left the Respondent's employ in November 2010, have Facebook accounts. On January 31 [2011], LaFrance posted the following "status update" to her Facebook page:

> Maybe someone should do the owners of Triple Play a favor and buy it from them. They can't even do the tax paperwork correctly!!! Now I OWE money. . . W-- [acronym for expletive]!!!!

The following comments were posted to LaFrance's page in response:

> KEN DESANTIS (a Facebook "friend" of LaFrance's and a customer): "You owe them money. . . that's f---ed up."
>
> DANIELLE MARIE PARENT (Triple Play employee): "I F---G OWE MONEY TOO!"
>
> LAFRANCE: "The state. Not Triple Play. would never give that place a penny of my money. Ralph [DelBuono] f---ed up the paperwork . . . as per usual."
>
> DESANTIS: "[Y]eah I really [don't] go to that place anymore."
>
> LAFRANCE: "It's all Ralph's fault. He didn't do the paperwork right. I'm calling the labor board to look into it [because] he still owes me about 2000 in paychecks."
>
> (At this juncture, employee Spinella selected the "Like" option under LaFrance's initial status update. The discussion continued as follows.)
>
> LAFRANCE: "We shouldn't have to pay it. It's every employee there that it[']s happening to."
>
> DESANTIS: "[Y]ou better get that money . . . that[']s b---it if that[']s the case [I']m sure he did it to other people too."
>
> PARENT: "Let me know what the board says because I owe $323 and [I']ve never owed."
>
> LAFRANCE: "I'm already getting my 2000 after writing to the labor board and them investigating but now I find out he f--ed up my taxes and I owe the state a bunch. Grrr."

PARENT: "I mentioned it to him and he said that we should want to owe."

LAFRANCE: "Hahahaha he's such a shady little man. He [pro[bab]ly pocketed it all from all our paychecks. I've never owed a penny in my life till I worked for him. Thank goodness I got outta there."

SANZONE: "I owe too. Such an a---le."

PARENT: "[Y]eah me neither, [I] told him we will be discussing it at the meeting."

SARAH BAUMBACH (Triple Play employee): "I have never had to owe money at any jobs . . . I hope I won[']t have to at TP . . . probably will have to seeing as everyone else does!"

LAFRANCE: "Well discuss good [because] I won't be there to hear it. And let me know what his excuse is;)."

JONATHAN FEELEY (a Facebook "friend" of LaFrance's and customer): "And the[y're] way to[o] expensive."

Sanzone added her comment from her cell phone on February 1. She testified that her Facebook privacy settings permit only her Facebook friends to view her posts. LaFrance's privacy settings are not in the record.

Co-owner Daddona learned about the Facebook discussion from his sister, who, in addition to being employed by the Respondent, is a Facebook friend of LaFrance. On February 2, when Sanzone reported to work, Daddona told her she was being discharged. When Sanzone asked why, Daddona responded that she was not loyal enough to be working for the Respondent because of her Facebook comment.

When Spinella reported for work on February 3, he was summoned to the Respondent's office, where Daddona and DelBuono were waiting; the Facebook comments from LaFrance's account were displayed on a computer screen in the office. After asking Spinella if he "had a problem with them, or the company," DelBuono and Daddona interrogated him about the Facebook discussion, the meaning of his "Like" selection, the identity of the other people who had participated in the conversation, and whether Spinella had written anything negative about DelBuono or Daddona. DelBuono told Daddona that the "Like" option meant that Spinella stood behind the other commenters [and] because he "liked the disparaging and defamatory comments," it was "apparent" that Spinella wanted to work somewhere else. . . .

B.

The judge found that the Facebook discussion was *concerted* activity because it involved four current employees (Danielle Marie Parent, Sarah Baumbach, Sanzone, Spinella) and was "part of an ongoing sequence" of discussions that began in the workplace about the Respondent's calculation of employees' tax withholding. Noting that the employees, in their Facebook conversation, discussed issues they intended to raise at an upcoming staff meeting as well as possible avenues for complaints to government entities, the judge found that the participants were seeking to initiate, induce, or prepare for group action. . . .

The judge further found that Sanzone and Spinella were engaged in *protected* concerted activity because the discussion concerned workplace complaints about tax liabilities, the Respondent's tax withholding calculations, and LaFrance's assertion that she was owed back wages. The judge found that Spinella's selection of the "Like" button expressed his support for the others who were sharing their concerns and "constituted participation in the discussion that was sufficiently meaningful as to rise to the level of" protected, concerted activity. . . . [T]he judge further found that they did not lose the Act's protection [and] concluded that the Respondent unlawfully discharged Sanzone and Spinella for their protected Facebook posts.

C.

The Respondent . . . contends that, as a result of their Facebook activities, Sanzone and Spinella adopted LaFrance's allegedly defamatory and disparaging comments and lost the protection of the Act. The Respondent asserts that the Facebook posts were made in a "public" forum accessible to both employees and customers and that, as a result, they undermined DelBuono's authority in the workplace and adversely affected the Respondent's public image. . . .

D.

The Board has long recognized that an employer has a legitimate interest in preventing the disparagement of its products or services and, relatedly, in protecting its reputation (and the reputations of its agents as to matters within the scope of their agency) from defamation. Section 7 rights are balanced against these interests, if and when they are implicated. In striking that balance, the Board applies these principles in accordance with the Supreme Court's decisions in *Jefferson Standard* and *Linn*.

In *Jefferson Standard*, the Court upheld the discharge of employees who publicly attacked the quality of their employer's product and its business practices without relating their criticisms to a labor controversy. The Court found that the employees' conduct amounted to disloyal disparagement of their employer and, as a result, fell outside the Act's protection.

In *Linn*, the Court limited the availability of State-law remedies for defamation in the course of a union organizing campaign "to those instances in which the complainant can show that the defamatory statements were circulated with malice and caused him damage." The Court indicated that the meaning of "malice," for these purposes, was that the statement was uttered "with knowledge of its falsity, or with reckless disregard of whether it was true or false."

Applying these precedents, the Board has held that "'employee communications to third parties in an effort to obtain their support are protected where the communication indicated it is related to an ongoing dispute between the employees and the employers and the communication is not so disloyal, reckless, or maliciously untrue as to lose the Act's protection.'"

Turning to the facts of this case, we first adopt the judge's finding that the only employee conduct to be analyzed is Sanzone's comment ("I owe too. Such an a---le.") and Spinella's indication that he "liked" LaFrance's initial status update ("Maybe someone should do the owners of Triple Play a favor and buy it from them. They can't even do the tax paperwork correctly!!! Now I OWE money . . . W-- [acronym for expletive]!!!!"). In agreement with the judge, we find that in the context of the ongoing dialogue among employees about tax withholding, Sanzone's comment effectively endorsed LaFrance's complaint that she owed money on her taxes due to a tax-withholding error on the Respondent's part. While Spinella's "like" is more ambiguous, we treat it for purposes of our analysis as expressing agreement with LaFrance's original complaint.

We reject the Respondent's contention that Sanzone or Spinella can be held responsible for any of the other comments posted in this exchange. Neither Sanzone nor Spinella accused the Respondent of pocketing employees' money or endorsed any comment by LaFrance to that effect. Assuming, arguendo, that such an accusation would have been unprotected, neither Sanzone nor Spinella would have lost the protection of the Act merely by participating in an otherwise protected discussion in which other persons made unprotected statements.

The comments at issue here are qualitatively different from the disparaging communications that lost protection in the *Jefferson Standard* case. First, the Facebook discussion here clearly disclosed the existence of an ongoing labor dispute concerning the Respondent's tax-withholding practices. Second, the evidence does not establish that the discussion in general, or Sanzone's and Spinella's participation in particular, was directed to the general public. The comments at issue were posted on an individual's personal page rather than, for example, a company page providing information about its products or services. Although the record does not establish the privacy settings of LaFrance's page, or of individuals other than Sanzone who commented . . ., we find that such discussions are clearly more comparable to a conversation that could potentially be overheard by a patron or other third party than the communications at issue in *Jefferson Standard*, which were clearly directed at the public.

In any event, we find that Spinella's and Sanzone's comments were not "so disloyal . . . as to lose the Act's protection" . . . . Where, as here, the purpose of employee communications is to seek and provide mutual support looking toward group action to encourage the employer to address problems in terms or conditions of employment, not to disparage its product or services or undermine its reputation, the communications are protected.

The comments at issue likewise were not defamatory. . . . [T]here is no basis for finding that the employees' claims that their withholding was insufficient to cover their tax liability, or that this shortfall was due to an error on the Respondent's part, were maliciously untrue. And Sanzone's characterization of DelBuono as an "a---le" in connection with the asserted tax-withholding errors cannot reasonably be read as a statement of fact; rather, Sanzone was merely (profanely) voicing a negative personal opinion of DelBuono. Accordingly, we find that these statements also did not lose protection under *Linn.*

[W]e adopt the judge's finding that the discharges of Sanzone and Spinella violated Section 8(a)(1). . . .

Questions

1. The NLRB concluded that the Facebook discussion was more like a conversation that could be overheard by a customer rather than communications "clearly directed at the public." Should Facebook discussions on workplace issues be treated the same as workplace conversations? Why or why not?
2. How did the administrative law judge ("the judge") view Spinella's "liking" of LaFrance's post? How did the NLRB view it? For purposes of the NLRA, should "liking" a coworker's Facebook post on a work condition be treated as supporting others' express comments on the post? Explain.
3. In affirming the NLRB's decision that the Facebook activity at issue did not lose the protection of the NLRA simply because it contained obscenities, the Second Circuit Court of Appeals cited the "reality of modern-day social media use." (See *Three D LLC v. NLRB*, 629 F. App'x 33 (2d Cir. 2015).

   a. Do you agree that obscenities are part of the "reality of modern-day social media use"? Should obscene language in otherwise protected, concerted activity *always* receive protection under the NLRA? Discuss.

   b. Two days before a union election at a catering company, while working as a server at a fund-raising event, a longtime employee got upset at his supervisor, Bob, for what he believed were Bob's disrespectful tone and comments towards the waitstaff. On break, the employee posted a message to his personal Facebook page: "Bob is such a nasty MO---ER F--ER don't know how to talk to people!!!!!! F--k his mother and his entire f---ng family!!!! What a LOSER!!!! Vote YES for the UNION!!!!!!" The post was visible to the employee's Facebook friends, who included some coworkers. The post was deleted the day after the election, but the employee was fired approximately two weeks later for the posting. Did the catering company violate the NLRA in terminating the employee? Decide. Explain. See *Pier Sixty, LLC*, 362 N.L.R.B. 59 (2015).

4. A school district's after-school center for high-school students that hires employees on an annual basis held a meeting in which staff anonymously identified the pros and cons of working at the center. Two employees who believed that management was not serious about addressing these concerns tried unsuccessfully to meet with their supervisor. These employees engaged in a Facebook conversation that advocated insubordination, such as not following specific school-district rules. Another employee forwarded the conversation to the center's management, and the two employees' reemployment offers were withdrawn. Did the center violate the NLRA in withdrawing those offers? Decide. Explain. See *Richmond District Neighborhood Center*, 361 N.L.R.B. No. 74 (2014).

Unfair Labor Practices by Unions

Section 8(b) lists activities constituting unfair labor practices by a labor organization. Some of these provisions mirror some of the activities prohibited to employers. Moreover, at least since the enactment of the Taft–Hartley Act, the law is not sympathetic to labor organizations that try to use certain coercive tactics, threats of the loss of livelihood, or any other strong-arm methods. Finally, Section 8(b) also regulates the union's collective bargaining practices, including economic action. Thus, a labor organization is not permitted to

1. Restrain or coerce any employee in the exercise of their rights as granted by Section 7.
2. Cause or attempt to cause an employer to discriminate against an employee who has chosen not to join a particular labor organization or has been denied membership in such an organization.
3. Refuse to bargain collectively with an employer on behalf of the bargaining unit it is certified to represent.
4. Induce or attempt to induce an employer to engage in secondary boycott activities, as will be discussed in Part Five.
5. Require employees to become union members and then charge them excessive or discriminatory dues.
6. Try to make an employer compensate workers for services not performed.
7. Picket or threaten to picket an employer in an attempt to force the employer to recognize or bargain with a labor organization that is not the duly certified representative of a bargaining unit.

LO 14-4 Explain the role of the National Labor Relations Board in enforcing the NLRA.

Representation Procedures

Section 9 of the NLRA specifies the election procedures by which employees may choose whether to be represented by a particular union or no union at all.

National Labor Relations Board

The National Labor Relations Board (NLRB) is a federal administrative agency responsible for regulating labor–management relations. Its primary tasks are designating appropriate bargaining units of workers (deciding which workers have a sufficient community of interest so that their needs can best be acknowledged and so that collective bargaining is efficient for the employer and the union); conducting elections for union representation within the chosen bargaining unit; certifying the results of such elections; and investigating, prosecuting, and adjudicating charges of unfair labor practices.[32]

Although the congressional mandate by which the NLRB was formed gives the agency jurisdiction theoretically to the full extent of the interstate commerce powers vested in Congress, the agency has neither the funding nor the staff to operate at that scope. Therefore, some smaller businesses, government employees, railroad and airline workers covered by the Railway Labor Act, agricultural workers, domestic workers, independent contractors, and supervisors and other managerial employees are not protected by the board.[33]

Over the years, the five-member NLRB has been criticized for sometimes reaching decisions based on political or philosophical considerations, rather than legal reasoning and board precedent. As successive presidential administrations appoint NLRB members, the board's decisions often "seesaw" according to the changes in Washington political power. [For more on the NLRB, see **www.nlrb.gov**].

Part Three—Elections

Choosing a Bargaining Representative

LO 14-5
Describe the process of union organizing and identify the related legal issues.

Representation elections are the process by which the NLRB achieves the first of the two statutory goals under the NLRA–employee freedom of choice. That goal, however, is sometimes in conflict with the other statutory goal–stable collective bargaining. The NLRB has devised rules to resolve such conflicts. In 2019, the NLRB adopted new election rules that went into effect in July 2020 (the "2020 rules").[34] The 2020 rules added back time in the election procedures the previous 2015 rules had reduced. The 2015 rules had been described by critics as "'ambush' NLRB election rules"[35] because they significantly shortened the timeline between petition and election, arguably harming an employers' ability to mount a defense to unionization. [For the AFL-CIO view of why workers should join unions, see **www.workingamerica.org/issues;** for the National Right to Work Legal Defense Foundation's information on employees' rights not to join a union, see **http://nrtw.org/know-your-rights**].

Election Petition

Employees, unions, and, under certain circumstances, employers[36] may file representation petitions asking the NLRB to conduct an election to determine if employees wish to be represented by a union for purposes of collective bargaining with their employer. The petition must be supported by at least 30 percent of the employees in the proposed bargaining unit.[37] The petitioner must also serve the petition on the other party. For example, the union must serve the petition on the employer. The NLRB will investigate the petition to assess whether an election should be conducted and will direct an election if appropriate.[38] The employer is free to simply acknowledge its employees' interest in joining a particular union and to engage in bargaining with that union, a decision normally called *voluntary recognition.*

The employer must post a notice of the election petition where other employee notices are posted so that employees are aware of it; if an employer typically communicates with employees through electronic means, then the notice also must be electronically distributed.[39]

Employees' support for a union had historically often been established by a *card check* method, in which employees signified their interest in the union simply by signing authorization cards, thus bypassing secret ballot elections and making union organizing easier. However, the NLRB overturned 40 years of precedent in 2007 and made the card check method less useful for union organizing. In *Dana Corporation/Metaldyne,*[40] the NLRB ruled that where an employer voluntarily recognizes a union based on a card check majority, anti-union employees have 45 days to petition the board for a federally supervised, secret ballot election to *decertify* the newly recognized union or to support a petition by a rival union.

Pre-election Hearings

If the parties do not agree to an election, the NLRB's regional office holds a pre-election hearing. The non-petitioning party (for example, the employer if the union filed the petition) must submit and serve on the petitioning party a Statement of Position. If an election is determined to be appropriate, the NLRB's regional office sets the election; unless the parties agree otherwise, the election will take place no sooner than 20 business days from the date the election was directed.[41]

The crucial issue to be addressed at this point, however, is normally whether the proposed bargaining unit (that is, the designated employee group–for example, all hourly workers at a facility, all welders, or all sales clerks) is appropriate for the election.

Appropriate Bargaining Unit

The key consideration in establishing an appropriate employee bargaining unit is the community of interest among the employees because collective bargaining will not be stable and efficient if it involves employees with diverse interests. Therefore, the bargaining unit may range from a portion of a plant to multiple employees in several plants. Similarly, a workplace may have more than one appropriate bargaining unit, depending on the composition of the workforce. In 2013, a federal appellate court upheld the NLRB's decision in S*pecialty Healthcare,*[42] in which a nursing home challenged the certification of Certified Nursing Assistants (CNAs) as a stand-alone bargaining unit. The employer argued that an appropriate bargaining unit would include all nonprofessional service and maintenance employees. The NLRB rejected the challenge, finding that a bargaining unit of a clearly identifiable group of employees is presumably appropriate. An employer challenging a bargaining unit as inappropriately excluding other employees must show that the excluded workers share an "overwhelming community of interest" with those included in the bargaining unit.[43]

Certain classes of employees, such as supervisors, are excluded from the bargaining unit. Supervisors are excluded because they act on behalf of the employer and, through their power to direct and assign work and to discipline and discharge employees, exert control over their subordinates, who are or may be in the bargaining unit. Often labor and management do not agree about the classification of workers as supervisors. In a 2006 decision that outraged union activists, the NLRB substantially expanded the range of employees who might lawfully be considered supervisors (and thus ineligible for union membership) to include those assigned supervisory duties just 10 or 15 percent of the time.[44]

Independent contractors are not protected under the NLRA. In 2009, a federal appeals court set aside the NLRB's decision that FedEx had unlawfully failed to bargain with a union that had been certified to represent drivers at two FedEx home terminals. The appeals court concluded that the drivers were independent contractors who had been misclassified as employees by the NLRB.[45]

Question

The Macy's store in Saugus, Massachusetts, is divided into 11 primary sales departments: juniors, ready-to-wear, women's shoes, handbags, furniture, housewares, men's clothing, bridal, fine jewelry, fashion jewelry, and cosmetics and fragrances. Local 1445 of the United Food and Commercial Workers Union filed a petition with the NLRB for a representation election among all cosmetics and fragrances employees of the Saugus Macy's store. Is the proposed bargaining unit appropriate? What facts would you want to know before making your decision? See *Macy's v. NLRB,* 824 F.3d 557 (5th Cir. 2016).

Union Solicitation, Email, and the Employer

Historically, unions relied on a physical presence on employers' property to organize employees. A 1992 U.S. Supreme Court decision in *Lechmere v. NLRB*[46] limited that presence by allowing employers to bar from their property union organizers who are not employees. This resulted in an increase in *salting,* the practice of union organizers applying for jobs with the intent of unionizing the other employees from the inside. The Supreme Court's 1995 *Town & Country* decision[47] held that salts are employees, thus affording them NLRA protection from discrimination based on union affiliation; an NLRB decision later clarified that only those salts who are "genuinely interested" in obtaining employment are protected.[48]

In 2019, the NLRB reversed its 2014 decision in *Purple Communications*[49] that had allowed union organizing via email. In the 2019 case, *Caesars Entertainment d/b/a Rio All-Suites Hotel and Casino,* the NLRB held that employees do not have the right to use employer-owned equipment, including email and other information technology systems, for purposes of Section 7 of the NLRA.[50]

The Election for Union Representation

Unionization requires a majority of the votes cast by the employees. The NLRB oversees the election to ensure the process is carried on under "laboratory conditions."[51] In other words, elections must be held under circumstances that, to the extent possible, are free from undue or unfair influence either by the employer or by unions vying for the right to represent the bargaining unit.

Employers have the right to speak out against unions in the form of ads, speeches, and the like. Section 8(c) of the Taft–Hartley Act is designed to ensure employers' and labor organizations' traditional First Amendment rights as long as they do not overstep certain bounds:

> The expressing of any views, argument, or opinion, or the dissemination thereof, whether in written, printed, graphic, or visual form, shall not constitute or be evidence of an unfair labor practice . . . if such expression contains no threat of reprisal or force or promise of benefit.

A "Punch in the Face" Is Not a Punchline

During a union election campaign for employees of a skilled-nursing facility, two bargaining unit nurses threatened to "punch people in the face," "beat people up and destroy their cars," and "slash their tires" if the union did not win. While these comments were made in a joking manner, other unit employees who were told about them believed the threats were serious. The employer provided additional security for several days after the election as a result, although the union had won by two votes. The employer challenged the election results due to the violent threats. The NLRB found the remarks to be casual jokes that had been distorted in their retelling among other employees, and not proper grounds for overturning an election. However, a federal appellate court agreed with the employer, finding the remarks to have disrupted the election, and noting that the speakers' joking intent was not relevant in evaluating the threats objectively.

Source: ManorCare of Kingston PA LLC v. NLRB, 823 F.3d 81 (D.C. Cir. 2016)."

Threats of Reprisal or Force

Employers cannot discriminate in employment to encourage or discourage union membership. Clearly, an employer who tells employees, for example, that they will all be discharged if they engage in union activity has interfered with their rights. Similarly, an employer who interrogates employees about their activities or spies on them while they attend union meetings has engaged in unlawful interference. Problems often arise, however, in determining whether anti-union arguments made by an employer contain veiled threats. Suppose, for instance, that a company owner tells their employees that, in a unionized workplace, they would have to go through the union representative to make their complaints, and it would be the representative who would decide whether to bring the complaints to the company's attention. The NLRB has determined that such a statement is not a threat but rather an accurate reflection of the nature of unionized workplaces.[52]

Promise of Benefit

Although threats of force or reprisal are clearly unlawful in union campaigns, the rationale behind the prohibition against promises of benefit is not as intuitively obvious.

> The union can't put any of those things in your envelope.

In a dispute that reached the U.S. Supreme Court, Exchange Parts sent its employees a letter shortly before a representation election that spoke of "the empty promises of the union." After mentioning a number of benefits, the letter said "The union can't put any of those things in your envelope–only the company can do that." Further on it stated "It didn't take a union to get any of those things and . . . it won't take a union to get additional improvements in the future." Accompanying the letter was a detailed statement of the benefits granted by the company and an estimate of the monetary value of such benefits to the employees.

In the representation election two weeks later, the union lost, but the outcome was challenged in court. Eventually the Supreme Court ruled that the employer's actions constituted an unfair labor practice, reasoning that "well-timed increases in benefits" provide a clear message that those who provide advantages are the same people who can withdraw those benefits should their wishes not be followed.[53]

Buying Votes?

An Atlantic City, New Jersey, limousine service held a union election-day raffle for a TV/VCR. The NLRB ruled, 3–2, that the raffle was an unfair labor practice that might reasonably be interpreted to be a reward that would influence voting. A new election was ordered. The NLRB order banned election-day raffles, but minor "gifts" such as food, drinks, and buttons would be considered case-by-case if an objection were lodged.

Source: *Atlantic Limousine,* 331 N.L.R.B. No. 134 (2000).

Union Persuasion

Unions, like employers, are restricted in the type of pre-election persuasion they employ. In cases involving promises of benefits made by the union, the NLRB has been more reluctant to set aside elections than it has when such promises have been made by management. The board's reasoning is that employees realize that union pre-election promises are merely expressions of a union platform, so to speak. Employees recognize that these are benefits for which the union intends to fight. Employers, on the other hand, really do hold the power to confer or withdraw benefits. Nonetheless, a union promise to employees to provide "the biggest party in the history of Texas" if the union won the next day's election was an unfair labor practice.[54]

> "The biggest party in the history of Texas."

Remedies for Election Misconduct

Unfair labor practices during a representation election can result in the imposition of penalties and remedies. If the union loses the election and the employer engaged in wrongful behavior, a new election or other remedies may be ordered.

Decertification

After a union has been certified or recognized, an employee or group of employees may continue to resist the union or may lose confidence in it. If so, they can file a decertification petition with the NLRB. The employees must be able to demonstrate at least 30 percent support for their petition. Once a decertification petition is properly filed with the board, the usual election rules are followed to determine whether the union enjoys continuing majority support. If not, the union is decertified. Ordinarily at least one year must pass before a new representation election can be conducted. [For management advice about decertification, see **www.nrtw.org/d/decert.htm**].

Withdrawal of Recognition

An employer may unilaterally withdraw recognition of a union that has lost the support of a majority of its members. Objective evidence such as a petition signed by a majority of unit employees is required. The NLRB will review the petition and its specific language, however, to make sure that it shows employees' desire to decline union representation. For example, a petition entitled "showing of interest for decertification" was found to be insufficient evidence, while a petition's statement of "wish for a vote to remove the Union" tends to show that employees no longer desire the union's representation.[55]

Escape the Union?

If a union clearly is about to win a representation election or already has done so, thus establishing its right to collective bargaining, management sometimes continues to resist. One strategy is to declare bankruptcy. That tactic may be lawful, but only after bargaining sincerely with the union and only after convincing the bankruptcy court that fairness requires modification or rejection of the collective-bargaining agreement. Similarly, a company may simply choose to shut down its business rather than engage in collective bargaining. Going out of business is fully lawful, unless the reason for doing so was to discourage union efforts at plants in other locations. Likewise, companies sometimes employ the *runaway shop* strategy, in which the about-to-be-unionized plant is simply shut down and replaced by another in a location less responsive to union interests. If that move was made for the purpose of thwarting union interests, it is an unfair labor practice, but if the move reflected legitimate economic goals such as reduced wages or taxes, the move is probably lawful.

Companies sometimes employ the *runaway shop* strategy.

The Union as Exclusive Bargaining Agent

Once a union has been certified as the representative of a bargaining unit, it becomes the exclusive agent for all employees within that bargaining unit, whether they voted for the union or not. The exclusivity of the union's authority has a number of implications, but one is particularly relevant in determining whether an employer has failed to demonstrate good faith at the bargaining table. Specifically, the employer must deal with the certified representative who acts on behalf of all employees in the bargaining unit. The employer commits an unfair labor practice if they attempt to deal directly with the employees or recognize someone other than the workers' chosen representative. In both instances, the issue is fairly straightforward. The employer is undermining the position of the representative by ignoring them.

Part Four—Collective Bargaining

Section 8(a)(5) of the NLRA requires an employer to engage in good-faith collective bargaining with a representative of the employees, and Section 8(b)(3) imposes the same duty on labor organizations. Failure to bargain by either an employer or a representative of the employees constitutes an unfair labor practice.

What is collective bargaining? What must one do to discharge the duty imposed? According to Section 8(d) of the NLRA

> [t]o bargain collectively is the performance of the mutual obligation of the employer and the representatives of the employees to meet at reasonable times and confer in good faith with respect to wages, hours, and other terms and conditions of employment . . . but such obligation does not compel either party to agree to a proposal or require the making of a concession.

Note what is *not* included: The parties are not required to reach an agreement. Thus, the NLRA governs only the process, not the result, of collective bargaining.

Bargaining in Good Faith

LO 14-6
Explain what constitutes "bargaining in good faith."

The duty to bargain in *good faith* obligates the union and employer to participate actively in the deliberations, showing a sincere and honest effort to reach common ground. Whether a party is bargaining in good faith is determined by the totality of the circumstances. Some of the objective criteria used by the NLRB in reviewing complaints asserting that this duty has been violated include whether the party is willing to meet at reasonable times and intervals, and whether the party is represented by someone who has the authority to make decisions at the table.[56]

Mandatory Bargaining Subjects

Although employers and labor representatives are free to discuss whatever lawful subjects they mutually choose, Section 8(d) of the NLRA clearly sets out some mandatory subjects over which the parties must bargain. These are wages, hours, and "other terms and conditions of employment." Although these topics for mandatory bargaining seem simple enough, questions still arise frequently. For example, suppose the union and employer bargain over wages and agree to institute merit increases for employees. Must the employer also bargain over which employees are entitled to receive these increases or who will make the decision at the time they are to be given? What about a decision to close a plant?

Generally, the NLRB and the courts will balance three factors. First, they look at the effect of a particular decision on the workers–how direct is it, and to what extent is the effect felt? Second, they consider the degree to which bargaining would constitute an intrusion into entrepreneurial interest or, from the opposite side, an intrusion into union affairs. Third, they examine the practice historically in the industry or the company itself.[57]

Permissive and Prohibited Bargaining Subjects

Those matters not directly related to wages, hours, and terms and conditions of employment and not falling within the category of prohibited subjects are considered permissive. Either party may raise permissive subjects during the bargaining process but neither may pursue them to the point of a bargaining impasse. Refusal to bargain over a permissive subject does not constitute an NLRA violation, and permissive subjects must simply be dropped if the parties do not reach an agreement.

Does a union have the right to bargain over management's placement of hidden surveillance cameras?

Permissive subjects ordinarily would include such items as alteration of a defined bargaining unit, internal union affairs, and strike settlement agreements. Prohibited bargaining subjects are those that are illegal under the NLRA or other laws. In the case that follows, the NLRB had to decide whether a union has a right to bargain over management's placement of hidden surveillance cameras in the workplace.

Colgate–Palmolive Co.

323 N.L.R.B. No. 82 (1997)

FACTS

Colgate-Palmolive's Jeffersonville, Indiana, plant employed approximately 750 workers. Colgate and the employees had a collective bargaining arrangement for over 20 years. In 1994 an employee discovered a surveillance camera in a restroom air vent. The union president later discussed the matter with Colgate's human resources officer, who indicated that the camera had been placed in the vent because of theft concerns and that the camera had been removed after employees objected to it. The Union filed a grievance over the matter, and the parties met for discussion where Colgate argued that it had the absolute right to install internal surveillance cameras. Later, the Union sent a letter to Colgate demanding to bargain over the subject of cameras within the plant. Colgate did not respond, and the Union filed an unfair labor practice charge. The case was heard by an administrative law judge. Evidence indicated that Colgate had installed 11 secret cameras over four years to address problems of theft and misconduct, including sleeping on the job. The cameras were placed in several offices, a fitness center, a restroom, and as a monitor for an overhead door that was not a proper exit from the building. The Union and some employees were aware of various "unhidden" cameras in the workplace and in some instances fortuitously discovered some of the hidden cameras.

The administrative law judge (ALJ) concluded that the use of hidden surveillance cameras is a mandatory subject of bargaining and by failing to do so, Colgate–Palmolive violated the National Labor Relations Act. The ALJ's ruling was then appealed to the National Labor Relations Board. The *NLRB* decision follows.

Chairman Gould and Members Fox and Higgins

In *Ford Motor Co. v. NLRB,* the Supreme Court described mandatory subjects of bargaining as such matters that are "plainly germane to the 'working environment'" and "not among those 'managerial decisions, which lie at the core of entrepreneurial control.'" As the judge found, the installation of surveillance cameras is both germane to the working environment and outside the scope of managerial decisions lying at the core of entrepreneurial control.

As to the first factor—germane to the working environment—the installation of surveillance cameras is analogous to physical examinations, drug/alcohol testing requirements, and polygraph testing, all of which the Board has found to be mandatory subjects of bargaining. They are all investigatory tools or methods used by an employer to ascertain whether any of its employees has engaged in misconduct.

The Respondent [Colgate–Palmolive] acknowledges that employees caught involved in theft and/or other misconduct are subject to discipline, including discharge. Accordingly, the installation and use of surveillance cameras has the potential to affect the continued employment of employees whose actions are being monitored.

Further, as the judge finds, the use of surveillance cameras in the restroom and fitness center raises privacy concerns which add to the potential effect upon employees. We agree that these areas are part of the work environment and that the use of hidden cameras in these areas raises privacy concerns which impinged upon the employees' working conditions. The use of cameras in these or similar circumstances is unquestionably germane to the working environment.

With regard to the second criterion, we agree with the judge that the decision is not a managerial decision that lies at the core of entrepreneurial control.

The use of surveillance cameras is not entrepreneurial in character, is not fundamental to the basic direction of the enterprise, and impinges directly upon employment security. It is a change in the Respondent's methods used to reduce workplace theft or detect other suspected employee misconduct with serious implications for its employees' job security, which in no way touches on the discretionary "core of entrepreneurial control."

The Respondent urges that bargaining before a hidden camera is actually installed would defeat the very purpose of the camera. The very existence of secret cameras, however, is a term and condition of employment, and is thus a legitimate concern for the employees' bargaining representative. Thus, the placing of cameras, and the extent to which they will be secret or hidden, if at all, is a proper subject of negotiations between the Respondent and the union. Concededly, the Respondent also has a legitimate concern. However, bargaining about hidden cameras can embrace a host of matters other than mere location. And, even as to location, mutual accommodations can and should be negotiated. The vice in the instant case was the respondent's refusal to bargain.

Accordingly, we affirm the judge's finding that the union has the statutory right to engage in collective bargaining over the installation and continued use of surveillance cameras, including the circumstances under which the cameras will be activated, the general areas in which they may be placed, and how affected employees will be disciplined if improper conduct is observed.

ORDER

The National Labor Relations Board adopts the recommended Order of the administrative law judge as modified and set forth in full below and orders that the Respondent, its officers, agents, successors, and assigns, shall

1. Cease and desist from
   a. Failing and refusing to bargain with Local 15, International Chemical Workers Union, AFL–CIO with respect to the

installation and use of surveillance cameras and other mandatory subjects of bargaining.

2. Take the following affirmative action necessary to effectuate the policies of the Act.

   a. On request, bargain collectively with the Union as the exclusive bargaining representative of the Respondent's employees with respect to the installation and use of surveillance cameras and other mandatory subjects of bargaining.

   b. Within 14 days after the service by the Region, post at its facility in Jeffersonville, Indiana, copies of the attached notice:

Notice to Employees
Posted by Order of the
National Labor Relations Board
An Agency of the United States Government

The National Labor Relations Board has found that we violated the National Labor Relations Act and has ordered us to post and abide by this notice. Section 7 of the Act gives employees these rights.

To organize

To form, join, or assist any union

To bargain collectively through representatives of their own choice

To act together for other mutual aid or protection

To choose not to engage in any of these protected concerted activities.

We will not fail and refuse to bargain with Local 15, International Chemical Workers Union, AFL–CIO over the installation and use of surveillance cameras within our facility and other mandatory subjects of bargaining.

We will not in any like or related manner interfere with, restrain, or coerce you in the exercise of the rights guaranteed you by Section 7 of the Act.

We will, on request, bargain collectively with the Union as the exclusive bargaining representative of our employees with respect to the installation and use of surveillance cameras within our facility and other mandatory subjects of bargaining.

Colgate–Palmolive Company.

Questions

1. What test did the ALJ and the NLRB employ to determine whether the placement of hidden surveillance cameras was a mandatory subject of bargaining?
2. Why did the union win this case?
3. If you were managing a workplace where theft, sleeping on the job, and other misconduct were at a worrisome level, would you employ hidden, secret cameras to monitor restrooms, fitness areas, and the like? Explain.
4. At an Anheuser-Busch brewing facility, a supervisor discovered a table, four chairs, a number of foam mattress pads, and cardboard in a room where only authorized personnel were to be, but which was next to a break area. Suspecting illicit activities including illegal drug use, the company installed two surveillance cameras pointed at the entrance and stairs leading to the room. The cameras led to the company identifying 16 employees who engaged in misconduct. The company took down the cameras on June 30, 1998, and then informed the union of their existence. The company fired and otherwise disciplined the employees in question. Did Anheuser-Busch violate the NLRA? Explain. *Brewers & Maltsters v. NLRB,* 414 F.3d 36 (D.C. Cir. 2005).

Administering the Agreement

Union–management bargaining does not end with the negotiation of a labor agreement. Rather, bargaining continues daily as the parties work out the disputes, confusions, and conflicting interpretations that are bound to arise and that cannot be entirely provided for in the labor agreement. Often this process of contract maintenance takes the form of resolving *grievances,* as in the *Colgate-Palmolive* case. Those problems are addressed through the grievance procedure that is included in collective-bargaining agreements. Often the grievance procedure involves a series of steps beginning with informal discussion mechanisms. Failing there, the dissatisfied employee typically files a written complaint (the grievance). Normally, grievances are presented to management by a union representative, often with the worker also present.

Arbitration

If, after negotiation, the parties cannot resolve their dispute, the collective-bargaining agreement ordinarily provides for *final and binding arbitration.* Many court decisions have vigorously supported the arbitration process as the means of settling labor–management contract maintenance disputes and tend to find disputes arbitrable unless the labor agreement explicitly and unambiguously exempts the subject at issue from the arbitration process. Furthermore, but for rare exceptions, neither the company nor the union can turn to the courts to set aside arbitration decisions. However, the U.S. Supreme Court held that a dispute between a union and an employer over the ratification date of a collective-bargaining agreement containing an arbitration clause should be resolved by a court rather than an arbitrator.[58]

Fair Representation

Because grievance processing is part of a union's bargaining responsibility, the union might breach its duty if it declined to represent an employee's grievance. An employee who feels wronged when a union does not process his or her grievance has the option of appealing to the NLRB or to the courts. Nevertheless, as the U.S. Supreme Court ruled in *14 Penn Plaza LLC v. Pyett,* a union may collectively bargain for an agreement providing that individual members' employment discrimination claims must be submitted to arbitration.[59]

Part Five—Labor Conflict

PRACTICING ETHICS Prisoners on Strike

Putting prisoners to work, for no or nominal wages, is a common practice. For example, an Alabama prisoner made $2 a day mopping floors and cutting license plates. The U.S. Constitution prohibits "involuntary servitude" but makes an exception for work done as part of criminal punishment. The Florida Department of Corrections declared that prisoners working in jobs that served state agencies saved taxpayers $45 million in taxes in 2014 and performed work valued at over $76 million. Private enterprises also benefited from prison labor, such as a furniture company that operated a factory at a South Carolina correctional facility where prisoners work without pay. In 2016 and in 2018, prisoners in several states staged work stoppages and hunger strikes to protest their wages and work conditions. The Industrial Workers of the World (IWW) helped organize the strikes.

Questions

1. Should prisoners be paid minimum wage for their work for state agencies? For their work for private enterprises using their labor? Why or why not?
2. From an ethical perspective, would it be right for a state to replace public sector workers with prison labor as a cost-cutting measure? Why or why not?
3. Should prisoners be allowed to form a union? If so, what barriers may exist to unionizing prisoners? Explain.

Sources: Jaweed Kaleem, "They're in Prison and on Strike," *Los Angeles Times,* November 2, 2016, pp. A1 & A12; Mike Elk, "The Next Step for Organized Labor: People in Prisons," *The Nation,* July 11, 2016 [**www.thenation.com**]; and Daniel A. Gross, "An Inside Account of the National Prisoners' Strike," *The New Yorker,* September 6, 2018 [**www.newyorker.com**].

Strikes

State Court Tort Lawsuits and Strikes

Glacier Northwest Inc. v. International Brotherhood of Teamsters

At this writing in March 2023, the U.S. Supreme Court is considering whether the National Labor Relations Act preempts an employer's state law tort claims against a union for allegedly intentionally destroying the employer's property during a labor dispute. Glacier Northwest, a corporation in the state of Washington that sells and delivers ready-mix concrete to businesses in the state, employs approximately 80 to 90 truck drivers to deliver concrete. Teamsters Local 174 represents the Glacier's truck drivers in King County. In 2017, during negotiations for a new collective bargaining agreement (CBA), Glacier truck drivers went on strike. Glacier's trucks had just been loaded with cement before the strike. The concrete hardens quickly, and because of the strike, the undelivered cement hardened inside the trucks. Glacier disposed of several batches of concrete that could not be delivered, resulting in significant loss.

Sources: Glacier Northwest, Inc. v. International Brotherhood of Teamsters. (n.d.). *Oyez.* Retrieved March 12, 2023 [**https://www.oyez.org/**]; and Fisher Phillips, "FP SCOTUS Predictions: Will the Supreme Court Make It Easier to Hold Unions Liable for Strike Misconduct," (January 31, 2023) [**https://www.fisherphillips.com/**].

LO 14-7 Distinguish between "unfair labor practice strikes" and "economic strikes."

The traditional image of a labor strike shows employees picketing a store or factory. A surge in labor strikes in 2019 may change that view to include public school teachers.[60] Uber drivers around the world have also participated in strikes.[61] Striking is a drastic measure under which employees must bear an immediate loss of wages and, in many instances, risk job loss. Similarly, employers bear the loss of a disruption to operations.

We will examine two kinds of strikes:

1. *Unfair labor practice strikes* are those instituted by workers in response to the employer's commission of an unfair labor practice such as interfering with legitimate union activities or failure to bargain in good faith. These strikers can be temporarily, but not permanently, replaced.
2. *Economic strikes* are those used purely as economic weapons to persuade employers to provide more favorable benefits or better working conditions. All strikes not involving unfair labor practices fall into this category. With some exceptions, economic strikers cannot be fired, but they can be permanently replaced. In what has been labeled "the most significant change in collective bargaining to occur since the passage of the Wagner Act in 1934," employers are now increasingly willing to permanently replace economic strikers.[62] Employers had enjoyed that right where necessary "in an effort to carry on the business" since a 1938 Supreme Court decision,[63] but for practical reasons they had rarely exercised it. Later decisions imposed some limitations on this right. For example, any striker who is permanently replaced is put on a preferential hiring list and will have priority to be selected to fill subsequent vacancies. President Reagan's 1981 dismissal of 11,300 striking air traffic controllers effectively crushed their union

(PATCO) and caused private-sector employers to reassess their long-standing reluctance to use replacements during and after strikes.[64] Thus, the use of, or threat to use, permanent replacements has become a powerful tool for employers facing economic strikes.

The following case examines when employers can legitimately decline to reinstate strikers.

LEGAL BRIEFCASE

Diamond Walnut Growers, Inc. v. NLRB 113 F.3d 1259 (D.C. Cir. 1997), *cert. denied*, 118 S. Ct. 1299 (1998)

Circuit Judge Silberman

I

Diamond Walnut processes and packages walnuts for national and international distribution. . . . Diamond's employees have for years been represented by Cannery Workers, Processors, Warehousemen, and Helpers Local 601 of the International Brotherhood of Teamsters, AFL-CIO (the union). In September of 1991, following expiration of the most recent collective-bargaining agreement between Diamond and the union, nearly 500 of Diamond's permanent and seasonal employees went on strike. Diamond hired replacement workers to allow it to continue operations.

By all accounts, the strike was, and remains, a bitter affair. The strikers are alleged to have engaged in various acts of violence against the replacement workers. . . . In addition, as part of its effort to exert economic pressure on Diamond, the union undertook an international boycott of its product. The boycott included a well-publicized national bus tour during which union members distributed to the public leaflets which described Diamond's workforce as composed of "scabs" who packaged walnuts contaminated with "mold, dirt, oil, worms, and debris."

Approximately one year into the strike, the Board held a representation election. The union lost the election, but its objections prompted the Board to order a rerun to be held in October of 1993. Just over two weeks prior to the new election, a group of four striking employees, represented by a union official, approached Diamond with an unconditional offer to return to work. According to the letter presented to the company at that time by their representative, the employees were convinced that "a fair election [was] simply impossible." Nonetheless, the employees "fe[lt] that it [was] important that the replacement workers . . . have an opportunity to hear from Union sympathizers." Thus, the group of strikers was "available and willing to return to immediate active employment." The following day, the union notified Diamond that pursuant to the above-quoted letter, two additional strikers were willing to return to work.

It is undisputed that for three of the returning strikers, neither the permanent jobs they held before the strike, nor substantially equivalent ones, were available at the time of their return. Diamond placed these three in various seasonal jobs. Prior to the strike, Willa Miller was a quality control supervisor; she was placed in a seasonal packing position even though a seasonal inspection job was available. Alfonsina Munoz had been employed as a lift truck operator and, despite the availability of a seasonal forklift job, was given a seasonal job cracking and inspecting nuts in the growers' inspection department at the front end of the production process. Mohammed Kussair, formerly an air separator machine operator, was, like Munoz, placed in a seasonal cracking and inspecting position in the growers' inspection department. . . .

The rerun election took place as scheduled, and the union lost. Following that election, the General Counsel filed a complaint alleging that Diamond had violated the National Labor Relations Act by unlawfully discriminating against Miller, Munoz, and Kussair. The General Counsel alleged that because of their protected activity, Diamond declined to put them in certain available seasonal positions for which they were qualified and that were preferable to the positions in which they were actually placed. After a hearing, an administrative law judge recommended that the charges be dismissed. He found that Diamond had "discriminated" insofar as it had placed the employees at least in part because of their protected activity, but he did not think that discrimination "unlawful."

[The NLRB reversed saying] "although [Diamond] was under no legal obligation . . . to reinstate the strikers . . ., once it voluntarily decided to reinstate them, it was required to act in a

still have to pay an agency fee to the union? This issue has reached the Supreme Court several times, culminating in the 2018 *Janus v. AFSCME* decision, discussed below.

First, in the 1977 *Abood* case,[76] the Supreme Court considered Detroit public school teachers' constitutional challenge of an agency shop clause in their school district's collective-bargaining agreement requiring nonunion members to pay service fees equal to union dues; the teachers, who did not believe in public-sector collective bargaining and did not support the union's ideological activities, argued that the fees requirement violated their freedoms of expression and association. Distinguishing between agency fees and voluntary union dues that could be used for political activity, the Court held that the teachers could prevent a share of their fees from supporting the union's unrelated ideological views, but the agency fees' impingement on constitutional rights was justified by the "union shop's" role in labor relations under federal legislation.[77]

Then in 2014, the Supreme Court held that health care workers who provided home care to Medicaid recipients under an Illinois program did not have to pay an agency fee required under state law to support the public union they did not wish to join.[78] The Court reached the decision on the narrow ground that the workers were only partial public employees, unlike public school teachers, and thus did not overturn *Abood,* although the Court's majority was critical of it.[79] Once again, in 2016, in the face of public school teachers challenging agency fees as violations of their freedom of speech, an "equally divided" Supreme Court, as a consequence of a vacancy following Justice Scalia's death, affirmed the application of *Abood.*[80]

The *Abood* decision was finally reversed in 2018 by the Supreme Court's decision in *Janus v. AFSCME.*[81] A child-support specialist for the state of Illinois who had opted out of the public union challenged the requirement that he pay partial dues to cover the union's collective bargaining and other costs. The Supreme Court's majority held that public union negotiations in collective bargaining are inherently political, erasing the distinction drawn between collective bargaining and other union activities made in *Abood.* The *Janus* court concluded that requiring public-sector nonunion members to pay any fees to a union in which they are not members is a violation of their First Amendment rights. In 2023, observers concluded that Janus had only minimally impacted public sector unions. In 2022, 34 percent of public employees were union members, approximately the same share that public unions held in 2018. One observer noted that any funds lost by the unions from nonmembers had been recovered through increased dues.[82]

Research Exercise

Go to the National Labor Relations Board's frequently asked questions [**www.nlrb.gov/resources/faq/nlrb**].

1. Explain what an employee at a unionized workplace who is "unhappy" with the union can do.
2. Explain how to file an unfair labor practice claim.

Chapter Questions

1. As an employee of a BMW car dealership, Becker complained on his Facebook page about his employer serving hot dogs and potato chips at the launch of the BMW 5 Series. On the day of the event, at the adjacent Land Rover dealership, also owned by

Becker's employer, a 13-year-old drove a Land Rover into a pond. Becker took photos of the accident, which he also posted on his Facebook page along with some sarcastic comments. After a meeting with the general manager and other supervisors, in which Becker was confronted about his Facebook postings, Becker was fired. Did his termination violate the NLRA? Explain. See *Karl Knaus Motors, Inc.,* 358 N.L.R.B. No. 164 (2012) [**www.nlrb.gov**].

2. The Eugene, Oregon, *Register-Guard* newspaper maintained a company policy prohibiting employees from using company communications systems such as email to "solicit or proselytize for commercial ventures, religious or political causes, outside organizations, or other nonjob-related solicitations." Employees, however, had not been disciplined for using the email system to invite coworkers to parties, sell sports tickets, and so on. Suzi Prozanski, an employee and union president, used the employer's email system to send three union-related messages to other employees at their work addresses. She was disciplined under the company policy. Did the *Register-Guard* violate the NLRA in disciplining Prozanski? Explain. See *Register-Guard v. NLRB,* 571 F.3d 53 (D.C. Cir. 2009).
3. You are the human resources manager for a manufacturing firm that presently is the subject of an organizing campaign by a union that filed an election petition with the NLRB 30 days ago. Your plant manager has come to you and said that she wishes to discharge one of her employees. She further explains that the employee in question has worked for the company for three years and throughout that time has had a terrible attendance record. She adds that, up to this point, the employee has not received any discipline for his attendance. Upon inquiry, the plant manager tells you that the employee has been seen on the plant floor wearing a button that says: "Union Yes!" In addition, the plant manager tells you that she knows that the employee is an outspoken union activist. How would you advise the plant manager? Explain.
4. ACE/CO, a Milwaukee automobile parts manufacturer, was accused of a series of unfair labor practices springing from company conduct both before and after a disputed union representation election. Among the charges were the following:
   - ACE/CO declined to grant its usual across-the-board wage increases and told employees that the union was responsible for the failure to grant a raise.
   - ACE/CO distributed a memorandum asking employees to inform supervisors whenever they felt pressured to sign a union authorization card. One employee testified that union representatives had visited his home 13 times and that he did feel "pressured" to support the union.
   - ACE/CO included in its employee handbook a statement indicating the company's "intention to do everything possible to maintain our company's union-free status for the benefit of both our employees and [the company]."

   a. Why might ACE/CO legitimately decline to offer a wage increase during an organizing campaign?

   b. Do any of these company behaviors constitute unfair labor practices? See *NLRB v. Aluminum Casting & Engineering Co.,* 230 F.3d 286 (7th Cir. 2000).
5. As part of an organizing campaign at a Jimmy John's sandwich-shop franchise, workers organized a sick leave campaign. The franchise's handbook stated that it did "not

allow people to simply call in sick!" and required employees who would be absent from a shift to find a replacement and notify the store manager; failure to do so would result in termination. As flu season approached, the union organizers designed and placed on stores' community bulletin boards posters that showed two identical Jimmy John's sandwiches, and two different messages: "Your sandwich made by a sick Jimmy John's worker" and "Your sandwich made by a healthy Jimmy John's worker" with the words "healthy" and "sick" in large red letters. Below the pictures, the posters stated: "Can't Tell the Difference? That's too bad because Jimmy John's workers don't get paid sick days. Shoot, we can't even call in sick." The poster then asked for help getting the workers paid sick days by going to a union website. The posters were removed, and the employees who distributed the posters were disciplined or discharged. Did the franchise violate the NLRA? Explain. See *MikLin Enterprises, Inc. v. NLRB,* 861 F.3d 812 (8th Cir. 2017).

6. The Yuwei Plastics and Hardware Product Company Ltd. in Dongguan, China, manufactures and exports auto parts to Ford. The Institute for Global Labour and Human Rights reported that Yuwei workers earn 80¢ an hour, work 14-hour shifts seven days a week, and are docked three days' wages if they miss one day's work. Managers' instructions to turn off safety mechanisms to increase workers' speed have resulted in serious injuries. Ford accounts for approximately four-fifths of Yuwei's total production. Should American corporations be held responsible for their global suppliers' oppressive working conditions? Explain. See Charles Kernaghan, *Dirty Parts: Where Lost Fingers Come Cheap: Ford in China,* Pittsburgh, PA: International Institute for Global Labour and Human Rights, March 2011, pp. 1, 11.

7. Midwestern Personnel Services provided truck drivers to employers in Indiana, Kentucky, and other locations. Midwestern wanted the drivers to join a union so they would be allowed to perform services for a unionized workplace, AK Steel. Midwestern management favored Teamsters Local 836 in Middletown, Ohio, for their drivers, but a majority of the drivers voted to join Teamsters Local 215 in Evansville, Indiana. Midwestern refused to recognize Local 215; management and the drivers could not reach an agreement about pension rights and contract length, and the drivers went on strike. The drivers later made an unconditional offer to return to work, but Midwestern would not allow them to return because, in its view, the drivers were economic strikers. The NLRB concluded that the drivers were motivated in part by unfair labor practices and thus should be reinstated to their jobs. Were the drivers entitled to reinstatement? Explain. See *NLRB v. Midwestern Personnel Services,* 322 F.3d 969 (7th Cir. 2003).

8. The collective-bargaining agreement between Ralphs Grocery and United Food & Commercial Workers Union Local 135 contained a union security clause. The union sent a new employee of Ralph's, a teenager who planned to work part-time, a letter stating that union membership was a condition of employment and that all new hires were required to come to one of the union's offices to affiliate with it. The new hire's mother called the union office to ask what his reduced dues would be if he objected to union membership and was told her son would have to visit the office in person to receive this information. Eventually, after further written and phone communication, the union sent the new employee information about the reduced fees. Did the union commit an

unfair labor practice? Discuss. See *United Food & Commercial Workers Union, Local 135,* NLRB Case 21-CB-112391 (February 19, 2015).

9. A crew member of the Havertown, Pennsylvania, Chipotle responded to a customer's tweet, "Free chipotle is the best thanks," by tweeting, "nothing is free, only cheap #labor. Crew members only make $8.50/hr how much is that steak bowl really?" In replying to a tweet about Chipotle guacamole posted by another customer, the crew member wrote, "it's extra not like #Qdoba, enjoy the extra $2." Under the direction of Chipotle's social media strategist, the regional manager told the employee to delete the tweets. Did Chipotle violate the NLRA? Decide. Explain. See *Chipotle Services LLC d/b/a Chipotle Mexican Grill and Pennsylvania Workers Organizing Committee,* 364 N.L.R.B. No. 72 (2016).
10. An employer, Ashley Furniture of Arcadia, Wisconsin, instructed its employees not to discuss such workplace issues as disciplinary infractions, the expiration of an employee's work permit, or the receipt of a "no-match" letter from the Social Security Administration. Did the employer violate the NLRA? Explain. See *Ashley Furniture Industries,* 353 N.L.R.B. 071 (2008).
11. Dick's Sporting Goods used a nonunion contractor to prepare for its opening in a Watertown, New York, shopping mall. The local carpenters' union requested permission from the shopping mall's operator to distribute literature in the mall protesting the use of a nonunion contractor. While the mall had previously allowed such charitable organizations as the American Cancer Society and the Boy Scouts to distribute materials on its property, it rejected the union's request. Did the shopping mall violate the NLRA? Explain. See *Salmon Run Shopping Center v. NLRB,* 534 F.3d 108 (2d Cir. 2008).
12. A Walmart store policy prohibited solicitation during employees' work time regardless of the cause or organization. An employee came to the store while off-duty with union authorization cards, wearing a union T-shirt that read: "Sign a card . . . ask me how!" on the back. A store manager escorted him out of the store. The next day, while on duty, the employee invited other employees to a union meeting. As a result of these two incidents, the employee was "verbally coached" that he violated the store's no-solicitation rule. Verbal coaching is the first step in Walmart's progressive discipline process. Were the employee's actions protected under the NLRA? Explain. See *Wal-Mart Store, Inc. v. NLRB,* 400 F.3d 1093 (8th Cir. 2005).
13. LaDonna, who drove a route for a vending machine company, mentioned to her fellow driver, Steve, that she had seen an employment ad online for a route driver, speculating that it had been posted by their employer, perhaps because one of the route drivers was about to be fired. Steve thought he might be the one about to get fired and inquired about it with the employer. LaDonna was then fired for, among other infractions, spreading gossip among employees about possible terminations. Did firing LaDonna violate the NLRA? Decide. Explain. See *Sabo, Inc. d/b/a Hoodview Vending Co.,* 362 N.L.R.B. No. 81 (2015).
14. In October 2022, after a cardboard compactor caught fire at an Amazon warehouse on Staten Island, New York, dozens of workers gathered in a break room and refused to work due to concerns with fire safety. Some worried that the air in the facility might not be safe to breathe because of smoke and fumes from the fire. Amazon fired more

than two dozen of the employees. Do these suspensions violate the NLRA? Explain. See Noam Scheiber, "Suspensions Follow Protest Over a Fire at Amazon," *The New York Times* (October 6, 2022, p. B3)

15. During a strike resulting from the failure to reach a collective-bargaining agreement, Pan American Grain laid off 15 striking workers, citing changing labor needs "due to economic reasons and as a result of a substantial decrease in production and sales." Where labor costs are one of multiple motives for a layoff, does the employer have a duty to bargain with the union over the decision to impose that layoff? Explain. See *Pan American Grain v. NLRB,* 558 F.3d 22 (1st Cir. 2009).
16. Should faculty at private universities be allowed to unionize, or are faculty members more like "managers" at the university? How about student teaching and research assistants? Discuss. See *Pacific Lutheran University,* 361 N.L.R.B. No. 157 (2014); and Danielle Douglas-Gabriel, "Harvard agrees to negotiate a contract with graduate-student union," *The Washington Post,* May 1, 2018 [**www.washingtonpost.com**].
17. Star Garden, a topless bar in North Hollywood, California, fired three exotic dancers and barred 15 others from working after they raised concerns about their health and safety at work. The dancers began picketing outside the bar and discouraging customers from entering by describing conditions they believed to be unsafe. The dancers' effort to unionize had stalled when a majority of ballots in their union election were challenged by Star Garden. Has Star Garden violated the NLRA? If so, what remedies could be granted to the dancers? Explain. See: Suhuana Hussain, "NoHo topless bar broke law by firing and locking out strippers, NLRB says, *Los Angeles Times* (December 10, 2022 p. A9).
18. In representing Broadway actors and stage managers in labor agreement negotiations, the Actors' Equity Association sought commitments to (a)employ technicians for certain hair styles, (b) consider gender identity in dressing rooms and bathrooms, (c) set up a committee to talk about onstage intimacy, and (d) improve casting notices for individuals with disabilities. Are these mandatory or permissive subjects of collective bargaining? Explain. See Michael Paulson, "Actors' Equity Ratifies a New Contract," *The New York Times* (December 21, 2022 p. C3).

Notes

1. David Yaffe-Bellany, "Labor Fight Collides with the Pandemic at Trader Joe's," *The New York Times,* April 2, 2020 [**www.nytimes.com**].
2. Jack Healy, "Uneasy Workers Risk Losing Jobs by Staying Home," *The New York Times,* June 5, 2020 [**www.nytimes.com**].
3. Ana Rocio Alvarez Brinez, "'A game changing decision': Why Louisville Trader Joe's employees voted to unionize," *Louisville Carrier Journal* (January 27, 2023) [**https://www.courier-journal.com/**].
4. Jeffrey M. Jones, "As Labor Day Turns 125, Union Approval Near 50-Year High," *Gallup,* August 28, 2019 [**https://news.gallup.com**].
5. Union Members Summary," *Bureau of Labor Statistics News,* January 19, 2023 [**www.bls.gov**].
6. Isaac A. Hourwich, *Immigration and Labor* (New York: Arno Press, 1969), pp. 125–45.
7. John J. Flagler, *The Labor Movement in the United States* (Minneapolis: Lerner Publications, 1972), pp. 26–28.

8. Alan Glassman, Naomi Berger Davidson, and Thomas Cummings, *Labor Relations: Reports from the Firing Line* (New York: Business Publications, 1988), pp. 5–6.
9. John J. Flagler, *The Labor Movement in the United States.*
10. Andria Taylor Hourwich and Gladys L. Palmer, eds., *I Am a Woman Worker* (Affiliated Schools for Workers, 1936), pp. 17ff, in *The American Worker in the Twentieth Century: A History Through Autobiographies,* by Eli Ginzberg and Hyman Berman (New York: Free Press, 1963), pp. 193–95.
11. Flagler, The Labor Movement in the United States, pp. 33, 36, quoting Frederick Lewis Allen, *The Big Change: America Transforms Itself, 1900–1950* (New York: Harper, 1952).
12. Flagler, *The Labor Movement in the United States,* p. 47.
13. J. David Greenstone, *Labor in American Politics* (New York: Alfred A. Knopf, 1969), p. 21.
14. Archibald Cox, with Derek Bok and Robert A. Gorman, *Cases and Materials in Labor Law,* 8th ed. (Mineola, NY: Foundation Press, 1977), pp. 7–8.
15. Greenstone, *Labor in American Politics,* p. 22.
16. Ibid., p. 23.
17. Patrick Hardin, *The Developing Labor Law* (Washington, DC: Bureau of National Affairs, 1992), pp. 31–32.
18. Ibid., p. 94.
19. Ibid., pp. 1, 108.
20. *Steele v. Louisville and Nashville Railroad,* 323 U.S. 192 (1944).
21. *Vaca v. Sipes,* 386 U.S. 171 (1967); and *Miranda Fuel Co.,* 140 N.L.R.B. 181 (1962).
22. 29 U.S.C. § 151 et seq.
23. National Labor Relations Board, GC 08-10, "Guideline Memorandum Concerning Unfair Labor Practice Charges Involving Political Advocacy," July 22, 2008 [**www.nlrb.gov**].
24. *Red Cross Arizona Blood Services Region,* 2012 NLRB LEXIS 43 (April 20, 2012).
25. Barry J. Kearney, Associate General Counsel, NLRB Advice Memorandum, SWH Corporation d/b/a Mimi's Café, October 31, 2012 [**www.nlrb.gov**].
26. Christian Schappel, "30 Employee Handbook Do's and Don'ts from the NLRB," *HR Morning,* July 18, 2018 [**www.hrmorning.com**].
27. *Bosch Imports, Inc. v. NLRB,* 826 F.3d 558 (1st Cir. 2016).
28. *Southern New England Telephone Company v. NLRB,* 793 F.3d 93 (D.C. Cir. 2015).
29. National Labor Relations Board, "The NLRB and Social Media," *NLRB Fact Sheets* [**www.nlrb.gov**].
30. *Costco Wholesale Corporation,* 358 NLRB No. 106 (2012) [**www.nlrb.gov**].
31. *Design Technology Group, d/b/a Bettie Page Clothing,* 359 NLRB No. 96 (2013) [**www.nlrb.gov**].
32. Cox, *Cases and Materials in Labor Law,* pp. 113–22.
33. Ibid., pp. 99–101.
34. Bradley M. Taormina, Bruce M. Bagdady, and Saniya Khare, "NLRB Curtails 'Quickie Election' Rules," *Hall Render,* January 2, 2020 [**www.hallrender.com**].
35. "NLRB 'Ambush' Election Rules Now in Effect," *The National Law Review,* April 14, 2015 [**www.natlawreview.com**]; and Frederick D. Braid, "NLRB Revises Election Rules Again," December 17, 2019 [**www.hklaw.com**].
36. National Labor Relations Board, "Employer-Filed Petitions—RM," accessed June 2020 [**www.nlrb.gov**].
37. National Labor Relations Board, "Conduct Elections," accessed June 2020 [**www.nlrb.gov**].
38. National Labor Relations Board, "NLRB Representation Case-Procedures Fact Sheet," accessed June 2020 [**www.nlrb.gov**].

39. National Labor Relations Board, "Conduct Elections."
40. 351 N.L.R.B. No. 28 (2007).
41. Braid, "NLRB Revises Election Rules Again."
42. 357 N.L.R.B. No. 83 (2011), *enforcement granted, Kindred Nursing Centers East v. NLRB,* 727 F.3d 552 (6th Cir. 2013).
43. Ibid.
44. *Oakwood Healthcare, Inc.,* 348 N.L.R.B. No. 37 (2006).
45. *FedEx Home Delivery v. NLRB,* 563 F.3d 492 (D.C. Cir. 2009).
46. 502 U.S. 527 (1992).
47. *Town & Country v. NLRB,* 516 U.S. 85 (1995).
48. *Toering Electric Company,* 351 N.L.R.B. No. 18 (2007).
49. 361 N.L.R.B. No. 126 (2014).
50. Howard M. Bloom and Philip B. Rosen, "NLRB Overrules Purple Communications," *National Law Review,* December 18, 2019 **[www.natlawreview.com]** citing Caesars Entertainment d/b/a Rio All-Suites Hotel and Casino, 368 N.L.R.B. No. 143 (Dec. 17, 2019).
51. See *Sewell Manufacturing Co.,* 138 N.L.R.B. 66 (1962), which states that the board's goal is to conduct elections "in a laboratory under conditions as nearly ideal as possible to determine the uninhibited desires of employees" and "to provide an atmosphere conducive to the sober and informed exercise of the franchise free from . . . elements which prevent or impede reasonable choice."
52. *Dish Network Corp.,* 359 N.L.R.B. No. 32 (2012) **[citing Tri-Cast, Inc., 274 N.L.R.B. 377 (1985)] [www.nlrb.gov]**.
53. *NLRB v. Exchange Parts Co.,* 375 U.S. 405 (1964).
54. *Trencor, Inc. v. National Labor Relations Board,* 110 F.3d 268 (5th Cir. 1997).
55. Ronald Meisburg, N.L.R.B. Office of the General Counsel, Memorandum GC 09-04, Guideline Memorandum Concerning Withdrawal of Recognition Based on Loss of Majority Support, November 26, 2008, p. 4 (citing *Highland Regional Medical Center,* 347 N.L.R.B. 1404, 1406 (2006), and *Wurtland Nursing,* 351 N.L.R.B. No. 50, slip op. at 2).
56. National Labor Relations Board, "Employer/Union Rights and Obligations," accessed June 2020 **[www.nlrb.gov]**.
57. See *First National Maintenance Corporation v. NLRB,* 101 S. Ct. 2573 (1981).
58. *Granite Rock v. International Brotherhood of Teamsters,* 130 S. Ct. 2847 (2010).
59. 129 S. Ct. 1456 (2009).
60. Becky Z. Dernbach, "Major Labor Strikes Surged in 2019," Mother Jones, February 13, 2020 **[www.motherjones.com]**.
61. Kate Conger, Vicky Ziuahong Xu, and Zach Wichter, "Uber Drivers' Day of Strikes Circles the Globe Before the Company's I.P.O.," *The New York Times,* May 8, 2019 **[www.nytimes.com]**.
62. Littler, Mendelson, Fastiff & Tichy, *The 1990 Employer* (San Francisco: Littler, Mendelson, Fastiff & Tichy, P.C., 1990), p. V6.
63. *NLRB v. Mackay Radio & Telegraph Co.,* 304 U.S. 333 (1938).
64. Littler, *The 1990 Employer,* p. V6.
65. Chase Hughes, "NBA's New Collective Bargaining Agreement Officially Signed," NBC Sports: Washington, January 19, 2017 **[www.nbcsports.com]**.
66. *United Steelworkers of America v. Sadlowski,* 457 U.S. 102 (1982).

67. 487 U.S. 735 (1988).
68. 132 S. Ct. 2277 (2012).
69. Jeffrey M. Jones, "Americans Approve of Unions but Support 'Right to Work,'" *Gallup,* August 28, 2014 [**www.gallup.com**].
70. Workplace Fairness Organization, "Right to Work Laws," accessed June 2020 [**www.workplace-fairness.org**].
71. *Int'l Union of Operating Eng'rs Local 139 v. Schimel,* 863 F.3d 674 (7th Cir. 2017).
72. *Sweeney v. Pence,* 767 F.3d 654 (7th Cir. 2014).
73. *Zoellers v. Sweeney,* 19 N.E.3d 749 (Ind. 2014).
74. Bureau of Labor Statistics, "Union Members Summary," *Bureau of Labor Statistics News,* January 22, 2020 [**www.bls.gov**].
75. David Madland and Alex Rowell, "Attacks on Public-Sector Unions Harm States: How ACT 10 Has Affected Education in Wisconsin," *Center for American Progress Action Fund,*" November 15, 2017 [**www.americanprogressaction.org**]; *Wisconsin Education Association Council v. Scott Walker,* 705 F.3d 640 (7th Cir. 2013); and Laborers Local 236, *AFL-CIO v. Scott Walker,* 749 F.3d 628 (7th Cir. 2014).
76. *Abood v. Detroit Board of Education,* 431 U.S. 209 (1977).
77. Ibid.; and Scott Horsley and Nina Totenberg, "Supreme Court Deals Blow to Government Unions," National Public Radio, June 27, 2018 [**www.npr.org**].
78. *Harris v. Quinn,* 134 S. Ct. 2618 (2014).
79. Ibid.
80. *Friedrichs v. California Teachers Association,* 136 S. Ct. 1083 (2016).
81. 138 S. Ct. 2448 (2018).
82. Mene Ukueberuwa, "Public Unions vs. The People," *The Wall Street Journal* (March 4-5, 2023 p. A 13).

Video icon credit: Comstock Images/Alamy Stock Photo

UNIT FIVE

Selected Topics in Government–Business Relations

CHAPTER FIFTEEN

Consumer Protection

After completing this chapter, students will be able to fulfill the following learning objectives:

15-1. Understand the business practices that have led to the adoption of consumer protection laws.

15-2. Be able to discuss the ethical obligations of businesses to the end-users of their goods and services.

15-3. Identify and describe the elements of the consumer protections offered under common law.

15-4. Be able to distinguish puffery from misrepresentation and fraud and give examples of each.

15-5. Be able to explain the difference between procedural and substantive unconscionability.

15-6. Describe “lemon laws” as an example of state consumer regulation.

15-7. Identify the major responsibilities of the FDA and discuss some of the challenges it faces in fulfilling them.

15-8. Discuss the regulatory challenge presented by e-cigarettes as both an on-ramp for nicotine addiction among young people and an off-ramp to reduce nicotine dependence in adult users.

15-9. Be able to identify the stakeholder groups which the FDA must consider in developing rules and processes to address food safety and articulate those groups’ disparate interests and concerns.

15-10. Be able to identify some of the consumer protection laws the FTC is charged with enforcing.

15-11. Identify and describe some of the actions the FTC may take against businesses that are in violation of the laws it enforces, as well as the types of relief it may seek for consumers.

15-12. Identify and describe the purposes for which the CPSC was established and some of the methods by which it accomplishes those purposes.

15-13. Identify and describe the purposes for which the CFPB was established and some of the methods by which it accomplishes those purposes.

15-14. Understand the way in which the debtor/creditor laws discussed in this part may impact you, now or in the future.

15-15. Identify the purposes of the Truth in Lending Act and Regulation Z.

15-16. Be able to identify one or more ways it might be argued to have disadvantaged them.

15-17. Identify protections offered under the Fair Credit Reporting Act.

15-18. Be able to identify the purpose of the Equal Credit Opportunity Act and give examples of facts which would be in violation of the Act.

15-19. Identify debt collection practices forbidden by the Fair Debt Collection Practices Act.

15-20. Understand the purpose for providing bankruptcy to individuals.

15-21. Be able to explain the effects and implications of the three bankruptcy options.

15-22. In light of the consumer protections discussed in this chapter, be able to proffer a reasoned evaluation of the necessity for consumer protection laws in relation to Adam Smith's "invisible hand" regulating the markets.

Introduction

LO 15-1
Understand the business practices that have led to the adoption of consumer protection laws.

LO 15-2
Be able to discuss the ethical obligations of businesses to the end-users of their goods and services.

Not that long ago many of the contexts in which the issues discussed in this chapter occur either did not exist or, if they did, they arose in face-to-face transactions, such as the denial of credit for the acquisition of consumer and household goods and services. If you look around you right now, most of you will be hard-pressed to identify anything that you use or consume in your daily life for which you know the person who grew it or made it. You might well know the company who manufactured it or the store you bought it from, but that is likely as much as you know. If you think about the company that manufactured one of the items you can see, that still does not mean that is the company who physically built it or who manufactured the parts from which is was made, and may or may not be the entity who designed or engineered it. For example, as many as 250,000 patents may be associated with your smartphone. Neither Apple, nor Microsoft, nor Google, even collectively, own all of them.[1]

The reverse is also true. Microsoft may know your name, your email address, and your phone number. But that is just data. Neither it or the people who work for it actually know you. That is the context in which most of the problems addressed by the laws in this chapter arise—through the operation of the invisible hand of the market consumers and producers come together. Consider the ethics discussions in Chapter Two. It is a lot easier to justify one's conclusions about ethical behavior in the abstract than feel the personal necessity to be ethically aware and put into practice the conclusions you reach. Distance does not make the ethical link grow stronger; it may make it almost vanish. That is where law steps in, often establishing not only laws, but agencies to oversee and enforce them.

Although we are going to spend most of this chapter looking at federal laws, we will start our discussion of the business-to-customer/client relationship with a brief look at state law, both common and statutory.

Part One—Common Law Consumer Protection

Later in this chapter we will explore legislative and regulatory efforts to protect consumers from deception, dangerous products, unfair lending practices, and the like. Before turning to those rules, we need to appreciate the common law that often preceded and, in some respects, provided the foundation for the many federal, state, and local government laws that now exist. In addition to the product liability claims (negligence, warranties, and

LO 15-3 Identify and describe the elements of the consumer protections offered under common law.

strict liability) discussed in Chapter Seven, injured consumers can look to several other common law protections, including actions for misrepresentation and unconscionability discussed here.

Pet Food Puffery?

Wysong, a pet food seller, brought a claim against some of its competitors that they had misled consumers by putting pictures on their packaging of delicious-looking lamb chops, chicken breasts, and so on, when the kibble inside is actually made from "trimmings" left over after the premium cuts have been sliced away. Many of the packages included mention of animal "meal" or animal "by-product" as ingredients. Wysong says its own products often do contain premium cuts of meat.

Question

Among other arguments, the defendants claimed the pictures on their packages constituted lawful puffing. How would you rule on the puffing defense? Explain.

Source: See *Wysong Corporation v. APN, Inc., et al.,* 889 F.3d 267 (6th Cir. 2018).

Misrepresentation

LO 15-4 Be able to distinguish puffery from misrepresentation and fraud and give examples of each.

In examining misrepresentation, the law distinguishes between statements of objective, verifiable facts, and expressions of opinion. The latter ordinarily are not fraudulent even if erroneous. Thus, normal sales *puffing,* illustrated in the preceding text box, is fully lawful, and consumers are expected to exercise good judgment in evaluating such claims.

If a misleading expression of opinion comes from an expert, however, and the other party does not share that expertise (such as in the sale of a diamond engagement ring), a court would likely offer a remedy.

Fraud

A 2022 report from the Federal Trade Commission (FTC) indicated that more than 2.8 million consumers had reported frauds that collectively caused losses of more than $5.8 billion, a 70 percent increase over 2020.[2] The five most commonly reported categories were imposter scams; online shopping scams; prizes, sweepstakes, and lotteries; internet services; and business and job opportunities.[3]

Fraud is an intentional deception related to a material fact designed to secure an unfair or unlawful gain. A victim of civil consumer fraud ordinarily is entitled to rescind the transaction in question and to seek damages, including penalties in some cases. Fraud also may constitute a crime. The elements that need to be shown to prove fraud were identified in Part One of Chapter Seven.

Other Forms of Misrepresentation

In addition to fraud, the law often recognizes claims of *negligent misrepresentation* and *innocent misrepresentation.* Negligent misrepresentation involves a false claim resulting not from an intentional untruth, as with fraud, but from a careless or baseless assertion. The false utterance was made without reasonable care. Innocent misrepresentation involves a false claim made in error. The wrongdoer reasonably believed the statement or conduct in question to be true, but they were mistaken.

Silence can constitute misrepresentation when material facts are not disclosed, as in the nondisclosure of a latent (hidden) defect during the sale of a house. Misrepresentation can involve false conduct as well as false expressions. A familiar example is the car seller who rolls back an odometer, with the result that the buyer is misled.

PRACTICING ETHICS Watery Beer?

Several class-action lawsuits were filed against Anheuser-Busch (AB) in 2013 claiming the brewing giant had intentionally watered down some of its beer products during the brewing process. The plaintiffs alleged that AB intentionally deceived buyers by selling beer such as Budweiser, Bud Ice, and Michelob with less alcohol than was indicated on product labels. Plaintiffs based their claims on AB whistleblowers, including a former operations director. Nonetheless, a federal district court in 2014 and a federal court of appeals in 2016 ruled for AB, saying that federal law allows a 0.3 percent tolerance between the true and the claimed alcohol content, and the plaintiffs had not alleged that AB beer exceeded that tolerance. Independent of the lawsuit, National Public Radio commissioned a laboratory report that concluded that the AB beers in question were "found to be in line with their advertised alcohol content."

Questions

1. If AB intentionally reduced alcohol content in some brands beneath the level advertised on the label but within the legal tolerance, did AB commit an ethical wrong? Explain.
2. Evidence indicates that many buyers do not read beer labels and perhaps do not care about precise alcohol content. Given that evidence, if AB did, in fact, dilute its beer, would that dilution constitute an ethical wrong? Explain.
3. Have you noticed other instances of arguable consumer fraud in your daily life? Explain.

Sources: Dan Bobkoff and Bill Chappell, "Budweiser May Seem Watery, but It Tests at Full Strength, Lab Says," *The Salt,* February 27, 2013 [**www.npr.org**]; Ben Bouckley, "Judge Throws Out Watered-Down Budweiser Beer Fraud Claims Against Anheuser-Busch," *BeverageDaily.com,* June 9, 2014 [**www.beveragedaily.com**]; and *In re Anheuser-Busch Beer Labeling,* 644 F. App'x 515 (6th Cir. 2016).

The following case involves a fraud claim against Harley-Davidson.

LEGAL BRIEFCASE

Tietsworth v. Harley–Davidson

677 N.W.2d 233 (Wis. 2004)

Justice Diane S. Sykes

The circuit court dismissed the entire action for failure to state a claim. [T]he court of appeals reinstated [the claims.]

FACTS AND PROCEDURAL HISTORY

Plaintiff Steven C. Tietsworth and the members of the proposed class own or lease 1999 or early-2000 model year Harley motorcycles equipped with Twin Cam 88 or Twin Cam 88B engines. Harley's marketing and advertising literature contained the following statement about the TC-88 engines:

> Developing [the TC-88s] was a six-year process. . . . The result is a masterpiece. We studied everything from the way oil moves through the inside, to the way a rocker cover does its job of staying oil-tight. Only 21 functional parts carry over into

the new design. What does carry over is the power of a Harley-Davidson™ engine, only more so.

Harley also stated that the motorcycles were "premium" quality, and described the TC-88 engine as "eighty-eight cubic inches filled to the brim with torque and ready to take you thundering down the road."

On January 22, 2001, Harley sent a letter to Tietsworth and other owners of Harley motorcycles informing them that "the rear cam bearing in a small number of Harley-Davidson's Twin Cam 88 engines has failed. While it is unlikely that you will ever have to worry about this situation, you have our assurance that Harley-Davidson is committed to your satisfaction." The letter went on to explain that the company was extending the warranty on the cam bearing from the standard one-year/unlimited mileage warranty to a five-year/50,000 mile warranty. Separately, Harley developed a $495 "cam bearing repair kit" and made the kit available to its dealers and service departments "to expedite rear cam bearing repair."

The amended complaint alleges that the cam bearing mechanism in the 1999 and early-2000 model year TC-88 engines is inherently defective, causing an unreasonably dangerous propensity for premature engine failure. [T]he amended complaint alleged that Harley's failure to disclose the cam bearing defect induced the plaintiffs to purchase their motorcycles by causing them to reasonably rely upon Harley's representations regarding the "premium" quality of the motorcycles.

The amended complaint further alleges that if the plaintiffs had known of the engine defect, they either would not have purchased the product or would have paid less for it. The amended complaint does not allege that the plaintiffs' motorcycles have actually suffered engine failure, have malfunctioned in any way, or are reasonably certain to fail or malfunction. Nor does the amended complaint allege any property damage or personal injury arising out of the engine defect. Rather, the amended complaint alleges that the plaintiffs' motorcycles have diminished value, including diminished resale value, because Harley motorcycles equipped with TC-88 engines have demonstrated a "propensity" for premature engine failure and/or fail prematurely.

DISCUSSION

Common-Law Fraud Claim

The plaintiffs' common-law fraud claim is premised on the allegation that Harley failed to disclose or concealed the existence of the cam bearing defect prior to the plaintiffs' purchases of their motorcycles. It is well established that a nondisclosure is not actionable as a misrepresentation tort unless there is a duty to disclose. *Ollerman v. O'Rourke Co., Inc.*, 94 Wis. 2d 17, 26, 288 N.W.2d 95 (1980). Our decision in *Ollerman* outlined the three categories of misrepresentation in Wisconsin law—intentional misrepresentation, negligent misrepresentation, and strict responsibility misrepresentation—and described the common and distinct elements of the three torts.

All misrepresentation claims share the following required elements: (1) the defendant must have made a representation of fact to the plaintiff; (2) the representation of fact must be false; and (3) the plaintiff must have believed and relied on the misrepresentation to his detriment or damage. The plaintiffs here allege intentional misrepresentation, which carries the following additional elements: (4) the defendant must have made the misrepresentation with knowledge that it was false or recklessly without caring whether it was true or false; and (5) the defendant must have made the misrepresentation with intent to deceive and to induce the plaintiff to act on it to his detriment or damage.

Ollerman reiterated the general rule that in a sales or business transaction, "silence, a failure to disclose a fact, is not an intentional misrepresentation unless the seller has a duty to disclose." The existence and scope of a duty to disclose are questions of law for the court. *Ollerman* held that "a subdivider–vendor of a residential lot has a duty to a 'noncommercial' purchaser to disclose facts which are known to the vendor, which are material to the transaction, and which are not readily discernible to the purchaser." We specified that this was a "narrow holding," premised on certain policy considerations present in noncommercial real estate transactions.

The transactions at issue here, however, are motorcycle purchases, not residential real estate purchases, and it is an open question whether the duty to disclose recognized in *Ollerman* extends more broadly to sales of consumer goods. . . .

No Legally Cognizable Injury

Ollerman also held that damages in intentional misrepresentation cases are measured according to the "benefit of the bargain" rule, "typically stated as the difference between the value of the property as represented and its actual value as purchased. . . ."

[W]e have generally held that a tort claim is not capable of present enforcement (and therefore does not accrue) unless the plaintiff has suffered actual damage. . . . Actual damage is harm that has already occurred or is "reasonably certain" to occur in the future. . . . Actual damage is not the mere possibility of future harm. . . . [T]he amended complaint must adequately plead an actual injury—a loss or damage that has already occurred or is reasonably certain to occur—in order to state an actionable fraud claim. . . .

The injury complained of here is diminution in value only—the plaintiffs allege that their motorcycles are worth less than they paid for them. However, the amended complaint does not allege that the plaintiffs' motorcycles have diminished value because their engines have failed, will fail, or are reasonably certain to fail as a result of the TC-88 cam bearing defect. The amended complaint does not allege that the plaintiffs have sold their motorcycles at a loss because of the alleged engine defect. The amended complaint alleges only that the motorcycles have diminished value—primarily diminished potential resale value—because Harley motorcycles equipped with TC-88 engines have demonstrated a "propensity" for premature engine failure and/or will fail as a result of the cam bearing defect. This is insufficient to state a legally cognizable injury for purposes of a fraud claim.

Diminished value premised upon a mere possibility of future product failure is too speculative and uncertain to support a fraud claim. The plaintiffs do not specifically allege that their particular motorcycles will fail prematurely, only that the Harley product line that consists of motorcycles with TC-88 engines has demonstrated a propensity for premature engine failure. An allegation that a particular product line fails prematurely does not constitute an allegation that the plaintiffs' particular motorcycles will do so, only that there is a possibility that they will do so.

We certainly agree with the court of appeals that the damage allegations in a fraud complaint are not evaluated against a standard of "absolute certainty" for purposes of a motion to dismiss for failure to state a claim. But an allegation that a product is diminished in value because of an event or circumstance that might—or might not—occur in the future is inherently conjectural and does not allege actual benefit-of-the-bargain damages with the "reasonable certainty" required to state a fraud claim.

[Reversed.] [The plaintiffs' additional claims are omitted.]

Questions

1. *a.* According to the Wisconsin Supreme Court, under what circumstances might the nondisclosure by a seller of a defect constitute misrepresentation?
   b. Did the court find that Harley–Davidson had a duty to disclose in this case? Explain.
2. *a.* What injury, if any, did the plaintiffs claim they suffered in this case?
   b. According to the Wisconsin Supreme Court, must a plaintiff in a fraud action prove that he or she has suffered actual damages prior to bringing a claim? Explain.
   c. What is the "benefit of the bargain" rule?
3. Why did the Wisconsin Supreme Court rule for defendant Harley-Davidson?
4. Robert McGlothlin, an employee of Thomson Consumer Electronics in Bloomington, Indiana, was injured while loading televisions into a semi-trailer when the trailer's "landing gear" (retractable legs that support the front of the trailer when it is not attached to the semi-tractor) collapsed. McGlothlin sued the owner of the trailer, among others, claiming that the defendants' repair and inspection procedures for *latent* (hidden) defects were inadequate. Should the court treat latent defects differently than *patent* (observable) defects in determining when a legal duty exists? Explain. See *McGlothlin v. M & U Trucking*, 688 N.E.2d 1243 (Ind. 1997).

Unconscionable Contracts

LO 15-5
Be able to explain the difference between procedural and substantive unconscionability.

Contracts that are shockingly unfair, oppressive, or one-sided may be considered unconscionable, and courts typically treat them as being unenforceable. (Unconscionability is also included in state statutory laws via the Uniform Commercial Code section 2-302.) The legal system is reluctant to intrude on contracts. Mere foolishness or lack of knowledge does not constitute grounds for unconscionability, nor is a contract unconscionable and hence unenforceable merely because one party is spectacularly clever and the other is not. Unconscionability can take either or both of two forms:

1. *Procedural unconscionability (how the contract was formed).* The bargaining power of the parties was so unequal that the agreement, as a practical matter, was not freely entered. Procedural unconscionability usually arises from lack of knowledge (such as being buried in fine print) or lack of choice (for example, urgent circumstances).
2. *Substantive unconscionability (the terms of the contract).* The clause or contract in question was so manifestly one-sided, oppressive, or unfair as to "shock the conscience of the court." Contract terms completely inconsistent with the relative risks assumed by the parties or a contract that does not provide a remedy for a breach are among the conditions that might lead to a finding of substantive unconscionability.

The classic example of an unconscionable contract was a seller-financed installment purchase of goods from a furniture store. If, prior to paying off the first contract the consumer purchased another item from the seller, all future payments were spread pro-rata among all items purchased under all outstanding contracts, even if only a small amount remained owing on the first contract at the time of the second purchase. Thus, if buyer defaulted, the contract allowed the seller to repossess all items purchased under any of the contracts. In essence, all items purchased were security for any outstanding balance. The District of Columbia Circuit Court held that "a contract is unconscionable when the contract terms are so extreme as to appear unconscionable according to the mores and business practices of the time and place."[4]

Part Two—The Consumer and Government Regulation of Business

State Laws

Having looked at the common law foundation, we turn to some of the many state laws and rules that provide consumer protection in the marketplace. Many states have enacted comprehensive consumer protection statutes. They may also have specific statutes addressing such problems as debtor protection and telemarketing fraud. We will look briefly at a pair of high-interest consumer loan situations, as well as state "lemon laws" which address the particularly frustrating problem of a hopelessly defective vehicle.

Payday, Auto Title, and Pawn Loans–Abusive, But Necessary?

Collectively, all of these loans are often referred to as alternative financial services, or AFS, because the lenders are not banks. The loan amounts are usually less that $1,000 and come with high interest rates and short-term durations. Typically the lender makes no credit check. Payday loans are provided in advance of the borrower's payday for a fee; the lender of an auto title loan takes custody of the title to the owner's car as collateral for repayment. Similarly, in a pawn loan, the item used to secure the loan, such as a computer or jewelry, is held by the lender as security for the payment. Using two surveys, in June 2019 and June 2020, the Consumer Finance Protection Bureau (CFPB) found, not surprisingly, that a "majority of AFS users have poor or very poor credit scores and are often turned down for mainstream credit or not granted the full requested amount."[5]

Jennifer Williams, a Cleveland, Mississippi, teacher borrowed $200 from a payday lender. Years later she said, "It sounds good in the beginning, and when you go in, they'll do all they can to get you in the system[.] . . ., But it's like quicksand: You try to get out, but you can't."[6] Ms. Williams ultimately paid off her loans with the help of financial literacy workshops and credit counseling offered by Southern Bancorp. Attendees of the workshops were able to receive low-interest loans on the completion of the coursework.

Eighteen states and Washington, D.C. have laws that prohibit payday loans or set interest rate limits so low that payday lenders do not operate there. The average annual percentage rate in states with payday lenders ranged from 114 percent (Colorado) to 652 percent (Idaho) based on research by the Pew Charitable Trusts.

Question

Do protective lending rules, as 18 states have enacted, advance consumer fairness or do they harm consumers most in need because they cannot meet the loan requirements of traditional lenders? Look at the full report from the CFPB and decide what you would want your state legislature to do.

Sources: Office of Research, "Consumer use of payday, auto title, and pawn loans," *Consumer Financial Protection Bureau,* May 2021 (**www.consumerfinance.gov**); Gretchen Morgenson, Lisa Cavazuti and Vicky Nguyen, *NBC News,* January 11, 2022 [**www.nbcnews.com**]; and "How Well Does Your State Protect Payday Loan Borrowers?," *The Pew Charitable Trusts,* July 26, 2022 [**www.pewtrusts.org**].

Lemon Laws

LO 15-6
Describe "lemon laws" as an example of state consumer regulation.

New vehicle purchases (and those of used vehicles in some states) are protected by warranty laws (see Part Two of Chapter Seven for a discussion of Uniform Commercial Code warranty provisions and the federal Magnuson-Moss Warranty Act).

In addition to warranty protection, all 50 states have some form of lemon law designed to provide recourse for consumers who purchase a new vehicle (car or truck) that turns out to be so defective that it cannot be repaired. Some states also cover leased and used cars. The quarrel, of course, is about how to determine when a vehicle truly is a lemon.

Lemon laws differ significantly from state to state, but they often cover new vehicles for one to two years or up to 24,000 miles after purchase. In addition, the laws will have standards with regard to such criteria as how many times a vehicle has been returned to the manufacturer, how substantially the defect impairs the safety or value of the vehicle, and how many days within a set period of time the vehicle has been unavailable for use by the owner. If the standard is met, the owner would be entitled to a replacement vehicle or a full refund of the price. In almost all states, the determination about whether a vehicle is a lemon is handled by an arbitration panel. If dissatisfied with the panel's ruling, the owner could still file a claim in court.

The quarrel is about how to determine when a vehicle truly is a lemon.

The case that follows examines Minnesota's lemon law requirements. [For lemon laws in all 50 states, see **www.kbb.com**].

LEGAL BRIEFCASE

Paul Sipe v. Workhorse Custom Chassis

572 F.3d 525 (8th Cir. 2009)

Circuit Judge Gruender

I. BACKGROUND

On September 18, 2004, Paul Sipe purchased a motor home manufactured by Fleetwood Motor Homes of Pennsylvania, Inc. ("Fleetwood"), from Brambillas, Inc. ("Brambillas"), an authorized Fleetwood motor home dealer and repair facility located in Minnesota. Workhorse manufactured the motor home's chassis, which included the motor home's supporting frame, engine, transmission, and certain electrical components. Sipe purchased the motor home for $105,616.75, and Brambillas delivered it to Sipe on October 21, 2004. Sipe received an owner's manual with the motor home that contained Workhorse's limited warranty for the chassis.

Sipe began experiencing problems with the motor home's engine shortly after he bought it. The engine stalled on three occasions while being driven by Sipe, once in October 2004, once in May 2005, and once in June 2005. Sipe brought the motor home to Brambillas for repairs after each stalling incident. After the first incident, Brambillas conducted diagnostic tests but made no repairs because it found no defect in the engine. Sipe testified in his deposition that after the second and third incidents, Brambillas claimed it performed diagnostic tests and found no defect but that the work order he received contained no indication that Brambillas performed any such tests. Sipe further testified that the last time the engine stalled was in June 2005 and that the engine problem has not prevented him from taking trips in the motor home.

In February 2006, Sipe listed the motor home for sale for the price of $94,900. After receiving only two offers at lower prices, Sipe reduced the listing price to $84,900, the Kelley Blue Book value of the motor home. Sipe testified that he ultimately decided to reduce the price because of a crack in the kitchen counter and that he did not recall any other defects that contributed to his decision to reduce the asking price. Sipe did not sell the motor home.

In January 2007 and December 2007, Sipe experienced problems with the motor home's transmission when he discovered that transmission fluid had leaked. Sipe testified that Brambillas refused to diagnose or repair the transmission after both incidents of fluid leakage.

Sipe brought this action against Workhorse and Fleetwood in the District Court for Hennepin County, Minnesota, alleging violations of Minnesota's lemon law. . . . The court dismissed Sipe's lemon law claims, finding that Sipe presented no evidence that the alleged engine defect required repair or that the defect substantially impaired the motor home and concluding that Sipe's claim regarding the transmission was time-barred.

II. DISCUSSION

A. Lemon Law

Sipe contends that the district court erred in granting summary judgment to Workhorse on his lemon law claim because Workhorse failed to repair his motor home's engine and transmission. Minnesota's lemon law provides:

> If the manufacturer, its agents, or its authorized dealers are unable to conform the new motor vehicle to any applicable express warranty by repairing or correcting any defect or condition which substantially impairs the use or market value of the motor vehicle to the consumer after a reasonable number of attempts, the manufacturer shall either replace the new motor vehicle with a comparable motor vehicle or accept return of the vehicle from the consumer and refund to the consumer the full purchase price. . . .

The manufacturer must make the required repairs if "the consumer reports the nonconformity to the manufacturer, its agents, or its authorized dealer during the term of the applicable express warranties or during the period of two years following the date of original delivery of the new motor vehicle to a consumer, whichever is the earlier date."

1. Engine Stalls

After thoroughly reviewing the record, we conclude that Sipe failed to present evidence showing a genuine issue of material fact about whether the engine stalls "substantially impair[ed] the use or market value of the motor [home]," as required by Minnesota's lemon law. In response to being asked if the engine defect "ever prevented [him] from going somewhere [or] taking a trip with [his] motor home," Sipe replied "no." In fact, Sipe traveled over 11,000 miles in the motor home since the first time the engine stalled. As Sipe explained, "I don't know if [the engine problem] affect[s] my use now because I know how to deal with it." Sipe also stated that he had not experienced an engine stall since June 2005. Thus, Sipe's own testimony shows that the engine defect has not impaired his use of the motor home; it follows that the defect has not substantially impaired his use.

With respect to the effect of the engine defect on the market value of the motor home, Sipe argues that the low number of offers he received for the motor home shows that its market value was substantially impaired. However, Sipe cannot avoid summary judgment by merely relying on his conclusory allegation that the engine defect caused the low number of offers. Sipe presented no evidence to suggest that his receipt of only two offers was in any way caused by the engine stalls and not some other factor, such as market conditions for used motor homes. He offered no evidence that potential buyers were even aware of the engine stalls, given that he described the motor home as being in "excellent condition" when he originally listed it for sale in February 2006. Sipe testified that he only reduced the original asking price to the Kelley Blue Book value because of a crack in the kitchen counter and that he did not recall any other defects "that played a role in reducing the price." Further, Sipe submitted no other evidence suggesting that the value of the motor home was impaired, such as expert testimony or an appraisal of the motor home. As with his testimony regarding his use of the motor home, Sipe's own testimony shows that the engine defect has not impaired, substantially or otherwise, the motor home's market value.

2. Transmission Fluid Leaks

When he received the motor home in October 2004, Sipe received a three-year limited warranty from Workhorse. Thus, to bring an actionable lemon law claim, Sipe must have reported any nonconformities within two years of the date of the original delivery of the motor home. *See* Minn. Stat. Section 325 F. 665, subdiv. 2 (requiring consumers to report a nonconformity "during the term of the applicable express warranties or during the period of two years following the date of original delivery of the new motor vehicle . . ., whichever is the earlier date"). Sipe first reported the transmission fluid leak to Brambillas in January 2007, which was more than two years after the delivery of the motor home. As such, we agree with the district court that Sipe's lemon law claim with respect to the transmission leaks is barred by statute.

[Affirmed.]

Questions

1. *a.* According to Minnesota's lemon law, what was Sipe required to show in order to win his engine defect claim?

   b. Why did Sipe lose his engine defect claim?
2. Why did Sipe lose his defective transmission claim?
3. Dieter and Hermes agreed to buy a new 1996 Dodge Ram pickup truck from Fascona Chrysler-Plymouth-Dodge Trucks on December 12, 1995. They requested the installation of some after-market accessories—a tonneau cover, a bug shield, and rust proofing. When Dieter and Hermes returned to take delivery of the truck, they noticed it had been scratched during the installation of the accessories. The salesperson told them the scratches would be repaired. Four months later, the dealership sent the truck to a body shop for repairs. After repair, Dieter and Hermes noticed swirl marks in the truck's finish. Dieter then demanded that Frascona repurchase the truck. Eight months later, Dieter and Hermes sued Chrysler Corporation under Wisconsin's lemon law.

   a. Make the argument that the lemon law does not apply to the facts of this case.

   b. Decide the case. Explain. See *Dieter and Hermes v. Chrysler Corporation,* 610 N.W.2d 832 (Wis. 2000).

Federal Laws and Consumer Protection Agencies

Much of the federal government's consumer protection authority rests in an array of powerful agencies that, in general, are given broad directives from and funded by Congress, occasionally with additional directives from the president. But the day-to-day work of developing standards, ensuring compliance, and investigating violations are carried out within the individual agencies. Conservatives and free market advocates frequently raise the argument that the agencies have too much power and often act as mini-legislatures imposing rules that reshape American life rather than allowing the market to render its judgments.

The direction taken by an agency depends, in part, on which party controls the Senate, which the House of Representatives, as well as the president's party affiliation. Changes in the composition of Congress, potentially every two years, can have noticeable impacts and sometimes cause complete reversals on key issues. See Chapter Eight, Part Three, "Controlling the Agencies."

The Food and Drug Administration

LO 15-7
Identify the major responsibilities of the FDA and discuss some of the challenges it faces in fulfilling them.

The FDA oversees much of America's health landscape to ensure the safety, effectiveness, and security of food, drugs (prescription and over-the-counter), medical devices, cosmetics, tobacco products, and more. It has the power to impose fines and remove dangerous drugs and other products from the market. The following are a few examples of recent actions taken by the FDA that illustrate some of the breadth of the agency's activities:

- Enabling the over-the-counter sales of a category of hearing aids for mild to moderate hearing impairment, which increases access and lowers the cost of the devices for many because neither a medical exam nor a fitting by an audiologist is required.[7]

- Proposing more stringent requirements before packaging can claim a product is "healthy."[8]
- Alerting the public to potential health hazards of an immediate nature, such as it did after an inspection of a Family Dollar distribution center revealed unsanitary conditions might have compromised food and drug products.[9]

Drug Approvals

You may already be aware that the FDA authorizes all new COVID boosters, such as the one that targeted Omicron subvariants.[10] It has also recently approved

- A drug for the treatment of Alzheimer's disease through an accelerated approval process.[11]
- The first gene therapy for treatment of certain bladder cancer.[12]
- The first drug that can delay onset of type 1 diabetes.[13]

Companies must undertake extensive testing before the FDA will consider approval of a new drug. Physicians and scientists working for the FDA review the company's evidence, which must demonstrate that the treatment is both safe and effective. Because the full approval process can take considerable time, both the federal government and about 40 states have passed "right to try" laws so that those with life-threatening diseases or conditions might gain early access to experimental drugs that have completed the first phase of testing. The laws do not, however, compel drug companies to provide those drugs. [For a look at the FDA Fact Sheet for those desiring access to such medications, see **www.fda.gov.**]

Scandalously high drug prices, in comparison to the cost of the same or comparable drugs in other countries, are beyond direct FDA authority. Congress, heavily influenced by drug industry lobbying and campaign donations, has struggled to find solutions. One method for reducing prices is to bring market forces to bear by getting more new drugs and generics to the market more quickly. But reduced regulation carries its own risks. A 2017 study found that nearly one out of three drugs have a significant safety issue subsequent to winning FDA approval.[14] On the other hand, reduced and more efficient regulation could increase medical innovation. Thus, to some the FDA imposes too many rules, to others too few.

LO 15-8
Discuss the regulatory challenge presented by e-cigarettes as both an on-ramp for nicotine addiction among young people and an off-ramp to reduce nicotine dependence in adult users.

Opioid Epidemic: Some Small Steps Being Taken

Opioid addiction in the U.S. is at epidemic levels, in no small part due to Purdue Pharma, as we saw in Part Three of Chapter Seven. Finding ways to effectively treat the addition continues to be challenging. A step forward was made in February 2022 with the FDA's announcement that one of its expedited programs may become available to companies in their development of nonaddictive alternatives to opioids for pain management.[15]

E-cigarettes And Other Tobacco Products

In December 2019, Congress raised the minimum age for sales of tobacco products to 21. The law applies to all states, even if state law permits sales at 18, and to all tobacco products, including e-cigarettes.[16] Of particular concern was the rise in vaping among high school students, which had nearly doubled, to 20.9 percent of seniors, from 2017 to 2018.[17] In early 2020, the FDA banned the manufacture, distribution, and sale of cartridge-based flavored vaping products, except tobacco and menthol. The banned flavors were believed

The rise in vaping among high school students nearly doubled from 2017 to 2018.

to be particularly appealing to young people.[18] On April 14, 2022, a federal law went into effect that clarified the FDA's authority to regulate tobacco products containing nicotine from any source, including synthetic nicotine.[19]

The vaping brand most in the news has been Juul Labs, often because of its particular popularity with teenagers, as well as its capture of 75 percent of the vaping market. In June 2022, the FDA ordered Juul to stop selling e-cigarettes completely. The order was based on a new concern about "potentially harmful chemicals that could leach out of Juul's e-liquid pods."[20]According to an article in *The New York Times* by Matt Richtel and Andrew Jacobs:

> Broadly, the F.D.A. is walking a fine line in remaking the landscape for nicotine products. It is trying to wean the public off traditional cigarettes while permitting less harmful vaping products that do not attract a new generation of users: The new devises must be appealing for smoking cessation but not so appealing that they lure young people en masse.[21]

Recent news is not comforting with regard to the continuing popularity of teen vaping. Data from the 2022 National Youth Tobacco Survey on e-cigarettes revealed that 2.5 million middle and high school students, or 9.4 percent, reported e-cigarette use within 30 days of taking the online survey. Nearly 85 percent used flavored e-cigarettes and more than 25 percent of those responding reported daily usage.[22]

In October 2022, the U.S. Department of Justice filed actions to obtain permanent injunctions against six e-cigarette manufacturers for their failure to submit premarket applications for their e-cigarettes while continuing to manufacture, distribute, and sell their devices.

> Between January 2021 through Sept. 9, 2022, the FDA issued nearly 300 warning letters, for firms that collectively have more than 17 million e-cigarettes listed with the agency, for failure to submit a timely premarket application. After receiving warning letters, a majority complied and removed their products from the market.[23]

Then in November 2022, the FDA warned an additional five firms for unauthorized marketing of e-cigarette products that

- Are designed to look like toys and youth-appealing electronics like glow sticks, Nintendo Game Boy, and walkie-talkies.
- Feature youth-appealing characters from TV shows, movies, and video game characters, including "The Simpsons," "Family Guy," "Squid Game," "Rick and Morty," "Minions," and "Baby Bus."
- Imitate foods like popsicles.[24]

Questions

1. Is it ethical for businesses to target nicotine products at young people who, by law, are not allowed to purchase them? Explain your response. Then provide the best argument for the opposite position.
2. The federal law prohibiting the sale of tobacco to anyone under the age of 21 was passed in 2019. The 2022 survey of middle and high school students on their usage of

e-cigarettes found 2.5 million students had used e-cigarettes within 30 days of the survey and more than 25 percent of those used them daily. Is it ethical for businesses to sell to those under 21? Is it ethical for their older friends to supply them with e-cigarettes?

Food Industry Oversight

LO 15-9
Be able to identify the stakeholder groups which the FDA must consider in developing rules and processes to address food safety and articulate those groups' disparate interests and concerns.

The FDA is also charged with protecting the public health by ensuring foods are safe and properly labeled. The 2011 Food Safety and Modernization Act (FSMA) gave the FDA greatly expanded authority to protect the safety of our food. These rules require food producers to maintain written safety plans, analyze hazards, and develop safety procedures. According to AskUSDA, dated November 21, 2022 posting on AskUSDA, every year about 3,000 Americans die and 128,000 are hospitalized because of food-borne illnesses.[25] Interestingly, these are the same figures that appeared in a 2017 government report from the Office of Inspector General in the Department of Health and Human Services, which found

> Although FDA is on track to meet the FSMA inspection mandates during the initial cycles, this did not result in a greater number of facilities being inspected. In fact, the overall number of food facilities FDA inspected . . . decreased over time.
>
> In addition, FDA did not always take action when it uncovered significant inspection violations that potentially threaten the safety of the food supply. When it did take action, it commonly relied on facilities to voluntarily correct the violations. Also, it rarely took advantage of the new administrative tools provided by FSMA. Moreover, FDA's advisory and enforcements actions were not always timely nor did they always result in the correction of the violations. Further, FDA did not consistently conduct timely followup inspections to ensure that facilities corrected the violations.[26]

The fault may lie not solely with the FDA, but at least partly with its funding. A February 2019 article, "Congress is still underfunding FSMA," stated that "Major parts of the FSMA have gone into effect, . . . but federal funding still lags behind estimates."[27] Apparently, that may still be the case, as the FDA's request for its fiscal year 2023 budget included $43 million for additional investments in food safety modernization, specifically referencing the FSMA and improving "prevention-oriented food safety practices . . . to more quickly respond to outbreaks and recalls for . . . food."[28]

Baby Food Safety

As of the time of this writing, two issues involving the FDA and the safety of baby food have been in the news. The first was a serious disruption in the availability of baby formula, ultimately necessitating the federal government airlifting formula from Europe and activating emergency rules to prioritize U.S. production.[29] The second is the lengthy process to deal with toxic metals in baby food that is on-going.

Closure of Abbott Laboratories' Baby Formula Plant

The cause of the sudden national shortage in baby formula was the shutdown of an Abbot Laboratories' plant in Sturgis, Michigan (which produces 20 percent of the infant formula made in the U.S.), following the recall in February 2022 of 70 million containers of Similac, the most popular brand on the market.[30] The full story illuminates both management and regulatory failures and involves a deadly cronobacter bacteria:

- In September 2021, FDA investigators began an annual inspection at the Sturgis plant. On the first day, the FDA received a report that a Michigan infant, who had been fed Similac, had been hospitalized for three weeks with a cronobacter infection. On the second day, the FDA notified Abbott about the case, but no one told the inspectors.
- In October a whistleblower report was filed with the FDA, alleging a management emphasis on productivity that at times compromised safety and that many violations were hidden. In months following, three infants receiving formula from Sturgis were infected, two of whom died and the third has brain damage.
- FDA inspectors again visited the Sturgis plant in January 2022, one month after the FDA had interviewed the whistleblower. Five different strains of cronobactor were found.
- Abbott's tests in February found cronobactor present 20 times.
- On February 15, the FDA recommended Abbott recall powdered formulas made at the Sturgis plant; the recommendation was reiterated the next day. On February 17, the FDA released a public warning advising the public against using formula made at the plant. That same day the company "voluntarily" recalled its formula.[31] Abbott shut down the factory.
- The FDA received over 100 complaints in the next few weeks, which included the death of seven infants. It closed its investigation of the plant in mid-May and Abbott agreed to a consent decree giving the FDA "extraordinary oversight" for five years.[32]
- In congressional testimony, the commissioner of the FDA gave an analogy to the conditions found in the plant:

> Let's say you had a next-door neighbor who had leaks in the roof, they didn't wash their hands, they have bacteria growing all over the kitchen. You walk in, and there was standing water on the counters and the floor, and the kids were walking through with mud on their shoes and no one cleaning it up. You probably wouldn't want your infant eating in that kitchen. And that's in essence what the inspection showed.[33]

In January 2023, the Justice Department opened a criminal investigation of Abbott Laboratories and the Sturgis plant.

Sources: Susan Berfield and Anna Edney, "How Deadly Bacteria Spread in a Similac Factory—and Caused the US Formula Shortage," *Bloomberg Businessweek,* August 29, 2022 [**www.bloomberg.com**]; Anna Edney, "What Happened at Abbott's Baby Formula Factory?" *Bloomberg Prognosis,* August 25, 2022 [**www.bloomberg.com**]; Laura Reiley, "New documents show more claims of baby formula illness and death," *The Washington Post,* June 10, 2022 [**www.washingtonpost.com**]; and Jacob Bogage, Dan Rosenzweig-Ziff, and Laura Riley, "Justice Department opens investigation into Abbott over baby formula," *The Washington Post,* January 21, 2023 [**www.washingtonpost.com**].

Closer to Zero—FDA's Action Plan to Reduce Heavy Metals in Food Consumed by Young Children

Following a February 2021 report of a subcommittee of the House of Representatives on Economic and Consumer Policy, a particular focus of the FDA has been on the reduction of heavy metals in foods commonly in diets of babies and young children. Unlike the problem with baby formula just discussed, toxic elements, including arsenic, lead, cadmium, and mercury, are found in the environment and enter our food through water, soil, and air. Levels of these elements in baby foods have been monitored by the FDA for some time. More recently, it developed its "Closer to Zero: Action Plan for Baby Foods" program, a continuous improvement cycle established to set interim standards for each element, consult with stakeholders on feasibility and best practices, finalize an action level, and continue thereafter with monitoring results, advancing the science, and ensuring compliance. In the first phase (April 2021–April 2022), the goal was to go through the stakeholder input process with lead, while also developing an initial proposal for arsenic. Phase two (April 2022–April 2024) is to establish the initial standard for lead, and go through the stakeholder process with arsenic, and set interim levels for cadmium and mercury. The third phase is set to begin in April 2024.

For a copy of the FDA's "Closer to Zero: Action Plan for Baby Foods," see **www.fda.gov/food/environmental-contaminants-food/closer-zero-action-plan-baby-foods.**

For a critique on the FDA's progress on the Closer to Zero program as of January 5, 2023, see Gary Harki, Celine Castonuovo, Julie Steinberg, Kaustuv Basu, and Alex Ruoff, "Baby Foods With Toxic Metals Stay on US Market While FDA Dithers," *Bloomberg Law,* January 5, 2023 [**https:news.bloomberglaw.com**].

Question

There is no easy solution for improving food safety. The food we eat comes from the full spectrum of providers–major corporations providing products for domestic and international consumption to family-run farms. Science and the footwork of physical inspections are both critical inputs for the FDA to fulfill its mandates. Both take time and money. Passing a law is only the first step–funding it and implementing it have to follow. The Research Exercise on Food Safety at the end of the chapter provides an opportunity to consider this challenge from your choice of viewpoints.

The Federal Trade Commission

LO 15-10
Be able to identify some of the consumer protection laws the FTC is charged with enforcing.

LO 15-11
Identify and describe some of the actions the FTC may take against businesses that are in violation of the laws it enforces, as well as the types of relief it may seek for consumers.

The Federal Trade Commission (FTC) was created to prevent "unfair methods of competition and unfair or deceptive acts or practices in and affecting commerce."[34] As part of its duties, it enforces the antitrust laws (see Chapters Ten and Eleven), has proposed a rule to ban noncompete clauses in most employment contracts (see Chapter Twelve, Part One, Employment Terms), and enforces the laws related to consumer privacy, identity theft, and information security, which include the Children's Online Privacy Protection Act (COPPA) (see Chapter Eighteen, Part Three, Privacy). In 2016, Congress passed the Consumer Review Fairness Act, which prohibits businesses from using form contracts to limit what their customers can say in online reviews or from directing websites to remove such reviews pursuant to a provision in their form contract transferring a customer's intellectual property rights in their reviews to the business. The FTC also enforces the provisions of this act.

The Federal Trade Commission Act specifically allows the FTC to seek *equitable relief.* Thus, it has been a long-standing practice of the FTC to seek equitable monetary relief through the courts in the form of restitution or disgorgement to obtain potentially sizable payments from defendants whose practices were found to violate the law and use those funds to compensate the victims of the defendant's actions. A brief look at press releases from the FTC illustrates the magnitude and types of recoveries sought:

- In 2023, the FTC started sending payments totaling more than $2.9 million to 20,402 people who paid thousands of dollars for Warrior Trading's investment programs. The company made misleading and unrealistic claims to sell a day-trading "system" that failed to pay off for most customers.[35]

- In 2022, it sent payments totaling more than $9.8 million to consumers who were harmed by Illinois-based Napleton Automotive Group's junk fees and discriminatory practices.[36]
- Payments totaling more than $415,000 were sent to 3,508 consumers who financed vehicles at a Tate's Auto dealerships in Arizona and New Mexico after January 1, 2013, and later had the vehicle repossessed. The company allegedly deceived consumers about payment information and falsified information on consumers' financing applications.[37]
- Payments of more than $1 million were also made to 1,966 consumers who were harmed by a debt collection scheme that conned them into paying debts they did not owe. The defendants used several names including GAFS Group, Global Mediation Group, and Mediation Services.[38]

Each of the above press releases contained the following language:

> The Commission's interactive dashboards for refund data provide a state-by-state breakdown of refunds in FTC cases. In 2021, Commission actions led to more than $472 million in refunds to consumers across the country, but these refunds were the result of cases resolved before the U.S. Supreme Court ruled in 2021 that the Commission lacks authority under Section 13(b) to seek monetary relief in federal court. Because of that ruling, the Commission no longer has its strongest tool to return money to consumers, and it will become harder to provide refunds to consumers harmed by deceptive and unfair conduct. The Commission has urged Congress to restore its ability to get money back for consumers.

The 2021 Supreme Court ruling referenced is *AMG Capital Management, LLC v. FTC*.[39] A unanimous Supreme Court held that the statutory words in the Federal Trade Commission Act "permanent injunction," which provides for "future injunctive relief, cannot be read to include retrospective monetary relief." Litigation finalized before the 2021 decision was not affected, but this provision cannot be used in that fashion prospectively. The FTC has asked Congress to pass legislation that will give it authority to seek monetary relief for consumers harmed by illegal business conduct.[40]

Recently, however, the FTC seems to be having some success in its quest for compensation for harmed customers through a two-prong settlement. An example is its settlement with Epic Games, the creator of Fortnite:

> The FTC's action against Epic involves two separate record-breaking settlements. As part of a proposed federal court order filed by the Department of Justice on behalf of the FTC, Epic will pay a $275 million monetary penalty for violating the COPPA Rule—the largest penalty ever obtained for violating an FTC rule. Additionally, in a first-of-its-kind provision, Epic will be required to adopt strong privacy default settings for children and teens, ensuring that voice and text communications are turned off by default. Under a separate proposed administrative order, Epic will pay $245 million to refund consumers for its dark patterns [design tricks that dupe players into making unintentional purchases-ed.] and billing practices, which is the FTC's largest refund amount in a gaming case, and its largest administrative order in history.[41]

The $275 million civil penalty will be paid to the U.S. Treasury; the $245 million will be refunded to consumers.[42]

LO 15-12
Identify and describe the purposes for which the CPSC was established and some of the methods by which it accomplishes those purposes.

The Consumer Product Safety Commission

The Consumer Product Safety Commission (CPSC) was created in 1972. It is responsible for reducing the risks in using consumer products such as furniture, toys, lawn mowers, washing machines, bicycles, fireworks, pools, portable heaters, and household chemicals.

The CPSC pursues product safety, initially, by collecting data and conducting research. Using its rule-making authority, it also mandates consumer product safety, performance, and labeling standards.

Manufacturers must certify before distribution that products meet federal safety standards. Manufacturing sites may be inspected, and specific product safety testing procedures can be mandated. Businesses other than retailers are required to keep product safety records. In cases of severe and imminent hazards, the CPSC has the power to enforce its decisions by seeking a court order to remove a product from the market. In less urgent circumstances, the commission may proceed with its own administrative remedies. Preferring voluntary compliance, it may also negotiate with companies to recall dangerous products. Where voluntary negotiations fail, the commission may proceed with an adjudicative hearing before an administrative law judge (ALJ) or members of the commission. ALJ decisions may be appealed to the full commission and thereafter, in most cases, to a federal court of appeals. Civil or criminal penalties may result. Despite these processes, as you will see below, many safety issues are not revealed until after a product is in the hands of consumers.

Over 70 infant deaths have been associated with all inclined sleepers.

Over 30 babies reportedly died in the Fisher-Price Rock 'n Play sleeper (an elevated and inclined sleeping "cot") in the decade between its introduction in 2009 and its recall in 2019.[43] In general, suffocation occurred when children rolled over from their backs to their stomach or sides while unrestrained. Fisher-Price issued a recall for all 4.7 million sleepers and told consumers to stop using them immediately. Later that same year the CPSC, noting over 70 infant deaths associated with all inclined sleepers, warned consumers to cease using any sleeper sloped at an angle greater than 10 degrees.[44]

After the 2019 recall, the U.S. Public Interest Research Group sponsored a survey of licensed daycares in a three-state area and found that 1 in 10 still used the sleepers with children under 12 months old.[45] On June 23, 2022, a new CPSC rule went into effect that makes it unlawful to sell noncompliant infant sleep products, but it applies only to products manufactured after June 22, 2022.[46]

Not Even Well-Known Stores Comply with Recalls

Not surprisingly, even after a recall, not all products get returned, even though consumers may receive repairs, refunds, or a new, safe model of the product. But sadly, if not shocking, some businesses continue to sell them. In August 2022, the CPSC announced that TJX Companies of Framingham, Massachusetts, had agreed to pay a $13 million civil penalty for selling and distributing previously recalled consumer products, the majority of which "were products recalled due to the risk of infant suffocation and death," including the Fisher-Price sleepers. TJX sold and distributed the recalled products through its retail stores, including T.J. Maxx, Marshalls, and HomeGoods, as well as online. In addition to the monetary penalty, TJX is required to maintain a compliance program to ensure it complies with the Consumer Product Safety Act.

Source: Press Release, "TJX Agrees to Pay $13 Million Civil Penalty for Selling, Offering for Sale and Distributing Recalled Products," Consumer Product Safety Commission, August 2, 2022.

NEISS

The CPSC maintains the National Electronic Injury Surveillance System (NEISS) that records, through a national sampling of hospital emergency visits, injuries, and deaths related to consumer products. A CPSC public database allows anyone to report dangerous products and to search complaints entered by others. It shows that in 2020, the latest annual report at the time of this writing, there were about 165,000 injuries associated with toys, about 29,000 with chain saws, and over 34,000 with televisions and their stands.[47] [For the CPSC's database of unsafe products see **http://saferproducts.gov**].

Online Robot

Because businesses often have difficulty in determining which CPSC regulations apply to their products, the agency has developed a regulatory "Robot." Businesses can input information to the online Robot and receive guidance about regulations, reporting obligations, and frequently asked questions. [To access CPSC's Regulatory Robot, see **https://www.cpsc.gov/Business–Manufacturing/Regulatory-Robot/Safer-Products-Start-Here.**]

Question

What does a manufacturer or importer of consumer products have to do to meet the safety requirements of the CPSC? The Research Exercise at the end of the chapter will give you an opportunity to discover the answer for a hypothetical new business you select.

Consumer Financial Protection Bureau

LO 15-13
Identify and describe the purposes for which the CFPB was established and some of the methods by which it accomplishes those purposes.

Broadly, the Consumer Financial Protection Bureau (CFPB), authorized by the 2010 Dodd–Frank Wall Street Reform and Consumer Protection Act (Dodd–Frank; see Chapter Eight), is expected to prohibit and prevent the commission of any "unfair, deceptive, or abusive act or practice" in conjunction with consumer financial products or services. In essence, CFPB's rules are intended to supplement market forces in order to enhance consumer welfare. Prohibited actions would include a wide array of dishonest practices, such as hidden credit card fees and misleading "teaser" rates for mortgages. The goal is to maximize fairness, transparency, and competitiveness for financial products and services. Another important element of the CFPB's charge is to provide financial education to support Americans' financial literacy. [For more information on the CFPB, see **www.consumerfinance.gov**].

To carry out its mission the CFPB has authority over financial services firms, including banks, thrifts, and credit unions, but it specifically excludes real estate brokerages, accountants, and lawyers, among others. It is also responsible for enforcing such finance laws as the Electronic Fund Transfer Act, the Equal Credit Opportunity Act, the Fair Credit Billing Act, and others which are discussed below in Part Three.

The CFPB maintains an online, searchable database where consumers can file complaints and examine others' complaints about credit cards, mortgages, banking, student loans, and more. [See **www.consumerfinance.gov/complain** to see how a complaint is submitted.]

PRACTICING ETHICS BIG BANKS, BIG DECEITS

Multiple consumer scandals have shaken Wells Fargo, one of the world's largest banks. In 2016, the CFPB fined Wells Fargo \$100 million for the widespread practice of secretly opening unauthorized deposit and credit card accounts for current customers. Employees covertly opened the accounts in order to meet sales targets and receive compensation incentives. It also had to pay full restitution to all of its victims, a \$35 million penalty to the Office of the Comptroller of the Currency, and \$50 million to the City and County of Los Angeles. It apparently did not learn much from the experience because in December 2022, it was required to pay \$2 billion to redress customers for systematic failures in servicing automobile loans across over 11 million accounts, causing cars to be wrongfully repossessed; improperly denying mortgage modification requests over a seven year period, causing some customers to lose their homes in wrongful foreclosures; and wrongfully charging overdraft fees when customers had enough funds on deposit to cover the transactions. It was assessed a \$1.7 billion fine to be paid to the CFPB' Civil Penalty Fund, to be used to provide relief to other victims of consumer financial law violations.

On the other hand, U.S. Bank apparently did learn from Wells Fargo's experience, but not the right lesson: in July 2022, the CFPB announced U.S. Bank had illegally accessed customers' credit reports and opened checking and savings accounts, credit cards, and lines of credit without the permission of their customers. Again, the motivation was pressure on and incentives to employees to sell multiple products and services through the imposition of sales goals as part of their job requirements. In addition to making its customers whole, a \$37.5 million penalty was imposed on U.S. Bank, to be paid into the CFPB's victims relief fund.

Questions

1. Assume the situation recurs and a member of your family works for a national bank and finds themselves in the position of those at Wells Fargo and U.S. Bank. Assume they tell you what is going on. What would you advise them to do and why?
2. Based on what you have read here, augmented by any additional information you obtain on your own, on balance, do you think the creation of the CFPB was an appropriate action for Congress to take? Provide your reasoning.

Sources: Press Release, "Consumer Financial Protection Bureau Fines Wells Fargo \$100 Million for Widespread Illegal Practice of Secretly Opening Unauthorized Accounts," *Consumer Financial Protection Bureau*, September 8, 2016 [**www.consumerfinance.gov**]; Press Release, "CFPB Orders Wells Fargo to Pay \$3.7 Billion for Widespread Mismanagement of Auto Loans, Mortgages, and Deposit Accounts," *Consumer Financial Protection Bureau*, December 20, 2022 [**www.consumerfinance.gov**]; and Press Release, "CFPB Fines U.S. Bank \$37.5 Million for Illegally Exploiting Personal Data to Open Sham Accounts for Unsuspecting Customers," *Consumer Financial Protection Bureau*, July 28, 2022 [**www.consumerfinance.gov**].

Part Three—Debtor/Creditor Law

LO 15-14 Understand the way in which the debtor/creditor laws discussed in this part may impact you, now or in the future.

Many of you reading this chapter likely already have some form of credit established, such as a credit card, if it is in your own name rather than a card on your parent's account. Likewise many of you may already have debt, possibly in the form of a car loan, unpaid principal on your personal credit card, or student loans. As you read the materials in this part, consider what you understand about the legal rules associated with those types of credit and debt.

If you have any of the above debt, can you answer the following questions about them?

1. What is the amount of principal owing as of your last statement or payment?
2. Is there any interest accruing on your outstanding principal and, if so, at what rate and how frequently does it compound?
3. If it is a student loan, on graduation what monthly payment would you need to make for your loan to be paid off in 5 years? In 10 years?

Now a brief look at student loan debt in the U.S.:

U.S. Student Loan Debt in September 2022 Totaled $1.76 Trillion

That total might shock you, but you might also be surprised by who owes it. Forty-five million Americans, or 17.4 percent of U.S. adults, have student loan debt. Those most likely to have student loan debt are 25- to 34-year-olds, but the largest amount of debt is owed by those from 35 to 49. That group owes $600 billion, which is 40 percent of the total. Fifty-five percent of the 2020 graduating class had student debt, with an average debt of $28,400.

The $1.76 trillion figure does not reflect the president's one-time debt cancellation announced in August 2022, which could potentially relieve qualifying borrowers of up to $20,000. The total debt has also likely been affected because of the automatic student loan payment pause that was put in place in March 2020 and has not been restarted as of this writing. During the pause, the interest rate on eligible federal student loans was set at 0% and, for most borrowers, unpaid interest will not be capitalized during the payment pause or for six months after the pause ends.

Questions

1. In a letter to *The Wall Street Journal,* a reader said: "[B]laming the [government loan] program for students' decisions to sign up for the loans leaves out one of the biggest factors: individual choice. . . . The answer isn't increased regulation of the loan program, but more personal responsibility, creative analysis of options and tough decision making."[48] Do you think the loan crisis is primarily a result of failed personal responsibility by students? By parents? By schools? Explain.
2. Do you see any evidence that colleges have unfairly and unnecessarily raised tuition in a manner that has significantly contributed to the student loan crisis? Explain.

Sources: Anna Helhoski, Ryan Lane, and Eliza Haverstock, "Student Loan Debt Statistics: 2023," *Nerdwallet,* January 13, 2023 [**www.nerdwallet.com**]; "COVID-19 Loan Payment Pause and 0%," *Federal Student Aid,* accessed January 22, 2023 [**https://studentaid.gov**]; and Josh Mitchell, "The Long Road to the Student Debt Crisis," *The Wall Street Journal,* June 7, 2019 [**www.wsj.com**].

Credit Regulations

For many Americans, paying for a modest, conventional life is becoming increasingly difficult. For many Americans, life is a daily, unremitting struggle to maintain a financial foothold. Seniors and working class people are often buried in debt. The middle class is shrinking.[49]

Personal discipline matters a great deal in this challenging financial landscape, but federal and state regulators have built some formidable legal shields to help consumers. Lending and credit abuse led Congress and state legislatures to enact an array of protective legislation. Earlier in this chapter, we introduced the CFPB which is designed, in part, to protect consumers from credit wrongs. Now we will turn to several other important pieces of federal law. [For a debtor/creditor law database, see **www.law.cornell.edu/wex/debtor_and_creditor**].

All of the credit regulations discussed in this part are overseen by the CFPB.

Truth in Lending Act (TILA)

LO 15-15 Identify the purposes of the Truth in Lending Act and Regulation Z.

Consumers often do not understand the full cost of buying on credit. The Truth in Lending Act (TILA) places a legal burden on lenders to assure full disclosure of credit terms in simple language. Most consumer borrowing, such as credit cards, vehicle loans, home mortgages and refinancing, and payday loans are governed by the TILA.

The TILA and Regulation Z, which interprets the act, are designed both to protect consumers from credit abuse and to assist them in becoming more informed about credit terms and costs so they can engage in comparison shopping. The heart of the act is the required clear, conspicuous disclosure of the amount financed, the finance charge (the actual dollar sum to be paid for credit), the annual percentage rate (APR–the total cost of the credit expressed as an annual rate), and the number of payments. The finance charge includes not just interest but also service charges, points, loan fees, carrying charges, and other costs. The federal Consumer Leasing Act and its related Regulation M provide protections similar to the TILA for consumer leases of personal property, such as cars.

TILA amendments in the Dodd–Frank Act gave extensive, additional attention to residential mortgages in recognition of the 2008 subprime mortgage crisis and its destructive impact on the entire American economy. For example, creditors are prohibited from making a higher priced residential mortgage loan without a good faith determination that the consumer has a reasonable "ability to repay."

Exemptions

While TILA and Regulation Z protect consumers, many types of loans are exempt from their requirements. For loans to be covered by them, the following criteria must be satisfied:

1. The debtor must be a "natural person" rather than an organization.
2. The creditor must be regularly engaged in extending credit and must be the person to whom the debt is initially payable.
3. The purpose of the credit must be "primarily for personal, family, or household purposes" involving transactions of $66,400 or less in 2023 (and adjusted annually for inflation), but loans secured by real property (such as home mortgages) are covered by the act regardless of the loan amounts.
4. The credit must be subject to a finance charge or payable in more than four installments.

The case that follows examines the application of the TILA to a credit card interest rate dispute.

Barrer v. Chase Bank USA

566 F.3d 883 (9th Cir. 2009)

Circuit Judge O'Scannlain

We must decide whether a credit card company violates the Truth in Lending Act when it fails to disclose potential risk factors that allow it to raise a cardholder's Annual Percentage Rate.

I

A

Walter and Cheryl Barrer held a credit card account with Chase. The Barrers received and accepted the Cardmember Agreement ("the Agreement") governing their relationship at the relevant time in late 2004. In February 2005, Chase mailed to the Barrers a Change in Terms Notice ("the Notice"), which purported to amend the terms of the Agreement, in particular to increase the Annual Percentage Rate ("APR") significantly. It also allowed the Barrers to reject the amendments in writing by a certain date. They did not do so, and continued to use the credit card. Within two months, the new, higher, APR became effective.

According to the Barrers' First Amended Complaint, they enjoyed a preferred APR of 8.99% under the Agreement. . . . In the event of default, the Agreement stated that Chase might increase the APR on the balance up to a stated default rate. The Agreement specified the following events of default: failure to pay at least a minimum payment by the due date; a credit card balance in excess of the credit limit on the account; failure to pay another creditor when required; the return, unpaid, of a payment to Chase by the customer's bank; or, should Chase close the account, the consumer's failure to pay the outstanding balance at the time Chase has appointed.

Another section entirely, entitled "Changes to the Agreement," provided that Chase "can change this agreement at any time, . . . by adding, deleting, or modifying any provision. [The] right to add, delete, or modify provisions includes financial terms, such as APRs and fees." The next section, entitled "Credit Information," stated that Chase "may periodically review your credit history by obtaining information from credit bureaus and others." These sections appeared five and six pages, respectively, after the "Finance Charge" section.

Around April 2005, the Barrers' noticed that their APR had "skyrocketed" from 8.99% to 24.24%, the latter a rate close to a non-preferred or default rate. None of the events of default specified in the Agreement, however, had occurred. When the Barrers contacted Chase to find out why their APR had increased, Chase responded in a letter citing judgments it had made on the basis of information obtained from a consumer credit reporting agency. In particular, Chase wrote that: "outstanding credit loan(s) on revolving accounts . . . [were] too high" and there were "too many recently opened installment/revolving accounts." The Barrers do not dispute the facts underlying Chase's judgments.

Despite the Barrers' surprise, the Notice they had received in February contained some indication of what would be forthcoming. Specifically, it disclosed that Chase would shortly increase the APR to 24.24%, a decision "based in whole or in part on the information obtained in a report from the consumer reporting agency."

The Barrers paid the interest on the credit account at the new rate for three months before they were able to pay off the balance. Then they sued Chase in federal district court.

B

The Barrers filed a class action lawsuit on their own behalf and on behalf of all Chase credit card customers similarly harmed and similarly situated. The complaint asserted one cause of action under the Truth in Lending Act ("the Act"), and Regulation Z. The Barrers claim to have been the victims of a practice they now call "adverse action repricing," which apparently means "raising . . . a preferred rate to an essentially non-preferred rate based upon information in a customer's credit report." Though the Barrers do not claim that the practice itself is illegal, they do claim that it was illegal for Chase not to disclose it fully to them or to the other members of the putative class.

[The federal district court dismissed the Barrers' cause of action. The Barrers appealed.]

II

The Truth in Lending Act is designed "to assure a meaningful disclosure of credit terms so that the consumer will be able to compare more readily the various credit terms available to him and avoid the uninformed use of credit." Rather than substantively regulate the terms creditors can offer or include in their financial products, the Act primarily requires disclosure.

* * * * *

Regulation Z, 12 C.F.R. Section 226, provides the precise regulations that the Barrers claim Chase violated. In general, these regulations establish two conditions a creditor must meet. "First, it must have disclosed all of the information required by the statute." That is, disclosures must be complete. . . .

Just as Section 226.6 states what must be disclosed, so Section 226 describes how to disclose it. Among other things, creditors must make the required disclosures "clearly and conspicuously in writing." . . .

* * * * *

III

The Barrers argue that . . . Chase failed to disclose completely under the Act why it would change the APRs of its cardholders, in violation of subsection 226.6(a)(2) of Regulation Z.

The Barrers do not argue that either the Agreement or the Notice failed to disclose the APR, which their complaint puts at 8.99% under the Agreement and 24.24% under the Notice. Rather, . . .

*****

Regulation Z requires that creditors disclose any APR "that *may* be used to compute the finance charge," and that they do so "clearly and conspicuously."

We are persuaded that Chase adequately disclosed the APRs that the Agreement permitted it to use simply by means of the change-in-terms provision. . . .

Even so, such disclosure must be clear and conspicuous. Neither the Act nor Regulation Z define clarity and conspicuousness in this context. The Staff Commentary explains only that "[t]he clear and conspicuous standard requires that disclosures be in a reasonably understandable form." . . .

Clear and conspicuous disclosures, therefore, are disclosures that a reasonable cardholder would notice and understand. No particular kind of formatting is magical, but, in this case, the document must have made it clear to a reasonable cardholder that Chase was permitted under the agreement to raise the APR not only for the events of default specified in the "Finance Terms" section, but for any reason at all.

. . . [T]he change-in-terms provision appears on pages 10–11 of the Agreement, five dense pages after the disclosure of the APR. It is neither referenced in nor clearly related to the "Finance Terms" section. This provision, as part of the APRs allowed under the contract, is buried too deeply in the fine print for a reasonable cardholder to realize that, in addition to the specific grounds for increasing the APR listed in the "Finance Charges" section, Chase could raise the APR for other reasons.

Therefore, the Barrers have stated a claim because Chase cannot show that, as a matter of law, the Agreement made clear and conspicuous disclosure of the APRs that Chase was permitted to use.

REVERSED and REMANDED.

[For a further ruling in this matter, see *Barrer v. Chase Bank, USA*, 2013 U.S. Dist. LEXIS 24268 (D. Or. February 21, 2013).]

Questions

1. *a.* How did Chase violate Regulation Z and the TILA?
   b. According to this decision, what is a "clear and conspicuous" disclosure?
2. If you have a credit card in your own name, find the paperwork you signed to obtain the card and compare its language to the language Chase Bank had in the above case. How do the terms for increasing the interest rate compare?
3. Sarah Hamm sued Ameriquest Mortgage Company claiming a violation of TILA. Hamm borrowed money secured by a 30-year mortgage from Ameriquest and signed a "Disclosure Statement" specifying, among other things, that she was responsible for 359 payments at a specified amount and one payment for the last month of a slightly smaller amount. The statement did not, however, explicitly specify, as required by TILA, the total payments due (360). Was the TILA violated? Explain. See *Hamm v. Ameriquest Mortgage,* 506 F.3d 525 (7th Cir. 2007).

Credit and Debit Cards

LO 15-16 Be able to identify one or more ways in which the CARD Act benefits college students, as well as one or more ways it might be argued to have disadvantaged them.

According to a September 2022 survey, 67 percent of undergraduate students have a credit card in their own name. Another 9 percent have a credit card as an authorized user.[50] Of those, 46 percent are carrying debt on the card.[51] Student debit card use has been consistently higher than credit cards, with around 80 percent of students using them.[52] However, if your college or university markets a particular card to students on campus, you might want to do some investigation before choosing that card.

The CFPB's 2022 report to Congress, entitled "College Banking and Credit Card Agreements," "raises questions about whether some marketing deals between colleges and financial institutions comply with Department of Education rules" and "also highlights a lack of transparency in the arrangements schools have made with financial institutions."[53]

> Many college students trust that schools have their best interests in mind. While colleges have substantial bargaining power to obtain superior terms and pricing for their students, we find that many college-sponsored financial products cost students more than accounts that are readily available on the open market," said CFPB Director Rohit Chopra. "Today's report

suggests that there is more work to do to ensure that students are not steered into school-endorsed products with junk fees. . . .

A small set of financial institutions partner with hundreds of colleges and universities in the United States to disburse federal financial aid and provide financial products to students, including credit cards and prepaid and debit accounts. These partnerships often claim to support students' financial health. However, the products marketed to students are often more costly than what students might otherwise find in the market.

*****

One entity dominates the market for financial aid disbursements, providing nearly 70% of the accounts offered in partnership with schools—and imposes surprise monthly fees: Under this provider, accountholders are charged monthly service fees on accounts with less than $300 in qualifying deposits per month, but financial aid disbursements that may comprise the bulk of a student's deposits do not count as qualifying deposits."[54]

Question

If you have a credit or debit card associated with your school, find the paperwork you signed to obtain the card. Does it have a monthly service fee if you do not have a qualifying deposit? If so, are financial aid deposits "qualifying deposits"? Now try going online to find out what interest rate you could qualify for if you selected a different credit card company.

CARD Act

The 2009 federal Credit Card Accountability, Responsibility, and Disclosure Act (CARD Act) forbids lenders from issuing credit cards to those under age 21 without a parent as cosigner or without proof the applicant can make payments.

Additional CARD Act provisions include

- Credit card companies are barred from increasing the annual percentage rate on existing account balances except when the cardholder's minimum payment is 60 days overdue.
- Issuers cannot charge interest on bills paid on time.
- Without specific agreement by the consumer, banks cannot accept charges where doing so puts creditors over their limits.
- Interest rates, with some exceptions, cannot be raised in the first year.

Other federal credit card rules provide additional consumer protection. For example, they cap fees for late payments, banish penalties for inactive accounts (although those accounts can still simply be closed), and limit consumer liability to $50 in the event of credit card loss or theft. Prior to these regulatory initiatives, card issuers could raise interest rates as they saw fit, charge unfair fees, and write the credit card terms in ways that made them nearly impossible to understand.

The CFPB's report to Congress excerpted above was also made under the CARD Act.

Question

How would you argue that government intervention in the credit card market is not in the best interest of consumers generally and college students in particular?

Consumer Credit Reports

Do you want some day to borrow money for a new car or a house? Perhaps you want a better job? Success in each of those efforts may depend to a considerable extent on your credit score. The three national credit information giants, Equifax, Experian, and TransUnion, as well as local credit bureaus, provide retailers, employers, insurance companies, and others with consumers' detailed credit histories. From those credit histories, a credit score is computed and sold to lenders.

LO 15-17 Identify protections offered under the Fair Credit Reporting Act.

The federal Fair Credit Reporting Act (FCRA) affords consumers the following credit reporting protections, among others:

- Anyone using information from a credit reporting agency (CRA), such as Equifax, and taking "adverse action" against you (for example, denying you credit, a job, insurance) must notify you and tell you where it secured the information.
- At your request, a CRA must give you the information in your file and reveal your credit score.
- If you claim that your credit file contains inaccurate information, the CRA must investigate your complaint unless your dispute is frivolous.
- All inaccurate information must be corrected or deleted, usually within 30 days.
- In most cases, negative information more than seven years old must not be reported.
- You must provide written consent before a CRA can provide information to your employer or prospective employer.
- You have a right to place a security freeze on your credit report that prohibits the CRA from releasing your information without your authorization.[55]

Online search engines may also be subject to the FCRA depending on what information they collect and how that information is used. Spokeo, a search engine for locating people, recently settled a longstanding lawsuit about alleged FCRA violations. Spokeo agreed, among other things, to post disclaimers indicating that it is not a consumer reporting agency as defined by the FCRA, and Spokeo customers must agree not to use the Spokeo website and its information for any FCRA purpose.[56]

Equal Credit Opportunity

LO 15-18 Be able to identify the purpose of the Equal Credit Opportunity Act and give examples of facts which would be in violation of the Act.

Honda agreed in 2015 to pay $24 million to affected minority car buyers to resolve allegations of discrimination in interest rates on car loans in violation of the federal Equal Credit Opportunity Act (ECOA). The CFPB and the Justice Department alleged that some local Honda dealers charged higher interest rates to thousands of African American, Hispanic, and Asian and Pacific Islander car buyers than to similarly qualified nonminority buyers. In addition to the payment, Honda agreed to reduce the amount of discretion local dealers have in marking up interest rates on auto loans.[57]

The ECOA is designed to combat bias in lending. Credit must be extended to all creditworthy applicants regardless of sex, marital status, age, race, color, religion, national origin, good-faith exercise of rights under the Consumer Credit Protection Act, and receipt of public assistance (like food stamps). Discrimination in credit against women was a primary stimulus for the ECOA. Historically, creditors often would not lend money to married women in their own names, or to single, divorced, and widowed women.

Does the ECOA provision forbidding sex-based credit discrimination also protect against credit discrimination based on gender identity and sexual orientation? The case that follows applies the ECOA to a "cross-dressing" male in the year 2000.

Lucas Rosa v. Park West Bank & Trust Co. 214 F.3d 213 (1st Cir. 2000)

Judge Lynch

I

[O]n July 21, 1998, [Lucas] Rosa came to the [Park West] Bank to apply for a loan. A biological male, he was dressed in traditionally feminine attire. He requested a loan application from Norma Brunelle, a bank employee. Brunelle asked Rosa for identification. Rosa produced three forms of photo identification: (1) a Massachusetts Department of Public Welfare Card; (2) a Massachusetts Identification Card; and (3) a Money Stop Check Cashing ID Card. Brunelle looked at the identification cards and told Rosa that she would not provide him with a loan application until he "went home and changed." She said that he had to be dressed like one of the identification cards in which he appeared in more traditionally male attire before she would provide him with a loan application and process his loan request.

II

Rosa sued the Bank. Rosa charged that "by requiring [him] to conform to sex stereotypes before proceeding with the credit transaction, [the Bank] unlawfully discriminated against [him] with respect to an aspect of a credit transaction on the basis of sex." He claims to have suffered emotional distress.

Without filing an answer to the complaint, the Bank moved to dismiss. . . . The district court granted the Bank's motion. The court stated,

> The issue in this case is not [Rosa's] sex, but rather how he chose to dress when applying for a loan. Because the Act does not prohibit discrimination based on the manner in which someone dresses, Park West's requirement that Rosa change his clothes does not give rise to claims of illegal discrimination. Further, even if Park West's statement or action were based upon Rosa's sexual orientation or perceived sexual orientation, the Act does not prohibit such discrimination.

PriceWaterhouse v. Hopkins, which Rosa relied on, was not to the contrary, according to the district court, because that case "neither holds, nor even suggests, that discrimination based merely on a person's attire is impermissible."

On appeal, Rosa says that the district court "fundamentally misconceived the law as applicable to the Plaintiff's claim by concluding that there may be no relationship, as a matter of law, between telling a bank customer what to wear and sex discrimination."

The Bank says that Rosa loses for two reasons. First, citing cases pertaining to gays and transsexuals, it says that the ECOA does not apply to cross-dressers. Second, the Bank says that its employee genuinely could not identify Rosa, which is why she asked him to go home and change.

III

The ECOA prohibits discrimination, "with respect to any aspect of a credit transaction[,] on the basis of race, color, religion, national origin, sex or marital status, or age." Thus to prevail, the alleged discrimination against Rosa must have been "on the basis of . . . sex."

While the district court was correct in saying that the prohibited bases of discrimination under the ECOA do not include style of dress or sexual orientation, that is not the discrimination alleged. It is alleged that the Bank's actions were taken, in whole or in part, "on the basis of . . . [the appellant's] sex." . . . Whatever facts emerge, and they may turn out to have nothing to do with sex-based discrimination, we cannot say at this point that the plaintiff has no viable theory of sex discrimination consistent with the facts alleged.

The evidence is not yet developed, and thus it is not yet clear why Brunelle told Rosa to go home and change. It may be that this case involves an instance of disparate treatment based on sex in the denial of credit. . . . It is reasonable to infer that Brunelle told Rosa to go home and change because she thought that Rosa's attire did not accord with his male gender: in other words, that Rosa did not receive the loan application because he was a man, whereas a similarly situated woman would have received the loan application. That is, the Bank may treat, for credit purposes, a woman who dresses like a man differently than a man who dresses like a woman. If so, the Bank concedes, Rosa may have a claim. Indeed, under *PriceWaterhouse,* "stereotyped remarks [including statements about dressing more 'femininely'] can certainly be evidence that gender played a part." It is also reasonable to infer, though, that Brunelle refused to give Rosa the loan application because she thought he was gay, confusing sexual orientation with cross-dressing. If so, Rosa concedes, our precedents dictate that he would have no recourse under the federal Act. It is reasonable to infer, as well, that Brunelle simply could not ascertain whether the person shown in the identification card photographs was the same person that appeared before her that day. If this were the case, Rosa again would be out of luck. It is reasonable to infer, finally, that Brunelle may have had mixed motives, some of which fall into the prohibited category.

It is too early to say what the facts will show; it is apparent, however, that, under some set of facts within the bounds of the allegations and nonconclusory facts in the complaint, Rosa may be able to prove a claim under the ECOA.

We reverse and remand.

Questions

1. *a.* Did the court of appeals find that Park West Bank had violated the ECOA? Explain.
   b. At trial, if the facts revealed that the bank employee thought Rosa was gay and demanded that he change clothes for that reason, who would have won this case in 2000? Would that result change today? Explain.
   c. According to the Court of Appeals, how did the lower court misunderstand this case?
2. *a.* Does federal law protect bank customers based on their style of dress? Explain.
   b. Should it offer that protection? Explain.

Debtor Protection

Millions of Americans are deeply in debt, a nightmare often magnified by the debt collection process. Stefanie Gray was paying interest as high as 14 percent on her $36,000 in private student loans serviced by Navient. She was on food stamps and had difficulty paying her rent. She defaulted on her debt after Navient would not grant her relief. Navient then filed four lawsuits against her. A lawyer from the New York Legal Assistance Group (designed to help low-income residents) came to her aid and was able to secure dismissal of the lawsuits on procedural grounds.[58]

In 2022, approximately 28 percent of Americans had a debt in collection (those that are more than 180 days past due and have been placed in the debt collection process).[59] All debtors may properly be expected to repay what they legitimately owe, but critics claim debtors are often wrongly and abusively pursued. Given these widespread concerns, both federal and most state governments have developed extensive legal protections for debtors.

> In 2022, approximately 28 percent of Americans had a debt in collection.

Debt Collection Law

LO 15-19 Identify debt collection practices forbidden by the Fair Debt Collection Practices Act.

Often employing very aggressive tactics, about 6,400 debt collection agencies nationwide pursue those who are delinquent in their debts. The federal Fair Debt Collection Practices Act (FDCPA), jointly administered by the CFPB and the FTC, is designed to shield debtors from unfair debt collection tactics by debt collection agencies and attorneys who routinely operate as debt collectors. The FDCPA does not extend to business debts or to creditors who are themselves trying to recover money owed to them. Most states also have fair debt collection practice laws, and wronged consumers may sue for damages.

The FDCPA protects consumers by forbidding, among others, the following practices:

- Use of obscene language.
- Contact with third parties other than for the purpose of locating the debtor. (This provision is an attempt to prevent harm to the debtor's reputation.)
- Use of, or threats to use, physical force.
- Contact with the debtor during "inconvenient" hours. For debtors who are employed during "normal" working hours, the period from 9 PM to 8 AM would probably be considered inconvenient.
- Repeated phone calls with the intent to harass.
- Contact with the debtor in an unfair, abusive, or deceptive manner.[60]

The case that follows suggests some of the confusion that can arise in the debt collection process.

Avila v. Riexinger & Associates, LLC 817 F.3d 72 (2d Cir. 2016)

Circuit Judge Pooler

BACKGROUND

Plaintiffs Annmarie Avila and Sara Elrod both received collection notices from defendant Riexinger & Associates, LLC. The notices stated that plaintiffs' accounts had been "placed with [the firm] for collection and such action as necessary." The notices stated each plaintiff's "current balance" but did not disclose that this balance was continuing to accrue interest or that, if plaintiffs failed to pay the debt within a certain amount of time, they would be charged a late fee. . . .

Plaintiffs filed this lawsuit, alleging that the collection notices violated the FDCPA. They claimed, among other things, that the collection notices were misleading because they stated the "current balance," but did not disclose that the balance might increase due to interest and fees. They alleged that they believed from reading the notice that the "current balance" was "static" and that their "payment of that amount would satisfy [the debt] irrespective of when [the] payment was remitted." Avila alleges that in fact interest was accruing daily at a rate equivalent to 500% per year and that defendants have tried to collect this interest from her.

Defendants moved to dismiss the complaint, and the district court granted the motion. . . .

DISCUSSION

. . . Section 1692e of the FDCPA provides that "[a] debt collector may not use any false, deceptive, or misleading representation or means in connection with the collection of any debt." The sixteen subsections of Section 1692e set forth a non-exhaustive list of practices that fall within this ban, including "the false representation of the character, amount, or legal status of any debt." "Because the list . . . is non-exhaustive, a debt collection practice can be a 'false, deceptive, or misleading' practice in violation of Section 1692e even if it does not fall within any of the subsections of Section 1692e."

The question presented is whether the sending of a collection notice that states a consumer's "current balance," but does not disclose that the balance may increase due to interest and fees, is a "false, misleading, or deceptive" practice . . . . In considering this question, we are guided by two principles of statutory construction.

The first principle is that, because the FDCPA is "primarily a consumer protection statute," we must construe its terms "in liberal fashion [to achieve] the underlying Congressional purpose." That purpose is to "eliminate abusive debt collection practices by debt collectors, to insure that those debt collectors who refrain from using abusive debt collection practices are not competitively disadvantaged, and to promote consistent State action to protect consumers against debt collection abuses." . . .

The second principle is that, in considering whether a collection notice violated Section 1692e, we apply the "least sophisticated consumer" standard. In other words, we ask how the least sophisticated consumer—"one not having the astuteness of a 'Philadelphia lawyer' or even the sophistication of the average, everyday, common consumer"—would understand the collection notice. Under this standard, a collection notice can be misleading if it is "open to more than one reasonable interpretation, at least one of which is inaccurate."

Applying these principles, we hold that plaintiffs have stated a claim that the collection notices at issue here are misleading within the meaning of Section 1692e. A reasonable consumer could read the notice and be misled into believing that she could pay her debt in full by paying the amount listed on the notice. In fact, however, if interest is accruing daily, or if there are undisclosed late fees, a consumer who pays the "current balance" stated on the notice will not know whether the debt has been paid in full. The debt collector could still seek the interest and fees that accumulated after the notice was sent but before the balance was paid, or sell the consumer's debt to a third party, which itself could seek the interest and fees from the consumer.

Because the statement of an amount due, without notice that the amount is already increasing due to accruing interest or other charges, can mislead the least sophisticated consumer into believing that payment of the amount stated will clear her account, we hold that the FDCPA requires debt collectors, when they notify consumers of their account balance, to disclose that the balance may increase due to interest and fees. We think that requiring such disclosure best achieves the Congressional purpose of full and fair disclosure to consumers that is embodied in Section 1692e. It also protects consumers such as plaintiffs who may hold the reasonable but mistaken belief that timely payment will satisfy their debts.

The district court . . . expressed a concern that requiring debt collectors to disclose this information might lead to more abusive practices, as debt collectors could use the threat of interest and fees to coerce consumers into paying their debts. This is a legitimate concern. To alleviate it, we adopt the "safe harbor" approach adopted by the Seventh Circuit in *Miller v. McCalla, Raymer, Padrick, Cobb, Nichols, & Clark, L.L.C.*, 214 F.3d 872 (7th Cir. 2000).

. . . The [*Miller*] court held that the following statement would satisfy a debt collector's duty to state the amount of debt in cases where the amount varies from day to day:

> As of the date of this letter, you owe $____ [the exact amount due]. Because of interest, late charges, and other charges that may vary from day to day, the amount due on the day you pay may be greater. Hence, if you pay the amount shown above, an adjustment may be necessary after we receive your check, in

which event we will inform you before depositing the check for collection. For further information, write the undersigned or call 1-800-[phone number].

The court held that a debt collector who used this form would not violate the "amount of the debt" provision, "provided, of course, that the information [the debt collector] furnishes is accurate and [the debt collector] does not obscure it by adding confusing other information (or misinformation)." . . .

We hold that a debt collector will not be subject to liability under Section 1692e for failing to disclose that the consumer's balance may increase due to interest and fees if the collection notice either accurately informs the consumer that the amount of the debt stated in the letter will increase over time, or clearly states that the holder of the debt will accept payment of the amount set forth in full satisfaction of the debt if payment is made by a specified date. Like the *Miller* court, we do not hold that a debt collector must use any particular disclaimer. Using the language set forth in *Miller* will qualify for safe harbor treatment. . . .

The collection notices at issue here stated only the "current balance" but did not disclose that the balance might increase due to interest and fees. Thus, plaintiffs have stated a claim that these notices were "misleading" within the meaning of Section 1692e. The district court's dismissal of this claim is vacated, and we remand for further proceedings consistent with this opinion.

Questions

1. *a.* Why did the *Avila* court rule for the plaintiffs?
   b. Do you agree with the court's decision to employ the "least sophisticated consumer" standard? Explain.
   c. How may debt collectors benefit from this decision?
2. Capital One Bank, in 2012, acquired about $28 billion in credit card accounts from HSBC (another bank). Capital One filed suit against Keith Davidson, whose overdue account was one of those acquired. Davidson filed suit claiming Capital One had violated the FDCPA in various ways. Capital One defended by arguing that it was not subject to the FDCPA.
   a. Why did Capital One claim the FDCPA did not reach its effort to collect the debt owed by Davidson?
   b. Decide the case. Explain. See *Davidson v. Capital One Bank*, 797 F.3d 1309 (11th Cir. 2015).
3. Why shouldn't debt collectors be able to use aggressive tactics to encourage payment of legitimate bills?

Part Four—Bankruptcy

Fresh Start for Consumers?

LO 15-20
Understand the purpose for providing bankruptcy to individuals.

In 2022, the average American household with debt owes about $165,388 (including mortgages). Among households with credit card debt, the average carried from one month to the next was about $7,500.[61] Many consumers struggle to meet their debt burdens.

Should we lend a hand to those consumers who are down on their luck? The bankruptcy laws are specifically designed to provide a fresh start for those whose financial problems are insurmountable. The idea is that both the debtor and society benefit from the new beginning.

Should we lend a hand to those down on their luck?

Bankruptcy Rules

Bankruptcy in the United States is governed exclusively by federal law; the states do not have the constitutional authority to enact bankruptcy legislation, but they do set their own rules within the limits provided by Congress. Our attention will be limited to the principal federal statute: the Bankruptcy Reform Act of 1978, as amended. Our focus will be on the law as it applies to individuals.

LO 15-21
Be able to explain the effects and implications of the three bankruptcy options.

Bankruptcy is an adjudication relieving a debtor of all or part of the debtor's liabilities. Any person or entity may seek debt relief. Our focus will be on the bankruptcy laws as they apply to individuals. Three forms of bankruptcy are important to us:

1. In a *liquidation* (Chapter 7 of the Bankruptcy Act) most debts are forgiven, all assets except those exempt are fairly distributed to creditors, and debtors receive a "fresh start."

2. A *reorganization* (Chapter 11) keeps creditors from using general debt collection mechanisms while the debtor, under the supervision of the court, works out a financial reorganization plan.
3. An *adjustment of debts* (Chapter 13) is an option for an individual with a regular income and somewhat limited debts to protect them from actions by creditors while they pay their debts in installments under an approved plan.

Liquidation

A Chapter 7 liquidation petition can be *voluntarily* filed in federal court by the debtor or creditors can seek an *involuntary* bankruptcy judgment. A Chapter 7 liquidation is commonly called a "straight" bankruptcy and is designed to relieve debtors of most debts, such as credit card and medical bills.

In a voluntary action, the debtor generally files a petition with the U.S. Bankruptcy Court. The court then has jurisdiction to proceed with the liquidation, and the petition becomes the *order for relief.* Creditors, however, can often compel an involuntary bankruptcy, which the debtor may challenge. The court will enter an order for relief if it finds the debtor has not been paying debts when due.

After an order for relief is made, voluntary and involuntary actions proceed in a similar manner. Creditors are restrained from reaching the debtor's assets. An interim bankruptcy trustee is appointed by the court. The creditors then hold a meeting at which a permanent trustee is elected. The trustee collects the debtor's property and converts it to cash, protects the interests of the debtor and creditors, may manage the debtor's business if there is one, and ultimately distributes the nonexempt estate to the creditors. Debtors are allowed to keep exempt property, which is determined under state but typically includes a car, some household and personal items, life insurance, and a small amount of additional assets. Normally a dollar maximum is attached to each allowed asset.

The debtor's nonexempt property is then divided among the creditors according to the priorities prescribed by statute. Secured creditors are paid first. If funds remain, "priority" claims, such as employees' wages and alimony and child support, are paid. Then, funds permitting, general creditors (such as credit card lenders) are paid. Each class must be paid in full before a class of lower priority will be compensated. Any remaining funds are returned to the debtor.

When the distribution is complete, the bankruptcy judge will issue an order discharging (relieving) the debtor of any remaining debts, except for certain statutorily specified claims. To that extent, the debtor is granted a "fresh start." One such "statutorily specified" claim is student loan debt, which can only be discharged by the establishment of "undue hardship." In late 2022, the Justice Department and the Department of Education announced the implementation of a new process that is intended to provide clear standards for discharge, enabling borrowers to determine whether they meet the criteria.[62]

Reorganization

Chapter 11 reorganizations are most commonly used by entities, but individuals may also seek a reorganization. An example might be an individual who operates a business in their own name as a sole proprietor. Such an individual would likely not qualify for an adjustment of debts under Chapter 13, discussed below, but might be able to develop a plan that would provide their creditors more than what they would receive under a liquidation.

If an individual files for a reorganization, whether or not they own a business, they will be required to file, with their petition, schedules showing their assets and liabilities, as well as current income and expenditures. A statement of their financial affairs must also be provided. Individual debtors or married couples filing jointly must also file a certificate of credit counseling and a copy of any debt repayment plan developed through credit counseling; evidence of payment from employers received 60 days before filing; and a statement of monthly net income including any anticipated increase in income or expenses after filing. Other information may also be required.

LO 15-22
In light of the consumer protections discussed in this chapter, be able to proffer a reasoned evaluation of the necessity for consumer protection laws in relation to Adam Smith's "invisible hand" regulating the markets.

A plan of reorganization will be developed by the debtor and be provided to the creditors, who may file objections to the confirmation of the plan. On confirmation of the plan by the court, the debtor is generally discharged of any debts that arose before the confirmation. After confirmation, the debtor is bound by the provisions of the plan and required to make plan payments.

Adjustment of Debts

Under Chapter 13 of the Bankruptcy Code, individuals can seek the protection of the court to arrange a debt adjustment plan. The use of Chapter 13 is restricted to those with steady incomes and somewhat limited debts. The process can begin only with a voluntary petition from the debtor. Creditors are restrained from reaching the debtor's assets. The debtor develops a repayment plan. If creditors' interests are sufficiently protected by the plan, the court will confirm it. The debtor then has generally three to five years to make the necessary payments, at which time the remaining debts are discharged.

[For more on all forms of bankruptcy, see **www.uscourts.gov/services-forms/bankruptcy**].

Bankruptcy Critique

Annual bankruptcy filings in 2021, both personal and business, were just under 400,000 (having declined annually since 2010), a numerical low not seen since 1985.[63] A full explanation may never be determined, but costs were driven up by the 2005 federal bankruptcy reform law that pushed more individuals into Chapter 13, as opposed to Chapter 7, but experts have pointed to debtors' inability to pay for the bankruptcy process and limited assets to protect as key reasons for the decline.[64] Supporters of the 2005 reform argue that it has reduced the cost of credit for all Americans while curbing bankruptcy abuse and unfairness.

PRACTICING ETHICS Bankruptcy—Who Is to Blame?

Commenting on the 2005 bankruptcy reform law, which in general made filing more difficult and bankruptcy less financially useful, Todd Zywicki, a George Mason University law professor, said, "This is a matter of morality and personal responsibility." Consumer advocates, on the other hand, say the bankruptcy problem lies with the "enablers"—the credit card companies and mortgage lenders that encourage deeper and deeper indebtedness.

QUESTION

Who bears the moral blame for America's bankruptcy struggles? Explain.

Source: Michael Schroeder and Suein Hwang, "Sweeping New Bankruptcy Law to Make Life Harder for Debtors," *The Wall Street Journal*, April 6, 2005, p. A1.

Epilogue

In this chapter we have focused on some of the many laws that protect consumers in their interactions with business. It is an appropriate time, then, to reflect back and consider why these protections are both important and necessary. We will end with one final question. Why do we have these laws for the protection of individuals? Why are they important?

Research Exercises

Research Exercise on Food Safety

There is no easy solution for ensuring food safety. The food we eat comes from both ends of the spectrum–major corporations providing products for domestic and international consumption to family-run farms. Science and footwork are both critical inputs for the FDA to fulfill its mandates. Both take time and money. Passing a law is only one step–funding it and implementing it have to follow. Everyone in the food chain associated with the impacted items potentially could help or hinder the effort. For example, think of one food item that is potentially hazardous. Then consider all of the people and businesses in the food chain before it gets to the final consumer. Many of these people and businesses will need help if the goal is going to be achieved–training, funding, testing, and problem-solving along the way.

Discuss the perspective (e.g., actor, food, and safety issue) you want to portray in your presentation or pick two contrasting perspectives. Create a presentation that illustrates the hurdles that will need to be overcome on the way to safer food.

Research Exercise on CPSC's Regulatory Robot

Imagine that you are going to start a small business that will manufacture or import consumer products. Develop a list of products you would like to have in your product line. Then access the CPSC's Regulatory Robot to find out what rules and regulations with which you will need to comply. Develop a presentation to give to potential financial backers of your business that explains the business and regulatory requirements it will face during start-up to ensure that your inventory meets those requirements.

Chapter Questions

1. A group of parents sued Gerber claiming its "Fruit Juice Snacks" product packaging was misleading. The words "Fruit Juice" appeared on the package beside images of fruits such as peaches and cherries. In fact, the only fruit juice in the "Snacks" was white grape from concentrate. A side panel statement said the product was made "with real fruit juice and other all natural ingredients," but the primary ingredients were corn syrup and sugar. The side panel also displayed the statement: "one of a variety of nutritious Gerber Graduates foods and juices that have been specifically designed to help toddlers grow up strong and healthy." The actual ingredients were correctly listed in "small print" on the side of the box. Is a "reasonable consumer" "likely to be deceived" by the Gerber packaging? Develop arguments to support both conclusions. Then provide an argument for the strength of one over the other. See *Williams v. Gerber Products,* 523 F.3d 934 (9th Cir. 2008) and, as amended, at *Williams v. Gerber Prods. Co.,* 552 F.3d 934 (9th Cir. 2008).
2. San Francisco Bay area consumers Wanda Greenwood, Ladelle Hatfield, and Deborah McCleese each signed up for an Aspire Visa credit card marketed by CompuCredit

Corp. of Atlanta, Georgia. The card was advertised as a means of rebuilding cardholders' credit histories as well as providing $300 in immediate credit, with no down payment. The consumers claimed that fees hidden in the fine print of the agreement used up much of the $300, with the result that they were misled about the card agreement's capacity to help restore their credit. The agreement also included language requiring both the consumer and the company to resolve disputes using binding arbitration. The federal Credit Repair Organizations Act (CROA) requires credit repair organizations to provide a disclosure statement to consumers saying: "You have a right to sue a credit repair organization that violates the [Act]." The three consumers brought a class-action lawsuit against CompuCredit alleging a violation of CROA, which, among other things, forbids deceptive practices in credit repair.

a. CompuCredit argued that the lawsuit was barred because of the arbitration provision. As you look at the facts, do you think the consumers can sue CompuCredit, or must they turn to binding arbitration? Explain.

b. How might a ruling favoring arbitration encourage fraud by credit card companies? See *CompuCredit Corp. v. Wanda Greenwood, et al.,* 132 S. Ct. 665 (2012).

3. A 2013 study found that over 4,400 children per year receive hospital care for injuries suffered at amusement parks and water parks, and 29 deaths from amusement rides were reported from 2010 to 2016. The Consumer Product Safety Commission is responsible for temporary parks such as traveling carnivals, while states are responsible for permanent amusement parks. Six states have no laws requiring inspections. Some states provide extensive inspection by state employees, while others allow amusement parks to hire private, licensed inspectors to check for safety problems.[65] Would you favor a federal law requiring uniform, comprehensive government inspection of all amusement parks and water parks? Explain.

4. Phusion Projects was accused by the Federal Trade Commission of mislabeling Four Loko, its flavored malt drink. The FTC investigated the company's implied claims that consumers could safely drink one 23.5-ounce can at a sitting because each can contained the alcoholic equivalent of one to two 12-ounce beers. It concluded that those claims were misleading. A single Four Loko can contained as much alcohol as four to five beers and drinking one can on a single occasion would amount to binge drinking. Several states banned the drink. In 2013, the FTC ordered Phusion to put on the back of Four Loko cans containing more than two servings (where one "serving" equals 0.6 ounce of alcohol) an "Alcohol Facts" panel that discloses alcohol content, serving size, and the number of servings per can.

a. Many public comments to the FTC called for banning Four Loko from the market. Should the FTC have done so? Explain.

b. From the FTC's point of view, what consumer benefit was achieved by the labeling order?

c. How would you have handled the Four Loko situation?

5. In 2018, less than 10 percent of Americans were "underwater" on their home mortgages; that is, they owed more than their homes were worth.[66] At the bottom of the Great Recession, about 30 percent of homeowners were underwater. Many of those "underwater" families walked away from their mortgage. Many declined to abandon

their mortgages because they feared the consequences on their credit records and wanted to avoid the cost of changing homes. Some continued to make payments simply because they believed defaulting would be immoral. While serving as U.S. Treasury Secretary, Henry Paulson said that anyone who walks away from their mortgage is "simply a speculator–and one who is not honoring his obligation."[67]

a. Make the argument that deliberately walking away from an underwater home mortgage is immoral.

b. Make the argument that walking away is not immoral.

c. What would you do? Explain. See Richard H. Thaler, "Underwater, but Will They Leave the Pool?" *The New York Times,* January 24, 2010 [**www.nytimes.com**]; and Brent T. White, "Buyers Have No Moral Duty to Lenders," *Arizona Republic,* April 25, 2010 [**www.azcentral.com**].

6. William Cohan, writing in *The New York Times,* objected to the federal government's consumer protection efforts in the Dodd-Frank Wall Street Reform and Consumer Protection Act, including the creation of the Consumer Financial Protection Bureau. Explain why Cohan and other critics would object to the government's efforts to protect consumers from "devious credit-card companies" and "dishonest mortgage lenders." See William D. Cohan, "The Elizabeth Warren Fallacy," *The New York Times,* September 30, 2010 [**http://opinionator.blogs.nytimes.com**].
7. Some studies suggest that consumer bankruptcies are much more common in some states than others. Aside from income levels, what socioeconomic factors would you expect to be closely correlated with high bankruptcy rates?
8. Perhaps you are among the masses of Americans who are annoyed by the seeming epidemic of underfilled potato chip bags and candy boxes and over-iced cold drinks. Starbucks was sued in 2018 on the grounds that it "uniformly underfills its lattes and mochas" to "save on the cost of milk." The plaintiffs claimed that Starbucks failed to fill its cups with the ounces of drinks specified on its menus and thus was guilty of breach of express warranty, false advertising, fraud, and more. Among other arguments, the plaintiffs said that Starbucks underfills its cups to accommodate milk foam, but milk foam should not count in the calculation of beverage volume. Assuming milk foam is included in Starbucks milk volume calculation, is Starbucks unlawfully deceiving its customers? Explain. See *Strumlauf v. Starbucks Corp.,* 2018 U.S. Dist. LEXIS 2409 (N.D. Cal. January 5, 2018).
9. Evan Parent sued MillerCoors for deceptively marketing its Blue Moon Belgian-style beer in violation of California consumer protection and false advertising laws. Parent argued that MillerCoors was marketing Blue Moon as a "craft beer" produced by Blue Moon Brewing, when in fact it is mass produced by MillerCoors. Parent pointed to the absence of references to MillerCoors on the Blue Moon website and to MillerCoors' use of its registered trademark "Artfully Crafted" on the label and in advertising. Parent also noted that Blue Moon is sold at a premium price like other craft brews, is stocked by retailers in their craft beer sections, and is listed in the craft beer section on the MillerCoors website. Do these allegations, if true, amount to deceptive, misleading marketing? See *Parent v. MillerCoors,* 2016 U.S. Dist. LEXIS 78764 (S.D. Cal. June 16, 2016).
10. Roseman resigned from the John Hancock Insurance Company following allegations that he misused his expense account. He reimbursed the company. Subsequently, he

was denied employment by another insurance firm after that firm read a Retail Credit Company credit report on him. The credit report included accurate information regarding Roseman's resignation. Was Retail Credit in violation of the Fair Credit Reporting Act in circulating information regarding the resignation? Explain. See *Roseman v. Retail Credit Co., Inc.,* 428 F. Supp. 643 (E.D. Pa. 1977).

11. Once the government decided to intervene in the free market on behalf of consumers, two broad product safety options presented themselves: (a) the government could have limited its effort to generating and distributing information to consumers, or (b) the government could have set safety standards for all products. Assuming the government was forced to choose one or the other but not elements of both, which option should it have chosen? Explain.
12. Consumers sometimes abuse sellers. One familiar technique is shoplifting. Shoplifting is a crime, but the criminal process is cumbersome and often does not result in monetary recoveries for sellers. As a result, state laws often permit store owners to impose civil fines, the collection of which is usually turned over to a lawyer or collection agency with a threat to sue in civil court, file criminal charges, or both if payment is not forthcoming. Fines may range from \$50 to \$5,000 or more, depending on the value of the item(s) stolen.
    a. Defense lawyers say this civil fine system is unfair. Why?
    b. On balance, is the civil fine approach to shoplifting a good idea? Explain.
    c. Cite some other examples of consumers abusing businesspeople.
13. Goswami failed to pay her \$900 credit card bill. A collection agency, ACEI, mailed her a collection letter with a blue bar across the envelope saying "Priority Letter." The letter did not, in fact, constitute priority mail. The purpose of the bar was to encourage Goswami to open the envelope. Was the bar a deceptive practice in violation of the Fair Debt Collection Practices Act? Explain. See *Goswami v. American Collections Enterprise, Inc.,* 377 F.3d 488 (5th Cir. 2004), *cert. denied,* 546 U.S. 811 (2005).

Notes

1. Jessie Yang, "The Use and Abuse of Patents in the Smartphone Wars: A Need for Change," *Journal of Law, Technology & the Internet,* Vol. 5 (2014), p. 239.
2. "Reported fraud losses increase more than 70 percent over 2020 to more than \$5.8 billion," Federal Trade Commission, February 22, 2023 [**www.ftc.gov**].
3. Ibid.
4. *Williams v. Walker-Thomas Furniture Co.,* 350 F.2d 445 (D.C. Cir. 1965).
5. Office of Research, "Consumer use of payday, auto title, and pawn loans," Consumer Financial Protection Bureau, May 2021 (**www.consumerfinance.gov**).
6. Gretchen Morgenson, Lisa Cavazuti, and Vicky Nguyen, "Payday lenders can send borrowers into tailspin. How one woman broke free," NBC News, January 11, 2022 [**www.nbcnews.com**].
7. "FDA Finalizes Historic Rule Enabling Access to Over-the-Counter Hearing Aids for Millions of Americans," U.S. Food & Drug Administration, August 16, 2022 [**www.fda.gov**].
8. "FDA Proposes Updated Definition of 'Healthy' Claim on Food Packages to Help Improve Diet, Reduce Chronic Disease," U.S. Food & Drug Administration, September 28, 2022 [**www.fda.gov**].
9. "FDA Alerts the Public to Potentially Contaminated Products from Family Dollar Stores in Six States," U.S. Food & Drug Administration, February 18, 2022 [**www.fda.gov**].

10. Noah Weiland and Sharon LaFraniere, "F.D.A. Authorizes Updated Covid Booster Shots Targeting Omicron Subvariants," *The New York Times,* August 31, 2022 [**nytimes.com**].
11. "FDA Grants Accelerated Approval for Alzheimer's Disease Treatment," U.S. Food & Drug Administration, January 6, 2023 [**www.fda.gov**].
12. "FDA Approves First Gene Therapy for the Treatment of High-Risk, Non-Muscle-Invasive Bladder Cancer," U.S. Food & Drug Administration, December 16, 2022 [**www.fda.gov**].
13. "FDA Approves First Drug That Can Delay Onset of Type 1 Diabetes," U.S. Food & Drug Administration, November 17, 2022 [**www.fda.gov**].
14. Associated Press, "The Odds of a Drug Having a Significant Safety Issue After Winning FDA Approval Are Nearly 1 in 3, Study Finds," *Los Angeles Times,* May 9, 2017 [**www.latimes.com**].
15. "FDA Takes Steps Aimed at Fostering Development of Non-Addictive Alternatives to Opioids for Acute Pain Management," U.S. Food & Drug Administration, February 9, 2022 [**www.fda.gov**].
16. "State System Minimum Legal Sales Age (MLSA) Laws for Tobacco Products Fact Sheet," Centers for Disease Control and Prevention, accessed January 18, 2023 (**www.cdc.gov).**
17. Ismail Shakil and Chris Kirkham, "E-Cigarette Usage Nearly Doubles in U.S. High-Schools: Survey," Health News, Reuters, December 16, 2018 [**www.reuters.com**].
18. Press Release, "FDA finalizes enforcement policy on unauthorized flavored cartridge-based e-cigarettes that appeal to children, including fruit and mint," U.S. Food & Drug Administration, January 2, 2020 [**www.fda.gov**].
19. "New Data Show More Than 2.5 Million U.S. Youth Currently Use E-Cigarettes," U.S. Food & Drug Administration, October 6, 2022 [**www.fda.gov**].
20. Matt Richtel and Andrew Jacobs, "F.D.A. Orders Juul to Stop Selling E-Cigarettes," *The New York Times,* June 23, 2022 [**www.nytimes.com**].
21. Ibid.
22. "New Data Show More Than 2.5 Million U.S. Youth Currently Use E-Cigarettes," U.S. Food & Drug Administration.
23. "FDA, DOJ Seek Permanent Injunctions Against Six E-cigarette Manufacturers," U.S. Food & Drug Administration, October 18, 2022 [**www.fda.gov**].
24. "FDA Warns Firms for Selling Illegal E-cigarettes That Look Like Toys, Food, and Cartoon Characters," U.S. Food & Drug Administration, November 16, 2022 [**www.fda.gov**].
25. "Have a Question? AskUSDA," U.S. Department of Agriculture, November 21, 2022 [**https://ask.usda.gov**], accessed January 18, 2023.
26. "Challenges Remain in FDA's Inspections of Domestic Food Facilities," U.S. Department of Health and Human Services, Office of Inspector General, September 25, 2017 [**https://oig.hhs.gov**].
27. Ryan McCrimmon, "Congress is still underfunding FSMA," *Politica,* February 11, 2019.
28. "FDA Seeks $8.4 Billion to Further Investments in Critical Public Health Modernization, Core Food and Medical Product Safety Programs," U.S. Food & Drug Administration, March 28, 2022 [**www.fda.gov**].
29. "Production resumes at troubled Abbott baby formula factory," CNBC, July 9, 2022 [**www.cnbc.com**].
30. Susan Berfield and Anna Edney, "How Deadly Bacteria Spread in a Similac Factory—and Caused the US Formula Shortage," *Bloomberg Businessweek,* August 29, 2022 [**www.bloomberg.com**].
31. Anna Edney, "What Happened at Abbott's Baby Formula Factory?" *Bloomberg Prognosis,* August 25, 2022 [**www.bloomberg.com**].

32. Susan Berfield and Anna Edney, "How Deadly Bacteria Spread in a Similac Factory."
33. Ibid.
34. Federal Trade Commission Act, §5(a).
35. Press Release, "FTC Returns More Than $2.9 Million To Consumers Harmed by Warrior Trading," January 10, 2023 [**www.ftc.gov**].
36. Press Release, "FTC Returns More Than $9.8 Million To Consumers Harmed by Napleton Auto's Junk Fees and Discriminatory Practices," November 14, 2022 [**www.ftc.gov**].
37. Press Release, "Federal Trade Commission Returns More Than $415,000 To Consumers Harmed by Deceptive Car Dealer Tate's Auto," September 15, 2022 [**www.ftc.gov**].
38. Press Release, "Federal Trade Commission Returns More Than $1 Million To Consumers Harmed by Global Asset Financial Services' Phantom Debt Collection Scheme," August 4, 2022 [**www.ftc.gov**].
39. 141 S.Ct. 1342 (2021).
40. Press Release, "FTC Asks Congress to Pass Legislation Reviving the Agency's Authority to Return Money to Consumers Harmed by Law Violations and Keep Illegal Conduct from Reoccurring," April 27, 2021 [**www.ftc.gov**].
41. Press Release, "Fortnite Video Game Maker Epic Games to Pay More Than Half a Billion Dollars over FTC Allegations of Privacy Violations and Unwanted Charges," December 19, 2022 [**www.ftc.gov**].
42. Ibid.
43. Claudia Koerner, "The Popular Rock 'N Play Baby Sleeper Has Been Recalled After Being Blamed for at Least 30 Infant Deaths," *BuzzFeed News,* April 12, 2019 [**www.buzzfeednews.com**].
44. Todd C. Frankel, "Stop Using All Inclined Sleepers, Warns Federal Safety Agency as Death Toll Hits 73," *The Washington Post,* November 1, 2019 [**www.washingtonpost.com**].
45. Jenny Gross, "100 Infant Deaths Linked to Recalled Fisher-Price Sleeper," *The New York Times,* January 10, 2023.
46. Press Release, "CPSC's New Federal Infant Sleep Products Safety Standard Takes Effect," Consumer Product Safety Commission, June 23, 2022.
47. Consumer Product Safety Commission, "2020 NEISS Data Highlights: Overview—All Products," accessed January 22, 2023 [**www.cpsc.gov**].
48. Eileen Carr, "Ending the Growing Student - Debt Problem," Letter to the Editor, *The Wall Street Journal,* June 14, 2019 [**www.wsj.com**].
49. "How the American Middle Class Has Changed in the Past Five Decades," *Trust Magazine,* September 20, 2022 [**www.pewtrusts.org**].
50. Beverly Harzog, "Survey: 46% of College Students With Credit Cards Have Debt," *U.S. News & World Report,* September 21, 2022 [**https://money.usnews.com**].
51. Ibid.
52. Bianca Peter, "Credit Card Activity for College Students, *WalletNews,* November 18, 2022 [**https://wallethub.com**].
53. Press Release, "CFPB Report Finds High Fees Charged on Student Banking Products Endorsed by Colleges," Consumer Financial Protection Board, October 13, 2022.
54. Ibid.
55. Federal Trade Commission, "A Summary of Your Rights Under the Fair Credit Reporting Act," accessed January 23, 2023 [**www.consumer.ftc.gov**].

56. H. Scott Kelly, David N. Anthony, and Tim J. St. George, "Spokeo Update: Parties Settle Long-Running FCRA Dispute," *Troutman Sanders,* March 15, 2019 [**www.consumerfinancialserviceslawmonitor.com**].
57. Keith Laing, "Feds Settle with Honda in Auto Racial Discrimination Case," *The Hill,* July 14, 2015 [**https://thehill.com**].
58. Stacy Cowley and Jessica Silver-Greenberg, "A Lawsuit Machine," *The New York Times,* November 14, 2017 [**www.nytimes.com**].
59. Capital Recovery Corporation, "Important Debt Collection Statistics to Know in 2022," *CRBlog,* May 8, 2022 [**www.capitalrecovery.net**].
60. Federal Trade Commission, "Debt Collection FAQs," Consumer Advice, May 2021 [**www.consumer.ftc.gov**].
61. Erin El Issa, "2022 American Household Credit Card Debt Study," NerdWallet, January 10, 2023 [**www.nerdwallet.com**].
62. Press Release, "Justice Department and Department of Education Announce a Fairer and More Accessible Bankruptcy Discharge Process for Student Loan Borrower," November 17, 2022 (updated August 10, 2023) [**www.justice.gov**].
63. Data from "Bankruptcy Statistics," American Bankruptcy Institute, accessed January 23, 2023 [**www.abi.org**].
64. Andrew Keshner, "Bankruptcy Filings Are at a 10-Year Low, but Not for the Reasons You Might Think," *MarketWatch,* January 8, 2019 [**www.marketwatch.com**].
65. See Kathleen Foody, Erik Schelzig, and Claire Galofaro, "Thrill-Ride Accidents Spark New Demands for Regulation," *The Des Moines Register,* August 23, 2016, p. 10A; and Rick Jervis, "Thousands of Kids Hurt Each Year on Thrill Rides," *The Des Moines Register,* August 10, 2016, p. 2B.
66. Zillow, "Less Than 10 Percent of Homeowners Are Underwater on Their Mortgages," Zillow Press Release, May 30, 2018 [**www.zillow.com**].
67. Ibid.

CHAPTER SIXTEEN

International Ethics and Law

After completing this chapter, students will be able to fulfill the following learning objectives:

16-1. Discuss the role of the World Trade Organization in reducing global trade barriers.

16-2. Discuss the interrelationship of religion, culture, and legal rules with comparisons to American and Islamic viewpoints.

16-3. Compare and contrast an American firm's social responsibility to its host country with its social responsibility to its home country.

16-4. Discuss the recent use of the Alien Tort Statute against corporate defendants.

16-5. Describe the basic forms of global business expansion.

16-6. Compare and contrast treaties, custom, and comity and give illustrations of each.

16-7. Describe examples of the law governing international business in sales of goods, trade in services, and employment.

16-8. Identify and describe the four main forms of intellectual property and the international agreements that govern them.

16-9. Discuss the challenges of governing multinational entities, in general, and state-owned companies, in particular.

16-10. Discuss the unique challenges MNEs face with regard to securities regulation and applicable accounting standards.

16-11. Identify the main regulators of MNEs with respect to anticompetitive behaviors generally and mergers specifically.

16-12. Discuss how and why nations regulate imports and exports.

16-13. Identify and evaluate the means for resolving international disputes.

16-14. Explain the act of state doctrine.

16-15. Describe the doctrine of sovereign immunity and its exceptions as codified under the Foreign Sovereign Immunities Act.

16-16. Identify some challenges to the enforcement of foreign judgments.

Introduction

The preceding chapters have addressed law and ethics, primarily in an American context. However, ours is undeniably a global economy, as painfully evidenced by the global economic recession triggered in 2008 and, even more so, by the COVID-19 pandemic.

> Globalization is the breaking down of national boundaries to allow free interchange of people, communications, services, goods, businesses, investments, and ideas.

The process of globalization is the breaking down of national boundaries and rules to allow free interchange around the world—the free interchange of people, communications, services, goods, businesses, investments, and ideas. Evidence of the global economy is everywhere. Travel the world and you can readily access automated teller machines (ATMs) for local currency that will be instantaneously charged to your domestic bank account. You will see such American logos as Starbucks, McDonald's, and Deloitte adorning shops and buildings. Back at home, on streets and in malls, you can see branches and outlets for HSBC (formerly the Hongkong and Shanghai Banking Corporation, now one of the world's largest banks, headquartered in London), Godiva Chocolatier (founded in Brussels), Hyundai cars (global headquarters in Korea), and H&M clothing stores (global headquarters in Sweden). As for the interchange of people, in addition to the millions of international temporary business and visiting travelers, there were 44.8 million immigrants living in the United States as of 2018, representing 13.7 percent of the population.[1] By comparison, the U.S. Department of State estimated there were 9 million U.S. citizens living abroad in 2016.[2]

How is business practice affected by this networked global economy? Which laws govern company behavior? The laws of the "home" country? The laws of the "host" country? The laws where the company's suppliers or customers reside? What happens if the laws of the host country and the home country conflict? And what happens when a corporation changes its home country? When the German corporation Daimler-Benz merged with Chrysler, becoming DaimlerChrysler, did the laws to which Chrysler was subject change? Did those changes have to be unwound when Daimler later sold Chrysler to Cerberus Capital Management, an American private equity fund, in 2007? In 2014, Chrysler became a wholly owned subsidiary of the Italian automaker Fiat, which then became known as Fiat Chrysler Automobiles. And in 2021, Fiat Chrysler merged with the Peugeot brand's parent company to form Stellantis, based in Amsterdam. What law governs the company now? As firms become companies of the world, rather than of one nation, ethical and legal complexities arise.

The International Environment

Ever since Adam Smith wrote *The Wealth of Nations* in 1776, many have argued that a decrease in trade barriers among countries will stimulate the total world economy, not only the economies of the countries involved in the specific trade agreement. Belief in this principle is affirmed each time a new nation joins the World Trade Organization (WTO). With the addition of three new countries in 2015 and 2016 (Afghanistan, Kazakhstan, and Liberia), the WTO now comprises 164 members.

LO 16-1
Discuss the role of the World Trade Organization in reducing global trade barriers.

A fundamental principle set forth in the preamble to the 1994 Marrakesh Agreement, which established the WTO effective January 1, 1995, is that a "substantial reduction of tariffs and other barriers to trade" will contribute to the objectives of "raising standards of living, ensuring full employment and a large and steadily growing volume of real income."[3] Member countries in the WTO represent a diverse array of the world's governments, from communist to socialist to capitalist, from Buddhist to Jewish to Christian to Muslim, and from all points around the globe. Thus, belief in the benefits of decreasing trade barriers has been widely shared in the international community, although a shift in this ideology has become more evident in recent years. [For more on the WTO, including full text documents, see **www.wto.org.**]

Trade Agreements

The desire to reach a common legal ground in international business is not a recent development. As early as 1778, U.S. commercial treaties have regulated shipping and trading rights and rules between U.S. citizens and those of other countries. Such agreements can be relatively simple—involving only two countries and only a few commodities—or they can be more complex, multilateral agreements involving three or more countries and governing broad areas of their trading relationships, such as the United States–Mexico–Canada Agreement, which replaced the North American Free Trade Agreement, effective July 1, 2020. The more countries involved and the more topics on the table, the more complex the agreement. The WTO is the prototypical multilateral agreement. The vast majority of countries are members, and conceivably any trade-related topic could become a topic for negotiation. In principle, involving the maximum number of state actors and addressing the universe of possible trade issues will result in the greatest economic stimulation. As a practical matter, that ideal may be very difficult to effectuate, as was manifestly illustrated by the WTO negotiations that concluded in December 2013.[4]

Those negotiations, known as the Doha Round after the city in Qatar where the round was initiated, began in 2001 and collapsed in 2008. Sticking points included the continuation of substantial agricultural subsidies for farmers in the United States and Europe, which negatively impact the competitive strength of agricultural products originating in other countries, and the relatively high import tariffs on manufactured goods imposed by some then-emerging economies like China and India. Another impediment to its conclusion was the dramatic change in the global trading environment over the 13 years the negotiations continued. Not only had major industrialized countries suffered substantial recessions, but emerging economies began contributing dramatically to the global growth in gross domestic product (GDP)—accounting for two-thirds of it in 2008.[5] Both realities contributed to a shift in the economic balance of power. The December 2013 agreement reflected a substantially modified agenda compared to that envisioned in 2001 and focuses primarily on the streamlining of international customs rules and procedures.

In light of the limited negotiating successes in recent years under the auspices of the WTO, the fear is that there will be a return to less comprehensive regional and bilateral negotiations in which the imbalance of power between rich and poor nations will be more pronounced. This imbalance of power may be further amplified by a recent trend in U.S. immigration policies and trade negotiations that reflect a more nationalistic ideology—a belief that globalization hurts American jobs and threatens the American way of life.

> "Globalism is an ideology, and its struggle with nationalism will shape the coming decade."

This is in sharp contrast to globalism, the belief that globalization is good and that national sovereignty should give way to global governance. Political debate during the 2016 U.S. presidential election was sharply divided on these issues, and there was a surge in nationalism in the United States under the Trump Administration, underscoring that "globalism is an ideology, and its struggle with nationalism will shape the coming decade."[6] Other countries, such as Britain and France, have been debating similar issues. "Globalization has gone into reverse gear. . . . In the boom years between 2003 and 2010 it appeared that a new era of openness and global supply chains would help emerging countries to grow at turbocharged rates for decades, closing the gap with the rich world. Today that idea is out of fashion."[7]

While WTO negotiations have proven difficult, regional trade agreements do seem to be on the rise, with more than 10 agreements reached on average each year from 1994 until 2018.[8] Until recent years, the United States had been attempting to negotiate two major regional compacts: one with the European Union, the Transatlantic Trade and Investment Partnership (TTIP), and the other with 11 countries circling the Pacific, the Trans-Pacific Partnership (TPP). These negotiations were not successful. However, after the United States abandoned the TPP following the 2016 presidential election of Donald Trump, the remaining countries, including Canada, Chile, Mexico, and New Zealand, continued negotiations and signed a new version of the pact in March 2018, known as the Comprehensive and Progressive Agreement for Trans-Pacific Partnership (CPTPP). Meanwhile, China–which was excluded from the TPP–sought to create a separate pact and ultimately launched the world's largest trading bloc, the Regional Comprehensive Economic Partnership (RCEP), with 14 other countries in 2022.[9]

European Union

One of the most well-known and most developed trade agreements is that of the European Union (EU). It is also quite significant for our purposes because the EU is the United States' largest trading partner, and vice versa. As of this writing, the EU is made up of 27 member countries, with eight candidate countries: Albania, Bosnia and Herzegovena, Moldova, Montenegro, North Macedonia, Serbia, Turkey, and Ukraine. The EU population far surpasses that of the United States–approximately 446.8 million compared with 333.3 million in 2022–but its combined gross domestic product was only an estimated $16.6 trillion compared to the United States' $24.2 trillion that same year. Like the United States, the European Union has a robust domestic regulatory regime that impacts foreign companies seeking to do business there. But their regulatory philosophies differ: Europe tends to take a precautionary approach, disallowing new products and technologies until they are proven safe, whereas the United States tends to weigh costs and benefits even while recognizing that unknowns exist.[10] These differing approaches were one of the challenges of TTIP negotiations, which ended unsuccessfully in 2016.

Like the WTO, the European Union has faced considerable challenges in recent years. As the 2008 financial crisis spread around the world through global financial and economic networks, not only were weak banks revealed but also weak countries. The very success of the EU in increasing trade and other economic ties among its member countries became a liability, with economically weaker countries acting as a drag on the EU's stronger economies.

Consider, for example, that some of the strongest economic ties in the European Union are those that link the 19 countries sharing the euro as their common currency. In the usual course, as a national economy deteriorates, its currency is devalued in relation to other currencies, and the economic hardship remains primarily a domestic problem. However, within the eurozone, for example, Greece's currency cannot fall to reflect the comparative degree of its economic difficulties because the value of the euro is tied to perceptions of the eurozone as a whole. What happens when the world sees weakness not just in Greece, but also in Spain, Portugal, Ireland, and Italy? Even the economically strong eurozone countries suffer the devaluation of their shared currency. If they provide support to prop up the weaker economies, then the issue becomes whether the recipient countries will institute changes that will strengthen their economies and prevent future negative impacts on the euro. If the stronger economies do not have faith in such change or cannot compel it as a condition of their support, they may determine that the better long-term choice is to abandon the euro. The European Union could ultimately disintegrate as a result.[11]

Brexit

Yet another challenge for the European Union was the withdrawal of the United Kingdom as a result of "Brexit," the referendum passed by voters in the UK in June 2016. Many voters believed that Britain was subject to too many rules, paid too much in membership fees, and received too little benefit from the EU. Many in the UK also wanted to pull back on immigration policies, believing the EU did not afford them enough control over the number of European nationals living and working within the United Kingdom's borders. Effective January 31, 2020, the UK is the first nation ever to withdraw from the EU (although a transition period was afforded through December 31, 2020, to help minimize uncertainty while the parties tried to negotiate a new trade deal). The United Kingdom's unwillingness to make concessions made negotiations particularly difficult. [For more on the EU, see EUROPA, the portal site of the European Union at **https://europa.eu/european-union/index_en**.]

Globalization and Countervailing Forces

Recall our definition of globalization: the breaking down of national boundaries to allow free interchange of people, communications, services, goods, businesses, investments, and ideas. Understanding what globalization is *not* may be just as important as knowing what it is. It is not homogenization; the goal is not to make us all the same. But the goals do include increased choice through the sharing of diversity, as well as appropriate protection of historical, social, and cultural identities. It is also not just about free trade. Consider some of the other issues on the table in the TTIP and TPP negotiations, such as standards for food safety, Internet freedom, labor, and acceptable environmental practices. The WTO's own website acknowledges, "the WTO is not just about liberalizing trade, and in some circumstances its rules support maintaining trade barriers–for example, to protect consumers or prevent the spread of disease. . . . The system's overriding purpose is to help trade flow as freely as possible–so long as there are no undesirable side-effects–because this is important for economic development and well-being."[12]

> Globalization has not been uniformly beneficial.

Unfortunately, the process of globalization has not been uniformly beneficial. "The real question isn't whether free markets are good or bad. It is why they are producing such wildly different results in different countries."[13] One reason for disparate results may be that not all governments develop in tandem with their economies and, therefore, do not capture an appropriate portion of the wealth created to use on behalf of their populations. Where that is not occurring, it has been argued that "multinationals–which account for the bulk of direct cross-border investment and one-third of trade–have social responsibilities in nations where the rule of law is weak. And this view dispenses with the erroneous notion that open markets will magically produce prosperity in all conditions."[14] The challenge is to find ways to correct the inequities as the world becomes increasingly interconnected. As a result, the global impact of multinationals is an important focus of this chapter.

Questions

1. Once the Brexit referendum passed in June 2016, the UK had two years after invoking Article 50 of the Lisbon Treaty on March 29, 2017, to negotiate its withdrawal from the EU. While many voters were in favor of leaving the EU, they were not uniformly decided on the laws and regulations that must be adopted in place of the European Union's. The UK has had to resolve some difficult issues in a relatively short amount of time. For instance, should it remain in the EU's single market but exercise sovereignty over its own immigration policies? Alternatively, as a member of the WTO, should the UK negotiate separate trade deals with the EU and with other members of the WTO? (This is the approach the UK has taken thus far.) Next, should it adopt the same labor and consumer safety standards currently enforced by the EU? If not, what effect would this have on compliance costs for multinational companies? What concerns would you have if you were operating a multinational company in Europe?
2. If multinational corporations have affirmative social responsibilities in "nations where the rule of law is weak," who should identify and impose those responsibilities? If you believe that it is a matter for corporate management, what forces might cause management to act more responsibly? What forces exist that might impede multinationals from adopting greater corporate social responsibility? On the other hand, if you believe that social responsibilities should be imposed on multinationals, what governing body should do so? How will that governing body obtain the power to legislate and enforce such responsibilities?

Part One—Ethics Across International Borders

The September 11, 2001, World Trade Center attack focused attention on ethical and legal tensions between certain aspects of American culture and the cultures of some nations in which Islam is the predominant religion. America's long presence in Iraq and Afghanistan kept these cultural divisions in the public eye, and polls indicated that many Americans believed the values of Islam were at odds with America's own.[15] Yet, the public protests of the Arab Spring in 2011 may have demonstrated that Islamic cultures are no more

LO 16-2
Discuss the interrelationship of religion, culture, and legal rules with comparisons to American and Islamic viewpoints.

homogeneous than America's. Many issues triggering the protests–such as human-rights violations, unemployment, and extreme poverty–are issues about which much of the American public was sympathetic and, perhaps, is even more so today. Bridging cultural differences is an essential first step in creating an effective working relationship. [For more on the Arab Spring, see **https://en.wikipedia.org/wiki/Arab_Spring**.]

Religion often provides the foundation for a culture's ethical structure. Thus, two countries with different religious heritages are likely to have divergent ethical and legal norms. In addition, cultures differ in their judgments about which rights are so important that they should be protected. For example, separation of church and state is a basic legal precept in the United States. The purpose of this legal separation was to permit individuals to practice their own religious traditions and prohibit the government from imposing a single belief system on everyone. By contrast, in some predominantly Islamic countries, religious law is also the law of the state.

In some Islamic countries, religious law is also the law of the state.

Laws and Social Norms Regarding Free Speech

Standards for appropriate speech are regulated by both societal norms and, in many cases, local law. The bounds of free speech vary considerably from country to country. The Internet magnifies the issue because its inherent nature allows speech to flow freely, divorced from political boundaries. Although Chapter 18 will cover the Internet and free speech primarily with regard to U.S. law, here we look at the issue from an international perspective, not with regard to the speaker, but rather to the service provider that facilitates transmission of the contested speech.

Because service providers such as Google, Facebook, and X (formerly known as Twitter) store the speech of others on their servers, one issue is whether these providers can, should, or must remove content that is offensive to portions of their audience, particularly after receiving notification of the specific content that is found objectionable. Governments around the world routinely make requests to block certain content, citing national security reasons or that the content violates local laws, including those regulating goods and services; prohibiting hate speech, bullying, defamation, obscenity, invasion of privacy, and certain political speech; and protecting trademarks or copyrights from infringement. For example, Google received government requests to remove 772,709 content items in the 12-month period ending June 30, 2022, and many of those requests were honored by blocking access from the respective countries under Google's policy of complying with lawful requests.[16] Other requests were denied after undergoing careful review. The United States made 3,088 of these requests; China made none.[17] The difference is not as surprising as it might seem when one considers that countries less tolerant of free speech block content more directly. China's "Great Firewall" is a case in point. What speech draws a red flag in Brazil? Racial issues, but also some political speech. Brazil "has strict electoral laws that limit criticism of candidates in the runup to elections."[18] [For Google's Transparency Report on government requests to block content, see **https://transparencyreport.google.com/government-removals/overview?hl=en**.]

A particularly difficult issue facing online providers is the restriction of hate speech. Lawmakers in Germany led the West on this front, demanding that Facebook enforce

specific jurisdiction," we explained, such contacts "do not warrant a determination that, based on those ties, the forum has *general* jurisdiction over a defendant." As *International Shoe* itself teaches, a corporation's "continuous activity of some sorts within a state is not enough to support the demand that the corporation be amenable to suits unrelated to that activity." Because Goodyear's foreign subsidiaries were "in no sense at home in North Carolina," we held, those subsidiaries could not be required to submit to the general jurisdiction of that State's courts.

IV

With this background, we turn directly to the question whether Daimler's affiliations with California are sufficient to subject it to the general (all-purpose) personal jurisdiction of that State's courts. . . . While plaintiffs ultimately persuaded the Ninth Circuit to impute MBUSA's California contacts to Daimler on an agency theory, at no point have they maintained that MBUSA is an alter ego of Daimler.

A

In sustaining the exercise of general jurisdiction over Daimler, the Ninth Circuit relied on an agency theory, determining that MBUSA acted as Daimler's agent for jurisdictional purposes and then attributing MBUSA's California contacts to Daimler. The Ninth Circuit's agency analysis derived from Circuit precedent considering principally whether the subsidiary "performs services that are sufficiently important to the foreign corporation that if it did not have a representative to perform them, the corporation's own officials would undertake to perform substantially similar services."

This Court has not yet addressed whether a foreign corporation may be subjected to a court's general jurisdiction based on the contacts of its in-state subsidiary. Daimler argues, and several Courts of Appeals have held, that a subsidiary's jurisdictional contacts can be imputed to its parent only when the former is so dominated by the latter as to be its alter ego. . . .

. . . The Ninth Circuit's agency theory thus appears to subject foreign corporations to general jurisdiction whenever they have an in-state subsidiary or affiliate, an outcome that would sweep beyond even the "sprawling view of general jurisdiction" we rejected in *Goodyear.*

B

Even if we were to assume that MBUSA is at home in California, and further to assume MBUSA's contacts are imputable to Daimler, there would still be no basis to subject Daimler to general jurisdiction in California, for Daimler's slim contacts with the State hardly render it at home there.

Goodyear made clear that only a limited set of affiliations with a forum will render a defendant amenable to all-purpose jurisdiction there. "For an individual, the paradigm forum for the exercise of general jurisdiction is the individual's domicile; for a corporation, it is an equivalent place, one in which the corporation is fairly regarded as at home." . . . These bases afford plaintiffs recourse to at least one clear and certain forum in which a corporate defendant may be sued on any and all claims.

. . . Accordingly, the inquiry under *Goodyear* is not whether a foreign corporation's in-forum contacts can be said to be in some sense "continuous and systematic," it is whether that corporation's "affiliations with the State are so 'continuous and systematic' as to render [it] essentially at home in the forum State."

Here, neither Daimler nor MBUSA is incorporated in California, nor does either entity have its principal place of business there. If Daimler's California activities sufficed to allow adjudication of this Argentina-rooted case in California, the same global reach would presumably be available in every other State in which MBUSA's sales are sizable. Such exorbitant exercises of all-purpose jurisdiction would scarcely permit out-of-state defendants "to structure their primary conduct with some minimum assurance as to where that conduct will and will not render them liable to suit."

It was therefore error for the Ninth Circuit to conclude that Daimler, even with MBUSA's contacts attributed to it, was at home in California, and hence subject to suit there on claims by foreign plaintiffs having nothing to do with anything that occurred or had its principal impact in California.

C

Finally, the transnational context of this dispute bears attention. The Court of Appeals emphasized, as supportive of the exercise of general jurisdiction, plaintiffs' assertion of claims under the Alien Tort Statute (ATS), 28 U.S.C. § 1350, and the Torture Victim Protection Act of 1991 (TVPA), 106 Stat. 73, note following 28 U.S.C. § 1350. Recent decisions of this Court, however, have rendered plaintiffs' ATS and TVPA claims infirm.

The Ninth Circuit, moreover, paid little heed to the risks to international comity its expansive view of general jurisdiction posed. Other nations do not share the uninhibited approach to personal jurisdiction advanced by the Court of Appeals in this case. In the European Union, for example, a corporation may generally be sued in the nation in which it is "domiciled," a term defined to refer only to the location of the corporation's "statutory seat," "central administration," or "principal place of business." The Solicitor General informs us, in this regard, that "foreign governments' objections to some domestic courts' expansive views of general jurisdiction have in the past impeded negotiations of international agreements on the reciprocal recognition and enforcement of judgments." See also U.S. Brief 2 (expressing concern that unpredictable applications of general jurisdiction based on activities of U.S.-based subsidiaries could discourage foreign investors); Brief for Respondents 35 (acknowledging that "doing business" basis for general jurisdiction has led to "international friction"). Considerations of international rapport thus reinforce our determination that subjecting Daimler to the general jurisdiction of courts in California would not accord with the "fair play and substantial justice" due process demands.

For the reasons stated, the judgment of the United States Court of Appeals for the Ninth Circuit is *Reversed.*

Questions

1. What were the facts in *Perkins,* and why did the Court rule that it was appropriate to exercise general jurisdiction over the foreign corporation in that case?
2. In contrast, what were the facts in *Goodyear,* and why did the Court rule that it was *not* appropriate to exercise general jurisdiction over the foreign corporation in that case?
3. Applying *Perkins* and *Goodyear,* what were the Court's reasons for finding that there was a lack of general jurisdiction over Daimler AG?
4. The Court proceeded to give public policy reasons reinforcing its denial of general jurisdiction in *Daimler AG.* What is the transnational context for the dispute, and of what did the Solicitor General inform the court?

The Foreign Corrupt Practices Act

Consider the problem of bribery and other forms of corruption. Some nations argue that bribery is acceptable behavior, whereas others criticize it severely. In July 2013, the Chinese minister who had overseen a substantial modernization of China's railways received a death sentence (which was suspended for two years and then statutorily commuted to a life sentence after no further convictions) for accepting $10.5 million in bribes.[28] How would you define bribery? What problems are created by a culture of bribery?

For years, U.S. firms have dealt with bribery issues in America and abroad. Congress has attempted to respond harshly to corruption in other governments and to support U.S. firms that do not participate in foreign corruption. As we saw in Chapter 2, the Foreign Corrupt Practices Act (FCPA) prohibits businesses from making certain payments or gifts to government officials for the purpose of influencing business decisions. In recent years, the United States has stepped up its enforcement of the FCPA, both through criminal suits brought by the Department of Justice and through civil cases brought by the Securities Exchange Commission.[29] Recent FCPA investigations include

- In 2023, Flutter Entertainment, PLC, agreed to pay a $4 million civil penalty to settle charges that it paid approximately $8.9 million to consultants in support of its operations in Russia and its efforts to have gambling legalized there.[30]
- Also in 2023, Rio Tinto, PLC, agreed to pay a $15 million civil penalty to settle charges that it paid approximately $10.5 million to a consultant to retain certain mining rights in Guinea by offering to pay or paying a government official.[31]

Some critics argue that the FCPA, although well-intentioned, unduly restricts American companies operating abroad and prevents them from competing effectively. However, the biggest settlements under the FCPA have actually been paid by foreign companies, a consequence of the act's application to any company that has securities listed on a U.S. stock exchange or does business in the United States.[32] Others argue the United States should not use foreign trade to unilaterally impose its sense of morality around the globe. Many other countries, however, are enforcing similar antibribery measures. [For more information on FCPA enforcement actions, see **www.fcpablog.com**.]

Questions

1. Is it ethical for the U.S. Congress to impose federal laws on the operations of U.S. corporations abroad? Why or why not?
2. Consider the scandal that broke in 2015 involving FIFA, soccer's international governing body. The U.S. Department of Justice (DOJ) brought charges against FIFA officials under both the Racketeer Influenced and Corrupt Organizations Act (RICO) and the Travel Act (which prohibits the engagement in interstate or foreign travel, or the use of any facility in interstate commerce, to carry out an illegal activity) for the alleged transaction of commercial bribes, estimated at $150 million. Russia's foreign ministry viewed this as "another case of the illegal extraterritorial application of U.S. laws" and an attempt "to set itself up as a judge far outside its borders."[33] Is it ethical for the U.S. to extraterritorially impose its values on foreign organizations? Is the U.S. unilaterally imposing its sense of morality around the globe?
3. Why did the DOJ did not charge FIFA under the FCPA? Explain. See **https://fcpaprofessor.com**.

Social Responsibility to Humanity?

Are we evolving toward a set of common international ethical standards that can be supported and implemented globally? Would international ethical standards simply represent a natural progression from national standards? At one time, agreements were achieved only at a city level, but state-level agreements followed, and those, in turn, evolved to agreements among federated states. Is a similar progression to global standards inevitable? Does a framework that divides ethical issues between those of the "host" country and those of the "home" country remain a useful analytical tool?

> If we are moving toward global social responsibility, can we do so without sacrificing the existence of wonderfully diverse and unique cultures?

If we are moving toward global social responsibility, can we do so without sacrificing the existence of wonderfully diverse and unique cultures? Do we have to become ever more uniform in our beliefs and practices? Can we agree on fundamentals but still appreciate diversity?

Consider the evidence. Not only are businesses interacting with stakeholders of ever more diverse nationalities (investors/owners/shareholders, customers/clients, suppliers, and general citizenry impacted by business decisions), but the cultural identity of businesses themselves may be unclear. Take, for example, Chrysler's changing ownership, as set forth in the chapter introduction.

We have growing evidence of voluntary international cooperation to establish acceptable business practices. This includes the celebration of World Standards Day on October 14 to honor the work of many nongovernmental international bodies that have developed a wide range of voluntary standards addressing global production and trade. Also consider the following:

- As far back as 1948, the UN General Assembly adopted its Universal Declaration of Human Rights. Inherent in the structure of the declaration is a recognition of the connection between work (and business, by extension) and the protection of fundamental human values. Article 23 declares that everyone has a right "to just and favourable conditions of work" and "to just and favourable remuneration ensuring for himself and his family an existence worthy of human dignity." [For a copy of the Declaration, see the University of Minnesota's Human Rights Library [**http://hrlibrary.umn.edu/instree/b1udhr.htm**].]

- In 2000, the United Nations launched a voluntary initiative to promote corporate social responsibility globally. The 10 principles of the *Global Compact* address human rights, labor standards, the environment, and corruption. Over 10,880 businesses and 12,000 total signatories from almost 160 countries have joined the Compact. [For more on the Global Compact, see **www.unglobalcompact.org**.]
- Social Accountability International has developed SA8000, a social accountability standard based on international norms (such as the Universal Declaration of Human Rights previously mentioned) that companies can adopt to develop and assure an equitable and safe workplace for their employees and those of their suppliers. A verification system was simultaneously developed so results are auditable. As of this writing, more than 5,125 facilities with over 2 million employees in 56 industries and 54 countries are certified. [For more on SAI and SA8000, see **www.sa-intl.org** and SA8000 Search–SAI (sa-intl.org).]

PRACTICING ETHICS Individual Social Responsibility to Humanity?

Consider the following excerpt from a speech delivered September 28, 2001, by Jose Ramos-Horta, Nobel Peace Prize Laureate (1996) and Minister for Foreign Affairs and Cooperation for the East Timor Transition Government:

> There is no dispute that abject poverty, child labor, and prostitution are a moral indictment of all humanity.
>
> However, poverty should not only touch our conscience: It is also a matter of peace and security because it destabilizes entire countries and regions. In turn it threatens the integration of the global economy that is vital if the rich are to stay rich or if the poor are to move up, if only an inch.
>
> Peace will be illusory as long as the rich ignore the clamor of the poor for a better life, as long as hundreds of millions of people live below the poverty line, cannot afford a meal a day, do not have access to clean water and a roof.

Question

Should most of us, not just active international businesses, accept a social responsibility to humanity? If we answer yes to this question, how might our actions as students, educators, employees, employers, and investors change?

Source: Jose Ramos-Horta, "Speech to the Northern Medical Foundation Tribute to Military Medicine and Lt-Gen. P. Cosgrove," Sydney, Australia, September 28, 2001.

Part Two—Laws Governing Cross-Border Business

All businesses must, of course, follow the laws of the countries in which they are physically present and operating. (Whether a business with no physical presence that solicits or performs business electronically in a foreign country must follow the laws of that country will be examined in Chapter 18.) Foreign firms often wish to establish operations in the United

States, in part because Americans are more inclined to buy goods made in this country. As a requirement of doing business in the United States, the foreign firm must comply with U.S. laws and regulations.

Conversely, when U.S. businesses operate abroad, they are required to follow the law of the host country. In 2006, when Google began operating its search engine in China, it accepted the government's requirement that it filter results to remove material the government deemed unsuitable for its citizens. In March 2010, Google ceased that practice and automatically redirected search requests coming from China to its uncensored site in Hong Kong. China then threatened Google with the loss of its license to provide other online services, such as its music, mapping, and translation. The license was renewed when Google proposed to stop automatically redirecting search requests and instead present would-be searchers with a clickable link to **google.com.hk**. While it appears that **google.com.hk** is still functioning in Hong Kong, that address may not be fully functional as of this writing from inside China.[34]

Even in their foreign operations, businesses may also be required to follow certain laws of their home country, as previously discussed. Notably, although there is a presumption against the extraterritorial application of U.S. criminal law, U.S. citizens can be held accountable in America for their criminal actions abroad where Congress has clearly indicated an intent to cover actions outside of the United States.[35]

Finally, businesses operating across national borders will also be subject to international law. The foundation and some examples of international business law will be discussed shortly, but first it will be useful to explore some of the different forms of business available to companies wishing to expand their operations into foreign countries.

Forms of Global Business Expansion

Multinational Enterprise

LO 16-5
Describe the basic forms of global business expansion.

The term *multinational enterprise* (MNE) traditionally refers to a company that conducts business in more than one country. Any of the following operations, except for a direct contract with a foreign purchaser, may qualify a company as an MNE.

Direct Contract

A firm may expand its business across territorial borders using a variety of methods. The simplest, from a contractual perspective, occurs where a firm in one country enters an agreement with a person in another country. For example, a UK firm may contract to sell its product to a foreign purchaser, say in Brazil. This is called a *direct sale.* The parties simply agree on the terms of the sale and record them in a contract.

When the contract is silent as to a term of the sale, the law that will apply to the missing term will be the law specified in the contract; when none is specified, the applicable law will depend on the country in which the parties would litigate their potential dispute in court. Some courts will employ the *vesting of rights doctrine,* applying the law of the jurisdiction in which the rights in the contract vested. Other courts may apply the *most significant relationship doctrine,* applying the law of the jurisdiction that has the most significant relationship to the contract and the parties. Finally, some courts will apply the *governmental interest doctrine,* applying the law of the jurisdiction that has the greatest interest in the issue's outcome.

Payment is one of the most complicated issues pertaining to direct sales.

Payment is one of the most complicated issues pertaining to direct sales. The seller should, and usually does, require an *irrevocable letter of credit,* which the buyer obtains after paying a specified amount to the bank (or securing that amount of credit). The bank then promises to pay the seller the contract amount after conforming goods have been shipped. The "irrevocable" component prohibits the bank from revoking the letter of credit without the consent of both the buyer and the seller. The seller is protected because the buyer has already provided adequate funds for the purchase, confirmed by a bank. The buyer is protected because the funds are not turned over to the seller until it has been determined that the goods conform to the contract. It is important to the buyer, however, that the letter of credit be specific as to the conformance of the goods because the bank will only ensure that the goods conform to the letter of credit and not to the contract itself.

Foreign Representation

A second type of foreign expansion is a sale through a distributor, agent, or other type of representative in a foreign country. A firm may decide to sell through an *agent*–that is, the firm hires an individual who will remain permanently in the foreign country, negotiate contracts on behalf of the firm, and assist in the firm's performance of the contracts. Agents are generally compensated on a commission basis. On the other hand, the firm may act through a *representative,* who may solicit and take orders but, unlike an agent, may not enter into contracts on behalf of the firm. In some countries, laws may substantially restrict the actions a representative may take. For example, in China, a representative may generally gather information and market research but may undertake no direct business activities.[36]

Distributors purchase goods from the seller, then negotiate sales to foreign buyers on their own behalf. In so doing, a distributor may be more likely to invest resources to develop the foreign market for the goods. *Exclusive dealing agreements* with distributors, in which a distributor agrees to sell only the goods of one manufacturer and the manufacturer, in turn, agrees to sell only to that distributor in a particular geographic area, are generally not allowed abroad, although they often are legal in the United States.

Export trading companies specialize in acting as the intermediary between a domestic business and foreign purchaser. The trading company will take title to the goods being sold and then complete the sale in the foreign country. *Export management companies,* on the other hand, merely manage the sale but do not take title to the goods; consequently, they do not share any of the risk associated with the sale.

Joint Venture

Foreign expansion may also occur through a *joint venture* agreement between two or more parties. This partnership-like agreement usually covers one or several specific projects and is in effect for a specified period. For instance, Toyota operated a joint venture with General Motors at a plant in Fremont, California, from 1984 to 2009, and with Subaru at a plant in Lafayette, Indiana, from 2007 to 2016. BMW Group and Great Wall Motor announced in November 2019 the opening of a joint venture plant in China to build electric Minis. In 2023, Honda Motor Co. and Sony Corporation announced their new joint venture, Sony Honda Mobility, Inc., which will manufacture Afeela brand electric vehicles.

Branch Office or Subsidiary

A *branch office* is simply an extension of a foreign corporation into the host country. A *subsidiary,* however, is a legally separate entity formed under the laws of the host country and substantially owned by the foreign parent company. For example, an Indian paper company may open a branch office in London to market and sell its products. That office would be a mere extension of the offices already established in India. On the other hand, the Indian firm could create a British subsidiary to handle its British business from its London offices. Either a subsidiary or branch office relationship can also be established by acquiring an existing firm in the host country.

The distinction between a subsidiary, which is a legal entity separate from its foreign parent, and a branch office, which is not, has a number of ramifications. For example, many countries require a local subsidiary to have in-country directors and/or shareholders. On the other hand, setting up a branch office will likely subject the parent company to taxation in the host country. Indeed, the parent company is legally liable for all obligations of the branch office. In contrast, when a subsidiary is sued, the parent company is not generally liable. For example, in *United States v. Philip Morris, Inc.,*[37] a U.S. district court dismissed British American Tobacco (BAT) from the federal government's suit against various cigarette manufacturers for recovery of health care expenses. BAT was the British parent of the U.S. company, Brown & Williamson (B&W). The subsidiary, B&W, remained part of the suit.

Licensing

When a company has no interest in commencing operations in a foreign country but instead merely wants to have its product or name in that market, the company may decide to license the rights to the name, or to manufacture the product, to a company in the target market. The benefit to this type of relationship is that the licensor (holder of the right) has the opportunity to enter the foreign market, but the licensee provides all of the capital for, and assumes all of the obligations and risks of running, the business.

Franchising

In a franchise agreement, the franchisee pays the franchisor for a license to use trademarks, formulas, and other trade secrets. The difference between a franchise agreement and a licensing contract is that the former is usually made up of a number of licensing arrangements, as well as other obligations. For instance, in a typical fast-food franchise agreement, the franchisor will license to the franchisee the right to use its trademark, tradename, logo, recipes, menus, and other intangible assets. Kentucky Fried Chicken has over 25,000 franchise locations in 147 countries and territories, with more than 928 in the United Kingdom and Ireland, and 7,166 in China.

Question

Assume that you are interested in importing silk blouses from Bangkok, Thailand, to France. What facts might persuade you to enter into an agency agreement with a Thai blouse manufacturer rather than a distributorship or vice versa? Explain.

Foundations of International Law

LO 16-6
Compare and contrast treaties, custom, and comity and give illustrations of each.

Suppose a firm with manufacturing plants in Argentina and Thailand and corporate headquarters in Bangkok enters into a contract with a French firm to distribute its products manufactured in the Argentinean plant. The French firm is not satisfied with the quality of the products being sent. What law would apply to this situation? Argentinean? Thai? French? Or are there, perhaps, specific provisions of international law that will govern? The answer to this question is not simple, even for seasoned lawyers, yet the firms involved will be greatly affected by the result.

The source of law applicable to an international dispute depends, in part, on the issue involved. In general, private parties are free to form agreements in whatever manner they wish. The parties can determine, for instance, which nation's law will govern the contract, where disagreements in connection with the contract will be resolved, and even in which language the transactions will be made. This is referred to as the *private law* of contracts. Whenever the parties to a transaction from different jurisdictions are involved in a lawsuit, the court will start by looking at the agreement of the parties to resolve these issues. When the contract is silent as to the choice of law, jurisdiction, and other questions, the court must identify the governing law. Generally, the law of the jurisdiction in which the transaction occurred is applied. If the contract is formed through a form of cross-border communication, as are many international trade negotiations, most often the law of the jurisdiction of the seller's place of business will apply.

What law would apply to this situation? Argentinean? Thai? French?

In contrast, *public law* includes each nation's rules that regulate contractual agreements between parties–for instance, import and export taxes, packaging requirements, and safety standards. In addition, it regulates the relationships among nations and derives from a number of sources. The most familiar source of international public law is a *treaty* or *convention* (essentially a contract between nations). For example, the United States–Mexico-Canada Agreement (USMCA) is a convention governing trade among the three largest countries in North America.

Some treaties and conventions are self-executing, which means that once a country has ratified them, a business can rely on and directly enforce the treaty terms in court. The United Nations Convention on Contracts for the International Sale of Goods (CISG), which will be discussed shortly, is an example of a self-executing convention. On the other hand, some treaties and conventions apply only to the government signatories and not directly to private parties. Such a convention may, for example, require an adopting country such as the United States to amend its domestic law so as to bind private parties, thereby accomplishing the purposes of the convention.

Public law can also be found in *international custom* or *generally accepted principles of law.* These terms refer to practices that are commonly accepted as appropriate business or commercial practices among nations. For instance, sovereign immunity, discussed later in this chapter, is an accepted principle of international law. A *custom,* on the other hand, is derived from consistent behavior over time that is accepted as binding by the countries that engage in that behavior.

Piracy on the High Seas

Events off the coast of Somalia, which hit a peak in 2011, raised public awareness of modern-day piracy. One might think that the international law against piracy would be clear, given that piracy has existed as a threat to security since well before Britain's Royal Navy returned to port in 1718 with the severed head of Blackbeard. The 2010 federal case *United States v. Said* attempts to prosecute raiders in other countries, however, suggested otherwise. What the *Said* case made clear is that generally accepted principles of international law give any country the right to capture pirates on the high seas. U.S. law merely states that "whoever on the high seas, commits the crime of piracy as defined by the law of nations . . . shall be imprisoned for life."

The Virginia court had before it several Somali men who, in an open boat, had approached a U.S. Navy amphibious dock landing ship in the Gulf of Aden in the early morning hours of July 7, 2010. One of the men shot an AK-47 rifle at the *USS Ashland,* which returned fire, sank the assailants' boat, and took the men into custody. The U.S. government argued that piracy under the law of nations does not require the active taking of property and that any unauthorized armed assault or direct violent act on the high seas is enough. The defense argued the charge could not stand because the defendants "did not board, take control, or otherwise rob the *USS Ashland.*" Relying on an 1820 U.S. Supreme Court decision defining piracy as robbery on the high seas, and holding that contemporary international law is unsettled on the definition of piracy, the court dismissed the piracy charge.

The case was appealed, as was a later federal district court opinion that upheld piracy charges against five other men who attacked another U.S. vessel off the coast of Somalia. Those defendants were sentenced to life in prison plus 80 years for piracy. The Fourth Circuit affirmed those sentences, vacated the *USS Ashland* decision, and held that the 1820 decision did not preclude conduct other than robbery, including acts of violence committed for private ends against persons on the high seas, from qualifying as piracy.

Sources: *United States v. Said,* 757 F. Supp. 2d 554 (E.D. Va. 2010) (dismissing the statutory piracy charge), *vacated and remanded,* 680 F.3d 374 (4th Cir. 2012) (**https://casetext.com**); *United States v. Dire,* 680 F.3d 446 (4th Cir. 2012) (**https://casetext.com**).

The Development of Customs

Historically, merchants followed certain accepted customs or principles in connection with the sale of goods. These customs or manners of dealing among merchants were often recognized and applied in court decisions and were later codified in the United States in Article 2 of the Uniform Commercial Code (UCC), previously studied in Chapter 6. Thus customs or practices traditionally followed by merchants have become accepted principles of law throughout the United States (except in Louisiana).

In the international legal arena, customary practices are still evolving. For instance, it was once common practice for personal information to move freely between countries, encouraging the efficient exchange of information in the business world. Then, in 1998, the

European Union adopted minimum standards for the protection of personal data. These standards were substantially strengthened with the implementation of the General Data Protection Regulation or GDPR in the EU in 2018. Any country receiving information from an EU country must comply with these revised standards. (See Chapter 18 for more on the GDPR.)

Two factors are used to determine whether an international custom exists: (1) consistency and repetition of the action or decision, and (2) recognition by nations that this custom is binding. The first merely establishes that the action or decision has been accepted by a number of nations for a long enough time to establish uniformity of application. The second dictates that the custom be accepted as binding by nations observing it. If the custom is accepted as merely persuasive, it does not rise to the level of a generally accepted principle of law. Through persistent objections, any nation may ensure that such custom is not applied to cases in which it is involved.

Generally, once a contract has been created, it is enforceable according to its terms by all parties to the contract. In the following case, read carefully to see what law the judge applied. Notice that he first considered the *private* law of the parties (that is, the express terms of the contract), then looked to custom, and finally applied the concept of *commercial impracticability.*

LEGAL BRIEFCASE

Transatlantic Financing Corporation v. United States

363 F.2d 312 (D.C. Cir. 1966)

Judge J. Skelly Wright

[In 1956, Transatlantic Financing, a steamship operator, contracted with the United States to ship wheat from Texas to Iran. Six days after the ship left port for Iran, the Egyptian government was at war with Israel and blocked the Suez Canal to shipping. The steamer therefore was forced to sail around the Cape of Good Hope. Transatlantic accordingly sued the United States for its added expenses as a result of this change of circumstances. Transatlantic contended that it had contracted only to travel the "usual and customary" route to Iran and that the United States had received a greater benefit than that for which it contracted. The district court held for the United States; Transatlantic appealed.]

Transatlantic's claim is based on the following train of argument. The charter was a contract for a voyage from a Gulf port to Iran. Admiralty principles and practices, especially stemming from the doctrine of deviation, require us to [infer] into the contract the term that the voyage was to be performed by the "usual and customary" route. The usual and customary route from Texas to Iran was, at the time of contract, via Suez, so the contract was for a voyage from Texas to Iran via Suez. When Suez was closed this contract became impossible to perform. Consequently, appellant's argument continues, when Transatlantic delivered the cargo by going around the Cape of Good Hope, in compliance with the Government's demand under claim of right, it conferred a benefit upon the United States for which it should be paid on quantum meruit.

The contract in this case does not expressly condition performance upon availability of the Suez route. Nor does it specify "via Suez" or, on the other hand, "via Suez or Cape of Good Hope." Nor are there provisions in the contract from which we may properly [infer] that the continued availability of Suez was a condition of performance. Nor is there anything in custom or trade usage, or in the surrounding circumstances generally, which would support our constructing a condition of performance. The numerous cases

considering such a reduction must consult in good faith with employees about avoiding or mitigating such an action, even if the reduction policy was set by the board of directors at its foreign headquarters.[48] Similar issues can face MNEs involved in international mergers or acquisitions.

Compulsory Retirement

In late 2007, the European Court of Justice ruled that the European Framework Directive on Equal Treatment, which prohibits unjustified age discrimination in the workplace, applied to national laws requiring age-based compulsory retirement. The case challenged a Spanish law permitting employers to impose a compulsory retirement age. Although the court held the directive applied to the Spanish law, it nevertheless ruled that the Spanish legislation was a lawful, appropriate means of achieving a legitimate government aim. The law had been passed during a period of high unemployment in Spain and was intended to further a national policy for a better distribution of work across generations.

As discussed in Chapter 13, in the United States, the Age Discrimination in Employment Act (ADEA) prohibits discrimination on the basis of age against individuals who are 40 or older. It applies to decisions to hire or fire, as well as to discriminatory compensation or other terms or conditions of employment. Interestingly, a narrow exception allows universities to require retirement of tenured faculty who reach the age of 70. The ADEA specifically applies to American citizens employed overseas by American companies.

Questions

1. A U.S. corporation operates a branch in Spain. Consistent with Spanish law, it adopts a compulsory retirement age of 62. Is this a violation of the ADEA?
2. Which policy do you favor–the Spanish or the American approach to compulsory retirement? Why? Is this an issue over which countries should be allowed to differ?

Source: Legal Week, "Age discrimination: Age shall not weary them," Law.com International, November 21, 2007 [**www.law.com**].

Intellectual Property Regulations

LO 16-8
Identify and describe the four main forms of intellectual property and the international agreements that govern them.

Intellectual property, most broadly, refers to creations of the mind. As used here, it refers more specifically to creations of the mind for which legal protection is given, especially trade secrets, trademarks, patents, and copyrights. It is a form of personal property or *personalty,* which is the legal term used to denote all forms of property, both tangible and intangible, other than real property or *realty.* Realty is comprised only of land and items permanently affixed to the land, such as buildings.

The commercial significance of intellectual property has grown tremendously. By one estimate, intangible assets made up 84 percent of the value of S&P 500 companies in 2018-five times greater than the value of their tangible assets.[49] Theft of intellectual property has also grown tremendously; dollar losses amount to approximately $600 billion annually, with China named as the world's largest source of theft.[50] Clearly, then, understanding the legal protections available for intellectual property is of significant importance to business managers. The greatest losses are suffered by U.S., European, and Japanese business; the largest threats originate from China, India, and Russia. Even though cybersecurity issues are often in the news, much of the theft occurs in other unpublicized ways by both malicious actors and insiders and includes the theft of trade secrets.[51] A *trade secret* can be virtually any information that has economic value; what information a business makes reasonable efforts to keep secret to secure an advantage over its competition is generally unknown. [For more information on the theft of intellectual property, see **http://ipcommission.org**.]

Trademarks

A *trademark* distinguishes the source of a particular good or service, whether by a trade name, packaging, logo, or other distinguishing mark. When the law protects a trademark, it grants a limited monopoly to the holder of the mark: no one else may use that mark without the holder's permission. Under the Tariff Act of 1930, it is unlawful to import goods bearing a trademark registered with the Patent and Trademark Office that is "owned by a citizen of, or by a corporation or association . . . organized within the United States" without the permission of the trademark holder.

This provision safeguards a U.S. trademark holder's rights in the United States from infringement by foreign actors. But what about an American company that wants to obtain trademark protection in other countries? Each country has distinct trademark regulations and offers different levels of protection to marks registered in other countries. For example, a battle that lasted nearly a century ended in early 2013 when the EU General Court in Luxembourg ruled that the Czech brewer Budvar could not assert exclusive use of either "Bud" or "Budweiser" throughout the EU, because its use of the names was not sufficiently widespread. Anheuser-Busch InBev had claimed use of the Budweiser name as early as 1876, almost 20 years before Budvar was formed.[52]

As of this writing, 179 countries, including the United States, are parties to a treaty that provides protection for trademarks, known as the *Paris Convention.*[53] More formally called the International Convention for the Protection of Industrial Property, it was originally signed by 11 countries in 1883. Member countries ensure trademark protection to marks registered in other member countries, with several exceptions. The convention also provides for *national treatment,* which requires that any individual claiming infringement must have the same protection as would a national of that country; a member country may not favor its own nationals over foreigners.

Another treaty, the Madrid Agreement Concerning the International Registration of Marks, attempts to create an international trademark system; if a holder registers a trademark with the World Intellectual Property Organization (WIPO) in Switzerland, that mark is protected in all member countries requested by the holder. A 1989 Protocol relating to the Madrid agreement aimed to render the Madrid system more flexible and more compatible with the domestic legislation of certain countries that had not been able to accede to the Agreement."[54] Notably, the United States is one of those countries. [For extensive information on WIPO, see **www.wipo.int**.]

Nevertheless, trademark issues still arise between countries, even when both are parties to the Paris Convention and to the Madrid Agreement or Protocol. For example, after two French courts found Google guilty of infringing on the Louis Vuitton trademark, the highest

French court sought a ruling under EU trademark law from the European Court of Justice (ECJ). At issue was Google's AdWords service, pursuant to which Google sold ad space to a Vuitton competitor that appeared next to the search results anytime "Louis Vuitton" was entered as a search phrase. The ECJ determined that Google had not impermissibly "used" the Louis Vuitton trademark if its role proved to be "merely technical, automatic and passive," and it had not been active in "drafting the commercial message" displayed by the competitor.[55]

Patents

A *patent* is a monopoly granted by a government on a product, process, or device which is an innovation that is unique, inventive, and useful. The Paris Convention covers patents as well as trademarks, but it does not establish a network of protection, even among member countries; patents granted in different member countries for the same invention are independent of each other. The convention does establish a *right of priority,* however, which gives a patent applicant one year from the date they first file in one member country to file in other member countries and have the subsequent filings treated as if made on the same date as the first filing. Nevertheless, because a patent must be original to be registered in any country, many countries hold that patents previously awarded elsewhere automatically preclude additional patent registration.

Other issues have made the international enforcement of patents quite challenging. For example, the United States historically awarded patents on a first-to-create basis, whereas most other nations have used a first-to-file rule. Through passage of the America Invents Act in 2011, the United States adopted the first-to-file rule. Europe has also simplified the patent process. In late 2012, the European Parliament voted in favor of creating a single patent, which is now recognized automatically in all EU countries (other than Croatia and Spain) without the need to file separately in each country.[56] These same contracting countries, except for Poland, also signed a Unified Patent Court Agreement. As of this writing, 16 of those countries have ratified the agreement; Germany is expected to be the 17th country to ratify it by the time the Unified Patent Court begins operating on June 1, 2023. [For more information on the EU's unitary patent system, see **https://single-market-economy.ec.europa.eu/industry/strategy/intellectual-property/patent-protection-eu/unitary-patent-system_en**.]

Copyrights

A *copyright* is a government grant giving the copyright holder exclusive control over the reproduction or use of a literary, musical, or artistic work. Most developed nations provide copyright protection within their borders, but many also belong to international copyright protection pacts. The Berne Convention of 1886 and the Universal Copyright Convention (UCC) of 1952 both provide a measure of international protection against the unauthorized reproduction of books, photos, drawings, movies, and the like. Copyright protection extends for a period provided by national law. For example, in the United States, a copyright generally spans the author's life plus 70 years (95 or 120 years for certain types of work). The United States is a party to the UCC and the Berne Convention.

The case below points out that formal accession to an international treaty does not necessarily lead to satisfactory compliance in the view of other signatories.

Justice Ginsburg

The Berne Convention . . . is the principal accord governing international copyright relations. Latecomer to the international copyright regime launched by Berne, the United States joined the Convention in 1989. To perfect U.S. implementation of Berne, . . . Congress, in 1994 [through enactment of] § 514 of the Uruguay Round Agreements Act (URAA) [, extended] copyright protection to preexisting works of Berne member countries, protected in their country of origin, but lacking protection in the United States for any of three reasons: The United States did not protect works from the country of origin at the time of publication; the United States did not protect sound recordings fixed before 1972; or the author had failed to comply with . . . formalities Congress no longer requires as prerequisites to copyright protection.

The URAA accords no protection to a foreign work after its full copyright term has expired, causing it to fall into the public domain, whether under the laws of the country of origin or of this country. Works encompassed by § 514 are granted the protection they would have enjoyed had the United States maintained copyright relations with the author's country or removed formalities incompatible with Berne. Foreign authors, however, gain no credit for the protection they lacked in years prior to § 514's enactment. They therefore enjoy fewer total years of exclusivity than do their U.S. counterparts. As a consequence of the barriers to U.S. copyright protection prior to the enactment of § 514, foreign works "restored" to protection by the measure had entered the public domain in this country. . . .

Petitioners include orchestra conductors, musicians, publishers, and others who formerly enjoyed free access to works § 514 removed from the public domain. They maintain that the Constitution's Copyright and Patent Clause, Art. I, § 8, cl. 8, and First Amendment both decree the invalidity of § 514. [All further reference to petitioners' First Amendment argument has been omitted.–ed.] Under those prescriptions of our highest law, petitioners assert, a work that has entered the public domain, for whatever reason, must forever remain there.

[W]e conclude that § 514 does not transgress constitutional limitations on Congress' authority. . . .

I

Members of the Berne Union agree to treat authors from other member countries as well as they treat their own. . . . Each country, moreover, must afford at least the minimum level of protection specified by Berne. The copyright term must span the author's lifetime, plus at least 50 additional years, whether or not the author has complied with a member state's legal formalities. And, as relevant here, a work must be protected abroad unless its copyright term has expired in either the country where protection is claimed or the country of origin.

A different system of transnational copyright protection long prevailed in this country. Until 1891, foreign works were categorically excluded from Copyright Act protection. Throughout most of the 20th century, the only eligible foreign authors were those whose countries granted reciprocal rights to U.S. authors and whose works were printed in the United States. For domestic and foreign authors alike, protection hinged on compliance with notice, registration, and renewal formalities.

The United States became party to Berne's multilateral, formality-free copyright regime in 1989. Initially, Congress adopted a "minimalist approach" to compliance with the Convention. The Berne Convention Implementation Act of 1988 (BCIA) . . . accorded no protection for "any work that is in the public domain in the United States." . . . Congress indicated, however, that it had not definitively rejected "retroactive" protection for preexisting foreign works; instead it had punted on this issue of Berne's implementation, deferring consideration until "a more thorough examination of Constitutional, commercial, and consumer considerations is possible."

The minimalist approach essayed by the United States did not sit well with other Berne members. . . . Mexican authorities complained about the United States' refusal to grant protection . . . to Mexican works that remained under copyright domestically. The Register of Copyrights also reported "questions" from Turkey, Egypt, and Austria. Thailand and Russia balked at protecting U.S. works, copyrighted here but in those countries' public domains, until the United States reciprocated with respect to their authors' works.

Berne, however, did not provide a potent enforcement mechanism. . . .

The landscape changed in 1994. The Uruguay round of multilateral trade negotiations produced the World Trade Organization (WTO) and the Agreement on Trade-Related Aspects of Intellectual Property Rights (TRIPS). The United States joined both. TRIPS mandates, on pain of WTO enforcement, implementation of Berne's first 21 articles. The WTO gave teeth to the Convention's requirements: Noncompliance with a WTO ruling could subject member countries to tariffs or cross-sector retaliation. The specter of WTO enforcement proceedings bolstered the credibility of our trading partners' threats to challenge the United States for inadequate compliance with Article 18.

Congress' response to the Uruguay agreements put to rest any questions concerning U.S. compliance with Article 18. Section 514 of the URAA extended copyright to works that garnered protection in their countries of origin, but had no right to exclusivity in the United States for any of [the previously listed] three reasons. . . .

. . . Copyrights "restored" under URAA § 514 "subsist for the remainder of the term of copyright that the work would have otherwise been granted . . . if the work never entered the public domain." Prospectively, restoration places foreign works on an equal footing with their U.S. counterparts; assuming a foreign and domestic author died the same day, their works will enter the public domain simultaneously. . . .

The URAA's disturbance of the public domain hardly escaped Congress' attention. Section 514 imposed no liability for any use of foreign works occurring before restoration. In addition, anyone remained free to copy and use restored works for one year following § 514's enactment. . . .

In 2001, petitioners filed this lawsuit challenging § 514. . . .

II

We first address petitioners' argument that Congress lacked authority, under the Copyright Clause, to enact § 514. The Constitution states that "Congress shall have Power . . . [t]o promote the Progress of Science . . . by securing for limited Times to Authors . . . the exclusive Right to their . . . Writings." Art. I, § 8, cl. 8. Petitioners find in this grant of authority an impenetrable barrier to the extension of copyright protection to authors whose writings, for whatever reason, are in the public domain. We see no such barrier in the text of the Copyright Clause, historical practice, or our precedents.

. . . Petitioners' contrary argument relies primarily on the Constitution's confinement of a copyright's lifespan to a "limited Tim[e]." "Removing works from the public domain," they contend, "violates the 'limited [t]imes' restriction by turning a fixed and predictable period into one that can be reset or resurrected at any time, even after it expires."

Our decision in *Eldred* [*v. Ashcroft*] is largely dispositive of petitioners' limited-time argument. There we addressed the question whether Congress violated the Copyright Clause when it extended, by 20 years, the terms of existing copyrights [in the Copyright Term Extension Act (CTEA)]. Ruling that Congress acted within constitutional bounds, we declined to infer from the text of the Copyright Clause "the command that a time prescription, once set, becomes forever 'fixed' or 'inalterable.'" "The word 'limited,'" we observed, . . . is best understood to mean "confine[d] within certain bounds," "restrain[ed]," or "circumscribed." . . .

The terms afforded works restored by § 514 are no less "limited" than those the CTEA lengthened. In light of *Eldred,* petitioners do not here contend that the term Congress has granted U.S. authors—their lifetimes, plus 70 years—is unlimited. Nor do petitioners explain why terms of the same duration, as applied to foreign works, are not equally "circumscribed" and "confined." . . .

The difference, petitioners say, is that the limited time had already passed for works in the public domain. What was that limited term for foreign works once excluded from U.S. copyright protection? Exactly "zero," petitioners respond. We find scant sense in this argument, for surely a "limited time" of exclusivity must begin before it may end. . . .

Historical practice corroborates our reading of the Copyright Clause to permit full U.S. compliance with Berne. . . .

On occasion . . . Congress has seen fit to protect works once freely available. Notably, the Copyright Act of 1790 granted protection to many works previously in the public domain. Before the Act launched a uniform national system, three States provided no statutory copyright protection at all. Of those that did afford some protection, seven failed to protect maps; eight did not cover previously published books; and all ten denied protection to works that failed to comply with formalities. The First Congress, it thus appears, did not view the public domain as inviolate. . . .

Congress has also passed generally applicable legislation granting patents and copyrights to inventions and works that had lost protection. An 1832 statute authorized a new patent for any inventor whose failure, "by inadvertence, accident, or mistake," to comply with statutory formalities rendered the original patent "invalid or inoperative." An 1893 measure similarly allowed authors who had not timely deposited their work to receive "all the rights and privileges" the Copyright Act affords, if they made the required deposit by March 1, 1893. And in 1919 and 1941, Congress authorized the President to issue proclamations granting protection to foreign works that had fallen into the public domain during World Wars I and II. . . .

Installing a federal copyright system and ameliorating the interruptions of global war, it is true, presented Congress with extraordinary situations. Yet the TRIPS accord, leading the United States to comply in full measure with Berne, was also a signal event. Given the authority we hold Congress has, we will not second-guess the political choice Congress made between leaving the public domain untouched and embracing Berne unstintingly.

Petitioners' ultimate argument as to the Copyright and Patent Clause concerns its initial words. Congress is empowered to "promote the Progress of Science and useful Arts" by enacting systems of copyright and patent protection. . . .

The "Progress of Science," petitioners acknowledge, refers broadly to "the creation and spread of knowledge and learning." They nevertheless argue that federal legislation cannot serve the Clause's aim unless the legislation "spur[s] the creation of . . . new works." . . .

. . . In *Eldred,* . . . we held that the Copyright Clause does not demand that each copyright provision, examined discretely, operate to induce new works. Rather, we explained, the Clause "empowers Congress to determine the intellectual property regimes that, overall, in that body's judgment, will serve the ends of the Clause." . . .

. . . Congress rationally could have concluded that adherence to Berne "promotes the diffusion of knowledge." A well-functioning international copyright system would likely encourage the dissemination of existing and future works. Full compliance with Berne, Congress had reason to believe, would expand the foreign markets available to U.S. authors and invigorate protection against piracy of U.S. works abroad, thereby benefitting copyright-intensive industries stateside and inducing greater investment in the creative process.

. . . Congress determined that exemplary adherence to Berne would serve the objectives of the Copyright Clause. We have no warrant to reject the rational judgment Congress made.

Affirmed.

Questions

1. What does it mean to say that a work is in the "public domain"?
2. *a.* If you were a Canadian composer in 1950 with a new orchestral piece, fully protected under the copyright laws of Canada (a Berne signatory), what would you have had to do to protect your work in the United States (based on the law as it is presented in *Golan*)?
   b. What would you have to do if you were a Canadian composer in 2005 under similar facts?
3. Before Congress passed § 514 of the URAA, what could petitioners do that, after the legislation, was no longer legal?
4. In the words of the Court, why did "Congress have reason to believe" that full compliance with the Berne Convention "would expand the foreign markets available to U.S. authors and invigorate protection against piracy of U.S. works abroad"?

Agreement on Trade-Related Aspects of Intellectual Property

It can be argued that a solid international system for effective protection of intellectual property does not yet exist. That said, the Agreement on Trade-Related Aspects of Intellectual Property (TRIPS) mentioned by the Court in *Golan v. Holder* is having a positive effect. As one of the foundation agreements to which all WTO member countries must subscribe, the provisions of TRIPS are enforceable through the WTO Dispute Settlement Body, which is discussed later in this chapter. TRIPS establishes certain minimum levels of protection for copyrights, trademarks, and patents and also requires WTO members to adopt effective enforcement measures. Whether members are effectively enforcing its provisions remains an issue regularly raised in WTO settings.

Regulation of Multinational Enterprises

LO 16-9
Discuss the challenges of governing multinational entities, in general, and state-owned companies, in particular.

With globalization, the number of multinational entities, or MNEs, has vastly expanded. Precisely because MNE operations span the globe, regulating their activities has become quite difficult. For example, the health risks from smoking tobacco have been well established, and there are now 182 parties to the Framework Convention on Tobacco Control, which was the first treaty negotiated under the auspices of the World Health Organization and addresses controls on ingredients, packaging, marketing, cessation programs, and smoke-free spaces, all proven to reduce smoking. Yet, tobacco companies have been "aggressively recruiting new customers in developing nations."[57] Philip Morris, whose annual sales were twice Uruguay's gross domestic product, even went as far as suing Uruguay in 2010, claiming that its regulations were excessive. As the head of the Convention's Tobacco Free Initiative stated, "[t]hey're using litigation to threaten low- and middle-income countries."[58] The case was dismissed in 2016, "demonstrat[ing] that small countries can win legal challenges brought by well-resourced multinational corporations."[59] [For more on the Convention, see **https://fctc.who.int/who-fctc/overview**.]

It is not uncommon for merger regulators to require accommodations to address national antitrust concerns before providing the required approval. Such national-level reviews and negotiations can pose a significant cost for mergers and acquisitions involving MNEs. Although some bilateral agreements among countries are in place, the approximately 70 countries with merger review systems do not have an agreement coordinating their processes as of yet–not even at the level of coordinating review thresholds, timetables, and required filings.[76]

Regulation of Trade

Import Tariffs

LO 16-12
Discuss how and why nations regulate imports and exports.

The General Agreement on Tariffs and Trade (GATT), now governed by the WTO, regulates import duties among signatory countries to reduce barriers to trade and to ensure fair treatment. Without GATT, it is argued, countries with stronger markets would be able to secure better deals on imports than would other countries. In addition, countries with strong market economies could use the threat of higher import taxes as a bargaining chip in other negotiations.

To limit such discriminatory practices, the concepts of MFN status and national treatment are integral to GATT, just as they are to GATS, as discussed earlier in the context of international trade in services. Thus, under GATT, a reduced tariff offered to one WTO member country must be offered to all WTO members, and once a good has been imported, it must be treated just as domestic goods are treated. That, at any rate, is the ideal. In practice, GATT has not actually done away with nonconforming tariffs. Rather, it prohibits countries from moving farther away from the ideal, while providing successive rounds of multilateral trade negotiations to encourage countries to collectively move forward on achieving these goals.

A Closer Look at U.S. Tariffs

Imposing tariffs runs counter to the avowed goal of free trade. In addition, there seems to be little logic behind some of the disparities in tariffs imposed by particular countries. Consider, for example, the United States' assessment of an 8.5 percent import duty on women's wool suits in 2007; no import duties were imposed on men's suits. Furthermore, when one considers all of the tariffs the United States assesses on imports, it is evident that the assessment across countries is neither even nor fair. In 2006, both France and Cambodia paid $367 million in duties to the United States; but for its payment, France was able to import $36.8 billion in goods, whereas Cambodia was able to import only $2.2 billion.

Questions

1. Who in the United States is hurt by the tariffs described above? Who in the United States is advantaged by them?
2. Why might U.S. tariffs be friendlier to French products than Cambodian goods?

Source: Editorial, "The Other Boot," *The New York Times,* May 4, 2007 [**www.nytimes.com**].

Export Restrictions

Imports are regulated to protect American businesses. Exports by American businesses, on the other hand, may be regulated for several reasons. Specifically, the U.S. Export Administration Act of 1979 permits restrictions on goods and technology where exportation would harm national security or where restriction would significantly advance U.S. foreign policy, prevent an excessive drain of scarce materials, or reduce serious inflationary impacts from foreign demand. [To learn more about U.S. import and export practices, see **www.cbp.gov/trade**.]

Rare Earth Elements

China supplied 80 percent of rare earth elements–metals less scarce than precious metals but still relatively rare–imported by the U.S. from 2014 to 2017. Its processing capacity to convert these elements to materials ready for manufacturing purposes represented 85 percent of worldwide capacity. Many of these metals have turned out to be important to a wide range of green technologies, such as those used in wind turbines and in the electric motors for the Toyota Prius and Chevrolet Volt. They are also used in computers, lasers, and fiber optics, as well as in some U.S. missile guidance systems.

China imposed substantial export restrictions on rare earth elements beginning in 2006, arguing reduced production was an environmental protection measure. The restrictions were challenged by the U.S., the EU, and Japan in the WTO, which ultimately led to China dropping the export quotas in 2015.

Recent tensions between the U.S. and China have raised concerns that China could again use its dominance in rare earth elements to achieve advantages–particularly in high-tech–over other global economies, including the U.S. and Japan. In fact, China is reportedly implementing a ban on these exports as early as 2023.

Question

If China and the U.S.'s positions in terms of importing and exporting rare earth metals were reversed, do you think such actions by the U.S. would be defensible under the Export Administration Act? Why or why not?

Sources: "U.S. Dependence on China's Rare Earth: Trade War Vulnerability," *Reuters,* June 27, 2019 [**www.reuters.com**]; Paul Geitner, "U.S., Europe and Japan Escalate Rare-Earth Dispute with China," *The New York Times,* June 27, 2012 [**www.nytimes.com**]; "Hands Slapped," *The Economist,* July 9, 2011 [**www.economist.com**]; Keith Bradsher, "China Tightens Grip on Rare Minerals," *The New York Times,* September 1, 2009 [**www.nytimes.com**]; and Tim Newcomb, "Why China is Banning Rare Earth Metals Exports," *Popular Mechanics,* April 17, 2023 [**www.popularmechanics.com**].

Fair Trade Regulations: Dumping and Subsidies

To promote fair trade, the WTO prohibits the practice of *dumping.* Dumping occurs when a manufacturer sells its goods in a foreign country for less than their normal value. If this practice causes or threatens material injury to a domestic or established foreign manufacturer in the foreign country, it is prohibited. The price is considered less than normal value if it is less than the price charged in the producer's home country.

A firm may want to dump its goods in a foreign market for two reasons. First, its home market may be saturated and cannot support any further supply. For example, the U.S. accused China of dumping cheap steel exports in an effort to keep China's steel mills running; there had been a downturn in China's economy, which could not support previous levels of production. Alternatively, a firm may wish to establish itself and even drive other firms out of the foreign market. To do so, it might sell its goods in the foreign market at a price below those of its competitors, and then support that price with higher prices in its home country. After its competitors are forced out, the firm might set its prices at or above the normal level. In either case, GATT permits retaliatory duties to be imposed on countries that have dumped goods in other member countries.

The WTO also prohibits the payment of *unfair subsidies* by governments. This occurs when a government, perhaps in an effort to encourage growth in a certain industry, offers subsidies to producers in that industry. The producers are then able to sell their goods at a price that is substantially lower than those of their competitors. Subsidies are considered unfair when governments use them to promote export trade that harms another country. When unfair subsidization is found, the WTO permits the harmed country to impose countervailing duties on those products in an amount sufficient to counteract the effect of the offending subsidy. If a country believes that *countervailing duties* have been illegally imposed, it must either sue in the courts of the country imposing the duties, and under that country's laws, or take the dispute through the adjudication process provided by the WTO, discussed later in this chapter.

A dispute over solar panels illustrates many of these fair-trade regulations. In what has been called "the world's largest antidumping and antisubsidy trade cases,"[77] both the United States and the European Union asserted that China had become the world's dominant producer of solar panels through the provision of subsidies in the form of favorable loans from state-owned banks and incentives provided by local and provincial governments to Chinese manufacturers.[78] They also argued that China was dumping its panels into Western markets at prices below its cost of production, resulting in more than 20 American and European manufacturers cutting back production or going bankrupt. In response, both the United States and the European Union imposed substantial tariffs on the importation of Chinese panels. China responded with a tariff of its own—on the importation of polysilicon, one of the main raw materials in the production of the panels. This was a move that didn't particularly harm Chinese panel producers because of the existence of an abundance of other sources for the polysilicon. The U.S. Commerce Department ultimately lowered import duties in 2015 for most Chinese solar panel manufacturers, perhaps because the tariffs were artificially inflating prices and could slow the growth of the U.S. solar industry; as of 2023, however, it looks as though the U.S. will expand import duties after discovering that Chinese manufacturers have been circumventing those still in place.[79]

Question

Why do developed countries such as the United States regulate trade through the mechanisms described in this section? Why might a less developed country do so?

Trade Restrictions—A Tangled Web

International trade has never been free of national barriers in modern times. For that reason, WTO negotiations start with existing historical protections. Member countries agree not to increase barriers, and they commit to participating in multilateral trade negotiations with the goal of lessening restrictions over time. New countries are admitted to the WTO only after sometimes prolonged negotiations with existing members over modifications deemed necessary to existing trade-related barriers. However, even

> Every country has companies and industries that benefit directly from existing barriers.

if everyone agreed that the world, as a whole, would be better off without trade restrictions, it does not follow that all countries or all persons would be better off, certainly not in the short run. Every country has companies and industries that benefit directly from existing barriers–businesses whose profits rely on, and sometimes depend on, protection. Each of these businesses, in turn, has employees, suppliers, and communities that benefit indirectly from those protections. Thus, any change in a nation's trade policies will have a negative effect on some segment of its economy, even if it can be demonstrated that the change will produce a positive effect on its economy as a whole.

Take a specific example: The United States has had an ongoing dispute with China over its protection of, and trade in, intellectual property. In 2009, a WTO dispute resolution panel ruled that China must permit foreign companies to sell music online in China. The panel said China's prohibition on downloaded music violates a promise China made upon joining the WTO that it would open access to foreign mass-produced art. China responded that it never promised to open markets in the electronic distribution of sound recordings in a nonphysical form and that the restriction was necessary to protect China's "public morals."[80] Interestingly, only once has the public morals defense previously been used before the WTO–by the United States when it argued in support of its ban on Internet gambling over the objections of Antigua. The United States lost. To succeed, a proponent must be able to show that the restriction is "necessary" to defend public morals.

Now consider more broadly the trade relationship between the United States and China. What other forces influence the resolution of a particular dispute? For example, China exported nearly $4.49 of goods to the United States in 2022 for every $1 of goods that the United States exported to China, which suggests that China is more dependent on trade with the United States than the reverse.[81] Conversely, in significant part because of China's large positive trade balance with the United States, China invests its abundance of U.S. dollars in U.S. Treasury bonds. China's demand for treasuries keeps the interest rates that the United States pays on those bonds significantly lower than they would otherwise be, thus reducing the cost of borrowing for the United States.

The United States has also had a trade dispute with Brazil. Brazil forced the United States into the WTO dispute resolution process, arguing that the $3 billion per year the United States has been paying to cotton growers (mostly large agribusinesses in the South) constitutes an unfair subsidy. U.S. companies accounted for about 40 percent of cotton exports globally. The WTO ruled in favor of Brazil and ultimately authorized the imposition of countervailing duties. In order to avoid the imposition of those duties, the United States negotiated a settlement in 2010 that allowed it to continue paying the $3 billion annual subsidy, at least until Congress passed a new farm bill, so long as the United States also paid Brazil $147.3 million per year. However, the parties negotiated a second agreement in 2014 that permitted the United States to continue paying the $3 billion annual subsidy until the passage of a new farm bill, in exchange for a final lump-sum payment to Brazil of $300 million.[82] When Congress approved a new support program for cotton farmers in 2018, Brazil threatened to bring a new challenge to the WTO, even though the United States remained confident the program did not violate the WTO's rules.[83] It does not appear that Brazil acted on its threat.

Questions

1. How would you challenge China's assertion that prohibiting music downloads is necessary to protect public morals in China? What facts might you look for to support your argument?
2. Is it ethical for the United States to dispute China's protectionist policies while spending years defending an enormous annual subsidy that it pays to a well-developed U.S. industry? Explain.
3. Note that the WTO had ruled in favor of Brazil that the United States' $3 billion annual payment to American cotton growers is an unfair subsidy. Were either or both the negotiated settlements the United States made with Brazil in 2010 and 2014 ethical? What effect does the subsidy have on the cotton industry in Brazil as well as other developing nations?[84]

Part Three—International Dispute Resolution

LO 16-13
Identify and evaluate the means for resolving international disputes.

As we have seen, international business relationships are highly complex. Disputes are inevitable. International dispute resolutions often face roadblocks. Three significant international dispute resolution bodies presently exist: the International Court of Justice, the European Court of Justice, and the WTO Dispute Settlement Body. Alternatively, parties to an international contract may agree to international arbitration in order to resolve their disputes.

International Dispute Resolution Bodies

International Court of Justice

The only court devoted entirely to hearing cases of international public law is the International Court of Justice (ICJ) in the United Nations. The ICJ is made up of 15 judges from 15 different member countries. It may issue two types of decisions: binding and nonbinding. It has advisory jurisdiction when the United Nations asks the court for an opinion on a matter of international law. These opinions do not bind any party. It has contentious jurisdiction where two or more nations (not individual parties) have consented to its jurisdiction and have requested a binding opinion. Such opinions are not, however, precedent for the ICJ in later cases. [For more information about the ICJ, see **www.icj-cij.org**.]

How Binding Are ICJ Decisions?

Just how binding an ICJ contentious case decision actually is on U.S. state and federal courts was called into question by the 2008 U.S. Supreme Court decision in *Medellín v. Texas*. The Court, in a 6–3 decision, held that a Texas court did not have to give effect to an ICJ ruling despite the fact that the case was submitted to the ICJ pursuant to a treaty obligation specifying that the ICJ has "compulsory jurisdiction" for all "disputes arising out of the interpretation or application" of the treaty. In the view of the majority, the "most natural reading" of the "compulsory jurisdiction" language is "as a bare grant of jurisdiction. . . . The [treaty] says nothing about the effect of an ICJ decision and does not itself commit signatories to comply with an ICJ judgment." In his dissent, Justice Breyer observed

> In the majority's view, the [treaty] simply sends the dispute to the ICJ . . . and the U.N. Charter contains no more than a promise to "undertak[e] to comply" with that judgment. Such a promise, the majority says, does not as a domestic law matter . . . "operat[e] of itself without the aid of any legislative provision." Rather, here (and presumably in any other ICJ judgment rendered pursuant to any of the approximately 70 U.S. treaties in force that contain similar provisions for submitting treaty-based disputes to the ICJ for decisions that bind the parties) Congress must enact specific legislation before ICJ judgments entered pursuant to our consent to compulsory ICJ jurisdiction can become domestic law. . . . In my view . . . we must look instead to our own domestic law, in particular, to the many treaty-related cases interpreting the Supremacy Clause. Those cases . . . lead to the conclusion that the ICJ judgment before us is enforceable as a matter of domestic law without further legislation.
>
> ***Source:*** *Medellín v. Texas,* 552 U.S. 491 (2008)[**https://supreme.justia.com**].

European Court of Justice

The European Court of Justice (ECJ) hears cases involving European Community law. Although not required, one judge from each member nation traditionally sits on the ECJ. At first glance, the ECJ may not seem a particularly important court for American business, but in an age of MNEs, its decisions can be critical. For example, the ECJ ruled whether Google's AdWord service violated the Louis Vuitton trademark under EU trademark law when Google sold an ad to a Vuitton competitor; the competitor's ad appeared next to the search results returned any time "Louis Vuitton" was entered as a search phrase.[85] The court held, with certain caveats, that it was not a violation. [For information on the ECJ, see **https://curia.europa.eu/jcms/jcms/Jo2_6999/en.**]

WTO Dispute Settlement Body

Although the WTO Dispute Settlement Body (DSB) is not a true court, it is a significant forum for the resolution of international trade disputes between WTO members. The DSB is made up of all member governments, usually represented by ambassadors or the equivalent. The DSB establishes a panel to hear a particular dispute brought by a member state. The panel then reports back to the DSB, which can either accept or reject the panel's findings. Either side can then appeal to the WTO Appellate Body. Again, the DSB can either accept or reject the appeals report. If a WTO member fails to comply with the final decision of the DSB, the opposing party may seek compensation. If the compensation is not agreed upon by the parties within 20 days, the complaining party can seek authorization for retaliation–that is, the suspension of favorable trade concessions to the noncompliant party. The reality of this power was demonstrated by the DSB's authorization of import duties against U.S. goods by Brazil as discussed above. In the years 2017–2019, 75 new cases were brought to the WTO. The number dropped significantly during 2020–2022 (perhaps due to the Covid19 pandemic): there were only 22. [For more information on the WTO dispute resolution function and dispute documents, see **www.wto.org/english/tratop_e/dispu_e/dispu_e.htm**.]

Other International Fora

In addition to the three institutions just discussed, particular treaties may implement specific resolution processes for disputes arising under that treaty between its signatories.

For example, NAFTA provided for special tribunals before which corporations could, and did, bring complaints against governments for actions perceived to be unfair or inequitable to them as foreign investors. However, the USMCA, the successor treaty to NAFTA, no longer provides for investor-state dispute settlement (ISDS) mechanisms between the U.S. and Canada, and ISDS proceedings between the United States and Mexico are limited to expropriation and nondiscrimination claims.[86]

National courts also rule on matters of international law and on matters involving business in international settings. In fact, because of the absence of any international courts of general jurisdiction, national courts are where most international business disputes are heard. When the underlying dispute seems to have little association with the forum state, but that state's national court agrees to rule on the substantive claim, legal commentators may lay charges of "judicial imperialism."[87] The principle of comity previously discussed also applies to the exercise of a national court's jurisdiction.

PRACTICING ETHICS The Long Road through Court

In the summer of 2007, 12 banana plantation workers from Nicaragua got their day or, rather, their four months in a California federal district court.

The workers were employed by Dole Food Co. on banana plantations in Nicaragua, where a pesticide known as DBCP, manufactured by Dow Chemical Co., was used to increase the weight of the banana harvest and help with rodent and pest control. In 1977, the U.S. government suspended the use of the chemical after complaints arose of sterility in California workers. When Dow informed Dole that it would no longer be producing the chemical, the two companies agreed that Dow would sell to Dole, for use in Central America, the more than 500,000 gallons that had been returned to it by other purchasers.

The plaintiffs were some of the workers who were exposed to DBCP while working for Dole in Nicaragua, workers who then became sterile.

After a successful suit was brought in the United States in the early 1980s on behalf of affected California workers, U.S. law firms began suing in U.S. courts on behalf of workers from other countries. Nearly every case ended when American courts ruled that the principle of *forum non conveniens* required the lawsuits to be maintained in the countries where the workers had suffered their injuries. Their view was that Nicaragua was a more appropriate forum for the dispute. So the workers tried again at home. After lengthy delays and, ultimately, a change in Nicaraguan law to facilitate the DBPC lawsuits, in 2002, a Nicaraguan court awarded nearly $490 million in damages, and other judgments followed. But so far Dole and Dow have successfully blocked all enforcement of the judgments in U.S. courts. The new laws in Nicaragua have meant, however, that Dole and Dow have ceased invoking the *forum non conveniens* argument against new suits in the United States.

After a month of deliberations in the 2007 case in California, the jury awarded six of the Nicaraguan workers a total of $3.3 million. Following a number of post-trial motions, the companies successfully reduced the award to $1.58 million to be shared among four of the plaintiffs. The jury decision as to one plaintiff was overturned, and Dole was granted a new trial as to another. In the years following, Dole filed post-trial motions to have the jury verdict thrown out; in 2011, the judgment was vacated. At the same time, each side accused the other of fraud, including fraud instigated by the opposing attorneys, but the California State Bar is no longer pursuing investigations of those attorneys.

Questions

1. Apart from whether Dole or Dow Chemical, or both, are liable for health issues associated with exposure to DBCP, was it ethical for Dole to use, and for Dow to supply, DBCP for use in Nicaragua and elsewhere after the chemical was banned in the United States? Explain.
2. Why do you think Dole and Dow did not object to the new suits brought in the United States after the plaintiffs' successful suit in Nicaragua?
3. Do you think the Nicaraguan judgments should be enforceable in the United States? Why or why not?

Sources: T. Christian Miller, "Plantation Workers Look for Justice in the North," *Los Angeles Times,* May 27, 2007 [**www.latimes.com**]; Justin Rebello, "U.S. District Court in Calif. Rules Against Dow Chemical in Pesticide Exposure Case," *Lawyers USA,* December 2007; "Dole Food Co. Inc. Wins Court Rulings," *Business Wire,* March 10, 2008; Victoria Kim, "Judge Throws Out Verdict Awarding Millions to Dole Workers," Los Angeles Times, July 16, 2010 [**www.latimes.com**]; Press Release, "Dole Food Company Announces That Court Enters Final Order Vacating Judgment, Dismissing Fraudulent Lawsuit Brought by Nicaraguans Claiming to Have Been Banana Workers," *Business Wire,* March 15, 2011 [**www.businesswire.com**]; Amada Bronstad, "California Bar Drops Complaint Against Dole's Lawyers," *Law.Com,* February 28, 2011 [**www.law.com**]; and Amanda Bronstad, "California State Bar Drops Complaint Against Attorney Who Sued Dole," *Law.Com,* accessed April 2023 [**www.law.com**].

Arbitration

In light of the difficulty of litigation between parties of diverse nationalities and the desire for more certainty and expediency in business transactions, parties to an international contract may prefer to insert a clause that calls for the international arbitration of any dispute. As discussed in Chapter 4, arbitration is a nonjudicial means to settle a conflict where the parties agree to a hearing in front of a neutral third party who will issue a binding award decision. [For more information on international arbitration, see **www.arbitration-adr.org.**]

Government Defenses

"Some evil acts don't violate international law unless they are performed by someone acting with government authority."[88] Even where government action is the source of the wrong, two additional doctrines accepted as general principles of international law may pose barriers to the judicial enforcement of a party's rights: the *act of state doctrine* and the *doctrine of sovereign immunity.*

Act of State Doctrine

LO 16-14
Explain the act of state doctrine.

It is generally accepted that a country has absolute rule over what occurs within its borders. Consequently, the act of state doctrine holds that a judge in one country does not have the authority to examine or challenge the acts of another country within that country's borders. For instance, an American court may not declare invalid the acts of the British government taken within its own jurisdiction, because it is presumed that the foreign country, Britain, acted legally within its own territory.

One government action that has caused a great deal of dispute in connection with the act of state doctrine is *expropriation.* Expropriation is the taking by a national government of property and/or rights of a foreign person within that government's borders without adequate compensation. The United States contends that international law requires compensation for the taking. Not all governments agree with the United States' position. Until 1999, YPF had been Argentina's state energy corporation. It was privatized in 1999, however, and became an affiliate of a Spanish oil company. Then in 2012, YPF discovered one of the world's largest deposits of shale oil and gas. Shortly thereafter, Argentina nationalized YPF as its state energy corporation and refused to give the Spanish oil company the

$9–10 billion compensation it was seeking. The somewhat dubious reason given for the 2012 nationalization was that YPF's production had fallen, causing Argentina to become a net importer of energy.[89]

Doctrine of Sovereign Immunity

LO 16-15
Describe the doctrine of sovereign immunity and its exceptions, as codified under the Foreign Sovereign Immunities Act.

The doctrine of sovereign immunity is based on the concept that "the king can do no wrong." In other words, if the king makes the rules, how could the king ever be wrong? As Chief Justice Marshall explained in *The Schooner Exchange v. McFaddon*:[90] "The jurisdiction of the nation within its own territory is necessarily exclusive and absolute. It is susceptible of no limitation not imposed by itself; deriving validity from an external source would imply a diminution of its sovereignty to the extent of the restriction, and an investment of that sovereignty to the same extent in that power which could impose such restriction."

The doctrine has been codified in the United States by the Foreign Sovereign Immunities Act of 1976 (FSIA), which provides that foreign countries may not be sued in American courts, subject to several exceptions. Accordingly, U.S. citizens usually would not be allowed to sue Britain in the U.S. courts, unless the claim falls into one of the following FSIA exceptions:

- The foreign country has waived its immunity (that is, it has consented to be sued in another country's courts).
- The legal action is based on a commercial activity by the foreign country in the United States or outside the United States but having a direct effect in the United States.
- The legal action is based on personal injuries "caused by an act of torture, extrajudicial killing, aircraft sabotage, hostage taking, or the provision of material support or resources" for such acts.[91]

Thus, a country that conducts a commercial activity in a foreign country may not hide behind sovereign immunity if sued. In recent years, however, the Supreme Court has effectively limited the jurisdiction of U.S. courts to preside over such cases, stressing that in order do so, the underlying commercial activity must have a sufficient connection to the United States.[92] For instance, in 2015, the Supreme Court held that a California woman who bought a Eurail pass from a Massachusetts-based travel agency and then lost her legs in an Austrian national railway accident could not sue for damages in a United States federal district court.[93] The court held that it was the accident in Austria–not the sale of the Eurail pass in Massachusetts–that was central to the case, and as such, the United States was not the proper forum. Note that a country acting on its own behalf and not for a commercial purpose may avail itself of sovereign immunity. However, the Supreme Court has held that the FSIA provides immunity only to a foreign state and not to a foreign official, even if that official is acting on behalf of the state.[94]

The "restrictive theory of immunity" recognized and applied by the United States is to be contrasted with the policies of some countries that contend that immunity is absolute–no exceptions exist. The following case examines sovereign immunity.

Chief Judge Wilkinson

Appellant Nyla Butters brought suit against her employer, Vance International, claiming that Vance discriminated against her on the basis of gender. The district court held that Vance was entitled to immunity from Butters' suit under the Foreign Sovereign Immunities Act because Vance's client, the Kingdom of Saudi Arabia, was responsible for Butters not being promoted.

I

Vance International, headquartered in Oakton, Virginia, provides security services to corporations and foreign sovereigns. In October 1994, Saudi Arabia hired Vance to augment the security provided to Princess Anud, a wife of Saudi King Fhad, while the Princess was undergoing medical treatments in California. The Saudi military was responsible for protecting Princess Anud. The Princess' residence in Bel Air, California, was referred to as "Gold." Saudi Arabian Colonel Mohammed Al-Ajiji supervised all security at the site—three Saudi military officers and the Vance agents. . . . The Saudi government paid Vance for its services.

In August 1995, Vance hired Nyla Butters as a part-time, at-will security agent. From 1995 until April 14, 1998 . . . [on] several occasions, Butters temporarily worked in Gold's command post.

In early April 1998, Vance supervisors at Gold recommended that Butters serve a full rotation in the command post. . . . Gregg Hall, the Vance detail leader, spoke with Mohammed. Colonel Mohammed denied Hall's request for Butters to serve a rotation in the command post. Colonel Mohammed told Hall that such an assignment was unacceptable under Islamic law, and Saudis would consider it inappropriate for their officers to spend long periods of time in a command post with a woman present. This in turn could have political ramifications at home for the Saudi royal family. Mohammed also informed Hall that the Princess and her contingent wanted to speak only to male officers when they called the command post. In total, three Vance supervisors recommended Butters for the assignment. Saudi military officers denied every request.

On May 28, 1998, Butters filed a charge of gender discrimination with the California Department of Fair Employment and Housing. On October 15, 1998, Butters filed suit . . . for discriminatory constructive termination, retaliatory constructive termination, and wrongful constructive termination in violation of public policy under California's Fair Employment and Housing Act. Vance filed a motion for summary judgment with respect to these counts.

On July 30, 1999, the district court granted Vance's motion, finding Vance immune from Butters' suit under the Foreign Sovereign Immunities Act (FSIA). . . . The district court held that derivative FSIA immunity attached to Vance because it was "acting under the direct military orders of Colonel Mohammed when [it] did not allow the plaintiff to work a full rotation in the command center." Butters appeals.

II

Butters first contends that FSIA immunity does not attach to Vance because the action here was a "commercial activity." . . .

The FSIA defines "commercial activity" as "a regular course of commercial conduct or a particular commercial transaction or act. The commercial character of an activity shall be determined by reference to the nature of the course of conduct or particular transaction or act, rather than by reference to its purpose." . . . The Court elaborated on the distinction: "[A] state engages in commercial activity . . . where it exercises 'only those powers that can also be exercised by private citizens,' as distinct from those 'powers peculiar to sovereigns.'"

The relevant act here—a foreign sovereign's decision as to how best to secure the safety of its leaders—is quintessentially an act "peculiar to sovereigns." . . . Indeed, it is difficult to imagine an act closer to the core of a nation's sovereignty. Providing security for the royal family in this country is not a commercial act in which the state is acting "in the manner of a private player within the market." . . .

III

Butters next argues that Vance is not entitled to immunity since Vance, as opposed to the Saudi officials, was responsible for the decision not to promote Butters.

A

If Vance was following Saudi Arabia's orders not to promote Butters, Vance would be entitled to derivative immunity under the FSIA. . . .

. . . To abrogate immunity would discourage American companies from entering lawful agreements with foreign governments and from respecting their wishes even as to sovereign acts. Under the circumstances here, imposing civil liability on the private agents of Saudi Arabia would significantly impede the Saudi government's sovereign interest in protecting its leaders while they are in the United States.

IV

Any type of governmental immunity reflects a trade-off between the possibility that an official's wrongdoing will remain unpunished and the risk that government functions will be impaired. FSIA immunity presupposes a tolerance for the sovereign decisions of other countries that may reflect legal norms and cultural values quite different from our own. Here Saudi Arabia made a decision to protect a member of its royal family in a manner consistent with Islamic law and custom. The Act requires not that we approve of the diverse cultural or political motivations that may underlie another sovereign's acts, but that we respect them. We thus affirm the judgment.

Questions

1. Why did the court hold that Vance, a U.S. corporation, could avoid Butters's claim of discrimination based on a claim of sovereign immunity? Why did Butters argue that sovereign immunity should not apply?
2. How do you feel about the end result of this decision? Did Butters suffer discrimination? Explain.

Subjecting MNEs to Compliance with the Law of Nations

The largest MNEs have economic strength equaling or exceeding that of some countries. In this chapter, we have seen how challenging it can be to effectively regulate their activities. That makes it worth asking whether MNEs should be held liable if, in furtherance of their economic objectives, they either (1) take advantage of foreign government actors willing to subdue a local population or (2) are complicit in a foreign government's perpetuation of its own dominance, where the action of the foreign government violates the law of nations.

Some foreign plaintiffs are attempting to hold MNEs liable under such circumstances in suits brought in U.S. federal courts under the Alien Tort Statute. In one sentence, this statute authorizes foreign nationals to file civil suits in the United States against those who violate "the law of nations or a treaty of the United States." Enacted in 1789, the statute began to be used in the 1990s to sue major corporations for alleged complicity in crimes violating human rights by foreign governments, including torture, extrajudicial killings, and war crimes.

Many such suits have withstood motions to dismiss by corporate defendants. In some cases, juries have found against the plaintiffs; a number of suits have been settled, subject generally to a restriction that the settlement terms not be publicly disclosed. An exception to such nondisclosure was a 2009 settlement for $15.5 million of claims against Royal Dutch Shell for its role in the Nigerian government's execution of local activists who protested the environmental damage caused by oil drilling in the Niger delta.

Other plaintiffs did not settle. On April 17, 2013, the U.S. Supreme Court foreclosed their claims, holding that the Alien Tort Statute was subject to the traditional presumption against extraterritorial application but suggesting that cases that "touch and concern the territory of the United States" might "displace the presumption." U.S. courts may not hear claims of foreign plaintiffs against foreign companies on foreign soil, but other claims—such as those of foreign plaintiffs against U.S. companies on foreign soil—perhaps are still viable.

Under EU law, a European company can be sued "at home for complicity in human-rights violations committed anywhere in the world."

Sources: Brent Kendal, "High Court Rejects Pfizer Appeal in Nigeria Drug-Trial Case," *The Wall Street Journal,* June 29, 2010 [**www.wsj.com**]; Nathan Koppel, "Arcane Law Brings Conflicts from Overseas to U.S. Courts," *The Wall Street Journal,* August 27, 2009 [**www.wsj.com**]; Jad Mouawad, "Shell to Pay $15.5 Million to Settle Nigerian Case," *The New York Times,* June 9, 2009 [**www.nytimes.com**]; Jad Mouawad, "Oil Industry Braces for Trial on Rights Abuses," *The New York Times,* May 22, 2009 [**www.nytimes.com**]; Russell Gold, "Chevron Case Weighs Extent of Overseas Liability," *The Wall Street Journal,* December 1, 2008 [**www.wsj.com**]; Warren Richey, "U.S. High Court Allows Apartheid Claims Against Multinationals," *The Christian Science Monitor,* May 13, 2008 [**www.csmonitor.com**]; *Kiobel v. Royal Dutch Petroleum Co.,* 569 U.S. 108 (2013) [**https://supreme.justia.com**]; Mark Walsh, "Global Warning," *ABA Journal,* July 2013, p. 17; and "Law's Long Arm," *The Economist,* October 6, 2012 [**www.economist.com**].

Enforcing Foreign Judgments

LO 16-16
Identify some challenges to the enforcement of foreign judgments.

As we have seen, even if a harmed party in an international dispute successfully initiates a judicial proceeding, many procedural hurdles are likely to be encountered. Recall the *forum non conveniens* principle that initially kept the Nicaraguan workers from obtaining substantive hearings in U.S. courts. But what happens after the successful conclusion of such a suit? Do challenges arise in the enforcement of the court's decision?

The answer is yes, particularly in those cases where the losing defendant has insufficient assets located in the same jurisdiction as the court awarding the plaintiff monetary relief. In those cases, the plaintiff may need to present the judgment to a court in a country where assets of the defendant are located and seek local enforcement. This is an added cost, in terms of both time and money, for successful plaintiffs. Furthermore, enforcement may be difficult or impossible to obtain.

When a plaintiff is successful in a California court, but the defendant's assets are in New York, the plaintiff may have to seek enforcement from a New York court. In that situation, the U.S. Constitution requires the New York court to give "full faith and credit" to the decision of the California court. No such broad policy exists in U.S. law with respect to decisions of foreign courts, nor does such a broad policy exist in international law. Instead, the court from which enforcement is being requested is likely to consider whether the original foreign judgment violates local notions of justice and morality, or is otherwise contrary to public policy, so as not to be entitled to enforcement. This is also true of foreign arbitration awards if the losing party has refused to satisfy the award—even if both countries are among the 158 current signatories of the United Nations Convention on the Recognition and Enforcement of Foreign Arbitral Awards (also known as the New York Convention). [For current information about the convention, see **www.uncitral.un.org/en/texts/arbitration/conventions/foreign_arbitral_awards**.]

To illustrate, consider the Nicaraguan banana plantation workers. After U.S. courts largely refused to allow substantive hearings in the 1980s based on *forum non conveniens,* the workers took their claims back to Nicaragua, which was exactly what U.S. courts had told them to do. Although resolution of claims in Nicaragua took a long time, some plaintiffs obtained substantial judgments there. In response to plaintiffs' applications to U.S. courts for recognition and enforcement of these Nicaraguan judgments, however, the defendant U.S. corporations have thus far been successful in avoiding the requested enforcement.

Enforcing U.S. Judgments

Similar problems can arise when a U.S. citizen obtains a judgment from a U.S. court against a foreign national, and the judgment is then sent for enforcement to the home courts of the foreign national. Consider the case of an Alabama 15-year-old who died in an accident when the buckle of his motorcycle helmet failed. The helmet was made by an Italian company. His mother sued in an Alabama court and won a $1 million judgment. The Italian company refused to pay, and the mother presented the judgment to an Italian court for enforcement. The Italian Supreme Court found the award of punitive damages so offensive to its notion of justice that it refused to enforce any of the award. Many countries share the Italian court's distaste for punitive damages in such situations.[95]

Question

Considering the effort and delay plaintiffs already undergo in obtaining judgments, do you think it would be better, on balance, for countries to simply agree to mutually enforce foreign judgments in favor of private citizens (both nationals and nonnationals) without applying culturally based notions of justice? Why or why not? If not, try generating a list of principles you think should permit a court to refuse enforcement of a foreign judgment.

Research Exercise

Identify a multinational firm that conducts business with suppliers in developing countries. Find its vendor code of conduct on its website and evaluate the areas of enforcement that might prove to be the most difficult. For more information about codes of conduct for MNEs, see James K. Jackson, "Codes of Conduct for Multinational Corporations: An Overview," *Congressional Research Service,* April 16, 2013 [**https://sgp.fas.org/crs/misc/RS20803.pdf**].

Chapter Questions

1. Thomas Friedman, in his 2005 book, *The World Is Flat: A Brief History of the Twenty-First Century,* argues that countries with connected manufacturing supply chains won't go to war with one another. He offers an example of Dell's multi-country supply chain for the manufacture of its laptops. On balance, do you think globalization is a catalyst for bringing world peace or a tinderbox that may set international disputes on fire through the collision of differing ideals and competing interests? Explain.
2. *a.* Why do you think China, one of the most communist of nations, wanted to join the WTO?

   b. Would it surprise you to learn that Iraq, Iran, and Syria, while not currently WTO members, are all formally enrolled as observer countries? This means they are (or are considering) pursuing accession negotiations to become WTO member states. Why might they be interested in joining the WTO?
3. From 2010 through 2012, many state legislatures considered or passed laws outlawing aspects of Islamic or Shariah law. Some of them would have prohibited the enforcement of private contracts in which a "butcher would no longer be able to enforce his contract for halal meat–contracts that, like deals for kosher or other faith-sanctioned foods, are regularly enforced around the country. Nor could a Muslim banker seek damages for violations of a financial instrument certified as 'Sharia compliant' since it pays no interest."[96]

   a. Develop an argument that laws prohibiting enforcement of such contracts would be unconstitutional.

   b. What historical parallels exist, in which laws in the United States were seen to deny certain constitutional rights to a subgroup of American citizens?
4. Different countries and cultures have different norms for dress. In the United States, for example, some restaurants require men to wear jackets and state law generally prohibits even partial public nudity. Public schools often have enforceable dress codes.

In the 1960s, those codes often prohibited female students from wearing pants. Consider the following:

- In 2010, the French Parliament passed a law forbidding people from concealing their faces in public, punishable by fines. Higher fines and prison sentences up to one year could be imposed on individuals who encouraged others to ignore the ban. Although freedom of religion is constitutionally protected in France, it is generally acknowledged that the purpose of the law was to prohibit Muslim women from wearing traditional head coverings and full-body robes. It has been estimated that fewer than 2,000 women in France, most of whom are French nationals, wear them. Some supporters of the ban have said that such robes are a means of forcing women to be submissive and are a sign of enslavement or debasement. Some of the wearers say that the dress is a method to concentrate on their religious faith.[97]
- Also in 2010, one province in Indonesia, the world's most populous Muslim-majority nation, banned Muslim women from wearing revealing clothes such as tight skirts and pants. After their third violation, women could be subject to two weeks' detention. Shopkeepers violating restrictions on selling inappropriate clothing could lose their business licenses.[98]

a. Do the laws discussed in the sections above seem logical to you? On what basis should you judge them?

b. Would conflicts with cultural issues, such as those addressed by the local laws above, impact your decision as a manager about where to conduct your business? Should they impact your decisions? Explain.

c. If your job required you to live in a country that had laws with which you disagreed on moral grounds, would you follow those laws? Explain.

5. *a.* What are the relative advantages and disadvantages of each form of doing business in a foreign country?

   b. Why would a firm choose one form over another?

6. The United States exports its values structure in a variety of ways, including through the extraterritorial application of its laws. For instance, American firms must maintain Title VII standards abroad and are therefore prohibited from discriminating against employees anywhere in the world on the basis of sex, race, color, national origin, and religion. Compare this with the Alien Tort Statute, which was enacted in 1789 and authorizes foreign nationals to file civil suits in the United States against those who violate "the law of nations or a treaty of the United States." In 2013, the U.S. Supreme Court held that the Alien Tort Statute (ATS) is subject to the traditional presumption *against* extraterritorial application and underscored the danger of judicial interference in foreign policy. It ruled that the ATS is presumed to cover only violations of international law occurring in the United States, unless the conduct overseas affects the United States "with sufficient force." The court thus dismissed the underlying action brought by foreign plaintiffs against Royal Dutch Shell (a foreign MNE) for its alleged complicity in the Nigerian government's execution of local activists.[99] What public policy interests are likely to have motivated the Court's decision? See *Kiobel v. Royal Dutch Petroleum Co.,* 569 U.S. 108 (2013) [**https://supreme.justia.com**].

7. In *Doe v. Nestlé USA, Inc.*, three former child slaves brought claims under the Alien Tort Statute against a number of defendants alleging they aided and abetted child slavery by providing assistance to farmers in the Ivory Coast. The defendants argued that the complaint should be dismissed based on the Supreme Court's ruling in *Kiobel v. Royal Dutch Petroleum Co.*, which held that ATS is subject to the traditional presumption against extraterritorial application. The Ninth Circuit Court of Appeals, however, allowed the case to proceed on the basis that the defendants acted with the purpose to facilitate slavery, a plan that starkly distinguished the case from other ATS decisions in which the defendants merely profited by doing business with known human rights violators. It also remanded the case to allow the plaintiffs to amend their complaints to allege that some of the activity underlying their ATS claim, such as planning the promotion of child slavery overseas, took place in the United States. One commentator had concerns that the Ninth Circuit's decision would open the doors to many other ATS claims, and that corporations could potentially be held liable under ATS for the tortious acts committed outside the United States by foreign actors with whom they do business, "so long as the company intended to turn a profit."[100] *See Doe v. Nestlé USA, Inc.*, 766 F.3d 1013 (9th Cir. 2015) [**https://casetext.com**] and *Kiobel v. Royal Dutch Petroleum Co.*, 569 U.S. 108 (2013) [**https://supreme.justia.com**].
   a. Do you agree with this characterization of Nestle's alleged actions–that it merely did business with foreign actors, who committed tortious acts, in order to turn a profit?
   b. Do you think that Nestlé should not be subject to an ATS claim in the United States if its alleged actions were limited to aiding and abetting child slavery overseas? See *Nestlé USA, Inc. v. Doe,* 593 U.S. _ (2021) [**https://supreme.justia.com**].
   c. What if the corporate defendant allegedly undertook planning in the United States to facilitate child slavery in order to maximize its profits? In that case, do you think Nestlé should or should not be subject to an ATS claim in the U.S.?
8. In 2016, the WTO ruled that a tax break given by Washington State for the aerospace industry was a prohibited subsidy. The tax cut was agreed to when Boeing was considering where to establish a new assembly base, and it was designed to help Boeing develop its new 777X jetliner. Explain how a tax break might serve as a subsidy and thus be prohibited by the WTO. Does it surprise you to learn that, for 17 years, Boeing (a U.S. corporation founded in Seattle, Washington and headquartered in Chicago) and Airbus (an EU corporation) accused one another of receiving tens of billions of dollars of illegal subsidies? Is it unethical for either of these two companies to have accepted state aid while attacking the other for doing so? Or is this behavior an acceptable means of maximizing profits and getting ahead of the competition? (Note that the U.S. and EU finally resolved their trade dispute in 2021, with both parties agreeing for five years to suspend tariffs stemming from the aircraft-subsidy dispute.[101])
9. Camel Manufacturing imported nylon tents to the United States. The tents held nine people and weighed over 30 pounds. The tents' floors ranged from 8 feet by 10 feet to 10 feet by 14 feet. The tents were to be used as shelter during camping. The importer categorized the goods as "sports equipment," which carried a 10 percent import duty, whereas the U.S. Customs Service considered the tents "textile articles not specifically

provided for," with a duty of $0.25 per pound plus a 15 percent import duty. The importer appealed the decision. What should be the result? Explain. See *Camel Manufacturing Co. v. United States,* 686 F. Supp. 912 (C.I.T. 1988), *aff'd,* 861 F.2d 1266 (Fed. Cir. 1988) [**https://law.justia.com**].

10. Should a Mexican citizen who bought a Chrysler vehicle in Mexico be allowed to sue the manufacturer in a U.S. court under U.S. product liability laws if the plaintiff's three-year-old son was killed when the passenger-side air bag deployed during an accident in Mexico? Explain. See *Gonzalez v. Chrysler Corp.,* 301 F.3d 377 (5th Cir. 2002) [**https://law.justia.com**], *cert. denied,* 538 U.S. 1012 (2003).
11. Prior to 1941, Kalmich owned a business in Yugoslavia. In 1941, the Nazis confiscated his property as a result of Kalmich's Jewish heritage and faith. Bruno purchased the business from the Nazis in 1942 without knowledge of the potential unlawful conversion. Kalmich contended that because the confiscation was in violation of well-defined principles of international law prior to the German occupation, the transfer to Bruno was ineffective. Kalmich sought to apply a 1946 Yugoslavian law called "Law Concerning the Treatment of Property Taken Away from the Owner" in a case in an American court. That law provided that where property is taken from its owners, the owner may bring an action against "responsible persons" for recovery.
    a. Should the act of state doctrine apply in this case? Explain.
    b. If not, what should be the result in an American court? Explain. See *Kalmich v. Bruno,* 450 F. Supp. 227 (N.D. Ill. 1978) [**https://law.justia.com**].
12. Zedan received a telephone call from a Saudi Arabian organization offering him an engineering position at a construction project in Saudi Arabia. The Ministry of Communications, an agency of the government, guaranteed payment to Zedan for any work he performed there, whether for the government or for a nonsovereign third party. After three years, Zedan left the country without being fully paid. After he returned to the United States, he filed an action in federal court seeking to enforce the ministry's guarantee. The ministry argued that it was protected under the Foreign Sovereign Immunities Act.
    a. Was Zedan's recruitment in the United States a commercial activity as required by the act? Explain.
    b. Did this action have a direct effect in the United States as required by the act? Explain. See *Fawwaz Zedan v. Kingdom of Saudi Arabia,* 849 F.2d 1511 (D.C. Cir. 1988) [**https://law.justia.com**].
13. From time to time, courts are called on to determine the enforceability of an arbitration clause contained in a contract. DiMercurio was injured in 1994 when the commercial fishing vessel in which he was working sank. The vessel was owned by R&M, which was found by a court to be liable to DiMercurio for his injuries and ordered to pay $350,000 in compensation. However, because R&M had no other assets, it assigned to DiMercurio all the rights it had against Sphere Drake, the London-based insurer of the fishing vessel. When DiMercurio looked to Sphere Drake for payment, it denied the claim and invoked the arbitration clause in its insurance policy with R&M, which required the arbitration to take place in England. Should DiMercurio be required to

pursue his claim through arbitration in England? Explain. See *DiMercurio v. Sphere Drake Insurance,* 202 F.3d 71 (1st Cir. 2000) [**https://law.justia.com**].

Notes

1. Abby Budiman, "Key findings about U.S. immigrants," *Pew Research Center,* August 20, 2020 [**www.pewresearch.org**].
2. Bureau of Consular Affairs, "CA by the Numbers," U.S. Department of State, January 2020 [**https://travel.state.gov**]. According to Wikipedia, the United States is "the only developed country that does not even attempt a formal enumeration of expatriate citizens. The State Department does not release what statistics it may have, citing 'security reasons.'" Wikipedia, "American Diaspora," accessed April 22, 2023 [**https://en.wikipedia.org**].
3. Marrakesh Agreement Establishing the World Trade Organization [**www.wto.org**].
4. "Trade Talks Produce a Deal," *The New York Times,* December 12, 2013 [**www.nytimes.com**].
5. "When Giants Slow Down," *The Economist,* July 27, 2013 [**www.economist.com**].
6. Greg Ip, "We Are Not the World," *The Wall Street Journal,* January 6, 2017 [**www.wsj.com**].
7. "The Long Road," *The Economist,* June 4, 2016 [**www.economist.com**].
8. "Game of Zones," *The Economist,* March 21, 2015 [**www.economist.com**]; and World Trade Organization, "Chart: Evolution of Regional Trade Agreements," accessed June 2020 [**www.wto.org**].
9. Opinion, "China Picks Up the U.S. Trade Fumble," *The Wall Street Journal,* November 17, 2016 [**www.wsj.com**]; and Yuka Hayashi, "U.S. on Sidelines as China and Other Asia-Pacific Nations Launch Trade Pact," *The Wall Street Journal,* January 1, 2022 [**www.wsj.com**].
10. "A Transatlantic Tipping Point," *The Economist,* April 27, 2013 [**www.economist.com**].
11. "Europe's Choice," *The Economist,* May 26, 2012 [**www.economist.com**].
12. World Trade Organization, "What is the World Trade Organization," accessed June 2020 [**https://www.wto.org**].
13. Pete Engardio, "Global Capitalism: Can It Be Made to Work Better?" *Bloomberg,* November 6, 2000 [**www.bloomberg.com**].
14. Ibid.
15. Christopher Ingraham, "What Most Americans Think of Islam Today," Wonkblog, *The Washington Post,* November 17, 2015 [**www.washingtonpost.com**].
16. Google, "Google Transparency Report: Government Requests to Remove Content," accessed April 2023 [**https://transparencyreport.google.com**].
17. Ibid.
18. Craig Timberg and Paula Moura, "In Brazil, Google Is in the Middle of a Battle over Free Speech," *The Washington Post,* October 3, 2012 [**www.washingtonpost.com**].
19. "Facebook Runs Up Against German Hate-Speech Laws," *The New York Times,* November 28, 2016 [**www.nytimes.com**].
20. Eric Pfanner and Somini Sengupta, "In a French Case, a Battle to Unmask Twitter Users," *The New York Times,* January 24, 2013 [**www.nytimes.com**]; and Somini Sengupta, "Twitter Yields to Pressure in Hate Case in France," *The New York Times,* July 12, 2013 [**www.nytimes.com**].
21. Steven Greenhouse, "U.S. Retailers See Big Risk in Safety Plan for Factories in Bangladesh," *The New York Times,* May 22, 2013 [**www.nytimes.com**]; and Julfikar Ali Manik and Jim Yardley, "Building Collapse in Bangladesh Leaves Scores Dead," *The New York Times,* April 24, 2013 [**www.nytimes.com**].

22. International Labour Organization, "Strengthening Workplace Safety and Labour Rights in the Bangladesh Ready-Made Garment Sector," April 2016 [**https://studylib.es**]. See also, Zobaer Ahmed, "Has Bangladesh made progress on the rights of garment workers?," *DW,* February 6, 2020 [**www.dw.com**].
23. Steven Greenhouse, "Under Pressure, Bangladesh Adopts New Labor Law," *The New York Times,* July 16, 2013 [**www.nytimes.com**]; and Jim Yardley, "Garment Trade Wields Power in Bangladesh," *The New York Times,* July 24, 2013 [**www.nytimes.com**].
24. Clifford J. Levy, "Microsoft Changes Policy over Russian Crackdown," *The New York Times,* September 13, 2010 [**www.nytimes.com**].
25. *EEOC v. Arabian American Oil Co.,* 499 U.S. 244 (1991) [**https://supreme.justia.com**].
26. Association of American Residents Overseas, "8.7 million Americans (excluding military) live in 160-plus countries," accessed April 2023 [**www.aaro.org**].
27. Robert Barnes, "Supreme Court Extends Protections for Multinational Companies," *The Washington Post,* January 14, 2014 [**www.washingtonpost.com**].
28. "The World This Week," *The Economist,* July 13, 2013 [**www.economist.com**]; and "China' s Former Railways Minister's Death Sentence Commuted to Life," *The Supreme People's Court of the People's Republic of China,* December 14, 2015 [**https://english.court.gov.cn/2015-12/14/c_767231.htm**].
29. Dionne Searcey, "Watergate-Era Law Revitalized in Pursuit of Corporate Corruption," *The Wall Street Journal,* October 15, 2010 [**www.wsj.com**].
30. SEC Enforcement Actions: FCPA Cases [**www.sec.gov**].
31. Ibid.
32. Leslie Wayne, "Foreign Firms Most Affected by a U.S. Law Barring Bribes," *The New York Times,* September 3, 2012 [**www.nytimes.com**].
33. "Russia Calls FIFA Probe an 'Illegal' Application of US Laws," Reuters, May 27, 2015 [**www.reuters.com**].
34. Amir Efrati and Andrew Batson, "Google to Alter Access to Its China Site," *The Wall Street Journal,* June 30, 2010 [**www.wsj.com**]; John C. Abell, "China Renews Google's License," *Wired,* July 9, 2010 [**www.wired.com**]; Ellen Nakashima, Shibani Mahtani, and Rachel Lerman, "Google ends direct cooperation with Hong Kong authorities on data requests," *The Washington Post* (August 14, 2020) [**www.washingtonpost.com**]; and "Is Google blocked in China," Comparitech, accessed April 2023 [**www.comparitech.com**].
35. For example, see *United States v. Kim,* 246 F.3d 186 (2d Cir. 2001) [**https://supreme.justia.com**], in which a New York resident was convicted of wire fraud while working for the United Nations in Croatia.
36. Mayer Brown JSM, *Guide to Doing Business in the PRC* (2010), p. 9.
37. 116. F. Supp. 2d 116 (D.D.C. 2000) [**https://law.justia.com**].
38. 192. F.3d 240 (2d Cir. 1999) [**https://supreme.justia.com**].
39. "At Your Service? The Promise of Services-Led Development," *World Factbook,* accessed April 2023 [**www.worldbanc.org**].
40. "Services, Value Added (% of GDP)-United States," *World Factbook,* accessed April 2023 [**www.worldbanc.org**].
41. Foreign Trade Division, "Annual 2022 Press Highlights," U.S. Census Bureau, accessed April 2023 [**www.census.gov/foreign-trade/statistics**]; and Bureau of Economic Analysis, "International Services, Expanded Detail," Department of Commerce, accessed April 2023 [**www.bea.gov/data/intl-trade-investment**].

42. "Global market of outsourced services from 2000 to 2019," *Statista,* accessed April 2023 [**www.statista.com**].
43. To browse or download the text of the General Agreement on Trade and Services, go to **www.wto.org/english/docs_e/legal_e/legal_e.htm#services**. For a summary of the agreement, go to **www.wto.org/english/docs_e/legal_e/ursum_e.htm#mAgreement**.
44. For a summary of the General Agreement on Tariffs and Trade, see **www.wto.org/english/docs_e/legal_e/ursum_e.htm#General**.
45. GATS, Art. I, para. 3(b), accessed April 2023 [**www.wto.org/english/docs_e/legal_e/26-gats.pdf**].
46. "Principles of the trading system," World Trade Organization, accessed April 2023 [**www.wto.org**].
47. U.S. Bureau of Labor Statistics, "Economic News Release, Union Membership (Annual) News Release," U.S. Department of Labor, January 19, 2023 [**www.bls.gov**].
48. Donald C. Dowling Jr., "Reductions-in-Force Outside the US," *White & Case LLP,* December 1, 2008 [**www.lexology.com**].
49. Bruce Berman, "$21 Trillion in U.S. Intangible Assets is 84% of S&P 500 Value-IP Rights and Reputation Included," *IP CloseUp,* June 4, 2019 [**https://ipcloseup.com**].
50. Eric Rosenbaum, "1 in 5 Companies Say China Has Stolen Their IP Within the Last Year: CNB CFO Survey," *CNBC,* March 1, 2019 [**www.cnbc.com**]; and Derek Scissors, "The Rising Risk of China's Intellectual-Property Theft," *The National Review,* July 16, 2021 [**www.aei.org**].
51. Juliana De Groot, "IP Theft: Definition and Examples," *Data Insider,* December 16, 2021 [**www.digitalguardian.com**].
52. "When You Say 'Bud,'" *ABA Journal,* July 2013, p. 12.
53. From the World Intellectual Property Organization, "WIPO-Administered Treaties" [**www.wipo.int**].
54. "Summary of the Madrid Agreement Concerning the International Registration of Marks (1891) and the Protocol Relating to That Agreement (1989)," WIPO, accessed April 2023 [**www.wipo.int**].
55. Case C-236/08, *Google Inc. v. Louis Vuitton Malletier SA,* 2010 E.C.R. I-02417 [**https://curia.europa.eu**].
56. "Yes, Ja, Oui, No, No," *The Economist,* December 15, 2012 [**www.economist.com**].
57. Duff Wilson, "Cigarette Giants in Global Fight on Tighter Rules," *The New York Times,* November 13, 2010 [**www.nytimes.com**].
58. Ibid.
59. Tobacco Tactics, "Philip Morris vs the Government of Uruguay," *University of Bath,* February 4, 2020 [**https://tobaccotactics.org**].
60. Michael Schroeder and Silvia Ascarelli, "New Role for SEC: Policing Companies beyond U.S. Borders," *The Wall Street Journal,* July 30, 2004 [**www.wsj.com**].
61. "European Imperialism," *The Wall Street Journal,* October 31, 2007 [**www.wsj.com**].
62. PwC, "State-Owned Enterprises: Catalysts for Public Value Creation?," accessed April 2023 [**www.pwc.com/gx/en/psrc/publications/assets/pwc-state-owned-enterprise-psrc.pdf**].
63. Qin Mei, "Fortune Favors the State-Owned: Three Years of Chinese Dominance on the Global 500 List," *Center for Strategic and International Studies,* October 7, 2022 [**www.csis.org**] and Clay Chandler and Grady McGregor, "Bigger Isn't Always Better for China's State-Owned Giants," *Fortune,* September 2, 2021 [**https://fortune.com**].

64. Michael Schroeder and Silvia Ascarelli, "New Role for SEC," *The Wall Street Journal,* July 30, 2004, p. A1.
65. *Morrison v. National Australia Bank Ltd.,* 561 U.S. 247 (2010) [**https://supreme.justia.com**].
66. Floyd Norris, "Accounting Détente Delayed," *The New York Times,* July 19, 2012 [**www.nytimes.com**]; and Kirsten Becker, Holger Daske, Christopher Pelger, and Stephen A. Zeff, "IFRS Adoption in the United States: An Analysis of the Role of the SEC's Chairs," *Journal of Accounting and Public Policy,* September 13, 2022 [**www.sciencedirect.com**].
67. David Reilly and Duncan Mavin, "Chinese Accounting Earns Tough Stance," *The Wall Street Journal,* August 7, 2012 [**www.wsj.com**].
68. Sofia Horta e Costa, "Two Accounting Scandals in China in One Week Burn Investors," *Bloomberg,* April 8, 2020 [**www.bloomberg.com**].
69. Michael Rapoport, "U.S., China Set Pact on Auditor Access," *The Wall Street Journal,* May 24, 2013 [**www.wsj.com**].
70. Dave Michaels, "U.S. Investors Have Another Reason to Fret over China Firms," *Bloomberg,* November 3, 2015 [**www.bloomberg.com**].
71. Dave Michaels and Akane Otani, "U.S. Moves to Audit Chinese Firms. Market Frets Over What Comes Next," *The Wall Street Journal,* May 26, 2020 [**www.wsj.com**]; Dave Michaels, "White House Seeks Crackdown on U.S.-Listed Chinese Firms," *The Wall Street Journal,* August 6, 2020 [**www.wsj.com**]; and Keith Zhai, Paul Kiernan, and Michelle Chan, "U.S. and China Reach Agreement on Chinese Company Audits," *The Wall Street Journal,* August 26, 2022 [**www.wsj.com**].
72. Brent Kendall and John D. McKinnon, "Justice Department is Preparing Antitrust Investigation of Google," *The Wall Street Journal,* June 1, 2019 [**www.wsj.com**]; and Lauren Feiner, "DOJ Files Second Antitrust Suit Against Google, Seeks to Break Up Its Ad Business," *CNBC,* January 24, 2023 [**www.cnbc.com**].
73. Lauren Hirsch and Lauren Feiner, "States' Massive Google Antitrust Probe Will Expand Into Search and Android Businesses," *CNBC,* November 14, 2019 [**www.cnbc.com**]; and Lauren Feiner, "DOJ Case Against Google Likely Won't Go to Trial Until Late 2023, Judge Says," *CNBC,* December 18, 2020 [**www.cnbc.com**].
74. Foo Yun Chee, "Google Loses Challenge Against EU Antitrust Decision, Other Probes Loom," *Reuters,* September 14, 2022 [**www.reuters.com**].
75. Press Release, "Mergers: Commission Approves AB InBev's Acquisition of SABMiller, Subject to Conditions," *European Commission,* May 24, 2016 [**https://docslib.org**].
76. For a good comparison of U.S. and EU merger analysis and enforcement, see Cento Veljanovski, "EC Merger Policy after GE/Honeywell and Airtours," *Antitrust Bulletin* 49 (Spring 2004), p. 153.
77. Keith Bradsher, "U.S. and Europe Prepare to Settle Chinese Solar Panel Cases," *The New York Times,* May 20, 2013 [**www.nytimes.com**].
78. James Kantor and Keith Bradsher, "Europe and China Agree to Settle Solar Panel Fight," *The New York Times,* July 27, 2013 [**www.nytimes.com**].
79. "U.S. Revises Tariffs and Duties on Chinese Solar Imports," *Bloomberg News,* July 9, 2015 [**www.bloomberg.com**]; and Nichola Groom, "U.S. to Expand Solar Panel Tariffs After Probe Finds Chinese Evasion," December 2, 2022 [**www.reuters.com**].
80. John W. Miller and Peter Fritsch, "Hollywood Upstages Beijing," *The Wall Street Journal,* August 13, 2009 [**www.wsj.com**].

81. Keith Bradsher, "China Moves to Retaliate Against U.S. Tire Tariff," *The New York Times,* September 14, 2009 [**www.nytimes.com**]; and "Total Value of U.S. Trade in Goods (Export and Import) With China From 2012-2022," *Statistica,* February 8, 2024 [**www.statistica.com**].
82. "Why the Deal to Pay Brazil $300 Million Just to Keep Subsidies Is Bad for the WTO, Poor Countries, and U.S. Taxpayers," *The Washington Post,* October 12, 2014 [**www.washingtonpost.com**].
83. Bill Tomson, "Brazil Ag Minister Vows New Challenge to US Cotton Subsidies," *Agri-Pulse,* May 2, 2018 [**www.agri-pulse.com**].
84. "Why the Deal to Pay Brazil $300 Million Just to Keep Subsidies Is Bad for the WTO, Poor Countries, and U.S. Taxpayers," *The Washington Post,* October 12, 2014 [**www.washingtonpost.com**].
85. Case C-236/08, *Google Inc. v. Louis Vuitton Malletier SA,* 2010 E.C.R. I-02417 [**https://curia.europa.eu**].
86. Nathalie Bernasconi-Osterwalder, "USMCA Curbs How Much Investors Can Sue Countries-Sort of," International Institute for Sustainable Development, October 2, 2018 [**www.iisd.org**].
87. Klaus-Heiner Lehne, "Hands Off Our Torts," *The Wall Street Journal,* November 18, 2003.
88. Steve Garmisa, "U.S. Courts Handle International Law," *Chicago Sun-Times,* September 24, 1997.
89. Juan Forero, "Seizure of Repsol Affiliate in Argentina Stuns Oil Markets," *The Washington Post,* April 26, 2012 [**www.washingtonpost.com**].
90. 11 U.S. 116 (1812) [**https://supreme.justia.com**].
91. *Sutherland v. Islamic Republic of Iran,* 151 F. Supp. 2d 27 (D.D.C. 2001) [**https://casetext.com**].
92. Richard Wolf, "Supreme Court Limits Reach of U.S. Courts," *USA TODAY,* December 1, 2015 [**www.usatoday.com**].
93. *OBB Personenverkehr AG v. Sachs,* 577 U.S. _ (2015) [**https://supreme.justia.com**].
94. *Samantar v. Yousuf,* 560 U.S. 305 (2010) [**https://supreme.justia.com**].
95. Adam Liptak, "Foreign Courts Wary of U.S. Punitive Damages," *The New York Times,* March 26, 2008 [**www.nytimes.com**].
96. Aziz Huq, "Defend Muslims, Defend America," *The New York Times,* June 19, 2011 [**www.nytimes.com**].
97. David Gauthier-Villars and Charles Forelle, "Burqa Is Banned in France," *The Wall Street Journal,* September 15, 2010 [**www.wsj.com**].
98. Fakhrurradzie Gade, "Indonesia's Aceh Province Enacted a Strict Muslim Law Thursday: A Tight Pants Ban," *The Christian Science Monitor,* May 27, 2010 [**www.csmonitor.com**].
99. John B. Bellinger III, "Lawsuits Force Foreign Governments to Navigate U.S. Court System," *The Washington Diplomat,* May 3, 2016 [**www.washdiplomat.com**].
100. Institute for Legal Reform,"SCOTUS Decides Not to Review 9th Circuit's Controversial Doe v. Nestlé Decision," *U.S. Chamber of Commerce,* January 12, 2016 [**www.instituteforlegalreform.com**].
101. Silvia Amaro and Leslie Josephs, "U.S. and EU Resolve 17-Year Boeing-Airbus Trade Dispute," *CNBC,* June 15, 2021 [**www.cnbc.com**].

Video icon credit: Comstock Images/Alamy Stock Photo

CHAPTER SEVENTEEN

Environmental Protection

After completing this chapter, students will be able to fulfill the following learning objectives:

17-1. Provide concrete examples of environmental degradation around the globe.

17-2. Explain some of the ways market incentives can be used to prevent or correct environmental problems.

17-3. Evaluate environmental problems using the concepts of coincidence, correlation, and causation; cost–benefit analysis; and incidence of costs.

17-4. Identify the primary goals and mechanisms of the National Environmental Policy Act.

17-5. Identify the duties of the Environmental Protection Agency.

17-6. Describe the uses of the Clean Air Act, including its application to greenhouse gas emissions.

17-7. Describe the main purposes of the Clean Water Act.

17-8. Explain the meaning and purpose of the term *navigable waters* and the scope of *covered waters* under the CWA.

17-9. Identify some of the major federal laws that address land pollution.

17-10. Discuss the purpose and effect of the Comprehensive Environmental Response, Compensation, and Liability Act of 1980, commonly known as "the Superfund."

17-11. Identify the penalties and other enforcement mechanisms available under federal regulations.

17-12. Identify and explain some of the challenges to protecting a species under the Endangered Species Act.

17-13. Describe the primary common law remedies for environmental damage.

17-14. Discuss the purpose of the Kyoto Protocol and the Paris Agreement.

Introduction

Global climate change has been described as "among the handful of most important public policy issues of our time,"[1] "one of the greatest challenges the world faces,"[2] and the "greatest market failure the world has ever seen."[3] At issue is the projected overall increase in surface and ocean temperatures around the globe. This phenomenon is substantially caused by the release of man-made carbon dioxide and other greenhouse gases into the atmosphere, largely through the burning of fossil fuels, especially in gasoline engines and coal-fired plants.

Both the politics and the science of climate change are controversial–a particularly potent and poignant example of the issues of coincidence, correlation, and causation discussed at the beginning of Part Two of this chapter. In 2013, the Intergovernmental Panel on Climate Change (IPCC) stated that it is "extremely likely that human influence has been the dominant cause of the observed warming since the mid-20th century" and that human influence "has been detected in warming of the atmosphere and the ocean, in changes in the global water cycle, in reductions in snow and ice, in global mean sea level rise, and in changes in some climate extremes."[4] "Extremely likely" refers to a probability of 95 to 100 percent. The U.S.' Fourth and Fifth National Climate Assessments and the European Climate Law, codifying the EU's goal to become climate neutral by 2050, reaffirm that conclusion.[5]

Because global average surface temperatures did not appreciably rise (despite significant global GHG emissions) between 1998 and 2012, some commentators recommended a hiatus in the implementation of emission reduction policies while we "see if the nonwarming trend continues."[6] Others pointed out, however, that the "current pause is consistent with numerous prior pauses" and that "it is a mistake to interpret a landing as the end of the climb."[7] In fact, 2016 was the third year in a row that average global temperatures set a new record high, and scientists blamed the trend, along with an El Niño, on man-made global warming.[8] And that trend continues, 2023 proving as of this writing to be the hottest year in recorded history. According to NASA, 2020 was tied (with 2016) for second. The 10 hottest years on record have all occurred since 2010.[9]

Scholar and activist Bill McKibben has argued that we no longer live on the same planet on which our parents grew up and that climate change has passed the tipping point. "The planet we inhabit has a finite number of huge physical features. Virtually all of them seem to be changing rapidly."[10] Consider, for example, that the Arctic ice cover had been the lowest ever in July 2020–26 percent below average, equivalent to an area 30 percent larger than Mexico. Every year, ice the size of North Dakota melts and never reforms. The Arctic is warming more than twice as fast as the rest of the planet, and the rate is accelerating. The shrinking temperature differential between the Arctic and the tropics is altering global wind patterns. As a result, storms are moving much slower (converting normal rains into deluges), and arid zones are becoming more parched.[11]

In June 2020, Siberia had its first 100-degree day (the highest temperature recorded above the Arctic Circle).[12] Unprecedented wildfires raged there in July, and melting permafrost led to a massive oil spill when the ground collapsed.[13] Events in the Arctic will cause global temperatures to rise, because the ice cover–which reflects solar radiation back into space—is rapidly disappearing; soot from wildfires will make the situation worse, because it darkens what ice remains.[14] "The ocean . . . bears the brunt of climate change"—as a carbon sink capturing greenhouse gases, its acidity has increased 30 percent.[15] It has absorbed 93 percent of the energy trapped by the greenhouse effect, leading to higher water temperatures.[16] The ramifications include coastal erosion, algae blooms, coral bleaching, widening dead zones, new marine diseases, ocean hotspots, and a redistribution of heat that alters weather patterns. Thermal expansion is responsible for 30 percent of the rise in sea level, the other 70 percent being attributable to melting ice.[17]

Sea level is expected to rise three feet by the end of the century. Island nations, such as Fiji (Pacific), the Maldives (Indian Ocean), and the Bahamas (Caribbean), are in jeopardy. The first expected to disappear is Kiribati, which has an elevation of just seven feet in the Pacific Ocean. Storm surges are already contaminating the fresh water, destroying crops, and flooding buildings. Major cities will also suffer severe flooding or inundation, including Rio de Janeiro, Shanghai, New Orleans, Miami, Houston, and Boston.[18]

[For a NASA video showing the decline in Arctic ice cover, see **www.youtube.com/watch?v=qHE0n5c6-6g.**] [For an award-winning 2012 Sundance Film Festival documentary recording receding glaciers throughout the world using time-lapse photography, see **www.chasingice.com.**]

Another feature of our landscape intrinsically linked to climate change is our forests. They hold more than one trillion tons of carbon—more than twice the total carbon emitted since the Industrial Revolution. Each year we emit 39 billion tons of CO_2, and forests absorb 28 percent of it. Yet humanity has reduced forestation by 60 percent; the forests lost each year would nearly cover Greece. A tipping point is being reached. Higher temperatures are making wildfires much more frequent and far more devastating. Growth cannot keep up with the rate of destruction. Higher temperatures also increase the impact of insects, fungi, and bacteria on tree death and impair photosynthesis, resulting in less carbon intake and smaller trees. If the temperature increases 2 degrees Celsius above preindustrial levels, huge swaths of forests will release more carbon than they capture. This is already occurring in portions of the Amazon.[19]

Regulating air pollution is critical to addressing climate change. Yet, it is only one aspect of environmental protection. Important regulatory schemes also govern water and land pollution.

LO-17-1
Provide concrete examples of environmental degradation around the world.

Because of the impact business operations have on our environment, it is important to understand the legal and ethical dimensions. In this chapter, we examine environmental protection laws and regulations in the United States, the role of the Environmental Protection Agency (EPA) in mounting a coordinated attack on environmental problems, and the concept of environmental justice. In addition, we also examine international treaties addressing climate change. But first, we consider the complexity of environmental issues and provide notable examples of environmental degradation around the globe.

A Global View

Environmental issues are complex for a variety of reasons. Consider the fact that a single action can have variable impacts on the environment—for example, reducing the emission of greenhouse gases (GHG), while at the same time adversely affecting water quality. In addition, the consequences of an action in one location may not manifest themselves for some time, or they may impact another location a substantial distance away. This is further complicated by the fact that scientific methodology requires a sufficient amount of time to pass to establish causation with a sufficient coefficient of probability to offset countervailing arguments that cessation of the act will cause economic harm.

Consider, too, that the Earth is a closed, complex, and unique system; no computer program can model it, and no lab can test possibilities under lifelike conditions. And no international body has the jurisdiction (or credibility) to make enforceable decisions (or persuasive recommendations) to balance competing national interests and protect against devastating harms to the world's delicate ecosystems, and possibly to life itself.

What observable evidence of this complexity do we have? Consider the following:

- In May 2020, a fuel reservoir at a Siberian power plant collapsed, releasing historic levels of oil–approximately 21,000 tons–into the Arctic Circle. Investigators claim that the metal company operating the power plant violated environmental safety rules by continuing to use the reservoir even though it was determined in 2018 that it needed repair. Company officials were taken into custody and face up to five years in prison if convicted.[20] Sadly, this was not an isolated event. In 2010, oil spewed out of British Petroleum's Macondo well in the Gulf of Mexico for 86 days straight. The long-term impacts on sea life, shorelines, and coastal communities from the roughly 200 million-gallon spill, as well as the effects of the nearly 2 million gallons of chemical dispersants used in the cleanup, are unknown.[21] By volume, it was far larger than the 1989 *Exxon Valdez* spill in Prince William Sound, Alaska. In the Niger delta, where Royal Dutch Shell, Chevron, and ExxonMobil all have significant drilling operations, as many as 546 million gallons of oil leaked into the waters during the 50-year period leading up to 2010,[22] averaging annually the rough equivalent of the *Exxon Valdez* spill.
- In January 2017, the poor air quality in London set a new modern record and was, at times, worse than the air quality in Beijing–a city notorious for dangerous levels of air pollution. Children in London were told to play indoors because pollution levels were double the legal hourly limit. It took only five days that summer for London to surpass its legal annual limit. A judge ordered Britain's ministers to address the issue, stating that they had broken the law by failing to do so. Pollution in the city was responsible for causing an estimated 9,400 premature deaths.[23]
- In June 2013, Singapore resorted to issuing face masks, and southern Malaysia declared a state of emergency, when air pollution in both regions peaked. The cause? The intentional burning of forests and peat wetland to expand palm oil plantations across the Strait of Malacca in Indonesia. Primarily because of this burning, Indonesia ranked as one of the world's largest emitters of carbon. The fires burned despite Indonesia's pledge to cut its carbon emissions by at least 26 percent by 2020 and a $1 billion agreement with Norway in support of a U.N. program to reduce deforestation. Both forest and wetlands are "huge absorbers of carbon," and the forests are home to Indonesia's endangered orangutans.[24]
- An earthquake and tsunami crippled Japan's Fukushima power plant in March 2011, melting three of its six nuclear reactors. As of May 2020, attempts to prevent the flow of groundwater into the buildings at the plant have proven unsuccessful despite Japan's investment of hundreds of millions of dollars. The government is now focusing its efforts

Until the issue is resolved, Japan's Fukushima nuclear plant—which was crippled by both an earthquake and a tsunami—will produce 400 tons of contaminated water each day.

on storing the contaminated water.[25] Until the groundwater issue is resolved, the plant will continue to produce 400 tons of contaminated water each day. In July 2013, 300 tons of this water were discovered to have drained into the sea. Yet another issue at the plant is the cleanup of the radioactive contamination that spread through the environment at the start of the disaster. The central government was in charge of cleanup efforts in the most heavily contaminated areas, but the rest has been left for local governments to handle; decommissioning work of the nuclear power station and widespread cleanup efforts are still ongoing today.[26]

- According to the World Health Organization, 663 million people rely on unimproved sources of drinking water, and in low- and middle-income countries, 38 percent of health care facilities lack an improved water source.[27] It is believed that 10 percent of the world's population consumes food that has been irrigated with wastewater, which contributes to the incidence of disease, malnutrition, and death.[28]
- Between 2030 and 2050, climate change is expected to cause approximately 250,000 additional deaths per year from malnutrition, malaria, diarrhea, and heat stress.[29]
- Current greenhouse gas emission trajectories are projected to cause the extinction of over 1 million, or one-third, of the Earth's animal and plant species by 2050. In September 2021, 20 species on the U.S. endangered list were officially declared extinct.[30]

PRACTICING ETHICS Global Environmental Justice

Environmental justice is "the fair treatment and meaningful involvement of all people regardless of race, color, national origin, or income with respect to the development, implementation and enforcement of environmental laws, regulations and policies. Fair treatment means no group of people should bear a disproportionate share of the negative environmental consequences resulting from industrial, governmental and commercial operations or policies."[31]

Studies in the United States have shown that at least some risks, such as proximity to hazardous waste disposal sites, are not equally distributed. Is the concept of equally distributed environmental risks a useful tool in assessing global environmental hazards? Consider the following:

- In Flint, Michigan, 38.8 percent of the population lives below the poverty line (the child poverty rate is 54.7 percent), and the median household income is $28,834. The city is 54.1 percent Black or African American.[32]
- The Flint River had been severely polluted in the 1970s. In 2001, Michigan ordered the monitoring and cleanup of 134 polluted sites within the Flint River watershed, but the state's Department of Environmental Quality allegedly failed to treat the water with an anticorrosive agent, in violation of federal law.
- In 2011, the state took over Flint's finances because of a projected $25 million deficit.
- To reduce the budget shortfall, in 2014, the state switched the city's water supply from Lake Huron to the Flint River while a new pipeline to Lake Huron was under construction.
- Residents started reporting changes to the water's color, smell, and taste. The river water was found to be 19 times more corrosive than the water from Lake Huron. As a result, lead from aging pipes began to leach into the water supply. Lead can cause heart, kidney, and neurological damage. In children, exposure can cause impaired cognition, behavioral disorders, hearing problems, and delayed puberty.
- In the summer of 2014, after receiving positive test results for the presence of certain bacteria, the city advised certain neighborhoods to boil their water before using it.

- In December 2014, the state's Department of Environmental Quality increased the chlorine in the water to control the level of dangerous bacteria. That same month, the General Motors plant in Flint stopped using the city's water because it was concerned about the high levels of chlorine corroding engine parts.
- In early 2015, the city warned residents that byproducts from disinfectants used to address the bacteria could cause health issues, including an increased risk of cancer. It also declined an offer from its former supplier to reconnect the city's water supply to Lake Huron citing concerns that water rates could increase by $12 million each year.
- In December 2015, Flint declared a state of emergency.
- In 2016, several lawsuits were filed, including a class action against the state and another against the EPA, alleging violations of the Safe Water Drinking Act, as well as criminal actions against various state employees.
- In 2017, a report, "The Flint Water Crisis: Systemic Racism Through the Lens of Flint," was issued by the Michigan Civil Rights Commission, the EPA awarded Flint $100 million for water infrastructure upgrades, and a $97 million settlement was reached requiring the state to replace lead water lines in Flint.
- In October 2019, the EPA proposed its first major revision of federal regulations on lead in drinking water in two decades as a direct response, in part, to the Flint water crisis.
- In August 2020, the state agreed to a $600 million settlement establishing a victims compensation fund providing direct payments to Flint residents.

Question

What factors might make a minority or low-income population more susceptible to environmental injustice? Explain.

Sources: "Learn About Environmental Justice," U.S. Environmental Protection Agency [**www.epa.gov**]; Amy Littlefield and Bettina Boxall, "EPA Looks at Effects of Waste Plants on Minorities, Poor," *Los Angeles Times*, July 27, 2009 [**www.latimes.com**]; and CNN Editorial Research, "Flint Water Crisis Fast Facts," *CNN*, updated December 13, 2022 [**www.cnn.com**].

Part One—A Return to Fundamentals: The Market, Government Regulation, and Self-Regulation

The first three chapters of this text set up the following framework for analyzing the substantive law topics we have discussed: (1) consideration of how well market forces achieve the goals we have for our society; (2) a brief investigation of whether government intervention can bring us closer to those societal goals; and (3) reflection on the role that self-regulation, through ethical decision-making and corporate social responsibility, can and does play in realizing our goals. This framework is also useful in evaluating the relationship between business and our natural environment.

Market Failure?

Without regulation, a firm might consider dumping its garbage into a nearby canal to be no problem. In fact, perhaps the slight amount of garbage it dumps is no big deal. However, if every firm were allowed to dump that same amount, the canal might become thoroughly polluted. Or consider the possibility that we may all prefer less costly cars that pollute more. Would future generations concur with the decisions we would make in the absence of regulation today?

As discussed in Chapter 8, these examples of water and air pollution would be categorized by economists as *negative externalities*. Wilfred Beckerman, a British economist, described the analysis as follows:

> [T]he costs of pollution are not always borne fully, if at all, by the polluter. . . . Naturally, he has no incentive to economize in the use [of the environment] in the same way that he has for

other factors of production that carry a cost, such as labor or capital. . . . This defect of the price mechanism needs to be corrected by governmental action in order to eliminate excessive pollution.[33]

Accordingly, environmentalists claim that regulation is necessary because the market fails to protect us. Lawmakers and the public apparently agree: A substantial number of environmental laws have been enacted since the early 1970s–laws that address pollution of our air and waterways; regulate the use, disposal, and cleanup of hazardous and toxic wastes; and protect rare plant and animal species. Many of these laws will be discussed in Part Two.

But as we shall see, our conceptualization of the problems we face may be too simplistic. The bulk of our environmental laws and regulations were drafted to address compartmentalized and discrete issues, including clean air, clean water, and hazardous waste, as well as particular contaminants, point sources, or individual species. They may be inadequate to address the interrelationships that characterize both our environment and our social and political structures.

Elinor Ostrom, a Nobel laureate in economics, was a leading scholar of common-pool resource management before her death in 2012. She studied how communities develop effective rules for governing depletable resources such as water, fishing grounds, and the atmosphere. Her conclusion? All arrangements–"government-controlled, privatized, or owned by a community–work in some places but not in others. The success or failure of a specific approach hinges on the match of the specific institutional arrangement, local culture, and particular problems involved, as well as how the approach is implemented. . . . [P]olicies for common resources should be considered experiments within complex systems."[34]

Market Incentives

LO 17-2

Explain some of the ways market incentives can be used to prevent or correct environmental problems.

One approach federal regulation has taken is to dictate standards with which businesses must comply. Such legislation has led to steady, and at times even spectacular, strides forward in environmental protection in the United States. But this progress has not dispelled the view, particularly among economists and those in business, that regulating standards may not be the best approach to tackle environmental problems. They believe that pollution control is not so much a matter of law as economics. It follows that, in some instances with proper incentives, the market will prove superior to traditional regulation in preventing and correcting environmental problems. Examples of these market incentives follow.

Cap-and-Trade Programs

The concept behind cap-and-trade incentives is that a government sets a cap on the total emissions of a particular pollutant that is lower than the existing level. It then issues pollution credits to the most significant emitters of that pollutant. Credit recipients can either reduce their discharge to within their credit limit or buy credits from other companies that have reduced their emissions below their own credit amounts. Such programs, therefore, allow the most cost-effective pollution reduction methods to be used to reach the desired environmental goals.

California hit its climate target in 2016, four years ahead of schedule.

The United States was very successful using this approach to reduce sulfur dioxide emissions that were a major factor in the creation of acid rain.[35] In 1995 alone, when the cap-and-trade program first took effect, emissions dropped nationally by 3 million tons, well ahead of the schedule required by law.[36] By 1999, electric utilities produced about 41 percent more electricity than they had in 1980, while emitting 25 percent fewer tons of sulfur dioxide.[37] In 2007, total sulfur dioxide emissions dropped below the long-term goal, well ahead of the 2010 statutory deadline.[38] When the House of Representatives passed a cap-and-trade bill in 2009 to address greenhouse gas (GHG) emissions, and the Senate declined to act on it, a coalition of nine Northeast and Mid-Atlantic states acted independently to set up a cap-and-trade program for carbon emissions from power plants within their jurisdictions. In the first three years, average annual emissions were reduced by 23 percent.[39] California began running its own carbon cap-and-trade program on January 1, 2013, as part of its program to cut GHG emissions to 1990 levels by 2020. It was the second largest such program in the world, following only the European Union's.[40] As a result, California hit its climate target in 2016, four years ahead of schedule.

Tax Laws

Tax provisions can also affect behavior, either by encouraging certain behaviors through tax incentives or by discouraging other behaviors through additional taxes. For example, federal income tax credits, which reduce the amount of tax owed, have been granted in various years for solar installations, the production of power from wind turbines, and purchasing certain new fuel-efficient cars, such as hybrids. Many in the United States favor the imposition of a new federal tax on carbon, such as a specified tax per ton of carbon dioxide emitted. Proponents argue that such a tax would promote a reduction in emissions and simultaneously raise revenues, which could be used to reduce the federal deficit, maintain lower corporate tax rates to make U.S. companies more competitive, or compensate lower-income citizens who, indirectly, would bear a heavier burden for the tax through higher gas prices and heating bills. According to some estimates, the poorest 20 percent of Americans spend 21.4 percent of their income on gas and utilities, whereas the richest 20 percent spend only 6.8 percent, and 34 of the richest industrialized countries collect an average of $68.4 in fuel taxes per metric ton of carbon dioxide, while the United States collects federal taxes on energy (including the federal gas tax) amounting to only $6.30 per ton.[41]

PRACTICING ETHICS The Ethical Stoplight

GHG cap-and-trade programs are more complex than the acid rain program in the United States because there are many different sources of GHG emissions and many varied ways to reduce global GHG. For example, forests and peat wetlands act as carbon sinks—naturally capturing atmospheric carbon and locking it up. Thus, a GHG emitter could cause global GHG emissions to decrease by paying a country such as Indonesia to prevent deforestation that would otherwise occur. Such an approach to controlling global GHG emissions raises complex valuation and verification issues. If country A pays country B to protect its forests, how many GHG credits should country A receive? How much carbon is captured by a square mile of Indonesian forest? How long should country B be required to protect that forest for a particular payment?

Some ecologists and economists are working to establish an analytical framework that would facilitate targeted conservation investments, yielding the highest ecological returns by systematically inventorying and valuing the services nature performs, such as carbon absorption. Others, such as foresters, chemists, and accountants, are developing ways to verify and audit different factors, such as the amount of carbon stored by a particular stand of trees.

This approach to controlling GHG has raised ethical issues. One commentator has argued that "farmers should not be paid to reduce their water pollution any more than I should be paid to stop mugging people." In contrast, another sees the possibility of a hybrid "stoplight" approach. "The red part is: Here's some things you can do to your land that are so bad that we're gonna take you to prison. The yellow light is: Here's . . . some minimal stuff that you really ought to do. Then the green light is: Here's some stuff that's above and beyond the stewardship obligation, and we're going to pay you for doing it, because it's to the benefit of society."*

Question

If burning fossil fuels is a major catalyst of global climate change, then the developed world is the major cause. But citizens of the least developed countries will suffer the most severe consequences. If you already suffer food and water insecurity, any further disruption is catastrophic. "Because hunger and misery cannot afford to make the distinctions of the well-fed—to choose between cutting a tree or saving it—poverty is among the greatest environmental threats in the world."[42] Does this reasoning provide a response to the argument that farmers should not be paid to reduce their water pollution? Explain.

Sources: *Matt Jenkins, "Mother Nature's Sum," *Pacific Standard*, October 2008 [**www.psmag.com**]; and Felicity Barringer, "A Grand Experiment to Rein in Climate Change," *The New York Times*, October 13, 2012 [**www.nytimes.com**].

Rebates and Loans

Other targeted market incentives have also been employed to address environmental issues. For example, direct subsidies in the nature of rebates are not uncommon. One example is the Clean Vehicle Rebate Project administered by The California Environment Protection Agency's Air Resources Board, which offers rebates for the purchase or lease of certain new zero-emission vehicles. To achieve greater equity, larger rebates are now available to lower-income applicants and for public fleets operated in disadvantaged communities. As of November 2022, 481,600 vehicles have been implemented under the program, with awarded rebates totaling $3.18 billion.[43]

Government agencies have also subsidized particular activities through guaranteed loan programs. For instance, in 2010 and 2011, the Department of Energy's Loan Programs Office financed the launch of five of the world's largest commercial-scale concentrating solar power plants, sources of clean energy that are "helping to better integrate renewable energy into the electric grid."[44]

Ethical Business Decision Making

What level of environmental concern can we expect from managers of publicly held corporations? Can we identify examples of environmental corporate social responsibility? The answer is a resounding yes–all one has to do is review a sample of corporate websites.

Why are corporate giants voluntarily doing now what they have not done in the past? In part, the answer may be that the market has changed, and market forces are operating to reward corporate responsibility. For example, a manager may believe that being "green," or at least being seen by consumers and investors as such, will improve their company's bottom line. Or they may believe that a proactive approach may lessen the likelihood of future regulation on an issue that is becoming increasingly visible.[45] This is an example of a pay-now-or-pay-later analysis. Managers may take a more environmentally responsible approach because they think the future cost of not doing so could be much larger–in negative publicity, the imposition of fines and penalties, or the cost of more stringent future regulation–than the present actual cost of responsible action.

In addition, business executives and managers, like the rest of the population, are becoming increasingly aware of the environmental direction the planet is heading and want to do what they can to put us on a better path. In Chapter 9, we saw evidence of that, both in the Business Roundtable's rejection of the notion that a corporate board's primary obligation is to make profit for the owners and in the increasing number of businesses voluntarily going through certification for B Corp status.

Does the market actually reward sound environmental practices? Surprisingly, it does. The most recent data, as discussed in Chapter 9, does make the case for considering Environmental, Social, and corporate Governance (ESG) factors, and then incorporating a long-term view of today's choices into a company's core strategies, to increase shareholder returns.

Green growth

There is also an ever-growing list of successful *green growth* examples–concrete illustrations that economic growth and environment protection are not mutually exclusive. By 1994, 60-year-old Ray Anderson had grown his 15-person carpet-tile company, Interface Inc., into the world's largest carpet-tile maker, but customers were pushing for the company to develop an environmental strategy. Anderson did. His goal for his company? By 2020, to produce no GHG emissions and no waste, and to consume no raw materials that could not be rapidly replenished. As of 2010, the company reduced its GHG emissions by 35 percent, water usage by 82 percent, fossil fuel consumption by 60 percent, and landfill waste by 82 percent. Company sales increased by 64 percent and, by avoiding over $450 million in costs, its earnings more than doubled. Ray Anderson dedicated the rest of his life to advocating for environmental stewardship and sustainability. He received numerous awards worldwide and, until his death in 2011, was widely sought after as a speaker and adviser on environmental issues.[46] In honor of the "noble qualities" he championed, The Ray C. Anderson Foundation was established to "help create a better world for future generations–tomorrow's child."[47]

[For a video of Ray Anderson's 2009 TED Talk, in which he shares his story, see **www.raycandersonfoundation.org/butterfly-effect**.] [For many other examples of environmentally responsible actions by business, see **www.bsr.org/en/about/in-the-new**.]

Questions

1. Consider the implications of two headlines in recent years: "Fiat Chrysler Shares Crash by a Fifth as It Is Drawn into Emissions Scandal by US Regulators"[48] and "FBI Arrests Volkswagen Executive in Emissions Scandal."[49] It appears that Fiat Chrysler and Volkswagen not only failed to act responsibly to comply with emissions regulations, but they also committed fraud to make government officials and the public believe they were in compliance. Do you think Fiat Chrysler and Volkswagen are regretting the decisions they made in the past to avoid compliance costs? What costs are they paying now?
2. A 2015 documentary, *The True Cost,* examines many troubling issues in the "fast fashion" industry, including soil and water pollution as a result of using cheap textiles and

toxic dyes to reduce manufacturing costs and speed up production. As a consumer, how do your clothing choices contribute to these environmental issues? Are your choices unethical? What can you do to reduce these environmental costs? [To view the movie trailer for *The True Cost*, see **https://truecostmovie.com.**]

Part Two—Laws and Regulations

LO 17-3 Evaluate environmental problems using the concepts of coincidence, correlation, and causation; cost–benefit analysis; and incidence of costs.

Having reviewed both market forces and ethical business decision making, we turn now to government regulation as an approach to meeting our environmental goals. The United States has developed a wide variety of environmental protection laws and remedies, some of which are covered in this section. These, in turn, have served as a model for environmental protection laws around the world. In evaluating a particular regulation, it will be helpful to keep in mind the following concepts:

- **Cost–Benefit Analysis.** Environmental protection can be expensive. How much as a society are we willing to pay? Do we want clean air at any cost? We may be able to estimate the cost of a particular environmental protection action, but we also need to consider its benefits. To that end, how do we value human life, represented by a statistical decrease in deaths or illness from exposure to environmental pollutants or from decreased human productivity? When does environmental protection sacrifice short-term economic development? Are there offsetting long-term economic benefits? Can these costs and benefits be measured? These are not easy questions. The answers will necessarily be inexact and require subjective judgments and the use of estimates. More attention, however, is being directed at this effort. The Group of Eight Industrialized (G-8) Nations (Canada, France, Germany, Italy, Japan, Russia, the United Kingdom, and the United States) was formed in 1975 and meets annually so that presidents, prime ministers, finance ministers, and foreign ministers can speak candidly about tough global issues, including energy and the environment. It initiated a project in 2007 to study environmental monetary values and estimated the cost of environmental degradation to the world economy at anywhere between $2.5 and $4 trillion annually, or up to five percent of global GDP.[50]

How do we value human life?

- **Impact on Future Generations.** When performing a cost-benefit analysis, how do we evaluate the cost to future generations of our failure to take action? How can we measure the value to those generations if we do take action? For example, how do we measure the impact of climate change on future generations? This is a complex question about which there is no scientific, economic, or political consensus.
- **Proving Causation.** If event A occurs, followed by event B, is it necessarily true that event A *caused* event B? It could simply be a coincidence that first A was observed and then B. Or there could, in fact, be a *correlation* between events A and B, but no actual causation. For example, event Z might cause both A and B, but no causal link may exist between A and B themselves. In the environmental area, issues of coincidence, correlation, and causation may be extremely difficult to determine. Does exposure to secondhand smoke cause lung cancer in some nonsmokers? Did the observed increase in greenhouse gases contribute to global warming such that sea

levels rose, increasing the intensity of Hurricane Katrina and, in turn, causing property damage to a degree that would not otherwise have occurred?[51] If, in the example of Z, A, and B, we focus our efforts to stop A in order to prevent B, we will be wasting our time and money. On the other hand, how long can we wait to determine definitively whether a causal link exists between A and B? Our answer may depend on the severity of the harm we believe is associated with B.

- **Who Pays?** If we decide to correct an environmental problem, who should pay for the corrective measure? If we require corporate America to invest in pollution control devices, the cost may be shared by consumers (through increased prices) and investors (through reduced corporate profits). If habitats of endangered species are to be preserved, current landowners may lose all or a portion of their investment, and workers employed on the land may lose their jobs. Sometimes the issue of who will pay is central to the controversy as to where a particular facility, such as a hazardous waste disposal site, should be located. Not surprisingly, a common response of those who live near a proposed location is: "Yes, it's necessary, but *not in my backyard!*"

"Yes . . . but *not in my backyard!*"

- **Politics.** Environmental protection in the United States is not just a matter of science, cost–benefit assessments, and social policy; it is also a matter of politics. California, for example, has historically received permission from the Environmental Protection Agency (EPA) to impose stricter vehicle emission standards than federal law requires. California sought similar permission in 2005, in part to add greenhouse gases to the list of regulated emissions. After delaying the decision for two years, the EPA denied California's request on the same day in 2007 that President Bush signed into law the federal 35-miles-per-gallon standard. California responded by taking the EPA to court. A year later, in his first month in the White House, President Obama directed the EPA to reconsider California's application, signaling a sharp break with the Bush Administration's less aggressive stance on climate change. The waiver was approved in June 2009.[52] President Trump's Administration subsequently resumed a much less aggressive stance on climate change. As he was sworn into office on January 20, 2017, the link to the original White House page dedicated to climate change was broken. The webpage was updated and, referencing specific administrative rulings that the former administration put in place to address climate change, stated: "Lifting these restrictions will greatly help American workers, increasing wages by more than $30 billion over the next 7 years."[53] President Biden, in turn, issued executive orders signaling his administration's commitment to both environmental protection and environmental justice.[54]

Question

What environmental issue do you care about most? Greenhouse gases? Deforestation? Drinkable water for the world's population? Protection of the polar bear? Select an issue you care about. (If it's climate change, select a specific potential response to it, such as sharing environmental technologies with developing countries, increasing mileage requirements, or requiring the use of energy-efficient light bulbs.) Do some online research for relevant data and explore your issue in light of the five concepts discussed above. Be careful to use reliable online resources in your research.

The Federal Role

The federal government has long maintained a role in the protection of the environment—some argue too great a role. As early as 1899, Congress enacted a law that required a permit to discharge refuse into navigable waters. When it became apparent that private, state, and local environmental efforts were not adequate to address the burgeoning problems, Congress enacted more aggressive legislation in the early 1970s. It began with the 1970 National Environmental Policy Act [NEPA], which proved to be a catalyst for environmental protection initiatives around the world.

National Environmental Policy Act

LO 17-4 Identify the primary goals and mechanisms of the National Environmental Policy Act.

The NEPA established a strong federal presence in the promotion of a clean and healthy environment and represents a general commitment by the federal government to "use all practicable means" to conduct federal affairs in a fashion that promotes "the general welfare" and operates in "harmony" with the environment. It established the Council on Environmental Quality (CEQ), which serves as an adviser to the president. The CEQ is a watchdog of sorts. It is required to conduct studies and collect information regarding the state of the environment. The council then develops policy and legislative proposals for the president and Congress. [For the CEQ's homepage, see **www.whitehouse.gov/ceq.**]

> The NEPA's primary influence results from its environment impact statement requirements.

The NEPA's primary influence, however, results from its *environmental impact statement* (EIS) requirements. With few exceptions, "proposals for legislation and other major federal action significantly affecting the quality of the human environment" must be accompanied by an EIS explaining the impact on the environment and detailing reasonable alternatives. Completing an EIS requires undertaking a cost-benefit analysis. It also requires consideration of cause-and-effect links. Major federal construction projects (such as highways, dams, and nuclear reactors) would normally require an EIS, but less visible federal programs (like ongoing timber management or the abandonment of a lengthy railway) may also require an EIS. Although the focus here is on federal actions, a major private-sector action supported by federal funding or by one of several varieties of federal permission may also require an EIS. Therefore, private companies receiving federal contracts, funding, licenses, and the like may be parties to the completion of an EIS.

Questions

Should a state be required to prepare an EIS if it wants to use federal funds to promote statewide tourism? Does it matter which state it is? Consider Iowa and then consider Hawaii. Can you identify factors that make one distinctly different from the other?[55]

Environmental Protection Agency

LO 17-5 Identify the duties of the Environmental Protection Agency.

The Environmental Protection Agency (EPA) was created in 1970 to mount a coordinated attack on environmental problems. EPA duties include, among other things: (1) gathering information, particularly by surveying pollution problems; (2) conducting research on pollution problems; (3) assisting state and local pollution control efforts; and (4) administering many of the federal laws directed to environmental concerns. [For the EPA home page, see **www.epa.gov.**]

Fracking: A Cautionary Tale

Hydraulic fracturing, commonly referred to as fracking, is a process in which a mixture of sand, fluids, and chemical additives are pumped under high pressure into wells to fracture shale rock, thereby releasing natural gas for extraction. Primarily as a result of fracking, the U.S. became the world's largest natural gas producer in 2018 and became a net fossil fuel exporter in 2019 for the first time in decades, restoring energy security to the nation.

But fracking's heyday may be over. A worldwide glut has driven natural gas prices so low that 80 percent of fracking operations are now unprofitable. Energy has long been the S&P 500's worst-performing sector. In the past five years, 240 fracking companies have gone bankrupt. The market values of the two largest frackers have dropped 90 percent or more as of this writing.

Investors are veering away from fracking not only because of poor financial performance, but also because of fears of regulatory changes on the horizon related to the impact of the fracking process (and of fossil fuels generally) on the environment and public health. In fact, New York State instituted the earliest global ban on fracking in 2014. Other bans in the U.S. and around the world have since followed. Consider the following:

- Methane: Methane is 80 times more harmful as a greenhouse gas than CO_2. Emissions have increased six percent largely as a result of the commencement of fracking in the mid-2000s. Satellites have mapped columns of the gas leaking from fracking sites in an amount equal to the total CO_2 released annually by all U.S. homes.
- Earthquakes: Quakes caused by fracking with magnitudes of up to 5.8 have been observed (a magnitude 5.8 quake is 60,000 times more powerful than a magnitude 1 quake). In the central United States, the number of earthquakes of at least magnitude 3 has increased 800 percent since fracking began.
- Water use: The EPA estimates that it takes 4 million gallons of water to start a fracking well, equal to Denver's total annual consumption. In Arkansas, 51 percent of the streams and rivers are dangerously depleted by water withdrawal for fracking.
- Water contamination: Wastewater disposed of on a large parcel of land killed all of the ground vegetation in less than a week and more than half of the trees in two years. The level of methane in drinking water in locations near fracking sites was found to be 17 times higher than that in locations distant from fracking. The entire groundwater resource of Wyoming's 7,400-square mile Wind River Basin has been contaminated by fracking.
- Health: Children born near fracking sites are more likely to be smaller and are 40 percent more likely to be premature. A significant association exists between proximity to a fracking site and the increased severity of asthma symptoms.

Sources: "Does the Production of Oil and Gas from Shales Cause Earthquakes? If So, How Are the Earthquakes Related to These Operations?", U.S. Geological Survey, accessed October 2020 [**www.usgs.gov**]; Judy Stone, "Fracking Is Dangerous To Your Health–Here's Why," *Forbes,* February 23, 2017 [**www.forbes.com**]; Gayathri Vaidyanathan, "Fracking Can Contaminate Drinking Water," *Scientific American,* April 4, 2016 [**www.scientificamerican.com**]; Adam Vaughan, "Fracking Wells in the US Are Leaking Loads of Planet-Warming Methane," *New Scientist,* April 22, 2020 [**www.newscientist.com**]; Quirin Schiermeier, "Global Methane Levels Soar to Record High," *Nature,* July 14, 2020 [**www.nature.com**]; Jed Graham, "Is the U.S. Shale Boom Over? Four Major Threats to the Fracking Revolution," *Investors Business Daily,* March 6, 2020 [**www.investors.com**]; Clark Williams-Derry, Kathy Hipple, Tom Sanzillo, "Pandemic Accelerates Dismal Financial Performance of U.S. Fracking Companies," *Institute for Energy Economics and Financial Analysis,* September 2020 [**https://ieefa.org**]; "Worldwide Shale Gas Industry to 2025 - Increasing Environmental Concerns Expected to Restrain the Market," *GlobeNewswire,* September 11, 2020 [**www.globenewswire.com**]; Andrew Nikiforuk, "The Fracking Industry Is Hurting. Its Future Should Be an Election Issue," *Resilience,* October 6, 2020 [**www.resilience.org**]; and Stephen Leahy, "Fracking Boom Tied to Methane Spike in Earth's Atmosphere," *National Geographic,* August 15, 2019 [**www.nationalgeographic.com**].

Regulation of Air Pollution

In the United States, we depend on (and, indeed, we emotionally embrace) the automobile. In doing so, we have opened vistas of opportunity not previously imagined. However, motor vehicles also discharge carbon monoxide, nitrogen oxide, and hydrocarbons as by-products of the combustion of fuel, thus polluting our air. Today we know they are significant emitters of greenhouse gases. Industrial production, manufacturing, the generation of electricity, and the use of fossil fuels in homes and businesses for heat and air conditioning are also significant contributors to air pollution and greenhouse gases.

Clean Air Act of 1990

LO 17-6
Describe the uses of the Clean Air Act, including its application to greenhouse gas emissions.

Early clean air legislation in 1963 and 1965 afforded the government limited authority. The Clean Air Act (CAA) amendments of 1970 and 1977 gave the EPA the power to set air quality standards and to ensure that those standards are achieved according to a timetable prescribed by the agency. Politics brought clean air to the forefront in 1990, and the Clean Air Act of 1990 followed. It phased in new standards over a period of years, generally requiring tougher auto emission controls, cleaner-burning gasoline, and new equipment to capture industrial and commercial pollution, all directed at the general goal of reducing airborne pollutants by about 50 percent. Under the CAA, air quality standards are set federally, but the states are required to establish implementation plans to achieve and maintain those standards.

In recent years, there has been considerable high-profile litigation over clean air standards. The Supreme Court's decision in *Massachusetts v. EPA,* presented below, has had the most profound effect. In this case, a number of states, cities, and private organizations joined as petitioners to argue that the EPA had abdicated its responsibility under Section 202(a)(1) of the CAA to "prescribe . . . standards applicable to the emission of any air pollutant" when it refused to regulate greenhouse gas emissions from new motor vehicles.

Massachusetts v. Environmental Protection Agency

LEGAL BRIEFCASE

127 S. Ct. 1438 (2007)

Justice Stevens

A well-documented rise in global temperatures has coincided with a significant increase in the concentration of carbon dioxide in the atmosphere. Respected scientists believe the two trends are related. For when carbon dioxide is released into the atmosphere, it acts like the ceiling of a greenhouse, trapping solar energy and retarding the escape of reflected heat. It is therefore a species—the most important species—of a "greenhouse gas."

Calling global warming "the most pressing environmental challenge of our time," a group of states, local governments, and private organizations, alleged . . . [that the] EPA has abdicated its responsibility under the Clean Air Act to regulate the emissions of four greenhouse gases, including carbon dioxide. Specifically, petitioners asked us to answer two questions concerning . . . the Act: whether EPA has the statutory authority to regulate greenhouse gas emissions from new motor vehicles; and if so, whether its stated reasons for refusing to do so are consistent with the statute.

I

Section 202(a)(1) of the Clean Air Act . . . provides:

> The [EPA] Administrator shall by regulation prescribe (and from time to time revise) . . . standards applicable to the emission of any air pollutant from any class or classes of new motor vehicles or new motor vehicle engines, which in his judgment cause, or contribute to, air pollution which may reasonably be anticipated to endanger public health or welfare. . . .

The Act defines "air pollutant" to include "any air pollution agent or combination of such agents, including any physical, chemical, biological, radioactive . . . substance or matter which is emitted into or otherwise enters the ambient air." "Welfare" is also defined broadly: among other things, it includes "effects on . . . weather . . . and climate."

II

On October 20, 1999, a group of 19 private organizations filed a rulemaking petition asking EPA to regulate "greenhouse gas emissions from new motor vehicles under Section 202 of the Clean Air Act." . . . As to EPA's statutory authority, the petition observed that the agency itself had already confirmed that it had the power to regulate carbon dioxide. In 1998, Jonathan Z. Cannon, then EPA's General Counsel, prepared a legal opinion concluding that "CO[2] emissions are within the scope of EPA's authority to regulate," even as he recognized that EPA had so far declined to exercise that authority. Cannon's successor, Gary S. Guzy, reiterated that opinion before a congressional committee just two weeks before the rulemaking petition was filed.

On September 8, 2003, EPA entered an order denying the rulemaking petition. The agency gave two reasons for its decision: (1) that contrary to the opinions of its former general counsels, the Clean Air Act does not authorize EPA to issue mandatory regulations to address global climate change; and (2) that even if the agency had the authority to set greenhouse gas emission standards, it would be unwise to do so at this time.

Having reached that conclusion, EPA believed it followed that greenhouse gases cannot be "air pollutants" within the meaning of the Act. . . . The agency bolstered this conclusion by explaining that if carbon dioxide were an air pollutant, the only feasible method of reducing tailpipe emissions would be to improve fuel economy. But because Congress has already created detailed mandatory fuel economy standards subject to Department of Transportation (DOT) administration, the agency concluded that EPA regulation would either conflict with those standards or be superfluous.

Even assuming that it had authority over greenhouse gases, EPA explained in detail why it would refuse to exercise that authority. The agency began by recognizing that the concentration of greenhouse gases has dramatically increased as a result of human activities, and acknowledged the attendant increase in global surface air temperatures. EPA nevertheless gave controlling importance to the [National Resource Council] Report's statement that a causal link between the two cannot be unequivocally established. Given that residual uncertainty, EPA concluded that regulating greenhouse gas emissions would be unwise.

The agency furthermore characterized any EPA regulation of motor-vehicle emissions as a "piecemeal approach" to climate change and stated that such regulation would conflict with the president's "comprehensive approach" to the problem. That approach involves additional support for technological innovation, the creation of nonregulatory programs to encourage voluntary private-sector reductions in greenhouse gas emissions, and further research on climate change—not actual regulation. According to EPA, unilateral EPA regulation of motor-vehicle greenhouse gas emissions might also hamper the president's ability to persuade key developing countries to reduce greenhouse gas emissions.

V [III–IV OMITTED]

[We] "may reverse any such action found to be . . . arbitrary, capricious, an abuse of discretion, or otherwise not in accordance with law."

VI

On the merits, the first question is whether Section 202(a)(1) of the Clean Air Act authorizes EPA to regulate greenhouse gas emissions from new motor vehicles in the event that it forms a "judgment" that such emissions contribute to climate change. We have little trouble concluding that it does. . . .

The statutory text forecloses EPA's reading. The Clean Air Act's sweeping definition of "air pollutant" includes "*any* air pollution agent or combination of such agents, including *any* physical, chemical . . . substance or matter which is emitted into or otherwise enters the ambient air. . . ." On its face, the definition embraces all airborne compounds of whatever stripe, and underscores that intent through the repeated use of the word "any." Carbon dioxide, methane, nitrous oxide, and hydrofluorocarbons are without a doubt "physical [and] chemical . . . substance[s] which [are] emitted into . . . the ambient air." The statute is unambiguous.

EPA finally argues that it cannot regulate carbon dioxide emissions from motor vehicles because doing so would require it to tighten mileage standards, a job (according to EPA) that Congress has assigned to DOT. But that DOT sets mileage standards in no way licenses EPA to shirk its environmental responsibilities. EPA has been charged with protecting the public's "health" and "welfare," a statutory obligation wholly independent of DOT's mandate to promote energy efficiency. The two obligations may overlap, but there is no reason to think the two agencies cannot both administer their obligations and yet avoid inconsistency.

VII

The alternative basis for EPA's decision—that even if it does have statutory authority to regulate greenhouse gases, it would be unwise to do so at this time—rests on reasoning divorced from the statutory text. While the statute does condition the exercise of EPA's authority on its formation of a "judgment," that judgment must relate to whether an air pollutant "cause[s], or contribute[s] to, air pollution which may reasonably be anticipated to endanger public health or welfare." Put another way, the use of the word "judgment" is not a roving license to ignore the statutory text. It is but a direction to exercise discretion within defined statutory limits.

If EPA makes a finding of endangerment, the Clean Air Act requires the agency to regulate emissions of the deleterious pollutant from new motor vehicles. . . . EPA no doubt has significant latitude as to the manner, timing, content, and coordination of its regulations with those of other agencies. But once EPA has responded to a petition for rulemaking, its reasons for action or inaction must conform to the authorizing statute. Under the clear terms of the Clean Air Act, EPA can avoid taking further action only if it determines that greenhouse gases do not contribute to climate change or if it provides some reasonable explanation as to why it cannot or will not exercise its discretion to determine whether they do. To the extent that this constrains agency discretion to pursue other priorities of the administrator or the president, this is the congressional design.

EPA has refused to comply with this clear statutory command. Instead, it has offered a laundry list of reasons not to regulate. For example, EPA said that a number of voluntary executive branch programs already provide an effective response to the threat of global warming, that regulating greenhouse gases might impair the president's ability to negotiate with "key developing nations" to reduce emissions, and that curtailing motor-vehicle emissions would reflect "an inefficient, piecemeal approach to address the climate change issue."

Although we have neither the expertise nor the authority to evaluate these policy judgments, it is evident they have nothing to do with whether greenhouse gas emissions contribute to climate change. Still less do they amount to a reasoned justification for declining to form a scientific judgment. . . .

Nor can EPA avoid its statutory obligation by noting the uncertainty surrounding various features of climate change and concluding that it would therefore be better not to regulate at this time. If the scientific uncertainty is so profound that it precludes EPA from making a reasoned judgment as to whether greenhouse gases contribute to global warming, EPA must say so. That EPA would prefer not to regulate greenhouse gases because of some residual uncertainty . . . is irrelevant. The statutory question is whether sufficient information exists to make an endangerment finding.

In short, EPA has offered no reasoned explanation for its refusal to decide whether greenhouse gases cause or contribute to climate change. Its action was therefore "arbitrary, capricious, . . . or otherwise not in accordance with law." . . .

[Reversed and remanded.]

AFTERWORD

Despite the Court's 2007 ruling in *Massachusetts v. EPA*, it was not until President Obama took office in 2009 that the EPA ruled GHG emissions are pollutants which threaten public health. Built on the foundation of its initial endangerment finding, the EPA then promulgated rules establishing fuel economy and greenhouse gas emission standards for cars and light trucks covering model years 2012–2016, as well as a timetable for controlling GHG emissions from power plants and other stationary sources and targeting those controls to cover only the largest emitters. Quickly, the EPA found itself back in court with various industry groups and 14 states arguing, in part, that the EPA had impermissibly relied on scientific findings from the U.N. Intergovernmental Panel on Climate Change, the National Research Council, and the U.S. Global Change Research Program. In a sharply worded opinion, the federal Circuit Court for the District of Columbia ruled on June 26, 2012, that:

> [the] EPA had before it substantial record evidence that anthropogenic emissions of greenhouse gases "very likely" caused warming of the climate over the last several decades. . . . Relying again upon substantial scientific evidence, EPA determined that anthropogenically induced climate change threatens both public health and public welfare. It found that extreme weather events, changes in air quality, increases in food- and water-borne pathogens, and increases in temperatures are likely to have adverse health effects. The record also supports EPA's conclusion that climate change endangers human welfare by creating risk to food production and agriculture, forestry, energy, infrastructure, ecosystems, and wildlife. Substantial evidence further supported EPA's conclusion that the warming resulting from the greenhouse gas emissions could be expected to create risks to water resources and in general to coastal areas as a result of expected increase in sea level.[56]

The Supreme Court granted *certiorari* and, on June 23, 2014, held that the EPA could regulate GHG emissions from stationary sources that were already subject to regulation, based on their emissions of conventional pollutants.[57]

Questions

1. Under what conditions did the Supreme Court say it had the power to reverse the EPA's decision not to regulate the carbon dioxide emissions of new vehicles?
2. What did the petitioners, including the Commonwealth of Massachusetts, want the EPA to do?
3. The EPA said that, even if it had the authority to regulate greenhouse gas emissions from motor vehicles, it would not do so. What reasons did the EPA give for this refusal? What did the Supreme Court say about those reasons?
4. Following this decision of the Supreme Court, what was the EPA required to do? Was the EPA required to set a standard for greenhouse gas emissions from new vehicles?
5. Look back at the discussion about proving causation at the start of this Part Two. Did the Supreme Court say that greenhouse gas emissions from vehicles caused global warming? What did the Court observe about causation?

Greenhouse Gas Regulations

Although many have argued that no amount of GHG regulation will be as effective as a federal climate bill, Congress has thus far chosen not to act. The Obama Administration, however, made curbing GHG emissions through administrative rule-making a priority during his second term. Among other initiatives, it established national standards for carbon dioxide pollution from U.S. power plants, the largest source of carbon pollution in the country. The goal was a 30 percent reduction by 2030 in the level of carbon dioxide that existed in 2005. Under the Clean Power Plan, states could, but were not required to, include cap-and-trade arrangements in their initiatives to control plant emissions. Such arrangements would permit more efficient plants to sell their excess credits to less efficient plants, thereby allowing mandated reductions to be achieved as cost-effectively as possible for the state as a whole. Between 2008 and 2015, there was a 9.4 percent decrease in carbon emissions.[58] However, the EPA's repeal of the Clean Power Plan rules in December 2016, just one month before President Trump took office, reflected his campaign promise to reduce regulations on American industry even at the expense of climate change.[59] Significant cuts to the EPA's budget reflected the Trump Administration's view that "American energy policy must balance environmental protection with economic growth in order to encourage innovation, discovery, and prosperity."[60] In August 2019, a coalition of nearly 30 states and cities challenged the EPA's repeal of the Clean Power Rules.[61] However, litigation stalled as President Biden prepared to take office and another shift in environmental policy was all but certain. As of this writing, the EPA has proposed aggressive new rules setting greenhouse gas emission performance standards for power plants, old and new alike.[62]

Non-GHG Air Quality Regulations

Greenhouse gases are not the only air pollutants hazardous to health. A 2022 "report card" from the American Lung Association noted that more than 137 million Americans live in counties that exceeded standards set for ozone and particulates, and that 9 million more Americans were impacted by potentially deadly particle matter than in the year prior; people of color are disproportionately affected.[63] In recent years, the EPA has issued stricter standards governing pollutants such as ozone (a substantial contributor to smog), fine particulate matter (also known as soot, which can enter the lungs and bloodstream and cause respiratory and heart ailments), and sulfur dioxide (which contributes to acid rain and smog).

The EPA has attempted to address another persistent problem through its issuance of the Cross-State Air Pollution Rule (CSAPR): Air pollution traveling into downwind states often impairs their capacity to attain federally mandated air standards. However, implementation of the rule was delayed four years, until January 1, 2015, after nearly 40 separate petitioners, including cities, states, power companies, and various trade organizations, challenged the EPA's statutory authority in designing the rule's provisions. The Supreme Court upheld the EPA's authority in April 2014.[64] Once implemented, CSAPR required power plants in 28 states to install new pollution controls or buy pollution credits under a limited cap-and-trade system.[65]

In the years following its implementation, the EPA has faced multiple lawsuits from downwind states alleging its failure to act.[66] In a unanimous decision in October 2019, the D.C. Circuit Court of Appeals struck down an EPA rule after determining its guidelines for monitoring pollution crossing states lines were too lax and effectively absolved upwind states from effectuating air quality improvements.[67] In the meantime, price competition from abundant natural gas has significantly reduced the amount of power contributed by coal-fired plants in the United States. At its peak in 1988, coal provided 60 percent of our electricity; that dropped almost in half by 2012.[68] In 2019, it was less than 20 percent.[69]

Motor Vehicle Emission Standards

The total gallons of gas consumed annually in the United States decreased gradually from its peak in 2007 through 2012, due, in part, to the 2008 financial crisis, higher gas prices, and increased vehicle fuel efficiency. Consumption in 2012 was about six percent below the 2007 peak, roughly on par with usage in 2003.[70] While steadily increasing after 2012, it came to a crashing halt in spring 2020–down to levels not seen since 1968–with the onset of COVID-19 and the travel restrictions that ensued.[71] Although gasoline consumption has increased since the pandemic, it is expected to remain less than in 2019 through the end of 2024, in large part because of increased fuel economy.[72]

Under the Obama Administration, a fuel economy standard of 29 miles per gallon (MPG) was established for new vehicles in 2012 and was set to increase about five percent annually, up to 54.5 MPG for the 2025 model year. Express GHG auto emission standards were also implemented for the first time. Although these standards were supported by most major auto manufacturers, they were scaled back by the Trump Administration for model years 2021-2026, with a mandated annual increase in fuel economy of only 1.5 percent. Further, the EPA announced that it was withdrawing California's waiver (in place for half a century), which allowed the state to enact stricter fuel economy rules than the national standards. California, joined by 22 other states that elected to follow its standards, challenged the withdrawal of the waiver in court. However, under the Biden Administration, the U.S. Department of Transportation announced new Corporate Average Fuel Economy standards in 2022, requiring annual increases of 8-10% in fuel efficiency for model years 2024 through 2026 and an industry-wide fleet average of nearly 49 MPG for passenger cars and light trucks in model year 2026.[73] Also in 2022, the EPA reinstated California's waiver, allowing it to resume its Clean Car Program.[74]

Regulation of Water Pollution

As with the air, we often treat our water resources as free goods. Rather than paying the full cost of producing goods and services, we have simply dumped a portion of that cost into the nearest body of water. The results range from malodorous to dangerous to tragic. The evidence can be found not only in our local rivers and lakes, but also in our global gulfs, seas, and oceans.

BP's 2010 oil spill in the Gulf of Mexico has done, and will do, untold damage, but the waters of the Gulf before the spill were hardly pristine. Ninety percent of America's offshore drilling occurs there, drilling that has gone on for over 85 years and that provides tens of thousands of jobs. Since 1964, more than 300 spills releasing over a half-million barrels of oil have occurred, not to mention the thousands of tons of "produced water"–a by-product of drilling that includes oil, grease, and heavy metals–that are dumped annually. Of the approximate 82,000 oil and gas wells drilled in the Gulf of Mexico coastal waters of Louisianna, Texas, and Alabama, 14,000 are inactive and remain unplugged, increasing the environmental risks. However, plugging these wells would cost more than $30 billion.[75] In addition, the Gulf was even used by the government after World War II to dispose of surplus mines, bombs, and ammunition.[76]

"You can fool people, but you can't fool the fish."

The debris of our modern lives–including light bulbs, bottle caps, toothbrushes, and all manner of plastics–also shows up in our oceans.[77] In both the Atlantic and Pacific, "garbage patches" involving millions of square miles exist, composed primarily of microplastics broken down from larger items, but also including larger objects, such as those already mentioned. We have ample evidence of the consequences for fish and other aquatic life. As one observer who has worked on the Gulf his whole life noted: "You can fool people, but you can't fool the fish." [For more on the Great Pacific Garbage Patch, see **https://theoceancleanup.com/great-pacific-garbage-patch.**]

The Clean Water Act

LO 17-7
Describe the main purposes of the Clean Water Act.

The 1972 Clean Water Act (CWA), designed to "restore and maintain the chemical, physical, and biological integrity of the nation's waters," established two national goals: (1) achieving water quality sufficient for the protection and propagation of fish, shellfish, and wildlife and for recreation in and on the water; and (2) eliminating the discharge of pollutants into navigable waters. The case below is the first to apply *Massachusetts v. EPA* to the CWA but with, perhaps, a surprisingly different outcome. It underscores the fact that states have the primary responsibility for enforcing the CWA and that the EPA may assume enforcement authority at its sole discretion.

LEGAL BRIEFCASE

Gulf Restoration Network v. Jackson 2016 WL7241473 (E.D. La., December 15, 2016)

Judge Jay C. Zainey

I. BACKGROUND

Plaintiffs are various not-for-profit environmental organizations that strive to protect the environment. Plaintiffs filed this action to assert alleged violations of the Administrative Procedure Act ("APA") by the EPA. The lawsuit derives from EPA's July 29, 2011 denial of a rule-making petition that Plaintiffs filed with the agency.

A. THE PETITION

[H]igh levels of nitrogen and phosphorous pollution are devastating the Gulf of Mexico as evidenced by a large "dead zone" or "hypoxic zone" in the northern Gulf. . . . [T]he states in the Mississippi River Basin have no numeric water quality standards for phosphorous in rivers or streams or for nitrogen in any waters. And most states do not attempt to limit nitrogen and phosphorous discharges in [National Pollutant Discharge Elimination System] permits. Because the States do not sufficiently limit levels of nitrogen and phosphorous in their own waters, the Mississippi River is inundated with excess levels of harmful nitrogen and phosphorous, thereby leading to the "dead zone" near the mouth of the river.

The crux of the Petition is Plaintiffs' dissatisfaction with what they characterize as EPA's "hands-off approach" to dealing with the problem of nitrogen and phosphorus pollution in the United States. Acknowledging that the Clean Water Act assigns responsibility for such pollution control to the States in the first instance, Plaintiffs contend that most states to date have done little or nothing to meaningfully control the levels of nitrogen and phosphorous that pollute their waters, and that they have even less political will to protect downstream waters. Plaintiffs explain that over the years EPA has offered many plans and methods for addressing the nitrogen and phosphorous pollution problem but those plans have failed because they have never been backed by direct action by EPA. Recognizing that Congress gave EPA the authority to step in and address the nitrogen/phosphorus problem in light of the States' clear failure to do so, Plaintiffs requested under section 4 of the APA, 5 U.S.C. § 553(e), that EPA use its rulemaking powers to promulgate federal standards to control nitrogen and phosphorous pollution.

The rulemaking powers referenced in the Petition derive from § 303(c)(4) of the Clean Water Act ("CWA"), 33 U.S.C. § 1251, *et seq.* Section 303(c)(4) provides:

> The Administrator shall promptly prepare and publish proposed regulations setting forth a revised or new water quality standard for the navigable waters involved—
>
> (A) if a revised or new water quality standard submitted by such State under paragraph (3) of this subsection for such waters is determined by the Administrator not to be consistent with the applicable requirements of this chapter, or
>
> ***(B) in any case where the Administrator determines that a revised or new standard is necessary to meet the requirements of this chapter.***

33 U.S.C. § 1313(c)(4)(A), (B) (emphasis added).

Specifically, Plaintiffs urged EPA to invoke its rulemaking authority under § 303(c)(4)(B), the emphasized language above, to impose federal numeric water quality standards for the portion of the ocean protected by the CWA but outside the jurisdiction of any state and for all water bodies in all states for which numeric water quality standards controlling nitrogen and phosphorous pollution have not yet been established. Alternatively, Plaintiffs proposed that EPA do this for the Northern Gulf of Mexico and for all waters of the United States within the Mississippi River Basin. At a minimum, Plaintiffs urged EPA to establish water quality standards to control nitrogen and phosphorous pollution in the mainstem of the Mississippi River and the Northern Gulf of Mexico. Additionally, Plaintiffs urged EPA to establish TMDLs [Total Maximum Daily Loads] for nitrogen and phosphorous for the Gulf of Mexico, the Mississippi River, and each Mississippi River tributary that fails to meet the numeric standards set for nitrogen and phosphorous for which a TMDL had not already been prepared. At the least, Plaintiffs suggested that EPA should prepare a TMDL for nitrogen and for phosphorous for the mainstem of the Mississippi River and the Northern Gulf of Mexico.

B. EPA'S DENIAL

EPA issued its formal response ("the Denial") on July 29, 2011. . . . EPA neither determined that a new or revised standard was necessary—a threshold determination which would have triggered EPA's non-discretionary duty under § 303(c)(4)(B) to promulgate federal standards—nor determined that a new or revised standard was not necessary—a conclusion that might have been difficult to reconcile with the undisputed evidence demonstrating the significant and serious water quality problems caused by nitrogen and phosphorous pollution. Instead, EPA declined to make a "necessity determination," essentially deciding not to decide. *See Gulf Restoration Network,* 783 F.3d [227,] 238 n.61 [5th Cir. 2015].

C. THE COMPLAINT

. . . Plaintiffs requested that the Court declare that EPA's denial of the Petition was arbitrary, capricious, an abuse of discretion, or otherwise not in accordance with law in violation of the APA, 5 U.S.C. § 706(2)(A), and the CWA, 33 U.S.C. § 1313(c)(4)(B). . . .

D. THE COURT'S RULING

. . . [T]he Court concluded that the Supreme Court's [2007] decision in *Massachusetts v. Environmental Protection Agency* . . . precluded EPA from refusing to make a § 303(c)(4)(B) necessity determination in response to Plaintiffs' petition for rulemaking. . . . The Court rejected, however, Plaintiffs' contention that . . . EPA could not rely on non-scientific factors when making a necessity determination under § 303(c)(4)(B). . . . The Court declined to grant Plaintiffs' motion insofar as they sought to have the Court rule as a matter of law that a necessity determination under § 303(c)(4)(B) would be limited solely to scientific data. The Court remanded the matter to EPA. . . .

E. THE APPEAL

EPA appealed the Court's ruling. . . . As to the second question of whether EPA was required to make a necessity determination, in other words whether EPA had discretion under § 303(c)(4)(B) of the CWA to choose not to make a determination, the Fifth Circuit disagreed with the Court. The appellate court was convinced that *Massachusetts v. EPA* did not deprive EPA of discretion to decline to make a necessity determination so long as it provided a "reasonable explanation" grounded in the statute for why it had elected not to do so. The Fifth Circuit vacated the ruling, and remanded the case to have this Court decide in the first instance whether EPA's explanation for why it declined to make a necessity determination was legally sufficient. In doing so, the appellate court not only explained the proper way to apply the *Massachusetts v. EPA* decision but also provided several legal principles to guide this Court's next course of action.

II. DISCUSSION

This Court's task on remand is a narrow one: To determine whether EPA's explanation for why it refused to make a necessity determination was legally sufficient. Per the Fifth Circuit's application of *Massachusetts v. EPA,* legal sufficiency turns on whether EPA has provided a "reasonable explanation," which must be grounded in the statute, as to why it declined to make a necessity determination. In reviewing EPA's refusal to make a necessity determination, the Court applies the arbitrary and capricious standard of review set out in the APA. This standard will be "at the high end of the range of deference" in this case, which while dealing specifically with a refusal to make a threshold determination, is analogous to a refusal to initiate rulemaking. This Court's review is therefore "extremely limited," and must be "highly deferential." EPA's burden is "slight."

Turning to the Denial, EPA did not take issue with Plaintiffs' contentions regarding the significant and serious water quality problems caused by nitrogen and phosphorous pollution. But EPA disagreed that use of its federal rulemaking authority would be the most effective or practical means of addressing the nitrogen/phosphorous problem at this time. Instead, EPA explained that in its judgment the most effective and sustainable way to address widespread and pervasive nutrient pollution in the Mississippi-Atchafalaya River Basin ("MARB") and elsewhere would be to build on its earlier efforts and to continue to work cooperatively with states and tribes to strengthen nutrient management programs. EPA characterized Plaintiffs' proposed rulemaking solution as "unprecedented and complex" as well as "highly resource and time intensive." EPA explained that efforts to promulgate federal numeric nutrient criteria ("NNC") for 50, 31, or even 10 states at one time would involve EPA staff from across the entire agency, as well as support from technical experts outside the agency. Then after the daunting task of completing a rulemaking process of the magnitude proposed, EPA would be faced with sizable regulatory and oversight burdens. EPA summarized its position by stating that it did not believe that the use of its rulemaking authority, especially in light of the sweeping scope of the Petition, would be a practical or efficient way to address nutrient pollution on a national or regional scale.

[T]he Denial was grounded primarily on EPA's assessment that working in partnership with the States to reduce nutrient pollution would be a more effective approach at present. In other words, EPA was not ready to give up on the cooperative states-first model upon which the CWA is based. EPA gave a thorough explanation as to why the agency believed that federal rulemaking would not be the most efficacious approach to the nitrogen/phosphorous problem. EPA also explained the non-rulemaking programs that it was implementing to address the problem with the states. EPA did not deny that rulemaking may become necessary at some point if continued efforts at the cooperative approach either fail to improve current water quality conditions appreciably or conditions worsen. EPA did explain the administrative burdens associated with the rulemaking that Plaintiffs were proposing but this explanation was given in light of the sweeping nature of the rulemaking that Plaintiffs were requesting.

The question then is whether the reasons given in the Denial are sufficiently "grounded in the statute" to pass muster as a "reasonable explanation" for EPA's refusal to render a necessity determination. The parties have opposite views as to what constitutes an explanation "grounded in the statute."

Plaintiffs argue that EPA's reasons for refusing to make a necessity determination—as provided in the Denial—are not "grounded in the statute," and reflect the very type of alternative policy arguments that the Supreme Court found unacceptable in *Massachusetts v. EPA*. Plaintiffs characterize the Denial as a "laundry list of reasons not to regulate," that like the unacceptable reasons at issue in *Massachusetts v. EPA*, reflect EPA's own policy preferences rather than the requirements of the CWA. Plaintiffs contend that the Fifth Circuit's opinion on appeal demonstrates that an explanation "grounded in the statute" must include the specific statutory and regulatory requirements of the CWA, which are incorporated by reference into § 303(c)(4)(B). Plaintiffs posit that the strongest evidence that the Denial is not "grounded in the statute" is that it barely mentions the law at all, and omits any analysis of how the specific statutory and regulatory "requirements" of the CWA informed EPA's decision.

EPA, on the other hand, argues that Plaintiffs' position reflects a far more demanding standard than what either *Massachusetts v. EPA* or the Fifth Circuit's opinion in this case requires. EPA contends that the type of detailed scientific and technical analysis that Plaintiffs want is more akin to what is required when EPA actually makes a necessity determination one way or the other. EPA argues that Plaintiffs are misreading the Fifth Circuit's opinion when they argue that the appellate court's discussion of the specific statutory requirements of the CWA—a discussion that was held to determine judicial reviewability—dictates the content of what a reasonable explanation "grounded in the statute" must contain.

This Court is convinced that the Denial, which again is grounded primarily on EPA's assessment that working in partnership with the States to reduce nutrient pollution would be a more effective approach at present, is sufficiently "grounded in the statute." Section 303(c)(4)(B) draws upon the entire body of the CWA, which itself is a broadly-worded statutory scheme. And as the Court previously explained, the CWA is by design a states-in-the-first-instance regulatory scheme. *See* 33 U.S.C. § 1251(b) ("It is the policy of Congress to recognize, preserve, and protect **the primary responsibilities and rights of States** to prevent, reduce, and eliminate pollution . . . and to consult with the Administrator in the exercise of his authority under this chapter.") (emphasis added). Under the CWA the States are charged with adopting water quality standards for their territorial waters, and EPA exercises oversight, stepping in only when the states demonstrate that they either cannot or will not comply. With the CWA the federal role is properly characterized as a secondary or backstop role. Focusing more narrowly on § 1313 to Title 33 or § 303 of the Act, the primacy of the States' role permeates the text. As a matter of law, the Denial is not based on reasons divorced from the statutory text of the CWA.

Plaintiffs argue that the Denial is deficient because it does not address the specific statutory considerations that the Fifth Circuit identified in its opinion as those that EPA must consider when it declines to make a necessity determination. *Gulf Restoration,* 783 F.3d at 240. The Court disagrees with this characterization of the Denial. As EPA detailed in its brief, the Denial and in particular the substance of EPA's Framework Memo, which is referenced in the Denial, demonstrates that EPA did consider the text of both § 303 and the CWA as a whole when formulating its partnership strategy with the States. A reasonable explanation grounded in a statute need not necessarily contain a verbatim recitation of a statute or parse its provisions to the letter.

Furthermore, *Massachusetts v. EPA* does not preclude EPA from relying on policy grounds in the Denial, only those without clear textual support in the statute. The "policy" of partnering with the States and maintaining a states-in-the-first-instance approach is not an alternative policy as was the case in *Massachusetts v. EPA* but rather is an integral part of the CWA as enacted by Congress. And as the Court previously explained, *Massachusetts v. EPA* does not stand for the broad proposition that every discretionary EPA determination that serves as a restraint or hurdle to federal action must be based on scientific data.

Of course, what Plaintiffs really question in this case is whether EPA's *continued* reliance on the CWA's states-first approach is reasonable in light of the undisputed scientific data surrounding the serious nature of the nitrogen and phosphorous pollution in the nation's waters. According to Plaintiffs, the state-driven approach upon which the CWA is built is simply not working and the scientific data proves it. Even if the Court were to disagree with EPA's stance on rulemaking the Court cannot properly substitute its own judgment for that of the agency. EPA's assessment that the best approach at this time is to continue in its comprehensive strategy of bringing the States along without the use of federal rule making is subject to the highly deferential and limited review that the Fifth Circuit described in its opinion. Presumably, there is a point in time at which the agency will have abused its great discretion by refusing to concede that the current approach—albeit the one of first choice under the CWA—is simply not going to work. But for now, Plaintiffs have not demonstrated that EPA's assessment was arbitrary, capricious, or contrary to law. EPA is entitled to judgment as a matter of law in its favor.

Accordingly, and for the foregoing reasons;

IT IS ORDERED that the **Motion for Summary Judgment** filed by Plaintiffs is **DENIED;**

IT IS FURTHER ORDERED that the **Cross Motion for Summary Judgment** filed by defendants Gina McCarthy, Administrator, and the United States Environmental Protection Agency is **GRANTED.** Judgment will be entered in favor of Defendants.

Questions

1. What did the plaintiffs want the EPA to do?
2. Did the EPA disagree with plaintiffs about the "significant and serious water quality problems" in the Mississippi River and the Northern Gulf of Mexico? Did it determine that a new or revised standard was necessary—or not necessary—to control the pollution? What exactly did it decide?
3. What reasons did the EPA give for refusing to use its federal rule making authority under the CWA to address the water quality problems at issue?
4. What narrow determination was the court tasked with making? How was *Massachusetts v. EPA* applied? What standard did the court use to evaluate whether the EPA's explanation was legally sufficient regarding its failure to make a necessity determination under the CWA? Did the court rule that the EPA's explanation was sufficiently grounded in the CWA statute? What was the court's reasoning?
5. What did the court ultimately rule? Is the court's decision consistent with the Supreme Court's ruling in *Massachusetts v. EPA*? Does the EPA's responsibility to regulate greenhouse gas emissions under the Clean Air Act differ from its responsibility to regulate pollution under the CWA? Explain.

There is no doubt the CWA has resulted in enormous improvements, but there are problems as well. The EPA conducts national surveys to evaluate water quality, sediment quality, coastal habitats, and fish-tissue contaminants. Its 2012 report rated the West Coast as fair to good; the Northeast, Southeast, and Gulf coasts as fair; and the Great Lakes as poor.[78] Yet there appears to be a decreasing trend in enforcement actions in the Great Lakes region since 2016, and an increasing number of facilities in the area in significant noncompliance with the CWA since 2017.[79]

Ideally, the goals of the CWA are implemented primarily by imposing limits on the amount of pollutants that may lawfully enter U.S. waters from any "point source" (typically a pipe). The National Pollutant Discharge Elimination System (NPDES) requires all dischargers to secure a permit, most often from the EPA, but at times from some other government agency, before pouring effluent into a navigable stream. The permit specifies maximum permissible levels of effluent and typically also mandates the use of a particular pollution control process or device to ensure that level is not exceeded. It also requires the permit holder to monitor its own performance and report the results to the state or the EPA. This allows the EPA to take effective action. For instance, the Justice Department and the EPA reached a settlement in 2017 with the Potomac Electric Power Company, which allegedly violated its CWA permit by exceeding the limit on certain metals and other pollutants allowed to enter its storm water drainage system. The storm drainage system empties into a major tributary to the Potomac River, which ultimately flows to the Chesapeake Bay. The company agreed to pay a civil penalty of $1.6 million, undertake a mitigation project at its plant, and implement "Best Management Practices."[80]

> In the Gulf, there is a dead zone the size of Massachusetts.

But regulation of point sources leaves many pollutants unmonitored. Surface water runoff is polluted with our lawn fertilizer, pet waste, and grease and oil from vehicles. Despite rules that were established in 1999, surface water is also polluted by runoff from large row crop, hog, cattle, and poultry farms. Nitrogen from fertilizers finds its way into the Mississippi River from sources hundreds of miles from the Gulf–1.5 million tons of it yearly. As a result, there was a dead zone in the Gulf in which little life could exist, that 10 years ago was larger in size than Connecticut.[81] Today, that dead zone is estimated to be the size of the land mass of Massachusetts.[82]

Discouragingly, even point sources covered by the NPDES violate the terms of their permits, often with impunity. *The New York Times* published an in-depth series of articles over the fall of 2009 through the first quarter of 2010 based on records received in response to Freedom of Information Act requests made to every state and the EPA. In them, journalist Charles Duhigg presented an alarming picture of CWA violations rising steadily across the nation affecting drinking water from municipal and other sources. Many violations were relatively minor, but about 60 percent were deemed to be in "significant noncompliance." Fewer than three percent resulted in fines or other substantial punishment. Some, but not all, of the rise was attributable to insufficient enforcement resources. The number of regulated facilities more than doubled in a 10-year span, but state enforcement budgets remained essentially flat. The EPA made promises to regulate the discharge of such toxic substances as arsenic, lead, and cadmium, but has never done so. [To read the articles in this series, go to **www.nytimes.com/toxicwaters**.]

LO 17-8
Explain the meaning and purpose of the term *navigable waters* and the scope of *covered waters* under the CWA.

Covered Waters

Decades after CWA enactment, it remains unclear exactly what waters are actually covered by the act and therefore subject to EPA regulation. In the 2001 *Northern Cook County* case that follows, the Supreme Court looked at what qualifies as "navigable waters" for purposes of the CWA. Only a bare majority (five) of the justices agreed with this decision; the remaining four dissented. In 2006 and 2023, the Supreme Court once again considered the scope of covered waters under the CWA. Those decisions will be discussed in the Afterword at the end of the case.

Solid Waste Agency of Northern Cook County v. U.S. Army Corps of Engineers 531 U.S. 159 (2001)

Chief Justice Rehnquist

Section 404(a) of the Clean Water Act (CWA or Act) regulates the discharge of dredged or fill material into "navigable waters." The United States Army Corps of Engineers (Corps) has interpreted Section 404(a) to confer federal authority over an abandoned sand and gravel pit in northern Illinois that provides habitat for migratory birds. We are asked to decide whether the provisions of Section 404(a) may be fairly extended to these waters, and, if so, whether Congress could exercise such authority consistent with the Commerce Clause. We answer the first question in the negative and therefore do not reach the second.

Petitioner, the Solid Waste Agency of Northern Cook County (SWANCC), is a consortium of 23 suburban Chicago cities and villages that united in an effort to locate and develop a disposal site for baled nonhazardous solid waste. The Chicago Gravel Company informed the municipalities of the availability of a 533-acre parcel, . . . which had been the site of a sand and gravel pit mining operation for three decades up until about 1960. Long since abandoned, the old mining site eventually gave way to a successional stage forest, with its remnant excavation trenches evolving into a scattering of permanent and seasonal ponds of varying size (from under one-tenth of an acre to several acres) and depth (from several inches to several feet).

The municipalities decided to purchase the site. . . .

Section 404(a) grants the Corps authority to issue permits "for the discharge of dredged or fill material into the navigable waters at specified disposal sites." The term "navigable waters" is defined under the Act as "the waters of the United States, including the territorial seas." The Corps has issued regulations defining the term "waters of the United States" to include

> waters such as intrastate lakes, rivers, streams (including intermittent streams), mudflats, sandflats, wetlands, sloughs, prairie potholes, wet meadows, playa lakes, or natural ponds, the use, degradation or destruction of which could affect interstate or foreign commerce. . . .

In 1986, in an attempt to "clarify" the reach of its jurisdiction, the Corps stated that Section 404(a) extends to intrastate waters:

a. Which are or would be used as habitat by birds protected by Migratory Bird Treaties; or

b. Which are or would be used as habitat by other migratory birds which cross state lines; or

c. Which are or would be used as habitat for endangered species; or

d. Used to irrigate crops sold in interstate commerce.

This last promulgation has been dubbed the "Migratory Bird Rule."

The Corps initially concluded that it had no jurisdiction over the site. . . . However, after the Illinois Nature Preserves Commission informed the Corps that a number of migratory bird species had been observed at the site, the Corps reconsidered and ultimately asserted jurisdiction over the balefill site pursuant to subpart (b) of the "Migratory Bird Rule." The Corps found that approximately 121 bird species had been observed at the site, including several known to depend upon aquatic environments for a significant portion of their life requirements. . . .

[The] Corps refused to issue a Section 404(a) permit. The Corps found that SWANCC had not established that its proposal was the "least environmentally damaging, most practicable alternative" for disposal of nonhazardous solid waste; that SWANCC's failure to set aside sufficient funds to remediate leaks posed an "unacceptable risk to the public's drinking water supply"; and that the impact of the project upon area-sensitive species was "unmitigatable since a landfill surface cannot be redeveloped into a forested habitat."

Petitioner filed suit. . . . Petitioner argued that respondents had exceeded their statutory authority in interpreting the CWA to cover nonnavigable, isolated, intrastate waters based upon the presence of migratory birds. . . .

The Court of Appeals [held] that respondents' "Migratory Bird Rule" was a reasonable interpretation of the Act.

We granted certiorari. . . .

Congress passed the CWA for the stated purpose of "restoring and maintaining the chemical, physical, and biological integrity of the Nation's waters." In so doing, Congress chose to "recognize, preserve, and protect the primary responsibilities and rights of States to prevent, reduce, and eliminate pollution, to plan the development and use (including restoration, preservation, and enhancement) of land and water resources, and to consult with the Administrator in the exercise of his authority under this chapter." Relevant here, Section 404(a) authorizes respondents to regulate the discharge of fill material into "navigable waters," which the statute defines as "the waters of the United States, including the territorial seas." Respondents have interpreted these words to cover the abandoned gravel pit at issue here because it is used as habitat for migratory birds. We conclude that the "Migratory Bird Rule" is not fairly supported by the CWA.

This is not the first time we have been called upon to evaluate the meaning of Section 404(a). In *United States v. Riverside Bayview Homes, Inc.*, 474 U.S. 121 (1985), we held that the Corps had Section 404(a) jurisdiction over wetlands that actually abutted on a navigable waterway. In so doing, we noted that the term "navigable" is of "limited import" and that Congress evidenced its intent to "regulate at least some waters that would not be deemed 'navigable' under the classical understanding of that term." But our holding was based in large measure upon Congress' unequivocal acquiescence to, and approval of, the Corps' regulations interpreting the CWA to cover wetlands adjacent to navigable waters. We found that Congress' concern for the protection of water quality and aquatic ecosystems indicated its intent to regulate wetlands "inseparably bound up with the 'waters' of the United States."

It was the significant nexus between the wetlands and "navigable waters" that informed our reading of the CWA in *Riverside Bayview Homes*. . . . In order to rule for respondents here, we would have to hold that the jurisdiction of the Corps extends to ponds that are *not* adjacent to open water. But we conclude that the text of the statute will not allow this.

Indeed, the Corps' *original* interpretation of the CWA, promulgated two years after its enactment, is inconsistent with that which it espouses here. Its 1974 regulations defined Section 404(a)'s "navigable waters" to mean "those waters of the United States which are subject to the ebb and flow of the tide, and/or are presently, or have been in the past, or may be in the future susceptible for use for purposes of interstate or foreign commerce." The Corps emphasized that "it is the water body's capability of use by the public for purposes of transportation or commerce which is the determinative factor." Respondents put forward no persuasive evidence that the Corps mistook Congress' intent in 1974.

We hold that [the regulations], as clarified and applied to petitioner's balefill site pursuant to the "Migratory Bird Rule," [exceed] the authority granted to respondents under Section 404(a) of the CWA. The judgment of the Court of Appeals for the Seventh Circuit is therefore

Reversed.

Questions

1. Summarize the arguments made by the Army Corps of Engineers for finding that the government had the power to regulate this site under the CWA.
2. Explain the Supreme Court's response to each of the Army Corps of Engineers' arguments previously identified.
3. Did the Supreme Court hold that the government could not regulate this type of site or only that Congress had not in fact sought to extend its regulation to this type of site?
4. In your view, should the federal government be able to regulate bodies of water that are of significant use by migratory birds? Explain.

AFTERWORD

In the *Northern Cook County* case, the Supreme Court evaluated a regulation of the Army Corps of Engineers and determined that the Corps exceeded its scope of authority under the CWA. All nine justices agreed that the term "navigable waters" should be interpreted more broadly than its literal meaning, but only four of the justices would have approved the Corps' expansive reading of the statute.

In the 2006 case *Repanos v. United States,* the Supreme Court again reviewed the term "navigable waters."[83] The same four justices dissented, arguing that the revised, but still broad authority asserted by the Corps was permissible under the statute. This time, however, the remaining five justices did not agree on the reach of the CWA, but only agreed that the Corps was still asserting an authority broader than allowable. The result was that the case was remanded for "further proceedings" but without a standard on which to base those proceedings. The bottom line was that the government was required once again to define the scope of its regulatory authority.

In 2023, the Supreme Court delivered a huge blow to the agency in *Sackett v. EPA,* severely limiting its ability to regulate wetlands.[84] Five conservative justices rejected the EPA's test that protected those wetlands having a "significant nexus" to nearby protected waters, affecting their chemical, biological, and physical integrity. The new test, the Court held, extends the CWA to only those wetlands with a surface continuously connected to bodies of water that are protected in their own right, making it difficult to determine where one begins and the other ends. In her dissent, Justice Elena Kagan blasted the Court's "vice" in appointing itself "the national decision-maker on environmental policy." Justice Brett Kavanaugh also dissented along with the Court's four liberal justices, writing that this new test "departs from the statutory text, from 45 years of consistent agency practice, and from this Court's precedents" and will have "significant repercussions for water quality and flood control throughout the United States."

Even before the Supreme Court's ruling in 2023, enforcement under the CWA was already substantially hampered. "In drier states, some polluters say the act no longer applies to them and are therefore refusing to renew or apply for permits, making it impossible to monitor what they are dumping." A case in point: Cannon Air Force Base in New Mexico informed the EPA that it "no longer considers itself subject to the act." According to *The New York Times,* it "dumps wastewater—containing bacteria and human sewage—into a lake on the base."[85]

In May 2015, the Obama administration announced a new administrative rule that expanded the scope of the EPA's reach to waters beyond those that are "navigable." The new Waters of the United States Rule (or "Clean Water Rule") met with opposition from many industry leaders. In October 2015, the U.S. Court of Appeals for the Sixth Circuit stayed the Clean Water Rule nationwide pending further action of the court. In addition, the day that President Trump was sworn into office, the White House website indicated that Trump was committed to "eliminating harmful and unnecessary policies such as . . . the Waters of the US Rule."[86] In September 2019, the EPA and the U.S. Army followed through on Trump's promise, announcing they had finalized a new rule, repealing the 2015 Clean Water Rule and re-codifying the regulatory scheme that previously existed.

Regulation of Land Pollution

Pollution does not fit into separate, tidy compartments (air, water, land) as might seemingly be suggested by the earlier sections of this chapter. Acid rain debases not only air and water, but also the fruits of the earth, such as our fish and trees. Land pollution likewise seeps into the soil and contaminates our groundwater, harming both plants and animals. This section addresses the laws governing land pollution and, more specifically, how we dispose of waste–solid, hazardous, and toxic.

LO 17-9 Identify some of the major federal laws that address land pollution.

Toxic Substances Control Act

Because our disposal laws vary based on the classification of the materials being disposed, the primary law governing classification is a good place to start. In 1976, Congress approved the Toxic Substances Control Act (TSCA) to identify toxic chemicals and assess their risks and to control dangerous chemicals. Under the terms of TSCA, the EPA is empowered to review and to limit or stop the introduction of new chemicals. Companies must notify the EPA before manufacturing or importing new industrial chemicals, but they need not provide any safety data unless the data they have suggest the substance poses a "substantial risk." The EPA has only 90 days to block the chemical, and it can only suspend the review and request company data if it can show a potential risk from the chemical.

The structure of TSCA results in a "safe until proven dangerous" presumption. Only a small fraction of the 85,000 industrial chemicals in use today have been tested for safety.[87] Some that have been tested, such as formaldehyde, are still widely used in a large range of products–from nail polish and hair straighteners to many building materials. The Department of Health and Human Services identified formaldehyde as a known carcinogen in June 2011, but as of this writing, the EPA has it listed as a "probable human carcinogen."[88] Perhaps more disconcerting, the names and physical properties of nearly 20 percent of the chemicals in use are secret from all but a handful of EPA employees, who are required by law to protect the trade secrets of the manufacturers.[89] That protection prohibits disclosure to other federal officials, state health and environmental regulators, and physicians, as well as the public. Although many of these unknown chemicals are likely harmless, in just one month "more than half of the 65 'substantial risk' reports filed" with the EPA by manufacturers "involved secret chemicals." Essentially, we have been withholding information about the potential risks in exchange for "ensuring the long-term competitiveness of the U.S. [chemical] industry."[90]

Congress responded to these concerns by enacting the landmark "Frank R. Lautenberg Chemical Safety for the 21st Century Act," which was signed into law in June 2016 with broad bipartisan support. It reforms the "badly broken" TCSA and focuses on offering greater protection to the public and to the environment from dangerous chemicals.[91] This includes increased transparency with the public about chemical information. In November 2016, the EPA announced ahead of schedule the first 10 chemicals–including asbestos–that it would review for potential risks in accordance with the new law. Although "there is ample evidence linking these chemicals to cancer and other severe health problems, they have been on the market largely unchecked and unregulated for decades."[92] As soon as it completes its review of a potentially dangerous chemical, the EPA must begin reviewing another. By the end of 2019, it must have 20 reviews underway at any given time. The law also calls on the Centers for Disease Control and Prevention to investigate and respond to cancer clusters and to improve communication among various government agencies. [For more about the TSCA and the Chemical Safety for the 21st Century Act, see **www.epa.gov**.]

Pollution in the Movies

Perhaps surprisingly, toxic pollution has provided the central theme in three major Hollywood movies: *Dark Waters, Erin Brockovich,* and *A Civil Action.* The 2019 movie *Dark Waters,* starring Mark Ruffalo, tells the true story of a lawyer's courageous battle against Dupont after discovering that it contaminated an Ohio town with dangerous chemicals used to make Teflon nonstick cooking surfaces. [For more information on perfluorooctanoic acid, one of the chemicals used to make Teflon, see **www.cdc.gov/biomonitoring/PFOA_FactSheet.html.**] [For movie trailer, see **www.youtube.com/watch?v=RvAOuhyunhY.**]

The 2000 movie *Erin Brockovich,* starring Julia Roberts, tells the true story of a California community's battle against Pacific Gas & Electric after it caused groundwater pollution that resulted in extensive illness. [For more information on hexavalent chromium, the carcinogen at issue in the movie, see **www.cdc.gov/niosh/topics/hexchrom**]. [For the movie trailer, see **www.youtube.com/watch?v=jjqUUxIy_yk.**]

In the 1998 Disney movie, *A Civil Action,* John Travolta depicted a plaintiff's lawyer in a true story in which several middle-class families sued two corporate giants, Beatrice Food and W. R. Grace & Co., for allegedly polluting the groundwater in East Woburn, Massachusetts, where eight children died of leukemia. A jury found Beatrice Foods not liable, while W.R. Grace settled with the plaintiffs for $8 million. [For more information on this specific pollutant, trichloroethylene, see **Trichloroethylene | Toxzine | ATSDR (cdc.gov).**] [For movie trailer, see **www.youtube.com/watch?v=fHRXGQhpib8.**]

Question

Look back at the discussion about proving causation at the start of Part Two. Using that terminology, describe the causation issues that had to be addressed in the real-life counterparts to these movies.

Resource Conservation and Recovery Act

By 1976, the dangers of hazardous substances were becoming apparent to all, and Congress complemented the TSCA with the Resource Conservation and Recovery Act (RCRA). The act addresses both nonhazardous and hazardous solid wastes. Its provisions for nonhazardous wastes are more supportive than punitive, in tone and approach. The federal government is authorized, among other strategies, to provide technical and financial assistance to states and localities, prohibit future open dumping, and establish cooperative federal, state, local, and private-enterprise programs to recover energy and valuable materials from solid waste.

Subtitle C of the RCRA is designed to ensure the safe movement and disposal of hazardous solid wastes. The generator of the waste must determine if that waste is hazardous under EPA guidelines. If that is the case, the waste generator must then create a manifest to be used in tracking the waste from its creation to its disposal. Along the cradle-to-grave path, all those with responsibility for it must sign the manifest and safely store and transport the waste. Once the waste reaches a licensed disposal facility, the owner or manager of that site must sign the manifest and return a copy of it to the generator. Disposal sites must be operated according to EPA standards, and remedial action must be taken should hazardous wastes escape from the sites. [For more information, see the EPA website at **Learn the Basics of Hazardous Waste | US EPA.**]

For cradle-to-grave tracking to apply, one preliminary statutory requirement is that the material must be "discarded" to qualify as waste. The U.S. Court of Appeals for the District of Columbia ruled that "discarded" means "disposed of," "abandoned," or "thrown away," and it has repeatedly held various versions of the EPA's rules as being overly broad because they improperly covered recycling practices when the materials were not discarded within the meaning of the statute.[93] Thus, recycled hazardous materials are not covered by RCRA, although they may be subject to other EPA regulations.[94]

Household Recycling

Our lifestyles result in mountains of waste that grow higher every year. On average, each of us produces 4.9 pounds of municipal solid waste everyday.[95] Of course, we pay an immediate price to dispose of all of that waste, but what risk does it pose to public health and safety? To the environment? Even state-of-the-art landfills can leak, with the result that toxic elements can enter our groundwater. Seventy percent of the toxic waste in our landfills comes from electronics (e-waste). The United States is the only industrialized country that has not ratified the Basel Convention, a treaty prohibiting exporting or trafficking in toxic e-waste, because it does not have the statutory authority to implement all its provisions. A part of the solution, of course, is to "reduce, reuse, recycle."

Seventy percent of the toxic waste in our landfills comes from electronics.

Recycling turns materials that would otherwise become waste into usable resources which can reduce dependence on new materials, thereby reducing deforestation, for example. It is now cheaper to recycle an aluminum can than it is to make one from new materials. The same is true of plastic bottles.[96] The EPA reports that more than 94 million tons of solid waste material were recycled and composted in 2018, equivalent to a 32.1 percent recycling rate, down from 35 percent in 2017.[97]

Increasingly, large food and beverage companies in the United States have voluntarily taken on the costs of recycling the consumer packaging of their goods, a process known as "extended producer responsibility." (In contrast, Europe has required packaged goods companies to take financial responsibility for package recycling for many years.) For instance, Coca-Cola has implemented recycling programs around the globe and is increasing the use of a first-ever fully recyclable lightweight PET bottle made partially from plants, which significantly cuts down the use of oil and carbon dioxide emissions.[98] And to help reach the company's goal of reducing waste by 50 percent by 2030, Starbucks is piloting a program that will allow every customer in the United States and Canada their own reusable cup at every visit. Their objective is to create a culture movement by 2025 toward reusables.[99]

Superfund—Comprehensive Environmental Response, Compensation, and Liability Act of 1980

LO 17-10
Discuss the purpose and effect of the Comprehensive Environmental Response, Compensation, and Liability Act of 1980, commonly known as "the Superfund."

The Comprehensive Environmental Response, Compensation, and Liability Act of 1980 (CERCLA), more commonly known as the Superfund, was enacted for the purpose of identifying and cleaning up abandoned hazardous waste sites. The process involves the assessment and ranking of proposed sites, followed by the development and implementation of cleanup plans for sites added to the National Priorities List. Cleanups may be carried out by the EPA or private parties, either of which may seek reimbursement of costs from those liable under CERCLA. Potentially responsible parties (PRPs) include present owners of the site as well as past owners who operated the site when the hazardous wastes were deposited; parent firms can be liable for the actions of subsidiaries; and transferors (successive owners of businesses discharging hazardous wastes) are also liable. Any parties found to be responsible are strictly liable–that is, liability attaches without proof of either intent or negligence.

Cleanup tends to be very expensive and generally requires considerable time to accomplish. The first listed Superfund site, Love Canal in Niagara Falls, New York, was finally clean enough to be delisted in 2004.[100] Originally, cleanup costs were paid from a trust fund created by taxes on chemicals and petroleum, but that taxing authority lapsed in 1995. At that point, the Superfund program was run on annual appropriations and reserve funds. In recent years, funding has come primarily from PRPs and funds are kept in site-specific, interest-bearing accounts. About $8.5 billion of deposited funds and interest from PRP settlements has been made available for Superfund site cleanups; $3.5 billion of it remains for ongoing or future site cleanup.[101] As of April 2023, there were 40 proposed new Superfund sites and 1,336 sites already on the national priorities list; only 453 sites had been delisted.[102]

> Any parties found to be responsible are strictly liable.

The Biggest Nuclear Waste Hazard in the Western World

Forty years after the passage of CERCLA, some of the country's most hazardous sites remain toxic. Until the earthquake and tsunami in Japan, the biggest nuclear waste hazard in the Western world was located in southeast Washington–the Hanford nuclear facility, a 586-square-mile site constructed as part of the Manhattan project to produce weapons-grade plutonium in nine nuclear reactors along the banks of the Columbia River. As of this writing, the highly toxic waste is still being stored in underground tanks, although it is being moved from single-shell tanks to double-shell tanks. The Waste Treatment and Immobilization Plant, which is currently under construction, will turn the waste into glass, which will then be stored in high-grade stainless steel casks. While the glass will still be radioactive, it will no longer be able to pollute air, water, or soil.[103] [For more information, about the Hanford cleanup efforts, see **https://ecology.wa.gov/Waste-Toxics/Nuclear-waste/Hanford-cleanup**.]

Question

Visit the following EPA site: **www.epa.gov/superfund/search-superfund-sites-where-you-live.** Do any Superfund sites exist in or near your community?

PRACTICING ETHICS Environmentally Aware Decision Making

Imagine you have just been hired as the business manager for a chain of restaurants in your state. During the interview process, you were told that part of your responsibilities would be to develop more environmentally friendly practices to be implemented at all 10 locations, while making sure that the changes overall have either a neutral or a positive impact on the business's bottom line. A local business school professor is interested in having her students do semester-long service learning projects on the feasibility of various green projects for local businesses. Develop a list of possible practices your restaurants could implement to share with the professor for further development by her students.

Small Business Liability Relief and Brownfields Revitalization Act

There has been considerable dissatisfaction over CERCLA over the years for a number of reasons, including the percentage of Superfund dollars that have gone to administration expenses and litigation, as well as the slow remediation process at most sites. Worried about liability risks, developers were often reluctant to buy and improve brownfield sites, which are sites not currently in use, but previously used or developed with known or suspected soil contamination from hazardous waste. The problem was alleviated with the passage of the 2002 Small Business Liability Relief and Brownfields Revitalization Act, which provides liability protection for prospective purchasers and contiguous property owners and authorizes increased funding for state and local programs that assess and clean up brownfields. [For more on brownfields, see **https://www.epa.gov/brownfields**.]

Part Three—Penalties and Enforcement under Federal Law

LO-17-11 Identify the penalties and other enforcement mechanisms available under federal regulations.

Many environmental statutes require companies to monitor their own environmental performance and report that information, including violations, to the government (although, as noted in our discussion of the Clean Water Act, such disclosure does not necessarily lead to any form of corrective or enforcement action). Government agencies also have broad authority to conduct environmental inspections of plants and company records as necessary, but they must obtain search warrants if criminal prosecutions are anticipated.

A broad range of enforcement actions is available to both state and federal agencies. Often, violators initially receive a simple warning, and a compliance schedule may be prescribed. If corrective action is not forthcoming, sterner measures may follow, including an administrative order to comply. Such orders are somewhat less effective now, given the Supreme Court's 2012 decision in *Sackett v. EPA*[104] and its 2016 decision in *U.S. Army Corps of Engineers v. Hawkes Co.*[105] In *Sackett,* the Court held that the issuance of a compliance order under the Clean Water Act, requiring the plaintiffs to restore wetlands on their property and subjecting them to a $75,000-per-day penalty for any noncompliance, was a final agency action that entitled them to immediate judicial review for declaratory relief. Likewise, the Court held in *Hawkes* that a jurisdictional determination issued by the Army Corp of Engineers under the CWA constitutes a final agency action that a landowner can challenge in court. These rulings will very likely impact the effectiveness of compliance orders under many other environmental programs as well.

Alternatively, the government may resort to litigation. It may seek an injunction to prevent continued or future violations, or to require the polluter to remediate the environmental damage that has occurred. Monetary civil penalties and fines may be imposed under most environmental statutes. If the government has incurred cleanup costs in response to a violation, it may seek recovery of those costs. Although many suits are brought, most are settled rather than litigated. Settlement opens the possibility of somewhat more creative solutions, sometimes including Supplemental Environmental Projects (SEPs). Such projects involve the violator undertaking some environmental "good work" or community service project. For example, in two separate settlements, Scotts Miracle-Gro agreed to pay $500 million in contributions to various charities dedicated to the protection of bird populations, and $2 million to acquire and protect 300 acres to prevent runoff of agricultural chemicals into nearby waterways.[106] [To find other examples of SEPs, explore the EPA's webpage at **www.epa.gov/enforcement/supplemental-environmental-projects-seps**.]

Many environmental laws also provide for the imposition of criminal penalties, including imprisonment. Individual corporate officers can be held criminally liable if they either had actual knowledge of the criminal action or they are held to be a "responsible person" under the appropriate law. To illustrate, in December 2016, Princess Cruises pleaded guilty to seven felony charges in federal court and was fined $40 million–the largest criminal penalty ever imposed for intentional vessel dumping. For over eight years, five Princess cruise ships employed several tactics, including a "magic pipe," to circumvent water cleaning mechanisms and devices that monitored oil. When a newly hired engineer observed over 4,000 gallons of contaminated waste being dumped into the ocean off England's coast, he reported it to officials and then quit as soon as the ship docked.[107] In January 2017, Volkswagen pled guilty to a conspiracy to keep U.S. officials from discovering that diesel vehicles it made were programmed to cheat on emissions tests, and it agreed to pay $4.3 billion in penalties. A number of employees, including a former CEO, have been indicted; at least two have pled guilty and been sentenced to prison terms.

BP Gulf Oil Spill: A Case Study

BP incurred costs of at least $53.8 billion as a result of the Gulf oil spill. Here are estimates of some of them:

- As of mid-2013, BP had spent $14 billion to plug the Macondo well and recover spilled oil.
- It pleaded guilty to 14 criminal charges and agreed to pay $4.5 billion in fines and other penalties.
- BP was subject to civil fines under the Clean Water Act and agreed to a $20 billion settlement, including $7.1 billion for natural resource damages, $5.5 billion for Clean Water Act fines, and $4.9 billion in state payments.
- The company set up a $20 billion compensation fund to address damages suffered by tens of thousands of Gulf Coast businesses and individuals.
- As of 2015, BP's legal fees were about $2 billion, including retaining experts.

Sources: Justin Scheck, Tom Fowler, and Selina Williams, "BP Says Spill Fund Is Running on Fumes," *The Wall Street Journal,* July 30, 2013 [**www.wsj.com**]; "Deepwater, Deep Pockets," *The Economist,* July 13, 2013 [**www.economist.com**]; Clifford Krauss and Stanley Reed, "Leaner BP Blanches at Bill for Cleanup," *The New York Times,* July 11, 2013 [**www.nytimes.com**]; Clifford Krauss and Barry Meier, "As Oil Spill Trial Opens, Push for a Deal Continues," *The New York Times,* February 25, 2013 [**www.nytimes.com**]; "Gulf of Mexico Oil Spill, 2010," *The New York Times,* April 25, 2011 [**www.nytimes.com**]; Associated Press, "Tallying the Spill's Cost," *The Des Moines Register,* December 30, 2010, p. 8B; and Susan Heavey, Patrick Rucker, and Emily Stephenson, "U.S. Says BP to Pay $20 Billion in Fines for 2010 Oil Spill," *Reuters,* October 5, 2015 [**www.reuters.com**].

Citizen Suits

In addition to the aforementioned mechanisms, many environmental statutes allow citizen suits, in which individuals may challenge government environmental decisions, such as the granting of a permit, and generally demand both governmental and private-sector compliance with the law. *Massachusetts v. EPA,* the Clean Air Act case previously presented, was brought by a group of states, local governments, and private organizations as a citizen suit.

Citizen suits have often been brought under the Endangered Species Act, which provides a federal program for the protection of threatened and endangered species and their habitats. Such suits may either seek greater protection for a species or argue that proposed protections exceed that which is necessary. The two cases that follow illustrate both types of concerns. In the first, more protection for the Cook Inlet beluga whale was sought; in the second, plaintiffs argued that too large an area had been designated for the protection of the Mexican spotted owl in the southeastern United States. In both cases, petitioners lost. When reading the cases, pay attention to the process required of the government in listing a species as threatened or endangered and in defining its protected habitat.

LEGAL BRIEFCASE

Cook Inlet Beluga Whale v. Daley 156 F. Supp. 2d 16 (D.C.D.C. 2001)

Judge James Robertson

The Cook Inlet Beluga Whale . . . is a genetically distinct, geographically isolated marine mammal with a remnant population that inhabits Cook Inlet from late April or early May until October or November. NMFS [National Marine Fisheries Service] estimates that in the mid-1980s, between 1,000 and 1,300 whales inhabited the inlet. Today, the population is estimated at between 300 and 400 whales. It is not disputed that the single most significant factor in the population decline has been Native American hunting. . . . That is why, in March 1999, the plaintiffs filed a petition to list the Cook Inlet Beluga Whale under the Endangered Species Act (ESA).

The Endangered Species Act delegates to the Secretary of Commerce the authority to determine whether fish, wildlife, or plant species should be listed as endangered or threatened. A species is "endangered" when it is in "danger of extinction throughout all or a significant part of its range," and it is "threatened" when it is "likely to become an endangered species within the foreseeable future." The Secretary's ESA determination is made on the basis of five statutorily prescribed factors, any one of which is sufficient to support a listing determination.

Within 30 days of plaintiffs' request for an ESA listing, the NMFS published formal notice that action under the ESA "may be warranted." That notice triggered a one-year status review period. On October 19, 1999, the NMFS published a proposed rule, not under the ESA, but under the Marine Mammal Protection Act (MMPA), to list the whale as "depleted." . . . Under the MMPA, the Secretary can designate a species as "depleted" . . . if the Secretary determines that the stock is below its Optimum Sustainable Population. Once a marine mammal has been listed as "depleted," the Secretary is authorized to promulgate regulations limiting takings by Native Americans, but a listing under the MMPA does not have the regulatory, economic, and environmental fallout of a listing as "threatened" or "endangered" under the ESA.

On June 22, 2000, the NMFS determined that an ESA listing was "not warranted." It is that determination which, in plaintiffs' submission, was "arbitrary, capricious, an abuse of discretion, or otherwise not in accordance with law."

ARGUMENT

"In exercising its narrowly defined duty . . . , the Court must consider whether the agency acted within the scope of its legal authority, adequately explained its decision, based its decision on facts in the record, and considered the relevant factors." Plaintiffs argue that the agency decision in this case improperly applied the law and facts to the five-factor determination; failed to apply the best scientific and commercial data available; and improperly considered political and economic factors.

I. STATUTORY FACTORS

A decision whether or not to list a species shall be made "solely on the basis of the best scientific and commercial data available . . . after conducting a review of the status of the species and after taking into account those efforts, if any, being made by any State or foreign nation." Applying this standard, the Secretary must list a species as endangered or threatened if "any of Section 1533(a)(1)'s five factors are sufficiently implicated." Each of the five factors is considered below.

(A) The Present or Threatened Destruction, Modification, or Curtailment of the Species' Habitat or Range The agency's conclusion that "no indication exists that the range has been, or is threatened with being modified or curtailed to an extent that appreciably diminishes the value of the habitat for both survival and recovery of the species," was not arbitrary or capricious. There is no dispute that the Cook Inlet, the whale's habitat, has changed over time in response to the increasing demand of municipal, industrial, and recreational activities, but there is no record basis for concluding that these changes have had a deleterious effect on the whale. Plaintiffs can point only to the fact that the whales have increasingly inhabited the upper inlet in recent decades. The agency concedes that this change in whale behavior might be in response to human activities, but no data suggest that the change threatens extinction. The agency is not required to conduct further testing to determine the effect of various environmental factors, such as oil drilling, on the whale population. "The 'best available data' requirement makes it clear that the Secretary has no obligation to conduct independent studies."

(B) Overutilization All agree that Native American harvesting has been the most significant factor in the declining whale population. The agency has found "that a failure to restrict the subsistence harvest would likely cause CI beluga whales to become in danger of extinction in the foreseeable future." But the agency has also concluded that "overutilization" does not support ESA listing because it has been stopped—by designating the whale as "depleted" under the MMPA. Plaintiffs attack that conclusion as unreasonable.

If the moratorium fails to control Native American harvesting in the future, ESA listing will be warranted. That much is agreed. But plaintiffs have been unable to point to anything in the record indicating that the current whale population is unsustainable if the harvest is indeed restricted successfully. . . .

[There] is no reason to believe that the MMPA's enforcement mechanisms, which are identical to those of the ESA, will be less effective in controlling illegal takings. Plaintiffs' concerns are reasonable, and enforcement should be carefully monitored, but the record contains support for the agency's conclusion that future takings will be minimal and that the current population is sustainable.

(C) Disease or Predation The agency concedes that both disease or predation "occur in the CI beluga population and may affect reproduction and survival," but it has concluded that these factors are not causing the stock to be threatened or endangered. Plaintiff has not shown that conclusion to be arbitrary or capricious. . . .

(D) Inadequacy of Existing Regulatory Mechanisms We have found nothing in the record, and plaintiff has identified nothing, showing that there are inadequacies in existing regulatory mechanisms or, if there were, what the effects of such inadequacies would be. Plaintiffs argue that the MMPA is inadequate to ensure that illegal hunting does not occur . . . , but that argument simply asserts plaintiffs' policy preference for a remedy under the ESA and begs the question of whether ESA listing is required.

(E) Other Natural or Manmade Factors Affecting Its Continued Existence Plaintiffs argue that there are many other factors—strandings, oil spills, takings through commercial fishing, effects of pollutants, ship strikes, noise, urban runoff, etc.—that put the species at risk and that it was arbitrary and capricious for the agency to determine that "the best available information . . . indicates that these activities, alone or cumulatively, have not caused the stock to be in danger of extinction and are not likely to do so in the foreseeable future." . . .

It is true that the absence of "conclusive evidence" of a real threat to a species does not justify an agency's finding that ESA listing is not warranted. But neither is listing required simply because the agency is unable to rule out factors that could contribute to a population decline. It was not arbitrary or capricious for the agency to place its principal reliance on the cessation of Native American hunts and the [study that concluded] that the Cook Inlet Beluga Whale population could sustain itself, even accounting for stochastic events.

[Plaintiffs' remaining arguments have been omitted.]

Ordered that defendant's motion for summary judgment is granted.

Questions

1. Why did the plaintiffs want the Cook Inlet Beluga Whale listed as endangered under the ESA?
2. What was the standard of review that the court applied to the agency's decision?
3. What five factors are to be considered in the listing of a species as endangered under the Endangered Species Act?

Judge Betty B. Fletcher

LITIGATION HISTORY

In 1993 the Mexican Spotted Owl was listed as a threatened species under the Endangered Species Act ("ESA"). The listing decision prompted a series of lawsuits alternately seeking to compel the FWS [U.S. Fish and Wildlife Service] to designate critical habitat for the owl and, following the FWS's designation of habitat, attacking that designation.

The first such lawsuit was in 1995 to compel the FWS to designate critical habitat and resulted in the FWS's issuing a final rule designating 4.6 million acres of critical owl habitat, a designation that was quickly challenged in court and then revoked in 1998. After another lawsuit was filed to compel the FWS to designate habitat, the FWS proposed a rule in 2000 to designate 13.5 million acres of critical habitat and in 2001 the agency promulgated a final rule that again designated 4.6 million acres. That rule was later struck down and . . . the FWS reopened the comment period on the rule it proposed in 2000. In 2004 the FWS designated approximately 8.6 million acres of critical habitat. It is this designation, the 2004 Final Rule, that Arizona Cattle [Growers' Association] challenges in the current action.

Arizona Cattle moved for summary judgment to set aside the 2004 Final Rule. . . . The District Court rejected Arizona Cattle's arguments. . . .

THE 2004 FINAL RULE

The FWS relied on three types of habitat management areas . . . as a starting point for the 2004 Final Rule: protected areas, restricted areas, and other forest and woodland types. Protected areas are those areas containing known owl sites, termed Protected Activity Centers ("PACs"); "steep slope" areas meeting certain forest conditions; and legally and administratively reserved lands. "PACs include a minimum of 600 acres . . . that includes the best nesting and roosting (i.e., resting) habitat in the area . . . and the most proximal and highly used foraging areas." However, PACs contain only 75% of necessary foraging areas for the owl. Restricted areas include non-steep slope areas with appropriate forest conditions that are "adjacent to or outside of protected areas." "Areas outside of PACs, including restricted areas, provide additional habitat appropriate for foraging." . . .

THE ESA AND THE DEFINITION OF "OCCUPIED"

The ESA defines a species' critical habitat as . . . "the specific areas within the geographical area occupied by the species, at the time it is listed. . . ."

The statute thus differentiates between "occupied" and "unoccupied" areas. . . . [We] face the preliminary issue of what it means for an area to be "occupied" under the ESA.

It is useful to unpack this inquiry into two components: uncertainty and frequency. Uncertainty is a factor when the FWS has reason to believe that owls are present in a given area, but lacks conclusive proof of their presence. Frequency is a factor when owls are shown to have only an intermittent presence in a given area. Occasionally, both factors will play a part in determining whether an area is "occupied." Because the ESA permits only one of two possible outcomes for this inquiry—occupied or unoccupied- . . . we must determine the scope of the FWS's authority to categorize as "occupied" those areas that may not fit neatly into either pigeonhole.

We have ample guidance on the "uncertainty" issue. The ESA provides that the agency must determine critical habitat using the "best scientific data available." This standard does not require that the FWS act only when it can justify its decision with absolute confidence. . . .

Turning to the "frequency" component, Arizona Cattle asserts that the word "occupied" is unambiguous and must be interpreted narrowly to mean areas that the species "resides in." In the context of the owl, they argue that such areas consist only of the 600-acre PACs. The FWS argues . . . that where a geographic area is used with such frequency that the owl is likely to be present, the agency may permissibly designate it as occupied. FWS contends that, at a minimum, this includes the owl's "home range" and may include other areas used for intermittent activities.

We cannot agree that "occupied" has an unambiguous, plain meaning as Arizona Cattle suggests. The word "occupied," standing alone, does not provide a clear standard for how frequently a species must use an area before the agency can designate it as critical habitat. Merely replacing the word "occupied" with the word "resides" does not resolve this ambiguity. . . . Viewed narrowly, an owl resides only in its nest; viewed more broadly, an owl resides in a PAC; and viewed more broadly still, an owl resides in its territory or home range. Determining whether a species uses an area with sufficient regularity that it is "occupied" is a highly contextual and fact-dependent inquiry. . . . Such factual questions are within the purview of the agency's unique expertise and are entitled to the standard deference afforded such agency determinations.

The FWS has authority to designate as "occupied" areas that the owl uses with sufficient regularity that it is likely to be present during any reasonable span of time. This interpretation is sensible. . . . Arizona Cattle's "reside in" interpretation would make little sense as applied to nonterritorial, mobile, or migratory animals—including the owl—for which it may be impossible to fix a determinate area in which the animal "resides." Such a narrow interpretation also would mesh poorly with the FWS's authority to act in the face of uncertainty.

It is possible for the FWS to go too far. Most obvious is that the agency may not determine that areas unused by owls are occupied merely because those areas are suitable for future occupancy. Such a position would ignore the ESA's distinction between occupied and unoccupied areas. . . . The fact that a member of the species is not present in an area at a given instant does not mean the area is suitable only for future occupancy if the species regularly uses the area.

Having thus framed the inquiry, we turn to the primary issue before the court: whether the FWS included unoccupied areas in its critical habitat designation.

THE FWS DID NOT DESIGNATE UNOCCUPIED AREAS AS CRITICAL HABITAT

. . . PACs are explicitly defined with reference to frequent owl presence, and non-PAC protected areas and restricted areas are "devised around" and "adjacent to" PACs. More to the point, we note significant record support for owl occupancy of these areas in the form of studies correlating the habitat characteristics of protected and restricted areas with owl presence.

The agency did not stop there. [Its] analysis proceeds, unit by unit, through the addition of areas to the critical habitat proposal on the basis of information about known owl locations. . . .

A point of recurring significance to our analysis is that PACs reflect only known owl sites. Although the 2004 Final Rule identified 1,176 PACs, owl populations have been estimated to be significantly greater than the maximum 2,352 owls reflected by this number of PACs. . . . Efforts by the FWS to identify other evidence of owl presence when it is unable to fix the location of a PAC with certainty are, therefore, highly significant.

Even more significant is the fact that the FWS excluded areas with evidence of few or no owls. . . . Finally, we note that . . . the FWS excluded the vast majority of critical habitat units that contained no PACs and refined the boundaries of the critical habitat units to exclude large areas that are distant from PACs.

The FWS's process for designating critical habitat gives us a strong foundation for our conclusion that the agency did not arbitrarily and capriciously treat areas in which owls are not found as "occupied." . . .

THE AMOUNT OF LAND DESIGNATED IS NOT DISPROPORTIONATE TO THE NUMBER OF OWLS

Arizona Cattle also argues that even using the owl's substantially larger home range as the appropriate measure for the territory occupied by the owl, the FWS has designated a grossly disproportionate amount of land compared to the amount the owl occupies. It ties this argument to a seemingly simple calculation: multiplying the 1,176 PACs by the maximum estimated home range size of the owl of 3,831 acres, the resultant area is only approximately 4.5 million acres, in contrast to the 8.6 million acres designated. This calculation, however, rests on a faulty assumption that the PACs represent all extant owls. We have already explained that PACs reflect only known owl sites and that there is record support for the existence of substantially greater numbers of owls and undiscovered sites. . . . Arizona Cattle's argument does not overcome the strong evidence that the FWS was focused on designating areas occupied by owls.

We find no fault with the FWS's designation of habitat for the Mexican Spotted Owl. . . .

Affirmed.

Questions

1. Identify the statutory language the court had to interpret to resolve this case.
2. How did the FWS select the areas included in its designation of 8.6 million acres as critical habitat for the owl?
3. What contrary arguments were made by Arizona Cattle?
4. What was the standard of review that the court applied to the agency's decision?
5. How many years elapsed between the first lawsuit over the designation of the Mexican spotted owl and the decision in this case?

LO-17-12

Identify and explain some of the challenges to protecting a species under the Endangered Species Act.

Endangered Species Act

The *Cook Inlet Beluga Whale* and *Arizona Cattle Grower's Association* decisions illustrate how complicated and time-consuming the legal process is for the protection of species. It is also costly—for citizen groups on both sides, for the government (and therefore all of us as taxpayers), for those whose lives and livelihoods may be substantially altered by the protections extended, and for the species and our world in the event necessary protections are not extended or are not effective.

Consider what is on the horizon. In 2019, an intergovernmental body (which includes the United States) issued the most comprehensive report on ecosystems ever undertaken. It found that 1 million of the planet's 8.7 million species are threatened with extinction, including 40 percent of amphibians and 25 percent of mammals. Extinction is occurring hundreds of times faster than before industrialization. "The essential interconnected web of life on Earth is getting smaller and increasingly frayed[.]"[108] The causes (discussed in order of importance) begin with human use of the world. We have altered 75 percent of the planet's land surface and significantly impacted 66 percent of its oceans[109] (dead zones exceed the area of Wyoming[110]). Eighty-seven percent of the wetlands are gone, as are almost 500,000 square miles of rain forests. The second cause is direct use. For example, more than one-third of all fish stocks are being harvested at unsustainable levels.[111] Climate change is the third cause. A recent study found that where the maximum temperature rose more than .9 degrees (F), 50 percent of the species became extinct; a whopping 95 percent became extinct when the increase exceeded 5.2 degrees.[112] Pollution and invasive alien species are the other two causes. A 2018 study indicates that the actual rate of future species extinction could be 10 times higher than projected due to domino effects: "[B]ecause all species are connected in the web of life[,] even the most tolerant species ultimately succumb to extinction when the less-tolerant species on which they depend disappear."[113]

[For photos of some endangered or threatened species in the United States, see **www.nytimes.com/interactive/2013/03/06/science/earth/endangered-species.html?ref=earth#index.**]

Part Four—Common Law Remedies

LO-17-13 Describe the primary common law remedies for environmental damage.

The remedies discussed in Part Three are based on statutory claims. But long before federal and state government became involved in environmental issues, courts were grappling with the problem and fashioning common law remedies. As early as the 1500s, city officials were ordered by a court to keep the streets clean of dung deposited by swine allowed to run loose; the air was said to be "corrupted and infected" by this practice. Legal arguments have typically revolved around the extent of a person's right to use and enjoy private property if such usage causes harm to a neighbor's property or the use of public property. More recently, tort actions for negligence and strict liability have been brought by those sustaining injuries. Successful plaintiffs may recover monetary damages for the harm they have suffered, or obtain an injunction to prevent similar conduct (and therefore harm) by the defendant in the future, or both.

Nuisance

A private ***nuisance*** is a substantial and unreasonable invasion of the private use and enjoyment of one's land; a public nuisance is an unreasonable interference with a right common to the public. Harmful conduct may be both a public and a private nuisance simultaneously; the case law distinctions between the two are often blurred. A classic nuisance dispute is the 1970 New York case *Boomer v. Atlantic Cement Co.*[114] Neighboring landowners sued the operator of a cement plant for injury to their properties from the plant's dirt, smoke, and vibration. The court recognized the wrong that was committed and ordered the operator to pay damages.

In the last decade, a number of nuisance cases were initiated in federal courts against emitters of significant greenhouse gases. For instance, in *Connecticut v. American Electric Power Co.,*[115] several states joined New York City and three land trusts in suing the operators of several coal-fired power plants, claiming their carbon emissions were a nuisance under federal common law. The plaintiffs sought an order requiring the utilities to cap, and then reduce, their carbon dioxide emissions. A unanimous Supreme Court ruled against the plaintiffs in 2011, finding that the Clean Air Act and the EPA's rule-making authority displaced any common law right to sue to curb carbon dioxide emissions from power plants. The decision affirms the power of the EPA under the CAA and encourages a single nationwide standard for addressing carbon emissions, rather than multiple court-imposed remedies. According to some commentators, it may also foreclose the use of the common law cause of action of nuisance for many other environmental harms under federal law. Some further believe it may hamper state law remedies, based on arguments that where federal law exists, federal environmental laws preempt state law causes of action.

Trespass

A ***trespass*** occurs, and liability is imposed, on any intentional invasion of individuals' right to the exclusive use of their own property. For example, in a 1959 Oregon case, *Martin v. Reynolds Metals Co.,*[116] the plaintiffs successfully sued in trespass for damages caused by the operation of an aluminum reduction plant, which caused certain fluoride compounds in the form of gases and particulates to become airborne, settle on the plaintiffs' land, contaminate their forage and water, and poison their cattle.

Negligence

The elements of ***negligence*** have been previously discussed in Chapter 7. In 2010, the Florida Supreme Court held that fishermen were entitled to recover for the damages they suffered when defendants' wastewater storage pond spilled into the Tampa Bay, killing fish, crabs, and other marine life. Defendants' negligence "interfered with the special interest of the commercial fishermen to use the public waters to earn their livelihood."[117]

Particularly troubling causation issues can arise in negligence cases based on environmental pollution, such as when a plaintiff claims injury from a toxic substance manufactured or otherwise supplied by a defendant. Recall the discussion of causation at the start of this chapter, as well as the bases for the movies *Dark Waters, Erin Brockovich,* and *A Class Action.* Think of the factual difficulties of proving that a particular substance causes certain medical conditions, that it was the cause of a particular individual's injury, and that the substance is traceable back to a particular defendant.

An organic compound, MTBE, is used around the world as an additive to gas. However, at least half of U.S. states have banned its use, and the EPA has classified it as a possible human carcinogen. Many lawsuits have been brought against oil companies by municipalities and other governmental bodies to recoup the costs of cleaning up water supplies contaminated with MTBE. New Hampshire brought such a suit against 16 oil companies, all of which, except ExxonMobil, settled with the state for a total of $136 million. In April 2013, a jury returned a $236 million verdict for the state, finding Exxon negligent for putting the additive in its gas and failing to warn the state of its risks. In 2015, the New Hampshire Supreme Court denied Exxon's appeal.[118]

Strict Liability

Certain activities, such as the use of toxic chemicals, may be seen as so abnormally dangerous or haphazard as to give rise to a ***strict liability*** claim (previously discussed in Chapter 7). In an environmental law context, strict liability has been considered where crop dusting contaminated adjacent properties,[119] toxic chemicals were improperly disposed of,[120] and oil contaminated a nearby water well.[121]

Several of the above claims can sometimes be triggered by the same set of facts. For instance, in a 2007 West Virginia case, a jury found DuPont negligent in its use of a 112-acre site that for 90 years had been a zinc-smelting plant. The jury also found that DuPont had created both a public and a private nuisance, had committed trespass, and should be held strictly liable for exposing local residents to various toxic substances. Residents and property owners had sued, claiming that the company had deliberately dumped toxic heavy metals, particularly zinc, on the site. The medical problems caused by such toxins include cancer, damage to internal organs, and decreased fertility.[122]

Part Five—International Treaties

LO-17-14 Discuss the purpose of the Kyoto Protocol and the Paris Agreement.

In 1997 the governments of the world, realizing that global action would be required to have any significant impact on overall emissions, adopted the Kyoto Protocol. Specifically, the protocol called for a five percent reduction from 1990 levels of greenhouse gas emissions to be achieved by 2012. The protocol acknowledged that developed countries were principally responsible for the GHG levels at that time. These countries agreed to legally binding emission reductions; developing countries did not take on binding reductions and were allowed to grow, consistent with their development needs. The protocol became binding when it was ratified by 180 countries; this occurred when Russia ratified the protocol in late 2004. The United States never ratified the protocol.

Although the protocol did bring climate change into the public's awareness, in terms of impact, it was a failure. In 1990, 38.2 million tons of greenhouse gases were emitted globally; by 2012, it was 53.6 million–sixty percent higher.[123] Despite assertions that the protocol reduced emissions by 12.5 percent, unrelated factors accounted for most of the improvement. The Great Recession occurred during this period and the USSR collapsed, causing a major decline in manufacturing. Crucially, the protocol didn't involve the United States (the then-second largest emitter, which never ratified the protocol), or the fastest-growing polluters, China and India (because developing economies were excluded).[124] Between 2005 and 2014, India's emissions increased 40 percent, China's by 70 percent. Among the reasons for U.S. nonparticipation was the 2010 target that would have mandated a 30 percent reduction–deemed impossible without inducing a major economic downturn.[125]

Formal discussions for a post-Kyoto international framework to reduce global emissions began in Bali, Indonesia, in December 2007, and a new global agreement was reached at the Paris Climate Change Conference in 2015. The so-called Paris Agreement has several key provisions in which governments agreed to keep the increase in global average temperature to well below 2°C above preindustrial levels and to pursue efforts to limit it to 1.5°C; to report every five years on their progress and ambitious new targets; and for the EU and other developed countries to provide financing to assist developing countries to reduce emissions and to build resilience to climate change impacts. Participating countries also submitted comprehensive national climate action plans.[126]

The United States is one of 195 countries to date that have ratified the Paris Agreement; it specifically agreed to lower its GHG emissions by 17.89 percent. Under the Trump Administration, the United States withdrew from the treaty effective November 4, 2020. However, it rejoined the agreement less than three months later, on January 20, 2021, President Biden's first day in office.

One integrated way to consider climate change is through the lens of global security. In 2020, an elite group assessed the threat climate change poses to civilization. They said that "even in scenarios of low warming, . . . the world will face severe risks[.] Higher levels of warming will pose catastrophic . . . and likely irreversible . . . risks[.] . . . [W]e stand on the precipice of some of the greatest . . . security threats the world has ever seen." Some of their projections for North America include "extreme heat, sea level rise, and disaster events . . . severely impact infrastructure[.] Increasing divisions within society–including ethnonationalist, anti-democratic . . . views[.]" They recommend that "we call for the world to achieve net-zero global emissions as soon as possible [and to] 'climate-proof' the . . . systems on which human security depends[.] . . . [W]e must act in a manner that is commensurate to the scale and scope of the threat."[127]

Research Exercise

One indication of the extent to which global climate change has become a grassroots issue in the United States is the entry of carbon footprint considerations into everyday conversation. A carbon footprint is a measurement of how much carbon dioxide is emitted into the atmosphere as the result of a particular product, activity, or lifestyle. It is a way to measure the carbon "cost" of a particular activity or the carbon "savings" of changing that activity.

What's your carbon footprint? Find out from **http://www.nature.org/greenliving/carbon calculator.** Compare that with your ecological footprint–that is, how many Earths we would have to have if everyone lived as you do. Go to **www.footprintcalculator.org**.

Chapter Questions

1. In 2016, 21 teenagers sued the federal government, alleging that it allowed, and even encouraged, carbon emissions to increase over the past 50 years and that the government's actions, and its failure to act, have so profoundly damaged the Earth that they threaten the plaintiffs' fundamental rights to due process under the Fifth Amendment. A federal district court judge in Oregon denied the government's motion to dismiss the case, finding that the plaintiffs sufficiently alleged that the government's conduct violated their constitutional right to a clean and healthy climate environment. The court's decision is the first of its kind in the environmental law arena. How might the government's actions and its failure to act constitute violations of due process under the Fifth Amendment? Do you agree with the judge's ruling that the plaintiffs should be allowed to proceed with their case? See *Juliana v. United States,* 217 F.Supp.3d 1224 (D. Or. Nov. 10, 2016) [**https://law.justia.com**]. The Ninth Circuit Court of Appeals reversed the lower court, holding that the plaintiffs' injuries were not of a nature for which the federal district court could offer redress. See *Juliana v. United States,* 947 F.3d 1159 (9th Cir 2020) [**https://law.justia.com**]. However, in June 2023, a U.S. District Court

judge granted the teenage plaintiffs their request to amend their complaint, clearing the way for case to go to trial. See E360 Digest, "Youth Climate Lawsuit Against Federal Government Headed to Trial," Yale Environment 360 [**https://e360.yale.edu**].

2. Consider the politics of environmental law. The Obama Administration utilized administrative rulings such as the Clean Power Plan rule in order to promote environmental protections in the absence of legislation. The EPA, however, withdrew the rule one month before President Trump took office, and he continued to cut back on regulation in order to promote American industry. Dismantling administrative rulings may be relatively easy. Undoing legislation is not, especially given the many moving parts of environmental law. What about market forces? Will the energy sector continue to transform even if regulation is reduced, moving further towards renewable energy? Clean gas-fired plants are already replacing coal-fired plants, and consumers are buying more energy-efficient homes and appliances. After studying this chapter, what are your thoughts about environmental protections? Should regulations be scaled back in favor of U.S. industry? What are the potential costs of deregulation? In light of the economic impacts of COVID-19, will consumers still want environmentally friendlier products and industry practices?
3. The Dakota Access Pipeline controversy highlights the issues of environmental justice that plague Native Americans. Although 99 percent of the pipeline had been constructed, the Standing Rock Sioux protested further construction in the vicinity of their reservation on the basis that the tribe was excluded from preapproval discussions with the Army Corps of Engineers before the necessary federal permits were issued. The pipeline is over 1,000 miles long and would be used to transport a half million barrels of oil each day past the reservation. Consider the devastating hazards posed by oil spills. During the protests, over 176,000 gallons of oil leaked from a pipeline 150 miles away, and 130,000 of those gallons spilled into a nearby creek.[128] There were over 3,300 incidents of oil or gas pipeline leaks and ruptures between 2010 and 2016.[129] Because of the level of controversy surrounding the pipeline, the District Court for the District of Columbia ordered the Army Corps of Engineers to prepare an Environmental Impact Survey, which is anticipated in 2023. Should the pipeline be allowed in such close proximity to the reservation? Should it be allowed, given the fact that the Standing Rock Sioux tribe was excluded, in violation of the rules, from preapproval discussions? What are the ethical considerations? the legal?
4. "The Aral Sea is going, gone. Once the world's fourth largest inland body of water, the Aral has shriveled to half its former area and a third of its volume. As for the region's drinking water, even the local vodka has a salty tang."[130] The Aral is the victim of the former Soviet Union's central planners, who decreed that the area would be the nation's main source of cotton. To achieve that goal, intense irrigation was required, with the result that only a trickle of fresh water was left to feed the Aral. Refilling the Aral would require tremendous dislocations in the agriculture of the vast region. If you were a member of a commission charged with developing a plan for the future of the Aral Sea, what issues would you want to address?
5. Professor and business ethics scholar Norman Bowie:

> Environmentalists frequently argue that business has special obligations to protect the environment. Although I agree with the environmentalists on this point, I do not

> agree with them as to where the obligations lie. Business does not have an obligation to protect the environment over and above what is required by law; however, business does have a moral obligation to avoid intervening in the political arena in order to defeat or weaken environmental legislation.[131]

a. Explain Professor Bowie's reasoning.

b. Do you agree with him? Explain.

6. Mexico is quickly running short of water:

> 85 percent of Mexico's economic growth and 75 percent of its 100 million people are in the north, and the water is far to the south. . . . [P]oliticians facing elections are reluctant to ask voters to spend more on any utility, let alone water. Agriculture uses 80 percent of the water and pays nothing, although it only ranks seventh in contribution to the gross national product. . . . Less than half of the capital's wastewater is treated. The rest sinks into underground lakes or flows toward the Gulf of Mexico, turning rivers into sewers. . . . Well over half of irrigation water is lost to evaporation or seepage.[132]

In one of its largest cities, Monterey, where temperatures often exceed 100 degrees in the summer, residents are allowed to use the water only 6 hours each day.[133] Brainstorm as many possible contributions to solving Mexico's water problem as you can. For a photo gallery, see Melissa Hogenboom, "How a City That Floods is Running Out of Water," BBC, May 14, 2018 [**https://www.bbc.com**].

7. Because of the spread of the West Nile virus in the state of New York, an insecticide spraying program was implemented to control the mosquitoes responsible for spreading the virus. Several groups sued, arguing that the spray was a pollutant that damaged waters in violation of the Clean Water Act. What criteria should the court use to decide the outcome? See *No Spray Coalition, Inc. v. The City of New York,* 2000 U.S. Dist. LEXIS 13919, 51 ERC (BNA) 1508 (S.D.N.Y. September 25, 2000).

8. Ott Chemical Co. polluted the ground at its Michigan plant. CPC International created a wholly owned subsidiary to buy Ott, which was accomplished in 1965. CPC retained the original Ott managers. Pollution continued through 1972 when CPC sold Ott. In 1981 the U.S. EPA began a cleanup of the site. To recover some of the tens of millions in cleanup costs, the EPA sued CPC (called Bestfoods) among other potentially responsible parties. The Superfund law places responsibility on anyone who "owned or operated" a property when pollution was deposited. The district court held that CPC was liable because of its active participation in Ott's business and its control of Ott's decisions in that it selected the Ott board of directors and placed some CPC managers as executives at Ott.

   a. Do you think CPC should be held liable? Why or why not?

   b. What test would you employ to determine whether a parent corporation should be liable for a subsidiary's pollution? See *United States v. Bestfoods,* 524 U.S. 51 (1998) [**https://law.justia.com**].

9. William Tucker said:

> [Environmentalism is] essentially aristocratic in its roots and derives from the land and nature-based ethic that has been championed by upper classes throughout history. Large landowners and titled aristocracies . . . have usually held a set of ideals

> that stresses "stewardship" and the husbanding of existing resources over exploration and discovery. This view favors handicrafts over mass production and the inheritance ethic over the business ethic.[134]

Tucker went on to argue that environmentalism favors the economic and social interests of the well-off. He said people of the upper middle class see their future in universities and the government bureaucracy, with little economic stake in industrial expansion. Indeed, such expansion might threaten their suburban property values. Do you agree with his assertions? Why or why not?

10. Americans' commitment to the car raises serious environmental problems. The vast spaces required to park those cars are themselves a significant environmental hazard. Consider some of the measures taken by cities around the world to ameliorate the problems: Mexico City bans the use of vehicles one Saturday each month; New Delhi assigns each driver certain designated days on which they are allowed to operate their car; Barcelona and Madrid transformed city blocks into playgrounds, gardens, and plazas with restricted vehicle access; and Norway converted parking spaces to bike lanes in its city center. What are some of the environmental problems created or encouraged by parking lots? Which of the possible measures to ameliorate the problems do you most favor? Why? Which of the measures do you think would get the best buy-in in your community? Explain.
11. The Endangered Species Act provides that all federal agency actions are to be designed so that they do not jeopardize endangered or threatened species. The act had been interpreted to reach federal agency work or funding in foreign countries, but the federal government changed that interpretation in 1986 to limit the act's reach to the United States and the high seas. A group labeled Defenders of Wildlife filed suit, seeking to reinstate the original interpretation. The case reached the U.S. Supreme Court, and Justice Scalia wrote that Defenders of Wildlife would have to submit evidence showing that at least one of its members would be "directly" affected by the interpretation. In response, one member of Defenders of Wildlife wrote that she had visited Egypt and observed the endangered Nile crocodile and hoped to return to do so again but feared that U.S. aid for the Aswan High Dam would harm the crocodiles. Do you think Defenders of Wildlife should have been permitted to sue? Why or why not? See *Lujan v. Defenders of Wildlife,* 504 U.S. 555 (1992) [**https://law.justia.com**].
12. Economist Robert Crandall said in 1982 (toward the beginning of Reagan's presidency):

    > [O]ur best chances for regulatory reform in certain environmental areas, particularly in air pollution policy, come from the states. Probably, responsibility for environmental regulation belongs with the states anyway, and most of it ought to be returned there.[135]

    a. What reasoning supports Crandall's notion that responsibility for environmental regulation belongs with the states?

    b. How might one reason to the contrary?

    c. If the power were yours, would environmental regulation rest primarily at the state, federal, or international level? Explain.
13. Airplanes are a significant contributor to greenhouse gases. What would cap-and-trade program to address this issue for consumer air travel look like?

Consider, on the other hand, that hydrogen planes may be a viable alternative in just another decade, but airports and airplanes will need to be redesigned at considerable expense, and hydrogen costs three to four times as much as conventional fuels.[136] As a consumer, do you favor a cap-and-trade system, paying more to fly to help cover the costs of converting to hydrogen fuel, or leaving things just as they are? Why?

Notes

1. David Markell and J. B. Ruhl, "An Empirical Survey of Climate Change Litigation in the United States," *Environmental Law Reporter* 40, no. 7 (2010), pp. 10644–55 [**https://papers.srnn.com**].
2. IPCC, 2007: Climate Change 2007: Synthesis Report *IPCC* (Geneva, Switzerland, p. 1) [**https://www.ipcc.ch**].
3. "Carbon Taxes Cut Debt, Cool Planet," *Bloomberg,* August 14, 2012 [**www.bloomberg.com**].
4. IPCC, 2013: Climate Change 2013: The Physical Science Basis, *IPCC* (Cambridge University Press, p. 1535) [**https://www.ipcc.ch**].
5. Tom DiChristopher, "White House-Approved Report Concludes Humans Are behind Climate Change," *CNBC,* November 3, 2017 [**www.cnbc.com**]; "The Fifth National Climate Assessment," *NCA5,* accessed January 2024 [**https://nca2023.globalchange.gov/**]; and "2050 Long-Term Strategy," *European Union* [**https://climate.ec.europa.eu**].
6. "Climate of Uncertainty," *The Wall Street Journal,* October 1, 2013 [**www.wsj.com**].
7. Richard A. Muller, "A Pause, Not an End, to Warming," *The New York Times,* September 25, 2013 [**www.nytimes.com**].
8. Justin Gillis, "Earth Sets a Temperature Record for the Third Straight Year," *The New York Times,* January 18, 2017 [**www.nytimes.com**].
9. NASA Global Climate Change: Vital Signs, "Global Temperature," accessed June 2023 [**https://climate.nasa.gov**]; and "NASA Analysis Confirms 2023 as Warmest Year on Record," NASA, accessed January 2024 [**https://www.nasa.gov**].
10. Bill McKibben, *Earth* (New York: Henry Holt, 2010), p. 45.
11. Alexandra Borunda, "Arctic Summer Sea Ice Could Disappear as Early as 2035," *National Geographic,* August 13, 2020 [**www.nationalgeographic.com**]; and "Drought or Deluge: Different Threats, Same Problems," *Watercalculator.org,* April 28, 2020 [**www.watercalculator.org**].
12. Jonathan Erdman, "100-Degree Fahrenheit Temperature Confirmed in Siberia; 90s Measured at Russian Arctic Coast," *The Weather Channel,* July 2, 2020 [**www.weather.com**].
13. Kate Ramsayer, "2020 Arctic Sea Ice Minimum at Second Lowest on Record," *NASA,* September 21, 2020 [**https://climate.nasa.gov**]; and Alejandra Borunda, "Arctic Summer Sea Ice Could Disappear as Early as 2035," August 13, 2020 [**www.nationalgeographic.com**].
14. Bob Henson, "Baked by Midsummer Sun, Arctic Sea Ice Could Face Worst Losses on Record," *Yale Climate Connections,* July 20, 2020 [**https://yaleclimateconnections.org**]; and Chelsea Harvey, "With Fires, Heat and a Cyclone, Arctic Breaks Noting Record," *Scientific American,* July 31, 2020 [**www.scientificamerican.com**].
15. "The Ocean and Climate Change," *The Ocean Foundation,* accessed June 2023 [**https://oceanfdn.org**].
16. "The Ocean and Climate Change," *International Union for Conservation of Nature,* accessed June 2023 [**www.iucn.org**].
17. Chris Mooney, "The World's Oceans are Speeding Up—Another Mega-Scale Consequence of Climate Change," *The Washington Post,* February 5, 2020 [**www.washingtonpost.com**]; "Multi-Agency Report Highlights Increasing Signs and Impacts of Climate Change in Atmosphere,

Land and Oceans," *World Meteorological Association,* March 10, 2020 [**https://public.wmo.int**]; and "Ocean and Climate Change," *The Ocean Foundation* [**https://oceanfdn.org**].

18. Josh Holder, Niko Kommenda, and Jonathan Watts, "The Three-Degree World: The Cities That Will Be Drowned by Global Warming," *The Guardian,* November 3, 2017 [**www.theguardian.com**]; Aria Bendix, "8 American Cities That Could Disappear by 2100," *Business Insider,* March 17, 2020 [**www.businessinsider.com**]; "Kiribati, the First Country Rising Sea Levels Will Swallow Up as a Result of Climate Change," *Iberdrola,* accessed September 2020 [**www.iberdrola.com**]; and Justin Worland, "The Leaders of These Sinking Countries Are Fighting to Stop Climate Change. Here's What the Rest of the World Can Learn," *Time,* June 13, 2019 [**https://time.com**].
19. Gabriel Popkin, "Will Climate Change Upend Projections of Future Forest Growth?" *YaleEnvironment360,* July 7, 2020 [**https://e360.yale.edu**]; James Conca, "Climate Change Driving Forests to Smaller and Younger Trees," *Forbes,* May 31, 2020 [**www.forbes.com**]; Max Wilbert, "46% of Forests Have Been Destroyed by Civilization . . . and Counting," *Deep Green Resistance News Service,* July 24, 2018 [**https://dgrnewsservice.org**]; Elizabeth Pennisi, "Tropical Forests Soak Up Huge Amounts of Greenhouse Gas. Climate Change Could End That," *Science,* May. 21, 2020 [**www.sciencemag.org**]; Ashley Junger, "Saving the Forest for the Trees," *Earthwatch,* accessed June 2023 [**https://earthwatch.org**]; and Statement from Scientist Signatories: "Five Reasons the Earth's Climate Depends on Forests," *Climate and Land Use Alliance,* accessed June 2023 [**www.climateandlandusealliance.org**].
20. "Officials in Siberia Have Warned Fuel Spill Could Take Years to Clean Up," *The Guardian,* June 10, 2020 [**www.theguardian.com**].
21. "A Decade After Deepwater Horizon," *The New York Times,* April 19, 2020 [**www.nytimes.com**]; and Henry Fountain, "Gulf Spill Sampling Questioned," *The New York Times,* August 19, 2013 [**www.nytimes.com**].
22. Adam Nossiter, "Far from Gulf, a Spill Scourge 5 Decades Old," *The New York Times,* June 16, 2010 [**www.nytimes.com**]; and "A Desperate Need for Reform," *The Economist,* October 20, 2012 [**www.economist.com**].
23. Lisa Fleisher and Anna Hirtenstein, "London Just Set a New Modern Pollution Record," *Bloomberg,* January 27, 2017 [**www.bloomberg.com**].
24. "Unspontaneous Combustion," *The Economist,* June 29, 2013 [**www.economist.com**]; "Logging the Good News," *The Economist,* May 25, 2013 [**www.economist.com**]; and "REDDY at Last," *The Economist,* December 8, 2012 [**www.economist.com**].
25. Martin Fackler, "Japan's $320 Million Gamble at Fukushima: An Underground Ice Wall," *The New York Times,* August 29, 2016 [**www.nytimes.com**]; and World Nuclear Association, "Fukushima Daiichi Accident," updated January 2023 [**www.world-nuclear.org**].
26. Fackler, "Errors Cast Doubt on Japan's Cleanup of Nuclear Accident Site," *The New York Times,* September 3, 2013 [**www.nytimes.com**] and Yamaguchi, "11 Years Later, Fate of Fukushima Reactor Cleanup Uncertain," *TechXplore,* March 11, 2022 [**https://techxplore.com**]. For updates on the decommissioning work, see "Fukushima Daiichi Status Updates," *International Atomic Energy Agency* [**https://www.iaea.org**].
27. World Health Organization, "Drinking-Water," March 21, 2022 [**www.who.int**].
28. World Health Organization, "Sanitation," March 21, 2022 [**www.who.int**].
29. "Climate Change and Health," *World Health Organization,* October 30, 2021 [**www.who.int**].
30. "The Global Extinction Crisis," *The New York Times,* September 29, 2021 [**www.nyt.com**]; and Benji Jones, "5 Signs of How Climate Change Is Unravelling Earth's Ecosystems," *Vox,* March 1, 2022 [**www.vox.com**].
31. "Learn About Environmental Justice," *U.S. Environmental Protection Agency* [**www.epa.gov**].

32. "Flint, Michigan Population History, 1920–2021," accessed June 2023 [**https://www.usbiggestcities.com**].
33. Wilfred Beckerman, cited in Robert Solomon, The New World of Business (Lanham, MD: Rowman & Littlefield, 1994), p. 319. "The Science of Sharing,"
34. "The Science of Sharing," *NYU Law Magazine,* 2012, p. 106.
35. Susan Lee, "How Much Is the Right to Pollute Worth?" *The Wall Street Journal,* August 1, 2001 [**www.wsj.com**].
36. Mark Golden, "Dirty Dealings," *The Wall Street Journal,* September 13, 1999 [**www.wsj.com**].
37. Ibid.
38. U.S. Environmental Protection Agency, "Acid Rain and Related Programs: 2007 Progress Report," accessed June 2023 [**www.epa.gov**].
39. Peter Shattuck and Daniel L. Sosland, "Northeast Faces Stark Choice on Climate Pollution," *The New York Times,* January 24, 2013 [**www.nytimes.com**].
40. "Gold and Green," *The Economist,* March 16, 2013 [**www.economist.com**].
41. Eduardo Porter, "In Energy Taxes, Tools to Help Tackle Climate Change," *The New York Times,* January 29, 2013 [**www.nytimes.com**].
42. Jeff Gersh, "*Seeds of Change,*" Amicus Journal 21, no. 2 (Summer 1999), p. 36.
43. Center for Sustainable Energy, "Clean Vehicle Rebate Project," *California Air Resources Board,* updated February 6, 2023 [**https://ww2.arb.ca.gov**].
44. Mark A. McCall, "Powering New Markets: Energy Storage Poised for Growth," Loan Programs Office, U.S. Department of Energy, October 2016 [**www.energy.gov**].
45. Jon J. Fialka and Jeffrey Ball, "Companies Get Ready for Greenhouse-Gas Limits," *The Wall Street Journal,* October 26, 2004 [**www.wsj.com**].
46. "Ray Anderson," *The Economist,* September 10, 2011 [**www.economist.com**]; and The Ray C. Anderson Foundation [**www.raycandersonfoundation.org**].
47. "Why We Exist," *Ray C. Anderson Foundation,* accessed June 2023 [**www.raycandersonfoundation.org**].
48. Alan Tovey, "Fiat Chrysler Shares Crash by a Fifth as It Is Drawn into Emissions Scandal by US Regulators," *The Telegraph,* January 12, 2017 [**www.telegraph.co.uk**].
49. William Boston, Arian Campo-Flores, and Aruna Viswanatha, "FBI Arrests Volkswagen Executive in Emissions Scandal," *The Wall Street Journal,* January 9, 2017 [**www.wsj.com**].
50. Katy Daigle, "Putting a Price on Clean Environment," *Des Moines Register,* June 18, 2012, p. 6A.
51. This was the essence of plaintiffs' nuisance suit against various large greenhouse gas emitters in *Comer v. Murphy Oil USA,* 2007 WL 6942285 (S.D. Miss. 2009). The district court dismissed the case; a three-judge panel for the 5th Circuit reversed. When defendants sought an *en banc* rehearing, a number of the circuit judges recused themselves, but the remaining quorum granted the request and vacated the panel decision. Another judge then recused herself, leaving the court without a quorum. It determined the rehearing could not proceed, nor could the panel decision be reinstated. Thus, the district court's dismissal is the final decision.
52. John M. Broder and Peter Baker, "Obama's Order Is Likely to Tighten Auto Standards," *The New York Times,* January 26, 2009 [**www.nytimes.com**]; and Editorial, "Cleaner Cars, a Safer Planet" *The New York Times,* October 5, 2010 [**www.nytimes.com**].
53. Rebecca Leber, "Donald Trump Just Replaced the White House Climate Website with . . . This," *Mother Jones,* January 20, 2017 [**www.motherjones.com**].
54. See, for example, "FACT SHEET: President Biden's Executive Actions on Climate to Address Extreme Heat and Boost Offshore Wind," *The White House,* July 20, 2022 [**www.whitehouse.gov**];

and "FACT SHEET: President Biden Signs Executive Order to Revitalize Our Nation's Commitment to Environmental Justice for All," *The White House,* April 21, 2023 [**www.whitehouse.gov**].

55. Ellen Goodman, "Can Tourists Love a Place to Death?" *Des Moines Register,* March 31, 2001, p. 7A.
56. Coalition for Responsible Regulation, Inc. v. Environmental Protection Agency, 684 F. 3d 102, 121 (D.C. Cir. 2012).
57. *Utility Air Regulatory Group v. Environmental Protection Agency,* 134 S. Ct. 2427 (2014) [**https://justia.supreme.com**], appealing *Coalition for Responsible Regulation,* 684 F.3d 102 (2012).
58. "A Historic Commitment to Protecting the Environment and Addressing the Impacts of Climate Change," *The Record* [**https://obamawhitehouse.archives.gov**]. See also Coral Davenport, "Obama to Take Action to Slash Coal Pollution," *The New York Times,* June 1, 2014 [**www.nytimes.com**].
59. Seth v.d.H. Cooley, "Formal Federal Government Withdrawal from Climate Change Regulation Begins," *Duane Morris LLP,* December 21, 2016 [**www.duanemorris.com**].
60. White House, "Energy & Environment," accessed June 2020 [**www.whitehouse.gov**].
61. Lisa Friedman, "States Sue Trump Administration Over Rollback of Obama-Era Climate Rule," *The New York Times,* August 13, 2019 [**www.nytimes.com**].
62. Proposed Rule, "New Performance Standards for Greenhouse Gas Emissions. . . ," *Federal Register,* May 23, 2023 [**www.federalregister.gov**].
63. "American Lung Association Report: Nearly 9 Million More Americans Impacted by Deadly Particle Pollution," *American Lung Association,* April 21, 2022 [**www.lung.org**].
64. *Environmental Protection Agency v. EME Homer City Generation,* 134 S. Ct. 1584 (2014) [**https://supreme.justia.com**].
65. U.S. Environmental Protection Agency, "Cross-State Air Pollution Rule (CSAPR)–Regulatory Actions and Litigation," accessed June 2023 [**www.epa.gov**].
66. See, *e.g.,* Maya Earls, "NY, Other States to Argue EPA Fails to Enforce Pollution 'Drift'," *Bloomberg Law,* May 6, 2020 [**https://news.bloomberglaw.com**].
67. *NY v. EPA,* 781 Fed. Appx 4, USCA No. 19-1019 (D.C. Cir. 2019) [**https://law.justia.com**]. See also Jack Rodgers, "DC Circuit Strikes Down Lax EPA Rules on Cross-Border Pollution," *Courthouse News Service,* October 1, 2019 [**www.courthousenews.com**].
68. "Coal in the Rich World: The Mixed Fortunes of a Fuel," *The Economist,* January 5, 2013 [**www.economist.com**].
69. Independent Statistics and Analysis, "Frequently Asked Questions, What is U.S. electricity generation by energy source?" *U.S. Energy Information Administration,* 2022 [**www.eia.gov**].
70. Janet Larsen, "Falling Gasoline Use Means United States Can Just Say No to New Pipelines and Food-to-Fuel," *Earth Policy Institute,* March 28, 2013 [**www.earth-policy.org**].
71. Tsvetana Parascova, "U.S. Gasoline Consumption Hasn't Been This Low Since the Vietnam War," *OilPrice.com,* April 23, 2020 [**https://oilprice.com**].
72. Today in Energy, "EIA Expects U.S. Gasoline and Diesel Retail Prices to Decline in 2024 and 2024," *Energy Information Administration,* January 12, 2023 [**www.eia.gov**].
73. "US DOT Announces New Vehicle Efficiency Standards for Model Year 2024-2026," U.S. Department of Transportation, April 1, 2022 [**www.transportation.gov**].
74. Lia Cattaneo, "EPA's Revived Clean Cars Waiver for California," *Harvard Law School Environmental and Energy Law Program,* April 6, 2022 [**https://eelp.law.harvard.edu**].
75. Julia Jacobo, "14,000 Inactive Wells in US Remain Unplugged, Posing Risks for Leaks, Researchers Say," A*BC News,* May 8, 2023 [**https://abcnews.go.com**].
76. Campbell Robertson, "Gulf of Mexico Has Long Been Dumping Site," *The New York Times,* July 29, 2010 [**www.nytimes.com**].

77. Lindsey Hoshaw, "Afloat in the Ocean, Expanding Islands of Trash," *The New York Times,* November 9, 2009 **[www.nytimes.com]**.
78. David Erickson and Mark Anstoetter, "EPA Rates U.S. Coastal Waters as 'Fair,'" *Association of Corporate Counsel,* May 4, 2012.
79. Danielle Kaeding, "Report: EPA's Environmental Enforcement Down in Great Lakes States," *Wisconsin Public Radi*o, April 22, 2020 **[www.wpr.org]**.
80. Press Release, "The Justice Department and EPA Reach Clean Water Act Settlement with Pepco to Reduce Pollution to Anacostia River," U.S. Department of Justice, January 13, 2017 **[www.justice.gov]**.
81. "Blooming Horrible," *The Economist,* June 23, 2012 **[www.economist.com]**; and Campbell Robertson, "Gulf of Mexico Has Long Been Dumping Site," *The New York Times,* July 29, 2010 **[www.nytimes.com]**.
82. National Oceanic and Atmospheric Administration, "NOAA forecasts very large 'dead zone' for Gulf of Mexico," U.S. Department of Commerce, updated June 12, 2019 **[www.noaa.gov]**.
83. 547 U.S. 715 (2006) **[https://supreme. justia.com]**.
84. 598 U.S. _____ (2023) **[https://supreme. justia.com]**.
85. Charles Duhigg and Janet Roberts, "Rulings Restrict Clean Water Act, Foiling E.P.A.," *The New York Times,* February 28, 2010 **[www.nytimes.com]**.
86. Rebecca Leber, "Donald Trump Just Replaced the White House Climate Website with . . . This," *Mother Jones,* January 20, 2017 **[www.motherjones.com]**.
87. Ian Urbina, "Think Those Chemicals Have Been Tested?" *The New York Times,* April 13, 2013 **[www.nytimes.com]**.
88. National Toxicology Program, "Formaldehyde," *U.S. Department of Health and Human Services,* June 2011 **[www.ntp.niehs.nih.gov]**; and National Center for Environmental Assessment, "Formaldehyde; CASRN 50-00-0," p. 7, *U.S. Environmental Protection Agency,* October 1989 (last revised September 1, 1990) **[https://cfpub.epa.gov]**.
89. Lyndsey Layton, "Use of Potentially Harmful Chemicals Kept Secret under Law," *The Washington Post,* January 4, 2010 **[www.washingtonpost.com]**.
90. Ibid.
91. Sen. Ed Markey, "Bipartisan Group of Senators Urge Smooth Transition for Chemical Safety Reform Implementation in New Administration," *Press Release,* November 30, 2016 **[www.markey.senate.gov]**.
92. Sen. Tom Udall, "Udall: With EPA Announcement of First 10 Chemicals for Review Under New Law, Historic Chemical Reform Bill Already Working to Keep American Safe," *Press Release,* November 29, 2016.
93. See, for example, *Safe Food and Fertilizer v. EPA,* 350 F.3d 1263 (D.C. Cir. 2003) **[https://law.justia.com]**.
94. U.S. Environmental Protection Agency, "Regulatory Exclusions and Alternative Standards for the Recycling of Materials, Solid Wastes and Hazardous Wastes," accessed June 2023 **[www.epa.gov]**.
95. U.S. Environmental Protection Agency, "National Overview: Facts and Figures on Materials, Wastes and Recycling," accessed June 2023 **[www.epa.gov]**.
96. Stephanie Strom, "Companies Pick Up Used Packaging, and Recycling's Cost," *The New York Times,* March 23, 2012 **[www.nytimes.com]**.
97. U.S. Environmental Protection Agency, "Advancing Sustainable Materials Management: 2018 Fact Sheet," December 2020 **[www.epa.gov]**.

98. Coca-Cola, "Sustainable Packaging," accessed June 2023 [**www.coca-colacompany.com**].
99. "Starbucks Affirms Commitment to a Planet Positive Future Through Innovation and Learnings from Store Partners," March 15, 2022 [**https://stories.starbucks.com**].
100. Anthony DePalma, "Love Canal Declared Clean, Ending Toxic Horror," *The New York Times,* March 18, 2004 [**www.nytimes.com**].
101. U.S. Environmental Protection Agency, "Superfund Special Accounts," accessed June 2023 [**www.epa.gov**].
102. U.S. Environmental Protection Agency, "Superfund: National Priorities List (NPL)," accessed June 2023 [**www.epa.gov**].
103. Department of Ecology, "Hanford Tank Waste Management," *State of Washington,* accessed June 2023 [**https://ecology.wa.gov**].
104. 566 U.S. 120 (2012) [**http://supreme.justia.com**].
105. 578 U.S. __ (2016) [**https://supreme.justia.com**].
106. May Wall and John Fehrenbach, "Scotts Miracle-Gro to Pay $10 Million in Criminal Fines and Civil Penalties, and Spend $2.5 Million on Environmental Projects, for Violations of Federal Pesticide Laws," *Association of Corporate Counsel,* September 10, 2012.
107. Katie Rogers, "Princess Cruise Lines to Pay $40 Million Fine for Illegal Dumping," *The New York Times,* December 2, 2016 [**www.nytimes.com**].
108. "Nature's Dangerous Decline 'Unprecedented'; Species Extinction Rates 'Accelerating'," United Nations, May 6, 2019 [**www.un.org**].
109. Stephen Leahy, "One Million Species at Risk of Extinction, UN Report Warns," *National Geographic,* May 6, 2019 [**www.nationalgeographic.com**].
110. Brad Plumer, "Humans Are Speeding Extinction and Altering the Natural World an 'Unprecedented' Pace," *The New York Times,* May 6, 2019 [**www.nytimes.com**].
111. Matt McGrath, "Nature Crisis: Humans 'Threaten 1m Species with Extinction,'" BBC, May 6, 2019 [**bbc.com**].
112. Doyle Rice, "One-Third of All Plant and Animal Species Could Be Extinct in 50 Years, Study Warns," *USA Today,* February 14, 2020 [**www.usatoday.com**].
113. "Climate Change Risks 'Extinction Domino Effect,'" *Science Daily,* November 29, 2018 [**www.sciencedaily.com**].
114. 257 N.E.2d 870 (N.Y. 1970) [**https://law.justia.com**].
115. *American Electric Power Co., Inc. v. Connecticut,* 564 U.S. 410 (2011) [**https://supreme.justia.com**].
116. 342 P.2d 790 (Or. 1959) [**https://law.justia.com**].
117. *Curd v. Mosaic Fertilizer LLC,* 39 So. 3d 1216 (Fla. 2010) [**https://law.justia.com**].
118. Julian Harrell, "Is Gasoline a Defective Product?" *Association of Corporate Counsel,* April 23, 2013; and Office of the Attorney General, N.H. Department of Justice, "MtBE Jury Verdict," press release, April 9, 2013. See also "Supreme Court Refuses Appeal of $236m Exxon Mobil Groundwater Contamination Case," *RT,* May 16, 2016 [**www.rt.com**].
119. *Langan v. Valicopters, Inc.,* 567 P.2d 218 (Wash. 1977) [**https://law.justia.com**].
120. *State Department of Environmental Protection v. Ventron,* 468 A.2d 150 (N.J. 1983) [**https://law.justia.com**].
121. *Branch v. Western Petroleum, Inc.,* 657 P.2d 267 (Utah 1982) [**https://law.justia.com**].
122. Associated Press, "DuPont Found Negligent in Waste-Site Lawsuit," *The Wall Street Journal,* October 3, 2007.

123. "Total Greenhouse Gas Emissions," The World Bank, accessed September 2020 [**https://data.worldbank.org**].

124. "The Kyoto Protocol: Climate Change Success or Global Warming Failure?" *Circular Ecology,* February 4, 2015 [**https://circularecology.com**].

125. Brad Plumer, "Past Climate Treaties Failed. So the Paris Deal Will Try Something Radically Different," *Vox,* December 14, 2015 [**www.vox.com**]; and David G. Victor, "The Collapse of the Kyoto Protocol and the Struggle to Slow Global Warming," Counsel on *Foreign Affairs,* May/June 2001 [**www.cfr.org**].

126. Council of the European Union, "International Agreements on Climate Action," June 2016.

127. The National Security, Military, and Intelligence Panel on Climate Change, "A Security Threat Assessment of Global Climate Change," The Center for Climate and Security, February 2020 [**https://climateandsecurity.org**].

128. Chandrika Narayan, "Pipeline 150 Miles from Dakota Access Protests Leaks 176,000 Gallons," CNN, December 13, 2016 [**www.cnn.com**].

129. Ibid.

130. Hugh Pope, "Uzbeks Manage to Endure Amid Ruins of the Aral Sea," *The Wall Street Journal,* February 5, 1998 [**www.wsj.com**].

131. Norman Bowie and Kenneth Goodpaster, "Corporate Conscience, Money and Motorcars," Business Ethics Report, Highlights of Bentley College's Eighth National Conference on Business Ethics (ed. Peter Kent 1989), pp. 4, 6.

132. "Progfligate Past, Poor Planning Created Mexican Water Crisis," Associated Press, August 22, 2002.

133. Scott Simon, "A Water Crisis Restricts Usage to 6 Hours a Day in One of Mexico's Largest Cities," July 16, 2022 [**www.npr.org**].

134. "Tucker Contra Sierra," Regulation, March–April 1983, pp. 48–49.

135. Robert Crandall, "The Environment," in "Regulation-The First Year," Regulation, January-February 1982, pp. 19, 29, 31.

136. Coco Khan, "Do We Need to Stop Flying to Save the Planet? We Asked an Expert," *The Guardian,* April 15, 2022 [**www.theguardian.com**].

Video icon credit: Comstock Images/Alamy Stock Photo

CHAPTER EIGHTEEN

Internet Law and Ethics

After completing this chapter, students will be able to fulfill the following learning objectives:

18-1. Be able to identify some of the ongoing and emerging challenges for businesses in their use of the Internet.

18-2. Be able to explain what stablecoins are, what distinguishes asset-backed stablecoins, and how stablecoins differ from other cryptocurrencies.

18-3. Explain the term *digital sovereignty* with respect to the jurisdiction to legislate and give examples.

18-4. Identify the three foundational laws governing the Internet in the EU and be able to describe the primary purpose of each of them.

18-5. Be able to compare and contrast the legal frameworks governing the Internet in the EU and in the United States.

18-6. Be able to apply the requirements of personal jurisdiction to a dispute arising in cyberspace, both where the parties are residents of different states and where they are residents of different countries.

18-7. Identify free speech issues that arise in the context of the Internet and present the competing interests that make each particular issue difficult to resolve.

18-8. Provide examples of online activities that raise privacy concerns and be able to identify those concerns.

18-9. Explain the differences in online privacy protection among the federal law of the United States, California's specific laws, and those of the EU.

18-10. Describe several Internet-related crimes—including ransomware, data theft, and control of physical assets—and identify how to protect against them.

18-11. Be able to classify specific items of property associated with the Internet as either real property or personal property, and either tangible property or intangible property.

18-12. Be able to explain what a stablecoin is and distinguish it from an asset-backed stablecoin, as well as how they both differ from other cryptocurrencies.

18-13. Be able to identify ways in which the Internet is dependent on the protection provided by patents, copyrights, and trademarks.

18-14. Explain the trademark issues affecting e-commerce facilitators like eBay.

18-15. Be able to describe the tax implications of mining, receiving, and spending cryptocurrencies.

18-16. Discuss several ethical issues raised by social media.

Part One—The Market, Law, and Ethics

Introduction: The Internet and Business

By its very nature, the Internet is a rapidly evolving space. It is also a unique and complex space for a number of reasons:

- It is potentially accessible by any person in the world:
  - According to the International Telecommunication Union, a United Nations specialized agency for information and communication technologies, as of November 2021, 4.9 billion people had used the Internet, or 63 percent of the population.[1] Ninety-six percent of the 2.9 billion who have not been online live in developing countries. The largest annual percentage increase in the number of users occurred in the first year of the pandemic.[2]
  - Not surprisingly, the least developed countries have the lowest percentage of usage, and the women in those countries have a lower percentage of usage than the men, 27 percent compared to 30 percent.[3]
- Some countries have put in place measures to restrict access beyond their national boundaries. As of this writing, China and North Korea have the most stringent controls. Iran, Myanmar, Turkmenistan, and the United Arab Emirates also exert substantial controls.[4]
- Every country can potentially develop standards that apply to residents of that country, which means, for the most part, individuals will be most highly impacted by the laws of the country in which they reside. In the EU, the most powerful laws are those enacted by the European Parliament, but there may be national laws that also apply. In the United States, federal laws are often supplemented by more stringent state laws, in addition to state laws governing areas in which Congress has not acted.

Where does all this leave businesses? They are left with the challenge of complying with the laws of all of the states and nations in which they operate. This may affect more businesses than you might initially realize. According to the International Organization for Economic Co-operation and Development (OECD), "about 70% of international trade today involves global value chains (GVCs), as services, raw materials, parts, and components cross borders–often numerous times. Once incorporated into final products they are shipped to consumers all over the world."[5]

> 4.9 billion people have used the Internet, or 63 percent of the population.

LO 18-1
Be able to identify some of the ongoing and emerging challenges for businesses in their use of the Internet.

The primary goal of this chapter is to explore some of the current, ongoing, and emerging challenges facing the full spectrum of entities (public or private, for-profit or non-profit) in their use of the Internet, as well as highlighting a few businesses that exist solely because of the Internet (for example, social networks and cryptocurrencies). We will also explore the perspectives of individuals in their dealings via the Internet with those entities.

That said, what we will cover is only the tip of the iceberg.

The roots of the Internet date back to the late 1960s when a small group of researchers sought a way to freely exchange digital information with colleagues at other institutions. By the end of the 1980s, a backbone system of networked computers had been created, and email use reached the general public. In the mid-1990s, the first browser was released and the World Wide Web was born.[6] Since then the cost of both technology and access has dropped and made the Internet a truly public, and international, space.

The growth in users and uses has created the most diverse community imaginable.

Originally, it was an open-access forum only lightly touched by regulation. The exponential growth in users and uses has now created the most diverse community imaginable–nearly as diverse as the human race itself. Unfortunately, along with volume and diversity come conflicting interests and disputes. No existing judicial or legislative body has obvious or natural jurisdiction over the Internet in its entirety. "[T]herein lies the central truth of globalization today: We're all connected and nobody is in charge."[7]

What choices do we have in this difficult situation? On one end of the spectrum, one might argue for the establishment and enforcement of globally applicable principles and processes. On the other end, one might predict complete balkanization with countries enforcing national standards by creating isolated domestic Internets. As with most aspects of our globalized world, the result to date falls in the middle: global standards where uniformity is critical to the functioning of the whole system and national regulation where fundamental cultural values and political choices differ, including in some cases the establishment of separate national Internets as already mentioned.

LO 18-2
Be able to describe some of the limitations of work produced by generative A.I. and steps that can be taken to correct for those limitations.

Practicing Ethics: ChatGPT and Other Generative A.I.

As this is being written, ChatGPT, a creation of OpenAI, is the first readily accessible generative artificial intelligence (A.I.) tool on the market. Like the initial releases of other technology, improvements will come. But people are already taking it out for a test drive to see what it can, and cannot (at least not yet), do. Examples tried, albeit not necessarily successfully, include composing an entire song, making a logo, and writing an entire book in one day. Others have used it to write homework assignments, both with and without the permission of the instructor.

The "with" permission submissions have come from instructors who are themselves experimenting with ways AI can aid in the educational process. One high school English teacher in Oregon had the class use ChatGPT to create outlines for essays comparing and contrasting two short stories. "The process, she said, had not only deepened students' understanding of the stories. It had also taught them about interacting with A.I. models, and how to coax a helpful response out of one."[8]

As a warning to those who use it for homework "without permission," best be aware that OpenAI has also released a tool to allow readers to identify text generated by ChatGPT. Turnitin, which many institutions use to check for plagiarism, has indicated that it is incorporating features in its software for identifying A.I. use in submitted papers.

Other appropriate cautions if you're going to experiment: the results may not have much grounding in truth. As many of us have discovered, much of what is searchable has only a tenuous relationship to reality and the language used could be either biased or just plain offensive. Finally, ChatGPT results are often not annotated, so you won't know the sources that were used, which means you are likely to have to do your own research to check the results.

One interesting question involves how A.I. programs are trained. What if you asked it to create a comic strip on a particular topic? You might think the result you get back looks rather like that your favorite webcomic, Sarah Anderson. Why? A.I. text-to-image generators "learned" how to create comic strips by creating data sets collected from images found on the Internet (called data scraping). Many artists, as identified by Ms. Anderson, have had "what amounted to our entire portfolios fed into the data set without our consent. This means that A.I. generators were built on the backs of our copyrighted work."[9] Further, since users can enter artists' names in with their request, their names can call up imitations, of varying quality and content, that the artist has not approved, while the implication is that the image represents their work.

Question

Artificial intelligence is powerful, but like all technology, it is ethically neutral. Our choices about how we use it present ethical issues. The Research Exercise on Ethics and A.I. at the end of the chapter will allow you to explore the application of ethics to the use of generative A.I.

Sources: Kalley Huang, "Alarmed by A.I. Chatbots, Universities Start Revamping How They Teach," *The New York Times,* January 16, 2023 [**www.nytimes.com**]; Alan Truly, "5 amazing things people have already done with ChatGPT," *digitaltrends,* December 29, 2022 [**www.digitaltrends.com**]; Kevin Roose, "Don't Ban ChatGPT in Schools. Teach With It," *The New York Times,* January 12, 2023 [**www.nytimes.com**]; Annie Chechitelli, "Sneak preview of Turnitin's AI writing and ChatGPT detection capability," *turnitin,* January 13, 2023 [**turnitin.com**]; Fionna Agomuoh, "ChatGPT has a new way to detect its own plagiarism," *digitaltrends,* February 1, 2023 [**www.digitaltrends.com**]; and Sarah Anderson, "The Alt-Right Manipulated My Comic. Then A.I. Claimed It." *The New York Times,* December 31, 2022 [**www.nytimes.com**].

Market Forces and Government Regulation

As we have seen throughout this text, markets rarely effectively self-regulate. One example occurred in early 2017 when rideshare company Uber suffered the loss of over 200,000 users due to public outcry over the company's perceived strike-breaking and support of President Trump's immigration ban. When New York City taxi drivers went on strike at John F. Kennedy International Airport to protest the ban, Uber announced that they would continue to provide service to the airport, leading to the viral hashtag #Delete Uber. Over the coming days, Lyft, Uber's top competitor, experienced an over 60 percent increase in ridesharing app activations, swiftly taking about 5 percent of Uber's market share. This breach of socially acceptable business behavior, as judged by the market, was followed quickly by numerous additional scandals, resulting in the resignation of Uber's co-founder and CEO.[10] Two years later, the fallout from these scandals continued to represent a notable risk factor for the company.[11]

In most instances, however, the market will not self-correct and regulation at some level may be necessary. For example, to regulate the actual functioning of the Internet and its component parts, global norms are required. Many norms, such as the assignment of top-level domain names (.com, .org, and so forth) and the system for routing digital traffic, had routinely been set by the United States. However, the European Union and Brazil successfully argued that matters of Internet governance should be globalized instead of resting with the United States.[12] The United States conceded. Effective October 1, 2016, it relinquished control of the Internet Corporation for Assigned Names and Numbers (ICANN). Originally established by the United States Department of Commerce, ICANN is now an independent organization that will continue to oversee the distribution of Internet addresses. ICANN also owns the database that stores all Internet domain names, the Internet Assigned Numbers Authority.[13]

Most Internet issues have not been resolved by establishing one rule applicable to all.

Most issues, however, have not been resolved by establishing one rule applicable to all Internet users. Instead we have a complicated patchwork in which some issues are resolved collectively by a subset of nations, such as the EU; some are resolved by individual nations; and in the United States, issues that have not been resolved by Congress have been left to the states individually to resolve. Examples of each of these will be discussed.

LO 18-3
Explain the term *digital sovereignty* with respect to the jurisdiction to legislate and give examples.

Jurisdiction to Legislate

Governmental bodies, including supranational bodies such as the European Union, only have power (in this context referred to as jurisdiction) to legislate the actions of their own citizens and those residing within their geographic boundaries. Thus, normally a rule adopted by the EU would not have force of law for an American citizen unless that person resides in the EU. However, if a United States business wishes to provide services to a person located in the EU, that business may be required to comply with some of the EU's laws. This is particularly germane to American and other non-EU businesses that provide services over the Internet to persons located in the EU. For example, all of the American Internet icons–Apple, Amazon, Alphabet, Microsoft, and Meta–are subject to EU regulation. In some instances, this has required profound changes in their services with respect to EU citizens. In essence, if those companies want to do business in Europe, they have to adhere to European rules.

LO 18-4
Identify the three foundational laws governing the Internet in the EU and be able to describe the primary purpose of each of them.

Countries within and outside the EU may also have national laws that govern the provision of services over the Internet to their citizens (such as those that set national data and privacy standards), which collectively are sometimes referred to as *digital sovereignty* laws.[14] For example, at least 140 countries have regulations requiring that the digital information of their residents be stored in that country;[15] France and Austria prohibit companies from using Google Analytics to collect audience information from those nations' websites;[16] the Netherlands is insisting that Apple permit multiple payment options for using apps on their residents' iPhones (issuing weekly fines of 25 million euros until Apple complies); it also required Google to add privacy protections to its tools for schools or have its products banned;[17] and Canada and Austria require that Alphabet and Meta pay Canadian and Austrian media outlets when those companies allow links to these outlets' news content to be posted on their platforms.[18]

LO 18-5
Be able to compare and contrast the legal frameworks governing the Internet in the EU and in the United States.

The European Union

For a new law to be adopted by the European Union, it must have the approval of three separate bodies: the European Commission must propose the law, then it has to be approved by both the European Parliament and the Council of Ministers. Parliament members are elected by the citizens of their home country, with members apportioned among the EU states in proportion to country populations. Each member country's minister for a particular policy area sits on the Council of Ministers. For example, agricultural issues would be addressed by the Ministers of Agriculture.

Consider the implications of this structure. The icons of American technology want to do business in the EU because it is a substantial and influential market. But that makes them subject to EU laws vis-à-vis their EU customers. Those laws require the agreement of three bodies, the membership of two of which are not elected (providing a partial explanation for the EU's lower susceptibility to American lobbying efforts).

The EU has adopted three major laws governing the tech industry, all of which are groundbreaking in their coverage and depth. They provide frameworks that other jurisdictions can emulate.

- In 2016, the EU adopted the General Data Protection Regulation (GDPR), the rules became enforceable on May 25, 2018. Its purpose is to protect the personal data of EU citizens and to regulate the movement of such data. It mandates that individuals must consent to having their person information collected or used, making it opt-in, rather than the opt-out structure used in the United States. It replaced the 1995 Data Protection Directive, which established similar principles but left it to each member state to translate the principles into national laws. In contrast, the GDPR is enforceable by national regulators in any of the 27 EU countries, in part through fines as high as 20 million euros or 4 percent of a company's global revenue, whichever is higher.[19] Over $2.4 billion has been levied collectively against Amazon, Instagram, Facebook, and Google through January 2023. This includes a $414 million fine on Meta imposed in January 2023 by the European Data Protection Board, which overruled the contrary decision of Ireland's data privacy board.[20] As of September 2022, about 160 countries have used the GDPR as a model for enacted legislation.[21]
- The 2022 Digital Services Act (DSA) regulates how platforms moderate content, advertise, and use algorithms for recommendation systems across online marketplaces, social networks, app stores, travel websites, and more. Service providers have until January 1, 2024 to become compliant. If notified by trusted flaggers, platforms will be required to remove illegal content "expeditiously." Transparency is one of the DSA's goals. Explanations must be provided for content removed. There must be a clear label on every ad users see, and the party who paid for the ad must be identified. The DSA imposes privacy protections, in part by prohibiting platforms from undertaking targeted advertising based on sensitive user information, such as ethnicity or sexual orientation. Platforms must explain in detail their content curation algorithms in user-friendly language and give users the option to choose a content curation algorithm that is not based on profiling. Very large online platforms (VLOPs) have greater obligations and will face oversight through independent annual audits.[22] Significantly, the DSA and the Digital Markets Act (discussed next) will be enforced by the European Commission, rather than by member states.
- The 2022 Digital Markets Act (DMA), in the words of the European Commission, "will put an end to unfair practices by companies that act as gatekeepers in the online platform economy."[23] The DMA defines these gatekeepers as digital platforms that provide gateways between business users and consumers whose market share gives them the power to act as private rulemakers. Data provided on Wikipedia's DMA

entry shows that "EU digital markets face a high level of concentration, with companies such as Google or Facebook controlling almost the entirety of a specific market segment."[24] The DMA prohibits such gatekeepers from engaging in certain behaviors, as described below.

- Gatekeepers are companies that operate services "such as app stores, online search engines, social networking services, certain messaging services, video sharing platform services, virtual assistants, web browsers, cloud computing services, operating systems, online marketplaces, and advertising services."[25] They must be of a size sufficient to impact the market based on a specified level of annual revenues. They must provide at least one of the services noted above in at least three EU member states to more than (in each of the prior three years) 45 million monthly active end-users and to more than 10,000 yearly active business users in the EU.[26] Penalties and fines up to 10 percent of worldwide revenues (20 percent in the case of repeated infringements) may be imposed, along with behavioral or structural remedies.[27] These latter could include: requiring the gatekeeper "to make their messaging services interoperable and provide business users access to their data," allowing business users "to promote competing products and services on the platform and reach deals with customers off the platforms," and prohibiting the gatekeeper from favoring "their own services over rivals' or prevent[ing] users from removing pre-installed software or apps."[28]
- The DMA prohibits "combining data collected from two different services belonging to the same company (for example, Facebook and WhatsApp);"[29] "bans targeted advertising aimed at children or based on sensitive data such as religion, gender, race and political opinions;" and forbids the use of "[d]ark patterns, which are tactics that mislead people into giving personal data to companies online."[30]

The United States

The United States has no general federal online data protection act such as the EU's GDPR. The closest Congress has ever come to enacting such a law occurred in July 2022 when the American Data Privacy and Protection Act became the first such law to be passed out of committee in either the House or the Senate. The vote in the House Energy and Commerce Committee was nearly unanimous, but the bill never came to a House floor vote, let alone advance to the Senate for consideration. Congress did pass the Children's Online Privacy Protection Act, which took effect in 2008 and was revised in 2013. Its provisions will be addressed in Part Three.

State Laws

California In the United States, California has been the leader in protecting personal online privacy. At this writing, it is in the process of establishing the California Privacy Protection Agency, the first government agency "in the United States with the sole job of regulating how Google, Facebook, Amazon and other companies collect and use data from millions of people."[31] California's first step was the enactment in 2004 of a law which requires commercial websites that collect personally identifiable information on California residents to conspicuously post a privacy policy on their websites. In 2020, it passed the California Consumer Privacy Act (CCPA), which has since been amended several times and, in general, gives California residents considerable control over what data is collected on them and how it is used, as well as the power to require its deletion. The CCPA applies to any business (whether it is a retailer, a phone company, a ride-hailing app, or any other kind of business) that operates in California and meets one or more of the following criteria:

- Has annual gross revenues greater than $25 million.
- Earns more than half of its annual revenues from selling consumers' information.
- Buys, receives, or sells the personal information of 50,000 or more consumers or households.[32]

Most recently, California's legislature passed the California Age-Appropriate Design Code Act, to take effect in 2024, which will require general-audience sites and apps that are "likely to be accessed" by children to install basic protections for users under 18.

The substantive provisions of these laws will be discussed in Part Three, as well as California's recently passed law imposing new rules to address child online safety.

Washington Somewhat ironically, Washington State's privacy bill, which failed to pass in 2022, has been and is being used as a template for privacy bills in several other states,[33] including Virginia, Colorado, Utah, and Connecticut–each of which became law in 2022.

Other States As of mid-January 2023, eight states were considering broad consumer data privacy laws; four had children's privacy laws before them; and two were considering biometric privacy bills. All of this activity is indicative of the need states feel for enforceable rules in the absence of federal legislation.[34]

[To check the status of state consumer data privacy legislation, see **https://www.huschblackwell.com/2023-state-privacy-law-tracker**. Insert the current year where "2023" appears in this link or go to **www.huschblackwell.com**, select Blogs from their dropdown menu, and then click on "Byte Back."]

Questions

1. Do you believe the Internet-based social media and e-commerce markets can be relied on to properly control their participants' behavior without government regulation? Explain.
2. The EU is widely considered to be far ahead of the United States with respect to regulating the Internet (for example, data privacy and transparency in advertising and content recommendation algorithms). What might be responsible for this situation?
3. If you were an EU resident who frequently used the Internet to locate information on healthy eating, dietary supplements, safe and effective exercise, maintaining good mental health, and surgical procedures to address physical problems, would you be glad the EU put the DSA in place? Explain your answer.
4. Why are California and other states becoming so active in the area of Internet data privacy?

Part Two—Jurisdiction to Adjudicate

LO 18-6
Be able to apply the requirements of personal jurisdiction to a dispute arising in cyberspace, both where the parties are residents of different states and where they are residents of different countries.

Business in the cyberworld raises puzzling legal problems. The Internet, after all, is borderless. We communicate and engage in transactions around the world. When a dispute arises from one of those billions of communications and transactions, where will that dispute be litigated? If an American website provides child pornography viewed by a resident of Germany, which nation will have the authority to prosecute the offense?[35] If a Massachusetts resident posts an arguably libelous article on a dedicated server sited in New York, may the Texas resident who claims harm from the libel sue the author and the host server in a Texas court?[36] These are *jurisdictional* questions. The party filing suit must take its claim to a court that has both *subject-matter jurisdiction* (the authority to address the particular kind of legal problem raised) and *personal jurisdiction* (the power to compel the defendant to respond). (For a general discussion of jurisdiction, see Chapter 4.)

In the United States, if both the plaintiff and defendant are residents of the forum state, personal jurisdiction ordinarily is not an issue. However, personal jurisdiction over nonresidents depends on the constitutional requirement of *due process.* In practice, the test is one of *minimum contacts:* Did the defendant have sufficient contact with the forum state that being sued there would be fair and just? Put another way, was the defendant's contact with the forum state of such a nature that it should expect to be subject to the state's courts? Thus, the more business a defendant does in a state, the more likely personal jurisdiction will be found. Internet business raises special problems because the "contacts" are often electronic and fleeting.

> Did the defendant have sufficient contact with the state that being sued there would be fair and just?

Several cases have arisen in the United States that begin to answer these personal jurisdiction questions. In one, the Fifth Circuit held in a case of alleged copyright violation that Texas did not have personal jurisdiction over a Vermont corporation merely because the corporation's website was accessible from Texas.[37] It reached this conclusion, in part, because there was no specific connection between the existence of the corporation's website and the harm complained of by the plaintiff. Thus, the Vermont corporation could be sued in Texas only if it had contacts with Texas that were sufficiently "continuous and systematic" as to subject the corporation to suit in Texas generally. A passive website was insufficient to do this. When the defendant has more contact with the forum state than the existence of a passive website reachable by forum state computer users, the due process analysis becomes more complex and hinges on an evaluation of the defendant's specific additional contacts with the state. The existing decisions are often hard to reconcile and many cases have been reversed on appeal, indicating that judgments as to personal jurisdiction are challenging and uncertain.[38]

Question

The operator of the dating service be2.com sued the CEO of a competing dating service, be2.net, for trademark infringement. The suit was brought in a federal district court in Illinois. The defendant was a New Jersey resident. The only evidence of his contact with Illinois was a list of 20 Illinois members of be2.net. After the court granted a default judgment when the defendant did not respond to the complaint, the defendant moved to vacate the judgment for lack of personal jurisdiction.[39] Should Illinois courts have jurisdiction? Explain.

Jurisdiction in International Suits

Similar jurisdictional issues arise across national boundaries. In 2010, an Italian court convicted three U.S.-based Google executives in absentia of violating Italian privacy laws based on a video posted by third parties on Google's system. The video showed three teenage boys harassing a boy with autism. Italian law holds executives responsible for company actions.[40] Google appealed, and the decision was overturned. The appellate court found that Google had not performed an editorial function. Under EU law at least at that time, mere hosting of user-generated content did not make the hosting service responsible for the content.[41]

> Most countries have long had laws that prohibit or regulate some forms of commerce, such as pornography, gambling, and alcohol.

In international contexts, it may be useful to distinguish among three types of jurisdiction: jurisdiction to prescribe (legislate), jurisdiction to adjudicate (judicial personal jurisdiction), and jurisdiction to enforce.[42] Most countries have long had laws that prohibit or regulate some forms of commerce, such as pornography, gambling, and alcohol. When a country seeks to apply those laws to foreigners, the question is whether the country has jurisdiction to adjudicate. The Restatement (Third) of Foreign Relations Law attempts to identify the circumstances under which countries have exercised their jurisdiction to adjudicate. It enumerates, among other circumstances: (1) when a person is present in the territory, other than transitorily; (2) when a person is domiciled, a resident, or a national of that country; (3) when a person regularly carries on business in that country; (4) when a person has carried on an activity in the country and that activity is the subject of the dispute; and (5) when a person has done something outside the country that has a "substantial, direct, and foreseeable effect within" the country and that effect forms the subject of the suit.

Questions

1. Based on the standards presented in the Restatement above, under which of the listed standards, if any, do you think the Italian courts would have had the jurisdiction to adjudicate with respect to Google's American executives?
2. In 2022, the attorney general for the state of Indiana sued TikTok, which is owned by the Chinese company ByteDance, for a violation of Indiana's consumer protection laws for its failure to disclose the Chinese government's ability to access sensitive customer information collected by the app. TikTok denied that it sends data belonging to Americans to the Chinese government. TikTok referenced its offices in Los Angeles and Singapore as evidence of its independence and said that the Chinese government has never tried to access data of U.S. users. Indiana's attorney general argued such assurances were not credible because Chinese law gives the government the authority to demand data from a U.S. affiliate. The attorney general also said that in Europe TikTok discloses that user data can be accessed by individuals, including those in China.[43]
   A. Under the circumstances enumerated in the Restatement above, do Indiana courts have jurisdiction hear the attorney general's case against TikTok? Explain your answer.
   B. Would Indiana have jurisdiction to include ByteDance as a defendant in the suit? Explain your answer.

Consider now both the French court's approach and the U.S. district court's approach to the issue of jurisdiction to adjudicate in the following dispute.

Yahoo! v. La Ligue Contre Le Racisme et L'Antisemitisme

169 F. Supp. 2D 1181 (N.D. Cal. 2001)

Judge Jeremy Fogel

I. PROCEDURAL HISTORY

[Defendant] La Ligue Contre Le Racisme Et L'Antisemitisme ("LICRA") [is a French nonprofit organization] dedicated to eliminating anti-Semitism. Plaintiff Yahoo!, Inc. ("Yahoo!") is a corporation organized under the laws of Delaware with its principal place of business in Santa Clara, California. . . . Yahoo! services ending in the suffix ".com," without an associated country code as a prefix or extension (collectively, "Yahoo!'s U.S. Services"), use the English language and target users who are residents of, utilize servers based in, and operate under the laws of the United States. Yahoo! subsidiary corporations operate regional Yahoo! sites and services in 20 other nations, including, for example, Yahoo! France, Yahoo! India, and Yahoo! Spain. Each of these regional websites contains the host nation's unique two-letter code as either a prefix or a suffix in its URL. Yahoo!'s regional sites use the local region's primary language, target the local citizenry, and operate under local laws.

Yahoo! provides a variety of means by which people from all over the world can communicate and interact with one another over the Internet. . . . As relevant here, Yahoo!'s auction site allows anyone to post an item for sale and solicit bids from any computer user from around the globe. Yahoo! records when a posting is made and after the requisite time period lapses sends an e-mail notification to the highest bidder and seller with their respective contact information. Yahoo! is never a party to a transaction, and the buyer and seller are responsible for arranging privately for payment and shipment of goods. Yahoo! monitors the transaction through limited regulation by prohibiting particular items from being sold (such as stolen goods, body parts, prescription and illegal drugs, weapons, and goods violating U.S. copyright laws or the Iranian and Cuban embargos). . . . Yahoo! informs auction sellers that they must comply with Yahoo!'s policies and may not offer items to buyers in jurisdictions in which the sale of such item violates the jurisdiction's applicable laws. Yahoo! does not actively regulate the content of each posting, and individuals are able to post, and have in fact posted, highly offensive matter, including Nazi-related propaganda and Third Reich memorabilia, on Yahoo!'s auction sites.

On or about April 5, 2000, LICRA sent a "cease and desist" letter to Yahoo!'s Santa Clara headquarters informing Yahoo! that the sale of Nazi and Third Reich–related goods through its auction services violates French law. LICRA threatened to take legal action unless Yahoo! took steps to prevent such sales within eight days. Defendants subsequently utilized the United States Marshal's Office to serve Yahoo! with process in California and filed a civil complaint against Yahoo! in the Tribunal de Grande Instance de Paris (the "French Court").

The French Court found that approximately 1,000 Nazi and Third Reich–related objects, including Adolf Hitler's *Mein Kampf, The Protocol of the Elders of Zion* (an infamous anti-Semitic report produced by the Czarist secret police in the early 1900s), and purported "evidence" that the gas chambers of the Holocaust did not exist, were being offered for sale on Yahoo.com's auction site. Because any French citizen is able to access these materials on Yahoo.com directly or through a link on Yahoo.fr, the French Court concluded that the Yahoo.com auction site violates Section R645-1 of the French Criminal Code, which prohibits exhibition of Nazi propaganda and artifacts for sale. On May 20, 2000, the French Court entered an order requiring Yahoo! to (1) eliminate French citizens' access to any material on the Yahoo.com auction site that offers for sale any Nazi objects, relics, insignia, emblems, and flags; (2) eliminate French citizens' access to Web pages on Yahoo.com displaying text, extracts, or quotations from *Mein Kampf* and *Protocol of the Elders of Zion;* (3) post a warning to French citizens on Yahoo.fr that any search through Yahoo.com may lead to sites containing material prohibited by Section R645-1 of the French Criminal Code, and that such viewing of the prohibited material may result in legal action against the Internet user; (4) remove from all browser directories accessible in the French Republic index headings entitled "negationists" and from all hypertext links the equation of "negationists" under the heading "Holocaust." The order subjects Yahoo! to a penalty of 100,000 Euros for each day that it fails to comply with the order. . . .

The French Court also provided that penalties assessed against Yahoo! Inc. may not be collected from Yahoo! France. Defendants again utilized the United States Marshal's Office to serve Yahoo! in California with the French Order.

Yahoo! subsequently posted the required warning and prohibited postings in violation of Section R645-1 of the French Criminal Code from appearing on Yahoo.fr. Yahoo! also amended the auction policy of Yahoo.com to prohibit individuals from auctioning:

> Any item that promotes, glorifies, or is directly associated with groups or individuals known principally for hateful or violent positions or acts, such as Nazis or the Ku Klux Klan. Official government-issue stamps and coins are not prohibited under this policy. Expressive media, such as books and films, may be subject to more permissive standards as determined by Yahoo! in its sole discretion.

Notwithstanding these actions, the Yahoo.com auction site still offers certain items for sale (such as stamps, coins, and a copy of *Mein Kampf*) which appear to violate the French Order. . . .

Yahoo! claims that because it lacks the technology to block French citizens from accessing the Yahoo.com auction site to view materials which violate the French order or from accessing other Nazi-based content of websites on Yahoo.com, it cannot comply with the French order without banning Nazi-related material from Yahoo.com altogether. Yahoo! contends that such a ban would infringe impermissibly upon its rights under the First Amendment to the United States Constitution. Accordingly, Yahoo! filed a complaint in this Court seeking a declaratory judgment that the French Court's orders are neither cognizable nor enforceable under the laws of the United States.

Defendants immediately moved to dismiss on the basis that this Court lacks personal jurisdiction over them. That motion was denied. . . .

II. OVERVIEW

As this Court and others have observed, the instant case presents novel and important issues arising from the global reach of the Internet. Indeed, the specific facts of this case implicate issues of policy, politics, and culture that are beyond the purview of one nation's judiciary. Thus it is critical that the Court define at the outset what is and is not at stake in the present proceeding.

This case is *not* about the moral acceptability of promoting the symbols or propaganda of Nazism. Most would agree that such acts are profoundly offensive. By any reasonable standard of morality, the Nazis were responsible for one of the worst displays of inhumanity in recorded history. . . .

Nor is this case about the right of France or any other nation to determine its own law and social policies. A basic function of a sovereign state is to determine by law what forms of speech and conduct are acceptable within its borders. . . .

What *is* at issue here is whether it is consistent with the Constitution and laws of the United States for another nation to regulate speech by a United States resident within the United States on the basis that such speech can be accessed by Internet users in that nation. In a world in which ideas and information transcend borders and the Internet in particular renders the physical distance between speaker and audience virtually meaningless, the implications of this question go far beyond the facts of this case. The modern world is home to widely varied cultures with radically divergent value systems. There is little doubt that Internet users in the United States routinely engage in speech that violates, for example, China's laws against religious expression, the laws of various nations against advocacy of gender equality or homosexuality, or even the United Kingdom's restrictions on freedom of the press.

The French order prohibits the sale or display of items based on their association with a particular political organization and bans the display of websites based on the authors' viewpoint with respect to the Holocaust and anti-Semitism. A United States court constitutionally could not make such an order. The First Amendment does not permit the government to engage in viewpoint-based regulation of speech absent a compelling governmental interest, such as averting a clear and present danger of imminent violence.

COMITY

No legal judgment has any effect, of its own force, beyond the limits of the sovereignty from which its authority is derived. . . . The extent to which the United States, or any state, honors the judicial decrees of foreign nations is a matter of choice, governed by "the comity of nations." United States courts generally recognize foreign judgments and decrees unless enforcement would be prejudicial or contrary to the country's interests.

As discussed previously, the French order's content and viewpoint-based regulation of the Web pages and auction site on Yahoo.com, while entitled to great deference as an articulation of French law, clearly would be inconsistent with the First Amendment if mandated by a court in the United States. . . . The reason for limiting comity in this area is sound. "The protection to free speech and the press embodied in [the First] amendment would be seriously jeopardized by the entry of foreign judgments granted pursuant to standards deemed appropriate in [another country] but considered antithetical to the protections afforded the press by the U.S. Constitution." Absent a body of law that establishes international standards with respect to speech on the Internet and an appropriate treaty or legislation addressing enforcement of such standards to speech originating within the United States, the principle of comity is outweighed by the Court's obligation to uphold the First Amendment.

CONCLUSION

Yahoo! seeks a declaration from this Court that the First Amendment precludes enforcement within the United States of a French order intended to regulate the content of its speech over the Internet. . . . [Yahoo!'s] motion for summary judgment will be granted.

AFTERWORD

On appeal in 2006, the Ninth Circuit Court of Appeals ruled by a vote of eight to three that the California district court had personal jurisdiction over the French defendants, but six judges also held that Yahoo! could not pursue its declaratory judgment action. Three of those six said the declaratory judgment action was not "ripe" for decision, while the other three were the minority that held that the court had no personal jurisdiction.[44] The Supreme Court declined to review the decision.[45]

Questions

1. We cannot tell from this opinion why the French court believed it had jurisdiction to adjudicate against Yahoo!, as opposed to Yahoo! France. Look back at the discussion of the Restatement (Third) of Foreign Relations Law immediately before this case. Why might the French court have had jurisdiction over Yahoo! France? Over Yahoo!?
2. If you were sitting on the Ninth Circuit, how would you have decided the jurisdiction question? Consider both the U.S. rule of minimum contacts and the Restatement provision.
3. Notice the court's conclusion that the principle of comity is outweighed by its constitutional obligation to uphold the freedom of speech. Is this approach to the requirements of comity consistent with the discussion of comity in Chapter 16?

Part Three—Speech and Privacy

Speech

Regulating Internet Speech

LO 18-7
Identify free speech issues that arise in the context of the Internet and present the competing interests that make each particular issue difficult to resolve.

The district court opinion in *Yahoo! v. La Ligue Contre Le Racisme et L'Antisemitisme* illustrates a free speech issue the Internet raises in an international context. Internet content has also raised free speech issues in the U.S. The Internet's seeming anonymity, ease of use, relatively low costs, and global reach make it a natural vehicle for transporting speech messages. As we saw in Chapter 5, the First Amendment protects us from government restraints on the *content* of speech, although reasonable restraints on the *context* (time, place, and manner) of that speech are sometimes constitutionally permissible. Thus, a court will not restrain free speech by enjoining someone from posting defamatory or copyrighted material, but the damaged party may sue for defamation or copyright infringement after the posting.[46]

[For articles on cyberlaw free speech, search for "free speech" at **http://repository.jmls.edu**. When the results appear, select "Internet Law" under "Discipline."]

The cases discussed in the text box below grapple with the question of when, if ever, the proprietary algorithms developed and used by social media platforms can be classified as speech and, as a result, the platforms classified as content providers. Those algorithms select and shape individualized responses to users' inquiries. For example, if a lover of classical music requests videos of pop-up concerts and a lover of jazz makes the same request, the results returned are apt to be quite different, as well as the ads that accompany them.

The 1996 Communications Decency Act and the Modern Internet

In early 2023, the Supreme Court had two cases from the Ninth Circuit before it that involved claims against Google, Twitter, and Facebook based on real-world impacts facilitated, in part, by the way their algorithms magnify the messages of terrorist organizations, such as ISIS. The cases were:

- *Gonzalez v. Google:*[47] Plaintiffs were family members of Nohemi Gonzalez, a 23-year-old American citizen studying in Paris, who was killed in one of the several attacks perpetrated there by ISIS on November 13, 2015, in which at least 130 people died.

- *Taamneh v. Twitter, Google, and Facebook*:[48] Plaintiffs were U.S. family members of Nawras Alassaf, a Jordanian citizen, who was with his wife in a nightclub in Istanbul, Turkey, to celebrate the 2017 New Year when an individual affiliated with and trained by ISIS entered the nightclub shortly after midnight and in seven minutes "fired more than 120 rounds into the crowd of 1700 people, killing 39 and injuring 69 others."[49]

Plaintiffs in both cases made claims under the Anti-Terrorism Act (ATA), as amended in 2016 to impose secondary liability upon anyone who "aids or abets" international terrorism "by knowingly providing substantial assistance."[50] [18 U.S.C. 2333(a) & (d)(2).] Plaintiffs alleged the defendants were directly and secondarily liable because their social media platforms "allowed ISIS to post videos and other content to communicate the terrorist group's message, to radicalize new recruits, and to generally further its mission."[51] [2 F.4th 880.] In addition, the plaintiffs alleged that "Google placed paid advertisements in proximity to ISIS-created content and shared the resulting ad revenue with ISIS."[52]

In each case the trial court granted defendants' motions to dismiss, which argued that the pleadings failed to state viable causes of action[.] No trials had begun. In both cases the appeals went to the 9th Circuit. The defendants argued that plaintiffs' claims were barred by § 230(c)(1) of the Communications Decency Act (CDA). The Ninth Circuit held that the CDA had no application to the portion of *Gonzalez* alleging that Google provided direct support to ISIS through its sharing of ad revenues[.] Thus, that issue will be discussed here only in the context of Taamneh.

Section 230(c)(1) of the CDA states: "No provider or user of an interactive computer service shall be treated as the publisher or speaker of any information provided by another information content provider." Congress passed the CDA in 1996, when the Internet was a vastly different place. For example, Google didn't exist until 1998, Facebook began in 2004, and Twitter was started in 2006. The Ninth Circuit described the original goal of § 230 as "modest." Then it went on to say, "By passing § 230, Congress sought to allow interactive computer services 'to perform some editing on user-generated content without thereby becoming liable for all defamatory or otherwise unlawful messages that they didn't edit or delete.'"[53]

Now turn the clock back to 1996, when Congress passed the CDA. As noted above, modern social media did not exist at the time. The first web browser usable by ordinary people (Netscape) had only become available in 1994.

Assume that, in 1994, a company (one of thousands seeking to explore the potential of the fledgling Internet) creates a subscription-only (no advertising) Internet platform that allows any subscriber to post any content desired under one of the company's 20 categories (for example: "cooking," "personal finance," "politics," "business," and "finding love"). The only action taken by the company related to the postings is to eliminate pornographic content (as defined by the Supreme Court). The postings are listed in chronological order within each category, but subscribers can perform basic text searches. This was the environment in which the CDA was enacted. Congress, academics, and business leaders all envisioned the nascent Internet's extraordinary possibilities and wanted to shield companies like this from tort liability to those offended by the posted content. Companies that engaged only in the minimalistic types of editing described above were excluded from the status "content provider;" they were merely "publishers." Plaintiffs seeking redress for harms allegedly caused by the content itself could sue only the actual content provider (the person posting the content).

The CDA case law under §230 emerged in that context. However, it became increasingly thorny as Internet platforms incrementally, but fundamentally, revised their business models, evolving into today's generally monetarily free-to-the-user, advertising-funded operations.

This was a dramatic change in the relationships among public users, content providers, advertisers, and platform companies. Among other things, platform providers devised sophisticated algorithms to route users revealing a particular interest to selected content posted by others with related content. Under this structure, advertisers seeking to reach those particular users pay the platform roughly in proportion to the number of viewers coming into contact with their messages, which the platforms place visually adjacent to the user's search results. With certain media content, the platforms also automatically start playing the next item in the search list without any further action on the part of the user, potentially multiplying contact with the advertiser's message many times over as a result of one search.

In significant part as a result of a precedent-structured judicial system, a substantial disjunct now exists between the cumulative case law that developed under the CDA (written in the context of a long-gone 1994 business model) and the potential dangers to society from the way Internet platforms now operate.

"The Gonzalez Plaintiffs argue that Google does more than merely republish content created by third parties; the TAC [Third Amended Complaint] alleges that Google 'creat[es]' and 'develop[s]' the ISIS content that appears on YouTube, at least in part, and therefore receives no protection under § 230."[54] The majority of the Ninth Circuit responded, "we disagree," immediately followed by, "This argument is **precluded by this court's § 230 precedents.**" (Emphasis added.)

However, the Ninth Circuit seems to have gone out of its way to emphasize that, if there had not been prior Ninth Circuit precedent, its decision in *Gonzalez* might well have been different. As it continued with its analysis under § 230, the Court wrote:

- "According to the Gonzalez TAC [Third Amended Complaint], Google makes a material contribution to the unlawfulness of ISIS content by pairing it with selected advertising and other videos because 'pairing' enhances user engagement with the underlying content. **Our case law forecloses the argument that this type of pairing vitiates § 230 immunity.**"[55] (Emphasis added.)
- "**Our precedent requires that we reach the same outcome** and we hold, **consistent with our case law,** that Google is entitled to § 230 immunity with respect to the Gonzalez Plaintiffs' theories of liability that are **not** directed to revenue-sharing."[56] (Emphasis added.)
- "[W]e do not hold that 'machine-learning algorithms can never produce content within the meaning of Section 230.' We only reiterate that a website's use of content-neutral algorithms, without more, does not expose it to liability for content posted by a third-party. **Under our existing case law, § 230 requires this result.**"[57] (Emphasis added.)
- "In sum, though we agree the Internet has grown into a sophisticated and powerful global engine the drafters of § 230 could not have foreseen, the **decision we reach is dictated by the fact that we are not writing on a blank slate.**"[58] (Emphasis added.)

The Supreme Court issued opinions in both the *Taamneh* and *Gonzalez* cases on May 18, 2023, which, in the words of the New York Times, "did not definitively resolve the question of what responsibility platforms should have for the content posted on and recommended by their sites."[59] No ruling was made by the Court with regard to secondary liability under the Anti-Terrorism Act.

Questions

1. From an ethical point of view, do you believe web browsers and social networks bear some responsibility for facilitating criminal activities by sending potentially like-minded individuals to web content that promotes illegal activities?
2. From a legal point of view, do you believe web browsers and social networks should risk legal consequences for facilitating criminal behavior by splitting revenues for ads that might attract more viewers to websites of entities known to be engaging in criminal activities, e.g., ISIS?
3. From an ethical point of view, do you believe social networks bear some level of responsibility for facilitating criminal activities by sending potentially like-minded individuals to related web content? Explain.

Sources: Gonzalez *v. Google* and *Taamneh v. Twitter, Google, and Facebook,* 2 F.4th 871 (9th Cir. 2021); Anna Rhoads, "Incitement and Social Media-Algorithmic Speech: Redefining Brandenburg for a Different Kind of Speech," 64 Wm. & Mary L. Rev. 525 (2022) [**https://scholarship.wm.edu**]; "The History of Web Browsers," *Mozilla,* accessed February 8, 2023 [**www.mozilla.org**]: *Twitter v. Taamneh,* 598 U.S.___ (2023); *Gonzalez v. Google,* 598 U.S.___ (2023); and Adam Liptak, "Supreme Court Won't Hold Tech Companies Liable for User Posts," *The New York Times,* May 18, 2023 [**www.nytimes.com**].

State Regulation of Social Media Platforms

In response to Facebook and Twitter barring President Trump from their platforms after the January 6, 2021, riot in Washington, D.C., both Texas and Florida passed laws designed to prohibit such actions in the future.[60] Florida's statute[61] prohibits social media from "deplatforming" political candidates. The Florida Elections Committee is authorized to fine platforms violating the rule $250,000 per day for candidates running for statewide offices and $25,000 per day for candidates for other offices.

The Texas statute[62] is much broader. It prohibits censoring any user or blocking a user's ability to receive communications from another based on the user's or other person's viewpoint or their location in Texas, without regard to the medium, social or otherwise, in which the viewpoint is expressed. The law only applies to users in Texas and expressions shared or received in Texas and only to social media platforms that have 50 million active U.S. users in a calendar month. It also permits requests intended to prevent the sexual exploitation of children or to protect the survivors of sexual abuse from harassment, as well as communications that directly incite criminal activity.

Groups representing the tech industry, the members of which include Facebook and YouTube, challenged the constitutionality of the laws. The 11th Circuit's decision on the Florida statute found much of that law violated internet platforms' First Amendment rights; the 5th Circuit upheld the Texas law. The Supreme Court has agreed to hear the cases and has prohibited the Texas law from taking effect while the litigation continues.[63]

Online Access to Pornography by Minors

Issues of free speech on the Internet can be far more complex than their analog counterparts. The issue of underage access to pornography illustrates this well. Whereas restricting underage access to pornography was relatively easy before the internet, doing so online may be impossible. Keeping minors away from online pornography, while simultaneously maintaining adult access to constitutionally protected content, has been an ongoing struggle. Congress has repeatedly and unsuccessfully attempted to enact legislation meeting the free

> Restricting underage access to pornography online may be impossible.

speech demands of the Constitution that would also effectively eliminate access by minors. In 1997, the Supreme Court held that critical provisions of the Communications Decency Act of 1996 were overbroad and therefore violated the First Amendment.[64] Then, in 2007, a federal district court found the Child Online Protection Act of 1998 unconstitutional and permanently enjoined its enforcement. In refusing to hear the government's appeal in 2009, the Supreme Court effectively left the permanent injunction in place.[65]

Somewhat more successfully, Congress has addressed a slightly different problem–the exploitation of children in the making of child pornography and its online accessibility to child predators. Its first legislative attempt was held unconstitutional by the Supreme Court,[66] but in 2008 the Court upheld the PROTECT Act of 2003. Nevertheless, child pornography remains one of the Internet's most intractable challenges: "too large for law enforcement, policymakers and child protection groups to handle on their own."[67] Major content hosters, such as YouTube, may enforce content standards, but online child pornography today hides and multiplies on the dark web[68] (a part of the Internet intentionally hidden from search engines and requiring a specific browser, Tor, to gain access).

Anonymous Speech

"[An] author's decision to remain anonymous, like other decisions concerning omissions or additions to the content of a publication, is an aspect of the freedom of speech protected by the First Amendment."[69] So held the U.S. Supreme Court in 1995.

A unique characteristic of the Internet and of electronic communication through the Internet is the ease with which a poster or sender can be anonymous and remain so without "fear of economic or official retaliation . . . [or] social ostracism."[70] Anonymity makes it more likely that individuals will feel free to say things about which they would otherwise keep silent. Thus, it can promote "the robust exchange of ideas."[71] Anonymity may, however, make individuals bolder about asserting untruths–misleading, fraudulent, or otherwise unprotected speech. For example, sites containing nonconsensual pornography on which exes can post explicit photos and videos of their former partners, colloquially known as "revenge porn," have proliferated, at times along with disparaging remarks, information on where the individuals work and live, and links to their social media accounts.

> Over one million people signed a petition to stop Pornhub from posting underage and other nonconsensual pornographic videos.

The victim of such a post can request that the hosting site remove the material, but it is largely up to that site whether the content will actually be removed. Even if the offending material is removed from the originating site, there is a significant chance that it has been copied and could reappear in other locations at any time. This occurs frequently on Pornhub, the most popular porn site in the world, where flagged content can take weeks to be removed. According to a report in 2020, over one million people signed a petition demanding that Pornhub stop posting underage and other nonconsensual pornographic videos, but the company, citing freedom of speech and freedom of expression, continues to allow these types of submissions.[72] As discussed previously, the Communications Decency Act makes it very unlikely that the hosting website will be held liable for such postings, particularly if it removes the material when requested by the subject of the posting to do so. The law rests liability on the "information content provider" and courts have generally held that website owners are not content providers on these facts. However, some lower courts seem willing to consider that some actions of a hosting website may result in liability–such as itself supplying responsive comments supportive of the original post or by naming the site in such a way as to encourage offensive, damaging, or defamatory posts.[73]

As of this writing, 48 states and Washington, D.C., have passed some form of nonconsensual pornography law, providing legal avenues for victims to directly hold perpetrators accountable,[74] although victims and legal professionals point to a myriad of problems and loopholes, including a requirement to prove malicious intent on the part of the perpetrator.[75] Victims have occasionally been successful bringing civil suits for damages, depending on their specific facts, based on copyright infringement, emotional distress, online impersonation, harassment, invasion of privacy, voyeurism, or stalking.[76] [For more on the campaign to end revenge porn, see **www.cybercivilrights.org**].

Before a victim of revenge porn or other forms of online harassment, defamation, and invasion of privacy can sue the content provider, the victim has to be able to prove who that is. Seeking the release of this information from the website or the ISP of the poster triggers First Amendment claims for anonymity on behalf of the original poster. In the case that follows, a Yahoo! poster argues that the First Amendment prohibits Yahoo! from responding to a subpoena from Immunomedics, a corporation claiming that the anonymous poster is, or was, an employee who violated the company's confidentiality agreement by posting company information on a Yahoo! message board.

LEGAL BRIEFCASE

Immunomedics v. Jean Doe

775 A.2d 773 (N.J. Super. 2001)

Judge Fall

Defendant Jean Doe, a/k/a "moonshine_fr," appeals from an order . . . denying her motion to quash a subpoena issued to Yahoo! by plaintiff, Immunomedics, Inc., seeking all personally identifiable information relating to the person or identity who posted messages on the Yahoo! Finance Message Board under the identifier "moonshine_fr" which may identify or lead to the identification of that person or entity.

Immunomedics is a publicly held biopharmaceutical Delaware corporation . . . focused on the development, manufacture, and commercialization of diagnostic imaging and therapeutic products for the detection and treatment of cancer and infectious diseases.

Yahoo! is an Internet Service Provider (ISP) that maintains a Web site that includes a section called Yahoo! Finance. Yahoo! Finance maintains a message board for every publicly traded company, including Immunomedics. Visitors to the Immunomedics site can obtain up-to-date information on the company, and can post and exchange messages about issues related to the operation or performance of the company.

On October 12, 2000, Immunomedics filed a complaint against Jean Doe, also known by the computer screen name "moonshine_fr" ("Moonshine"). The complaint alleged that Moonshine had "posted a message on Yahoo! Finance." Immunomedics claimed that message contained information confidential and proprietary to Immunomedics. As a result, Immunomedics asserted it had sustained injury and that Moonshine should be held liable under theories of breach of contract, breach of duty of loyalty, and negligently revealing confidential and proprietary information.

Of the two messages in question, the first, with Moonshine describing herself as "[a] worried employee," stated that Immunomedics was "out of stock for diagnostic products in Europe" and claimed that there would be "no more sales if [the] situation [did] not change." The second message, allegedly posted by Moonshine after the initial complaint was filed, reported that Chairman of the Company Dr. Goldenberg was going to fire the Immunomedics "european manager." In her certification to the trial court, Immunomedics' Executive Vice President and Chief Operations Officer Cynthia L. Sullivan admitted that the statements were true, but that, as an employee,

Moonshine had violated the company's confidentiality agreement and "several provisions" of the company's Employee Handbook.

On or about October 20, 2000, Immunomedics served a subpoena on Yahoo!, seeking discovery of Moonshine's true identity. Yahoo!, in turn, contacted Moonshine. In response, Moonshine filed a motion to quash the subpoena on or about November 15, 2000.

. . . After considering the arguments, the judge denied Moonshine's motion, stating, in pertinent part,

> We have two issues here. We have an issue, she's an employee, she signed a confidential document saying that she was not going to speak freely about information she learned at the company. So she contracted away her right of free speech if she's an employee. Number two, free speech, anonymous, but if it harms another individual, that is another way that we have a little bit of a dent in our rights for free speech.

Moonshine contends the motion judge erred in denying her motion to quash the subpoena, as anonymous speech is constitutionally protected and Immunomedics' complaint is insufficient to warrant a breach of that anonymity. Immunomedics argues that, while anonymous speech is constitutionally protected, that protection can be overcome if a defendant uses that freedom in an unlawful manner. . . .

In another case involving an application for expedited discovery to disclose the identity of an anonymous user of an ISP message board, we concluded that courts must decide such applications by striking a balance between the First Amendment right of an individual to speak anonymously and the right of a company to protect its proprietary interest in the pursuit of claims based on actionable conduct by the ISP message board user.

We hold that . . . the trial court should first require the plaintiff to undertake efforts to notify the anonymous posters that they are the subject of a subpoena or application for an order of disclosure, and withhold action to afford the fictitiously named defendants a reasonable opportunity to file and serve opposition to the application. . . .

The court shall also require the plaintiff to identify and set forth the exact statements purportedly made by each anonymous poster that plaintiff alleges constitute actionable speech.

The complaint and all information provided to the court should be carefully reviewed to determine whether plaintiff has set forth a prima facie cause of action against the fictitiously named anonymous defendants. In addition . . . , the plaintiff must produce sufficient evidence supporting each element of its cause of action, on a prima facie basis, prior to a court ordering the disclosure of the identity of the unnamed defendant.

Finally, assuming the court concludes that the plaintiff has presented a prima facie cause of action, the court must balance the defendant's First Amendment right of anonymous free speech against the strength of the prima facie case presented and the necessity for the disclosure of the anonymous defendant's identity to allow the plaintiff to properly proceed.

Applying the procedure and test outlined, we conclude Judge Zucker-Zarett properly analyzed the disclosure issue, and we affirm substantially for the reasons articulated by the judge in her oral opinion. . . . We add the following. Immunomedics presented sufficient evidence that Moonshine is, or was, an employee of Immunomedics. Ms. Sullivan indicated in her certification that "all employees are bound by several Company policies and a confidentiality agreement." Within its "Confidentiality and Assignment Agreement," Immunomedics includes the following language:

> This Agreement and any disputes arising under or in connection with it shall be governed by the laws of the State of New Jersey and each of the parties hereto hereby submits to the jurisdiction of any Federal or state court sitting in the State of New Jersey over any such dispute.

Accordingly, Immunomedics clearly established a prima facie cause of action for breach of the confidentiality agreement founded on the content of Moonshine's posted messages.

In balancing Moonshine's right of anonymous free speech against the strength of the prima facie case presented and the necessity for disclosure, it is clear that the motion judge struck the proper balance in favor of identity disclosure. . . . Although anonymous speech on the Internet is protected, there must be an avenue for redress for those who are wronged. Individuals choosing to harm another or violate an agreement through speech on the Internet cannot hope to shield their identity and avoid punishment through invocation of the First Amendment.

Affirmed.

Questions

1. In your opinion, should employers, victimized individuals, and others who have been damaged by anonymous postings be able to obtain the identity of the poster from the hosting site or the poster's ISP? Explain.
2. An FBI agent monitored an AOL chat room suspected of being a site for exchanging child pornography. The agent did not participate in the chat room conversations. Charbonneau allegedly distributed child pornography to the chat room participants, including the FBI agent. Charbonneau was arrested. Did Charbonneau have a First Amendment free speech right to transmit child pornography online? Explain. See *U.S. v. Kenneth Charbonneau,* 979 F. Supp. 1177 (S.D. Ohio 1997).
3. Having read these materials on freedom of speech and the limits on the right to anonymity, what would you advise a friend who was a regular blogger? A classmate posting comments on **www.ratemyprofessors.com**? Your middle school cousin who is an avid Facebook user? Explain.

Commercial Speech

Remember from Chapter 5 that commercial speech has been accorded reduced, but significant First Amendment protection. Thus, online advertising is subject to the same kinds of government oversight as that in print and on television. Perhaps the most well-known and irritating form of online commercial messaging is spam. Though this electronic junk mail is often a legitimate form of commercial message, it is also a regular annoyance and can contain deceptive or fraudulent information and objectionable content. In January 2023, the U.S. had the highest number of spam emails sent daily (8 billion). Second and third were Czechia and the Netherlands, with 7.7 billion and 7.6 billion, respectively.[77] Overall, 24.77 percent of the global spam volume originated from IPs based in Russia. Germany ranked second with 14.12 percent, and the U.S. followed, accounting for 10.46 percent.[78]

The federal CAN-SPAM Act of 2003 establishes both civil and criminal penalties for violations of its provisions and is enforced by the Federal Trade Commission (FTC). One of its provisions requires that email recipients be able to opt out of receiving future commercial emails.[79] This rule allows users to reduce or avoid the spam they receive from legitimate sources but does little to discourage spam from illegitimate sources, of which the quality and personalization has increased dramatically over time. Early era spam of this type was essentially a low-grade version of legitimate spam marketing emails, selling products like male enhancement pills and work-from-home schemes. They have been transformed into highly targeted, professionally crafted schemes that play off of recipients' fears. Two common types are phishing emails and ransomware.

[To file a complaint with the FTC about spam or other online fraud, go to **https://ftc.gov** and click on "Report Fraud."

PRACTICING ETHICS "The Internet is not a Civil-Rights-Free Space."

It is well known that Internet platforms, such as Google and Facebook, collect data on individuals that is used to provide ads targeted to particular demographics. Facebook has gone further by providing services that do the reverse—services that enable advertisers to exclude their ads from reaching particular demographics.

In 2018, the National Fair Housing Alliance was one of several groups that sued Facebook for creating "pre-populated lists that made it possible for its housing advertisers to 'exclude' (in Facebook terminology) home seekers from viewing or receiving rental or sales ads because of protected characteristics, including race, family status, and sex." Facebook settled the suit in March 2019 for about $5 million and an agreement to remove age, gender, zip code, and a criteria it labeled "ethnic affinity" as ad filters with regard to housing, employment, and credit. Geographic targets for such ads will now have a minimum 15-mile radius from a specific location, and its "lookalike audience" tool will not use additional factors, such as religious views or membership in specific Facebook Groups. As stated by counsel for plaintiffs: "The internet is not a civil-rights-free space."

Question

Is race ever an acceptable demographic to use for targeted advertising campaigns? Explain. If you answer in the affirmative, identify when it is acceptable and when it is not.

Sources: Press Release, "Fair Housing Groups Settle Historic Lawsuit with Facebook: Transforms Facebook's Ad Platform Impacting Millions of Users," *National Fair Housing Alliance*, March 19, 2019 [**https://nationalfairhousing.org**]; Nat Ives, "Facebook Axes Age, Gender and Other Targeting for Some Sensitive Ads," *Wall Street Journal*, March 19, 2019 [**www.wsj.com**]; and Noam Scheiber and Mike Isaac, "Facebook Halts Ad Targeting Cited in Bias Complaints," *The New York Times*, March 19, 2019 [**www.nytimes.com**].

Privacy

LO 18-8
Provide examples of online activities that raise privacy concerns and be able to identify those concerns.

Before going further, check your knowledge about online privacy by answering true, false, or "don't know" to the following questions:

- When I go to a website, it can collect information about my online behaviors even if I don't register using my name or email address.
- A Smart TV can help advertisers send an ad to a viewer's smartphone based on the show they are watching.
- A company can tell that I have opened its email even if I don't click on any links.
- The federal government requires that companies ask Internet users to opt-in to being tracked.
- In the United States, the federal government regulates the types of digital information companies collect about individuals.
- The Health Insurance Portability and Accountability Act prevents apps that provide information about health from selling data collected about app users to marketers.[80]

Federal judge rules room scan before online exam violated student's 4th Amendment privacy right

Even before Covid, Cleveland State University offered remote classes, for which it had published guidelines. One policy mandated that students taking remote classes have a photograph in the university's database at the time of registration "to eliminate impersonation" and ensure that the enrolled student "is attending the online lectures and taking the exams." However, the university did not enforce that rule. Some enrolled students did not even have a photograph in the database. The guidelines also provided recommended practices, but left them "to the faculty member's discretion" to use or not. Faculty had access to proctoring tools such as Respondus (including its LockDown Browser) and Honorlock, which uses a student's camera and artificial intelligence monitoring. The university had no written policy requiring or recommending the use of a room scan. However, both Respondus and Honorlock have a required room scan as part of their prerecorded instructions.

During the spring 2021 semester, Cleveland State required students to complete and pass a "Daily Health Assessment" to attend classes in-person. That was not an option for plaintiff, who, due to issues impacting his immune system, could not pass the Daily Health Assessment.

At the start of the January 2021 semester, the syllabus for the student's chemistry class stated:

> The proctors and I reserve the right to ask any student, before, during, or after an exam to show their surroundings, screen, and/or work area. We will send you a private chat to ask you to do this. If you do not see the chat message, I will use the microphone to ask you to check the chat.

After reading the syllabus, the student "disputed" the policy and, three days later, the policy was removed from the syllabus by the professor. Nonetheless, slightly less than two hours before an exam, the university testing center sent him an email saying that the proctor would be "checking your ID, your surroundings and your materials." Although he responded back, making it clear that he did not want to have the scan, at the start of the exam, the proctor asked the scan to be done and the student complied. The scan was recorded and retained by the software vendor.

The 4th Amendment applies to States, and thus to state universities, via the 14th Amendment. The court found that the remote virtual room scan qualified as a "search" within the meaning of the 4th Amendment and noted that homes are given "heightened protection" over other searches. It further noted that the university had "a variable policy–enforced, unevenly, in the discretion of a combination of proctors and professors–of using remote scans that make a student's home visible, including to other students." The 4th Amendment, said the court, "generally prohibits suspicionless searches," except in circumstances where the government has "special needs, beyond the normal need for law enforcement." In this setting, "it is difficult to see how enrollment in a higher educational institution would limit the core protections of the home. . . . Although the intrusion at issue might not strike a person as especially problematic, particularly in the nascent Zoom era, the core protection afforded to the home, the lack of options [available to this student], inconsistency in application of the policy, and short notice of the scan weigh in Plaintiff's favor." It held that his "privacy interest in his home outweighs Cleveland State's interests in scanning his room. Accordingly, the Court determines that Cleveland State's practice of conducting room scans is unreasonable under the Fourth Amendment."

Question

1. Based on the court's statements, what changes could Cleveland State University make to the scan policy so that its enforcement would not violate the 4th Amendment?
2. Assume the same facts occurred in the context of a small, private liberal arts college. Could the student have brought a 4th Amendment case? Explain your answer.

Sources: *Ogletree v. Cleveland State University,* N.D. Ohio, Eastern Division, August 22, 2022; and Amanda Holpuch and April Rubin, "Remote Scan of Student's Room Before Test Violated His Privacy, Judge Rules," *The New York Times,* August 25, 2022 [**www.nytimes.com**].

Privacy Overview

The correct answer (as of this writing) for each of the first three questions posed above the text box is true; the answer for the last three questions is false. Researchers at the University of Pennsylvania posed these questions, along with 11 others, to 2,014 people in the U.S. Of those, 77 percent got 9 or fewer right (9 being slightly above 50 percent correct). Only one person would have received an A (90 percent or higher), answering 16 questions correctly. No one got all 17 answers right.[81]

The Internet has brought with it an explosion of accessible data, including personal data. Some of the information now available online has, in fact, been public for decades, but most people were not aware that it was public, did not know how to obtain it, or simply never bothered. For example, local governments keep information such as property ownership, tax assessments, criminal, and court records, often housed in the local courthouse, but not easily searchable. Now many, if not most, of these public records are available online, just a Google search away to anyone who is simply curious.

Public records are just the tip of the iceberg regarding personal information and the Internet. There are countless data-brokering websites, such as Whitepages, Spokeo, and BeenVerified, the sole purpose of which is to scour the Internet for information about individuals and provide it to anyone who is interested, generally for a fee. And, as we are all aware, the use of most websites, social media platforms, online services, and mobile apps requires giving consent to their privacy policies, essentially making it impossible to be connected without constantly compromising our privacy. And then there is the information we volunteer ourselves–things like photos and posts on social media platforms, reviews we post, blog entries, and comments on online forums.[82]

Consider, however, the following items, some of which may, in fact, surprise and, perhaps, disturb you:

- It is likely to be fairly easy to identify where you and your family live, work, and go to school. It may also be possible to identify your regular coffee shop, the dog park you like to visit, and your favorite restaurants. Stalking someone has never been easier.
- Photos and videos of you, your family, and friends are also likely to be found, often provided knowingly by you via social media, but in many cases posted without your knowledge, such as from events such as school reunions, pictures posted by friends and relatives and sometimes by complete strangers. Even then, with facial recognition software, someone may simply add your name as well.
- The ability to hack computer webcams is so well known that covering them when not in use has become commonplace, but smartphone cameras pose perhaps an even greater privacy risk since they tend to travel everywhere with us. In 2019, bugs were detected that caused both Android and iPhone cameras to become vulnerable to hacking. Though the bugs were patched, it is reasonable to assume these will not be isolated incidents.[83]
- In 2018, the Supreme Court, in a 5:4 decision, held that an individual has "a legitimate expectation of privacy in the record of his physical movements as captured through CELI" (cell-site location information).[84] Thus, a warrant is required for police to seek location data from cellphone providers. That said, a September 2022 article in Time magazine reported that both Immigration and Customs Enforcement (ICE) and the Department of Homeland Security (DHS) bought app location data from commercial brokers to use in immigration enforcement[85] under the theory that there is no "legitimate expectation of privacy" in our physical movements if they are captured through apps running on our phones. A bill entitled the Fourth Amendment Is Not For Sale Act was introduced in Congress in 2021 to address this problem, but as of this writing has not been passed.[86]

For $160 a full week's data disclosing all those who had visited any Planned Parenthood location was provided, as well as their prior locations and where they went afterward.

- After the draft of the Supreme Court's abortion decision in *Dobbs v. Jackson Women's Health Organization* was leaked, a reporter paid a location collector $160 for a full week's data disclosing all those who had visited any of the over 600 Planned Parenthood locations in the U.S. This information included where they were before and after the visit. The information came from apps on the phones they were carrying.[87] Does law enforcement have to have a warrant to obtain information in this manner?

Data Mining

> Whenever I see one of those billboards that read: "Privacy. That's iPhone," I'm overcome by the urge to cast my own iPhone into a river. Of lava.
>
> That's not because the iPhone is any better or worse than other smartphones when it comes to digital privacy. . . .
>
> What's infuriating is the idea that carrying around the most sophisticated tracking and monitoring device ever forged by the hand of man is consistent with any understanding of privacy.[88]

With regard to data privacy, this is a time of heightened concern: as of this writing, 18 states have passed laws banning abortions or prohibiting abortions after a set gestational period has passed. Courts in another six states have blocked, some temporarily and some indefinitely, abortion bans from going into effect.[89] The FTC has filed a lawsuit against Kochava Inc. for selling geolocation data that can, among other things, identify individuals' visits to "reproductive health clinics, places of worship, and homeless and domestic violence shelters."[90] The complaint states, "The sale of such data poses an unwarranted intrusion into the most private areas of consumers' lives and . . . is likely to cause substantial injury."[91] At the time of this writing, the FTC also has under consideration a rule expanding online privacy protection by reining in online surveillance and requiring technology companies to strengthen their data-security practices.[92] The FTC's announcement of the proposed rulemaking states that its purpose is to address harms from the "business of collecting, analyzing, and monetizing information about people."[93]

For updates on state legislation and judicial decisions concerning this issue, visit the *New York Times* tracker, "Tracking the States Where Abortion Is Now Banned," **https://www.nytimes.com/interactive/2022/us/abortion-laws-roe-v-wade.html.**

Consider for a moment the amount of information residing in the databases of institutions with which we regularly deal: credit card companies, online vendors such as Amazon and Netflix, social media, schools, pharmacies, medical service providers, our ISPs, phone companies, and so forth. ***Data mining*** is the process of compiling profiles of individuals by organizing millions of discrete pieces of information gleaned from proprietary databases and from tracking connected devices as individuals browse the Internet and move around carrying connected devices. Those profiles can be used to provide better services to repeat customers–from the pizza outlet that knows what you ordered last time (and how often, how much you spend and, possibly, whether you tip), to Netflix which knows all your historical downloads and rentals (and how you rated them), as well as everything listed in your queue.

But those same profiles permit fair housing laws to be circumvented and facilitate price discrimination that can mimic the geographical restrictions of offline shopping, such as higher prices for customers from zip code locations where less competition exists (rural and poor areas).[94] Even children have been targeted, a practice for which Google was fined in 2019, despite laws like the Children's Online Privacy Protection Act that prohibit such activities.[95] In one test of 80 Apple apps, "[a]ll but one used third-party trackers for marketing, ads or analytics. The apps averaged four trackers apiece."[96] And the information often ends up with mobile marketers, Google, and

> Facebook keeps data on nonusers, creating "shadow profiles."

Facebook (even if you have never joined Facebook). "Billions of web pages (including those of the New York Times) and mobile apps contain code from [Facebook]–tracking pixels–that collect detailed data, and communicate them back to Facebook. They . . . keep it even for nonusers, creating what's called 'shadow profiles.'"[97]

Even when some progress seems to made, such as Apple's new App Tracking Transparency feature[98] (which requires the owner to give an app express permission to track them, send targeted ads, share their location data or any other personal identifiers with third parties), ever more privacy invasions are revealed. Here are just a few examples:

- You think you are in the privacy of your own home when you are talking to Alexa, Siri, or Google Assistant? Think again. "[W]histle-blowers recently said they had listened in on Siri recordings and Alexa activations that inadvertently recorded couples having sex and criminals making drug deals. . . . [a news outlet] chronicled how a Google subcontractor shared more than 1,000 excerpts from Google recordings, which journalists then used to identify some individuals."[99]
- You can get a credit card from Apple or through Google Pay, or choose a credit or debit card from Amazon. Why do they all want to be in the finance business? It is all about the data. Through these mechanisms they get "a treasure trove of information, including how much money people make, where they shop, and what bills they pay.[100]
- Amazon just bought Roomba, a maker of robot vacuum cleaners, for $1.7 billion. Why? From their point of view, they were not buying a vacuum cleaner, they were buying a company that will map your home and send them the details. "The size of your house is a pretty good proxy for wealth. A floor covered with toys means you likely have kids. A household without much furniture is a household to which you can try to sell more furniture."[101] Similarly, Amazon purchased Whole Foods in 2017 to give it an in-depth view of the grocery business and Amazon Prime members' shopping habits.

Now consider the ways in which Google and Amazon have become involved in the medical field.

Google

In November 2019, Google and the country's second-largest health information system, Ascension, publicly announced a joint endeavor, Project Nightingale. Ascension "aims in part to improve patient care," is "eager to have a system that is faster than its existing decentralized electronic record-keeping," and "hopes to mine data to identify additional tests that could be necessary or other ways in which the system could generate more revenue from patients."[102] Google's "end goal is to create an omnibus search tool to aggregate disparate patient data and host it all in one place." It "has assigned dozens of engineers" to the project "without charging for the work because it hopes to use the framework to sell similar products to other health systems."[103]

The agreement ostensibly did not violate U.S. law regarding health data, which can be shared "with business partners [but] only to help the covered entity carry out its health-care functions."[104] Nevertheless, the way in which it was managed does raise privacy issues. Before the new venture was announced, Ascension had already started sharing medical records with Google. Neither patients nor doctors had been notified. The data shared was not anonymized but was essentially a complete history, including patient names, birth dates, all lab results, diagnoses, and hospitalizations.

Questions

1. From a patient-privacy viewpoint, provide the basis for arguing that the arrangement between Google and Ascension was unethical. Then determine whether there were steps the parties could have taken to better ensure patient privacy.
2. The legal rule allowing the sharing of health data is that it can be shared with business partners but "only to help the covered entity carry out its health-care functions." Based on the information given, did Ascension contract with Google "only" to carry out its health-care functions? Did Google? Explain.

Amazon

Amazon has also gone into the medical field by buying the primary care network One Medical, which has 190 clinics, a subscription telehealth service, and contracts with thousands of employers. Unlike Google's Project Nightingale, which is essentially a data processing activity for Google, when Amazon's acquisition is finalized, Amazon will be in the medical business. Because One Medical has five clinics in Portland, the Oregon Health Authority (OHA) had to approve it. One of the conditions for approval is that One Medical submit reports to the OHA every six months for the first five years covering, among other things, the quality of the care provided and any governance or organizational changes. The acquisition also has to be approved by the FTC, which approval is still pending as of this writing.[105]

Question

Compare the ways in which Google and Amazon have entered the medical field. Which would you rather be, a patient of Ascension or a patient of One Medical? Why?

PRACTICING ETHICS — Where were you on February 12, 2023? We Know How to Find Out.

Location tracking is the most invasive, and probably one of the least understood, forms of data mining. As part of its larger Privacy Project, *The New York Times* obtained one data file, not "from a telecom or giant tech company, nor . . . from a government surveillance operation. It originated from a location data company, one of dozens quietly collecting precise movements using software slipped onto mobile phone apps." It contained "more than 50 billion location pings" from the phones of over 12 million people living in such cities as Los Angeles, New York, San Francisco, and Washington, D.C., for portions of 2016 and 2017. Each piece of information discloses the exact location of a single smart phone. The file, containing the largest data set ever made available to a news organization, nevertheless "represents just a small slice of what's collected and sold every day by the location tracking industry." It is surveillance data so precise and specific that it reveals the exact time and location of tens of millions of people, regardless of age or wealth. That data is in the hands of corporations that sell such data, which are unregulated at the state level except, as of the time of this writing, in California, Colorado, and Virginia. "Only internal company policies and the decency of individual employees" prevent its misuse. True, if one believes that using the data to sell you products, services, and political candidates is not misuse.

"The companies that collect all this information on your movements justify their business on the basis of three claims: People consent to be tracked, the data is anonymous and the data is secure." With regard to anonymity, consider the following:

- "[I]t's child's play to connect real names to the dots that appear on the maps."
- "Consider your daily commute: Would any other smartphone travel directly between your house and your office every day?"
- "Really precise, longitudinal geolocation information is absolutely impossible to anonymize."
- "Our privacy is only as secure as the least secure app on our device."

The data obtained by *The New York Times* included inauguration week in 2017 and "yielded a trove of personal stories" from attendees at presidential ceremonies to protesters participating in the Women's March the next day. It revealed a senior official from the Department of Defense in the mall that day and then going home. There the spouse's phone was identified, after which both were tracked both back and forward in time–tracked at work, at home, and to a high school. In truth, the full data set was "large enough that it surely points to scandal and crime" and "sometimes revealed hints of faltering marriages, evidence of drug addiction, [and] visits to psychological facilities."

> If you lived in one of the cities the dataset covers and use apps that share your location—anything from weather apps to local news apps to coupon savers—you could be in there, too.
>
> If you could see the full trove, you might never use your phone the same way again.

To read more of the articles from *The New York Times* Privacy Project, see "Opinion: The Privacy Project," *The New York Times,* 2019-2020 [**www.nytimes.com/series/new-york-times-privacy-project**].

Questions

1. How does a location data company, also referred to as a location collector, generate income? Is location data collection a regulated industry?
2. If you have a weather app on your phone, do you know if it has a location tracker? Do you know how to find out? "Weather apps can give you an accurate weather reading for New York even if you are sitting in California at the time, so such tight location surveillance is not necessary for the app to work properly."[106]
3. Do you carry a smartphone? Is it ethical for companies to collect, buy, and sell data that identifies not only where you were on February 12, 2023, but everywhere you were at every moment of the day, as well as for months before and after, moment-to-moment and place-to-place? Explain your answer.
4. In the midst of the COVID-19 pandemic, some western democracies such as Germany and Italy started using contact tracing apps to mitigate or avoid new waves of infection.[107] Apple and Google announced a joint project to release such a tool usable in their phones worldwide. Individuals would be able to choose to opt in and voluntarily report if they became infected.[108] If such an app had become available in the United States, do you think people should have used it? Would you opt in to such a program? Explain.

Source: Stuart A. Thompson and Charlie Warzel, "Twelve Million Phones, One Dataset, Zero Privacy," *The New York Times,* December 19, 2019 [**www.nytimes.com**] and Theodore F. Claypoole, "State Laws Shift Geolocation's Spot On The Privacy Map," *Womble Bond Dickinson,* March 8, 2022 [**www.womblebonddickinson.com**].

Facial Recognition

One of the most concerning developments in the online world, resulting from the combined extraordinary increase in computing power, emergence of the cloud, and explosive advancement in artificial intelligence, is facial recognition–the use of technology to identify a human face.

In May 2020, the American Civil Liberties Union filed a lawsuit against Clearview AI (a leading provider of facial-recognition software), claiming that it was engaging in "unlawful, privacy-destroying surveillance activities." The complaint described the company's business model as "embody[ing] the nightmare scenario [of a] private company capturing untold quantities of biometric data for purposes of surveillance and tracking without notice to the individuals affected, much less their consent."[109] The ACLU brought the suit on behalf of "groups representing survivors of domestic violence and sexual assault, undocumented immigrants, current and former sex workers, and other vulnerable communities uniquely harmed by face recognition surveillance."[110]

There are clearly circumstances in which, properly constrained, facial recognition can be of great benefit. The police can use it to find an abducted child, track a fleeing terrorist suspect, or locate a person known to be carrying a deadly virus. Employers and apartment building owners can utilize it to restrict access to facilities. It can be provided as an option for logging into computers and smartphones. It could even be used in lieu of a key to authorize the use of motor vehicles.

But facial recognition can also be employed by governments to suppress their people, as is occurring in China. An investigative team from *The New York Times* was given unprecedented access to more than 100,000 government bidding documents for the provision of surveillance technology, the study of which allowed the team to conclude, "The Chinese government's goal is clear: designing a system to maximize what the state can find out about a person's identity, activities and social connections, which could ultimately help the government maintain its authoritarian rule."[111]

> Microsoft President Brad Smith: "artificial intelligence [software] is too important and potentially dangerous to permit tech giants to police themselves."

Back in the U.S., in December 2010, Facebook introduced its own facial recognition system. Without the authorization of nonusers who appeared in user-uploaded photographs, Facebook applied facial-recognition technology to identify nonusers and scan for their presence in other photographs on the platform. It then sold the data, as well as used it for its own purposes. The company was repeatedly sued for these privacy violations, to no avail.[112]

But then the environment started to change. By July 2018, Microsoft president Brad Smith urged lawmakers to step in, saying that "such artificial intelligence is too important and potentially dangerous to permit tech giants to police themselves."[113] In 2019, the FTC fined Facebook $5 billion to settle a variety of privacy complaints, including concerns about its facial recognition software.[114] Also in 2019, San Francisco became the first major American city to block the use of facial-recognition technology by law enforcement[115] and California placed a three-year moratorium on the use of facial recognition with police body cameras.[116]

Then, in early 2020, Facebook paid $550 million to settle a facial recognition suit.[117] It had been brought under Illinois' biometric privacy law, which "requires companies to obtain written permission before collecting a person's fingerprints, facial scans or other identifying biological characteristics."[118] It also provides a private right to sue, which means class actions can be brought in Illinois, rather than requiring all enforcement to originate with the state attorney general, which is one of the reasons Illinois is considered to provide the strongest protection of biometric data in the U.S.

In the wake of the Black Lives Matter protests which began in May 2020, Amazon, Google, and IBM joined in advocating for strong government regulation.[119] Further, Amazon suspended police use of its facial-recognition software.[120]

In November 2021, Facebook announced its plans to delete the face scans of over a billion users, a feature introduced a decade earlier.[121]

What about the ACLU suit against Clearview AI mentioned at the top of this section? It won. Under the settlement agreement, among other requirements, "Clearview will be permanently banned from granting paid or free access to its gargantuan face recognition database to private entities (including both private companies and private individuals) nationwide, subject to narrow exceptions contained in Illinois' biometric privacy law under which the suit was brought" and it "will end its practice of offering free trial accounts to individual police officers, without the knowledge or approval of their employers."[122]

Question

A new, very large, mixed-use indoor mall is being planned. The first two floors will be standard retail with 400 stores, augmented with a movie theater complex, an ice-skating rink, a video game arcade, a swimming pool, and a small "amusement park" area with a dozen rides intended for children under 12. The third and fourth floors will be residential rental with 650 apartments. The mall owner has asked the local government, for which you work, to permit it to install extensive facial-recognition technology throughout the mall, including in the underground parking facility and the elevators, as well as the common areas of the residential floors. You have been assigned the task of identifying and explaining the pros and cons of this proposal for the government's consideration. What will your report cover? Explain.

Privacy Laws Revisited

LO 18-9
Explain the differences in online privacy protection among the federal law of the U.S., California's specific laws, and those of the EU.

The material below calls upon the foundation built at the end of Part One of this chapter, which presented both EU and U.S. laws governing the Internet, which you may wish to briefly review before continuing.

Many U.S. companies may not be required by law to have a general online privacy policy if their operations do not bring them within the jurisdiction of California or the EU (which after Brexit, still includes Ireland). However, if they want to take advantage of Google's AdSense, AdWords, Google Play, or Google Analytics, Google will require them to have a privacy policy that conforms to those laws, as will Apple if they want their product to appear in the Apple Store.

Whether required to have a privacy policy or not, if a company does have a stated privacy policy, the FTC can bring an action to ensure the company follows that policy. In addition, individual states may have general consumer protection laws that would also apply to online transactions to sales to citizens in those states.

> In 2017, . . . the Massachusetts Attorney General reached a settlement with marketing company Copley Advertising, LLC, and its principal for using location technology to identify when people crossed a secret digital "fence" near a clinic offering abortion services. Based on that data, the company sent targeted ads to their phones with links to websites with information about alternatives to abortion. The Massachusetts AG asserted that the practice violated state consumer protection law.[123]

The California Consumer Privacy Act (CCPA) entered into effect in 2020. It gives California residents the rights to

- On request, receive data collected on them without charge, including predictions or categorizations that relate to their behavior, attitudes, intelligence, and so forth.
- Have their data deleted.

- Easily opt out of having their data sold.
- Sue for data breaches.

California's new Age-Appropriate Design Code (AADC) takes effect in 2024. It extends the affected businesses beyond those covered by the federal COPPA, (further discussed below), because COPPA defines a child as under age 13, while the AADC's coverage includes services likely to be accessed by 13–17-year-olds, which will pull in many websites also used by adults. In general terms, the code requires that covered entities set default privacy settings to a "high level of privacy;" imposes new limits on profiling; prohibits collecting, sharing, or selling geolocation data by default (except where necessary for the service and then it is limited to that necessity), and prohibits the use of manipulative design (also referred to as "dark patterns"). Covered entities are required to complete a data protection impact statement on any service, product, or feature likely to be accessed by a child.

Additional federal regulations may be forthcoming. The FTC announced in August 2022 that it was exploring whether to create new rules to address online commercial surveillance and data security practices.[124]

For the FTC's "Fact Sheet on the FTC's Commercial Surveillance and Data Security Rulemaking,' see **https://www.ftc.gov/system/files/ftc_gov/pdf/Commercial%20Surveillance%20and%20Data%20Security%20Rulemaking%20Fact%20Sheet_1.pdf.**

For a clickable list of privacy and security enforcement cases brought by the FTC, see **https://www.ftc.gov/news-events/topics/protecting-consumer-privacy-security/privacy-security-enforcement.**

Questions

> Our own information–from the everyday to the deeply personal–is being weaponized against us with military efficiency.[125]
>
> Tim Cook, CEO, Apple Inc., October 24, 2018
> Speech before EU privacy regulators

1. Having read the materials on privacy in this section, do you believe that the personal information about you out on the web "is being weaponized against" you? Explain.
2. Which approach to data collection on Internet users do you prefer: the current situation in the United States in which we do not know who is storing our personal information, nor what they are doing with it; or California's law requiring companies that collect personal data, on request, to identify it, delete it, and stop its collection; or the EU's approach, requiring companies to disclose what they have collected, remove it on request, and collect nothing in the future, unless the individual is told the use that will be made of it and gives express permission? Explain.

> The federal Children's Online Privacy Protection Act prohibits websites from collecting personal information from children under 13.

Child Online Privacy

The United States does have a separate law addressing the privacy of children online. The 1998 Children's Online Privacy Protection Act

(COPPA) prohibits websites from collecting personal information from children under 13 without parental permission and requires that parents be allowed to review and correct any information collected about their children. The FTC is charged with primary enforcement of COPPA. Its initial implementation rule was revised effective July 1, 2013. It expanded the definition of "personal information" to include not just names, phone numbers, and home and e-mail addresses, but also mobile phone serial numbers. It extended the rule's application to cover social media sites, interactive gaming sites, and smartphone and tablet apps. It also increased restrictions on the use of behavior-based online advertising.

Some examples of its enforcement are

- A $170 million fine imposed on Google for advertising targeted at children and was linked to YouTube videos designed for children.[126]
- A $2 million settlement with OpenX Technologies for collecting personal information from children under 13 and passing that information along to third parties to use in creating targeted ads for child-directed apps. OpenX was also required to delete the data that was collected and institute a review process to ensure that child-directed apps stay banned from their ad exchange.[127]
- A $275 million penalty levied on Epic, the maker of Fortnite video games for violating COPPA. Epic also had to refund $245 million because of the schemes it deployed to trick users into buying items they did not want. It was also ordered to ensure that live text and voice are off by default to reduce the opportunity for child-to-stranger communications that have resulted in harassment while playing the game.[128]

For more information about COPPA, see [**www.ftc.gov/tips-advice/business-center/guidance/complying-coppa-frequently-asked-questions**].

As mentioned in Part One, Market Forces and Government Regulation, California has passed the California Age-Appropriate Design Act, which is broader than COPPA. It protects minors under the age of 18, rather than 13. It applies to all general-audience sites and apps; for example, by requiring them to turn on the highest level of privacy settings by default for minors and by prohibiting platforms from collecting minors' precise locations without "providing an obvious sign to the child" whenever their locations are being tracked. The covered platforms, sites and apps will have to proactively analyze and mitigate privacy risks their services may present to minors, including the use of "manipulative techniques to prod them to spend hours on end online."[129]

Questions

1. You have always liked little known fun facts. So you have been amused by an app you downloaded a few months ago, Curious World. You generally leave it running in the background so you can click through it while you wait in line at the drive through. After reading about online privacy, you decide to check your apps and, yes, Curious World has been sending out your location data pretty much 24/7 for months. You are miffed. Would you be successful suing the app developer for stealing your location data? Explain.
2. What if Curious World was a children's app starring a cute little monkey[130] and you discovered it on your four-year-old cousin's tablet? Should the app developer be more worried now? Explain.

Part Four—Cybercrime, Cyberattacks, and Cybersecurity

Cyberattacks

LO 18-10

Describe several Internet-related crimes—including ransomware, data theft, and control of physical assets—and identify how to protect against them.

The statistics are sobering:[131]

- Phishing is the most common form of online crime. In 2021, one in five Internet users were presented with a phishing email. That same year, half of all data breaches were a result of a phishing attack. Russian-based phishing attacks via U.S. and European email addresses increased by a factor of 8 since Russia invaded Ukraine. On a per-event basis, however, phishing has the lowest loss per victim, averaging $136.
- In 2022, online investment fraud had the highest loss per victim–an average of $70,811.
- Over 236 million ransomware attacks were reported in the first half of 2022 worldwide. There were 623 million total attacks in 2021. (These numbers are for attempted breaches, not successful attacks.) This suggests that businesses have had some success adapting to remote working environments that increased dramatically and without warning during the COVID-19 pandemic. The attackers are also adapting: instead of just charging a fee for the decryption key, the release or sale of data is threatened if the ransom is not paid. The year-over-year increase in the average ransomware payment was 171 percent from 2019 to 2020 and another 82 percent from 2020 to 2021, in which year it was $570,000.
    - These numbers reflect the cost paid to the perpetrators. Significant collateral costs are also incurred, such as brand reputation damage.
    - The reported numbers are also quite likely to be much lower than the actual payments made. In a survey of 900 senior management and directors, only 42 percent said they would report a ransomware attack to both law enforcement and a cyber security response service. Sixty-four percent indicated their company had already been the victim of an attack; of those, 79 percent paid the perpetrators.
    - Ransomware is itself a business: some data suggests that one group was behind 37 percent of all ransomware attacks during 2021, allowing the direct perpetrators to use its software on a subscription basis.
    - One interesting statistic is that the incident rate of ransomware attacks in the U.S. during 2022 was 7 percent, while the worldwide average was 37 percent. However, U.S. targets may be less likely to report the attacks.

The FBI maintains an Internet Crime Complaint Center (IC3), which allows filing reports online and also reports annual statistics. At the time of this writing, 2022 figures were not available. Over the years 2017-2021, IC3 "received a total of 2,760,004 complaints, reporting a loss of $18.7 billion."[132]

Cybersecurity

Data Theft

In the attacks described below, the object of the theft was data rather than money. These are, of course, just a few data points from among many.

- The largest data breach uncovered to date was the theft of user information from three billion accounts on Yahoo in 2013, although when the breach was first discovered in

2016 it was believed that "only" one billion accounts had been compromised. The full scale of the breach was not identified until 2017.[133]

- Healthcare is one of the top three industries for which the most data breaches were recorded in 2021. The other two were financial services and manufacturing.[134]
- The FTC filed a complaint in October 2022 charging Chegg, a homework help app students can use for a monthly fee, with unfair and deceptive business practices. One of the occurrences cited referred to a former Chegg contractor who used company-issued credentials to steal names, addresses, and passwords for about 40 million users. In settling the dispute, Chegg agreed to adopt a comprehensive data security program.[135]
- In September 2022, some of Uber's internal systems were hacked, including its internal communications, a finance tool for invoices, and the dashboard where their security researchers report bugs and potential vulnerabilities in their systems. The hack was likely accomplished through a corporate password obtained through a contractor. A teenager was arrested in London and the belief was at the time that the hack was related to an organized group, Lapsus$.[136]

Bruce Schneier has been a Lecturer in Public Policy at the Harvard Kennedy School and a Fellow at the Berkman Klein Center for Internet & Society. He wrote an article for the New York Times after the Uber hack mentioned above which illustrates how start-up businesses that are built around tech solutions, such as Uber, can find themselves unprotected and victims of hacking. He describes the trade-offs in getting a new high-tech venture up and running:

> [Y]our primary focus is to earn customers and grow quickly, enough to remain in business when your venture capital runs out. Anything that isn't absolutely essential to making the business work is left for later, and that includes security culture and practices. . . . Security can be improved later, but only if necessary. . . . You're now an established company, and you had better look and act that way. . . .
>
> But in all that, you've never had incentive to upgrade your security. . . . [I]t's expensive and time-consuming to rebuild everything from the ground up with security in mind.[137]

The bottom line is that crucial security often is not timely put in place, at least not until the company suffers reputation and monetary damage–both of which may be very large.

Controlling Physical Assets

Cyberattacks have also been directed at taking control of physical assets, which can create very dangerous conditions. For example, on Thursday, April 29, 2021, a hacker accessed the Colonial Pipeline Company's virtual private network (VPN) through an employee VPN account that was no longer in use. The password had not been deactivated and was not protected by a multifactor identification process. Entry of a single password was enough to get into the company's internal network.

Just a little over a week after the as-yet-undiscovered breach occurred, an employee working in the control room at 5 a.m. encountered a ransom note containing a cryptocurrency demand. An operations supervisor immediately began the process of shutting down the entire pipeline, for the first time in its 57-year history. It was not reopened until five days later. Before that happened, not only were the hacker's movements through the internal network tracked, but the company examined the entire length of the 29,000-mile pipeline, both

While the plant operator was watching, his mouse moved and began clicking through the plant's controls.

on the ground and by air, to ensure no physical damage had been done. The network investigation found no breach of the critical operational technology systems. Rather, the hackers had stolen about 100 gigabytes of data and had threatened to leak it if they were not paid.

In a meeting before a U.S. Senate Committee, the CEO of Colonial Pipeline, Joseph Blount, told the Senators that the stolen password was a complicated password, "not a Colonial123-type password."[138] Although the company had notified the FBI within hours, some of the senators questioned the ransom payment without more consultation with the government. "It was our understanding that the decision was solely ours to make about whether to pay the ransom," Blount said.[139] Of the nearly $5 million paid, the Justice Department was able to recover about $2.3 million (about 60 of the 75 bitcoin paid). Much of the difference was caused by a substantial drop in the value of bitcoin in the interim.

In early February 2021, a hacker successfully took control of a water treatment plant in Oldsmar, Florida. While the plant operator was watching, his mouse moved and "began clicking through the . . . plant's controls[,] . . . attempting to change the water supply's levels of sodium hydroxide, also known as lye . . . , moving the setting from 100 parts per million to 11,100 parts per million. . . . In low concentrations the corrosive chemical regulates the PH level of potable water. At high levels, it severely damages any human tissue it touches."[140] "After the hacker exited the computer, the operator immediately reduced the sodium hydroxide back to its normal level and then notified his supervisor, [the] Pinellas County sheriff."[141] Even if the change had not occurred while the operator was watching, such systems routinely have testing equipment at several stages of the purification process that would have reported the change well before the water reached the public.

The perpetrator had accessed the system through software that provided remote access to targeted computers. Best practices would restrict remote access solely to a monitoring function, with devices controlling actual operations fully disconnected from any network. "About 52,000 community water systems operate in the United States, providing water to more than 286 million people year round. Most systems are run by local governments; many are very small. . . . Small water utilities often don't have their own IT or cybersecurity staff."[142]

In 2017, Russian actors nearly got access to a large portion of the U.S. electricity grid. As we saw when discussing data thefts, the weak point was an outside contractor, in this case one of the private company supply chain participants. The computers of subcontractors were hacked using strategies such as planting malware on the sites of online publications frequently read by utility engineers and sending fake job-seeker resumes with infected attachments. Having gained access to computers inside the companies, the hackers exploited the linkages to reach the networks controlling the physical systems themselves. At least 60 utilities were targeted; about two dozen were breached all the way to the control systems. Ominously, *The Wall Street Journal* reported: "Industry experts say Russian government hackers likely remain inside some systems, undetected and awaiting further orders."[143] Other infrastructures, such as the air traffic control system, communication microwave towers, and dams are also vulnerable.

Hospitals have discovered that Internet-connected equipment, like infusion pumps and respirators, is also vulnerable to being hacked and taken over.

Hospitals have discovered that Internet-connected equipment, like infusion pumps and respirators, is also vulnerable to being hacked and taken over. Two cyberattacks in 2017 disrupted operations at several hospitals, forcing the cancellation of surgeries. In 2018, the Department of Homeland Security issued 30 advisories about cybersecurity weaknesses in medical devices. Vizient Inc., which negotiates equipment and supply purchase contracts for over 3000 hospitals, has now added sophisticated cybersecurity questions to the screening process. Vendors are often required to submit their proprietary firmware for review.[144]

Other attacks seek to interfere with, rather than seize control of, physical assets. In 2017, more than 20 commercial ships near Crimea discovered that their GPS equipment was reporting their location to be dozens of kilometers from where they actually were. A University of Texas expert concluded: "There is incontrovertible evidence that spoofing occurred."[145] The consequences could have been devastating.

TikTok: A Cool App for Teens and Twenty-Somethings or a Weapon for Global Turmoil?

TikTok is owned by ByteDance, a Chinese corporation which had its headquarters in Singapore until recently. It was largely the creation of Zhang Yiming, started in early 2012, which Zhang initially ran out of two apartments in Beijing. He had looked for financial backers in China, but without much success, until a friend sent a visiting American venture capitalist to take a look at what ByteDance was doing. That infusion of capital was exactly what it took to propel the company forward. The same year, ByteDance launched the first generation of its original app, named Jinri Toutiao (Today's Headlines). Jinri Toutiao reached one million daily average users in four months. By 2017 its annual revenue was $2.5 billion.

Between 2012 and 2017, Xi Jinping was elected president by the 12th National People's Congress. China was changing.

Zhang had been watching the progress of Musical.ly, a lip-syncing app started in Shanghai by two Chinese entrepreneurs. It was becoming a hit in the U.S. In March 2016, Zhang started a few employees working on replicating Musical.ly. When the new app that resulted, named Douyin (Shaking Sound), was launched, they targeted it at young people in China's large cities. Growth "exploded" in early 2017 when some of the videos went viral on other social media. On opening the app, a 15-second video would immediately start playing. By swiping up, one could scroll through a virtually never-ending feed of these very short videos, shown in full-screen mode. If the video did not capture your taste, you could continue scrolling up. The built-in algorithm would learn your preferences from your passes and selections. The more you watched, the more it learned. By May, Douyin had over a million daily average users.

At that point, Zhang contacted Musical.ly to propose an acquisition. The purpose would be to wed ByteDance's algorithm with Musical.ly's established American user base. The app that resulted from this combination of strengths took the name TikTok.

ByteDance moved its offices to Singapore in 2020.

By 2021, "TikTok had more site visits than Google, and more watch minutes in the United States than YouTube. Facebook took almost nine years to reach one billion users; TikTok did it in five."[146] It is most known for its viral dance videos, but has become more than that for many. When Auburn University, a state school in Alabama banned it from the campus Wi-Fi network, students were surprised–it had been "woven into campus life." For example, students use "its short-form videos to highlight the school's football team."[147] When Ezra Klein, co-founder of Vox and the host of his own podcast, spoke in the spring of 2022 at a college in South Carolina, he "asked some of the students where they liked to get their news. Almost every one said TikTok."[148]

Yet, at the time of this writing, 34 states have banned TikTok on state devices. Montana has passed legislation banning TikTok from operating in state, and TikTok has file suit against the state in the Montana Federal District Court. What happened?

In 2017, the Chinese Cybersecurity Law and the National Intelligence Law took effect. Together they "created affirmative legal responsibilities for Chinese companies and citizens to assist the investigative and intelligence-gathering activities of state organs. 'Any organization or citizen shall support, assist and cooperate with state intelligence work in accordance with the law . . . and maintain the secrecy of all knowledge of state intelligence work.' In 2021, two new laws on data security asserted the extraterritorial reach of the Chinese state over any data on Chinese citizens anywhere in the world."[149]

ByteDance, although headquartered in Singapore, is still a Chinese corporation; and, as already noted, the U.S. has no national privacy law requiring users to be able to opt out of programs collecting their personal data.

This is the dilemma we face as a nation with TikTok:

- As identified in an executive order from President Biden, TikTok "can access and capture vast swaths of information from users, including United States persons' personal information and proprietary business information. This data collection threatens to provide foreign adversaries with access to that information."[150] Ezra Klein refers to this as the "data espionage problem."[151]
- Then there is the success of the app with teens and young adults in America. Why is it so successful? One reason is that TikTok experimented with what appealed to its intended audience, which was different in different countries: "Thai users liked videos of people dancing at school," Japanese users liked funny videos about people obsessed with anime and manga; "Americans, it turned out, had an unusual attachment to memes."[152] In other words, TikTok found the precise algorithm to capture and increase time spent on its app by American youth, an algorithm it would be possible to put to an entirely different purpose–like "tweaking . . . to increase exposure to divisive content, or adjusting the platform to seed or encourage disinformation campaigns."[153] Ezra Klein refers to this as "the manipulation problem."

In his opinion column in *The New York Times,* Klein wrote

> TikTok has been thick with videos backing the Russian narrative on the war in Ukraine. Media Matters, for instance, tracked an apparently coordinated campaign driven by 186 Russian TikTok influencers who normally post beauty tips, prank videos and fluff. . . .
>
> Imagine a world in which the United States has a contested presidential election. . . If one candidate was friendlier to Chinese interests, might the Chinese Communist Party insist that ByteDance give a nudge to content favoring that candidate? Or . . . maybe TikTok begins serving up more and more videos with election conspiracies, sowing chaos at a moment when the country is near fracture.
>
> None of this is far-fetched. . . . We know that other foreign countries–Russia comes to mind–have used American social networks to drive division and doubt.
>
> It is telling that China sees such dangers as obvious enough to have built a firewall against them internally: They've banned Facebook and Google and Twitter and, yes, TikTok.[154]

Although still working for TikTok, on November 4, 2021, Zhang stepped down as CEO of ByteDance and is now living in Singapore. The ByteDance headquarters are back in Beijing. ByteDance has multiple subsidiaries, in one of which the Chinese government has taken an ownership interest, although a small one–only 1 percent.[155] The CEO of TikTok is now Chew

Shouzi, a former CFO of Xiaomi (a Chinese designer and manufacturer of consumer electronics and related software). Xiaomi is the second largest manufacturer of cellphones in the world.

TikTok had been in talks with the Committee on Foreign Investment in the United States (CFIUS) for two years. It submitted a written proposal to the CFIUS in August 2022. In that proposal, TikTok would remain owned by ByteDance, steps would be taken to prevent the Chinese government from access to data on U.S. users and to allow the U.S. government oversight of the platform. All U.S. data would be transferred onto servers owned by Oracle and located in the U.S. Data would not be allowed to be transferred out of the U.S. and would not be accessible to ByteDance or TikTok employees not also located in the U.S. It also proposed regular audits by CFIUS. Further, TikTok's source code would be reviewed by Oracle and a third-party inspector. As of this writing TikTok had not received any responses to its proposal.

Thus, as of this writing, TikTok's future in the U.S. is still unknown.

Question

You are having lunch with some friends and one of them starts talking about TikTok. Imagine what they might say. How would your contributions to that conversation change, or the conversation itself change, as a result of what you've read here?

Sources: Alex W. Palmer, "How TikTok Became a Diplomatic Crisis," *The New York Times,* December 20, 2022 [**www.nytimes.com**]; Ezra Klein, "TikTok May Be More Dangerous Than It Looks": Sapna Maheshwari, "Montana Governor Signs Total Ban of TikTok in the State," *The New York Times,* May 17, 2023 [**www.nytimes.com**]; Sapna Maheshwari and David McCabe, "TikTok Users Sue Montana, Calling State Ban Users Sue Montana, Calling State Ban Unconstitutional," *The New York Times,* May 18, 2023 [**www.nytimes.com**]; David Shepardson, "Montana's TikTok ban faces skeptical U.S. judge," Reuters, October 12, 2023 [**www.reuters.com**]; *The New York Times,* May 8, 2022 [**www.nytimes.com**]; Cecilia Kang, Sapna Maheshwari, and David McCabe, "TikTok's New Defense in Washington: Going on the Offense," *The New York Times,* January 26, 2023 [**www.nytimes.com**]; Sawdah Bhaimiya, "Here's a full list of the US states that have introduced full or partial TikTok bans on government devices over mounting security concerns," *Insider,* January 15, 2023 [**www.businessinsider.com**]; and Sapna Maheshwari, "Auburn Banned TikTok, and Students Can't Stop Talking About It," *The New York Times,* January 15, 2023 [**www.nytimes.com**].

Questions—Part Four

1. Think back to the cybercrimes discussed in this Part. Have you experienced a cybercrime or do you know someone who has? Did it turn out to be just an annoyance or did it result it greater harm? Was the harm monetary or of some other type?
2. How serious an issue do you think cybercrime is? What do you think the most effective tools to combat cybercrime are? Explain.

Part Five—Cryptocurrencies and Related Intangible Assets

Intangible Assets

What exactly do you own if you own a cryptocurrency or an NFT?

Both cryptocurrencies and nonfungible tokens (NFTs) are products of blockchain technology. From a common law perspective, anything you can own is property. So humans are not property, but nearly everything else is. Property can be divided into different categories. For example, something can be classified as real property or personal property. Real property is land and most items physically connected to it, such as buildings. Personal property is

Cryptocurrencies and NFTs are intangible personalty.

anything that is not real property. Therefore cryptocurrencies and NFTs are personal property.

LO 18-11
Be able to classify specific items of property as either real property or personal property, and either tangible property or intangible property.

Property can also be classified as tangible or intangible. Nearly all of the things you can touch are tangible property. (A gold doubloon is tangible property; the quarter in your wallet is intangible property–its value is what it will purchase, not its value as a physical object.) Anything you can own that has no physical substance is intangible property. Ownership of intangible property is usually proven through documents. Such documents could also be tangible (on paper) or intangible (electronic records).

Cryptocurrencies are intangible personalty. Each unique cryptocurrency is associated with its own blockchain. Each block of the chain contains a data element–a fungible token for a digital currency–and a timestamp with the date and time the data was added to the blockchain. Each block is called a "token." Also built into the blockchain is a mechanism to ensure that only one party (actually a web address) can be considered the owner of that token.

An NFT is also a piece of data on a blockchain and thus also intangible personalty. However, each NFT is linked to a particular, unique, asset. Again, each token is uniquely identifiable and is generally owned by a single address on the blockchain, but it can also be easily exchanged, as is true with cryptocurrency transactions. One of the most well-known NFTs is actually a collection of NFTs, the Bored Ape collection, each token of which links to a unique (hence, nonfungible), but similar, digital representation of an ape. An NFT could also be linked to a physical asset, but that is beyond the scope of this chapter.

For a wealth of information on blockchains, including their classification as intellectual property which may be patentable or copyrighted, see **www.bitlaw.com.**

If you own Bitcoins, you likely have an account with a custodial platform, such as Coinbase or Kraken, which holds your Bitcoins for you until you direct it to transfer them to someone else or cash them in and deposit the dollars into the bank account you used when you set up your Bitcoin account. This is quite similar to the dollars you own. Only a small amount of the dollars people own are in the form of paper money, which we have just noted is intangible property, despite its physical manifestation. When you pay most bills, you likely direct your bank to transfer funds to, for example, pay your rent.

Cryptocurrencies are not actually currencies.

Despite the name, cryptocurrencies are not actually currencies because they are not issued and backed by the full faith and credit of a sovereign government. Currencies constitute legal tender in the country of issuance. If you are in the U.S. and someone owes you money, you cannot refuse to accept dollars in fulfillment of that obligation.

LO 18-12
Be able to explain what stablecoins are, what distinguishes asset-backed stablecoins, and how stablecoins differ from other cryptocurrencies.

Bitcoins are worth only what someone is willing to pay for them. That makes their value very volatile, which is not a good characteristic for a medium of exchange. To build a stable crypto environment, crypto owners need to have some sense that they are not investing their actual currency in something that overnight could become worthless. Hence, crypto companies started creating asset-backed cryptocurrencies. For example, Pexos has a cryptocurrency that is backed by gold–a commodity. Potential buyers interested in buying a gold-backed cryptocurrency will, of course, want proof that there is gold on deposit in the declared amount, preferably held by a third party to ensure it does not vanish. Because the value of gold varies, the value of the related cryptocurrency will also vary, but the value of the pegged asset (here gold) provides a floor. The strongest cryptocurrency would be one matched 1-for-1 with U.S. dollars held in a secure deposit. This "pegging" makes the cryptocurrency almost as good as the same amount of actual U.S. dollars. Asset-backed cryptocurrencies that are pegged to U.S. dollars or other world currency (or high-grade commercial paper denominated in U.S. dollars or other stable-value world currency, such as euros) are called ***stablecoins***.

Why still just "almost as good" as actual dollars? If the U.S. bank holding your checking account fails, your deposits are insured by the Federal Deposit Insurance Corporation (FDIC) up to $250,000. (If you have more than that, you would be well advised to open a second account at a different bank.) U.S. banks are subject to stringent regulation, in part so the government is willing to provide that insurance. If your US dollar-backed stablecoin cryptocurrency platform fails, the FDIC insurance would not be in your name, but in the name of your cryptocurrency platform.

Regulation of Cryptocurrencies

> Our national hands-off relationship with cryptocurrencies has abruptly come to an end.

The failure of FTX is a sharp demarcation line in the legal environment of cryptocurrencies in the U.S. From the first mining of Bitcoin in 2009 until FTX's bankruptcy filing on November 11, 2022, government regulation of the cryptocurrency industry was relatively modest. Our national hands-off relationship with cryptocurrencies has abruptly come to an end. Before continuing, you might want to refresh your memory of the collapse of FTX, which was covered in Chapter 9, Part Two, "Modern corporate governance failures: FTX (2022).

Prior to the FTX collapse, there was a growing awareness of a need for change. An example of that could be seen in an article from *The New York Times* on November 1, 2022, discussing a report just issued, prepared jointly by the President's Working Group on Financial Markets, the FDIC, and the Office of the Comptroller of Currency.

> The report . . . called on Congress to pass a law that makes issuers of stable coins subject to requirements like those of traditional banks and financial institutions. Such a change would require that those institutions hold adequate reserves to ensure they can meet the demands of customers to cash out quickly.[156]

Although Congress has been noticeably quiet on the subject, since the FTX failure there has been a veritable flood of legal action initiated regarding the world of cryptocurrencies and actions which had begun before FTX's collapse are gathering momentum. To illustrate, but not exhaust, this point, Here are some examples:

- The new chair of the SEC, Gary Gensler, had been studying the cryptocurrency industry even before arriving at the SEC in April 2021. Once there, he made it a major focus, as is evidenced by a near doubling of the number of people–to 50–employed in enforcing existing rules on the cryptocurrency industry.[157] It is the position of the SEC that cryptocurrencies are securities and therefore cannot be legally issued or sold without registration under the federal securities law, discussed in Part Three of Chapter 9.
- Less than three weeks after the collapse of FTX, Block-Fi, which is a cryptocurrency exchange platform, as well as an "interest-bearing custodial service for cryptocurrencies," filed for bankruptcy.[158]
- The ongoing case of *SEC v. Ripple* in the U.S. District Court for the Southern District of New York may turn out to be the first judicial ruling on whether the XRP token, and by

extension cryptocurrencies issued by others, is a "security" under federal law subject to SEC regulation. Ripple is arguing that XRP does not meet the requirements of the test set forth in *SEC v. W.J. Howey Co.,*[159] which is the case covered in the Legal Briefcase in Part Three of Chapter 9.

- On February 17, 2023, the SEC issued a statement announcing that it was bringing charges against Hall of Fame NBA player Paul Pierce "for touting EMAX tokens," a crypto asset sold by EthereumMax, without disclosing that he had been paid for the promotion and for making "false and misleading" statements about the tokens. Pierce agreed to settle the matter by paying "$1.409 million in penalties, disgorgement, and interest."[160]
- New York State's Department of Financial Services (NYDFS) regulates New York businesses issuing, transferring, purchasing, or selling certain currency-backed stablecoins through its establishment of a "BitLicense."[161] All BitLicensed stablecoins must be fully backed by bankruptcy-shielded reserves of U.S. dollars or their equivalents (such as U.S. government debt instruments). These reserves are regularly verified through audits, which also attest to compliance with NYDFS stablecoin guidance and bespoke (tailored specifically to the company) supervisory agreements. Paxos' "pax dollar" (USDP), for example, has secured New York BitLicensing and presently has a market capitalization of about $900 million.[162] Such value-stable, low-risk cryptocurrencies offer real promise for bringing access to banking services to the world's unbanked. They can also reduce the processing time and lower the cost of financial transactions for anyone because of the absence of a "clearing" process as exists with checks or online bank transfers. This can be even more important for intercountry transfers.

Questions

1. Can you identify any other well-known people facing lawsuits for their promotion of cryptocurrencies?
2. As mentioned previously, Bitcoin is not asset-backed, but Paxos' USDP is. What cryptocurrency would you buy if your objective is
   A. To speculate in, and hopefully generate large gains from, the cryptocurrency market? Why?
   B. To make transfers of 30 percent of your earnings as a farm laborer in Texas to your financially desperate family members in Madagascar? Why?
3. Go to **www.coindesk.com/price/bitcoin** and select "ALL" to fully expand the graph.
   A. Describe Bitcoin's price volatility.
   B. How much, based on the current Bitcoin price, would you gain or lose if you sold today a Bitcoin you had purchased on September 27, 2020? What would the result be if you had purchased it on November 10, 2021?

LO 18-13
Be able to identify ways in which the Internet is dependent on the protection provided by patents, copyrights, and trademarks.

Intellectual Property and the Internet

The expansion of electronic commerce has depended to a significant extent on the business community's success in protecting its technology from theft and infringement. Intellectual property is essentially composed of creative ideas that are the products of the human mind. Songs, computer programs, the formulas for new medicines, and novels are examples of intellectual property. Recalling the discussion of market failure in Chapter 8, you may recognize that intellectual property, from an economics point of view, is a public good.

Intellectual property is the product of human minds.

Intellectual property laws have been developed to provide creators a measure of protection from theft and exploitation. Under the Western view of intellectual property, the goal is to reward those whose ingenuity and hard work have produced results, such as movies, new methods production, and the like, as an incentive for them and others to continue doing so. Some cultures remain reluctant to recognize property rights of this kind, but globalization seems likely to promote relatively consistent intellectual property laws throughout most of the world. The inclusion of the Agreement on Trade-Related Aspects of Intellectual Property Rights as one of the WTO's foundation agreements supports this projection.

Patents

The grant of some early patents associated with basic methods of doing business online–such as Amazon.com's "one-click" method for making Internet purchases and Priceline.com's process of "reverse" auctions–raised considerable controversy, ultimately resulting in a 2000 revision of the way the U.S. Patent and Trademark Office processes and awards patents for many online processes.[163] [For more on business methods patents, see **www.uspto.gov/patents-getting-started/patent-basics/types-patent-applications/utility-patent/patent-business.html**].

The Current Patent Race

The revision of the patent process seems to have been successful. An article published in 2018 stated, "a few blockchain patents have already been granted. For example, Goldman Sachs has been awarded a patent for its proposed SETLcoin cryptocurrency settlement system, which envisions a system for settling securities trades using a built-in cryptocurrency.[164] However, two recent reports raise concern.

The first showed that as of early December 2021, 5,745 patents had been issued by the U.S. Patent and Trademark Office that specifically address blockchain technology.[165] The second, published in mid-July 2022, looked at which companies were applying for the most patents involving "blockchain" or "distributed ledger." IBM had filed the most applications, but in the top ten there were three companies affiliated with the Chinese business Alibaba Group Holding Company. Collectively, their filings were 25 percent higher than IBM's. Four of the top ten patent recipients were linked to Alibaba Group Holding Company, together holding more patents than the next largest holder, IBM (2493 patents versus 399). The researchers' ending observation was, "The substantial investment in U.S. blockchain patents by Alibaba and other Chinese companies could mean an intent to move more aggressively into blockchain businesses in the U.S., as U.S. patents are only enforceable with the United States."[166]

The Patent Wars

In the prior decade, the most prominent Internet-related patent legal issues involved disputes over the thousands of patents associated with mobile devices, such as smartphones and tablets, referred to as "a tsunami of patent-related lawsuits."[167] The disputes, primarily between Apple and Samsung, focused on patent infringement allegations with regard to design and functionality characteristics. Both companies were asserting the other had infringed.

The battle began in a California federal district court in April 2011 when Apple sued Samsung for copying patented aspects of Apple's iPhones, including their distinctive look (a rectangle with rounded corners) and a number of their software and hardware features. Samsung counterclaimed, charging Apple with violations of some of Samsung's standard-essential patents, which address matters of basic communication and data handling that support and permit industrywide standards. For example, the technology behind wireless communication requires standardization so smartphones made by any company can interact appropriately with Wi-Fi hotspots. These battles were fought not just in California, but also in Germany, South Korea, the Netherlands, and the United Kingdom. The war ended in 2018 after a jury decision resulted in an order for Samsung to pay Apple $539 million for infringing on its smartphone patents and the companies settled all their remaining lawsuits.[168] It is worthy of note that even in the midst of their smartphone battle, in other contexts, Apple and Samsung worked in concert. Apple is still a substantial customer for components manufactured by Samsung.[169]

Copyrights

Copyrights have only a modest application to new works posted on the Internet because only works that have been fixed in a tangible (physical) form are protectable. However, if original art is created in a tangible form and then a digital reproduction is posted on the Internet without the creator's permission, that would violate the creator's copyright. Damages could be quite high because once the digital content is posted, it can be reproduced an infinite number of times.

If an artist wished to create an NFT based on the original physical work, they could do so and it would be protected because they hold the copyright. If the artist wanted to sell the NFT version, they could contractually agree with the buyer that no more virtual copies would be permitted. The NFT purchaser would have the only legal virtual image.

Copyright infringement is rampant.

Copyright infringement, on the other hand, is rampant, and the Internet is responsible for its exponential growth. What is not clear is what can be done about it. Content owners individually have very little ability to stop infringement from happening. Reviewing and removing all the potentially infringing material could be a herculean task, and likely ineffective because offending content could be posted in any part of the world and still be accessible in nearly any other part.[170] Further, even if a particular infringement is stopped, a new one (or 10) could pop up immediately in another location. Who has the power and the right to assert jurisdiction over what is a worldwide problem? The answer is no one. However, if the infringement creates jurisdiction in any U.S. court and infringement is found, the potential costs to the infringer could be substantial:

- Statutory damages from $750 to $30,000 for each item infringed upon.
- Civil penalties up to $150,000 per piece if willful infringement is found.
- Surrender of any profits made on the work by the infringer.
- Criminal penalties up to $250,000 for each offense, in addition to up to five years in prison.[171]

One of the most visible Internet intellectual property disputes was the ongoing battle of the music recording industry to protect its copyrights. Music file sharing took off in the late 1990s through the use of the Napster website, where users could swap digital music. The recording industry successfully obtained an injunction against Napster's facilitation of such file sharing,[172] but the practice continued, aided by peer-to-peer computer programs such as KaZaA and Grokster, which were installed on users' computers. The recording industry sued Grokster and other file-sharing software distributors. The defendants prevailed at the district and circuit court levels. Then, in a unanimous Supreme Court decision in *Metro-Goldwyn-Mayer Studios v. Grokster,*[173] the recording industry achieved a major victory:

> In addition to intent to bring about infringement and distribution of a device suitable for infringing use, the inducement theory of course requires evidence of actual infringement by recipients of the device, the software in this case. As the account of the facts indicates, there is evidence of infringement on a gigantic scale, and there is no serious issue of the adequacy of MGM's showing on this point. . . There is substantial evidence in MGM's favor on all elements of inducement, and summary judgment in favor of Grokster and StreamCast was error.[174]

Concurrently with suing file-sharing facilitators such as Grokster and StreamCast, the recording industry pursued the file sharers as well–35,000 of them between 2003 and 2008, including many university students.[175] According to one source, in 2006 "college students illegally obtained two-thirds of their music and accounted for 1.3 billion illegal downloads."[176] Under the Digital Millennium Copyright Act, copyright holders can subpoena ISPs, including universities, to obtain the identity of those believed to be infringing. Of the 35,000 identified file sharers mentioned above, 12,000 lawsuits were filed, with two ultimately proceeding to trial. In one, a jury set damages against a former graduate student of $22,500 per song. The $675,000 award became final after the Supreme Court declined to hear the student's petition in 2012.[177] Just one month later, the Eighth Circuit reinstated a jury verdict of $220,000 in a second case.[178]

Questions

1. Based on your experience and knowledge, did these decisions effectively stopped illegal downloading of copyrighted material? Explain.
2. In your judgment, did Grokster and other peer-to-peer software distributors have a moral responsibility regarding the unlawful use of their products by third parties? Explain.
3. Go to Grokster.com. What if anything did you find?

Trademarks

LO 18-14
Explain the trademark issues affecting e-commerce facilitators like eBay.

The Internet has created new opportunities for trademark infringement. One company that has had to repeatedly defend trademark infringement suits is eBay. Individuals sometimes try to sell counterfeit goods on its site. For some luxury goods manufacturers, the quantities have been quite high. The issue is the extent to which eBay has a duty to weed out counterfeit goods. The company has improved its processes to substantially reduce the problem and it is sheltered from liability if it quickly removes any items when advised by the trademark holder that the goods are counterfeit. This places a duty of discovery on the trademark holder.

Question

Are you aware of any other websites that, like eBay, might have problems under our intellectual property laws similar to those eBay faces? If so, identify them.

Tax Implications of Cryptocurrencies

Creating, Selling, and Making Purchases with Cryptocurrencies

LO 18-15
Be able to describe the tax implications of mining, receiving, and spending cryptocurrencies.

The Internal Revenue Service (IRS) announced that, for income tax purposes, cryptocurrencies (referred to by the agency as *digital assets*) are treated as property, not as currency. It defines currency as "the . . . money of the United States or of any other country that is designated as legal tender . . . in the country of issuance[.]"[179]

Because cryptocurrencies are deemed to be property, income tax consequences can arise when

- Cryptocurrencies are mined and then converted into a currency or exchanged for property (including a different cryptocurrency or an NFT).
- Cryptocurrencies are received in exchange for services rendered or property sold.
- Cryptocurrencies are surrendered in exchange for services or property received.

Mining Cryptocurrencies

A U.S. taxpayer who mines cryptocurrencies and converts them into a currency or exchanges them for property is deemed to have business income equal to the fair market value of the currency or property received. If the miner is an individual, the combined income and self-employment taxes could be 25–40 percent.[180]

Receiving Cryptocurrencies in Exchange for Services or Property

If cryptocurrency is received in exchange for services performed, the fair market value of cryptocurrency is treated as income and must be reported on the recipient's tax return. If cryptocurrency is received in exchange for property, the tax gain or loss must be computed. The cost of the property given up is subtracted from the fair market value of the cryptocurrency received. The result must be reported on the service provider's or property seller's tax return.

Using Cryptocurrencies to Acquire Services or Property

The analytical model used by the IRS is

- The owner sells the cryptocurrency for cash, after which
- That cash is used to purchase the services or property.

A tax gain or loss must be computed as follows: the cost of the cryptocurrency is subtracted from the fair market value of the services or property received. That gain or loss must be reported on the cryptocurrency owner's tax return.

Audits, Interest, and Penalties

As a general rule, the IRS has three years to audit a filed tax return. However, if a return is fraudulent (for example, the return was prepared deliberately to exclude cryptocurrency dealings), there is no deadline for an audit. Many U.S. taxpayers have engaged in cryptocurrency dealings and not reported them on their tax returns; they are thus at risk of an IRS audit at any time.

Interest and potentially very large penalties can be imposed where cryptocurrency-related income has been omitted from a tax return. In egregious cases, criminal fines and imprisonment for up to five years are possible.

The IRS's new, aggressive enforcement actions, discussed below, pose a real threat for those who have ignored their cryptocurrency activities when preparing their tax returns.

Tax Law Enforcement

In testimony before Congress, former IRS Commissioner Charles Rettig estimated that the U.S. could annually be losing an astonishing $1 trillion in tax revenues (about 25 percent of all federal tax collections)–the so-called *tax gap*–due to tax evasion, taxpayer unfamiliarity with the tax laws leading to noncriminal underpayments, and inadequacies in the IRS's enforcement mechanisms. He attributed a significant and growing portion of the tax gap to the rise of cryptocurrencies.[181]

Convinced of the problem, Congress gave the IRS $45 billion in 2022 to increase cryptocurrency tax compliance. It will be hiring at least 500 employees to do so, 360 of whom will be IRS criminal investigation division (CID) special agents. Some of the funds will be used to improve the IRS's artificial intelligence capacities in forensic accounting to better trace cryptocurrency movements.[182]

The IRS accelerated its enhanced cryptocurrency enforcement activities in 2016 when it obtained a court order requiring Coinbase, a cryptocurrency exchange, to identify all U.S. persons who had engaged in cryptocurrency dealings in excess of $20,000 (in the aggregate) from 2013 to 2015. In 2018, Coinbase surrendered information on 13,000 accounts, after which the IRS sent over 10,000 letters to the identified taxpayers inquiring about their cryptocurrency activities. In 2021, the IRS obtained similar court orders against Kraken and Circle. Another court ordered SFOX, a digital currency broker, to provide such information in 2022.[183]

CID successes in 2022 included tax evasion convictions against the founders of Bitqyck, Samuel Mendez and Bruce Bise, both of whom were sentenced to eight years in prison. Collections from cryptocurrency tax evaders reached $7 billion, twice the amount from 2021. Criminal cases were commenced against Ilya Lichtenstein and Heather Morgan for conspiracy to launder cryptocurrencies.[184]

Information Returns

The IRS uses information returns to ensure that income is reported. Employees are likely quite familiar with Form W-2, which is sent both to the IRS and to the employee by the employer. Those who provide services as independent contractors receive Form 1099, issued by the service recipient. Investors who receive interest or dividends are sent Form 1099-INT or Form 1099-DIV.

A major flaw in this system is the lack of a Form 1099 related to cryptocurrency dealings. This weakness is being addressed by a new information return requirement for those parties who facilitate the storage or movement of cryptocurrencies. Although the law imposing the requirement was passed in 2021, problems associated with preparing the cryptocurrency industry to comply led to a temporary deferral set for early 2023 at the time of this writing.[185] The information return requirement will likely go into effect in 2024.

Questions

1. Bitcoin's own webpage (**bitcoin.com**), accessed on February 23, 2023, states that the cost to mine one bitcoin is $19,662. The value of one bitcoin on that day is $23,903.
   A. Assume you personally mine one bitcoin on February 23, 2023, and immediately convert it into its fair market value, $23,903 (U.S. dollars). Determine the tax consequences assuming a combined income and self-employment tax rate of 30 percent.
   B. Determine the tax consequences if, alternatively, you used that one bitcoin to purchase a car worth $23,903. Assume the tax rate is 23 percent (no self-employment tax).
2. You have been involved in cryptocurrency transactions for the last five years, each year generating a gain of $100,000, none of which has appeared on any of your tax returns.
   A. When will the IRS's power to audit your tax returns for these five years terminate?
   B. Assume you are audited by the IRS and the Justice Department is successful in obtaining a criminal tax evasion conviction against you. What are the potential consequences?
3. How could the IRS discover that you have been involved in cryptocurrency transactions:
   A. Before the information return requirement goes into effect?
   B. After the information return requirement goes into effect?

Part Six—Reprise: Who Governs Cyberspace?

A few short years ago, the world was in the midst of a global pandemic the economic impacts of which were unknown. Our collective impact on the ecosystem might have been temporarily lessened during the pandemic, but that alone would not materially alter the climate crisis trajectory presented in Part Five of Chapter 17. All 50 states had experienced massive protests, driven by the cry that Black lives do indeed matter. And, for the first time in about four decades, a genuine debate was occurring about whether shareholder primacy should be superseded by a balancing of the interests of all stakeholders.

In an economic system founded on capitalism, business is a potent force for assembling ideas, skills, and economic resources to find creative, cost-effective solutions to address our collective needs. Consider, in this respect, the husband and wife team in Ohio, an engineer and a doctor, who, over dinner in March 2020, envisioned a method for decontaminating N95 masks, so crucial to protect the health of medical personnel during the pandemic. Three days later, executives from the hospital system where she worked and engineers from his employer met. By the end of March, the FDA granted emergency authorization to deploy the new machines, which were able to process 80,000 masks per day.[186]

Throughout this text you, the readers, have been asked to examine the relationships among business, society, and government. Chapter 18 has explored these relationships in the context of the Internet, a tool created with government funding and transformed into a global communication network by business.

LO 18-16
Discuss several ethical issues raised by social media.

The Internet's contributions are many; but at the moment, it may be inflicting as much harm on society as the benefits it produces. To explore that proposition, we end the book with a final Practicing Ethics topic.

PRACTICING ETHICS The Dark Side of Social Media

To be able to weigh the benefits and costs of social media, we first need to understand its business model: what it was designed to do and why.

WE ARE NOT THEIR CUSTOMERS; THEIR ADVERTISERS ARE THEIR CUSTOMERS.

First, it is important to understand that we, the users, are not the customers of Google, Facebook, TikTok, Twitter, and YouTube. In truth, we are their products—our attention is what they are selling. The real business of these companies is to sell advertising. Their customers are their advertisers. To succeed in this business, their highest priority is to seize and retain users' attention.

Once they have a user's attention, they strive to hold onto it for as long as they can, because the longer they retain the user on site, the more data they collect about the user's interests and preferences. The more data they collect, the more targeted ads they can sell. The more targeted ads they sell, the more refined their user data becomes, and around it goes.

The algorithms they apply to the data collected (or purchased from others) allows them to deliver the content that most closely aligns with what will capture the user's attention, which results in the user staying longer and visiting more often. A corollary is that these companies go to great lengths to avoid presenting content inconsistent with a user's preferences.

SOCIAL MEDIA COMPANIES DID NOT JUST HAPPEN ONTO THIS GOLDMINE; SEIZING USERS' ATTENTION WAS THE DESIGN FROM THE BEGINNING.

The founding president of Facebook, Sean Parker, acknowledged this intentional design, when he said that, from the very beginning:

> The thought process that went into building these applications, Facebook being the first . . . , was all about: '**How do we consume as much of your time and conscious attention as possible?**' . . . This means that we need to . . . give you a . . . dopamine hit every once in a while . . . because someone liked your comment or post or whatever. . . . [T]hat's going to get you to contribute more content, and that's going to get you . . . more likes . . . [187] (Emphasis added.)

In other words, the attention-capturing techniques used on the sites are intended to trigger the brain's dopamine system, which creates a chemical inducement to repeat an action. This chemical inducement does not discriminate between good and bad actions (eating quality food versus engaging in behavior that thrills, like gambling with stakes that are unaffordable). Notifications and alerts, themselves, can produce a dopamine effect from the mere anticipation of engaging with the media.

HOW THEY PULL USERS INTO THEIR WORLD

To engage users, social media platforms and apps are designed to take advantage of human tendencies related to where attention is directed. Each company does its utmost to grasp more of that attention than its competitors. Author and New York University psychologist Adam Alter said: "There is an arms race for attention. [I]f you don't use every tool at your disposal to ensnare consumers, you will be left behind."[188]

Essential to capturing and holding users' attention is ensuring that the content most likely to induce engagement is presented at the top of the screen or, for TikTok, the first in the sequence. Captured (or purchased) data is used to create a profile of preferences—what is liked or disliked—for each user. Algorithms then locate and prioritize content for that user, which is shown in descending order of alignment with their preferences. Other techniques include:

- Pull-to-refresh (dragging the screen downward to prompt it to refresh): This takes advantage of individuals' attraction to unpredictability (known as intermittent reinforcement)—sometimes there is a "reward" (in this context, an item of interest) waiting, other times there is not; the uncertainty keeps the user coming back to find out.
- Infinite scrolling: App designers do not want the user to look away or disengage; they want to preclude any possibility of encountering stopping cues (moments like reaching the bottom of the screen that suggest it may be time to move on; having to take an affirmative action (like a click) to continue, which is eliminated when, for example, YouTube automatically starts the next video it has selected for the user within a few seconds of finishing the last video) and TikTok's 15-second videos, which run automatically, one after the other.
- Self-validation: Leah Pearlman, the co-inventor of Facebook's "Like," said it was added to pull users in by creating a sense of self-worth. She included herself: "When I need validation, I go to check Facebook."[189]

- Apps that indicate how many days in a row the user has engaged with it, creating a compulsion to sustain the "streak" by constantly returning.
- Exploiting fear-of-missing-out reactions ("I need to check in now so I know things as soon as everyone else does").
- Creating circumstances where a reciprocation is felt required (for example, WhatsApp's double-checkmark system and "user-is-typing" notification), which keeps the user engaged with the app to avoid giving offense.
- Endowment effect: The more time an app can get the user to invest in it, the harder it is for the user to detach from it.
- Utilizing imagery, action, and words known to attract and hold attention, as well as to induce actions (for instance, user clicks are strongly encouraged by phrases like "Princess . . . reveals . . . ," "Now we finally know why . . . ," and "Breaking News").

THINGS THEY DO TO ATTRACT ADVERTISING REVENUES

Everything they do to keep users coming back and staying as long as possible is specifically intended to better serve their real customers—their advertisers.

ADVERSE CONSEQUENCES OF THEIR SUCCESS: NEGATIVE EXTERNALITIES THAT ARE RENDING THE VERY FABRIC OF OUR SOCIETY.

Large swaths of today's online media carry content that is anything but even-handed, which poses a problem. The algorithms that drive social media sites are calibrated to deliver people only the information they like—only what they want to see or hear, with a powerful preference for the sensational. And the experience is designed to keep them immersed in what they like for as long as possible. Neither accuracy, balance, nor context are prerequisites for the information disseminated.

This all provides an opportunity to reconsider a core theme of this book: When businesses sell goods or render services with a view to generating a profit that provides an adequate return on investment to owners, negative externalities—costs to third parties resulting from the business's actions that are not born by the business or its customers—can result. The question is, how can these externalities be eliminated?

> Core principles of democracy, such as civil discourse between opposing views to reach sound compromises, are in jeopardy.

The negative externalities being generated by social media platforms threaten to rend the social fabric. Core principles of democracy, such as civil discourse between opposing views to reach sound compromises, are in jeopardy. Trust in essential, long-standing institutions like science and legitimate news sources is being eroded. Opinion, belief, and rumor are acquiring the same stature as fact. Titillating but baseless conspiracy theories are growing more ubiquitous and are gaining credibility among those who hear them. Extreme positions on issues are becoming impenetrable, with adherents isolating themselves from alternative views of reality; indeed, sometimes rejecting them with rage.

In May 2020, *The Wall Street Journal* explored Facebook's role in creating the extreme divisiveness of the current political landscape. "Facebook is under fire for making the world more divided. Many of its own experts appeared to agree—and to believe Facebook could mitigate many of the problems. The company chose not to. . . . Fixing the polarization problem would be difficult, requiring Facebook to rethink some of its core products. Most notably, [doing so would] force[ ] Facebook to consider how it prioritized 'user engagement'—a metric involving time spent, likes, shares and comments that for years has been the lodestar of its system."[190]

Facebook's former vice president for user growth, Chamath Palihapitiya, said: "I feel tremendous guilt. . . . **[W]e have created tools that are ripping apart the social fabric**[.]"[191] (Emphasis added.)

> Because of social media's influence, trust in bona fide news sources is waning.

Because of social media's influence, trust in bona fide news sources is waning. Overall, 35 percent of Americans believe at least some of the major news sources are biased. The more extreme the political views held, the more biased opposition-view news sources are deemed. Of those who describe themselves as either very liberal or very conservative, 43 percent felt such sources are biased. Only 31 percent of those who viewed themselves as moderate felt that way. The only news source to fare reasonably well was the Public Broadcasting System; yet 14 percent of Americans still felt its content was biased.

An echo chamber is commonly described as a situation in which individuals self-select into a group, all of the members of which share the individual's core beliefs. The group provides those beliefs legitimacy and promotes a tribal, us-versus-them mentality. Technically, this description of echo chambers is incorrect. An epistemic bubble arises when "insiders aren't exposed to people from the opposite side," whereas an echo chamber results when "insiders come to distrust everybody on the outside."[192] Divisiveness is usually not the result of insiders being unfamiliar with the outsiders' arguments. Rather, it occurs when the insiders' self-reinforcing version of reality becomes unassailable because its adherents profoundly distrust the outsiders and therefore dismiss their contradictory views.

Once individuals segregate themselves into echo chambers, they become especially vulnerable to fake news (that is, stories which appear to be news, but are disseminated either as jokes or maliciously with the intent of impacting a reader's understanding of the truth of the matter.)[193] Fake news can be used by bad actors to sow dissent, manufacture consensus, impair the community's ability to act responsibly, incite violence, and otherwise adversely impact the target. Once fake news is incorporated into the belief structure of an echo chamber, contrary new information is discarded to maintain cognitive consistency. It can reach the point that even highly dubious information is viewed as bona fide simply because it disparages opposing views. The mere exposure to outside opinions can elicit violent reactions, sometimes physical, which can disrupt familial and other personal relationships. Such encounters with opposing views intensify the cyberbalkanization.

Plaintiffs in two independent cases are arguing before the U.S. Supreme Court that, under the Anti-Terrorism Act, Google, Twitter, and Facebook can be held liable because their platforms allowed ISIS to post videos to communicate with and radicalize new recruits, who then committed mass murders which plaintiffs' family members were killed. These cases are discussed in Part Three above.

Perhaps most terrifying in an era of fake news are developments in artificial intelligence that provide the capacity to generate entirely fabricated pictures, videos, and sound recordings, collectively known as deepfakes. Illustrations have been presented by various news services using phony videos, for example, of Mark Zuckerberg and Vladimir Putin. It is not yet impossible to distinguish the real from the fake, but the fabrication technology has gotten so good that it can take hours or days to perform the verification analysis. In a world of instantaneous, far-reaching, uncurated communication and increasingly credulous and angry viewers, fake videos of political assassinations, terrorist attacks, tsunamis, or stock market crashes could have a catastrophic impact before they can be debunked. The implications for political campaigns are distressing, especially given the tinderbox state of American politics. Fortunately, some Silicon Valley leaders are finally recognizing how dangerous this technology is and, contrary to their usual stance, are calling for federal regulation. They realize that an appropriate solution cannot be achieved by the high-tech industry itself—regulation is required.

EVEN KNOWING THE HARM THEY ARE DOING, USERS DO NOT LEAVE.

Unsurprisingly, the various revelations about privacy breaches, political interference, fake news, extremism, the risk of addiction-like behavior, and other troubling matters have led the public to question the integrity of the social media platforms. A 2018 Pew Research Center survey found that 57 percent of those who get information from social media expect the bulk of it to be inaccurate. A 2019 Wall Street Journal/NBC poll found that the majority of Americans believe social media is divisive, a threat to privacy, and should be subjected to greater federal regulation. Remarkably, however, those polled admitted that they could not bring themselves to detach from these sites. Whether or not it is appropriate to label this as an "addiction," it is a testimony to the platforms' design that even those with strong negative views of social media in the aggregate find engaging with it indispensable to their daily lives.

HOW THEY CAN BE CONTROLLED

One force that could eliminate these negative externalities is social responsibility. A single business could simply choose to unilaterally change its behavior so the externalities it creates are eliminated or it could decide to bear the cost of those externalities. As a general rule, the responsibly acting business will experience reduced profitability by taking this step, which must be acceptable to the owners. Especially in the context of a publicly traded company, expecting an inclination toward social responsibility by an individual business to be the force that eliminates negative externalities is unrealistic.

Market forces could eliminate these externalities. For this to occur, there must be some factor that economically motivates a business generating negative externalities to either desist or internally absorb the cost. Market forces will only cause a business to change its behavior if doing so increases a competitive advantage or decreases a competitive disadvantage. For example, a business might take the step of reducing its carbon footprint if it believes that sourcing closer will produce a competitive advantage, as with a grocer that can increase its profits by catering to the subset of buyers attracted to "locally sourced" food.

The only market force that could induce social media platforms to change their behavior would be widespread, fervent, sustained outrage by the user community. Users would need to withdraw from the sites and vigorously press for change. It is highly improbable that these globe-spanning companies, collectively worth over $1.5 trillion, with extraordinary lobbying power will succumb to any plausible effort by users to compel a reconsideration of their fundamental business model. Recall that users cannot even bring themselves to disengage from these sites despite belief that the platforms are harming society.

Thus, we are left with the final choice: either endure the externalities or impose government regulation. Given the grave implications to society of allowing the externalities to continue, regulation would seem imperative. But that will be no easy task, especially in the United States with its constitutionally enshrined freedom of speech. The most realistic, and perhaps only, chance of government regulation in the United States is California's adoption of the California Consumer Privacy Act discussed in Part One, Market Forces and Government Regulation. Given the size of the California market, this law, which went into effect in July 2020, will force the big social media companies to provide effective opt-out paths for the collection and retention of users' personal data. To date, however, it has not spawned similar legislation in other states or by Congress.

It is not likely, however, that enhancements to privacy protection, alone, will suffice to redress all of harms social media is imposing on society. More will be needed. Nonetheless, perhaps its wider adoption would be an indication that a turning point is approaching where intense dissatisfaction with privacy violations, election interference, market domination, extremism, fear for the mental health of our families, fear of ever-increasing incidences of mass shootings, and dread of the social fabric unraveling will suffice to pressure more states or the federal government to act.

Questions

1. Do you agree that social media platforms are threatening the foundation of U.S. democracy? Explain.
2. Are you comfortable with the ways social media platforms strive to keep users from disengaging and moving on to other activities in their lives? Why or why not?
3. What is the difference between an epistemic bubble and an echo chamber? Which do you think is more likely to be the cause of the social dissension evidenced on social media platforms? Explain.
4. Assume that social media platforms cannot be permitted to continue to operate as they presently do. Which of the three forces (social responsibility, the market, government regulation) do you think is most likely to bring about the needed change? Explain your response.

Sources: Farhad Manjoo, "We Might Never Know How Much the Internet Is Hiding From Us," *The New York Times*, August 25, 2022 [**www.nytimes.com**]; David Lee, "Facebook founding president sounds alarm," *BBC*, November 9, 2017 [**www.bbc.com**]; Hilary Andersson, "Social media apps are 'deliberately' addictive to users," *BBC*, July 4, 2018 [**www.bbc.com**]; Catherine Price, "Trapped—the secret ways social media is built to be addictive (and what you can do to fight back)," *BBC Science Focus*, October 29, 2018 [**www.sciencefocus.com**]; Christian Montag, Bernd Lachmann, Marc Herrlich, and Katharina Zweig, "Addictive Features of Social Media/Messenger Platforms and Freemium Games against the Background of Psychological and Economic Theories," *International Journal of Environmental Research and Public Health*, July 23, 2019; Lee Rainie, Janna Anderson, and Jonathan Albright, "The Future of Free Speech, Trolls, Anonymity and Fake News Online," *Pew Research Center*, March 19, 2017 [**www.pewresearch.org**]; Jeff Horwitz and Deepa Seetharaman, "Facebook Executives Shut down Efforts to Make the Site Less Divisive," *The Wall Street Journal*, May 26, 2020 [**www.wsj.com**]; "Former Facebook and Google employees fight tech 'addiction,'" *BBC*, February 6, 2018 [**www.bbc.com**]; Jonathan Rothwell, "Biased News Media or Biased Readers? An Experiment on Trust," *The New York Times*, September 26, 2018 [**www.nytimes.com**]; C. Thi Nguyen, "The problem of living inside echo chambers," *The Conversation*, September 11, 2019 [**https://theconversation.com**]; Tonya Mosley, "How Social Media Echo Chambers Drown out the Voices in the Middle," *KQED*, November 5, 2018 [**www.kqed.org**]; Jeff Stibel, "Take news: How our brains lead us into echo chambers that promote racism and sexism," *USA Today*, May 15, 2018 [**www.usatoday.com**]; Ian Sample, "What are deep fakes—and how can you spot them?," *The Guardian*, January 13, 2020 [**www.guardian.com**]; Philip Ewing, "What You Need to Know about Fake Video, Audio and the 2020 Election," *National Public Radio*, September 2, 2019 [**www.npr.org**]. Sebastian Herrera, "Tech Giants' New Appeal to Governments: Please Regulate Us," *The Wall Street Journal*, January 27, 2020 [**www.wsj.com**]; "Apple investors urge action on 'smartphone addiction,'" *BBC*, January 8, 2018 [**www.bbc.com**]; Frank Solvato, "How Social Media Echo Chambers Dupe the Public," *Conservative Daily News*, February 24, 2020 [**www.conservativedailynews.com**]; and Jon McKinnon and Danny Dougherty, "Americans Hate Social Media but Can't Give It up, WSJ/NBC News Poll Finds," *The Wall Street Journal*, April 5, 2019 [**www.wsj.com**].

Research Exercise on Ethics and A.I.

Artificial intelligence is powerful. Like all technology, it is ethically neutral. Our choices of how we use it can present ethical issues. Do some research about the power of generative A.I., such as ChatGPT, and its use and abuse. How have they been used for positive ends? How have they been used for less-than-noble purposes? Then use ChatGPG, or whatever accessible generative AI program you prefer, to do the same research. Evaluate the two processes and results and turn that into a presentation. (You could even use AI to help create the presentation based on your results, but be sure to disclose that fact and check its results for accuracy!)

Chapter Questions

1. The United Nations has warned that the worldwide growth of e-commerce may constitute a threat to the well-being of the world's developing nations, as well as parts of Europe. Explain the UN's concerns.
2. Psychologists are worried that the Internet will make shopping too easy. Explain their concern.
3. In March 1992, Danish police seized the business records of BAMSE, a computer bulletin board system based in Denmark that sold child pornography over the Internet. The records included information that Mohrbacher, who lived in Paradise, California, had downloaded two graphic interface format (GIF) images from BAMSE in January 1992.

   In March 1993, police executed a search warrant at Mohrbacher's workplace and found, among other images, two files that had been downloaded from BAMSE, one of a nude girl and one of a girl engaged in a sex act with an adult; both girls were under 12. During the execution of the warrant, Mohrbacher was cooperative, confessing that he had downloaded the two images from BAMSE. Mohrbacher was charged with *transporting* or *shipping* images by computer as prohibited by 18 U.S.C. § 2252(a)(1). Mohrbacher argued that downloading is properly characterized as *receiving* images by computer, which is proscribed by section 2252(a)(2). He was not charged under section 2252(a)(2).

   Should downloading from a computer bulletin board constitute shipping or transporting within the meaning of 18 U.S.C. § 2252(a)(1)? Explain. See *U.S. v. Mohrbacher,* 182 F.3d 1041 (9th Cir. 1999).
4. To answer the following questions, compare *Apple Computer v. Doe,* 2005 WL 578641 (Cal. Super. Ct. Mar. 11, 2005) (requiring disclosure) with *O'Grady v. Superior Ct.,* 44 Cal. Rptr. 3d 72 (Cal. App. 2006) (reversing on appeal).
   a. Should online bloggers be entitled to protection as journalists under the First Amendment with regard to the confidentiality of their sources?
   b. What if those sources have illegally revealed corporate trade secrets?
5. America Online (AOL), an ISP, sued TSF Marketing and Joseph Melle, who founded TSF. AOL claimed that Melle and TSF sent spam to AOL subscribers. The e-mail contained the letters "aol.com" in the headers. AOL claimed that the e-mail totaled some 60 million messages over a 10-month period. Melle allegedly continued the mailings after he was notified in writing by AOL to stop. AOL received over 50,000 complaints from subscribers. AOL claimed, among other things, that Melle had diluted its trademark. The case arose before the passage of the CAN-SPAM Act. Would Melle have been liable under that act? Explain. See *America Online, Inc. v. IMS,* 24 F. Supp. 2d 548 (E.D. Va. 1998).

6. McLaren was an employee of Microsoft Corporation. In December 1996, Microsoft suspended McLaren's employment pending an investigation into accusations of sexual harassment and "inventory questions." McLaren requested access to his electronic mail to disprove the allegations against him. According to McLaren, he was told he could access his e-mail only by requesting it through company officials and telling them the location of a particular message. By memorandum, McLaren requested that no one tamper with his Microsoft office workstation or his e-mail. McLaren's employment was terminated on December 11, 1996.

   Following the termination of his employment, McLaren filed suit against the company alleging, as his sole cause of action, a claim for invasion of privacy. In support of his claim, McLaren alleged that, on information and belief, Microsoft had invaded his privacy by "breaking into" some or all of the personal folders maintained on his office computer and releasing the contents of the folders to third parties. According to McLaren, the personal folders were part of a computer application created by Microsoft in which e-mail messages could be stored. Access to the e-mail system was obtained through a network password. Access to personal folders could be additionally restricted by a "personal store" password created by the individual user. McLaren created and used a personal store password to restrict access to his personal folders.

   McLaren concedes in his petition that it was possible for Microsoft to "decrypt" his personal store password. McLaren alleges, however, that "[b]y allowing [him] to have a personal store password for his personal folders, [McLaren] manifested and [Microsoft] recognized an expectation that the personal folders would be free from intrusion and interference." McLaren characterizes Microsoft's decrypting or otherwise "breaking in" to his personal folders as an intentional, unjustified, and unlawful invasion of privacy.

   Did Microsoft unlawfully invade McLaren's privacy? Explain. See *McLaren v. Microsoft,* 1999 Texas App. LEXIS 4103 (Tex. Ct. App. May 28, 1999).

7. Bensusan Restaurant Corporation owns the famous New York City jazz club "The Blue Note," and in 1985 it registered the name as a federal trademark. Since 1980, King has operated a small club in Columbia, Missouri, also named "The Blue Note." Around 1993, Bensusan wrote to King demanding that he discontinue use of "The Blue Note" name. King's attorney responded by saying that Bensusan had no legal right to make the demand. In 1996, King created, in Missouri, a website for "The Blue Note," which also contained a hyperlink to the New York club's website. Bensusan then sued in the Southern District of New York, alleging Lanham Act and trademark violations, among other things. The New York court dismissed the case for lack of personal jurisdiction. Bensusan appealed. Decide. Explain. See *Bensusan Restaurant Corp. v. King,* 126 F.3d 25 (2d Cir. 1997).

8. Journalist John Snell remarked: "Not long ago you couldn't turn around in cyberspace without bumping into a tech geek. Now you're no more than a mouse click away from a lawyer. Attorneys are everywhere."[194] What factors account for the dramatic increase in lawyers addressing Internet issues?

Notes

1. "Facts and Figures 2021: 2.9 billion people still offline," *International Telecommunications Union,* November 29, 2021 **[www.itu.int]**.
2. Ibid.
3. Ibid.

4. Paul Bischoff, "Internet Censorship 2023: A Global Map of Internet Restrictions," *comparitech,* January 26, 2023 [**www.comparitech.com**].
5. "Global value chains and trade," *OECD,* accessed January 30, 2023 [**www.oecd.org**].
6. Anick Jesdanun, "As Internet Turns 40, Barriers Run Contrary to Creators' Aims," *Des Moines Register,* August 31, 2009, p. 1A.
7. Thomas L. Friedman, "The Great Iceland Meltdown," *The New York Times,* October 19, 2008 [**www.nytimes.com**]. Although this statement was offered in a somewhat different context–the financial crisis of 2008–it is equally applicable to this discussion of the Internet.
8. Kevin Roose, "Don't Ban ChatGPT in Schools. Teach With It." *The New York Times,* January 12, 2023 [**www.nytimes.com**].
9. Sarah Anderson, "The Alt-Right Manipulated My Comic. Then A.I. Claimed It.," *The New York Times,* December 31, 2022 [**www.nytimes.com**].
10. Katy Steinmetz, "How Lyft Is Capitalizing on Uber's Scandals," *Time,* March 28, 2017 [**https://time.com**].
11. Paige Leskin, "Uber says the #DeleteUber movement led to 'hundreds of thousands' of people quitting the app," *Business Insider,* April 11, 2019 [**www.businessinsider.com**].
12. "Doing the ICANN-can," *The Economist,* March 22, 2014 [**www.economist.com**].
13. Klint Finley, "The Internet Finally Belongs to Everyone," *Wired,* October 3, 2016 [**www.wired.com**].
14. David McCabe and Adam Satariano, "The Era of Borderless Data Is Ending," *The New York Times,* May 23, 2022 [**www.nytimes.com**].
15. Ibid.
16. Ibid.
17. Shira Ovide, "Why Apple's Fight in the Netherlands Matters," *The New York Times,* February 22, 2022 [**www.nytimes.com**] and Natasha Singer, "How the Netherlands Is Taming Big Tech," *The New York Times,* January 19, 2023 [**www.nytimes.com**].
18. Ian Austen and Vjosa Isia, "Canada Introduces Bill Requiring Online Giants to Share Revenues With Publishers," *The New York Times,* April 5, 2022 [**www.nytimes.com**].
19. Katie Collins, "GDPR Fines: The Biggest Privacy Penalties Handed Out So Far," *CNET,* February 21, 2022 [**www.cnet.com**].
20. Florian Zandt, "GDPR Breaches," *statista,* January 6, 2023 [**www.statista.com**] and Adam Satariano, "Meta's Ad Practices Ruled Illegal Under E.U. Law, *The New York Times,* January 4, 2023 [**www.nytimes.com**].
21. "Is the EU overreaching with new digital regulations?," *The Economist,* September 1, 2022 [**www.economist.com**].
22. "Here's how the Digital Services Act changes content moderation," *World Economic Forum,* December 13, 2022 [**www.weforum.org**] and Christoph Schmon and Paige Collings, "The Adoption of the EU's Digital Services Act: A Landmark Year for Platform Regulation: 2022 In Review," *Electronic Frontier Foundation,* December 26, 2022 [**www.eff.org**].
23. Press Release, "Digital Markets Act: rules for digital gatekeepers to ensure open markets enter into force," *European Commission,* October 31, 2022 [**https://ec.europa.eu**].
24. "Digital Markets Act," *Wikipedia,* accessed February 4, 2023 [**https://en.wikipedia.org**].
25. Press Release, "Digital Markets Act: rules for digital gatekeepers to ensure open markets enter into force."
26. Ibid.
27. Ibid.

28. Foo Yun Chee, "EU lawmakers pass landmark tech rules, but enforcement a worry," *Reuters,* July 5 2022 [**www.reuters.com**].
29. "Digital Markets Act," *Wikipedia,* accessed February 4, 2023 [**https://en.wikipedia.org**].
30. Foo Yun Chee, "EU lawmakers pass landmark tech rules, but enforcement a worry."
31. David McCabe, "How California Is Building the Nation's First Privacy Police," *The New York Times,* March 15, 2022 [**www.nytimes.com**].
32. "California Consumer Privacy Act," *Wikipedia,* accessed February 5, 2023 [**https://en.wikipedia.org**].
33. Isha Marathe, "Washington State's Privacy Bill Emerges as National Model, Despite Failure Over Private Right of Action," *Law.com,* May 6, 2022 [**www.law.com**].
34. David Strauss, "Proposed State Privacy Law Update: January 30, 2023," *Byte Back,* February 4, 2023 [**https://www.bytebacklaw.com**].
35. "Ex-CompuServe Chief's Conviction Overturned; German Case Involved Child Porn Sites," *Houston Chronicle,* November 18, 1999, p. 3. The head of CompuServe Germany was convicted in 1998 of violating German law by failing to block CompuServe's customers' access to child pornography websites. At the time, the only technical way for CompuServe to comply was to block all of its worldwide users from access. The conviction was reversed in 1999.
36. See *Revell v. Lidov,* 317 F.3d 467 (5th Cir. 2002). Lidov posted an article he wrote on the bombing of Pan Am Flight 103 over Lockerbie, Scotland, in 1988. He alleged that a broad politically motivated conspiracy within the Reagan administration intentionally failed to stop the bombing despite advance warnings. The article singled out Oliver "Buck" Revell, then Associate Deputy Director of the FBI. It was posted on an Internet bulletin board maintained by Columbia University's School of Journalism. Lidov had never been to Texas, except possibly to change planes, or conducted business there, and was apparently unaware that Revell then resided in Texas. Columbia had never received more than 20 Internet subscriptions to the *Columbia Journalism Review* from Texas residents. The Fifth Circuit found that neither general nor specific jurisdiction existed in the Texas courts.
37. *Mink v. AAAA Development,* 190 F.3d 333 (5th Cir. 1999).
38. See, for example, *Pavlovich v. DVD Copy Control Association.* The California Supreme Court reversed a state appeals court which had held that a Texas resident was subject to California's jurisdiction for the knowing posting of trade secrets of a California company on an Indiana website. 58 P.3d 2 (Cal.2002). See also *Gator.com Corp. v. L. L. Bean, Inc.,* in which the Ninth Circuit reversed the district court's decision that L. L. Bean could not be sued in California where it had no stores or agents, even though it regularly sold merchandise to California residents through its website. The volume of Internet business done by L. L. Bean with California residents made it subject to California's jurisdiction. 341 F.3d 1072 (9th Cir. 2003). That decision was vacated, however, when the Ninth Circuit decided to rehear the case en banc. 366 F.3d 789 (9th Cir. 2004). After the oral argument, Gator.com and L. L. Bean settled their substantive dispute and the Ninth Circuit dismissed the appeal as moot. 398 F.3d 1125 (9th Cir. 2005).
39. Ryan Davis, "7th Circ. Lets Bulgarian Dating Site Off Hook in IP Row," *Law 360,* April 27, 2011 [**www.law360.com**].
40. Rachel Donadio, "Larger Threat Is Seen in Google Case," *The New York Times,* February 25, 2010 [**www.nytimes.com**].
41. Eric Pfanner, "Italian Appeals Court Acquits 3 Google Executives in Privacy Case," *The New York Times,* December 21, 2012 [**www.nytimes.com**].
42. Stephan Wilske and Teresa Schiller, "International Jurisdiction in Cyberspace: Which States May Regulate the Internet?" *Federal Communications Law Journal* 50, December 1997 [**www.fclj.org**].
43. Ceclia Kang, "Indiana Sues TikTok for Security and Child Safety Violations," *The New York Times,* December 7, 2022 [**www.nytimes.com**].

44. *Yahoo! Inc. v. La Ligue Contre Le Racisme et L'Antisemitisme,* 433 F.3d 1199 (9th Cir. 2006).
45. *La Ligue Contre Le Racisme v. Yahoo!,* 126 S. Ct. 2332 (2006).
46. *Obsidian Finance Group v. Cox,* 740 F.3d 1284 (9th Cir. 2014). At trial, a federal jury found a Montana-based blogger had defamed both an Oregon attorney and the finance firm of which he was a principal, awarding damages to both plaintiffs. In her blog, defendant had asserted the attorney, a court-appointed trustee in a bankruptcy proceeding, had committed tax fraud. The Ninth Circuit held that unlawful acts of a person in such a position was a matter of public concern. Thus, plaintiffs could not prevail simply by proving the assertion to be false but were also required to prove negligence on plaintiff's part. In addition, any damage award would require proof of actual damages. The case was remanded for a new trial.
47. 2 F.4th 871 (9th Cir. 2021).
48. Ibid. Note: The Ninth Circuit issued one opinion covering both cases.
49. Id. at 882.
50. 18 U.S.C. 2333.
51. Id. at 880.
52. Ibid.
53. 2 F.4th 871, 887 (quoting an earlier case).
54. Id. at 892.
55. Id. at 893.
56. Id. at 895.
57. Id. at 896.
58. Id. at 897.
59. *Twitter v. Taamneh,* 598 U.S. ___ (2023), *Gonzalez v. Google,* 598 U.S. ___ (2023); and Adam Liptak, "Supreme Court Won't Hold Tech Companies Liable for User Posts," *The New York Times*, May 18, 2023 [**www.nytimes.com**].
60. David McCabe, "Supreme Court Poised to Reconsider Key Tenets of Online Speech," *The New York Times,* January 19, 2023 [**www.nytimes.com**].
61. 106.072 Fla. Stat. (2022).
62. Tex. Civ. Prac. & Rem. Code §§ 143A.001-.007.
63. Ann E. Marimow and Cat Zakrzewski, "U.S. Supreme Court to rule on Texas law limiting social media content removal," *The Texas Tribune*, September 29, 2023 [**www.texastribune.org**] and David McCabe, "Supreme Court Poised to Reconsider Key Tenets of Online Speech."
64. *Reno v. ACLU,* 521 U.S. 844 (1997).
65. *ACLU v. Gonzales,* 478 F. Supp. 2d 775 (E.D. Pa. 2007); *Mukasey v. ACLU,* 139 S. Ct. 1032 (2009).
66. *Ashcroft v. Free Speech Coalition,* 122 S. Ct. 1389 (2002).
67. Christine Arena, "Child Porn Too Big for Law Enforcement? Microsoft Steps In," *The Christian Science Monitor,* June 13, 2010.
68. Cyrus Farivar and Andrew Blankstein, "Feds take down the world's 'largest dark web child porn marketplace'," *NBC News,* October 16, 2019 [**www.nbcnews.com**].
69. *McIntyre v. Ohio Elections Commission,* 514 U.S. 334, 342 (1995).
70. Ibid.
71. *In re Anonymous Online Speakers v. U.S. Dist. Ct. for the Dist. of Nevada, Reno,* 661 F.3d 1168 (9th Cir. 2011).

72. Kate Isaacs, "Pornhub needs to change – or shut down," *The Guardian,* March 9, 2020 [**www.theguardian.com**].
73. Robert L. Rogers III, "Two Federal Cases Hold Website 'Responsible' for Postings on *thedirty.com,*" Association of Corporate Counsel, January 31, 2013.
74. "How do revenge porn laws work in the US?," *McAllister Olivarius,* accessed February 9, 2023 [**http://mcolaw.com**]. South Carolina and Massachusetts are the two states without such laws.
75. Melissa Rowley, "There are revenge porn laws on the books in 46 states, but victims say not enough is being done to protect them online," *Insider,* November 11, 2019 [**www.insider.com**].
76. Christine Hauser, "$6.4 Million Judgment in Revenge Porn Case Is Among Largest Ever," *The New York Times,* April 11, 2018 [**www.nytimes.com**].
77. S. Dixon, "Highest number of spam emails sent daily by country January 2023," *statistica,* January 16, 2023 [**www.statista.com**].
78. L. Ceci, "Spam e-mail: leading countries of origin of spam 2021," *statistica,* January 2, 2023 [**www.statista.com**].
79. Federal Trade Commission, "FTC Completes Review of CAN-SPAM Rule," February 12, 2019 [**www.ftc.gov**].
80. Natasha Singer and Jason Karaian, "Americans Flunked This Test on Online Privacy," *The New York Times,* February 7, 2023 [**www.nytimes.com**].
81. Ibid.
82. Zoe Schiffer, "How to erase your personal information from the internet (it's not impossible!)," *Vox,* September 11, 2019 [**www.vox.com**].
83. Alyssa Newcomb, "Big Tech's Bugs Beg the Question: Should You Cover Your Smartphone Camera?," *Fortune Magazine,* November 19, 2019 [**https://fortune.com**].
84. *Carpenter v. United States,* 138 S.Ct. 2206 (2018).
85. Sidney Fussell, "The Most Important Things to Know About Apps That Track Your Location," *Time,* September 1, 2022 [**https://time.com**].
86. Zeynep Tufekci, "We Need to Take Back Our Privacy," *The New York Times,* May 19, 2022 [**www.nytimes.com**].
87. Ibid.
88. Alex Kingsbury, "We're About to Find Out What Happens When Privacy Is All but Gone," *The New York Times,* August 23, 2022 [**www.nytimes.com**].
89. Kashmir Hill, "Deleting Your Period Tracker Won't Protect You," *The New York Times,* June 30, 2022 [**www.nytimes.com**].
90. Press Release, "FTC Sues Kochava for Selling Data That Tracks People at Reproductive Health Clinics, Places of Worship, and Other Sensitive Locations," *Federal Trade Commission*, August 29, 2022 [**www.ftc.gov**].
91. Natasha Singer, "F.T.C. sues over tracking data that could expose visits to abortion clinics," *The New York Times,* August 29, 2022 [**www.nytimes.com**].
92. John D. McKinnon, "Google Reaches $391.5 Million Settlement With States Over Location Tracking Practices," *The Wall Street Journal,* November 14, 2022 [**www.wsj.com**].
93. Press Release, "FTC Explores Rules Cracking Down on Commercial Surveillance and Lax Data Security Practices," *Federal Trade Commission*, August 11, 2022 [**www.ftc.gov**].
94. Jennifer Valentino-Devries, Jeremy Singer-Vine, and Ashkan Soltani, "Websites Vary Prices, Deals Based on Users' Information," *The Wall Street Journal,* December 24, 2012 [**www.wsj.com**].
95. John D. McKinnon and Rob Copeland, "Google to Pay Millions in Fines Over Children's Privacy Issues at YouTube," *The Wall Street Journal,* August 30, 2019 [**www.wsj.com**] and Natasha Singer and Kate Conger, "Google Is Fined $170 Million for Violating Children's Privacy on YouTube," *The New York Times,* September 4, 2019 [**www.nytimes.com**].

96. Joanna Stern, "iPhone Privacy Is Broken . . . and Apps Are to Blame," *The Wall Street Journal,* May 31, 2019 [**www.wsj.com**].
97. Zeynep Tufekci, "We Need to Take Back Our Privacy."
98. Alison DeNisco Rayome, "Change This Setting to Stop iPhone Apps From Tracking You," *CNET,* December 26, 2022 [**www.cnet.com**].
99. Brian X. Chen, "Hi, Alexa. How Do I Stop You From Listening In On Me?," *The New York Times,* August 21, 2019 [**www.nytimes.com**].
100. Peter Rudegeair and Liz Hoffman, "Next in Google's Quest for Consumer Dominance: Banking," *The Wall Street Journal,* November 13, 2019 [**www.wsj.com**].
101. Alex Webb, "Amazon's Roomba Deal Is Really About Mapping Your Home," *Bloomberg,* August 5, 2022 [**www.bloomberg.com**].
102. Rob Copeland, "Google's Project Nightingale' Gathers Personal Health Data on Millions of Americans," *The Wall Street Journal,* November 11, 2019 [**www.wjs.com**].
103. Ibid.
104. Rob Copeland and Sarah E. Needleman, "Google's 'Project Nightingale' Triggers Federal Inquiry," *The Wall Street Journal,* November 12, 2019 [**www.wsj.com**].
105. Susan Morse, "Amazon's $3.9 billion acquisition of One Medical moves a step forward," *Healthcare Finance,* January 4, 2023 [**www.healthcarefinancenews.com**].
106. Theodore F. Claypoole, "State Laws Shift Geolocation's Spot On The Privacy Map," *Womble Bond Dickinson,* March 8, 2022 [**www.womblebonddickinson.com**].
107. Jason Horowitz and Adam Satariano, "Europe Rolls Out Contact Tracing Apps, With Hope and Trepidation, *The New York Times,* June 16, 2020 [**www.nytimes.com**].
108. Jack Nicas and Daisuke Wakabayashi, "Apple and Google Team Up to 'Contact Trace' the Coronavirus," *The New York Times,* April 10, 2020 [**www.nytimes.com**].
109. Davey Alba, "ACLU Accuses Clearview AI of Privacy 'Nightmare Scenario'," *The New York Times,* May 28, 2020 [**www.nytimes.com**].
110. Press Release, "In Big Win, Settlement Ensures Clearview AI Complies With Groundbreaking Illinois Biometric Privacy Law," *ACLU,* May 9, 2022 [**www.aclu.org**].
111. Isabelle Qian, Muyi Xiao, Paul Mozur and Alexander Cardia, "Four Takeaways From a Times Investigation Into China's Expanding Surveillance State," *The New York Times,* June 21, 2022 [**www.nytimes.com**].
112. John McKinnon, "Facebook's Facial Recognition Feature Violates Users' Privacy Rights, Groups Allege," *The Wall Street Journal,* April 6, 2018 [**www.wsj.com**].
113. Drew Harwell, "Microsoft calls for regulation of facial recognition, saying it's too risky to leave to industry alone," *The Washington Post,* July 13, 2018 [**www.washingtonpost.com**].
114. Press Release, "FTC Imposes $5 Billion Penalty and Sweeping New Privacy Restrictions on Facebook," *Federal Trade Commission*, July 24, 2019 [**www.ftc.gov**].
115. Kate Conger, Richard Fausset, and Serge Kovaleski, "San Francisco Bans Facial Recognition Technology," *The New York Times,* May 14, 2019 [**www.nytimes.com**].
116. Matt O'Brien, "Why some cities, states and lawmakers want to curb facial recognition technology," *USA Today,* December 17, 2019 [**www.usatoday.com**].
117. Natasha Singer and Mike Issac, "Facebook to Pay $550 Million to Settle Facial Recognition Suit," *The New York Times,* January 29, 2020 [**www.nytimes.com**].
118. Ibid.
119. Shira Ovide, "A case for banning facial recognition," *The New York Times,* June 9, 2020 [**www.nytimes.com**].

120. Asa Fitch, "Amazon Suspends Police Use of Its Facial-Recognition Technology," *The Wall Street Journal,* June 10, 2020 [**www.wsj.com**].
121. Kashmir Hill and Ryan Mac, "Facebook, Citing Societal Concerns, Plans to Shut Down Facial Recognition System," *The New York Times,* November 2, 2021 [**www.nytimes.com**].
122. Press Release, "In Big Win, Settlement Ensures Clearview AI Complies With Groundbreaking Illinois Biometric Privacy Law."
123. Kristin Cohen, "Location, health, and other sensitive information: FTC committed to fully enforcing the law against illegal use and sharing of highly sensitive data," *Federal Trade Commission*, July 11, 2022 [**www.ftc.gov**].
124. Press Release, "FTC Explores Rules Cracking Down on Commercial Surveillance and Lax Data Security Practices," *Federal Trade Commission*, August 11, 2022 [**www.ftc.gov**].
125. Sam Schechner and Emre Peker, "Apple CEO Condemns 'Data-Industrial Complex'," *The Wall Street Journal,* October 24, 2018 [**www.wsj.com**].
126. John D. McKinnon and Rob Copeland, "Google to Pay Millions in Fines Over Children's Privacy Issues at YouTube."
127. Press Release, "Advertising Platform OpenX Will Pay $2 Million for Collecting Personal Information from Children in Violation of Children's Privacy Law," *Federal Trade Commission,* December 15, 2021 [**www.ftc.gov**].
128. Press Release, Fortnite Game Maker Epic Games to Pay More Than Half a Billion Dollars over FTC Allegations of Privacy Violations and Unwanted Charges," *Federal Trade Commission,* December 19, 2022 [**www.ftc.gov**].
129. Natasha Singer, "Sweeping Children's Online Safety Bill Is Passed in California," *The New York Times,* August 30, 2022 [**www.nytimes.com**].
130. Joanna Stern, "iPhone Privacy Is Broken . . . and Apps Are to Blame."
131. The items on this list were reported in Charles Griffiths, "The Latest 2023 Cyber Crime Statistics (updated February 2023)," *AAG,* February 10, 2023 [**https://aag-it.com**] and Charles Griffiths, "The Latest 2023 Ransomware Statistics (updated February 2023), *AAG,* February 10, 2023 [**https://aag-it.com**].
132. "Complaints and Losses over the Last Five Years," Internet Crime Complaint Center (IC3), accessed February 16, 2023 [**www.ic3.gov**].
133. Ani Petrosyan, "Cyber crime: number of compromises and impacted individuals in U.S. 2005–2022," *Statista,* February 7, 2023 [**www.statista.com**].
134. Ibid.
135. Press Release, "FTC Brings Action Against Ed Tech Provider Chegg for Careless Security that Exposed Personal Data of Millions of Customers," *Federal Trade Commission*, October 31, 2022 [**www.ftc.gov**].
136. Bruce Schneier, "The Uber Hack Exposes More Than Failed Data Security," *The New York Times,* September 26, 2022 [**www.nytimes.com**].
137. Ibid.
138. Stephanie Kelly and Jessica Resnick-ault, "One password allowed hackers to disrupt Colonial Pipeline, CEO tells senators," *Reuters,* June 8, 2021 [**www.reuters.com**].
139. Ibid.
140. Andy Greenberg, "A Hacker Tried to Poison a Florida City's Water Supply, Officials Say," *Wired,* February 8, 2021 [**www.wired.com**].
141. Jenni Bergal, "Florida Hack Exposes Danger to Water Systems," *Pew,* March 10, 2021 [**www.pewtrusts.org**].
142. Ibid.

143. Rebecca Smith and Rob Barry, "America's Electric Grid Has a Vulnerable Back Door—and Russia Walked through It," *The Wall Street Journal,* January 10, 2019 [**www.wsj.com**].
144. Melanie Evans and Peter Loftus, "Rattled by Cyberattacks, Hospitals Push Device Makers to Improve Security," *The Wall Street Journal,* May 12, 2019 [**www.wsj.com**].
145. Nicholas Barrett, "Hacking Gets Physical," *The Economist,* November 30, 2017 [**www.economist.com**].
146. Alex W. Palmer, "How TikTok Became a Diplomatic Crisis," *The New York Times,* December 20, 2022 [**www.nytimes.com**].
147. Sapna Maheshwari, "Auburn Banned TikTok, and Students Can't Stop Talking About It," *The New York Times,* January 15, 2023 [**www.nytimes.com**].
148. Ezra Klein, "TikTok May Be More Dangerous Than It Looks," *The New York Times,* May 8, 2022 [**www.nytimes.com**].
149. Alex W. Palmer, "How TikTok Became A Diplomatic Crisis."
150. Ezra Klein, "TikTok May Be More Dangerous Than It Looks."
151. Ibid.
152. Alex W. Palmer, "How TikTok Became a Diplomatic Crisis."
153. Ezra Klein, "TikTok May Be More Dangerous Than It Looks."
154. Ibid.
155. Alex W. Palmer, "How TikTok Became a Diplomatic Crisis."
156. Ephrat Livni and Eric Lipton, "Regulators Ask Congress to Create New Rules for Cryptocurrencies," *The New York Times,* November 1, 2022 [**www.nytimes.com**].
157. David Yaffe-Bellany, "Inside a Crypto Nemesis' Campaign to Rein in the Industry," *The New York Times,* November 21, 2022 [**www.nytimes.com**].
158. Greg Iacurci, "As BlockFi files for bankruptcy, what to know about crypto investor protections," CNBC, November 28, 2022 [**www.cnbc.com**].
159. Kevin George, "SEC vs. Ripple," *Investopedia,* January 23, 2023 [**www.investopedia.com**].
160. Press Release, "SEC Charges NBA Hall of Famer Paul Pierce for Unlawfully Touting and Making Misleading Statements about Crypto Security," U.S. Securities and Exchange Commission, February 17, 2023 [**www.sec.gov**].
161. "Cryptocurrency Laws and Regulations by State," *Bloomberg Law,* updated May 26, 2022 [**https://pro.bloomberglaw.com**].
162. Jamie Redman, "Paxos Receives Wells Notice from SEC, NYDFS Orders Issuer to Stop Minting BUSD," *Bitcoin.com,* February 13, 2023 [**https://news.bitcoin.com**].
163. Anna Mathews, "U.S. Will Give Web Patents More Scrutiny," *The Wall Street Journal,* March 29, 2000 [**www.wsj.com**].
164. Inayat Chaudhry, "The Patentability of Blockchain Technology and the Future of Innovation," *Landslide,* Vol. 10, No. 4, March/April 2018 [**www.americanbar.org**].
165. Kristopher B. Kastens and Timothy Layden, "Blockchain Patents and Litigation," *Kramer Levin,* December 8, 2021 [**www.kramerlevin.com**].
166. Kristopher B. Kastens and Timothy Layden, "Top Holders of Blockchain Patents," *Kramer Levin,* July 21, 2022 [**www.kramerlevin.com**].
167. "Swipe, Pinch and Zoom to the Courtroom," *The Economist,* September 1, 2012 [**www.economist.com**].
168. Jack Nicas, "Apple and Samsung End Smartphone Patent Wars," *The New York Times,* June 27, 2018 [**www.nytimes.com**].
169. Omar Sohail, "Apple To Start Sourcing iPhone Memory Chips From Samsung as Chinese Supplier Unable to Comply Due to Trade Ban," *wccftech,* November 21, 2022 [**https://wccftech.com**].

170. Michael Davis-Wilson, "The Burden of Online Misdeeds: Who Should Be Responsible?" Association of Corporate Counsel, March 19, 2012 [**www.lexology.com**] and "Stopping SOPA," *The Economist,* January 21, 2012 [**www.economist.com**].
171. River Braun, "What to do if you get a copyright infringement notice," *LegalZoom,* February 7, 2023 [**www.legalzoom.com**].
172. *A & M Records, Inc. v. Napster, Inc.,* 284 F.3d 1091 (9th Cir. 2002) and *A & M Records, Inc. v. Napster, Inc.,* 239 F.3d 1004 (9th Cir. 2001).
173. 125 S. Ct. 2764 (2005).
174. Ibid. at 2782.
175. Sarah McBride and Ethan Smith, "Music Industry to Abandon Mass Suits," *The Wall Street Journal,* December 19, 2008 [**www.wsj.com**].
176. Amy Brittain, "Universities Strike Back in Battle over Illegal Downloads," *The Christian Science Monitor,* June 18, 2007 [**www.csmonitor.com**].
177. Susan Neuberger Weller, "Are You Willing to Pay $22,500 to Download a Song?" Association of Corporate Counsel, August 28, 2012 [**www.lexology.com**]; and Ben Sisario, "Supreme Court Passes on File-Sharing Case, but Still No End Is in Sight," *The New York Times,* May 21, 2012 [**www.nytimes.com**].
178. *Capitol Records v. Thomas-Rasset,* 692 F.3d 899 (8th Cir. 2012).
179. Internal Revenue Service Notice 2014-21 and Internal Revenue Service Revenue Ruling 2019-24.
180. "How the IRS is trying to nail crypto tax dodgers," *CNBC,* July 15, 2021 [**www.cnbc.com**].
181. Ibid.
182. "Looking to 2023, IRS Cryptocurrency Enforcement Is Just Beginning," *Bloomberg Tax,* December 30, 2022 [**www.bloombergtax.com**].
183. Ibid.; "How the IRS is trying to nail crypto tax dodgers," *CNBC*; and Laura Sanders and Britton O'Daly, "IRS Sending Warning Letters to More Than 10,000 Cryptocurrency Holders," *The Wall Street Journal,* July 26, 2019 [**www.wsj.com**].
184. "Looking to 2023, IRS Cryptocurrency Enforcement Is Just Beginning," *Bloomberg Tax.*
185. Internal Revenue Service Announcement 2023-2.
186. Didi Martinez, Brenda Breslauer, and Stephanie Gosk, "A dinner table chat between husband and wife may help solve the coronavirus mask shortage," *NBC News,* April 14, 2020 [**www.nbcnews.com**].
187. David Lee, "Facebook founding president sounds alarm," BBC, November 9, 2017 [**www.bbc.com**].
188. Catherine Price, "Trapped-the secret ways social media is built to be addictive (and what you can do to fight back)," *BBC Science Focus,* October 29, 2018 [**www.sciencefocus.com**].
189. Hilary Andersson, "Social media apps are 'deliberately' addictive to users," BBC, July 4, 2018 [**www.bbc.com**].
190. Jeff Horwitz and Deepa Seetharaman, "Facebook Executives Shut Down Efforts to Make the Site Less Divisive," *The Wall Street Journal,* May 26, 2020 [**www.wsj.com**].
191. "Former Facebook and Google employees fight tech 'addiction'," BBC, February 6, 2018 [**www.bbc.com**].
192. C. Thi Nguyen, "The problem of living inside echo chambers," *The Conversation,* September 11, 2019 [**https://theconversation.com**].
193. See, for example, *Cambridge Dictionary,* accessed June 2020 [**https://dictionary.cambridge.org**].
194. John Snell, "Lawyers Drawn to Unsettled Internet; Lots of Legal Issues, Large and Small, Must Be Sorted Out," *Minneapolis Star Tribune,* November 29, 1999, p. 6D.

Video icon credit: Comstock Images/Alamy Stock Photo

The Constitution of the United States of America

Preamble

We the People of the United States, in Order to form a more perfect Union, establish Justice, insure domestic Tranquility, provide for the common defence, promote the general Welfare, and secure the Blessings of Liberty to ourselves and our Posterity, do ordain and establish this Constitution for the United States of America.

Article I

Section 1. All legislative Powers herein granted shall be vested in a Congress of the United States, which shall consist of a Senate and House of Representatives.

Section 2. (1) The House of Representatives shall be composed of Members chosen every second Year by the People of the several States, and the Electors in each State shall have the Qualifications requisite for Electors of the most numerous Branch of the State Legislature.

(2) No Person shall be a Representative who shall not have attained to the Age of twenty-five Years, and been seven Years a Citizen of the United States, and who shall not, when elected, be an Inhabitant of that State in which he shall be chosen.

(3) Representatives and direct Taxes shall be apportioned among the several States which may be included within this Union, according to their respective Numbers, which shall be determined by adding to the whole Number of free Persons, including those bound to Service for a Term of Years, and excluding Indians not taxed, three fifths of all other Persons.[1] The actual Enumeration shall be made within three Years after the first Meeting of the Congress of the United States, and within every subsequent Term of ten Years, in such Manner as they shall by Law direct. The Number of Representatives shall not exceed one for every thirty Thousand, but each State shall have at Least one Representative; and until such enumeration shall be made, the State of New Hampshire shall be entitled to chuse three, Massachusetts eight, Rhode Island and Providence Plantations one, Connecticut five,

[1]Refer to the Fourteenth Amendment.

New York six, New Jersey four, Pennsylvania eight, Delaware one, Maryland six, Virginia ten, North Carolina five, South Carolina five, and Georgia three.

(4) When vacancies happen in the Representation from any State, the Executive Authority thereof shall issue Writs of Election to fill such Vacancies.

(5) The House of Representatives shall chuse their Speaker and other Officers; and shall have the sole Power of Impeachment.

Section 3. (1) The Senate of the United States shall be composed of two Senators from each State, chosen by the Legislature thereof,[2] for six Years; and each Senator shall have one Vote.

(2) Immediately after they shall be assembled in Consequence of the first Election, they shall be divided as equally as may be into three Classes. The Seats of the Senators of the first Class shall be vacated at the Expiration of the Second Year, of the second Class at the Expiration of the fourth Year, and of the third Class at the Expiration of the sixth Year, so that one third may be chosen every second Year; and if Vacancies happen by Resignation, or otherwise, during the Recess of the Legislature of any State, the Executive thereof may make temporary Appointments until the next Meeting of the Legislature, which shall then fill such Vacancies.[3]

(3) No Person shall be a Senator who shall not have attained to the Age of thirty Years, and been nine Years a Citizen of the United States, and who shall not, when elected, be an Inhabitant of that State for which he shall be chosen.

(4) The Vice President of the United States shall be President of the Senate, but shall have no Vote, unless they be equally divided.

(5) The Senate shall chuse their other Officers, and also a President pro tempore, in the Absence of the Vice President, or when he shall exercise the Office of President of the United States.

(6) The Senate shall have the sole Power to try all Impeachments. When sitting for that Purpose, they shall be on Oath or Affirmation. When the President of the United States is tried, the Chief Justice shall preside: And no Person shall be convicted without the Concurrence of two thirds of the Members present.

(7) Judgment in Cases of Impeachment shall not extend further than to removal from Office, and disqualification to hold and enjoy any Office of honor, Trust, or Profit under the United States: but the Party convicted shall nevertheless be liable and subject to Indictment, Trial, Judgment, and Punishment, according to Law.

Section 4. (1) The Times, Places and Manner of holding Elections for Senators and Representatives, shall be prescribed in each State by the Legislature thereof; but the Congress may at any time by Law make or alter such Regulations, except as to the Places of chusing Senators.

(2) The Congress shall assemble at least once in every year, and such Meeting shall be on the first Monday in December, unless they shall by Law appoint a different Day.[4]

[2]Refer to the Seventeenth Amendment.

[3]Ibid.

[4]Refer to the Twentieth Amendment.

Section 5. (1) Each House shall be the Judge of the Elections, Returns, and Qualifications of its own Members, and a Majority of each shall constitute a Quorum to do Business; but a smaller Number may adjourn from day to day, and may be authorized to compel the Attendance of absent Members, in such Manner, and under such Penalties as each House may provide.

(2) Each House may determine the Rules of its Proceedings, punish its Members for disorderly Behavior, and, with the Concurrence of two thirds, expel a Member.

(3) Each House shall keep a Journal of its Proceedings, and from time to time publish the same, excepting such Parts as may in their Judgment require Secrecy; and the Yeas and Nays of the Members of either House on any question shall, at the Desire of one fifth of those Present, be entered on the Journal.

(4) Neither House, during the Session of Congress, shall, without the Consent of the other, adjourn for more than three days, nor to any other Place than that in which the two Houses shall be sitting.

Section 6. (1) The Senators and Representatives shall receive a Compensation for their Services, to be ascertained by Law, and paid out of the Treasury of the United States. They shall in all Cases, except Treason, Felony and Breach of the Peace, be privileged from Arrest during their Attendance at the Session of their respective Houses, and in going to and returning from the same; and for any Speech or Debate in either House, they shall not be questioned in any other Place.

(2) No Senator or Representative shall, during the Time for which he was elected, be appointed to any civil Office under the Authority of the United States, which shall have been created, or the Emoluments whereof shall have been encreased during such time; and no Person holding any Office under the United States, shall be a Member of either House during his Continuance in Office.

Section 7. (1) All Bills for raising Revenue shall originate in the House of Representatives; but the Senate may propose or concur with Amendments as on other Bills.

(2) Every Bill which shall have passed the House of Representatives and the Senate, shall, before it becomes a Law, be presented to the President of the United States; If he approve he shall sign it, but if not he shall return it, with his Objections to the House in which it shall have originated, who shall enter the Objections at large on their Journal, and proceed to reconsider it. If after such Reconsideration two thirds of that House shall agree to pass the Bill, it shall be sent together with the Objections, to the other House, by which it shall likewise be reconsidered, and if approved by two thirds of that House, it shall become a Law. But in all such Cases the Votes of both Houses shall be determined by yeas and Nays, and the Names of the Persons voting for and against the Bill shall be entered on the Journal of each House respectively. If any Bill shall not be returned by the President within ten Days (Sundays excepted) after it shall have been presented to him, the Same shall be a Law, in like Manner as if he had signed it, unless the Congress by their Adjournment prevent its Return in which Case it shall not be a Law.

(3) Every Order, Resolution, or Vote, to Which the Concurrence of the Senate and House of Representatives may be necessary (except on a question of Adjournment) shall be presented to the President of the United States; and before the same shall take Effect, shall be approved by him, or being disapproved by him, shall be repassed by two thirds of the Senate and House of Representatives, according to the Rules and Limitations prescribed in the Case of a Bill.

Section 8. (1) The Congress shall have Power To lay and collect Taxes, Duties, Imposts and Excises, to pay the Debts and provide for the common Defence and general Welfare of the United States; but all Duties, Imposts and Excises shall be uniform throughout the United States;

(2) To borrow money on the credit of the United States;

(3) To regulate Commerce with foreign Nations, and among the several States, and with the Indian Tribes;

(4) To establish a uniform Rule of Naturalization, and uniform Laws on the subject of Bankruptcies throughout the United States;

(5) To coin Money, regulate the Value thereof, and of foreign Coin, and fix the Standard of Weights and Measures;

(6) To provide for the Punishment of counterfeiting the Securities and current Coin of the United States;

(7) To Establish Post Offices and Post Roads;

(8) To promote the Progress of Science and useful Arts, by securing for limited Times to Authors and Inventors the exclusive Right to their respective Writings and Discoveries;

(9) To constitute Tribunals inferior to the Supreme Court;

(10) To define and punish Piracies and Felonies committed on the high Seas, and Offenses against the Law of Nations;

(11) To declare War, grant Letters of Marque and Reprisal, and make Rules concerning Captures on Land and Water;

(12) To raise and support Armies, but no Appropriation of Money to that Use shall be for a longer Term than two Years;

(13) To provide and maintain a Navy;

(14) To make Rules for the Government and Regulation of the land and naval Forces;

(15) To provide for calling forth the Militia to execute the Laws of the Union, suppress Insurrections and repel Invasions;

(16) To provide for organizing, arming, and disciplining, the Militia, and for governing such Part of them as may be employed in the Service of the United States, reserving to the States respectively, the Appointment of the Officers, and the Authority of training the Militia according to the discipline prescribed by Congress;

(17) To exercise exclusive Legislation in all Cases whatsoever, over such District (not exceeding ten Miles square) as may, by Cession of particular States, and the Acceptance of Congress, become the Seat of the Government of the United States, and to exercise like Authority over all Places purchased by the Consent of the Legislature of the State in which the Same shall be, for the Erection of Forts, Magazines, Arsenals, dock-Yards, and other needful Buildings;–And

(18) To make all Laws which shall be necessary and proper for carrying into Execution the foregoing Powers, and all other Powers vested by this Constitution in the Government of the United States, or in any Department or Officer thereof.

Section 9. (1) The Migration or Importation of Such Persons as any of the States now existing shall think proper to admit, shall not be prohibited by the Congress prior to the Year one thousand eight hundred and eight, but a Tax or duty may be imposed on such Importation, not exceeding ten dollars for each Person.

(2) The privilege of the Writ of Habeas Corpus shall not be suspended, unless when in Cases of Rebellion or Invasion the public Safety may require it.

(3) No Bill of Attainder or ex post facto Law shall be passed.

(4) No Capitation, or other direct, Tax shall be laid, unless in proportion to the Census or Enumeration herein before directed to the taken.[5]

(5) No Tax or Duty shall be laid on Articles exported from any state.

(6) No Preference shall be given by any Regulation of Commerce or Revenue to the Ports of one State over those of another; nor shall Vessels bound to, or from, one State be obliged to enter, clear, or pay Duties in another.

(7) No money shall be drawn from the Treasury, but in Consequence of Appropriations made by Law; and a regular Statement and Account of the Receipts and Expenditures of all public Money shall be published from time to time.

(8) No Title of Nobility shall be granted by the United States; And no person holding any Office of Profit or Trust under them, shall, without the Consent of the Congress, accept of any present, Emolument, Office or Title, of any kind whatever, from any King, Prince, or foreign State.

Section 10. (1) No State shall enter into any Treaty, Alliance, or Confederation; grant Letters of Marque and Reprisal; coin Money; emit Bills of Credit; make any Thing but gold and silver Coin a Tender in Payment of Debts; pass any Bill of Attainder, ex post facto Law, or Law impairing the Obligation of Contracts, or grant any Title of Nobility.

(2) No State shall, without the Consent of the Congress, lay any Imposts or Duties on Imports or Exports, except what may be absolutely necessary for executing its inspection Laws: and the net Produce of all Duties and Imposts, laid by any State on Imports or Exports, shall be for the Use of the Treasury of the United States; and all such Laws shall be subject to the Revision and Controul of the Congress.

(3) No State shall, without the Consent of Congress, lay any Duty of Tonnage, keep Troops, or Ships of War in time of Peace, enter into any Agreement or Compact with another State, or with a foreign Power, or engage in War, unless actually invaded, or in such imminent Danger as will not admit of delay.

Article II

Section 1. (1) The executive Power shall be vested in a President of the United States of America. He shall hold his Office during the Term of four Years, and, together with the Vice President, chosen for the same Term, be elected as follows:

(2) Each State shall appoint, in such Manner as the Legislature thereof may direct, a Number of Electors, equal to the whole Number of Senators and Representatives to which the State may be entitled in the Congress; but no Senator or Representative, or Person holding an Office of Trust or Profit under the United States, shall be appointed an Elector.

(3) The Electors shall meet in their respective States, and vote by Ballot for two Persons, of whom one at least shall not be an Inhabitant of the same State with themselves. And they shall make a list of all the Persons voted for, and of the Number of Votes for each; which List they shall sign and certify, and transmit sealed to the Seat of the Government of the United States, directed to the President of the Senate. The President of the Senate shall, in

[5]Refer to the Sixteenth Amendment.

the Presence of the Senate and House of Representatives, open all the Certificates, and the Votes shall then be counted. The Person having the greatest Number of Votes shall be the President, if such Number be a Majority of the whole Number of Electors appointed; and if there be more than one who have such Majority, and have an equal Number of Votes, then the House of Representatives shall immediately chuse by Ballot one of them for President; and if no Person have a Majority, then from the five highest on the List the said House shall in like Manner chuse the President. But in chusing the President, the Votes shall be taken by States, the Representation from each State have one Vote; A quorum for this Purpose shall consist of a Member or Members from two thirds of the States, and a Majority of all the States shall be necessary to a Choice. In every Case, after the Choice of the President, the Person having the greater Number of Votes of the Electors shall be the Vice President. But if there should remain two or more who have equal Votes, the Senate shall chuse from them by Ballot the Vice President.[6]

(4) The Congress may determine the Time of chusing the Electors, and the Day on which they shall give their Votes; which Day shall be the same throughout the United States.

(5) No person except a natural born Citizen, or a Citizen of the United States, at the time of the Adoption of this Constitution, shall be eligible to the Office of President; neither shall any Person be eligible to that Office who shall not have attained to the Age of thirty-five Years, and been fourteen Years a Resident within the United States.

(6) In case of the removal of the President from Office, or of his Death, Resignation or Inability to discharge the Powers and Duties of the said Office, the Same shall devolve on the Vice President, and the Congress may by Law provide for the Case of Removal, Death, Resignation or Inability, both of the President and Vice President, declaring what Officer shall then act as President, and such Officer shall act accordingly, until the Disability be removed, or a President shall be elected.[7]

(7) The President shall, at stated Times, receive for his Services, a Compensation, which shall neither be encreased nor diminished during the Period for which he shall have been elected, and he shall not receive within that Period any other Emolument from the United States, or any of them.

(8) Before he enter on the Execution of his Office, he shall take the following Oath or Affirmation: "I do solemnly swear (or affirm) that I will faithfully execute the Office of President of the United States, and will to the best of my Ability, preserve, protect, and defend the Constitution of the United States."

Section 2. (1) The President shall be Commander in Chief of the Army and Navy of the United States, and of the militia of the several States, when called into the actual Service of the United States; he may require the Opinion, in writing, of the principal Officer in each of the executive Departments, upon any Subject relating to the Duties of their respective Offices, and he shall have Power to grant Reprieves and Pardons for Offenses against the United States, except in Cases of Impeachment.

(2) He shall have Power, by and with the Advice and Consent of the Senate, to make Treaties, provided two thirds of the Senators present concur; and he shall nominate, and by and

[6]Refer to the Twelfth Amendment.

[7]Refer to the Twenty-Fifth Amendment.

with the Advice and Consent of the Senate, shall appoint Ambassadors, other public Ministers and Consuls, Judges of the supreme Court, and all other Officers of the United States, whose Appointments are not herein otherwise provided for, and which shall be established by Law; but the Congress may by Law vest the Appointment of such inferior Officers, as they think proper, in the President alone, in the Courts of Law, or in the Heads of Departments.

(3) The President shall have Power to fill up all Vacancies that may happen during the Recess of the Senate, by granting Commissions which shall expire at the End of their next Session.

Section 3. He shall from time to time give to the Congress Information of the State of the Union, and recommend to their Consideration such Measures as he shall judge necessary and expedient; he may, on extraordinary Occasions, convene both Houses, or either of them, and in Case of Disagreement between them, with Respect to the Time of Adjournment, he may adjourn them to such Time as he shall think proper; he shall receive Ambassadors and other public Ministers; he shall take Care that the Laws be faithfully executed, and shall Commission all the Officers of the United States.

Section 4. The President, Vice President and all civil Officers of the United States, shall be removed from Office on Impeachment for, and Conviction of, Treason, Bribery, or other high Crimes and Misdemeanors.

Article III

Section 1. The judicial Power of the United States, shall be vested in one supreme Court, and in such inferior Courts as the Congress may from time to time ordain and establish. The Judges, both of the supreme and inferior Courts, shall hold their Offices during good Behaviour, and shall, at stated Times, receive for their Services a Compensation, which shall not be diminished during their Continuance in Office.

Section 2. (1) The judicial Power shall extend to all Cases, in Law and Equity, arising under this Constitution, the Laws of the United States, and Treaties made, or which shall be made, under their Authority;–to all Cases affecting Ambassadors, other public Ministers and Consuls;–to all Cases of admiralty and maritime Jurisdiction;–to Controversies to which the United States shall be a Party;–to Controversies between two or more States;–between a State and Citizens of another State,[8]–between Citizens of different states;–between Citizens of the same State claiming Lands under the Grants of different States, and between a State, or the Citizens thereof, and foreign States, Citizens or Subjects.

(2) In all Cases affecting Ambassadors, other public Ministers and Consuls, and those in which a State shall be a Party, the supreme Court shall have original Jurisdiction. In all the other Cases before mentioned, the supreme Court shall have appellate Jurisdiction, both as to Law and Fact, with such Exceptions, and under such Regulations as the Congress shall make.

(3) The trial of all Crimes, except in Cases of Impeachment, shall be by Jury; and such Trial shall be held in the State where the said Crimes shall have been committed; but when not committed within any State, the Trial shall be at such Place or Places as the Congress may by Law have directed.

[8]Refer to the Eleventh Amendment.

Section 3. (1) Treason against the United States, shall consist only in levying War against them, or, in adhering to their enemies, giving them Aid and Comfort. No Person shall be convicted of Treason unless on the Testimony of two Witnesses to the same overt Act, or on Confession in open Court.

(2) The Congress shall have Power to declare the Punishment of Treason, but no Attainder of Treason shall work Corruption of Blood, or Forfeiture except during the Life of the Person attainted.

Article IV

Section 1. Full Faith and Credit shall be given in each State to the public Acts, Records, and judicial Proceedings of every other State. And the Congress may by general Laws prescribe the Manner in which such Acts, Records and Proceedings shall be proved, and the Effect thereof.

Section 2. (1) The Citizens of each State shall be entitled to all Privileges and Immunities of Citizens in the several States.

(2) A Person charged in any State with Treason, Felony, or other Crime, who shall flee from Justice, and be found in another State, shall on demand of the executive Authority of the State from which he fled, be delivered up, to be removed to the State having Jurisdiction of the Crime.

(3) No Person held to Service or Labour in one State, under the Laws thereof, escaping into another, shall, in Consequence of any Law or Regulation therein, be discharged from such Service or Labour, but shall be delivered up on Claim of the Party to whom such Service or Labour may be due.[9]

Section 3. (1) New States may be admitted by the Congress into this Union; but no new State shall be formed or erected within the Jurisdiction of any other State; nor any State be formed by the Junction of two or more States, or Parts of States without the Consent of the Legislatures of the States concerned as well as of the Congress.

(2) The Congress shall have Power to dispose of and make all needful Rules and Regulations respecting the Territory or other Property belonging to the United States; and nothing in this Constitution shall be so construed as to Prejudice any Claims of the United States, or of any particular State.

Section 4. The United States shall guarantee to every State in this Union a Republican Form of Government, and shall protect each of them against Invasion; and on Application of the Legislature, or of the Executive (when the Legislature cannot be convened) against domestic Violence.

Article V

The Congress, whenever two thirds of both Houses shall deem it necessary, shall propose Amendments to this Constitution, or, on the Application of the Legislatures of two thirds of the several States, shall call a Convention for proposing Amendments, which, in either Case, shall be valid to all Intents and Purposes, as part of this Constitution, when ratified by the

[9]Refer to the Thirteenth Amendment.

Legislatures of three fourths of the several States, or by Conventions in three fourths thereof, as the one or the other Mode of Ratification may be proposed by the Congress; Provided that no Amendment which may be made prior to the Year One thousand eight hundred and eight shall in any Manner affect the first and fourth Clauses in the Ninth Section of the first Article; and that no State, without its Consent, shall be deprived of its equal Suffrage in the Senate.

Article VI

(1) All Debts contracted and Engagements entered into, before the Adoption of this Constitution shall be as valid against the United States under this Constitution, as under the Confederation.

(2) This Constitution, and the Laws of the United States which shall be made in Pursuance thereof; and all Treaties made, or which shall be made, under the Authority of the United States, shall be the supreme Law of the Land; and the Judges in every State shall be bound thereby, any Thing in the Constitution or Laws of any State to the Contrary notwithstanding.

(3) The Senators and Representatives before mentioned, and the Members of the several State Legislatures, and all executive and judicial Officers, both of the United States and of the several States, shall be bound by Oath or Affirmation, to support this Constitution, but no religious Test shall ever be required as a Qualification to any Office or public Trust under the United States.

Article VII

The Ratification of the Conventions of nine States shall be sufficient for the Establishment of this Constitution between the States so ratifying the Same.

[Amendments 1 to 10, the Bill of Rights, were ratified in 1791.]

Amendment I

Congress shall make no law respecting an establishment of religion, or prohibiting the free exercise thereof; or abridging the freedom of speech, or of the press; or the right of the people peaceably to assemble, and to petition the Government for a redress of grievances.

Amendment II

A well regulated Militia, being necessary to the security of a free State, the right of the people to keep and bear Arms, shall not be infringed.

Amendment III

No Soldier shall, in time of peace be quartered in any house, without the consent of the Owner, nor in time of war, but in a manner to be prescribed by law.

Amendment IV

The right of the people to be secure in their persons, houses, papers, and effects, against unreasonable searches and seizures, shall not be violated, and no Warrants shall issue, but upon probable cause, supported by Oath or affirmation, and particularly describing the place to be searched, and the persons or things to be seized.

Amendment V

No person shall be held to answer for a capital, or otherwise infamous crime, unless on a presentment or indictment of a Grand Jury, except in cases arising in the land or naval forces, or in the Militia, when in actual service in time of War or public danger; nor shall any person be subject for the same offence to be twice put in jeopardy of life or limb; nor shall be compelled in any criminal case to be a witness against himself, nor be deprived of life, liberty, or property, without due process of law; nor shall private property be taken for public use, without just compensation.

Amendment VI

In all criminal prosecutions, the accused shall enjoy the right to a speedy and public trial, by an impartial jury of the State and district wherein the crime shall have been committed, which district shall have been previously ascertained by law, and to be informed of the nature and cause of the accusation; to be confronted with the witness against him; to have compulsory process for obtaining witnesses in his favor, and to have the Assistance of Counsel for his defence.

Amendment VII

In Suits at common law, where the value in controversy shall exceed twenty dollars, the right of trial by jury shall be preserved, and no fact tried by jury, shall be otherwise reexamined in any Court of the United States, than according to the rules of the common law.

Amendment VIII

Excessive bail shall not be required, nor excessive fines imposed, nor cruel and unusual punishments inflicted.

Amendment IX

The enumeration in the Constitution, of certain rights, shall not be construed to deny or disparage others retained by the people.

Amendment X

The powers not delegated to the United States by the Constitution, nor prohibited by it to the States, are reserved to the States respectively, or to the people.

Amendment XI [1798]

The Judicial power of the United States shall not be construed to extend to any suit in law or equity, commenced or prosecuted against one of the United States by Citizens of another State, or by Citizens or Subjects of any Foreign State.

Amendment XII [1804]

The Electors shall meet in their respective states and vote by ballot for President and Vice-President, one of whom, at least, shall not be an inhabitant of the same state with themselves; they shall name in their ballots the person voted for as President, and in distinct ballots the person voted for as Vice-President, and they shall make distinct lists of all persons voted for as President, and of all persons voted for as Vice-President, and of the number of votes for each, which lists they shall sign and certify, and transmit sealed to the seat of the government of the United States, directed to the President of the Senate;–The President of the Senate shall, in the presence of the Senate and House of Representatives, open all the certificates and the votes shall then be counted;–The person having the greatest number of votes for President, shall be the President, if such number be a majority of the whole number of Electors appointed; and if no person have such majority, then from the persons having the highest numbers not exceeding three on the list of those voted for as President, the House of Representatives shall choose immediately, by ballot, the President. But in choosing the President, the votes shall be taken by states, the representation from each state having one vote; a quorum for this purpose shall consist of a member or members from two-thirds of the states, and a majority of all the states shall be necessary to a choice. And if the House of Representatives shall not choose a President whenever the right of choice shall devolve upon them before the fourth day of March next following, then the Vice-President shall act as President, as in the case of the death or other constitutional disability of the President.[10]–The person having the greatest number of votes as Vice-President, shall be the Vice-President, if such number be a majority of the whole number of Electors appointed, and if no person have a majority, then from the two highest numbers on the list, the Senate shall choose the Vice-President; a quorum for the purpose shall consist of two-thirds of the whole number of Senators, and a majority of the whole number shall be necessary to a choice. But no person constitutionally ineligible to the office of President shall be eligible to that of Vice-President of the United States.

[10]Refer to the Twentieth Amendment.

Amendment XIII [1865]

Section 1. Neither slavery nor involuntary servitude, except as a punishment for crime whereof the party shall have been duly convicted, shall exist within the United States, or any place subject to their jurisdiction.

Section 2. Congress shall have power to enforce this article by appropriate legislation.

Amendment XIV [1868]

Section 1. All persons born or naturalized in the United States, and subject to the jurisdiction thereof, are citizens of the United States and of the State wherein they reside. No State shall make or enforce any law which shall abridge the privileges or immunities of citizens of the United States; nor shall any State deprive any person of life, liberty, or property, without due process of law; nor deny to any person within its jurisdiction the equal protection of the laws.

Section 2. Representatives shall be apportioned among the several States according to their respective numbers, counting the whole number of persons in each State, excluding Indians not taxed. But when the right to vote at any election for the choice of electors for President and Vice President of the United States, Representatives in Congress, the Executive and Judicial officers of a State, or the members of the Legislature thereof, is denied to any of the male inhabitants of such State, being twenty-one years of age,[11] and citizens of the United States, or in any way abridged, except for participation in rebellion, or other crime, the basis of representation therein shall be reduced in the proportion which the number of such male citizens shall bear to the whole number of male citizens twenty-one years of age in such State.

Section 3. No person shall be a Senator or Representative in Congress, or elector of President and Vice President, or hold any office, civil or military, under the United States, or under any State, who having previously taken an oath, as a member of Congress, or as an officer of the United States, or as a member of any State legislature, or as an executive or judicial officer of any State, to support the Constitution of the United States, shall have engaged in insurrection or rebellion against the same, or given aid or comfort to the enemies thereof. But Congress may by a vote of two thirds of each House, remove such disability.

Section 4. The validity of the public debt of the United States, authorized by law, including debts incurred for payment of pensions and bounties for services in suppressing insurrection or rebellion, shall not be questioned. But neither the United States nor any State shall assume or pay any debt or obligation incurred in aid of insurrection or rebellion against the United States, or any claim for the loss or emancipation of any slave; but all such debts, obligations and claims shall be held illegal and void.

Section 5. The Congress shall have power to enforce, by appropriate legislation, the provisions of this article.

[11] Refer to the Twenty-Sixth Amendment.

Amendment XV [1870]

Section 1. The right of citizens of the United States to vote shall not be denied or abridged by the United States or by any State on account of race, color, or previous condition of servitude.

Section 2. The Congress shall have power to enforce this article by appropriate legislation.

Amendment XVI [1913]

The Congress shall have power to lay and collect taxes on incomes, from whatever source derived, without apportionment among the several States, and without regard to any census or enumeration.

Amendment XVII [1913]

(1) The Senate of the United States shall be composed of two Senators from each State, elected by the people thereof, for six years; and each Senator shall have one vote. The electors in each State shall have the qualifications requisite for electors of the most numerous branch of the State legislatures.

(2) When vacancies happen in the representation of any State in the Senate, the executive authority of such State shall issue writs of election to fill such vacancies:*Provided,* That the legislature of any State may empower the executive thereof to make temporary appointments until the people fill the vacancies by election as the legislature may direct.

(3) This amendment shall not be so construed as to affect the election or term of any Senator chosen before it becomes valid as part of the Constitution.

Amendment XVIII [1919]

Section 1. After one year from the ratification of this article the manufacture, sale, or transportation of intoxicating liquors within, the importation thereof into, or the exportation thereof from the United States and all territory subject to the jurisdiction thereof for beverage purposes is hereby prohibited.

Section 2. The Congress and the several States shall have concurrent power to enforce this article by appropriate legislation.

Section 3. This article shall be inoperative unless it shall have been ratified as an amendment to the Constitution by the legislatures of the several States, as provided in the Constitution, within seven years from the date of the submission hereof to the States by the Congress.[12]

[12]Refer to the Twenty-First Amendment.

Amendment XIX [1920]

(1) The right of citizens of the United States to vote shall not be denied or abridged by the United States or by any State on account of sex.

(2) Congress shall have power to enforce this article by appropriate legislation.

Amendment XX [1933]

Section 1. The terms of the President and Vice President shall end at noon on the 20th day of January, and the terms of Senators and Representatives at noon on the 3rd day of January, of the years in which such terms would have ended if this article had not been ratified; and the terms of their successors shall then begin.

Section 2. The Congress shall assemble at least once in every year, and such meeting shall begin at noon on the 3rd day of January, unless they shall by law appoint a different day.

Section 3. If, at the time fixed for the beginning of the term of the President, the President elect shall have died, the Vice President elect shall become President. If the President shall not have been chosen before the time fixed for the beginning of his term or if the President elect shall have failed to qualify, then the Vice President elect shall act as President until a President shall have qualified; and the Congress may by law provide for the case wherein neither a President elect nor a Vice President elect shall have qualified, declaring who shall then act as President, or the manner in which one is to act shall be selected, and such person shall act accordingly until a President or Vice President shall have qualified.

Section 4. The Congress may by law provide for the case of the death of any of the persons from whom the House of Representatives may choose a President whenever the right of choice shall have devolved upon them, and for the case of the death of any of the persons from whom the Senate may choose a Vice President whenever the right of choice shall have devolved upon them.

Section 5. Sections 1 and 2 shall take effect on the 15th day of October following the ratification of this article.

Section 6. This article shall be inoperative unless it shall have been ratified as an amendment to the Constitution by the legislatures of three-fourths of the several States within seven years from the date of its submission.

Amendment XXI [1933]

Section 1. The eighteenth article of amendment to the Constitution of the United States is hereby repealed.

Section 2. The transportation or importation into any State, Territory, or possession of the United States for delivery or use therein of intoxicating liquors, in violation of the laws thereof, is hereby prohibited.

Section 3. This article shall be inoperative unless it shall have been ratified as an amendment to the Constitution by conventions in the several States, as provided in the Constitution, within seven years from the date of the submission hereof to the States by the Congress.

Amendment XXII [1951]

Section 1. No person shall be elected to the office of the President more than twice, and no person who has held the office of President, or acted as President, for more than two years of a term to which some other person was elected President shall be elected to the office of President more than once. But this Article shall not apply to any person holding the office of President when this Article was proposed by the Congress, and shall not prevent any person who may be holding the office of President, or acting as President, during the term within which this Article becomes operative from holding the office of President or acting as president during the remainder of such term.

Section 2. This article shall be inoperative unless it shall have been ratified as an amendment to the Constitution by the legislatures of three-fourths of the several States within seven years from the date of its submission to the States by the Congress.

Amendment XXIII [1961]

Section 1. The District constituting the seat of Government of the United States shall appoint in such manner as the Congress may direct:

> A number of electors of President and Vice President equal to the whole number of Senators and Representatives in Congress to which the District would be entitled if it were a State, but in no event more than the least populous state; they shall be in addition to those appointed by the states, but they shall be considered, for the purposes of the election of President and Vice President, to be electors appointed by a state; and they shall meet in the District and perform such duties as provided by the twelfth article of amendment.

Section 2. The Congress shall have power to enforce this article by appropriate legislation.

Amendment XXIV [1964]

Section 1. The right of citizens of the United States to vote in any primary or other election for President or Vice President, for electors for President or Vice President, or for Senator or Representative in Congress, shall not be denied or abridged by the United States or any State by reason of failure to pay any poll tax or other tax.

Section 2. The Congress shall have power to enforce this article by appropriate legislation.

Amendment XXV [1967]

Section 1. In case of the removal of the President from office or of his death or resignation, the Vice President shall become President.

Section 2. Whenever there is a vacancy in the office of the Vice President, the President shall nominate a Vice President who shall take office upon confirmation by a majority vote of both Houses of Congress.

Section 3. Whenever the President transmits to the President pro tempore of the Senate and the Speaker of the House of Representatives his written declaration that he is unable to discharge the powers and duties of his office, and until he transmits to them a written declaration to the contrary, such powers and duties shall be discharged by the Vice President as Acting President.

Section 4. Whenever the Vice President and a majority of either the principal officers of the executive departments or of such other body as Congress may by law provide, transmit to the President pro tempore of the Senate and the Speaker of the House of Representatives their written declaration that the President is unable to discharge the powers and duties of his office, the Vice President shall immediately assume the powers and duties of the office as Acting President.

Thereafter, when the President transmits to the President pro tempore of the Senate and the Speaker of the House of Representatives his written declaration that no inability exists, he shall resume the powers and duties of his office unless the Vice President and a majority of either the principal officers of the executive departments or of such other body as Congress may by law provide, transmit within four days to the President pro tempore of the Senate and the Speaker of the House of Representatives their written declaration that the President is unable to discharge the powers and duties of his office. Thereupon Congress shall decide the issue, assembling within forty-eight hours for that purpose if not in session. If the Congress, within twenty-one days after receipt of the latter written declaration, or, if Congress is not in session, within twenty-one days after Congress is required to assemble, determines by two-thirds vote of both Houses that the President is unable to discharge the powers and duties of his office, the Vice President shall continue to discharge the same as Acting President; otherwise, the President shall resume the powers and duties of his office.

Amendment XXVI [1971]

Section 1. The right of citizens of the United States, who are eighteen years of age or older, to vote shall not be denied or abridged by the United States or by any State on account of age.

Section 2. The Congress shall have power to enforce this article by appropriate legislation.

Amendment XXVII [1992]

No law, varying the compensation for the services of the Senators and Representatives, shall take effect, until an election of Representatives shall have intervened.

The Uniform Commercial Code

The Uniform Commercial Code, or UCC, was developed by the American Law Institute (ALI) and the National Conference of Commissioners on Uniform State Laws (NCCUSL) as a body of rules intended to make the application of law to commercial transactions consistent across fifty states. The UCC has been adopted in whole by all but one state legislature, Louisiana, which adopts only certain sections. Such widespread use of the UCC, even with the minor deviations some jurisdictions make from the official code, makes possible more efficient and more confident transactions across state lines.

We reference UCC Articles 2 and 2(A) when discussing sales and leases of goods, respectively. These Articles, along with the rest of the UCC, can be accessed here: **https://www.law.cornell.edu/ucc**.

GLOSSARY

A

absolute privilege In libel and slander law, situations where a defendant is entirely excused from liability for defamatory statements because of the circumstances under which the statements were made.

acceptance The actual or implied receipt and retention of that which is tendered or offered.

accord and satisfaction A legally binding agreement to settle a disputed claim for a definite amount.

accounting In the partnership context, "an accounting" is the legal determination of a partnership interest's value.

accredited investor Financial institutions, charities, directors and officers of the issuer, individuals with demonstrated expertise in securities (such as those holding Series 7 or Series 65 licenses), and individuals with annual net income of at least $200,000 and/or net worth of at least $1,000,000 (excluding their personal residence). Such persons are presumed to understand, and be able to withstand the risk associated with, securities investments.

actus reus Wrongful act or omission.

adjustment of debts Individuals with limited debts are protected from creditors while paying their debts in installments (Chapter 13 bankruptcy).

affirmative action A government or private-sector program, springing from the civil rights movement, designed to actively promote the employment or educational opportunities of protected classes rather than merely forbidding discrimination.

affirmative defense A portion of a defendant's answer to a complaint in which defendant presents contentions that, if proved true, will relieve the defendant of liability even if the assertions in the complaint are correct.

agent An individual authorized to act for another within a given scope. For example, employees are agents of their employers.

agreement A meeting of the minds based on an offer by one party and acceptance by another.

answer The defendant's first pleading in a lawsuit, in which the defendant responds to the allegations raised in the plaintiff's complaint.

appellant The party filing an appeal.

appellee The party against whom an appeal is filed.

arbitration An extrajudicial process in which a dispute is submitted to a mutually agreeable third party for a decision.

arraignment A criminal law proceeding in which a defendant is brought before a judge to be informed of the charges and to file a plea.

articles of dissolution The document filed with the state to dissolve a corporation.

articles of incorporation The document filed with a state to create a corporation.

articles of organization The document filed with a state to create a limited liability company.

assault A show of force that would cause reasonable persons to believe that they are about to receive an intentional, unwanted, harmful physical touching.

assignee The person to whom an assignment is made.

assignment A transfer of property, or some right or interest therein, from one person to another.

assignor The maker of an assignment.

assumption of risk An affirmative defense in a negligence case in which the defendant seeks to bar recovery by the plaintiff by showing that the plaintiff knowingly exposed himself or herself to the danger that resulted in injury.

assumption of the risk A defense that precludes recovery by a plaintiff in a negligence action if the plaintiff willingly and knowingly undertook the unreasonable risk presented by the activity and is injured as a result.

audit committee A committee of the board of directors charged with ensuring the accuracy of the company's financial statements.

audited financial statements Income statement, balance sheet, statement of cash flows, and other items prepared by management and audited (pursuant to generally accepted auditing standards) by an independent certified public accountant to ensure the disclosures are made in accordance with generally accepted accounting principles.

B

balance sheet Financial statement showing a business's assets, liabilities, and equity at a point in time.

battery Any intentional, unwanted, harmful physical touching.

beneficiary In the context of fiduciary duties, the person on whose behalf the fiduciary is acting.

beyond a reasonable doubt The level of proof required for conviction in a criminal case.

bilateral contract A contract formed by an offer requiring a reciprocal promise.

blue laws Laws forbidding certain kinds of business on Sundays.

blue sky laws State laws regulating the purchase and sale of securities in a manner similar to federal securities regulation. Unlike federal securities law, however, some states engage in a substantive review intended to evaluate the economic merits of the investment.

board of directors The body elected by the shareholders to govern the corporation on their behalf.

bona fide occupational qualification (BFOQ) A defense in a discrimination claim where the employer argues that a particular religion, sex, or national origin is a necessary qualification for a particular job.

bonds A long-term debt security issued to raise capital for a venture.

breach of contract Failure, without legal excuse, to perform any promise that forms the whole or part of a contract.

bribe In the context of the Foreign Corrupt Practices Act of 1977, anything of value given or taken with the corrupt intent to influence an official in the performance of her or his duties.

broker A person who acts as a sales agent in the purchase or sale of a security.

business judgment rule A rule protecting business managers from liability for making bad decisions when they have acted in accordance with the fiduciary duties of loyalty and due care.

buy-sell agreement A contract under which a shareholder is required to sell (or offer to sell) its stock to the corporation or another shareholder before selling it to a third party.

bylaws The document that governs the management and operation of an organization.

C

C corporation All corporations that have not elected to be taxed as an S corporation. All corporations are C corporations by default.

capacity The ability to incur legal obligations and acquire legal rights.

capital In the finance context, the resources required by a venture to acquire its assets and operate. It comprises debt capital and equity capital.

capital structure The relative use of debt and equity capital in financing a venture.

cease and desist order A directive from an agency ordering a party to refrain from engaging in specified conduct.

centralized management A pyramidal hierarchy of executive authority similar to that used in military organizations.

certificate of limited partnership The document filed with a state to create a limited partnership.

certified public accountant An accounting professional licensed by a state to perform auditing and high-level tax services.

Chapter 7 bankruptcy A proceeding before the U.S. Bankruptcy Court in which the debtor asks the court to discharge (eliminate liability for) all debts (except those which, by law, cannot be discharged–such as loans obtained by fraud and student loans) remaining after all of the debtor's assets (other than exempt assets–such as a limited amount of equity in an automobile and certain items of clothing and jewelry of modest value) have been used to settle as many of the debts as possible.

civil law The branch of law dealing with private rights. Contrast with **criminal law.**

closely held corporation A corporation with relatively few shareholders, the stock of which is not traded on a public market. Also referred to as a *close corporation.*

common law Judge-made law. To be distinguished from statutory law as created by legislative bodies.

common stock The residual ownership interest in a corporation. It carries the rights to participate in control, earnings, and assets upon liquidation.

compensatory damages Damages that will compensate a party for actual losses due to an injury suffered.

complaint The first pleading filed by the plaintiff in a civil lawsuit.

consideration A required element in an enforceable contract. The thing of value passing between the parties that results in a benefit to the one making the promise or a detriment to the one receiving the promise.

consumer-expectations test In the context of product liability, the principle that a manufacturer has a duty to design its products so that they are safe not only for their intended use but also for any reasonably foreseeable use.

contributory negligence A defense that precludes recovery by a plaintiff in a negligence action if the plaintiff's conduct, even to a miniscule degree, contributed to the harm suffered.

conversion Wrongfully exercising control over the personal property of another.

corporate governance The system of rules and processes by which the board of directors governs a corporation.

corporation A form of business created under state law that is owned by shareholders who have no inherent right to manage the business. Corporations are governed by a board of directors elected by the shareholders and managed by a cadre of executives appointed by the board. A corporation is a legal entity separate from its owners.

counterclaim A cause of action filed by the defendant in a lawsuit against the plaintiff in the same suit.

counteroffer Response by the offeree that, in its legal effect, constitutes a rejection of the original offer and proposes a new offer to the offeror.

crime A public wrong; an act punishable by the state.

criminal law Wrongs against society that the state has seen fit to label as crimes and that may result in penalties against the perpetrator(s). Contrast with **civil law.**

crown jewel defense A hostile takeover defense in which the target corporation prearranges to sell critical assets to a friendly third party, which will make them available should management successfully resist the takeover.

D

data mining The process of compiling profiles of individuals by organizing millions of discrete pieces of information gleaned from proprietary databases and from tracking their connected devices as they browse the Internet.

day trading Purchasing and selling securities in rapid succession to exploit small, highly time-sensitive changes in market price.

dealer In the securities context, a person who purchases securities hoping to profit from their resale.

debt capital Resources obtained by the entity from lenders to acquire assets and conduct operations.

debt covenant Promises made by a borrower in a lending agreement for the protection of the creditors.

deceit A tort involving intentional misrepresentation to deceive or trick another.

defamation False statement, intended to be taken as fact, negligently or maliciously made to a third a party, which impugns the reputation of and results in damage to the subject of the statement.

default judgment A judgment entered by the court in favor of the plaintiff because the defendant failed to respond to the plaintiff's complaint.

deposition A discovery procedure wherein a witness's sworn testimony is taken out of court, prior to trial, for subsequent use at trial.

directed verdict A party to a lawsuit makes a motion asking the judge to instruct the jury to reach a particular decision because reasonable minds could not differ about the correct outcome of the case.

director A person elected by the shareholders to govern, along with the other members of the board, the corporation. Individual directors have no authority; only when they act as a board do directors have the power to govern.

discovery Legal procedures by which one party to a litigation may obtain information from the other party. Depositions and interrogatories are examples of discovery procedures.

disgorgement The forfeiture of ill-gotten gains.

dissociation The cessation of a person's status as a partner without causing the partnership's dissolution.

dissolution The termination of an entity's existence.

dividend A distribution by a corporation to a shareholder, typically out of earnings.

double jeopardy The U.S. Constitution provides that the same individual may not be tried twice in the same tribunal for the same criminal offense.

double taxation The fact that a corporation is first taxed on its income, after which the shareholders are taxed again on that income (less the taxes paid by the corporation) when it is distributed to them as dividends.

due diligence A defense in a securities action involving a materially misleading statement or omission in an SEC filings, such as a registration statement. The defendant must demonstrate that a reasonable investigation was undertaken to provide a plausible basis for believing the accuracy of the statements in the filing. Proving due diligence depends on whether the defendant is an expert; experts are held to a significantly higher standard.

duress Overpowering of the will of a person by force or fear.

duty of due care The standard of conduct expected of a reasonable, prudent person in the conduct of their affairs under the given circumstances.

duty of loyalty The standard of conduct that requires a person to act in the best interests of another.

E

earnings per share In essence, the net income of a corporation divided by the number of shares of common stock outstanding (in actuality, the calculation is much more complex than the preceding suggests).

ECG ESG refers to the environmental, social and governance factors that impact a business's performance. While a consensus definition has yet to emerge, the following have been identified as coming within its province: environmental (climate change, water use, waste management, natural resource scarcity), social (diversity of and relationship with workforce, supply chain management, innovation, product and workforce safety, consumer engagement, relationships with communities, human rights), and governance (code and values; transparency and reporting; cyber risk and security; executive compensation; political contributions; board independence, composition and oversight effectiveness).

effective tax rate Although the computation is actually quite complex, the effective tax rate is basically determined by dividing a company's income tax expense by its net income before income tax.

equity Fairness; a system of courts that developed in England. A chancellor presided to mete out fairness in cases that were not traditionally assigned to the law courts headed by the king.

equity capital Resources obtained by an entity from owners to acquire assets and conduct operations.

exculpatory clause Portion of a contract that seeks to relieve one of the parties to the contract from any liability for breach of duty under that contract.

executed In contract law, full performance of the terms of the bargain.

executed contract Contract for which performance is complete.

executory contract Contract that is not yet fully performed or completed.

exempt security A security that is not required to satisfy the full registration requirements under the 1933 Securities Act because of the nature of the issuer; for example, a government or financial institution.

exempt transaction A form of security issuance that is not required to satisfy the full registration requirements under the 1933 Securities Act; for example, a private placement restricted to accredited investors.

express authorization In contract law, the offeror specifies a means of communication by which the offeree can accept.

F

false imprisonment Tort of intentionally restricting the freedom of movement of another.

false light Falsely and publicly attributing certain characteristics, conduct, or beliefs to another such that a reasonable person would be highly offended.

felony A crime of a serious nature ordinarily involving punishment by death or imprisonment in a penitentiary.

fiduciary One who holds a relationship of trust with another (beneficiary) and has an obligation to act in the other's best interests. For example, the executor is the fiduciary of the estate's beneficiaries.

fiduciary duty The responsibility of a person (fiduciary) in a position of trust to act in the best interests of another person (beneficiary).

firm offer Under the Uniform Commercial Code (UCC), a signed, written offer by a merchant containing assurances that it will be held open, and which is not revocable for the time stated in the offer, or for a reasonable time if no such time is stated.

Force Majeure French term describing an event resulting from natural occurrences, as opposed to human conduct or behavior.

foreign corporation Any corporation formed in a jurisdiction other than that in which it is conducting business or otherwise taking action.

Form 10-K The principal annual required filing with the SEC by entities whose securities are publicly traded. Contents include audited financial statements and management commentary on past performance and future prospects.

Form 10-Q The required quarterly filing with the SEC by entities whose securities are publicly traded. Unaudited interim financial statements are presented along with limited management commentary.

Form 8-K The required filing with the SEC anytime an entity whose securities are publicly traded has a major event, such as the resignation of a director, a change in certified public accountant, or the breach of a bond covenant.

franchise An arrangement in which the franchisor permits the franchisee to produce, distribute, and/or sell the franchisor's products or services using the franchisor's name, trademark, and other intangibles, including the rights to participate in the franchisor's supply chain and marketing programs, and to obtain consultation in franchise operation.

franchisee The holder of a franchise.

franchisor The party granting a franchise.

fraud An intentional misrepresentation of a material fact with intent to deceive where the misrepresentation is justifiably relied on by another and damages result.

fraud-on-the-market theory Misleading statements or omissions distort the market and thus defraud a securities buyer or seller regardless of whether that party relied on the actual misstatement or omission. The theory is based on the assumption that a stock's price reflects all information available to the market (a core tenet of the efficient markets hypothesis).

G

general jurisdiction A court's authority to hear cases that arise within the geographical region over which the court has power. For example, California state courts have general jurisdiction over cases that arise in California.

general partner A partner who participates in management and has unlimited liability for partnership obligations.

general partnership A partnership in which all partners are general partners.

generally accepted accounting principles In the context of publicly held companies, legally mandated rules for measuring and disclosing the amounts shown on financial statements.

generally accepted auditing standards Legally mandated rules for performing audits.

genuineness of assent In contract law, the parties knowingly agreed to the same thing.

going private A transaction in which private investors buy all of the equity securities of a publicly held corporation.

going public A reference to the first time an entity, typically a corporation, sells its equity interests (for example, corporate stock) in the public market.

golden parachute An employment contract clause granting a generous severance package to an executive ousted in a hostile takeover.

greenmail A hostile takeover defense involving the target corporation's repurchase of a takeover raider's stock at a premium not offered to other shareholders.

H

hostile takeover The acquisition of control of a corporation by outsiders over the strong opposition of management.

hybrid form A form of business that combines the characteristics of corporations and general partnerships.

I

implied authorization In contract law, where the offeror's behavior or previous dealings with the offeree suggest an agreeable means of communicating an acceptance.

implied-in-fact conditions Conditions derived from the parties' conduct and the circumstances of the bargain.

implied-in-fact contract Contract whose terms are implicitly understood based on the behavior of the parties.

implied-in-law conditions or constructive conditions Conditions imposed by the court to avoid unfairness.

in personam jurisdiction The power of the court over a person.

income statement Financial statement showing revenues, expenses, gains, and losses, ultimately displaying net income or net loss.

incorporator The person who files the articles of incorporation with a state to create a corporation.

indemnification A corporate policy to compensate officers and directors for losses and costs sustained in defending themselves against litigation associated with their professional duties where those duties were performed in accordance with their fiduciary duties.

independent director An outside director who has no relationship with the corporation that would improperly align the director's interests with those of management.

indictment A grand jury's formal accusation of a crime.

information A prosecutor's formal accusation of a crime.

initial public offering A security offered for sale to the public for the first time.

injunction A court order commanding a person to do or not do a specified action.

injurious falsehood Intentional tort based on a false statement made with malice that disparages the property of another.

inside director A director who is an officer or employee of the corporation.

insider In the securities law context, anyone under a fiduciary duty who has knowledge of material facts not available to the general public.

insider trading Trading securities while in possession of material nonpublic information in violation of a fiduciary duty.

intent A conscious and purposeful state of mind.

intentional tort Voluntary civil wrong causing harm to a protected interest.

interrogatories An ingredient in the discovery process wherein one party in a lawsuit directs written questions to another party in the lawsuit.

Intersectional Discrimination Occurs when an individual is discriminated against on combined protected bases such as national origin and religion.

interstate offering Offering to sell a security to persons residing in states other than that in which the issuer is incorporated.

intrastate offering Offering to sell a security only to persons residing in the same state as that in which the issuer is incorporated.

intrusion Wrongfully entering on or prying into the solitude or property of another.

invasion of privacy Violation of the right to be left alone.

investment contract A form of security that comprises a contract, transaction, or scheme whereby a person invests money in a common enterprise and is led to expect profits primarily from the efforts of someone else, usually the promoter.

issuer An entity, typically a corporation, that is offering to sell, or has already sold, a security to the public.

J

joint and several liability The nature of a liability of a group of persons such that the plaintiff has the choice of suing all members of the group collectively, or only one member, or any subset of members, for the entire amount.

judgment notwithstanding the verdict (judgment n.o.v.) A judge's decision overruling the finding of the jury.

jurisdiction The power of a judicial body to adjudicate a dispute. Also, the geographical area within which that judicial body has authority to operate.

L

lease A contract for the possession and use of land or other property, including goods, on one side, and a recompense of rent or other income on the other.

legal detriment Any act or forbearance by a promisee.

legal impossibility A party to a contract is relieved of his or her duty to perform when that performance has become objectively impossible because of the occurrence of an event unforeseen at the time of contracting.

legality of purpose The object of the contract does not violate law or public policy.

libel A false published statement damaging to a person's reputation.

limited liability The circumstance in which the owners' loss when an entity becomes insolvent is limited to the amount invested. Entity liabilities in excess of its assets are a loss borne by the creditors, not the owners.

limited liability company A hybrid form of business combining the economic flexibility and tax advantages of a general partnership with the limited liability and other operating advantages of a corporation.

limited liability partnership A partnership form providing enhanced limited liability.

limited partner A partner in a limited partnership who does not participate in management and enjoys limited liability.

limited partnership A partnership with at least one general partner and at least one limited partner. The general partner(s) manages(manage) the business and has(have) unlimited liability for partnership obligations. The limited partner(s) plays(play) no role in management, provides(provide) equity capital, and enjoys(enjoy) limited liability.

liquidated damages Damages made certain by the prior agreement of the parties.

liquidation In the *business form context,* the distribution of all of the entity's assets, first to creditors and then to owners, followed by the termination of the entity's existence. In the *bankruptcy context* (Chapter 7 bankruptcy), an action in which a debtor's assets (except those that are exempt) are used to settle the creditors' claims. In the unlikely event that any assets remain, they are returned to the debtor. In the normal situation in which the liabilities exceed the assets, the loss is suffered by the creditors.

M

mailbox rule Rule holding that a mailed acceptance is effective upon dispatch when the offeror has used the mail to invite acceptance; the rule has been expanded to include the use of any reasonable manner of acceptance.

malice A required element of proof in a libel or slander claim by a public figure. Proof of a defamatory statement expressed with actual knowledge of its falsity or with reckless disregard for the truth would establish malice.

management committee In the partnership context, a committee composed of a subset of partners to which the other partners have delegated most or all of their rights to participate in control.

managing partner A partner to whom the other partners have delegated most or all of their rights to participate in control.

market share liability Product liability action by which plaintiffs may be able to recover against manufacturers of defective products based on those manufacturers' market shares even though proof of causation cannot be established.

materially misleading A statement or omission of information by an issuer that has a high likelihood of leading a reasonable investor to form an incorrect judgment about a security.

mediation An extrajudicial proceeding in which a third party (the mediator) attempts to assist disputing parties to reach an agreeable, voluntary resolution of their differences.

member In the context of limited liability companies, an owner.

member's interest The ownership interest of a limited liability company member. In the corporate context, this would be called a share of stock.

mens rea Evil intent.

misappropriation In the securities law context, taking material, nonpublic information, and engaging in insider trading in violation of a fiduciary duty. In the context of torts, wrongfully using an individual's name or image without permission for commercial purposes.

misdemeanor A criminal offense less serious than a felony, normally requiring a fine or less than a year in a jail other than a penitentiary.

mutual agency The power of a general partner to bind the partnership in business matters.

mutual mistake An error about a material fact made by both parties to the contract.

N

necessaries That which is reasonably necessary for a minor's proper and suitable maintenance.

negligence Failure to do something that a reasonable person would do under the circumstances, or an action that a reasonable and prudent person would not take under the circumstances.

nominating committee A subset of the board of directors charged with nominating board candidates to be elected at the next shareholders' meeting.

nuisance A class of wrongs that arise from the unreasonable, unwarrantable, or unlawful use by a person of his or her property that produces material annoyance, inconvenience, discomfort, or hurt.

O

offer A proposal by one person to another that is intended to create legal relations on acceptance by the person to whom it is made.

offeree In the contract law context, one to whom an offer is made. In the securities law context, a person to whom a security is offered for sale.

officer A person holding executive authority in an organization.

operating agreement The governing instrument of a limited liability company.

option contract A separate contract in which an offeror agrees not to revoke her or his offer for a stated period in exchange for some valuable consideration.

ordinance A law, rule, or regulation enacted by a local unit of government (such as a town or city).

outside director A director who is neither an officer nor an employee of the corporation.

over-the-counter market A computer network linking dealers to effectuate the purchase and sale of securities.

P

partner An owner of a partnership.

partner A person who owns an equity interest in a partnership.

partnership An association of two or more persons who carry on as co-owners of a business for profit.

partnership agreement The governing instrument of a partnership.

partnership interest The ownership interest of a partner. The analogous term in the corporate context is a share of stock.

past consideration Performance that is not bargained for and was not given in exchange for the promise.

peremptory challenge An attorney's authority to dismiss prospective members of the jury without offering any justification for that dismissal.

personal property All property other than real property, including all intangible property rights, such as contracts, copyrights, and trademarks.

physical exchange A physical location at which agents of buyers and sellers deal directly with each other to effectuate the purchases and sales of securities.

piercing the corporate veil Holding a shareholder responsible for acts of a corporation because of the shareholder's domination and improper use thereof.

pleadings The formal entry of written statements by which the parties to a lawsuit set out their contentions and thereby formulate the issues on which the litigation will be based.

poison pill defense A tactic to resist a hostile takeover, one version of which involves the target corporation prearranging a new issuance of a significant amount of common stock to existing shareholders at a discounted price, triggered by the commencement of a tender offer.

post-effective period In the securities law context, the period beginning after the SEC has approved the issuer's registration statement during which securities sales can be solicited and consummated.

preferred stock Corporate ownership interests that enjoy a priority over common stock with respect to the rights to participate in earnings and assets upon liquidation but that typically lack the right to participate in control.

prefiling period In the securities law context, the time before the registration statement has been filed with the SEC during which securities sales can be neither solicited nor consummated.

principal The person on whose behalf an agent acts.

private law Individually determined agreement of the parties relating to choice of laws, where disagreements shall be settled, and the language of the transactions.

private placements Securities sold without a public offering, thus eliminating most of the registration requirements of the Securities Act of 1933.

promisee The person to whom a promise is made.

promisor A person who makes a promise to another.

promissory estoppel An equitable doctrine that protects those who foreseeably and reasonably rely on the promises of others by enforcing such promises when enforcement is necessary to avoid injustice.

prospectus A communication, usually in the form of a pamphlet, offering a security for sale and summarizing the information needed for a prospective buyer to evaluate it. It is the principal portion of the registration statement.

proximate cause Occurrences that in a natural sequence, unbroken by potent intervening forces, produce an injury that would not have resulted in the absence of those occurrences.

proxy Written permission from a stockholder for another person to vote that stockholder's shares at a stockholders' meeting.

proxy fight An attempt to oust corporate management by securing a sufficient number of shareholder voting proxies to take control of the board of directors.

public disclosure of private facts Public disclosure of private facts where disclosure of the matter in question would be highly offensive to a reasonable person.

public law Rules of national law that regulate transactions between parties, as well as the relationships between nations.

public policy That which is good for the general public, as gleaned from a state's constitution, statutes, and case law.

publicly held corporation A corporation with publicly traded shares; hence, also referred to as a *publicly traded corporation.*

punitive damages Damages designed to punish flagrant wrongdoers and to deter them and others from engaging in similar conduct in the future.

Q

qualified privilege In libel and slander law, situations where a defendant is excused from liability for defamatory statements except where the statements were motivated by malice.

quasi-contract The doctrine by which courts imply, as a matter of law, a promise to pay the reasonable value of goods or services when the party receiving such goods or services has knowingly done so under circumstances that make it unfair to retain them without paying for them.

R

ratify Adopting or affirming a prior, nonbinding act.

real property Land, buildings, and things permanently attached to land or buildings.

reasonable person Fictitious being the law constructs to determine whether a person's behavior falls short of what a "reasonable person" would do under the circumstances.

red herring prospectus The draft securities prospectus included in the registration statement filed with the SEC. It does not constitute an offer to sell the security.

redemption value The amount received by a preferred shareholder if the corporation liquidates. The amount is stated on the stock certificate.

registration statement The document filed with the SEC with respect to a proposed issuance detailing the information needed to evaluate the security.

Regulation A+ The term used to describe the greatly expanded Regulation A. For example, the $5 million annual cap was raised to $75 million.

release Agreement to relinquish a right or a claim. Sometimes labeled a *waiver* or a *hold harmless clause.*

remand To send back. For example, a higher court sends a case back to the lower court from which it came.

reorganization A bankruptcy action in which creditors are kept from the debtor's assets while the debtor, under court supervision, works out a repayment plan and continues operations (Chapter 11 bankruptcy).

res ipsa loquitur The thing speaks for itself. Rule of evidence establishing a presumption of negligence if the instrumentality causing the injury was in the exclusive control of the defendant, the injury would not ordinarily occur unless someone was negligent, and there is no evidence of other causes.

respondeat superior "Let the master answer." The doctrine holding employers liable for acts (especially negligent acts) committed by employees when acting for the employer.

reverse Overturn the decision of a court.

right of contribution The right of a partner to be reimbursed by the other partners for its payment of a disproportionate amount of a partnership obligation.

risk-utility test In the context of product liability, the principle that a product is negligently designed if the benefits of that product's design are outweighed by the risks that accompany that design.

S

S corporation A closely held corporation whose shareholders have elected to be taxed in a manner similar to the way partners are taxed. Also referred to as a *subchapter S corporation.*

Securities and Exchange Commission The federal regulatory agency, created in 1934, that is responsible for overseeing the securities markets.

securities crowdfunding Raising equity and interest-paying debt capital from a large number of investors in relatively small amounts using the Internet and SEC-approved intermediaries to solicit and consummate the issuance of the security.

security In the securities law context, stock, bonds, and investment contracts. In the debtor-creditor context, it refers to liens, promises, mortgages, etc., given by a debtor to assure payment or performance on a debt.

shareholder An owner of a corporation. Also referred to as a **stockholder.**

shareholder derivative suit An action brought on behalf of a harmed corporation by a shareholder, usually for wrongs done to the corporation by directors or officers. All relief obtained inures to the benefit of the corporation, not to the shareholder bringing the action. However, the plaintiff-shareholder is reimbursed for all reasonable costs incurred.

shelf registration A registration that permits the issuer to hold the securities for sale until favorable market conditions emerge or the issuer needs the proceeds.

short-swing profits Any profits made by an insider through the sale of a security within six months of acquisition. Insider trading is conclusively presumed.

slander A false spoken statement damaging to a person's reputation.

slander per se Category of oral defamation not requiring proof of actual harm to recover.

small claims courts Courts of limited powers designed to hear cases involving modest sums of money (typically limited to $2,000–$7,500, but some states permit recoveries of $15,000 or more) in hearings free of many of the formalities and burdens associated with the more conventional judicial process.

social business A business form that is unique compared with for-profit to not-for-profit entities. Unlike a for-profit business, it is formed primarily to further a social objective, rather than to seek profit maximization. It is distinct from a not-for-profit enterprise because (1) it is intended to be economically self-sustaining and (2) its start-up capital is to be returned without interest.

sole proprietorship A form of business in which one person owns and controls the business. The business is legally indistinguishable from the owner. The proprietorship's assets are owned personally by the proprietor. The proprietorship's liabilities are the personal liabilities of the proprietor. The business per se cannot be sold. The proprietor must personally sell each of the individual assets.

solicitation Offering to sell a security.

sophisticated investor A person with sufficient knowledge and experience in financial matters to need less protection under the securities laws (or a person advised by such a person).

specific performance A contract remedy whereby the defendant is ordered to perform precisely according to the terms of her contract.

stablecoin A cryptocurrency that is pegged to a currency or a currency-denominated asset.

stare decisis Let the decision stand. A doctrine of judicial procedure expecting a court to follow precedent in all cases involving substantially similar issues unless extremely compelling circumstances dictate a change in judicial direction.

stateless income Income purportedly subject to taxation nowhere in the world.

statement of cash flows Financial statement that identifies the reasons the cash balance changed over a period of time.

statement of qualification The document filed with a state that creates a limited liability partnership.

Statute of Frauds A statute specifying that certain contracts must be in writing to be enforceable.

statute of limitations A statute requiring that certain classes of lawsuits must be brought within defined limits of time after the right to begin them accrued or the right is lost.

stock The ownership interest of a shareholder.

stockholder An owner of a corporation. Also referred to as a **shareholder.**

strict liability Civil wrong springing from defective products and "unreasonably dangerous" products or activities where responsibility automatically attaches without proof of blame or fault.

subchapter S corporation A closely held corporation whose shareholders have elected to be taxed in a manner similar to the way partners are taxed. Also referred to as an S corporation.

Subchapter S corporation A closely held corporation whose shareholders have elected to be taxed in a manner similar to the way partners are taxed. Also referred to as an *S corporation.*

subject-matter jurisdiction The authority of a particular court to judge a particular kind of dispute.

supplemental information All information in the registration statement other than the prospectus.

T

tax avoidance Minimizing taxes by lawful means.

tax evasion Minimizing taxes by unlawful means.

tender offer A public offer to buy common stock at a specified price for a specified period of time.

tippee One who receives inside information about a security from another.

tipper One who conveys inside information about a security to another.

tombstone ad A securities advertisement that does not constitute an offer to sell, but rather informs the public that the security might be offered for sale in the future.

torts A civil wrong against persons or property not based on a contractual relationship.

trading suspension The SEC-mandated suspension of trading in a security when serious misconduct or material misrepresentation is suspected.

trespass Entering the property of another without any right, lawful authority, or invitation.

tying arrangement Dealer agrees to sell or lease a product (the tying product) only on the condition that the buyer also purchases or leases another product (the tied product).

U

unconscionability a contract that is so thoroughly one-sided that fairness precludes their enforcement.

underwriter A finance professional who acts as the issuer's sales agent in a securities offering (best-efforts underwriter) or who buys the securities from the issuer hoping to profit from their resale to the public (firm-commitment underwriter).

unenforceable contract A contract that meets basic requirements but remains faulty.

unilateral contract A contract wherein the only acceptance of the offer that is necessary is the performance of the act.

unilateral mistake An error about a material fact made by only one party to the contract.

unjust enrichment An unearned benefit knowingly accepted.

usury Charging an interest rate exceeding the legally permissible maximum.

V

valid contract A contract that is effective; sufficient in law.

venture capitalists Those who invest in new, risky business ventures.

venue The specific geographic location in which a court holding jurisdiction should properly hear a case, given the convenience of the parties and other relevant considerations.

void contract No contract at all; entirely null.

voidable contract Contract that is capable of being made void; enforceable but can be canceled.

voir dire The portion of a trial in which prospective jurors are questioned to determine their qualifications, including absence of bias, to sit in judgment in the case.

W

waiting period The time between filing the registration statement and SEC approval during which securities sales may not be consummated, but limited solicitation of interest may be undertaken.

warranty A contract-based guarantee regarding the character or quality of goods.

word Glossary definition for word goes here.

CASE INDEX

SUBJECT INDEX

C

E

F

G

N

O

Q

R

S

ओं श्रीः

अथ श्रीआकाशभैरवकल्पाख्य-सिद्धग्रन्थस्याध्यायानुसारो विषयानुक्रमः

ओ३म् श्रीः

आकाश भैरव कल्प तंत्रम्

(श्री शिवशक्तिसम्वादात्मकम्)

ओ३म् देवो यः सवितास्माकं प्रेरयत्यनिशं धियः ।
वरेण्यं तस्य यद्भर्गस्तद्वयं समुपास्महे ॥

नील प्रवाहरुचिरं विलसत् त्रिनेत्रं
पाशारुणोत्पल-कपाल-त्रिशूल-हस्तम् ।
अर्द्धाम्बिकेशमनिशं प्रविभक्तभूषं
बालेन्दु-बद्धमुकुटं प्रणमामि रूपम् ॥ शा० ति०

आध्यात्मिक-आधिदैविक-आधिमानसिकादि बहुविध दुःखों से आक्रान्त इस मानव जीव का अन्तिम लक्ष्य किसी न किसी तरह दुःखों से निवृत्ति एवं शान्ति प्राप्त करना है, जिसके लिए वह स्थान-स्थान पर भटक रहा होता है । मायावी गुरुओं का बोलबाला, गली गली में नकली देवी-माताएं (क्या दुर्गा क्या काली और क्या वैष्णवी) भैरव-हनुमान्-सिद्ध-पीर-जिन्नात, शैतान और न जाने क्या क्या और किन किन की चौकियों (अड्डों) पर वह बेचारा क्या नहीं करता । अनगिनत नक्षत्रसूचक (नाम के राजज्योत्तिषी) और एक के बाद एक ऐसे ही तांत्रिक, काला जादू जानने वाले उस बेचारे की परेशानियों, भोलेपन और अज्ञान का लाभ उठाते हुए अपनी वाक्पटुता के प्रभाव से अपने माया जाल में घेर कर उसे कई बार शिकार बना चुके होते हैं, किन्तु वह फिर भी काम-क्रोध-लोभ-मोह-अहंकारादि विकार-रूपी तम से आवृत होने के कारण अपने उद्देश्यों की प्राप्ति के लिए अज्ञानवश इतर धर्मावलम्बी ओझाओं-झाड़ फूंक करने वालों, नाम के महात्माओं-बाबाओं-मठाधीशों-सन्तों-नव्वाबों-मुल्लाओं और पीरों तक के द्वार पर मस्तक रगड़ता रहता है, किन्तु "ढाक के वही तीन पात", उसके हाथ फिर भी कुछ नहीं लगता—

"दुर्लभा चित्तविश्रान्तिर्विना गुरुकृपां पराम् ।"

सैकड़ों वर्ष पूर्व तत्कालीन शासन द्वारा संरक्षणप्राप्त विविध धर्मप्रचारकों ने अत्यन्त चतुराई से सावरी मंत्रों से मिलते जुलते ऊटपटांग छूमन्त्रों किन्तु वास्तव में हाथ की सफाई, युक्ति अथवा रासायनिक द्रव्यादिकों के बल पर विशेष प्रकार के चमत्कारों के प्रदर्शन से देश के असंख्य लोगों को प्रभावित करके दूसरे धर्मों में परिवर्तित किया था । इन लोगों के केन्द्र ऐसे स्थानों पर बनाए गए थे जहां लोग अत्यन्त गरीब, तथा अविद्या—अज्ञान और अन्धविश्वास से आवृत थे, अतः उन्हें वहां अच्छी

सफलता मिली। इन ही में से अधिकांश गोसाईं-सिद्ध-फकीर-औलिया-पीर-हज़रत नवाब तथा कुछ मठाधीश बन गए। इन ही लोगों द्वारा देश की जनता में हीन भावना उत्पन्न करने के लिए बहुत से ऐसे मनघड़न्त मन्त्रों की रचना की गई थी—

गज़ना से आए महमूद ने हमारे देश के परस्पर विरोध का लाभ उठाते हुए भारत पर आक्रमण करके तत्कालीन श्री सोमनाथ के प्रसिद्ध मन्दिर को लूटने में सफलता प्राप्त की थी, वापिसी पर वह मार्ग में ही मर गया, वह महमूद-गज़नवी कोई फ़रिश्ता या पैगम्बर नहीं था; किन्तु आज वह कुछ इसी प्रकार के मन्त्रों का नायक है, और ओझा लोग उन लोगों के कथनानुसार उसकी प्रेतात्मा (रूह—spirit) को बुलाकर उससे विविध काम लेते हैं और मजे की बात तो यह है कि ऐसे मन्त्रों के आरम्भ में "ओ३म् या "ओं नमो आदेश गुरू को" तथा अन्त में "फुरो मन्त्र ईश्वरो वाचा भी जोड़ा हुआ है ताकि भोली भाली जनता उन की चाल को समझ न सके। उदाहरण के लिए ऐसे कुछ मंत्रों के कुछ खण्ड दे रहा हूं—

"ओं नमो आ हां कंत जुगराज. ए गढ़ गजनी के महमदा वीर—भूत को बांध, प्रेत को बांध, देव को बांध, अ सठ कला को बांध, चौंसठ योगिनी को बांध भैरू को बांध, काली को बांध,——शब्द सांचा, पिण्डकांचा, फुरो मन्त्र ईश्वरो वाचा।" "ओं नमो आदेश गुरु को, लड़गढ़ी (गजनी) से महम्मूद पठान चढ़िया—चौंसठ योगिनी बांध, हनुमान वीर को बांध, लूना चमारी करे, सहमूद पीर—तुरकनी के पूत की बुहाई।"

और कुछ इस प्रकार के दूसरे मंत्र जो इसी तरह के मठाधीशों तथा उनकी प्रेमिकाओं के नाम पर रचे गए तथा जो दूरदृष्टि के अभाव के कारण कुछ इसी प्रकार के आचार्यों द्वारा संग्रह कर के प्रकाशित कर दिए गए थे—

"ओं नमो आदेश गुरू को—कामरूप देश कामाक्षा देवी, जहां बसे इस्माईल जोगी·········चूके उमा, सुखे लोना चमारी······फुरो मंत्र ईश्वरो वाचा।"

"ओं काला कलवा चौंसठ वीर"० इत्यादि

और कुछ एक ही प्रकार के ऐसे मंत्रों की भी रचना की गई, जिस में दो प्रकार के धर्मावलम्बियों का परस्पर विरोध या मुकाबला दृष्ट होता है, यथा—एक सम्प्रदाय का मन्त्र

"बन में आए बांदरी जो आधा फल खाय।
खड़े मुहम्मद हांक दें आधा सीसी जाए॥

यही मन्त्र दूसरे धर्मानुयाईयों ने इस प्रकार लिखा—

"बन में जाए बानरी जो आधा फल खाय।
खड़े हनुमत हांक दें आधा सीसी जाए॥

यह कोई तांत्रिक मंत्र नहीं हैं और न ही यह कोई सावरि मंत्र हैं और न ही इनमें कुछ प्रभाव है, अपितु यह केवल मात्र स्वार्थ और कनिष्ठ भावनाओं के छींटों से आप्लावित नाम मात्र के मंत्र हैं और इसी प्रकार के ग्रन्थों में से कुछ थोड़े-थोड़े अंश संग्रह कर के कुछ आधुनिक अदूरदर्शक ग्रंथकार "कहीं की ईंट कहीं का रोड़ा। भानमती ने कुनबा जोड़ा" के वाक्यानुसार छोटे छोटे (नाम मात्र के) तंत्र ग्रन्थों को अपनी लेखपटुता के सहारे प्रकाशित कराके वस्तुतः तंत्रक्षेत्र पर कोई उपकार नहीं कर रहे हैं। तंत्र-मंत्र-यंत्रादिकों के उनके इस प्रकार के संग्रहग्रन्थों ने तो मूल-तंत्र-ग्रन्थों को इस प्रकार आच्छादित कर दिया है, जिस तरह राख के ढेर में सुलगते अंगारे। इस से जहाँ मूल विद्याओं का लोप हो रहा है, वहाँ व्यर्थ में लोगों का परिश्रम, समय और धन नष्ट होता है और इसके साथ ही केवलमात्र तंत्रशास्त्र ही नहीं, अपने धर्म पर से भी श्रद्धा हटते हुए हमारा न केवल अपना, अपितु अपनी सभ्यता एवं पूर्वजों की पुरा-उपलब्धियों का क्रमशः ह्रास हो रहा होता है।

विदेशियों द्वारा हमारे पुरा-साहित्य का बहुमूल्य भाग किसी भी मूल्य पर ले जाने के अभियान से जागृत तत्कालीन कुछ राष्ट्र नेताओं, नरेशों, धनपतियों और विद्वानों के भरसक प्रयत्नों ने गुह्य तथा गुप्त ग्रंथों के संकलन-संग्रह एवं पुनः प्रकाशन में निःसन्देह बहुमूल्य सहयोग दिया है। जम्मू, काश्मीर, बीकानेर, राजस्थान, त्रिवेन्द्रम, वड़ोदा, तंजोर, पूना प्रभृति भूतपूर्व राज्यों के नरेशों से आश्रित लाइब्रेरियों के अतिरिक्त नेपाल दरबार, एशियाटिक-सोसाईटी आफ बंगाल, मद्रास राजकीय पुस्तकालय, संस्कृत कालेज लायब्रेरी-संस्कृत विश्वविद्यालय बनारस, भण्डारकर रीसर्च संस्थान, बिहार अनुसन्धान समिति प्रभृति बहुत से संस्थानों ने तो लुप्त हो रहे सहस्रों दुर्लभ ग्रंथों का संकलन एवं अधिकांश का प्रकाशन करके भारतीय साहित्य के क्षेत्र पर अत्यन्त उपकार किया है। इसके अतिरिक्त श्री खेमराज श्रीकृष्णदास श्री वैंकटेश्वर प्रेस, निर्णयसागर प्रेस मुंबई, श्री मोतीलाल बनारसी दास, श्री मेहर चन्द लक्ष्मण दास तथा चौखम्बा बनारस प्रभृति बहुत से प्रकाशकों ने साहित्य को निःसन्देह पुनर्जीवन दिया है।

इस डेढ़-शताब्दी में सर आर्थर-एवलेन, श्री प्रबोधचन्द्र जी बागची, श्री चिन्ताहरण चक्रवर्ती तथा डाक्टर गोपीनाथ कविराज ऐसे महान् विद्वानों ने तंत्र के बहुमूल्य, आर्ष एवं गुप्त ग्रंथों के प्रकाशन के साथ साथ उन पर जो विशेष शोध कार्य किया है उसकी प्रशंसा के लिए शब्द नहीं हो सकते, तथा उन का यह अनुसन्धान कार्य भविष्य में भी तंत्र पर गवेषणा करने वालों के लिए सुमार्गदर्शक रहेगा।

महामहोपाध्याय डाक्टर गोपीनाथ जी कविराज महोदय ने **श्री आकाश भैरव-कल्पाख्य** इस तन्त्रग्रन्थ का अपने लिखे **"तंत्र साहित्य"** नामक ग्रंथ, जो उत्तर प्रदेश शासन के सूचना-विभाग की हिन्दी समिति द्वारा १९७२ ई० में प्रकाशित हुआ, में पष्ठ संख्या २३ पर इस प्रकार वर्णन किया है—

आकाशभैरव कल्प

लि० (१) प्रत्यक्ष सिद्धिप्रद उमा महेश्वरसम्वाद रूप—श्लोक संख्या २००० और ७८ अध्यायों में पूर्ण ।

यह मंत्रशास्त्र सांग, सलक्षण, वेदसारभूत तथा सब जीव-जन्तुओं का अभीष्ट प्रद और ज्ञानप्रदायक एवं साधक-सुखदायी कहा गया है । देवी पार्वती जी के महेश्वर से यह प्रार्थना करने पर कि हे दयानिधे, जो शास्त्र लोक में अत्यन्त गुप्त हो, जो सब अभीष्टों को देने वाला हो, और जो साधक श्रेष्ठों का हितकारी हो, उसे आप कहने की कृपा करें—महेश्वर ने इस का उपदेश किया । इसके ७८ अध्यायों के मुख्य विषय यह हैं—उत्साह-प्रक्रम, यजन विधि, उत्साहाभिषेक, मंत्र यंत्र प्रक्रम, चित्रमाला मंत्र, वश्य और आकर्षण प्रयोग, मोहन एवं द्रावण प्रयोग, स्तंभन और विद्वेषण तथा प्रयोग, उच्चाटन-निग्रह प्रयोग, भोगप्रद विधि, आशुताक्ष्र्य विधि, आशुगरुड़ प्रयोग, शिष्याचार विधि, शरभ-सालुव-पक्षिराज कल्प, शरभेशाष्टक स्तोत्रादि, रक्षाभिषेक विधि, बलिविधान, माया प्रयोग विधि, आचार विधि, मातृका-वर्णन, भद्रकाली विधि, औषध विधि, शूलिनि-दुर्गा-कल्प, शूलिनि विधि, वीरभद्रकल्प, जगत्क्षोभण-माला मंत्र, त्रपाविधि, भैरव विधि, दिक्पाल विधि, व्याधिकल्पन, मृत्यु विधि, मन्मथ विधि, चामुंडा विधि, मोहिनीविधि, द्राविणीविधि, शब्दार्काषिणी प्रयोग, माया-सरस्वती प्रयोग, महालक्ष्मी प्रयोग, माया विधि, पुलिन्दिनी विधि, महाशान्त (न्ति ?) विधि, संक्षोभिणी विधि, धूमावती प्रयोग, चित्रविद्या-विधि, देशिक-स्तोत्र, दुःस्वप्ननाशन-मंत्र विधि, पाशविमोचन-विधि, औषधिमन्त्र-विधि, कालमंत्र-विधि, षण्मुखमंत्र-विधि, त्वरिता-विधि, वड़वानल-भैरव-विधि, ब्राह्मी प्रभृति सप्तमातृ-विधि, नारसिंही-विधि, एवं शरभहृदयादि

(१) (नेपाल दर्बार पुस्तकालय) ने० द० ३१२४६ (ग)

(२) (क) श्लोक सं० २४०० अध्याय ७८, उपदेश शङ्कर

(ख) श्लोक सं० १००० अध्याय ३६ अ० ब० (बड़ोदा पुस्तकालय का अकारादि सूचीपत्र (क) ५६०१ (ख) १०६६८

(३) महार्शव तंत्र से गृहीत । २० उपदेशों में पूर्ण—कैट० कैट (कैटा लागस कैटालागोरस) एन अलफाबेटीकल रजिस्टर आफ सं० वर्क्स एंड आथर्स, इन थ्री पार्ट्स ।

(४) श्लोक संख्या १३७५ अध्याय १-४५ तक-महार्शव तंत्रांतर्गत-सं० वि० (संस्कृत विश्वविद्यालय पुस्तकालय वाराणसी का सूचीपत्र)—२६३७८ अपूर्ण (उल्लिखित) उ०-प्राणतोषिणी में ।

देश विभाजन से पूर्व भारत के पश्चिमोत्तरीय सीमाप्रान्त में स्थित एवं वस्तुतः पश्चिम-काशी कहलाए जाने वाले "हरिपुर हज़ारा" नगर वास्तव्य भरद्वाज कुलोत्पन्न परमशाक्त श्री पं० देवीदासजी धम्मी के सुपुत्र मेरे श्री पिता राजज्योतिषी

तथा राजवैद्य पं० लक्ष्मीनारायण जी धम्मी के ज्येष्ट भ्राता एवं मेरे श्री गुरु सर्वतंत्रस्वतंत्र, वेद-शास्त्र-ज्योतिष-ग्रायुर्वेद-तंत्रादि बहुविध विद्याओं में पारंगत, तथा वास्तविकता में विद्यावारिधि श्री श्री श्री १००८ श्री पण्डित लालचन्द्र जी धम्मी ने बहुत परिश्रम और अमूल्य समय लगा कर ज्योतिष-तंत्र तथा आयुर्वेद के हस्तलिखित दुर्लभ ग्रन्थों का, जिनमें बहुत से ग्रन्थ हमारे यहाँ भी कुलपरम्परा से सुरक्षित चले आ रहे थे और कुछ विशेष दुर्लभ ग्रंथों की प्रतिलिपियां स्वयं अपने हाथों द्वारा तैयार की थीं, का एक विशाल भण्डार संग्रह किया था, जिनमें से अधिकांश ग्रंथ हरिपुर हज़ारा में उनके मूल-निवासस्थान में तथा कुछ भाग मेरे पूज्य पिता जी के पास इसी ज़िल्ला में वहां से कोई सांठ मील पश्चिमोत्तर-दिशा-स्थित "बफा" उपनगर में सुरक्षित रखे थे, परम पूज्य श्री गुरु जी का स्वर्गारोहण विक्रम संख्या १९९५ में हो गया था अत: उन बहुमूल्य ग्रंथों का अधिकांश भाग उनके एक मात्र सुपुत्र दिवंगत राजज्योतिषी पं० दुर्गादत्तजी धम्मी तथा पौत्र राजज्योतिषी पं० डेवलचन्दजी धम्मी, जो आजकल बंठिण्डा पंजाब में निवास रखे हुए हैं, के पास हरिपुर हज़ारा (मूल घर) में रह गया। देश विभाजन के समय भागदौड़ में दुर्लभ ग्रन्थों का वह अनमोल खज़ाना उन से नहीं लाया जा सका, किन्तु मैं अपने श्री पिता जी की प्रेरणा तथा दृढ़ प्रोत्साहन से कुछ डेढ़ हज़ार के लगभग ग्रन्थ लाने में सफल हो गया था। तन्त्रशास्त्र सम्बन्धित महत्वपूर्ण ग्रंथों में श्री आकाशभैरवकल्प, श्री गुरु जी कृत संस्कृतानुवाद-सहित श्री शिवताण्डव-तंत्र, श्री भूतडामर-तंत्र, श्री देवीरहस्य, श्री साहिबकौल-कृत श्रीविद्या-पूजापद्धति, श्री दक्षिणकालिका पूजन पद्धति, श्री भुवनेश्वरी रहस्य, श्री गायत्रीपंचाङ्ग तथा ज्योतिष से सम्बन्धित ग्रन्थों में महाराजा रणजीतसिंह जी के राजपण्डित द्वारा अर्घ-ज्ञान एवं भावीफल-ज्ञान पर लिखा हुआ "**भावीज्ञान नामक महाग्रंथ**" तथा आयुर्वेद से सम्बन्धित सुखपुराणादि ग्रन्थों की प्रतिलिपियां मेरे पास सुरक्षित पड़ी हैं, इसके अतिरिक्त पूज्यपाद श्री गुरु जी द्वारा लिखित जैमिनीयसूत्र (ज्यो०) के चारों अध्यायों की संस्कृत टीका तथा उस पर मेरे श्री पिता जी द्वारा कृत सविस्तृत सोदाहरण हिन्दी टीका, श्री पञ्चस्वरा की सोदाहरण संस्कृत हिन्दी टीका, गणितशास्त्र से सम्बन्धित श्री मकरन्दोत्पत्ति तथा शष्कुली-पक्व-ग्रहण सारिणी आदि के अतिरिक्त और बहुत से ग्रन्थ जिनमें पारसीक (फारसी) भाषा में अनुवादित श्री वाल्मीकि-रामायण की भी एक प्रति है, हमारे संग्रहालय में मौजूद हैं, यदि श्री जगदीश्वर की कृपा हुई और विद्वानों से प्रोत्साहन मिला तो बहुत शीघ्र ही उनका प्रकाशन हो जाएगा।

तंत्रशास्त्र कोई अनियमित या ऊटपटांग कल्पना नहीं है, वरन् शब्द, हेतु तथा विज्ञान द्वारा दृढ़ निश्चित, निखिल-शास्त्र-प्रमाणित एवं सर्वसिद्ध विद्याएं तंत्र कहलाती हैं, और इसमें व्यवहृत मंत्रबीज, श्रुति की ऋचाओं के स्वर व्यञ्जनादि अक्षरों के क्षेपकांक जो श्वेत-रक्त-श्यामादि विविध महाविद्याओं के आधार पर दूरद्रष्टा ऋषियों ने विशेष नियमानुसार निश्चय किए थे, परस्पर जोड़कर यथोक्त

अङ्क द्वारा सविधि संस्कार करते हुए शेषांकों से फलस्वरूप निकाले जाते हैं। यथा-प्रसिद्ध ब्रह्मगायत्री ऋचा के आद्यपद "तत्सवितुर्वरेण्यं" से "अ", "भर्गोदेवस्य धीमहि" से "उ" "धियो यो नः प्रचोदयात्" से "म्"। इस प्रकार मंत्र के पदक्रमानुसार वीजाक्षर अ+उ+म् होने से उस का बीजमंत्र ओम् निकलता है। इसी प्रकार विशेष ऋचाओं का उपरोक्त विधि से बीज संस्कार द्वारा 'ऐं'—'ह्रीं'—"श्रीं"—"क्लीं" 'जूं'—'सः'—सौः, "क्ष्म्र्यैं" आदि विविध मंत्रबीज निकाले गए हैं, जो तंत्रशास्त्र का आधार हैं।

गुरु परम्परा से प्राप्त इस प्रकार की बीज-साधन-विधि को यदि ईश्वरेच्छा हुई तो इस ग्रन्थ के बाद प्रकाशित होने वाले तंत्र ग्रन्थ श्री शिवताण्डव तंत्र तथा भूतडामर तंत्र के साथ-साथ प्रकाशित करने का यत्न करूंगा।

श्री आकाश-भैरव-कल्पाख्य यह ग्रन्थ वेदमूलक है, अतः इस ग्रन्थ में दी गई सिद्ध ऋचाओं के प्रयोग करने से पहिले अपने आपका ब्रह्मगायत्री मंत्र द्वारा यथा-शक्ति पुरश्चरण करके विद्युतीकरण कर लेना चाहिए॥

"गायत्र्याः परं नास्ति इह लोके परत्र च।"

श्री गुरू जी के उपदेशानुसार गायत्रीमंत्र का जप या पुरश्चरण कोई कामना रख कर नहीं करना चाहिये। कार्यानुसार उपयोगी ऋचाएं गायत्री मंत्र के अभ्यासी को ठीक उसी प्रकार फलदायक होती हैं, जिस प्रकार विद्युत-संचारित कमरे में विद्युत उपकरण—पंखा, हीटर या रीफ्रेजेटरादि।

वेद मंत्र किस प्रकार यथोक्त तथा इच्छानुकूल फल देते हैं, इस सम्बन्ध में श्री मेरुतंत्र में इस प्रकार उपदेश दिया गया है—

"अथ गोप्यं प्रवक्ष्यामि गोप्यं मातरिजारवत्।
सर्वेषां वेदमंत्राणां यच्च संसिद्धिकारकम्॥
लोलुपाय कृतघ्नाय नास्तिकाय शठाय च।
सगर्वाय गुरुद्वेष्ट्रे प्रोक्त्वा शापमवाप्नुयात्॥
येषां वैदिकमंत्राणां चलनं कर्मसूचितम्।
तानादि-पाद-सहितान् गायत्र्यास्तु सदा जपेत्॥
अष्टोत्तरसहस्रन्तु तद्वत् पालनमन्त्रकान्।
मध्यपादेन संयुक्तानन्तिमेन तु नाशनम्॥
अवश्यं जायते सिद्धिर्गायत्री तेजसा इति॥"

इस प्रकार महर्षियों ने पाद-भेद से गायत्री-मंत्र को सृष्टि, स्थिति, लयानुसार तीन भागों में व्यक्त किया है। सकाम-कार्यों में कार्यभेदानुसार वेद-विधानोक्त अथवा तंत्रशास्त्र में दर्शित ऋचाओं के साथ शीर्ष स्थान पर "ओं भूर्भुवः स्वः" के साथ गायत्री मंत्र के उक्त व अनुकूल भाग को लगा कर शास्त्रानुकूल-विधानोक्त

पुरश्चरण किया जाये, तो निःसन्देह शीघ्र सिद्धि होती है। मंत्र गुरुमुख से ग्रहण करना चाहिये, इस प्रकार श्री गुरु की आज्ञानुसार श्री गुरु की पूजन-प्रणामादि-पूर्वक कार्य करने से यथेष्ट फल की प्राप्ति होती है। यद्यपि गुरुपूजन का सर्वत्र महत्व है, किन्तु तंत्र-शास्त्र में तो श्री गुरु के बिना एक पग भी नहीं उठाया जा सकता, इसीलिये तो जिस तरह अच्छे प्रकार परख कर शिष्य को दीक्षा देने का विधान है, वहाँ शिष्य को भी सुयोग्य एवं सिद्धिप्राप्त गुरु से ही मंत्रोपदेश लेना चाहिए और यदि भूल से किसी ऐसे मायावी-गुरु से दीक्षा ली गई थी जो स्वयं सिद्धि प्राप्त नहीं कर सका, तो शिष्य को दूसरा गुरु अपनाने के लिये भी शास्त्र आज्ञा देता है।

"असिद्धत्वात् गुरोर्देवाः शिष्यसिद्धिर्नजायते ।।"

"मधुभुक् च यथाभृङ्गः पुष्पात्पुष्पान्तरं व्रजेत् ।
ज्ञानलुब्धस्तथा शिष्यो गुरोगुर्वन्तरं व्रजेत् ।।"

तंत्रशास्त्र में दीक्षाप्राप्त मनुष्य अपने श्री गुरु में साक्षात् ब्रह्म, मन्त्र ध्वनियों में ईश्वरीय शक्ति की विविध लीलाएं और प्राणप्रतिष्ठाकृत-प्रतिमा में नाना प्रकार की शक्तियां तथा उन की अर्चना के साधन देखता है, यदि ऐसा नहीं कर पाता तो वह सफलताओं से कोसों दूर अशान्त मन होता हुआ दुःख सागर में पतित होता है, इसीलिये शास्त्र कहता है—

'गुरौ मनुष्यबुद्धिश्च मंत्रे वाक्षरशेमुषीम् ।
प्रतिमासु शिला बुद्धि कुर्वाणो नरकं व्रजेत् ।।"

इसी प्रकार यदि गुरु किसी तरह की लालसा-भय या धन लेने देने की इच्छा से शास्त्रोक्त योग्यताओं से हीन किसी व्यक्ति को सिद्धविद्या की दीक्षा देता है तो देवता उसको विपरीत फल देते हुए शाप देता है, तथा उसका अपना एवं शिष्य दोनों का किया कराया सब विफल हो जाता है।

'धनेच्छा-भय लोभाद्वा अयोग्यं यदि दीक्षयेत् ।
देवताशापमाप्नोति कृतं च विफलं भवेत् ।।"

अतः पूजन-क्रियादि कार्यों में अपने श्री गुरु से आदेश लेकर गुरु के निर्दिष्ट मार्ग से साध्य-देवता को अनन्य भाव से स्मरण करता हुआ यथोक्त मंत्र का जपानुष्ठान करने से निःसन्देह विस्मयजनक लाभ होता है।

जीवों के नाना प्रकार के भोग कल्याण एवं पुरुषार्थ सिद्धि के लिये सर्वत्र व्यापक ब्रह्म श्रीशिव के ऊर्ध्व-पूर्व-दक्षिण-पश्चिम और उत्तरादि पञ्च मुखस्रोतों द्वारा करोड़ों विद्याओं के श्रवण की रहस्यमय-कल्पना अति गूढ़ विज्ञान से ओत प्रोत है, तथा इन स्रोतों द्वारा तंत्र की असंख्य विद्याओं का प्रकाश उनके उपास्य देवता की कलाओं के अनुरूप उनका कई श्रेणियों में विभाजन शास्त्रसिद्ध

है, इन ही श्रेणियों में एक प्रसिद्ध श्रेणी है—"क्रान्ता," जिसके अनुसार जगत्स्रष्टा शिव ने इस त्रिलोकी जगत की तंत्र सम्बन्धित विद्याओं को 'अश्वक्रान्ता'-'रथक्रान्ता-'विष्णुक्रान्ता' तीन भागों में विभक्त कर दिया था, इनमें रथक्रान्ता भाग के ८४ प्रसिद्ध तंत्रों में श्री आकाश-भैरव-कल्प का नाम सर्वप्रथम है। इस सिद्ध ग्रन्थ के योग थोड़े ही परिश्रम से शीघ्र ही प्रत्यक्ष फल देते हैं, इसके बहुत से योग मेरे परिवार में परम्परा से चलते आ रहे हैं, तथा इनसे यथा आवश्यकता मनोवाञ्छित कार्यों में आश्चर्य की सफलता प्राप्त की जाती रही है, इन प्रयोगों से असम्भव को भी सम्भव में बदलते देखा है, यहां तक कि इसके विधिवत् प्रयोग-क्रियाओं से साधारण व्यक्ति से राजा तक के भाग्य में उलट पलट हो सकती है, तथा किसी भी व्यक्ति को गतिशील, उसके विविध कार्यों में सफलता, अथवा किसी का गतिरोध तक किया जा सकता है, विजय प्राप्ति तथा शत्रुनिग्रह कार्यों में तो आकाशभैरव, वनदुर्गा महाकाली, शूलिनी तथा श्री वाराही आदि महाविद्याओं को मैंने हस्तामलकवत् सिद्ध देखा है।

शिवशक्ति सम्वादात्मक **श्री आकाश-भैरव-कल्पाख्य** इस तंत्र का तांत्रिक क्षेत्र में बहुत सम्मान है, इसके **निग्रह-दारुण-सप्तक** की तो इतनी प्रसिद्धि है, कि कई तंत्र-ग्रन्थकारों ने अपनी रचनाओं में इसका विशेष प्रशंसा पूर्वक वर्णन किया है, वर्तमान काल में भी श्री पीताम्बरा-पीठ के अधीश्वर राष्ट्रगुरु सर्वतंत्रस्वतन्त्र निगमागम तंत्रपारीण परमहंस परिव्राजकाचार्य श्री स्वामी जी ने स्वकृति श्री बगलामुखी रहस्य में इसके निग्रह-दारुण-सप्तक को उसके महत्व को समझते हुए अत्यन्त सुन्दर भाष्य सहित उपयुक्त स्थान दिया है ॥

अतिबलवान् तेजस्वी तथा आततायी हिरण्यकश्यपु के संहार, धर्म मर्यादा के संरक्षण, वैष्णव-धर्म के पुनः संस्थापन तथा विष्णुभक्त प्रह्लाद को बचाने के लिए भगवान् विष्णु अंशात्मक-अवतार श्री नृसिंह के रूप में प्रकट हुए थे, तथा उस कार्य की समाप्ति के बाद उन्हें उसी प्रकार विष्णु के तेज में लीन हो जाना चाहिये था, किन्तु उस के स्थान में नरसिंह-रूपधारी वह महाशक्तिमान् अपने कर्त्तव्य को भूलते हुए अहंकार में प्रवृत हो कर अपनी क्रोध-ज्वालाओं के दहकते तेज से विश्व भर को जलाने लगे, तथा उस तेज द्वारा उत्तप्त प्रणी त्राहि त्राहि एवं शान्तिः शान्तिः के लिये परं-ब्रह्म जगदीश्वर से निरन्तर प्रार्थनारत थे, तब प्राणीमात्र के त्राता, त्रिलोकी के विधाता, परम-कैलाश-वासी, भगवान् सदाशिव ने अपने तृतीय-नेत्र से उत्पन्न स्वांशरूप परम तेज और सामर्थ्य युक्त महान् बली श्री वीरभद्र को आदेश दिया कि वह श्री विष्णु के उन अंशावतार श्री नृसिंह के पास जा कर उन्हें समझाएं कि जिस कार्य के लिये उनका प्रादुर्भाव हुआ था वह समाप्त हो चुका है, अतः उन्हें अपने उत्तरदायित्व को ध्यान में रखते हुए अब विश्व भर को दुःख-संतप्त करने की बजाय विश्व की स्थिति की ओर ध्यान देने के लिये परम विष्णु के तेज में अपने आप

को लीन कर लेना चाहिये, और यदि वह फिर भी अहंकार-जाल से आवृत होने के कारण न मानें, तो उन्हें किसी भी तरह उस दिव्य एवं भयानक शरीर से मुक्त कर दिया जाये, श्री शिवमहापुराण तथा लिङ्गपुराणादिकों में इस कथा का सविस्तार वर्णन है। श्री नृसिंह ने श्री वीरभद्र की एक नहीं सुनी और उन्हें ही मारने के लिये दौड़े, तब साक्षात् सदाशिव-रूपी वीरभद्र सूक्ष्मातिसूक्ष्म रूप धारण करके अदृश्य हो गये, और क्षण भर में शरभ रूपी भयानक पक्षी, जिनका एक पंख श्री महाकाली और दूसरा पंख श्री दुर्गा की महान् शक्ति से युक्त था, के रूप में प्रकट हो कर आकाश मार्ग से एक ही चोंच के वार से श्री नृसिंह की बाह्यत्वचा खींच कर ले गये। यही शिव-रूपी वीरभद्र शरभावतार तथा आकाशभैरवादि नाम से प्रसिद्ध हैं। आदिशिवकृत इस प्रस्तुत ग्रन्थ में यही शंकरावतार-शरभ, खगपति, शरभेश्वर तथा आकाश-भैरवादि बहुत से नामों से सम्बोधित इस तंत्र के मुख्य देवता हैं। वेद प्रधान इस तंत्रग्रन्थ में इनकी साधना तथा शूलिनी आदि इनकी बहुविध शक्तियों द्वारा मारण-उच्चाटन-स्तंभन-मोहन-वशीकंरणादि षट्कर्म-सिद्धि के लिए इक्यासी अध्यायों में आशु एवं प्रत्यक्ष फल कारक सिद्ध विधान दिये हैं।

जब किसी सुसंस्कृत विधि से सृष्टि, स्थिति एवं लयकरी असंख्य ईश्वरीय शक्तियों द्वारा सञ्चालित विविध क्रियाओं को मनोवाञ्छित मार्ग पर लाकर मनोरथ सिद्ध कर लिये जाते हैं, अथवा शब्द, ध्वनि, औषधि, सङ्कल्प एवं भावनाओं द्वारा दृश्यादृश्य ईश्वरीय-शक्तियों को ग्रहण कर के उनके द्वारा लौकिकालौकिक विविध प्रकार के मनोवाञ्छित कार्यों पर सफलता प्राप्त की जाती है, तो उस की अधिष्ठात्री-विद्या तंत्र कहलाती है। तंत्र, विज्ञान रूपी एक विशाल समुद्र है और नाना प्रकार की विद्याएं इस की तरङ्गें। यह एक बड़ा भारी विज्ञान है, इस में पूजा पद्धति भी है, यौगिक क्रियायें भी हैं, जप पाठ भी हैं, मातृका, शब्द, ध्वनि, स्वर, वर्ण, विन्दु, नादादि से नियमसिद्ध मंत्र भी हैं और मंत्ररहित क्रियाएं भी—स्वरों से रासायनिक द्रव्य, वर्णों से धातु उपधातु तथा मातृकाओं के शेष वर्णों एवं उनके मिलान से विविध औषधि तथा रासायनिक द्रव्यों के भी सङ्केत मिलते हैं। यंत्रावलियां रहस्यों से भरी हैं इन में पूजा पद्धति भी है, धारणा एवं प्रयोग क्रियाएं भी हैं और इनमें विशेष मशीनरी बनाने के भी सङ्केत हैं। जिस तरह दो प्रकार की वायु (गैसें) मिलकर या परस्पर रगड़ खाकर आर्द्रता-शुष्कता या शीतलता ले आती हैं, अथवा उन से अग्नि की ज्वालाएं या विद्युत सरीखा तेज एवं शक्ति उत्पन्न हो सकती है, ठीक उसी प्रकार मातृकाओं तथा उनसे मिश्रित अक्षरों के उच्चारण से उत्पन्न नाना प्रकार की ध्वनियों के परस्पर मिलान या घर्षण से प्रकृति एवं वातावरण में अमृत और प्रेम की लहरें तरङ्गित हो रही होती हैं, और कभी विरुद्ध-मिलान से द्वेष, परस्पर विरोध, सूनापन एवं संहारात्मक भयानक वातावरण।

जैसा कि पहिले बताया जा चुका है, कि तंत्र विद्या का एक बहुत विशाल

क्षेत्र है और नाना प्रकार के विषय इसके अन्तर्गत आ जाते हैं। तन्त्र विद्या से सम्बन्धित श्री आकाशभैरवकल्पाख्य इस ग्रन्थ में आदिनाथ श्री शिवमुख द्वारा प्रकाश में आई हुई विद्याओं के प्रयोग से राजा से लेकर एक साधारण व्यक्ति तक के राज्य सम्बन्धित, सांसारिक, व्यवहारिक अथवा गार्हस्थ्य से सम्बन्ध रखने वाली विविध समस्याओं के निवारण के लिय सिद्ध तथा सरल विधियां दी हुई हैं, इसीलिये इस ग्रन्थ की विशेष महानता है। देश भर के पूर्व से पश्चिम एवं दक्षिण से उत्तर तक इस ग्रन्थ के विषयों का विद्वानों में समादर पाना इस ग्रन्थ की विशेष उपादेयता तथा प्राचीनता सिद्ध करता है। प्राचीन हस्तलिखित प्रतिलिपियों पर क्रमशः सैकड़ों सहस्रों बार प्रतिलिपि लिखते समय अशुद्धियों का हो जाना स्वाभाविक है, इस ग्रन्थ में कतिपय ऐसा देखा गया है अथवा कहीं कहीं तो उनका अभिप्राय अच्छे प्रकार स्पष्ट न समझा जा सकने के कारण उनको उसी प्रकार लिखा गया था। यद्यपि मैंने कई स्थानों पर उनको शुद्ध करने का यत्न किया है, किन्तु बहुत क्लिष्ट एवं कुछ स्थानों पर अप्रासंगिक होने के कारण उनको उसी प्रकार छोड़ दिया गया है। और दो एक स्थानों पर अक्षर मिटे होने के कारण मूल प्रतिलिपि में भी वह श्लोक अधूरे ही छोड़ दिए गए थे, उनको भी तद्वत् लिखते हुए पुनः पूर्ण कर सकने के सङ्कल्प के साथ छोड़ दिया गया है। यदि किसी विद्वान् महोदय के पास यह ग्रन्थ मौजूद हो, तो आशा है कि वह हमें इस उत्क्षेप से हुई क्षति को पूर्ण कराने में सहायक होंगे। फिर भी बहुत सी अशुद्धियां अभी भी हैं, जिन्हें मैं ठीक नहीं कर पाया हूं। आशा है कि विद्वान् अगले संस्करण में उनके निवारणार्थ मार्ग दर्शक बनेंगे ॥

आभार प्रदर्शन

मुझ जैसा साधनरहित, चिकित्सादि कार्यों में व्यस्त एवं प्रकाशन-कार्य से सर्वथा अनुभवहीन व्यक्ति इतने बड़े कार्य को कभी भी न कर पाता, यदि मुझे इस ग्रंथ के सम्पादन, संशोधनादि कार्यों के लिए गीर्वाण-भारती-क्षेत्र के प्रकाण्ड तथा प्रसिद्ध विद्वान् श्रीयुत पं० युधिष्ठिरजी मीमांसक के सुपुत्र चिरञ्जीव डा० वाचस्पति शास्त्री, साहित्याचार्य, एम० ए०, पी० एच० डी० का हार्दिक एवं पूर्ण सहयोग प्राप्त न होता। श्री डाक्टर साहिब ने अत्यधिक समय, अनथक परिश्रम तथा विशेष योग्यता के बल पर इस कठिन और महान् कार्य में जो मेरी सहायता की है, उसके लिए मेरे पास उनके तथा उनके परिवार के लिए आशीर्वाद से अधिक कोई शब्द नहीं, जगदीश्वर उनके कुल में उत्तरोत्तर वृद्धि देता हुआ उनको श्री मार्तण्डवत् प्रकाशमान् रखें, और वह अपने जीवन में भरपूर सफलताएं प्राप्त करें।

इसी प्रकार लाजपतनगर निवासी श्री पं० ज्ञानचन्दजी शास्त्री एम० ए० ने भी कुछ दो तीन फर्मों के संशोधन कार्य में सहायता की थी, मैं उनका भी आभारी हूं।

इसके अतिरिक्त मेरे ज्येष्ठ भ्राता श्री पं० फकीरचन्द्र जी धम्मी शास्त्री के

आशीर्वाद तथा मेरे अनुज भ्राता पं० पद्मनाभ जी धम्मी शास्त्री, कनिष्ठ भ्राता पं० शिवकुमार धम्मी तथा भ्रातृव्य राजज्योतिषी पं० देवलचन्द्र जी धम्मी तथा पं० सूर्यकुमार जी धम्मी का सौहार्द एवं सहयोग मेरे साथ रहा है। मेरी पुत्री श्रीमती राजरानी शर्मा एम० ए० बी० एड० आयुर्वेदाचार्य, एम० ए० एम० एस० ने भी इस ग्रन्थ की भूमिका-लेखन तथा सम्पादन में मुझे भरसक सहयोग दिया है।

किसी किसी के हाथ से कोई कोई कार्य आरम्भ करा दिया जाए तो वह पूर्णता को प्राप्त होता है। यह श्रेय मेरी शिष्या श्रीमती स्वदेश अरोड़ा एम० ए० संस्कृत को है, जिसने मेरे संग्रहालय में रखी हुई मूल प्रतिलिपि से अपना बहुत समय देते हुए बहुत श्रम पूर्वक मुद्रण कार्य के लिए नई प्रतिलिपि बनाई।

निगमागम विद्याओं के परम श्रद्धालु, धर्ममूर्ति श्री लाला देसराज जी गुप्त तथा उनके सुपुत्र आयुष्मान् श्री शीतल प्रसाद जी गुप्त ने इस ग्रन्थ के मुद्रण तथा प्रकाशन एवं प्राचीन भारतीय वाङ्मय की विद्याओं विशेषतया-वेद, वेदांग तथा तंत्र साहित्य के अभ्यर्चन एवं प्रकाशन के लिए निरन्तर उद्यमशील। परम विदुषी श्रीमती शान्ति देवी जी मल्होत्रा तथा उनके सुपुत्र आदर्शरत्न मल्होत्रा तथा श्री दिव्यरत्न मल्होत्रा ने इस ग्रन्थ की जिल्द बन्दी के सारे खर्चे का भार अपने ऊपर लिया है, उन सब को कोटिशः आशीर्वाद देता हुआ इन सबके लिए आभार प्रदर्शन करता हूं।

नानक चन्द्र शर्मा (धम्मी-भारद्वाज)
(वैद्य कविराज)

॥ ॐ श्री ॥

आकाश-भैरव-कल्प (तंत्रम्)

(अध्यायानुसार संक्षिप्त-हिन्दी-सारांश)

अध्याय १-२

श्री आकाशभैरव कल्प के प्रथम अध्याय में श्री देवी जी सभी विश्व के कल्याण एवं हितार्थ निखिल संसार की मनःकामनाओं और कार्यों में सफलता प्राप्त करने के लिए भगवान् श्री सदाशिव से परम गुह्य विद्या के उपदेश के लिए प्रार्थना करती हैं तथा भगवान् शिव ने प्रत्युत्तर में उन्हें सभी कार्यों के आरम्भ में सर्व प्रथम ब्रह्मरूपी श्री गुरु को नमस्कार करने के बाद एकान्त स्थान में पीठस्थापना करके देव-द्विजादिकों का आशीर्वाद लेकर भूतादि शुद्धि-अङ्गन्यासादि के साथ साथ सभी प्रकार के विघ्न-नाशन एवं सर्वप्रकार के मनोरथों में सिद्धि प्राप्ति के लिए पञ्चाक्षर, द्वयक्षर, एकविंशाक्षर अथवा अट्ठाईसाक्षर मन्त्र से श्री महागणपति की पूजन करने की विधि बतलाई।

साधक पीठासीन-कर्णिकान्तर्गत श्रीगणेश जी की नवशक्तियों "तीव्रा-ज्वालिनी-नन्दा-भोगदा-कामरूपिणी-उग्रा-तेजोवती-सत्या-विघ्नविनाशिनी" जो सभी रक्त वर्ण वाली—रक्त वस्त्र धारण किए हुए एवं सिन्दूरादि आभरणों से विभूषित हैं और वर तथा अभय दान की मुद्रा में हैं, की सुगन्धित पुष्पों द्वारा पूजन करे। अब इनके मध्य में श्री गणेश-महायन्त्र की "बिन्दु-त्रिकोण-षट्कोण-अष्टदल-चतुरस्रादि" के अनुसार यथाविधि कल्पना करके बिन्दु में श्री गणेश तथा त्रिकोण की बाह्य दिशा में श्री लक्ष्मी जी का पूजन करे, तदनन्तर पूर्व में श्री सहित श्रीपति, दक्षिण में अम्बिका सहित अम्बिकापति, पश्चिम में रति सहित काम, तथा उत्तर दिशा में मही सहित महीपति की पूजन करनी चाहिए। इसके अनन्तर षट्कोण में देवता के अग्रभाग से क्रमपूर्वक पूर्वदक्षिणादि प्रदक्षिणा क्रम से ऋद्धयामोद, समृद्धि-प्रमोद कान्ति-सुमुख-मदनावती दुर्मुख, मदद्रवा-अविघ्न, द्राविणी विघ्नकर्तृ की पूजन करके दक्षिण की ओर पार्श्व में वसुधारा-शंखनिधि तथा वाम पार्श्व में वसुमती-पद्मनिधि की पूजन करे। इसके अनन्तर अग्न्यादि चारों कोणों और पूर्वादि चारों दिशाओं में धर्मादिकों तथा अष्टदल-कमल पर पूर्वादि क्रम से यथाविधि ब्राह्मी, माहेश्वरी, कौमारी, वैष्णवी, वाराही, इन्द्राणी, सिद्धचामुण्डा आदि अष्टमातृकाओं तथा अङ्गदेवियों की पूजन करनी चाहिए, और फिर क्रमपूर्वक दिशाओं में लोकपालों की पूजन करते हुए यंत्र के बाहिर की ओर 'अ' से 'क्ष' तक पच्चासों मातृकाओं के अधीशों की अर्चना करे और तदनन्तर यंत्र के बाहिर दो भूचक्रों पर क्रम से श्री गणेश के अस्त्रों पाश और अङ्कुश का

समर्चन करता हुआ गन्ध-माल्य-धूप-दीपादि उपचारों द्वारा चक्रराज की पूजन करे, और फिर श्रीगणेश जी की उनके ध्यानपूर्वक, यथाशक्ति आराधना एवं जप करे, और फिर श्रद्धाभाव से श्री गणेशजी के सोलह (१६) नामों का स्मरण करे। इस प्रकार श्री गणेश की आराधना से विघ्न नहीं होते तथा सभी कार्यों में सफलता मिला करती है।

यहां इस ग्रन्थ में "सुमुखश्चैकदन्तश्च०" इस प्रसिद्ध पौराणिक मन्त्र में "द्वादशैतानि नामानि०" के स्थान पर "षोडशैतानि नामानि०" देते हुए "वक्रतुण्ड-शूर्पकर्ण-हेरम्ब और स्कन्द" चार नाम अधिक दिए हैं, तथा इसके बाद नवकोष्ठात्मक पीठ पर श्री आकाशभैरव की आराधना के आदेश दिए हैं।

अध्याय ३-४

इस अध्याय में श्री शिव ने लोककल्याणार्थ श्री भैरव का आकाशभैरव-आशुगरुड़ तथा शरभेश्वर तीन रूपों में विभक्त होने का वर्णन किया है, इसी प्रकार श्री शरभेश्वर के पुनः तीन रूप शरभ-सालुव तथा पक्षिराज बतलाते हुए श्री शिव ने उन की ऋषि-छन्दादि विनियोग तथा ध्यानादि पूर्वक आराधना करने के लिए उपदेश दिया। तदनन्तर सर्वत्र व्यापक श्री आदिशिव श्री भैरव का ध्यान करते हुए गुरु-मुख से प्राप्त षोडशाक्षर मंत्र का जपाङ्गों के सहित एक लक्ष जप करने का कहा। यहीं श्री भैरव यन्त्र, उसके पूजन की विधि बताते हुए मनोवाञ्छित कामनाओं में सफलता प्राप्ति के लिए पूजनानन्तर वेदोक्त श्री रुद्रसूक्त के पाठ का विधान दिया है। रुद्रसूक्त के तीन बार पाठ करने से देवता प्रसन्न होते हैं, तथा भिन्न भिन्न संख्या में रुद्रसूक्त का जप पाठ कई प्रकार की सिद्धियां एवं मनोरथ पूर्ण करता है। रुद्रसूक्त से शिवलिंग का अभिषेचन (रुद्राभिषेक) चतुर्थ अध्याय में दर्शित विधि द्वारा एकादश बार करने से असाध्य कार्य भी सिद्ध हो जाते हैं।

रुद्राभिषेक के लिए वेद-मन्त्रों द्वारा यथाविधि कलश स्थापना कर के साधक, मातृका बीज सहित पुरुषसूक्त मंत्रों से अङ्गन्यास करे तथा **"इमं में गङ्गे०"** इस वेद मंत्र द्वारा जल पूर्णशङ्ख से अपने शरीर पर मार्जन करे, तदनन्तर श्री रुद्र महादेव का वैदिक ऋचाओं द्वारा आवाहनादि करता हुआ इष्ट-देवता की पूजन करे, तदनन्तर **श्री सूक्त-घृत सूक्त-भूसूक्त-पुरुष सूक्त-ब्रह्म सूक्त-विष्णु सूक्तादिकों** का पाठ करने के पश्चात् **श्री रुद्रपञ्चक** का यथादर्शित विधि से पाठ करके **"सोऽहं" "सोऽहं"** प्राणमंत्र का स्मरण करते हुए श्री गुरुचरण सूक्त से श्री गुरुचरणों को श्रद्धापूर्वक प्रणाम करता हुआ तीन बार श्री गुरुचरणोदक का पान करे।

"अविद्या-मूल-नाशाय जन्म-कर्म-निवृत्तये।
ज्ञान-सौभाग्य-सिद्ध्यर्थं गुरुपादोदकं शुभम्॥"

श्री **गुरुचरणोदक** अज्ञान रूपी अन्धकार को समूल नष्ट करता है, तथा बुद्धि, ज्ञान, सौभाग्य और सर्वत्र सिद्धि-प्रदायक है इस प्रकार श्री भैरव की महदाराधना श्री गुरुमुख से ही शिक्षा ले कर करनी चाहिए, ऐसा आदेश दिया गया है।

अध्याय ५

इस अध्याय में निग्रहानुग्रहादि सभी कार्यों में यथेष्ट सफलता प्राप्त करने के लिये श्री शरभ यंत्रराज का वर्णन किया है। यथाविधि तीन सीधी और तीन तिरछी रेखाएं एक दूसरे को काटती हुई लिख कर रेखाओं के अग्रसिरों पर त्रिशूल बनाएं और उसके कोष्ठों में "धूं कुरु कुरु फट्" क्रम से लिखें। अब इस यंत्र पर आकाश भैरव श्री शरभ का आवाहन करके अपना मनोवांछित अभिप्राय लिख कर इसकी यथाविधि स्थापना कर दें, फलस्वरूप इस यंत्र द्वारा निग्रहानुग्रहाख्य सभी प्रकार के मनोरथों की सिद्धि होती है। तथा भूत-प्रेत-पिशाच और वैरियों का दमन होता है।

इसके अनंतर इसी अध्याय में सप्तकूटात्मक श्री चिन्तामणि मंत्र कथन किया गया है—

क्ष्म्र्यौं

यहां इस श्लोक में "मरीचिकाश्यपि" से अभिप्राय ऋग्वेद की बहुप्रसिद्ध ऋचा "जातवेदसे०" से सम्बन्धित अग्निबीज "र" लिया है, चिन्तामणि महामंत्र तंत्रशास्त्र में विशेष प्रसिद्ध है तथा सभी प्रकार के चिन्तित कामनाओं को पूरा करता है। इस एक रक्षामंत्र के विविध संख्या में जप-प्रयोगादि करने से नाना प्रकार के कार्य सिद्ध होते हैं।

इस के अनन्तर श्री कामराज के चतुष्कूटात्मक प्रसिद्ध बीज "क्लीं" तथा महामाया का चतुष्कूटात्मक बहुप्रसिद्ध बीज "ह्रीं" का वर्णन किया है, जिनके स्वतन्त्र रूप में या मंत्र यंत्रों से युक्त या सम्पुटित करके यथोचित संख्या में जपानुष्ठानादि करने से नाना प्रकार के कार्यों में सफलता प्राप्त होती है।

तदनन्तर सभी प्रकार की समृद्धि देने वाला एवं राज या राजकार्यों में जय, यश, सिद्धि तथा समृद्धि देने वाला चतुष्कूटात्मक लक्ष्मी बीज "स्त्रैं"[2] का वर्णन है। इसी प्रकार द्रावण बीज "सां" जो पत्थर हृदयों को भी द्रवित कर देता है तथा सभी प्रकार की व्याधि एवं रोग निवारक भगवान् सूर्य के चतुष्कूटात्मक प्रसिद्ध "ह्रां" बीज का भी वर्णन किया है, जिस के दो लक्ष जप से कुष्ठ, तीन लक्ष जप से राज-यक्ष्मा और चार लक्ष जप से सभी प्रकार के भयंकर तथा असाध्य रोग नष्ट हो जाते हैं।

---

१. चिन्तामणि मंत्र को कुछ टीकाकारों ने "क्ष्म्र्यौं" और कुछ ने क्ष्म्र्यीं, कहीं कहीं क्ष्म्र्यैं—क्ष्म्र्यां भी लिया गया है।

तंत्रसार संग्रह में ब्रह्ममज्जा विषाग्नित्वक् सद्यान्तार्घीश बिन्दुमान्।
पावक कांक्षितानर्थान् दद्याच्चिन्तामणिर्यथा ॥

तथा तत्रसार में अग्नि: संवर्तकादित्यचानिलो षष्ठ विन्दुमत्।
चिन्तामणिरिति ख्यातं बीजं सर्वसमृद्धिदम् ॥

२. "श्रीं"

(अध्याय ६-७-८-९-१०)

छठे अध्याय में **चित्रमाला नाम** का श्री आकाशभैरव का प्रसिद्ध मंत्र दिया गया है, जिसे गुरुस्मरण पूर्वक एकाग्रमन से सर्वार्थसिद्धि के लिए एक सौ बार पढ़ने का विधान है और दूसरे साधारण कार्यों में सफलता तथा विजय प्राप्ति के लिए केवल ३ बार ही पाठ करना पर्याप्त होता है।

सातवें अध्याय में वशीकरण एवं आकर्षण कार्यों में सिद्धि के लिए देवता के ध्यान सहित विधि बतलाई गई है। वशीकरणादि कार्यों में मंत्रराज को "क्लीं" बीज से एवं आकर्षण कार्यों में "ग्रां" बीज से सम्पुटित कर के साध्यनामाक्षर सहित मंत्र का स्मरण करना चाहिये, ऐसा विधान है।

आठवें अध्याय में मोहन तथा द्रावण कार्यों के लिए विशेष विधि का उपदेश दिया गया है। श्री आकाश भैरव के विशेष प्रकार के ध्यान पूर्वक उसके मंत्रराज को "ह्रीं" बीज से सम्पुटित करके "साध्यं विमोहय २ स्वाहा" इस प्रकार अपने मनोरथात्मक शब्दों सहित स्मरण करें, और द्रावण कार्यों में "साध्यं द्रावय द्रावय स्वाहा" शब्दयुक्त मंत्रराज का अनुष्ठान करना चाहिए, इस प्रकार क्रिया करने से कामवश आकर्षित हुई स्त्रियां सम्मोहित होकर इस तरह द्रवीभूत हो जाती हैं, जिस तरह कि अग्नि के पास रखा हुआ घृत।

नौवें अध्याय के अनुसार स्तंभन-विद्वेषादि कार्यों में श्री आकाशभैरव के विशेष रूप का ध्यान करते हुए स्तंभन के लिए "लं" तथा द्वेषकार्यों में 'हुं' बीज से सम्पुटित करके स्वाहान्त मंत्रराज का पुरश्चरण करने का विधान है—इससे दश दिनों के अन्दर ही वैरी पक्ष आपस में लड़ पड़ते हैं।

शत्रु-निग्रह एवं उच्चाटन कार्यों में श्री आकाशभैरव के दशमाध्याय में दिये गये ध्यान के अनुसार रूप का स्मरण करते हुए क्रम से "यं" तथा हुं इन बीज मंत्रों से महामंत्र को सम्पुटित करके यथाविधि ५०० बार नित्य दस रात्रि तक प्रयोग करने का उपदेश दिया है, इस से यथेष्ट फल प्राप्त होता है।

(अध्याय ११)

इस अध्याय में **सारस्वत मंत्र** का वर्णन किया है, जिसके प्रयोग से जिह्वा पर साक्षात् सरस्वती बैठती है तथा गंगाप्रवाहवत् मुख से वाणी का निःसरण होता है, इस विद्या के विधिवत् प्रयोग से भोग और मोक्ष दोनों की प्राप्ति होती है।

वाणी और वाक्सिद्धि के लिए श्री आकाशभैरव महामंत्र को 'वं' बीज से सम्पुटित कर के अन्त में स्वाहा शब्द लगाया जाए तथा चिन्तितार्थ प्राप्ति के लिए चिन्तामणिमंत्र, मोक्ष सिद्धि के लिए 'ओं' बीज और समृद्धि के लिए श्रीं बीज से सम्पुटित करना चाहिए। आरोग्य-प्राप्ति के लिए "घृणि" बीज, रोगनाशन के लिए "स्वौं" (इं) तथा विषनाशन के लिए ठं बीज-सम्पुटित स्वाहान्त मंत्र का जप किया जाए। इस तरह साधक थोड़े प्रयास से मनोवांच्छित फल प्राप्त कर सकता है।

(अध्याय १२)

इस अध्याय में **आशुताक्ष्यं मंत्र** की विधि बताई गई है, जिसके प्रयोग से सकल जगम तथा अनंगम विष तथा विषजनित उपद्रव दूर होते हैं तथा आवश्यकता पड़ने पर इसे शत्रुनिग्रह के लिए भी प्रयोग किया जा सकता है। विनियोग के लिए मंत्र के ऋषि—छन्दादिकों का वर्णन करते हुए आशुताक्ष्यं का ध्यान एवं मंत्र का उपदेश दिया गया है। यहीं प्रयोग और हवनविधि बताते हुए पूजन और धारणादि के लिए आशुताक्ष्यं यंत्र का विधान दिया है जिससे सर्पादि का भय नहीं होता तथा सभी प्रकार से सिद्धि और विजय की प्राप्ति होती है।

(अध्याय १३)

इस अध्याय में कामना भेद से यथानिर्दिष्ट बीजों से सम्पुटित कर के आशुगरुड़ के प्रयोग कहे गए हैं। इसके अनन्तर सम्मोहन—महासिद्धिकर आकर्षण यंत्र—वशीकरण यंत्र—पवनाग्निस्तंभनकर—स्तंभन—स्तोभन—भाषण—विद्वेषण—सर्वदण्डकारण—सर्वसंक्रामणसिद्धिप्रद—विजयकर—सर्पादिजंगम-विषनाशन—शत्रु-मारण तथा अतुल-सौभाग्यदायक—धनप्रद—सर्ववशीकर एवं सत्पुत्र-प्रदायक कई प्रकार के यंत्र लिखने तथा उनकी प्रयोगविधि का वर्णन किया गया है।

(अध्याय १४)

इस अध्याय में **आशुताक्ष्यं कवच** तथा उस के जप-पाठ का विधान दिखलाया गया है। इससे कुलवृद्धि एवं पुत्रप्राप्ति होती है। श्री आशुताक्ष्यं का अतिगुप्त यंत्र जो सभी प्रकार की सिद्धि देने वाला है तथा जिसके धारणादि से मृतवत्सा जीवित पुत्रा—बन्ध्या सन्तानयुक्त एवं कन्या ही जन्मने वाली के पुत्र होता है, का उपदेश दिया गया है। शुक्रवार से ३ दिन तक १० बार नित्य कवच पाठ तथा भल्लातक अथवा देव-सर्षप से हवनादि करना चाहिए एवं अभिषेकादि क्रिया करके एक बार फिर जल में डुबकी लगवा कर रक्षाबंधन विधान किया जाय।

(अध्याय १५)

इस अध्याय में **शिष्याचार विधि** का उपदेश है। किस प्रकार के व्यक्ति दीक्षा लेने के योग्य नहीं है, और यदि प्रमादवश या किसी भूल से कभी किसी अग्राह्यशिष्य को दीक्षा दी गई है अथवा शिष्य की बुद्धि में गुरु या विद्या के प्रति कोई विरोध या विकृति उत्पन्न होने से हानि का संशय हो रहा है तो उस शिष्य के विद्रावण के लिए श्री शिव ने विशेष विधि की मंत्रक्रिया बताई है। इसके अतिरिक्त दीक्षाविधि, गुरु ही आराध्य देव हैं—गुरु ही परम ज्योति हैं, गुरु ही सर्वोत्तरोत्तर हैं, इत्यादि गुरु की महानता और महिमा का वर्णन किया है। गुरु के आसन—गुरु के सामने ऊंचा या मुकाबले पर अथवा गुरुयान पर नहीं बैठना चाहिए—इत्यादि बहुत से शिक्षाएं दी हैं। अपने सर्वस्व समेत अपने आपको सदैव गुरु का ही समझना चाहिए। निग्रहानुग्रहात्मक सभी अनुष्ठान-क्रियाओं में सदैव श्री गुरु को अपने साथ ही समझना चाहिए तथा निर्भीक होकर सभी क्रियाएं करनी चाहिएं।

(अध्याय १६)

श्री देवी ने श्री शिव से समस्त जन्तुओं के कष्ट-विनाशन, रक्षा एवं लोकोपकार की दृष्टि से सभी मंत्रों का साररूप महामंत्र जानने की इच्छा प्रकट की इस पर श्री शिव ने सभी प्रकार से रक्षा करने वाला, भोग और मोक्ष को देने वाला, सभी प्रकार के पाप फल का निवारक, अपस्मारादि सभी प्रकार के कठिन मानसिक रोगों को नष्ट करने वाला, ज्वर-रोग-अपमृत्यु आदि नाना प्रकार के कष्टों को हरने वाला तथा सर्व शत्रुकुलविनाशक **श्री शरभेश्वर के महामंत्र** का उपदेश दिया। श्री शरभेश्वर महामन्त्र के कालाग्निरुद्र ऋषि हैं, जगती छन्द और देवता स्वयं भगवान् शरभेश्वर हैं, मंत्र का बीज "खं" तथा उसकी शक्ति "स्वाहा" रूपिणी है तथा इसका प्रयोग मनोवांछित सभी कार्यों की सिद्धि के लिए किया जाता है। इस प्रकार विनियोग करने के बाद साधक '४२' अक्षर वाले इस महामंत्र के क्रमपूर्वक ३-२-१२-६-७-६ अक्षरों से करन्यास तथा हृदयादि न्यास करने के अनन्तर देवता के साथ एक भावना युक्त तथा श्री शरभेश्वर को अग्निरूप एवं तेजोरूप समझते हुए मंत्र वर्णों से निर्दिष्ट शरीरांगों पर न्यासकरे। अब श्री शरभेश्वर का यथोक्त दिव्य ध्यान करते हुए मूलमन्त्र का यथोक्तविधि से जप करे (मंत्रोद्धार मूल ग्रन्थ के ३२ पृष्ठ पर कर दिया गया है)। इस विधि से इस मन्त्र के ४२००० जप से सिद्धि हो जाती है, जपान्त में मनोरथानुसार निर्दिष्ट होमद्रव्यों से दशांश तर्पण तथा ब्राह्मण-भोजनादि अवश्य करना चाहिए, तथा हवन के बाद तीन बार इस से अगले १७ अध्याय में बतलाये गये स्तोत्र सहित श्री शरभेशाष्टक का पाठ करने से मनोवांछित कार्य सिद्ध होते हैं।

तदनन्तर श्री **शरभेश्वर महायन्त्र** विधि बतलाई गई है, जिसके धारण करने से साधक मनोभीष्ट कार्यों में सिद्धि-समृद्धि-सौभाग्य-सर्वत्रविजय और सर्वसम्पत्ति आदि को प्राप्त कर सकता है, और सभी प्रकार के पाप और बाधाओं का निवारण होता है, नाना प्रकार के कठिन रोग, न समझे जा सकने वाले रोग, क्षुद्र रोग तथा भूत-पिशाचादादिकों के प्रकोपों का शमन होता है।

यहीं **शरभेश्वर चक्र** का विधान दिया है, छ और सात सीधी और तिरछी रेखाएं खेंच कर रेखाओं के अग्रभाग पर त्रिशूल बनाए और शूल के अग्रभाग पर साध्य का नाम लिख कर यंत्र के बाहिर गोलाकार चक्र में "**ओं ह्रीं**" शब्द लिखे कोष्ठों में मन्त्राक्षर लिखे—यह यंत्र सभी प्रकार से विजयादि देने वाला है।

(अध्याय १७)

इस अध्याय में श्री **शरभेश्वर का ध्यान** वर्णन करते हुए स्तोत्र-सहित श्री शरभेश्वराष्टक तथा इस स्तोत्र के पाठ फलादि का वर्णन किया है, इसके नित्य पाठ से सभी प्रकार की कामनाओं को प्राप्त करते हुए अन्त में शिवलोक की प्राप्ति होती है, साधक की चोर, अग्नि, व्याघ्र, हाथी आदि हिंसक जीवों तथा भूत, पिशाच

राक्षसादिकों के उपद्रव से रक्षा होती है, सभी पापों से निवृत्ति हो कर राजयक्ष्मादि नाना प्रकार के कठिन रोगों से छुटकारा मिलता है ।

(अध्याय १८)

इस अध्याय में श्री शरभेश्वर के माला-मंत्र पर प्रकाश डाला गया है, जिस के स्मरण-मात्र से सभी प्रकार की सिद्धियां साधक के करस्थ होती है ।।

वश्याकर्षणादि कार्यों में श्री शरभेश्वर का किस प्रकार ध्यान किया जाय, यह बताते हुए प्रथम श्लोक में आकर्षण मंत्र की विधि बताई गई हैं, जिस के द्वारा सभी संसार का मोहन, योषिताओं का आकर्षण और वशीकरण, साम्राज्य और लक्ष्मी की प्राप्ति एवं शत्रुओं पर विजय होती है ।।

दूसरे श्लोक में आकर्षण कार्यों के लिये अन्य यंत्र बनाने का विधान दिया गया है, जिस के द्वारा अदृष्ट स्त्री भी साधक के पास खिंची आती है और उसका वशीकरण होता है ।।

तदनन्तर स्तंभन-विद्वेषणादि कार्यों में श्री शरभेश्वर का किस प्रकार ध्यान करके प्रयोगारंभ किया जाए, बतलाते हुए चतुर्थ श्लोक में स्तंभन-यंत्र लिखने का रहस्य बताया गया है, जिसके प्रयोग से शत्रुओं की जिव्हा, दृष्टि, कर्ण, हनु, मति, गति आदि का स्तंभन होता है ।।

इसी प्रकार पञ्चम श्लोक में विद्वेषण यंत्र की विधि बताई गई है जिस के प्रभाव से दो घनिष्ठ मित्र भी एक दूसरे के जीवन के शत्रु बन जाते हैं ।।

मारणोच्चाटनादि कार्यों में श्री शरभेश्वर का स्मरण किस रूप में करना चाहिए, यह बतलाते हुए सातवें श्लोक में सभी शत्रुओं के उच्चाटन के लिये यंत्र विधि वर्णन की गई है । इससे शत्रु भूत, रोग, पिशाचादि-ग्रह, कलहादि विविध कारणों से आक्रांत और परेशान हो कर उच्चाट मन से भाग जाता है ।

आठवें श्लोक में श्री शिव ने सर्वसंहारातमक मारण-यंत्र बनाने की विधि बताई है, यंत्र में साध्य का नाम लिख कर यथाविधि प्रयोग करने से यथेष्ट फल होता है ।

यंत्र लिखते समय एवं प्रयोग-काल में नवम श्लोकोक्त श्री शरभेश्वर अस्त्र विद्या (श्री शरभेश्वर गायत्री) का पाठ करना चाहिये । श्री शरभास्त्र-विद्या के प्रभाव से साधक को देवता और राक्षस तक भी नहीं देख पाते साधारण मनुष्यों और पिशाचादिकों का तो कहना ही क्या है ।।

विषवृक्ष प्रयोग

रात्रि काल में विषवृक्ष के काष्ठ और पत्रादिक पर श्लोक १५ के अनुसार साध्य नाम-युक्त मंत्र लिख कर यंत्र पर साध्य के प्राण प्रतिष्ठापित करे, तथा श्री शरभेश्वर यंत्र का १००८ जप करके बलिपूर्वक दक्षिण दिशा में (श्मशानादि में) गाड़ दे, तदनन्तर स्नान कर के फिर १००८ बार जप करे, इस प्रयोग से निःसंदेह शत्रुओं का मरण होता है ।।

सूर्य ग्रहण से १० दिन पहिले शत्रु की यथापूर्व प्रतिमा बना कर प्राण प्रतिष्ठा कर लें और उसे सूर्यमण्डल में भावना-दृष्टि से स्थित मनन करते हुए श्री शरभेश्वर-मंत्र का यथोक्त विधि से १००८ पाठ नित्य करें, १० दिनों के बाद सूर्यग्रहण काल में शत्रु को अधोमुख और कृष्ण-वर्ण से आक्रान्त समझते हुए श्री शरभेश्वर मंत्र का १००८ बार जप करें, तथा जपांत में सूर्य को तीन बार अर्घ प्रदान करे, इस विधि से उसी दिन शत्रु मर जाता है ।।

श्लोक २२ के अनुसार इसी प्रकार शत्रु का नाम लेकर शरभेश्वर मंत्र का १०० बार दक्षिणाभिमुख होकर घृत-युक्त हवन करने से भी शत्रु दिनावसान तक विनाश को प्राप्त होता है ।

२३वें श्लोक में श्री शरभेश्वर के अन्य सिद्ध यंत्र का भी वर्णन है तथा २४वें श्लोक में सभी प्रकार की रक्षा, सौभाग्य-वर्द्धन और सर्वत्र विजय प्राप्ति के लिये श्री शरभ का विशेष मंत्र दिया गया है—जिसे अथर्वण विद्याओं से सम्बन्धित कहा गया है—और जिसे यंत्र कार्यों में भी प्रयोग किया जाता है ।

२७वें श्लोक में शत्रुकृत तंत्राभिचार एवं क्षुद्रों से संरक्षण एवं तज्जात दुष्टफल-निवारण के लिये यंत्र विधि बतलाई गई है ।

(अध्याय १९)

निग्रह कार्य कहां करना चाहिये या कहां नहीं करना चाहिये, इस अध्याय में श्री शिव ने बहुत सुन्दर शब्दों में वर्णन किया है ।

जो व्यक्ति अपने तथा पराये दोषों को गुप्त रखते हैं ऐसे उत्तम पुरुष के लिये निग्रह के लिये मन में कल्पना तक नहीं करना चाहिये । इसी प्रकार द्रव्य के लोभ अथवा दूषण के भय से किसी भी वधू के लिये निग्रह-कार्य निन्दनीय है, एवं गुरु, गुरु पुत्र, वन्द्य, दीक्षित, सत्यवादी, सन्यासी, योगी अथवा व्रतानुष्ठानादि-निष्ठ व्यक्ति के लिये मारण कर्म कदापि नहीं करना चाहिए ।

अत्यन्त दु:खी, भयभीत, क्रोधावेश से या राजा की आज्ञा से यदि कोई किसी को गालीगलोचादि या कभी दण्ड देता है या तिरस्कार करता है, किन्तु बाद में अपनी गलती या मजबूरी का अनुभव करते हुए क्षमा याचना कर लेता है तो ऐसे व्यक्ति के विरुद्ध भी निग्रह कार्य कदापि न किया जाय, अन्यथा श्री शरभेश्वर विपरीत फल भी तत्काल देते हैं। इस प्रकार बहुत सी शिक्षा दी हैं ।।

(अध्याय २०)

इस अध्याय में विविध प्रकार की कामनाओं में सिद्धि प्राप्त करने के लिये होमार्थ विविध प्रकार के हवन-द्रव्य, समिधादि लेने का विधान दिया है, स्थण्डिल विधि का भी निर्देश है। इस प्रकार पिशाचादि निवारण, उन्माद, ताप, ज्वरशूलादि से निवृत्ति, सर्पापत्ति-निवारण, चातुर्थिक ज्वर शान्ति, आयु-आरोग्य-प्राप्ति, बुद्धिवर्द्धन रोगनिवारण, मैत्रीकरण, अनन्त-धन-प्राप्ति, पुत्रकामना, प्रासाद-कामना, वशीकरण

कार्य, आकर्षण-कर्म, विद्वेषण-कर्म, स्तंभन-कर्म, उच्चाटन-कर्म, संहार-कर्म, शत्रुओं का उन्मादीकरण एवं उन्माद विमुक्ति, वाक्‌सिद्धि, धन-प्राप्ति, धान्य-वर्द्धन, शाप-निवारण, भाग्य-सम्वर्द्धन, द्रव्यलाभ, शक्ति, पुष्टि, रूप, कामशक्ति आदि की प्राप्ति, अभीष्ट-प्राप्ति, प्रसन्नता-प्राप्ति तथा शत्रु-क्षय कार्यों के लिए विविध प्रकार की होम-विधि बताई गई है तथा श्री सालुवेश यंत्र का विवरण देते हुए कुछ सिद्ध प्रयोग भी दिये गए हैं, जिनके विधिवत् करने से शत्रु सद्यः यमपुरी में चला जाता है ।।

(अध्याय २१)

निग्रह-कार्यों में श्री सालुवेश का ध्यान वर्णन करते हुए शत्रुओं को पीड़ित करने के लिए पुत्तलिका विधि बताई गई है । शत्रु जहां भूमि पर पांव धरे, वहां से थोड़ी मृत्तिका उठा लें, और उसमें चतुष्पथ (चौराहे) की मिट्टी मिला कर शत्रु की पुत्तली (प्रतिमा) बनाएं । अब इस पुत्तली में शत्रु के प्राण यथाविधि प्राण-प्रतिष्ठा मंत्रों से स्थापित करके उसे एक सौ बार प्राण-प्रतिष्ठा मंत्र से ही अभिमंत्रित कर लें, अब इस पर १००० बार श्री शरभेश्वर-मंत्र पढ़ कर मूलमंत्र से ही उस मूर्ति के जिस जिस अङ्ग में सूई आदि नोकदार कोई वस्तु चुभोकर बींध दिया जाए तो उस व्यक्ति के उस अङ्ग में तत्क्षण तीव्र पीड़ा होती है । और यदि उस पुत्तली को अग्नि ताप दिया जाए या अग्नि के निकट चूल्हा आदि में दबा दिया जाए तो उक्त शत्रु दाह-ज्वर से तत्काल पीड़ित होता है । और यदि उसी पुत्तलिका को त्रिकुटा और अर्कक्षार सहित अग्नि में जला दिया जाए तो शत्रु की तत्काल मृत्यु होती है ।

इस प्रकार श्लोक ४ में बतलाए गए अन्य पुत्तलिका विधान में शत्रु सपरिवार पीड़ाओं से आक्रान्त हो जाता है । पांचवें श्लोक में शत्रुमारण के लिए एक और पुत्तलिका विधान भी दिया है । इसी तरह छठे सातवें श्लोक में भी शत्रुनाशन के लिए प्रतिमा विधियां दी है आठवें श्लोक में किसी शत्रु-स्त्री को पीड़ित करने तथा नौवें श्लोक में आवश्यकता समझने पर उसके मारण कर्म के लिए भी विधि दी गई है ।

(अध्याय २२)

इस अध्याय में रक्षाभिषेक विधि का विशेष वर्णन किया गया है चतुरस्र भूमि को गोमय से लिप्त करके निर्दिष्ट द्रव्यों से नव-कोष्ठ बनाएं, तथा उसके मध्य कोष्ठ में एक वृत्ताकार लिख कर उसके मध्य में चतुरस्र बनाएं, अब उसके प्रत्येक कोष्ठ में यथाविधि पुष्पादि स्थापन करके उन पर नौ कुंभ रखें, प्रत्येक कुंभ पर नये दुपट्टे रख कर लाल धागे से लपेट दें अब इन को धूप-दीप प्रदर्शन तथा गन्ध पुष्पादि से अलंकृत कर के घड़ों में पानी भर दें अब इन घड़ों में जिस कामना के लिए अभिषेक कार्य करना है, उसके अनुसार श्लोक ६-७ में निर्दिष्ट रत्न डाल दिए जाएं । उन कुंभों पर दूर्वा और आम के पत्ते रखकर उस पर अलंकारों सहित नारियल रखकर उसे देवता के वाहन-रूप में कल्पना करें उस पर पुष्पासनादि रख कर १००८ बार श्री शरभेश्वर मंत्र का जप करें । अब स्नानादि से निवृत्ति के पश्चात् यजमान पूर्वाभिमुख

होकर बैठे तथा आचार्य उत्तर मुख होकर तीन दिन तक यथाविधि अभिषेक-कर्म करे इससे क्षुद्र रोगों से शीघ्र ही मुक्ति हो जाती है। पांच बार अभिषेक कार्य करने से वात रोग, पन्द्रह दिन तक अभिषेक कार्य करने से वात-शूल नष्ट हो जाते हैं, सर्व रोगों के नाशन के लिए १ मास तक, असाध्य शिरोरोगों के लिए भी १ मास तक— बिलासी पिशाचादिकों की पीड़ा निवारण के लिए ३ मास तक अभिषेक करना चाहिए इसी प्रकार राजयक्ष्मा तथा अपस्मारादि कठिन रोगों के लिए १ वर्ष तक रुद्राभिषेक करना चाहिए, इस से सब रोग निश्चय ही ठीक हो जाते हैं।

इसी अध्याय में अभिषेक कर्म द्वारा **वन्ध्या चिकित्सा** भी कही गई है। ऋतुस्नाता शुद्ध तथा स्वस्थ वधू को दस दिन—काक वन्ध्या को बारह दिन—मृतवत्सा को सोलह दिन तक अभिषिञ्चित करके यथानिर्दिष्ट धातु या भूर्जपत्र पर यंत्र लिखें अब इस यन्त्र की प्राण-प्रतिष्ठा करा के धारण करादें, इस प्रकार यथाविधि करवाने से अवश्य ही सन्तान होती है।

कार्त्तिक—ज्येष्ठ—भाद्रपद—चैत्र—फाल्गुन एवं मार्गशीर्ष में रक्षाभिषेक आरम्भ करने का विधान है, शेष महीनों में इसका आरंभ शुभ फलदायक नहीं होता।

अभिषेक विधि से गर्भ में पुत्र कन्या का भी ज्ञान हो सकता है।

(अध्याय २३)

इस अध्याय में **मनुष्य-मात्र के कष्ट निवारण,** सभी प्रकार की परेशानियों से मुक्ति तथा अपना मनोबल बढ़ाने, शत्रु-पक्ष द्वारा देश पर आक्रमण-जात संकट के मोचन एवं शत्रु-कृत नानाभिचार-कर्मादिकों से उत्पन्न ज्वरादि विविध रोग एवं महामारी आदि रोगों के शमन के लिए **बलि-विधान** दिया गया है।

ज्वरादि रोगों के शमन के लिए एक नया मिट्टी का बर्तन ले कर उसमें जल भर दें, अब उस पर कपास की जड़ और बीज, सैंधा नमक तथा नीम के पत्ते रखकर देव-भाव से इसे ३ बार प्रणाम करें, तथा यथाविधि पूजन करके तोरणमन्दिर में ले जाएं इसके बाद सायंकाल होने पर चौराहे (चतुष्पथ) में रख दें, इस प्रकार तीन सायंकाल क्रिया करने से रोगी ज्वरमुक्त हो जाता है।

इसी प्रकार और भी बहुत से बलि-विधान दिए गए हैं, जिनको विधिवत् करने से भूत, प्रेत, पिशाचादि ग्रहों के प्रकोप का निवारण होता है तथा शत्रु द्वारा प्रयोग की गई घोर क्रियाओं द्वारा जनित दुष्ट प्रभाव नष्ट होकर कष्ट और आपत्तियों से शान्ति मिलती है, और शत्रु-पक्ष का दमन होता है।

इसी अध्याय में एक विशेष बलिविधान भी है, जिसमें देवता स्वयं प्रत्यक्ष होकर बलि ग्रहण करते हैं।

इसके अतिरिक्त महारोग, ज्वर, क्षुद्र, भूत, दुष्कृति आदि निवारण के लिए बलिदान की विधि भी हैं। तथा अध्यायान्त में बलि कर्म के लिए श्मशानरुद्र का विशेष मन्त्र भी दिया है, जिसके स्मरण से बलिकर्मादि विविध क्रियाओं में अपनी भी सभी प्रकार से **रक्षा होती है।**

(अध्याय २४)

इस अध्याय में साधक के लिए सदाचार-विधि का वर्णन किया गया है। साधक ब्राह्म मुहूर्त में उठकर अपने गुरुदेव को प्रणाम करके **शरभेशाष्टक** स्तोत्र का ३ बार मन में स्मरण करें, फिर श्रीगणेश और श्रीशरभेश्वर का ध्यान करते हुए यथोक्त विधान से स्नान—संध्या—तर्पणादि से निवृत्त होकर एक सौ आठ या बयालीस बार श्री शरभेश्वर मंत्र का जप करे। अब इसके अनन्तर नदीतट, देवालय या निर्जन किन्तु रम्य स्थान में सुखासन पर आसीन होकर श्री शिवादि को प्रणाम कर के भूतादि शुद्धि पूर्वक ४२००० मूलमंत्र का जप करे, इस प्रकार दशांश विधि से हवन—तर्पण—मार्जन—ब्राह्मण-भोजनादि करना चाहिए। हवन, तर्पण, मार्जन, ब्राह्मण भोजनादि के बिना मंत्र फलदायक नहीं होते। अपितु इस से मनोवाञ्छित कार्य शीघ्र सिद्ध होते हैं, संग्राम में शत्रुओं पर विजय होती है, दुर्भाग्य सौभाग्य में परिवर्तित हो जाता है, अनावृष्टि से महावृष्टि आदि कई प्रकार के असाध्य कार्य सिद्ध हो जाते हैं। इस प्रकार की पुरश्चर्या विशेष संख्या में करने से विविध प्रकार के मनोरथ प्राप्त होते हैं तथा अतुल सिद्धि मिलती है, इस प्रकार सविस्तर विवरण दिया गया है। एवं सूर्य-चन्द्रग्रहणादि काल में इसके पुरश्चरण से विशेष फल होने का संकेत दिया गया है।

तदुपरान्त पुरश्चरण क्रिया के साथ साथ कुछ विशेष वैदिक ऋचाओं के प्रयोग द्वारा शीघ्र विविध प्रकार के मनोरथ सिद्धि के लिए सहज उपाय बतलाए गए है।

यथा—व्यक्ति-विशेष से अपेक्षित धन प्राप्ति के लिए "**किं ते कृण्वन्ति कीकटेषु०** ऋचा का जप-पाठ किया जाए तो वह व्यक्ति बिना मांगे ही स्वयं आकर यथेच्छित धन दे जाता है।

निर्जन वन या स्थान में अथवा भयावह जगह में राजा, चौर, डाकू अथवा शत्रु आदि की ओर से आई हुई आपत्ति के निवारण के लिए "**अभिव्ययस्व खदिरस्य०**" इस ऋचा का जप किया जाए तो सभी तरह के भय से साधक को मुक्ति मिलती है।

युद्ध, संग्राम, मल्लादि-युद्ध तथा विवादादिकों में जब परेशानियां अधिक हों और घबराहट बढ़ रही हो तो "**बलं धेहि०**" इस ऋचा का स्मरण करने से मनोबल और उद्यम सहित शक्ति बढ़कर प्रत्यक्ष विजय होती है।

शत्रु के साथ महान् युद्ध एवं शत्रु सेना से घिर जाने पर "वयः सुपर्णाः०" इस ऋचा का १०८ बार पाठ करें तो जिस प्रकार सूर्योदय होते ही अन्धकार नष्ट ही जाता है ठीक इसी प्रकार शत्रु के पराक्रम को जीत कर युद्ध को जीत लिया जाता है।

जल में डूब गए व्यक्ति की रक्षा एवं जलापत्ति शमन के लिए '**उदगादित्य०** :इस ऋचा का स्मरण करना चाहिये, इससे भयंकर मगरमच्छादिकों से युक्त अथवा

दुर्गम तथा भयानक नदी में से भी सुख पूर्वक तैर कर पार हो जाता है अथवा साधक तैर कर पार हो सकता है।

सुख-प्रसव के लिए **"विजहीष्व०"** इस सूक्त से एक सौ बार अभिमंत्रित तैल यदि स्त्री को पान कराया जाए तो सुख पूर्वक बच्चा होता है और यदि कोई स्त्री इस प्रकार के अभिमंत्रित तैल को गर्भ के प्रथम पांचवें तीसरे तथा सप्तम मास में भी पी ले तो उसका तत्क्षण गर्भस्राव या गर्भपात हो जाता है।

यदि आपत्ति काल में कहीं वन में निवास करना पड़े तो **"अयमस्मान् वनस्पति.०"** इस ऋचा के नित्य पाठ से हिंसक तथा अनिष्ट कर जीव कष्ट नहीं दे सकते तथा वनाधीश उसकी दिन रात स्वयं रक्षा करता है।

वन्ध्या स्त्री अथवा ऐसी स्त्री जो कन्याओं को ही जन्म देती है, को **"विष्णु-र्योनिं कल्पयतु०"** इस ऋचा से सहस्रवार अभिमंत्रित घृत १ मास तक पान कराया जाए, तो वन्ध्या सन्तान युक्त तथा कन्या जन्मने वाली के निश्चय पुत्र होता है।

जब बार बार बनते हुए कार्यों में विघ्न पड़ कर रुकावटें परेशान कर रही हों तो **"गणानां त्वा०"** इस ऋचा के जप से सभी प्रकार के विघ्न शान्त हो जाते है।

आत्म संरक्षण के लिए निम्न ऋचा से रक्षा-बन्धन तैयार किया जाए—

"बृहत्साम क्षत्रभृद्वृद्ध वृष्णियं त्रिष्टुभौजा शुभितमुग्रवीरम् ।
इन्द्रस्तोमेन पञ्चदशेन मध्यमिदं वातेन सगरेण रक्ष ।।

तैत्तिरीय सं० ४-४-१२

रक्त वर्ण के सूत को यथाविधि अभिमंत्रित करते हुए ३-४-७ अथवा ११ गांठें (ग्रन्थियां) रक्षाविधि के अनुसार डालकर रक्षासूत्र को शिर में धारण करने से यक्ष-गंधर्व-राक्षसादि भी भयभीत होकर भाग जाते है, भूत-प्रेत-पिशाचादिक ग्रहों का तो कहना ही क्या; दुष्ट हिंसक जानवरों तथा जंगमादि सब विषैले एवं दुःखदाई जन्तुओं से भी रक्षा होती है—अध्यायान्त में शत्रुओं पर विजय पाने एवं शत्रुसंहार के लिए विशेष प्रकार का यंत्र, प्रयोग विधि सहित बतलाया गया है। श्री शिव का कथन है, कि यह सब क्रियाएं गुरुमुख द्वारा जानकर ही करने से सिद्धि होती है, अन्यथा नहीं।

अध्याय २५-२६-२७-२८

२५वें अध्याय में माया-मंत्र तथा उसका पूजन-यंत्र, प्रयोगविधि के सहित दिया गया है, इस के विधिवत् पुरश्चरण से साधक मायावी हो जाता है, युद्धकाल में योद्धाओं को विजय दिलाने वाले इस यन्त्र के प्रभाव से शत्रु-पक्ष को हाथ पांव हिलाने की भी सूझ बूझ नहीं रहती।

२६वें अध्याय में श्री आकाश-भैरव के दिव्य यंत्र तथा उसकी सांगोपांग पूजन तथा पुरश्चरण की विधि दी गई है, जो सभी प्रकार से सिद्धि देने वाली, भोग-मोक्षप्रद तथा शत्रु, भूत, पिशाचादिकों को विशेषतया नष्ट करती है।

२७वें अध्याय में "अ" से "क्ष" तक मातृका अक्षर, उनके अधिष्ठातृ देवता,

रूप तथा गुणादि का विशेष महत्व, जपफलादि अति स्पष्ट एवं विज्ञानपूर्ण शब्दों के साथ वर्णन किया गया है। भगवान् शिव का कथन है कि मनोवाञ्छित कार्यों में सिद्धि के लिए साधक-श्रेष्ठ को यन्त्र मन्त्र और तंत्र तीनों क्रियाओं का प्रयोग करना चाहिए। इसी प्रकार पचास मातृका-वर्णों से युक्त श्री शरभेश मंत्र के पुरश्चरण का फलसहित वर्णन किया गया है। सौभाग्य सिद्धि के लिए भी मातृकावर्णों से पुटित अथवा युक्त श्री शरभेश-मन्त्र विशेष विधि द्वारा सफलताएं देता है। किन्तु शत्रुनाशन कर्म में मातृका-वर्णों को विलोम विधि से जोड़कर शरभेश मंत्र से पुरश्चर्या करनी चाहिए। मंत्रान्त में अपना मनोरथ और अभिप्राय बोलते हुए "स्वाहा" शब्द कह कर प्रयोग किया जाए, इस प्रकार सभी कामनाओं की सिद्धि के लिए मंत्र के साथ तन्त्र और यन्त्र क्रिया भी साथ साथ सुचारु रखनी चाहिए और यदि साधक विलोमार्णों से देवता के मन्त्र को ओतप्रोत करके यथोक्त विधि द्वारा दस हजार पाठ करता है तो दशों दिक्पालों की शक्तियां शत्रु के पराक्रम को छीन लेती है जिससे वह शीघ्र पराजित हो जाता है।

२८वें अध्याय में श्री भद्रकाली-मन्त्र, पूजन यन्त्र तथा उनके प्रयोग की विधि दर्शायी गई हैं। श्री भद्रकाली का मन्त्र इस प्रकार है—

"ईं ॐ काली ह्रीं कंकाली मह्यं सदा त्वं कल्याणी मनोहरी, इह कवितां अव्याहतं सौभाग्यं देहि, अस्मिन् पर-मन्त्र हारिणी रं, पर-यन्त्र-हारिणी रं, अहो पर-विद्याच्छेदिनी रं, ह्रीं स्वाहा।"

भद्रकाली के इस मन्त्र तथा यन्त्र के प्रभाव से शत्रु द्वारा फैलाया गया जाल नष्ट होकर शत्रुपक्ष का ही नाश हो जाता है। तथा साधक को अखण्ड सौभाग्य की प्राप्ति होती है।

नीम के वृक्ष में स्थित कौवे का घोंसला अमावस्या के दिन लेकर उसे भस्म कर लें, अब इस भस्म को फैलाकर श्लोक ५-६ के अनुसार उस पर भद्रकाली का यन्त्र बना लें तथा काले या नीले पुष्पों से उसकी पूजन करें, तदनन्तर दक्षिणाभिमुख होकर १००८ बार भद्रकाली-मन्त्र का जप करें। अब उस भस्म द्वारा शत्रु की पुतली बना कर उस पर शत्रु की प्राणप्रतिष्ठा करें, फिर उसे काले वस्त्र में लपेट कर शत्रु स्थान में भूमि में गाड़ दें, इस प्रकार करने से शत्रु निश्चय ही मर जाता है, और यदि शत्रु अधिक बलवान् हो या उस पर पूरा प्रभाव न हो सका हो तो उपरोक्त क्रिया एक बार और दुहरायी जाए, इस से निश्चय ही शत्रु का शीघ्र पञ्चत्व होता है।

मारण कार्य सम्पन्न हो जाने पर पुतली को उखाड़कर अवरोहण मन्त्रों से अभिमंत्रित करके ज़ल में डाल देना चाहिए। तदनन्तर साधक अपने वित्तानुसार देशिक-स्तोत्र पाठादिकों से श्री भद्रकाली को सन्तुष्ट करे, और भगवती से कृपा की याचना करे।

इसी प्रकार श्री भद्रकाली मन्त्र को ६४ कलाबीजों से ओतप्रोत करके जप करने से साधक सपरिवार सभी प्रकार की सिद्धि और समृद्धि से सम्पन्न जीवन व्यतीत करता हुआ देहान्त होने पर मुक्ति को प्राप्त होता है।

(अध्याय २९)

इस अध्याय में चिकित्सा की दृष्टि से कई प्रकार के सिद्ध-तैल और अंजनादि बनाने की विधियाँ दी हुई हैं, जिन के प्रयोग से कई प्रकार के दुःसाध्य रोग और भयंकर सर्प विष भी नष्ट हो जाते हैं।

शंकाक्षुद्र नामक मानसिकरोग से ग्रसित रोगी जो प्रत्येक वस्तु को संशयात्मक दृष्टि से देखता है, इन में किसी किसी को सब कुछ अपवित्र दृष्ट होता है, कोई सदैव प्रत्येक अथवा विशेष वस्तु वा व्यक्ति से भयभीत रहते हैं, अथवा सदैव अपने आपको रोगग्रस्त समझते हैं, ऐसे रोगियों के लिए रक्त अपामार्ग की मूल, वचा, लसुन समभाग लेकर महुआ, नीम तथा एरण्ड बीज के तैलों के साथ तैलपाक विधि से काली मिरच का प्रक्षेप देते हुए तैल सिद्ध करें। इस तैल के रोगानुसार पान, वस्ति, लेपादि से शंकाक्षुद्र रोग से शीघ्र निवृत्ति होती है।

नारियल की गरी तथा मायाफल दोनों समभाग लेकर नारियल के तैल में ही तैलपाक विधि से तैल सिद्ध करें, इस तैल के खान पान से गुह्यद्वार-गुह्योष्ठ ओष्ठ तथा हृदयादि से सम्बन्धित क्षुद्र रोग शान्त हो जाते हैं।

काले वर्ण के कुत्ते के नख और रोम तथा कम्बल नामक मृग विशेष के रोम लेकर अन्तर्धूम विधि से जला दें। अब इस भस्म को थोड़ी हींग मिला कर यथोचित मात्रा में गरम पानी से सेवन कराएं। इस प्रयोग से हृद्रोग (हृदय पीड़ादि) शान्त हो जाते हैं।

गन्धमांसी (जटामांसी विशेष), अपामार्ग, पुनर्नवा, हरिद्रा, शतावरी, लज्जालु, वचा, प्लाण्डु इन सब का मूलभाग-भूमिआमला-सोहांजना का सार (गोन्द) सब समभाग लेकर एरण्डतैल के साथ यथाविधि तैल सिद्ध करें, इस तैल के अभ्यङ्गादि से मस्तिष्क, नासा, हृदय, कर्ण, हाथ और पांव के बहुत से क्षुद्र रोग शान्त हो जाते हैं।

धत्तूर, बेर, पाटला, चित्रक, अर्क, गन्ध-पालाश सब का मूल भाग, गन्धमांसी, पीली सरसों, अपामार्ग-मूल, लाक्षा, शतावरी, गाजर बीज, लसुन, वचा—प्रत्येक १-१ पल (लगभग ४० ग्राम) जल ४ प्रस्थ (लगभग ५.१२० लिटर) निर्गुण्डी और आक के पत्र और पुष्पादिकों का स्वरस ४-४ प्रस्थ (५ लिटर १२० मि० लि०) सब को अग्नि पर चढ़ा कर यथाविधि क्वाथ करें। क्वाथ-शेष चतुर्थांश रहने पर इसके पांच भाग कर लें प्रत्येक भाग को क्रम से समभाग तिल, अलसी, सरसों, एरण्ड और नीम के तैलों के साथ कड़ाही में चढ़ा कर मंदाग्नि पर पाक करें, तैल मात्र शेष रहने पर छान कर अलग अलग रखें। रोगानुसार इन तैलों को अकेले या परस्पर मिलाकर सन्ध्या काल में गुग्गलु आदि से धूपादि-पूर्वक शिर से पांव तक या रोग युक्त अंग पर नरम हाथों से अभ्यङ्ग किया जाय, तो नाना प्रकार के वातादि कठिन रोगों से शीघ्र ही निवृत्ति मिलती है।

चौलाई के पत्ते, एकाब्ज (भूकदम्ब), गिलोय, शीतला, शमी (अथवा कदम्ब) की कोपलें, आकाशबेल, पुष्करमूल, मूली, कदम्ब, कमलकंद तथा वटजटा यह सब समान

भाग लेकर यथाविधि १६ गुण जल में क्वाथ करें, चतुर्थांश शेष रहने पर समभाग तिलतैल मिला कर पाक करें, सिद्ध होने पर प्रयोग करें, रक्तपित्त तथा त्वचा के रोगों के लिये अत्यन्त लाभदायक है।

कस्तूरी, गिलोय, पुष्करमूल, रुद्रजटा, लाल कमल की जड़, इलायची, लवङ्ग, महुआबीज, कुठ, वनचम्पक के पुष्प, मृगभृङ्ग की भस्म, श्वेत चम्पक—सब औषधियों का पृथक् पृथक् चूर्ण करके एकत्र मिला लें, अब इनमें से क्वाथौषधियों का यथाविधि क्वाथ सिद्ध करें, चतुर्थांश शेष रहने पर मृगशृङ्ग की भस्म मिलाएं, अब इसमें क्वाथ के बराबर तिलतैल-घृत-आमलास्वरस-गोदुग्ध और कत्तृण (रोहिष घास) का रस-तथा शर्करा मिलाकर मध्यम आँच पर तैल सिद्ध करें। कस्तूरी अन्त में मिलाएं। यह तैल प्राणोन्मुख नाना प्रकार के रोगियों को भी पुनः जीवन दान देता है तथा रसायन है, इसके प्रयोग से सौन्दर्य बढ़ता है, शरीर को पुष्ट करता हुआ पुनः कुमारावस्था देता है, स्त्रियों के रजोधर्म के विकार नष्ट होते हैं तथा पुरुषों की कामशक्ति बढ़ाता है। इसके अतिरिक्त यह तैल वातपित्तनाशक, दुःसाध्य रक्तचापादि रोग, अति अङ्गताप, पित्त की अति वृद्धि, और इस प्रकार के नाना रोग इसके प्रयोग से शान्त हो जाते हैं। वातपित्त नाशक यह योग सभी प्रकार के रोगों में दिया जा सकता है। इसे लेप, लेहन तथा अभ्यङ्ग सभी प्रकार से प्रयोग किया जा सकता है।

सर्वविष नाशन के लिये सिद्धाञ्जन योग दिया गया है—सुहागा-सैन्धानमक-हींग-हरिताल-कालीमिरच-पिप्पली-रसौत (अथवा पारद) कर्पूर, इन सब को आक के दुग्ध में खरल करके वर्ती बना कर रखें, इसे शीतल पानी से घिस कर आंखों में आंजने से भयङ्कर सर्प का कटा भी विषरहित होकर जी जाता है।

शंख, तगर, तुत्थ, कालासुरमा, मनःशिला, कुक्कुटाण्डत्वक्, विष, त्रिकुटा, सफेद कोयल को नन्द्यावर्त (जल पिप्पली) की कलियों अथवा कोंपलों के स्वरस से १० दिन तक खरल किया जाए तथा वर्तिका बनाकर छाया में सुखा लें। रुद्रांजन नाम की यह अगद-रूपी महौषधि आवश्यकता पड़ने पर नंद्यावर्त की कलियों के स्वरस से घिस कर आंजने से सर्प विषादि के महावेगों को नष्ट करती है, तथा मूर्च्छा मोहादि नष्ट हो कर रोगी बच जाता है, इसके अतिरिक्त—ज्वर तथा जङ्गम कीटादि के विषों को नष्ट करता है। एवं अक्षिवात-पिल्ल-काच-कुकूल-मांस-पटल-पुष्पादि नेत्र के अनेक रोग भी दूर होते हैं।

भृङ्गी, लोमशफला[1] (शशुण्डली), ताम्रवल्ली, कमलमूल, सैन्धवनमक, तरुष्क, त्रिकुटा सब सम भाग—त्रिफला क्वाथ से तीन दिन तक खरल कर के अंजन तैयार कर लें, इस के आंखों में आंजने से आंखें बन्द नहीं हो पातीं, पलक खुले के खुले रहं

---

१. शशुण्डली बहुफला तण्डुली क्षेत्रसंभवा। क्षुद्राम्ला लोमशफला धूम्रवृत्त फला च सा॥ धन्वन्तरिनिघण्टु।

जाते हैं। विष तो इससे नष्ट होती ही है, किन्तु शत्रु, कूटग्रह, पिशाच तथा भूतादिकों को परेशान करने के लिए यह अत्यन्त बढ़िया अस्त्र है, इसे पुन: ठीक करना अभीष्ट हो तो सुहांजना पुष्प के रस अथवा-क्वाथ से नेत्र धो लें।

तालग्रन्थि, तालपत्र, तिलमूल, पुष्कर मूल इन सब को समभाग लेकर किसी हण्डिया में बन्द कर के लघुपुट में भस्म कर लें। इस भस्म को गुड़ में मिला कर खाने से पन्द्रह दिन के अन्दर उदरगतशल्य का निवारण होता है।

अपामार्ग के छिलके-रहित बीज गोक्षीर में भिगो दें, फिर इन्हें गोक्षीर में ही रगड़ कर उचित मात्रा में ३ मास तक प्रयोग करायें। इससे कुष्ठ-रोग का निवारण होता है, कीटदंशादि से उत्पन्न लूतादि त्वचा के विविध विकार, मण्डलकुष्ठादि शान्त हो जाते हैं।

त्रिकुटा, पद्मकेसर, तुत्थ, गन्धमांसी, बीज बीजक (असन के बीज), सब सम भाग, जम्मीरी के फल के रस से सात दिन तक खरल करें। इस औषध को आंखों में आंजने से नाना प्रकार के सर्प-विष एवं भूत, पिशाचादि नष्ट होते हैं इसी योग की वर्तिका बना कर रख लें—इसे कौमारिका-अंजन कहते हैं। नेत्रपुष्प (नेत्र के फोले) पर इसे निंबू रस से आंजने से फोला कट जाता है, कार्श्य (बड़हर अथवा कचूर) के रस से घिस कर आंजने से पिल्ल रोग नष्ट होता है, इसी प्रकार दुग्ध से घिस कर आंजने से पित्त जनित काच, गोमूत्र से घिस कर आंजने से कुकूनादि रोग छूट जाते हैं। तैल में घिस कर लगाने से पड़वाल रोग नष्ट होकर पलकों पर बाल फिर उग आते हैं। सुहांजने के रस से लगाने से माला रोग तथा सफेद चन्दन के साथ घिस कर नेत्रों में आंजने से तापज्वर से छुटकारा मिलता है। लवङ्ग के साथ रगड़ कर आंजने से चातुर्थिक ज्वर से मुक्ति मिलती है। बकरी के मूत्र से घिस कर आंजने से त्रिदोष ज्वर और ताल-दण्ड के रस से वातपित्त ज्वर नष्ट होता है, इसी प्रकार पान के रस से रगड़ कर आंजने से सूतिका-ज्वर नष्ट होता है। बच्चों के अपने ही मूत्र के साथ रगड़ कर आंजने से बालग्रह शान्त होते हैं इसी प्रकार कष्ट-प्रसवा के लिए मुख की लार से रगड़ कर अंजन किया जाए।

चावल तक्र में भिगो दें, दूसरे दिन उन्हें निकाल कर महीन पीस लें, इस योग को युक्ति से अग्निदग्ध-व्रण पर लगाने (लेपादि करने) से पीड़ा शीघ्र शान्त होती है।

कृष्ण-गुग्गुलु तिलतैल में अग्नि पर इतना पकावें, कि मरहम सी तैयार हो जाए, इसे रूई के फोहे से व्रण के मुख पर रखने से कच्चा फोड़ा स्वयं बैठ जाता है, यदि उसमें पीवादि पड़ गई हो तो शीघ्र ही पक कर फूट जाता है, घाव व क्षत पर लगाने से भी इसे यह ठीक करता है। इसी (प्रकार कुचला और मैन फल) को जल से रगड़ कर न पके हुए दुष्ट फोड़े पर लेप करें और उसके सूखने के बाद उपरोक्त गुग्गुलु मलहर का गरम फोहा रखें, और ऊपर पट्टी बांध दें, इस प्रकार तीन बार यह क्रिया करने से दुष्ट-व्रण, विद्रधि आदि वहीं शान्त हो जाते हैं।

आम्लिका (चिञ्चा-वृक्षाम्ल) का कन्द ले कर दूध के साथ महीन पीस कर प्रयोग कराने से जिन स्त्रियों को रजोदर्शन नहीं हो रहा होता, उनका सद्यः रक्त प्रवर्तन होता है।

तिलाक्षिणी-जटा (रुद्रजटा) की जटा लेकर उषःकाल में दूध के साथ पिलाने से जिन स्त्रियों को ऋतु धर्म बिल्कुल नहीं होता, उनको भी रजोदर्शन होने लगता है।

कालीमिरच के चूर्ण को जम्भीरी निम्बू के उदर में भर दें और उसे फिर निर्गुण्डी रस में डुबो कर रख लें। चातुर्थिक ज्वर में बारी के दिन इस निम्बू का एक छोटा सा टुकड़ा रोगी को खिला दिया जाय तो चातुर्थिक ज्वर नहीं होता। इस औषध के स्वाद-मात्र से चातुर्थिकज्वर कोसों दूर भाग जाता है।

सूर्य-चन्द्रादि-ग्रहण काल में उत्तराभिमुख-गामिनी "गन्धमांसी" की जड़ निकाल कर अङ्गूठी की तरह अङ्गुली में लपेट लें, अथवा धारण कर लें, इस प्रकार इसे धारण करने से अखिल दुर्गम भूत-प्रेत पिशाचादि निकट नहीं आ सकते।

(अध्याय ३०-३१)

इस अध्याय में श्री शिव ने भगवती दुर्गा के "अग्निदुर्गा-महादुर्गा-जलदुर्गा वनदुर्गा-शूलदुर्गा तथा शूलिनी" छः भेद बताए हैं। इनमें मारणोच्चाटनादि कार्यों में शीघ्र सिद्धि प्राप्ति के लिये **श्री शूलिनी दुर्गा** की विशेषता बताते हुए मंत्र के ऋषि आदि कराङ्गन्यास, विशेष न्यास तथा ध्यानादि पूर्वक **श्री शूलिनी** का मंत्र बतलाया है।

"श्रीं ह्रीं क्लीं ओं नमः शूलिनि, नत जनस्य चिन्तामणे, ज्वल ज्वल, त्वमिह चास्मान्पाहि, समस्त-रिपु-दुष्टग्रह हुं फट् स्वाहा। ४२ अक्षरात्मकः

"ज्वल ज्वल शूलिनि दुष्ट ग्रह हुं फट् स्वाहा" ग्रन्थान्तरात्।

[1]"ज्वल ज्वल शूलिनि दुष्ट-निग्रहे हुं फट् स्वाहा" ग्रन्थान्तरे।

षट्कर्म साधना में अतिश्रेष्ठ इस विद्या को गुप्त रखना चाहिए। विशेष विशेष कार्यों में भगवती के रूप और ध्यान की विधि बताते हुए श्री भगवान् ने कहा कि वश्याकर्षणादि कार्यों में इसे रक्त वर्ण, स्तम्भन-विद्वेषण में श्याम वर्ण, निग्रहोच्चाटनादि कार्यों में गहरा कृष्ण वर्ण, मोक्षादि सिद्धि के लिये श्वेत वर्ण तथा सारस्वतादि कार्यों में इसे मोती की तरह चमकदार, श्वेत आभा-युक्तादि रूप में ध्यान करना चाहिये।

शूलिनी दुर्गा की उपासना भोग और मोक्ष दोनों देती है। तथा अणिमादि अष्ट-सिद्धियां प्रदान करती हुई साधक के सभी मनोरथ पूर्ण करती है। मातृकोष्ठ और श्मशानादि में इसके अनुष्ठान से विशेष सिद्धि प्राप्त होती है। मंत्र सिद्धि के लिये जप के विशेष अंग—तर्पण, होम, विप्रभोजनादि क्रियाएं अत्यन्त आवश्यक हैं। वश्यादि शुभ कार्य शुक्रवारादि सौम्य-वारों में तथा उच्चाटन-मारणादि पाप कार्य

---

१. "श्रीं ह्रीं क्लीं ओं नमः (शूलिनि) क्ष्म्र्यौं ज्वल ज्वल शूलिनि समस्त-रिपु-दुष्ट-ग्रह हुं फट स्वाहा"

अष्टमी-मङ्गलवारादि पाप वारों में करने की विधि है। इसी अध्याय में श्लोक ३०-३१ तथा ३२ में श्री शूलिनी भगवती का पूजनयंत्र तथा पूजन एवं श्लोक ४६ में दूसरा सिद्ध-यंत्र लिखने का विधान है इसी प्रकार अध्याय ३१ में श्री शूलिनी दुर्गा के यंत्र की पूजन विधि, बलि विधान, भगवती सुमुखी का विशेष सिद्धिदायक स्तोत्र तथा उसके अनन्तर क्रिया-भेद शीर्षक से षट्कर्मों से सम्बन्धित क्रियाओं में भेदात्मक विधि, विधि सहित **आकर्षण-सिद्धिप्रद कंकाली-काल रात्रि के** यंत्र सहित महामंत्र, शत्रु वशीकरण-शत्रुनाशन एवं **सर्वाभीष्टप्रद वटुक-भैरव सहित महाकाली** का यंत्र तथा महामंत्र एवं भगवती की कला को शत्रु देह में प्रविष्ट करा के शत्रु से अपनी इच्छानुसार सभी कार्य करवाने के लिये **रुद्रकाली-सप्तमातृका** महामंत्र दिये गए हैं। इसके अनन्तर **शत्रु मारण** यंत्र, उच्चाटन यंत्र, मारण यंत्रविशेष, सप्ताहान्तर शत्रु मारण प्रयोगादि का प्रकाश किया किया गया है। शत्रुमारण प्रयोगों में श्री **शूलिनि दुर्गा का विशेष ध्यान** बतलाते हुए श्री शिव ने स्पष्ट कहा है कि यह सिद्ध विद्या किसी भी हालत में किसी नास्तिक अथवा कृतघ्न को नहीं देनी चाहिये।

अध्यायान्त में महाभूत-पिशाचादि निवारण तथा शत्रुनाशन के लिये दो विशेष यंत्र बनाने एवं उनके द्वारा सकाम प्रयोग की विधि बताई गई है। शत्रुनाशक यंत्र मंत्रों के प्रयोगानुष्ठानादि के प्रभाव से शत्रुकुल-क्षय—शत्रु-उच्चाटन तथा शत्रु-राज्यादि का उसके गणों सहित सर्वनाश होता है।

(अध्याय ३२ से ३५)

३२ वें अध्याय में शत्रुदल को पराजित एवं नष्ट करने के लिये शूलिनी ध्यान, शूलिनी के मंत्र की विलोम जप-विधि, सर्व रोग, सर्वभूतादि-बाधा निवारण के लिए यंत्र पूजन विधि बताते हुए श्री शूलिनी दुर्गा से ही सम्बन्धित अतिसिद्ध एवं शत्रु दल-नाशक श्री वीर भद्र का मंत्र बतलाया गया है। तथा इसके अनुष्ठानारम्भ में पूजन विधि एवं जपविधि का विवरण देते हुए सर्वत्र जय एवं सफलता प्राप्ति के लिये प्रयोग दिया गया है।

३३ वें अध्याय में सर्व जगत् के क्षोभण के लिये श्री शरभेश्वर का माला मंत्र वर्णित है, जिसका नित्य पाठ अनुष्ठानादि सभी प्रकार की मनोकामनाएं पूर्ण करता हुआ शत्रुपक्ष तथा भूत-प्रेत-पिशाचादिकों को भी नष्ट करता है। अध्यायान्त में सर्वसंक्षोभण यंत्र एवं मंत्र तथा जप का फलादि वर्णन किया गया है।

३४वें अध्याय में ऋषिः, छन्द, ध्यान, मंत्रादि पूर्वक सर्वार्थ सिद्धि प्रद श्री भैरव जी के मन्त्र की प्रयोगविधि वर्णन की गई है। यहीं श्री **उग्रभैरवमन्त्र** बताते हुए नाना प्रकार के कार्यों में अभीष्ट सफलता के लिए **भैरवी** सहित श्री **भैरव** के विविध रूपों एवं प्रकारों की पूजन विधि का वर्णन किया गया है। विशेष कार्यों में होम द्रव्यों का भेद बतलाते हुए शत्रुओं के विशेष नाशन के लिए **वैरिवज्राख्य भैरव यंत्र** तथा उस चक्र में श्री भैरव की पूजन विधि पूजन मन्त्रों सहित वर्णन की गई है।

३५वें अध्याय में भूतादिकों के **आवेश कार्यों में सिद्धि** प्राप्ति के लिए **श्री विजय भैरव** का मन्त्र ऋषि, छन्द, न्यास, ध्यानादि पूर्वक वर्णन किया गया है, आवेश लाने के लिए मंत्र विधि भी दी गई है। तथा सभी प्रकार की आपत्ति, कष्ट एवं दुस्साध्य-रोगादि के निवारण और शमन के लिए **रुद्राख्या सिद्ध-भैरव-बलि** का विधान बतलाया है, रुद्र बलि में ग्राह्य द्रव्य और मंत्र भी बताए हैं। यहां पर श्री शिव का आदेश है कि अधीर (धैर्य रहित) एवं मन्त्रविद्या-ज्ञानरहित व्यक्ति को बलि कर्म नहीं करना चाहिये, अन्यथा उसे लाभ के स्थान पर हानि हो सकती है।

(अध्याय ३६)

इस अध्याय में सर्व कार्य सिद्धि एवं सर्वत्र विजय प्राप्ति के लिए श्री क्षेत्रपाल के अष्टाक्षर मंत्र का ऋषि, छन्द, षडङ्गन्यास, ध्यानादि पूर्वक वर्णन है, जिसका निर्दिष्टविधि से अनुष्ठानपूर्वक लक्ष जप करने से सिद्धि होती है। इसके अनन्तर चक्र तथा चक्र पूजन विधि तथा क्षेत्रपाल बलिदान विधि बतलाते हुये श्री क्षेत्रपाल के सूक्त का वर्णन किया गया है, जिसके केवल तीन बार जपने से विदेश में भी आजीविका के साधन प्राप्त होते हैं तथा शत्रुओं पर विजय प्राप्ति होती है। शत्रुमारण कार्य-सिद्धि के लिये श्मशान में यंत्रादि खनन-विधि, शुभ कार्यों तथा सर्व प्रकार के दुःखनिवारण, पुष्टि, सुख, वश्य, सुसन्तति प्राप्ति के लिये क्षेत्रपाल की **विशेषानुष्ठान-विधि** आदि बतलाई गई है। इसके अनन्तर चोरी गई वस्तु की प्राप्ति के लिये **क्षेत्रपाल-मंत्र-प्रयोग**, नष्ट वस्तु के शीघ्र लाभार्थ जपविधि से द्वितीय प्रयोग और यदि वह चोर फिर भी चौरित धन सम्पत्ति नहीं देता तो उसे, उसके परिवार तथा उसकी वंश तक को कष्ट एवं मारण के लिए श्री क्षेत्रपाल मंत्र के ही विशेष प्रयोगादि दिये गये हैं।

(अध्याय ३७-३८)

इस अध्याय में ऋषि-छन्द-ध्यानादि पूर्वक श्री वडवानल भैरव का यन्त्र और वेदऋचात्मक मंत्र, तथा उसकी पूजन, जप और प्रयोगविधि बतलाई गई है, इस विद्या का साधक जहां चाहे वहीं अग्नि की भड़कती हुई ज्वालाएं निकल सकती हैं तथा इस प्रकार शत्रुपक्ष का दहन करके अभीष्ट सफलता एवं शत्रु पर विजय पाई जा सकती है, यहां आगे जाकर शत्रु-सम्पत्ति के दहन के लिये '**अग्नि**' के प्रार्थनामन्त्र दिये हैं, तथा श्मशानादि की क्रिया बतलाई है। इसके अनन्तर अग्निप्रकोप को पुनः शान्त करने की विधि बताते हुए इस क्रिया द्वारा जनित पाप-निवारण के लिये १०८ बार उपसंहार मंत्र का विधान ब्राह्मण-भोजनादि सहित बतलाया गया है।

इसके अनन्तर आग्नेयास्त्र विद्या, ऋषि-छन्द-षडङ्ग-ध्यानादि सहित वर्णन करते हुये चक्र पूजन विधि बतलाई गई है, जिस के अनुसार आवाहनपूर्वक मन्त्र-स्मरण मात्र से ही शत्रु यमपुरी को चला जाता है।

३८वें अध्याय में अष्ट-कर्म-सिद्धि के लिए इन्द्रादि दशदिक्पालों के मंत्र एवं उनकी अर्चना और प्रयोग विधि बतलाई गई है।

(अध्याय ३६-४०)

इस अध्याय में **महाव्याधिकर रुद्र मंत्र** की ऋषि-छन्द-षडङ्ग-ध्यानादि सहित प्रयोग विधि का वर्णन किया गया है, तथा विशेष प्रकार का यंत्र बना कर बलिपूर्वक श्मशानादि में दबाने का विधान बतलाया है, जिसके केवल मात्र तीन दिन प्रयोग करने से प्रबल शत्रु भी महाव्याधि से अकस्मात् ग्रस्त होकर पंचत्व को प्राप्त होता है, साधक, शत्रु के लिए जिस प्रकार की महाव्याधि की कल्पना करना चाहे वह निर्दिष्ट यंत्र पर अंकित कर देनी चाहिए।

इसी प्रकार ४०वें अध्याय में शत्रु को अति शीघ्र विनाश करने के लिये ऋषि-छन्द-षडङ्गन्यास-ध्यानादि पूर्वक **"मृत्यु मन्त्र"** और उसका यंत्र तथा प्रयोग विधि बतलाई गई है। रात्रि के समय सहस्रबार शत्रु के नाम सहित यथाविधि जप करने से जपावसान काल में शत्रु की मृत्यु हो जाती है। यदि मूलमंत्र को पचास हजार बार पहिले जप करके सिद्ध कर लिया जाए तो केवल मात्र पांच सौ बार पढ़ने से शत्रु का देहावसान होता है और यदि साधक एक लक्ष जप कर ले तो केवल एक शत बार जप करने से ही शत्रु का कालग्रास हो जाता है।

(अध्याय ४१)

इस अध्याय में ऋषि-छन्द-ध्यानादि पूर्वक **वज्रपंजराख्य श्री शरभ-सालुव-पक्षिराज कवच** यंत्र विधि सहित दिया गया है, अध्यायान्त में कवच पाठ का फल बतलाते हुये श्रीशिव ने कथन किया है कि इस दिव्य कवच के त्रिकाल पाठ करने वाले की सर्वत्र रक्षा होती है और उसके मनोवांछित कार्य अपने आप सिद्ध होते रहते हैं।

(अध्याय ४२)

इस अध्याय में **जगद्वश्यकर श्री कामराज** के महामन्त्र का ऋषि-छन्द-कराङ्ग न्यास-ध्यानादि-पूर्वक उपदेश दिया गया है। श्री **कामराज-गायत्री** भी वर्णित है। मन्त्र सिद्धि के लिये श्री कामराज का अनुष्ठान तथा यंत्र विधान भी बतलाया गया है। तदुपरान्त जगत्क्षोभण कर, श्रीप्रद, मनोवांछित फलप्रदायक श्रीकामराज के दूसरे यंत्र का विधान दिया गया है, जिसके धारण करने से सभी प्रकार के सौभाग्यों की प्राप्ति होती है। तदनन्तर श्री **कामराज के पाचों बाणों के मंत्र, पंच बाणवृक्ष** तथा उनकी विधि बताते हुए **त्रैलोक्य-क्षोभकरी एकाक्षरी कामदेव-विद्या**, उसका जपविधान, पीठ शक्तियों के नाम, कामपीठ मंत्र, जगन्मोहन बाणन्यास के साथ साथ **मन्मथ (श्री कामदेव)** के प्रयोग का फल वर्णन किया है। जिससे सभी विश्व का सम्मोहन तथा यथेष्ट धन विभवादि की प्राप्ति होती है।

(अध्याय ४३-४५)

४३वें अध्याय में महासिद्धि-प्रदायिनी, निग्रहानुग्रह-फलप्रदा, शान्तिप्रदा, वश्याकर्षणादि विविध-कार्यकरी जगन्मोहनी भगवती **"रक्त-चामुण्डी"** का ऋषि, छन्द, न्यास, ध्यान, मंत्र, पूजनविधि सहित सिद्ध-मंत्र दिया गया है, इस बलिपूर्वक विधान से भगवती साक्षात् दर्शन भी देती है तथा साधक को यथेष्ट फल भी।

४४वें अध्याय में ऋष्यादि-ध्यानान्त **श्री मोहिनी भगवती** का महामंत्र तथा उसका विधान दिया है, तथा पूजनादि के लिए यंत्र बनाने की विधि भी; इस में भगवती कौतूहलपूर्ण विचित्र रूप दर्शाती हुई सब जगत् का सम्मोहन करके सर्वत्र विजय देती है।

४५वें अध्याय में पत्थर-दिलों तक को मोम कर देने वाली **भगवती द्राविणी की** विद्या का ऋष्यादि ध्यानपूर्वक उपदेश दिया गया है, तथा पूजनादि यंत्रविधि भी बतलाई गई है। द्राविणी विद्या के सिद्ध होने के पश्चात् केवल तीन बार मंत्रस्मरण से कठोर हृदय वाले भी द्रवित होकर वशीभूत होते हैं।

(अध्याय ४६-५०)

४६वें अध्याय में ऋष्यादि स्मरण ध्यानपूर्वक **श्री भगवती शब्दाकर्षिणी** के मंत्र तथा यंत्र का उपदेश दिया गया है जिसकी सिद्धि के पश्चात् विधिवत् प्रयोग से अतीतानागत तथा वर्तमान का साधक को सम्यक् ज्ञान हो जाता है तथा देवी उसके कान में सब कुछ कह देती है।

४७वें अध्याय में सर्वसिद्धिदायिनी भगवती सरस्वती का मंत्र ऋषि षडङ्ग-ध्यानादिपूर्वक सिद्धिकरण-विधि सहित दिया गया है, जिसके स्मरण से भगवती प्रसन्न होकर साधक की जिह्वा पर आसीन होती हुई असीम वाक्शक्ति देती है तथा सभी प्रकार के वाद-विवाद तथा सभा आदिकों में विजय प्रदान करती है।

४८वें अध्याय में सभी प्रकार से सौभाग्यवर्द्धन, स्वास्थ्य-संरक्षण, आयु संवर्द्धन आदि पुष्टिकर कार्यों के लिए **महावश्यकरी भगवती लक्ष्मी** का ऋषि-न्यास-ध्यानादि पूर्वक यंत्र सहित सिद्ध मंत्र वर्णित किया गया है, जिसके सिद्ध होने के पश्चात् साधक नित्य अष्टोत्तर जप से सभी प्रकार की समृद्धि से युक्त रहता है तथा उसे यथेष्ट धन की प्राप्ति होती है।

४९वें अध्याय में **माया मन्त्र** का सिद्ध प्रयोग वर्णन किया गया है, जो सारे जगत् को साधक की इच्छानुसार सम्मोहित करता हुआ मनोवांछित सिद्धि देता है। ऋषि छन्द ध्यानादि के सदुपदेश के अनंतर मंत्र सिद्ध करने की विधि का भी उपदेश दिया है, माया मंत्र के सिद्ध होने पर मनुष्य लोकदृष्टि से स्वेच्छापूर्वक अदृश्य हो सकता है।

५०वें अध्याय में **भगवती पुलन्दिनी** की सिद्धविद्या ऋषि-छन्द-षडङ्गन्यास ध्यानादिपूर्वक वर्णन की गई है। मंत्र सिद्ध करने की विधि बताते हुए जप-होमादि विधान का भी आदेश दिया है—मंत्र सिद्धि के बाद स्मरणपूर्वक, देवी, स्वप्न में शुभाशुभ सब कुछ कह देती है।

(अध्याय ५१)

इस अध्याय के तीन खण्डों में **महाशास्ता** जो सभी प्रकार से भोग, मोक्ष, आयु, आरोग्य, पुष्टि, हृष्टि तथा आनंद देने वाले हैं, पुत्र संतान दाता हैं एवं सभी प्रकार के अरिष्ट, अपमृत्यु आदि का निवारण करते हैं, का ऋषि, छन्द तथा नाना कार्यों के

लिए नाना प्रकार के ध्यानपूर्वक, सिद्ध मंत्र का उपदेश दिया गया है। मंत्रसिद्धि के लिए अनुष्ठान विधि बताते हुए सकाम कार्यों के साधनार्थ विशेष क्रिया वर्णित की गई है। इसके अनन्तर महाशास्ता का यंत्र बतलाया गया है जिससे सभी प्रकार के सुख और आनंद, सर्व सिद्धि, सर्वजगत्-वशीकरण तथा सभी प्रकार के भोग और अंत में मोक्ष की प्राप्ति होती है।

पति यदि क्रुद्ध हो या अनासक्त, अथवा रुष्ट हो गया हो तो इस यंत्र को निर्दिष्ट विधि से लिख कर यदि पत्नी धारण करे तो विरक्त पति भी उसके दर्शन मात्र से कामविह्वल होकर मोहित हुआ उस के वश में हो जाता है।

इसी यन्त्र के धारण से भूत, प्रेत, पिशाच, सर्प, सिंह, व्याघ्र, हिंस्र पक्षी तथा जल-ग्राहादिक जन्तुओं से संरक्षण होता है।

द्वितीय खण्ड में महाशास्तृ की पूजन विधि देते हुए पात्र शुद्धि, आवरण पूजन, यन्त्र के कोष्ठों पर अंगदेवताओं का स्थापन तथा उनकी पूजन, महाशास्तृ गायत्री तथा महाशास्ता की सांगोपांग पूजन-विधि तथा पूजन-फलादि का वर्णन किया गया है।

तृतीय खण्ड में महाशास्ता का ध्यान, आवाहन, एकविंशत्युपचारों सहित समांत्रिक पूजन तथा नमस्कार-मन्त्रादि दिए गए हैं।

(अध्याय ५२)

इस अध्याय में **भगवती संक्षोभिणी** का ऋषि-छन्द-ध्यानादि-पूर्वक मन्त्र वर्णन किया गया है, जिसके विधिवत् अनुष्ठान से सभी जीव क्षुभित होकर परास्त हो जाते हैं। शत्रुनामयुक्त इस मन्त्र के एक सहस्र जप से शत्रु भ्रष्टचित्त होकर घूमता रहता है। और यदि थोड़ी सी भस्म हाथ में लेकर संक्षोभिणी मन्त्र से एक सौ बार अभिमन्त्रित करके अपने मकान की आठों दिशाओं में फेंक दें अथवा गाड़ दें, तो उस मकान के निकट भी चौर, शत्रु, जंगली हिंसक-जानवरादि स्वप्न में भी नहीं आ सकते।

(अध्याय ५३)

शत्रुओं का संहार करने में अतिप्रसिद्ध, आशुफल देने वाली, **भगवती धूमावती** के ऋषि-छन्द-ध्यानादि पूर्वक सिद्धमन्त्र का उपदेश देते हुए मन्त्र सिद्धि के लिए केवल सात हजार जप तथा उसके अनन्तर हवन, तर्पण, ब्राह्मण भोजनादि करना चाहिए, इस प्रकार भगवान् शिव ने बताया; भगवती धूमावती का श्लोकोक्त विधि से यंत्र बना कर उसकी यथाविधि पूजन करके १००० बार मन्त्र का जप करें, फिर उसे बलिदान पूर्वक श्मशान में गाड़ दें और यदि शत्रु के घर भूमि में गाड़ सकने का साधन बन सके तो वहां बलिदान की आवश्यकता नहीं होती है। इस प्रकार तीन रात्रि तक शत्रु के निवास की ओर मुख करके जप नित्य करें, इस तरह शत्रु के लिए स्तंभन, उच्चाटन, निग्रह (पीड़ाकरण, मारण), चित्तविभ्रम, सर्वसम्पत्ति-विनाशन अथवा विद्वेषणादि जिस भी संकल्प से क्रिया की गई है, तीन दिन में ही उसका प्रभाव हो जाता है। इस प्रकार के क्रूर प्रयोगारम्भ काल में श्री **शरभेश्वर कवच** से अपना

संरक्षण कर लेना चाहिए, अन्यथा भगवती **ज्येष्ठा-लक्ष्मी** (क्षुत्पिपासामला ज्येष्ठा—दरिद्रता की देवी) क्रुद्ध होकर साधक के ही भाग्यों का क्षय कर देती है। शत्रु नाशन, शत्रुचित्त-भ्रष्टीकरण, शत्रुभाग्यक्षय-करण, शत्रुस्तम्भनादि विविध प्रकार के प्रयोगों के लिए श्लोक ११ से १४ तक निर्दिष्ट उपदेश के अनुसार देवी का ध्यान करना चाहिए।

५४वें अध्याय में श्री शिव ने विद्वेषण-मारण अथवा दूसरे क्रूर कर्मों के लिए श्री **ज्येष्ठालक्ष्मी (धूमावती)** के सिद्ध यत्र तथा उसकी प्रयोग विधि का उपदेश दिया है। इस यन्त्र की यथाविधि अर्चना करके उसे बलिपूर्वक आधीरात में श्मशान में गाड़ दिया जाए तथा देवीमंत्र का १००८ बार जप किया जाए तो शत्रु की शीघ्र ही मृत्यु होती है। इसी प्रकार **विद्वेषणादि** कार्यों में भी उसी प्रकार निर्दिष्ट विधि से ध्यानादि पूर्वक १००८ बार जप किया जाए तो दो घनिष्ठ मित्रों में भी परस्पर कलह ही केवल नहीं होती अपितु वह एक दूसरे के जीवन के शत्रु हो जाते हैं। और यदि साधक के मन में दया आ जाती है, अथवा साध्य-शत्रु उस की शरण में आ जाता है तो उस मन्त्र-पाठ का विलोम-विधि से जप किया जाए तो उसकी निवृत्ति हो जाती है और अन्य किसी भी उपाय से वह ठीक नहीं हो सकता।

इसके अतिरिक्त महाव्याधि, महारोग, महाभूत (दुष्ट-पिशाचादि), महोन्मादादि कठिन रोगों के निवारण के लिए भगवती धूमावती तथा शरभ-सालुव-पक्षिराज का मालामंत्र बतलाया गया है, जिस से अभिमंत्रित कर के ओषधि अथवा जलादि दिया जाए तो उसके प्रयोग से उन कष्टों का शीघ्र निवारण होता है।

(अध्याय ५५)

इस अध्याय में जलभय दूर करने, जलयात्रा में सभी प्रकार से सुरक्षित एवं सकुशल रहने तथा गहरे और भयानक जलमार्गों तथा नदी समुद्रादिकों में तरण-सिद्धि के लिए श्री **शरभेश्वर के यंत्र का विधान** दिया है, इसके साथ साथ श्री शरभेश्वर के दो मंत्र भी, जिन के विधिवत् अनुष्ठान करने से वह मन्त्र सिद्ध हो जाते हैं। सिद्धि के पश्चात् स्मरणमात्र से ही जल में डूबा हुआ मनुष्य भी क्षणभर में सुरक्षा पूर्वक तैर कर नदी के किनारे आ जाता है। नदी-समुद्रादि की यात्रा के समय इस के मन्त्र तथा यन्त्र दोनों का सदा स्मरण करना चाहिए।

(अध्याय ५६)

इस अध्याय में सिद्ध-विद्याओं में श्रेष्ठ अत्याश्चर्यंकरी श्री **चित्रविद्या** का उपदेश दिया गया गया है, जिस की सिद्धि के फलस्वरूप सभी प्रकार की आपत्तियां तथा कष्टादि दूर हो जाते हैं। पैत्योन्माद, अग्नि की भयंकर ज्वालाओं से घिर जाना अथवा किसी भी प्रकार का अग्नि प्रकोप आदि आपत्तियों के निवारण के लिए इस विद्या का सदैव स्मरण करना चाहिए। मन्त्र इस प्रकार है—

"वं रं घूं सं जुं ठं ह्लीं श्रीं ओं नमो भगवती चित्रविद्ये महामाये अमृतेश्वरी

सर्वविषं नाशय नाशय, सर्वतापज्वरं हन हन, सर्वपैत्योन्मादं मोचय मोचय, आज्योष्णं शमय शमय, सर्वजनं मोहय मोहय, मां पालय पालय, श्रीं ह्लीं ठं जुं सं धूं ह्रं वं स्वाहा ।

इसके दस हज़ार जप से मंत्र की सिद्धि हो जाती है । तथा सिद्धि के अनन्तर इसके केवल १००० जपादि प्रयोग से सभी प्रकार के ज्वर, विष, अनिद्रा, क्षुद्ररोग, महोन्माद, हृदयविग्रह, सर्वांगदाह आदि नाना प्रकार के कष्टों का अतिशीघ्र निवारण होता है । इसके अनन्तर श्री **चित्रविद्या का यन्त्र** बतलाया गया है, जिसे भगवती के मंत्र और देशिक-स्तोत्र स्मरणपूर्वक यथाकार्य धारण-सेचनादि से निखिल कार्यों में सफलता मिलती है तथा पैत्योन्माद में शान्ति होती है ।

उदम्बर-बीज (अथवा कमलगट्टे के बीज की गिरी) १ भाग-चम्पक पुष्प की कली-२ भाग, दोनों मिला कर अथवा इनमें से कोई एक लेकर, अथवा अवस्थानुसार अनुक्रम से थोड़े-थोड़े समय के बाद उचित मात्रा में रोगी को एक दिन देते रहें, दूसरे दिन प्रातः काल से रोगी को पञ्चगव्य दिलाते रहें और उधर कुंभ में जल भर कर पञ्चद्रव्य एवं पञ्चगव्य भी उस कुंभ में डाल दें और एक बार **चित्रविद्या** मंत्र से अभिमंत्रित करके उत्तराभिमुख ब्राह्मणों द्वारा दक्षिणाभिमुख साध्य रोगी को एक हजार बार अभिषिञ्चत करायें और इसके अनन्तर ३ दिन और बिना पञ्चगव्य पान कराए अभिषेचन किया जाय तो इस से पित्तविकार, पैत्योन्माद, उन्माद, अनिद्रा, अंगमर्दन क्षुद्रोन्माद, उन्मत्त-ग्रह तथा उसके द्वारा जनित हृदय-विग्रह, सर्वांगदाहादि नाना रोग नष्ट हो जाते है, यहां पथ्य के रूप में केवल दूधभात ही दिया जाए और कुछ न दिया जाए, और यदि और कुछ खाने को दिया जाए तो सारी क्रिया व्यर्थ हो जाती है और रोग में वृद्धि होती है ।

कमलनाल (बिस) को जौ की दूधीके साथ रगड़ कर अच्छे प्रकार मिला कर पीस ले, उसमें नींबू का रस और आमलास्वरस मिलाकर देवता के मंत्र द्वारा प्रार्थना-पूर्वक उचित मात्रा में मूर्च्छित (मूर्च्छा युक्त) रोगी को युक्ति से पिलाया जाए, तो वह बुलाने से चेतना में आ जाता है ।

और यदि चित्रमाला मंत्र से पान या इलायची को अभिमंत्रित करके किसी कामिनी को खिलाया जाए, तो उसका वशीकरण होता है तथा उस मनुष्य के बिना वह क्षण भर भी नहीं रह सकती है ।

तदुपरांत चित्रविद्या के दूसरे यन्त्र का विधान दिया गया है जिसे मन्त्रस्मरण पूर्वक स्पर्श करके देवता के वाहनादि उपचारों की पूजन पूर्वक १०० बार चित्रविद्या से अभिमंत्रित मंत्र जप करे फिर उस यन्त्र के कागज या पत्र को गुड़ में लपेट कर निगल ले, अब यदि साधक तीव्र-ज्वालाओं से आवृत वह्नि में प्रवेश करे तो उसके लिए अग्नि शीतल-पुष्पों की तरह सुख देने वाली हो जाती है और यदि उस यन्त्र को कण्ठ, हाथ या शिर पर धारण करें तो अग्नि भय नहीं होता, अग्नि से उबलता घी भी उसको नहीं जला सकता, तथा रोगादि का भय नहीं होता, इस प्रकार के पुरुष को देखकर

युवतियां मोहित होकर उसे प्राप्त करने के लिए यत्नशील होती हैं तथा सभी जगत् उसके वश में होता है और यदि कोई स्त्री इस प्रकार का प्रयोग करे तो सकल युवक उसके लिए लालायित रहते हैं।

चित्रविद्या के इस महागुह्य तथा गुप्त मन्त्र को उषःकाल में ३ बार नित्य पाठ करने से साधक विचित्र गुणों वाला हो जाता है। उसके लिए सूर्य की तीव्र किरणें चन्द्रमा और उसकी हथेली में रखा जल अमृत की तरह शीतल एवं शान्ति पहुंचाने वाला होता है। भूर्भुवः-स्वाधिपति श्री आकाशभैरव का ध्यान करते हुए नित्य अष्टोत्तरशत संख्या में चित्रविद्या का जप करके उससे अभिमंत्रित उषःकाल की सूर्य रश्मियों से युक्त जलपान करने से साधक मानसिक तौर पर पवित्र हो जाता है, तथा उसको किसी प्रकार की बाधाएं नहीं सतातीं।

चित्रविद्या के मंत्र से अभिमंत्रित करके ओषधि, तैल, घृत, दूधादि प्रातः काल नित्य पीने से मनुष्य का कायाकल्प होता है तथा कायासिद्धि होती हैं।

अध्याय ५७

इस अध्याय में भगवान् शरभेश्वर का देशिक स्तोत्र दिया गया है, जिसके नित्य पाठ से श्री गुरु की कृपा, स्वात्म-ज्ञान, सभी मंत्रों की सिद्धि, शत्रुओं पर विजय आयु, आरोग्य, विवादादिकों में जय, भोग, ऐश्वर्य और मोक्ष की प्राप्ति होती है तथा साधक को सर्व प्रकार से सुख और विश्रान्ति प्राप्त होती है।

अध्याय ५८-५९

५८वें अध्याय में दुःस्वप्न नाशन के लिए ऋग्वेद का सिद्ध मन्त्र जिसे मंत्रोद्धार पृष्ठों में दे दिया गया है, का वर्णन किया गया है, इसे ओं भूर्भुवः स्वः से विलोमानुलोम विधि से सम्पुट किया जाना चाहिए। इसके साथ ही दुःस्वप्ननाशन यन्त्र का भी विधान दिया गया है, जिस के धारण करने से स्त्रियों को गर्भ कालीन परेशानियां नहीं होतीं, तथा गर्भ की रक्षा होती है, गर्भपात नहीं होता। दुःस्वप्न-नाशन के लिए यह विद्या अत्युत्तम कही गई है।

५९वें अध्याय में सभी प्रकार के बन्धनों से मुक्ति प्राप्त करने के लिए ऋग्वेदोक्त "ध्रुवासु त्वासु०" मंत्र का विधान दिया गया है। इस मंत्र के आरम्भ में भी ओं भूर्भुवः स्वः तथा अन्त में स्वाहा लगाना चाहिए। इसके प्रयोग से सभी प्रकार के बन्धनों एवं पाश से छुटकारा मिलता है, तथा बन्दी कैद से छूट जाता है। सर्प दंश से मृतप्राय व्यक्ति भी इस मन्त्र के प्रभाव से विषरहित होकर पुनर्जीवन प्राप्त करता है। इसके अतिरिक्त तापज्वर, सभी प्रकार के उन्माद, कठिन रोग तथा शत्रुकृत-अभिचार, तथा उससे जनित दुष्टप्रभाव एव दुष्ट और क्षुद्र रोगादि बहुविध व्याधियां नष्ट हो जाती हैं। सर्व सौभाग्यप्रद इस महामंत्र का साधक अनावृष्टि काल में भी वर्षा करा सकता है।

अध्याय ६०-६१-६२

इन अध्यायों में श्री महागणपति विद्या, यंत्र, तर्पण, प्रयोग तथा श्री गणपति मंत्र की क्रिया से सम्बन्धित औषधि-विधि तथा औषधि मूलादिकों से षट्कर्म साधन की तांत्रिक क्रियाएं बतलाई गई हैं। श्री महागणपतिविद्या के नित्यानुष्ठान से साधक को सभी प्रकार की सिद्धि-समृद्धि-निर्विघ्नता तथा कल्याण मिलता है। इसके साधक की अकाल मृत्यु नहीं होती तथा उसे मनोवांछित फल की प्राप्ति होती रहती है।

६२वें अध्याय में सर्वप्रथम श्री गणपति के यंत्र का विधान दिया गया है, तथा इसके साथ श्री महागणपति मंत्र की जप क्रिया भी, जिसके प्रभाव से स्त्रियों का आकर्षण और वशीकरण होता है।

वशीकरण कार्यों के लिए श्वेतार्क, अपामार्ग—जो श्मशानादि भूमि पर उगे हों का विशेष विधान इस प्रकार बतलाया गया है, जिसके स्पर्श मात्र से जीवमात्र का महावशीकरण होता है, मुहूर्त शास्त्र के नियमानुसार सिद्ध योग से पहिले दिन श्मशान भूमि में उगे हुए श्वेतार्क और अपामार्ग की गन्ध-पुष्प-धूपादिकों द्वारा पूजन करे, तदुपरान्त बलिदानपूर्वक साधक छठे श्लोकानुसार नमस्कार करके उन्हें कच्चे सूत (अथवा कुमारी कन्या के हाथ से कते सूत) से तीन बार लपेटते हुए श्री महागणपति विद्या का दश बार पाठ करे। दूसरे दिन शुभ मुहूर्त में उन्हें बिना टूटे हुए (अखण्ड एवं पूर्ण) जड़ समेत उखाड़ लें। अब उनकी शाखा से इच्छानुसार कड़ा या अंगूठी बना कर रख ले। इसे धारण कर के साधक स्पर्शमात्र से सब को वशीभूत कर लेता है।

राजनीति आदि सम्बन्धित कार्यों में यदि दो परम मित्रों में परस्पर विरोध या लड़ाई करवाना अभिप्राय हो, अथवा दो महाविरोधियों में परस्पर मैत्री कराना उद्देश्य हो, तो उसके लिए भी इसी अध्याय में विशेष सिद्ध तथा अचूक योग दिये गये हैं;

शुभ कार्यों के आरम्भ के लिए शुभ वार-नक्षत्रादि एवं मारणोच्चाटनादि पाप प्रभाव वाले कार्यों के लिए तद्विपरीत पाप नक्षत्र-वारादि मुहूर्त लेना चाहिए, वशीकरणादि कार्यों में औषधि के पुष्प पुष्य नक्षत्र में, फल भरणी नक्षत्र में, शाखा विशाखा में, पत्रादि हस्त नक्षत्र में तथा मूला नक्षत्र में मूल लेनी चाहिए, ऐसा नियम है।

स्त्री वशीकरण—काले धत्तूरे का पञ्चाङ्ग उपरोक्तविधि के अनुसार लेकर उसका रस निकाल लें, अब इसमें से थोड़ा सा रस लेकर उसमें केसर-गोरोचन और कर्पूर मिला कर अच्छी तरह घिस लें या रगड़ लें। श्री महागणपति का मंत्र स्मरण करते हुए इसका तिलक करें, इस प्रकार के मनुष्य को देखते ही बड़ी से बड़ी अभिमानिनी स्त्री भी वशीभूत हो जाती है।

इसी प्रकार पुष्पादि सहित लज्जालु तथा श्वेतापराजिता की मूल ग्रहण करके गोरोचन के साथ पीसकर अभिमंत्रित करके तिलक लगा कर राजा के सम्मुख जाने से राजा वशीभूत होता है।

६२वें अध्याय में भी सभी जगत् के वशीकरण एवं सभी प्रकार के मनोरथ और कार्यादि साधन के लिए विशेष औषधियों के मूल द्वारा प्रयोग वर्णन किए गए हैं।

मूलिका ग्रहण के लिये भी शुभाशुभ कार्यों के अनुसार मुहूर्त के कुछ विशेष नियम बताए गए हैं—यथा गुटिका तैयार करना हो तो सिद्ध-योग में, पेय बनाना हो तो अमृत-योग में, द्वेष कार्यों में दग्ध-योग, मारणोच्चाटनादि कार्यों में मृत्यु-योग, तथा रोग-निवारणादि कार्यों में अमृत-योग।

मूलिका ग्रहण विधिः—

साधक रक्षाबन्धनादि पूर्वक यथोक्त मुहुर्त में निर्दिष्ट-विधि से भूमि को खोदकर औषध-मूल को बिना टूटे हुए निकाले, और फिर मंत्र से अभिमंत्रित करते हुए शास्त्रादेशानुसार उसे प्रयोग में ले।

स्त्री वशीकरणः—उपरोक्त नियमानुसार अश्वगन्धा-मूल उखाड़ कर कर्पूर और दारचीनी मिला कर जिस स्त्री को भी खान-पान में दी जाए, उसका वशीकरण होता है। और इन ही औषधियों में जायफल मिला कर अच्छे प्रकार पीस कर १-१ माशा (ग्राम) भर की गुटिका बना लें, अब इसे अङ्गूठी में नगीने के स्थान पर रखकर अङ्गुली में धारण करें अथवा उस पिष्टि का वलय बनाकर अंगुली में धारण करें। इसे जब तक धारण किया जाएगा, उस समय तक वीर्य स्तंभन होता है। तथा इसके धारण किए रहने से बार बार कामोत्तेजना होती है।

इसी प्रकार उद्धमिनी (नलिका) के मूल-चूर्ण के प्रयोग से विष, पाण्डु तथा कुष्ठादि नाश होते हैं, इसके अतिरिक्त इस औषधि के प्रयोग से स्तंभन, गुह्यस्तम्भ-नादि तथा तन्मोक्षीकरणादि विविध कार्य सिद्ध होते हैं।

कुछ औषध-मूलों के प्रयोग से विचित्र कार्य भी होते हैं, यथा काकमाची से नाग सिद्धि, लज्जालु द्वारा किसी को नपुंसक बना देना तथा इच्छानुसार उसका पुनः स्वस्थीकरण आदि। श्यामा नामक औषधि-मूल से सर्प-विष से मृतप्राय व्यक्ति भी बच जाता है, तथा एरण्ड बीज के प्रयोग से पति **न्यस्तचित्त** हो जाता है।

मारण—श्मशान भूमि में मार्ग के दोनों ओर आमने सामने उगे हुए अर्क वृक्षों की पश्चिम-दिक्गामिनी मूल को बलि पूर्वक उखाड़ कर मंत्र का १००० जप करें, तो शत्रु की मृत्यु होती है।

स्तम्भन—दो आमने सामने लगे विष वृक्षों (कनेर-आक-कुचलादि) की मूल यथा नियम ग्रहण करके साध्य की प्रतिमा बनावें, और उसके जिन्हा-नयन-हृदय-कान-ठोड़ी-पांव-हाथ आदि के चिन्ह बनाकर उस पर शत्रु की प्राण-प्रतिष्ठा करें, और इस पर[1] "लं" बीज मंत्र का एक सहस्र जप कर के देवस्थान-मातृकोष्ठ या शत्रु के द्वार के निकट भूमि में गाड़ दें, तो उस व्यक्ति का सब प्रकार से स्तंभन होता है।

---

(१) मघवाख्यं सहस्रकम्।

अध्याय ६३ से ६८

इस अध्याय में शत्रुनाशन के लिये "**काल**" का ३५ अक्षर का मंत्र दिया गया है, जिसके विधिवत् सहस्र जप से शत्रु काल के मुख में चला जाता है।

६४वें अध्याय में यंत्र सहित **श्री षण्मुख स्कन्द** का मंत्र वर्णित है, जिसके ऋषि-छन्द-ध्यानादि पूर्वक विधिवत् तीन हज़ार नित्य जप से साधक को अखिलार्थ लाभ, सर्वत्र सफलता एवं मनोवाञ्छित सिद्धि प्राप्त होती है।

६५वें अध्याय में **श्री महाभैरव (वटुक भैरव)** का मंत्र और यंत्र दोनों दिए गए हैं, सभी प्रकार की सिद्धि के लिये इस मंत्र के अन्त में "नमः" लगाना चाहिए तथा शत्रु के वशीकरण, शत्रु-निग्रह तथा उच्चाटनादि कर्मों में इसे स्वाहान्त कर देना चाहिए तथा यंत्र में अपना मनोवाञ्छित कार्य साध्य-नाम के सहित लिखना चाहिये। इससे अतुल-सिद्धि तथा अभीष्ट कार्यों में सफलता मिलती है।

६६वें अध्याय में अतिशीघ्र-सिद्धिप्रदा भगवती त्वरिता का सैंतीस अक्षर का मंत्र उसके यंत्र के सहित दिया गया है, ऋषि-छन्द-ध्यानादि स्मरण पूर्वक यथा-विधि इस मंत्र को अक्षर-सहस्र (३७०००) जप करके सिद्ध कर लेना चाहिये। इस सिद्धि के बाद मंत्र के १००० जप से भगवती स्वयं दर्शन देकर विहिताविहित सभी कार्य सिद्ध करती है, इसके अतिरिक्त यह गुह्य विद्या परम-सौभाग्य-प्रदा, सर्व-दोष-निवारक, भूत, ग्रह, शत्रु आदि नष्ट करने वाली, अभीष्ट फलप्रद—तथा सभी प्रकार से संरक्षण देती है।

६७वें अध्याय में निग्रहानुग्रह-कारक, सर्व-शत्रु-निवारक तथा सर्वत्र विजय-प्रद **श्री वीरभद्र** का यंत्र एवं मन्त्र दोनों बतलाये गये हैं, मंत्र के ऋषि-छन्द-षडङ्ग न्यास-ध्यानादि स्मरण पूर्वक अक्षर-सहस्र जप करने से सिद्धि हो जाती है, तदनन्तर विधिवत् स्मरण, जप और यंत्र धारण से सर्वार्थ-लाभ और मनोवांछित प्राप्ति होती है।

६८वें अध्याय में सम्पूर्ण विश्व के संहार करने में भी समर्थ **श्री वडवानल भैरव** का दारुण मंत्र दिया गया है, ऋष्यादि ध्यानान्त नियमित क्रियाओं के बाद इसका निर्दिष्ट विधि से कवचोक्त-यंत्र बना कर उस पर शत्रु का नाम लिखें, और उसके अनंतर ३००० बार नित्यप्रति तीन रात्रि तक मंत्र का जप करें, इसके प्रभाव से शत्रु अतिशीघ्र अग्नि से जल कर नाश को प्राप्त होता है तथा उसका सर्वस्व भी स्वाहा हो जाता है।

अध्याय ६९ से ७६

इन अध्यायों में **ब्राह्मी—माहेश्वरी—कौमारी—वैष्णवी—वाराही—नारसिंही—इन्द्राणी—चामुण्डी** इन अष्ट महाशक्तियों के यंत्र और मंत्र विधान दिये गये हैं। सभी देवियों के मन्त्रोद्धार मूल ग्रन्थ में उनके पाठ के साथ साथ ही कर दिये गये हैं।

यहां **श्रों भूर्भुवः स्वः सहित वेदोक्त गायत्री ही ब्राह्मी का मंत्र** है, जिसका एक सहस्र नित्य जप करने से मनुष्य दीर्घायु तथा इच्छाशक्ति प्राप्त कर लेता है। गायत्री मंत्र का साधक गायत्री के साथ किसी भी मंत्र को रख कर अनुष्ठान द्वारा उस मंत्र के फल को प्रत्यक्ष एवं त्वरित प्राप्त कर लेता है।

ब्राह्मी-मन्त्र के साथ आरम्भ में "ओं भुवः" अधिक बढ़ाया जाए तो सर्वत्र विजय और सौभाग्य देने वाला माहेश्वरी का मन्त्र कहलाता है।

कौमारी पूजन और दूसरी क्रियाओं के लिये शरभ चक्र पर ही विधान करने का आदेश है. **कौमारी मन्त्र** के जप, अनुष्ठान से शत्रु शीघ्र ही विनाश को प्राप्त होते हैं।

"ओं भूर्भुवः स्वः" के स्थान पर "ओं वं सं ओं" लगाकर **वेदोक्त गायत्री** मंत्र ही **भगवती वैष्णवी** का सर्वसौभाग्य, धन-धान्य, और अभीष्टार्थप्रद मंत्र बन जाता है। यंत्र-मंत्र-विधि-ज्ञाता इस मंत्र का यथोक्त विधान से नित्यप्रति सहस्र जप करे तो भगवती वैष्णवी सम्पूर्ण मनोरथ सिद्ध करती रहती है।

भगवती **वाराही** के षडक्षर मंत्र का जप, दक्षिणाभिमुख बैठ कर, भगवती वाराही के विशेष यंत्र की पूजन पूर्वक, रात्रि के समय तीन हज़ार बार करना चाहिये, (न दिवा स्मरेत् वार्तालीं), शत्रु नाशन के लिये भगवती वाराही प्रत्यक्ष फल तत्क्षण ही देती है।

नारसिही का मंत्र, यंत्र पूजन पूर्वक, नित्यं प्रति सहस्र संख्या में पचास दिन तक जपानुष्ठान विधि द्वारा करने से शत्रु विविध प्रकार की परेशानियों में फंस जाता है, तथा दस दिन के अन्दर ही अपना स्थान छोड़ कर दूसरे स्थान अथवा देशांतर में भाग जाता है।

व्याहृतित्रय-सम्पुटित भगवती **इन्द्राणी की** वैदिक-ऋचा (मंत्र) का ग्रन्थोक्त विधि से यंत्र की पूजन पूर्वक पुरश्चरण करने से सभी प्रकार के रोग नष्ट होते हैं, तथा साधक को सर्व प्रकार से अभीष्ट सिद्धि होती है।

इसी प्रकार **भगवती चामुण्डी मंत्र का** उसके अध्यायोक्त यंत्र की विधिवत् अर्चनापूर्वक एक सहस्र संख्या में रात्रि के समय, जप किया जाए, और उस यंत्र को श्मशान-चतुष्पथ, अथवा शत्रु की देहलीज़ आदि में दबा दिया जाए, तो निश्चय ही उस शत्रु की पराजय, विनाश और साधक के सभी मनोरथ सिद्ध होते हैं।

अध्याय ७७-७८

७७ वें अध्याय में श्री शरभेश्वर का भुजङ्ग-प्रयात-स्तोत्र दिया गया है, तथा उससे अगले अध्याय (७८ वें अध्याय) में श्री शरभ-हृदय का वर्णन है। इन दोनों स्तोत्रों का श्री शरभेश्वर की पूजन के अन्त में नित्य पाठ करने से नाना प्रकार की सिद्धियां, सभी प्रकार के कष्टों से निवृत्ति, तथा सभी प्रकार की दुर्गम समस्याओं का सुलझाव हो जाता है, इसके अतिरिक्त दूसरे देवी देवताओं के मंत्र भी सिद्ध होते हुए शीघ्र-फल-दायक होते हैं।

अध्याय ७९-८०

इन दोनों अध्यायों में भगवान् श्री शरभेश्वर का अष्टोत्तर-शतनाम तथा सहस्र-नाम सांगोपांग दिए गए हैं, जो पुण्यफल कारक, सर्वदुःख-निवारक, शत्रु समूह-विनाशक तथा सर्वत्र विजय देने वाले हैं।

अध्याय ८१

इस अध्याय में श्री शरभेश्वर का बहुप्रसिद्ध निग्रह-दारुण-सप्तक दिया गया है, जिसे उसकी सत्वर एवं प्रत्यक्ष सिद्धि तथा अचूक फलदायक होने के कारण बहुत से आधुनिक तंत्र-ग्रन्थ-सङ्कलन कर्ताओं ने अपने ग्रन्थ की उपादेयता बढ़ाने एवं विद्वानों को आकर्षित करने के लिये, अपने ग्रन्थ में उचित स्थान दिया है। यह सद्यः फलदायक स्तोत्र दिव्यशक्ति वाला, निग्रहानुग्रह-फलदायक, यथाविधि जपानुष्ठान पाठ करने से तीन दिन में ही शत्रु का नाश कर देता है तथा निर्दिष्ट मंत्रों द्वारा सम्पुटानुष्ठान करने से तत्तदनुरूप फल देता है। ग्रन्थान्त में कुछ और सिद्ध ऋचाओं और मंत्रों का भी वर्णन है, जिनके विधि-पूर्वक अनुष्ठान से साधक मनोऽभीष्ट फल प्राप्त करता है।

परिशिष्टम्

परिशिष्टाध्यायों में मेरुतंत्रोक्त श्री शरभेश्वर का मन्त्र, श्री कालभैरव कृत श्री शरभ-मंत्रराज, मेरुतंत्रोक्त श्री शरभ मालामंत्र, और श्री आकाशभैरव-कल्प नाम से ही लिखित कुछ उपलब्ध पत्रों से श्री शरभेश्वर मंत्रानुष्ठान तथा उस से सम्बन्धित विविध काम्य प्रयोग दिये गए हैं। पाठकों की सुगमता के लिये परिशिष्ट के अनंतर श्री आकाश-भैरव-कल्पाख्य महान् तंत्र में वर्णित वैदिक-ऋचाओं का पूरा विवरण मंत्रपाठ सहित दे दिया है। प्रायः सभी मंत्रों का यथा स्थान उद्धार कर दिया गया है, जो वहां किसी प्रकार लिखने से रह गये थे उन्हें हिन्दी व्याख्या में उद्धृत करने का यथामति यत्न किया है॥ आशा है कि विद्वान् अगले संस्करण में त्रुटियों और अशुद्धियों के लिए मार्गदर्शक बनने की कृपा करेंगे।

प्रक्षेप :—अन्त में प्रक्षेप के रूप में मैंने श्री शारदा तिलक, श्री मेरुतंत्र, श्री प्रपञ्चसार तंत्र, श्री मंत्रमहोदधि, श्री नित्योत्सव आदि विशेष प्रसिद्ध ग्रन्थों से संग्रह करके तंत्रासक्तचेतस् विद्वानों के पुनः संस्मरण एवं सर्व साधारण विद्वानों के ज्ञान की वृद्धि के लिये, अतीत से आज तक महर्षियों, सिद्धों एवं विद्या-मनीषियों द्वारा बहुशः अनुभूत श्री गायत्री, सावित्री और सरस्वती (ब्रह्म-गायत्री, आग्नेयास्त्र और त्र्यम्बक) के विधान, महामृत्युंजय और श्री शताक्षरा विधि भी दी है। इनमें आग्नेयास्त्र के साथ प्रकाशित दो अङ्ग दिनास्त्र और कृत्यास्त्र स्थानाभाव के कारण छोड़ दिये हैं, जिन्हें फिर कभी विस्तृत विधान सहित प्रकाशित करने का यत्न करूंगा।

आशा है कि विद्वान् ब्रह्मास्त्र-धारण के साथ साथ इन सिद्ध विद्याओं को विश्व के कल्याण के लिये उपयोग में लायेंगे।

नई दिल्ली-५ — नानकचन्द्र शर्मा
१ वैशाख २०३९ — धम्मी (भारद्वाज)

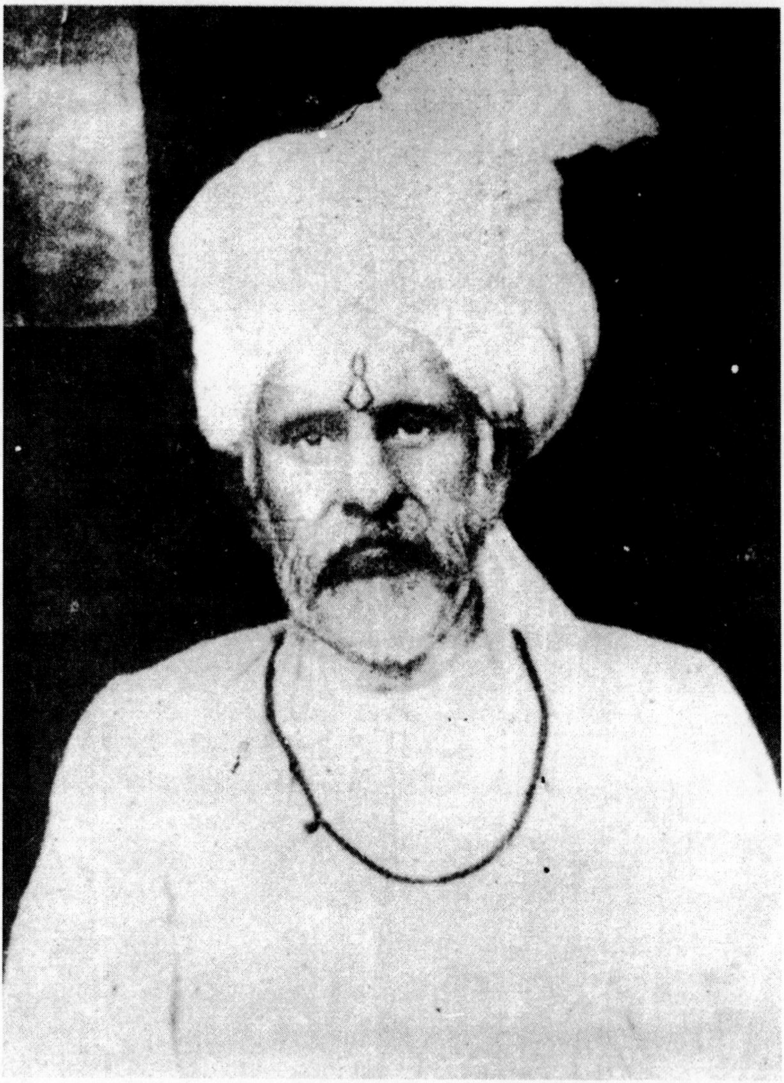

राजज्योतिषी तथा राजवैद्य श्री श्री श्री १०८

श्री पं० लक्ष्मीनारायण जी धर्म्मी (भारद्वाज)

जन्म स्थान—हरिपुर हज़ारा तथा स्वर्गारोहण स्थान—दिल्ली

परम पूज्य पितृवर,

आप की ही अपार कृपा तथा आशीर्वाद से मैं प्रत्येक कठिनाई को लांघ सका हूं।

॥ श्रों श्रीगणेशाय नमः ॥

श्राकाश-भैरव-तंत्रम्

शिवशक्तिसम्वादात्मकम्

प्रथमोऽध्यायः

श्रों श्रीगणेशाय नमः

गुरुं गणपतिं देवीं भैरवं शरभेश्वरम् ।
नमस्कृत्य प्रवक्ष्यामि मंत्रशास्त्रं विभूतये ॥१॥
सांगं सलक्षणं सर्वं वेदसारमभीष्टदम् ।
ज्ञानदं जीवजन्तूनां साधकानां सुखावहम् ॥२॥

श्रीदेव्युवाच ॥

श्रीशिवेशान देवेश श्रीनाथ जगतां पते ।
श्रीकाल-गल-चिद्रूप श्रीमते भवते नमः ॥३॥
श्रन्यथा शरणं नास्ति त्वमेव शरणं मम ।
तस्मात्कारुण्यभावेन रक्ष रक्ष महेश्वर ॥४॥
यद् गुह्यं परमं लोके यच्छास्त्रमखिलप्रदम् ।
यद्धितं साधकेन्द्राणां तद्वदस्व दयानिधे ॥५॥

श्रीशिव उवाच ॥

श्रीमत्परम-सौभाग्य-मंत्र-यंत्रागमादिनाम् ।
त्रयाणामपि वेदानां श्रृणु गुह्यतमं परम् ॥६॥
महामंत्रं क्रियाशास्त्रं महासिद्धिप्रदायकम् ।
सर्व-दोष-प्रशमनं पावनं लोकजीवनम् ॥७॥
धर्मार्थ-काम-मोक्षाणां फलदानप्रगल्भितम् ।
सर्व-ज्ञान-प्रदं ब्रह्म ज्ञानदं ब्रह्मसिद्धिदम् ॥८॥
तादृशं कल्पमागोप्यं सर्ववेदागमोद्भवम् ।
शीघ्र-सिद्धि-प्रदं श्रेष्ठं श्रृणु सर्वमयेऽम्बिके ॥९॥
वक्ष्यमाणं महाशास्त्रं पठतां शृण्वतामपि ।
तथालोकयतां पुंसां वनितानां विशेषतः ॥१०॥

क्षिप्र-सिद्धि-प्रदं दिव्यं कथयामि जगन्मयम् ।
प्रणम्य परया भक्त्या ब्रह्माख्यं योऽवलोकते ॥११॥

सहसा तस्य सौभाग्यमस्तु ज्ञानं च भूयकम् ।
लब्ध्वाशिषः समुत्थाय विभाते देशिकं स्मरन् ॥१२॥

वक्ष्यमाणेन शास्त्रेण साध्यं कर्म समाध्य सः ।
यथातथं पुरा युक्तमेकान्तं भवने शुभे ॥१३॥

यथाविधि समाविश्य भूतोच्चाटं चरेत् स्थितः ।
अपसर्पन्तु ते भूता ये भूता भुवि संस्थिताः ॥१४॥

ये भूता विघ्नकर्तारस्ते नश्यन्तु शिवाज्ञया ।
इति जप्त्वा करास्फोटं त्रिधाघातं पदा तथा ॥१५॥

ततो मन्त्रैर्नमस्कृत्य लोकपालांश्च मण्डपम् ॥

मुक्ता-विद्रुम-रत्न-कांति-रुचिरं हैमं विचित्रं परम्,
नाना-दिव्य-सुगन्धि-गन्ध-निवहं नानाप्रसूनार्चितम् ।
पञ्चाशल्लिपिशोभितं परसुधा-धाराभिरासेचयन्,
पञ्चानन्दमयं प्रसन्नसुखदं भद्राय पीठं नमः ॥१६॥

आब्रह्मलोकादाशेषादालोकालोकपर्वतात् ।
ये वसन्ति द्विजा देवास्तेभ्यो नित्यं नमो नमः ॥१७॥

इति नत्वा समासीनः सर्वालंकरणान्वितः ।
आराधनोपयोगानि संपाद्य तदनन्तरम् ॥१८॥

ब्रह्मरंध्रे यजेन्नाथं ब्रह्मानंदमयं विभुम् ।
परम्पराक्रमेणैव गन्धपुष्पाक्षतादिभिः ॥१९॥

चिरं ध्यात्वा ततो देवि भूतशुद्धिं यथाविधि ।
ऋषिन्यासादिकं कुर्यात् प्रसन्नात्मा यथाविधि ॥२०॥

सर्वकार्यार्थसिध्यै च सर्व-विघ्न-निवृत्तये ।
पंचद्व्यर्णकविंशेन यजेद्वै नायकं पुनः ॥२१॥

इति श्रीआकाशभैरवकल्पे प्रत्यक्षसिद्धिप्रदे उमामहेश्वरसम्वादे उत्साहप्रक्रमो नाम प्रथमोऽध्यायः ॥१॥

द्वितीयोऽध्यायः

अथ विघ्नविनाशाय मंत्रिणां सर्वसिद्धये ।
गणेशाराधनं वक्ष्ये सर्व-काम-फल-प्रदम् ॥१॥

पीठासनेऽष्ट-पत्रेऽब्जे नव-शक्तीर्गणेशि तु ।
प्रागादितो यजेद्देवि नवमीं कर्णिकान्तरे ॥२॥

तीव्रां च ज्वालिनीं नन्दां भोगदां कामरूपिणीम् ।
उग्रां तेजोवतीं सत्यां ततो विघ्नविनाशिनीम् ॥३॥

रक्तांग-राग-वसन-माल्याभरण-भूषिताः ।
वराभीतिकराः सर्वाः प्रसूनादिभिरर्चयेत् ॥४॥

तस्योपरि महायंत्रं कल्पयित्वा यथाविधि ।
आवाहनादिपुष्पांतं कृत्वा नत्वाथ पंचधा ॥५॥

गुरुं प्रथममाराध्य पारंपर्यविधानतः ।
विघ्नेश्वरं सावरणं विभुं संविन्मयं यजेत् ॥६॥

आराध्य योऽखिलान् देवानेक-चत्वारि-पंचभिः ।
यजेत्तस्य त्वरं सिद्धिं तन्वन्त्यखिलदेवताः ॥७॥

बिन्दौ गणेश्वरं लक्ष्मीं त्रिकोणे दिक्षु बाह्यतः ।
श्रियं च श्रीपतिं पूर्वे चांबिकामंबिकापतिम् ॥८॥

दक्षिणेऽथ रतिं कामं पश्चिमे चोत्तरेत्ततः ।
महीं महीपतिं चैव भूयो लक्ष्मीं गणेश्वरम् ॥९॥

परतो ऋतुकोणाग्रमादितस्तान्यजेत् क्रमात् ।
ऋद्ध्यामोदौ समृद्धिं च प्रमोदा-कान्ति-सौमुखौ ॥१०॥

मदनावती समायुक्तं दुर्मुखं च ततः परम् ।
मदद्रवामप्यविघ्नं द्राविणीं विघ्नकारकम् ॥११॥

वसुधारां शंखनिधिं बाह्ये दक्षिणपार्श्वके ।
वसुमतीं पद्मनिधिं वामपार्श्वे यजेत्ततः ॥१२॥

पावकेशानदैत्येय-पवमानेन्द्र-पाशिषु ।
अङ्गदेवीर्यजेदष्टपत्रे प्रागादिमातृकाः ॥१३॥
लोकपालांस्ततः पश्चाद्यजेद्दिक्षु यथाक्रमम् ।
पंचाशदक्षराधीशांस्ततः पाशांकुशौ यजेत् ॥१४॥
चक्रराजं महीकोणद्वन्द्वेन परिवेष्टितम् ।
चिरं ध्यात्वा गणेशं च गणेशाभिमुखं स्थिताः ॥१५॥
गन्धमाल्यैः समभ्यर्च्य धूपदीपादिकं यजेत् ।
हुत्वा तदर्घ्यमात्माग्नौ शतवाराभिमर्शितम् ॥१६॥
आत्मन्युद्वास्य देवेशं मस्तकाराधनं चरेत् ।
सुमुखश्चैकदन्तश्च कपिलो गजकर्णकः ॥१७॥
लम्बोदरश्च विकटो विघ्नराजो विनायकः ।
धूम्रकेतुर्गणाध्यक्षो भालचन्द्रो गजाननः ॥१८॥
वक्रतुण्डः शूर्पकर्णो हेरम्बः स्कन्दपूर्वजः ।
षोडशैतानि नामानि यः पठेच्छृणुयादपि ॥१९॥
विद्यारंभे विवाहे च प्रवेशे निर्गमे तथा ।
संग्रामे संकटे चैव विघ्नस्तस्य न जायते ॥२०॥
एवं स्तुत्वाथ नवकैर्देवमिष्ट्वा यथाविधि ।
सवने तत्र तत्स्थाने यजेदाकाशभैरवम् ॥२१॥

इति श्रीआकाशभैरवकल्पे प्रत्यक्षसिद्धिप्रदे उमामहेश्वरसम्वादे गणेशयजनविधिर्नाम द्वितीयोऽध्यायः ॥२॥

तृतीयोऽध्यायः

श्रीशिव उवाच ॥

रहस्यं श्रृणु कल्याणि भैरवस्य महात्मनः।
सर्वलोकैकरक्षार्थं तव वक्ष्यामि तत्त्वतः ॥१॥

कदा लोकहितार्थाय लीलयाकाशभैरवम्।
त्रिधा विभज्य चात्मानं रक्षते सर्वदाखिलम् ॥२॥

आकाशभैरवं पूर्वं द्वितीयं चाशु गारुडम्।
शरभं तु तृतीयं स्याद्रूपत्रयमिहोच्यते ॥३॥

तस्य तार्तीयरूपस्य त्रिधा रूपं विशेषतः।
शरभं सालुवं चैव पक्षिराजं तृतीयकम् ॥४॥

तत्र मूलत्रिरूपेषु यजेदेवं यथादृढम्।
आदिदेवोस्य मंत्रस्य विद्या ऋषिरिहोच्यते ॥५॥

तथाछंदस्तथादेवी देव आकाशभैरवः।
प्रणवं मां च मायां च बीजशक्ती च कीलकम् ॥६॥

स्वेच्छा-कार्यार्थ-सिद्ध्यर्थं विनियोगोऽथ मायया।
करांगन्यासजालानि क्रमात्कृत्वाथ भावना ॥७॥

नानाहेति सहस्र-वाह-सहितं नानास्थिमालाधरम्
नानावर्ण-सहस्र-पाद-कमलं नानाविधालंकृतम्।
नाना-नाग-विभूषणं पृथुतरग्रीवं सहस्राननम्
नानारातिहरं करालवदनं नौम्यावसानं शिवम् ॥८॥

एवं ध्यात्वा जपेन्मंत्रं षोडशाक्षरपूर्वकम्।
जपेद् गुरुमुखाल्लब्ध्वा लक्षं सर्वांग संयुतम् ॥९॥

भूकोणवृत्तांतरवह्निकोणे संपादितं कल्प्य यथाविधानम्।
आराध्य तत्स्थामखिलोपचारैराराध्य तद्वह्निशि बाह्यदेशे ॥१०॥
तत्कोणमध्ये सकलोपचारैस्ततो जपेन्मंत्रमभीष्टसिद्धये।
यामार्धकालार्जितकार्यजालः प्रादुर्भवत्यंबरभैरवः स्वयम् ॥११॥

निवेद्य तस्याखिलमात्मनाथं धृत्वा तदास्यः प्रणिपत्य तिष्ठेत् ।
श्रीरुद्रसूक्तं प्रजपेत् त्रिवारं ततोऽखिलेशं परितुष्टहृत्स्यात् ॥१२॥

चतुष्टयेन तं पश्येदपांगेन दयापरः ।
सप्तकेन लभेत्पूर्णवीक्षणं भाषणं तथा ॥१३॥

एकादशेन वाक्सिद्धिं षोडशेनामरत्वकम् ।
अष्टादशेन सौभाग्यं चतुर्विंशेन विग्रहम् ॥१४॥

अष्टाविंशेन देवत्वं त्रिंशेनेन्द्रत्वमाप्नुयात् ।
चत्वारिंशेन वेधस्त्वं स्वर्गभेदं च सर्वसु ॥१५॥

पंचाशता रमेशत्वमष्टाशीत्याथ रौद्रकम् ।
शतेन शिवसालोक्यं सहस्रेण स्वरूपकम् ॥१६॥

सामीप्यमयुतेनैव नियुतेन विशेषतः ।
लक्षेण शिवसायुज्यं चमकं तत्परं यजेत् ॥१७॥

चमकोक्ताखिलं भाग्यं ततस्त्वाकाशभैरवम् ।
संतुष्टहृदयस्तस्मै ददात्येव न संशयः ॥१८॥

तेन श्रीरुद्रसूक्तेन शिवलिंगाभिषेचनम् ।
कृत्वैकादशधा मंत्री पूजयेत्सर्वसिद्धये ॥१९॥

इति श्रीआकाशभैरवकल्पे प्रत्यक्षसिद्धिप्रदे उमामहेश्वरसम्वादे उत्साहयजनं नाम तृतीयोऽध्यायः ॥३॥

चतुर्थोऽध्यायः

श्रीशिव उवाच ॥

अथ रुद्राभिषेकस्य विधिं वक्ष्यामि तेऽम्बिके।
येनाखिलापराधं च क्षमते शृणु भैरवः ॥१॥

समाप्य साध्यकं कर्म ब्रह्मयज्ञमुपासनम्।
संगवानंतरं गेहं जनो रम्यं प्रविश्य सः ॥२॥

पूर्ववत्कलशं कृत्वा नमस्कृत्वा महेश्वरम्।
ततः पौरुषसूक्तेन पादर्चेन शिखादिकम् ॥३॥

मातृकासहितेनैव न्यसेत् सव्यापकः क्रमात्।
मंडपं विकरेत्पश्चाद्यज्ञेनेति ऋचाक्षतान् ॥४॥

सुगंधगंधिपयसा पूर्णकुंभमलंकृतम्।
संस्पृशंश्च जपेन्मंत्री गायत्रीं व्याहृतियुताम ॥५॥

वेदादींश्चतुरो मंत्रानापोहिष्टात्यृचो नव।
शन्नइन्द्रेति सूक्तं च एतोन्विंद्रमिति तृचः ॥६॥

तरत्समंदीतिचतुःपवस्वसोमसूक्तकं।
आपो वेति महासूक्तं जप्त्वाभ्यर्च्य सुमादिभिः ॥७॥

आपूर्य्य शंखमभ्यर्च्येमं मे गङ्गेत्यृचं जपेत्।
ऋतं चेति ऋचं पश्चात् त्रिवारं मनसा ततः ॥८॥

गंगे च यमुने चैव गोदावरि सरस्वति।
नर्मदे सिन्धु कावेरि जलेऽस्मिन् संनिधिं कुरु ॥९॥

इति जप्त्वा त्रिधात्मानं प्रोक्ष्योपकरणानि च।
ततः सहस्त्रशीर्षेति देवमावाह्य लिङ्गके ॥१०॥

पीठं पुरुष एवेदं एतावानस्यपाद्यकम्।
त्रिपादूर्ध्वं उदैदर्घ्यं तस्मादाचमनीयकम् ॥११॥

यत्पुरुषेण हविषा मधुपर्कं ततश्चरेत्।
ततो विशेषसूक्तेन स्नानं तं यज्ञमित्यृचा ॥१२॥

श्रीरुद्रपंचके चैव पंचशांतीस्ततः परम्।
श्रीसूक्तं घृतसूक्तं च भूसूक्तं पुरुषसूक्तकम् ॥१३॥

ब्रह्मसूक्तं विष्णुसूक्तं पंचरौद्रं ततः परम्।
तस्मादिति ततो वस्त्रं तस्मादौत्तर्यकं ततः ॥१४॥
तस्मादित्युपवीतं च मूलेनाभरणानि च।
यत्पुरुषमिति गंधं ब्राह्मणोऽस्येति पुष्पकम् ॥१५॥
चन्द्रमामनसो धूपं नाभ्या आसीत्तु दीपकम्।
सप्तास्यासन्नित्यनया नैवेद्यमखिलान्वितम् ॥१६॥
अहमस्मीति सूक्तेन स्पृशन् जप्त्वा ततः परम्।
परिषेचनमुख्यानि कृत्वा पुष्पेण संस्पृशन् ॥१७॥
निवेदयेत्ततः पश्चान्मधुवाता इति तृचा।
धूरसीति ततो धूपं श्रिये जातस्तु दीपकम् ॥१८॥
यज्ञेनेति च तांबूलं त्र्यंबकेन प्रसूनकम्।
सद्योजातेन छत्रं तु वामदेवेन चामरम् ॥१९॥
त्वमापोवषट् त इति शंखतीर्थनिवेदनम्।
व्यजनं च त्वघोरेण नीराजनं तदित्यथ ॥२०॥
सर्वं समाचरेद्देवमीशान इति दर्पणम्।
नमस्कृत्वा ततः स्तुत्वा त्रिधा स्वाद्याभिषिक्तकम् ॥२१॥
यथेष्टं प्रार्थ्य देवेशं स्वात्मन्युद्वास्य भैरवम्।
चिरं ध्यात्वा ततो मंत्री सोऽहं सोऽहमिति स्मरन् ॥२२॥
गुरोः समीपमागत्य गंधपुष्पाक्षतादिभिः।
अभ्यर्च्य तत्पदद्वंद्वं प्रक्षाल्य शुभवारिणा ॥२३॥
तत्कं चरणसूक्तेन प्रोक्षयेत् त्रिः स्वमूर्धनि।
ततस्तत्तीर्थमादाय स्मरन्मंत्रं त्रिधा पिबेत् ॥२४॥
अविद्यामूलनाशाय जन्म-कर्म-निवृत्तये।
ज्ञानसौभाग्यसिद्ध्यर्थं गुरुपादोदकं शुभम् ॥२५॥
ततो गंधप्रसूनाद्यैश्चिरं संपूज्य देशिकम्।
यथा सस्योदनेनैव सत्कारसहितेन तु ॥२६॥
संपूज्य परया भक्त्या स्वयं भुज्यात्ततः परम्।
इति तु श्रीभैरवस्य महदाराधनार्थकम्।
ज्ञात्वा गुरुमुखान्मंत्री प्रतिवासरमाचरेत् ॥२७॥

इति श्रीआकाशभैरवकल्पे प्रत्यक्षसिद्धिप्रदे उमामहेश्वरसम्वादे उत्साहाभिषेकविधिर्नाम चतुर्थोऽध्यायः ॥४॥

पंचमोऽध्यायः

श्रीशिव उवाच ॥

अथ यंत्रप्रयोगं तु कल्याणि शृणु वच्म्यहम् ।
नानासिद्धिप्रदं श्रेष्ठं नानाकार्यजयप्रदम् ॥१॥

वेधसेनं त्रिमूर्धानं परिविष्ट्याभिवेष्ट्य तत् ।
ऊर्ध्वंशूलं तु तन्मध्ये लिखेद् धुं-कुरुतेति फट् ॥२॥

संपूज्य विधिवद्देवमावाह्याकाशभैरवम् ।
तद्दले स्वेष्टमालिख्य स्थापयेत द्विकोष्ठके ॥३॥

यद्वा चक्रप्रकारेण सिद्ध्यत्याशु न संशयः ।
निग्रहानुग्रहे चैव तथा षट्कर्मसु ज्वरे ॥४॥

भूत-प्रेत-पिशाचेषु वैरिष्वपि चरेच्छिवे ।
मरीचिं काश्यपिं भानुं नायकं वह्नि मारुतौ ॥५॥

सूकरं च सूरीं चैव विदुश्च तदनंतरम् ।
चिंतामणिरिति ख्यातं सप्तकूटं महामनुम् ॥६॥

हेमपत्रे समालिख्यावाह्य संपूज्य भैरवम् ।
जपं साहस्त्रकं कुर्याद्रक्षाबंधं यथाविधि ॥७॥

तेन सर्वसमृद्धिं च सर्वकार्यजयं लभेत् ।
अयुतेन वशीकारं नियुतेन धनागमम् ॥८॥

चत्वारिंशेन वाक्सिद्धिं मोहनं चतुरुत्तरात् ।
पंचाशता जगत्क्षोभं षष्ट्याऽकर्षणमद्भुतम् ॥९॥

उच्चाटनं तु सप्तत्या नवत्या स्तंभनं भवेत् ।
निग्रहं षण्णवत्या तु लक्षेणाखिलदर्शनम् ॥१०॥

सप्तलक्षेण देवेशि सर्वाभीष्टं लभेद् ध्रुवम् ।
चिंतामणिमहामंत्रं चिंतितार्थप्रदायकम् ॥११॥

एकाक्षरं महामंत्रं (वीर्यं) यत्नेनापि जपांबिके ।
यंत्ररूपेण मंत्रं च मंत्ररूपेण यंत्रकम् ॥१२॥
यंत्रमंत्राक्षरं तस्मात्क्षिप्रसिद्धिप्रदं भवेत् ।
ब्रह्माणं वसुधां विष्णुं मायाबीजं समुद्धरेत् ॥१३॥
कामराजमितिख्यातं चतुष्कूटं महामनुम् ।
महामायां तु तेनैव वेष्टितं मंत्ररूपकम् ॥१४॥
तस्मिन्मंत्रे महायंत्रे देवमाकाशभैरवम् ।
आवाह्यानेन संपूज्य जपेदेकाग्रमानसः ॥१५॥
चतुःसहस्रं वश्याय भर्तुः स्त्रीणामथायुतम् ।
सेनाया नियुतं राज्ञः प्रयुतं द्व्यधिकं नृणाम् ॥१६॥
देवतानां चतुःषष्टिः मुनीनां सप्तसप्ततिः ।
हरेरशीतिर्नवति विष्णोर्लक्षं तु वेधसः ॥१७॥
चतुर्लक्षं महेशस्य सर्वंयजनपूर्वकम् ।
सर्वे ह्यनेन मंत्रेण प्रीता भवंति सिद्धिदाः ॥१८॥
अनंतं च बृहद्भानुं नारायणमतः परम् ।
महामायां ततो बिन्दुं संयोज्याशेषमुद्धरेत् ॥१९॥
महामायेति विख्याता चतुष्कूटाक्षरात्मिका ।
तत्कूटं मंत्रयंत्राख्यं सर्वकार्यार्थसिद्धिदम् ॥२०॥
तस्मिन्नावाह्य देवेशमिष्ट्वा पंचसहस्रकम् ।
मोहनाय जपेन्मंत्रं जंतूनामयुतं नृणाम् ॥२१॥
स्त्रियं द्वादशसाहस्रं नियुतं रोगशांतये ।
पंचविंशतिसाहस्रं द्रव्यलाभाय मानुषात् ॥२२॥
त्रयस्त्रिंशत्सहस्रं तु पुत्रलाभाय योषितम् ।
सप्तत्रिंशत्सहस्रं तु महावैरस्य शांतये ॥२३॥
षट्चत्वारिंसहस्रं तु विद्वेषोच्चाटसिद्धये ।
षट्पंचाशत्सहस्रं तु मृतकोत्थापनाय वै ॥२४॥
चतुःषष्टिसहस्रं तु सर्वाकर्षणसिद्धये ।
अष्टाशीतिसहस्रं तु देवताकर्षसिद्धये ॥२५॥
सप्तनवतिसाहस्रं सर्वसौभाग्यसिद्धये ।
सर्वस्तंभाय लक्षं तु मारणाय द्विलक्षकम् ॥२६॥

चतुर्लक्षं प्रसादाय पंचलक्षं विशेषतः ।
इन्द्रत्वं दशलक्षेण त्रिंशलक्षेण तत्त्वकम् ॥२७॥
षष्टिलक्षेण विष्णुत्वं रुद्रत्वं दशलक्षतः ।
चतुःशतेन लक्षेण महामायात्वमम्बिके ॥२८॥
रुद्रं वैश्वानरं विष्णुमायां बिंदुमतः परम् ।
उद्धरेदखिलं योज्य चतुष्कूटं परात्परम् ॥२९॥
लक्ष्मीबीजमितिख्यातं सर्वसंपत्समृद्धिदम् ।
महामायावदखिलं विशेषाद्राज्यसिद्धिदम् ॥३०॥
अश्विनीमंत्रमुद्धृत्य महामायां च बिंदुकम् ।
द्राविणीयमितिख्यातं त्रिकूटं द्रावकारकम् ॥३१॥
एतन्मंत्रमये यंत्रे विधिवत्पूज्य पूर्ववत् ।
लक्षत्रयं जपं कुर्यादखिलं कामराजवत् ॥३२॥
ईशानं पावकं विष्णुं नारायणमतः परम् ।
बिन्दुद्वयम् च संयोज्य चोद्धरेद्भास्कराख्यकम् ॥३३॥
चतुष्कूटं महामंत्रं सर्वव्याधिहरं परम् ।
चिंतामणिवदखिलं द्विलक्षात्कुष्ठनाशनम् ॥३४॥
यक्ष्माहरं त्रिलक्षं तु सर्वलक्षचतुष्टयम् ॥३५॥

इति श्रीआकाशभैरवकल्पे प्रत्यक्षसिद्धिप्रदे उमामहेश्वरसम्वादे मंत्र-यंत्र-प्रक्रमं नाम पंचमोऽध्यायः ॥५॥

षष्ठोऽध्यायः

श्रीशिव उवाच ॥

चित्रमालां प्रवक्ष्यामि शीघ्रसिद्धिप्रदायिनीम् ।
सर्वसौभाग्यदां तुर्यां चतुर्वर्गफलप्रदाम् ॥१॥
आकाशभैरवस्यास्य मंत्रस्यानंदभैरवः ।
ऋषिः छंदस्तु गायत्री देवताकाशभैरवः ॥२॥
ह्रींकारं बीजमित्युक्तं हुङ्कारं शक्तिरुच्यते ।
सर्वाभीष्टार्थसिद्ध्यर्थे विनियोगस्तु मायया ।
करांगन्यासजालानि क्रमात्कृत्वाथ भावयेत् ।
सहस्रपाणिपद्मवक्त्रं सहस्रत्रयलोचनम् ॥
सर्वाभीष्टप्रदं देवं स्मरेदाकाशभैरवम् ॥३॥

ओं नमो भगवते आकाशभैरवाय निखिललोकप्रियाय प्रणत जन-परिताप-विमोचनाय सकल-भूत-निवारणाय सर्वाभीष्टप्रदाय नित्याय सच्चिदानंदविग्रहाय सहस्रबाहवे सहस्रमुखाय सहस्र-त्रिलोचनाय सहस्र-चरणाय करालाय अखिलरिपु-संहारकारणाय अनेक-कोटि-ब्रह्म-कपाल-मालालंकृताय नररुधिरमांसभक्षणाय महाबलपराक्रमाय महदन्तराय विष-मोचनाय पर-मंत्र-यंत्र-तंत्र-विद्या-विच्छेदनाय प्रसन्नवदनाम्बुजाय एह्येहि आगच्छागच्छ ममाभीष्टमाकर्षयाकर्षय आवेशयावेशय मोहय २ भ्रामय २ द्रावय २ तापय २ साधय २ बंधय २ भाषय २ क्षोभय २ भूतप्रेतादि पिशा-चान्मर्दय २ कुर्दय २ पाटय २ मोटय २ गुंफय २ कंपय २ ताडय २ त्रोटय २ भेदय २ छेदय २ चंडवातातिवेगाय संतत-गंभीर-विजृंभणाय संकर्षय २ संक्रामय २ प्रवेशय २ स्तोभय २ स्तंभय २ तोदय २ खेदय २ तर्जय २ गर्जय २ नादय २ रोदय २ घातय २ वेतय २ सकल-रिपु-जनाञ्छिन्धि २ भिन्दय २ अंधयं २ रुन्धय २ नर्दय २ बंदय २ श्रीं ह्रीं क्लीं कल्याणकारणाय श्मशा-नानंदमहाभोगप्रियाय देवदत्तं आनय २ दूनय २ केलय २ मेलय २ प्रपन्न वत्सलाय प्रतिवदन-दहनामृत-किरणनयनाय सहस्रकोटि-वेताल-परिवृताय मम रिपूनुच्चाटयोच्चाटय नेपय २ तापय २ सेचय २ मोचय २ लोटय २ स्फोटय २ गृहाण २ अनंत-वासुकि-तक्षक-कर्कोटक-पद्म-महापद्म-शंख-

गुलिक-महानाग-भूषणाय स्थावर-जंगमानां विषं नाशय २ प्राशय २ भस्मीकुरु २ भक्तजनवल्लभाय सर्गस्थितिसंहारकारणाय कथय २ सर्वं शत्रून् उद्रेकय २ विद्वेषय २ उत्सादय २ उत्पादय २ बाधय २ साधय २ दह २ पच २ शोषय २ पोषय २ दूरय २ मारय २ भक्षय २ शिक्षय २ समस्तभूतं शिक्षय २ श्रीं ह्रीं क्लीं क्ष्म्र्यैं अनवरत-तांडवाय आपदुद्धारणाय साधुजनान् तोषय २ भूषय २ पालय २ शीलय २ काम-क्रोध-लोभ-मोह-मद-मात्सर्यं शमय २ दमय २ त्रासय २ शासय २ क्षिति-जल-दहन-मारुत-गगन-तरणि-सोमात्मशरीराय शम-दमोपरति तितिक्षा समाधान श्रद्धां दापय २ प्रापय २ विघ्न विच्छेदनं कुरु २ रक्ष २ क्ष्म्र्यैं क्लीं ह्रीं श्रीं ब्रह्मणे स्वाहा।

इति गोप्यं महामंत्रं परमाकाशभैरवम्।
यस्य स्मरणमात्रेण नंवंत्यखिलदेवताः॥
शतवारमिमं मंत्रं जपेत्सर्वार्थसिद्धये।
त्रिवारं कार्यसिद्ध्यर्थं जपेदेकाग्रमानसः॥
प्रथमं तु त्रिधा मृश्य गुरुं स्वेष्टं यदा स्मरेत्।
तत्काम्यसिद्धये शक्तौ जुहुयात्स्वात्मपावके॥७॥

इति श्रीआकाशभैरवकल्पे प्रत्यक्षसिद्धिप्रदे उमामहेश्वरसम्वादे चित्रमालामंत्रं नाम षष्ठोऽध्यायः॥६॥

सप्तमोऽध्यायः

श्रीशिव उवाच ॥

श्रृणु देवि क्रियाभेदं शीघ्रसिद्धिप्रदायकम् ।
नानाकर्मसमोपेतं साधकानां विवेकिनम् ॥१॥
रक्तांबरं सुमलेप भूषणं रक्तलोचनम् ।
रक्तवर्णलसद्ग्रीवं रक्तकुंडलसंयुतम् ॥२॥
रत्नकेयूरमुकुटं लसच्चांद्रार्धशेखरम् ।
प्रसन्नममृतोन्मत्तं प्रणताभीष्टसिद्धिदम् ॥३॥
इक्षुकोदडंपुष्पेषु पूर्णबाहुसहस्रकम् ।
कार्मुकोत्थशरैर्दिव्यैः पूरिताशावकाशकम् ॥४॥
चिरं ध्यात्वा जपेदेवं जगद्वश्याय साधकः ।
काममादौ ततो मंत्रं पुनः कामं सपल्लवम् ॥५॥
त्रिसहस्रं ततो मंत्री (मौनी) देशिकाज्ञामनुस्मरन् ।
ततः सर्ववशीकारं साध्ययुक्तं विशेषतः ॥६॥
आकर्षे तु तथा ध्यानं पाश-बाहु-सहस्रकम् ।
तत्पाशपूरिताशेषककुभः कर्षंताखिलम् ॥७॥
ध्यात्वा जपेत्तथा मंत्रं साधकः स्थिरमानसः ।
आंकारं च ततो मंत्रं पुनरां सहपल्लवम् ॥८॥
आकर्षणे विशेषज्ञः ससाध्यं तस्य सिद्धये ।
राजचौरारिनारीणाम् देवतानां विशेषतः ॥९॥
चेतनाचेतनानां च भूत-प्रेत-गणादिनाम् ।
तस्य शीघ्रं लभेद्देवि सर्वाकर्षणमद्भुतम् ॥१०॥
सर्वलोकवशीकारं सर्वकार्यजयं तथा ।
ते सर्वे तद्वशं प्राप्य दासभूता भवंति हि ॥११॥
यं यं मनसि संचित्य जपेद्भवति साध्ययुक् ।
ते सर्वे तद्वशं प्राप्य दासभूता भवंति हि ॥१२॥

इति श्रीआकाशभैरवकल्पे प्रत्यक्षसिद्धिप्रदे उमामहेश्वरसम्वादे वश्याकर्षणप्रयोगो नाम सप्तमोऽध्यायः ॥७॥

अष्टमोऽध्यायः

श्रीशिव उवाच ॥

पीताम्बरं प्रसन्नाक्षं कुंकुमारुणवक्षसम् ।
मुक्ताहार-लसद्ग्रीवं रत्नशिंजितनूपुरम् ॥१॥
उत्तुंग-रत्नमुकुटमुद्यद्भानुसमप्रभम्।
अमृतानंद-संभोग-लीलमद्भुत-विग्रहम् ॥२॥
स्वच्छंदमात्मवैलास्यं मोहिताखिललोककम् ।
ध्यात्वा जपेत्ततो मंत्रं प्रसन्नात्मा जितेन्द्रियः ॥३॥
तस्य दार्ढ्यप्रभावेन देव-दानव-राक्षसाः ।
भूत-प्रेत-पिशाचाश्च योषितोऽखिलमानुषाः ॥४॥
मन्मथानलनिर्दग्धास्त्यक्ताचेष्टांबराशनाः ।
दिदृक्षवस्त्यक्तलज्जा मुह्यंत्यखिलजंतवः ॥५॥
महामायां ततो मंत्रं मायां साध्यं विमोहय ।
ततःस्वाहेति माहेशि द्रावय द्रावयेति वै ॥६॥
विशेषान्मन्मथस्थानात् स्मरपारवशाः स्त्रियः ।
द्रवंति बहुरेतांसि वह्नेराज्यमिव स्वयम् ॥७॥

इति श्रीआकाशभैरवकल्पे प्रत्यक्षसिद्धिप्रदे उमामहेश्वरसम्वादे मोहन-द्रावक-प्रयोगो नामाष्टमोऽध्यायः ॥८॥

नवमोऽध्यायः

श्रीशिव उवाच ।।

वक्ष्यामि तव देवेशि स्तंभनद्वेषकर्मणि ।
जंगमस्थावराणां च क्षिप्राश्चर्यनिदर्शनम् ।।१।।

महाकालघनश्यामं वज्रदंतमुखांबुजम् ।
कपिलाक्षं बृहत्स्कंधं करालं कृष्णवाससम् ।।२।।

गंगास्थिमालाचंद्रार्धशेखरं विषमेक्षणम् ।
महाकायं महावेगं व्यालयज्ञोपवीतिनम् ।।३ ।।

वामहस्तै रिपोरास्यं भीषयंतं प्रतिक्षणम् ।
सत्वरं दक्षहस्ताग्रैस्ताडयंतं मुखस्थले ।।४ ।।

एवं ध्यात्वा जपेन्मंत्री चिरमाकाशभैरवम् ।
पूर्वसंख्यामहामंत्रमर्धरात्रौ यथाविधि ।।५ ।।

चराचर-गति-स्वांत-लोचनास्य-करांघ्रिणाम् ।
गुह्य-लिंग-श्रुति-स्तंभं स्तंभयंति न संशयः ।।६।।

वासवं मूलमंत्रं च पुनरिन्द्रं सपल्लवम् ।
रुद्रमंत्रं पुना रुद्रं पल्लवम् द्वेषसिद्धये ।।७।।

विद्वेषणप्रभावेण स्वप्रतापपराक्रमैः ।
वैरिणां मन्युमन्योन्यमेधयंतमहेतुकम् ।।८।।

तयोरैश्वर्यजालानां क्षयं कुर्वीत तत्परम् ।
तयोर्दशदिनात्पश्चान्महद्युद्धं भवेद् ध्रुवम् ।।९।।

इति श्रीआकाशभैरवकल्पे प्रत्यक्षसिद्धिप्रदे उमामहेश्वरसम्वादे स्तंभ-विद्वेष-प्रयोगो नाम नवमोऽध्यायः ।।९।।

दशमोऽध्यायः

श्रीशिव उवाच ।।

निग्रहोच्चाटने वक्ष्ये नितरां परिपंथिनाम् ।
महाक्रूरतरं गुह्यं श्रृणु सर्वं वरानने ।।१।।
करालमुग्रदंष्ट्रं च कालांजनसमप्रभम् ।
अनेक-कोटि-ब्रह्मास्थि-मुंड-मालाविभूषितम् ।।२।।
घोराट्टहास-भिन्नांड-गोलकं कृत्तिवाससम् ।
सहस्र-मुख-हस्तांघ्रि मुकुटं नागभूषणम् ।।३।।
सहस्र-कोटि-वेताल-गण-संघसमावृतम् ।
नानाविध-शिलाभेदैर्वर्षयंतं स्वकिंकरैः ।।४।।
महावीर्यमतिक्रुद्धं महाभीतपराक्रमम् ।
भक्षयंतं निजैर्भूतैः परिपन्थिकुलं बलात् ।।५ ।।
एवं रूपं चिरं ध्यात्वा स्मरेदाकाशभैरवम् ।
दशरात्रं जपेन्मंत्री जपन्पंचशतं मनुम् ।।६।।
उच्चाटनं च संहारं दशाहात्परतो लभेत् ।
वायुबीजं च मंत्रं च पुनर्वायुं सपल्लवम् ।।७।।
हुङ्कारं च पुनर्मंत्रं पुनर्हुङ्कारपल्लवम् ।
इति प्रयोगद्वितयं कुर्याद्यत्नेन चाम्बिके ।।८।।
सहस्राल्लभते सिद्धिं संशयो नास्ति शोभने ।

इति श्रीआकाशभैरवकल्पे प्रत्यक्षसिद्धिप्रदे उमामहेश्वरसम्वादे उच्चाटन-निग्रहप्रयोगो नामदशमोऽध्यायः ।।१०।।

एकादशोऽध्यायः

श्रीशिव उवाच ॥

मोक्षसारस्वतं वक्ष्ये सर्वेषामपि यत्नतः ।
समाहितेन मनसा शृणु कल्याणि शोभने ॥१॥
स्फटिकाभं महादेवं प्रसन्नवदनांबुजम् ।
अमृतांशु कलाचूड़मग्नि-सूर्येन्दु-लोचनम् ॥२॥
व्याघ्रचर्माम्बरं शांतं व्यालयज्ञोपवीतनम् ।
वैडूर्यहार-शोभाढ्यं मंदस्मित-मनोहरम् ॥३॥
मुक्ता-विद्रुम-रत्नानुसांगदंसु-विभूषितम् ।
स्वर्णनूपुरपादाब्जं श्वेत-कुंडल मंडितम् ॥४॥
वीणां व्याख्यानमुद्रां च पुस्तकं स्फटिकस्रजम् ।
भस्म-भस्त्रं-गदां-पद्मं-सुधाकुंभं करांबुजैः ॥५॥
बिभ्राणममलं ब्रह्मज्ञानमुद्रा-स्वरूपिणम् ।
चन्द्रमंडल-मध्यस्थं सच्चिदानंदमव्ययम् ॥६॥
ध्यात्वा जपेत्ततो मंत्रमयुतं तत्त्ववित्तमः ।
विजृंभते महाबाणी वियद्गंगाप्रवाहवत् ॥७॥
तद्वाणीं दूरतः श्रुत्वा प्रकंपंते कवीश्वराः ।
तस्य भोगं च मोक्षं च भुक्तिर्मुक्तिश्च लभ्यते ॥८॥
भूतले पूजितः सर्वैर्भुक्त्वा भोगान् यथेप्सितान् ।
अनेनैव शरीरेण जीवन्मुक्तो भवेच्छिवे ॥९॥
भाषा मंत्रं पुनर्भाषां स्वाहांतं मंत्रमुच्यते ।
चिंतामणिं ततो मंत्रं पुनश्चिंतामणिं नमः ॥१०॥
मोक्षाय प्रणवाद्यंतं धारणाय विशेषतः ।
श्रियै श्री पुटितं स्वाहा घृणिरारोग्यबृद्धये ॥११॥
चंद्रं रोगविनाशाय विषनाशाय ठं-युतम् ।
इति गुह्यतमं शास्त्रं लघुसिद्धिप्रदायकम् ॥१२॥
यत्नेनापि यजेद्देवि सर्वकामार्थसिद्धये ।

इति श्रीआकाशभैरवकल्पे प्रत्यक्षसिद्धिप्रदे उमामहेश्वरसम्वादे भोगप्रदो नामैकादशोऽध्यायः ॥११॥

द्वादशोऽध्यायः

श्रीदेव्युवाच ॥

देवादिदेव लोकेश शशिचूड़महेश्वर ।
त्राहि मां जगतां नाथ शश्वदानन्दशाश्वत ॥१॥

श्रीशिव उवाच ॥

आशुतार्क्ष्यप्रयोगस्य रहस्यं शृणु वच्म्यहम् ।
सर्वकामप्रदं दिव्यं चतुर्वर्ग-फल-प्रदम् ॥२॥
आशुतार्क्ष्याख्य-मंत्रस्य शंकरः ऋषिरुच्यते ।
छन्दस्तु जगती देव आशुतार्क्ष्याख्य-भैरवः ॥३॥
गं बीजमाहुतिः शक्तिरभीष्टे विनियोगकम् ।
गां श्रीं इति करन्यासं षडंगं चाथ भावना ॥४॥

आजानोस्तप्तहेम-प्रभममलमय-प्रख्यमानाभि तस्मा-
दाकर्णंकुंकमाभं भ्रमरकुलमिव श्याममामूर्ध्व-केशम्
ब्रह्मांडं व्याप्त-देहं द्विभुजमभिवरैर्भूषणैर्भूषितांगम्
पिंगाक्षं तीक्ष्णदंष्ट्रं वरदमभयदं तार्क्ष्यमुग्रं नमामि ॥५॥

श्रीं गं गरुडाय गरुडाय महागरुडाय समस्तांडाय त्रैलोक्यनायकाय नागशोणितदिग्धांगाय ओं पक्षिराजाय विष्णुवाहनाय सर्वसर्पान् संहर २ मर्दय २ मोदय २ लोटय २ त्रोटय २ भ्रामय २ मुंच २ आकर्ष २ आवेशय २ सिद्धय २ शीघ्रय २ समस्तभूतवेतालान् नाशय २ सर्वग्रहान् नाशय २ सर्वशत्रून् नाशय २ सर्वसर्पान् संहर २ स्वाहा ।

षट्षष्टिशतमेवैतं मंत्रं यत् आशुतार्क्ष्यकम् ।
मोहनाकर्षणावेश-स्तंभ-वश्यानि भाषणम् ॥६॥
दंड-विद्वेष-संक्राम-स्तंभोच्चाटारिनिगृहम् ।
एवं नानाप्रयोगं च योग्यं कर्मादि-मस्तके ॥७॥
कुर्यादतंद्रितो मंत्री सर्वकार्यार्थसिद्धये ।
देवभूत-ग्रहादीनां नाना रोग नृणां शिवे ॥८॥

एवं नानाविधाख्यानां नाशायानुग्रहाय च ।
दृढव्रतः क्रियां कुर्यात्सकलां पल्लवान्विताम् ॥६॥
अयुतं तु पुरश्चर्या संख्या सांगं समाचरेत् ।
पिष्टान्नांगंतिलांल्लाजान् पायसं च घृतान्वितम् ।
अश्वत्थ वह्नि शाखे चागरून्मद्धोममुच्यते ॥१०॥

षट्कोणांतरतोऽग्नि-वायु-लिपियुङ्मायां च सप्तार्णकम् ।
कोणेष्वष्टसु साध्य वह्नि लिपियुक् तद्बाह्य चिंतामणिम् ॥
पाशं शक्तिमथांकुशं प्रणवकं संवेष्टच तारायुतं ।
कुर्यात्सर्पभयापहं जयकरं सर्वार्थ-सिद्धि-प्रदम् ॥११॥

इति श्रीआकाशभैरवकल्पे प्रत्यक्षसिद्धिप्रदे उमामहेश्वरसम्वादे आशुतार्क्ष्यविधिर्नाम द्वादशोऽध्यायः ॥१२॥

त्रयोदशोऽध्यायः

श्रीशिव उवाच ॥

अथ प्रयोगभेदानि वक्ष्यामि शृणु शोभने ।
प्रयोग स्मरणादेव सर्वान् कामानवाप्नुयात् ॥१॥
मोहाकर्षवशीकारस्तंभ-स्तोभेषु भाषणे ।
विद्वेष-दंड-संक्राम-प्रें-खोच्चाटेषु मारणे ॥२॥
सोमाग्निकामदेवेशावन्यभ्रांशं भृगूनि च ।
[1]श्रीं ह्रीं यं तत्क्रमादांदौ मंत्रस्योच्चारणे तथा ॥३॥
मायां कृशानौ चतुष्पत्रकेसरं लक्ष्मी ऋतौ तत्त्रिशूलेषूनाम् ॥
यंत्रं प्रशस्तं स्थिरजंगमानां संमोहनं देवग्रहादिकानाम् ॥४॥
इति गुह्यं महामंत्रं संमोहनमनुत्तमम् ।
मंत्र-स्मरण-मात्रेण मुह्यं त्यक्त्वां वरानने ॥५॥
बिन्दौ वह्नि ऋतौ लक्ष्मीं कुलतारात्तु नामकम् ।
शूलकोणांतरालेजां श्री मायाभ्यां विवेष्टयेत् ॥६॥
एतद् गुह्यं महावीर्य्यं भीममत्याशुसिद्धिदम् ।
जंगमाजंगमानां च लभेदाकर्षणं शिवे ॥७॥
तारं मध्येऽष्टपत्रेमां मू ह्वं ह्वे नाम मन्मथम् ।
मायावृतमिदं श्रेष्ठं स्वेच्छावश्यकरं परम् ॥८॥
बिंदौ सुरेशमथ वह्निगृहे कृशानुं
भूकोण-युग्म-विलसत्क्षमयाभिवीतम् ।
मायांकवाह्य मथ तच्छ्रुतिराजभृंगं
स्तंभ-प्रशस्तमतुलं पवनाग्निकानाम् ॥९॥
मध्येनामवसप्तारेत्वष्टास्त्रे मामजामपि ।
कामावृतमिदं यंत्रं स्तंभनं स्तोभनं शिवे ॥१०॥
बिंदौ वायुं दशारे तु भूकारं नाम बाह्यकम् ।
मायावृत्तं महायंत्रं भूतभावनलंपटम् ॥११॥

1(वा) ऊं ह्रूं यं ह्रूं

देव-ग्रहाणां साध्यानां भूत-प्रेत-ग्रहादिनाम् ।
विशेषतो हि मूकानां भाषणं लभते क्षणात् ।।१२।।

राशिकोष्ठे लिखेद्राशिं मध्ये वह्नौ यशार्णके ।
कोणाग्रशूलके साध्यं स्वेच्छाविद्वेषणं परम् ।।१३।।

मध्ये नाम शिखौ वह्निं शकारं रुद्रपत्रके ।
शूलाग्रेषु क्रिया साध्यं मूलं मूलोर्ध्वकोणके ।।१४।।

यंत्रमेतन्महावीर्यं सर्व-दंडन-कारणम् ।
यस्य दर्शनमात्रेण बिभ्यतेऽखिलमूर्त्तयः ।।१५।।

बंधने त्रोटने चैव तापने पाटने तथा ।
वर्तने नर्तने तापे रोदने नादने प्लवे ।।१६।।

नानाविलासा दोषेषु दृढस्त्वं च क्रियां चरेत् ।
तत्क्षणादेव सिद्धिः स्यात् संशयो नास्ति शोभने ।।१७।।

ह्रूंकारं वृत्तमध्ये मरुदृतुभवने तत्कलापे कृशानुं
हंकारं शूलमूले तदनुपरिवृतं स्वेष्टकं कामसाध्यम् ।
कृत्वा तस्मिन् प्रकल्पे गृहकलितमथो साध्य वक्त्रात् प्रसर्प-
द्धूमो बभ्रं समेत्य द्रुतमरिवदने संविशंतं विचिंत्यात् ।।१८।।

एतद् गुह्यतमं मंत्रं सर्व-संक्राम-लंपटम् ।
देवभूत-ग्रह-क्ष्वेड-गर्भ-प्राण-ज्वराणि च ।।१९।।

बहुनात्र किमुक्तेन सर्वसंक्रामणं लभेत् ।
यत्नेनापि जपेत्तस्माच्छीघ्रसंक्रामसिद्धये ।।२०।।

एकादशविधा मंत्राः स्वरकोष्टोर्ध्वपंक्तिकम् ।
रेखा शूलाग्रनामार्णं प्रें खं दुःसहमद्भुतम् ।।२१।।

भूमौ निधाय तद्यंत्रं निविष्टः शिवदिङ्मुखः ।
जपेदाशुप्रतिध्वंसं रिपुं जित्वोपशांतये ।।२२।।

मध्ये मायां षडस्रे पवनमथ वहिः पंचकोणे फडर्णम्
बाह्ये शूलाग्र नाम प्रणवमथ बहिर्मायया वेष्ट्य पश्चात् ।
तालीपत्रे तु ताम्रे लिखितमथ जपेत्क्षिप्रताक्ष्यं समंत्रं
सर्पोच्चाटं तदेतत्किमुह विचरतां जंगमानां पशूनाम् ।।२३।।

ऊर्ध्वं तिर्यक् च पंचत्रितय-मनुगृहं रिष्ट-संख्यं विलिख्य
वर्णान्मंत्रस्य बाह्ये त्रिशिख-गृहयुगे क्रूरषट्कं च हुं हुम् ।
साध्यं शूलाग्रदेशे कटु-युग-लिपितं-नागदुग्धं प्रसिक्तम्
जप्त्वा मंत्रं लिखित्वा द्विशतमथ तथा वैरिणां ध्वंसनाय ॥२४॥

यंत्रमेतन्महावीर्यं रिपु-तूल-महानलम् ।
दृढचित्तः क्रियां कुर्यात्सहसा साधकोत्तमः ॥२५॥

शशि-रवि-शिखि-युक्तं ठाद्बहिः साध्यनाम्
महियुगमनुषंग प्रक्रिया-चक्रमेतत् ।
... ...
प्रतिवशमतुलं सत्पुत्र - भाग्यप्रदं च ॥२६॥

इति श्रीआकाशभैरवकल्पे प्रत्यक्षसिद्धिप्रदे उमामहेश्वरसम्वादे आशुगारुड-प्रयोगभेदो नाम त्रयोदशोऽध्यायः ॥१३॥

चतुर्दशोऽध्यायः

श्रीदेव्युवाच ।।

देव देव महादेव सर्वज्ञ करुणानिधे ।
पाहि मां कृपया शंभो परमानंदशंकर ।।१।।
यत्तु गुह्यं शुभतरं सर्व-रक्षा-करं परम् ।
गरुत्मान्येन मंत्रेण संतुष्यति हि तद्वद ।।२।।

श्रीशिव उवाच ।।

साधु देवि महाप्राज्ञे ज्ञानं वक्ष्यामि शंकरि ।
आशुतार्क्ष्यस्य कवचं महामंत्रं वदाम्यहम् ।।३।।
भोग-मोक्ष-दम-ज्ञान-तिमिरांधस्य तौलिकम् ।
भुक्ति मुक्ति प्रदं श्रेष्ठं सिद्धिदं सर्वसिद्धिदम् ।।४।।
ऋषि-न्यास-प्रभावाश्च शंकरादिति मंत्रवित् ।
समाहितेन मनसा जपेन्मंत्रोत्तमोत्तमम् ।।५।।
तार्क्ष्यो मे पुरतः पातु गरुडः पातु पृष्टतः ।
सोमः पातु च मे वामं वैनतेयस्तु दक्षिणम् ।।६।।
शिखायां गरुडः पातु निटिलं त्वहिसंधरः ।
नासिकाग्रं विभुः पातु नयने विनतासुतः ।।७।।
तेजिष्ठः श्रोत्रयोः पातु मुखं संतापमोचनः ।
ओष्ठयोः पातु नागारिः पातु तालू प्रजाकरः ।।८।।
जिह्वां खगेश्वरः पातु दंतान्पात्वरुणानुजः ।
सीरुकश्चिबुकं पातु पातु चोग्रः कपोलयोः ।।९।।
महारिहा गलं पातु चांसयोः कृतविक्रमः ।
करौ पातु च रक्ताक्षः कराग्रे तु महाबलः ।।१०।।
अंगुष्ठौ च हरिः पातु तर्जन्यौ हरिवाहनः ।
मध्यमे सुमुखः पातु चानामिके त्रिलोचनः ।।११।।
कनिष्ठिके महोत्साहः स्वात्मांगः पातु दोः स्तनम् ।
करपृष्ठं कलातीतो नखान्यमृत-संधरः ।।१२।।

हृदयं पातु सर्वज्ञः कक्षे पक्षिविराट् ततः ।
उरःस्थलं कलाधारः पातु मे जठरं परम् ॥१३॥
परात्परः कटिं पातु पातु नाभिं हरिप्रियः ।
गुह्यं पातु मनोवेगः जघनं खगपन्नजः ॥१४॥
जितेन्द्रियो गुदं पातु मेढ्रं संतानवर्धनः ।
ऊरू पशुपतिः पातु जानुनी भक्तवत्सलः ॥१५॥
जंघे पातु वषट्कारः सर्वलोकवशंकरः ।
गुल्फौ नीलशिरः पातु पादपृष्ठं मुरारिधृक् ॥१६॥
धीरः पादतलं पातु चांगुलीः परमंत्रतुत् ।
रोमकूपाणि मे पातु मंत्र-बंधिविमोचकः ॥१७॥
स्वाहाकारस्त्वचं पातु रुधिरं वेदपारगः ।
साक्षिकः पातु मे मांसं मेदांसि पातु यज्ञभुक् ॥१८॥
सामगः पातु मे चास्थि शुक्रं तु हविवर्धनः ।
शोभनः पातु मे मज्जां बुद्धिं भक्तवरप्रदः ॥१९॥
मूलाधारं खगः पातु स्वाधिष्ठानमथात्मवित् ।
मणिपूरकमत्युग्रः कलधी पात्वनाहतम् ॥२०॥
विशुद्धिमपरः पातु चाज्ञामाखंडलप्रियः ।
द्रुतताक्ष्यों महाभीमो ब्रह्मरंध्रं स पातु मे ॥२१॥
ऐंद्रं फणिभुजः पातु आग्नेयं कलिदोषभित् ।
याम्यं लघुगतिः पातु नैर्ऋतं सुरवैरिजित् ॥२२॥
पश्चिमं पातु लोकेशो धौतोरुः पातु मारुतम् ।
गुलिकाशीति कौवेरं पातु चैशान्यमोजसः ॥२३॥
ऊर्ध्वं पातु सदानंद-गीत-नृत्यप्रियस्तथा ।
गरुडः पातु पातालं गरलाशी तनुं तथा ॥२४॥
धन धान्यादिकं पातु ताक्ष्यों राक्षस-वैरिधृक् ।
भीषणः कन्यकाः पातु भार्यामग्निकणेक्षणः ॥२५॥
त्वरितः पातु चात्मानं धर्म-कर्म-क्रतूत्तमः ।
पुत्रानायुष्करः पातु वंशं रिपुनिषूदनः ॥२६॥

संग्रामे विजयः पातु माग्रं शत्रुविमर्दनः ।
सिद्धि पातु महादेवो भगवान्भुजगाशनः ॥२७॥

सततं पातु मां श्रेष्ठं स्वस्तिदः साधकात्मवान् ।
जाग्रत्स्वप्नसुषुप्तौ च कुंकुमारुणवक्षसः ॥२८॥

सर्व-संपत्प्रदः पातु स्तुतिमंत्रस्य सिद्धिषु ।
इदं तु तार्क्ष्यकवचं पुरुषार्थप्रदं परम् ॥२६॥

स्वस्तिदं पुत्रदं सर्वरक्षाकरमनुत्तमम् ।
युद्धे वह्निभये चैव राज-चोर-समागमे ॥३०॥

महाभूतारिसंघट्टे निजपेत् कवचं शिवे ।
स्मरणादेव नश्यंति प्रचंडानलतूलवत् ॥३१॥

आशुतार्क्ष्याख्य-कवचं परमं पुण्यवर्धनम् ।
महागुह्यं महामंत्रं महामोहन-संज्ञकम् ॥३२॥

सर्वदेवमयं मंत्रं सर्वायुधकरं परम् ।
सर्वमृत्यु-प्रशमनं सर्वसौभाग्य-वर्धनम् ॥३३॥

पावनं परमायुष्यं पाप-पाश-प्रमोचनम् ।
मुनीश्वरैश्च यमिभिर्नाभिजाद्यमरैः परैः ॥३४॥

गुह्यकैश्च सुरश्रेष्ठैः स्तूयमानं महोज्ज्वलम् ।
त्रिकालं प्रजपेद् ध्यानपूर्वकं कवचं शिवे ॥३५॥

सहसा सर्वसिद्धिः स्याद्वाग्विभूतिर्विशेषतः ।
मुनीनामपि संपूज्यः कवचेनावृतः पुमान् ॥३६॥

चतुर्दशसु लोकेषु संचरेन्मारवत्तु सः ।
अनेनैव तु कायेन भूतले बहुसंपदम् ॥३७॥

चिरं प्राप्य तु देहांते विष्णुसायुज्यमाप्नुयात् ॥३८॥

शिखि-ऋतु-वसु-कोणं चाष्टपत्रं भुवं च ।
ऋतु-शत-शशिचाग्निं भास्कर-व्योमकं च ॥
सकलमनिलयुक्तं तद्बहिः साध्यशक्तिं ।
धृत-मृत-सुत-वंध्या-पुत्रदं तार्क्ष्यमेतत् ॥३९॥

इदं चक्रं महाख्यातं सर्ववक्त्रोक्तमुत्तमम् ।
महागुह्यं महाभीमं महासिद्धिकरं परम् ॥३९॥
शुक्रवासरमारभ्य पूज्य जप्त्वा दिनत्रयम् ।
अनेन कवचेनैव जपेदष्टोत्तरं शतम् ॥४०॥
तज्जलेनाभिषिच्याथ होमं कृत्वा हि रक्षकैः ।
निमज्जतां जले देवि बंधयेत्पुत्रकामिनाम् ॥४१॥

इति श्रीआकाशभैरवकल्पे प्रत्यक्षसिद्धिप्रदे उमामहेश्वरसम्वादे आशुगारुडकवचं नाम चतुर्दशोऽध्यायः ॥१४॥

पंचदशोऽध्यायः

श्रीशिव उवाच ॥

रहस्यं श्रृणु वक्ष्यामि शिष्यबोध्यमनुत्तमम् ।
साधकानां हितार्थाय शोभने मंत्रसिद्धये ॥१॥
उदासीनं विटं दुष्टं लब्धास्यं रोगिणं जडम् ।
लब्धमूर्खमसत्याढ्यमभक्तं भीममभंकम् ॥२॥
मानहीनं वधूसक्तं विषयातुरमक्रमम् ।
अंगहीनमनाचारं शिष्यं नैव परिग्रहेत् ॥३॥
गृह्णीयाद्यदि हानिः स्यात्सिद्धेर्मंत्रस्य तत्त्वतः ।
महादेवो भवेत्क्रुद्धस्तस्याशुभकरं भवेत् ॥४॥
लब्धोपदेशं च कृतापराधं संबोधयित्वा बहुशः प्रयत्नात् ।
तत्रापि दुष्टं प्रसमीक्ष्य मंत्रं जपेत्ससाध्यं प्रतिलोमतो वाक् ॥५॥
सहस्रमेकं त्रिदिनं क्षपायां सदेशिकः क्रूरतरोऽधमः स्यात् ।
तमस्तु शिष्यस्य भवेद्दरिद्रं भ्रांतिश्च रोगो मरणं क्रमेण ॥६॥
तस्माद् गुरुः शिष्यमदर्पवित्तं सुभक्तमर्थाभिरतेर्निवृत्तम् ।
स्नातं समाहूय पवित्रहस्तं मंत्रेण संमंत्रित-तोयसिक्तम् ॥७॥
ध्यात्वा गुरुं दक्षिणकर्णरंध्रे कृत्वोपदेशं हृषिभावपूर्वम् ।
ततः प्रयोगांतरमप्यशेषं विधानपूर्वं स्वगुरूदिष्टम् ।
लब्ध्वाथ शिष्यः सकलं क्रमेण यथानुरूपं कलयेत्स्वनाथम् ॥८॥
गुरुरेव परं ज्योति र्गुरुः सर्वोत्तरोत्तरः ।
गुरुरेव जगत्साक्षी तस्मादाराधयेद्गुरुम् ॥९॥
देवो गुरुर्गुरुर्देवो गुरुर्मंत्रो मनुर्गुरुः ।
देवो मनुर्मनुर्देवस्तस्मादाराधयेद् गुरुम् ॥१०॥
देवता-गुरु-मंत्राणामैक्यभावमनुस्मरन् ।
निर्भयः सुतले भूते जपं कुर्यात्समाहितः ॥११॥
गुर्वासने गुरोरग्रे गुरुयाने च वेश्मके ।
गुरोरुपरि भागे च निवसेन्न कदाचन ॥१२॥

ज्येष्ठान्पितामहान्बंधून् तेषांपत्नींश्च वंशजान् ।
न नमेदात्मनाथस्य संन्निधौ पितरौ नमेत् ॥१३॥

नैव वंद्यो भवेदेतैरेताभिर्गुरुसंनिधौ ।
पुत्रैः सुतादिभिर्वर्गैः स्निग्धैश्चापि कदाचन ॥१४॥

मास्तु मास्त्विति वक्तव्यं कृते यदि यथातथैः ।
नमस्कारस्तथा मंत्री नाथायेति निवेदयेत् ॥१५॥

यथा स्वयं नमस्कुर्याद् गुरुबुद्धया तु पूर्वजान् ।
सर्वानपि विशेषज्ञाननुध्यायंश्च देवताः ॥१६॥

जप-होमादि-पूजादि न प्रसार्यं गुरोर्बुधः ।
वाक्यस्य श्रवणादर्वागुत्तिष्ठेदपि दर्शनात् ॥१७॥

गुरुवाक्यांतरे वाक्यं न वदेदप्यपांशु सः ।
तुं-कारमपि हुङ्कारं न चैकवचनं तथा ॥१८॥

निंदत्वखिलसुहृज्जनोऽपि वंश्यो निंदत्वनुजसुतप्रणामकाद्याः ।
निंदत्वनिशमंनिंदिता च भार्या नूनं यच्छरणमहं भजामि नाथम् ॥१६॥

इति निश्चित्य चित्तःसन् गुरोराज्ञानुपालनम् ।
कुर्यादतंद्रितो मंत्री यद्विधिस्तद्दिवानिशम् ॥२०॥

गुरुणोक्तं यदाचारं तदाचारं समाचरेत् ।
विहिताविहितं वापि गुर्वाचारस्तु चाचरेत् ॥२१॥

निग्रहानुग्रहे चैव तथाकर्म-विभेदके ।
गुरुध्यानपरः कुर्याज्जपं सर्वार्थसिद्धये ॥२२॥

शरीरं जीवितं धान्यं गृहं क्षेत्रं गवादिकम् ।
अभिमानादिकं सर्वं गुर्वर्थमिति भावयेत् ॥२३॥

वाजिनां दानदानानि नाथायेति स्मरेद् बुधः ।
कुर्यादनभिमानज्ञो निर्विकारो निराकुलः ॥२४॥

उपास्यन्नात्मनाथेन स्वात्मानं योज्य कातरात् ।
ऐक्यं तु चिंतयेत्किंचित्स्वप्नेऽपि न कदाचन ॥२५॥

ब्रह्मणा विष्णुना चैव मयोपास्यो हि देशिकः ।
तं कृपाम्भो निधिर्नाथं बुद्धिश्रांतं विभावयेत् ॥२६॥

सुकरं दुष्करं वापि सुखं वा दुःखमेव वा ।
सर्वं नाथाज्ञया प्राप्तमिति मत्वा गुरुं यजेत् ॥२७॥
स्वकीयं परकीयं वा यवदर्शि मनोहरम् ।
तद्वस्तु देशिकायैव तत्क्षणादेव वेदयेत् ॥२८॥
अखिल-निगम-शास्त्र-प्राप्त-सूत्रोपशाखो-
पनिषद तुलवाक्यं ज्ञानसारानुसारम् ।
विदितविहितपात्रज्ञानमाचारमार्गम्
विदित-गुरु-कटाक्षोद्भूतसर्वात्मबोधम् ॥२९॥

इति श्रीआकाशभैरवकल्पे प्रत्यक्षसिद्धिप्रदे उमामहेश्वरसम्वादे शिष्याचारविधिर्नाम पंचदशोऽध्यायः ॥१५॥

षोडशोऽध्यायः

श्रीदेव्युवाच ॥

देव देव महादेव गिरीश गिरिजापते ।
त्राहि मां दयया नाथ सच्चिदानंदशाश्वत ॥१॥

मंत्राणामपि यत्सारं सर्वलोकैक-शिक्षणं ।
रक्षणं सर्वजंतूनां ब्रूहि मे तं विभो मनुम् ॥२॥

श्रीशिव उवाच ॥

रहस्यं शृणु देवेशि सर्वरक्षाकरं परम् ।
यस्य स्मरणमात्रेण वैरिणां कुल-नाशनम् ॥३॥

भोगमोक्षप्रदं दिव्यं भुक्ति-मुक्तिप्रदायकम् ।
सर्व-पाप-प्रशमनं सर्वापस्मारनाशनम् ॥४॥

राजचौरादि-मृत्यूनां नाशनं जयवर्धनम् ।
ज्वर रोगघ्नमापद्घ्नं मनुं वक्ष्यामि तत्त्वतः ॥५॥

शरभेश्वर मंत्रस्य ऋषिः कालाग्निरुद्रकः ।
छंदस्तु जगती, देवो भगवान् शरभेश्वरः ॥६॥

'खं' कारं बीजमित्युक्तं स्वाहा शक्तिरतः परम् ।
स्वेच्छा-प्रयोगसिध्यर्थे विनियोगस्तथांबिके ॥७॥

त्रि द्वि द्वादश नवकं सप्तकं तु नव क्रमात् ।
मंत्राक्षरैः करन्यासं मातृका सहितं मनुम् ॥८॥

केशादिके न्यसेन्मंत्री करवत्तु षडंगकम् ।
शिरो-ललाट-भ्रूमध्ये नेत्रयोः श्रोत्रयोर्नसोः ॥९॥

गंडयोरंसयोः कंठे बाह्वोः संधिषु च क्रमात् ।
स्तनयोः पार्श्वयोर्नाभौ लिंगे पायौ क्रमान्न्यसेत् ॥१०॥

पदोः संधिषु सर्वांगे मंत्र-वर्णान्प्रविन्यसेत् ।
ब्रह्मरंध्रे च केशांते भाले चाज्ञाप्रदेशके ॥११॥

विशुद्धे नाहते चैव मणिपूरे च लिंगके ।
आधारे च त्रिभिर्द्वाभ्यां पंचभिः सप्तभिः पुनः ॥१२॥
नवभिर्मुनिभिर्बाणैर्द्वाभ्यां द्वाभ्यां विभागतः ।
पदानि विन्यसेत्पश्चान्मूलेन व्यापकं न्यसेत् ।
न्यासद्वयं विधायैवं ध्यायेत्तं शरभेश्वरम् ॥१३॥

चंद्रादित्याग्निदृष्टिः कुलिश-वर-नखश्चंचुरत्युग्रजिह्वः
काली दुर्गा च पक्षौ हृदय जठरगौ भैरवो वाडवाग्निः ।
ऊरुस्थौ व्याधि-मृत्यू शरभ-वर-खगश्चंडवातातिवेगः-
संहर्ता सर्वशत्रून्विजयतु शरभः सालुवः पक्षिराजः ॥१४॥

विमल-नभमहोद्यत्कृत्तिवासो वसानम्
द्रुहिण-सुरमुनीन्द्रैः स्तूयमानं गिरीशम् ।
स्फटिकमणि जपास्रक् पुस्तकोद्यत्कराब्जम्
शरभमहमुपासे सालुवेशं खगेशम् ॥१५॥

तारं प्रथममुच्चार्यं खें-खां-खं फडनंतरम् ।
प्राणग्रहासि द्वितयं हुं-फट् तु तदनंतरम् ॥१६॥
सर्वेति पदमुक्त्वाऽथ शत्रुसंहारणाय च ।
शरभ-सालुवायेति पक्षिराजाय इत्यपि ॥१७॥
हुं-फट् स्वाहेति मंत्रं तु द्विचत्वारिंशदक्षरम्[१] ।
जपेद्वर्णसहस्राणि संख्यानि च महेश्वरि ॥१८॥
दशांशं तर्पणं होमं शतांशं द्विजभोजनम् ।
सहस्रांशमथो देवि क्रमादेवं समाचरेत् ॥१९॥
होमद्रव्याण्यहं वक्ष्ये अधुना शृणु पार्वति ।
स्वगृहे दक्षिणे भागे कल्पिते त्र्यस्रकुंडके ॥२०॥
स्वसूत्रोक्तविधानेन त्वाज्य भागांतमाचरेत् ।
तत्र दूर्वां गुडूचीं च तिलांल्लाजांश्च पायसम् ॥२१॥
अपूपं च यवं चाज्यं क्रमात्सौम्यं समाचरेत् ।
अपामार्गं च वह्निं च खादिरं च कटुत्रयम् ॥२२॥

---

१ मंत्रोद्धारो यथा :—ओं खें खां खं फट् प्राणग्रहासि प्राणग्रहासि हुं फट् सर्व-शत्रु-संहारणाय शरभ-सालुवाय पक्षिराजाय हुं फट् स्वाहा ।

सैन्धवं सर्षपं चाज्यं क्रमात्क्षौद्रं हुनेत्सुधीः ।
होमेन विधिना देवि क्रूर-सौम्य-क्रियादिषु ॥२३॥

होमे जपेऽस्मिन्सद्भक्तिरवश्यं क्रियतां न चेत् ।
विपरीतं भवेत्तस्मादुदासीनं न कारयेत् ॥२४॥

स्वयं शिवमयं ध्यात्वा पावकं शरभेश्वरम् ।
होमांते तु जपेन्मंत्री त्रिवारं शरभाष्टकम् ॥२५॥

तेनाष्टकेन मंत्रेण भगवान्वरदो भवेत् ।
त्रिकोणं विलिखेत्पूर्वं तद्बाह्ये तु दलद्वयम् ॥२६॥

द्वादशारं तु तद्बाह्ये तद्बाह्ये तु नवास्रकम् ।
सप्तास्रं च चतुः पंच भूपुरं च क्रमाल्लिखेत् ॥२७॥

पावकादि-पृथिव्यंतं लिखेन्मंत्रं यथाक्रमम् ।
तद्बहिः कोणषट्केतु प्रागारभ्य मनुं लिखेत् ॥२८॥

खट् फट् जहि तथा छिन्धि भिन्धि हंधि लिखेत्क्रमात् ।
अकारादि क्षकारांतं वेष्टयेद्बिन्दु-संयुतम् ॥२९॥

महायंत्रमिदं पुण्यं सप्तावरणकं परम् ।
सर्व-सिद्धि-प्रदं श्रेष्ठं सर्वसंपत्प्रदायकम् ॥३०॥

सर्व-रोग-प्रशमनं सर्वसौभाग्यदायकम् ।
सर्व-बाधा-प्रशमनं सर्व-शत्रु-जयं शुभम् ॥३१॥

सर्व-भूतवशीकारं सर्वपापविमोचनम् ।
नानाज्वरहरं यंत्रं नाना क्षुद्र-निवारणम् ॥३२॥

य इदं धारयेद्भक्त्या नासाध्यं तस्य विद्यते ।
अनेनैव तु मंत्रेण साक्षाच्छिवमयो भवेत् ॥३३॥

षट् सप्तकोष्ठेषु विलिख्य शारभं रेखाग्रशूलं च तदग्रसाध्यम् ।
बाह्ये तु मायावृत-तारवेष्टितं जयादिकं साधितुमाशुचक्रम् ॥३४॥

इति श्रीआकाशभैरवकल्पे प्रत्यक्षसिद्धिप्रदे उमामहेश्वरसम्वादे शरभ-सालुव-पक्षिराज-कल्पं नाम षोडशोऽध्यायः ॥१६॥

सप्तदशोऽध्यायः

श्रीशिव उवाच ॥

श्रृणु देवि महागुह्यं परं पुण्यविवर्धनम् ।
शरभेशाष्टकं मंत्रं वक्ष्यामि तव तत्त्वतः ॥१॥

ऋषि-न्यासादिकं यत्तत्सर्वं पूर्ववदाचरेत् ।
ध्यान-भेदं विशेषेण वक्ष्याम्यहमतः शिवे ॥२॥

ज्वलन कुटिलकेशं सूर्यचंद्राग्नि नेत्रम्
निशित-तर-नखाग्रोद्धूतहेमापि देहम् ।
शरभमथ मुनीन्द्रैः सेव्यमानं सितांगम्
प्रणतभयविनाशं भावयेत्पक्षिराजम् ॥३॥

देवादिदेवाय जगन्मयाय शिवाय नालीक-निभाननाय ।
शर्वाय भीष्माय शराधिपाय नमोऽस्तु तुभ्यं शरभेश्वराय ॥४॥

हराय भीमाय हरिप्रियाय भवाय शांताय परात्पराय ।
मृडाय रुद्राय विलोचनाय नमोऽस्तु तुभ्यं शरभेश्वराय ॥५॥

शीतांशुचूडाय दिगंबराय सृष्टि-स्थिति-ध्वंसनकारणाय ।
जटाकलापाय जितेन्द्रियाय नमोऽस्तु तुभ्यं शरभेश्वराय ॥६॥

कलंक-कंठाय भवांतकाय कपाल-शूलात्तकरांबुजाय ।
भुजंगभूषाय पुरांतकाय नमोऽस्तु तुभ्यं शरभेश्वराय ॥७॥

शमादिषट्काय यमांतकाय यमादि-योगाष्टकसिद्धिदाय ।
उमाधिनाथाय पुरातनाय नमोऽस्तु तुभ्यं शरभेश्वराय ॥८॥

घृणादि-पाशाष्टक-वर्जिताय खिलीकृतास्मत्पथि पूर्वगाय ।
गुणादि-हीनाय गुणत्रयाय नमोऽस्तु तुभ्यं शरभेश्वराय ॥९॥

कालाय वेदामृत-कंदलाय कल्याण-कौतूहल-कारणाय ।
स्थूलाय सूक्ष्माय स्वरूपगाय नमोऽस्तु तुभ्यं शरभेश्वराय ॥१०॥

पंचाननायानिलभास्कराय पंचाशदर्णाद्यपराक्षराय ।
पंचाक्षरेशाय जगद्धिताय नमोऽस्तु तुभ्यं शरभेश्वराय ॥११॥

नीलकंठाय रुद्राय शिवाय शशिमौलिने ।
भवाय भवनाशाय पक्षिराजाय ते नमः ॥१२॥

परात्पराय घोराय शंभवे परमात्मने ।
शर्वाय निर्मलांगाय सालुवाय नमो नमः ॥१३॥

गंगाधराय सांबाय परमानंदतेजसे ।
सर्वेश्वराय शांताय शरभाय नमो नमः ॥१४॥

वरदाय वरांगाय वामदेवाय शूलिने ।
गिरिशाय गिरीशाय गिरिंजापतये नमः ॥१५॥

कनक-जठरकोद्यद्रक्त-पानोन्मदेन
प्रथित-निखिल-पीडा नारसिंहेन जाता ॥
शरभ हर शिवेश त्राहि नः सर्वपापा-
दनिशमिह कृपाब्धे सालुवेश प्रभो त्वम् ॥१६॥

सर्वेश सर्वाधिकशांतमूर्त्ते कृतापराधानमरानथान्यान् ।
विनीयविश्व-विधायि नीते नमोऽस्तु तुभ्यं शरभेश्वराय ॥१७॥

दंष्ट्रानखोग्रः शरभः सपक्षश्चतुर्भुजश्चाष्टपदः सहेतिः ।
कोटीर-गंगेन्दुधरो नृसिंहक्षोभापहोस्मद्रिपुहास्तु शंभुः ॥१८॥

हुङ्कारी शरभेश्वरोष्टचरणः पक्षीचतुर्बाहुकः
पादाकृष्ट-नृसिंह-विग्रहधरः कालाग्नि-कोटि-द्युतिः ॥
विश्व-क्षोभहरः सहेतिरनिशं ब्रह्मेन्द्र मुख्यैः स्तुतो
गंगाचंद्रधरः पुरत्रयहरः सद्यो रिपुघ्नोऽस्तु नः ॥१९॥

मृगांग लांगूल सचंचु-पक्षो दंष्ट्राननांघ्रिश्च भुजासहस्रः ।
त्रिनेत्र गंगेन्दुधरः प्रभाढ्यः पायादपायाच्छरभेश्वरो नः ॥२०॥

नृसिंहमत्युग्रमतीवतेजः प्रकाशितं दानव-भंग-दक्षम् ।
प्रशांतिमंतं विदधाति यो मां सोऽस्मानपायाच्छरभेश्वरो नः ॥२१॥

योऽभूत्सहस्रांशु-शत-प्रकाशः स पक्षि-सिंहाकृतिरष्टपादः ।
नृसिंह-संक्षोभशमात्तरूपः पायादपयाच्छरभेश्वरो नः ॥२२॥

त्वां मन्युमंतं प्रवदंति वेदास्त्वां शांतिमंतं मुनयो गृणन्ति ।
दुष्टे नृसिंहजगदीश्वरे ते सर्वापराधं शरभ क्षमस्व ॥२३॥

कर-चरण कृतं वाक्-कर्मजं कायजं वा
श्रवण नयनजं वा मानसं वापराधम्।
विहितमविहितं वा सर्वमेतत्क्षमस्व
शिव शिव करुणाब्धे श्रीमहादेव शंभो ॥२४॥
रुद्रः शंकर ईश्वरः पशुपतिः स्थाणुः कपर्दी शिवो
वागीशो वृषभध्वजः स्मरहरो भक्तप्रियस्त्र्यंबकः ॥
भूतेशो जगदीश्वरश्च वृषभो मृत्युंजयः श्रीपति-
र्योऽस्मान् कालगलोऽवतात्पुरहरः शंभुः पिनाकी हरः ॥२५॥

यतो नृसिंहं हरसि हर इत्युच्यते बुधैः।
यतो बिभर्ति सकलं विभज्य तनुमष्टधा ॥२६॥
अतोऽस्मान्पाहि भगवन्प्रसीद च पुनः पुनः।
इति स्तुतो महादेवः प्रसन्नो भक्तवत्सलः ॥२७॥
सुरानाह्लादयामास वरदानैरभीप्सितैः।
प्रसन्नोऽस्मि स्तवेनाहमनेन विबुधेश्वराः ॥२८॥
मयि रुद्रे महादेवे भयत्वं भक्तिमूर्जितम्।
ममांशोऽयं नृसिंहोऽयं मयि भक्तमस्त्विह ॥२९॥
इमं स्तवं जपेद्यस्तु शरभेशाष्टकं नरः।
तस्य नश्यंति पापानि रिपवश्च सुरोत्तमाः ॥३०॥
नश्यंति सर्वरोगाणि क्षयरोगादिकानि च।
अशेष-ग्रह-भूतानि कृत्रिमाणि ज्वराणि च ॥३१॥
सर्प-चौराग्नि-शार्दूल गजपोत्रिमुखानि च।
अन्यानि च वनस्थानि नास्ति भीतिर्न संशयः ॥३२॥
इत्युक्त्वान्तर्दधे देवि देवान् शरभ सालुवः।
ततस्ते स्व-स्वधामानि ययुराह्लादपूर्वकम् ॥३३॥
एतच्छरभकं स्तोत्रं मंत्रभूतं जपेन्नरः।
सर्वान्कामानवाप्नोति शिवलोकं च गच्छति ॥३४॥

इति श्रीआकाशभैरवकल्पे प्रत्यक्षसिद्धिप्रदे उमामहेश्वरसम्वादे शरभेशाष्टक-स्तोत्र-मंत्रो नाम सप्तदशोऽध्यायः ॥१७॥

अष्टादशोऽध्यायः

श्रीशिव उवाच ॥

माला-मंत्रं प्रवक्ष्यामि रहस्यं शृणु शोभने।
मंत्र-स्मरण-मात्रेण करस्थाः सर्वसिद्धयः ॥१॥

ओं नमः पक्षिराजाय निशि-कुलिश-वर-दंष्ट्रा-नखायानेक-कोटि-ब्रह्म-कपाल-मालालंकृताय सकल-कुल-महानागभूषणाय सर्वभूतनिवारणाय नृसिंह-गर्व-निर्वापण-कारणाय सकलरिपु-रंभाटवी-विमोटन-महानिलाय शरभ-सालुवाय ह्लां ह्लीं ह्लूं प्रवेशय २ रोग-ग्रहं बंधय २ बालग्रहं बंधय २ आवेशय २ भाषय २ मोहय २ कंपय २ बंधय २ भूतग्रहं बंधय रोगग्रहं बंधय यक्षग्रहं बंधय पातालग्रहं बंधय चातुर्थग्रहं बंधय भीमग्रहं बंधयापस्मार-ग्रहं बंधय उन्मत्तग्रहं बंधय राक्षसग्रहं बंधय ज्वालाग्रहं बंधय ज्वालामुखग्रहं बंधय तमोहारग्रहं बंधय भूचरग्रहं बंधय खेचरग्रहं बंधय बेतालग्रहं बंधय कूष्मांडग्रहं बंधय स्त्रीग्रहं बंधय पापग्रहं बंधय विक्रमग्रहं बंधय व्युत्क्रमग्रहं बंधय प्रेतग्रहं बंधय पिशाचग्रहं बंधयावेशग्रहं बंधय अनावेशग्रहं बंधय सर्वग्रहान्मर्दय सर्वग्रहान् त्रोटय त्रोटय प्रें त्रें हैं मारय शीघ्रं मारय मुंच २ दह २ पच २ नाशय २ सर्वदुष्टान्नाशय ह्लूं फट् स्वाहा।

अरुणमरुणमालालंकृता संकराग्रै-
र्विधृत-परशु-शक्ति पुष्प-बाणेक्षु-चापम्।
विविध-फणफणीन्द्रैर्भूषणैर्भूषितांगं
शरभमखिलनाथं नौम्यहं सालुवेशम्।

आकर्षणादिप्रयोगाः ॥

मारं वर्त्तुलमध्यगे वसुदले मायां च लक्ष्मीं तथा
बाह्ये क्षोणि-पुटे लिखेत्प्रतिदिशं ब्लूं कारकं भूपुरे।
मारं साध्य-समन्वितं रिपुजयं लोकाय मोहाकरं
नारीवश्यमहोविचित्रमचिरात्साम्राज्यलक्ष्मीप्रदम् ॥१॥

आलेख्यं वृत्तमध्ये मरुदनलगृहं द्वंद्वके शक्तिलक्ष्मीं
तद्बाह्ये षट्दलान्तः शरभ-मनुमथो सप्तकं सप्तकं च ।
ओंकारं तस्य बाह्ये तदनु परिवृतं साध्यमाकर्षयेत्तां
त्रैलोक्यस्थामदृष्टां स्त्रियमपि विविधान्याशु-भूतानि चैतत् ॥२॥

त्रिनयनमथ शुकाभं श्याममालावतंसं,
मुसल-हल-रथांगं-मुष्टिदाभीतिहस्तं ।
ग्रहगण-रिपु-पिशाच-स्तंभ-विद्वेष-सिद्ध्यै,
प्रतिदिनमथ मंत्रं भावयेत्सालुवेशम् ॥३॥

मध्ये शक्ति सभूमिं बहिरपि पृथिवी कोणके शक्तिबीज
तद्बाह्ये कोणषट्के शरभमनुमथो बाह्यके भूमिकोणे ।
भूमिं शक्ति च बाह्ये प्रणवमथ बहिस्साधकं स्तंभनाख्यम्
शत्रूणामास्य-दृष्टि-श्रुति-मुख-हनु-पत्प्राणिनां यंत्रमेतत् ॥४॥

खंकारं वृत्तमध्ये तदुपरि कमले लांतकं शक्तियुक्तम्
तद्बाह्ये शक्तिकोणे त्वज-वृषभ-मुखान्यालिखेत्कोणशूले ।
आलेख्यं साध्यमेतत्सकलमपि ततस्तारमायाभिवीतम्
विद्वेषं यंत्रमेतत्त्रिभुवनमपि किं स्वल्पकानां नराणाम् ॥५॥

ज्वलदनलसमाभं सूर्य-चंद्राग्नि-नेत्रं
स्वकरकलित-शूलं-खड्ग-खेटं-कपालम् ।
सकलरिपु-जनानां कर्ण-हृद्वाग्विभिन्नम्
स्मरतु शरभमेवं मारणोच्चाटनाय ॥६॥

वायुं सद्वृत्तमध्ये तदनु भृगुगृहे पावकं तस्य बाह्ये
षट्कोणे सालुवेशं त्रिशिखमथ बहिस्तस्य रेखाग्रसाध्यम् ।
तद्बाह्ये शक्तिबीजं जय-विजय-युतं दीपिकावीतमंत्रम्
शत्रूणां भूत-रोग-ग्रह-गण-समरोच्चाटनं चैवमेतत् ॥७॥

बीजं स्वाहेशकोणे ऋतुगृह-विवरे वायु-बीजंससाध्यम्
तद्बीजं साष्टकोणे शिखि-सहितमथो साध्यकं चाष्टपत्रे ।
वह्न्यर्णं साध्य-पूर्णं भुवि भुवनमथो साध्ययुक्तं दशारे
व्योमाख्यं साध्य-युक्तं शरभमनुवृतं सर्वसंहारचक्रम् ॥८॥

सालुवेशाय विद्महे पक्षिराजाय
धीमहि। तन्नो रुद्रः प्रचोदयात्॥९॥
एतदस्त्रं महामंत्रं जपेन्मंत्रं सदांबिके।
तस्य सर्वभयं नास्ति स्वप्नेऽपि च कदाचन॥१०॥
शरभास्त्रमिदं प्रोक्तममोघं जयवर्धनम्।
तत्प्रभावं दृशा द्रष्टुं न सहंतेऽमरासुराः॥११॥
कुतो नर-पिशाचाश्च क्षुद्र-भूताभिचारकाः।
ग्रहग्रामवृताः क्लिष्टाः खेचराः पृथिवीचराः॥१२॥
तस्मादेवं जपेन्नित्यमष्टोत्तरशतं सुधीः।
मंत्रपूतं समाक्रष्टुं कालेनापि न शक्यते॥१३॥
बुद्धिमान् शरभं घोरमस्त्रराजं महामनुम्।
न्यास-भावं-जपं कुर्यादिन्वहं-पाप-मुक्तये॥१४॥

विषवृक्षप्रयोगः।

ऊर्ध्वं च तिर्यग्ग्रह-वेद-रेखां लिखेत्क्रमाद्यंत्रमनन्यमंत्रम्।
बाह्येषु शूलं विलिखेत्ससाध्यं त्रैलोक्यसंहारकरं त्वमोघम्॥१५॥
विषवृक्षे समालिख्य प्राणानावाह्य पूज्य तत्।
अष्टोत्तराख्य-साहस्रं जपेदेकाग्रमानसः॥१६॥
बलि-पूर्वं क्षपामध्ये दक्षिणस्यां खनेद्दिशि।
ततः स्नात्वा जपेन्मंत्रमष्टोत्तर-सहस्रकम्॥१७॥
रिपवो मरणं यांति संशयो नास्ति सुंदरि।
भानुमण्डल-मध्यस्थं वैरिणं दशकेऽहनि॥१८॥
राहु-संग्रहणादेव कृष्णवर्णमधोमुखम्।
पुट-पाक-तनुं क्लांतं निर्वाणं प्राणसंकटम्॥१९॥
चिरं ध्यात्वा जपेन्मंत्री अष्टोत्तर-सहस्रकम्।
जपांतेऽर्घ्य-त्रयं कुर्यात्सूर्यमालोकयन्सुधीः॥२०॥
भूयो जपेत्सहस्रं तु कृत्वा भस्मीकृतं रिपुम्।
सरिपुस्तद्दिनादेव मरणं यात्यहेतुकम्॥२१॥
द्विषंतमुद्दिश्य सहस्रवारं जप्त्वा घृतं तेन हुनेद् हुताशे।
दिनावसानात्पुरतो रिपूणां शरीर-नाशाय सुसिद्धमंत्री॥२२॥

बिन्दु-वह्नि-रसकोणमथाष्टद्वं द्वकं सचतुर्दशपत्रम् ।
भूपुरं च विलिखेदथ मंत्रं मध्यमादि-बहि-नाम-सतारम् ॥२३॥

पायान्नो देवः शरभस्त्वपायात्
संहारि-रोगाद्विपिनोरगाभ्याम् ।
वैश्वानराखु-करि-ऋक्षकेभ्यः
परेभ्यो भूतेभ्यो ह्यषितात्कृतांतात् ॥२४॥

आथर्वणमिमं मंत्रममोघदुरितापहम् ।
सर्व-संरक्षणं श्रेष्ठं सर्व-सौभाग्य-दायकम् ॥२५॥

एतद्यंत्रं समालिख्य हेमपट्टादिके शुभे ।
विधिना धारयेद्योऽयं सर्वत्र विजयी भवेत् ॥२६॥

बिन्दौ बीजं ऋताब्जे यम-बटुक-महावीर-दुर्गा-विकार्णान्
वश्यादीनष्टपत्रे शतमख-मुखतो भैरवान्क्ष्माष्टकोणे ।
दिक्पालान्साध्य-पूर्वान्ननिल-रिपुकृता-शेषतंत्राभिचार-
क्षुद्रैस्तत्तत्प्रयोक्तं प्रमथननद्यं शारभं-घोरमेतत् ॥२७॥

इति श्रीआकाशभैरवकल्पे प्रत्यक्षसिद्धिप्रदे उमामहेश्वरसम्वादे अष्टादशोऽध्यायः ॥१८॥

एकोनविंशोऽध्यायः

निग्रह-प्रयोगः

श्रीशिव उवाच ॥

निग्रहं कर्म वक्ष्यामि मंत्राणां सर्वदा कलौ ।
उचितानुचितं वेत्तुमुपायं सिद्धि-हेतुकम् ॥१॥
क्रियांतरमुपालभ्य क्रियते योऽयमत्र तु ।
तं प्रतिक्रियया जेतुं कालं नैव विचारयेत् ॥२॥
अपवादं ब्रुवन् यं यः सभायां नैव हेतुना ।
तं नरं क्रियया हन्तुं दोषो नास्ति कदाचन ॥३॥
गुरु-मातृ-पितृ-द्रोही धर्मिणी मर्म-सूचकः ।
यस्तं मारयितुं देवि दोषो नास्ति कदाचन ॥४॥
धन-धान्य-गृह-क्षेत्र-धेनु-पुस्तक-तस्करम् ।
कुरुते यस्तमाहतुं दोषो नास्ति कदाचन ॥५॥
अभाषमाणं पुरुषं हठात्कारेण ताडयेत् ।
यस्तमाहर्तुमीशानि दोषो नास्ति कदाचन ॥६॥
भाषमाणं च तन्नारीं ब्रूयात्कोपादवाच्यकम् ।
तं नरं देवि संहतुं दोषो नास्ति कदाचन ॥७॥
वनितां वृन्द-मध्यस्थां मान-भंगं करोति यः ।
गिरिजे तं नरं हतुं दोषो नास्ति कदाचन ॥८॥
व्यभिचारीमपि वधूं बलात्कारं करोति यः ।
तं मारयितुं देवि दोषो नास्ति कदाचन ॥९॥
दंपती-मेलनं-कालं प्रकाशं यः करोति च ।
नराधमं तमाहतुं दोषो नास्ति कदाचन ॥१०॥
स्वकीयं परकीयं च दोषं यत्नेन गोपयेत् ।
नरोत्तमं तमाहतुं मनसापि न चिंतयेत् ॥११॥

भूषणं दूषणं वापि ब्रुवंती या तु तां वधूम् ।
यद्वा तद्वापि संहर्तुं मनसापि न चिंतयेत् ॥१२॥

गुरुपुत्रं गुरोर्वन्द्यं दीक्षितं सत्यवादिनम् ।
योगिनं व्रतमध्यस्थं मनसापि न चिंतयेत् ॥१३॥

दुःखातिरेकाच्च भयाच्चकोपाद्वाजाज्ञया भाषणमावभाष्य ।
पश्चात्क्षमध्वं विवशान्मयोक्तमिति ब्रुवंतं पुरुषं न कार्य्यम् ॥१४॥
एतद्रहस्यं सुबुधः समीक्ष्य क्रियाविधानं स करोति लोके ।
तदेव नूनं शरभेश्वराज्ञा नान्यत्र सर्वं विपरीतमेति ॥१५॥

इति श्रीआकाशभैरवकल्पे प्रत्यक्षसिद्धिप्रदे उमामहेश्वरसम्वादे एकोनविंशोऽध्यायः ॥१६॥

विंशोऽध्यायः

अथ होमभेद-प्रयोगः

श्रीशिव उवाच ॥

वदाम्यशेषं शृणु होम-भेदं क्रियाविधानं गिरिराज कल्पे ।
नूनं महाभूत-पिशाच-रोग-ज्वराहि-दुष्टौघवियोगशांत्यै ॥१॥
मधुं मधूकं मधुकं दशाहं सहस्रमेकैकदिनं वरेण्ये ।
होमं प्रकुर्यात्प्रयतो मनीषी समस्तदुर्वार-भयाद्विमुक्त्यै ॥२॥
लवंगमेकं मधुकं च कोष्ठं तिलं घृतं चंपककुड्मलं च ।
दिनं सहस्रं प्रयतो दशाहमुन्माद-ताप-ज्वर-शूलशांत्यै ॥३॥
श्रीभार्गवीभिर्नवरात्रहोमैः प्रयांति शांतिं कुपिताश्च देवाः ।
आयुष्करं मृत्युहरं समस्त-दोषापहं-श्रीकरमापदघ्नम् ॥४॥
पलाश-शाखाभिरभीष्टसिध्यै रक्षाय कुर्यादथ खादिरोत्थैः ।
तत्तद्दिनर्क्षस्य समिद्वरैस्तु ज्वरादि-शांत्यै जुहुयात्त्रिरात्रम् ॥५॥
उदुम्बराश्वत्थ-समित्सहस्रैः कुर्याच्चतुर्थज्वर-होम-शांत्यै ।
प्रतापसोत्थैः कुसुमैर्घृताक्तैश्चिरायुरारोग्य-बलाय कुर्यात् ॥६॥
मेधासमिद्भिस्त्वथ बुद्धिकामस्त्वरोगकामो नगराजजाभिः ।
उदुंबरोत्थैर्बहुमित्र-कामस्त्वनंतरायाय शमीसमिद्भिः ॥७॥
पुत्राय कुर्यादथ दीपिकाभिः प्रसाद-सिध्यै करवीरपुष्पैः ।
वश्याय कुर्यान्मधु-सिक्त-पद्मै राकर्षणाय स्मर-पंच-बाणैः॥८॥
विद्वेषणायाथ विषांघ्रिपोत्थैः स्तंभक्रियाया कपिजाप्रसूनैः ।
उच्चाटनाय स्नुहि-सालपत्रैः संहारणायार्क-कटु-स्नुहीभिः ॥९॥
धत्तूर-शाखा-फल-पत्र-पुष्पैरुन्मादनायास्यशिफां विमुक्त्यैः ।
वाक्सिद्धयेऽर्क मधुकं प्रकुर्याद्धनाय शान्ताङ्कुर शाखिपुष्पैः ॥१०॥
यद्धान्यहोमं हुतमस्य शीघ्रं तद्धान्य-राशेस्तनुतेऽभिवृद्धिम् ।
अन्नेन चान्नं पयसा घृतौघं घृतेन भाग्यं मधुना धनं स्यात् ॥११॥
तैलेन सारं दधिनाथपुष्टिं चूतप्रवालैरपि रूपसिद्धिम् ।
दाडिमीकुसुमजालकैर्नरो मन्मथत्वमुपयाति सुभ्रुवाम् ॥१२॥

एवमेवमयुतं रवौ दिने कारयेदखिल-कार्य-सिद्धये।
देह्यभीष्टमिति याचितुं पुरैर्वा मुदं परिदधाति सायकैः ॥१३॥
दानवारिभिरहर्निशं यथा पारिजात इव मानवैः शिवः।
त्रिकटु-सर्षप-हिंग्वजमोदकान्युरग-मौलि-ससैंधव-जीरकम्।
सुघृत-पारद-टंकण-संयुतं शरभ होममरिक्षयायेव तत् ॥१४॥

शिखिपुरयुगमध्ये शक्तिबीजं च कोणे
प्रतिगृहमथ मंत्रं सप्तवर्णं लिखित्वा॥
इषुमनुमथ बाह्ये षोडशारे त्रिवर्णं
महि-युग-युगमेतत्सालुवेशस्य यंत्रम् ॥१५॥

एतत्तु संपूज्य तदग्रभूमौ रिपुमलातेन लिखेद्यमस्य।
मध्ये तु रूपं विलिखेद्यथाङ्गं तदंग-देशे सुमनः पुमांसम् ॥१६॥
मुखाक्षि-नासापुट-कर्ण-जिह्वा-गलांस-वक्षोदर-नाभि-लिंगम्।
प्रत्यंग-साध्यं विलिखेत्समानं वह्नि ससाधाय हुनेत्सहस्रम् ॥१७॥
तत्साल-शाखाभिरथाष्ट-चूर्ण-युक्ताज्य-सिक्ताभिरनन्यचेताः।
दिनत्रयादेव पुरं यमाख्यमगाद्रिपुर्धाम इव स्वगेहान् ॥१८॥
साध्य-द्रुकृत्ति परिकल्प्य तस्मिन् वायुं समापाद्य मनोः शतेन।
श्वेतार्क-दुग्धेन ततोऽष्ट चूर्णं पिष्ट्वापि संलिप्य वितप्य वह्नौ ॥१९॥
लेप्यप्रताप्याथ पुनः प्रलेप्य प्रताप्य लिप्त्वा निखनेत् श्मशाने।
दत्वा बलिं मंत्रमथ त्रिवारं जप्त्वा ततः स्नानमथाचरित्वा ॥२०॥
जपेत्सहस्रं यम-दिङ्मुखः-सन्मंत्रावसाने रिपु-साध्य-मुक्त्वा।
वर्मादि शेषं तु ततः प्रयोज्य सद्योऽथ रात्रं शरभेश्वराख्यम् ॥२१॥
शरीरपिंडं तरसा विहाय सद्यो रिपुः कालपुरं प्रयाति।
संहृत्य तत्साध्य-विहङ्गमांगं सूत्रेण कोदडंमिवाथ बद्ध्वा ॥२२॥
साध्यं गजाद्दक्षपदांगमृद्भिः कृत्वाथ कृत्ति परिकल्प्य वायुम्।
मांजिष्टमालिप्य मुखे च कर्णे त्वलातचूर्णं ह्यवशेषदेहे ॥२३॥
तदस्थिशेषेण शरेण कर्णे मंत्रं समुच्चार्य विचार्य्य चैवम्।
शतप्रयोगात्सरिपुः स्वदेहात्प्रयाति याम्यं पुरमाशु घोरम् ॥२४॥

इति श्रीआकाशभैरवकल्पे प्रत्यक्षसिद्धिप्रदे उमामहेश्वरसम्वादे विंशोऽध्यायः ॥२०॥

एकविंशोऽध्यायः

श्रीशिव उवाच ॥

सजल-जलद-नीलं चाष्टबाहुं त्रिनेत्रम् ।
विविध-चटुलपक्षं दीप्यमानोर्ध्वकेशम् ॥
मनसि निहित-कोप-स्पंदमानाधरोष्ठं ।
सकलरिपु-विनाशं सालुवेशं नमामि ॥१॥

कृत्वा साध्य-चतुष्पदो स्थितिपथेषूत्कृष्णिकां मृत्तिकाम् ।
तस्मात्क्वाणक-वस्त्र-भूष-सुमनालेप्रांजनैश्चंदनैः ॥
आभूष्यास्य-करेण-मूर्ध्नि-निकटे स्पृष्ट्वा शतं मारुतम् ।
जप्त्वा मंत्र-सहस्रकं च विधिवत् खड्गेन तां पीडयेत् ॥२॥

यस्मिन्पीडितमत्र शत्रुतनुषु क्षिप्रं तु तस्मिन्स्थले ।
पीडां कुर्वंति नूनमग्नितपनादाविर्ज्वरांगो भवेत् ॥
अर्कक्षीरकटुत्रयेण-सहितां वह्नौ प्रदग्ध्वा तदा ।
शत्रुः कालपुरं प्रयाति तरसा श्रीसालुवाज्ञावशात् ॥३॥

कृत्तिं कृत्वाथ साध्यक्षितिमुचिततरोः क्षीरमालिप्य तस्याम् ।
वायुं प्रस्थाप्य जप्त्वा मनुमथ शतकं क्षारतोयेन लाक्ते ॥
कुर्यान्निक्षिप्य मंत्र-प्रवचन-करणैः शत्रुलोकास्तदानीम् ।
प्रायः संतानपूर्वं जनवरसहिताः सम्यगार्ताः भवंति ॥४॥

साध्यांबरेक्षीरसिक्त-प्रतिकृतिमथ तत् शालिपिष्टेन कृत्वा ।
संस्थाप्य प्राणवायुं शरभ-मनु-शतं संजपित्वाथ मंत्री ॥
तस्यां तस्योदरे तु प्रथित-कटुपरास्यस्य चत्वारि विश्य ।
त्वस्याग्रक्षारमध्ये पथि भुविनिखने द्वैरिणां मारणाय ॥५॥

साध्यस्य-कृत्तिकायां पवनमभिनिवेश्यावृताशीति मंत्रम् ।
तस्यां वै पीलिकानां द्व्यधिकदशशतं संनिवेश्यांगसंधौ ॥
कापित्थैः कंटकेन्द्रैः श्रुति-नयन-शिरोभाल-नासाग्र-जिह्वा ।
कर्णादिष्वंगकेषु प्रतिभिदि-खननं शत्रुनाशाय कुर्यात् ॥६॥

साध्याम्बरे मनोज्ञां द्विविधकृतियुतां तंतुनैकीकृतांताम्
वायुं संस्थाप्य तस्याः शिरसि तनयकं जंतुमावेशयित्वा ।।
नासांगंडे च कर्णे भ्रमरयुगमथो जाठरे त्वाशुसूतम्
जप्त्वा मंत्रं तु मंत्री द्विशतमथ खनेद्वैरिनाशाय कोष्ठे ।।७।।

तालं-क्ष्मारुहां समूलां महिपरिवृतं सालराजस्य मूलम्
हृत्वा ते गर्भ-नारी-मलयुग-सहितं नारिकेलस्य मध्ये ।।
क्षिप्त्वा मंत्री जपित्वा शतमनुमथ तं मार्गदेशे खनित्वा
पश्चात्तत्संख्यमेवं प्रजपतु स मनुं योषितां वेदनाय ।।८।।
गृह्णीयात्तं प्रसूत्यै पुनरपि नयनां मारणाय प्रताड्यद्
गर्भस्थं मृत्युमेतच्छिथिलितमकरोत्स्रावितुं धारयेत्तम् ।।
एवं मंत्री क्रियाणां कृतिमकलंयत स्वात्मताढ्य-प्रभावै-
र्निःशंकं क्ष्मासुदेशे शरभ-शिव-वशात्सर्वदा सिद्धिमेति ।।९।।

इति श्रीआकाशभैरवकल्पे प्रत्यक्षसिद्धिप्रदे उमामहेश्वरसम्वादे एकविंशोऽध्यायः ।।२१।।

द्वाविंशोऽध्यायः

अथाभिषेक-विधिः

श्रीदेव्युवाच ॥

शंभो शिव जगन्नाथ सर्वजीव दयापर ।
अभिषेक-विधिं श्रोतुमिच्छाम्यहं वद प्रभो ॥१॥

श्रीशिव उवाच ॥

अभिषेक-विधिं वक्ष्येऽलंकृते मंडपे शुभे ।
गोमयेनाथ संलिप्य पृथिवीं चतुरस्रकाम् ॥२॥
गंधाक्षतैस्तु संकीर्य तंदुलेनासितेन तु ।
नवकोष्ठं समालिख्यालंकृत्य कुसुमादिभिः ॥३॥
मध्यकोष्ठे लिखेद्वृत्तं तन्मध्ये चतुरस्रकम् ।
नवकुंभं च तन्मध्ये प्रतिष्ठाप्य नवांशुकम् ॥४॥
तंतुना परिवेष्टयाथ धूपदीपं प्रदर्शयेत् ।
गंध-माल्यैरलंकृत्य पूरयेद् घटमंभसा ॥५॥
पद्मरागं प्रजा-कामस्त्वायुष्कामस्य मौक्तिकम् ।
रजतं वृद्धिकामस्तु तेजस्कामस्तु विद्रुमम् ॥६॥
वैडूर्यं वीर्यकामस्तु सर्वकामस्त्वशेषकम् ।
हिरण्यं वा तु तत्स्थाने घटमध्ये विनिःक्षिपेत् ॥७॥
तस्योपरि च दूर्वाम्र-पल्लवानि प्रकल्पयेत् ।
नारीकेलं ततः पश्चात्सालंकारं प्रकल्पयेत् ॥८॥
देवता-वाहनं तत्र प्रकुर्यादासनादिकम् ।
विश्वामित्रेण तत्कुंभं दूर्वया संस्पृशेत्ततः ॥९॥
अष्टोत्तरसहस्रं तु जपेन्मंत्रं समाहितः ।
कृतस्नानं समाकृष्ट-भूतांगंत्वार्द्रवाससम् ॥१०॥
प्राङ्मुखं देवदत्तं तं कुंभ-पाणिरुदङ्मुखः ।
अभिषेकं त्वहं कुर्यात्क्षुद्र-रोग-विमुक्तये ॥११॥

पंचाहं वात-रोगस्य वात-शूलस्य पक्षकम् ।
मासं तु सर्वरोगस्य शिरोरोगस्य मंडलम् ।।१२।।
ग्रनुभोगपिशाचस्य त्रिमासं चाभिषेचयेत् ।
तथैव क्षय-रोगस्य त्वपस्मारस्य वत्सरम् ।।१३।।
ग्रभिषेकस्य तत्सर्वं शमनं याति सुन्दरि ।
तस्मात्सर्वप्रयत्नेन ग्रभिषेकं समाचरेत् ।।१४।।
ग्रथ वंध्याचिकित्साख्यमभिषेकं वदाम्यहम् ।
वीर्यवन्तीं वधूं शुद्धां ऋतुस्नानदिनात् ततः ।।१५।।
दशाहं जन्म-वंध्याख्यां द्व्यधिकं काकवंध्यकाम् ।
मृत-वंध्यां षोडशाहं तदंते तु विशेषतः ।।१६।।
ऋतं चेति त्यृचा कुंभं शत-वाराभि-मंत्रितम् ।
ग्रभिषिच्य ततः पश्चाद्रक्षां कुर्वीत बुद्धिमान् ।।१७।।
सीसं षण्मास-वीर्यं तु ताम्रं वत्सर-वीर्यकम् ।
त्रिलोहं च वत्सरार्धं तु राजतं च त्रिवर्षकम् ।।१८।।
भूर्जपत्रं चतुर्वर्षं पंचाब्दं पंचलोहकम् ।
दशवर्षं तु काश्णीयं कांचनं यावदायुषम् ।।१९।।
तस्माद्धिरण्मये पत्रे साध्ययंत्रं विलिख्य तु ।
तद्यंत्रमक्षरं यद्यत्तत्तदावाह्य देवतम् ।।२०।।
प्रत्येकं शतवारं तु प्राणमंत्रं जपेद् बुधः ।
षोडशाद्युपचारं तु कुर्यात्सर्वं यथाक्रमम् ।।२१।।
मूलेन च सहस्रं तु प्रत्यहं प्रजपेच्छिवे ।
ग्रभिषेकावसाने तु प्रमज्जन्तीं वधूं जले ।।२२।।
बद्ध्वा तु पत्रिकां कंठे पश्चादुत्थापयेच्छिवे ।
ग्रयसा शुद्ध-सिक्ताख्या शुद्धांगा शुद्ध-वाससी ।।२३।।
ततस्तदादि षण्मासे निम्नगां नातिलंघयेत् ।
भृगुवारे तु संस्नानं तदा यंत्रस्य धूपनम् ।।२४।।
ब्राह्मणान्भोजयेद्देवि ऋतुस्नानदिने दिने ।
तदा घृत-पयोक्तान्नमृतुस्नाता विपेध्य च ।
भित्वा तदष्टकं पिंडमुपलेपित-भूतले ।।२५।।

निक्षिप्य च करं[1] स्नात्वा तोयेन परिषेच्य च ॥२६॥
आकाश-भूतल-स्वर्गचारिणो देवताः स्वयम् ।
इहागत्य तदाकालं वदंत्याशु सितां सुतम् ॥२७॥
दशवारमिदं जप्त्वा स्फोटयेत्तु करं पुनः ।
ततः पश्चात्प्रदेशस्थो जपेन्मंत्रं पुनः पुनः ॥२८॥
प्रथमं काक आगत्य भक्षितं यत्तु पिंडकम् ।
तद्दक्षिणादियुग्मश्चेत्पुत्री भवति निश्चयः ॥२६॥
पुत्रं तु युग्मकं नूनं पिंडे चेत् स्याद्विशेषतः ।
प्रथमं प्रथमे मासि द्वितीयादि तथा क्रमात् ॥३०॥
तत्तल्लक्षणकाले तु सा नारी गर्भिणी भवेत् ।
एतद्विधानकं गुह्यं सर्वशास्त्रोत्तमोत्तमम् ॥३१॥
इत्थं ज्ञात्वा कलौ मंत्री सर्वकार्याणि साधयेत् ।
तुलायां वृषभे सिंहे मीने कुंभे च वृश्चिके ॥३२॥
रक्षाभिषेकौ कर्तव्यौ नान्ये मासि शुभावहौ ॥३३॥

इति श्रीआकाशभैरवकल्पे प्रत्यक्षसिद्धिप्रदे उमामहेश्वरसम्वादे रक्षाभिषेकविधिर्नाम द्वाविंशोऽध्यायः ॥२२॥

---

१ (खरं खात्वा इति मूल पाठे)

त्रयोविंशोऽध्यायः

बलिकर्म-प्रयोगः

श्रीशिव उवाच ॥

रहस्यं श्रृणु देवि त्वं सर्वलोकार्थसाधकम् ।
सर्वजीवात्म-संताप-मोचनं प्राणवर्धनम् ॥१॥
मंत्रे यंत्रे तथा तंत्रे प्रयोगे कृत्रिमे यदा ।
संकटे पूर्ण-संपाते त्वभिचार-महाज्वरे ॥२॥
नाना-निर्याण-संजाते ग्राम-गोग्रहणे रणे ।
प्रवर्तते महाक्रूरे रोगे पापसमाकुले ॥३॥
तदा तच्छमनार्थं तु बलिकर्म वदाम्यहम् ।
नवपात्रं समादाय मृण्मयं विधि-पूरितम् ॥४॥
कर्पासमूलबीजं च सैंधवं निम्ब-पल्लवम् ।
स्थापयित्वाऽनले देवि परिणीय त्रिवारकम् ॥५॥
ततस्तत्पश्चिमे भागे नयेत्तोरणमंदिरे ।
एतदेव त्र्यहं कुर्यात्केवलं ज्वरशांतये ॥६॥
प्रोक्तोऽयं बलि-कर्माख्यः सायंकाले समाचरेत् ।
शिखा-कर्णयुगे दोः पत्संधौ संधौ स्तनद्वये ॥७॥
नारिकेलं प्रणीयाऽथ छादयेन्नव-वाससा ।
प्रदर्श्य च महाधूपं माला मंत्रं स्मरेद् बुधः ॥८॥
नारिकेरं शिराग्रस्तं गृहीत्वा परिणीयतम् ।
दत्त्वा बलिं ततो वस्त्रं सकर्णं स विपाटयेत् ॥९॥
एवं क्रमेण पादांतं कृत्वा कुंभाभिषेचनम् ।
तद्बलिं नैर्ऋते भागे निनयेज्जल-वर्जिते ॥१०॥
कर्मारकमिदं प्रोक्तं नानाक्षुद्र-विमुक्तये ।
नाना-रोग-निवृत्त्यै स्यादेकाह-ज्वर-शांतये ॥११॥
प्रस्थद्वयं समुद्धृत्य त्रिधान्नं संविभज्य तत् ।
कृत्वा तु मध्यमं पिंडं पुत्तलिकाँ यथाविधि ॥१२॥

नानावर्णैरलंकृत्य नानावर्ण-प्रसूनकैः ।
आद्यंत पिंडं तद्बाह्ये न्यसेत्साध्यं समुच्चरन् ॥१३॥
केशाक्षिश्रुति-नासास्य कर्ण-हृन्नाभि-गुह्यके ।
पाणि-पत्संधि-भेदैश्च कुर्याद्दीपं पृथक् पृथक् ॥१४॥
साध्यप्राणमनु मंत्री जपांते नाभि नीयताम् ।
नालिकेर-बलिं दत्वा पश्चादीशान-दिङ्नयेत् ॥१५॥
प्रोक्तो घोरकृतिर्देवि सर्व-पैशाच-शांतये ।
ताम्रपात्रेऽम्भसा पूर्णे गंध-पुष्पाद्यालंकृते ॥१६॥
देवदत्त पुरो भागे तस्य छायाऽभिवेशिते ।
मालामंत्रेण संमृश्य शालिपिष्टेन छादयेत् ॥१७॥
नवदीपं तदग्रे तु कुर्याद्धि तं विचक्षणः ।
अभितो नीयते नैवं दिशि वायव्यके नयेत् ॥१८॥
कक्षपाल्यमिदं प्रोक्तं नानाज्वर-विमुक्तये ।
आदाय चोदकं पात्रं पूर्णोदक-बहिर्युतम् ॥१९॥
तिलाक्षत-समंगानां रजोभिस्तंडुलोन्मुखैः ।
अलंकृत्य चतुः पार्श्वं पंचदीपं प्रकल्पयेत् ॥२०॥
धूपं संवेशयित्वाथ लाजेनाभ्यर्च्य पेषयेत् ।
बलिं दत्त्वोत्तरे भागे नयेत्पैशाचशांतये ॥२१॥
एवं त्र्यहं समाकुर्याद्भीषणाख्यं विचक्षणम् ॥२२॥
भांडं शिरोविनादाय पादलोलूख-पूर्वकैः ।
क्रमाल्लिप्योरुलूखाग्रे दीपमादाय मध्यतः ॥२३॥
अष्टपद्माकृतिं कृत्वा त्वलंकृत्वा त्रिवर्णकैः ।
दलांतरं तु लाजेन दीपं पात्रे च मध्यगे ॥२४॥
दलाद्बहिस्तिलैः पुष्पैरलंकृत्यविचक्षणः ।
दल-केशं तु निर्वाणमुलमुकालेपनाननम् ॥२५॥
चूर्णं बिंदुं समायुक्तं तेन शेषावृतांगकम् ।
साधकं निर्भयं खड्ग-पाणिनं कालरात्रिके ॥२६॥
वरयेत्सोऽपि तद्गृह्य देवदत्तं प्रदक्षिणम् ।
त्रिधा कृत्वा तमालोक्य खड्गं कर्णे निधाय च ॥२७॥

आगच्छेद्दिवं गच्छेदट्टहासं समन्वितम् ।
सेवकैर्वाद्यघोषैश्च श्मशाने बलिपूर्वकम् ॥२८॥
श्मशाने रौद्रकं मंत्रं जपित्वा तत्त्रिवारकम् ।
निधाय च ततः स्नात्वा स गच्छेद् गेहकं विना ॥२९॥
अभिनीय कपालाख्यं बलिमेवं समाचरेत् ।
महारोग-ज्वर-क्षुद्र-भूत-कृत्रिमशांतये ॥३०॥
.........................ग्रह ग्राहोवधूम्रकम् ।
इतराण्यपि भूतानि यावंति बलि-दर्शनात् ॥३१॥

ओं नमो भगवते श्मशानरुद्राय नररुधिर मांसभक्षणाय कपालमालाधराय प्रेतवाहनाय खड्गकपालहस्ताय सर्वभूताधिपतये क्लां दां ह्रां एह्येहि आगच्छागच्छ समस्त-भूतरोगान् नाशय २ सर्वरिपून् नाशय २ क्लें दें ह्लें श्रीं इदं भुंक्ष्व २ क्लूं ब्लूं ह्लूं सर्वसौभाग्यं देहि देहि स्वाहा ।

इति श्रीआकाशभैरवकल्पे प्रत्यक्षसिद्धिप्रदे उमामहेश्वरसम्वादे बलिकर्मविधानं नाम त्रयोविंशोऽध्यायः ॥२३॥

चतुर्विंशोऽध्यायः

आचारविधिप्रयोगः

श्रीशिव उवाच ।।

सदाचारविधिं वक्ष्ये साधकानां वरानने ।
ब्राह्मे मुहूर्त्ते चोत्थाय प्रणम्य गुरुमात्मनः ।।१।।
शरभेशाष्टकं मंत्रं त्रिवारं मनसा जपेत् ।
नमस्कृत्वा ततो मंत्री गणेशं शरभेश्वरम् ।।२।।
ततस्तीर्थं समाश्रित्य मुखनासाक्षिशोधनम् ।
कृत्वा मंत्री ततः स्नात्वा मूलमंत्रं त्रिधा जपेत् ।।३।।
त्रिधाऽऽचम्य त्रिधा प्रोक्ष्य त्रिरर्घ्यं तर्पणत्रयम् ।
त्रिधा संमंत्र्य तद्भस्म ललाटादिषु विन्यसेत् ।।४।।
किरीट-कुंडलैर्युक्तं सर्वाभरण-भूषितम् ।
अथवा भस्मनाऽऽभूष्य सांध्यकर्म समाचरेत् ।।५।।
सूर्य-मंडल-मध्यस्थ ज्योतिर्मय-मुखांबुजम् ।
चारु-कुंडल-संयुक्तं चन्द्रमालावतंसिनम् ।।६।।
दशबाहुं महाकायं सुवर्ण-सदृश-प्रभम् ।
चक्र-शूल-गदा-खड्ग-बाण-कार्मुक-खेटकम् ।।७।।
घंटा-कपाल-शंखैश्च भासमान-करांबुजम् ।
दिव्याभरण-संयुक्तं दिव्यवासं त्रिलोचनम् ।।८।।
चिरं ध्यात्वा जपेन्मंत्रमष्टोत्तरशतं शिवे ।
द्विचत्वारिंशदथवा जपित्वा वाग्युतः सुधीः ।।९ ।।

पुरश्चरणविधिप्रयोगः ।।

शिलोच्चये नदी-तीरे वने देवालयेऽपि वा ।
विजने मंदिरे रम्ये प्राङ्मुखोदङ्मुखोऽथवा ।।१०।।
सुखासने समासीनः प्राणानायम्य तत्त्वतः ।
दुष्टोच्चाटं तु दिग्बंधं भूतशुद्धिं दृढासनः ।।११।।

प्राणायामत्रयं कृत्वा ऋषि-न्यासादि-पूर्वकम् ।
सहस्रद्वय-संयुक्तं चत्वारिंशज्जपं चरेत् ॥१२॥
तर्पणैरुक्तहोमैश्च सिद्धमंत्री तथा भवेत् ।
तर्पणस्य च होमस्य द्विजानां भोजनस्य च ॥१३॥
तद्दशांश-क्रमेणैव कुर्यादेकैकशः क्रमात् ।
तत्स्थानेष्वथवा मंत्री मनोः संख्यं पृथग् जपेत् ॥१४॥
विना तर्पण-होमैश्च विना ब्राह्मण-भोजनैः ।
पुरश्चर्यां च यः कुर्यात्तस्य मंत्रो न सिध्यति ॥१५॥
जपं च तर्पणं होमं ब्राह्मणाराधनं तथा ।
चतुरंगमिति ख्यातं तस्माद्यत्नेन कारयेत् ॥१६॥
स्वात्मनाभिमुखं मंत्रं सुश्रुवे विधिवद्यदा ।
यत्तथा सिद्धि-पर्यंतं गर्भस्थो मंत्र-दैवतः ॥१७॥
जपे पूर्णे ततः स्वांते जायते मंत्र-देवता ।
तज्जने दर्शनाद्यत्तत्प्रथमांगं वरानने ॥१८॥
संजात-तर्पणात्पूर्णमंत्रदेवो न सिध्यति ।
वरेण्यं तर्पणं तस्माद्यत्नेनापि समाचरेत् ॥१९॥
वर्धमानो मंत्र-देवस्तर्पणारंभणादितः ।
समाप्तौ विद्धि तं यत्तद्द्वितीयांगमुदीरितम् ॥२०॥
विधिनोक्तेन होमेन मनोर्देवः प्रभुर्भवेत् ।
सर्वाधिकं प्रभुत्वं यत्तत्तृतीयमुदाहृतम् ॥२१॥
ब्राह्मणाराधनाद्देवोदयावान् वरदो भवेत् ।
तेन लब्धं प्रसादं यत्तच्चतुर्थमुदाहृतम् ॥२२॥
मंत्रिणां मंत्रसिध्यर्थं चतुरंगमुदीरितम् ।
चतुरंगपुरश्चर्यां कारयेन्मंत्रसिद्धये ॥२३॥
एवं प्रयोग-सिध्यर्थं पुरश्चर्याद्वियं भवेत् ।
ततः स्वेच्छा-प्रयोगांस्तु भूत-वैरिषु कारयेत् ॥२४॥
पुरश्चर्यात्रयेणैव सर्वभूतवशी भवेत् ।
विशेषादनभिज्ञोऽपि बुध्याबुध्य समो भवेत् ॥२५॥

चतुष्टयेन देवेशि सारस्वतमवाप्नुयात् ।
अष्टादशसु भाषासु स्वनंदीव विजृंभते ॥२६॥
जपेल्लक्षत्रयं नूनं क्षुभ्यंत्यखिल-योषितः ।
देव-गंधर्व-भूतादि-वनिताकर्षणं भवेत् ॥२७॥
चतुष्टयेन लक्षेण बार्हस्पत्यं भवेन्नृणाम् ।
विशेषाद् द्रुम-सर्पादि स्मर-रूपत्वमंबिके ॥२८॥
षट्लक्षेण जपेनैव विषहंता गदं किमु ।
रिपूणां कालरूपत्वमंबिके संभविष्यति ॥२९॥
मंत्रिणां सप्तलक्षेण वरुणत्वं भविष्यति ।
स्वेच्छा-हानि महावृष्टिद्रुतं वर्षयितुं· किमु ॥३०॥
लक्षाष्टकेन संमंत्री श्रीदो भवति पार्वति ।
तथा नवनिधीनां च पतित्वं किं पुनः स्वयम् ॥३१॥
नवलक्ष-जपादेव कंपंत्यखिल-देवताः ।
चतुर्दशसु लोकेषु तस्यासाध्यं न विद्यते ॥३२॥
दशलक्षात् सुरेशत्वं मंत्रिणां संभविष्यति ।
निग्रहानुग्रहं सर्वं स्मरणादेव सिध्यति ॥३३॥
द्वादशाह्येन लक्षेण साक्षाद् ब्रह्मसमो भवेत् ।
स तदा विविधान्स्रष्टुमधिकारी भवेत्स्वयम् ॥३४॥
षोडशादेव लक्षाणां नरो नारायणो भवेत् ।
तत्र माया जयं तस्य विश्वरूपत्वमंबिके ॥३५॥
देव-दानव-गंधर्व-खेचराः पृथिवीचराः ।
भूत-प्रेत-पिशाचाद्याः स्थावरं जंगमं तथा ॥३६॥
तस्य मायावशं प्राप्य स्फुटितं नैव कौशलम् ।
अर्धयामेन तत्कोपान्नाशतां संप्रयांति ते ॥३७॥
पंचविंशति-लक्षेण पंचशीर्षो भवेन्नरः ।
तस्य सर्व-जयं तस्य वीक्षणान्निग्रहं तथा ॥३८॥
अनंत-कोट्यंड-डंभः अहंकारं च दारुणम् ।
स्वर्ग-स्थिति-लयादीनां कर्तृत्वं तस्य जायते ॥३९॥

पंचाशल्लक्षमात्रेण परब्रह्म भवेत्तु सः ।
चित्स्वरूपं समाश्रित्य चिदानंदो भवेत्तदा ॥४०॥
अतः परं फलं नास्ति स्वात्मलाभादिति श्रुतिः ।
स्व-स्वरूपानुसंधानं कुर्यादेवं पुनः पुनः ॥४१॥
सूर्य चंद्रोपरागे च विषुवे चायने तथा ।
दर्शके चाथ पूर्णायां संक्रांतौ पातिके परे ॥४२॥
याममात्रं व्रती भूत्वा जपेदालोक्य भास्करम् ।
सर्वसिद्धिमवाप्नोति मंत्री नूनं वरानने ॥४३॥
यस्मान्नराद्धनापेक्षा तं स्मरन् हि जपेदिमाम् ।
किं ते कृण्वन्त्यृचां मंत्री शतोत्तर-सहस्रकम् ॥४४॥
स्वयमेव स संतुष्टः सर्वस्वमपिदो भवेत् ।
तद्धनं सहसा लब्ध्वा सुखी भवति निश्चितम् ॥४५॥
विजने कानने घोरे राज-चौरारि-संकुले ।
अभिव्ययस्वेति ऋचं जपेत्तद्भीति-शांतये ॥४६॥
संग्रामे तुमुले प्राप्ते बलं धेहीत्यृचं जपेत् ।
स क्रंदनबलं प्राप्य सहसा विजयी भवेत् ॥४७॥
संग्रामे च महद्युद्धे शत्रूणां सेनयावृते ।
वयः सुपर्णेति ऋचं शतमष्टोत्तरं जपेत् ॥४८॥
तरसा वैरिणां माया क्षपा-सूर्य-इवोदये ।
जपित्वा स्वप्रभावेण स मंत्री विजयी भवेत् ॥४९॥
निमग्न-तरणे काले ह्युदगादित्यृचं जपेत् ।
महा-ग्राह-युतां घोरां नदीं तीर्त्वा सुखं व्रजेत् ॥५०॥
विजहीष्वेति सूक्तेन शतवाराभिमर्शनम् ।
तत्तैलं पाययेद्देवि सा नारी सूयते द्रुतम् ॥५१॥
प्रथमे पंचमे मासि तृतीये सप्तमेऽथवा ।
यदा पीतं तदा नारी तत्क्षणादेव सूयते ॥५२॥
विपत्ति-काले संप्राप्ते विपिने निवसेद्यदि ।
तदायमस्मान्नित्यृचं जप्त्वा शीर्विनिवृत्तये ॥५३॥

तत्रैव काननाधीशो रक्षत्यनिशमंबिके ।
तस्मात् सर्व-प्रयत्नेन जपेत्सौख्यं लभेत्तदा ॥५४॥
विष्णुरित्यादिसूक्तेन नारीणां पुत्र-सिद्धये ।
सहस्रवारं संमंत्र्य तदाज्यं प्राशयेच्छिवे ॥५५॥

एवं दिनत्रयं कुर्यान्मासात्पुत्रफलं लभेत् ।
तदादि-रक्षा कर्तव्या नारीणां गर्भवृद्धये ॥५६॥

गणानां त्वेत्यृचं मंत्री जपेद्विघ्न-निवृत्तये ।
तस्य विघ्न-भयं नास्ति जाग्रत्स्वप्न-सुषुप्तिषु ॥५७॥

बृहत्सामेत्यृचं मंत्री रक्षां संमृज्य पार्वति ।
तद्रक्षा-धारणं कुर्यादुत्तमांगे वरानने ॥५८॥

तथाविधं समालोक्य यक्ष-गंधर्व-राक्षसाः ।
बहुशो भीतिमालोक्य संनिकर्षं न यांति ते ॥५९॥

भूत-प्रेत-पिशाचानां किमु सर्वग्रहादिनाम् ।
नराणामितराणां च जंगमानां वरानने ॥६०॥

आलेख्यं तिर्यगूर्ध्वं स्ववसु-महि-तले शूलयुक्तां च रेखाम्
प्रदाक्षिण्येन बाह्या पृथगृतु-लिखितेन्द्रोतिभिः सूक्तमादौ ॥
शिष्टे-कोष्ठेऽरि-नाम त्रिशिख-बहिरपि क्रूरपूर्णाभिलिप्त्वा
स्पृष्ट्वाजप्त्वा च स्मृत्वा सह शशि-भवने कल्पयेच्छंसनाय ॥ ६१ ॥

संहारेऽस्मिन्प्रयोगे सकल विधिषु चेन्द्रोतिभिः सूक्त-मंत्र
मेकैकं वासमेतं निजगुरुवदनाद्यो न जानाति भूमौ ॥
सोऽविद्यामूल-दृष्टि कलयति कुपितः किं नु षूत्पातकर्म
ज्ञातस्तत्साध्य-कृत्ति कटुवर लिपितं तापितं निग्रहाय ॥६२॥

इति श्रीआकाशभैरवकल्पे प्रत्यक्षसिद्धिप्रदे उमामहेश्वरसम्वादे आचारविधिर्नाम चतुर्विंशोऽध्यायः ॥२४॥

पंचविंशोऽध्यायः

मायाप्रयोगः

श्रीशिव उवाच ।।

अथ मायाप्रयोगं च वक्ष्यामि तव पार्वति ।
मंत्र-स्मरण-मात्रेण महामायी भवेच्छिवे ।।१।।
अथास्य माया-मंत्रस्य परब्रह्म ऋषिः स्मृतः ।
त्रिष्टुप्छंदस्तथा देवि परशक्तिस्तु देवता ।।२।।
पुष्करं पावकं माया रामराजं च कीलकम् ।
माया-प्रयोग-सिद्ध्यर्थे विनियोगो वरानने
माययैव षडंगं स्यान्मंत्रमाथर्वणं परम् ।।३।।
तापिच्छ-नीलां शर-चाप-हस्तां सर्वाधिकां श्याम-रथाधिरूढाम्।
नमामि रुद्रावसनेन लोकान् सर्वान् सलोकामपि मोहयंतीम् ।।४।।
प्रथमं च महामायां व्याहृतेः प्रथमाक्षरम् ।
मायां द्वितीयं मायां च तृतीयं मायया सह ।।५।।
आथर्वणं ततः पश्चादंत्येऽपि प्रणवादिकम् ।
अवरोहानिवृत्तिः स्यादेवं शास्त्र-विनिर्णयः ।।६।।
"ओं ह्रीं भूः ह्रीं भुवः ह्रीं स्वः ह्रीं शिवांघ्रि
युग्मे विनिविष्टचित्तं सर्वेषां दृष्टयो हृदयस्य बालम् ।
रिपूणां निद्रां विवशं करोति महामाये मां परिरक्ष नित्यम्
ह्रीं स्वः ह्रीं भुवः ह्रीं भूः ह्रीं ओं स्वाहा" ।।७।।
त्रिकोणं विलिखेत्पूर्वं तद्बहिर्वृत्तमालिखेत् ।
तद्बहिश्चाथ मन्वंस्रं तद्बहिर्भूपुर-द्वयम् ।।८।।
मध्ये तारयुतं माया व्याहृती युक् त्रिकोणके ।
चतुर्दश-दले मंत्रं विलिखेत्पदशः क्रमात् ।।९।।
भूपुरे विलिखेत्साध्यं द्वं द्व द्वष्टदिशं प्रति ।
कृष्ण-पुष्पैश्च गंधाढ्यैः पराशक्तिं यथाविधि ।।१०।।

आवाह्याभ्यर्च्य संपूज्य जपेत्स्पृष्ट्वायुतं मनुम् ।
तन्मंत्र-धारणादेव माया-निधि-विधिर्भवेत् ॥११॥
धृत्वा यंत्रं ततो मंत्री स्मरेन्मंत्रं यथाविधि ।
ततस्तत्स्मरणादेव मायालोके विजृंभते ॥१२॥
तस्य मायावशेनैव देव-दानव-राक्षसाः ।
न पश्यंति समाजातं किं पुनः प्राणयो ग्रहाः ॥१३॥
युद्ध-भूमि समागत्य स्वसेना-मध्य-भूतले ।
कार्ष्णायवृक्ष-पुष्पोत्थैः समिद्भिः सघृतैस्तिलैः ॥१४॥
पायसैः पिशितं नृणां दक्षिणाभिमुखो हुनेत् ।
प्रत्येकं विधिवद्देवि षष्ट्युत्तर-शत-त्रयम् ॥१५॥
होमांते तु जपेन्मंत्री भानुमालोक्य पंचधा ।
युद्धं प्रति यदागच्छेत्तदा निर्विवशो भवेत् ॥१६॥
यथा युद्ध-दिने प्राप्ते तथा होमं तदा हुनेत् ।
प्रत्यहं विजयार्थाय यः कुर्यात्स जयी भवेत् ॥१७॥
समिद्भिः समरेऽन्यैश्च यः सहस्राहुतिं हुनेत् ।
तस्याग्निः पुरतः साक्षात्स्थित्वा दत्तवरो भवेत् ॥१८॥
तद्वरं देवलोकानां संहृतिर्नाशनं व्रजेत् ।
तद्वरं ब्राह्मणाभेद्यं तत्तुल्यं न कदाचन् ॥१९॥
विष्णुना च मया चैव नैव तस्याग्रतः स्थितः ॥२०॥

इति श्रीआकाशभैरवकल्पे प्रत्यक्षसिद्धिप्रदे उमामहेश्वरसम्वादे मायाविधिर्नाम पंचविंशोऽध्यायः ॥२५॥

षड्विंशोऽध्यायः

पूजाविधिः

श्रीशिव उवाच ॥

आराधनं प्रवक्ष्यामि सर्वसिद्धिप्रदायकम् ।
भोग-मोक्ष-प्रदं-दिव्यं-भुक्ति-मुक्त्यैक-हेतुकम् ॥१॥

विषुवकालेऽयने पुण्ये पूर्णायां दर्शके तथा ।
एकादश्यां च द्वादश्यां शुक्र-सौम्येन्दु-वासरे ॥२॥

जन्मर्क्षे च विपदृक्षे प्रत्यरौ च वधर्क्षके ।
शोभने पातिके ब्राह्मे दंडयोग-विवर्जिते ॥३॥

सिद्धयोगे तथाकाश-पाताल-रहिते दिने ।
विजने मंडपे रम्ये गोमयेनानुलेपिते ॥४॥

वितान लंबि-संयुक्ते धूप-दीप-समाकुले ।
स्नात्वा-पवित्र-पाणिः-सन् शुद्धो मौनी दृढव्रतः ॥५॥

प्राङ्मुखोदङ्मुखो वाथ सुखासीनः स्वलंकृतः ।
दिव्यगंधेन युक्तेन भस्मना रत्नि-मात्रकम् ॥६॥

चतुरस्रं ततः कृत्वा तस्मिन्भस्मनि बुद्धिमान् ।
त्रिकोणं विलिखेत्पूर्वं तद्बहिर्वृत्तमालिखेत् ॥७॥

तद्बहिश्चाष्टपत्रं तु द्वादशारं ततः परम् ।
षोडशारं ततः पश्चात्ततो भूपुर-युग्मकम् ॥८॥

त्रिकोण-मध्ये देवेशंशरभं सालुवेश्वरम् ।
चिरं ध्यात्वा ततो मंत्री गुरुपादयुगं स्मरन् ॥९॥

मूलेन गंध-पुष्पाद्यैरग्रंथिभिरकंडुभिः ।
आवाहनादि-पुष्पांतमुपचारान्समर्पयेत् ॥१०॥

चंद्रं सूर्यं च वह्निं च त्रिकोणे तु यजेत्क्रमात् ।
भैरवं वाडवाग्निं च दुर्गां कालीं यथाक्रमम् ॥११॥

त्रिकोणे वृत्त-मध्ये तु चतुर्दिक्षु यजेत्क्रमात् ।
इन्द्रमग्नि यमं चैव निर्ऋतिं वरुणं तथा ॥१२॥
वायुं सोमं तथेशानं दलेष्वष्टसु पूजयेत् ।
पार्श्वद्वये यजेद्देवि व्याधि मृत्युमतः परम् ॥१३॥
मदनं रक्तचामुंडीं मोहिनीं द्राविणीं तथा ।
शब्दाकर्षणिकां वाणीं रमां मायां पुलिंदिनीम् ॥१४॥
शास्तारं क्षोभिणीं ज्येष्ठां द्वादशारेयजेत्क्रमात् ।
पूजयेन्मूल-मंत्रेण स्व-स्व-यंत्रेण चांबिके ॥१५॥
षोडशारे यजेत्पश्चात्षोडश-स्वर-देवताः ।
गणेश्वरं यमं स्कंदं भैरवं च महादिशि ॥१६॥
प्रागादितो यजेन्मंत्री मूलेनैव पृथक् पृथक् ।
त्वरितां वीरभद्रं च वडवानल-भैरवम् ॥१७॥
महामायां यजेद्देवि वायव्यादि-विदिक्षु सः ।
आरभ्य चाग्रतो मंत्री ब्रह्माण्याद्यष्टमातरः ॥१८॥
परितस्तु यजेद्देवं ककाराद्यर्ण-देवताः ।
मूलेन सालुवं भूयो धूप-दीपादिकं यजेत् ॥१९॥
स्तुतिभिस्तोषयित्वाथ यथोक्तं प्रणिपत्य सः ।
मूलमंत्रं जपेन्मंत्री अष्टोत्तरसहस्रकम् ॥२०॥
आचार्यं पूजयेन्मंत्रं यथाशक्ति यथा-बलम् ।
शरभं हृदयथोद्वास्य शिवोऽहमिति भावयेत् ॥२१॥
इत्येवं सततं कुर्यात्स्वयमेव शिवो भवेत् ।
तद्भूस्मागमनं श्रुत्वा कंपंते विग्रहा ग्रहाः ॥२२॥
किं पुनर्दर्शनादस्य भूत-प्रेतादि-राक्षसाः ॥२३॥

इति श्रीआकाशभैरवकल्पे प्रत्यक्षसिद्धिप्रदे उमामहेश्वरसम्वादे पूजाविधिर्नाम षड्विंशोऽध्यायः ॥२६॥

सप्तविंशोऽध्यायः

मातृकाप्रयोगः

श्रीशिव उवाच ॥

अकारं ब्रह्म-दैवत्यं श्वेतं सर्ववशंकरम् ।
सर्वज्ञत्वं मनोज्ञत्वं कामरूपत्वमंबिके ॥१॥

आकारं तु पराशक्ति-श्वेतमाकर्षसिद्धिदम् ।
इच्छासिद्धिर्ज्ञानसिद्धिः स्वात्मसिद्धिर्वरानने ॥२॥

इकारं विष्णु-दैवत्यं श्यामं रक्षाकरं भवेत् ।
रूप-कांति-प्रदं-श्रेष्ठं-वरेण्यं-मोक्ष-सिद्धिदम् ॥३॥

मायादैवतमीकारं श्यामं मोहकरं परम् ।
वीराणां वनितानां च वशीकारं वरानने ॥४॥

उकारं कोल-दैवत्यं श्यामं लोकवशंकरम् ।
मृत्तकोत्थापनं पुण्यं क्रूरं रोगविनाशनम् ॥५॥

ऊकारं पृथिवी बीजं श्यामं रक्षाकरं परम् ।
भूत-प्रेत-पिशाचानां नाशनं रिपु-नाशनम् ॥६॥

ऋकारं विधि दैवत्यं पीतं सर्वार्थ-सिद्धिदम् ।
चिरायुष्यं तपःसिद्धं पराभोगं वरानने ॥७॥

ॠकारं शिव-दैवत्यं रक्तं सर्व-वशंकरम् ।
जन्म-मृत्यु-जरा-व्याधि-वर्जितं श्री-जयप्रदम् ॥८॥

अश्विभ्यां लृ लॄ रक्तं रोग-लोक-वशंकरम् ।
तीव्रसिद्धि भिषक्-सिद्धि मोक्ष-धी-सिद्धिदं भवेत् ॥९॥

एकारं वीरभद्रं स्यात्पीतं सर्वार्थ-सिद्धिदम् ।
निग्रहानुग्रह-करं भीषणं जयवर्धनम् ॥१०॥

ऐकारं भारती विद्यात्स्फटिकं ज्ञानसिद्धिदम् ।
चतुःषष्टि-कला सिद्धिदायकं परमं शिवे ॥११॥

ओकारं शिव-दैवत्यं ज्योतिर्मयमनुग्रहम् ।
मनोवेग-प्रदं श्रेष्ठं शांतं सर्वफलप्रदम् ॥१२॥
औकारं शांकरीविद्या स्फाटिकं सर्वसिद्धिदम् ।
सारस्वतं विशेषेण शत्रूणां कोप-नाशनम् ॥१३॥
अंकारं रुद्र-बीजं स्याद्रक्तं देव-वशंकरम् ।
सर्व-लोक-जयं कार्यसिद्धिदं चित्तशुद्धिदम् ॥१४॥
अःकारं कालरुद्रं स्याद्रक्तं पाशनिकृन्तनम् ।
स्व-प्रपंचोपसंहारं परमात्म-प्रयोजकम् ॥१५॥
ककारं ब्रह्मणो बीजं पीतं वृष्टिकरं परम् ।
संजीवनमशेषाणां लोकानां वृद्धिदायकम् ॥१६॥
खकारं जाह्नवी बीजं स्फटिकं पाप-नाशनम् ।
भोग मोक्ष-प्रदं पुण्यं भुक्ति-मुक्ति-प्रदायकम् ॥१७॥
गकारं तु गणेशं स्यात्पीताभं विघ्न-नाशनम् ।
पूर्वापरस्थितं ज्ञानं भू-लोक-विजयं-शुभम् ॥१८॥
घकारं भैरवं विद्याद्रक्ताभं शत्रुनाशनम् ।
महाघोर-ग्रहहरं-सारूप्यं जयवर्धनम् ॥१९॥
ङकारं कालबीजं स्यात्कृष्णं जीवजयं परम् ।
महाभीमं जगत्क्षोभ्यं मरणापत्ति-भंजनम् ॥२०॥
चकारं भद्रकालीयं रक्तांगं स्तोभनं भवेत् ।
स्वेच्छाकर्षण-सिद्धिस्तत्स्वस्थावेशमयत्नतः ॥२१॥
छकारं भीम-कालीयं रक्ताभं वैरिनाशनम् ।
संक्रामणं त्रिलोकेऽस्मिन्समरे विजय-प्रदम् ॥२२॥
जकारं जातवेदाख्यं तुर्यं सौदामिनी-प्रभम् ।
अभिचारं महाघोरमपमृत्यु भयापहम् ॥२३॥
झकारमर्धनारीशं श्यामं रक्त-समाकुलम् ।
सर्वसौख्यकरं श्रेष्ठं भोग-मोक्ष-फल-प्रदम् ॥२४॥
ञकारं परमात्मीयमवाङ्मनसगोचरं ।
सर्वज्ञानप्रदं ब्रह्मज्ञानदं श्री-जयप्रदम् ॥२५॥
टकारं पृथिवी-बीजं श्वेतं संहार-कारणम् ।
कृत्यादावौषधी वृद्धिः पाताल-निधि-दर्शनम् ॥२६॥

ठकारं चंद्र-बीजं स्यात्स्फाटिकं शत्रु-नाशनम् ।
रोग-क्ष्वेडहरं दिव्यं महाज्वर-हरं परम् ॥२७॥
डकारं शुक्रबीजं स्यात्पीताभं विजयं भवेत् ।
मृतसंजीवनं तत्स्यान्महामाया वशं शिवे ॥२८॥
ढकारं वैष्णवं विद्यात्पीतं सर्वार्थ-सिद्धिदम् ।
बलप्रदं जल-स्तंभं पातालस्यापि दर्शनम् ॥२९॥
णकारं बलभद्रीयं श्वेतं बल-विवर्धनम् ।
नित्यत्वं बुद्धि-वीर्यत्वं रिपु-दर्प विनाशनम् ॥३०॥
तकारं धनदं विद्यात्पीतमैश्वर्य-वर्धनम् ।
यक्ष-किन्नर-सिद्धानां वशीकारं जगद्वशम् ॥३१॥
थकारं तु पराशक्ति-रक्तं काल-जयं भवेत् ।
शांतिकं पौष्टिकं चैव भोग्यमायुष्य-वर्धनम् ॥३२॥
दकारं दौर्ग-बीजं स्याच्छ्यामं सर्वार्थ-साधनम् ।
निग्रहानुग्रह-करं भोग-मोक्षैकसाधनम् ॥३३॥
धकारं धर्मबीजं स्याच्छ्वेतं पुण्यविवर्धनम् ।
सदादेवमयं दिव्यं सर्वदर्शनदर्शकम् ॥३४॥
नकारं निर्विकल्पं स्यादप्रमेयाभमक्षरम् ।
वायुवेग-मनोवेगमिच्छा-रूपं भवेद् ध्रुवम् ॥३५॥
पकारमग्निबीजं स्याद्रक्तं सर्पहरं क्षणात् ।
स्त्री-पुं-नपुंसकादीनां भवेदाकर्षणं शिवे ॥३६॥
फकारं भैरवं विद्याद्रक्ताभं विजयं ततः ।
महाग्रह-हरं सर्व-ज्वर-रोग-विनाशनम् ॥३७॥
बकारमश्विनी-बीजं पीतं रोगहरं परम् ।
औषधस्य महावीर्यवृद्धिदं जयवर्धनम् ॥३८॥
भकारं भार्गवं ज्ञेयं ज्योतिष्प्रभमनामयम् ।
आयुरारोग्यदं श्रेष्ठमशेष-स्त्री-विवर्धनम् ॥३९॥
मकारमीश्वरं विद्याज्ज्योती रक्तं सुखावहम् ।
वश्याकर्षण-संतान-सिद्धिदानैक-तत्परम् ॥४०॥
यकारं वायु-बीजं स्यात्कृष्णं बलविवर्धनम् ।
सर्वोच्चाट-करं क्रूरं संग्रामे जयवर्धनम् ॥४१॥

रेफं कृशानुबीजं स्याद्रक्ताभं सर्पनाशनम् ।
जंगमाकर्षणं युद्धे द्विषां सेनाबलं तथा ।।४२।।
लकारं शक्रबीजं स्यात्पीतं सर्वफलप्रदम् ।
अग्निस्तंभं जलस्तंभं स्वेच्छास्तंभं विशेषतः ।।४३।।
वकारं वारुणं विद्याच्छ्वेतं स्वेच्छाभिवृष्टिदम् ।
आकर्षणं जलस्थानामशेषज्वरनाशनम् ।।४४।।
शकारं शंकरं विद्यात्तेजः सौभाग्य-सिद्धिदम् ।
अन्योऽन्यकलहादेव वैरिणां नाशनं भवेत् ।।४५।।
षकारं द्वादशादित्यं ज्योतिरारोग्यवर्धनम् ।
शमनं सर्वरोगाणामायुर्विद्याभिवर्धितम् ।।४६।।
सकारं भारतीबीजं श्वेतं सारस्वतप्रदम् ।
प्रतिविद्वज्जनजयं वराणां वनितावशम् ।।४७।।
सदाशिवं हकारं स्याद्धूम्रं ज्ञानार्थसिद्धिदम् ।
अणिमाद्यष्टसिद्धिः स्याच्चतुःषष्टिः कला अपि ।।४८।।
लकारं पृथिवीबीजं श्यामं सिद्धिकरं परम् ।
स भवेदोषधीवृद्धिः रिपु-भू-द्रव्यदर्शनम् ।।४९।।
क्षकारं श्रीनृसिंहं स्यात्स्फाटिकं मोक्षसिद्धिदम् ।
रिपुवर्गहरं सर्वलोकक्षोभहरं परम् ।।५०।।

इति सुमतिरहर्यो मातृका देवताया
द्युति-बल-महिमादीन्यादितःस्वामिवक्त्रात् ।
सकलमपि च लब्ध्वा सालुवाराधनांते
जयतु विविधसिद्धयै हेतुबीजेन मंत्रम् ।।५१।।
दशशतमभिमंत्री सावधानः प्रहृष्टः
प्रवणित-दृढ-भावः प्राकृतारंभशून्यः ।
जपमिति विधिपूर्वं मातृकायाश्च वर्णान्
प्रथममभिनियोज्य त्वेकमेकं च कुर्यात् ।।५२।।

पंचाशद्वर्णान् प्रथमं प्रयोक्त्वा जपेत्सहस्रं शरभेशमंत्रम् ।
स मानुषः सर्वकलाप्रवीणः प्रयाति तूर्णं पदमीश्वरस्य ।।५३।।
आदाय लब्धं य-ञा-हेः पंचाशद्भिरतः परम् ।
पृथग्वर्णैः तपः पश्चाज्जपेत्सौभाग्यसिद्धये ।।५४।।

साध्य-नाम विलोमार्णान्मंत्राणां चाऽसिध्य तत् ।
त्रिसहस्रं जपेनैव जंतुः कालपुरं व्रजेत् ॥५५॥
यदि मंत्री नरस्तस्य देवतामंत्रवर्णकम् ।
अनुविध्य विलोमेन संजपेदयुतं मनुम् ॥५६॥
दिग्देवताश्च लीयंते पराजेतुं महाबले ।
तस्मात्सर्वप्रयत्नेन जपेदेवं वरानने ॥५७॥
मंत्रांते योजयित्वाथ क्रियासाध्यं सपल्लवम् ।
विविधेषु प्रयोगेषु निजपेत्सर्वसिद्धये ॥५८॥
यंत्रं तंत्रं विना वापि यो जपेन्मंत्रमुत्तमः ।
सर्वसिद्धि जपेनैव सहसा नाप्नुयाच्छिवे ॥५९॥

श्रीदेव्युवाच ॥

ननु त्वत्र कथं शंभो नैव स्याद्यंत्रतंत्रकम् ।
यदि स्याद्यंत्रतंत्राभ्यां किं प्रयोजनमाविभो ॥६०॥

श्रीशिव उवाच ॥

शृणु साधु शिवे वच्म्यहं पुरश्चर्यैकया ।
यंत्र-तंत्र-क्रियापूर्वं यदि कुर्याल्लभेत्तदा ॥६१॥
चिरकालं जपैः क्रूरैर्यैः करोत्यंगशोषणैः ।
सिद्धि सोऽथ न वाऽप्नोति यंत्र-तंत्र-विवर्जितात् ॥६२॥
पुरश्चर्याद्वयेनैव स्मरणात्सिद्धिमेति सः ।
यंत्र-तंत्रं विना देवि सकलं जायते जपात् ॥६३॥
सर्वथा मनुजो मंत्री पुरश्चर्याद्वयं चरेत् ।
स्मरणात्तेन सिद्धिः स्यान्नानाकर्मक्रियाविषु ॥६४॥
सर्वेषां मंत्र-जालानां यदि साध्यं युगे युगे ।
तत्सर्वं स्मरणादेव सिद्धिर्भवति तत्वतः ॥६५॥

इति श्रीआकाशभैरवकल्पे प्रत्यक्षसिद्धिप्रदे उमामहेश्वरसम्वादे मातृकावर्णनं नाम सप्तविंशोऽध्यायः ॥२७॥

अष्टाविंशोऽध्यायः

भद्रकालीप्रयोगः

श्रीशिव उवाच ॥

भद्रकाल्याश्च मंत्रस्य सद्योजात ऋषिः स्मृतः ।
ततस्तु जगती छंदो भद्रकाली च देवता ॥१॥
ह्रींकारं बीजमित्युक्तं स्वाहा शक्तिरतः परम् ।
मोक्षे च विविधे कार्ये विनियोगो वरानने ॥
ह्रामित्यादि षडंगं स्यादथ ध्यानमिहोच्यते ॥२॥

अथ ध्यानम् ॥

नीलाभा हेमवस्त्रा नररुधिर-वसा-मांसनिर्भिष्यवक्त्रा
शूलं-कुंतं-रथांगं-फणि-मुसल-गदा-तोमरं-पट्टिशं च ।
पाशं शक्तिं च शंखं ध्वज-हल-दहनं वज्रखेटं कराब्जै-
र्बिभ्राणा भीमवेषा विजयतु भुवने विद्रुता भद्रकाली ॥३॥

अथ भद्रकाली-मंत्रोद्धारविधिः ॥

मायां मोचय तारकालिपुटितः कंकालि मह्यं सदा
त्वं कल्याणि मनोहरीह कवितां सौभाग्यमव्याहतम् ।
देह्यस्मिन् परमंत्रहारिणि शुभे तद्यंत्रहारिण्यहो
विद्याच्छेदिनि पूर्ववद्धृतभुजस्त्वयंते जगत्क्षोभिणि ॥४॥
सीसे ताम्रे त्रिलोहे रजत-कनकयोः पंच-लोहेऽथ भूर्जे
कृत्वा षट्-सप्त-कोष्ठं हरिहरसहितं भद्रकाल्याश्च मंत्रम् ।
संधौ पंचाशदर्णान्विजय-जययुतं सर्व-रेखाग्रशूलम्
बाह्ये साध्यं सतारं प्रणतरिपुजनप्राणसंहारदक्षम् ॥५॥
संपूज्य यंत्रं विधिवत्स्वगेहे जपेत्सहस्रं प्रयतो मनीषी ।
पश्चात्सहस्त्रद्वयमादरेण कुर्याज्जपं गौरि विशेषसिद्ध्यै ॥६॥
निंब-वृक्षे स्थितं काकनीडमादाय दर्शके ।
भस्मीकृत्य ततः सर्वं तस्मिन्भस्मनि मंत्रवित् ॥७॥

समालिख्य महायंत्रं सर्वलोकभयंकरम् ।
कृष्णपुष्पैः समभ्यर्च्य विधिवत्पूज्यतां सुधीः ॥८॥
अष्टोत्तरसहस्रं तु दक्षिणास्यो जपेन्निशि ।
दृढचित्तस्ततो बद्ध्वा कृष्णवस्त्रेण पुत्तलीम् ॥९॥
वैरिक्षेत्रे खनेन्मंत्री मरणं नात्र संशयः ।
पुनस्त्वेवं जपेन्मंत्री तद्रिपुर्बलवान्यदि ॥१०॥
सांत्ववादः कृतस्तेन मंत्रेण साधकोत्तमः ।
पुत्तलीमंभसि क्षिप्यावरोहेण जपेन्मनुम् ॥११॥
भद्रकाली ततः शत्रुमुक्त्वा कोपं च सीदति ।
पुनः संपूज्य तां मंत्री यथावित्तेन देशिकम् ॥१२॥
संतोष्य परया भक्त्या तत्प्रसादं च याचताम् ।
चतुःषष्टिकलास्वेवं योजयेन्मंत्रवित्तमः ॥१३॥
सर्वसिद्धिसमोपेतश्चिरं मंत्री महीतले ।
अनुभुज्य महायोगानप्रमेयाननर्गलान् ।
बांधवैः सह देहांते भर्गं सायुज्यमाप्नुयात् ॥१४॥

इति श्रीआकाशभैरवकल्पे प्रत्यक्षसिद्धिप्रदे उमामहेश्वरसम्वादे भद्रकालीविधिर्नामाष्टाविंशोऽध्यायः ॥२८॥

एकोनत्रिंशोऽध्यायः

तैलविधिः

श्रीशिव उवाच ।।

अथो वक्ष्यामि देवेशि तैलं सर्वार्थसाधकम् ।
नानाक्षुद्रहरं दिव्यं नानावातनिवारणम् ।।१।।

रक्तापामार्गकं मूलं वचा-लसुन-संयुतम् ।
मधूक-निंब-एरंड-तैल-पाकं यथोचितम् ।।२।।

त्रिधा विभज्य शाकाङ्गं त्र्यहं हन्मध्यया क्रमात् ।
वस्ति-लेपादिकं कुर्याच्छंकाक्षुद्र-निवृत्तये ।।३ ।।

नारिकेलफलं छिद्रं पक्वतैले स्वतैलके ।
पायु-गुह्योष्ठ-हृत्क्षुद्रशांतये भक्षयेच्छिवे ।।४ ।।

कृष्णश्वा-नख-रोमाणि दग्ध्वा कंबल-लोम च ।
हिंगूष्णवारिसंयुक्तं पिबेद्धृत्क्षुद्रमुक्तये ।।५ ।।

पैशाचभ्रमणीमूलमपामार्गं पुनर्नवम् ।
नक्तं सूरिं च भूधात्रीं लज्जां शिग्रुरसं तथा ।।७।।

वचोलिलसहितं पक्त्वा लिपेदेरंडतैलकैः ।
मूर्धाङ्गनासाहृत्कर्ण-कर-पत्क्षुद्र-शांतये ।।८।।

धत्तूरकं तथा कोलं पाटलाग्निं प्रतापसम् ।
पातालतिक्तमूलीं च पैशाचभ्रमकं तथा ।।९।।

दुराधर्षादपामार्गमलक्तशतमूलिकां ।
लशुनं तु वचायुक्तं प्रत्येकं पलमात्रकम् ।।१०।।

सांगनारंगजं बीजं नीरं प्रस्थचतुष्टयम् ।
पत्र-सारं चतुःप्रस्थं निर्गुण्डयर्कदलाब्जयोः ।।११ ।।

पंचतैलं चतुःप्रस्थं प्रत्येकं सुपदे पचेत् ।
केशादिपादपर्यंतमंगमंगं शनैः शनैः ।।१२।।

श्रालिप्य धूपयेत्संध्यारागे पंचदिनं तथा।
नानाक्षुद्रं च वातं च नश्यत्याशु न संशयः ॥१३॥
मेघनाददलैकाब्जं गुडूचीं शीतलीं तथा।
नौरुत्पलांकनिर्मुक्ता (म) मूलं मूलीशिफां तथा ॥१४॥
प्रस्थ-द्वयपरिमाणं कृत्वा सर्वं कषायकम्।
....॥१५॥

सहस्रवेधीममृताख्यवल्लीमूलं शिखां कोकनदस्य मूलम्
एलालवंगं मधुकं च कोष्ठं वनाकृषं चंपककुड्मलं च।
मृगस्य श्रृंगं सितचंदनं च पिष्ट्वैकमेकं लकुचप्रमाणम्।
घृतं च तैलं च शिवं च धेनोर्द्रोणं पयः पाटलनालिकांबु ॥१६॥
सशर्करं दिव्यपदे तु पक्त्वा लिहेल्लिपेत्प्राणतदुन्मुखः सन्।
क्षुद्रांगतापोल्वणपैत्यनाशं सौंदर्यदं पुष्टिकरं च बाल्यम् ॥१७॥
रेतोरजोवृद्धिकरं समस्त-रोगापहं पावक-वातनाशम्। ॥१८॥

टंकणं सैन्धवं हिंगु हरितालं कटुद्वयम्।
रसयुक्तं च पैशाचीहिमसारेण पेषितम्।
श्रंजयेदर्कदुग्धेन कालदष्टोऽपि जीवति ॥१९॥
शंखं च तगरं तुत्थमंजनं च मनःशिलाम्।
कुक्कुटांडं बिसं (षं)व्योषं श्वेतां च गिरिकर्णिकाम् ॥२०॥
नंद्यावर्त-प्रसूनस्य सारेण दशरात्रकम्।
पिष्ट्वा तु गुलिकां कृत्वा नातपेनैव धूसरे ॥२१॥
श्रंजयेत्तस्य सारेण स्तनदुग्धेन वांबिके ॥२२॥
रुद्रांजनमिति प्रोक्तं महावेगं सुखावहम्।
सर्वभूतहरं क्षुद्र-मोह-ज्वरविनाशनम् ॥२३॥
विषघ्नं चाक्षिवातघ्नं पिल्लकाचस्य पोहनम्।
कुकूणमांस-पटल-पुष्पापहमनुत्तमम् ॥२४॥

इन्दुखंड-फल-लोम च ताली-पत्रपद्म च ससैन्धव-धूमम्।
व्योषयुक्तमथजं फलसारैः पेषितं त्र्यहमनंतरमेतत् ॥२५॥
श्रंजनेन विषनाशनं पुनः शत्रुभूतनयनोद्घटोल्वणम्।
उग्रवेगजमिदं भ्रमरांजनशिग्रुपुष्पसुरसैर्विमोचनम् ॥२६॥

तालग्रंथिं च पत्रं च तिलमूलं समूलकम्।
भस्मीकृत्य तु तद्भस्म भक्षयेद् गुडमध्यकम् ॥२७॥

पक्षादेवोदरं शल्यं प्रणश्यति न संशयः ।
अपामार्गस्य सद्बीजं गोक्षीरेणान्वहं शिवे ॥२८॥
पिष्ट्वा पिबेद्यथासह्यं त्रिमासात्कुष्ठनाशनम् ।
मंडलात्कीटलूतादेर्वंशदंश-विषापहम् ॥२९॥
व्योषं धूलिकातुत्थं च पूतना-बीज-बीजकम् ।
जम्बीरफलसारेण पिष्ट्वा तत्सप्तरात्रकम् ॥३०॥
नानाभूतहरं क्रूर-नानासर्पविषापहम्
वर्त्तिकासुमसारेण कुर्यात्पुष्पस्य चांजनम् ॥३१॥
इतीदं गुलिका-श्रेष्ठं प्रोक्तं कौमारिकांजनम् ।
रसे जंभस्य कार्श्यस्य पिल्लस्यास्य जलेन च ॥३२॥
स्तन्येन पित्तकाचस्य कुकूणस्य च गोजलैः ।
निर्लोमस्य च तैलेन मालायां शिग्रुजारसैः ॥३३॥
सितचंदनतोयेन ताप-ज्वरविमुक्तये ।
लक्ष्मीपुष्पस्य सारेण चातुर्थ-ज्वर-मुक्तये ॥३४॥
तालीदंड-जलेनैव वातपैत्त्यज्वरं हरेत् ।
त्रिदोषस्याजमूत्रेण सूति-वातस्य चांबिके ॥३५॥
तांबूल-दल-सारेण मक्षबालग्रहस्य च ।
आत्मांभसा विघ्नसूतां आरोग्यस्यास्यबिन्दुना ॥३६॥
अक्षतं तक्रमध्यस्थमपरेऽह्नि निपेष्य तत् ।
स्थले लिहेद् गृहं तस्मिन्वह्नितप्तार्तिशांतये ॥३७॥
कृष्णगुग्गुलुचूर्णेन तिलतैलं पचेत्पदे ।
तैलेनार्द्रीकृतं तूलं स्थापयेद् व्रणशांतये ॥३८॥
तत्तैलाघ्राणतो यांति खड्गाद्याःव्रणकोटयः ।
कुंदा-श्रवण-संयोगे कटुं संपेष्य मध्यमम् ॥३९॥
तद्व्रणे लिप्य संबद्ध्वा तृतीयाहे विमुच्य तत् ।
त्रिविधं बंधनादेवमुच्यते तद्व्रणं नरः ॥४०॥
आम्लिकाकंदमाहृत्य पिष्ट्वा क्षीरेण पाययेत् ।
गतार्त्तवानां नारीणां सद्यो रक्तं प्रवर्तते ॥४१॥

तिलाक्षिणीशिफां पिष्ट्वा क्षीरेणोर्षसि पाययेत् ।
अनार्तवा तु या योषित् सार्तवा भवति ध्रुवम् ॥४२॥
मरीचचूर्णं प्रक्षिप्य जंबीरस्य फलोदरे ।
तस्य खंडादधोभागं स्नानं निर्गुंडिकारसे ॥४३॥
अपरेऽहनि तद्वारे भक्षयेत्प्रातरुत्थितः ।
तत्फलास्वादनाद्यांति ज्वराश्चातुर्थिका ध्रुवम् ॥४४॥
पैशाचभ्रमणीमूलं उपरागावसानके ॥
गृहीत्वोत्तरभागस्थं कृत्वासक्तांगुलीयकम् ॥४५॥
तेन युक्तकरं दृष्ट्वा धावंत्यखिलदुर्गमाः ।
भूतप्रेतपिचाशानां कुतस्तस्याग्रतः स्थितिः ॥४६॥

इति श्रीआकाशभैरवकल्पे प्रत्यक्षसिद्धिप्रदे उमामहेश्वरसम्वादे औषधविधिर्नामैकोनत्रिंशोऽध्यायः ॥२९॥

त्रिंशोऽध्यायः

शूलिनीप्रयोगः

श्रीशिव उवाच ॥

अथो वच्म्यंबिकां दुर्गां सर्वातीतपराक्रमाम् ।
चराचरमयीं देवीं सर्वकामफलप्रदाम् ॥१॥
बहुरूपां महोत्साहां भेदवादिकरां पराम् ।
शब्दब्रह्ममयीं दिव्यां सावधानमनाः शृणु ॥२॥
विभक्ता षड्विधा दुर्गा स्वात्मना करणेच्छया ।
अग्निदुर्गा महादुर्गा जलदुर्गेति नामतः ॥३॥
वनदुर्गा ततः पश्चाच्छूलदुर्गा च शूलिनी ।
तासां तु शूलिनी देवी महाक्रूरेति कीर्तिता ॥४॥
अथातः संप्रवक्ष्यामि शूलिनीं तु विशेषतः ।
समाहितेन मनसा शृणु सर्वं वरानने ॥५॥
ब्रह्मा तु शूलिनीदुर्गामंत्रस्य ऋषिरुच्यते ।
गायत्री छंद इत्युक्तं देवता शूलिनीश्वरी ॥६॥
दुंकारं बीजमित्युक्तं स्वाहाशक्तिस्ततः परम् ।
स्वेच्छाप्रयोगसिद्ध्यर्थे विनियोगो वरानने ॥७॥
ह्रामित्यादि करन्यासः षडंगं तु ततः प्रिये ।
लक्ष्मीबीजं समुच्चार्य बिंदुशूलिनीतत्परम् ॥८॥
देवसिद्धपदं चोक्त्वा पूजितेति पदं वदेत् ।
नंदिनीति पदं मां च रक्ष रक्ष पदं वदेत् ॥९॥
महायोगेश्वरि हुं फट् हृदयादि नमो न्यसेत् ।
नामतो वरदे देवसिद्धादिशिरसे तथा ॥१०॥
युद्धप्रिये शिखायै स्याद्विंध्यवासिनि मां तथा ।
द्विःत्रायस्वेति कवचं तथा महिषमर्दिनि ॥११॥
देवसिद्धादिफट्कारान्नेत्रत्रयमुदाहृतम् ।
बीजादिनामतः पश्चात्सर्वसिद्धिप्रदायिनि ॥१२॥

देवसिद्धादिफट्कारादस्त्राय फडितीरितम् ।१३।।

ॐ श्रीं शूलिनि दुर्गे देवसिद्धसुपूजिते नंदिनि मां रक्ष रक्ष महायोगेश्वरि हुं फट्—हृदयाय नमः ।

श्रीं शूलिनि वरदे देवसिद्धसुपूजिते हुं फट् स्वाहा—शिरसे स्वाहा ।।

श्रीं शूलिनि युद्धप्रिये देवसिद्धपूजिते हुं फट् स्वाहा—शिखायै वषट् ।

ओं श्रीं शूलिनि विंध्यवासिनि मां त्रायस्व त्रायस्व देवसिद्धसुपूजिते हुं फट् स्वाहा—कवचाय हुम् ।

ओं श्रीं शूलिनि महिषासुरमर्दिनि देवसिद्धसुपूजिते हुं फट् स्वाहा—नेत्रत्रयाय वौषट् ।

ओं श्रीं शूलिनि सर्वसिद्धिप्रदायिनि देवसिद्धसुपूजिते हुं फट् स्वाहा—अस्त्रायफट् ।

ओं भूर्भुवः स्वरोमिति दिग्बंधः ।।

ध्यानम् ।

अध्यारूढा मृगेन्द्रं सजलजलधर-श्यामलां हस्तपद्मैः
शूलं बाणं कृपाणं त्वरिजलजगदाचापपाशान्वहंतीं ।
चंद्रोत्तंसां त्रिनेत्रां चतसृभिरसिखेटान्विताभिः परीतां
कन्याभिः सेव्यमानां प्रतिभटभयदां शूलिनीं भावयामि ।।
नमः प्रणवपूर्विके नतजनस्य चिंतामणे
ज्वल ज्वलतु शूलिनी त्वमिह पाहि चास्मान्सदा ।
समस्तरिपु दुष्टग्रह हुं फडित्यक्षरैः शिखि-
स्त्रिशक्तियुङ्मनोहरे जननि तुभ्यमव्याहते ।।१४।।

शूलिनीयं महामंत्रं दुर्वारं सर्वजंतुभिः ।
गुह्याद् गुह्यतरंश्रेष्ठं गोपनीयं प्रयत्नतः ।।१५।।
वश्याकर्षणयो रक्ता श्यामा स्तंभविरोधयोः ।
निग्रहोच्चाटयोः कृष्णा श्वेता मोक्षपरोक्षयोः ।।१६।।
सारस्वतप्रयोगे तु मुक्ताधवलरूपिणी ।
एवं ध्यात्वा जपेद्देवीं शूलिनीं सर्वसिद्धये ।।१७।।
वश्याकर्षणविद्वेषस्तंभनोच्चाटनिग्रहं ।
अन्यानि च प्रयोगाणि सिध्यंति स्मरणादपि ।।१८।।

यस्यैहिकफलं न स्यात्तत्र स्यात्पारलौकिकम् ।
यत्र न स्यात्परं लोकं तत्रैहिकफलं लभेत् ॥१९॥

मंत्राणां तु द्विजातीनां रहस्यं तु युगे युगे ।
शूलिनीं देवतायां तु भोगमोक्षं च विद्यते ॥२०॥

तत्राणिमादिसिद्धिः स्याच्चतुःषष्टिःकलास्तथा ।
जपतर्पणहोमादौ सांगो भूमौ कृते यदि ॥२१॥

मातृकोष्ठे श्मशाने वा प्रोक्तदेशे मनोरमे ।
जपेत्षोडशसाहस्रं विधिपूर्वं जितेन्द्रियः ॥२२॥

दशांशं तर्पणं तस्य शतांशं होमयेत्ततः ।
सहस्रांशमथो देवि ब्राह्मणांस्तर्पयेत्ततः ॥२३॥

त्रिकोणं कल्पयेत्कुंडमथात्माभिमुखाग्रकम् ।
स्वसूत्रोक्तविधानेन कुर्याद्धोमं समाचरेत् ॥२४॥

शुक्रवारे तथा सौम्ये सौम्यहोमं समाचरेत् ।
कुजवारे तथाष्टम्यां क्रूरहोमं समाचरेत् ॥२५॥

पायसं च तिलापूपं घृतं दधि मधु तथा ।
क्षीरं गुडं च तैलं च कदलीं च फलत्रयम् ॥२६॥

मुद्गं सर्षप-यष्टिं च वर्णैकैकविधानतः ।
तत्तद्वर्णादिमंत्रेण कुर्यादिकैकशः क्रमात् ॥२७॥

दक्षिणाभ्यंगपूर्वं तु कारयेद् द्विजभोजनम् ।
देवपूजागृहे रम्ये धूपदीपसमाकुले ॥२८॥

चंदनागरुकर्पूरकुंकुमारोचनैर्युते ।
धातुदारुमये पीठे यजेद्यंत्रं सुशोभनम् ॥२९॥

त्रिकोणं विलिखेत्पूर्वं तद्बहिर्वृत्तमालिखेत् ।
तद्बहिश्चाष्टपत्रं तु पुटीकृत्य च भूपुरम् ॥३०॥

भूपुरं द्वंद्वबाह्ये तु षट्कोणं विलिखेत्ततः ।
कोणाग्रे शूलमालिख्य तद्बाह्ये पृथिवीं लिखेत् ॥३१॥

अनुलोमविलोमाभ्यां बहिः प्रणवमालिखेत् ।
जया च विजया चैव अजिता चापराजिता ॥३२॥

अंतरावरणे पूज्याश्चतस्रो वीरशक्तयः ।
पूर्वे त्वैंकारमालिख्य दक्षिणे मन्मथाक्षरम् ॥३३॥
श्रींकारं पश्चिमे भागे मायाबीजं तथोत्तरे ।
त्रिकोण-मध्ये देवीं तां ज्वालमालां विभावयेत् ॥३४॥
श्रीशक्ति-सहितं मंत्रं मनसा बहुशः स्मरन् ।
आवाहनादि-पुष्पांतमुपचारान्समर्पयेत् ॥३५॥
ब्राह्मी माहेश्वरी चैव कौमारी वैष्णवी तथा ।
वाराही नारसिंही च इन्द्राणी चंडिका क्रमात् ॥३६॥
श्रीशक्ति-बीजयुक्तेन मंत्रेणानेन पूजयेत् ।
प्रागादितो यजेद्देवि दलेष्वष्टसु मंत्रवित् ॥३७॥
इन्द्राग्नि-यम-रक्षेश-जलेश-पवनादिकान् ।
धनेशेशान-पर्यंतान् लोकपालान् यथाक्रमम् ॥३८॥
स्व-स्व-मंत्रेण युक्तेन मूलमंत्रेण भक्तिमान् ।
पूर्वकोणे तु शुंभं च निशुंभं पश्चिमे तथा ॥३९॥
नैर्ऋते धर्मसिंहं च वायव्ये महिषं तथा ।
आग्नेय्यां वीरभद्रं च ऐशान्यां क्षेत्रपालकम् ॥४०॥
श्रियं शक्ति च षट्कोणे संधावुत्तरदक्षिणे ।
श्रीशक्ति-सहितं बीजं षट्कोणायतनस्थितान् ॥४१॥
महावीरान् यजेन्मर्त्यो महाबल-पराक्रमान् ।
पूर्वद्वारे गणेशं च दक्षिणे रुद्ररूपिणं ॥४२॥
पश्चिमे कालरूपं च द्वारे षण्मुखमुत्तरे ।
रमामायार्णयुक्तेन मूलमंत्रेण भक्तिमान् ॥४३॥
एतानेव द्वारपालान् पृथगाराधयेत्ततः ।
मूलेन शूलिनीदुर्गां धूपदीपादिकं चरेत् ॥४४॥
कृत्वा ततो जपेन्मंत्रमष्टोत्तरसहस्रकम् ।
अकारादि क्षकारांतं वेष्टयेद्बिन्दु-संयुतम् ॥४५॥
एतद्यंत्रं महावीर्यं सर्वकाम-फल-प्रदम् ।
युद्धे शत्रुभये चैव रोगोत्पन्ने च संकटे ॥४६॥

समाराध्य महादुर्गां सर्व-कर्माणि साधयेत् ।
महादुर्गाप्रसादेन सर्वत्र लभते जयम् ॥४७॥
विशेषात्पुत्रकामश्च सद्यः पुत्रफलं लभेत् ।
वैरिणां मारणे कामः सद्यो नश्यंति वैरिणः ।
तरसा सर्वसिद्धिः स्यात्संहृतिस्तु विशेषतः ॥४८॥

मध्ये शक्तिं वसुदललसच्छूलिनीवर्णयुग्मम्
किंजल्कोद्यन्महिषमथिनी मंत्रवर्णं बहिश्च।
त्रिष्टुब्दुर्गालिपिपरिवृतं भूपुरश्चांतरस्थं
दुर्गाबीजं धर्मसमहितं शूलिनीयंत्रमेतत् ॥४९॥

इति श्रीआकाशभैरवकल्पे प्रत्यक्षसिद्धिप्रदे उमामहेश्वरसम्वादे शूलिनीदुर्गाकल्पनं नाम त्रिंशोऽध्यायः ॥३०॥

एकत्रिंशोऽध्यायः

पूजाविधिः

श्रीशिव उवाच ॥

(क) अथ सर्वाभीष्टप्रसिद्धयर्थं शूलिनीदुर्गापूजां करिष्ये—

गुरुवंदनादिदेवेशि मातृकांतं समाचरेत् ।
शिरो-ललाट-भ्रूमध्यं मुख-कर्ण-हृदस्तथा ॥१॥
कुक्षि-नाभि-कटिर्गुह्य आधारश्चोरुजानुके ।
जंघ-पादद्वये देवि अक्षराणि क्रमान्न्यसेत् ॥२॥
कुंभशंखौ च संपूज्य प्राकारं नवरत्नकम् ।
यजेत्सहस्रस्तंभं च महाभृंगारकं ततः ॥३॥
धर्माद्यष्टकमभ्यर्च्य सत्त्वं रजस्तमस्ततः ।
पद्मं चैव शिवे नालं धर्मं कंदं तथैव च ॥४॥
ततः शिवे ज्ञाननालं यजेद्वैराग्यकर्णिकाम् ।
मंडलत्रयमभ्यर्च्य आत्मत्रयमतः परम् ॥५॥
ज्ञानात्मानं ततः पश्चादिच्छा-ज्ञाना-क्रिया तथा ।
दुर्गा च वरदा विंध्यवासिन्यसुरमर्दिनी ॥६॥
युद्धप्रिया पञ्चमी च षष्ठी चासुरमर्दिनी ।
सर्वसिद्धिप्रदायिनी देवसिद्धसुपूजिता ॥७॥
नंदिनी चैव नवमी महायोगिनी उच्यते ।
पीठशक्तीः सुसंपूज्याः पीठमभ्यर्च्य देशिकम् ॥८॥
ओं नमो भगवते वज्रनखदंष्ट्रमहासिंहासनाय दुर्गापीठाय नमः ॥९॥
वस्तुशुद्ध्यादि संस्कार-बलिपात्रांतमेव च ।
शंखमध्यं भोगपूजां बलिपात्रं तथैव च ॥१०॥
आत्मभैरवनामानि सप्तपात्राणि साधयेत् ।
विद्यापद्धतिवद्देवि सर्वं पूर्ववदाचरेत् ॥११॥
अन्तर्यागं पुरा कृत्वा बहिर्यागं समाचरेत् ।
न्यसेद्गुरुं च मूर्धनि मध्ये श्रीशूलिनीं पराम् ॥१२॥

ऋषिच्छंदो देवताश्च षडंगं ध्यानपूर्वकम् ।
आवाह्य देवीं हृत्पद्मे मुद्रास्त्वावाहनादिकाः ॥१३॥
प्रदर्श्य पंचोपचारैरुपचर्य्याथ शूलिनीम् ।
हृत्पंकजात्समुत्थाप्य वामनासाविनिर्गताम् ॥१४॥
ज्योतीरूपां परां दुर्गां परमानन्द-रूपिणीम् ।
त्रिखंडमुद्रयाऽऽवाह्य चक्रेऽभ्यर्च्य यथाविधि ॥१५॥
देवेशि भक्तिरित्याद्या आवाहनमुदीरितम् ।
आवाहनी स्थापनी च संनिधि संनिरुध्य च ॥१६॥
अवगुंठित-सव्यापस्वामत प्रसीदेति च ।
अष्टमुद्रेति विख्याता देवता भावसिद्धिदा ॥१७॥
षोडशैरुपचर्याथ मूलेनाभ्यर्च्यं ह्यष्टधा ।
पश्चादावरणानीष्ट्वा श्रीशक्ति-सहितं यजेत् ॥१८॥
जया च विजया चैव अजिता चापराजिता ।
सरस्वती मन्मथश्च महालक्ष्मीश्च मायया ॥१९॥
इति पूर्वाद्युत्तरांतं मूलैर्देवीं समर्चयेत् ।
ब्रह्मादीः पूजयेत्पत्रे लोकेशानष्टपत्रके ॥२०॥
पूर्वकोणे तु शुंभं च पश्चिमे तु निशुंभकम् ।
राक्षसे धर्मसिंहं च वायव्ये महिषं तथा ॥२१॥
आग्नेय्यां वीरभद्रं च क्षेत्रेशं चेशकोणके ।
महालक्ष्मीं दक्षपार्श्वे मायामुत्तरपार्श्वके ॥२२॥
गणेशरुद्रकालाश्च सुब्रह्मण्यादि च क्रमात् ।
पूर्वद्वाराद्युत्तरांतं पूज्यमूलेन पूजयेत् ॥२३॥
मूलेनाष्टोत्तरशतं देवीं संपूजयेत्सुधीः ।
धूपदीपादिनैवेद्यं तांबूलं छत्रदर्पणे ॥२४॥
चामरं व्यजनं चैते उपचाराष्टकं क्रमात् ।
प्रदक्षिणां नमस्कारं कृत्वा शांतिस्तवं पठेत् ॥२५॥
बलिकर्म तथैशान्ये सर्वावरणसंयुताम् ।
सांगां च शूलिनीं दुर्गां हृन्मुद्रास्य हृदयांबुजे ॥२६॥

(ख) अथ सुमुखीकरणस्तोत्रम् ।।

सर्वकार्याभिविजयं सदारोग्यं शिवे शृणु ।
ओं सर्वविघ्नकृद्भ्यः सर्वभूतेभ्यो हुं फट् स्वाहा ।

इति मंत्रं त्रिःपठित्वा यथाविधि देव्यै बलिं निवेद्य स्तुवीत—

सुमुखीकरणस्तोत्रमंत्रस्य दीर्घतमा ऋषिः
ककुब्छन्दः शूलिनी देवता तत्प्रसादसिद्ध्यर्थे जपे विनियोगः

ध्यानम् ।।

ध्यायेद्धेमसहोपलासनपरे कन्याजनालंकृते
पंचब्रह्ममुखामरैर्मुनिगणैः सेव्ये जगन्मंगले ।
आसीनां स्मितभाषणां शिवसखीं कल्याणवेषोज्ज्वलां
भक्ताभीष्टवरप्रदाननिरतां विश्वात्मिकां शूलिनीम् ।।

ओंकारपीठमध्यस्थे ओषधीशमहोज्ज्वले ।
ऐश्वर्य्यमायुरारोग्यमिष्टसिद्धिं च देहि मे ।।१।।
श्रीपूर्णे श्रीपरे श्रीशे श्रीप्रदे श्रीविवर्धने ।
ऐश्वर्यमायुरारोग्यमिष्टसिद्धिं च देहि मे ।।२।।
कामेशि कामरसिके कामितार्थफलप्रदे ।
ऐश्वर्य्यमायुरारोग्यमिष्टसिद्धिं च देहि मे ।।३।।
मायाविलासचतुरे माये मायाधिमायिके ।
ऐश्वर्य्यमायुरारोग्यमिष्टसिद्धिं च देहि मे ।।४।।
चिंतामणेऽखिलाभीष्टसिद्धिदे विश्वमंगले ।
ऐश्वर्य्यमायुरारोग्यमिष्टसिद्धिं च देहि मे ।।५।।
सर्वबीजाधिपे सर्वसिद्धिदे सर्वरूपिणि ।
ऐश्वर्य्यमायुरारोग्यमिष्टसिद्धिं च देहि मे ।।६।।
ज्वलत्तेजस्त्रयानंत-कोटि-कोटिसमद्युते ।
ऐश्वर्यमायुरारोग्यमिष्टसिद्धिं च देहि मे ।।७।।
लसच्चंद्रार्धमुकुटे लयजन्मविमोचिके ।
ऐश्वर्य्यमायुरारोग्यमिष्टसिद्धिं च देहि मे ।।८।।
ज्वररोगमुखापत्ति-भंजनैकधुरंधरे ।
ऐश्वर्य्यमायुरारोग्यमिष्टसिद्धिं च देहि मे ।।९।।

लक्ष्यलक्ष्ये लयातीते लक्ष्मीवर्गधरेक्षणे ।
ऐश्वर्य्यमायुरारोग्यमिष्टसिद्धिं च देहि मे ॥१०॥
शूरांगनानंतकोटिव्यावृताशेषजालके ।
ऐश्वर्य्यमायुरारोग्यमिष्टसिद्धिं च देहि मे ॥११॥
पिलीलिंगादि दिक्-स्थाननियंताराधनप्रिये ।
ऐश्वर्य्यमायुरारोग्यमिष्टसिद्धिं च देहि मे ॥१२॥
निर्मले निर्गुणे नित्ये निष्कले निरुपद्रवे ।
ऐश्वर्य्यमायुरारोग्यमिष्टसिद्धिं च देहि मे ॥१३॥
दुर्गे दुरित-संहारे दुष्टतूलांत्यपावके ।
ऐश्वर्य्यमायुरारोग्यमिष्टसिद्धिं च देहि मे ॥१४॥
टमामये टमासेव्य-टमावर्धनतत्परे ।
ऐश्वर्य्यमायुरारोग्यमिष्टसिद्धिं च देहि मे ॥१५॥
ग्रसिताशेषभुवने ग्रंथिसंध्यर्णशोभिते ।
ऐश्वर्य्यमायुरारोग्यमिष्टसिद्धिं च देहि मे ॥१६॥
हंस-तार्क्ष्य-वृषारूढैराराधित-पद-द्वये ।
ऐश्वर्य्यमायुरारोग्यमिष्टसिद्धिं च देहि मे ॥१७॥
हुंकार-काल दहन-भस्मीकृत-जगत्त्रये ।
ऐश्वर्य्यमायुरारोग्यमिष्टसिद्धिं च देहि मे ॥१८॥
फट्कार-चंडपवनोद्वासिताखिलविग्रहे ।
ऐश्वर्य्यमायुरारोग्यमिष्टसिद्धिं च देहि मे ॥१९॥
स्वाकृते वामिपादाब्जभक्तानां स्वाभिवृद्धये ।
ऐश्वर्य्यमायुरारोग्यमिष्टसिद्धिं च देहि मे ॥२०॥
हालाहलविषाकारे हाटकारुणपीठके ।
ऐश्वर्य्यमायुरारोग्यमिष्टसिद्धिं च देहि मे ॥२१॥
मूलादिब्रह्मरंध्रांतं मूलज्वालास्वरूपिणि ।
ऐश्वर्य्यमायुरारोग्यमिष्टसिद्धिं च देहि मे ॥२२॥
वषडादि-क्रियाषट्क-महासिद्धिप्रदे परे ।
ऐश्वर्य्यमायुरारोग्यमिष्टसिद्धिं च देहि मे ॥२३॥

सर्वविद्वन्मुखांभोज-दिवाकर-समुद्युते ।
ऐश्वर्य्यमायुरारोग्यमिष्टसिद्धिं च देहि मे ॥२४॥
नानामहीप-हृदय-नवनीतद्रवानले ।
ऐश्वर्य्यमायुरारोग्यमिष्टसिद्धिं च देहि मे ॥२५॥
अशेषज्वर-सर्पादि-चंद्रोपल-शशिद्युते ।
ऐश्वर्य्यमायुरारोग्यमिष्टसिद्धिं च देहि मे ॥२६॥
महापापौघ-कलुषक्षालनामृतवाहिनि ।
ऐश्वर्य्यमायुरारोग्यमिष्टसिद्धिं च देहि मे ॥२७॥
अशेष-काय-संभूत-रोगतूलानलाकृते ।
ऐश्वर्य्यमायुरारोग्यमिष्टसिद्धिं च देहि मे ॥२८॥
औषधि-कोटि-दावाग्नि-शांतिसंपूर्णवर्षिणि ।
ऐश्वर्य्यमायुरारोग्यमिष्टसिद्धिं च देहि मे ॥२९॥
तिमिरारातिसंहार-दिवानाथ-शताकृते ।
ऐश्वर्य्यमायुरारोग्यमिष्टसिद्धिं च देहि मे ॥३०॥
सुधाग्रजिह्वावर्त्यग्र-सुदीपे विश्ववाक्प्रदे ।
ऐश्वर्य्यमायुरारोग्यमिष्टसिद्धिं च देहि मे ॥३१॥
अरात्यवनिपानीक-तूलोच्चाट-महानिले ।
ऐश्वर्यमायुरारोग्यमिष्टसिद्धिं च देहि मे ॥३२॥
समस्तमृत्यु-तुहिन-सहस्रकिरणोपमे ।
ऐश्वर्य्यमायुरारोग्यमिष्टसिद्धिं च देहि मे ॥३३॥
जगत्सौभाग्यफलदे जंगम-स्थावरात्मके ।
ऐश्वर्य्यमायुरारोग्यमिष्टसिद्धिं च देहि मे ॥३४॥
सुभक्तहृदयानंद-सुख-संवित्स्वरूपिणि ।
ऐश्वर्य्यमायुरारोग्यमिष्टसिद्धिं च देहि मे ॥३५॥
धनधान्याब्धिसंवृद्धिचंद्रकोटिसमोदये ।
ऐश्वर्य्यमायुरारोग्यमिष्टसिद्धिं च देहि मे ॥३६॥
सर्वजीवात्मधेन्वग्र-समुच्चयानिलवत्सके ।
ऐश्वर्य्यमायुरारोग्यमिष्टसिद्धिं च देहि मे ॥३७॥
तेजःकण-महावीर-समावीतांत्यपावके ।
ऐश्वर्य्यमायुरारोग्यमिष्टसिद्धिं च देहि मे ॥३८॥

नानाचराचराविष्ट-दाहोपशमनामृते ।
ऐश्वर्य्यमायुरारोग्यमिष्टसिद्धिं च देहि मे ॥३९॥
सर्व-कल्याण-कल्याणे सर्वसिद्धिविवर्धने ।
ऐश्वर्य्यमायुरारोग्यमिष्टसिद्धिं च देहि मे ॥४०॥
सर्वेशि सर्वहृदये सर्वाकारे निराकृते ।
ऐश्वर्य्यमायुरारोग्यमिष्टसिद्धिं च देहि मे ॥४१
अनंतानंतजनके अभूते आत्मनायिके ।
ऐश्वर्य्यमायुरारोग्यमिष्टसिद्धिं च देहि मे ॥४२॥
रहस्यादि-रहस्यात्म-रहस्यागमपालके ।
ऐश्वर्य्यमायुरारोग्यमिष्टसिद्धिं च देहि म ॥४३॥
आचारकरणातीते आचार्यकरुणामये ।
ऐश्वर्य्यमायुरारोग्यमिष्टसिद्धिं च देहि मे ॥४४॥
सर्वरक्षाकरे भद्रे सर्वरक्षाकरेऽतुले ।
ऐश्वर्य्यमायुरारोग्यमिष्टसिद्धिं च देहि मे ॥४५॥
सर्वलोके सर्वदेशे सर्वकाले सतांबिके ।
ऐश्वर्य्यमायुरारोग्यमिष्टसिद्धिं च देहि मे ॥४६॥

आद्येऽनादिकलाविशेषविवृतेऽनंताखिलात्माकृते ।
आचार्यांघ्रि-सरोजयुग्मशिरसामापूरिताशामृते ॥
संसारार्णवतारणोद्यत-कृपा-संपूर्ण वृष्ट्यानिशम् ।
दुर्गे शूलिनि शंकरि स्नपय मां त्वं भाव-संसिद्धये ॥४७॥

इति परमशिवाया सुमुखी महाशक्तयः
स्तुतिमतिशय सौख्यप्राप्तये यो नु वाऽत्र ।
स्मरति जपति विद्वत्संवृतो शेषलोकं-
निखिल-सुखमवाप्य श्रीशिवाकारमेति ॥४८॥

क्रियाभेदः

श्रीशिव उवाच ॥

अथातः संप्रवक्ष्यामि क्रियाभेदं तु पार्वति ।
अभक्तानामगम्यं तु भक्तानां सुलभोत्तमम् ॥१॥

सवातवृत्तं ऋतुकोणकोणे लक्ष्मीं च मायामथ तारसाध्यम् ।
आराध्य यंत्रं प्रजपेत्सहस्रमाकर्षणं त्वाशु चराचराणाम् ॥२॥

एतद्यंत्रं महावीर्यं सर्वलोकेषु दुर्लभम् ।
सुतरां सर्वजंतूनां स्त्रीणामाकर्षणं भवेत् ॥३॥
यक्ष-गंधर्व-सिद्धादीन् देवान्देवस्त्रियः तथा ।
आकर्षति महाभूतान् किमु भूलोकवासिनः ॥४॥

ओं नमो भगवते दिग्बंधनाय कंकालि कालरात्रि दुं दुर्गे शूं शूलिनि वं वटुकभैरवी अर्धरात्रविलासिनि महानिशि-प्रताप-केलिनि महाज्ञाधारिणि महाशक्ति मम सर्व भूत-प्रेत-पिशाच-सर्वज्वर-शांतिनि मदभीष्टमाकर्षयाकर्षय वटुक-भैरवि भैरवेश्वरि हुं फट् स्वाहा ॥

क्लींकारं वृत्तमध्ये तदनु वसुदले शक्ति-लक्ष्मीं लिखित्वा
बाह्ये भूकोण-युग्मे दिशि दिशि मदनं तद्बहिस्तार-साध्यम् ।
लोहे ताम्रे तु पूज्य-प्रयत-नरवरस्तत्सहस्रं जपित्वा
खन्याद्यंत्रं नलिन्यां मधु-कमलयुतं होमकं कर्म कुर्यात् ॥५॥

ततस्त्वादाय तद्भस्म तस्मिन्यंत्रं विलिख्य तु ।
संपूज्य विधिवद्देवीं सहस्रं प्रजपेत् पुनः ॥६॥
तद्भस्म रोचना गंधं कुंकुमेन ललाटके ।
तिलकं मंत्रवित्कुर्यात्सर्वलोकवशंकरम् ॥७॥

ओं नमो भगवते क्षांक्षां र र र र हुं रं लं वं वटुकाय ऐं ह्रीं क्लीं हर २ महाकालीपति एह्येहि संहर २ महाकालि सर्वाभीष्टसिद्धिप्रदे शं सर्वशत्रून् नाशय २ शोषय २ नर-भूत-प्रेत-पिशाचादिसर्वग्रहान् नाशय २ दह २ पच २ सर्वस्त्रीपुरुषवशंकरि सर्वलोकभुवनेश्वरि तद्वशं भ्रंशय २ मद्वशमानय स्वाहा ॥

त्रिकोण-कोणेश्वथ वह्नि बीजं बाह्येषु वृत्तं परितो धरिण्याः ।
कोणेषु धात्रीमभितोऽथ तारं साध्यावृत्तं स्तंभनयंत्रमेतत् ॥८॥
लोहे तु ताम्रे तु विषद्रुमे वा आलिख्य मंत्रं परिपूज्य जप्त्वा ।
सहस्रवारं प्रजपेत्क्षपायां दृढासनस्थो रिपुदिङ्मुखः सन् ॥९॥
सभाकूटे रिपोश्छत्रे द्वारे तोरणमंदिरे ।
मातृस्थानेऽथवा प्राच्यां दिशि ज्येष्ठागृहेऽथ वा ॥१०॥

जिह्वास्तंभं हनुस्तंभं भुज-पल्लिंग-गुह्ययोः ।
चक्षुर्हृच्छ्रवणस्तंभं सर्वलोकेष्वथ प्रिये ॥११॥

ओं नमो भगवति रुद्रकालि कालकूटमोहिनि ऐं क्लीं ह्रीं इष्ट कामसिद्धिप्रदायिनि सकलाज्ञापिनि संक्रामिणि ब्राह्मी माहेश्वरी कौमारी वैष्णवी वाराहि इंद्राणि चामुंडी बटुकभैरवेश्वरि आकर्षय २ आवेशय २ देवदत्तदेहं प्रवेशय २ केलय २ भाषय २ ह्रीं क्लीं ऐं हन २ सप्तमातृके हुं फट् स्वाहा ॥

सबिंदुकं पावकदीर्घबीजं बाह्ये सलग्नाक्षर-राशि-कोष्ठे ।
प्रत्येक-रेखा-त्रिशिखाख्यसाध्यं विद्वेषणं क्षोभकरं तदेतत् १२॥
एतत्समाराध्य जपेत्सहस्रं कृत्वा निशायां रिपुके श्मशाने ।
पुनर्जपेदेवमथो द्विषंतश्चान्योन्ययुद्धान्मरणं प्रयांति ॥१३॥
दशाहमेवं प्रजपेद्रिपूणां कुलक्षयाय प्रलयाय मंत्री ।
ततस्तथा शत्रु कुलोद्भवानां भवेद्यमाख्या नगरी प्रसन्ना ॥१४॥
पंचास्त्रमालिख्य तदग्रशूलं मध्ये तु वृत्तं पवनं च कोणे ।
माया फडर्णं त्रिशिखाग्रसाध्यं तारं तदोच्चाटनयंत्रमेतत् ॥१५॥
संपूज्य जप्त्वा विधिवत्सहस्रं खनेत् श्मशाने रिपु-गेह-कोष्टे ।
शत्रुः सबंधुः सगणः सवर्गः प्रयाति देशांतरमाशु गेहात् ॥१६॥
भवेद् विनाशो गृहमध्यगानां भूतादिचेष्टा बहुशो भवंति ।
स्वप्नार्भटि क्रूरगणोल्वणं च पाषाणवृष्टिः पतनं च पक्षात् ॥१७॥

त्रिकोणं विलिखेत्पूर्वं पंचकोणं ततः परम् ।
वसुकोणं ततः पश्चादृतुकोणं बहिस्ततः ॥१८॥
भूकोण-त्रितयं बाह्ये लिखेद्यंत्रं महोज्ज्वलम् ।
तारसाध्यं त्रिकोणांतर्वह्नि-बीजेन योजयेत् ॥१९॥
पंचारेषु ठकारांतं विलिखेत्साध्य-मारुतम् ।
बहिरष्टसु कोणेषु साध्यं चिंतामणिं लिखेत् ॥२०॥
ततः षट्कोण-कोणेषु झिंटीशं साध्यसंयुतम् ।
चतुष्कोणे देवदत्तं मारयेति पृथक् पृथक् ॥२१॥
लोहे संलिख्य तत्कृष्णपुष्पेणाभ्यर्च्य पूजयेत् ।
अष्टोत्तर सहस्रं तु स्पृष्ट्वा जप्त्वा जितेंद्रियः ॥२२॥

पर्वमारभ्य पर्वान्ते निशायां दक्षिणदिशि।
दक्षिणाभिमुखो मंत्री खनित्वा बलिपूर्वकम् ॥२३॥
पुनः स्नात्वा जपेन्मंत्रमष्टोतरसहस्रकम् ।
तत्पश्चाद्रिपवः सर्वे प्रयांत्यव्याजमारणम् ॥२४॥
अथवा साध्यवृक्षस्य समिन्मधुघृतैर्युतम् ।
तिल-सर्षप-संयुक्तम् कुर्याद्धोमं यथाविधि ॥२५॥
कृष्णवर्णां ज्वलत्केशां शूलहस्तां कपालिनीम् ।
खड्ग-चर्मधरां बाण-धनुर्हस्तां महाभुजाम् ॥२६॥
अग्निज्वालामयीं दुर्गां संभाव्य शरभः स्वयम् ।
मंत्रांते साध्यमारोप्य मारयेति हुनेच्छिवे ॥२७॥
सप्ताहान्मरणं याति स शत्रु नैव-संशयः ।
स्वर्ग-भूतल-पातालवासिनोऽमर्त्य-मर्त्यकाः ॥२८॥
शूलिनी-दर्शनादेव मरणं यांति निश्चयम् ।
एतदेव महाबीजं स्मरणात्पापनाशनम् ॥२९॥
जपतः सर्वसिद्धिः स्याद् भूयोभूयो युगे युगे ।
संभावनात्क्रियासिद्धिः पूजनाद्भाषणाद् भवेत् ॥३०॥
नास्तिकाय कृतघ्नाय नाभक्ताय कदाचन ।
विटाय कुलहीनाय न देयं चंडिकामनुम् ॥३१॥
त्रि-पंच-कोष्ठेषु विलिख्य शूलिनीं ससाध्य-नामांकित-मध्यबीजम् ।
रेखाशिरः कल्पित-शूल-युक्तं यंत्रं महाभूत-पिशाचहारि ॥३२॥
त्रयोदश-गृहे ह्यथ दिनकर-त्रिशूलांकिते
नवानल गृहोल्लसच्छरभ-मूलवर्णाब्जयोः ।
चतुर्ग्रह ऋगर्णथाशिखि समन्विता........
....॥३३॥

इति श्रीआकाशभैरवकल्पे प्रत्यक्षसिद्धिप्रदे उमामहेश्वरसम्वादे शूलिनीविधिर्नाम एकत्रिंशोऽध्यायः ॥३१॥

द्वात्रिंशोऽध्यायः

वीरभद्रकल्पः

अथ ध्यानम् ॥

अध्यारूढां मृगेन्द्रं सजल-जलधर-श्यामलां हस्त-पद्मः
शूलं-बाणं-कृपाणं-त्वरिजलज-गदा-चाप-पाशान्वहंतीम् ।
चन्द्राचूडां त्रिनेत्रां चतसृभिरसिना खेटकं बिभ्रतीभिः
कन्याभिः सेव्यमानां प्रति-भट-भयदां शूलिनीं भावयामि ॥१॥

एवं ध्यात्वा—

जपेन्मंत्रं विलोमेन रिपुनाम-विमिश्रितम् ।
अष्टोत्तरशतमेवं भवेद्वैरि पराजितः ॥२॥

आलिख्य शांतत्रितयावृतांतर्बहिः शिरोधस्त्रिशिखं दलादौ ।
स्वकीयकार्योचितवाचकांते दुर्गेति तत्पूज्य तु मात्रशत्रोः ? ॥३॥
द्वारेऽथवा रोगिकलेवरे वा नयेल्लभेदिष्टफलार्थसिद्धिम् ।
भूतामयघ्नं च द्विपाच्चतुश्पाच्चराचराणामचरं च नूनम् ॥४॥

सृंकारं वेदमूलं जितरिपु-बहु (लं) श्यामलं वीरभद्रं
फट्कारं व्योमकेशं घृणि घृणि निनदं खड्ग-खेटोग्रहस्तम् ।
हुंकारं भीमनादं हुतवह-नयनो दग्धमानाखिलाशं
फट्कारं वज्रदंष्ट्रं प्रणत-रिपुजन-प्राणसंहारमीडे ॥५॥

सृंखं विद्वेष-हननाय वीरभद्राय खड्गहं ह्रीं दक्षध्वंसनाय
द्रां ह्रां र र र र हुं फट् स्वाहा ।

एतं मंत्रं महावीर्यं वीरभद्रं महोज्ज्वलम् ।
सहस्रं प्रजपेच्छक्त्या निग्रहेऽनुग्रहे तथा ॥६॥
मूलमंत्रावसाने तु ब्रह्माण्याद्यष्टमातृकाः ।
दिक्पालांश्च श्रियं मायां मत्त शुंभ-निशुंभकम् ॥७॥

महिषं धर्मं सिंहं च वीरेशं क्षेत्रपालकम् ।
विघ्नेश्वरं च रुद्रं च कालं स्कंदं पृथक् पृथक् ॥८॥
स्व स्व बीजेन मंत्रेण योजयित्वाऽथ साध्यकम् ।
सहस्रं प्रजपेन्मंत्री तत्तत्काम्यार्थसिद्धये ॥९॥
शत वारं जपेन्नित्यं पंचाशद्वर्णं पूर्वकम् ।
सर्वसिद्धि समाश्रित्य स मंत्री सुखमेधते ॥१०॥
भानुमालोकयन्मंत्री भानु-बीज-युतं मनुम् ।
भानुवारे जपेत्सद्यो भानुवद्भाति भूतले ॥११॥
ठं वं त्रं भं चं जूं सं च योजयित्वाऽथ पूर्ववत् ।
भानुमालोकयन्मंत्री प्रजपेत्सोमवासरे ॥१२॥
निवेद्याग्रेलतापुष्प-फल-पूर्णमुखादयः ।
तद्भानुदर्शनादेव सफलं जायते ध्रुवम् ॥१३॥
विशेषदिवसे भानुं येन बीजेन योजयेत् ।
तत्सिद्धि लभते तस्य संशयो नास्ति तत्त्वतः ॥१४॥

इति श्रीआकाशभैरवकल्पे प्रत्यक्षसिद्धिप्रदे उमामहेश्वरसम्वादे वीरभद्रकल्पं नाम द्वात्रिंशोऽध्यायः ॥३२॥

त्रयस्त्रिंशोऽध्यायः

जगत्क्षोभणप्रयोगः

श्रीशिव उवाच ।।

अथ शृणु कथयामः प्रार्थ्यमानं मुनीन्द्रै-
रधिगतरिपुलोकानावृतानाधृतास्त्रान् ।
हरि-विधि-मुख-वीरानप्रमेयानसह्या-
नपि विषु-मृतयोधान् यत्करोति द्रुतं तत् ।।१।।

जगत्क्षोभण-मंत्रस्य ऋषिस्तत्पुरुषेश्वरः ।
तथातिजगती छंदो देवता शरभेश्वरः ।।२।।

खं बीजं फट् ततः शक्तिर्विनियोगस्तु निग्रहे ।
खामित्यादि षडंगंस्यान्मूलन्यासं समाचरेत् ।।३।।

ध्यात्वा जपेन्महामंत्रं सहस्रं सर्वसिद्धये ।

अथ ध्यानम् ।।

दूर्वाश्यामं महोग्रं स्फुट चलदधरं सूर्यचन्द्राग्निनेत्रम्
चक्रं वज्रं त्रिशूलं शर मुसल-गदा-शक्त्यभीतिर्विहंतम् ।
शंखं खेटं कपालं सधनु-हल-फणि-त्रोट-दानानि हस्तैः
सिंहारिं सालुवेशं नमत रिपुजन-प्राणसंहार-दक्षम् ।।४।।

ओं नमो भगवते विश्वशरीराय पंचमुखभंजनाय प्रणतार्ति-विनाशनाय उग्राय उग्रदंष्ट्राय उरग-मणि-भूषणाय उद्दंड-कोलाहलाय सर्वलोकप्रियाय सकल-भूतनिवारणाय शतधृतिकपालमालालंकृताय शार्दूल-चर्मवसनाय शरभ-सालुवाय सूर्यसोमाग्निलोचनाय-दुर्निवारण-वारणाय दूर्वादलश्यामलाय दुरितहराय ओं श्रीं ह्लीं प्रीं सर्वभूतानाकर्षयाकर्षय सर्वग्रहाण्याकर्षयाकर्षय श्लां भ्रां ह्लां भूतग्रह पिशाचग्रह यक्षग्रह राक्षसग्रह सर्पग्रह दर्पग्रह अपस्मारग्रह भीमग्रह ब्रह्मराक्षसग्रह पातालग्रह कौमारग्रहापातालग्रह खेचरग्रह भूचरग्रह कूष्मांडग्रह ज्वालास्यग्रह तामसग्रह तमोहारग्रह स्त्रीग्रह पर्वतग्रह पापग्रह पापविक्रमग्रह बालग्रह

निशाचरग्रह अहोरात्रग्रह सप्तरात्रग्रह पक्षग्रह मासग्रह मंडलग्रह त्रिमासग्रह षण्मासग्रह वत्सरग्रहानुभोगग्रहानुसारग्रहाभिचारग्रहाभिमुक्तग्रह जीवग्रह दावग्रह वातग्रह पातकग्रह ज्वरग्रह रोगग्रह चेतनग्रहाचेतनग्रह स्फोटकग्रह दंशग्रह वांतिग्रह भ्रांतिग्रह हिक्वारग्रह धिक्वारग्रह संघातिकग्रह सन्निपातग्रह शोषणग्रह पोषणग्रह अविद्याग्रह विज्ञानग्रह लौकिकग्रह वैदिकग्रह रणग्रह राजग्रह कीटग्रह लूटग्रह सात्त्विकग्रह सार्वत्रिकग्रहाण्यावेशयावेशय प्रवेशय शीघ्रं प्रवेशय २ क्षोभय २ कंपय २ सकल-शैलं चालय २ सकल-सालं घातय २ सकलदिशां शोधय २ सकल-पदवीं भ्रंशय २ सकलदोषान् नाशय २ सकलसेनां ध्वंसय २ श्रीं ह्रीं क्लीं ह्लूं मोहय २ भ्रामय २ भाषय २ सर्वशूलग्रहं भाषय २ सर्वपिशाच ग्रहं भाषय २ सर्वयक्षग्रहं भाषय २ सर्वराक्षसग्रहं भाषय २ सर्वसर्पग्रहं भाषय २ सर्वदर्पग्रहं भाषय २ सर्वापस्मारग्रहं भाषय २ सर्व भीमग्रहं भाषय २ सर्व ब्रह्मराक्षसग्रहं भाषय २ सर्ववेतालग्रहं भाषय २ सर्वकौमार-ग्रहं भाषय २ सर्वपातालग्रहं भाषय २ सर्वखेचरग्रहं भाषय २ सर्वभूचर ग्रहं भाषय २ सर्वकूष्मांडग्रहं भाषय २ सर्वज्वालास्यग्रहं भाषय २ सर्वतामसग्रहं भाषय २ सर्वतमोहारग्रहं भाषय २ सर्वस्त्रीग्रहं भाषय २ सर्वपर्वग्रहं भाषय २ सर्वपापग्रहं भाषय २ सर्वपापविक्रमग्रहं भाषय २ सर्व बालग्रहं भाषय २ सर्वचातुर्थग्रहं भाषय २ सर्वमिथ्याग्रहं भाषय २ सर्वमिथ्या-पिशाचग्रहं भाषय २ सर्वघटिकाग्रहं भाषय २ सर्वयामग्रहं भाषय २ सर्वदिवाचरग्रहं भाषय २ सर्वनिशाचरग्रहं भाषय २ सर्वाहोरात्रग्रहं भाषय २ सर्वसप्तरात्रग्रहं भाषय २ सर्वपक्षग्रहं भाषय २ सर्वमासग्रहं भाषय २ सर्वमंडलग्रहं भाषय २ सर्वद्विमासग्रहं भाषय २ सर्वत्रिमासग्रहं भाषय २ सर्वषाण्मासग्रहं भाषय २ सर्ववत्सरग्रहं भाषय २ सर्वानुभोगग्रहं भाषय २ सर्वानुसारग्रहं भाषय २ सर्वाभिचारग्रहं भाषय२ सर्वाभिमुक्तग्रहं भाषय२ सर्वजीवग्रहं भाषय२ सर्वदावग्रहं भाषय२ सर्ववातग्रहं भाषय२ सर्व-पावकग्रहं भाषय २ सर्वज्वरग्रहं भाषय २ सर्वरोगग्रहं भाषय २ सर्वचेतनग्रहं भाषय२ सर्वाचेतनग्रहं भाषय२ सर्वस्फोटकग्रहं भाषय२ सर्वदंशग्रहं भाषय२ सर्ववांतिकग्रहं भाषय२ सर्वभ्रांतिकग्रहं भाषय२ सर्वहिक्वाग्रहं भाषय२ सर्व-धिक्वाग्रहं भाषय२ सर्वसंघातग्रहं भाषय२ सर्वसान्निपातकग्रहं भाषय२ सर्व-शोषणग्रहं भाषय२ सर्वपोषणग्रहं भाषय२ सर्वविद्याग्रहं भाषय२ सर्वविज्ञान

ग्रहं भाषय२सर्वलौकिकग्रहं भाषय२सर्ववैदिकग्रहं भाषय२सर्वरणग्रहं भाषय२ सर्वराजग्रहं भाषय२ सर्वकीटग्रहं भाषय२ सर्वमोटग्रहं भाषय२ सर्वसात्विक ग्रहं भाषय २ सर्वसार्वत्रिकग्रहं भाषय २ ग्रां ह्लीं ह्लां बंधय २ खं खं रुंधय २ ताटय २ पाटय २ क्रोशय २ कुर्दय २ रोदय २ खादय २ स्त्रौं ह्लौं ग्रंधय २ भद्रकालि-दुर्गाकलित-पक्षद्वयाय तिट्टवरि ग्लौ त्रां स्तंभय २ त्रों क्रौं त्रोटय २ रं रं ह्लूं प्रां दाहय २ त्रं ह्लीं ठं वं जुं सं पालय २ सर्वसंहार कारणाय सालुवपक्षिराजाय चंडवातातिवेगाय प्रें प्रीं यं यं संक्रामय २ खं खं रुंधय २ ताटय २ पाटय २ क्रोशय २ कुर्दय २ रोदय२ खादय २ स्त्रौं ह्लौं ग्रंधय २ भद्रकालि दुर्गा कलित पक्षद्वयाय प्रं खं ह्लं श्रौं उच्चाटय २ त्रैं परमंत्रभेदनाय जहय २ स्फोटय २ प्रैं परमंत्र प्रमोटनाय छिंदय २ र र र र भैं परतंत्रविच्छेदनाय भिंदय २ ठं ठं छें परविद्याविध्वंसनाय कालानल भैरवाय श्रितोदरोनुरुस्थलाय नाशय नाशय २ सर्वग्रहं नाशय सर्वभूतग्रहं नाशय सर्वपिशाचग्रहं नाशय २ सर्वसात्विकग्रहं नाशय २ प्रें परयंत्रतंत्र भेदनाय व्याधिकालो-रुद्रद्वयाय सर्वशत्रून् मारय २ भक्षय २ ह्लीं हुं फट् श्रीं ह्लीं क्लीं शरणागतवत्सलाय सामगानप्रियाय शंकराय चंद्रशेखराय ग्रथर्वणपारायणाय ग्रमृतोद्भाषणाय क्लीं श्रीं ह्लीं संतान-सिद्ध-प्रदाय श्रीं क्लीं श्रीं सर्वसंपत्समृद्धिदाय जं रं सर्वसम्मोहनाय सर्वमायां मोचय २ एं ऐं सोः कालाय भाषां ज्ञापय लृं लृं सर्वरोगहराय रूपं जनय २ विज्ञानं दापय २ हं हं वामदेवाय ग्रात्मानं दर्शय २ ग्रों खं श्रीं ह्लीं क्लीं ग्रभिवृद्धि देहि मे स्वाहा।

ग्रालेख्य वृत्तं बहिरष्टशूलं मध्ये च मायां त्रिशिखांतराले।
साध्यावृतं सर्वजयोपयोगं संक्षोभणं चक्रममोघमेतत् ।।५।।

एतन्मंत्रं महावीर्यं सर्वलोकेषु दुर्लभम्।
यस्य स्मरणमात्रेण तरसा विजयी भवेत् ।।६।।

य इमं प्रजपेद्भक्त्या नासाध्यं तत्र विद्यते।
मंत्राणां राजराजोऽयं तस्मात्त्वं जप सर्वदा ।।७।।

शत्रुमृत्यु जयं वांछन् सततं मंत्रवित्तमः।
सकृद्वा प्रत्यहं कुर्याज्जपेदेकाग्रमानसः ।।८।।

जयैषी मनसा स्मृत्वा वैरिणां नाम पूर्वकम् ।
तत्स्थानाभिमुखो मंत्री रात्रावष्टादशं जपेत् ।।६।।
देवतानां यमीनां च मानिनां च नृणां तथा ।
यदसाध्यं युगे सर्वे सर्वरोगे वरानने १०।।
मंत्रिणां जातरोषाणां मानिनां स्थानवासिनां ।
तत्सर्वं सहसा मंत्र-स्मरणात्साध्यमाप्नुयात् ।।११।।
यो जपेन्मनसा सोऽहमिति यावत्पदे पदे ।
सर्वलोकाश्च कंपंते किं पुनः शत्रुभाविनाम् ।।१२।।
किमत्र बहुनोक्तेन वक्ष्याम्यार्ये यथा तथम् ।
मंत्रस्मरणमात्रेण शरभेशो भवेद् ध्रुवम् ।।१३।।

इति श्रीआकाशभैरवकल्पे प्रत्यक्षसिद्धिप्रदे उमामहेश्वरसम्वादे जगत्क्षोभणमालामंत्रंनाम त्रयस्त्रिंशोऽध्यायः ।।३३।।

चतुस्त्रिंशोऽध्यायः

भैरवप्रयोगः

श्रीशिव उवाच ॥

अथ वच्मि महामंत्रं भैरवं लोकभैरवम् ।
किमत्र बहुनोक्तेन वक्ष्याम्यार्ये यथातथम् ॥१॥
सर्वसिद्धिप्रदं श्रेष्ठं सर्वविघ्ननिवारणम् ।
सर्वशत्रुंजयं दिव्यं सर्वरोगहरं शुभम् ॥२॥
सर्वार्थ-साधकं नृणां भोग-मोक्षैकसाधनम् ।
प्रत्यंगदेवतां चैतच्छृणु सम्यग्वरानने ॥३॥
भैरवस्यास्यमंत्रस्य अघोरो ऋषिरुच्यते ।
विराट्छंदस्तथा देवो भैरवः सर्वजिद्वरः ॥४॥
भंकारं बीजमित्युक्तं फट्कारं शक्तिरुच्यते ।
स्वेच्छा-संहार-सिध्यर्थे विनियोगस्तथांबिके ।
भामित्यादि करन्यासं षडंगं च ततस्तथा ॥५॥
कालांबुद-श्यामलमायतास्यं करालमव्याहतमप्रमेयम् ॥
लोल्लालकं लोकविनाशहेतुं लुठद्रिपुं नौमि धृताट्टहासम् ॥६॥

"ओं नमो भगवते उग्रभैरवाय सर्वविघ्ननाशाय ठ ठ स्वाहा" ।
(वर्ण २४)

चतुर्विंशतिसाहस्रं जपेन्मंत्रं यथाविधि ।
जप-तर्पण-होमानि द्विजानां भोजनस्य च ॥७॥
तद्दशांश-क्रमेणैव कुर्यात्पूर्ववदंबिके ।
कृसरं पायसं चाज्यमपूपं नवनीतकम् ॥८॥
महामुद्गं च सक्तुं च कुर्यात्सौम्यं पृथक् पृथक् ।
अष्टचूर्णं च तैलं च, सर्षपं क्रूरमुच्यते ॥९॥
अनल-भवन-मध्ये शक्तिबीजं फडर्णं
हरि-हर-जय हुं फट् साष्ट कोणे-ससाध्यम् ।

बहिरथ वसुपत्रे मूलमंत्रान् त्रिवर्णान्
सकलरिपुविनाशं भैरवं वैरिवज्रम् ।।१०।।

एतच्चक्रं तस्य पूज्यं जपेदष्टोत्तरं शतम् ।
भैरवं वह्निकोणे च वसुकोणेऽग्निमादितम् ।।११।।
भैरवीमप्यघोरं च गणेशं शिखिवाहनम् ।
विष्णुं च दक्षिणामूर्ति चंडोद्दंडगणेश्वरम् ।।१२।।
आपदुद्धारणं पश्चाद्यजेन्मंत्री यथाक्रमम् ।
तत्तन्मंत्रैः पृथक् पश्चान्मूलेनाप्यग्निदिङ्मुखः ।।१३।।

ह्रीं भैरवी देवि देवदत्त-कोपशमनं कुरु कुरु स्वाहा ।

ह्रीं रीं अघोर-भैरवाय देवदत्तं मोहय २ हुं फट् स्वाहा ।।

हुं ह्लां गं विघ्नराजाय देवदत्तकर्मविघ्नं कुरु कुरु स्वाहा ।

ओं ह्लां सुं रं सुब्रह्मण्याय वैरिधैर्यं चलय २ स्वाहा ।

श्रीं ह्रीं ओं जं सुदर्शनकराय रिपुचित्तं भ्रामय २ स्वाहा ।

ह्रीं ज्रं दक्षिणामूर्तये सुरसाध्य-मेधां समुत्कर्षय स्वाहा ।

ओं ह्लुं चंडोद्दंडाय शत्रून् घातय घातय स्वाहा ।

ओं ह्लः षः स्वं क्षं लं आपदुद्धारणाय देवदत्तचक्षु-श्रोत्र-जिह्वा घ्राण मनः-प्राण-हनुस्तंभं कुरु कुरु लं क्षं स्वं षः ह्लः ओं स्वाहा

दलांते केचित्प्राच्यादि मातृकाः पूजयेत्क्रमात् । ।।१४।।
नरांतकं महाभीमं विजयं रक्तभैरवम् ।
पश्चिमादि यजेद् भूमौ तत्तन्मंत्रैः पृथक् पृथक् ।।१५।।

ओं नमो भगवते नरमृगशरीराय सकलनरांतकाय रिपु-शरीरं नाशय २ हुं फट् स्वाहा ।

ह्रीं नमो महाभीमभैरवाय सर्वलोकभयंकराय सर्वश-शत्रून् संहार-कारणाय ह्लुं ह्लुं देवदत्तं ध्वंसय २ स्वाहा ।

वीरं हूं ओं नमो भगवते विजयभैरवाय सर्वशत्रून् विनाशनाय विधुरिताधराय नररुधिरमांसभक्षणाय देवदत्तमुच्चाटयोच्चाटय ताडय २ संहर २ भस्मीकुरु कुरु स्वाहा ।

ओं ह्रीं स्फ्रं रक्तभैरवाय नवशवकपालमालालंकृताय नवांबुद-श्यामलाय एहि एहि शीघ्रमेहि मां पाहि एं ऐं आगामिकार्यं वद वद अखिलोपाधि हर हर सौभाग्यं देहि मे स्वाहा ।

भैरवं पुनरिष्ट्वाऽथ मूलमंत्रं शतं जपेत् ।
तथा क्षयो भवेन्नूनं तद्दिनादेव वैरिणाम् ॥१६॥

इति श्रीआकाशभैरवकल्पे प्रत्यक्षसिद्धिप्रदे उमामहेश्वरसम्वादे भैरवमंत्रविधिर्नाम चतुस्त्रिंशोध्यायः ॥३४॥

पंचत्रिंशोऽध्यायः

सिद्धभैरवप्रयोगः

श्रीशिव उवाच ।।

रहस्यं वच्मि ते देवि सर्वकाम्यार्थसिद्धिदम् ।
मंत्रस्य स्मरणादेव मुह्यंत्यखिलजंतवः ।।१।।
सिद्धभैरवमंत्रस्य ऋषिः शंकर उच्यते ।
संकृतिश्छंद इत्युक्तं देवता सिद्धभैरवः ।।२।।
भं बीजं तु ततः शक्तिर्विनियोगस्तु मोहने ।
भां ह्लामित्यादिना पाणिन्यासं सर्वस्य चांबिके ।।३।।

अथ ध्यानम् ।।

जलद पटलनीलं दीप्यमानोर्ध्वकेशं
त्रिशिख-डमरु-हस्तं चद्रंरेखावतंसम् ।
विमल वृषभरुढं चित्रशार्दूलवासं
विजयमनिशमीडे विक्रमोद्दंडचण्डम् ।।४।।

ओं नमो भगवते विजय-भैरवाय प्रलयांतकाय महाभैरव्यै महाभैरवाय सर्वविघ्ननिवारणाय शक्तिधराय चक्रपाणये बटमूलनिषण्णाय अखिलगणनायकाय आपदुद्धारणाय आकर्षय २ आवेशय २ मोहय २ भ्रामय २ भाषय २ शीघ्रं भाषय शीघ्रं भाषय ह्लां ह्लीं त्रिपुरताण्डवाय अष्टभैरवाय भाषय स्वाहा ।।

आवेशम्

शांतं त्रिमुखमालिख्य तेन संवेष्ट्य सर्वतः ।
अधोशूला-द्विपार्श्वे च यंत्रं विजयमद्भुतम् ।।५।।
एतेद्यंत्रं लिखित्वाऽथ मंत्रेणानेन मंत्र्य तत् ।
भस्मदर्शनमात्रेण क्षणादावेशमाप्नुयात् ।।६।।
त्रिभांडकं विनादाय प्रत्येकं प्रस्थषट्ककम् ।
उद्धृत्यमागताद्भांडादन्नमादाय कृत्तिकम् ।।७।।

कृत्वालंकृत्य पूर्वोक्तं स्थानदीपं प्रकल्प्य च।
अन्य भांडद्वयं चापि नियतः कल्प्य तत्त्वतः ॥८॥
रक्तपुष्पोपाहारैस्तानलंकृत्य विशेषतः।
घटिका कृष्णजभस्मानां विपिनं सस्यरूपकम् ॥९॥
झष-सस्यं च शाकं च सर्वं संमिश्रितं तथा।
शालिपिष्ट्चे न्यसेत्पीठे त्ववृतं षट्शतं क्रमात् ॥१०॥
मोदकं नारिकेलं च कदलीं च गुलं तथा।
लाजं-मुद्गं-तिलं-सक्तुं-लोकसस्यं यथोचितम् ॥११॥
सर्वाण्येकानि विन्यस्य कृत्तिकाग्र भुविन्यसेत्।
भांडद्वयं तु तत्पार्श्वे नयेदात्ताभिधं मुखम् ॥१२॥
उलूखले समासीनं वेत्र-छत्रोत्तमांगकम्।
आर्द्रवासोपस्थवीत पश्येत्युक्त्वा तु तत्क्षणात् ॥१३॥
निर्धूमं निर्ज्वलंतं च किरेदुपरि पावकम्।
आहूय साधकान्धीरानलंकृत्याभिनीयवत् ॥१४॥
दत्त्वा तैरुद्धृतेकाले अट्टहास-युतं-बलिम्।
साधकैः सेवकैर्युक्तोवाद्य-घोष-युतोनरम् ॥१५॥
संवृतास्ते निशामध्ये नयेद्रुद्रभुवं ततः।
दत्त्वा रुद्रबलिं तत्र त्रिवारं जप्यतं मनुम् ॥१६॥
ततस्तद्ग्रामसीमांतमाग्नेयीं ककुभं नयेत्।
संजपन्भैरवं मंत्रं दशवारं दृढस्तथा ॥१७॥
तत्र रक्तं बलिं दद्यात्स पुर्नानियतः स्वयम्।
स्नात्वा तीर्थेऽथ संवृक्तान्नयेयुस्ते क्षपात्यये ॥१८॥
अथ बलिगमनादुलूखलस्थं दृढतरमनघो जपेन पश्चात्।
परिग्रहमथवा कणांतरं वा शुभयुत भवने नयेयुरन्ये ॥१९॥
तमभिनिहितदीपं तत्क्षणादेव शांतम्
पथ भुवि धृत सर्वानन्वकृत्वापि कुर्युः।
तदनु सतल भूमिं गोमयेनानुलिप्य
प्रसव-कुसुम-धूपैरंगबल्यादि कुर्यात् ॥२०॥
तदनु दिनमुहूर्ते भोजनैर्होममन्यै-
र्विधियुतमथ मंत्री कारयेद्वत्तमेव।

सकलशमनवृक्ता विद्यया पार्श्वया वा।
सरिवर-विनिशातान्त्स्यात्प्रतापेन सिद्ध्यै ॥२१॥
एष रुद्रबलिर्नाम प्रशस्तं बलिकर्मणाम्।
नंद्युर्देवासुरगणा-यक्ष गंधर्व-राक्षसाः।
सर्वभूतपिशाचाद्याः सर्वरोगाश्च दारुणाः।
स्वयमेव हि संयांति होमेनापि विशेषतः ॥२२॥
अधीरोऽपण्डितो मंत्री बलि कर्म न कारयेत्।
कारयेद्यदि तस्यैव कालः स्निग्धो भवेच्छिवे। ॥२३॥

ओं ह्रीं श्रीं हालाहल-भैरव अखिल-लोक भैरव आं भैरव देवदत्तेऽस्मिस्तस्य साध्यस्य वाङ्मनस्त्वक्-चक्षुः-श्रोत्र-जिह्वा-घ्राण-प्राणानाकर्षयाकर्षय तोषय २ गर्जय २ साधय२ बोधय२ नादय२ सीदय२ ह्लः उच्चाटय२ शीघ्रमुच्चाटय एह्येहि मां रक्ष २ ममैतद्बलिं भक्ष २ ओंकार-भैरव भक्ष२ उन्मत्तभैरव भक्ष २ नीलभैरव भक्ष २ त्वरितं भक्ष २ ओं ह्लां ह्लीं स्वाहा।

कुक्कुटस्य पलं मीनमन्नं लाजं गुलं तथा।
नालिकेरं श्मशाने तु रुद्रस्य बलिमाहरेत् ॥२४॥

इति श्रीआकाशभैरवकल्पे प्रत्यक्षसिद्धिप्रदे उमामहेश्वरसम्वादे बलिविधिर्नाम पंचत्रिंशोऽध्यायः ॥३५॥

षट्त्रिंशोऽध्यायः

श्रीशिव उवाच ॥

ब्रह्मा-ऋषिश्चगायत्री-छंदो देवतमुच्यते ।
क्षेत्रपाल-भैरवश्च क्ष्रीं बीजं वह्निजायया ॥१॥
शक्तिः सर्वार्थसिद्ध्यर्थे विनियोगो वरानने ।
क्षामित्यादि करन्यासमंगन्यासं च कारयेत् ॥२॥
शिरोमुखे तथा कर्णे-हृन्नाभ्याधार-जानुके ।
पादयोर्मंत्रवर्णांस्तु विन्यसेन्मंत्रवित्तमः ॥३॥

अथ ध्यानम् ॥

नीलांजनाद्रिनिभमूर्ध्वपिशंगकेश
वृत्ताग्निलोचनमुपात्त-गदा-कपालम् ।
आशां-वरं-भुजगभूषणमुग्रदंष्ट्रं
क्षेत्रेशमद्भु त-तनुं प्रणमामि देवम् ॥४॥

रक्तज्वाल-जटाधरं शशिधरं रक्तांग तेजोनिधि
हस्तैः शूल-कपाल-पाश-डमरु लोकस्य रक्षाकरम् ।
निर्बाणं शुनवाहनं भुजहरमानंद कोलाहलम्
वन्दे भूत-पिशाच नाथमनिशं क्षेत्रस्यपालं शिवे ॥५॥

क्षां बीजं पूर्वमुच्चार्य क्षेत्रपालाय वै पुनः ।
नम इत्युच्यते देवि अष्टाक्षरमिहोच्यते ॥६॥
लक्षमेकं जपेन्मंत्रं जुहुयात्तद्दशांशकम् ।
चरुणाघृत सिक्तेन ततः क्षेत्रेशमर्चयेत् ॥७॥
ब्राह्मे मुहूर्ते उत्थाय ध्यायेन्नाथपदांबुजम् ।
देहशुद्धादिकं कृत्वा स्नानं संध्यां समाप्य च ॥८॥
यागभूमिं ततोगत्वा अर्चयेन्मंडपं पुनः ।
"क्षां क्षेत्रपाल-अर्चनमंडपाय नमः"—इत्यभ्यर्च्य ।
"पृथिव्यै नमः"—इति भूमिमभ्यर्च्य ।
आसनं परिकल्प्याऽथ स्थित्वा तच्छोषणादिकम् ।
मातृकान्तं सुविन्यस्य ततः संकल्प्य पूजयेत् ॥९॥

संवित्सेवां ततः कृत्वा कलशं पूजयेत्सुधीः ।
शंख-पूजां समारम्य प्रोक्ष्य पीठार्चनं चरेत् ॥१०॥
श्राधार-शक्तिमारभ्य दिग्गजांतं समर्चयेत् ।
श्रष्ट-कुल-पर्वतं च रत्नभूमिं ततः परम् ।
श्वेतच्छत्र चामरे च धर्माद्यष्टकमेव च ।
गुणत्रयं च पद्मं च कंद-नालसपद्मकम् ॥१२॥
शिव-धर्मकंदमर्च्य तच्छिव-ज्ञाननालकम् ।
वैराग्यकर्णिकां चैव निध्यष्टकमतःपरम् ॥१३॥
इच्छा-ज्ञानक्रियामेतच्छैव-पीठंततोऽर्चयेत् ।
षट्कोणाष्टदलं लिख्य चतुर्द्वार-युतं प्रिये ॥१४॥
भूपुरं विलिखेद्देवि क्षेत्रपालमनुक्रमात् ।
मूलमध्ये सुसंपूज्य उपचारैस्तु षोडशैः ॥१५॥
षट्कोणायनमभ्यर्च्य सर्वज्ञादि षडंग-षट् ।
क्षं पूर्वमनुलिख्याऽथ भैरवाय नमस्ततः ॥१६॥
श्रग्निकेशं करालं च घंटारवमतः परम् ।
महाकोपमतः पश्चात्पिशिताशनमेवच ॥१७॥
पिंगलाक्षं चोर्ध्वकेशं श्रष्टपत्रे समर्चयेत् ।
चतुर्द्वारसमायुक्त चतुरस्रं ततोऽर्चयेत् ॥१८॥
बीजं स्वबीज-युक्तं च ऐंद्रादीशांतकं यजेत् ।
भूपुरद्वयमध्ये तु वज्राद्यष्टकमर्चयेत् ॥१९॥
तत्त्वावरणांते तु मूलं मध्ये त्रिरर्चयेत् ।
षोडशैरुपचर्याऽथ सर्वं मूलेन पूजयेत् ॥२०॥
गंधं पुष्पं च धूपं च दीपं नैवेद्यमेव च ।
तांबूलं बलिदानं च क्षेत्रेशोद्वासनं क्रमात् ॥२१॥

श्रों क्षां भिक्ति २ तुष्ट २ कुरु २ कुल २ भंजय २ नर्तय २ विश २ महाभैरव क्षेत्रपाल बलिं ग्रहण २ हुं फट् स्वाहा।

क्षेत्रपालं समुद्वास्य शिवोऽहमिति भावयेत्।
शृणु वक्ष्यामि ते देवि रहस्यं सावधानतः ।
गृहे ग्रामांतरे चैव देशे वेशांतरेषु च ॥१॥

मंत्री प्रवेशकाले तु शुद्धोऽशुद्धोऽथवापि स :
त्रिवारं प्रजपेद्भक्त्या क्षेत्रपालस्य सूक्तकम् ।।२।।
जप्तमंत्रस्तु यो गच्छेद्विदेशे यत्र कुत्रचित् ।
तत्राप्यपजयं नास्ति स्वप्नेऽपि च न संशयः ।।३ ।।

सूक्तेन संमंत्र्य सहस्रवारं तत्कुक्कुटांडं लवणांबु मध्ये।
संस्थाप्य शत्रोर्द्विमलं च रात्रौ खनेत् श्मशाने रिपुमारणाय ।।४।।
आदाय नीरं त्वभिमंत्र्य मंत्री सहस्रमेकैक-दिनं त्रिरात्रम् ।
सन्तानदं तापहरं-समस्तदोषापहं पुष्टिकरं च वश्यम् ।।५।।

अभयाष्टकमादाय सवर्णं सप्रमाणकम् ।
"क्षेत्रस्यपतिना वयं हितेनेव यजामसि
गामश्वं पोषयित्वा सनो मृडातीदृशे"[1] ।
संस्थाप्याभ्यर्च्य कट्वाद्यैर्नवपात्रे तु मृण्मये ।।६।।
चौरेणापि हृतं वस्तु तरसा दापयेत्स्वयम्।
उक्तेति साध्यमाकर्ष पल्लवं तदनंतरम् ।।७।।
मंत्रावसाने संयोज्य जपेत्सूक्तं सहस्रकम् ।
पंचांगं प्रजपेद्देवं पश्चिमाभिमुखं स्पृशन् ।।८।।
स चौरः पीडितोऽनेन स्वयं दास्यति निश्चयम् ।
न दत्तश्चेत्पुनः कुर्याज्जपेदेकाग्रमानसः ।।९।।
सचौरस्तद्दिनादेव ज्वरग्रस्तो भवेद् ध्रुवम् ।
प्लोष्यते द्विदिनाच्चोरस्त्रिदिनान्म्रियते ध्रुवम् ।।१०।।
तत्पालनं च पंचाहात्तद्भ्राताष्टदिनात्पिता ।
दशाहात्तस्य बंशस्य मरणं याति सुंदरि ।।११।।
तस्मादेवं प्रयत्नेन जपेत्सूक्तमिति क्रमात् ।
यस्तस्य सर्वसिद्धिः स्यात् सर्वदेशे च सर्वदा ।।१२ ।।

इति श्रीआकाशभैरवकल्पे प्रत्यक्षसिद्धिप्रदे उमामहेश्वरसम्वादे क्षेत्रपालविधिर्नाम षट्त्रिंशोऽध्यायः ।।३६।।

---

१ ऋक् ३-८-६ ।

सप्तत्रिंशोऽध्यायः

अथ वडवानलभैरव प्रयोगः

श्रीशिव उवाच ॥

वडवानल मंत्रस्य रहस्यं वच्मि तेऽम्बिके।
मंत्रस्मरणमात्रेण वह्निरुज्जृंभते ध्रुवम् ॥१॥
जये कृतेऽखिलान् लोकान्दहत्येव हि निश्चयः।
तादृशं दुःसहं मंत्रं सावधानमनाः शृणु ॥२॥
वडवानल-मंत्रस्य भास्करो ऋषिरुच्यते।
पंक्तिःछंदस्तथा देवो भगवान्वडवानलः ॥३॥
रं बीजमाहुतिः शक्तिर्विनियोगस्त्वभीष्टके।
रामित्यादि करन्यासं षडंगं च तथाम्बिके ॥४॥

अथ ध्यानम् ॥

त्रिनयनमरुणंत्वाबद्धमौलिं सुशुक्लां
शुकमरुणमनेका-कल्पमंभोजसंस्थम् ॥
अभिमत वर शक्ति स्वस्तिकाभीतिहस्तं
नमत कनकमालालंकृतांसं कृशानुम् ॥५॥
ओं '[1]त्वमग्नेद्युभिस्त्वमाशुशुक्षणि०—ऋक् ॥
पंचाष्टकोष्ठेषु यथाक्रमेण वैश्वानरं मंत्रमथो लिखित्वा।
रेखाग्रशूलं च तदग्र-साध्यं तारावृतं तद्वडवाग्नि-चक्रम् ॥६॥
एतद्यंत्रं समालिख्य लोहे ताम्रेऽथ सीसके।
आवाह्य पूजयेद्वह्नि आग्नेयाभिमुखांबिके ॥७॥
शत्रुवसून्संहराग्ने तद्देहं दह सत्वरम्।
फट् स्वाहेत्यग्नि-मंत्रस्य पल्लवं समुदीरितम् ॥८॥
सपल्लवं जपेन्नूनमष्टोत्तरसहस्रकम्।
दग्धयोगे खनेद्रात्रौ श्मशाने बलिपूर्वकम् ॥९॥

---

१ ऋक् २-५-१७

ततः स्नात्वा जपेत् मंत्रमष्टोत्तरसहस्रकम् ।
तत्क्षणाद्वैरि-वेश्मानि निर्दग्धानि भवंति हि ।।१०।।
तत्पश्चादुपसंहारः कर्तव्यश्च वरानने ।
उपसंहार-मंत्रस्य सविता-ऋषिरुच्यते ।।११।।
छंदोऽत्यष्टि ततो देवोभगवान्-हव्यवाहनः ।
ऋकारं बीजमित्युक्तं शक्तिर्वैश्वानरी-जया ।।१२।।
अनलास्त्रोपसंहारे विनियोगस्ततः प्रिये ।
पादैरर्धैः करन्यासं षडंगन्यासकं तथा ।।१३।।
सशराय सशार्ङ्गाय शक्तिहस्ताय वन्हये ।
कपालिने नमस्तुभ्यं मत्पापं दह मुंच तम् ।।१४।।

"ओं भूर्भुवः स्वः [1]अग्निरस्मि जन्मना जातवेदा:० —ऋक् ।।
भूर्भुवः स्वरों मत्पापं दह मुंच तं स्वाहा" ।

जपेदष्टोत्तरशतं ब्राह्मणान्भोजयेत्ततः ।
आग्नेयास्त्रस्य मंत्रस्य परब्रह्म ऋषिः स्मृतः ।
छंदस्तु देवी गायत्री देवता पावकोंऽबिके ।।१५।।
ओंकारं बीजमित्युक्तं शक्तिर्व्याहृतिरुच्यते ।
स्वेच्छा-संहार-सिद्ध्यर्थे विनियोगस्ततः परम् ।।१६ ।।
सतारव्याहृतिवर्णैरनुलोम विलोमकैः ।
षड्भिरेतैः करन्यासं षडंगं च यथाविधि ।।१७।।

बाणाग्रेकोणस्थितमेध्मानं परान्दहंतं स्वमरीचिकोणैः ।
शोणाबरं चन्द्रकलावतंसं नमामि देवं वडवामुखाग्निम् ।।१८।।

"शोचिष्केशाय विद्महे वैश्वानराय धीमहि तन्नः शुकः प्रचोदयात्" ।।१६।।

त्रिकोणे वह्नि बीजं च वसुकोणेऽस्त्र मंत्रकम् ।
पदशोवाह्यके साध्यः प्राणनावाह्य पावकम् ।।२०।।
मनसा तरसा साध्य पश्चादस्त्र-मनुं जपेत् ।
मंत्र स्मरण-मात्रेण वैरिणां मरणं भवेत् ।।२१।।
एतदेवं महाघोरं अव्याहत-मनुत्तमम् ।
अतंत्रितोरिदुष्टानाममोघं जयवर्धनम् ।।२२ ।।

---

१ ऋक् ३-१-२७

यः सकृत्प्रजपेत्तस्य सर्वं सिध्यति निश्चयः ।
पर्वते विपिने घोरे विजने दुर्गमे तथा ॥२३॥
आग्नेयास्त्रं जपेन्मंत्री तस्य नैवास्ति तद्भयम् ।
जाज्वल्यमानैस्तु बर्हिर्भटैस्तु संजातवेदाभिवृतस्तदानीम् ।
सर्वत्ररक्षेदथ सोऽपि पश्चात् कुर्याद्दिने ब्राह्मणभोजनं च ॥२४॥

इति श्रीआकाशभैरवकल्पे प्रत्यक्षसिद्धिप्रदे उमामहेश्वर सम्वादे वडवानल-भैरव-विधिर्नाम सप्तत्रिंशोऽध्यायः ॥३७॥

अष्टत्रिंशोऽध्यायः

दिक्पालप्रयोगः

श्रीशिव उवाच ॥

वक्ष्यामीन्द्रादि-दिक्पालान्महाबल-पराक्रमान् ।
सर्वलोकेश्वरान्वीरान् साधकाभीष्टदायकान् ॥१॥
मंत्रस्य लोकपालानां घोररुद्र ऋषिः स्मृतः ।
अनुष्टुबुष्णिक् त्रिष्टुप्-प्रकृतिर्गायत्रमेव च ॥२॥
जगती-बृहती-पंक्तिः क्रमाच्छंदोऽभिधीयते ।
देवतास्त्वथ दिक्पालास्तथा बीजानि शांभवि ॥३ ॥
स्व-स्व-वाहन-संरूढान् स्व-स्वायुध समन्वितान् ।
स्व-स्वालंकार संयुक्तान् स्तौम्यहं लोकनायकान् ॥४॥

"ओं नमो भगवते लां इन्द्राय वज्रहस्ताय सुराधिपतये ऐरावत-वाहनाय सशक्तिकाय सपरिवाराय हुं फट् स्वाहा" ॥१ ॥

"ओं नमो भगवते रामग्नये शक्ति-हस्ताय तेजोऽधिपतये मेषवाहनाय सशक्तिकाय सपरिवाराय हुं फट स्वाहा" ॥२॥

"ओं नमो भगवते हां (टां) यमाय दंडहस्ताय प्रेताधिपतये महिषवाहनाय सशक्ति० हुं फट् स्वाहा" ॥३॥

"ओं नमो भगवते षां (क्षां) निर्ऋतये खड्गहस्ताय रक्षोऽधिपतये नरवाहनाय सशक्ति० हुं फट् स्वाहा" ॥४॥

"ओं नमो भगवते वां वरुणाय पाशहस्ताय पयोऽधिपतये मकरवाहनाय सशक्ति० हुं फट् स्वाहा" ॥५॥

"ओं नमो भगवते यां वायवे ध्वजहस्ताय प्राणाधिपतये रुरू-वाहनाय सशक्ति० हुं फट् स्वाहा" ॥६॥

"ओं नमो भगवते सां सोमाय गदा-हस्ताय नक्षत्राधिपतये अश्ववाहनाय सशक्ति० हुं फट् स्वाहा" ॥७॥

"ओं नमो भगवते शं (हां) ईशानाय त्रिशूलहस्ताय विद्याऽधिपतये वृषभवाहनाय सशक्तिकाय सपरिवाराय० हुं फट् स्वाहा" ॥८॥

एतानि दिव्यमंत्राणि स्वेष्ट-मंत्रावसानके ।
योज्य मंत्री जपेदेवं प्रयोगाष्टक-सिद्धये ।

आदौ बीजानि संयोज्य जपेन्मंत्रं यथाविधि ।
तत्रैवाष्ट-महाकर्म-सिद्धयः सिध्यंति ध्रुवम् ।।६।।

स्तंभनाकर्ष-संहार-विद्वेष-प्लावनानि च ।
उच्चाट-मोह-दंडानि वासवादि शिवांतकम् ।।७।।

मूलं विनानेन दिशापतीनां मंत्रप्रयोगेण सपल्लेवन ।
कुर्यान्मनीषी सततं वरेण्ये कर्मस्वशेषेषु यथाक्रमेण ।।८।।

इति श्रीआकाशभैरवकल्पे प्रत्यक्षसिद्धिप्रदे उमामहेश्वरसम्वादे दिक्पालविधिर्नामाष्टत्रिंशोऽध्यायः ।।३८।।

एकोनचत्वारिंशोऽध्यायः

अथ व्याधिप्रयोगः

श्रीशिव उवाच ॥

अथ वक्ष्यामि गुह्यं ते दारुणं व्याधिकारणम्।
सर्ववैरिहरं देवि सर्वजंतुविनाशनम् ॥१॥
अतोऽस्य व्याधिमंत्रस्य वीरभद्रोऋषिः स्मृतः।
छंदोऽनुष्टप् तथा देवो महाव्याधिकरः शिवः ॥२॥
व्यांकारं बीजमित्युक्तं हुं शक्तिस्तदनंतरम्।
विनियोगोऽनिशं भक्त-शत्रुनाशाय-पीडने ॥३॥
व्यामित्यादि करन्यासं षडंगं तदनंतरम्।
त्रिपादं त्रिभुजं भीमं त्रिमूर्धानं त्रिलोचनम् ॥४॥
त्रिशूलासि-कपालाढ्यं ज्वालास्यं वक्त्रदंष्ट्रकम्।
सप्तशृंगं वसा-मांस-श्वचर्माम्बरधारिणम् ॥५॥
अशेषांग-व्रणोद्भूत-कृमिजाल-समाकुलम्।
वक्रनासं बृहत्स्कन्धं क्षुधया पीडितोदरम् ॥६॥
वैरिणां देहमालिग्यमक्षयंतं-विकर्णकम्।
कषाय कुसुमानीलं महाव्याधिकरं शुभे ॥
चिरं ध्यात्वा जपेन्मंत्रं सहस्रं शत्रुदिङ्मुखः ॥७॥

"ओं नमो भगवते रुद्राय महाव्याधिकराय देवदत्तं पीडय हुं फट् स्वाहा"।

तिर्यगूर्ध्वं चतुर्दश रेखा मध्यतोविलिखेदथ मंत्रम्।
बाह्य शूल तदग्रक साध्यं रोग चक्रमिदं रिपु नाशम् ॥८॥
यंत्रमालिख्य सीसे वा साध्यवृक्षेऽथवांबिके।
आराध्य चाष्टचूर्णेन लिप्त्वा जप्त्वा खनेन्निशि।
श्मशाने बलिपूर्वंतु पुनः स्नात्वा जपेत्तथा ॥१०॥

जपमेवं त्र्यहं कुर्याच्छत्रूणां रोगवृद्धये ।
अहेतुकं महारोगं रिपुः संप्राप्य नश्यति ।।११

यत्साध्यं लिख्यतं व्याधेस्तत्तद् व्याधिर्भविष्यति ।
तद्रोगं रिपुराश्रित्य सुभगोऽनुभवेद् ध्रुवम् ।।१२।।

इति श्रीआकाशभैरवकल्पे प्रत्यक्षसिद्धिप्रदे उमामहेश्वरसम्वादे व्याधिकल्पनं-नामैकोनचत्वारिंशोऽध्यायः ।।३९।।

चत्वारिंशोऽध्यायः

अथ मृत्युप्रयोगः

श्रीशिव उवाच ।।

अथ मृत्यु-प्रयोगस्य रहस्यं वच्मि तेऽम्बिके ।
स्मरणादस्य मंत्रस्य मृत्युराविर्भवेद् ध्रुवम् ।।१।।
अतोऽस्य मृत्युमंत्रस्य ऋषिर्नारायणः स्मृतः ।
उष्णिग्छंदस्तथा देवो मृत्युर्जीवांतको यमः ।।२।।
हुं कारं बीजमित्युक्तं ह्लैं कारं शक्तिरीरितम् ।
नियोगो जीवसंहारे ङामित्यादि करांगकम् ।।३।।

रक्ताक्षं भीमदंष्ट्रं प्रकटितवदनं वक्रनासं कराब्जैः
शूलं-पाशं-कपालं-फणि-मुसल-हल-वज्र-खेटं वहंतम् ।
भीमं कालाभ्रनीलं भृकुटितनयनं सैरिभोत्स्कंधरूढं
नाना-भूतैः-करालैः-परिवृतमखिल-प्राणकालं भजामि ।।४।।

"ओं नमो भगवते ङा मृत्यवे यमाय सर्वजीवहरणाय उग्राय दण्डहस्ताय ङ्गं ह्लैं देवदत्तं गृह्ण २ सर्वलोक भयंकराय नाशय २ ह्लैं ह्लुं फट् स्वाहा" ।

य इदं कालमंत्रं तु निशामध्ये युतं पुनः ।
जप्त्वा ततो जपेन्मंत्रं सहस्रं नामपूर्वकम् ।
तज्जपस्यावसाने तु स रिपुर्मरणं व्रजेत् ।
कृते पंचायुते मंत्रे रिपोः पंचशतान्मृतिः ।
लक्षे कृते शतादेव तद्द्वये स्मरणाद्भवेत् ।।६।।

इति श्रीआकाशभैरवकल्पे प्रत्यक्षसिद्धिप्रदे उमामहेश्वरसम्वादे मृत्युविधिर्नाम चत्वारिंशोऽध्यायः ।।४०।।

एकचत्वारिंशोऽध्यायः

श्री देव्युवाच ।।

सर्वज्ञ सर्वमंत्रस्य सर्वाचार्य शिव प्रभो ।
शारभं कवचं दिव्यं सर्वरक्षाकरं परम् ।।१।।
वज्रपंजर नामाख्यं वद मे करुणाकर ।

श्रीशिव उवाच ।।

वक्ष्यामि शृणु देवेशि सर्वं लक्षणमद्भुतम् ।
शारभं कवचं नाम्ना चतुर्वर्गफलप्रदम् ।।२।।
शरभ-सालुव-पक्षिराजाख्य कवचस्य तु ।
सदाशिव ऋषिश्छंदो बृहती शरभेश्वरः ।।३ ।।
देवता प्रणवं बीजं प्रकृतिः शक्तिरुच्यते ।
कीलकं पक्षिराजाय सर्वरक्षाकरोविभुः ।।४।।
पर-प्रयोग-शांत्यर्थं सर्वशत्रुनिवृत्तये ।
चतुर्वर्गार्थ-सिद्ध्यर्थे विनियोगोऽथ भावना ।।५ ।।

ध्यानम् ।।

रक्ताभं सुप्रसन्नं त्रिनयनममृतोन्मत्त-भाषाभिरामम्
कारुण्यांभोधिमीशं वरदमभयदं चन्द्ररेखावतंसम् ।
शंख-ध्माताखिलाशा प्रतिहतविधिना भासमानात्म-भावम्
सर्वेशं सालुवेशं प्रणतभयहरं पक्षिराजं नमामि ।।६।।

ओं श्री शिवः पुरतः पातु मायाधीशस्तु पृष्ठतः ।
पिनाकी दक्षिणं पातु वामपार्श्वं महेश्वरः ।।१।।
शिखाग्रं पातु मे शंभुर्निटिलं पातु शंकरः ।
ईश्वरो वदनं पातु भ्रुवोर्मध्यं पुरांतकः ।।२ ।।
भ्रुवौ पातु मम स्थाणुः कपर्दी पातु लोचने ।
शर्वो मे श्रोत्रयोः पातु वागीशः पातु लंबिकाम् ।।३।।

नासयोर्मे वृषारूढो नासाग्रं वृषभध्वजः ।
स्मरारिः पातु मे ताल्वोरोष्ठयोर्भक्तवत्सलः ॥४॥
जिह्वां मम सदा पातु सर्वविद्या प्रदायकः ।
पातु मृत्युंजयो दन्तान् चिबुकं पातु भूतराट् ॥५॥
परमेशः कपोलौ मे त्रिकं पातु कपाल भृत् ।
कंठं पशुपतिः पातु शूली पातु हनू मम ॥६॥
स्कंधद्वयं हरः पातु धूर्जटि पातु मे भुजौ ।
भुजसंधि महादेव ईशानो मे प्रकूपरे ॥७॥
मध्यसंधी जगन्नाथः प्रकोष्ठे चन्द्रशेखरः ।
मणिबन्धौ त्रिनेत्रो मे भीमः पातु करस्थले ॥८॥
करपृष्ठे मृडः पातु रुद्रोंऽगुष्ठद्वये मम ।
उमासहायस्तर्जन्यौ भर्गो मे पातु मध्यमे ॥९॥
अनामिके करालास्यः कालकंठः कनिष्ठिके ।
गंगाधरोऽङ्गुलीपर्वाण्यप्रमेयोनखानि मे ॥१०॥
वक्षस्तत्पुरुषः पातु कक्षे दक्षाध्वरांतकः ।
अघोरो हृदयं पातु वामदेव स्तनद्वयम् ॥११॥
भालदृक् जठरं पातु नाभिं नारायणप्रियः ।
कुक्षौ प्रजाकरः पातु कुक्षिपार्श्वे महाबलः ॥१२॥
सद्योजातः कटी पातु पृष्ठभागं तु भैरवः ।
मोहनो जघनं पातु गुदं मम जितेन्द्रियः ॥१३॥
ऊर्ध्वरेता लिङ्गदेशं वृषणं विश्वमोहनः ।
ऊरूद्वयं भवः पातु जानुयुग्मं भवांतकः ॥१४॥
हुंकारः पातु मे जंघे फट्कारो मम गुल्फके ।
वषट्कारः पादपृष्ठे वौषट्कारोंऽघ्रिणस्तले ॥१५॥
स्वाहाकारोंऽगुलीपार्श्वे स्वधाकारोङ्गुलीर्मम ।
त्वरितः सर्वसंधीन्मे रोमकूपाणि सिंहजित् ॥१६॥
त्वचं पातु मनोवेगः कालजिद् रुधिरं मम ।
पुष्टिदः पातु मे मांसं मेदो मे स्वस्तिदोऽवतु ॥१७॥

सर्वात्मास्थिचयं पातु मज्जानं मे जगत्प्रभु ।
शुक्रं वृद्धिकरः पातु बुद्धिं वाचामधीश्वरः ॥१८॥

मूलाधारांबुजं पातु भगवान् शरभेश्वरः ।
स्वाधिष्ठानमजः पातु मणिपूरं हरिप्रियः ॥१९॥

अनाहतं सालुवेशोविशुद्धं जीवनायकः ।
सर्वज्ञानप्रदोह्याज्ञां ललाटं मे सदाशिवः ॥२०॥

ब्रह्मरंध्रं महादेवः पक्षिराजोऽखिलात्मवान् ।
सर्वलोकवशीकारः पातु मां परगर्वजित् ॥२१॥

वज्र-मुष्टि-वराभीतिहस्तः कालाभ्रसन्निभः ।
विजया सहितः पातु चैंद्रीं ककुभमग्निजित् ॥२२॥

शक्ति-शूल-कपालासिहस्तः सौदामिनीप्रभः ।
जयायुतो महाभीमः पातु वैश्वानरीं दिशम् ॥२३॥

दंडासि-मुसलं-हाल-पाशांकुश-करांबुजः ।
यमांतकोऽजितायुक्तोयाम्यीं पातु दिशं मम ॥२४॥

खड्ग-खेटासि-परशुहस्त-शत्रुविमर्दनः ।
अपराजितया युक्तः सदाव्यान्नैर्ऋतिं दिशम् ॥२५॥

पाशांकुश-धनुर्बाण-पाणि-घोणियुतोऽग्रकः ।
हरिद्राभोऽनिशं पायाद्वारुणीं दिशमात्मजित् ॥२६॥

ध्वज-चक्रयुतोदारिभुजो दुर्गा युतोऽर्गलः ।
चंडवेगः शिवः पायात्सततं मारुतीं दिशं ॥२७॥

गदास्त्रग्वरदाभीति करांभोज श्रियायुतः ।
कनकाभो महातेजः पातु कौबेरकीदिशम् ॥२८॥

त्रिशूलाहि-कपालाग्निदोस्तलोविद्ययायुतः ।
भस्मोद्धूलितसर्वांग ऐशीं पात्वपराजितः ॥२९॥

जपास्त्रक्-पुस्तकांभोज कमण्डलुं करांबुजः ।
ऊर्ध्वं पातु गिरायुक्तः सर्वभूतहितेरतः ॥३०॥

शंख-चक्र-गदाऽभीति-हस्तः पद्मायुतोऽव्ययः ।
कालांजनसमोनीलः पातालं पात्वनारतम् ॥३१॥

अनुक्ता विदिशः पातु सालुवो नारसिंहजित् ।
शरभः पातु संग्रामे युद्धे वैरिकुलांतकः ३२॥
सर्वसौभाग्यदः पातु जाग्रत्स्वप्न-सुषुप्तिषु ।
सर्वसंपत्प्रदः पातु धनधान्यादिकं मम ॥३३॥
संतानदः सुतान्पातु दारानायुष्करोऽनिशम् ।
बंधून्वृद्धिकरः पातु गृहं सर्ववशंकरः ॥३४॥
ग्रामं ग्रामेश्वरः पातु राज्यं पातु दिगंबरः ।
राष्ट्रं शांतिकरः पातु राजानं धर्मशासकः ३५॥
मार्गं दुष्टहरः पातु धर्मकर्माणि भैरवः ।
बटुकः पातु मे सर्वं अवस्थासु भयेषु च ॥३६॥
स्पर्श-वीक्षण-संयुक्तः प्राणरक्षां मनोजवः ।
[1]प्रधानमूर्तिभावश्च प्रासादेष्वाशुसिद्धिकृत् ॥३७॥
साधकः प्रणवं बीजं नमो भगवतेति च ।
प्रतिनाम चतुर्थ्यंतं स्पर्श इत्यभिधीयते ॥३८॥
द्विर्ज्वल-प्रज्वले साध्यं साधय द्विर्द्वि रक्ष तत् ।
सर्वदुष्टेभ्यो हुं फट् स्वाहान्तं युग्-वीक्षणम् ॥३९॥
स्पृशन् पश्यन् जपं कृत्वा प्रतिस्थानं समाहितः ।
प्रार्थयेदखिलं स्वेष्टं हृद्रिस्थं सालुवेश्वरम् ॥४०॥
ये ग्रामघातकाः क्रूराः कपटा दौष्टिका भटाः ।
तस्कराः शत्रवः क्रुद्धा वधे सक्ताः पलाशनाः ॥४१॥
छद्मचाराः विटाः भ्रष्टास्दिवाचर-निशाचराः ।
ते सर्वे पक्षिराजस्य पक्षवातपराहताः ॥४२॥
स्त्री-बाल-सहिताः क्षिप्रं पितृ-मातृ कुलान्विताः ।
भग्नचित्ता गतस्थाना यांतु देशांतरं स्वयम् ॥४३॥
ये च दुष्टग्रहा रक्षः-पिशाचाः देवयोनयः ।
चतुःषष्टिगणाः सप्तसप्तत्युन्मादका ग्रहाः ॥४४॥
अष्टाशीति महाभूताः सप्तकोटि महाग्रहाः ।
नवति ज्वरभेदाश्च शत-भेदाश्च कृत्तिकाः ॥४५॥

---

१. ओं नमो भगवते श्री शिवाय मम पुरतः ज्वल २ प्रज्वल २ साध्यं साधय २ सर्वदुष्टेभ्यो हुं फट् स्वाहा—श्री शिवः पुरतः पातु ॥ एवं सर्वत्र० ।

पंचाशद् गणनाथाश्च नियुता कृत्रिमा ग्रहाः ।
प्रेतारूढास्त्रयस्त्रिंशत्पिंडदानपरायणाः ।।४६।।

अयुतं क्षुद्र-भेदाश्च चत्वारिंशच्छिवाह्वयाः ।
द्वात्रिंशद्वह्निवक्त्राश्च त्रिंशन्मार्जारवक्त्रकाः ।।४७।।

चतुःषष्ट्याखुरूपाश्च ये चान्ये क्षुद्रयोनयः ।
ते सर्वे सालुवेशस्य शंख-निःस्वन-मोहिताः ।।४८।।

विषण्णाः खिलतःस्वांताः प्राण-त्राण-परायणाः ।
गच्छंतु संप्रयोक्तारो देशांतरमनिच्छया ।।४९।।

ये च मूषक-वैडालाः शुनकोरगवृश्चिकाः ।
आशीविषाः शिवा व्याला व्याघ्र-ऋक्षेभसूकराः ।।५०।।

गृध्राः श्येनाः खगाः कंका दंशका भ्रंशका मृगाः ।
एते शरभहस्ताग्र-नख-क्षतविमोक्षगाः ।।५१।।

स्रवद्रक्ततलासिक्ताः शिलातलनिपीडिताः ।
संभिन्नतनवः शीघ्रं नश्यंत्वखिलदुश्चराः ।।५२।।

न दंशंतूरगाः क्वापि नातिवातोऽपि वीजतु ।
न दहत्वसहो वह्निरायांत्वापो न चाधिकाः ।।५३।।

न वर्षत्वतिवृष्टिश्च न पतत्वशनिः क्वचित् ।
नाक्रामत्वपमृत्युश्च नास्त्युत्पातं कदाचन ।।५४।।

न स्त्रियंत्वंभसि जना न भवत्वशुभं क्वचित् ।
न वदंत्वसहं वाक्यं जंतवो मम देशके ।।५५।।

नास्ति वैरं तु जंतूनामन्योऽयं राजके मम ।
भवंतु सुखिनः सर्वे नार्यः संतु पतिव्रताः ।।५६।।

सर्वाः सूयंतां सत्पुत्रान् पुत्रीश्च शुभलक्षणाः ।
सर्वे देवाश्च नंदंतु संतु कल्याणकारकाः ।।५७।।

राजन्वती मही चास्तु राजा भवतु धार्मिकः ।
ससंस्रवं-पयोगावः फलंत्वोषधयोऽधिकम् ।।५८।।

भवंतु फलदा वृक्षाः सिद्धिर्भवतु मेऽखिला ।
ममास्तु तरसा नूनमात्मज्ञानमचंचलम् ।।५९।।

महाक्रोध-महालोभाः समदा लोभ मत्सराः ।
न संतु क्वापि मे सर्वे भगवन्करुणानिधे ॥६०॥
शरभेश्वर विश्वेश पक्षिराज दयानिधे ।
देहि मे ह्यचलां भक्तिं प्रणतोऽस्मि पुनः पुनः ॥६१॥
गौरिवल्लभ कामारे कालकूटविषादन ।
मामुद्धरापदंभोधेस्त्रिपुरघ्नांतकांतक ॥६२॥
सालुवेश जगन्नाथ सर्वभूतहिते रत ।
पाहि मां तरसा चौरान् दुष्टान्नाशय नाशय ॥६३॥
कालभैरव विश्वेश विश्वरक्षापरायण ।
रक्ष मूषक-चौरेभ्यो धान्यराशिमिमं प्रभो ॥६४॥
पक्षिराज महादेव प्रणतार्तिविनाशन ।
मदीयानि पदार्थानि नित्यं पालय पालय ॥६५॥
सर्वज्ञ सर्वलोकेश सर्वदुष्टविनाशन ।
तस्करेण हृतं वस्तु द्रुतं दापय दापय ॥६६॥
ये मर्मवादिनः क्षुद्राः छिद्रोपद्रवकारकाः ।
सर्वाचार-परिभ्रष्टा मानहीनाश्च रोधकाः ॥६७॥
ते सर्वे सालुवेशस्य मुसलायुधचूर्णिताः ।
नश्यंतु निमिषार्धेन पावकावृततूलवत् ॥६८॥
ये जना द्रोहिणोऽश्लाघ्यास्त्वकालोचितभाषणाः ।
सत्कर्म विघ्नकर्तारः शांत भर्त्सापरायणाः ॥६९॥
ते सालुवेश हस्ताग्र-खड्ग निर्भिन्नदेहिनः ।
पतंतु भूतले याम्यां प्राणास्तेषां प्रयांत्वरम् ॥७०॥
त्वदंघ्रि ध्यान निर्दग्ध पापकोशाय मंत्रिणे ।
मह्यं द्रुह्यंति ये तेषां विभवानि क्षयंत्वरम् ॥७१॥
त्वदाचारं परं भक्तं साधकानां विवेकिनम् ।
य आक्रमंति संग्रामे ते गच्छंतु पराहताः ॥७२॥
त्वदीयेनैव मार्गेण संचरंतं जपातुरम् ।
ये वदंति परीवादं भ्रांताः शीघ्रं भवंतु ते ॥७३॥

त्वद्धासममलं धीरं ये मां तर्जयितुं बलात् ।
मनसा ये न मन्यंते तत्स्वांतं भ्रमतु क्षणात् ॥७४॥
मनसा कर्मणा वाचा ये कुर्वंत्यतिदुःसहम् ।
ते महाशोक रोगाब्धौ पतंत्वाशु शिवाज्ञया ॥७५॥
मदीयानि पदार्थानि ग्रहीतुं योऽवलोकते ।
तत्क्षणादेव नष्टाक्षो भवत्वाश्वीश्वराज्ञया ॥७६॥
मदीयं द्रव्यमादाय ये गच्छंतीह तस्कराः ।
सिंहारि-पाश-संबद्धास्ते चरंतु प्रदक्षिणम् ॥७७॥
सीमातीताश्च ये चौरा गृहीतद्रव्यसंचयाः ।
अवशावयवास्ते तु आगच्छंतु शिवाज्ञया ॥७८॥
तस्कराः निम्नगातीताः स्वांत-धान्य-धनाधिकाः ।
पक्षिराजांकुशाकृष्टाः समागच्छन्तु मद्गृहम् ॥७९॥
समाहृत-पदार्थाद्या देशातीताश्च तस्कराः ।
शरभेश-हलाकृष्टास्ते आगच्छंतु वै द्रुतम् ॥८०॥
चौरा ग्रहीतुमुद्युक्ताः समागच्छंति मद्गृहे ।
ते सालुवेशपक्षोत्थवातैर्गच्छंतु सत्वरम् ॥८१॥
शांतं विवेकिनं भक्तं त्वदंघ्रि ध्यानतत्परम् ।
ब्रुवंति ये सहप्राणास्तेषां यांति यमीं पुरीम् ॥८२॥
षट्त्रिंशत्कोष्टके यंत्रे रेखाशूलाग्रसाध्यके ।
स्वेच्छामंत्रं लिखित्वा तु जपेदाराध्य साधकः ॥८३॥
मध्ये पाशांकुशे वह्नि साध्य नाम लिखेत्क्रमात् ।
उदङ्मुखः सहस्रं तु रक्षणाय जपेन्निशि ॥८४॥
नष्टाहरणके पंचरात्रं पश्चिम-दिङ्मुखः ।
मारणे सप्तरात्रं तु दक्षिणाभिमुखो जपेत् ॥८५॥
रोगनिग्रहणे चाष्टरात्रमाग्नेयदिङ्मुखः ।
इति गुह्यं महामंत्रं परमं सर्वसिद्धिदम् ॥८६॥
शरभेशाख्य-कवचं चतुर्वर्गफलप्रदम् ।
प्रत्यहं प्रतिपक्षं वा प्रतिमासमथापि वा ॥८७॥

यो जपेत्प्रतिवर्षं वा वरेण्यः स शिवो भवेत् ।
एवं हि जपतः पुंसां पातकं चोपपातकम् ॥८८॥
तत्सर्वं लयमाप्नोति रविणा तिमिरं यथा ।
दशाब्दं यो जपेन्नित्यं प्रातरुत्थाय साधकः ॥८९॥
सर्वसिद्धि समाश्लिष्य देहांते स शिवो भवेत् ।
त्रिकालं ध्यानपूर्वं तु जपेद् द्वादश-वार्षिकम् ॥
कायेनानेन सो देवि जीवन्मुक्तो भवेन्नरः ॥९०॥
शतवारं जपेन्नित्यं मंडलं यो वरानने ।
सोऽणिमादिगुणान् प्राप्य विचरेत्स्वेच्छया सदा ॥९१॥
अतलादिधरण्यादि भुवनानि चतुर्दश ।
विचरेत्कामतः सर्वैः पूज्यमानो यथासुखम् ॥९२॥
त्रिमासं यो जपेन्नित्यमष्टोत्तरसहस्रकम् ।
सहसा शरमेशस्य सारूप्यं लभतेऽम्बिके ॥९३॥
षण्मासं यो जपेद्देवि प्रयतस्तु दृढव्रतः ।
मद्रूपधारको मर्त्यः सर्वसिद्धिप्रदायकम् ॥९४॥
मम लोके च संपूज्यो विष्णुलोके विशेषतः ।
ब्रह्मलोके च रमते सर्वत्र न निवार्य्यंते ॥९५॥
इंद्राग्नियमरक्षेशजलेशपवनैः सह ।
सोमेशैः सह रुद्रैर्दिशांपालैः स पूज्यते ॥९६॥
आदित्य-सोम-पृथ्वीज-बुध-श्री-गुरु-भार्गवैः ।
पूज्यते स ग्रहैः सर्वैस्सशनि-राहु-केतुभिः ॥९७॥
भृग्वंगिरः-पुलस्त्यैश्च पुलहात्रि-मरीचिभिः ।
दक्ष-कश्यप-भृग्वाद्यैर्योगिभिश्च स पूज्यते ॥९८॥
भैरवैर्वसुभी रुद्रैरादित्यैर्बालखिल्यकैः ।
दिग्गजैश्च महानागैर्दिव्यास्त्रैर्दिव्यवाहनैः ॥९९॥
माहेश्वरैर्महारत्नैः कामधेनु-सुरद्रुमैः ।
सरिद्भिः सागरैः शैलैर्देवताभिस्तपोधनैः ॥१००॥
दानवै राक्षसैः क्रूरैः सिद्ध-गंधर्व-किन्नरैः ।
यक्ष-विद्याधरैर्नागैरप्सरोभिश्च पूज्यते ॥१०१॥

अपस्मार-ग्रहैर्भीमैरुन्मत्तैर्ब्रह्मराक्षसैः ।
वेतालैः खेचरैर्मर्त्यैः कूष्मांडै राक्षसग्रहैः ॥१०२॥
ज्वालावक्त्रैस्तमोहारैः स्त्रीग्रहैः पावकग्रहैः ।
भूत-प्रेत-पिशाचाद्यैर्ग्रहैः सर्वैः स पूज्यते ॥१०३॥
ब्राह्मणैः क्षत्रियैर्वैश्यैः शूद्रैरन्यैश्च जातिभिः ।
पशु-पक्षि-मृग-व्यालैः पूज्यते सर्वजंतुभिः ॥१०४॥
किमत्र बहुना देवि तव वक्ष्येऽहं यथातथम् ।
मया च विष्णुना चैव विश्वकर्त्रा च कल्प्यते ॥१०५॥
भवत्या च गिरा लक्ष्म्या ब्रह्माण्याद्यष्टमातृभिः ।
गणेश्वरादियोगीन्द्रैर्योगिनीभिः स पाल्यते ॥१०६॥
य इदं प्रजपेद्भक्त्या तस्यासाध्यं न विद्यते ।
कवचेन्द्रं महामंत्रं जपेत्तस्मादनुत्तमम् ॥१०७॥
उच्चाटने मरुद्वक्त्रो विद्वेषे राक्षसाननः ।
प्रागाननोऽभिवृद्धौ तु सर्वेष्वीशानदिङ्मुखः ॥१०८॥
यो जपेत्कवचं नित्यं त्रिकालं ध्यान-पूर्वकम् ।
सर्वसिद्धिमवाप्नोति सहसा साधकोत्तमः ॥१०९॥

श्रीदेव्युवाच ॥

देवदेव महादेव शिव कारुण्यवारिधे ।
पाहि मां प्रणतं स्वामिन्प्रसीद सततं मम ॥११०॥
सर्वार्थसाधनोपाय सर्वैश्वर्य-प्रदायक ।
समस्तापत्प्रतीकार चंद्रशेखर ते नमः ॥१११॥
यत्कृत्यं यन्न कृत्यं तत्तदाचरितम् ।
उभयोः प्रायश्चित्तं शिव तव नामाक्षर-द्वयोच्चरितम् ॥११२॥

इति श्रीआकाशभैरवकल्पे प्रत्यक्षसिद्धिप्रदे उमामहेश्वरसम्वादे शरभकवचं नामैकचत्वारिंशोऽध्यायः ॥४१॥

द्विचत्वारिंशोऽध्यायः

श्रीशिव उवाच ।।

अथ वच्मो वयं देवि कामराजं महामनुं ।
यस्य स्मरण मात्रेण मुह्यंत्यखिल-जंतवः ।।१।।

विशेषतोऽखिला देवा यक्ष-किन्नर-राक्षसाः ।
गणा गण-पिशाचाश्च भूत-प्रेतादयोऽम्बिके ।।२।।

श्रीकामराजमंत्रस्य संमोहन ऋषिः स्मृतः ।
तस्यच्छंदस्तु गायत्री मन्मथोदेवता स्वयम् ।।३।।

क्लंकारं बीजमीकारः शक्तिर्योगस्तु मोहने ।
क्लामित्यादि करन्यासं षडंगं च ततस्तथा ।।४।।

ध्यानम् ।।

अरुणमरुणवासो माल्यदामांगरागं
स्वकर कलितपाशं सांकुशास्त्रेक्षु चापं ।
मणिमय मुकुटाद्यं र्दीप्तमाकल्पजालै-
ररुणनलिनसंस्थैश्चिन्तयेदंगयोनिम् ।।५।।

कामराज-गायत्री ।।

कामदेवाय विद्महे पुष्पवाणाय धीमहि ।
तन्नोऽनंगः प्रचोदयात् ।।६।।

महामंत्रमिमं दिव्यं तन्नोऽनंगः प्रचोदयात् ।
चतुर्विंशतिसाहस्रं जपेन्मंत्रं दृढव्रतः ।।७।।

ततः सिद्धिमवाप्नोति साधकेन्द्रोऽखिलां शिवे ।।

आलेख्यं कर्णिकायामनलपुरपुटे मारबीजं ससाध्यं
तद्बंध्रेष्वंग-षट्कं बहिरथ गुणशो मारगायत्रि-वर्णान् ।
मालामंत्रं दलाग्रेष्वथ गुह-मुखशः पार्थिवाश्रिष्वनंगं
कुर्याद्यंत्रं तदेतद्भुवनमपि वशेत्का कथा मानुषेषु ।।८।।

[१]क्लींकारं पूर्वमुच्चार्य कामदेवाय तत्परम् ।
रतिवल्लभाय सर्वजनसंमोहनाय च ॥६॥
ज्वल ज्वल प्रज्वलेति स्यात्सर्वजनदृष्टि च ।
तत्पश्चान्मुखं हृदयं पश्चान्मम वशं कुरु ॥१०॥
कुरु स्वाहेति मंत्र एकोनपंचाशदक्षरः
विविधेषु प्रयोगेषु साध्यनामसु पल्लवम् ॥११॥
एतद्यंत्रं समालिख्य जपेत्स्पृष्ट्वाऽर्थसिद्धये

वह्नेर्गेहपुरांतरस्थमदनं मायालिखेद्वाग्भवम्
षट्कोणेष्वथ संधिषु प्रविलिखेत् ब्लूंकारमावेष्टयेत् ।
स्त्रीबीजेन समीरितं त्रिभुवनं क्षोभाकरं श्रीप्रदम्
यंत्रं पंचमनोभवात्मकमिदं सौंदर्यसंपत्प्रदम् ॥१२॥

यंत्रमेतद्वरं श्रेष्ठं सर्वसौभाग्यदायकम्—
तस्य धारणमात्रेण सर्वलोकजयं लभेत् ॥१३॥

एकारौकारयुक्ता हरि-हरज-हराः पंचबाणाः स्मरस्य
ख्याता लक्ष्म्याण्यमीषा हृदय-कुच-दृशोर्मूर्ध्नि गुह्यक्रमेण ।
मर्मस्वेतेषु भूयो निजनयनधनुःप्रेरितस्तैश्चतुर्भिः
स्पंदंते सुंदरीणां मदनपरिवशाद्वह्नि-वक्त्राद्यथाऽज्यम् ॥१४॥

हृदयं कमलं चैव स्तनौ चूतस्तथैव च ।
नेत्रमशोकपुष्पं च शिरसि मल्लिकास्तथा ॥१५॥
योनिं नीलोत्पलं चैव इत्येते पंचबाणयोः ।
कामैकाक्षरविद्या तु त्रैलोक्यक्षोभकारणम् ॥१६॥
लक्षत्रयं जपेन्मंत्री मधुरत्रयसंयुतैः ।
फुल्लैः किंशुकजैः पुष्पैर्जुहुयात्तद्दशांशकम् ॥१७॥
आधार-शक्तिमारभ्य पीठमंत्रान्तमंबिके ।
मोहिनी क्षोभिणी चैव त्रासिनी जंभिनी तथा ॥१८॥
आकर्षिणी द्राविणी च ह्लाविनी च ततः परम् ।
क्लिन्ना च क्लेदिनी चैव पीठशक्तय ईरिताः ॥१९॥

---

१. मंत्रोद्धार :—क्लीं कामदेवाय रतिवल्लभाय सर्वजनसम्मोहनाय ज्वल ज्वल प्रज्वल सर्वजनदृष्टि-मुख-हृदयं मम वशं कुरु कुरु स्वाहा ।

"श्रों नमो भगवते जगन्मोहनरूपाय कामपीठाय नमः" ।
इष्ट्वांगावरणं पूर्वं मध्ये दिक्ष्वर्चयेच्छरान् ।
शोषणं मोहनं चैव संदीपनमतः परम् ॥२०॥
संतापनोन्मादनं च पंचबीजयुतं क्रमात् ।
प्रणामबाणहस्ताब्जा ध्येयास्ता बाणदेवताः ॥२१॥
संपूज्याः पत्रमध्ये तु शक्तयोऽष्टौयथाक्रमम् ।
प्रथमाऽनंगरूपा च द्वितीयाऽनंगमन्मथा ॥२२॥
अनंगकुसुमानंगशीर्षाह्यनंगवेगिनी ।
अनंगांकुशा चानंग मेखलाऽनंगदीपिका ॥२३॥
लीलाकमलधारिण्यःस्मेर-वक्त्राः सुभूषिताः ।
बहिः षोडशपत्रेषु पूज्याः षोडश शक्तयः ॥२४॥
युवती विप्रलंभान्या ज्योत्स्ना सुभ्रूर्मदद्रवा ।
सुरता गुरणी लोल्या कांतिः सौदामिनी पुनः ॥२५॥
कामच्छत्रा चन्द्रलेखा शुकी स्यान्मदना पुनः ।
योनिर्मायावती ताः स्युः कल्हार-विलसत्कराः ॥२६॥
स्मेर-वक्त्रा युवतयो मदविह्वलमंथराः ।
दलाग्रेषु पुनः पूज्याः स्मेरस्य परिचारिकाः ॥२७॥
शोको मोहो विलास्यन्यो विभ्रमो मदनातुरः ।
अपत्रपो युवा कामी चूतपुष्पो रतिप्रियः ॥२८॥
ग्रीष्मतपान्तानुजोऽन्यो हेमंतः शिशिरोमदः
इक्षु-कार्मुक-पुष्पेषु धरासक्ता सुभूषितः ॥२९॥
अपरा अंगनांगस्था वनितासक्त-मानसाः
रतिप्रियानष्टदिक्षु यजेदष्टौ विशिष्टधीः ॥३०॥
परभृत्सारसौ पश्चाच्छुकमेका स्वयौ पुनः ।
अनंगभ्रूविलासौ द्वौ भाषाभावौ प्रकीर्तितौ ॥३१॥
चतुरस्रस्य कोणेषु पूज्यास्तत्परिचारिकाः ।
माधवीमावृती पश्चाद् धरणी-क्ष्मा-मदोत्कटा ॥३२॥
सित चामरधारिण्यः सर्वाभरणभूषिताः ।
बाह्ये लोकेश्वरान् पश्चात्तदस्त्राण्यर्चयेत्ततः ॥३३॥

इत्थं यो भजते देवं सुगंध-कुसुमादिभिः ।
स भवेल्लब्धसौभाग्यो लक्ष्म्यादित-धरेश्वरः ॥३४॥

नेत्रघ्राणमुखेषु पाणिपदयोः साग्रेषु संधिष्वथो
मूलाधारसलिंगनाभ्युदर-हृत्पार्श्वा परांग-स्तने ।
कर्णांसत्रिकवक्त्रग्रोष्ठरसनाघ्राणाक्षिकर्णाब्जिके
एतान्विन्यसतु क्रमेण दशधा बाणान् जगन्मोहनान् ॥३५॥

इति श्रीआकाशभैरवकल्पे प्रत्यक्षसिद्धिप्रदे उमामहेश्वरसम्वादे मन्मथप्रयोगो नाम द्विचत्वारिंशोऽध्यायः ॥४२॥

त्रिचत्वारिंशोऽध्यायः

श्रीशिव उवाच ॥

वक्ष्यामि रक्तचामुंडीं महासिद्धिप्रदायिनीम् ।
निग्रहानुग्रहाकर्षदक्षामद्भुतमोहिनीम् ॥१॥
मंत्रस्य रक्तचामुंडाया ऋषिः शंकर ईरितः ।
छंदोऽनुष्टुप् तथा रक्तचामुंडी देवताऽम्बिके ॥२॥
[1]लक्ष्मीं बीजं ततः शक्ति (ह्रीं) र्महामायेष्टसिद्धये ।
विनियोगः करांगस्य न्यासं ताभ्यां यथाविधि ॥३॥

ध्यानम् ॥

रक्ताभां पीतवस्त्रां स्मित-मुख-कमलामिन्दुरेखावतंसां
दिव्यैर्माणिक्य-मुक्ता-मणिगण-खचितैर्भूषणैर्दीप्यमानाम् ।
पुष्पेष्विक्ष्वास-बाणानरिजलजभुजां फुल्लपद्मायताक्षीं
चामुंडासृङ्नृमुंडीं रिपु-कुल-मथनां शाकिनीं[2] भावयामि ॥
[3]लक्ष्मीं मायां समुच्चार्य वर्जितापकरं ततः ।
रक्तचामुंडीश्वरीति शत्रु जीवविनाशिनी ॥४॥
एह्येहि च ततः शीघ्रमिष्टानाकर्षयाथ तु ।
आकर्षय ततः स्वाहा चतुस्त्रिंशल्लिपिः क्रमात् ॥५॥
वृत्तं च सप्तच्छदमष्टपत्रं ततः पदं सप्तदशास्रकं च
मध्ये द्विबीजं क्रमशस्तु मंत्रं दलेषु साध्यं परतो द्विबीजम् ॥६॥
एतत्तु रक्तचामुंडी-यंत्रमाकर्ष-मोहयोः ।
महावीर्यमयत्नारि-जय-वश्य-करं परम् ॥७॥
आकर्षं सर्वजंतूनां वनितानां विशेषतः ।
चतुस्त्रिंशत्सहस्रेण मंत्रसिद्धिर्जपेन्मनुम् ॥८॥

---

१. श्रीं

२. शांकरीं

३. मंत्रोद्धार :—श्रीं ह्रीं कट् रक्तचामुण्डीश्वरी शत्रुजीवविनाशिनी एह्येहि शीघ्रं इष्टानाकर्षयाकर्षय स्वाहा ।

तर्पणं च तथा कुर्यादंते भौमदिनेऽम्बिके ।
मध्याह्ने च बलिं दत्वा मातृ-कोष्ठे तु साधकः ॥९॥
तद्वारिवस्त्रसूत्राग्र-पलालात्यग्रमध्यतः ।
बंधनेन तु मंत्रेणाबध्द्वान्यस्योपरि स्थले ॥१०॥
निराहारान् द्विजान्वृत्वा संपूज्य च चतुष्टयान् ।
तस्मिन्कोष्ठे स्पृशन्हेतुं निशां वा संगवात्परम् ॥११॥
सहस्रं प्रजपेद्देवि दृढचित्तो निर्मीलितः ।
ततो देवी समागत्य हठात्कारासिताथ मम ॥१२॥
आहूयसे भवानत्र किमर्थं वद सत्वरम् ।
इति ब्रूयात्ततो मंत्री निर्भयस्तिष्ठ तिष्ठ सः ॥१३॥
त्वयि कार्यं ममास्तीहेत्युक्त्वा गृह्णेति तत्वतः ।
दद्यात्स शकलं हेतुं सा चांगीकृत्य तं प्रति ॥१४॥
तुष्टाहं तु किमिष्टं ते वद सत्यं ददामि तत् ।
इति वक्ष्ये ततो मंत्री गुरुसान्निध्यमन्वहम् ॥१५॥
समादानानुदानं च मोहाकर्षवशानि मे ।
श्रुत्वा देवी ततः सर्वं तथैवाहं करोमि च ॥१६॥
देहि मे च बलिं हेतुं प्रति संततिमित्यथो
तथा भवतु चामुंडी सततं त्वं प्रसीद मे ॥१७॥
इति दृष्ट्वा ततो देवी दत्वा वरं करांबुजम् ।
अंगुलीयं च गृह्णीयात्तस्यहस्ताब्जसंस्थितम् ।
ततः स्वेच्छाक्रियां कुर्यान्नित्यालंकृतविग्रहः ॥१८॥

इति श्रीआकाशभैरवकल्पे प्रत्यक्षसिद्धिप्रदे उमामहेश्वरसम्वादे चामुण्डी-विधिर्नाम त्रिचत्वारिंशोऽध्यायः ॥४३॥

चतुश्चत्वारिंशोऽध्यायः

श्रीशिव उवाच ।।

मंत्रस्य मोहिनी देव्या ऋषिरीशान उच्यते
छंदस्तु जगती-देवी मोहिनी देवतांबिके ।।१।।
ऐं बीजं ह्लीमथोशक्तिर्मदनं कीलकं ततः
विनियोगस्तु लोकानां चित्तसंमोहने तथा ।।२।।
ऐंकारसहितैर्मायाभेदवर्णैः षडंगकम् ।

ध्यानम्

भुवन-विजयदक्षा पुष्प-बाणेक्षु-चापा,
जगति विविधरूपान् दर्शयंती जनानाम्,
तरुणतरणिशोभाश्वेतवासो वसाना,
जयति निखिललोकाञ्जीविनी मोहिनीयम् ।।३।।
[1]बीजं-शक्ति समुच्चार्य कीलकं-हृत्ततः परम् ।
श्रों नमो भगवति महामोहिन्यतः परम् ।।४।।
महामाये ततः पश्चात्सर्वलोक वशंकरि ।
देवदत्तस्य वाक्-चक्षुश्चित्तं मोहय मोहय ।।५।।
नानारूपाकृतिं शीघ्रं पश्चाद्दर्शय दर्शय ।
ह्रीं स्वाहेति महामंत्रं पंचाशद्वर्ण रूपकम् (षष्टि वर्णात्मकं परम्) ।।६।।
प्रजपेत्पंचसाहस्रं सिद्धये तर्पणं तथा ।
पंचकोणे लिखित्वा तन्मध्यबीजेन वेष्टयेत् ।।७।।
पंचकोणे लिखेच्छक्ति बाह्ये साध्यं समन्मथम् ।
देवदत्ते मुखे यंत्रं दर्शयन्प्रजपेन्मनुम् ।।८।।
जंगमाजंगमानां च देवभूतादिरक्षसाम् ।
पुरतो विविधं रूपं दर्शनं विस्मयं भवेत् ।।९।।
कौतूहलं महामंत्रं स्वेच्छादर्शनसिद्धिदम् ।
सर्वसंमोहनं श्रेष्ठं साध्यभेदैरदर्शनम् ।।१०।।
सर्वलोक-वशीकारं सर्व-विद्वेष-कारणम् ।
सर्वशत्रुजयं दिव्यं सर्वाकर्षण-सिद्धिदम् ।।११।।
सहस्रं प्रजपेन्नित्यं योऽम्बिके सावधानतः ।
सर्वलोक-जयं तस्य लभते नात्र संशयः ।।१२।।

इति श्रीआकाशभैरवकल्पे प्रत्यक्षसिद्धिप्रदे उमामहेश्वरसम्वादे मोहिनीविधिर्नाम चतुश्चत्वारिंशोऽध्यायः ।।४४।।

---

१. मंत्रोद्धार :—ऐं ह्रीं क्लीं श्रों नमो भगवति महामोहिनि महामाये सर्वलोक वशंकरि देवदत्तस्य वाक् चक्षुश्चित्तं मोहय२ नानारूपाकृतीः शीघ्रं दर्शय२ ह्रीं स्वाहा ।

पंचचत्वारिंशोऽध्यायः

अथ द्राविणीप्रयोगः

श्रीशिव उवाच ।।

मंत्रस्य द्राविणीदेव्या वरुणो ऋषिरुच्यते ।
बृहती छंद इत्युक्तो द्राविणी देवता ततः ।।१।।
द्रांकारं बीजमित्युक्तं स्वाहा शक्तिरतः परम् ।
स्वेच्छा-द्रावक-सिद्ध्यर्थे विनियोगो वरानने ।।२।।
द्रामित्यादि षडंगं स्यात्करन्यासपुरःसरम् ।

ध्यानम्

चंद्रार्धचूडां शतपत्रनेत्रां शरासपुष्पेषुकरां नराणाम् ।
वृगास्य-चित्त-श्रवणांडलक्ष्म्यां श्रीद्राविणीं नौमि सुधार्द्र-वाणीम् ।।३।।

[1]भ्रीं ठं प्रथममुच्चार्यं द्रां नमो भगवत्यथ ।
जगन्मोहिनि तत्पश्चात्सोमेश्वरि ततः परम् ।।४।।
सर्वलोकाक्षि-हृच्छ्रोत्रं द्रावय द्वितयं द्वि ठः ।
प्रोक्तोर्णानां चतुस्त्रिंशद् द्राविणीमंत्रमव्ययम् ।।५।।
जपेदक्षरसाहस्त्रं तर्पणाहुति भोजनात् ।
तद्दशांश-क्रमेणैव कुर्यात्सर्वंसमर्पकम् ।।६।।
शिखि-ऋतु-मणि-कोणं षोडशारं क्रमेण
प्रतिगृहमथ मंत्रं वर्णमेकं लिखित्वा ।
बहिरपि व्रतसाध्यं कामराजं च चंद्रं
सकल-मनुज-चित्त-द्रावकं यंत्रमेतत् ।।७।।
वदने हृदये गुह्ये दर्शयित्वाऽथ यंत्रकम् ।
त्रिवारं प्रजपेन्मंत्रं द्रावकस्य वरानने ।।८।।
नराश्च विविधा योगा महामोहवशाः वशाः ।
स्वयमेव सदा देवी क्षिप्रं तद्वशमाप्नुयात् ।।९।।

इति श्रीआकाशभैरवकल्पे प्रत्यक्षसिद्धिप्रदे उमामहेश्वरसम्वादे द्राविणी-प्रयोग-विधिर्नामपंचचत्वारिंशोऽध्यायः ।।४५।।

---

१. मंत्रोद्धार :—भ्रीं ठं द्रां नमो भगवति जगन्मोहिनि सोमेश्वरि सर्व लोकाक्षि-हृच्छ्रोत्रं द्रावय द्रावय स्वाहा ।

षट्चत्वारिंशोऽध्यायः

अथ शब्दार्काषिणी प्रयोगः

श्रीशिव उवाच ॥

शब्दाकर्षणिकायास्तु बल-प्रमथनो ऋषिः ।
जगती छंद इत्युक्तं देवता सैव सुंदरी ॥१॥
पंकारं बीजमित्युक्तं स्वाहाशक्तिरतः परम् ।
शब्दाकर्षणसिद्ध्यर्थे विनियोगस्ततोऽम्बिके ॥२॥
पामित्यादि षडंगं स्यात्करन्यासं कृशानुना ।
पाशांकुश-धनुर्बाणपाणिमेणांक-संनिभाम् ॥३॥
चंडवातादिगमनां शब्दाकर्षण-तत्पराम् ।
महामायां विशेषज्ञां मंद-स्मित-मुखांबुजाम् ॥४॥
भक्तेष्टदाननिरतां प्रणमामि जगन्मयीम् ।
[1]पामों नमो भगवति शब्दार्काषिणि चेश्वरि ॥५॥
अभीष्ट-वरदे सर्वलोकमोहिन्यनंतरम् ।
ततः पश्चात्सर्वमये शब्दानाकर्षयाथ तु ॥६॥
स्वाहेति मंत्ररूपं तु चत्वारिंशन्महार्णकम् ।
आलिख्य नव-षट्-तिर्यगूर्ध्वमंत्रं यथाक्रमम् ॥७॥
बाह्ये तु साध्यमालिख्य रेखाग्रेषु रं तथा ।
मायावृतं महायंत्रं शब्दाकर्षणमद्भुतम् ॥८॥
चत्वारिंशतसहस्रं तु साधकः सिद्धये जपेत् ।
पश्चाद्यंत्रं भुवो लिख्य शतवारं जपेन्मनुम् ॥९॥
अतीतानागता स्वस्था स्वस्थानि श्रुतितोऽम्बिके ।
यमुद्दिश्य जपेद्देवं तद्वाक्य-श्रवणं भवेत् ॥१०॥
यः पूज्यानुदिनं मंत्री शतवारं जपेन्मनुम् ।
इति गुह्यं महामंत्रं सर्वज्ञानप्रदं परम् ॥११॥
सर्वदा सर्वकार्येषु जपेन्मंत्री वरानने ॥१२॥

इति श्रीआकाशभैरवकल्पे प्रत्यक्षसिद्धिप्रदे उमामहेश्वरसम्वादे शब्दार्काषिणीप्रयोगोनाम षट्चत्वारिंशोऽध्यायः ॥४६॥

---

१. मंत्रोद्धार :—पामों नमो भगवति शब्दार्काषिणि देवि अभीष्ट वरदे सर्वलोक मोहिनि सर्वमये शब्दानाकर्षय स्वाहा ।

सप्तचत्वारिंशोऽध्यायः

अथ भाषाप्रयोगः

श्रीशिव उवाच ॥

वदामि शृणु ते गुह्यं भाषामंत्रमनुत्तमम् ।
यस्य स्मरणमात्रेण सुप्रसन्ना सरस्वती ॥१॥

ऋषिर्मंत्रस्य भारत्या ब्रह्मा गायत्रमुच्यते ।
छंदो देवी महावाणी देवता यां तमद्भुतम् ॥२॥
बीजं शक्तिस्तथा स्वाहा विनियोगो विशेषतः ।
सर्वशब्दार्थविज्ञानसिध्य·सारस्वताप्तये ।
समित्यादि करन्यासमंगन्यास-विधानतः ॥३॥

ध्यानम्

नव-नलिन-निरूढा वल्लभा पद्मजस्य
द्युतिविहसित-चंद्रोद्दाम-कांतिप्रसन्ना ।
विहरतु मम चित्ते सर्वबोधप्रदात्री
वितरतु सुकवित्वं सर्वलोके प्रसिद्धम् ॥४॥

ओं सं प्रथममुच्चार्य ततः पश्चात्सरस्वति ।
वह्निजाया युतं मंत्रं सर्वसिद्धिप्रदायकम्[1] ॥५॥

सिद्धये सप्त सहस्रं जपं कुर्याद्विचक्षणः ।
तद्दशांशक्रमेणैव तर्पणाहुतिभोजनात् ॥६॥

बिन्दौ बीजं षडस्रे मनुमथ परितो मातृका-वर्णजालं
कृत्वा यंत्रं हिरण्ये सकल-विधियुतं भारतीं सम्यगिष्ट्वा ।
बिन्दौ पद्मादि देवी ऋतु-दल-विवरे सावधानः स्वनाथं
ध्यायन् शीतांशुपीठे जपतु नरवरः सर्वसिद्ध्यै समृद्ध्यै ॥७॥

पश्चादपि शतं नित्यं यो जपेत्स तु भूतले ।
कविताचक्रवर्ती स्यात्तस्य साम्यं न विद्यते ॥८॥
सभासंवेशने काले प्रतिवादिसमाकुले ।
मनसा संजपेन्मंत्री विजयाय गुरुं स्मरन् ॥९॥

इति श्रीआकाशभैरवकल्पे प्रत्यक्षसिद्धिप्रदे उमामहेश्वरसम्वादे भाषा-सरस्वती-प्रयोगो नाम सप्तचत्वारिंशोऽध्यायः ॥४७॥

---

१. ओं सं सरस्वति स्वाहा ।

अष्टचत्वारिंशोऽध्यायः

अथ लक्ष्मीप्रयोगः

श्रीशिव उवाच ॥

लक्ष्मीमंत्रं प्रवक्ष्यामि सर्व-सौभाग्य-वर्धनम् ।
आयुष्करं महावश्यममोघ-जयवर्धनम् ॥१॥
लक्ष्मी-मंत्रस्य वामेशो ऋषिः छंदस्तु बार्हती ।
महालक्ष्म्याः प्रसादस्य सिद्ध्यै सर्वसमृद्धये ॥२॥
सर्वलोक-वशीकारे विनियोगस्तथाम्बिके ।
लक्ष्मीबीजस्य भेदेन करांगन्यासमाचरेत् ॥३॥

ध्यानम्—

या सा पद्मासनस्था विपुल-कटि तटी पद्मपत्रायताक्षी
गंभीरावर्त-नाभि-स्तनभर-नमित शुभ्रवस्त्रोत्तरीया ।
लक्ष्मीर्दिव्यैर्गजेन्द्रैर्मणिगण-खचितैः स्नापिता हेमकुंभै-
र्नित्यं सा पद्महस्ता मम वसतु गृहे सर्वमांगल्ययुक्ता ॥४॥
[1]प्रणवं च रमां मारं महालक्ष्मी-पद-द्वयम् ।
एह्येहि सर्व-सौभाग्यं देहि मे तु ततः परम् ॥५॥
स्वाहेति मंत्ररूपं च चतुर्विंशति वर्णकम् ।
चतुर्विंशति-साहस्रं जपेत्सर्व-समृद्धये ॥६॥
दशांशं क्रमशः कुर्यादंगत्रयमतः परम् ।
त्रिकोणे तु त्रिबीजं स्याद्वसुकोणे परं लिखेत् ॥७॥
त्रयोदशदले शेषं बाह्ये पंचाशदर्णकम् ।
लक्ष्मी बीजावृतं यंत्रं सर्वसौभाग्यदायकम् ॥८॥
सर्व-संपत्समृद्धि च सर्वलोकवशंकरम् ।
यो जपेदन्वहं प्रातरष्टोत्तरशतं सुधीः ।
तस्य सर्वसमृद्धिः स्यात्संशयो नास्ति सुन्दरी ॥९॥

इति श्रीआकाशभैरवकल्पे प्रत्यक्षसिद्धिप्रदे उमामहेश्वरसम्वादे महालक्ष्मी-प्रयोगो नामाष्टचत्वारिंशोऽध्यायः ॥४८॥

---

१. ओं श्रीं क्लीं महालक्ष्मी महालक्ष्मी एह्येहि सर्वसौभाग्यं देहि मे स्वाहा ॥

एकोनपंचाशोऽध्यायः

अथ मायाप्रयोगः

श्रीशिव उवाच ॥

ऋषिस्तु मायामंत्रस्य भगवान्मंकणः स्मृतः ।
उष्णिक् छंदस्ततो देवो महामाया तु देवता ॥१॥
मायाबीजं च मायैव शक्तिः स्यात्तदनंतरम् ।
सर्वाकर्षणसिद्ध्यर्थे विनियोगोऽथ पार्वति ।
माययैव षडंगं स्याद्ध्यान-मेव इहोच्यते ॥२॥

माया पुटेन जगतां विवशं च मोहम्
माया कुतूहल-मनोरथमाकरोति ।
नारायणप्रियतमा सुतमालनीला
शूलायुधा विजयते तुरगाधिरूढा ॥३॥

'ह्रीं कारं च महामाये जगन्मोहिनि तत्परम् ।
ततः परं सर्वजन-वाङ्-मनः-काय-चक्षुः च ॥४॥
श्रोत्र-घ्राण पदं पश्चात्प्राणान्मोहय मोहय ।
स्वेच्छा-कुतूहलं शीघ्रं दर्शयेति द्वयं ततः ॥५॥
ह्रींकारं स्वाहया युक्तं मंत्रः पंचाशदक्षरः ।
श्री पंचाशतसहस्रं तु सिद्ध्यै मंत्रं जपेद् बुधः ॥६॥
कुर्यात्तर्पण-होमे च ब्राह्मणाराधनं ततः ।
ततः स्वेच्छाक्रियां कुर्यान्माया चास्य क्रियादिषु ॥७॥
दर्शनादर्शनं चैव तथादर्शन-दर्शनम् ।
मंत्र-स्मरण-मात्रेण भवेद्देवि न संशयः ॥८॥

इति श्रीआकाशभैरवकल्पे प्रत्यक्षसिद्धिप्रदे उमामहेश्वरसम्वादे मायाविधिर्नाम एकोनपंचाशोऽध्यायः ॥४९॥

मंत्रोद्धारः—ह्रीं महामाये जगन्मोहिनी सर्व-जन-वाङ्-मनः-काय-चक्षुः-श्रोत्र-घ्राण-प्राणान्मोहय मोहय स्वेच्छा-कुतूहलं शीघ्रं दर्शय दर्शय ह्रीं स्वाहा ।

पंचाशोऽध्यायः

अथ पुलिंदिनी प्रयोगः

श्रीशिव उवाच ॥

पुलिंदिन्याश्च मंत्रस्य शंकरो ऋषिरीरितः ।
छंदस्तु जगती देवी देवता सा पुलिंदिनी ॥१॥
ईङ्कारं बीजमित्युक्तं स्वाहा शक्तिरनंतरम् ।
पुलिंदिन्याः प्रसादस्य सिद्ध्यर्थे विनियोगकम् ॥२॥
आमित्यादि करं न्यासं षडंगं तदनंतरम् ।

वर्हापीड कचाभिरामचिकुरां बिंबोज्ज्वलच्चंद्रिकाम्
गुंजाहार-लतांशु-जालविलसद् ग्रीवामधीरेक्षणाम् ।
माकंद-द्रुमपल्लवारुणपटां मंदेन्दु-बिंबाननाम्
देवीं सर्वमयीं प्रसन्नहृदयां ध्यायेत्किरातामृताम् ॥३॥

[1]ईं ओं नमो भगवति श्री बीजमथ मंडि च ।
शारदादेवि तत्पश्चात्त्यक्त-कौतूल-भोज्यकम्[2] ॥४॥
देहि देहि ततस्त्वेहि त्वागच्छागच्छ तत्परः ।
आगंतुकं हृदयस्थं कार्यं सत्यमनंतरम् ॥५॥
ब्रूहि सत्यं ततो ब्रूहि ततः पश्चात्पुलिंदिनीम् ।
ईं स्वाहेति महामंत्रं पंचाशद्वर्ण-मिश्रितम् ॥६॥
पंचाशच्छतमात्रं तु जपेन्मंत्रस्य सिद्धये ।
शिष्टांगं पूर्ववत्कुर्याद्विधिपूर्वं दृढव्रतः ॥७॥
कार्याकार्य-विवेकार्थं रात्रावष्टोत्तरं शतम् ।
जप्त्वा शयीत यस्तस्य स्वप्ने वदति सांबिके ॥८॥
साधकस्तद्वचः श्रुत्वा तथैवान्वहमाचरेत् ।
तस्य नास्ति भयं क्वापि सर्वकालं सुखी भवेत् ॥९॥

इति श्रीआकाशभैरवकल्पे प्रत्यक्षसिद्धिप्रदे उमामहेश्वरसम्वादे पुलिंदिनी-विधिर्नाम पंचाशोऽध्यायः ॥५०॥

---

१. मंत्रोद्धार :—ईं ओं नमो भगवति श्रीं ह्रीं शारदा देवि क्रीं (अनन्तातुल भोज्यं) देहि देहि एह्यागच्छागच्छागन्तुकं हृदयस्थं कार्यं सत्यं ब्रूहि सत्यं ब्रूहि पुलिन्दिनि ईं स्वाहा ।

२. त्यक्त-कौन्तुला बीजकम् । (वा पाठः)

एकपंचाशोऽध्यायः

श्रीशिव उवाच ।।

शृणु गुह्यं महामंत्रं महाशास्तुर्वदाम्यहम् ।
भोग-मोक्ष-प्रदं दिव्यं पुत्रसंपत्प्रदं परम् ।।१।।

अष्ट-कर्म-क्रियादक्षममोघं पुण्यवर्धनम् ।
आयुरारोग्यदं सौम्यमपमृत्युभयापहम् ।।२।।
ऋषिरस्यार्धनारीशः छंदोऽनुष्टुप् ततः परम् ।
देवता तु महाशास्ता देवो हरिहरात्मजः ।।३।।
मायावर्णं तु बीजं स्यान्नमः शक्तिरतः परम् ।
मम सर्वार्थ-सिद्ध्यर्थे विनियोगो वरानने ।।४।।
मूलेन तु करन्यासं षडंगं पदशः क्रमात् ।
आश्याम कोमल विशाल तनुं विचित्र
वासोवसानमरुणोत्पलदानहस्तम् ।
उत्तुंगरत्नमुकुटं कुटिलालकेशम्
शास्तारमिष्टवरदं शरणं प्रपद्ये ।।५।।
शांतं शारद-चंद्र-कांति-धवलं चंद्राभिरामाननम्
चंद्रार्कोपल-कांति-कुंडलधरं चंद्राभिरामाननम् ।
वीणा-पुस्तकमक्ष-सूत्रवलय-व्याख्यानमुद्राः करै-
र्बिभ्राणं कलये सदा हृदि महाशास्तं हि वाक्सिद्धये ।।६।।
तेजो मंडलमध्यगं त्रिनयनं दिव्यांबरालंकृतम्
देवं पुष्प-शरेक्षु-कार्मुक-लसन्माणिक्यपात्राभयान् ।
बिभ्राणं करपंकजैर्मदगज-स्कंधाधिरुढं महा-
शास्तारं सततं भजामि वरदं त्रैलोक्यसंमोहनम् ।।७।।
कल्हारोज्ज्वल नीलकुण्डलधरं कालांबुद-श्यामलम्
कर्पूराकलिताभिरामतिलकं कांतेन्दु-बिंबाननम् ।
श्रीवंडांकुश-पाश-शूलविलसत्पाणिं मदोद्धद्-द्विपा-
रुढं शत्रुविमर्दनं हृदि महाशास्तेशमाद्यं भजे ।।८।।

जंबूमूलतले सुमेरुशिखरे माणिक्यसिंहासने
रुढं विश्वविमोहनं निरुपमं बंधूकपुष्पारुणम् ।
बाणेष्वास-गदासि-पाश फणिदाभीतीः-करांभोरुहै-
र्बिभ्राणं नततापहं हृदि महाशास्तारमाद्यं भजे ।।९।।

नौमि वक्रमधिष्ठित-कुंडलं, श्याममुत्पलदक्षकरांबुजम् ।
योगपट्टित-पद्मसुखासनं, वाम दक्षिण-पुष्कल-पूर्णयोः ।।१०।।

पुष्करं शुचिसंयुक्तं चतुर्थस्वरभूषितम् ।
सबिंदुं पूर्वमुद्धृत्य हरि हरेति तत्परम् ।।११।।

पुत्राय पुत्रलाभाय शत्रुनाशाय तत्परम् ।
मदाथ गज तत्पश्चाद्वाहनाय ततः परम् ।।१२।।

महाशास्ताय तत्पश्चान्नमोऽन्त मंत्रमुत्तमम् ।
एतदेव परं गुह्यं त्रयस्त्रिंशन्महार्णकम् ।।१३।।

त्रयस्त्रिंशत्सहस्रं तु चतुरंगयुतं जपेत् ।
बीजं विना त्रिंशदर्णान् परं साध्यं नियोजयेत् ।।१४।।

सपल्लवं सहस्रं तु जपेत्तत्काम्यसिद्धये ।

षट्कोण-मिश्र-रि पुटं परितो द्विवृत्तम्
कर्णे च मन्मथमथांसयुगे मुखे माम् ।
कक्षद्वये च पवनं हृदयेऽजमायाम्
नाभौ च तारमनुतारमथो द्विकुक्षौ ।।१५।।

कट्योश्च पार्श्वयुगले मणिबीजवर्णं
गुह्येऽमृतं हरिहरेति युगं द्विकोणे ।
साध्यं द्विबिंदुयुगले मनुमंतराले
हंसेति पार्श्वयुगले विवृतद्विवृत्ते ।।१६।।

ऊर्ध्वाध-सादिश-सहादितमंतराले
चत्वार वह्नि भवने कमलां च मायाम् ।
पंचाशदर्ण सहितं परमं च शास्तु-
र्यंत्रं समस्त सुखदं वश-मोक्ष दक्षम् ।।१७।।

एतद्यंत्रं महावीर्यं पुरुषार्थप्रदायकम् ।
करस्थाः सिद्धयः सर्वाः सर्वलोकः युगे युगे ।।१८।।

कुंकुमारोचनाभ्यां तु लिखित्वाग्रपटोऽग्रतः ।
कृत्वा भर्तुर्गृहं गच्छेत्स्मित-भाषण-पूर्वकम् ।।१९।।

क्रुद्धोऽपि वान्यसक्तोऽपि विरक्तोऽपि सनाथकः ।
तस्यास्तु दर्शनात्कामपीडितो मोहितो वशः ॥२०॥
तद्वशं समुदं याति चूतपुष्पमलिर्यथा ।
राजसेनारिनारीणां वश्यं कनकपत्रिके ॥२१॥
भूत-प्रेत-पिशाचानां जंतूनामुरगादिनाम् ।
सिंहादीनां मृगाणां च ग्राहादि-जलजन्मनाम् ॥२२॥
कार्ष्णायसे-पत्रके यंत्रमालिख्य निवहेद् बुधः ।
संपद्यं च समृद्धि च प्रसादेऽनुग्रहे परे ॥२३॥
तन्मे कुरु कुरु स्वाहेत्यखिलं प्रजपेद् बुधः ॥२४॥

(इति प्रथम खण्डः)

पूजाविधि

अथ पूजाविधि वक्ष्ये साधकानां हिताय वै ।
बिंबे वा यंत्रमध्ये वा महाशास्तं प्रपूजयेत् ॥१॥
पादप्रक्षालनं कृत्वा देवपूजागृहं विशेत् ।
तत्र प्राङ्मुख आसीनः प्राणानायम्य मूलतः ॥२॥
आसनं कल्पयित्वा तु गुरु-वंदनपूर्वकम् ।
दिग्देवतानमस्कृत्य भूतशुद्धि समाचरेत् ॥३॥
भक्त्या च मातृकान्यासं प्राण-न्यास-समन्वितः ।
पश्चान्मंत्रऋषिन्यास छंदसा न्यासमाचरेत् ॥४॥
पादं न्यासं षडंगं च पंचांगं वा सुविन्यसेत् ।
ध्यानयोगोपयुक्तः सन् मुद्रां चैव प्रदर्शयेत् ॥५॥
आत्मानं देवतारूपं ध्यात्वा देविस्वरूपिणी ।
अष्टोत्तरसहस्रं तु शतमष्टोत्तरं तु वा ॥६॥
अष्टाविंशतिकं वापि यथाशक्ति जपेत्सुधीः ।
पात्रशुद्धि ततः कुर्याद् द्रव्यसंस्कार-पूर्वकम् ॥७॥
बीजासनं समभ्यर्च्य आसने तान्समर्चयेत् ।
आधारादिपृथिव्यंतमासने तान्समर्चयेत् ॥८॥
भानुबिंबात्समाहूय मूलेनावाहयेच्छिवे ।
सांगावरणमभ्यचर्य देवं संपूजयेद् बुधः ॥९॥
योगारूढमथो वापि गजारूढमथोऽपि वा ।
भावयेन्मनसा नित्यं ध्यानगम्यं परात्परम् ॥१०॥

साक्षिणं सर्वलोकानामंतर्यामिनमव्ययम् ।
देवस्य दक्षिणे पार्श्वे पुष्कलं च समर्चयेत् ॥११॥
वामे पूर्णार्चनं कृत्वा गजाननमथार्चयेत् ।
सिंहार्चनं प्रकुर्वीत हयार्चन शुनार्चनम् ॥१२॥
गुरुं गणपतिं दुर्गां स्कंदं भैरवमर्चयेत् ।
ऋषिश्छंदस्तथा भानुमर्चयेद्वह्नि-कोणके ॥१३॥
पश्चादावरणे देवमभीष्ट-परिवारकम् ।
षडंग-देवताद्याश्च गंध-पुष्पाक्षतादिभिः ॥१४॥
षट्कोणे देवताषट्कं हृदयादीन्समर्चयेत् ।
महाशास्ता जगच्छास्ता शत्रुशास्तारमेव च ॥१५॥
अग्निशास्ता बालशास्ता प्रशास्ता च क्रमादमून् ।
अष्टकोणे महादेवि भैरवाष्टकमर्चयेत् ॥१६॥
असितांगो रुरुश्चंडः क्रोध उन्मत्तभैरवः ।
कपाली भीषणश्चैव संहारश्चाष्टमः क्रमात् ॥१७॥
पश्चाद् ब्राह्म्याद्यष्टशक्तीः कोणाग्रेषु समर्चयेत् ।
दलेष्वष्टसु देवेशि गायत्रीं च समर्चयेत् ॥१८॥
भूताधिपाय विद्महे हरिहरपुत्राय धीमहि ।
तन्नः शास्ता प्रचोदयात् ॥१९॥
गायत्र्येषा समुद्दिष्टा महाशास्तृ-स्वरूपिणी ।
महादिक्षु दलाग्रेषु भूतादीन्क्रमशोऽर्चयेत् ॥२०॥
भूत-प्रेत-पिशाचानां-गणानां च समर्चयेत् ।
यक्ष-राक्षस-वेताल-सिद्धानां च समर्चयेत् ॥२१॥
षोडशारे पुनर्देवि शक्तिषोडशमर्चयेत् ।
दुर्गा च भैरवी देवी त्वरिता भुवनेश्वरी ॥२२॥
नारायणी भद्रकाली रुद्राणी चंडिकान्विता ।
वाराही सिद्धलक्ष्मीश्च मातंगी च मनोन्मनी ॥२३॥
कालरात्रिर्महामाया महिषासुरमर्दिनी ।
निशाचरी च नामानि नित्या षोडश-शक्तयः ॥२४॥

लोकपालान्पुनर्देवि ह्यष्टदिक्षु समर्चयेत् ।
देवताग्रे महापीठे कल्पयित्वा जलं बुधः ।।२५।।
अग्रपीठ-स्थित-सिद्ध-विद्याधर सकिन्नराः ।
किम्पुरुषाः सर्वसंपन्नः पीठोपरि समर्चयेत् ।।२६।।
लोकपाल-समौ द्वारपालौ सम्यक् समर्चयेत् ।
सर्वं श्रीमायया युक्तं नाममंत्रं समर्चने ।।२७।।
हरिशंम्वोः सुपुत्रस्य पूजैषा भुवि दुर्लभा ।
सर्वोपचारान्मूलेन कल्पयेन्मंत्रनायिके ।।२८।।
जपं पश्चात्प्रकुर्वीत ध्यानयोग-परायणः ।
प्रदक्षिणं परिक्रम्य देवं सम्यक् प्रणम्य च ।।२९।।
देवस्य चरणौ सम्यक् पूजयेद्भक्ति-पूर्वकम् ।
कामरूपधरः स स्यादणिमादिफलप्रदः ।।३०।।
वेद शास्त्रेषु भरत शास्त्रार्थेषु विचक्षणः ।
सर्वज्ञः सर्वसंपन्नः सर्वदेवैरभिष्टुतः ।।३१।।
विचरंति महात्मानो महाशास्तृ-प्रसादतः ।
महाशास्तृपदासक्तः सर्वदा प्रीतिमानसः ।।३२।।
भक्तोपकारकाः सर्वे परमानन्द-विग्रहाः ।
सर्वान्कामानवाप्येह यथेष्टं फलमाप्नुयात् ।।३३।।
इहलोके महाशास्ता सर्वशास्त्राणि साध्येत् ।
पुत्र पौत्रवरैश्चान्यैर्मोहनं भुवि मोदते ।।३४।।
(इति द्वितीय खण्डः)

अथ पूजा-प्रकार उच्यते ।।

हस्ते पुस्तकमक्षसूत्रवलयं मुद्रां च सच्चिन्मयीं ।
बिभ्राणं कमल-प्रवाल-रुचिरैः स्वर्णोज्ज्वलां लेखिनीम् ।।
मुक्ताभा-मणि-भूषणैर्विलसितं व्याख्यान-पीठ-स्थितम् ।
व्यासाद्यैर्मुनिपुंगवैः परिवृतं शास्तारमंतर्भजे ।।१।।
महाशास्तर्गजारुढ-गणेशान सुरेश्वर ।
विश्वेश्वर सुरश्रेष्ठ लोकनाथ नमोऽस्तु ते ।।२।।
आवाहनं चासनं च पाद्यार्घ्याचमनं तथा ।
स्नानं वस्त्रं चोत्तरीयमुपवीतं सुगंधतः ।।३।।

ग्रक्षतं पुष्प धूपं च दीपं नैवेद्यमेव च ।
तांबूलं प्रदक्षिणं च नमस्कारं तथैव च ।।४।।

मंत्र-पुष्पं महादेवि क्रमादुपचरेद्विभुम् ।
महाशास्तर्गणाधीश ऋषीन्द्र-यमिनां-वर ।।
गृह्यतामासनं देव मया दत्तं सुरेश्वर ।।५।।

महाशास्ताय देवाय नित्याय निधनात्मने ।
समस्त-लोक-नाथाय नाथाय प्रभवे नमः ।।६।।

महाशास्ताय शांताय सर्वज्ञाय महात्मने ।
योगनिष्ठाय नित्याय नित्यशुद्धाय ते नमः ।।७।।

सर्वात्मन् सर्वदेवेश सर्वव्यापिन्महेश्वर ।
गृहाणाचमनं देव महाशास्त्र नमोऽस्तु ते ।।८।।

महाशास्ताय वीराय नित्याय निखिलात्मने ।
नरकासुरहंत्रे च श्रीशगर्भाय ते नमः ।।९।।

हरि-शंभु-हृदानंदकराय च महात्मने ।
महाराज-वसिष्ठाय महाशास्त्राय ते नमः ।।१०।।

दामोदरेश-पुत्राय नमस्ते भक्त-पालिने ।
शुभ्रवस्त्रोत्तरीये च गृहाण पुरुषोत्तमः ।।११।।

हरि-शंभु-हृदानंदकराय च महात्मने ।
महाराज-वसिष्ठाय महाशास्ताय ते नमः ।।१२।।

श्रीखंडं रोचनायुक्तं कुंकुमेन समन्वितम् ।
विलेपनं महाशास्तः प्रीत्यर्थं प्रतिगृह्यताम् ।।१३।।

ग्रनर्घ्यमक्षतं श्रेष्ठं धनारोग्य-विवर्धनम् ।
दास्यामि माधवेशान-सूनो प्रीत्यै तवोपरि ।।१४।।

कल्पवृक्ष-सुपुष्पाणि माल्यानि विविधानि च ।
मयार्पितानि पूजार्थं गृहाण सर्वनंदन ।।१५।।

चन्दनागुरु-कर्पूर-घृत-गुग्गुल-संयुतम् ।
वह्निना रचितं धूपं गृहाण सुरनायक ।।१६।।

ग्राज्याक्तं वर्ति-संयुक्तं वह्निना योजितं शुभम् ।
गृहाण दीपं देवेश श्रीश-गौरीपतेः सुत ।।१७।।

अन्नं चतुर्विधं ज्ञेयं रसैः षड्भिः समन्वितम् ।
मया निवेदितं तुभ्यं गृह्यतां दैत्यसूदन ॥१८॥
अपूपानि निवेद्यानि भक्ष्याणि विविधानि च ।
मयार्पितानि सर्वाणि गृह्यतां गजवाहन ॥१९॥
पूगीफल-समायुक्तं नाग-वल्लीदलैर्युतम् ।
कर्पूर-चूर्ण-संयुक्तं तांबूलं प्रतिगृह्यताम् ॥२०॥
हरिशंभु-स्तुतः पायादपायान्मां सदा पुनः ।
हरीशपुत्र विश्वेश जगदानंददायक ॥२१॥
विश्वरूपव्रतस्थाय कारुण्याय नमोऽस्तु ते ।
नमोऽस्तु सुप्रसन्नाय पुरुषाय महात्मने ॥२२॥
योगानंद-स्वरूपाय महाशास्ताय ते नमः ।
नमो हरीश-पुत्राय नमस्तेऽनंतसाक्षिणे ॥२३॥
आनंदरूपिणे तुभ्यं महाशास्त्रे नमो नमः ।
योगारुढाय नित्याय योगगम्याय योगिने ॥२४॥
योगाध्यक्षाय गूढाय महाशास्ताय ते नमः ।
उक्तोपचारैः संपूज्य देवेशं पुनरुद्वहेत् ॥२५॥

(इति तृतीय खण्डः)

इति श्रीआकाशभैरवकल्पे प्रत्यक्षसिद्धिप्रदे उमामहेश्वरसम्वादे महाशास्तृविधिर्नाम एकपंचाशोऽध्यायः ॥५१॥

मंत्रोद्धार :—प्रथम खण्ड—श्लोक ११-१३—पत्रांक १३३

ह्रीं हरिहर-पुत्राय पुत्र-लाभाय शत्रुनाशाय मद-गज-वाहनाय महाशास्ताय नमः ।

द्विपंचाशोऽध्यायः

संक्षोभिणीप्रयोगः

श्रीशिव उवाच ॥

संक्षोभिण्या महामंत्रं तव वक्ष्यामि पार्वति ।
मंत्रोच्चारणमात्रेण क्षुभ्यंत्यखिलजंतवः ॥१॥
संक्षोभिण्यास्तु मंत्रस्य अगस्त्यो भगवानृषि ।
पंक्तिश्छन्दस्तथा देवी सर्वसंक्षोभिणी शिवा ॥२॥
क्षंकारं बीजमित्युक्तं माया शक्तिरनंतरम् ।
सर्वसंक्षोभणार्थं तु विनियोगो वरानने ॥३॥
क्षामित्यादि षडंगं स्यात्करन्यासं तथा पुनः ।

ध्यानम् ॥

पर्वा पंचमुखारूढा परिघासि करांबुजा ॥४॥
सर्वारि-हृदय-क्षोभ-कारिणी पातु सर्वदा ।
[1]क्षामों नमो भगवति चापवादहरे परे ॥५॥
महाक्रूरेति तत्पश्चात्सर्वशत्रुविमर्दिनि ।
देवदत्तमनःक्षोभं कुरु कुर्वनलप्रियाम् ॥६॥
तदंते तु समुद्धृत्य जपेन्मंत्रं समाहितः ।
दृढव्रतोऽर्णसाहस्रं सांगं ब्राह्ममुहूर्तके ॥७॥
मंत्रावसानके वैरि-नाम-मिश्रित-पल्लवम् ।
सहस्रं प्रजपेन्मंत्रं भ्रष्टचित्तो भवेद्रिपुः ॥८॥
शताभिमंत्रितं भस्मं निखनेदष्टदिक्षु सः ।
भवनं परितो मंत्री रक्षणाय स्वकीयकम् ॥९॥
तस्कर-शत्रु-पीडा च जंतु-भूतादि-पीडनम् ।
स्वप्नकालेऽपि नैव स्याद्वरेण्यो नात्र संशयः ॥१०॥

इति श्रीआकाशभैरवकल्पे प्रत्यक्षसिद्धिप्रदे उमामहेश्वरसम्वादे संक्षोभिणी-विधिर्नाम द्विपंचाशोऽध्यायः ॥५२॥

---

१. मंत्रोद्धार :—क्षां श्रों नमो भगवति अपवाद-हरे परे महा-क्रूरे सर्वशत्रु-विमर्दिनी देवदत्तमनः क्षोभं कुरु कुरु स्वाहा ।

त्रिपंचाशोऽध्यायः

अथ धूमावतीप्रयोगः

श्रीशिव उवाच ॥

धूमावत्या महादेव्या नारसिंहो ऋषिः स्मृतः ।
पंक्तिश्छंदस्तथा देवी ज्येष्ठादेवी तु देवता ॥१॥
धूंबीजं तु ततः स्वाहा शक्तिर्योगस्तु निग्रहे ।
धामित्यादि करन्यासं षडंगं च तथाऽम्बिके ॥२॥
ध्यायेत्कालाभ्रनीलां विलिखित-वदनां काकनासां विकर्णीं
संमार्जन्युल्क-शूर्पैर्युत-मुसलकरां वक्रदंताविषास्याम् ॥
ज्येष्ठां निर्वाणवेषां भ्रुकुटितनयनां मुक्तकेशामुदाराम्
शुष्कोत्तुङ्गातितिर्यक्-स्तनभरयुगलां निष्कृपां शत्रुहंत्रीम् ॥३॥
[1]प्रथमं धूं समुच्चार्य पश्चाद् धूमावती तथा ।
स्वाहेति मंत्ररूपं तु सप्ताक्षरमनुत्तमम् ॥४॥
जपेत्सप्तसहस्रं तु सांगं धूमरमाहुतीः ।
ऋतुकोणस्थ वृत्तांतर्बीजं कोणे मनुं लिखेत् ॥५॥
कोणत्रिशूलके साध्यं ज्येष्ठायंत्रमिहोच्यते ।
संपूज्य विधिवद्यंत्रं जपित्वा तु सहस्रकम् ॥६॥
शमशाने तु निशामध्ये निखनेद्बलिपूर्वकम् ।
रिपुगेहेऽथवा कुर्यात् खननं बलिवर्जितम् ॥७॥
भूयो जपेत्त्रिरात्रं तु तत्कार्यो रिपुदिङ्मुखः ।
स्तंभनोच्चाटने चैव निग्रहे चित्तविभ्रमे ॥८॥
संपत्क्षये च विद्वेषे प्रकुर्यात्सावधानतः ।
कवचं शरभेशस्य स्वांगे विन्यस्य तत्वतः ॥९॥
पश्चाज्जपेदिमां ज्येष्ठामतिक्रूरां दृढव्रतः ।
धूमावत्याश्च मंत्रं तु यो जपेत्कवचं विना ॥१०॥
स्वयं क्रुध्यति सा ज्येष्ठा तस्य भाग्यक्षयंकरी ।
अनात्माऽभिमुखं ध्यात्वा गच्छंतीं वैरिणां प्रति ॥११॥

---

१. मंत्रोद्धार :—धूं धूमावती स्वाहा ।

योो जपेन्निशि साहस्त्रं तस्य शत्रुर्विनश्यति ।
ताडयंतीं महावेगाच्छूर्पेण रिपुवक्षसि ।।१२।।
ध्यात्वा जपेत्सहस्त्रं तु भ्रष्टचित्तो भवेद्रिपुः ।
मार्जयंतीं क्षणाच्छत्रोर्धन-धान्यादिकं चिरम् ।।१३।।
ध्यात्वाष्टोत्तर-साहस्त्रं जपेद्भाग्यक्षयाय सः ।
दीप्यमानोल्मुकेनैव दहंतीं वाचि वैरिणाम् ।।
ध्यात्वा जपेत्तदा मंत्रं स्तंभनायांबिके बुधः ।।१४।।

इति श्रीआकाशभैरवकल्पे प्रत्यक्षसिद्धिप्रदे उमामहेश्वरसम्वादे धूमावती-विधिर्नाम त्रिपंचाशोऽध्यायः ।।५३।।

चतुःपंचाशोऽध्यायः

श्रीशिव उवाच

वक्ष्येऽहं शृणु ते यंत्रं धूमावत्या विशेषतः ।
विद्वेषे मारणे चैव क्रूरमत्याशुसिद्धिदम् ॥१॥
त्रिकोणं विलिखेत्पूर्वं तन्मध्ये बीजमालिखेत् ।
कोणाग्रे तु लिखेच्छूलं तच्छूलांतर्लिखेन्मनुम् ॥२॥
तदग्रे विलिखेत्साध्यं ज्येष्ठायंत्रं वरानने ।
संपूज्य विधिवद्यंत्रं निशामध्ये श्मशानके ॥३॥
बलिपूर्वं खनित्वा तु पुनः स्नात्वा जपेन्मनुम् ।
अष्टोत्तराष्ट-साहस्रं दृढचित्तोऽरिदिङ्मुखः ॥४॥
वैरिणस्तत्क्षणादेव यांति वैवस्वतं पुरम् ।
विद्वेषणे तथा देवि जपेदेकाग्रमानसः ॥५॥
अन्योन्य-कलहं क्षिप्रं शत्रूणां जायते ध्रुवम् ।
विलोमेन जपेनैव निवृत्तिः स्यात्सहस्रधा ॥
नान्यमंत्रैर्निवृत्तिः स्यात्प्रयत्नेन कृतेऽम्बिके ॥६॥

ओं नमो भगवति शत्रु-संहारिणि सर्वरोगप्रशमनि सकलरिपु-धन-धान्य-क्षयं कुरु कुरु धूमावतीश्वरि शरभ सालुवपक्षिराजप्रिये अमृत-कलश वरदाभय-कमल करांबुजे जगत्क्षोभिणि देवदत्तस्य शरीरे वर्तमान वर्तिष्यमाण सकल रोगं मोचय २ समस्त-भूतं नाशय २ सर्वोन्मादशमनं कुरु कुरु स्वाहा ।

मालामंत्रमिमं गुह्यं महारोग-प्रशांतिदम् ।
महाभूतहरं श्रेष्ठं महोन्मादहरं परम् ॥७॥
मंत्रेणानेन संमंत्र्य दशवारं तु संस्पृशन् ।
पाययेदौषधं यत्तत्सर्वव्याधिहरं भवेत् ॥८॥

इति श्रीआकाशभैरवकल्पे प्रत्यक्षसिद्धिप्रदे उमामहेश्वरसम्वादे धूमावती-प्रयोगो नाम चतुःपंचाशोऽध्यायः ॥५४॥

पंचपंचाशोऽध्यायः

श्रीशिव उवाच

अथ देवि प्रवक्ष्यामि मंत्रं तरणसिद्धिदम् ।
रक्षाकरं महासौख्यं शारभं तीव्रमद्भुतम् ।।१।।
भूपुरद्वयमालिख्य मध्ये पार्थिवमक्षरम् ।
चतुष्कोणे तु लंकारं अष्टदिक्षु तदा लिखेत् ।।२।।
परितो वायुबीजं च नैरंतर्य्यन्तु संमुखम् ।
प्रतिष्ठाप्यानिलं यंत्रं तोये संतारयेद् बुधः ।।३ ।।
कृत्वा यंत्रं जले देवि तत्परं निम्नगान्तरे ।
यंत्रोपरि स्वयं स्थित्वा देवदत्तं प्रकल्प्यवान् ।।४।।
त्रिवारं मनसा मंत्रं जपेदेकाग्रमानसः ।
निम्नगांतरसा तीर्त्वा सुखं गच्छति मानवः ।।५।।

ओं नमः शरभ-सालुव-पक्षिराजाय सर्वभूतमयाय सर्वमूर्तये रक्ष २ शीघ्रं तारय २ ओं श्रीं ह्री क्षं लं टं लं यं प्रतरणाय स्वाहा ।।

ओं नमो भगवते महाशरभ-सालुवाय पक्षिराजाय वरवर अष्टमूर्तये अखिलमयाय पालय २ भक्तवत्सलाय प्रणातार्तिविनाशनाय उत्तारय २ शीघ्रमुत्तारय श्रां ह्रां ओं हां देवदेवाय उत्तारणाय स्वाहा ।।

इमं मंत्रं महावीर्यं विचित्रं सर्वसाधकम्
जंतुमंभसि मज्जंतं क्षणादुत्कर्षयेच्छिवे ।।
पंचवारं जपेनैव सालुवेशो जगन्मयः
तस्य केशं समुद्धृत्य तत्क्षणादुद्धरेज्जलात् ।।६।।
एतदेव महागुह्यं जगतोद्भुतदर्शकम् ।
भक्तानां सर्वजंतूनां तोयोत्तरणकं शिवे ।
तस्मात्सर्वप्रयत्नेन साधकेन्द्रो जपेदिदम् ।।७।।

इति श्रीआकाशभैरवकल्पे प्रत्यक्षसिद्धिप्रदे उमामहेश्वरसम्वादे चामुण्डी-विधिर्नाम पंचपंचाशोऽध्यायः ।।५५।।

षट्पंचाशोऽध्यायः

श्रीशिव उवाच

वयं ते शृणु वक्ष्यामश्चित्रविद्यां विशेषतः ।
अत्याश्चर्यकरीं श्रेष्ठामतिगुह्यां वरानने ॥१॥
श्री चित्रविद्या मंत्रस्य ऋषिः संवर्त उच्यते ।
छंदस्तु शक्वरी देवी चित्रविद्या तु देवता ॥२॥
अमृतार्णं च रुंकार बीजं शक्तिर्यथाक्रमम् ।
घृतस्पृष्टौ शुचिःस्पृष्टौ ज्वरमुक्तौ विपत्क्षये ॥३॥
पैत्योन्माद-प्रशमने कायासिद्धौ निषेकके ।
अग्निप्रवेशने वाऽपि तज्जयार्थे नियोजयेत् ।
ताभ्यां न्यासं करांगस्य ततो मूलेन मातृकाम् ॥४॥

ध्यानम् ॥

अमलकमलमध्ये चंद्रपीठे निषण्णा-
ममृतकलशदानाभीतिमुद्राग्र-हस्ताम् ।
प्रणतशिरसि पूरं सत्रवंतं सुधायाः
शरणमहमुपैमि श्रीशिवां चित्रविद्याम् ॥५॥
'वं रुं ध्रूं स च जुं ठं ह्लीं श्रीमों नमो भगवतीति च ।
चित्रविद्ये महामाये अमृतेश्वरि तत्परे ॥६॥
सर्वविषं नाशय द्विः सर्वतापज्वरं ततः ।
हन-द्वयं ततः सर्वपैत्योन्मादमतः परम् ॥७॥
मोचयेति द्वयं पश्चादाज्योष्णं शमय द्वयम् ।
सर्वजनं मोहय द्विर्मां ततः पालय द्वयम् ॥८॥
विलोमेनाष्टबीजं च स्वाहांतो मंत्र उच्यते ।
विद्यामंत्रमिदं गुह्यं साधकस्त्वयुतं जपेत् ॥९॥
सहस्रं वा जपेद्देवि सर्वकार्यार्थसिद्धये ।
वृत्तमालिख्य तन्मध्ये बीजषट्कं लिखेत्ततः ॥१०॥

---

१. सं इति ग्रंथे ।

मायया च श्रियावेष्ट्य मनसा साध्यमूर्धनि ।
तत्सुतासेवितं ध्यात्वा देशिकं मूर्ध्नि चिन्तयेत् ॥११॥
विशेत्स्पृशेद्धरेन्सेचेच्चित्रविद्यामनुस्मरन् ।
कारयेद्वाखिलं चान्यैः पैत्योन्मादे तु सुंदरि ॥१२॥
पिष्ट्वाऽथ सौम्यकं बीजं द्विमात्रं वाऽथ काचकम् ।
सोऽप्यद्वयं समाहृत्य चैकं संयोज्य पाययेत् ॥१३॥
तूष्णीमेव तयोरन्यं पाययेत्तदनंतरम् ।
अपरेऽह्नि तथा कृत्वा प्रातर्यामादनंतरम् ॥१४॥
पंचगव्यं तथा पंचद्रव्य-युक्तं घटोदकम् ।
मंत्रेणानेन संमंत्र्य चैकवारमुदङ्मुखः ॥१५॥
किंचित्किंचिद्युगैस्तस्मादन्यैः कुंभोदकैर्द्विजैः ।
दक्षिणाभिमुखं साध्यं सहस्रमभिषेचयेत् ॥१६॥
पानं विना ऽप्यहं कुर्यादभिषेकं वरानने ।
पैत्यं च केवलोन्मादं ह्यनिद्रां चांगमर्दनम् ॥१७॥
क्षुद्रोन्मादं तथोन्मत्तग्रहे-हृदयविग्रहम् ।
सर्वांगि-दाह-रोगं च नश्यत्याशु न संशयः ॥१८॥
पथ्यं तु पयसा मिश्रमोदनं नान्यमंबिके ।
दत्ते यदि वृथा स्यात्तद्रोग-वृद्धि च तत्त्वतः ॥१९॥
विसं-थावा पया पिष्ट्वा जंबीराम्बुसमाम्लकम् ।
पाययेद्यदि मूर्च्छास्ति प्रार्थयेद्बहुधा मिथः ॥२०॥
संमंत्र्यानेन तांबूलमंगनानां समर्पयत् ।
तांबूलभक्षणादेव बहुमारद्रवं भवेत् ॥२१॥
न सहत्यंगना स्थातुं क्षणमात्रं च तं बिना ।
कामार्दिता चलच्चित्ता भवेदुत्तानचित्स्वयम् ॥२२॥
वृत्तद्वयं समालिख्य बहिः शूलाष्टकं लिखेत् ।
वृत्तमध्येऽष्टबीजं च मंत्रं तस्यांतरालके ॥२३॥
शूलाग्रे तु लिखेत्साध्यमष्टबीजं द्विधा ततः ।
स्पृशन्मंत्रं त्रिधा जप्त्वा वाहनाद्युपचारकान् ॥२४॥

कृत्वा तच्छतवारं तु मंत्रस्य चित्रविद्यया।
तत्पत्रं गुडमध्यस्थं खादयित्वा प्रवेशयेत् ॥२५॥
पुष्पवत्संधरेज्जंतुं प्रविष्टं हव्यवाहनम्।
यंत्रं गले करे मूर्ध्नि धत्ते यस्तस्य तत्त्वतः ॥२६॥
नास्ति वह्निभयं क्वापि सर्वज्वरभये तथा।
घृतस्पर्शन-भीतिश्च रोग-भीतिश्च सुन्दरि ॥२७॥
तादृशं पुरुषं दृष्ट्वा मुह्यंत्यखिलयोषितः।
प्रापयेयुः स्वयं तास्तत्तथा तादृग्विधा नराः ॥२८॥
महागुह्यं महामंत्रमतिचित्रं मनोहरम्।
त्रिधोषसि जपेन्मंत्रं यः स चित्री भवेच्छिवे ॥२९॥
भानुमालोक्य शीतांशुस्तत्करामृतशीतलम्।
जगत्त्रयं चिरं ध्यात्वा जपेदष्टोत्तरं शतम् ॥३०॥
सूर्यरश्मियुतायाम······स्तस्यामनः शुचिः।
न बाधतेऽखिलान्भक्तान्स्पृशतः सत्यवादिनः ॥३१॥
मंत्रेण संमंत्रितमौषधं वा तैलं घृतं वा भुवनं पयं वा।
दिनं पिबेत्प्रातरुदङ्मुखो यः स कायसिद्धिं लभते दशाहात् ॥३२॥

इति श्रीआकाशभैरवकल्पे प्रत्यक्षसिद्धिप्रदे उमामहेश्वरसम्वादे चित्रविद्या-विधिर्नाम षट्पंचाशोऽध्यायः ॥५६॥

सप्तपंचाशोऽध्यायः

श्रीशिव उवाच ॥

अथ देवि महागुह्यं श्रृणु सर्वार्थसाधकम् ।
शांतिकं देशिकं स्तोत्रं सारभूतं वदामि ते ॥१॥
देशिक-स्तोत्रमंत्रस्य परब्रह्म ऋषिः स्मृतः ।
छंदस्तु देवी गायत्री देवता देशिकोत्तमः ॥२॥
प्रणवं बीजमित्युक्तं लक्ष्मी शक्तिस्ततः परम् ।
श्री देशिक-प्रसादार्थे सिद्ध्यर्थे विनियुज्यते ॥३॥
ओमित्यादि करन्यासं तथा गौरी षडंगकम् ।
मायया वा करांगस्य न्यासं कुर्यात्समाहितः ॥४॥

शान्तं सर्वमयं प्रसन्नवदनं सर्वोत्तरं शाश्वतम् ।
सत्यं निश्चलमव्ययं विभुमजं तुर्यं चिदंशं वरम् ॥
एकं निर्मलमिन्दुपीठनिलयं ह्रींकारगम्यं शिवम् ।
कार्यं निर्मलमप्रमेयमकलं वन्देऽनिशं देशिकम् ॥५॥

समस्त-भुवनेशाय सच्चिदानंदतेजसे ।
नमः शरभरूपाय गुरुवे करुणानिधे ॥६॥
अनाद्यायाखिलाद्याय मायिने गतमायिने ।
अरूपाय स्वरूपाय शिवाय गुरवे नमः ॥७॥
सालुवाय महेशाय सर्वजीवनिवासिने ।
व्यवस्थातीतकालाय शिवाय गुरवे नमः ॥८॥
विभवे पक्षिराजाय ब्रह्मणे गणनात्मने ।
प्रकाशानंदरूपाय शिवाय गुरवे नमः ॥९॥
वेदवेद्यांतवेद्याय योगिने ब्रह्मवर्चसे ।
सदसद्दृश्यभावाय शिवाय गुरवे नमः ॥१०॥
संसाराब्धिपोताय शंभवे मृत्युमृत्यवे ।
परात्परतरेशाय शिवाय गुरवे नमः ॥११॥

षट्कोशमध्यसंस्थाय सर्वकारणमूर्तये ।
कारणातीतपीठाय शिवाय गुरवे नमः ॥१२॥
प्रणवार्थप्रबोधाय प्रपंचातीततेजसे ।
शब्दब्रह्मस्वरूपाय शिवाय गुरवे नमः ॥१३॥

अज्ञान-तिमिरांधस्य ज्ञानांजनशलाकया ।
चक्षुरुन्मीलितं येन तस्मै श्रीगुरवे नमः ॥१४॥
अज्ञानपाशसंबद्ध-तिमिरावृत-मानसः ।
कृपया श्वासितो यस्य तस्मै श्रीगुरवे नमः ॥१५॥
देश-काल-स्थलं व्याज-संवृत-ध्वांतमात्मनाम् ।
येनामलीकृतं सद्यः तस्मै श्रीगुरवे नमः ॥१६॥

अखण्डमण्डलाकारं व्याप्तं येन चराचरम् ।
तत्पदं दर्शितं येन तस्मै श्रीगुरवे नमः ॥१७॥
गुरुर्ब्रह्मा गुरुर्विष्णुर्गुरुर्देवो महेश्वरः ।
गुरुरेव परं ब्रह्म तस्मै श्रीगुरवे नमः ॥१८॥
सर्ग-स्थिति-लयादीनामादिकर्तारमीश्वरम् ।
नमामि शिरसा देवि देशिकं शरभेश्वरम् ॥१९॥
नमामि सोमसूर्याग्नि-रूपिणं दिव्यतेजसम् ।
ज्ञानदं जीव-लोकानां गुरुनाथं परात्परम् ॥२०॥
भैरवाय नमस्तुभ्यं नमस्ते वडवाग्नये ।
नमोऽस्तु दुर्गादेव्यै च भद्रकाल्यै नमो नमः ॥२१॥
नमस्ते लोकपालाय सहस्राक्षाय वह्नये ।
यमाय राक्षसेशाय वरुणाय पवस्वते ॥२२॥
किन्नरेन्द्राय रुद्राय व्याधये मृत्यवे नमः ।
कामाय रक्तचामुण्डयै मोहिन्यै च नमो नमः ॥२३॥
द्राविण्यै च नमः शब्दाकर्षिण्यै च गिरे नमः ।
नमो रमायै मायायै पुलिंदिन्यै नमो नमः ॥२४॥
महाशास्ताय क्षोभिण्यै ज्येष्ठादेव्यै नमो नमः ।
ब्रह्मणे च पराशक्त्यै नमो नारायणाय च ॥२५॥

मायायै घोणिने वाण्यै वेधसे बटुकाय च ।
अश्विनीभ्यां नमो वीरभद्राय च नमो नमः ॥२६॥
भाषायै दक्षिणामूर्त्त्यै कात्यायन्यै नमो नमः ।
नमस्ते घोररूपाय कालरुद्राय ते नमः ॥२७॥
गणेश्वराय कालाय पार्वतीनंदनाय च ।
भैरवाय नमस्तुभ्यं त्वरितायै नमो नमः ॥२८॥
निर्वाणवीरभद्राय वडवानल-शम्भवे ।
नमोऽस्तु वीरमायायै ब्रह्माण्यै च नमो नमः ॥२९॥
माहेश्वर्यै च कौमार्यै वैष्णव्यै च नमो नमः ।
नमः सूकरमुख्यै च सिंहमुख्यै नमो नमः ॥३०॥
इन्द्राण्यै चंडिकायै च मरीच्यै कश्यपाय च ।
नमोऽस्तु भागीरथ्यै च नमो विघ्नेश्वराय च ॥३१॥
ईशानायै कृतांताय भद्रकाल्यै नमो नमः ।
हुंकाल्यै जातवेदाग्नि-दुर्गादेव्यै नमो नमः ॥३२॥
अर्द्धनारीशरूपाय नमस्ते परमात्मने ।
श्वेतभूम्यै च सोमाय नमः शुक्राय विष्णवे ॥३३॥
नमोऽस्तु बलभद्राय कुबेराय नमो नमः ।
परात्परायै दुर्गायै धर्माय परशंभवे ॥३४॥
नमोऽग्नये भैरवाय चाश्विन्यै भार्गवाय च ।
नायकाय नमस्तेऽस्तु वायवे पावकाय च ॥३५॥
इन्द्राय जलनाथाय रुद्रैकादशमूर्तये ।
द्वादशादित्य-रूपाय भारत्यै तांडवाय च ॥३६॥
श्यामभूम्यै नृसिंहाय भूयोभूयो नमाम्यहम् ।
नमः शरभ-सालुव-पक्षिराजाय शंभवे ॥३७॥
ज्ञानमुद्रा-स्वरूपाय गुरवे करुणानिधे ।
देशिकाय नमः सर्वसिद्ध्यै सर्वान्तरात्मने ॥३८॥
बिन्दुनादस्वरूपाय ब्रह्मणेऽनंतशक्तये ।
नमोस्वरूपाय जगन्मयाय जगन्निवासाय हिरण्मयाय ।
भूतावसानाय पुरातनाय नवाय नाथाय नमो नमस्ते ॥३९॥

त्वमेव माता च पिता त्वमेव त्वमेव बंधुश्च गुरुस्त्वमेव ।
त्वमेव विद्या द्रविणं त्वमेव त्वमेव सर्वं मम देव-देव ॥४०॥

सुमतिरखिल-विद्या कंदली-कंद-कंदम् ।
दिवसमनु निपश्यन् चंद्र-पीठे स्वनाथम् ॥
उषसि शरभ-पूजा-सद्विधानं विधाय ।
जपतु सकल-सिद्ध्यै देशिक-स्तोत्र-मंत्रम् ॥४१॥

यो जपेत्प्रत्यहं तस्य सुप्रसन्नो भवेद् गुरुः ।
स्वात्मज्ञानं च लभते सर्वशत्रुजयं तथा ॥४२॥

मंत्राणां सिद्धिभेदं च भोग-भोग्यं जयं तथा ।
आयुरारोग्यवृद्धि च सर्वसौख्यं लभेद् ध्रुवम् ॥४३॥

इति श्रीआकाशभैरवकल्पे प्रत्यक्षसिद्धिप्रदे उमामहेश्वरसम्वादे देशिक-स्तोत्रं नाम सप्तपंचाशोऽध्यायः ॥५७॥

अथ अष्टपंचाशोऽध्यायः

श्रीशिव उवाच ॥

अथ देवि प्रवक्ष्यामि मंत्रं दुःस्वप्ननाशनम्।
अनुभोगानुसाराख्यं पिशाचानां विशेषतः ॥१॥
दुःस्वप्ननाशमंत्रस्य ऋषिः सिद्धामृतेश्वरः।
छंदस्तु बृहती देवो वरुणो लांतमक्षरम् ॥२॥
बीजं शक्तिर्व्याहृती च तथा दुःस्वप्ननाशने।
विनियोगस्ततः पश्चाद्व्याहृत्या सह मंत्रकम् ॥३॥
पादैरर्धैः करांगस्य न्यासमेकैकशः क्रमात्।

ध्यानम् ॥

पाशांकुश-धनुर्बाण-वरदाभय-दोस्तलम् ॥४॥
सिचंतममृतैर्लोकान्वन्दे देवं प्रचेतसम्।
[1]यो मे राजन्समुच्चार्य भूर्भुवः स्वरनन्तरम् ॥५॥
दुःस्वप्न नाशनं मंत्रं पश्चाद् बीजं विलोमतः।
जपेदक्षर-साहस्रं संपुटीकृत्य बीजयुक् ॥६॥
तत्क्रमादेव शिष्टांगं कुर्यादेकैकशोऽम्बिके।
पंचाशत्कोष्टके यंत्रे विना तारं शिखिस्त्रियुक् ॥७॥
रेखा-रेखाग्र-शूलेषु साध्यं तारेण-वेष्टितम्।
सारावर्णां प्रयोगाग्नि-घृत-तैलौषधानि च ॥८॥
पुरस्कृत्वा यथा शास्त्रमभिषेकं ततः परम्।
कृत्वा ततःपरं रक्षां बंधयेत्स्वप्नमुक्तये ॥९॥
अभिषेकं ततः पश्चाद् गर्भलाभाय योषिताम्।
गर्भरक्षां च तद्वृद्ध्यै कुर्यात्तैल-घृतं तथा ॥१०॥

इति श्रीआकाशभैरवकल्पे प्रत्यक्षसिद्धिप्रदे उमामहेश्वरसम्वादे दुःस्वप्ननाशन-मंत्रविधिर्नामष्टपंचाशोऽध्यायः ॥५८॥

---

१. ऋक्—२-७-१० ।

नवपंचाशोऽध्यायः

श्रीशिव उवाच ।।

अथान्यं संप्रवक्ष्यामि मंत्रं पाशविमोचकम् ।
पूर्ववदृषि-भावादि मंत्रभेदमिहोच्यते ।।१।।
प्रथमं त्वनुलोमेन व्याहृतीः प्रणवं ततः ।
[1]ध्रुवासु त्वेत्यृचं पश्चात्स्वरादि-व्याहृतीस्तथा ।।२।।
ओं स्वाहेति महामंत्रः सर्वपाशविमोचनः ।
पूर्ववत्तु पुरश्चर्यां मंत्री कुर्याद्यथाविधि ।।३।।
सर्पदष्ट-मृतं जंतुं पुनरुत्थापनाय च ।
तापज्वर-विनाशाय सर्वव्याधि-विमुक्तये ।।४।।
शत्रु-कृति-विनाशाय सर्वोन्माद-विमुक्तये ।
महावर्षाकर्षणाय सर्वसौभाग्यसिद्धये ।।५।।
चतुर्विंशतिधा भद्रे जपेदेकाग्रमानसः ।
तत्क्षणादेव सो देवि तत्तत्सिद्धिमवाप्नुयात् ।।६।।
अविश्वासो न कर्तव्यः कृते सर्वं विनश्यति ।
तस्मात्सर्व-प्रयत्नेन जपेत्सिध्यति निश्चयः ।।७।।

इति श्रीआकाशभैरवकल्पे प्रत्यक्षसिद्धिप्रदे उमामहेश्वरसम्वादे पाशविमोचनं नाम एकोनषष्टितमोऽध्यायः ।।५९।।

---

१. ऋक्—५-६-१० ।

अथ षष्टितमोऽध्यायः

अथ गणपतिप्रयोगः

श्रीशिव उवाच ।।

शृणु देवि महागुह्यं मंत्रं सर्वार्थसाधकम् ।
काल-मृत्यु-प्रशमनं चतुर्वर्ग-फलप्रदम् ।।१।।
यस्य स्मरण-मात्रेण क्षुभ्यंत्यखिलमूर्त्तयः ।
तादृशं भीषणं शान्तं गाणपत्यं वदामि ते ।।२।।
अथो महागणपति-मंत्रस्य गणको ऋषिः ।
छन्दस्तु गायत्रं महागणेशो देवतांबिके ।।३।।
पंच पंच तथा पंच द्वि-त्रि-द्विस्तु यथाक्रमम् ।। (करांग-क्रिया)

ध्यानम् ।।

बीजापूरगदेषुकार्मुकरुजा चक्राब्जपाशोत्पल
व्रीह्यग्रस्व-विषाणरत्नकलशप्रोद्यत्करांभोरुहः ।।
ध्येयो वल्लभया सपद्मकरया श्लिष्टोज्वलद्भूषयः ।
विश्वोत्पत्ति-विपत्ति-संस्थिति-करो विघ्नो विशिष्टार्थदः ।।४।।
प्रणवं च महालक्ष्मीं मायां कामं क्ष्मां स्वयम् ।
गणपतये तत्पश्चाद्वर वरद तत्परम् ।।५।।
सर्वजनं मे वशं स्यादानयेति ततः परम् ।
स्वाहेति मंत्र-रूपं तु देव्यष्टाविंशदक्षरम् ।।६।।
चतुर्लक्षं जपेन्मंत्रमेकलक्षमथापि वा ।
चतुरंग-समोपेतं मंत्री सर्वार्थसिद्धये ।।७।।
तर्पणेऽत्र विशेषोऽस्ति चतुरावृतिरित्यथ ।
नारिकेरं तिलं गुंजा मोदकं पृथु सक्तु च ।।८।।
ऐक्षवं कदलीं चैव पृथक् सर्वं वरानने ।
नैवेद्यं च तथा होमे नित्यहोममथाद्यकम् ।।९।।
बीजं षट्कोणमध्ये स्फुरदनलपुरे तारकं दिक्षु लक्ष्मी ।
माया-कंदर्प-भूमी तदनु रसपुटेष्वालिखेद् बीजषट्कम् ।

मंत्रोद्धार :—श्रों श्रीं ह्रीं क्लीं ग्लौं गं गणपतये वर वरद सर्व जनं मे वशमानय स्वाहा ।

तत्संधिश्वंगमंत्रान्वसुदल-कमले मूलमंत्रस्य वर्णा-
न्छिष्टान्पत्रेषु विद्वान्विलिखितु गुणशश्चांत्यमंत्ये पलाशे ॥१०॥
आवीतं लिपिभिः क्रमोत्क्रम-वशात्पाशांकुशाभ्यामपि।
क्ष्मा-कोण-द्वितयेन संवृतमिदं यंत्रं गणाधीशितुः ॥
मध्ये षड्भवनेऽष्ट-पत्रपृथिवी बाह्ये त्रिकोणांतरे।
वश्याकर्षण-मारणं-चलगति-ग्रामांतिकं चेष्टदम् ॥११॥

आलिख्य यंत्रं वरशातपत्रे गणेश्वरं सावरणं प्रसन्नम्।
एकोत्तरंविंशति वासरं यः संपूजयेत्सिद्ध्यति तस्य भोगम् ॥१२॥
आदौ गणेशं शिखि-कोणमध्ये त्वावाह्य सर्वं मनसा निवेद्य।
ध्यात्वा चिरं मूर्धनि भानुवारं संतर्पयित्वा स्वकरद्वयाभ्याम् ॥१३॥

अग्रेऽथ बिल्वमभितश्च रमेरमेशौ तद्दक्षिणे वटजुषौ गिरिजावृषांकौ।
पृष्ठे तु पिप्पलजुषौ रति-पुष्प-बाणौ सव्ये प्रियंगुमभितश्च महीकराहौ ॥१४॥

देवीमेकां चतुर्वारं मूलमंत्रं यथा पुरा।
तर्पयेच्चतुरो युग्मानृतु-वह्नि-गृहांतरे ॥१५॥
महालक्ष्मीं गणेशं च बिंदौ वह्नि-गृहे ततः।
कोण-षट्केऽग्रमारभ्य ऋद्ध्यामोदौ तु तर्पयेत् ॥१६॥
श्री समृद्धि-प्रमोदौ च कांति-श्रीसुमुखौ ततः।
तत्पश्चान्महादेवि मदनावति-दुर्मुखौ ॥१७॥
पश्चान्मदद्रवाविघ्नौ द्राविणी विघ्नकारकौ।
षट्कोणाष्टास्रयोर्मध्ये वाम-दक्षिण-पार्श्वके ॥१८॥
वसुधारा-शंखनिधि तर्पयेद् वामपार्श्वके।
वसुमत्या युतं पद्मनिधिं संतर्पयेच्छिवे ॥१९॥
तर्पयेदष्टपत्रे तु ब्राह्म्याद्यष्टमातरः।
अष्टविंशतिवर्णानां चैकमेकं चतुर्विधम् ॥२०॥
मूलं च तर्पणं कुर्याच्चतुर्वारं यथाक्रमम्।
चतुश्चत्वारिंशदधिकं चतुःशतमथो भवेत् ॥२१॥
चतुश्चत्वारिंशद्वारं कुर्यादेवमतंद्रितः।
तस्य सर्वसमृद्धिः स्याद्विघ्नेशस्य प्रसादतः ॥२२॥

इति श्रीआकाशभैरवकल्पे प्रत्यक्षसिद्धिप्रदे उमामहेश्वरसम्वादे गणपतिविधिर्नाम षष्टितमोऽध्यायः ॥६०॥

अथ एकषष्टितमोऽध्यायः

श्रीशिव उवाच ॥

अथान्यं वच्मि ते यंत्रं सर्व-कामफलप्रदम् ।
साध्यर्क्षफलके लोहे तालपत्रेऽथ ताम्रके ॥१॥
लिखेत्सप्तचतुःकोष्ठे रेखा-रेखाग्र-शूलके ।
क्रमान्मंत्रं बहिः साध्यमावाह्यात्र गणेश्वरम् ॥२॥
संपूज्य विधिवच्चक्रं स्पृशन्मंत्रं सहस्रधा ।
जपावसानात्पूर्वं तु स्त्रीणामाकर्षणं भवेत् ॥३॥
राज-मित्र-वधूनां च तथा वश्यं च तादृशम् ।

प्रयोगान्तरम् ॥

श्वेतार्कं चाप्यपामार्गं परेत-पृथिवीरुहम् ॥४॥
सिद्धयोगदिनात्पूर्वं शुक्र-सौम्येन्दुवासरे ।
गंधं-पुष्पं च धूपं च बलिं दत्त्वा प्रणम्य तत् ॥५॥
यदर्थं केन सृष्टाऽसि भूतले सांप्रतं वयं ।
आगतस्त्वत्र त्वत्सिद्ध्यै तिष्ठ तिष्ठ महौषधे ॥६॥
इति सूत्रं त्रिधावेष्ट्य दशवारं जपन्मनुम् ।
सिद्ध्ययोगे समुत्पाट्य तन्मूलं छिद्रमादितः[१] ॥७॥
सक्तांगुलीयकं कृत्वा चेष्टा तस्मिन्गणेश्वरम् ।
अष्टोत्तरसहस्रं तु जप्त्वा धृत्वांगुलीयकम् ॥८॥
तेन हस्तेन जंतूनां कराग्रं संस्पृशेद् बुधः ।
तस्य स्पर्शन-मात्रेण महावश्यं भवेद् ध्रुवम् ॥९॥
जंतवस्तद्वशं प्राप्य दास्यन्ति प्राणमप्यहो ।
मूलमंगांभसा बीजमिन्द्रियेणास्त्रबिंदुना ॥१०॥
पुष्पमास्यांबुना पत्रे रक्तेनागमनस्पिकम् ।
उत्पाट्य पूर्ववत्स्पृष्ट्वा कृष्णधत्तूरकं शिवे ॥११॥

---

१. अच्छिद्र मूलमित्यर्थः ।

सर्वं गुंजापरीमाणं कृत्वामचटकं पृथक् ।
संस्पृशत्पूर्ववत्स्पृष्ट्वा खाने पाने प्रदापयेत् ॥१२॥
प्राणिनस्तद्वशं गत्वा सर्वे सर्वस्वदा भवेत् ।
मित्रयोः प्रत्ययुर्द्भूत साल-मूलं तथोद्धरेत् ॥१३॥
द्विधा भित्त्वाऽथ मूलानि विपरीतं तु बंधयेत् ।
स्पृष्ट्वा तु पूर्ववज्जप्त्वा श्मशाने कोष्ट-सीमसु ॥१४॥
खनित्वा बलिपूर्वं तु जपेदष्टोतरंशतम् ।
तत्क्षणादेव देवेशि मित्रयोः शत्रुता भवेत् ॥१५॥
मैत्रं जन्मभयोर्मूलं तथा बद्ध्वा खनेद् गृहे ।
तस्मिन्स्थले जपं कुर्यादाशु-मेलन-सिद्धये ॥१६॥
विपज्जन्माङ्गयोर्मूलं विपत्यैकं (?) श्मशानके ।
जन्मसाध्ययोः साध्याय वधाय वधजन्मनोः ॥१७॥
एकीकरणयोर्मूलं द्वयोः परममैत्रयोः ।
शुभाय सिद्धयोगे च दग्धयोगेऽशुभाय च ॥१८॥
पापवारे शुभाय स्याच्छुभाय पापवासरे ।
पुष्पं पुष्यदिने हार्यं फलं च भरणीदिने ॥१९॥
शाखा विशाखा-दिवसे पत्रं हस्त-दिने तथा ।
मूलं मूले तथा कृष्णधत्तूरस्य यथाक्रमम् ॥२०॥
कर्पूरसहितं पिष्ट्वा समे कुंकुम-रोचने ।
मंत्रं तु पूर्ववज्जप्त्वा तिलकं धारयेद् बुधः ॥२१॥
तिलकात्स्त्री वशं याति यथा साक्षादरुन्धती ।
अथो पुष्पलतां लज्जां श्वेताख्य-गिरिकर्णिकाम् ॥२२॥
यथा सरोचनं पिष्टं तिलकं राजमोहनम् ।
याकपूकाष्टकं कृत्वा बाल्यखिल्योदरस्थितम् ॥२३॥
स्वामृतेनाभिमृश्याथ खादयेद्वश्यसिद्धये ।
समंत्राणि तथा कुर्यादनुक्तान्यौषधानि च ।
यस्तस्य सर्वसिद्धिः स्यात्संशयो नास्ति शोभने ॥२४॥

इति श्रीआकाशभैरवकल्पे प्रत्यक्षसिद्धिप्रदे उमामहेश्वरसम्वादे औषधिमंत्रविधिर्नाम एकषष्टितमोऽध्यायः ॥६१॥

अथ द्विषष्टितमोऽध्यायः

श्रीशिव उवाच ॥

अथान्यं वच्मि ते देवि मूलिका-सिद्धि संग्रहम् ।
सर्व-लोक-जयं चैव सर्वकार्यार्थ-साधकम् ॥१॥

गुलिका सिद्धियोगेन पेयं चामृतयोगके ।
द्वेषणं दग्धयोगे च मृत्युयोगे च निग्रहम् ॥२॥

विशेषाद्रोगनाशायामृतयोगेऽथ सिद्धके ।
स्तंभनायापरे पक्षे धृति-योग-समन्विते ॥३॥

पंचम्यां शुक्रवारे वा सोमार्कदिवसेऽथवा ।
एकदेशयुतेनापि धृतियोगेऽथ वज्रके ॥४॥

रक्षाबन्धनपूर्वं तु यथोक्त-दिवसे ततः ।
मूलोत्पाटनमंत्रेण साध्यलग्ने समुद्धरेत् ॥५॥

सिद्धौषधे महावीर्ये जगत्कारण-संभवे ।
नाथाज्ञया हरामि त्वां कार्यसिद्धि प्रयच्छ मे ॥६॥

दशवारमिदं जप्त्वा हरेदच्छिद्रमादितः ।
यथायोगे ततः कृत्वा पूर्ववत्कल्पयेत्सुधीः ॥७॥

अश्वगंधा समूलं-त्वक् पिष्ट्वा कर्पूर-संयुतम् ।
पाने खाने प्रदातव्यं रंभा रामा वशंकरम् ॥८॥

जातीफलयुतं पिष्ट्वा वटकं माषमात्रकम् ।
कृत्वांगुलीयकं मूलहेतावारोप्य मेलने ॥९॥

कुर्यादनुक्षणं भाव (?) निषेकं च शनैः शनैः ।
प्रासेद्यदि तथा मोक्षमवसार्य निधाय च ॥१०॥

भावेदमंगुलीयं यत्तस्य वीर्य-जयं भवेत् ।
हृच्छ्वास-धारणात्पूर्वं कुर्यात्स्तंभस्य सिद्धये ॥११॥

किं च त्रिकं च मूर्धा च हेतुरित्यभिधीयते ।
कच्छपं मङ्गलेवारे मातृकोष्ठेऽग्रमंडपे ॥१२॥

दत्त्वा बलिं समादाय तस्य रक्तं पटांतरे।
योषिद्बाह्यांशुकगं च समं तद्वसनं ततः ॥१३॥
पूर्व-पिष्ट-युतं योज्यं नाराचमभिवर्तनम्।
कार्पास-सूत्र-निर्बद्धं वीत-नाराचमर्बुदे ॥१४॥
विद्धे संलभते देवि तादृशं गुह्यबंधनम्।
मोचनामोचनं क्षीरक्षालनं गुह्यवस्त्रयोः ॥१५॥
दिवसे वैधृतियुते पूर्णलक्षणसंयुते।
उत्पाट्य कुलिशं कृत्वा जिह्वामारोप्य मंत्रितम् ॥१६॥
प्रणापयेत्कवाटानि सद्यो मुंचति निश्चयः।
बद्धउद्धमना देवी नीयते तत्कवाटकम् ॥१७॥
उद्ध-मनिरिति ख्यातं तच्चूर्णं कार्यसिद्धिदम्।
विषघ्नं पाण्डुरोगघ्नं विशेषात्कुष्ठनाशनम् ॥१८॥

कांगोणी ॥

काकमाचि-शिखां हृत्वा कृत्वा तु कुलिशं ततः।
संपूज्य पूर्ववज्जप्त्वा सर्पावासबिले न्यसेत् ॥१९॥
सर्पं आगत्य कुलिशमाघ्राणति वरानने।
आदाय कुलिशं पश्चाद् गच्छेदारोप्य मूर्धनि ॥२०॥
सहैव सर्पं आगच्छेद्देश-देशांतरेष्वपि।
सर्पं निर्वर्तितुं देवि कुलिशं भूतले न्यसेत्।
सर्पो वसति तत्रैव गंध-तोयाभिषेचनात् ॥२१॥

अवला ॥

व्याघात-योग-सहिते लज्जामूलं यथा पुरा।
सक्तांगुलीयकं कृत्वा धृत्वानामिकयांबिके ॥२२॥
मेलने पुरुषं योषा स्पृशेद्वक्षसि तेन तु।
तत्क्षणादेव षण्डत्वं जायते मोचने सुखम् ॥२३॥
दर्शे चैत्ररथं मूलमादायोत्तरगं तथा।
पाटल-व्रीहि-युक् पक्त्वा कृत्वा तु तुषतण्डुलम् ॥२४॥

संपेष्य पयसा मूलमादद्यात्तुष-तण्डुले ।
स्पृष्ट्वा जप्त्वा यथापूर्वं तुषं तुष्टकुलालयोः ॥२५॥
अथो मृत्तापके वह्नौ युज्पत्रावोद्भवे दलम् ।
धुलु धुलायमानेत्रे (?) योजयेत्तण्डुलं तथा ॥२६॥
सुपक्वान्नं भवेत्क्वापि षण्मासमपि निश्चयम् ।
वर्द्धते केसरी बाभूलु ? कांदा भुरंग मुदानि ? ॥२७॥

कालीशेवरी ॥

श्यामोरगस्य सम्भूता कृष्ण-काष्ठविमोचनम् ।
आहृत्य पूर्ववन्मूलमुपरागावसानके ॥२८॥
धृत्वा तु कुलिशं जप्त्वा धृत्वानामिकयाम्बिके ।
तेनादाय करेणांबु-विषग्रस्त-मुखेऽर्पयेत्
त्रिवारार्पणमात्रेण मृतजीवोऽपि जीवति ॥३०॥

हलद ॥

एरण्ड ॥

एरण्ड-पक्व-सुफलं रक्षापूर्वं यथा पुरा ।
उपरागे तयोर्हृत्वा नग्नवेषस्तु निर्भयः ॥३१॥
तस्य बीजं सुबीजिन पेषतां वरवर्णिनि ।
संमृज्य पूर्ववत्तेनालिप्तस्नातां वधूं पुनः ॥३२॥
पश्येद्यदि पतिस्तस्यां न्यस्तचित्तो भवेद् ध्रुवम्
अवसान कृतेनैव तयोर्विद्वेषणं भवेत् ॥३३॥

मारणम् ॥

विपक्षगार्कयोर्मूलमाहृत्य यमदिग्गतम् ।
समस्तं पूर्ववत्कृत्वा श्मशाने बलिपूर्वकम् ॥३४॥
भूयो जपेत्सहस्रं तु जपाद्याम्यं व्रजेद्रिपुः ।
वेध-वैनाशयोर्मूलं ? शिवार्काग्निशिफां तथा ॥३५॥
आहृत्य पूर्ववत्कृत्वा निशायां दक्षिणामुखः ।
दक्षिणस्यां खनेन्मंत्री नग्नरूपः पुनर्जपेत् ॥३६॥

नामपूर्वं त्रिसाहस्रं देशिकाज्ञामनुस्मरन् ।
त्रिदिनाद्वै रिपुर्याति याम्यं घोरतरं पुरम् ॥३७॥

स्तंभनम् ॥

आदाय पूर्ववन्मूलं विष-प्रत्ययवृक्षयोः ।
जिह्वा-नयन-हृच्छ्रोत्र-हनु-पत्करसाध्ययुक् ॥३८॥
मातृकोष्ठे यथा द्वारे चित्रे-तोरण-मन्दिरे ।
खनित्वा तु जपेद्भूयो मघवास्य सहस्रकम् ॥३९॥
सर्वस्तंभमिति ख्यातं संशयो नास्ति सर्वदा ।
प्राणप्रतिष्ठा पूर्वं तु कुर्यात्सर्वमतंद्रितः ।
यस्तस्य सर्वसिद्धिः स्यान्न चेत्सर्वं न सिद्ध्यति ॥४०॥

इति श्रीआकाशभैरवकल्पे प्रत्यक्षसिद्धिप्रदे उमामहेश्वरसम्वादे मूलिकाविधिर्नाम द्विषष्टितमोऽध्यायः ॥६२॥

अथ त्रिषष्टितमोऽध्यायः

श्रीशिव उवाच ।।

अस्य श्रीकालमंत्रस्य पुलस्त्यो भगवानृषिः ।
छंदस्तु जगती प्रोक्ता देवता काल उच्यते ।।१।।

द्रां बीजं प्रकृतिः शक्तिर्नियोगः [1]सर्वनाशने ।
द्रामित्यादि करांगस्य न्यासं मूलेन वाम्बिके ।।२।।

ध्यानम् ।।

आरुढं सैरिभेन्द्रं ज्वलदनलशिखं मुंड-मांसास्थिमालाम् ।
प्रासं शूलं च वज्रं मुसलमथ हलं चर्मपात्रं च पाशम् ।।
हस्तैर्बिभ्राणमंसस्थ-नमितमुखं भीमकायं त्रिनेत्रम् ।
कालं घोराट्टहासं रिपुकुलमथनं खर्वगर्वं नमामि ।।३।।

मंत्रः—

ओं नमो भगवते कालाय घोराय वज्रदंष्ट्राय
शत्रुनाशाय सर्वभूतवमनाय हुं फट् स्वाहा ।
एतन्मंत्रं महावीर्यं सर्वभूतारिनाशनम् ।
पंचत्रिंशल्लिपिमयं पशूनां भीतिदायकम् ।।४।।
कवचोक्त-महायंत्रे मंत्रमालिख्य साधकः ।
सम्पूज्य [2]पंचभांतेन जपं कुर्यात्सहस्रकम् ।।५।।
जपावसाने देवेशि कालकृष्टो भवेद्रिपुः ।
शकलं हेतुसंयुक्तं पुनः कालाय वेदयेत् ।।६।।

इति श्रीआकाशभैरवकल्पे प्रत्यक्षसिद्धिप्रदे उमामहेश्वरसम्वादे कालविधिर्नाम त्रिषष्टितमोऽध्यायः ।।६३।।

---

१. शत्रुनाशने ।

२. पञ्चतिक्तेन-पञ्चतत्त्वेन ।

अथ चतुःषष्टितमोऽध्यायः

श्रीशिव उवाच ॥

अथ षण्मुख-मन्त्रस्य भगवान्काश्यपो ऋषिः ।
त्रिष्टुबृछंदस्तथा देवः सुब्रह्मण्योऽथ देवता ॥१॥
सुं बीजं सं ततः शक्तिर्नियोगो विजयाय वै ।
सामित्यादि करांगस्य न्यासं मूलयुतं शिवे ॥२॥

ध्यानम् ॥

शक्तिहस्तं विरूपाख्यं शिखिवाहं षडाननम् ।
दारणं रिपुरोगघ्नं भावयेत् कुक्कुटध्वजम् ॥३॥

मंत्रः—

[1]सुंकारं पूर्वमुच्चार्य्य सुब्रह्मण्याय तत्परम् ।
वह्नि जाया-समोपेतं मंत्रमष्टाक्षरं परम् ॥४॥
अष्टाष्ट-कोष्टके यंत्रे रेखा-शूलाग्र साध्यके ।
आदौ सुं वर्जयित्वाऽथ लिखेन्मंत्रं परात्परम् ॥५॥
अंत्यकोष्ठे लिखेत्सुं च बाह्यवीथीं विना ततः ।
मातृका ल-क्षहीना च लिखेत्संधौ यथाक्रमम् ॥६॥
पादि-क्षांतं बहिर्वीथ्यां प्रकृतित्रिशिखां ततः ।
अकारादि नकारान्तं बाह्यरेखान्तरालके ॥७॥
पाशावृतं महायंत्रं परमं सर्वसिद्धिदम् ।
गुहमाराध्य यंत्रे तु जपेत्स्वेष्टार्थसिद्धये ॥८॥
त्रिसहस्रं जपादेव साधकस्याखिलं लभेत् ।
अण्डादि मेरुपर्यन्तं कार्येषु सकलेषु च ।
तत्तत्कार्यार्थ-सिद्ध्यर्थं त्रिसाहस्रं जपेच्छिवे ॥९॥

इति श्रीआकाशभैरवकल्पे प्रत्यक्षसिद्धिप्रदे उमामहेश्वरसम्वादे षण्मुखमंत्रविधिर्नाम चतुश्षष्टितमोऽध्यायः ॥६४॥

---

१. मन्त्रोद्धार :—सुं सुब्रह्मण्याय स्वाहा ।

अथ पंचषष्टितमोऽध्यायः

श्रीशिव उवाच ॥

अथ वक्ष्यामि देवेशि भैरवस्य महात्मनः
रक्षणाय समस्तानां मंत्रं सर्वार्थसिद्धये ॥१॥
महाभैरवमंत्रस्य वामदेव ऋषिः स्मृतः ।
अत्यनुष्टुप् तथा छंदो देवता वटुकः शिवः ॥२॥
वंकारं बीजमित्युक्तं हुंकारं शक्तिरुच्यते ।
सर्व-विघ्न विनाशार्थे विनियोगस्ततः परम् ॥३॥
वां-हामित्यादिना देवि करांगन्यासमाचरेत् ।

ध्यानम् ॥

करकलितकपालः कुंडली दंडपाणि-
स्तरुणतिमिरनीलो व्यालयज्ञोपवीती ।
कृत-समय-सपर्या विघ्नविच्छेदहेतुः
जयतु वटुकनाथः सिद्धिदः साधकानाम् ॥४॥

मंत्रः—

[1]प्रणवं च महालक्ष्मीं महामायां च मन्मथम् ।
चिंतामणिं च वंकारं वटुकाय द्वयं ततः ॥५॥
आपदुद्धारणाय कुरु कुर्विति ततःपरम् ।
वटुकाय ततः पश्चान्नमोऽन्तं सर्वसिद्धये ॥६॥
द्वात्रिंशदक्षरं मंत्रं नमः स्थाने तु पल्लवे ।
निग्रहोच्चाट-वश्यानां [2]द्विठं शेषं यथातथम् ॥७॥
चतुरंगयुतं कुर्यात्पुरश्चर्यां यथा पुरा ।

---

१. मन्त्रोद्धार:—ओं श्रीं ह्रीं क्लीं र्क्ष्म्र्यां वं वटुकाय वटुकाय आपदुद्धारणाय कुरु कुरु वटुकाय ह्रीं नमः ।

२. स्वाहा ।

श्रीर्माया-स्मर-कूटमंत्र विलिखेन्मध्ये दलेष्वष्टसु ।
द्विःप्रोक्तं वटुकाय शब्दमपरान्मंत्रस्य वर्गान्बहिः ।।
अ्रष्ट-द्वंद्व-दलेषु तद्बहिचरस्तत्पत्रसंख्येषु च ।
द्वात्रिंशद्दलकादि-सांत-सहितं यंत्रं लिखेद् भूपुरे ।।८।।

अनुक्तानामथो नाम यंत्रस्योपरि कर्म च ।
साध्यमालिख्य तत्पश्चात्कुर्याद्यंत्रप्रयोगकम् ।।९।।
चतुःषष्टिक्रियास्वेव यो जपेन्मंत्रवित्तमः ।।१०।।

इति श्रीआकाशभैरवकल्पे प्रत्यक्षसिद्धिप्रदे उमामहेश्वरसम्वादे भैरव-विधिर्नाम पंचषष्टितमोऽध्यायः ।।६५।।

अथ षट्षष्टितमोऽध्यायः

श्रीशिव उवाच ।।

वदामि शृणु ते देवि त्वरितां क्षिप्रसिद्धिदाम् ।
सप्तत्रिंशल्लिपिमयीं सर्वशत्रूनिवर्हणाम् ।।१।।
त्वरितायाश्च मंत्रस्य सद्योजात ऋषिः स्मृतः ।
अतित्रिष्टुप् तथा छंदो देवता त्वरितेश्वरी ।।२।।
त्वंकारं बीजमित्युक्तं भंकारं शक्तिरुच्यते ।
स्वेच्छाकरणसिद्ध्यर्थे विनियोगस्ततः परम् ।
भामित्यादि करन्यासं त्वामिति स्यात्षडंगकम् ।।३।।

ध्यानम् ।।

पिच्छामंडित-कुंडलांत-विलसच्छीतांशुलेखां पराम् ।
गुंजाहारविभूषणां कुचभरक्लान्तां प्रवालांबराम् ।।
वन्दे तां खचरेश्वरप्रियतमां बाणालसत्कार्मुकाम् ।
नित्यानंदमयीं प्रसन्नवदनां नीलोत्पलश्यामलाम् ।।४।।

मंत्रः—

[1]आदौ हसतु तत्पश्चात्तथा सरटु तत्परम् ।
पश्चात्करटु तत्पश्चात्करापयिटु तत्परम् ।।५।।
टभिमयस्तु तत्पश्चादलुट्टद्यमुमुक् घ च ।
रभसं विपटु तथा हानपिट्थ तत्परम् ।।६।।
स्वाहेति मंत्ररूपार्णं त्रिंशदुत्तरसप्तकम् ।
अशेषांगयुता देवि पुरश्चर्या यथापुरा ।।७।।
जपांते सिद्धयोगे तु संपदादि शुभर्क्षके ।
कवचस्थं महायंत्रं हेमपत्रे विलिख्य तु ।।८।।
त्वरितामंत्रवर्णानि लिखेत्तस्मिन्यथाक्रमम् ।
हाकारमर्धसंधौ तु तत्रावाह्य महेश्वरीम् ।।९।।

---

१. मन्त्रोद्धार :—हसतु सरटु करटु करापयिटु टभिमयस्त्वलुट्टद्यमुमुक्घरभसं विपटु हान पिट्थ स्वाहा ।

आराध्याथ परैः सम्यक् जपेन्मंत्रं सहस्त्रधा ।
तदा तस्य महेशानि त्वरिता सुप्रसीदति ॥१०॥
उपस्थां त्वरितां धीरः साधको देशिकं स्मरन् ।
आगच्छेति त्रिधा ब्रूयात्सर्वसिद्धिप्रदायिनीम् ॥११॥
चिरं ध्यात्वा महादेवीं कुर्यादावाहनादिकम् ।
क्रमशो मूलमंत्रेण धूपदीपावसानके ॥१२॥
निवेद्य तस्याः प्रथमं पुनर्धूपादिकं यजेत् ।
त्वरिता तस्य तुष्टाहं किं करोमीति ते वद ॥१३॥
संवदे बहुशो देवी दृढचित्तस्तु साधकः ।
अभीष्टं प्रार्थयेत्तत्र भक्तिपूर्वं यथोचितम् ॥१४॥
ततो देवी महातुष्टा साधकेन यदीरितम् ।
विहिताविहितं वापि ददात्येव न संशयः ॥१५॥
एतद्विधानकं श्रेष्ठं गुह्याद् गुह्यतरं परम् ।
सर्वदोषहरं सौम्यं सर्व-सौभाग्य-साधकम् ॥१६॥
सर्वभूत-ग्रहादीनां नाशनं वैरिनाशनम् ।
सर्वोत्पातहरं दिव्यं सर्वचित्र-विचित्रदम् ॥१७॥
सर्वरक्षाकरं क्रूरं सर्वोच्चाटकरं तथा ।
साधकाभीष्टदं देवि संशयो नास्ति सर्वथा ॥१८॥

इति श्रीआकाशभैरवकल्पे प्रत्यक्षसिद्धिप्रदे उमामहेश्वरसम्वादे त्वरिताविधिर्नाम षट्षष्टितमोऽध्यायः ॥६६॥

अथ सप्तषष्टितमोऽध्यायः

श्रीशिव उवाच ।।

वक्ष्यामि वीरभद्रस्य मंत्रं सर्वार्थसाधकम् ।
निग्रहानुग्रहकरं साधकानां जयप्रदम् ।।१।।
श्री वीरभद्र मंत्रस्य कालरुद्र ऋषिः स्मृतः ।
जगती छंद इत्युक्तं वीरभद्रस्तु देवता ।।२।।
वीं बीजं हुं ततः शक्ति विनियोगस्तु निग्रहे ।
व्यामित्यादि करांगस्य न्यासं कृत्वाऽथ भावयेत् ।।३।।

ध्यानम्—

मरकतमणिनील किंकिणीजालमालम्
प्रकटितमुखमीशं भानु-सोमाग्नि-नेत्रम् ।
अरिवरमसि-खेटत्यग्रमुंडाग्रहस्तम्
विधुधरमहिभूषं वीरभद्रं नमामि ।।४।।

मंत्रः—

ओं नमः पुर्वमुद्धृत्य वीरभद्राय तत्परम् ।
वैरिवंश-विनाशाय सर्वलोकभयं तथा
कराय भीमवेषाय हुं फट् च विजयद्वयम् ।।५।।
ह्रीं खं फट् च रिपून् फट् च स्वाहांतो मंत्र उच्यते ।
जपेदक्षरसाहस्रमशेषांगयुतं शिवे ।।६।।
ठकारमध्ये परिलिख्य मंत्रं बाह्येषु पत्रेषु च हुंफडर्णम् ।
संवेष्ट्य पाशांकुश-मातृकार्णान्नाराधयेच्छ्यामल-वीरभद्रम् ।।७।।
आराधनावसाने तु मातृकावर्णपूर्वकम् ।
सर्वकार्यार्थसिद्ध्यर्थं जपेत्सिध्यति शोभने ।।८।।

इति श्रीआकाशभैरवकल्पे प्रत्यक्षसिद्धिप्रदे उमामहेश्वरसम्वादे वीरभद्रविधिर्नाम सप्तषष्टितमोऽध्यायः ।।६७।।

---

१. मंत्रोद्धार :—ओं वीरभद्राय वैरिवंशविनाशाय सर्वलोकभयंकराय भीमवेषाय हुं फट् श्रों श्रों ह्रीं खं फट् रिपून् फट् स्वाहा ।

अथ अ्रष्टषष्टितमोऽध्यायः

श्रीशिव उवाच ।।

वदामि ते महेशानि वडवानल-भैरवम् ।
सर्वलोकैक-संहारकारणं दारुणं परम् ।।१।।
अ्रस्य देवस्य मंत्रस्य ऋषिर्ब्रह्मा तदुच्यते ।
छंदस्तु गायत्री देवो वडवानलभैरवः ।।२।।
प्रं बीजं च ततः स्वाहा शक्तिर्योगस्तु दाहने ।
प्रामित्यादिकरांगस्य न्यासं ध्यानमनन्तरम् ।।३।।

ध्यानम् ।।

ज्वालामालाभमंत्य-प्रलय-विभवजा-ज्वल्यमानोर्ध्वकेशम् ।
धूमं-शक्ति-कपालं-त्रिशिखमथकरैरुद्वहंतं त्रिनेत्रम् ।।
प्राणाधीशं प्रसन्नं प्रणतभयहरं स्पंदमानाधरोष्ठम् ।
वन्दे सर्वारिलोक-प्रसनपटुतरं भैरवं वाडवाग्निम् ।।४।।

मंत्रः—

[1]प्रामों नमो भगवते वडवानल तत्परम् ।
भैरवाय ततः पश्चात् ज्वल द्विः प्रज्वलेति च ।।५।।
तत्परं वैरिलोकं च दहद्विर्वह्निधर्मिणी ।
श्री चतुस्त्रिंशदर्णं च पुरश्चर्यां यथा पुरा ।।६।।
कवचोक्त यंत्रे परिलिख्य मंत्रं हरकोष्टयुग्मे त्रिशिखाग्र-नाम ।
अ्रभिवेष्ट्य मायामभिमृश्य मंत्रं निखनेत् श्मशाने रिपुमारणाय ।।७।।
यमुद्दिश्य जपेन्मंत्रं त्रिसहस्रं यमाननः ।
त्रिरात्रं निशितं देवो दहत्याशु न संशयः ।।८।।

इति श्रीआकाशभैरवकल्पे प्रत्यक्षसिद्धिप्रदे उमामहेश्वरसम्वादे वडवानलभैरवप्रयोगोनाम अष्टषष्टितमोऽध्यायः ।।६८।।

---

१. मन्त्रोद्धार :—प्रामों नमो भगवते वडवानल-भैरवाय ज्वल ज्वल प्रज्वल वैरि-लोकं दह दह स्वाहा ।

अथ एकोनसप्ततितमोऽध्यायः

मायाप्रयोगस्तु पंचविंशेऽध्याये लिखितः ॥

अथ ब्राह्मी

श्रीशिव उवाच ॥

अथ ब्राह्म्यास्तु मंत्रस्य ब्रह्मा गायत्रमुच्यते ।
ऋषिः छंदस्तु गायत्री देवता भूस्तु बीजकम् ॥१॥
ततस्तु शक्तिर्गायत्री विनियोगः प्रसादके ।
न्यासद्वयं मंत्रवर्णैर्भागशो भावनोच्यते ॥२॥

ध्यानम् ॥

रक्तां रक्तसुमाल्य-लेप-वसनां भूषादिभिर्भूषिताम्
शुद्धां स्मेरचतुर्मुखीं शुभतरग्रीवां द्विनेत्रांचलाम् ।
देवीं दण्ड-कमंडलुं स्रुव-स्रुचाक्षस्त्रक्करांभोरुहाम्
ब्राह्मींभक्तजनेष्टदाननिरतां वन्दे सुहंसाननाम् ॥३॥

मंत्रः—

[1]तारं च बीजमुद्धृत्य गायत्रीं तदनंतरम् ।
जपेदक्षरलक्षन्तु तदर्धं वा सहस्रकम् ॥
सर्वांग-सहितं देवि चतुर्वर्गार्थसिद्धये ॥४॥

शक्तेर्बाह्य-कृशानुकोण-विलसद् भूरादिसत्कर्णिकम् ।
वस्वब्ज-स्वरयुग्मकेसर-दलैर्वर्गैस्त्रिवर्णैर्मनोः ॥
चूडामंत्र-तुरीय-वेष्टितमिदं क्ष्माकोण-तारांकितम् ।
गायत्र्याः कथितं महः प्रभृतिभिर्यंत्रं तु दिक्ष्वंकितम् ॥५॥

चक्रमध्ये स्थितां ब्राह्मीं प्रातर्हृदयमध्यगाम् ।
दृढचित्तः स्थिरं ध्यात्वा सप्तव्याहृतिपूर्वकम् ॥६॥
सहस्रं यो जपेन्नित्यं ब्रह्मकल्पो भवेत्तु सः ।
चूडामंत्रयुतं मंत्रं योजयेद्देवमंबिके ॥७॥
सर्गादि-पंच-कार्याणां कर्ता भवति निश्चयः ॥८॥

इति श्रीआकाशभैरवकल्पे प्रत्यक्षसिद्धिप्रदे उमामहेश्वरसम्वादे ब्राह्मीविधिर्नामैकोन-सप्ततितमोऽध्यायः ॥६९॥

---

१. मन्त्रोद्धारः—ओं भूर्भुवः स्वः तत्सवितुर्वरेण्यं भर्गो देवस्य धीमहि । धियो यो नः प्रचोदयात् ॥

अथ सप्ततितमोऽध्यायः

श्रीशिव उवाच ॥

माहेश्वर्य्यास्तु मंत्रस्य तथा रुद्रःऋषिः स्मृतः ।
छंदस्तु देवी गायत्री देवता सा महेश्वरी ॥१॥
भुवो बीजं ततः शक्तिर्गायत्री स्वेष्टयोगकम् ।
न्यासादिकं यथापूर्वं ध्यानभेदमिहोच्यते ॥२॥

ध्यानम् ॥

श्वेताभां श्वेतवस्त्रां कुचभरनमितां श्वेतमाल्याभिरामाम् ।
त्रेधा शूलं-कपालं-कनकमणिजपस्रवहंतीं कराब्जैः ॥
वन्देऽनड्वाहरूढां स्मित-विशद-चतुर्वक्त्र-पद्मां त्रिनेत्राम् ।
माहेशीं स्निग्धकेशीं मणिमयवलयां मन्यु-युक्तां प्रसन्नाम् ॥३॥

मंत्रः—

प्रणवं च भुवः पश्चात्ततः पूर्वोक्तमंत्रकम् ।
पुरश्चर्यां च योगं च सर्वं पूर्ववदाचरेत् ॥४॥

मध्ये शक्तिं भुवश्च प्रणवमथ वसोः पत्रके क्षेत्रवर्णम् ।
बाह्ये भूस्वर्महस्तवृतुगृहविवरे षोडशारे स्वरांश्च ॥
बाह्ये चूडाख्यमंत्रं कचटतपयशहं तुर्यं मंत्रं च तारम् ।
साविञ्या यंत्रमेतत्सकलविजयदं सर्व-सौभाग्य-हेतुः ॥५॥

इति श्रीआकाशभैरवकल्पे प्रत्यक्षसिद्धिप्रदे उमामहेश्वरसम्वादे माहेश्वरी विधिर्नाम सप्ततितमोऽध्यायः ॥७०॥

---

१. मन्त्रोद्धार :—ओं भुवः ओं भूर्भुवः स्वः तत्सवितुर्वरेण्यं भर्गो देवस्य धीमहि । धियो यो नः प्रचोदयात् ॥

अथैकसप्ततिमोऽध्यायः

श्रीशिव उवाच ।।

कौमार्यास्त्वथ मंत्रस्य भरद्वाजः ऋषिः स्मृतः ।
पंक्तिश्छंदस्तथा देवी कौमारी देवताम्बिके ।।१।।
कं बीजं चाथ हुंशक्तिः प्रसादार्थे नियोगकम् ।
क्वामित्यादि करांगस्य न्यासं कुर्यात्समाहितः ।।२।।

ध्यानम् ।।

पीताभां शक्ति-खड्गाभय-वरसुभुजां पीतमाल्यां शुकाढ्याम् ।
देवीं बर्हाधिरूढां हिमकरशकला बद्ध-नीलालकांताम् ।।
नानारत्नै-र्विचित्रैरनु खचित महाभूषणैर्भूषितांगाम् ।
ध्यायेत् सर्वार्थसिद्ध्यै प्रणतभवहरां दिव्यहारां कुमारीम् ।।३।।

मंत्रः—

[1]क्वामों नमो भगवति कौमारि शिखिवाहने ।
मां पालय ततः पश्चात्सकलासुरमर्दिनि ।।४।।
एह्येहि च ततः पश्चाद्रिपून्मर्दय मर्दय ।
हुं हुं फट् च ततः स्वाहा चतुश्चत्वारिंशदक्षरम् ।।५।।
यथापूर्वं पुरश्चर्यां कृत्वा शरभ-चक्रके ।
क्रमादालिख्य मंत्रन्तु कुर्यात्स्वेच्छा-क्रियादिषु ।।६।।

इति श्रीआकाशभैरवकल्पे प्रत्यक्षसिद्धिप्रदे उमामहेश्वरसम्वादे कौमारीविधिर्नामैकसप्ततितमोऽध्यायः ।।७१।।

---

१. मंत्रोद्धार:—क्वामों नमो भगवति कौमारि शिखिवाहने मां पालय सकलासुरमर्दिनि एह्येहि रिपून् मर्दय मर्दय हुं हुं फट् स्वाहा ।

अथ द्विसप्ततितमोऽध्यायः

श्रीशिव उवाच ॥

अथ मन्त्रस्य वैष्णव्या ऋषिर्विष्णुरनंतरम् ।
गायत्रं-छंद इत्युक्तं वैष्णवी देवता ततः ॥१॥
वं बीजं चाथ सं शक्तिर्विनियोगस्त्वभीष्टके ।
वां सामित्यादि हृस्तस्य न्यासमंगस्य तत्परम् ॥२॥

ध्यानम् ॥

मरकत-मणि-नीला नीलवासोवसाना ।
विधृत मणि-जपस्त्रक्-कंबु-चक्राम्बुजाढ्या ॥
चपलगरुडरूढा सर्वतो वक्त्रपद्मा-
दिशतु दिनमघघ्नी जीवनी वैष्णवी नः ॥३॥

मंत्रः—

[1]तारं वं सं समुच्चार्य गायत्रीं तदनंतरम् ।
सप्तविंशति वर्णं तु पुरश्चर्या यथा पुरा ॥४॥

मध्ये तारं वसस्वो हुतवहभवने कोणषट्के नभोक्ता-
मष्टारे मंत्रवर्णं लिपिभिरभिवृते भूपुरे तुर्य-मंत्रम् ।
चूडामंत्रं स्वनाब्जे हनि-हन-सहित-वैष्णवीयंत्रमेतत् ।
भक्ताभीष्टार्थ-दान-प्रचुरतर-महो प्राणिनां भाग्यधेयम् ॥५॥
आराध्य देवीमनुवासरं यो जपेत्सहस्रं प्रयतः प्रदोषे ।
तस्याशुसिद्धि धनधान्यवृद्धि सौभाग्यजालं तनुते तु लक्ष्मीः ॥६॥

इति श्रीआकाशभैरवकल्पे प्रत्यक्षसिद्धिप्रदे उमामहेश्वरसम्वादे वैष्णवीमंत्रविधिर्नाम द्विसप्ततितमोऽध्यायः ॥७२॥

---

१. मन्त्रोद्धार :—ओं वं सं तत्सवितुर्वरेण्यं भर्गो देवस्य धीमहि । धियो यो नः प्रचोदयात् ॥

अथ त्रिसप्ततितमोऽध्यायः

श्रीशिव उवाच ॥

अथ मन्त्रस्य वाराह्या ऋषिरत्रिर्जितेन्द्रियः ।
छन्दोऽनुष्टुप् ततो देवी वाराही देवतांबिके ॥१॥
वं बीजमथ हुं शक्तिरभीष्टे विनियोगकम् ।
वामित्यादि करांगस्य न्यासं मूलेन चांबिके ॥२॥

ध्यानम् ॥

वज्रोपलसमां नीलां प्रसन्नां महिषासनाम् ।
सर्वदुःखहरां घोरां स्तब्धलोमाननां नुमः ॥३॥

मंत्रः—

[1]वंकारं पूर्वमुच्चार्य वाराहीति ततः परम् ।
स्वाहेति मंत्ररूपं तु सर्वदुष्टहरं परम् ॥४॥
अक्षरस्य त्रिसाहस्रं जपेत्सांगमथो निशि ।
पंचकोणे लिखेन्मंत्रं मध्ये बीजं तदग्रके ॥५॥
साध्यं मायावृतं यंत्रं सर्वदुष्टनिवारणम् ।
सम्पूज्य विधिवद्देवीं जपेदष्टसहस्रकम् ।
दक्षिणाभिमुखं देवि तत्क्षणाद्रिपुनाशनम् ॥६॥

इति श्रीआकाशभैरवकल्पे प्रत्यक्षसिद्धिप्रदे उमामहेश्वरसम्वादे वाराहीविधिर्नाम त्रिसप्ततितमोऽध्यायः ॥७३॥

---

१. मन्त्रः—वं वाराही स्वाहा ।

अथ चतुःसप्ततितमोऽध्यायः

श्रीशिव उवाच ।।

नारसिंह्याश्च मंत्रस्य ऋषिर्घोरतमाः स्मृतः ।
छंदः पंक्तिस्तथा देवि नारसिंही तु देवता ।।१।।
नं बीजमथ फट् शक्तिः सर्वोच्चाटे नियोगकः ।
नामित्यादि षडंगं स्यात्करन्यास-पुरःसरम् ।।२।।

ध्यानम् ।।

अश्वाधिरूढामतिभीमगात्रीमराति-वर्गानति-घातयंतीम् ।
शिलाविभंगैर्विविधैः कुचाभिर्नमामि घोरां वरदां नृसिंहीम् ।।३।।

मंत्रः—

नमो नमो भगवति नारसिंहि सर्वलोकेश्वरी
सकलासुरमर्दिनि समस्तरिपूनुच्चाटयोच्चाटय स्वाहा ।
शरभेश्वरचक्रे तु क्रामां मंत्रं विलिख्य तु ।
मध्ये कोष्ठे द्वये वायुं तत्रावाह्य यजेत्ततः ।।४।।
सहस्रं प्रजपेन्नित्यं पंचाशन्निशि साधकः ।
ग्रावाण-पीडितः शत्रुः क्षणभोग्यो मृतप्रजः ।।५।।
दशाहाद्बंधुभिः सार्धं देशांतरगतो भवेत् ।।

इति श्रीआकाशभैरवकल्पे प्रत्यक्षसिद्धिप्रदे उमामहेश्वरसम्वादे नारसिंहीविधिर्नाम चतुःसप्ततितमोऽध्यायः ।।७४।।

अथ पंचसप्ततितमोऽध्यायः

श्रीशिव उवाच ॥

मंत्रस्य ऋषिरिंद्राण्यश्छन्दोऽनुष्टुप् पुरंदरः ।
इंद्राणी देवता प्रोक्ता मां माये बीज-शक्तिके ॥१॥
ओंकारः कीलकं योगः स्वेष्टकार्यार्थसिद्धये ।
त्रिभिर्बीजैरथो न्यासं त्वदीयस्यापि तत् क्रमात् ॥२॥

ध्यानम् ॥

हेमाभां वरमालिकाभिरचितां हेमां प्रसन्नाननाम् ।
नानारत्नविभूषितां नवनवां नाथां हरीशादिनाम् ॥
मायातीतपराक्रमां मदगजस्कंधे-निबद्धासनाम् ।
वंदे नागविनाशिनीं वनकरां वज्रायुधोद्यतकराम् ॥३॥

[1]बीजादीनि समुच्चार्य इन्द्राणीमास्वृचं ततः ।
इन्द्राणीमासुनारिषु सुपत्नीमहमश्रवम् ॥४॥
न ह्यस्याऽअपरं च न जरसामरते पतिः ।
विलोमानि च बीजानि स्वाहान्तो मंत्र उच्यते ॥५॥
नव सप्तोर्ध्वतिर्यासु रेखासु श्र्यग्रनाम च ।
मंत्रकोष्ठं महायंत्रं सर्वकार्यार्थ-साधकम् ॥६॥
सर्वरोगहरं श्रेष्ठं सर्वकामफलप्रदम् ।
पुरश्चर्या यथा पूर्वं कार्यार्थमयुतं जपेत् ॥७॥
इच्छासिद्धिमवाप्नोति साधको नैव संशयः ॥

इति श्रीआकाशभैरवकल्पे प्रत्यक्षसिद्धिप्रदे उमामहेश्वरसम्वादे इन्द्राणीविधिर्नाम पंचसप्ततितमोऽध्यायः ॥७५॥

---

१. मन्त्रोद्धार :—ओं भूर्भुवः स्वः इन्द्राणीमासु नारिषु सुपत्नी महमश्रवम । न ह्यस्याऽअपरं च न जरसामरते पतिः विश्वस्मादिन्द्रऽउत्तरः ॥ स्वः भुवः भूरोम् स्वाहा ॥ ऋग्वेद ०८।०४।०३ ॥

अथ षट्सप्ततितमोऽध्यायः

श्रीशिव उवाच ।।

ऋषिर्वसिष्ठश्चामुंडयाश्छंदोऽतिजगती तथा ।
देवता सैव ह्रीं बीजं हुं फट् शक्तिस्तु निग्रहे ।।१।।
विनियोगस्तु ह्रामित्यादि करांग-न्यासकं ततः ।

ध्यानम् ।।

ध्यायेत्प्रेतासनस्थां मुसल-शर-गदा-खड्ग-कुतास्यभीतीः ।
गोत्रादानं-शरासं-परिघ-जलधिकं-पाश-खेटं-वरं च ।।
हस्तांभोजैर्वहंतीं शशि-रवि-नयनामक्षवर्णात्मरूपाम् ।
चामुण्डीं मुण्डमालां सकलरिपुहरां श्यामलां कोमलांगीम् ।।२।।

मंत्रः—

ह्रीं नमो भगवति चामुण्डीश्वरि सर्वशत्रुविनाशनि सर्वलोकभयंकरि एह्येहि मां रक्ष रक्ष मम शत्रून्भक्षय भक्षय हुं फट् स्वाहा ।।

एतद्वीर्यं महामंत्रं पंचाशद्वर्ण-संमितम् ।
पूर्ववत्तु पुरश्चर्यां कृत्वा देवीं यजेत्ततः ।।३।।
लेख्यं षण्नवकोष्ठके मनुमथो मध्ये चतुष्के च ह्रीं ।
बाह्ये शूलशिखाग्रके रिपुलिपिः पंचाशदर्णावृतम् ।।
देवीं पूज्य विधानतो निशि बुधो जप्त्वा सहस्रं खने-
द्यंत्रं वैरिकुलांतकं विजयदं चेष्टार्थ-सिद्धिप्रदम् ।।४।।

इति श्रीआकाशभैरवकल्पे प्रत्यक्षसिद्धिप्रदे उमामहेश्वरसम्वादे चामुण्डीविधिर्नाम षट्सप्ततितमोऽध्यायः ।।७६।।

अथ सप्तसप्ततितमोऽध्यायः

अथ शरभ-भुजंगप्रयात-स्तोत्रम्

श्रीशिव उवाच ॥

नमो विघ्नराजाय वागीश्वराय शिवाय विरञ्चाय नारायणाय ।
नमश्चंद्रचूडाय नाथाय तुभ्यं प्रसीद प्रसीद प्रसीदार्थिनो मे ॥१॥
कुठार-त्रिशूलाभिबाणास्यभीतीन् मृगाब्जाग्नि-घंटा-धनुश्चर्मदानि ।
कराब्जैर्वहंतं निरंतं हर त्वां कदा नाथ पश्याम्यहं सालुवेशम् ॥२॥
[1]लसद्वासवर्णांक वेदास्त्रमध्ये जपासंनिभे हंसपीठे निषण्णम् ।
जयंतं चिदानंदकंदं प्रसन्नं जगत्कारणं त्वां नमस्यामि शंभो ॥३॥
षडस्त्रेऽम्बुजे बादिलांतार्ण-युक्ते स्फुरच्चंचलाह्वे वसंतं भवं त्वाम् ।
कृपापूरपूर्णेक्षणंत्याधिनाहं प्रहृष्टोऽस्मि हृष्टोऽस्मि पुष्टोऽस्मि शंभो ॥४॥
दशारेऽम्बुजे दिव्यरत्नप्रभाढ्ये महाहंसपीठे समासीनमाद्यम् ।
जगत्त्राणदक्षं चिदात्मानमेकं शिवं त्वा विनाऽहं न मन्येऽन्यदेवम् ॥५॥
हृदि द्वादशारे हिरण्यप्रभेऽब्जे विराजं महाहंसपीठे प्रतिष्ठम् ।
गुणोपेतमीशं कनत्कादिठांते परं सालुवेशं शरण्यं प्रपद्ये ॥६॥
विशुद्धांबुजे षोडशारे कलाढ्ये निबद्धासनं जीवनाथं वरेण्यम् ।
क्षपाराजचूडं वराभीतिहस्तं पुराणं भजाम्यच्युतं सालुवेशम् ॥७॥
ललाटे हलक्षे दलद्वंद्वपत्रे ज्वलन्मौक्तिकाभे सुहंसासनस्थम् ।
परीतेश-सोमाग्निनेत्रं पवित्रं परं शंभुमीडे पराशक्तिमित्रम् ॥८॥
चतुः-षड्-दश-द्वादशाशास्त्र-युग्मान्यतीताष्टपत्रे लिखार्णावृतेऽब्जे ।
नमो वाग्भवानी-विसर्गान्तिरस्थं नमः सालुवेशं परं मातृकाख्यम् ॥९॥
चतुर्मातृका-पंचपंचाशदर्ण-प्रपूर्णे सहस्रच्छदे स्फाटिकाब्जे ।
प्रणौमि ध्रुवस्थं जगत्साक्षिभूतं प्रकाश-प्रपंच-प्रबोधस्वरूपम् ॥१०॥
नमो दुर्गया भद्रकाल्या च शश्वत्सदासेव्यमानं दयासिंधु-राजम् ।
प्रसन्नं शुभाक्षं शिवं तत्त्वरूपं परं सालुवेशं नुमः पक्षिराजम् ॥११॥
नमस्त्वालिकाक्षं भयत्राणदक्षं चिताभस्मनोद्धूलिताशेष-कायम् ।
महानागभूषं महेशं गिरीशं मदीयं सदानंदयत्वादि शंभो ॥१२॥

---

१. वादि सान्तांक

महीनीरशुक्रानिलव्योमसोमाहरीशात्ममूर्त्यष्टभेदस्वरूपम् ।
प्रसीदेति रक्षेति वक्तुं भवन्तं वयं के जगन्नाथ शंभो प्रसीद ॥१३॥

सहस्रेष्टकास्रे द्विपत्रे स्वराब्जे लसद् द्वादशारे दशारे षडस्रे ।
चतुष्पत्रमध्ये च मिथ्यासनस्थं जगद्रूपिणं नौमि संवित्स्वरूपम् ॥१४॥

समध्यात्मपूर्वाधिदैवाधिभूतं परं पूरुषं योगिनो यं यजंति ।
तमाद्यंतशून्यं जगद्भासयंतं महायोगशीलं सदाहं भजामि ॥१५॥

निवृत्तिः प्रतिष्ठा च विद्येति शांतिस्ततोऽतीतशांतिः कलेति स्वशक्तिम् ।
विभज्य प्रपंच-परिभ्राजयंतं नमः सालुवेशं भजेत्वाखिलेशम् ॥१६॥

यदा पुत्रमित्रानुज-भ्रातृवर्गं पिता सद्म माता धनंधान्यजालम् ।
तनुक्ष्मा च पत्नीति सर्वं कृपालो जहत्याशु मां त्वं त्वमेव प्रसीद ॥१७॥

भव त्राणनाशं पिता सुप्रसादान्यनुस्पूतमीहं तमात्मप्रभावैः ।
शिव त्वाखिलाधारमूर्ते दयाब्धेऽनिशं भावयेऽहं हृदंभोजमध्ये ॥१८॥

नमः कालकालाय रुद्राय तुभ्यं नमः पक्षिराजाय देवेश्वराय ।
नमः सालुवेशाय घोराय तुभ्यं नमो मुण्डमालाय चर्माम्बराय ॥१९॥

इति स्तोत्रमेतद्भुजंगप्रयातं जपंतं पठंतं प्रगायंतमीशम् ।
समस्तापदं प्राक् समुधृद्त्य हस्तैः पुरस्ताच्छिवत्वं ददात्येव सत्यम् ॥२०॥

इति श्रीआकाशभैरवकल्पे प्रत्यक्षसिद्धिप्रदे उमामहेश्वरसम्वादे सालुवभुजंगप्रयातस्तोत्रं नाम सप्तसप्ततितमोऽध्यायः ॥७७॥

अथ अष्टसप्ततितमोऽध्यायः

शरभहृदयम्

श्रीदेव्युवाच ॥

भगवन्देवदेवेश सर्वशास्त्रार्थवादक ।
ब्रूहि मे सर्वपापघ्नं किं मंत्रमिष्टकामदम् ॥१॥
केन पुण्यप्रभावेन शत्रूणां प्राणनाशनम् ।
सर्वपापप्रशमनं धन्यमायुष्यवर्धनम् ।
ब्रूहि मे कृपया शंभो त्वत्पादकमलं नमः ॥२॥

ईश्वर उवाच ॥

शृणु वक्ष्यामि देवेशि सर्वपापहरं परम् ॥३॥
सर्वशत्रुहरं दिव्यं हृदयं शरभस्य च ।
सालुवं सर्वरोगघ्नं हृदयं परमाद्भुतम् ॥४॥
गुह्याद्गुह्यतरं गुह्यं गोपनीयं प्रयत्नतः ।
पुरा नारायणः श्रीमान् क्षीराब्धौ मथनं ततः ॥५॥
तस्य प्रारंभसमये हृदयं शरभस्य च ।
प्रातः कालेऽजपन्नित्यं विंशदावर्त्तिकं मुदा ॥६॥
एवं मासत्रयं कृत्वा प्रादुर्बभूव सालुवः ।
तस्य सोदंडवद्भूमौ प्रणम्य च पुनः पुनः ॥७॥
तमुत्थाप्य महातेजा मूर्ध्न्युपाघ्राय सालुवः ।
संतुष्टः प्रत्युवाचेदं निर्विघ्नेनामृतं भवेत् ॥८॥
इत्युक्त्वा प्रददौ तस्मै रक्षणं सर्वविश्वकम् ।
ततो नारायणो देवः प्रणमानोऽब्रवीद्वचः ॥९॥

नारायण उवाच ॥

देव देव महादेव पक्षिराज महाप्रभो ।
हृदयं तव देवेश तस्य को वा ऋषिर्वद ॥१०॥

श्री शरभेश्वर उवाच ॥

छंदः किं बीजशक्ति च किं फलं वद मे प्रभो ।
श्रृणु वक्ष्याम्यहं विष्णो हृदयं मम सालुवम् ॥११॥
सर्वपापक्षयं पुण्यं सर्वशत्रुविनाशनम् ।
सर्वक्लेशविनाशं च सर्वसंतोषकारणम् ॥१२॥
सर्वसौभाग्यदं शांतं सर्वमंगलवर्धनम् ।
ऋषिः कालाग्निरुद्रस्तु जगती छंद ईरितम् ॥१३॥
खं बीजं च महं देव शक्तिः स्वाहेत्युदीरितम् ।
कीलकं नम इत्याहुरिष्टार्थे विनियोगकम् ॥१४॥
मूल-न्यासादिकं कृत्वा ध्यायेच्छरभ सालुवम् ।
प्रथमं पक्षिराजं च द्वितीयं शरभं तथा ॥१५॥
तृतीयं सालुवं प्रोक्तं चतुर्थं लोकनायकम् ।
पंचमं रेणुकानाथं षष्ठं कालाग्निरुद्रकम् ॥१६॥
सप्तमं नारसिंहारिमष्टमं विश्वमोहनम् ।
श्रीं ह्रीं क्लीं नवमं चैव हुं हुं हुं दशमं तथा ॥१७॥
क्लीं ह्रीं क्लामेकादशं च द्वादशं सर्वमंत्रवित् ।
त्रयोदशं तु यंत्रेशं चतुर्दशं महाबलः ॥१८॥
पंचदशं पापनाशं षोडशं च करालकम् ।
सप्तदशं महारौद्रं भीममष्टादशं तथा ॥१९॥
एकोनविंशं सांबं च विंशं च शंकरं तथा ।
विंशोत्तरैकं सर्वेशं द्वाविंशं पार्वतीपतिम् ॥२०॥
त्रयोविंशं च ह्लूं ह्लूं ह्लूं चतुर्विंशमनन्तकम् ।
पंचविंशं वृषारूढं षड्विंशं विश्वलोचनम् ॥२१॥
त्रिलोचनं सप्तविंशमष्टाविंशं खगेन्द्रकम् ।
पं पं पं नवविंशं च त्रिंशं भुजगभूषणम् ॥२२॥
एकत्रिंशं च लं लं लं द्वात्रिंशं पंचवक्त्रकम् ।
त्रयस्त्रिंशं च आनंदं चतुस्त्रिंशं परात्परम् ॥२३॥
पंचत्रिंशं च भं भं भं षट्त्रिंशं शत्रुनाशनम् ।
सप्तत्रिंशं स्वयंभूजं विभमष्टत्रिगुंठितम् ॥२४॥

शूलपाणि नवत्रिंशं चत्वारिंशं कलाधरम् ।
एकचत्वारिंशं सं सं (सं) द्विचत्वारिंश हंसकम् ॥२५॥
एतद् हृदयमायुष्यं मंत्रं सर्वार्थसाधकम् ।
अनेकरत्नलंबानी जटा-मुकुटधारिणम् ॥२६॥
अनेकरत्नसंयुक्तं सुवर्णांचितमौलिनम् ।
तक्षकादि-महानाग-कुंडलद्वय-शोभितम् ॥२७॥
त्रि पंचनयनं पंचवक्त्र-तुंडधरं प्रभुम् ।
करालं भृकुटीभीमं शंखतुल्य-कपोलकम् ॥२८॥
कालीकलित-दुर्गा च पक्षद्वय-विराजितम् ।
दशायुधधरं दीप्तं दशबाहुं त्रिलोचनम् ॥२९॥
नीलकण्ठधरं भोग-सर्पहारोपशोभितम् ।
विशालवक्षः विश्वेशं विश्वमोहनमव्ययम् ॥३०॥
त्रिपुरारिं त्रिशूलादिधारिणं मृगधारणम् ।
व्याघ्रचर्माम्बरधरं वाडवाग्निस्थितोदरम् ॥३१॥
मृत्यु-व्याधिस्थितोरुं च वज्र-जानुप्रदेशकम् ।
पादपंकजयुग्मं च तीक्ष्णवज्र-नखाग्रकम् ॥३२॥
झणि-नूपुर-मंजीरझणंतिककिणि-जंघकम् ।
वज्रतुण्ड-महादीप्तं कालकालं कृपानिधिम् ॥३३
एवं ध्यात्वा च हृदयं त्रिंशदावृतिकं क्रमात् ।
नित्यं जप्त्वा सालुवेशं हृदयं सर्वकामदम् ॥३४॥
सर्वपुण्यफलश्रेष्ठं सर्वशत्रुविनाशनम् ।
सर्वरोगहरं दिव्यं भजतां पापनाशनम् ॥३५॥
इहैव सकलान्भोगानंते शिवपदं व्रजेत् ।
इत्युक्त्वान्तर्दधे देवः शरभः पक्षिराजकः ॥३६॥
ततो नारायणं ध्यात्वा श्रुत्वा रूपं च विस्मितः ।
एतत्ते कथितं देवि हृदयं शरभस्य च ।
पठतां शृण्वतां चैव सर्वमंत्रार्थसिद्धिदम् ॥३७॥

इति श्रीआकाशभैरवकल्पे प्रत्यक्षसिद्धिप्रदे उमामहेश्वरसम्वादे शरभहृदयं नामाष्टसप्ततितमोऽध्यायः ॥७८॥

अथ एकोनाशीतितमोऽध्यायः

श्रीशिव उवाच ॥

अस्य श्रीशरभाष्टोत्तरशतनाम-महामंत्रस्य योगानंद ऋषिः अनुष्टुबछंदः श्रीमदघोर-वीर-शरभेश्वरो देवता खं बीजं स्वाहाशक्तिः फट्कीलकम् श्रीमच्छरभ-सालुव अष्टोत्तरशतनाम[1] सिद्ध्यर्थे जपे विनियोगः ।

ध्यानम् ॥

अष्टांघ्रिश्च सहस्रबाहुरनलच्छाया शिरोयुग्मधृग्-
यस्त्र्यक्षो द्विखु[2]...पुच्छउदितः साक्षान्नृसिंहासनः ॥
अर्धेनापि मृगाकृतिः पुनरथाप्यर्धेन पक्ष्याकृतिः ।
श्री वीरः शलभः स पातु शलभश्चिन्त्यः सदा मां हृदि ॥१॥

सदा शिवोग्ररूपाय पक्षविक्षिप्तभूभृते ।
नमो रुद्राय रौद्राय महोग्रा[3]साय जिष्णवे ॥२॥
नम उग्राय भीमाय नमः क्रुद्धाय मन्यवे ।
नमो भवाय शर्वाय शंकराय शिवाय च ॥३॥
कालाय कालकालाय महाकालाय मृत्यवे ।
वीराय वीरभद्राय क्षयद्वीराय शूलिने ॥४॥
महादेवाय महते पशूनां पतये नमः ।
एकाय नीलकंठाय श्रीकंठाय पिनाकिने ॥५॥
नमोऽनंताय सूक्ष्माय नमस्ते मृत्यु-मृत्यवे ।
पराय परमेशाय तत्पराय परात्मने ॥६॥
परात्पराय विश्वाय नमस्ते विश्वमूर्तये ।
नमो विष्णुकलत्राय विष्णुक्षेत्राय भानवे ॥७॥
वैकर्ताय किराताय महाव्याधाय शाश्वते ।
भैरवाय शरण्याय महाभैरवरूपिणे ॥८॥
नमो नृसिंह-संहर्त्रे काम-काल-पुरारये ।
कर्मपाशौघसंहर्त्रे विष्णुमायांतकारिणे ॥९॥

---

१. प्रसाद   ३. महोग्रास्याय
२. द्विखुरप्र

त्र्यंबकाय च त्र्यक्षाय शिपिविष्टाय मीढुषे ।
मृत्युञ्जयाय रुद्राय सर्वज्ञाय मखारये ॥१०॥
खखोल्काय वरेण्याय नमस्ते वाग्भिरेतसे ।
महाप्राणाय देवाय प्राणापानप्रवर्तिने ॥११॥
त्रिगुणाय त्रिशूलाय गुणातीताय योगिने ।
संसारचक्रवाहाय महायंत्रप्रवर्तिने ॥१२॥
तमस्विद्व्योमसूर्याय मुक्तिवैचित्र्यहेतवे ।
वरदाय विकाराय सर्वकारणहेतवे ॥१३॥
कपालिने करालाय पतये पुण्यकीर्तये ।
अमोघायाग्निनेत्राय नकुलीशाय शंभवे ॥१४॥
भीषांबराय चंडाय दंडिने घोररूपिणे ।
मेघवाहाय देवाय पार्वतीपतये नमः ॥१५॥
अव्यक्तायाप्यशोकाय स्थिराय स्थिरधन्विने ।
स्थाणवे कृत्तिवासाय नमश्चंद्रार्द्धमौलये ॥१६॥
नमस्तेऽध्वरराजाय वचसां पतये नमः ।
योगीश्वराय नित्याय सत्याय परमात्मने ॥१७॥
सर्वात्मने नमस्तुभ्यं नमः सर्वस्वराय च ।
एक-द्विस्त्रि-चतुः-पंच-सृष्टिकृत्यस्तुते नमः ॥१८॥
दशकृत्वः शतकृत्वः सहस्रकृत्वो नमो नमः ।
नमो परिमिते कृत्वो नमः कृत्वो नमो नमः ॥१९॥
नमो भूयो नमो भूयो पुनर्भूयो नमो नमः ।

सूत उवाच ॥

नाम्नामष्टशतेनैव स्तुत्वामृतमयेन च ॥२०॥
तथा तथा विनीतव्यस्त्वयैव परमेश्वर ।
एवं विज्ञाप्य सव्रीडं शंकरं नरकेसरम् ॥२१॥
ततः स्तुत्वा च भगवान् जीवितं सापराधतः ।
तद्वक्त्रशेषं तद्गात्रं कृत्वा शरभ-विग्रहः ॥२२॥
अतीन्द्रियत्वमगमद्वीरभद्रेक्षणात्ततः ।
अद्य ब्रह्मादयः सर्वे वीरभद्रस्य तेजसा ॥२३॥

देवा ऊचुः ॥

जीवितास्स्मो वयं देवाः पर्जन्येनैव पादपाः ।
अस्माद्भीषादहत्यग्निरुदेति च रविः शशी ॥२४॥
वातो वाति च भीषास्य मृत्युर्धावति पंचमः ।
तद्व्यक्तं परमं व्योम कलातीतं सदाशिवः ॥२५॥
भवंतमेव भगवान्वदंति ब्रह्मवादिनः ।
किं वयं तव पादाब्ज-वदने परमेश्वरः ॥२६॥
नांगीकुर्वन्यजात्यंधं रूपलावण्यदर्शने ।
उपसर्गेषु सर्वेषु त्रायस्वास्मान्नराधिप ॥२७॥
एकादशात्मभगवन् दुःखं नः कृपया हर ।
ईदृशान्यवताराणि दृष्ट्वापि बहुशस्तव ॥२८॥
न विद्मस्ते परं भावं वंचितास्तव मायया ।
देव देव महादेव भीतान्नः पाहि सर्वशः ॥२९॥
त्वं पिता सर्वलोकनां नाथस्त्वं त्वं गुरुः सुहृत् ।
विश्वेश्वर विरूपाक्ष भगवन्करुणाकर ॥३०॥
अस्माभिः सह गंतव्यं तत्क्षंतव्यं परात्पर ।
द्वे तनू तव रुद्रस्य वेदज्ञा ब्राह्मणा विदुः ॥३१॥
घोर एका शिवा अन्या ते प्रत्येकमनेकधा ।
घोरा तव तनू ब्रह्मन् सूर्यो विष्णुर्हुताशनः ॥३२॥
शिवा तव तनू ब्रह्मा आपो धर्मश्च चंद्रमाः ।
उभाभ्यां पाहि भगवन्भीतिभ्योऽस्मान्महाबलः ॥३३॥
भवतेदं जगत्सर्वं व्याप्तं स्वेनैव तेजसा ।
ब्रह्माविष्ण्वर्कशक्राग्नि-जलधर्मपुरोगमाः ॥३४॥
सुरासुराः सुप्रभूतास्त्वत्तः सर्वं महेश्वर ।
ब्रह्माणमिंद्रं विष्णुं च यान्तु मृत्युं सुरा नराः ॥३५॥
यतो निगृह्य हरसि हर इत्युक्तं वेदवित् ।
इदं परममाख्यानं पुण्यं सर्वाघनाशनम् ॥३६॥

इति श्रीआकाशभैरवकल्पे प्रत्यक्षसिद्धिप्रदे उमामहेश्वरसम्वादे शरभाष्टोत्तरशतनाम एकोनाशीतितमोऽध्यायः ॥७९॥

अथ अशीतितमोऽध्यायः

श्रीशिव उवाच ॥

अस्य श्री शरभ सहस्रनाम-स्तोत्र-मंत्रस्य कालाग्नि-रुद्रो-वामदेव ऋषिः अनुष्टुब्छन्दः शरभ-सालुवो देवता ह्स्रां बीजं स्वाहा शक्तिः फट्-कीलकं शरभ-सालुव प्रसादसिद्ध्यर्थे जपे विनियोगः ॥

ओं ह्स्रां अंगुष्ठाभ्यां नमः———हृदयाय नमः
ओं ह्स्रीं तर्जनीभ्यां नमः———शिरसे स्वाहा
ओं ह्स्रूं मध्यमाभ्यां नमः———शिखायै वषट्
ओं ह्स्रैं अनामिकाभ्यां नमः———कवचाय हुम्
ओं ह्स्रौं कनिष्ठिकाभ्यां नमः———नेत्रत्रयाय वौषट्
ओं ह्स्रः करतल-करपृष्ठाभ्यां नमः———अस्त्राय फट्
ओं भूर्भुवः स्वरोम् इति दिग्बन्धः ।

ध्यानम् ॥

क्वाकाशः क्व समीरणः क्व दहनः क्वापः क्व विश्वंभरः
क्व ब्रह्मा क्व जनार्दनः क्व तरणिः क्वेन्दुः क्व देवासुराः ।
कल्पांते शरभेश्वरः प्रमुदितः श्रीसिद्धयोगीश्वरः
क्रीडा-नाटक-नायको विजयते देवो महासालुवः ॥१॥

लं पृथिव्यादि पंचोपचारैः संपूज्य—

श्री भैरव उवाच ॥

श्री नाथो रेणुकानाथो जगन्नाथो जगाश्रयः ।
श्रीगुरुर्गुरुगम्यश्च गुरुरूपः कृपानिधिः ॥१॥
हिरण्यबाहुः सेनानी दिक्पतिस्तरुराट्टरः ।
हरिकेशः पशुपतिर्महांसःपिंजरो मृडः ॥२॥
गणेशो गणनाथश्च गणपूज्यो गणाश्रयः ।
विव्याधिर्बभ्लशः श्रेष्ठः परमात्मा सनातनः ॥३॥
पीठेशः पीठरूपश्च पीठपूज्यः सुखावहः ।
सर्वाधिको जगत्कर्ता पुष्टेशो नंदिकेश्वरः ॥४॥
भैरवो भैरव-श्रेष्ठो भैरवायुधधारकः ।
आततायी महारुद्रः संसारार्क-सुरेश्वरः ॥५॥

सिद्धःसिद्धिप्रदः साध्यः सिद्धमंडलपूजितः ।
उपवीती महानात्मा क्षेत्रेशो वननायकः ॥६॥
बहुरूपो बहुस्वामी बहुपालनकारणः ।
रोहितः स्थपतिः सूतो वाणिजो मंत्रिरुन्नतः ॥७॥
पदरूपः पदप्राप्तः पदेशः पदनायकः ।
कक्षेशोऽहुः भूतदेवो भुवं तिर्वारिवस्कृतः ॥८॥
दूतिक्रमो दूतिनाथः शांभवः शंकरः प्रभुः ।
उच्चैर्घोषो घोषरूपः पत्तीशः पापमोचकः ॥९॥
वीरो वीर्यप्रदः शूरो वीरेशो वीरदायकः ।
श्रोषधीशः पंचवक्त्रः कृत्स्नवीतो भयानकः ॥१०॥
वीरनाथो वीररूपो वीर-श्रायुधधारकः ।
सहमानः स्वर्णरेतो निर्व्याधि निरुपप्लवः ॥११॥
चतुराश्रमनिष्ठश्च चतुर्मूर्तिश्चतुर्भुजः ।
श्राव्याधिनीशः ककुभो निषंगी स्तेनरक्षकः ॥१२॥
षष्टीशो घटिकारूपः फलसंकेतवर्धकः ।
मंत्रात्मा तस्कराध्यक्षो वंचकः परिवंचकः ॥१३॥
नवनाथो नवांकस्थो नवचक्रेश्वरो विभुः ।
अरण्येशः परिचरो निचेयुस्तायुरक्षकः ॥१४॥
वीरावलीप्रियः शांतो युद्ध-विक्रम-दर्शकः ।
प्रकृतेशो गिरिचरः कुलिचेशो गुहेष्टदः ॥१५॥
पंचपंचकतत्वस्थस्तत्वातीत स्वरूपकः ।
भवः शर्वो नीलकंठः कपर्दी त्रिपुरांतकः ॥१६॥
श्रीमंत्र श्रीकलानाथः श्रेयदः श्रेयवारिधिः ।
मुक्तकेशो गिरिशयः सहस्राक्षः सहस्रपात् १७॥
मालाधरो मनःश्रेष्ठो मुनिमानसहंसगः ।
शिपिविष्टश्चंद्रमौली हंसो मीढुष्टमोऽनघः ॥१८॥
मंत्रराजो मंत्ररूपो मंत्रपुण्यफलप्रदः ।
उर्व्यः सूर्म्योद्‌ग्रीयशीभ्यः प्रथम-पावकाकृतिः ॥१९॥

गुरुमंडलरूपस्थो गुरुमंडलकारणः ।
अचरस्तारकस्तारो वस्वन्योऽनंतविग्रहः ॥२०॥
तिथि-मंडल-रूपश्च वृद्धि-क्षयविवर्जितः ।
द्वीप्यः स्रोतस्य ईशानो धुर्यो गव्य-यतोमयः ॥२१॥
प्रथमः प्रथमाकारो द्वितीयः शक्तिसंयुतः ।
गुणत्रय—तृतीयोऽसौ युगरूपश्चतुर्थकः ॥२२॥
पूर्वजो वरजो ज्येष्ठः कनिष्ठो विश्वलोचनः ।
पंचभूतात्मा साक्षीशो ऋतुःषड्गुणभावनः ॥२३॥
अप्रगल्भो मध्यमोर्म्योजघन्योऽजघन्यः शुभः ।
सप्तधातुस्वरूपश्च अष्टमः सिद्धिसिद्धिदः ॥२४॥
प्रतिसर्पोऽनन्तरूपो सोम्यो याम्य सुराश्रयः ।
नवनाथ-नवम्यस्थो दिशदिग्रूपधारकः ॥२५॥
रुद्र एकादशाकारो द्वादशादित्यरूपकः ।
वन्यो वसान्यः पूतात्मा श्रवः कक्षः प्रतिश्रवाः ॥२६॥
व्यंजनो व्यंजनातीतो विसर्गः स्वरभूषणः ।
आशुषेणो महासेनो महावीरो महारथः ॥२७॥
अनंतो अव्ययो आद्यो आदिशक्ति-वरप्रदः
श्रुतसेन-श्रुतसाक्षी कवची वशकृद्वशः ॥२८॥
आनंदश्चाद्यसंस्थान आद्याकारणलक्षणः ।
आहनन्योऽनन्यनाथो दुंदुम्यो दुष्टनाशनः ॥२९॥
कर्ता कारयिता कार्यः कार्यकारणभावगः ।
धृष्ण-प्रमृश ईड्यात्मा वदान्यो वेदसम्मतः ॥३०॥
कलानाथः कलातीतः काव्य-नाटक-बोधकः ।
तीक्ष्णेषुपाणिः प्रहितः स्वायुधः शस्त्रविक्रमः ॥३१॥
कालहन्ता कालसाध्यः कालचक्रप्रवर्तकः ।
सुधन्वा सुप्रसन्नात्मा प्रविविक्तः सदागतिः ॥३२॥
कालाग्निरुद्र-संदीप्तः कालांतकभयंकरः ।
खड्गीशः खड्गनाथश्च खड्गशक्तिः परायणः ॥३३॥

गर्वघ्नः शत्रुसंहर्ता गमागमविवर्जितः ।
यज्ञकर्मफलाध्यक्षो यज्ञमूर्तिरनातुरः ॥३४॥

घनश्यामो घनानंदी घनाधारप्रवर्तकः ।
घनकर्ता घनत्राता घनबीजसमुत्थितः ॥३५॥

लोप्यो लुप्यः पर्णसद्यः पण्यः पूर्ण पुरातनः ।
डकारसंधि-साध्यानो वेदवर्णनसांगकः ॥३६॥

भूतो भूतपतिर्भूपो भूधरो भूधरायुधः ।
छंदःसारः छंदकर्ता छंद-अन्वयधारकः ॥३७॥

भूतसंगो भूतमूर्तिर्भूतिहा भूतिभूषणः ।
छत्रसिंहासनाधीशो भक्तछत्रसमृद्धिमान् ॥३८॥

मदनो मादको माद्यो मधुहा मधुरप्रियः ।
जपो जपप्रियो जप्यो जपसिद्धिप्रदायकः ॥३९॥

जपसंख्यो जपाकारः सर्वमंत्रजपप्रियः ।
मधुर्मधुकरः शूरो मधुरो मदनांतकः ॥४०॥

झषरूपधरो देवो झषवृद्धिविवर्धकः ।
यमशासनकर्ता च यमपूज्यो यमाधिपः ॥४१॥

निरंजनो निराधारो निर्लिप्तो निरुपाधिकः ।
टंकायुधः शिवप्रीतष्टंकारो लांगलाश्रयः ॥४२॥

निष्प्रपंचो निराकारो निरीहो निरुपद्रवः ।
सपर्याप्रतिडामर्यो मंत्रडामरस्थापकः ॥४३॥

सत्त्व-सत्त्वगुणोपेत सत्त्ववित्सत्त्ववित्प्रियः ।
सदाशिवोह्य प्ररूपश्च पक्षविक्षिप्तभूभृत् ॥४४॥

धनदो धननाथश्च धनधान्यप्रदायकः ।
"ओं नमो रुद्राय रौद्राय महोग्राय च मीढुषे" ॥४५॥

नाद-ज्ञानरतो नित्यो नादांत-पद-दायकः ।
फलरूपः फलातीतः फल-अक्षर-लक्षणः ॥४६॥

ओं श्रीं ह्रीं क्लीं सर्वभूतान्यो भूतिहा भूतिभूषणः ।
रुद्राक्षमालाभरणो रुद्राक्षप्रियवत्सलः ॥४७॥

रुद्राक्षवक्षो रुद्राक्षरूपो रुद्राक्षभक्षकः ।
फलदः फलदाता च फलकर्ता फलप्रियः ॥४८॥
फलाश्रयः फलातीतः फलमूर्तिर्निरंजनः ।
बलानंदो बलग्रामो बलीशो बलनायकः ॥४९॥
ओं खें खां घ्रां ह्लां वीरभद्रः सम्राट्-दक्ष-मखांतकः ।
भविष्यज्ञो भयत्राता भयकर्ता भयारिहा ॥५०॥
विघ्नेश्वरो विघ्नहर्ता गुरुर्देवशिखामणिः ।
भावनारूपध्यानस्थो भावार्थफलदायकः ॥५१॥
ओं श्रां ह्लां कल्पित-कल्पस्थो कल्पना-पूरणालयः ।
भुजंग-विलसत्कंठो भुजंगाभरणप्रियः ॥५२॥
ओं ह्लीं ह्लूं मोहनोत्कर्ता छन्द मानसतोषकः ।
नानातीतः स्वयं वान्यो भक्तमानंदसंश्रयः ॥५३॥
नागेन्द्र-चर्म-वसनो नारसिंह-निपातनः ।
रकारो अग्निबीजस्थो अपमृत्युविनाशनः ॥५४॥
ओं प्रें प्रें प्रें प्रें ह्लां दुष्टेष्टा मृत्युहा मृत्युपूजितः ।
व्यक्तो व्यक्ततमो व्यक्तो रतिलावण्य-सुंदरः ॥५५॥
रतिनाथो रतिप्रीतो निधनेशो धनाधिपः ।
रमाप्रियकरो रम्यो लिंगो लिंगात्मविग्रहः ॥५६॥
ओं क्ष्रों क्ष्रों क्ष्रों क्ष्रों ग्रहाकारो रत्नविक्रयविग्रहः ।
ग्रहकृद् ग्रहभृद् ग्राही गृहाद् गृहविलक्षणः ॥५७॥
"ओं नमः पक्षिराजाय दावाग्निरूपरूपकाय
घोरपातकनाशाय [1]सूर्यलसु—प्रभुः" ? ॥५८॥
पवनः पावको वामो महाकालो महापहः ।
वर्धमानो वृद्धिरूपो विश्वभक्तिप्रियोत्तमः ॥५९॥
ओं ह्लूं ह्लूं सर्वगः सर्वः सर्वजित्सर्वनायकः ।
जगदेकप्रभुः स्वामी जगद्वंद्यो जगन्मयः ॥६०॥
सर्वान्तरः सर्वव्यापी सर्वकर्मप्रवर्तकः ।
जगदानंददो जन्म-जरा-मरण-वर्जितः ॥६१॥

---

१. शलभ-शाल्वाय हुं फट् ।"

सर्वार्थसाधकः साध्य-सिद्धिः साधक-साधकः ।
खट्वांगी नीतिमान्सत्यो देवतात्मात्मसंभवः ॥६२॥
हविर्भोक्ता हविः प्रीतो हव्यवाहनहव्यकृत् ।
कपालमालाभरणः कपाली विष्णुवल्लभः ॥६३॥
ओं ह्रीं [1](प्रवेश रोगाय) स्थूलास्थूलविशारदः ।
कलाधीशस्त्रिकालज्ञो दुष्टावग्रहकारकः ॥६४॥
ओं हुं हुं हुं हुं नटवरो महानाट्यविशारदः ।
क्षमाकरः क्षमानाथः क्षमापूरितलोचनः ॥६५॥
वृषांको वृषभाधीशः क्षमासाधनसाधकः ।
क्षमाचिंतनप्रीतस्थो वृषात्मा वृषभध्वजः ॥६६॥
ओं क्रों क्रों क्रों क्रों महाकायो महावक्षो महाभुजः ।
मूलाधारनिवासश्च गणेशः सिद्धिदायकः ॥६७॥
महास्कंधो महाग्रीवो महद्वक्त्रो महच्छिरः ।
महदोष्ठो [2]महदार्यो महादंष्ट्रो महाहनुः ॥६८॥
सुंदरभ्रूः सुनयनः षट्चक्रो वर्णलक्षणः ।
मणिपूरो महाविष्णुः सुललाटः सुकंधरः ॥६९॥
सत्यवाक्यो धर्मवेत्ता प्रजासृजन-कारणः ।
स्वाधिष्ठाने रुद्ररूपः सत्यज्ञः सत्यविक्रमः ॥७०॥
ओं ग्लों ग्लों ग्लों ग्लों महादेव द्रव्य-शक्ति-समाहितः ।
कृतज्ञः कृतकृत्यात्मा कृतकृत्यः कृतागमः ॥७१॥
ओं हं हं हं हं गुरुरूपो हंस-मंत्रार्थ मंत्रकः ।
व्रतकृद् व्रतविच्छ्रेष्ठो व्रतविद्वान्महाव्रती ॥७२॥
सहस्रारे-सहस्राक्षः व्रताधारो वृतेश्वरः ।
वृतप्रीतो वृताकारो वृतनिर्वाणदर्शकः ॥७३॥
"ओं ह्रीं ह्रूं क्लीं श्रीं क्लीं ह्रीं फट् स्वाहा" ।
अतिरागी वीतरागः कैलासोऽनाहतध्वनिः ।
मायापूरकयंत्रस्थो रोगहेतुर्विरागवित् ॥७४॥
रागघ्नो रागशमनो लंबकाश्यभिषिञ्चनः ।
सहस्रदलगर्भस्थः चंद्रिकाद्रवसंयुतः ॥७५॥

१· प्रें वं शं शरण्यः २. महदास्यो

अंतनिष्ठो महाबुद्धिःप्रदाता नीतिवित्प्रियः ।
नीतिकृन्नीतिविन्नीतिरंतर्याग-स्वयंसुखीन् ॥७६॥
विनीतवत्सलो नीतिस्वरूपो नीतिसंश्रयः ।
स्वभावो यंत्रसंचारस्तन्तुरूपोऽमलच्छविः ॥७७॥
क्षेत्रकर्मप्रवीणश्च क्षेत्रकीर्तनवर्धनः ।
क्रोधजित्क्रोधनः क्रोधीजनवित् क्रोधरूपधृक् ॥७८॥
विश्वरूपो विश्वकर्ता चैतन्यो ग्रंत्रमालिकः ।
मुनिध्येयो मुनित्राता शिवधर्मधुरंधरः ॥७९॥
धर्मज्ञो धर्मसंबंधो ध्वांतघ्नो ध्वांतसंशयः ।
इच्छा-ज्ञान-क्रियातीत-प्रभावः पार्वतीपतिः ॥८०॥
हं हं हं हं लतारूपः कल्पनावांछितप्रदः ।
कल्पवृक्षः कल्पनस्थः पुण्यश्लोकप्रयोजकः ॥८१॥
प्रदीप-निर्मल-प्रौढः परमः परमागमः ।
ओं ज्रं ज्रं ज्रं सर्वसंक्षोभ सर्वसंहारकारकः ॥८२॥
क्रोधदः क्रोधहा क्रोधी जनहा क्रोधकारणः ।
गुणवान् गुणविच्छ्रेष्ठो वीर्यविद्वीर्यसंश्रयः ॥८३॥
गुणाधारो गुणाकारः सत्त्व-कल्याणदेशिकः ।
सत्वरः सत्त्वविद्भावः सत्य-विज्ञान-लोचनः ॥८४॥
"ओं ह्रां ह्रीं ह्रू क्लीं श्रीं ब्लू प्रों [1]ओं ह्रीं क्रों हुं फट् स्वाहा" ॥
वीर्याकारो वीर्यकरच्छंनमूलो महाजयः ।
अविच्छिन्न-प्रभावश्री वीर्यहा वीर्यवर्धकः ॥८५॥
कालवित्कालकृत्कालो बलप्रमथनो बली ।
छिन्नपापश्छिन्नपाशो विच्छिन्नभययातनः ॥८६॥
मनोन्मनो मनोरूपो विच्छिन्नभयनाशनः ।
विच्छिन्नसंगसंकल्पो बलप्रमथनो बलः ॥८७॥
विद्याप्रदाता विद्येशः शुद्धबोधः सदोदितः ।
शुद्धबोधो विशुद्धात्मा विद्यामात्रैकसंश्रयः ॥८८॥
शुद्धसत्त्वो विशुद्धांतविद्यावेद्यो विशारदः ।
गुणाधारो गुणाकारः सत्त्वकल्याणदेशिकाः ॥८९॥

---

१. प्रों

सत्त्वरः सत्त्वसद्भावः सत्त्वविज्ञानलोचनः ।
वीर्यवान्वीर्यविच्छ्रेष्ठः सत्त्वविद्यावबोधकः ॥९०॥
अविनाशो निराभासः विशुद्धज्ञानगोचरः ।
"ओं ह्रीं श्रीं ऐं सौः शिवं कुरु कुरु स्वाहा ।
संसार-यंत्र-वाहाय महायंत्रप्रवर्तिने ॥९१॥
नमः श्री-व्योम-सूर्याय मूर्ति वैचित्र्यहेतवे" ।
जगज्जीवो जगत्प्राणो जगदात्मा जगद्गुरुः ॥९२॥
आनंदरूप-नित्यस्थः प्रकाशानंदरूपकः ।
योग-ज्ञान-महाराजो योगज्ञान-महाशिवः ॥९३॥
अखंडानंददाता च पूर्णानंद-स्वरूपवान् ।
"वरदायाविकाराय सर्वकारणहेतवे ॥९४॥
कपालिने करालाय पतये पुण्यकीर्तये ।
अघोरायाग्निनेत्राय दंडिने घोररूपिणे ॥९५॥
भिषग्गण्याय चंडाय अकुलीशाय शंभवे ।
ह्लं क्षुं रूं क्लीं सिद्धाय नमः" ।
[1]घंडारवः सिद्धगंडो गजघंटा-ध्वनिप्रियः ॥९६॥
गगनाख्यो गजावासो गरलांशो गणेश्वरः ।
सर्वपक्षि-मृगाकारः सर्वपक्षिमृगाधिपः ॥९७॥
चित्रो विचित्रसंकल्पो विचित्रो विशदोदयः ।
निर्भवो भवनाशश्च निर्विकल्पो विकल्पकृत् ॥९८॥
कक्षाविसलकः कर्त्ता कोविदः काऽमशासनः ।
[2](शुद्धबोधो विशुद्धात्मा विद्यामात्रैकसंश्रयः ॥९९॥
शुद्धसत्त्वो विशुद्धांत-विद्या-वैद्यो विशारदः ।)
प्रलयानलकृद्धव्यः . प्रलयानलशासनः ॥१००॥
त्रियंबकोऽरिषड्वर्गनाशको धनदः प्रियः ।
अक्षोभ्यः क्षोभरहितः क्षोभदः क्षोभनाशकः ॥१०१॥
"ओं प्रां प्रीं प्रूं प्रैं प्रौं प्रः मणिमंत्रौषधादीनां शक्तिरूपाय शंभवे
अप्रमेयाय देवाय वषट् स्वाहा स्वधात्मने" ॥१०२॥

---

१. घण्टारवः २. श्लोक-पाद पुनरुक्ति ८८-८९

द्यौर्मूर्धा-दशदिग्बाहुश्चन्द्रसूर्याग्निलोचनः।
पातालांघ्रिरिलाकुक्षिः खंमुखो गगनोदरः ॥१०३॥
कलानादः कलाबिंदुः कलाज्योतिः सनातनः।
अलौकिकः कलोदारः कैवल्यपददायकः ॥१०४॥
कौल्यः कुलेशः कुलजः कविः कर्पूरभास्वरः।
कामेश्वरः कृपासिंधुः कुशलः कुलभूषणः ॥१०५॥
कौपीनवसनः कांतः केवलः कल्पपादपः।
कुन्देन्दु-शंखधवलो भस्मोद्धूलितविग्रहः ॥१०६॥
भस्माभरणहृष्टात्मा तुष्टः पुष्टोऽरिषूदनः।
स्थाणुर्दिगंबरो भर्गो भगनेत्रभिदुज्ज्वलः ॥१०७॥
त्रिकाग्निकालः कालाग्निरद्वितीयो महायशाः।
सामप्रियः सामकर्ता सामगः सामगप्रियः ॥१०८॥
धीरो दांतो महाधीरो धैर्यदो धैर्यवर्धकः।
लावण्यराशिः सर्वज्ञः सुबुद्धिर्बुद्धिमद्वरः ॥१०९॥
तारणाश्रयरूपस्थस्तारणाश्रयदायकः।
तारकस्तारकस्वामी तारणस्तारणप्रियः ॥११०॥
एकतारो द्वितारश्च तृतीयो मंत्र-आश्रयः।
एकरूपश्चैकनाथो बहुरूपः स्वरूपवान् ॥१११॥
लोकसाक्षी त्रिलोकेशस्त्रिगुणातीतमूर्तिमान्।
बालस्तारुण्यरूपस्थो वृद्धरूपप्रदर्शकः ॥११२॥
अवस्थात्रय-भूतस्थो अवस्था-त्रयवर्जितः।
वाच्य-वाचक-भावार्थो वाक्यार्थप्रियमानसः ॥११३॥
ओऽस्त्रो वाक्यप्रमाणस्थो महावाक्यार्थबोधकः।
परमाणु प्रमाणस्थः कोटिब्रह्माण्डनायकः ॥११४॥
"ओं हं हं हं हं ह्रीं वामदेवाय नमः"
कक्षवित्पालकः कर्ता कोविदः कामशासनः।
कपर्दी केसरी कालः कल्पनारहिताकृतिः ॥११५॥
खं खेलः खेचरः ख्यातः खन्यवादी खमुद्गतः।
खांबरः खंडपरशुः खचक्षुः खड्गलोचनः ॥११६॥

अखंडब्रह्म खंडश्रीरखंडज्योतिरव्ययः ।
षट्चक्रखेलनः स्रष्टा षट्ज्योति-षट्गिरार्चितः ॥११७॥

गरिष्ठो गोपतिर्गोप्ता गंभीरो ब्रह्मगोलकः ।
गोवर्धनगतिर्गोविद् गवातीतो गुणाकरः ॥११८॥

गंगाधरोऽङ्गसंगम्यो गंकारो गट्करागमः ।
कर्पूरगौरो गौरीशो गौरी-गुरु-गुहाशयः ॥११९॥

धूर्जटिः पिंगलजटो जटामंडलमण्डितः ।
मनोजवो जीवहेतुरंधकासुरसूदनः ॥१२०॥

लोकबन्धुः कलाधारः पाण्डुरः प्रमथाधिपः ।
अव्यक्तलक्षणो योगी योगीशो योगिपुंगवः ॥१२१॥

भूतावासो जनावासः सुरावासः सुमंगलः ।
भववैद्यो योगिवैद्यो योगीसिंहहृद्वासनः ॥१२२॥

युगावासो युगाधीशो युगकृद्युगवन्दितः ।
किरीटलेटिबालेन्दु मणिकंकणभूषितः ॥१२३॥

रत्नांगरागौ रत्नेशो रत्नरंजितपादुकः ।
नवरत्नगुणोपेत किरीटो रत्नकञ्चुकः ॥१२४॥

नानाविधानेकरत्नलसत्कुण्डलमंडितः ।
दिव्यरत्नगणोत्कीर्णं कंठाभरणभूषितः ॥१२५॥

नवफालामणिर्नासापुटभ्राजित-मौक्तिकः ।
रत्नांगुलीयविलसत्करशाखा-नखप्रभः ॥२२६॥

रत्नभ्राजद्धेमसूत्र-लसत्कटितटः पटुः ।
वामांगभागविलसत्पार्वती-वीक्षणः-प्रियः ॥१२७॥

लीलाविलंबितवपुर्भक्तमानसमंदिरः ।
मंद-मंदार-पुष्पौघ-लसद्वायुनिषेवितः ॥१२८॥

कस्तूरी विलसत्फालोदिव्यवेषविराजितः ।
दिव्यदेहप्रभाकूट-संदीपित-दिगंतरः ॥१२९॥

देवासुरगुरुस्तव्यो देवासुरनमस्कृतः ।
हंसराजः प्रभाकूट-पुण्डरीकनिभेक्षणः ॥१३०॥

सर्वाशाहगुणोमयः सर्व-लोकेष्ट-भूषणः ।
सर्वेष्टदाता सर्वेष्टस्फुरन्मंगलविग्रहः ॥१३१॥
अविद्यालेशरहितो नानाविद्यैकसंश्रयः ।
मूर्तिभावःकृपापूरो भक्तेष्टफलपूरकः ॥१३२॥
संपूर्णकामः सौभाग्यनिधिः सौभाग्यदायकः ।
हितैषी हितकृत्सौम्यः परार्थैकप्रयोजकः ॥१३३॥
शरणागत दीनार्तपरित्राणपरायणः ।
विष्वंचिता वषट्कारो भ्राजिष्णुर्भोजनंहविः ॥१३४॥
भोक्ता भोजयिता जेता जितारिर्जितमानसः ।
अक्षरः कारणो रिद्धः शमदः शारदाप्लवः ॥१३५॥
आज्ञापकश्च गंभीरः कविर्दुःस्वप्ननाशनः ।
पंचब्रह्मसमुत्पत्तिः क्षेत्रज्ञः क्षेत्रपालकः ॥१३६॥
व्योमकेशो भीमवेषो गौरीपतिरनामयः ।
भवाब्धितरणोपायोभगवान्भक्तवत्सलः ॥१३७॥
वरो वरिष्ठ-तेजिष्ठः प्रियाप्रियवधः सुधीः ।
यंताऽयविष्ठः क्षोदिष्ठो यविष्ठो यमशासनः ॥१३८॥
हिरण्यगर्भो हेमांगो हेमरूपो हिरण्यदः ।
ब्रह्मज्योतिरनावेक्ष्यश्चामुण्डाजनको रवि ॥१३९॥
मोक्षार्थीजनकःसेव्यो मोक्षदो मोक्षनायकः ।
महाश्मशान-निलयो वेदाश्वाभूरथस्थिरः ॥१४०॥
मृगव्याधो धर्मधामप्रच्छन्नस्फटिकःप्रभः ।
सर्वज्ञः परमात्मा च ब्रह्मानंदाश्रयो विभुः ॥१४१॥
शरभेशो महादेवः परब्रह्मसदाशिवः ।
स्वराविकृतिकर्तार स्वरातीत स्वयंविभुः ॥१४२॥
स्वर्गतः स्वर्गतिर्दाता नियंता नियताश्रयः ।
भूमिरूपो भूमिकर्ता भूधरो भूधराश्रयः ॥१४३॥
भूतनाथो भूतकर्ता भूतसंहारकारकः ।
भविष्यज्ञो भवत्राता भवदो भवहारकः ॥१४४॥

वरदो वरदाता च वरप्रीतो वरप्रदः ।
कूटस्थः कूटरूपश्च त्रिकूटो मंत्रविग्रहः ॥१४५॥
मंत्रार्थो मंत्रगम्यश्च मंत्रेशो मंत्रभागकः ।
सिद्धिमंत्रः सिद्धिदाता जपसिद्धिः स्वभावकः ॥१४६॥
नामातिगो नामरूपो नामरूपगुणाश्रयः ।
गुणकर्ता गुणत्राता गुणातीता गुणारिहा ॥१४७॥
गुणग्रामो गुणाधीशः गुणनिर्गुणकारकः ।
अकार-मातृकारूपो अकारातीतभावनः ॥१४८॥
परमैश्वर्यदाता च परमप्रीतिदायकः ।
परमः परमानंदः परानंदः परात्परः ॥१४९॥
वैकुण्ठपीठमध्यस्थो वैकुण्ठो विष्णुविग्रहः ।
कैलाशवासी कैलाशः शिवरूपः शिवप्रदः ॥१५०॥
जटाजूटो भूषितांगो भस्म-धूसरभूषणः ।
दिग्वाससो दिग्विभागो दिगंतरनिवासकः ॥१५१॥
ध्यानकर्ता ध्यानमूर्तिर्धारणाधारणप्रियः ।
जीवन्मुक्तिपुरीनाथो द्वादशांतस्थितप्रभुः ॥१५२॥
तत्त्वस्थस्तत्त्वरूपस्थस्तत्त्वातीतोऽति-तत्त्वतः ।
तत्त्वासाम्यस्तत्त्वगम्यस्तत्त्वार्थसर्वदर्शकः ॥१५३॥
तत्त्वासनस्तत्त्वमार्गस्तत्त्वांतस्तत्त्वविग्रहः ।
दर्शनादतिगो दृश्यो दृश्यातीतोऽतिदर्शकः ॥१५४॥
दर्शनो दर्शनातीतो भावनाकाररूपकृत् ।
मणिपर्वतसंस्थामो मणिभूषणभूषितः ॥१५५॥
मणिप्रीतो मणिश्रेष्ठो मणिस्थो मणिरूपकः ।
चिंतामणिगृहांतस्थः सर्वचिंताविवर्जितः ॥१५६॥
चिंताक्रांतो भक्तचिंत्यो चिंतनाकार-चिंतकः ।
अचिंत्यश्चिन्त्यरूपश्च निश्चिन्त्यो निश्चयात्मकः ॥१५७॥
निश्चयो निश्चयाधीशो निश्चयात्मकदर्शकः ।
त्रिविक्रमस्त्रिकालज्ञस्त्रिमूर्तिस्त्रिपुरान्तकः ॥१५८॥

ब्रह्मचारी व्रतप्रीतो गृहस्थो गृहवासकः।
परंधाम परंब्रह्म परमात्मा परात्परः ॥१५९॥
सर्वेश्वरः सर्वमयः सर्वसाक्षी विलक्षणः।
मणिद्वीपो द्वीपनाथो द्वीपांतो द्वीपलक्षणः॥१६०॥
सप्तसागरकर्ता च सप्तसागरनायकः।
महीधरो महीभर्ता महीपालो मनस्विनः॥१६१॥
महीव्याप्तो व्यक्तरूपः सुव्यक्तो व्यक्तभावनः।
सुवेषाढ्यः सुखप्रीतः सुगमः सुगमाश्रयः॥१६२॥
तापत्रयाग्निसन्तप्त समाह्लादन-चन्द्रमाः।
तारणस्तापसाराध्यस्तनुमध्यस्तमोमहः ॥१६३॥
पररूपः परध्येयः परदैवतदैवतः।
ब्रह्मपूज्यो जगत्पूज्यो भक्तपूज्यो वरप्रदः॥१६४॥
अद्वैतो द्वैतचित्तश्च द्वैतोऽद्वैतविवर्जितः।
अभेद्यः सर्वभेद्यश्चभिद्यभेदकवेधकः॥१६५॥
लाक्षारसः सुवर्णाभः प्लवंगमप्रियोत्तमः।
शत्रुसंहारकर्ता च अवतारपरो हरः॥१६६॥
संविदेशः संविदात्मा संविज्ञानप्रदायकः।
संवित्कर्ता च भक्तश्च संविदानंदरूपवान्॥१६७॥
संज्ञायातीत संहार्या सर्वसंशयहारकः।
निःसंशयो मनोध्येयः संशयात्मातिदूरगः॥१६८॥
शैवमंत्र शिवप्रीत दीक्षा शैवस्वभावकः।
भूपतिः क्ष्माकृतो भूपो भूप-भूपत्वदायकः॥१६९॥
सर्वधर्मसमायुक्तः सर्वधर्मविवर्धकः।
सर्वशास्त्रः सर्ववेदा सर्ववेत्ता सतृप्तिमान्॥१७०॥
भक्तभावावतारश्च भुक्ति-मुक्ति-फलप्रदः।
भक्त-सिद्धार्थ-सिद्धिश्च सिद्धि-बुद्धि-प्रदायकः॥१७१॥
वाराणसी-वासदाता वाराणसीवरप्रदः।
वाराणसीनाथरूपो गंगामस्तकधारकः॥१७२॥

पर्वताश्रयकर्ता च लिंग-पर्वत-त्र्यंबकः ।
लिंग-देहो लिंगपतिर्लिङ्गपूज्योऽतिदुर्लभः ॥१७३॥
रुद्रप्रियो रुद्रसेव्य उग्ररुप विराड्कृत् ।
मालारुद्राक्षभूषांगो जपरुद्राक्षतोषकः ॥१७४॥
सत्यसत्यः सत्यदाता सत्यकर्ता सदाश्रयः ।
सत्यसाक्षी सत्यलक्ष्मी लक्ष्म्यातीतमनोहरः ॥१७५॥
जनको जगताधीशो जनिता जननिश्चयः ।
सृष्टिस्थितः सृष्टिरूपी सृष्टिरुपस्थितिप्रदः ॥१७६॥
संहाररूपः कालाग्निः कालसंहाररूपकः ।
सप्तपाताल-पादस्थो महदाकाश-शीर्षवान् ॥१७७॥
अमृतो अमृताकारो अमृतामृतरूपकः ।
अमृताकारचित्तिस्थ अमृतोद्भवकारणः ॥१७८॥
अमृताहारनित्यस्थस्त्वमृतोद्भवरूपिणः ।
अमृतांशोऽमृताधीशोऽमृतप्रीतिविवर्धनः ॥१७९॥
अनिर्देश्यो अनिर्वाच्यो अनंगो अंग-आश्रयः ।
श्रेयदः श्रेयरूपश्च श्रेयातीतफलोत्तमः ॥१८०॥
सारः संसारसाक्षिश्च सारासारविचक्षणः ।
धारणातीतभावस्थो धारणान्वयगोचरः ॥१८१॥
गोचरो गोचरातीतो अतीवप्रियगोचरः ।
प्रिय-प्रिय तथा स्वार्थी स्वार्थः अर्थफलप्रदः ॥१८२॥
अर्थार्थिसाक्षी लक्षांशो लक्ष्यलक्षणविग्रहः ।
जगदीशो जगत्त्राता जगन्मयोजगद्गुरुः ॥१८३॥
गुरुमूर्तिः स्वयंवेद्यो वेद्यवेदकरूपकः ।
रूपातीतो रूपकर्ता सर्वरूपार्थदायकः ॥१८४॥
अर्थवस्त्वर्थमान्यश्च अर्थार्थी अर्थदायकः ।
विभवो वैभवः श्रेष्ठ सर्ववैभवदायकः ॥१८५॥
चतुःषष्टि-कला-सूत्र चतुःषष्टिकलामयः ।
पुराणश्रवणाकारः पुराणपुरुषोत्तमः ॥१८६॥

पुरातन-पुराख्यातः पूर्वजः पूर्वपूर्वकः ।
मंत्रतंत्रार्थसर्वज्ञः सर्वतंत्र प्रकाशकः ॥१८७॥
तन्त्रवेता तंत्रकर्ता तंत्रांतरनिवासकः ।
तंत्रगम्यस्तंत्रमान्यस्तंत्रयंत्रफलप्रदः ॥१८८॥
सर्वतंत्रार्थतत्त्वज्ञस्तंत्रराजः स्वतंत्रकः ।
ब्रह्मांडकोटिकर्ता च ब्रह्मांडोदरपूरकः ॥१८९॥
ब्रह्मांडदेशदाता च ब्रह्मज्ञान परायणः ।
स्वयंभूः शम्भुरूपश्च हंसविग्रह निस्पृहः ॥१९०॥
श्वास-निःश्वास-उच्छ्वासः-सर्वसंशयहारकः ।
सोऽहंरूपः स्वभावश्च सोऽहंरूपप्रदर्शकः ॥१९१॥
सोऽहमस्मीति नित्यस्थः सोऽहं-हंसः-स्वरूपवान् ।
हंसोहंसः-स्वरूपश्च हंसविग्रह-निस्पृहः ।
श्वास-निश्वास-उच्छ्वासः-पक्षिराजो निरंजनः ॥१९२॥
अष्टाधिकसहस्रन्तु नाम साहस्रमुत्तमम् ।
नित्यं संकीर्तनासक्तः कीर्तयेत्पुण्यवासरे ॥१९३॥
संक्रांतौ विषुवे चैव पौर्णमास्यां विशेषतः ।
अमावास्यां रविवारे त्रिःसप्तवारपाठकः ॥१९४॥
स्वप्ने दर्शनमाप्नोति कार्याकार्येऽपि दृश्यते ।
रविवारे दशावृत्या रोगनाशो भविष्यति ॥१९५॥
सर्वदा सर्वकामार्थी जपेदेतत्तु सर्वदा ।
यस्य स्मरण मात्रेण वैरिणां-कुलनाशनम् ॥१९६॥
भोग-मोक्षप्रदं श्रेष्ठं भुक्ति-मुक्ति-फलप्रदम् ।
सर्वपापप्रशमनं सर्वापस्मारनाशनम् ॥१९७॥
राजचौरारि-मृत्यूनां-नाशनं जयवर्धनम् ।
मारणे सप्तरात्रं तु दक्षिणाभिमुखो जपेत् ॥१९८॥
उदङ्मुखः सहस्रं तु रक्षणाय जपेन्निशि ।
पठतां शृण्वतां चैव सर्वदुःखविनाशकृत् ॥१९९॥
धन्यं यशस्यमायुष्यमारोग्यं पुत्रवर्धनम् ।
योगसिद्धिप्रदं सम्यक् शिवं ज्ञानप्रकाशितम् ॥२००॥

शिवलोकैकसोपानं वांछितार्थैकसाधनम् ।
विष-ग्रह-क्षयकरं पुत्रपौत्राभिवर्धनम् ॥२०१॥
सदा दुःस्वप्नशमनं सर्वोत्पातनिवारणम् ।
यावन्न दृश्यते देवि शरभो भयनाशकः ॥२०२॥
तावन्न दृश्यते जाप्यं बृहदारण्यको भवेत् ।
सहस्रनाम नाम्न्यस्मिन्नैकैकोच्चारणात्पृथक् ॥२०३॥
स्नातो भवति जाह्नव्यां दिव्यां दृष्टिः स्थिरो भुवि ।
सहस्रनाम सद्विद्यां शिवस्य परमात्मनः ॥२०४॥
यो निष्ठास्यति कल्पान्ते शिवकल्पो भविष्यति ।
हिताय सर्वलोकानां शरभेश्वर भाषितम् ॥२०५॥
स ब्रह्मा स हरिः सोऽर्कः स शक्रो वरुणो यमः ।
धनाध्यक्षः स भगवान् स चैकः सकलं जगत् ॥२०६॥
सुखाराध्यो महादेवस्तपसा येन तोषितः ।
सर्वदा सर्वकामार्थं जपेत्सिध्यति सर्वदा ॥२०७॥
धनार्थी धनमाप्नोति यशोर्थी यशमाप्नुयात् ।
निष्कामः कीर्तयेन्नित्यं ब्रह्मज्ञानमयो भवेत् ॥२०८॥
बिल्वैर्वा तुलसीपुष्पैश्चंपकैर्बकुलादिभिः ।
कल्हारैर्जातिकुसुमैरंबुजैर्वा तिलाक्षतैः ॥२०९॥
एभिर्नाम सहस्रैस्तु पूजयेद् भक्तिमान्नरः ।
कुलं तारयते तेषां कल्पे कोटिशतैरपि ॥२१०॥

इति श्रीआकाशभैरवकल्पे प्रत्यक्षसिद्धिप्रदे उमामहेश्वरसम्वादे श्री मच्छरभ-सहस्रनाम-स्तोत्रंनाम अशीतितमोऽध्यायः ॥८०॥

अथ एकाशीतितमोऽध्यायः

निग्रह-दारुण-सप्तकम्

अस्य श्री निग्रह-दारुण-सप्तक स्तोत्रस्य वासुदेवो ऋषिः स्रग्धरा छंदः श्री शरभेश्वरो देवता तत्प्रसादसिद्ध्यर्थे सर्वशत्रुनाशने विनियोगः—

हरिः ओम्—

कोपोग्रे कातितिर्यक् पटल चरिचरत्तारवर्णप्रभूत-
ज्वालामालाप्रदग्धस्मरतनुशकलं त्वामहं सालुवेश ।
याचे त्वत्पादपद्मप्रणतिभिरनिशं वेष्टि मां यः क्रियाभि-
स्तस्य प्राणप्रयाणं परशिव भवतः शूलभिन्नस्य तूर्णम् ॥१॥
शम्भो त्वद्धस्तकुंत-क्षत-रिपुहृदयान्निःस्रवल्लोहितौघं
पीत्वा पीत्वाऽतिदर्पाद्दिशि दिशि विचरास्त्वद्गणाश्चण्डमुख्याः ।
गर्जन्तु क्षिप्रवेगं निखिलजयकराः खेललीलाः सलीलाः
संत्रस्ता ब्रह्मदेवाः शरभखगपते त्राहि नः सालुवेश ॥२॥
सर्वाद्यं सर्वनिष्ठं सकलभयकरं तत्त्वरूपं शरण्यम्
याचेऽहं त्वाममोघं परिकरमिह ते द्वेष्टये तस्य यो माम् ।
श्रीशंभो त्वत्कराब्जस्थित हल-कठिणाघातवक्षःस्थलस्य
प्राणाः प्रेतेशदूत ग्रहण-परिभव क्रोधपूर्वं प्रयान्तु ॥३॥
क्षिप्मः क्षोण्यां वयं यं तवपदयुगलध्याननिर्दग्धपापाः
कृत्याकृत्यैर्विमुक्ता विहगकुलपते खेलया बद्धमूर्ते ।
तूर्णं त्वत्पाणिपद्मप्रधृतपरशुना तुंडखंडीकृतांगः
स द्वेषी यातु याम्यंपुरमतिकलुषः कालपाशाप्रबद्धः ॥४॥
भीम श्रीसालुवेश प्रणतभयहर प्राणिजिद्दुर्मदानां
या ते पंचास्य गर्वं प्रशमनविहितः स्वेच्छया बद्धमूर्ते ।
त्वामेवाशु त्वङ्घ्रघष्टक-नखविलुठद्ग्रीवजिह्वोदरस्य
प्राणोत्क्राम-प्रमाद-प्रकुटितहृदयस्यायुरव्याहतेश ॥५॥
श्रीशूलिन् ते भुजाग्रस्थितदृढमुसलावर्तवाताभिघातै-
र्याता-यातारियूथस्त्वरितविघटनो भूतरक्तच्छटार्द्राम् ।

तां दृष्ट्वाऽऽयो धनेज्यामखिलसुरगणाश्चाशु नंदंतु भूता
नाना वेतालपूगः पिबंतु तदखिलं प्रीतचित्तः प्रमत्तः ॥६॥
त्वद् दोर्दण्डाग्रमुण्ड प्रकटित विनमच्चंडकोदंडमुक्तै-
बार्णैर्दिव्यैरनेकैः शिथिलितवपुषः क्षीणकोलाहलस्य ।
तस्य प्राणावसानं शरभरिपुरिपोऽहंत्वदाज्ञा प्रभावै-
स्तूर्णं पश्यामि यो मां परिहसति सभास्वादिमध्यांतहेतो ॥७॥
इति निशि प्रयतस्तु निराशनो यममुखः शिवभावमनुस्मरन् ।
दशदिन प्रतिवार-शतद्वयं जपतु निग्रह-दारुण-सप्तकम् ॥८॥

इति गुह्यं महावीर्यं परमं रिपुनाशनम् ।
भानुवासरमारभ्य मंगलांतं जपेत्सुधीः ॥९॥
आदावंते च मूलांते पल्लवेन सुसंपुटम् ।
प्रतिश्लोकं पठेद्भक्तया मण्डलाच्छत्रुनाशनम् ॥१०॥
शरभानुष्टुभारोग्यं संपुटेन जपाच्छिवे ।
सर्वरोगा विनश्यंति गौरीवल्लभसम्पुटात् ॥११॥
सालुवेश-पुटाच्चौरनाशनं च स्वरक्षणम् ।
स्वधान्यरक्षणार्थाय कालभैरव-संपुटम् ॥१२॥
पदार्थरक्षणार्थाय पक्षिराजेति-संपुटम् ।
सर्वज्ञ संपुटाद्देवि हृतवस्तुधनागमम् ॥१३॥
आकृष्टं रक्तचामुंड्या मोहिन्या मोहनं भवेत् ।
शास्तार संपुटाद्देवि पुत्रलाभो भवेद् ध्रुवम् ॥१४॥
नारसिंह्या तथोच्चाटे वीरभद्रेण वा शिवे ।
वडवानलमंत्रेण संपुटाद्वैरिनाशनम् ॥१५॥
चामुण्डी संपुटाद्देवि सर्वशत्रुविनाशनम् ।
निशायाँ बिल्वमूले च स्थित्वा तत्र दिशामुखः ॥१६॥

ऋग्विधाने ॥

विश्वेत्ताते ऋचंमंत्रं देवकोष्ठं विलिख्यतु । "विश्वेत्ताते स० बधवे" ।
चिंतामणि सर्वसंधौ साध्यं शूलान्तरालके ॥१॥

मायावृतमिदं यंत्रं मरणावर्तभंजनम् ।
बद्धयो रोगमुक्तस्य सर्वरक्षाकराय वै ॥२॥

कुषुंभकमृचा-तोयं दशवाराभिमंत्रितम् ।
पाययेदागलं सद्यो वृश्चिकाखुविषापहम् ॥३॥

शं न इन्द्राग्नी-सूक्तेन पचेत्तैलं स्पृशेत्तथा ।
तत्तत्तैलविधानोक्त फलं सद्यो लभेद् ध्रुवम् ॥४॥

लेह-पानक-खानानि रसपिष्टबटानि च ।
सूक्तेनानेन संस्पृष्टवा कुर्यात्तत्तत्फलाप्तये ॥५॥

भेषजे व्यवहारे च मंत्रवादेऽर्थवादके ।
संसृष्टमित्यृचं मंत्री विजयाय शतं जपेत् ॥६॥

स्वप्नः स्वप्नाधिकरण इत्याथर्वणसूक्तकम् ।
त्रिवारं यो जपेन्नित्यं तस्य नास्त्यहिजं भयं ॥७॥

स्वकृत्यगोपनार्थं च परवर्त्मसुशांतये ।
कारयेच्छतमेकेन "य आस्त" इति ऋक् जपम् ॥८॥

आवहंतीति सूक्तेन शतवाराभिमंत्रितम् ।
अन्नं प्रसादयेन्मंत्री भवेदर्घाधिकं गुणम् ॥९॥

द्रव्यं स्पृशन्नन्नभांडं पचेन्मंत्री सदा जपन् ।
तस्मादादाय च कस्मै दत्वा शेषं पुनर्न्यसेत् ॥१०॥

एवं चरेत्क्रमेणैव पृथिव्युद्धृत्य मंत्रवित् ।
तत्काल वर्तमानानामन्नं पूर्णतरं भवेत् ॥११॥

जपेद्वर्णशतं सिद्धिर्योबायास्तस्य शोभने ।
सिद्धिस्तु नित्यभोक्तृणां तादृशी भांडदर्शनात् ॥१२॥

चतुर्भिः पंचभिः षड्भिः स्वाहा पंचभिरेव च ।
द्वाभ्यां चतुर्भिः सर्वैश्चावहंती होममुच्यते ॥१३॥

जपेदक्षरसाहस्रं नित्यहोमसमन्वितम् ।
स्मरणादन्नवृद्धिः स्यात्तस्य तद्राज्य-वंशयोः ॥१४॥

इति गुह्यं महाशास्त्रमभीष्टफलदायकम् ।
सतामनुग्रहतरमसतां निग्रहं परम् ॥१५॥

अमोघं परमंगुह्यं परमाकाशभैरवम्।
तादृशं सिद्धिदं श्रेष्ठं कल्पं सत्समयोचितम् ॥१६॥
योगिनां योगदं तत्त्वं कर्मिणां कर्मसिद्धिदम् ।
तत्त्वसिद्धिप्रदं तत्त्ववादिनां लक्षधारिणाम् ॥१७॥
सत्यं सर्वमयानां वै सर्वसिद्धिप्रदायकम् ।
यः स्मरेत्परया भक्तया प्रजपेच्छृणुयात्पठेत् ॥१८॥
लिखेद्वा निवहेत्कल्पं सकृन्मासाच्छिवो भवेत् ।
शुश्रूषा वर्तते यस्य कल्पे त्वाकाशभैरवे ॥१९॥
तस्मै च धर्मसायुज्यं दत्तमेव सनातनम् ।
पुस्तकं वा स्मरेत्पश्येन्नित्यं यद्यज्जनोऽम्बिके ॥२०॥
भुक्त्वा यथेप्सितान्भोगान्भूयः शैवपदं व्रजेत् ।
आदि-क्षांतार्ण-मंत्र-प्रभव बहुकुलाकार शास्त्रोक्तमार्गम्
शर्वाग्न्यावित्यतत्त्व प्रसवलयकरं भैरवं ब्रह्मकल्पम् ।
रम्यं मैत्री समीक्ष्य स्वमतिविभवतो निर्णयं स्वात्मबोधम्
कर्णे शिष्यस्य कस्यापि च दृढमनसोऽनल्पबुद्धे रहस्यम् ॥२१॥

इति श्रीआकाशभैरवकल्पे प्रत्यक्षसिद्धिप्रदे उमामहेश्वरसम्वादे शरभ-सालुव-पक्षिराजकल्पाख्यं निग्रह-दारुणसप्तकं-नाम एकाशीतितमोऽध्यायः ॥८१॥

अथ परिशिष्टम्

शास्त्रान्तरे शरभ-मंत्राणि

शरभ मंत्रम्—(मेरुतन्त्रोक्तम्)

अथातः सम्प्रवक्ष्यामि नृसिंहाद्बलिनो मम ।
मंत्रं शरभ-संज्ञस्य द्रुतसिद्धिप्रदायकम् ॥१॥
"ओं खं खां खं फडुच्चार्य्य द्विःशत्रून्-प्रससीति च ।
तथा हुं फट् सर्वास्त्र संहरणाय शरभेति (शरभाय) च ॥२॥
[1]शान्ताय पक्षिराजाय हुं फट् स्वाहा नमो मनुः ।
एकचत्वारिंशदर्णो वासुदेवो मुनिर्मतः ॥३॥
कालाग्निरुद्रः शरभो देवता परिकीर्तितः ।
छन्दस्तु जगती स्वाहा शक्तिर्बीजं स्वमुच्यते ॥४॥
वेदाङ्कः दश सप्तांग सागरैरंगकल्पनम् ।
पुनः समस्त मन्त्रेण दिग्बन्धं तु समाचरेत् ॥५॥

ध्यानम्--

चन्द्रार्काग्नि त्रिनयनं काली दुर्गा द्विपक्षकम् ।
विद्युज्जिव्हं वज्रनखं वडवाग्न्युदरन्तथा ॥६॥
व्याधि-मृत्यु-रिपुघ्नं च चण्डवातातिवेगिनम् ।
हुङ्कार रव-स्वरूपं च वैरिवृन्दनिषूदनम् ॥७॥
मृगेन्द्रत्वक्शरीरोऽस्य पक्षाभ्यां चञ्चुनारवः ।
अधोवक्त्रश्चतुष्पादा ऊर्ध्वंदृष्टिश्चतुर्भुजः ॥८॥
कालान्त-दहन-प्रख्यो नीलजीमूत-निःस्वनः ।
अरिर्यद्दर्शनादेव विनष्ट-बल-विक्रमः ॥९॥
शलाख्य ग्रहरूपाय पक्ष-विक्षिप्त-भूभृते ।
अष्टपादाय रुद्राय नमः शलभमूर्त्तये ॥१०॥
एवं ध्यायेत् सहस्रं तु प्रजपेत् पायसं हुनेत् ।
प्रत्यहं मासषट्केन मन्त्रसिद्धिः प्रजायते ॥११॥
तदा जेयस्तु सङ्ग्रामे भूत-प्रेत-पिशाचकाः ।
नश्यन्ति दर्शनादेव चाधयो व्याधयस्तथा ॥१२॥

इति श्री महामाया-महाकालानुमते मेरुतंत्रे शिवप्रणीते द्रुतसिद्धि प्रदायकोनाम शरभ-मंत्रम् ॥

मंत्रोद्धारो यथा :—ओं खं खां खं फट् शत्रून् प्रससि प्रससि हुं फट् सर्वास्त्र संहरणाय शरभाय शान्ताय पक्षिराजाय हुं फट् स्वाहा नमः ॥

1. शाल्वाय ।

शरभ-मन्त्रराज

(ग्रन्थान्तरे)

अमृतानन्दनाथाय कृष्णानन्द योगिने ।
विमलानन्दनाथाय शिवाय गुरवे नमः ।।

ओं आं ह्रीं क्रों एहि एहि शरभ-शाल्वाय स्फुर् स्फुर् पक्षिराजाय प्रस्फुर् प्रस्फुर् शत्रुणां शोणितं पिब पिब ओं ऐं ग्लौं ग्लौं ग्लौं ओं ह्रीं ह्रीं ह्रीं ॐ ऐं ग्लौं ग्लौं ग्लौं ग्लौं ग्लौं आवेशय आवेशय आगच्छ आगच्छ स्थिरोभव स्थिरोभव रोगान्नाशय नाशय कृत्रिमान् खाहि खाहि चटकान् खादय खादय ओं ह्रीं क्षीं क्रों (अमुकस्य) रोगान् सुशीघ्रेण छेदय छेदय खेदय खेदय खड्गेन छेदय छेदय आं पाशेन बन्धय बन्धय ह्रीं वं आरोग्यं कुरु कुरु रं खें शत्रुणां रक्तं पिब पिब शीघ्रं शीघ्रं कृत्रिमान् खादय खादय ओं ह्रीं क्रों खें खां खं फट् प्राणग्रहासि प्राणग्रहासि हुं फट् सर्वशत्रुसंहारणाय शरभ-शाल्वाय पक्षिराजाय हुं फट् स्वाहा—ओं नमो भगवते अष्टपादाय सहस्रबाहवे द्विशीर्षाय द्विनेत्राय द्विपक्षाय रुद्ररूपाय रौद्रमृगविहङ्ग-वेषधारिणे योगनृसिंह-वेष-संहारणाय उद्दण्डखण्डनाय ज्वाला-नृसिंह हताय-शमनाय लक्ष्मी-नृसिंह-मथनकराय जगन्नृसिंह सुदर्शनाय अनेक विघ्नरूपछेदनाय अखिल-देवता-वन्दनाय निखिलदेवता परिपालनाय क्षयरोगादि सकल-रोग-निवारणाय ह्रीं ह्रीं महाचित्ररथादि गन्धर्व प्रतिष्ठिताय अन्तरिक्षग्रह आकाशग्रह वसुन्धराग्रह क्षिप्रग्रह मंत्रग्रह यक्षग्रह कामिनीग्रह मोहिनीग्रहोच्चाटनाय सकल-ब्रह्मराक्षस-वेताल कूष्माण्डादि महाप्रबलग्रहोच्चाटनाय सकलदुष्टग्रहनिवारणाय महा-वीरभद्राय परमंत्र-परयंत्र-परतंत्रादिकानां मूलछेदनाय शिष्यपरिपालनाय महापशुरूपिणे शरभ-शाल्वाय पक्षिराजाय हुं फट् स्वाहा ।।

इति श्री कालभैरवकृत शरभमंत्रराजः।

अथ श्री शरभमालामन्त्रम्

(मेरुतन्त्रोक्तम्)

श्रीशिव उवाच ।।

अथातः सम्प्रवक्ष्यामि मालामन्त्रं सुसिद्धिदम् ।
तारो नमो भगवते ङेन्तं शलभ शाल्व च ।।१।।
सर्वं भूतोच्चाटनाय ग्रह-राक्षसचोच्चरेत् ।
निवारणाय ज्वालेति ङेन्तं माला स्वरूप च ।।२।।
दक्षनिष्काशनायेति साक्षादिति पदं वदेत् ।
कालरुद्र-स्वरूपाष्टमूर्त्तये च तथा चरेत् ।।३।।
कृशानुरेतसे चेति महेति पदमुच्चरेत् ।
क्रूर भूतोच्चाटनायेत्यप्रतिशयनाय च ।।४।।
शत्रूंश्च नाशय द्वन्द्वं वदेच्छत्रुपशूंस्ततः ।
गृह्ण-युग्मं खादययुग्मं तारं हुं च वसुप्रियाम् ।।५।।
अष्टोत्तरशतार्णोऽयमष्टोत्तरशतं जपेत् ।
प्रत्यहं मासषट्केन सिद्धः स्यात्तत्फलं शृणुः ।।६ ।।
पात्रे पूतं जलं स्थाप्य सप्तवाराभिमन्त्रितम् ।
पानार्थं यत्प्रसादेन दातव्यं लापयेत्तथा ।।७।।
प्रयान्ति सर्वभूतानि ज्वराश्चातुर्थिकादयः ।
सप्ताहात्तत्प्रयोगेण नात्र कार्य्या विचारणा ।।८ ।।

मन्त्रोद्धारः—ओं नमो भगवते शलभाय शाल्वाय सर्वभूतोच्चाटनाय ग्रह-राक्षस-निवारणाय ज्वालामाला-स्वरूपाय दक्ष-निष्काशनाय साक्षात्-कालरुद्रस्वरूपायाष्टमूर्त्तये कृशानुरेतसे महाक्रूर-भूतोच्चाटनाय प्रतिशयनाय शत्रून्नाशय नाशय शत्रुपशून् गृह्ण गृह्ण खादय खादय ओं हुं फट् ।।

इति श्री महामायामहाकालानुमते मेरुतन्त्रे शिवप्रणीते शरभ मालामंत्रम् ।।

तंत्रान्तरे—१. ओं नमो भगवते प्रलय कालाग्निरुद्राय दक्षाध्वर-ध्वंसकाय महाशरभाय मम शत्रुच्छेदनं कुरु स्वाहा—

२. ओं खें खां खं फट् प्राणग्रहासि प्राणग्रहासि हुंफट्, सर्वशत्रुसंहारकारकाय शरभ-साल्वाय पक्षिराजाय हुं फट् स्वाहा ।

अथ काम्य प्रयोगानि लिख्यन्ते

ठकारं पूर्वमालिख्य तद्बाह्ये वर्तुलं लिखेत् ।
तद्बाह्ये चतुरस्रं च तद्बाह्येऽष्टदलं तथा ॥१॥
तद्बाह्ये षोडशदलं तद्बाह्ये वृत्तमालिखेत् ।
तद्बाह्ये पञ्च कोणं च ठकारे साध्य नाम च ॥२॥
वर्तुले मूल मालिख्य स्वरान् षोडश पार्वती ।
वृत्तेचाभिमतं सार्द्धं बाणस्य पंचकोणके ॥३॥
एवमालिख्य यंत्रं तु तालपत्रे प्रयत्नतः ।
स्नुहिक्षीरं जले क्षिप्त्वा यंत्रं तत्रैव निक्षिपेत् ॥४॥
चुल्लोपरि चिरं स्थाप्य क्वाथैः सर्वत्र शत्रवः ।
व्यवहिताः पलायन्ते प्रसादात्सालुवस्य च ॥५॥
साधके सर्वसिद्धिः स्याद्रिपुर्देशान्तरं व्रजेत् ।
सालुवं पक्षिराजानं यो ध्यायेल्लोकपूजितम् ॥६॥
शत्रूणां सर्व संघाता नोत्पद्यन्ते कदाचन ।
चन्दनं च सकर्पूरं कस्तूरी कुङ्कुमान्वितम् ॥७॥
वामावर्तं लिखेन्मंत्रं शरभं चिन्तयेन्नरः ।
ललाटे तिलकं कृत्वा त्रैलोक्यं मोहयेत् क्षणात् ॥८॥
देवांश्चापि वशं कुर्यात् किं पुनर्मानवादयः ।
गोरोचनं च गोक्षीरं गोघृतं गोमयं तथा ॥९॥
शन्यर्काङ्गारवारे तु मूलनैव तु होमयेत् ।
देवासुर मनुष्याणां स्त्रीणां वशकृद् भवेत् ॥१०॥
अजामाहिषकं चैव नवनीतं तथाऽगरुः ।
मूलमुच्चार्यत्वाद्यन्ते साध्यनाम पुरस्सरम्
असाध्यमपि वशं कुर्यात्पक्षिराजप्रभावतः ॥११॥
अजामानुषाकानां च रुधिरं प्रेतवाससा ।

संवेष्ट्य पुत्तलीं चैव साध्यनाम-विगर्भितम् ।
शत्रुप्राणान् प्रतिष्ठाप्य प्रेतकेशैश्च वेष्टयेत् ॥१२॥
शरभेनाभिमंत्र्य वै निखनेत् प्रेतभूमिषु ।
निखनेद्वा रिपोर्द्वारे सद्यः शत्रोर्मृतिर्भवेत् ॥१३॥
सालुवं पक्षिराजानं यो ध्यायेच्च दिने दिने ।
जपेद् दशसहस्रन्तु शतमष्टोत्तरं तु वा ॥१४॥
कृष्णाष्टमी समारभ्य यावत् कृष्णचतुर्दशी ।
मासांतसमये प्राप्ते वैरिपक्षक्षयो भवेत् ।
कारस्करं तु भल्लातं तैलेनाष्टशतं हुनेत् ॥१५॥
मासान्ते शत्रवस्तस्य पलायन्ते न संशयः ।
शमी-दर्भादि-पयसा चाष्टोत्तरशतं हुनेत् ॥१६॥
दिनत्रयं महेशानि सर्वरोगैः प्रमुच्यते ।
विभीतकतरोरष्ट-प्रादेश-परिमाणकम् ॥१७॥
काष्ठमादाय यत्नेन सालुवं च स्मरन्निशि ।
यन्नाम्ना कटुतैलाक्तं शतमष्टोत्तरं हुनेत् ॥१८॥
मासान्ते मृत्युमाप्नोति यदि त्राता शिवः स्वयम् ।
अपामार्गस्य समिधा पायसं सघृतं हुनेत् ॥१९॥
रात्रौ भर्ग्यं स्मरन्[1] खाख्यं नश्यन्ति ते पदातिनः ।
पञ्चस्नुहि समिद्भिर्वा होमयेत् सर्षपैस्तिलैः ॥२०॥
महानिशार्द्धे साहस्रं शरभमंत्रेण संयुतम् ।
रात्र्यां यन्नाम्ना जुहुयात् पञ्चाहे स प्रणश्यति ॥२१॥
सगोत्रः सपरिवारो बन्धुर्मित्रगणैः सह ।
सालुवं पक्षिराजं च पूजयेत् साधकोत्तमः ॥२२॥
सार्ष्टविंशति संख्याकान् ब्राह्मणान् भोजयेत्सुधीः ।
शुक्लप्रतिपदारभ्य पौर्णमायां तु नित्यशः ॥२३॥
यो जपेदष्टसाहस्रं मुच्यते सर्वपातकैः ।
शरभं शालुवं ध्यात्वा एतद्विधिवदाचरेत् ॥२४॥
पुत्तलीं च विधायाथ कुलालचक्रमृण्मयीम् ।
वायुं सम्यग्विधानेन कृत्वा स्थाणुं समाहितः ॥२५॥

---

१. आकाशभैरवमित्यर्थः ।

स्नुहिक्षीरेण संप्लुष्य स्पृष्टस्तवयुतं जपेत् ।
उन्मत्तमूले निखनेदपस्मारी भवेद् रिपुः ॥२६॥
सालुवं शिवरूपं च ध्यात्वा सम्यक् समाहितः ।
निम्बमूलेन कृत्वा तु पुत्तलीं च यथाविधि ॥२७॥
पुत्तल्यां वायुमारोप्य स्पृष्टवाताऽयुतं जपेत् ।
श्मशाने निखनेद्देवी पुत्तलीं शत्रुचालने ॥२८॥
उन्मत्तमूले पुत्तल्यां वायुमारोप्य साधकः ।
रिपुनामांकितं शारभं-मंत्रं सहस्रं जपेत् ॥२९॥
शन्यार-रवि-रात्र्यां च निक्षिपेत्तां चतुष्पथे ।
उच्चाटनं भवेद्देवि त्रयोर्मासांतरे खलु ॥३०॥
शन्यर्काङ्गारवारे तु जपेदयुतसंख्यया ।
त्रिदिनान्ते रिपून् बद्ध्वा चालयेदाशु साधकः ॥३१॥
दूर्वाङ्कुरैर्घृताक्तैश्च गोमयैश्च विशेषतः ।
तिल-लाजास्सर्षपाश्च मिश्रीकृत्य हुनेत्तदा ॥३२॥
त्रिदिनान्ते शत्रुसंघाः पलायन्ते न संशयः ।
पिष्टेन पुत्तलीं कृत्वा मूलेनैव तु पूजयेत् ॥३३॥
मांसयुक्तं तु नैवेद्यं तांबूलं तु निवेदयेत् ।
लाक्षारसेन संयुक्तं बिम्बस्य च शिरोगले ॥३४॥
साध्यनाम च संयुक्तं लिखित्वा चैव पुत्तलीम् ।
सदा पचेत्तदा वन्हौ समिद्भिर्पिचुमन्दकैः ॥३५॥
गणनायकमंत्रेण होमं कृत्वा विधानतः ।
जपादयुतमात्रेण पलायन्ते सर्वशत्रवः ॥३६॥
अर्कमूलं समादाय पुत्तलीं च यथाविधि ।
शत्रोः प्राणस्य पवनं विदधीत यथोदितम् ॥३७॥
तस्याश्च हृद्देशे च माया बीजं समालिखेत् ।
तस्या शिरसि चालिख्य वह्निबीजं सबिन्दुकम् ॥३८॥
पादयोश्च तथाऽऽलिख्य पृथ्वीबीजं च भैरवम् ।
उभयोः स्कन्धयोश्चैव वायुः बीजं च भार्गवम् ॥३९॥
भार्गवं वदने पृष्ठे श्री बीजं भुवनेश्वरीम् ।
पूजां च विधिवत्कृत्वा नैवेद्यं तु निवेदयेत् ॥४०॥

निखनादर्कमूले च शत्रोर्पलायनं खलु ।
ततः शत्रुशरीरे च पीडनं स्फोटकैर्ज्वरैः ॥४१॥
सप्ताहाच्च यमस्थाने रिपुः गच्छेन्न संशयः ।
श्मशानमृत्तिकया वा पुत्तलीं कारयेद् बुधः ॥४२॥
श्मशानाङ्गारमादाय उन्मत्तरससंयुतम् ।
पुत्तली-हृदि खेंकारं पार्श्वे चिन्तामणिं लिखेत् ॥४३॥
मस्तके कामराजं च हंस-बीजं च मूर्धनि ।
स्नुहिक्षीराभिषेकं च विधिवत् प्राणपूर्वकम् ॥४४॥
स्नुहिवृक्षस्याधोभागे खनेत् प्रादेशमात्रकम् ।
शुक्ल-प्रतिपदारम्य त्वष्टम्यन्तं जपेत् सुधीः ॥४५॥
यो द्विजः सततं ध्यायेत् पलायन्ते तस्य शत्रवः ।
खादिरं पुत्तलीं कृत्वा पवनं च यथाविधि ॥४६॥
तत्स्पृष्ट्वा चायुतं मंत्रं यो जपेन्निशि साधकः ।
राज-चौर-भयान्मुक्तः सर्वत्र स्याद्धि पूजितः ॥४७॥
पुत्तलीं खादिरमूले निक्षिपेद् यस्य नामतः ।
पुत्र-मित्र-कलत्रादींस्त्यक्त्वा देशान्तरं व्रजेत् ॥४८॥
पराजिताः पलायन्ते शत्रवो नैव संशयः ।
शालुवं पक्षिराजानं शरभं शिवरूपिणम् ॥४९॥
राजवृक्षस्य पुत्तल्यां भूर्बीजं स्मरवह्निना ।
वाग्भवं वायु बीजं च श्री बीजं भुवनेश्वरी ॥५०॥
प्रदाक्षिण्येन वेष्टव्यं पुत्तल्योपरि संलिखन् ।
मूलेन राजवृक्षस्य समिद्धोमो विधीयते ॥५१॥
अष्टोत्तरसहस्रं च शतमष्टोत्तरं च वै ।
हुनेच्च विधिवन्मंत्रं चतुष्पथे विधानतः ॥५२॥
त्रिदिनान्ते च विद्वेषं शत्रूणां च परस्परम् ।
रिपवः संक्षयं यान्ति पलायन्ते न संशयः ॥५३॥

इति श्री आकाशभैरवे समुपलब्धातिरिक्तपत्रेषु शरभमंत्रप्रयोगविधिः ॥

अथ आकाशभैरवस्थ-वैदिक-मंत्राः

ओ३म् गणानां त्वा गणपतिं हवामहे कविं कवीनामुपमश्रवस्तमम् ।
ज्येष्ठराजं ब्रह्मणां ब्रह्मणस्पत आ नः शृण्वन्नूतिभिः
सीद सादनम् ॥ (ऋक्) २।६।२९

एतो न्विन्द्रं स्तवाम सखायः स्तोम्यं नरम् ।
कृष्टीर्यो विश्वा अभ्यस्त्येक इत ॥ (ऋक्) ६।२।१६

एतो न्विन्द्रं स्तवामेशानं वस्वः स्वराजम् ।
न राधसा मर्धिषन्नः ॥ (ऋक्) ६।५।३८

एतो न्विन्द्रं स्तवाम शुद्धं शुद्धेन साम्ना ।
शुद्धैरुक्थैर्वावृध्वांसं शुद्ध आशीर्वान्ममत्तु ॥१॥
इंद्र शुद्धो न आ गहि शुद्धः शुद्धाभिरूतिभिः ।
शुद्धो रयिं नि धारय शुद्धो ममद्धि सोम्यः ॥२॥
इंद्र शुद्धो हि नो रयिं शुद्धो रत्नानि दाशुषे ।
शुद्धो वृत्राणि जिघ्नसे शुद्धो वाजं सिषाससि ॥३॥ (ऋक्) ६।६।३१

तरत्स मंदी धावति धारा सुतस्यांधसः ।
तरत्सं मंदी धावति ॥१॥
उस्रा वेद वसूनां मर्तस्य देव्यवसः ।
तरत्स मंदी धावति ॥२॥
ध्वस्रयोः पुरुषंत्योरा सहस्राणि दद्महे ।
तरत्स मंदी धावति ॥३॥
आ ययोस्त्रिंशतं तना सहस्राणि च दद्महे ।
तरत्स मंदी धावति ॥४॥ (ऋक्) ७।१।१५

इमं मे गङ्गे यमुने सरस्वति शुतुद्रि स्तोमं सचता परुष्ण्या ।
असिक्न्या मरुद्वृधे वितस्तयार्जीकीये शृणुह्या सुषोमया
(ऋक्) ॥ ८।३।६

अहमस्मि महामहोऽभिनभ्यमुदीषितः ।
कुवित्सोमस्यापामिति ।। (ऋक्) ८।६।२७

अहमस्मि सहमानाथ त्वमसि सासहिः ।
उभे सहस्वती भूत्वी सपत्नीं मे सहावहै ।। (ऋक्) ८।८।३

ऋषभं मा समानानां सपत्नानां विषासहिम् ।
हंतारं शत्रूणां कृधि विराजं गोपतिं गवाम् ।।१।।

अहमस्मि सपत्नहेन्द्र इवारिष्टो अक्षतः ।
अधः सपत्ना मे पदोरिमे सर्वे अभिष्ठिताः ।।२।।
अत्रैव वोऽपि नह्याम्युभे आर्त्नी इव ज्यया ।
वाचस्पते नि षेधेमान्यथा मदधरं वदान् ।।३।।
अभिभूरहमागमं विश्वकर्मेण धाम्ना ।
आ वश्चित्तमा वो व्रतमा वोऽहं समितिं ददे ।।४।।
योगक्षेमं व आदायाहं भूयासमुत्तम आ वो मूर्धानमक्रमीम् ।
अधस्पदान्म उद्वदत मण्डूका इवोदकान्मंडूका उदकादिव ।।५।।
(ऋक्) ८।८।२४ ।

श्रिये जातः श्रिय आ निरियाय श्रियं वयो जरितृभ्यो दधाति ।
श्रियं वसाना अमृतत्वमायन्भवंति सत्या समिथामितद्रौ ।।
(ऋक्) ७।४।४

किं ते कृण्वन्ति कीकटेषु गावो नाशिरं दुह्रे न तपंति घर्मम् ।।
आ नो भर प्रमगंदस्य वेदो नैचाशाखं मघवन् रन्धया नः ।।
(ऋक्) ३।३।२१

बलं धेहि तनुषु नो बलमिन्द्रानळुत्सुनः ।
बलं तोकाय तनयाय जीवसे त्वं हि बलदा असि ।।१।।
अभि व्ययस्व खदिरस्य सारमोजो धेहि स्पंदने शिंशपायाम् ।
अक्ष वीलो वीलित वीलयस्व मा यामादस्मादव जीहिपो नः ।।२।।

अयमस्मान्वनस्पतिर्मा च हा मा च रीरिषत् ।
स्वस्त्या गृहेभ्य आवसा आ विमोचनात् ॥३॥
(ऋक्) ३।३।२२ ॥

वयः सुपर्णा उप सेदुरिन्द्रं प्रियमेधा ऋषयो नाधमानाः ।
अप ध्वांतमूर्णुं हि पूर्धि चक्षुर्मुमुग्ध्यस्मान्निधयेव बद्धान् ॥४॥
(ऋक्) ८।३।४

उदगादयमादित्यो विश्वेन सहसा सह ।
द्विषन्तं मह्यं रंधयन्मो अहं द्विषते रधम् ॥ (ऋक्) १।४।८

वि जिहीष्व वनस्पते योनिः सूष्यन्त्या इव ।
श्रुतं मे अश्विना हवं सप्तवध्रिं च मुञ्चतम् ॥१॥
भीताय नाधमानाय ऋषये सप्तवध्रये ।
मायाभिरश्विना युवं वृक्षं सं च वि चाचथः ॥२॥
यथा वातः पुष्करिणीं समिङ्गयति सर्वतः ।
एवा ते गर्भ एजतु निरैतु दशमास्यः ॥३॥
यथा वातो यथा वनं यथा समुद्र एजति ।
एवा त्वं दशमास्य सहावेहि जरायुणा ॥४॥
दश मासाञ्छशयानः कुमारो अधि मातरि ।
निरैतु जीवो अक्षतो जीवो जीवंत्या अधि ॥५॥
(ऋक्) ४।४।२०

अयमस्मान्वनस्पतिर्मा च हा मा च रीरिषत् ।
स्वस्त्या गृहेभ्य आवसा आ विमोचनात् ॥ (ऋक्) ३।३।२२

इंद्रोतिभिर्बहुलाभिर्नो अद्य याच्छ्रेष्ठाभिर्मघवञ्छूर जिन्व ।
यो नो द्वेष्टयधरः सस्पदीष्ट यमु द्विष्मस्तमु प्राणो जहातु ॥१॥
परशुं चिद्वि तपति शिम्बलं चिद्वि वृश्चति ।
उखा चिदिन्द्र येषंती प्रयस्ता फेनमस्यति ॥२॥
न सायकस्य चिकिते जनासो लोधं नयंति पशुमन्यमानाः ।
नावाजिनं वाजिना हासयंति न गर्दभं पुरो अश्वान्नयंति ॥३॥

इम इन्द्र भरतस्य पुत्रा अपपित्वं चिकितुर्न प्रपित्वम् ।
हिन्वंत्यश्वमरणं न नित्यं ज्यावाजं परि णयन्त्याजौ ॥४॥
(ऋक्) ३।३।२३

क्षेत्रस्य पतिना वयं हितेनेव जयामसि ।
गामश्वं पोषयित्न्वा स नो मृलातीदृशे ॥१॥

क्षेत्रस्य पते मधुमंतमूर्मिं धेनुरिव पयो अस्मासु धुक्ष्व ।
मधुश्चुतं घृतमिव सुपूतमृतस्य नः पतयो मृलयंतु ॥२॥

मधुमतीरोषधीर्द्याव आपो मधुमन्नो भवत्वंतरिक्षम् ।
क्षेत्रस्य पतिर्मधुमान्नो अस्त्वरिष्यंतो अन्वेनं चरेम ॥३॥

शुनं वाहाः शुनं नरः शुनं कृषतु लांगलम् ।
शुनं वरत्रा बध्यंतां शुनमष्ट्रामुदिंगय ॥४॥
शुनासीराविमां वाचं जुषेथां यद्दिवि चक्रथुः पयः ।
तेनेमामुप सिंचतम् ॥५॥

अर्वाची सुभगे भव सीते वंदामहे त्वा ।
यथा नः सुभगाससि यथा नः सुफलाससि ॥६॥

इंद्रः सीतां नि गृह्णातु तां पूषानु यच्छतु ।
सा नः पयस्वती दुहामुत्तरामुत्तरां समाम् ॥७॥
शुनं नः फाला वि कृषंतु भूमिं शुनं कीनाशा अभियंतु वाहैः ।
शुनं पर्जन्यो मधुना पयोभिः शुनासीरा शुनमस्मासु धत्तम् ॥८॥
(ऋक्) ३।८।६

त्वमग्ने द्युभिस्त्वमाशुशुक्षणिस्त्वमद्भ्यस्त्वमश्मनस्परि ।
त्वं वनेभ्यस्त्वमोषधीभ्यस्त्वं नृणां नृपते जायसे शुचिः ॥
(ऋक्) २।५।१७

अग्निरस्मि जन्मना जातवेदा घृतं मे चक्षुरमृतं म आसन् ।
अर्कस्त्रिधातू रजसो विमानोऽजस्रो घर्मो हविरस्मि नाम ॥
(ऋक्) ३।१।२७

ध्रुवासु त्वासु क्षितिषु क्षियंतो व्यस्मत्पाशं वरुणो मुमोचत् ।
अवो वन्वाना अदितेरुपस्थाद्यूयं पात स्वस्तिभिः सदा नः ॥
(ऋक्) ५।६।१०

इंद्राणीमासु नारिषु सुभगामहमश्रवम् ।
नह्यस्या अपरं चन जरसा मरते पतिर्विश्वस्मादिन्द्र उत्तरः ॥
(ऋक्) ८।४।३

यो मे राजन्युज्यो वा सखा वा स्वप्ने भयं भीरवे मह्यमाह ।
स्तेनो वा यो दिप्सति नो वृको वा त्वं तस्माद्वरुण पाह्यस्मान् ॥
(ऋक्) २।७।१०

विश्वेत्ता ते सवनेषु प्रवाच्या या चकर्थ मघवन्निंद्र सुन्वते ।
पारावतं यत्पुरुसंभृतं वस्वपावृणोः शरभाय ऋषिबंधवे ॥
(ऋक्) ६।७।४

कुषुंभकस्तदब्रवीद्गिरेः प्रवर्तमानकः ।
वृश्चिकस्यारसं विषमरसं वृश्चिक ते विषम् । (ऋक्) २।५।१६

संसृष्टं धनमुभयं समाकृतमस्मभ्यं दत्तां वरुणश्च मन्युः ।
भियं दधाना हृदयेषु शत्रवः पराजितासो अप नि लयंताम् ॥
(ऋक्) ८।३।१९।

य आस्ते यश्च चरति यश्च पश्यति नो जनः ।
तेषां सं हन्मो अक्षाणि यथेदं हर्म्यं तथा ॥ (ऋक्) ५।४।२२

आवहंती पोष्या वार्याणि चित्रं केतुं कृणुते चेकिताना ।
ईयुषीणामुपमा शश्वतीनां विभातीनां प्रथमोषा व्यश्वैत् ॥
(ऋक्) १।८।३

आवहंत्यरुणीर्ज्योतिषागान्मही चित्रा रश्मिभिश्चेकिताना ।
प्रबोधयंती सुविताय देव्यु१ षा ईयते सुयुजा रथेन ॥
(ऋक्) ३।५।१४

ओ षु स्वसारः कारवे शृणोत ययौ वो दूरादनसा रथेन ।
नि षू नमध्वं भवता सुपारा अधो अक्षाः सिंधवः
स्रोत्याभिः ॥ (ऋक्) ३।२।१३

स्वप्नः स्वप्नाधिकरणे सर्वं नि ष्वापया जनम् ।
आ सूर्यमन्यान् स्वापय[1] व्युषं जागृयादहम् ॥१॥
अजगरो नाम सर्पः सर्पिरविषो महान् ।
तस्मिन् हि सर्पः सुधितस्तेन त्वा स्वापयामसि ॥२॥
सर्पः सर्पो अजगरः सर्पिरविषो महान् ।
तस्य सर्पात्सिंधवस्तस्य गाधमशीमहि ॥३॥
कालिको नाम सर्पो नवनागसहस्रबलः ।
यमुनह्लदे ह सो जातो ३ यो नारायणवाहनः ॥४॥
यदि कालिकदूतस्य यदि काः कालिकाद्भयम् ।
जन्मभूमिमतिक्रांतो निर्विषो याति कालिकः ॥५॥
आ याहींद्र पथिभिरीलितेभिर्यज्ञमिमं नो भागधेयं जुषस्व ।
तृप्तां जुहुर्मातुलस्येव योषा भागस्ते पैतृष्वसेयी वपामिव ॥६॥
यशस्करं बलवंतं प्रभुत्वं तमेव राजाधिपतिर्बभूव ।
संकीर्णनागाश्वपतिर्नराणां सुमंगल्यं सततं दीर्घमायुः ॥७॥
कर्कोटको नाम सर्पो यो दृष्टिविष उच्यते ।
तस्य सर्पस्य सर्पत्वं तस्मै सर्प नमोऽस्तु ते ॥८॥

(ऋक्) खिल सूक्तम् (परिशिष्टे)

अपश्यं त्वा मनसा चेकितानं तपसो जातं तपसो विभूतम् ।
इह प्रजामिह रयिं रराणः प्र जायस्व प्रजया पुत्रकाम ॥१॥
अपश्यं त्वा मनसा दीध्यानां स्वायां तनू ऋत्व्ये नाधमानाम् ।
उप मामुच्चा युवतिर्बभूयाः प्र जायस्व प्रजया पुत्रकामे ॥२॥
अहं गर्भमदधामोषधीष्वहं विश्वेषु भुवनेष्वंतः ।
अयं प्रजा अजनयं पृथिव्यामहं जनिभ्यो अपरीषु पुत्रान् ॥

(ऋक्) ८।८।४१

विष्णुर्योनिं कल्पयतु त्वष्टा रूपाणि पिंशतु ।
आ सिंचतु प्रजापतिर्धाता गर्भं दधातु ते ॥१॥

---

१. स्वापयाव्यु ।

गर्भं धेहि सिनीवालि गर्भं धेहि सरस्वति।
गर्भं ते अश्विनौ देवावाधत्तां पुष्करस्रजा ॥२॥
हिरण्ययी अरणी यं निर्मन्थतो अश्विना।
तं ते गर्भं हवामहे दशमे मासि सूतवे ॥३॥
(ऋक्) ८।८।४३

परिशिष्टं—नेजमेष परा पत सुपुत्रः पुनरा पत।
अस्यै मे पुत्रकामायै गर्भमाधेहि यः पुमान् ॥१॥
यथेयं पृथिवी मह्यु त्ताना गर्भमा दधे।
एवं तं गर्भमाधेहि दशमे मासि सूतवे ॥२॥
विष्णोः श्रैष्ठ्येन रूपेणास्यां नार्यां गवीन्याम्।
पुमांसं पुत्रमाधेहि दशमे मासि सूतवे ॥३॥
(ऋक्) खिल सूक्तम्

पवस्व सोम मंदयन्निंद्राय मधुमत्तमः ॥१॥
असृग्रन् देववीतये वाजयंतो रथा इव ॥२॥
ते सुतासो मदिन्तमाः शुक्रा वायुमसृक्षत ॥३॥
ग्राव्णा तुन्नो अभिष्टुतः पवित्रं सोम गच्छसि।
दधत्स्तोत्रे सुवीर्यम् ॥४॥
एष तुन्नो अभिष्टुतः पवित्रमति गाहते।
रक्षोहा वारमव्ययम् ॥५॥ (ऋक्) ७।२।१६।

आपी वो अस्मे पितरेव पुत्रोग्रेव रुचा नृपतीव तुर्यै।
इर्येव पुष्ट्यै किरणेव भुज्यै श्रुष्टीवानेव हवमा गमिष्टम् ॥
(ऋक्) ८।६।१

इति श्रीआकाशभैरव महातन्त्रे वैदिक-मन्त्राः ॥

॥ समाप्तश्चायं ग्रन्थः ॥

अथ गायत्री-विधिः

(तन्त्रान्तरे)

अथो वक्ष्यामि गायत्रीं तत्त्वरूपां त्रयीमयीम्।
यया प्रकाश्यते ब्रह्म-सच्चिदानन्द-लक्षणम् ॥१॥
प्रणवाद्या व्याहृतयः [1]सप्त स्युस्तत्पदादिका।
चतुर्विंशत्यक्षरात्मा गायत्री शिरसाऽन्विता [2]॥२॥
सर्ववेदोद्धृतःसारो मन्त्रोऽयं समुदाहृतः।
प्राणायामान् पुरा कृत्वा गायत्रीं सन्ध्ययोर्जपेत् ॥३॥

प्राणायामविधिः ॥

सप्तव्याहृति संयुक्तां गायत्रीं शिरसाऽन्विताम्।
त्रिरुच्चरन् धिया प्राणान् धारयेद्यतमानसः ॥४॥
प्राणायामोऽयमाख्यातः समस्त-दुरितापहः ॥५॥

ऋषिः छन्ददेवतादयः ॥

(क) ओङ्कारस्य प्रजापति ऋषिः गायत्रीछन्दः श्री परमात्मा देवता

(ख) सप्तव्याहृतीनां जमदग्नि-भरद्वाज-भृगु-गौतम-काश्यप-विश्वामित्र-वसिष्ठाः ऋषयः गायत्र्युष्णिगनुष्टुब्-बृहती-पंक्तिः-त्रिष्टुब्-जगत्यः छंदांसि, सप्तार्चिरनिलः सूर्यो वाक्पतिर्वरुणो वृषभो विश्वेदेवाः देवता :—

(ग) गायत्र्या विश्वामित्र ऋषिर्गायत्री छंदः सविता देवता :—

(घ) आपो ज्योतीति शिरसाऽस्य ब्रह्माऋषिर्गायत्री छंदः श्री परमात्मा देवता।

---

१. ओं भूः ओं भुवः ओं स्वः ओं महः ओं जनः ओं तपः ओं सत्यम्।

२. ओं तत्सवितुर्वरेण्यं भर्गोदेवस्य धीमहि। धियो यो नः प्रचोदयात् ॥

३. ओं आपो ज्योतीरसोऽमृतं ब्रह्म भूर्भुवः स्वः सोऽहमोम् (स्वरोम्) ॥

४. ओं भूर्भुवः स्वः ओं तत्सवितुर्वरेण्यं भर्गो देवस्य धीमहि। धियो यो नः प्रचोदयात् ॥

अथ जपमंत्रः ॥

व्याहृतित्रयसंयुक्तां गायत्रीं दीक्षितो जपेत् ।
चतुर्विंशतिलक्षाणि पुरश्चरणमुच्यते ॥६॥
क्षीरौदनं तिलान्दूर्वा-सिद्धौदन-समिद्वरान् ।
पृथग्द्रव्यं सहस्रं तु जुहुयात् मंत्रसिद्धये ॥७॥
तर्पणादि ततः कृत्वा गुरुं संतोष्य यत्नतः ।
प्रयोगानाचरेद्विद्वांस्तदनुज्ञा-पुरस्सरम् ॥८॥
तत्त्वसंख्या सहस्राणि मंत्री प्रजुहुयात्तिलैः ।
सर्वपापविनिर्मुक्तो दीर्घमायुस्स विन्दति ॥९॥

गायत्र्याः तुर्यपादः ॥

जपेन्मुमुक्षुर्गायत्रीं तुर्य्यपादेन संयुताम् ।
परा रजसे सावदो३मिति तुर्य्यः प्रकीर्तितः ॥१०॥

तुर्यपादस्य ऋष्यादयः ॥

विमलोऽस्य ऋषिश्छंदो गायत्रं देवता प्रभुः ॥११॥

"ओं भूर्भुवः स्वः ओं तत्सवितुर्वरेण्यं भर्गोदेवस्य धीमहि धियो यो नः प्रचोदयात्-परो रजसे सावदो३म्—"

नातः परतरो मंत्रो नातः परतरं तपः ।
तृणायन्ते महाविद्यादयः सर्वा यदग्रतः ॥१२॥

अथ तेजोमयं सदाशिवोरूपं भावयन् आत्मानं ओं भू र्भुवः स्वः पूर्वकं मातृका-वर्ण-षडङ्गादिन्यासान्विधाय मूलाधारादाब्रह्मबिलं विलसन्ती बिसतन्तुतनीयसीं विद्युत्पुञ्जपिंजरां विवस्वदयुतभास्वत्प्रकाशां परश्शतसुधा मयूख-शीतल-तेजो दण्डरूपां परचितिं भावयन्, मूलाधारात्-स्वाधिष्ठानात् नाभिगत, मणिपूरक-सरोज-कर्णिकया वा ओङ्कारं समुत्थाय, वक्ष्यमाण दिव्यरूपात्मिकां परंदेवतां ध्यायन्-गुरुरुपदिष्टमार्गेण मानस-यौगिक-योग-वाचक-योगमानसिक-वाङ्मानसिक यौगिकविधिना वा सकलवेदसाररूपां तुर्यपादसहितां चतुर्विंशतिवर्णात्मिकां प्रणवसहितव्याहृतित्रययुतां गायत्रीं जपेदिति विधिः ।

ध्यानम् ।।

"मुक्ता-विद्रुम-हेम-नील-धवलच्छायैर्मुखैस्त्रीक्षणै-
र्युक्तामिन्दुनिबद्धरत्नमुकुटां तत्त्वात्मवर्णात्मिकाम् ।
सावित्रीं वरदाभयाङ्कुशकशाः शुभ्रं कपालं गुणम्
शङ्खं चक्रमथाऽरविंदयुगलं हस्तैर्वहन्तीं भजे ।।१३।।

आयुषे साज्यहविषा केवलेनाऽथ सर्पिषा ।
दूर्वात्रिकैस्तिलैर्मन्त्री जुहुयात् त्रिसहस्रकम् ।।१४।।
अरुणाब्जैस्त्रिमध्वक्तैर्जुहुयादयुतं ततः ।
महालक्ष्मीर्भवेत्तस्य षण्मासान्नाऽत्र संशयः ।।१५।।
ब्रह्मश्रिये प्रजुहुयात् प्रसूनैर्ब्रह्मवृक्षजैः ।
बहुना किमिहोक्तेन यथावत् साधुसाधिता ।।१६।।
द्विजन्मिनामियं विद्या सिद्धा कामदुघा मता ।।१७।।

इति गायत्रीविधिः
(शारदातिलकात्)

अथ सावित्री-विधिः

(आग्नेयास्त्रम्)

श्रीशिव उवाच ।।

सर्वार्थसाधकं वक्ष्ये सङ्ग्रामविजयप्रदम् ।
(सर्वार्ति-रोग-शत्रूणां नाशनं च सुखप्रदम्) ।।१।।

"ओ३म् जातवेदसे सुनवाम सोममरातीयतो निदहाति वेदः ।
स नः पर्षदति दुर्गाणि विश्वा नावेव सिंधुं दुरितात्यग्निः" ।।२।।
(ऋक्)

मारीचःकाश्यपः प्रोक्तो मुनिरस्य महामनोः ।
त्रिष्टुबछंदो देवताऽत्र जातवेदोऽग्निरीरितः ।।३।।
नवभिः सप्तभिः षड्भिः सप्तभिः पुनरष्टभिः ।
सप्तभिर्मूलमंत्रार्णैः षडङ्गविधिरीरितः ।।४।।
अङ्गुष्ठ-गुल्फ जंघासु-जानुनोरूरुयुग्मके ।
कट्यन्धु नाभिषु हृदि स्तनयो पार्श्वयोर्द्वयोः ।।५।।
पृष्ठतः स्कंधयोर्मध्ये बाहुमूलोपबाहुषु ।
प्रकूर्पर-प्रकोष्ठेषु मणिबंधतलेषु च ।।६।।
मुख-नासाक्षि-कर्णेषु-मस्त-मस्तिष्क-मूर्धसु ।
क्रमेण विन्यसेद्वर्णान्मंत्री मंत्रसमुद्भवान् ।।७।।
शिखा-ललाट-नयन-कर्णोष्ठ-रसनास्वथ ।
सकण्ठ-बाहु-हृत्कुक्षि-कटिगुह्योरू-जानुषु ।।८।।
जङ्घयोः पादयोर्न्यस्येदथ विश्वेश्वरीं स्मरेत् ।।९।।

ध्यानम् ।।

उद्यद्विद्युत्कराला कुलहरिगल संस्थाऽरिशंखासिखेट-
ष्विश्वासाख्य त्रिशूलानरिगणभयदां तर्जनीञ्चाऽऽदधाना ।
चर्मास्युद्घूर्णदोर्भिः प्रहरण-निपुणाभिर्वृता कन्यकाभि-
र्वंद्यात्काशानवीष्टांस्त्रिनयनलसिता चापि कात्यायनी वः ।।१०।।

दीक्षा प्रवर्त्यंते पूर्वं यथावद्देशिकोत्तमैः ।
ततोऽस्त्रक्लृप्तिः सम्प्रोक्ता स्यात्प्रयोगविधिस्ततः ॥११॥
दीक्षकाख्याक्षराण्यादौ शक्त्यावेष्टय ततो बहिः ।
यंत्रं षड्गुणितं कृत्वा दुर्वर्णलसितास्त्रकम् ॥१२॥
बहिरष्टदलं पद्मं प्रोक्त-लक्षण-लक्षितम् ।
अत्र पीठे यजेन्मंत्री नवशक्ति-सह-शिवाम् ॥१३॥
जयां च विजयां भद्रां रुद्रां कालीं च पूर्वतः ।
सुमुखीं दुर्मुखीं चन्द्रमुखीं सिंहमुखीं तथा ॥१४॥
मध्ये दुर्गां यजेत्पश्चादासनं सिंहमंत्रतः ।
तारमुक्त्वा वज्रनखदंष्ट्राय च महाततः ॥१५॥
सिंहाय हुं फट् हृच्चेति[1] मंत्रः सप्तदशाक्षरः ।
मूर्ति मूलेन सङ्कल्प्य तस्यामावाह्य पूजयेत् ॥१६॥
केशरेषु षडङ्गानि पूर्वतोऽष्टदले पुनः ।
जातवेदः सप्तजिह्वो द्वितीयो हव्यवाहनः ॥१७॥
ततोऽश्वोदरजं वैश्वानरं कौमारतेजसम् ।
विश्वमुखं देवमुखं पीठे कोष्ठचतुष्टये ॥१८॥
धरात्मानं जलात्मानं वह्न्यात्मानं निरात्मकम् ।
निवृत्तिश्च प्रतिष्ठा च विद्या शांतिश्च गौणकाः ॥१९॥
पूषा-वाण्यौ ततो वीथी शचीतोयात्मिका तथा ।
नित्या दयावती चैव अष्टमी कारिणी मता ॥२०॥
तथैव नवमी नामा प्रोक्ता चैव तिरस्क्रिया ।
[2]देवमाता च दमनप्रिया पश्चान्निरूप्यते ॥२१॥
समाराध्य नंदिनी च परा रिपुविमर्दिनी ।
पद्माख्या दण्डिनी तिग्मा दुर्गा गायत्र्यतः परम् ॥२२॥
निरवद्या विशालाक्षी सौम्या सायं निरूप्यते ।
स्वरोद्वाहा नादिनी च वेदना वह्निगर्भिणी ॥२३॥

---

१. मन्त्रोद्धार—ओं वज्र नखदंष्ट्राय महासिंहाय हुं फट् नमः ।
२. वेदमाता ।

सिंहवासा च धूम्रा च दुर्विषंहारिरंसुका ।
तापहरा त्यक्तदोषा निःसपत्नेति तद्वहिः ॥२४॥
लोकपालांस्तदास्त्राणि पूजयेच्च यथाविधि ।
एवं शिष्यमभिषिच्य कुम्भादीन् गुरुराहरेत् ॥२५॥
ईदृशं यंत्रमारुह्य जपेच्छिष्यः सुयन्त्रितः ।
मंत्रं वर्णसहस्राणि सिद्ध्यर्थं गुरुसन्निधौ ॥२६॥
सर्वं जापेषु चाग्नेय्या गायत्र्या द्विगुणो जपः ।
कर्तव्यो वाञ्छितावाप्त्यै रक्षायै कार्यसिद्धये ॥२७॥
वेद-वेदाब्धि-संख्याकं तिलसिद्धार्थ-चित्रजैः ।
मूलैश्च समिधाभिश्च वटोदुम्बर-पैप्पलैः ॥२८॥
अर्क-प्लक्षोद्भवैश्चापि घृतेन हविषान्नकैः ।
सर्वैर्घृताक्तैर्जुहुयात्तिलैश्चान्ते घृताहुतीः ॥२९॥
ततस्सन्तर्प्य सतिलैः कृत्वा चात्माभिषेचनम् ।
समाराध्य धरादेवीं तोषयेद् गुरुमात्मनः ॥३०॥
इच्छब्जपादिभिः सिद्धे मंत्रेऽस्मिन् साधकोत्तमः ।
आग्नेयास्त्राधिकारी स्यात्तद्विधानमितीर्य्यते ॥३१॥
आग्नेयास्त्रमिति प्रोक्तं विलोमप्रथितो मनुः ।
पूर्वोक्ता एव मुन्याद्याः षडङ्गानि विलोमतः ॥३२॥
ग्नि त्य तारि वु धुं सि हृदयाय नमः ।
व वे ना श्वा विणिर्गा दु-शिरसे स्वाहा ॥३३॥
ति द ष रि प नः स-शिखायै वषट् ।
दः वे ति हा द नि-कवचाय हुम् ॥३४॥
तो य ती रा म म सो-नेत्रत्रयाय वौषट् ।
म वा न सु से द वे त जा अस्त्राय फट् ॥३५॥
पूर्वोक्त संख्यकैर्वर्णैर्वर्णन्यासस्तथैव च ।
तथैव च पदन्यासो जपः पूजा च पूर्ववत् ॥३६॥
पञ्चगव्य-सुपक्वेन चरुणा तस्य सिद्धये ।
चतुस्साहस्रं च शतं चत्वारिंशच्चतुष्टयम् ॥३७॥

होमयेदर्चनं प्राग्वज्जपश्च प्रतिलोमतः ।
क्रूरकर्मणि कुर्वीत प्रतिलोमविधानतः ॥३८॥
शान्तिकं पौष्टिकं कर्म्मं कर्त्तव्यमनुलोमतः ॥३९॥
ग्न्याद्यः पञ्चाक्षरः पादो ज्ञेयो ज्ञानेन्द्रियात्मकः ।
धुमाद्यः पञ्चवर्णो द्वितीयः कर्म्मेन्द्रियात्मकः ॥४०॥
श्वाद्यस्तृतीयः पञ्चार्णः सर्वभूतमयः स्मृतः ।
त्याद्यः सप्ताक्षरः पादश्चतुर्थो धातुरूपकः ॥४१॥
दः पूर्वः पञ्चमः पाद ऊर्मिरूपः षडक्षरः ।
तोवर्णादिः षडर्णोऽन्यः षट् कौशिकमयो मतः ॥४२॥
सोपूर्वः पञ्चवर्णोऽन्यः शब्दादिमय ईरितः ।
से वर्णाद्योऽष्टमो ज्ञेयः पञ्चार्णो वचनादिकः ॥४३॥
एवं तत्त्व समायोगात्परिक्लृप्तिरुदीरिता ।
तत्तत्पादाक्षरोत्पन्नास्ताराद्या वह्निदेवताः ॥४४॥
प्रधानमूर्तिप्रतिमाः स्व-स्वकर्मेरितप्रभा ।
प्रज्वलत्केशवदना भीमदंष्ट्रा भयापहाः ॥४५॥
देवता इन्द्रियोत्पन्ना ऊर्ध्वदृष्टय ईरिताः ।
देवता भूतपादोत्थास्तिर्यग्नेत्राः प्रकीर्त्तिताः ॥४६॥
धातुरूपाक्षरोत्पन्ना उभयात्मदृशोमताः ।
ऊर्म्मिजा ऊर्ध्ववदनाः कोशोत्थास्तिर्यगाननाः ॥४७॥
अर्थसंख्या समुत्पन्ना देवता द्विदिगाननाः ।
एताः सर्वाः स्मृता क्लीवा इन्द्रियार्थो भवाः स्त्रियः ॥४८॥
याभिर्मन्त्री दहेच्छत्रो राष्ट्रं सगिरिकाननम् ।
अस्त्रं मनुष्यनक्षत्रे प्रारभेत विचक्षणः ॥४९॥
आसुरेषु प्रयुञ्जीयात् देवतासु शुभं हरेत् ।
उपक्रमेत नन्दासु रिक्तास्वस्त्रं विसर्जयेत् ॥५०॥
भद्रास्वाहरणं कुर्याज्जपाहे कार्य्यमुत्तमम् ।
उपक्रमो भौमवारे शनिवारे विसर्जयेत् ॥५१॥

प्रतिसंहरणं वारे गुरो शुक्रस्य वा भवेत् ।
स्थिरेषु राशिष्वारंभश्चरेषु स्याद्विसर्जनम् ।।५२।।
अस्त्रसंहरणं कुर्यादुभयेषु विचक्षणः ।
कृष्णपक्षे चरेदस्त्रं विसृजेच्छशिना पुनः ।।५३।।
शुक्लपक्षे क्रमादस्त्रं पुनरात्मनि संहरेत् ।
भानुना मोक्षसंहारौ कुर्यात्पक्षद्वये सुधीः ।।५४।।

मारणं—पश्चिमाभि मुखो भूत्वा सर्वकर्माणि साधयेत् ।
नक्षत्रवृक्षशकलान्साध्याख्यान्कर्म्मसंयुतान् ॥ ५५ ॥
राजी तैलेनसंलिप्तान् पृथक् सप्तसहस्रकम् ।
जुहुयात्संयतो भूत्वा रिपुर्यमपुरं व्रजेत् ।।५६।।

ज्वरकरणं—सप्तरात्रं प्रजुहुयात्सिद्धार्थस्नेहसंयुतैः ।
आर्द्र वस्त्रो विष्टिकाले मरीचैर्मनुनाऽमुना ।।५७।।
निगृह्यते ज्वरेणाऽरिः प्रलयाग्निसमेन सः ।

पुनः ज्वरकरणं—ताल पत्रे समालिख्य शत्रुनाम यथाविधि ।।५८।।
आग्नेयास्त्रेण संवेष्ट्य कुण्डमध्ये निखन्यते ।
मरिचैश्च हुनेत्क्रुद्धो ज्वराक्रान्तः सजायते ।।५९।।

वशीकरणम्—तदादाय क्षिपेत्तोये शीतले स वशो भवेत् ।

मारणे पुत्तलि विधि—सामुद्रे सलिले हिङ्गु-विष-जीरकलोलिते ।।६०।।
क्वथिते पुत्तलिं साध्यनक्षत्रतरुनिर्मिताम् ।
अधोवक्त्रां विनिक्षिप्य यष्ट्या विषतरूत्थया ।।६१।।
तच्छिरस्ताड़नं कुर्याज्जपन्मंत्रं विलोमतः ।
सप्ताहान्मरणं याति शत्रुर्ज्वरविमोहितः ।।६२।।

शत्रोरुच्चाटनम्—आदित्यरथनागेन्द्रप्रस्तांघ्रि तद्विषाहतम् ।
नग्नं तैलेन लिप्ताङ्गं दग्धं भानुमरीचिभिः ।।६३।।
अधोमुखं निजरिपुं ध्यात्वा क्वथित देशिकः ।
विभ्राणां गर्जनीं शूलं ध्यात्वा दुर्गां भयङ्करीम् ।।६४।।
महिषीघृतसंसिक्तैः पल्लवैर्विषवृक्षजैः ।
हुत्वा रिपोर्महासेनामुच्चाटयति मन्त्रवित् ।।६५।।

रिपुसेना उच्चाटनम्—ध्यात्वा देवीं पुरा-प्रोक्तां चरुभिर्मरिचान्वितैः।
अजारुधिरसंसिक्तैर्जुहुयाद् दिवसत्रयम् ॥६६॥
रिपोरुच्चाटनं कुर्यात् सेनाया नाऽत्र संशयः।

शत्रुमोहनम्—अग्निशूलकरां दुर्गां ज्वलन्तीं प्रलयाग्निवत् ॥६७॥
ध्यात्वा सर्षपतैलाढ्यैर्बीजैर्धत्तूरसम्भवैः।
हुत्वा विमोहयेच्छत्रून्मरीचैर्वा ससर्षपैः ॥६८॥

शत्रुमारणम्—कालाञ्जननिभां दुर्गां शूलखड्गकरां स्मरन्।
नक्षत्रवृक्षसम्भूतै व्रणवृक्षजसंज्ञकैः ॥६९॥
समिद्वरैः प्रजुहुयाद्धन्यान्मासेन वैरिणम्।

शत्रोरुच्चाटनम्—सिंहारूढां-प्रधावन्तीं-धावमानं रिपुं प्रति ॥७०॥
शरान्कार्मुकनिर्मुक्तान्वह्नि-ज्वालामुखाकुलान्।
मुञ्चन्तीं संस्मरन्दुर्गां तर्पयेदुष्णवारिणा ॥७१॥
भानुबिम्बं समालोक्य शत्रोरुच्चाटनं भवेत्।
(अतिदुर्गादयः पञ्च वक्ष्ये षट्कर्मसाधने) ॥७२॥

१. अतिदुर्गा—ओं अति दुर्गाणि विश्वानावेव सिन्धुं दुरितात्यग्निः।
जातवेदसे सुनवाम सोममरातीयतो नि दहातिवेदः।
स नः पर्षत् स्वाहा ॥७३॥

२. गाणि दुर्गा—ओं गाणि विश्वा नावेव सिन्धुं दुरितात्याग्निः।
जातवेदसे सुनवाम सोममरातीयतो नि दहाति वेदः।
स नः पर्षदति दुः स्वाहा ॥७४॥

३. विश्वा दुर्गा—ओं विश्वा नावेव सिन्धुं दुरितात्यग्निः जातवेदसे।
सुनवाम सोममरातीयतो नि दहाति वेदः। स नः पर्षदति
दुर्गाणि स्वाहा ॥७५॥

४. सिन्धु दुर्गा—ओं सिन्धुं दुरितात्यग्निः। जातवेदसे सुनवाम
सोममरातीयतो नि दहाति वेदः।
स नः पर्षदति दुर्गाणि विश्वा नावेव स्वाहा ॥७६॥

५. अग्नि दुर्गा—ओं अग्निः जातवेदसे सुनुवाम
सोममरातीयतो नि दहाति वेदः ।
स नः पर्षदति दुर्गाणि विश्वा नावेव सिन्धुं दुरितातित
स्वाहा ॥७७॥

[1]अतिदुर्गामयोमुष्टिगदाहस्तां विचिन्तयेत् ।
विद्युद्दामसमानाभां महिषीघृतसंयुतैः ॥७८॥
[2]पुलाकैर्जुहुयान्निम्ब-विभीतक-समिद्वरैः ।
कोद्रवैरथशत्रोश्च सेनाया स्तंभनं भवेत् ॥७९॥
[3]आत्तपाशाङ्कुशां रक्तां गाणि-दुर्गामनु स्मरेत् ।
लोणैः समधुरैः साध्यवृक्षकाष्ठैधितेऽनले ॥८०॥
जुहुयान्निशि सप्ताहान्मन्त्रविद्वशयेन्नृपान् ।
(लभते वांच्छितानर्थान् साम्राज्यं च न संशयः) ॥८१॥
पाशाङ्कुशधरां रक्तां विश्वदुर्गां विचिन्तयेत् ।
फलिनीकुसुमैः फुल्लैश्चन्दनाम्भःसमुक्षितैः ॥८२॥
जुहुयान्निशि यो मंत्री तस्य विश्वं वशं भवेत् ।
शरच्चन्द्रनिभां देवीं विगलत्परमामृताम् ॥८३॥
पाशाङ्कुशधरां ध्यायन् सिन्धुदुर्गां समिद्वरैः ।
वैतसैर्मधुरासिक्तैर्जुहुयात् (वृत्ति) वृष्टिसिद्धये ॥८४॥
कपालं त्रिशिखं पाशमङ्कुशं बिभ्रतीं करैः ।
जवाकुसुमसङ्काशामग्निदुर्गां विचिन्तयन् ॥८५॥
हुत्वा लवणपुत्तल्या मधुरत्रययुक्तया ।
आकर्षेद्वांच्छितान् साध्यान्मंत्रविन्नाऽत्रसंशयः ॥८६॥
अङ्गणे स्थण्डिलं कृत्वा सुगन्धिकुसुमादिभिः ।
देवीमभ्यर्च्य नित्यं प्रागुक्तेनैव वर्त्मना ॥८७॥
आहरेद्रात्रिषु बलिं चरुणा सर्वसिद्धिदम् ।
कृत्या-रोग-भय-द्रोह-भूतादीन्नाऽत्रसंशयः ॥८८॥
यथावदग्निमाराध्य गंधैः पुष्पैर्मनोरमैः ।
स्थित्वा तस्याग्रतो मंत्री जपेन्मंत्रमनन्यधीः ॥८९॥

---

१. ममोर्धष्टि, २. पुरोक्तैः, ३. इषु जालांकुशाढ्यां च ।

जपोऽयं सर्वसिद्धयै स्यान्नाऽत्र कार्या विचारणा ।
लवणैर्मधुरासिक्तैर्जुहुयात्पश्चिमामुखः ॥९०॥
मंत्रार्णसंख्यया मंत्री रिपुमात्मवशं नयेत् ।
शालीन् प्रक्षाल्य संशोष्य शुद्धान् कुर्वीत तण्डुलान् ॥९१॥
जपित्वा पञ्चगव्येषु संस्कृते हव्यवाहने ।
चरुं पचेज्जपन्मंत्रमवतार्य पुनः सुधीः ॥९२॥
अर्चयित्वा विशदधीर्देवीमग्नौ यथा पुरा ।
जुहुयाच्चरुणाऽनेन साज्येनाष्टसहस्रकम् ॥९३॥
पात्रे सम्पातनं कुर्वन् साध्यं तत् प्राशयेत् सुधीः ।
शेषं तं निखनेद् वारिसम्पातं प्राङ्गणान्तरे ॥९४॥
कृत्या-रोगा विनश्यन्ति सहभूतग्रहामयैः ।
परैरुत्पादिता कृत्या पुनस्तानेव भक्षयेत् ॥९५॥
व्रीहिभिर्हविषाक्षीरै पयोवृक्षसमिद्वरैः ।
आज्यैर्मधुत्रयोपेतैरेतैर्दशशतं पृथक् ॥९६॥
जुहुयात्सम्पदां भूमिः साधको भवति ध्रुवम् ।
भास्करे मेषराशिस्थे मंत्रज्ञोऽनुगुणे दिने ॥९७॥
नद्यां सागरगामिन्यां सततं पुश्कलांभसि ।
उद्धृत्यादाय सिक्ताः संशोष्य परिशोधयेत् ॥९८॥
न्यस्य ताः पञ्चगव्येषु संस्कृते हव्यवाहने ।
भर्ज्येन्मनुना सिद्धचै दर्व्या ब्रह्मरुहोत्थया ॥९९॥
सिंहमेषधनुस्थेऽर्के कृष्णपक्षेऽष्टमी तिथौ ।
विशाखाकृतिकामूलहस्तोत्तरमघास्वथ ॥१००॥
रोहिण्यां श्रवणे वारौ मन्दवाक्पतिदैवतौ ।
विहायाऽन्येषु कुर्वीत सिक्तास्थापनं सुधीः ॥१०१॥
गृहग्रामादिराष्ट्राणां रक्षार्थं सिक्ताः शुभाः ।
प्रस्थाढकघटोन्माना मध्यादिष्ववटेष्विमाः ॥१०२॥
नवसु प्रक्षिपेज्जप्तास्तेषु सम्पूजयेत् क्रमात् ।
मध्यादि देवीशस्त्राणि कपालान्तानि देशिकः ॥१०३॥

चक्रं शङ्खमसिं खेटं वाणञ्चापं त्रिशूलकम् ।
कपालं स्वस्वमंत्रेण सम्पूज्याऽन्ते बलिं हरेत् ॥१०४॥
नक्षत्र-ग्रह-राशीनां लोकेशानां बलिं हरेत् ।
विहिता यत्र रक्षेयं वर्धन्ते तत्र सम्पदः ॥१०५॥
क्षुद्रग्रहमहारोगसौरभूतसरीसृपाः ।
अमुना विलयं यान्ति विधिना नाऽत्र संशयः ॥१०६॥
सिकतानां विशुद्धानां कुडवांश्चापि षोडश ।
पञ्चगव्ययुते पात्रे ब्रह्मवृक्षेण निर्मिते ॥१०७॥
निक्षिपेद्विधिना यत्र स्थापयेत्तत्र सम्पदः ।
दिने दिने प्रवर्धन्ते कालवृष्ट्यादिभिः सह ॥१०८॥
महोत्पाता विनश्यन्ति कृत्याद्रोहमहाग्रहाः ।
चरुगव्याशमनां कुर्यात् स्थापनं विधिनामुना ॥१०९॥
गोमूत्रं प्रस्थमात्रं स्याद् गोमयाम्भस्तदर्धकम् ।
आज्यात्सप्तगुणं क्षीरं गोमूत्रात्त्रिगुणं दधि ॥११०॥
गोमूत्रेण समं सर्पिः सर्वं वा सममुच्यते ।
गावः स्युः कपिलाश्वेतसितधूम्रारुणप्रभाः ॥१११॥
अभावे च सिताः सर्वाः सर्वं वा कपिलोद्भवम् ।
एकोनपञ्चाशत्कोष्ठे फलके ब्रह्मशाखिनः ॥११२॥
विहाय कोणकोष्ठानि मध्यकोष्ठे लिखेच्च ह्रीम् ।
तदूर्ध्वकोष्ठमारभ्य प्रादक्षिण्येन संलिखेत् ॥११३॥
देवीं तत्र समावाह्य पूजयेदुपचारकैः ।
कृत्वा होमं तु सम्पातं निखनेत्तद्यथापुरा ॥११४॥
दद्याद्बलिं यथा पूर्वं तस्य पूर्वोदितं फलम् ।
नवकोष्ठान्वितं लेख्यं चतुरस्रं सुशोभनम् ॥११५॥
साध्यनामान्वितां मायां मध्यकोष्ठे तु संलिखेत् ।
तदधःकोष्ठमारभ्य प्रादक्षिण्येन संलिखेत् ॥११६॥
मूलमंत्रस्य पूर्वोक्तानष्टौ पादांश्च तद्बहिः ।
वृत्तद्वयान्तराले तु मातृकार्णैः प्रवेष्टयेत् ॥११७॥
तद्बहिश्चतुरस्रं स्याद्धारणायंत्रमद्भुतम् ।
सर्वभूतभयहरं श्रीकीर्त्यायुःप्रदं शुभम् ॥११८॥
आग्नेयास्त्रस्य ज्ञानानि विसर्गादान कर्मणी ।
यः पुमान् गुरुणाशिष्टस्तस्याधीनं जगत्त्रयम् ॥११९॥

इति सावित्री विधिः (तंत्रान्तरात्)

अथ सरस्वती विधिः

(त्र्यम्बक-मन्त्र-विधिः)

अथ त्रैयम्बकं मंत्रमभिधास्याम्यनुष्टुभम् ।
यं भजन्तं नरं कालः स्वयं वीक्षितुमक्षमः ।।१।।

अथ प्रयोगः ।।

आदौ स्वस्तिवाचनम् विष्णुस्मरणं च,

प्रतिज्ञा—अद्य तत्सद्ब्रह्मेत्यादि० अमुकगोत्रः अमुक शर्मा-वर्मा-गुप्तोऽहं मम आत्मनः जन्मलग्नादि द्वारा दुष्टस्थानस्थित ग्रहजन्याशेषोपसर्गापमृत्यु-पीड़ा-निवृतिपूर्वक आयुरारोग्य-सुख-सौभाग्य-धन-धान्य-स्त्री पुत्र-सम्पत्प्रवृद्धि-कुलानन्द दीर्घजीवित्वकामनया श्रीमतो मृत्युञ्जय देवस्य पूजनं, तदङ्गतया निर्विघ्नतार्थे श्री गणपत्यादिनां पूजनं च करिष्ये ।।

ततो गणेशादीन्सम्पूज्य कलशस्थापनं कृत्वा देवस्य पूजनं कुर्यात् । आदौ मातृकान्यासं कृत्वा पश्चान्मंत्रन्यासं—यथा

त्र्यम्बकमित्यस्य वसिष्ठ ऋषिरनुष्टुब्छंदस्त्र्यम्बको देवता मम (अमुकस्य वा) अपमृत्यु-प्रशमन-दीर्घजीवित्व-धन-धान्य-पुत्रादि प्राप्तये जपे विनियोगः ।।

अथ ऋष्यादि न्यासं कृत्वा—

ओं त्र्यम्बकं—अंगुष्ठाभ्यां नमः, ओं यजामहे—तर्जनीभ्यां नमः,
ओं सुगन्धिं पुष्टिवर्द्धनम्—मध्यमाभ्यां नमः, ओं उर्वारुकमिव
बन्धनात्—अनामिकाभ्यां नमः, ओं मृत्योर्मुक्षीय—कनिष्ठिकाभ्यां
नमः, ओं मामृतात्—करतलकरपृष्ठाभ्यां नमः ।।

—एवं हृदयादिषु न्यस्य

ओं त्र्यं नमः—पूर्व मुखे, ओं बं नमः—पश्चिमं मुखे ।
ओं कं नमः—दक्षिण मुखे, ओं यं नमः—उत्तर मुखे ।
ओं जां नमः—वक्षसि, ओं मं नमः—गले ।

श्रों हें नमः—ऊर्ध्व मुखे, श्रों सु ं नमः—नाभौ ।
श्रों गं नमः—हृदि, श्रों धि नमः—पृष्ठे ।
श्रों पु ं नमः—कुक्षौ, श्रों ष्टि नमः—लिंगे ।
श्रों वं नमः—गुदे, श्रों द्धं नमः—दक्षिणोरुमूले ।
श्रों नं नमः—वामोरुमूले, श्रों उं नमः—दक्षोरुपान्ते ।
श्रों र्वां नमः—वामोरुपान्ते, श्रों रु ं नमः—दक्षजानुनि ।
ओं कं नमः—वामजानुनि, श्रों मि नमः—दक्षगुल्फे ।
श्रों वं नमः—वामगुल्फे, श्रों बं नमः—दक्षस्तने ।
श्रों धं नमः—वामस्तने, श्रों नात् नमः—दक्षपार्श्वे ।
श्रों मृ ं नमः—वामपार्श्वे, श्रों त्यों नमः दक्षपादे ।
श्रों मु ं नमः—वामपादे, श्रों क्षीं नमः—दक्षहस्ते ।
श्रों यं नमः—वामहस्ते, श्रों मां नमः—दक्षिण नासायां
श्रों मृ ं नमः—वामनासायाम्, श्रों तात् नमः—शीर्षे ।।

श्रों त्र्यम्बकं नमः—शिरसि, श्रों यजामहे नमः—भ्रू युगले ।
श्रों सुगन्धिं नमः—श्रक्षिद्वये, श्रों पुष्टि नमः—वक्त्रे ।
श्रों वर्धनं नमः—गण्डयुगले, श्रों उर्वारुक नमः—हृदये ।
श्रों मिव नमः—जठरे, श्रों बंधनात् नमः—गुह्ये ।
श्रों मृत्योः नमः—ऊरुद्वये, ओं मुक्षीय नमः—जानुद्वये ।
श्रों मामृतात् नमः—पादयोः ।।इति।।

श्रथ ध्यानम् :—

हस्ताभ्यां कलशद्वयामृतरसैराप्लावयन्तं शिरो
द्वाभ्यां तौ दधतं मृगाक्षवलये द्वाभ्यां वहन्तं परम् ।
अङ्कन्यस्तकरद्वयामृत घटं कैलाशकान्तं शिवम्
स्वच्छाम्भोजगतं नवेन्दुमुकुटं देवं त्रिनेत्रं भजे ।।

—एवं ध्यात्वा

स्वकीय यजमानस्य वा मध्यमांगुलिसम दीर्घ चतुरस्त्रे षडष्टास्त्र भू गृहां कुंकुम कस्तूरी चन्दनैर्यन्त्रतनुं ताम्र, रौप्य, स्वर्ण भाजनोपरि सम्पाद्य तत्र पञ्चाक्षरोदितेपीठे वषभध्वजं पूजयेत् ।।तत्रैव देवमावाह्य, पुष्पां-

ञ्जलि निक्षिप्य, पाद्यादि षोडशोपचारैः सम्पूज्य—आवरण पूजनंच कुर्यात् ।

अथ षट्कोणेषु हृदयादि षडङ्गं सम्पूज्येत्—प्रथमावरणं ॥

अथाष्टदलेषु—ओं अर्कमूर्तये नमः, ओं सोममूर्तये नमः, ओं पृथिवी मूर्तये नमः, ओं जलमूर्तये नमः, ओं अग्निमूर्तये नमः, ओं वायुमूर्तये नमः, ओं आकाशमूर्तये नमः, ओं यजमानमूर्तये नमः ॥इति द्वितीयावरणम् ॥

अथ मध्ये—ओं रमायै नमः, ओं राकायै नमः, ओं प्रभायै नमः, ओं ज्योत्स्नायै नमः, ओं पूर्णायै नमः, ओं [1]उमायै नमः, ओं [2]पूषायै नमः, ओं [3]स्वधायै नमः—॥इति तृतीया वरणम् ॥

ओं विश्वायै नमः, ओं विद्यायै नमः, ओं सितायै नमः, ओं [4]शुद्धायै नमः, ओं सारायै नमः, ओं संध्यायै नमः, ओं शिवायै नमः, ओं निशायै नमः—॥इति चतुर्थावरणम् ॥

ओं आर्यायै नमः, ओं प्रज्ञायै नमः, ओं प्रभायै नमः, ओं मेधायै नमः, ओं शांत्यै नमः, ओं [5]काल्यै नमः, ओं धृत्यै नमः, ओं मत्यै नमः ॥

॥इति पञ्चमावरणम् ॥

ओं [6]उमायै नमः, ओं मायायै नमः, ओं [7]अवन्यै नमः, ओं पद्मायै नमः, ओं शान्तायै नमः, ओं मेधायै नमः ओं जयायै नमः, ओं अमलायै नमः ।

॥इति षष्ठावरणम्॥

एवं सम्पूज्य चतुरस्रे इन्द्रादि लोकपालान् यथा पूर्वादितः—

ओं इन्द्राय वज्रहस्ताय नमः, ओं अग्नये शक्तिहस्ताय नमः, ओं यमाय दण्डहस्ताय नमः, ओं निर्ऋतये खड्गहस्ताय नमः, ओं वरुणाय पाश हस्ताय नमः, ओं वायवे ध्वजहस्ताय नमः, ओं सोमाय गदाहस्ताय नमः, ओं ईशानाय शूलहस्ताय नमः, ऊर्ध्वे—ओं ब्रह्मणे पद्महस्ताय नमः, अधः-ओं अनन्ताय चक्रहस्ताय नमः ॥इति सप्तमावरणम्॥

एवं कृते प्रयोगार्हो जायतेऽयं महामनुः ।
जपेन्मंत्रमिमं लक्षमेवं ध्यायन् जितेन्द्रियः ॥२॥
जुहुयाद्दशभिर्द्रव्यैरयुतं घृतसम्प्लुतैः ।
विल्वं पलाशं खदिरं वटं च तिल सर्षपौ ॥३॥

१—उषायै, २—पूरण्यै, ३—सुधायै, ४—प्रह्वायै ५—कान्त्यै
६—धरायै, ७—पावन्यै । (तन्त्रान्तरे पाठभेदः)

दौग्धं दुग्धं दधि पुनर्दूर्वान्तानि विबुर्बुधाः ।
अयुतं जुहुयाद्बिल्वसमिद्भिः सम्पदे सुधीः ॥४॥
जुहुयाद् ब्रह्मवृक्षस्य समिद्भिर्ब्रह्मतेजसे ।
खादिरैरयुतं हुत्वा कान्तिपुष्टिमवाप्नुयात् ॥५॥
वटवृक्षस्य समिधो जुहुयादयुतावधि ।
धन-धान्य-समृद्धः स्यादचिरेणैव साधकः ॥६॥
तिलैस्तत् संख्यया हुत्वा सर्वपापैः प्रमुच्यते ।
सिद्धार्थैरयुतं हुत्वा शत्रून्विजयते नृपः ॥७॥
अनेनैव विधानेन नश्येत् मृत्युरकालजः ।
पायसेन कृतो होमो रक्षाश्रीकीर्तिकान्तिदः ॥८॥
पशुदुग्धेन सिद्धान्नं हुत्वा कृत्यां विनाशयेत् ।
अयमेवमतो होमः शान्तिश्रीसम्पदावहः ॥९॥
दधिहोमेन सम्वादं कुर्याद्विद्वेषिणोर्मिथः ।
प्रत्यहं जुहुयान्मंत्री दूर्वामष्टोत्तरं शतम् ॥१०॥
आमयान्निखिलान् जित्वा दीर्घमायुरवाप्नुयात् ।
जुहुयाज्जन्मदिवसे पायसान्नैर्घृतान्वितैः ॥११॥
इच्छन्ननिन्दितां लक्ष्मीमारोग्यमतुलं यशः ।
गव्यदुग्धघृताक्ताभिर्दूर्वाभिर्जुहुयाद्वशी ॥१२॥
सविंशतिशतं सम्यक् स्वजन्मदिवसे सुधीः ।
आमयैः सकलैर्मुक्तो जीवेद्वर्षशतं खलु ॥१३॥
काश्मरीसमिधस्तिस्रः पयोऽन्नं त्रिशतं पृथक् ।
जुहुयाद्ब्राह्मणानन्ते भोजयेन्मधुरान्वितम् ॥१४॥
प्रीणयेद्धनधान्याद्यैरात्मनो गुरुमादरात् ।
अनामयमवाप्नोति दीर्घमायुः श्रिया सह ॥१५॥
सघृतेन पयोऽन्नेन हुत्वा पर्वणि पर्वणि ।
राज्यश्रियमवाप्नोति षण्मासान्नाऽत्र संशयः ॥१६॥
लाजैर्विशुद्धैर्जुहुयात् कन्याप्त्यै सा वराप्त्यै ।
क्षीरद्रुमसमिद्धोमाद् ब्राह्मणादीन्वशं नयेत् ॥१७॥
स्नात्वा सहस्रं प्रजपेदादित्याभिमुखो मनुम् ।
आधिव्याधिविनिर्मुक्तो दीर्घमायुरवाप्नुयात् ॥१८॥
अनेन मनुना सर्वं साधयेदिष्टमात्मनः ॥१९॥

इति त्र्यम्बक विधिः

अथ प्रसंगान्महामृत्युंजय महामंत्रः

(मंत्र महोदधौ)

महामृत्युंजयं वक्ष्ये दुरितापन्निवारणम् ।
यं प्राप्य भार्गवः शम्भोर्मृतान्दैत्यानजीवयत् ॥१॥
तारः खं व्यापिनो चन्द्रयुक्तारश्चतुराननः ।
अर्घीश बिन्दुसंयुक्तो हंसः सर्गी च भूर्भुवः ॥२॥
सकारो बालसर्गाढ्यस्त्र्यम्बकं वैदिकं मनुः ।
भूर्भुवः स्वर्भुजङ्गेशस्तारी जूं सर्गवान् भृगुः ॥३॥
आकाशो मुनि बिन्द्वाढ्यः प्रणवान्तो मनूत्तमः ।
महामृत्युंजयाख्योऽयं पञ्चाशद्वर्ण निर्मितः ॥४॥

मंत्रो यथा :—

ओं हौं ओं जूं सः भूर्भुवः स्वः त्र्यम्बकं यजामहे सुगन्धिं पुष्टिवर्द्धनम् । उर्वारुकमिव बन्धनान्मृत्योर्मुक्षीय मामृतात्, भूर्भुवः स्वरों जूं सः हौं ओं ॥

अस्य श्री महामृत्युंजयमंत्रस्य वामदेव-कहोल वसिष्ठा ऋषयः पंक्तिगायत्र्यनुष्टुभश्छंदांसि सदाशिव महामृत्युंजय रुद्रोदेवता ह्रीं शक्ति श्रीं बीजम् मम सर्वाभीष्टसिद्धयर्थे जपे विनियोगः

मूर्ध्नि वक्त्रे हृदि लिङ्गे पदोर्मुन्यादिकान्न्यसेत् ॥५॥

अथ षडङ्गानि :—

ओं हौं ओं जूं सः भूर्भुवः स्वः-त्र्यम्बकं ओं नमो भगवते रुद्राय शूलपाणये स्वाहा—हृदि ।

ओं हौं यजामहे ओं अमृतमूर्तये मां जीवय—शिरसि ।

ओं हौं सुगन्धिं पुष्टिवर्द्धनम्—ओं चन्द्रशिरसे जटिने स्वाहा—शिखायां ।

ओं हौं उर्वारुक मिव बन्धनात् ओं त्रिपुरान्तकाय हां हीं—कवचम् ।

ओं हौं मृत्योर्मुक्षीय ओं नमः त्रिलोचनाय ऋग्यजुः साम मन्त्राय-नेत्रत्रये ।

ओं हौं मामृतात् ओं नमो भगवते रुद्राय अग्निरूपाय ज्वल ज्वल मां रक्ष रक्ष ओं अघोरास्त्राय—अस्त्राय फट् ॥

एवं—द्वात्रिंशत्त्र्यम्बकान् वर्णान् नमोऽतान् विन्दुसंयुतान् ।
तारादि नववर्णाद्यानंगेश्वेषु प्रविन्यसेत् ॥६॥
मूलेन व्यापकं कृत्वा ततो ध्यायेत्त्रिलोचनम् ॥७॥

अथ ध्यानम्—

हस्ताम्भोज युगस्थ कुम्भयुगलादुद्धृत्य तोयं शिरः
सिंचंतं करयोर्युगेन दधतं स्वांके सकुंभौ करौ ।
अक्षस्रङ्मृगहस्तमंबुजगतं मूर्द्धस्थचंद्रस्रवत्,
पीयूषोन्नतनुं भजे सगिरिजा मृत्युंजयं त्र्यम्बकम् ॥८॥

शेषं सर्वं त्र्यम्बक मंत्रविधिवत्

इति महामृत्युंजय मंत्र-विधिः

अथ शताक्षरा गायत्री मन्त्र विधिः

(शारदा-तिलके)

गायत्री त्रिष्टुबनुष्टुब्वर्णैः प्रोक्तः शताक्षरः ।
पूर्वोक्ता एव मुनयाद्याः परं तेजोऽस्य देवता ॥१॥

ओं अस्य शताक्षरा महामंत्रस्य प्रजापतिर्जमदग्निर्भरद्वाजोभृगु र्विश्वामित्राः ऋषयः, गायत्री-त्रिष्टुबनुष्टपाख्य-त्रिपादात्मको गायत्रीछंदः, परंतेजो देवता तत्प्रसाद सिद्ध्यर्थे जपे विनियोगः ॥

मंत्रो यथा :—

(ओं भूर्भुवः स्वः) ओं तत्सवितुर्वरेण्यं भर्गो देवस्य धीमहि । धियो यो नः प्रचोदयात् ॥ (परो रजसे सावदो३म्) जातवेदसे सुनवाम सोम-मरातीयतो नि दहाति वेदः । स न पर्षदति दुर्गाणि विश्वा नावेव सिन्धुं दुरितात्यग्निः ॥ त्र्यम्बकं यजामहे सुगन्धिम्पुष्टि वर्द्धनम् । उर्वारुक मिव बंधनान्मृत्योर्मुक्षीयमामृतात् ॥

अथ मूलमंत्रेण त्रिर्व्यापकं कृत्वा षडङ्गमन्त्रैः हृदयादिषु न्यसेत्—

यथा—

ओं भूर्भुवः स्वः ओं तत्सवितुर्वरेण्यं भर्गो देवस्य —हृदयाय नमः
" ओं धीमहि धियो यो नः प्रचोदयात् —शिरसे स्वाहा
" ओ३म् जातवेदसे सुनवाम सोममरातीयतो
नि दहातिवेदः —शिखायै वषट्
" ओ३म् स न पर्षदति दुर्गाणि विश्वानावेव सिंधुं
दुरितात्यग्नि ॥ —कवचाय हुम्
" ओ३म् त्र्यम्बकं यजामहे सुगन्धिं पुष्टिवर्द्धनम्
—नेत्रत्रयाय वौषट्
" ओ३म् उर्वारुक मिव बंधनान्मृत्योर्मुक्षीयमामृतात्
—अस्त्राय फट्

एवं वर्णन्यासादिकं सर्वं कुर्यात् पूर्वोक्त वर्त्मना ॥

अथ ध्यानम् ॥

सत्यं मानविवर्जितं श्रुतिगिरामाद्यं जगत्कारणं
व्याप्तं स्थावरजङ्गमं मुनिवरैर्ध्यातं निरुद्धेन्द्रियैः ॥
अर्काग्नीन्दुमयं शताक्षरवपुस्तारात्मकं संततं
नित्यानंदगुणालयं गुणपरं वंदामहे तन्महः ॥२॥

लक्षमानं जपेदेनमयुतं पायसान्धसा ।
जुहुयात् घृतसिक्तेन मंत्रविद्विजितेन्द्रियः ॥३॥
सौरे पीठे यजेत्सम्यक् वक्ष्यमाणविधानतः ।
आद्यामावृत्तिमभ्यर्चेत् षडङ्गैर्देशिकोत्तमः ॥४॥
गायत्रीशक्तिभिस्तिस्रः पूजयेदावृतीः क्रमात् ।
आवृत्तिः पञ्चमी प्रोक्ता त्रिष्टुबुद्भूतशक्तिभिः ॥५॥
अनुष्टुप्शक्तिभिः प्रोक्तमावृतीनां चतुष्टयम् ।
इंद्राद्यैर्दशमी प्रोक्ता वज्राद्यैस्तत्परा मता ॥६॥
एवं सिद्धे मनौ मंत्री भवेद्भास्करसन्निभः ।
सुधालतोद्भवैं खण्डैर्जुहुयात्क्षीरसंयुतैः ॥७॥
दीर्घमायुरवाप्नोति निराधिर्व्याधिवर्जितः ।
दूर्वाभिर्घृतसिक्ताभिस्तदेव फलमाप्नुयात् ॥८॥
मधुरत्रयसंसिक्तैर्जुहुयादरुणाम्बुजैः ।
महालक्ष्मीमवाप्नोति षड्भिर्मासैर्विधानवित् ॥९॥
रक्तोत्पलैस्त्रिमध्वक्तैर्जुहुयात्सर्वसम्पदे ।
श्रीप्रसूनै प्रजुहुयाद्रमाया वसतिर्भवेत् ॥१०॥
सहस्रं जुहुयान्नित्यं मासमेकं तिलैः शुभैः ।
भानुसंख्यान् द्विजान्नित्यं भोजयेन्मधुरान्वितैः ॥११॥
सर्वपापैर्विनिर्मुक्तः सर्वरोगविवर्जितः ।
कृत्याद्रोह ग्रहद्रोहान् जित्वा दीर्घं स जीवति ॥१२॥
प्रातःस्नानरतो मंत्री जपेन्नित्यं शतं शतम् ।
भानुमालोकयन् सम्यक् स जीवेच्छरदां शतम् ॥१३॥
तारव्याहृतिसंरुद्धं जपेन्मंत्रं शताक्षरम् ।
नित्यमष्टोत्तरशतं निःश्रेयस फलाप्तये ॥१४॥
गायत्र्याद्यं जपेन्मंत्रं सर्वपापविमुक्तये ।
सर्वशत्रुविनाशाय त्रिष्टुबाद्यमिमं जपेत् ॥१५॥
अनुष्ठुबाद्यं प्रजपेदायुरारोग्यसिद्धये ।
शताक्षरो मनुः प्रोक्तः समस्तपुरुषार्थदः ॥१६॥

इति शताक्षरा विधिः ॥